D1088653

Teacher's Wraparound Edition

Working with Young Children

Dr. Judy Herr
Professor, Early Childhood Education
School of Education
University of Wisconsin-Stout
Menomonie, Wisconsin

Annotations written by
Gail Dughi
Woodstock, Illinois

Publisher
The Goodheart-Willcox Company, Inc.
Tinley Park, Illinois
www.g-w.com

Copyright © 2008
by
The Goodheart-Willcox Company, Inc.

All rights reserved. No part of this work may be reproduced, stored, or transmitted in any form or by any electronic or mechanical means, including information storage and retrieval systems, without the prior written permission of The Goodheart-Willcox Company, Inc.

Manufactured in the United States of America.

Printed in Canada

ISBN: 978-1-59070-814-9
1 2 3 4 5 6 7 8 9 – 08 – 12 11 10 09 08

Cover photo: Penny Gentieu/Babystock/Jupiterimages

Contents

Working with Young Children

Prepare your students for the challenges of working in early childhood education!

Topics include

- children's physical, intellectual, social, and emotional development
- characteristics of infants, toddlers, preschoolers, school-age children, and children with special needs
- practical guidance techniques
- creating safe, healthful environments
- curriculum planning and development
- family involvement
- career planning for early childhood education

The Building Blocks of the Package

A complete package of support materials is available to aid you in teaching these important topics.

Student Text

Colorful headings, readable typeface, and logical organization facilitate reading comprehension and learning.

Teacher's Wraparound Edition

A variety of teaching aids in the margins of the pages guide you in reviewing and reinforcing the chapter content. Answer keys appear next to review questions.

Student Activity Guide

Includes numerous activities to help students review and apply chapter concepts.

Observation Guide

Designed for observing, planning, and evaluating classroom experiences.

Teacher's Resource Portfolio

Everything you need for teaching a chapter in *Working with Young Children* is conveniently grouped in an easy-to-use binder! Includes color transparencies.

Teacher's Resource Guide

Contains all of the items in the *Teacher's Resource Portfolio* except the color transparencies.

Teacher's Resource CD

This powerful electronic tool allows you to easily access the content of the *Portfolio* and the *Teacher's Wraparound Edition,* and create daily lesson plans.

ExamView® Assessment Suite

This test generator CD allows you to quickly and easily create and print tests from a test bank of hundreds of questions.

Teacher's PowerPoint® Presentations

Includes a PowerPoint presentation in both English and Spanish for each chapter.

Mastering CDA Competencies

Prepares students for obtaining their Child Development Associate Credential.

Student Edition

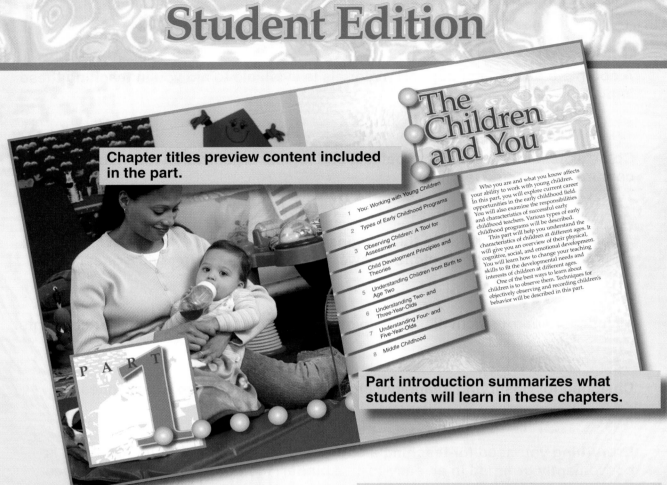

Chapter titles preview content included in the part.

The Children and You

1 You: Working with Young Children
2 Types of Early Childhood Programs
3 Observing Children: A Tool for Assessment
4 Child Development Principles and Theories
5 Understanding Children from Birth to Age Two
6 Understanding Two- and Three-Year-Olds
7 Understanding Four- and Five-Year-Olds
8 Middle Childhood

Who you are and what you know affects your ability to work with young children. In this part, you will explore current career opportunities in the early childhood field. You will also examine the responsibilities and characteristics of successful early childhood teachers. Various types of early childhood programs will be described.

This part will help you understand the characteristics of children at different ages. It will give you an overview of their physical, cognitive, social, and emotional development. You will learn how to change your teaching skills to fit the developmental needs and interests of children at different ages.

One of the best ways to learn about children is to observe them. Techniques for objectively observing and recording children's behavior will be described in this part.

Part introduction summarizes what students will learn in these chapters.

Bright, contemporary design and chapter-opening photos will interest students in reading the chapter.

Health and Safety boxes alert students to important facts about maintaining healthful environments.

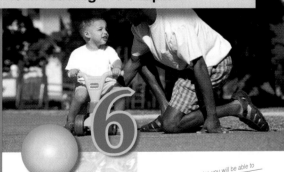

Health and Safety

The Human Need for Safety

According to psychologist Abraham Maslow, the human need for safety must be met before growth and development occurs in other areas. This is especially true for young children. What does this mean for early childhood teachers? Be alert to what causes children in your care to feel unsafe or have fear. Some children may cling to you for security. Others may act out by hitting or biting. Still others may react negatively to "strangers" in the room. On a continuing basis, look for ways to keep children feeling secure. For example, this may mean standing close to a child who fears strangers when a new person is in the room.

expression of feelings. Trust, fear, confidence, pride, friendship, and humor are all part of social-emotional development. Other emotional traits include timidity, interest, and pleasure. See 4-3. Learning to express emotions in appropriate ways begins early. Caregivers promote this learning when they positively model these skills. A person's self-concept and self-esteem are also part of this area. As children have success with all skills, confidence flourishes. This leads to a healthy self-concept and sense of worth.

The physical, cognitive, and social-emotional areas of development are linked to one another. Development in one area can strongly influence another. For instance, writing words requires fine-motor skills. It also requires cognitive development. Language, a part of cognitive development, is needed to communicate with others. It is also necessary for growing socially and emotionally.

Just as research has made known the *areas* of development, it also shows that development follows key patterns, or principles. Think about how these principles might influence how you care for children.

processes people use to gain knowledge. Language, thought, reasoning, and imagination are all included. Identifying colors and knowing the difference between *one* and *many* are examples of cognitive tasks.

Language and thought are a result of cognitive development. These two skills are closely related. Both are needed for planning, remembering, and problem solving. As children mature and gain experience with their world, these skills develop.

The th... social-em... areas are g... so interrela... social deve... on the other hand, involves feelings and

4-3

6

Understanding Two- and Three-Year-Olds

After studying this chapter, you will be able to

- describe the physical, cognitive, and social-emotional development of two-year-olds.
- explain how three-year-olds develop physically, cognitively, socially, and emotionally.
- relate how the development of two- and three-year-olds will affect your role as a teacher.

Objectives make students aware of the skills they are building as they read the topic.

New terms appear in boldface where they are defined.

Chapter Review features:

Summary

Two-year-olds grow and change in many ways. Their motor skills improve so they can run, jump, and balance. They can also scribble, drink, and undress. Children of this age are also learning to control their elimination.

Two-year-olds are able to understand and say many words. They can answer simple questions and follow simple directions. They are beginning to learn basic math concepts related to size, number, shape, and color.

Socially and emotionally, these children are striving to be independent. They want to do things their own way, and when they can't, they may have temper tantrums. These children still need affection and attention from adults.

Three-year-olds grow out of many of the problems of two-year-olds. They have better muscle control and coordination. Children of this age can draw, cut with scissors, and work simple puzzles. They can dress themselves without much help from adults.

The thinking abilities of three-year-olds is improving. These children have a growing understanding and use of language. They have a better understanding of questions and instructions. They are using more complex sentences to communicate. They are beginning to learn grammar rules for past tense. At this age, children are also developing more refined concepts of number and size.

Socially, three-year-olds are beginning to reach out. They seek and favor adults, and they are starting to make friends with other children. These children have strong emotions, but they are learning appropriate ways to express these emotions.

Review and Reflect

1. List three motor skills of two-year-olds.

2. True or false. Most two-year-olds can dress themselves without help from adults.

3. Language comprehension is _____ advanced than expressive language in two-year-olds.

4. Compare the language strategies of expansion and feeding-in.

5. Which sentence is typical of a two-year-old?
   A. "Mommy."
   B. "Mommy go."
   C. "Mommy go and I go too."
   D. "Is Mommy going?"

6. How do most two-year-olds express their anger?

7. When working with two-year-olds, why do you need to allow plenty of time for transitions between activities?

8. True or false. Three-year-olds can climb and descend stairs easily.

9. Describe two self-help skills of three-year-olds.

10. Most three-year-old children can count to _____ while pointing to corresponding objects.

11. Why are three-year-olds less likely to become angry than two-year-olds?

Apply and Explore

1. Design a toy, activity, or teaching aid to help improve the self-help skills of a two- or three-year-old.

2. Interview a child care teacher about the differences in expression of emotions between two-year-olds and three-year-olds.

3. Visit a children's library and find books designed to help young children express their feelings in positive ways. Write a report on one of these books.

Cross-Curricular Link

Writing

1. Visit a child care center and observe the motor skills of two- and three-year-olds. Write a report comparing the motor skills of the two age groups based on your observations.

Technology

2. Visit the Web site for the National Network for Child Care (www.nncc.org) to review the development of two- and three-year-olds.

3. Review the developmental milestones for preschool children at the Web site for Early Childhood Development (www.ecdgroup.com).

Workplace Link

Construct a book, doll, or activity board that contains buttons and buttonholes, zippers, shoelaces and eyelets, snaps, buckles, and hook-and-loop closures. These can be made using recycled clothing. You might want to look at equipment catalogs for early childhood programs for ideas. Demonstrate the project for three-year-olds and observe how they practice these self-help skills.

Summary highlights major chapter concepts.

Review and Reflect questions help students recall important information.

Apply and Explore questions engage the higher-level thinking skills of analysis, synthesis, and evaluation.

Cross-Curricular Link activities aim to strengthen students' performance in core academic subjects. The activities also stress the relationship between these subjects and early childhood education.

Workplace Link activities prompt students to apply chapter material to a work setting. This helps them connect chapter material with real-life applications.

Teacher's Wraparound Edition

A wide variety of teaching ideas and techniques make it easy to offer stimulating discussion questions and activities!

Vocabulary—Reinforcement activities such as defining or comparing terms, using in sentences, or using the glossary.

Discuss—Questions to stimulate learning.

Reflect—Questions that apply content to the students' lives. Can be used for journaling.

Resource—Tells when to use related material from the *Student Activity Guide, Observation Guide,* or *Teacher's Resources.*

Activity—Reteaches and reinforces chapter concepts.

Enrich—Challenging activities that involve role-playing, research topics, and field trips.

Note—Additional statistics, facts, historical notes, quotes, and notes to the teacher.

Side-margin teaching aids provide ideas to help you introduce, reinforce, enhance, and extend learning.

Challenging chapter activities appear at the bottom of most pages.

Review and Reflect Answer Key—Answers to the chapter review questions are conveniently placed next to the questions in the side and bottom page margins.

Meeting Special Needs—Suggestions to reinforce learning among students with special needs and pose challenging activities for gifted students.

Putting Technology to Use—Ways to incorporate the Internet, computer software programs, and other types of technical equipment for learning.

Cross-Curricular Activity—Ideas to relate the chapter content to other curriculum areas, such as history, math, science, language arts, and social studies.

Workplace Connection—Activities that help students connect chapter concepts to career opportunities, job skills, workplace issues, and career planning.

Portfolio Project—Creative ideas for work samples and documents to submit during college program interviews or job interviews.

Teacher's Resources

Teacher's Resource Portfolio

 Child Development Principles and Theories

Objectives

After studying this chapter, the students will be able to

- describe the areas and principles of development.
- define *windows of opportunity* as related to brain development.
- summarize how theories about development can be used as practical guides to early care and education.
- contrast the developmental theories of Erikson, Piaget, Vygotsky, and Gardner.

Teaching Materials

Text, pages 68–87
Terms to Know
Review and Reflect
Apply and Explore
Cross-Curricular Link
Workplace Link

Student Activity Guide
- A. *Understanding Development*
- B. *Erikson's Psychosocial Theory*
- C. *Dialing for Answers to Piaget's Theory*
- D. *Applying Multiple Intelligence Theory*
- E. *Check Your Theory IQ*

Teacher's Resources
Characteristics of Development, transparency master 4-1
Brain Research Tells Us…, transparency master 4-2
Applying Piaget's Theory of Cognitive Development, transparency master 4 -3
Gardner's Multiple Intelligences, reproducible master 4-4
Chapter Test

The Observation Guide
Mastering CDA Competencies

Introductory Activities

1. Have the students discuss the meaning of the term *development*. Students should try to explain how and why the term is used to describe the growth of children.

Instructional Concepts and Student Learning Experiences

Child Development

2. Have the students explain the differences among the areas of development.
3. *Understanding Development,* Activity A, SAG. Have the student identify the correct term to complete each of the statements.
4. Have the students explain the following concepts in their own words: *cephalocaudal principle, proximodistal principle,* and *maturation.*
5. *Characteristics of Development,* transparency master 4-1, TR. Use the master to review and discuss the characteristics of development with the class.

Brain Development

6. Discuss with students why both nature and nurture are critical to brain development.
7. *Brain Research Tells Us…,* transparency master 4-2, TR. Review the master and have students describe the ideal environment for a young child.
8. Have the students discuss types of overstimulation that might produce high levels of cortisol.
9. Have the students explain how warm, nurturing, consistent, and responsive care causes positive changes in the brain.
10. Have the students describe the type of caregiver needed to promote emotional control.

The **three-ring binder** makes it easy to add your own materials to each chapter. The portfolio has a Velcro closure and a handle, making it easy to transport.

National Standards Correlation Chart indicates where topics related to the National Standards for Early Childhood, Education, and Services are covered in the text.

Scope and Sequence Chart identifies major concepts presented in each chapter of the text.

Instructional Concepts and Student Learning Experiences for each major concept include diverse experiences—debates, field trips, and speaker presentations. Many activities promote critical thinking, problem solving, and decision-making skills.

Transparency Master 10-6A

Playground Equipment Dangers

Pinch-Crush Parts
Moving parts, particularly on gliders and seesaws, can pinch or crush fingers.

S-Rings
Open-ended hooks, especially on swings, which can catch ski ing, should be avoided. If a se hooks, pinch the ends in tightly of pliers.

Rings
Swinging exercise rings with a diameter between 5 and 10 inches can entrap a child's head. Remove such rings and discard them where children will not find and play with them.

Hard, Heavy Swing Sea
Hard, heavy swing seats can st gerous blow. Choose a set with l seats or purchase such seats sepa replace the hard seats. Metal se have smooth, rolled edges.

Source: U.S. consumer Product

Copyright Goodheart-Willcox Co., Inc.
Permission granted to reproduce for educational use only.

Working with You

Transparency or reproducible masters include student handouts, blackline transparencies, and chapter test masters.

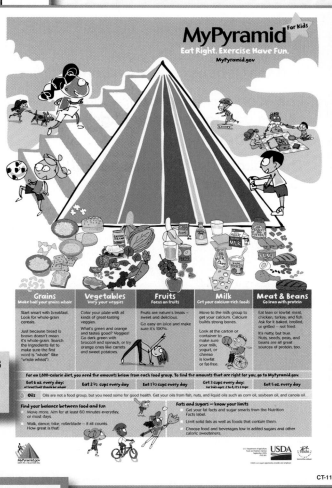

CT-11

A set of ready-to-use **color transparencies** presents chapter concepts visually to stimulate classroom discussion.

The Teacher's Resource Guide

A bound version of the *Teacher's Resource Portfolio* includes all the materials in the portfolio except the color transparencies.

Some teachers like to keep a copy of the *Teacher's Resource Guide* at home and a copy of the *Teacher's Resource Portfolio* at school.

Technology Resources for *Working with Young Children*

Teacher's Resource CD

This exciting ancillary puts all the contents of the *Teacher's Resource Portfolio* and the *Teacher's Wraparound Edition* on one CD-ROM!

The *Working with Young Children Teacher's Resource Portfolio* in PDF format allows you to see each page exactly as it appears in the *Portfolio* and print it from your computer.

The *Teacher's Wraparound Edition* also can be viewed in its entirety in PDF format on the TRCD

Transparencies in PowerPoint®. All the color and blackline transparencies from the Teacher's Resource Portfolio are presented as PowerPoint presentations and listed by chapter.

Lesson Plans. Quickly prepare customized daily lesson plans using our click-and-print format. Begin with publisher-prepared resources and add your own time-tested resources. Lesson plans can be saved and modified using Microsoft Word.

Related Web Sites. A direct Internet link is provided for numerous content-related Web sites.

Teacher's Resource CD

Working with Young Children

Judy Herr

- Teacher's Wraparound Edition
- Teacher's Resource Portfolio
- Lesson Plans
- Transparencies in PowerPoint®

ExamView® Assessment Suite.

This software suite includes the Test Generator, Test Player, and Test Manager.

- *Test Generator* easily creates and prints tests and answer keys.
- The database includes all the questions from chapter tests in the *Teacher's Resources* plus 25 percent additional questions for more complete coverage of chapter concepts.
- Choose specific questions to make customized tests or generate a test with randomly selected questions.
- Add your own questions to meet your classroom's needs.
- Generate different versions of the same test for different class periods.
- *Test Player* enables you to deliver tests on a local area network (LAN)
- *Test Manager* allows you to keep track of student's test scores and print reports.

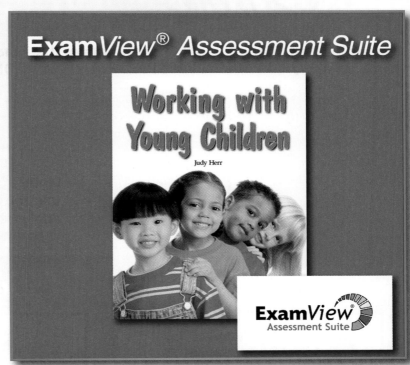

Teacher's PowerPoint® Presentations CD in English and Spanish

Includes objectives, definitions of new terms, discussion questions, and critical thinking strategies.

Present each chapter entirely in English, entirely in Spanish, or with alternating English/Spanish slides.

The Student Activity Guide

Some activities further develop the concepts presented in the text.

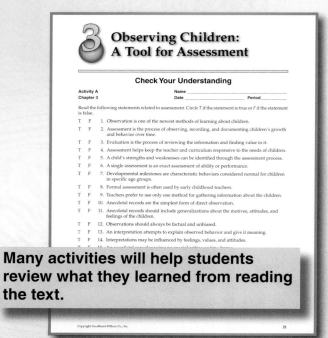

Rating Play Dough

Activity E
Chapter 10

Name _____
Date _____   Period _____

...pes included in the text: refrigerator play dough, sawdust play ...k them according to the criteria listed. Use a scale of 1 to 3 with 1 ...s for each play dough. The play dough with the lowest rating has

	Stickiness	Softness	Odor	Texture	Visual Appeal	Keeping Quality	Total Score
Refrigerator Play Dough General Reaction:							
Sawdust Play Dough General Reaction:							
Cooked Play Dough General Reaction:							

Which play dough would you prefer to use in the classroom and ...

106 *Working with Young Children Student Activity Guide*   Copyright Goodheart-Willcox Co., Inc.

Many activities require students to use the higher-order thinking skills of analysis, synthesis, and evaluation.

---

3 Observing Children: A Tool for Assessment

Check Your Understanding

Activity A
Chapter 3

Name _____
Date _____   Period _____

Read the following statements related to assessment. Circle *T* if the statement is true or *F* if the statement is false.

T F 1. Observation is one of the newest methods of learning about children.
T F 2. Assessment is the process of observing, recording, and documenting children's growth and behavior over time.
T F 3. Evaluation is the process of reviewing the information and finding value in it.
T F 4. Assessment helps keep the teacher and curriculum responsive to the needs of children.
T F 5. A child's strengths and weaknesses can be identified through the assessment process.
T F 6. A single assessment is an exact assessment of ability or performance.
T F 7. Developmental milestones are characteristic behaviors considered normal for children in specific age groups.
T F 8. Formal assessment is often used by early childhood teachers.
T F 9. Teachers prefer to use only one method for gathering information about the children.
T F 10. Anecdotal records are the simplest form of direct observation.
T F 11. Anecdotal records should include generalizations about the motives, attitudes, and feelings of the children.
T F 12. Observations should always be factual and unbiased.
T F 13. An interpretation attempts to explain observed behavior and give it meaning.
T F 14. Interpretations may be influenced by feelings, values, and attitudes.
T F 15. An anecdotal record requires no special setting or time frame.

Many activities will help students review what they learned from reading the text.

Copyright Goodheart-Willcox Co., Inc.   21

Managing Conflicts

Activity C
Chapter 17

Name _____
Date _____   Period _____

Read each of the following situations. Then work in small groups to discuss them. Write a suggestion for solving each of the conflicts in a positive way.

1. Four-year-old Shyrell refuses to take off her coat. When she arrived at school, she went directly to the art area, picked up a paintbrush, and began to paint. How could you handle this situation?
_____
_____
_____

2. Luis had a birthday last week. He is now four years old. He still depends on the teacher to help him put on his outdoor clothing. Will this cause Luis to become more dependent or more independent? What advice do you have for the teacher?
_____
_____
_____

3. Blanca does not appear to have an interest in food. Every day her teacher reminds her to eat during mealtime. Blanca does not seem to take the teacher's advice. Sometimes the teacher even tries to feed Blanca, but this does not appear to be effective. What advice do you have for Blanca's teacher?
_____
_____
_____

4. All children are expected to remain at the table until everyone is finished eating. However, Andi usually leaves the table before her peers have finished. So far her teacher has been ignoring this behavior. How may Andi's behavior affect the other children? What actions should Andi's teacher take?
_____
_____
_____

Students may be asked to present their own ideas, opinions, evaluations, and conclusions.

94 *Working with Young Children Student Activity Guide*   Copyright Goodheart-Willcox Co., Inc.

Observation Guide

Includes forms for:
Observing • Planning • Evaluating

Observing Developmental Characteristics of Five-Year-Olds

Activity D
Chapter 7

Name _____
Date _____ Period _____

• **Objectives**
After completing this activity, you will be able to
- identify gross-motor, fine-motor, self-help, social, and language skills of a five-year-old child.
- report specific information about the observation setting.

• **Preparation**
1. Make arrangements to observe a five-year-old child. (More than one visit may be needed to complete the activity.)
2. Review the skills on the following chart.

• **Setting**
Place _____
Address _____
Telephone number _____
Contact person _____ Title _____
Date(s) _____ Time(s) _____ to _____
_____
_____
Child's name _____ Birthdate _____
Description of observational setting _____

Other information _____

Attempts to jump rope.

(Continued)

Copyright Goodheart-Willcox Co., Inc.   Understanding Four- and Five-Year-Olds   77

Observing Developmental Characteristics of Five-Year-Olds (cont.)   Name _____

Gross-Motor Skills	Date Observed
Attempts to skate.	
Walks forward, backward, and sideways on balance beam.	
Uses hands to catch ball.	
Fine-Motor Skills	
Copies a triangle.	
Prints first name.	
Prints simple words.	
Dials telephone numbers correctly.	
Models objects with clay.	
Colors within lines.	
Draws recognizable people, houses, and vehicles.	
Self-Help Skills	
Dresses and undresses without assistance.	
Washes self.	
Puts shoes on correct feet.	
Unbuttons back buttons.	
Language Skills	
Uses third person irregular verbs. (*He has a ball.*)	
Uses compound sentences. (*I went to the grocery store and I went to my grandmother's house.*)	
Uses descriptions in telling a story.	
Uses some pronouns correctly.	
Uses words to describe sizes, distances, weather, time, and location.	
Asks the meaning of words.	

78   *Working with Young Children Observation Guide*   Copyright Goodheart-Willcox Co., Inc.

Helps students become familiar with observation and recording techniques.

Observation activities include objectives, preparation steps, setting, "To Do" instructions, and "To Review" questions.

Planning a Math Activity

Activity E
Chapter 23

Name _____
Date _____ Peri

• **Objectives**
After completing this activity, you will be able to
- plan a math activity.
- develop a lesson plan for the activity.
- introduce the activity to a group of children.
- evaluate the activity.

• **Preparation**
1. Make arrangements to present a math activity in an early childhood center.
2. Find out the number and ages of children with whom you will be working.
3. Review the chapter material on math activities.
4. Review the sample lesson plan and evaluation in Chapter 18.
5. Think of an appropriate math activity that you could introduce to the children.

• **Setting**
Place _____
Address _____
Telephone number _____
Contact person _____ Title _____

I. The Lesson Plan
Name of Activity _____
Time Scheduled _____
Classroom Area _____

Copyright Goodheart-Willcox Co., Inc.   Guiding Math

Planning a Math Activity (cont.)   Name _____

Goals (This is the purpose of the activity. What skills and knowledge will the childre

Introduction (This should include how the children's attention is gained. What will

Procedures (List what is said and done step-by-step.)

ll be ended.)

Materials (What equipment and/or supplies are needed to carry out the activity?)

220   *Working with Young Children Observation Guide*

Planning a Math Activity (cont.)   Name _____

II. Evaluation of the Activity
A. Is the content worth knowing? Justify your response.

B. Was it developmentally appropriate? Explain.

C. Was it interesting to the children? How do you know?

D. Did the activity include opportunities for the children to test their knowledge? Explain.

III. The Children's Responses
A. Did all the children reach the objective(s)? If not, why?

B. Were there behavior problems? If so, what do you think might have caused them?

IV. The Teacher Strategies
A. Were you well organized? Explain.

In later chapters, students plan and conduct their own classroom activities with the children.

Self-evaluation of the student's classroom activity is an important part of the process.

Mastering CDA Competencies Using *Working with Young Children*

Encourage the students in your program to obtain their Child Development Associate (CDA) Credential. The CDA program is a national effort to credential qualified caregivers who work with children from birth to age five. In order to receive the CDA Credential, applicants must complete a fieldwork requirement, attend 120 hours of formal course work, and then receive a final evaluation, which includes a Parent Opinion Questionnaire. Another option for receiving the Credential involves a written assessment and interview by a Council representative. Either way, the text *Working with Young Children* can aid in obtaining the CDA Credential.

The CDA *Competency Standards* define the skills needed by child care providers. Six statements of skill called Competency Goals establish the framework for caregiver behavior. These goals are divided into 13 Functional Areas. These are listed in the Introduction to *Mastering CDA Competencies,* followed by a list of related text chapters. The Functional Areas are further broken down into major tasks caregivers must accomplish to satisfy the Competency Goals. These are also listed in the Introduction to the book.

CDA Competency Goals and Functional Areas	Related Chapters in *Working with Young Children*
I. To establish and maintain a safe, healthy learning environment	9, 10, 11, 12, 13, 16, 17, 26, 29, 30, 31
1. **Safe:** Candidate provides a safe environment to prevent and reduce injuries.	11, 12, 16, 28, 29
2. **Healthy:** Candidate promotes good health and nutrition and provides an environment that contributes to the prevention of illness.	11, 12, 13, 17, 26, 29
3. **Learning Environment:** Candidate uses space, relationships, materials, and routines as resources for constructing an interesting, secure, and enjoyable environment that encourages play, exploration, and learning.	9, 10, 11, 12, 17, 29, 30, 31
II. To advance physical and intellectual competence	20, 21, 22, 23, 24, 25, 27, 28, 29, 30
4. **Physical:** Candidate provides a variety of equipment, activities, and opportunities to promote the physical development of children.	3, 5, 6, 7, 8, 17, 18, 19, 20, 21, 22, 27, 28, 29
5. **Cognitive:** Candidate provides activities and opportunities that encourage curiosity, exploration, and problem solving appropriate to the developmental levels and learning styles of children.	4, 5, 6, 7, 8, 17, 18, 19, 20, 21, 22, 23, 24, 25, 26, 27, 28, 29, 30
6. **Communication:** Candidate actively communicates with children and provides opportunities and support for children to understand, acquire, and use verbal and nonverbal means of communicating thoughts and feelings.	14, 15, 18, 19, 20, 21, 22, 24, 25, 26, 27, 28, 29, 30
7. **Creative:** Candidate provides opportunities that stimulate children to play with sound, rhythm, language, materials, space, and ideas in individual ways and to express their creative abilities.	18, 19, 20, 21, 27, 29, 30
III. To support social and emotional development and provide positive guidance	5, 6, 7, 8, 15, 17, 29, 30
8. **Self:** Candidate provides physical and emotional security for each child and helps each child to know, accept, and take pride in himself or herself and to develop a sense of independence.	1, 3, 4, 14, 16, 25, 29, 30
9. **Social:** Candidate helps each child feel accepted in the group, helps children learn to communicate and get along with others, and encourages feelings of empathy and mutual respect among children and adults.	3, 4, 5, 6, 7, 8, 14, 16, 18, 25, 28, 29, 30
10. **Guidance:** Candidate provides a supportive environment in which children can begin to learn and practice appropriate and acceptable behaviors as individuals and as a group.	4, 5, 8, 9, 14, 15, 16, 17, 29, 30
IV. To establish positive and productive relationships with families	26, 32
11. **Families:** Candidate maintains an open, friendly, and cooperative relationship with each child's family; encourages their involvement in the program; and supports the child's relationship with his or her family.	26, 32
V. To ensure a well-run, purposeful program responsive to participant needs	1, 3, 4, 18, 29, 30
12. **Program Management:** Candidate is a manager who uses all available resources to ensure an effective operation. The Candidate is a competent organizer, planner, record keeper, communicator, and a cooperative coworker.	1, 3, 4, 18, 29
VI. To maintain a commitment to professionalism	1, 2, 3, 4, 33
13. **Professionalism:** Candidate makes decisions based on knowledge of early childhood theories and practices; promotes quality in child care services; and takes advantage of opportunities to improve competence, both for personal and professional growth and for the benefit of children and families.	1, 2, 3, 4, 33

COMPETENCY GOAL I:
To establish and maintain a safe, healthy learning environment

	Pretraining Self-Assessment			Postraining Self-Assessment		
	Regularly	Sometimes	Never	Regularly	Sometimes	Never
1. Functional Area: Safe						
I keep both the inside of the center and the outdoor play area free of debris; structural hazards; unguarded space heaters; tools; and dangerous substances, such as medicine, cleaning products, matches, chipped paint, toxic plants, small objects, balloons, and plastic bags.						
I ensure that safety equipment, such as fire extinguishers and smoke detectors, is in place and operable and that someone knows how to use it.						
I maintain a current list of phone numbers for contacting parents and emergency services, such as poison control, fire company, and medical help.						
I use diagrams, pictures, and words that are easy for children and adults to understand. I post instructions and practice emergency procedures, including safety procedures for disabled children.						
I plan and practice monthly fire drills with children in my care.						
I check daily that outdoor equipment is safe for children and is in good repair.						
I respond immediately and sympathetically to a child's injury or fear of injury, and I encourage the same response by the children.						
I take safety precautions in a reassuring manner without overprotecting or making children fearful.						
I anticipate and plan to prevent potentially dangerous situations, such as leaving sleeping children unattended.						
I maintain first aid supplies—gauze, tape, syrup of ipecac, tweezers, scissors, and soap—and know basic first aid procedures appropriate for young children, such as how to handle choking and treat cuts.						
I use safe auto and bus travel procedures, including appropriate car seats for children.						
I discuss safety information with parents and tell them about resources, such as poison control centers.						
I supervise all children's indoor and outdoor activities.						
I know current information about safety standards for toys and equipment and share this information with parents and the center staff.						
I adapt the indoor and outdoor environments to enhance disabled children's independence.						
I require written parental authorization before allowing people other than parents to pick up children from the center.						
2. Functional Area: Healthy						
I conduct activities in a positive, relaxed, and pleasant atmosphere to reduce tension and stress.						
I wash my hands before and after helping children toilet, blow their noses, and before preparing food and eating.						
I attend to each child's physical needs, such as toileting, eating, exercising, and napping.						

(Continued)

Mastering CDA Competencies, designed for use with the text *Working with Young Children,* can help students earn their CDA Credential. Each chapter corresponds to a text chapter. The chapters begin by listing CDA Competency Goals and Functional Areas the reading and exercises address. Each chapter of *Mastering CDA Competencies* is divided into the following four parts:

Read from *Working with Young Children*

Review What You Have Read

Observe What You Have Learned

Apply What You Have Learned

Mastering CDA Competencies prepares students to become competent caregivers and will benefit anyone involved in training for the CDA program.

Introduction

Working with Young Children is an early childhood education text designed to make students competent early childhood caregivers and teachers.

Strategies for Successful Teaching

You can make the *Working with Young Children* subject matter exciting and relevant for your students by using a variety of teaching strategies. Many suggestions for planning classroom activities are given in the various teaching supplements that accompany this text. As you plan your lessons, you might also want to keep the following points in mind.

Helping Your Students Develop Critical Thinking Skills

As today's students leave their classrooms behind, they will face a world of complexity and change. They are likely to work in several career areas and hold many different jobs. Providing young people with a base of knowledge consisting only of facts, principles, and procedures will be doing them a disservice. They must, in addition, be prepared to solve complex problems, make difficult decisions, and assess ethical implications. In other words, students must be able to use critical thinking skills. These skills are often

referred to as the higher-order thinking skills. Benjamin Bloom listed these as

- analysis—breaking down material into its component parts so that its organizational structure may be understood;
- synthesis—putting parts together to form a new whole; and
- evaluation—judging the value of material for a given purpose.

In a broader perspective, students must be able to use reflective thinking in order to decide what to believe and do. According to Robert Ennis, students should be able to

- define and clarify problems, issues, conclusions, reasons, and assumptions;
- judge the credibility, relevance, and consistency of information; and
- infer or solve problems and draw reasonable conclusions.

Students have the right to be taught how to think critically—it cannot be an option. To think critically, one must have knowledge. However, critical thinking goes beyond memorizing or recalling information. Critical thinking cannot occur in a vacuum; it requires individuals to apply what they know about the subject matter. It requires students to use their common sense and experience. It may also involve controversy.

Critical thinking also requires *creative thinking* to construct all the reasonable alternatives, consequences, influencing factors, and supporting arguments. Unusual ideas are valued and perspectives outside the obvious are sought.

Finally, the teaching of critical thinking does not require exotic and highly unusual classroom approaches. Complex thought processes can be incorporated in the most ordinary and basic activities, even reading, writing, and listening, if these activities are carefully planned and skillfully executed.

Help your students develop their analytical and judgmental skills and to go beyond what they see on the surface. Rather than allowing students to blindly accept what they read or hear, encourage them to examine ideas in ways that show respect for others' opinions and different perspectives. Encourage students to think about points raised by others. Ask them to evaluate how new ideas relate to their attitudes about various subjects.

Debate is an excellent way to explore opposite sides of an issue. You may want to divide the class into two groups, each to take an opposing side of the issue. You can also ask students to work in smaller groups and explore opposing sides of different issues. Each group can select students from the group to present the points for their side.

Problem-Solving and Decision-Making Skills

An important aspect in the development of critical thinking skills is learning how to solve problems and make decisions. Some very important decisions lie ahead for your students, particularly those related to their future education and career choices.

Simulation games and role-plays allow students to practice solving problems and making decisions under nonthreatening circumstances. Role-playing allows students to examine others' feelings as well as their own. It can help them learn effective ways to react or cope when confronted with similar situations in real life.

Using Cooperative Learning

Because of the new emphasis on teamwork in the workplace, the use of cooperative learning groups in your classroom will give students an opportunity to practice teamwork skills. During cooperative learning, students learn interpersonal and small-group skills that will allow them to function as part of a team. These skills include leadership, decision making, trust building, communication, and conflict management.

When planning for cooperative learning, you will have a particular goal or task in mind. You will first specify the objectives for the lesson. Small groups of learners are matched for the purpose of completing the task or goal, and each person in the group is assigned a role. The success of the group is measured not only in terms of outcome, but also in terms of the successful performance of each member in his or her role.

In cooperative learning groups, students learn to work together toward a group goal. Each member is dependent on others for the outcome. This interdependence is a basic component of any cooperative learning group. Students understand one person cannot succeed unless everyone succeeds. The value of each group member is affirmed as learners work toward their goal.

The success of the group depends on individual performance. Groups should be mixed in terms of abilities and talents so there are opportunities for the students to learn from one another. Also, as groups work together over time, the roles should be rotated so everyone has an opportunity to practice and develop different skills.

You will also need to monitor the effectiveness of the groups, intervening as necessary to provide task assistance or help with interpersonal and group skills. Finally, evaluate students' achievement and help them discuss how well they collaborated with each other.

Helping Students Recognize and Value Diversity

Your students will be entering a rapidly changing workplace—not only in the area of technology, but also in the diverse nature of its workforce. Years ago, the workforce was dominated by white males, but 85 percent of the new entrants into the workforce at the start of this century are women, minorities, and immigrants. The workforce is also aging. Over half of the workforce will be people between the ages of 35 and 54. Because of these changes, young workers will need to be able to interact effectively with those who are different from themselves.

The appreciation and understanding of diversity is an ongoing process. The earlier and more frequently young people are exposed to diversity, the better able they will be to bridge cultural differences. If your students are exposed to different cultures within your classroom, they can begin the process of understanding cultural differences. This is the best preparation for success in a diverse society. In addition, teachers have found the following strategies to be helpful:

- Actively promote a spirit of openness, consideration, respect, and tolerance in your classroom.

- Use a variety of teaching styles and assessment strategies.

- Use cooperative learning activities whenever possible. Make sure group roles are rotated so everyone has leadership opportunities.

- When grouping students, make sure the composition of each group is as diverse as possible with regard to gender, race, and nationality. If the groups present information to the class, make sure all members have a speaking part.

- Make sure one group's opinions are not over-represented during class discussions. Seek opinions of under-represented persons/groups if necessary.

- If a student makes a sexist, racist, or other comment that is likely to be offensive, ask the student to rephrase the comment in a manner that will not offend other members of the class. Remind students that offensive statements and behavior are inappropriate in the workplace as well as the classroom.

- If a difficult classroom situation arises based on a diversity issue, ask for a time out and have everyone write down their thoughts and opinions about the incident. This allows everyone to cool down and allows you to plan a response.

- Arrange for guest speakers who represent diversity in gender, race, and ethnicity even though the topic does not relate to diversity.

- Have students change seats from time to time throughout the course, having them sit next to people they do not know well.

- Several times during the course, have students do anonymous evaluations of the class, asking them if there are any problems with which you are unaware.

Assessment Techniques

Various forms of assessment need to be used with students in order to evaluate their achievement. Written tests have traditionally been used to evaluate performance. This method of evaluation is good to use when assessing knowledge and comprehension. Other methods of assessment are preferable for measuring the achievement of the higher-level skills of application, analysis, synthesis, and evaluation.

Included in the *Working with Young Children Teacher's Resource Guide, Portfolio,* and *CD* are objective tests for each chapter in the text. The *Review and Reflect* sections in the text can be used to evaluate students' recall of key concepts. The activities suggested in *Apply and Explore, Cross-Curricular Link,* and *Workplace Link* will provide opportunities for you to assess your students' abilities to use critical thinking, problem solving, and application.

Performance Assessment

When you assign students some of the projects described in the text, a different form of assessing mastery or achievement is required. One method that teachers have successfully used is a rubric. A *rubric* consists of a set of criteria that includes specific descriptors or standards that can be used to arrive at performance scores for students. A point value is given for each set of descriptors, leading to a range of possible points to be assigned, usually from 1 to 5. The criteria can also be weighted. This method of assessment reduces the guesswork involved in grading, leading to fair and consistent scoring. The standards clearly indicate to students the various levels of mastery of a task. Students are even able to assess their own achievement based on the criteria.

When using rubrics, students should see the criteria at the beginning of the assignment. Then they can focus their effort on what needs to be done to reach a certain level of performance or quality of project. They have a clear understanding of your expectations of achievement.

Though you will want to design many of your own rubrics, several generic ones are included in the front section of the *Working with Young Children Teacher's Resource Guide, Teacher's Resource Portfolio,* and *Teacher's Resource CD.* These are designed to assess the following:

- Individual Participation
- Individual Reports
- Group Participation

These rubrics allow you to assess a student's performance and arrive at a performance score. Students can see what levels they have surpassed and what levels they can still strive to reach.

Portfolios

Another type of performance assessment that is frequently used by teachers today is the portfolio. A *portfolio* consists of a selection of materials that students choose to document their performance over a period of time. Students select their best work samples to showcase their achievement. These items might provide evidence of employability skills as well as academic skills. Some of the items students might include in portfolios are

- work samples (including photographs, videotapes, assessments, etc.) that show mastery of specific skills
- writing samples that show communication skills

- a resume
- letters of recommendation that document specific career-related skills
- certificates of completion
- awards and recognition

The portfolio is assembled at the culmination of a course to provide evidence of learning. A self-assessment summary report should be included that explains what has been accomplished, what has been learned, what strengths the student has gained, and any areas that need improvement. Portfolios may be presented to the class by the students. The items in the portfolio can also be discussed with the teacher in light of educational goals and outcomes. Portfolios should remain the property of students when they leave the course. They may be used for interviews with potential employers.

Portfolio assessment is only one of several evaluation methods teachers can use, but it is a powerful tool for both students and teachers. It encourages self-reflection and self-assessment of a more global nature. Traditional evaluation methods of tests, quizzes, and papers have their place in measuring the achievement of some course objectives, but other assessment tools should also be used to fairly assess the achievement of all desired outcomes.

Teaching the Learner with Special Needs

The students in your classroom will represent a wide range of ability levels and needs. Special needs students in your classes will require unique teaching strategies. The chart on the next page provides descriptions of several of the types of special needs students you may find in your classes, followed by some strategies and techniques to keep in mind as you work with these students. You will be asked to meet the needs of all your students in the same classroom setting. It is a challenge to adapt daily lessons to meet the demands of all your students.

	Learning Disabled*	Mentally Disabled*	Behaviorally Emotionally Disabled*
Description	Students with learning disabilities (LD) have neurological disorders that interfere with their ability to store, process, or produce information, creating a "gap" between ability and performance. These students are generally of average or above-average intelligence. Examples of learning disabilities or distractibility, spatial problems, and reading comprehension problems.	The mentally disabled student has subaverage general intellectual functioning that exists with deficits in adaptive behavior. These students are slower than others their age in using memory effectively, associating and classifying information, reasoning, and making judgments.	These students exhibit undesirable behaviors or emotions that may, over time, adversely affect educational performance. Their inability to learn cannot be explained by intellectual, social, or health factors. They may be inattentive, withdrawn, timid, restless, defiant, impatient, unhappy, fearful, and unreflective; lack initiative; have negative feelings and actions; and blame others.
Teaching Strategies	• Assist students in getting organized. • Give short oral directions. • Use drill exercises. • Give prompt cues during student performance. • Let students with poor writing skills use a computer. • Break assignments into small segments and assign only one segment at a time. • Demonstrate skills and have students model them. • Give prompt feedback. • Use continuous assessment to mark students' daily progress. • Prepare materials at varying levels of ability. • Shorten the number of items on exercises, tests, and quizzes. • Provide more hands-on activities.	• Use concrete examples to introduce concepts. • Make learning activities consistent. • Use repetition and drills spread over time. • Provide work folders for daily assignments. • Use behavior management techniques, such as behavior modification, in the area of adaptive behavior. • Encourage students to function independently. • Give students extra time to both ask and answer questions while giving hints to answers. • Avoid doing much walking around while talking to MD students as this is distracting for them. • Give simple directions and read them over with students. • Use objective test items and hands-on activities because students generally have poor writing skills and difficulty with sentence structure and spelling.	• Call students' names or ask them questions when you see their attention wandering. • Call on students randomly rather than in a predictable sequence. • Move around the room frequently. • Improve students' self-esteem by giving them tasks they can perform well, increasing the number of successful achievement experiences. • Decrease the length of time for each activity. • Use hands-on activities instead of using words and abstract symbols. • Decrease the size of the group so each student can actively participate. • Make verbal instructions clear, short, and to the point.

*We appreciate the assistance of Dr. Debra O. Parker, North Carolina Central University, with this section.

Academically Gifted	Limited English Proficiency	Physical Disabilities
Academically gifted students are capable of high performance as a result of general intellectual ability, specific academic aptitude, and/or creative or productive thinking. Such students have a vast fund of general knowledge and high levels of vocabulary, memory, abstract word knowledge, and abstract reasoning.	These students have a limited proficiency in the English language. English is generally their second language. Such students may be academically quite capable, but they lack the language skills needed to reason and comprehend abstract concepts.	Includes individuals who are orthopedically impaired, visually impaired, speech impaired, deaf, hard-of-hearing, hearing impaired, and health impaired (cystic fibrosis, epilepsy). Strategies will depend on the specific disability.
<ul><li>Provide ample opportunities for creative behavior.</li><li>Make assignments that call for original work, independent learning, critical thinking, problem solving, and experimentation.</li><li>Show appreciation for creative efforts.</li><li>Respect unusual questions, ideas, and solutions these students provide.</li><li>Encourage students to test their ideas.</li><li>Provide opportunities and give credit for self-initiated learning.</li><li>Avoid overly detailed supervision and too much reliance on prescribed curricula.</li><li>Allow time for reflection.</li><li>Resist immediate and constant evaluation. This causes students to be afraid to use their creativity.</li><li>Avoid comparisons with other students, which applies subtle pressure to conform.</li></ul>	<ul><li>Use a slow but natural rate of speech; speak clearly; use shorter sentences; repeat concepts in several ways.</li><li>Act out questions using gestures with hands, arms, and the whole body. Use demonstrations and pantomime. Ask questions that can be answered by a physical movement such as pointing, nodding, or manipulation of materials.</li><li>When possible, use pictures, photos, and charts.</li><li>Write key terms on the board. As they are used, point to them.</li><li>Corrections should be limited and appropriate. Do not correct grammar or usage errors in front of the class, causing embarrassment.</li><li>Give honest praise and positive feedback through your voice tones and visual articulation whenever possible.</li><li>Encourage students to use language to communicate, allowing them to use their native language to ask/answer questions when they are unable to do so in English.</li><li>Integrate students' cultural background into class discussions.</li><li>Use cooperative learning where students have opportunities to practice expressing ideas without risking language errors in front of the entire class.</li></ul>	<ul><li>For visually and hearing-impaired students, seat them near the front of the classroom. Speak clearly and say out loud what you are writing on the board.</li><li>In lab settings, in order to reduce the risk of injury, ask students about any conditions that could affect their ability to learn or perform.</li><li>Rearrange lab equipment or the classroom and make modifications as needed to accommodate any special need.</li><li>Investigate assistive technology devices that can improve students' functional capabilities.</li><li>Discuss solutions or modifications with the student who has experience with overcoming his or her disability and may have suggestions you may not have considered.</li><li>Let the student know when classroom modifications are being made and allow him or her to test them out before class.</li><li>Ask advice from special education teachers, the school nurse, or physical therapist.</li><li>Plan field trips that can include all students.</li></ul>

Using Other Resources

Much student learning in this class can be reinforced and expanded by exposing your students to a variety of viewpoints and teaching methods. Your providing guest speakers, panel presentations, field trip experiences, and access to media resources related to child care can greatly enhance student learning.

Current magazines and journals are good sources of articles on various aspects of early childhood education. Having copies in the classroom will encourage students to use them for research and ideas as they study early childhood education. Information can also be obtained from the Internet.

Publications

The Black Child Advocate
http://nbcdi.org

Child and Youth Quarterly
(212) 620-8000
http://springerlink.com

Child Development and Child Development Abstracts and Bibliography
(734) 926-0600
http://srcd.org

Child Health Alert
(781) 239-1762
www.childhealthalert.com

Childhood Education
http://acei.org/jour.htm

Children Today
http://catalog.gpo.gov

Child Welfare
http://cwla.org

Clearinghouse on Early Education and Parenting
http://ceep.crc.uiuc.edu/pubs.html

Developmental Psychology
http://apa.org/journals/dev

Dimensions of Early Childhood
http://southernearlychildhood.org/dimensions.html

Early Child Development and Care
www.tandf.co.uk/journals

Early Childhood News
www.earlychildhoodnews.com

Early Childhood Research Quarterly
(800) 424-2460
http://naeyc.org

Educational Leadership
(800) 933-ASCD
http://ascd.org

Educational Researcher
(202) 238-3200
http://aera.net

Education Resources Information Center (ERIC)
(800) LET-ERIC
http://eric.ed.gov

Exceptional Children
www.cec.sped.org

Gifted Child Quarterly
http://nagc.org

Head Start Policy Book—The White House
www.whitehouse.gov/infocus/earlychildhood

Instructor
http://scholastic.com/instructor

Journal of Family and Consumer Sciences
http://aafcs.org

Journal of Research in Childhood Education
http://acei.org/jrcehp.htm

Parent's Magazine
http://parents.com

Young Children
http://naeyc.org

Publications for School-Age Children

Cricket, Ladybug, and *Spider* magazines
http://cricketmag.com

Highlights for Children, Inc.
www.highlights.com

Ranger Rick and *Your Big Back Yard* magazines
http://nwf.org

Sesame Family Newsletter
(212) 595-3456
http://sesameworkshop.org

Stone Soup
http://stonesoup.com

Turtle and *Children's Digest* magazines
http://cbhi.org

Professional Organizations

Administration for Children and Families (ACF)
www.acf.hhs.gov

American Academy of Pediatrics
http://aap.org

American Association for Gifted Children—Duke University
(919) 783-6152
http://aagc.org

American Association of Family and Consumer Sciences
http://aafcs.org

American Association of School Administrators
http://aasa.org

American Council on Education (ACE)
www.acenet.edu

American Educational Research Association (AERA)
http://aera.net

American Federation of Teachers (AFT)
http://aft.org

American Foundation for the Blind
http://afb.org

American Medical Association
www.ama-assn.org

American Montessori Society Bulletin
http://amshq.org

American Public Health Association (APHA)
http://apha.org

American Society for Deaf Children
www.deafchildren.org

American Speech, Language and Hearing Association
http://asha.org

The Annie Casey Foundation
www.aecf.org

Appalachian Regional Commission
http://arc.gov

Association for Childhood Education International (ACEI)
http://acei.org

Association for Library Service to Children
http://ala.org/alsc

Association for Supervision and Curriculum Development (ASCD)
http://ascd.org

Association Montessori Internationale
http://montessori-ami.org

Bank Street College of Education
www.bnkst.edu

California Child Care Resource and Referral Network
http://rrnetwork.org

Center for Child Care Workforce
http://ccw.org

Center for Early Childhood Leadership
http://cecl.nl.edu

Center for Nutrition Policy and Promotion
www.cnpp.usda.gov

Center for Policy Alternatives
http://cfpa.org

Centers for Disease Control & Prevention
http://cdc.gov

Child Care Information Exchange
http://childcareexchange.com

Child Care in Health Care
www.childcareinhealthcare.org

Child Care Law Center
http://childcarelaw.org

Child Care Services Association
http://childcareservices.org

The Children's Book Council
http://cbcbooks.org

Children's Defense Fund
www.childrensdefense.org

Child Welfare League of America (CWLA)
http://cwla.org

Community Development Institute Head Start
http://cdiheadstart.org

Council for Exceptional Children
www.cec.sped.org

Council for Indian Education
http://cie-mt.org

Council for Professional Recognition
www.cdacouncil.org

Council of Chief State School Officers
www.ccsso.org

Director's Network, Child Care Information Exchange Press, Inc.
http://ccie.com

Division for Early Childhood
http://dec-sped.org

Early Childhood and Parenting (ECAP) Collaborative
(217) 333-1386
http://ecap.crc.uiuc.edu

Education Development Center (EDC)
http://edc.org

Families and Work Institute
(212) 465-2044
http://familiesandwork.org

The Feminist Press at the Graduate Center, CUNY
http://feministpress.org

Forum for Early Childhood Organization and Leadership Development
(800) 474-1170
http://bloch.umkc.edu/mwcnl/forum/forum.htm

The Foundation Center
http://fdncenter.org

Foundation for Child Development
http://fcd-us.org

Head Start—Johnson and Johnson Management Fellows Program
www.anderson.ucla.edu/x320.xml

High/Scope Educational Research Foundation
(734) 485-2000
http://highscope.org

Innovations in Early Education: The International Reggio Exchange
http://reggioalliance.org

International Child Resource Institute
http://icrichild.org

International Reading Association
http://reading.org

Jean Piaget Society
http://piaget.org

Kids and the Power of Work
http://kapow.org

Leadership Development Program—Bank Street College of Education
www.bnkst.edu

Learning Disabilities Association of America
http://ldaamerica.org

National After School Association
http://naaweb.org

National Association for Bilingual Education
http://nabe.org

National Association for Family Child Care
http://nafcc.org

National Association for Sick Child Daycare
http://nascd.com

National Association for the Education of Young Children (NAEYC)
http://naeyc.org

National Association of Child Care Professionals
http://naccp.org

National Association of Child Care Resource and Referral Agencies
www.naccrra.org

National Association of Elementary School Principals
http://naesp.org

National Association of State Boards of Education
http://nasbe.org

National Association of State Directors of Special Education (NASDSE)
http://nasdse.org

National Black Child Development Institute
http://nbcdi.org

National Center for Children in Poverty
http://nccp.org

National Child Care Association
http://nccanet.org

National Coalition for Campus Children's Centers
www.campuschildren.org

National Council of Jewish Women
http://ncjw.org

National Council on Family Relations
www.ncfr.org

National Down Syndrome Society
http://ndss.org

National Education Association
http://nea.org

National Food Service Management Institute (NFSMI)
http://olemiss.edu/depts/nfsmi

National Head Start Association
www.nhsa.org

National Institute of Child Health and Human Development
www.nichd.nih.gov

National Institute on Out-of-School Time
http://niost.org

National League of Cities
http://nlc.org

National PTA
www.pta.org

National Resource Center for Health and Safety in Child Care
http://nrc.uchsc.edu

National Science Teachers Association
www.nsta.org

National Women's Law Center
http://nwlc.org

North American Montessori Teachers Association (NAMTA)
www.montessori-namta.org

North Carolina Adult Education Association
http://rtpnet.org/~ncaea/

Office of Head Start—U.S. Department of Health and Human Services
www.acf.hhs.gov/programs/hsb/

Opportunity Finance Network
http://opportunityfinance.net

Organisation Mondiale pour L'Education Préscholaire (OMEP)
(World Organization for Early Childhood Education)
http://omep-ong.net

Parent Cooperative Preschools International—U.S. Office
http://preschools.coop

Parents Anonymous, Inc.
www.parentsanonymous.org

Prevent Child Abuse America
http://preventchildabuse.com

Puerto Rican Association for Community Affairs (ASPIRA)
http://aspira.org

Save the Children Federation
http://savethechildren.org

School-Age NOTES
http://schoolagenotes.com

Society for Research in Child Development
(734) 926-0600
http://srcd.org

Southern Early Childhood Association
http://southernearlychildhood.org/raising_intro.html

Southern Institute on Children and Families
www.kidsouth.org

Superintendent of Documents
www.gpoaccess.gov

Teaching Pre K-8
http://teachingk-8.com

Texas Child Care
www.dfps.state.tx.us/child_care

The Trust for Early Education
http://trustforearlyed.org

USA Child Care
http://usachildcare.org

USDA Communication and Governmental Affairs Office
www.usda.gov

U.S. Consumer Product Safety
http://cpsc.gov

U.S. Department of Agriculture
www.usda.gov

U.S. Department of Education
www.ed.gov

U.S. Department of Health and Human Services
http://hhs.gov

Work and Family Life Studies, Research Division
Bank Street College
www.bnkst.edu

Worthy Wage Campaign
National Center for the Early Childhood Work Force
http://ccw.org

Zero to Three
www.zerotothree.org

Integrating Academics

No matter what career path a student chooses, academic skills will be critical to his or her success. The *No Child Left Behind Act of 2001* brought to national attention the importance of reading and mathematics to academic and personal success. The Act also instituted a program of accountability testing, placing high stakes on student achievement in key areas. The *No Child Left Behind Act* lists the following as core academic subjects in high school: English, reading, language arts, math, science, foreign languages, civics and government, economics, arts, history, and geography.

Because achieving in these areas is so important, many career and technical education teachers are asked to incorporate academic standards into their curriculum. An early childhood course can support the core subjects by including subject matter from these areas as appropriate. Co-curricular projects with core subject teachers can also support students' growth and achievement in these areas.

The *Working with Young Children* program supports student growth and achievement in key academic areas in several ways. Some subjects are covered as background or supporting information to early childhood concepts (reading, language arts, math, science, social studies). Each chapter contains at least one *Cross-Curricular Link* activity to promote connection to academic areas. In addition, *Cross-Curricular Activities* are provided in the *Teacher's Wraparound Edition.*

Reading/English/Language Arts

The entire student text of *Working with Young Children* is designed to encourage reading and understanding. The *Teacher's Wraparound Edition* includes activities to strengthen students' vocabulary. There are also *Cross-Curricular Activity* annotations that strengthen reading and writing skills. The *Student Activity Guide* provides vocabulary activities for the chapters. Both the *Student Activity Guide* and *Teacher's Resources* have activities designed to develop skills in English/Language Arts.

Math

Mathematics is a tool necessary for success in business as well as in managing personal finances. Unfortunately, some of our high school students have not learned the basics of arithmetic and using numbers. *Cross-Curricular Link* activities in the text and *Cross-Curricular Activities* in the *Teacher's Wraparound Edition* strengthen these skills.

Art

Art is a key element of early childhood education. Many chapters in the text discuss the many art activities children can experience. In addition, early childhood teachers must be creative in the way they present classroom learning (for example, bulletin boards). The *Cross-Curricular Links* in the student text and the *Cross-Curricular Activities* in the *Teacher's Wraparound Edition* will reinforce these talents.

Social Studies—History, Psychology

Social Studies is an integral part of early childhood education. Psychology is especially important in reference to child development theorists. In addition, the teaching and promotion of all cultures is extremely important in a child care setting. Emphasis on these areas can be found throughout the text, as well as in *Cross-Curricular Links* in the text and *Cross-Curricular Activities* in the *Teacher's Wraparound Edition.* Appropriate activities may also be found in the *Teacher's Resources.*

Science

Science is all around us. The text activities *Cross-Curricular Link*, the *Teacher's Wraparound Edition* annotation *Cross-Curricular Activities*, and some *Teacher's Resources* activities provide science. Internet activities are provided at the end of each chapter in the student text. Mentions of science occur as appropriate in the student text.

Incorporating Career and Technical Student Organizations

Career and Technical Student Organizations (CTSOs) have been a vital part of career and technical education since 1918. Currently, the U.S. Department of Education recognizes several CTSOs.

CTSOs Officially Recognized by the U.S. Department of Education

Short Name	Full Name	Web Site
BPA	Business Professionals of America	www.bpa.org
DECA	DECA—An Association of Marketing Students	www.deca.org
FBLA/PBL	Future Business Leaders of America/Phi Beta Lambda	www.fbla-pbl.org
FCCLA	Family, Career and Community Leaders of America	www.fcclainc.org
FFA	National FFA Organization	www.ffa.org
HOSA	Health Occupations Students of America	www.hosa.org
SkillsUSA	Formerly VICA–Vocational Industrial Clubs of America	www.skillsusa.org
TSA	Technology Student Association	www.tsaweb.org

Federal career and technical education funds can be used to support activities of these CTSOs. Many states require that CTSOs be incorporated as a cocurricular activity in career and technical subjects. The CTSOs offer a wide variety of activities, which can be adapted to almost any school and classroom situation. A brief introduction to CTSOs follows. If you would like more details, visit their Web sites.

Purpose

The purpose of CTSOs is to assist students in acquiring knowledge and skills in career and technical areas as well as leadership skills and experience. These organizations achieve these goals by enlisting teacher-advisors to start chapters in their schools. Support for teacher-advisors and the chapters is often coordinated through each state Department of Education. The chapters elect officers and establish a program of work. This program of work can include a variety of activities, including community service, co-curricular projects, and competition preparation. Student achievement in specified areas is recognized with certificates and/or public acknowledgement through awards ceremonies. Competition is the most visible activity of CTSOs, but not the only one.

Competitive Events

Competitive events are a main feature of most CTSOs. The CTSO develops events that enable students to showcase the content they have learned and their decision-making, problem-solving, and leadership skills. The competitive events also give the winners the opportunity for public recognition of their achievements. Each CTSO has its own list of competitive events and activities. Members develop career and leadership skills even though they may not participate or win at the competitions.

FCCLA Star Events

Family, Career and Community Leaders of America (FCCLA) is a national student organization that helps students address personal, family, work, and societal issues through Family and Consumer Sciences Education. STAR Events (Students Taking Action with Recognition) are part of the FCCLA program. Participants may perform
- individually
- cooperatively (within a team)
- competitively (judged against established criteria)

The STAR Events are intended to promote achievement in areas of individual skills, leadership skills, and career preparation. These ideals correspond to the FCCLA mission of encouraging excellence in multiple roles (as a family member, wage earner, and community leader). Evaluators include members of business and industry, so participants may begin making future career network connections through their performance. Participants also gain experience in areas such as teamwork, communication, cooperation, critical thinking, and problem solving.

STAR Events that may be of interest to students in early childhood education include the following:

- Early Childhood—preparing a portfolio and resources, then planning and presenting an activity
- Focus on Children—planning and conducting a child development project
- Applied Technology—using technology to address a concern related to family and consumer sciences occupations
- Career Investigation—researching careers and setting career goals
- Chapter Service Project—executing a service project that contributes to families, schools, and communities
- Chapter Showcase—recognizing FCCLA chapters whose program promotes family and consumer sciences occupation skills in the community
- Entrepreneurship—preparing a plan for starting a small family and consumer sciences-related business
- Illustrated Talk—using visuals in an oral presentation on issues related to family and consumer sciences occupations
- Interpersonal Communications—strengthening communications with community, coworkers, family, or peers
- Job Interview—developing a portfolio, participating in a job interview, and showing an understanding of job requirements
- National Programs in Action—using the planning process to plan and implement a national program project
- Parliamentary Procedure—conducting an FCCLA business meeting using parliamentary procedure

National Standards for Family and Consumer Sciences Education

In 1998, the National Standards for Family and Consumer Sciences Education were written, and they were updated in 2008. This comprehensive guide provides family and consumer sciences educators with a structure for identifying what learners should be able to do. This structure is based on knowledge and skills needed for work life and family life, as well as family and consumer sciences careers. The National Standards Components include 16 areas of study, each with a comprehensive standard that describes the overall content of the area. Each comprehensive standard is then broken down into content standards that describe what is expected of the learner. Competencies further define the knowledge, skills, and practices of the content standards and provide the basis for measurement criteria.

By studying the text *Working with Young Children*, students will be prepared to master the competencies listed for the area of study called Early Childhood, Education, and Services. To help you see how this can be accomplished, a *Correlation of National Standards for Early Childhood, Education, and Services with Working with Young Children* has been included in the *Teacher's Wraparound Edition* and *Teacher's Resources* products. This chart appears at the end of this introduction. If you want to make sure you prepare students to meet the National Standards for Family and Consumer Sciences Education, this chart should interest you.

Scope and Sequence Chart

A *Scope and Sequence Chart*, located at the end of the introduction, identifies the major concepts presented in each chapter of the text. This special resource is provided to help you select for study those topics that meet your curriculum needs. Bold numbers indicate chapters in which concepts are found.

Marketing Your Program

Your class is likely to be the first early childhood education class some of your students have taken. Many students and their parents may have preconceived ideas about what this curriculum includes. You need to identify these preconceptions and, if necessary, gently alter them to give students and their parents a more accurate idea of what your class entails. You may need to make them aware of the value early childhood education classes hold for students at a variety of levels.

To get your public relations campaign started, create a newsletter to inform parents about what their children will be studying in your class. You can also use copies of these promotionally to encourage students to enroll in your class. Post copies of flyers around your school or pass them out to students. You might ask some of your former students what they feel they have gained from taking your class and add some of their ideas to the flyer. (If you decide to use direct quotations, be sure to get permission from your students.)

Students and their parents are not likely to be the only ones who are not totally aware of the importance of early childhood education classes. You can make people more aware through good public relations. It pays to make the student body, faculty, and community aware of your program. With good public relations, you can increase your enrollment, gain support from administrators and other teachers, and achieve recognition in the community. Following are some ways to market your program:

- Create visibility. It is important to let people know what is going on in your program. Ways to do this include announcements of projects and activities at faculty meetings and in school bulletins or newspapers, displays in school showcases or on bulletin boards, and articles and press releases in school and community newspapers. Talk up your program with administrators, other teachers, and students. Invite them to visit your classes.

- Interact with other subject matter areas. Early childhood education information is related to many fields of learning. You can strengthen your program and contribute to other disciplines by cooperating with other teachers. For example, you can work with a science teacher to present information on the scientific principles involved in cooking food. The teaching elements through this *Teacher's Wraparound Edition* include *Cross-Curricular Activities* in each chapter. These suggestions will help you coordinate the teaching of chapter material with other departments in your school that might be covering related information. The more interaction you can generate, the more you promote your class.

- Contribute to the education objectives of the school. If your school follows stated educational objectives and strives to strengthen specific skills, include these overall goals in your teaching. For example if students need special help in developing verbal or writing skills, select projects and assignments that will help them in these areas. Show administrators examples of work that indicate student improvement in needed skills.

- Serve as a resource center. Early childhood education information is of practical use and interest to almost everyone. You can sell your program by making your department a resources center of materials related to child care. Invite faculty members, students, and parents to tap into the wealth of information available in your classroom.

- Generate involvement and activity in the community. You are teaching concepts students can apply in their everyday life. You can involve students in community life and bring the community into your classroom through field trips, interviews with businesspeople and community leaders, surveys, and presentations from guest speakers. You may be able to set up cooperative projects between the school and community organizations around a variety of topics.

- Connect with parents. If you can get them involved, parents may be your best allies in teaching early childhood education classes. Let parents know when their children have done good work. Moms and dads have had experiences related to many of the issues you discuss in class. Call on them to share individually or as part of a panel addressing a specific topic. Parents can be a rich source of real-life experience. Keep them informed about classroom activities and invite them to participate as they are able.

- Establish a student sales staff. Enthusiastic students will be your best salespeople. Encourage them to tell their parents and friends what they are learning in your classes. You might create bulletin boards or write letters to parents that focus on what students are learning in your classes. Ask students to put together a newsletter

highlighting their experiences in your early childhood education class. Students could write a column from your department for the school paper.

Goodheart-Willcox Welcomes Your Comments

We welcome your comments and suggestions regarding *Working with Young Children* and its supplements. Please send any comments you may have to the editor by visiting our Web site at www.g-w.com or writing to

Editorial Department
Goodheart-Willcox Publisher
18604 West Creek Drive
Tinley Park, IL 60477-6243

Correlation of National Standards for

Early Childhood, Education, and Services

with

Working with Young Children

In planning your program, you may want to use the correlation chart below. This chart correlates the Family and Consumer Sciences Education National Standards with the content of *Working with Young Children*. It lists the competencies for each of the content standards for Early Childhood, Education, and Services. It also identifies the major text concepts that relate to each competency. Bold numbers indicate chapters in which concepts are found.

After studying the content of this text, students will be able to achieve the following comprehensive standard:

4.0 Integrate knowledge, skills, and practices required for careers in early childhood education and services.

Content Standard 4.1	
Analyze career paths within early childhood, education, and services.	
Competencies	**Text Concepts**
4.1.1 Explain the roles and functions of individuals engaged in early childhood, education, and services.	**1:** Social and economic changes; Career opportunities in early childhood; Other career opportunities; The teacher's responsibilities; Characteristics of successful teachers
	2: Family child care homes; Child care centers; Montessori schools; Head Start: Kindergarten; School-age child care; Parent cooperatives; Laboratory schools; High school child care programs; Universal pre-kindergarten; Center accreditation
	3: Assessment
	9: Organizing basic activity areas; Planning the playground
	10: Selection criteria; Using technology in the classroom; Selecting safe toys; Selecting playground equipment
	11: Safety objectives; Reporting child abuse; Protection education; Liability
	12: Meeting special nutritional needs; Planning meals and snacks; Serving meals
	13: Administering medications; Personal hygiene; Controlling foodborne illness; First aid; Caring for children who become ill
	14: Guidance and you; Preparing for guidance
	15: Communicating with families about stress; Helping children cope; Handling negativism, stealing, anger, biting, tattling, exploring the body, thumbsucking, and fear
	16: Establishing, enforcing, and communicating limits

(Continued)

Content Standard 4.1 (cont.)
Analyze career paths within early childhood, education, and services.

Competencies	Text Concepts
4.1.1 Explain the roles and functions of individuals engaged in early childhood, education, and services.	**17:** The daily schedule; Daily routines **18:** Developing program goals; Written plans **19:** Techniques for guiding art experiences **20:** Selecting books for children; Reading stories to children; Achieving variety in storytelling; Displaying books **21:** Socio-dramatic play; The teacher's role **22:** Techniques for encouraging writing **23:** Assessing math ability **24:** Planning science activities; Role of the teacher **25:** The teacher's role in social studies **26:** Working with parents **27:** The teacher's role; Building rhythm instruments; Teacher preparation; Teaching movements **28:** Selecting trips; Planning a field trip **29:** Characteristics of infant and toddler caregivers; Guidelines for infant and toddler care; Caring for infants and toddlers **30:** Characteristics of staff; Planning curriculum; Scheduling **31:** Teacher's roles; Identification; Teaching suggestions; Integrating children with special needs **32:** Parent-teacher conferences; Home visits; Volunteers **33:** Abilities; Values; Employee responsibilities
4.1.2 Analyze opportunities for employments and entrepreneurial endeavors.	**1:** Career opportunities in early childhood; Nannies and au pairs; Kindergarten teachers; Early childhood assistant and associate teachers; Child care teachers and directors; Family child care home; Licensing specialists; Other career opportunities **2:** Family child care homes; Child care centers; Montessori schools; Head Start: Kindergarten; School-age child care; Parent cooperatives; Laboratory schools; High school child care programs; Universal pre-kindergarten; Sponsorship of early childhood centers; Private sponsorship; Center accreditation **33:** Choosing a career; Résumés; Avenues for seeking employment; Preparing for an interview; The interview; Employee rights and responsibilities
4.1.3 Summarize education and training requirements and opportunities for career paths in early childhood, education, and services.	**1:** Education and training needed to work with young children; To continue to learn **2:** Center accreditation
4.1.4 Analyze the impact of early childhood, education, and services occupations on local, state, national, and global economics.	**1:** Social and economic changes; Changes in families; Changes in employers' attitudes; Benefits to the economy

(Continued)

Content Standard 4.1 (cont.)

Analyze career paths within early childhood, education, and services.

Competencies	Text Concepts
4.1.5 Create an employment portfolio for use with applying for internships and work-based learning opportunities in early childhood.	**3:** Portfolios **33:** Teaching portfolio
4.1.6 Analyze the role of professional organizations in early childhood.	**1:** To participate in professional organizations

Content Standard 4.2

Analyze developmentally appropriate practices to plan for early childhood, education, and services.

Competencies	Text Concepts
4.2.1 Analyze child development theories and their implications for educational and childcare practices.	**1:** To know how children grow and develop; To plan a developmentally appropriate curriculum **3:** Assessment; Formal and informal observation **4:** Child development; Brain development; Theories of development **5:** Physical development in the first two years; Cognitive development in the first two years; Social-emotional development in the first two years **21:** Stages of play; Stages of material use in play
4.2.2 Apply a variety of assessment methods to observe and interpret children's growth and development.	**3:** Assessment; Formal and informal observation; Choosing a method of assessment; Assessment tools; Anecdotal records; Checklists; Participation chart; Rating scales; Collecting samples of children's products; Using technology for assessment; Visual documentation; Portfolios; Guidelines for observing children **18:** Assessment: an important step in curriculum planning; Emergent curriculum **23:** Assessing math ability; Assessment by observation; Specific task assessment **30:** Assessing interests
4.2.3 Analyze cultural and environmental influences when assessing children's development.	**1:** Social and economic changes; Changes in families **3:** Assessment; Formal and informal observation; Anecdotal records **14:** Cultural variations **32:** Home visits
4.2.4 Analyze abilities and needs of children and their impact on children's growth and development.	**31:** Individualized Education Plans; Teacher's roles; Hearing disorders; Speech and language disorders; Vision disorders; Physical disabilities; Health disorders; Cognitive disabilities; Learning disabilities; Social or emotional impairment; Integrating children with special needs; Gifted children

(Continued)

Content Standard 4.2 (cont.)

Analyze developmentally appropriate practices to plan for early childhood, education, and services.

Competencies	Text Concepts
4.2.5 Analyze strategies that promote children's growth and development.	**6:** Teaching two-year-olds; Teaching three-year-olds **7:** Teaching four- and five-year-olds **14:** Techniques for effective guidance **16:** Establishing, enforcing, and communicating limits **19:** Techniques for guiding art experiences **20:** Reading stories to children; Displaying books **24:** Planning science activities; Role of the teacher; Care of the earth **25:** Importance of social studies **26:** First experiences; Eating habits **29:** Caring for infants and toddlers **30:** Planning curriculum; Assessing interests; Scheduling

Content Standard 4.3

Demonstrate integration of curriculum and instruction to meet children's developmental needs and interests.

Competencies	Text Concepts
4.3.1 Analyze a variety of curriculum and instructional models.	**18:** Developing program goals; The content and process-centered approach; Themes; Written plans **29:** Curriculum **30:** Program models
4.3.2 Implement learning activities in all curriculum areas that meet the developmental needs of children.	**1:** To plan a developmentally appropriate curriculum **18:** The content and process-centered curriculum; Factors to consider in curriculum planning **19:** Techniques for guiding art experiences; Painting activities; Molding; Cutting; Collages; Blockbuilding; Sensory experiences: sand and water play; Woodworking **20:** Selecting books for children; Reading stories to children; Achieving variety in storytelling; Displaying books **21:** Socio-dramatic play; Puppetry **22:** Prewriting skills; Building writing skills; Early experiences in writing **23:** Mathematical activities **24:** Planning science activities; Using senses, color, water, foods, child's own body, gardening, air, magnets, wheels, field trips, and animals to teach science concepts **26:** Cooking experiences **27:** A music center; Rhythm instruments; Music activities; Movement experiences; Movement activities **28:** First field trips; Selecting trips; Planning a field trip **29:** Infant environments; Toddler environments; Toys for infants and toddlers; Curriculum **30:** Planning curriculum; Scheduling

(Continued)

Content Standard 4.3 (cont.)

Demonstrate integration of curriculum and instruction to meet children's developmental needs and interests.

Competencies	Text Concepts
4.3.3 Implement an integrated curriculum that incorporates a child's language, learning styles, early experiences, and cultural values.	**10:** Selection criteria; Multicultural toys and materials **12:** Food preferences; Multicultural experiences **18:** Developing program goals; The content and process-centered curriculum; Factors to consider in curriculum planning; Emergent curriculum **20:** Selecting books for children **21:** Equipment and setup for socio-dramatic play; Puppetry **25:** Importance of social studies; The teacher's role in social studies; Multicultural concepts; Intergenerational concepts; Change concepts; Holiday concepts **27:** A music center **28:** Resource people; Planning a field trip **30:** Promote respect for cultural diversity; Mealtimes
4.3.4 Demonstrate a variety of teaching methods to meet individual needs of children.	**18:** The content and process-centered curriculum; Emergent curriculum **19:** Techniques for guiding art experiences; Painting activities; Molding; Cutting; Collages; Blockbuilding; Sensory experiences: sand and water play; Woodworking **20:** Reading stories to children; Achieving variety in storytelling **21:** Socio-dramatic play; Puppetry **22:** Manuscript writing systems; Building writing skills; Techniques for encouraging writing **23:** Mathematical activities **24:** Role of the teacher **27:** The teacher's role **28:** The importance of field trips; First field trips **30:** Planning curriculum; Assessing interests; Group planning sessions; Scheduling
4.3.5 Arrange learning centers that provide for children's exploration, discovery, and development.	**1:** To prepare the environment **9:** Organizing basic activity areas; Outdoor play environments **16:** Limits for specific areas and activities **19:** Art supplies and tools **20:** Selecting books for children; Displaying books **21:** Socio-dramatic play; Puppetry **22:** Space for writing **23:** Mathematical activities **24:** Planning science activities **26:** The "cooks" corner **27:** A music center **29:** Infant environments; Toddler environments; Toys for infants and toddlers **30:** Indoor space; Outdoor space

(Continued)

Content Standard 4.3 (cont.)

Demonstrate integration of curriculum and instruction to meet children's developmental needs and interests.

Competencies	Text Concepts
4.3.6 Establish activities, routines, and transitions.	**17:** The daily schedule; Daily routines; Transitions **19:** Painting activities; Blockbuilding; Sensory experiences: sand and water play **20:** Reading stories to children **21:** Socio-dramatic play; Puppetry **23:** Mathematical activities **24:** Planning science activities; Using senses, color, water, foods, child's own body, gardening, air, magnets, wheels, field trips, and animals to teach science concepts **27:** The teacher's role; Scheduling music; Music activities; Movement experiences; Movement activities **29:** Caring for infants and toddlers; Infant environments; Toddler environments **30:** Planning curriculum; Scheduling

Content Standard 4.4

Demonstrate a safe and healthy learning environment for children.

Competencies	Text Concepts
4.4.1 Manage physical space to maintain a learning environment that is safe and healthy and encourages physical activity.	**1:** To prepare the environment **9:** Value of planned space; Physical space; Factors that affect space organization **10:** Safe playgrounds **11:** Supervise the children at all times; Develop safety limits; Provide a safe environment **13:** Health policies **29:** Infant environments; Toddler environments; Toys for infants and toddlers; Safety issues **30:** The environment
4.4.2 Apply safe and healthy practices that comply with state regulations.	**9:** Isolation area; Bathrooms; Indoor environment; Licensing requirements; Outdoor play environments **10:** Selecting safe toys; Safe playgrounds; Selecting playground equipment **11:** Maintain minimum adult-child ratios; Playground equipment; Transportation; Fire drills and evacuation procedures; Reporting child abuse; Protection education; Liability; Privacy law **12:** Meeting special nutritional needs; Serving safe meals and snacks **13:** Healthy children; Objectives for guiding health; Health policies; Controlling foodborne illness; First aid; Wounds and their treatment; Burns and their treatment; Splinters; Insect stings; Choking; Oral hygiene; Dental emergencies; Head lice; Caring for children who become ill; Special health concerns **29:** Safety issues

(Continued)

Content Standard 4.4 (cont.)

Demonstrate a safe and healthy learning environment for children.

Competencies	Text Concepts
4.4.3 Implement strategies to teach children health, safety, and sanitation habits.	**8:** Health concerns **11:** Develop safety limits; Playground equipment; Fire drills and evacuation procedures; Sun safety; Weather or disaster emergencies; Protection education **13:** Controlling foodborne illness; Personal hygiene **17:** Eating; Napping; Toileting **26:** Nutrition concepts; Cooking experiences; Eating habits **29:** Feeding toddlers; Diapering and toileting
4.4.4 Plan healthy meals and snacks.	**12:** Nutrition; MyPyramid; Meeting special nutritional needs; Planning meals and snacks; Serving meals; Serving safe meals and snacks **13:** Controlling foodborne illness **26:** Eating habits; Setting the table **29:** Feeding infants; Feeding toddlers
4.4.5 Document symptoms of child abuse and neglect and use appropriate procedures to report suspected abuse or neglect to the designated authorities.	**11:** Neglect and abuse; Nonaccidental physical injury; Neglect; Emotional abuse; Sexual abuse; Reporting child abuse; Background checks; Protection education; Helping families
4.4.6 Implement basic health practices and prevention procedures regarding childhood illness and communicable diseases.	**13:** Healthy children; Objectives for guiding health; Health policies; Environmental control; Sanitizing and disinfecting; Controlling foodborne illness; Wounds and their treatment; Burns and their treatment; Splinters; Insect stings; Choking; Oral hygiene; Dental emergencies; Head lice; Caring for children who become ill; Temperature emergency; Special health concerns **29:** Diapering and toileting; Maintaining the environment to prevent illness

Content Standard 4.5

Demonstrate techniques for positive collaborative relationships with children.

Competencies	Text Concepts
4.5.1 Establish developmentally appropriate guidelines for behavior.	**14:** Guidance and you; Preparing for guidance; Direct guidance; Indirect guidance; Techniques for effective guidance **15:** Causes of behavioral problems; Specific problem behaviors; Handling negativism, stealing, anger, biting, tattling, exploring the body, thumbsucking, and fear **16:** Establishing limits; Enforcing limits; Limits for specific areas and activities; Communicating limits
4.5.2 Demonstrate problem-solving skills with children.	**11:** Develop safety limits **14:** Techniques for effective guidance; Promoting a positive self-concept **15:** Stress; Helping children cope; Handling negativism, stealing, anger, biting, tattling, exploring the body, thumbsucking, and fear **21:** Puppetry; "Me" puppets

(Continued)

Content Standard 4.5 (cont.)

Demonstrate techniques for positive collaborative relationships with children.

Competencies	Text Concepts
4.5.3 Demonstrate interpersonal skills that promote positive and productive relationships with children.	**1:** Characteristics of successful teachers **14:** Techniques for effective guidance; Promoting a positive self-concept **16:** Communicating limits **21:** Puppetry **24:** Role of the teacher **25:** Multicultural concepts **29:** Caring for infants and toddlers **33:** Positive attitude; Confidentiality
4.5.4 Implement strategies for constructive and supportive interactions between children and families.	**2:** Head Start; Parental involvement; Parent cooperatives; Sponsorship of early childhood centers; Selecting a child care program **13:** Contacting parents **25:** Multicultural concepts; Intergenerational concepts **26:** Working with parents **28:** Resource people; Adult-child ratios; Parent preparation **29:** Parent involvement; Record keeping **32:** Objectives for parent involvement; Written communication; Class videos; Home visits; Parent-teacher conferences; Discussion groups; Other methods of involvement; Volunteers
4.5.5 Analyze children's developmental progress and summarize developmental issues and concerns.	**3:** Assessment; Formal and informal observation; Choosing a method of assessment; Assessment tools; Anecdotal records; Checklists; Participation chart; Rating scales; Collecting samples of children's products; Using technology for assessment; Visual documentation; Portfolios; Guidelines for observing children **31:** Individualized Education Plans; Teacher's roles

Content Standard 4.6

Demonstrate professional practices and standards related to working with young children.

Competencies	Text Concepts
4.6.1 Utilize opportunities for continuing training and education.	**1:** Education and training needed to work with young children; The teacher's responsibilities; To participate in professional organizations; To continue to learn
4.6.2 Apply professional ethical standards as accepted by the recognized professional organizations.	**1:** The teacher's responsibilities; To communicate effectively; To demonstrate teamwork; To follow ethical standards; Characteristics of successful teachers **2:** Center accreditation **3:** Assessment; Assessment tools; Anecdotal records; Guidelines for observing children **30:** Accreditation and standards **33:** Employee rights and responsibilities; Confidentiality

(Continued)

Content Standard 4.6 (cont)	
Demonstrate professional practices and standards related to working with young children.	
Competencies	**Text Concepts**
4.6.3 Implement federal, state, and local standards, policies, regulations, and laws which impact children, families, and programs.	**1:** Licensing specialists **2:** Child care centers; Head Start; Sponsorship of early childhood centers; Center accreditation **9:** Isolation area; Bathrooms; Indoor environment; Licensing requirements; Outdoor play environment **10:** Selecting safe toys; Safe playgrounds **11:** Reporting child abuse; Liability; Privacy law **12:** Serving meals **13:** Health policies; Caring for children who become ill **30:** Adult-child ratios **33:** Legal problems in interviewing; Employee rights and responsibilities
4.6.4 Demonstrate enthusiasm, initiative, and commitment to program goals and improvements.	**1:** Characteristics of successful teachers **9:** Program goals **18:** Developing program goals **30:** Characteristics of staff **33:** Positive attitude
4.6.5 Apply business management skills to planning businesses in early childhood, education, and services.	**1:** The teacher's responsibilities; To manage time wisely **2:** Center accreditation **10:** Selection criteria; Budget **11:** Forms **18:** Developing program goals; Who plans the curriculum **33:** Employee rights and responsibilities; Attendance and Punctuality; Professional appearance; Confidentiality

Scope and Sequence

In planning your program, you may want to use the *Scope and Sequence Chart*. This chart identifies the major concepts presented in each chapter of the text. Refer to the chart to find the material that meets your curriculum needs. Bold numbers indicate chapters in which concepts are found.

Part 1   The Children and You

Careers and Professionalism
1: Social and economic changes; Career opportunities in early childhood; Education and training needed to work with young children; Teacher's responsibilities; Characteristics of successful teachers
2: Family child care homes; Child care centers; Montessori schools; Head Start; Kindergarten; School-age child care; Parent cooperatives; Laboratory schools; High school child care programs; Universal pre-kindergarten

Child Growth and Development
3: Assessment; Assessment tools; Using technology for assessment; Portfolios; Guidelines for observing children
4: Child development; Brain development; Theories of development
5: Physical, cognitive, and social-emotional development in the first two years
6: Physical, cognitive, and social-emotional development of two-year-olds; Physical, cognitive, and social-emotional development of three-year-olds
7: Physical, cognitive, and social-emotional development of four- and five-year-olds
8: Physical, cognitive, social-emotional, and moral development of school-age children

Curriculum Development
3: Assessment; Assessment tools; Using technology for assessment; Portfolios; Guidelines for observing children

Guidance and Discipline
6: Teaching two-year-olds; Teaching three-year-olds
7: Teaching four- and five-year olds

Health, Safety, and Nutrition
8:   Health concerns

Parent/Teacher and Community Relationships
2:   Parent cooperatives; Sponsorship of early childhood centers; Selecting a child care program

Part 2   Creating a Safe and Healthful Environment

Health, Safety, and Nutrition
10:   Selecting safe toys; Safe playgrounds; Selecting playground equipment
11:   Safety objectives; Neglect and abuse; Liability
12:   Nutrition; Meeting special nutritional needs; Planning meals and snacks; Serving meals
13:   Healthy children; Objectives for guiding health; Health policies; Controlling foodborne illness; First aid; Caring for children who become ill; Special health concerns

Physical Space and Equipment
9:   Value of planned space; Physical space; Furniture; Color choices for child care centers; Factors that affect space organization; Organizing basic activity areas; Outdoor play environments
10:   Selection criteria; Using technology in the classroom; Selecting safe toys; Safe playgrounds; Selecting playground equipment; Sources for toys and equipment

Part 3   Guiding Children

Guidance and Discipline
14:   Goals of guidance; Guidance and you; Preparing for guidance; Direct and indirect guidance; Techniques for effective guidance
15:   Causes of behavioral problems; Stress; Specific problem behaviors
16:   Establishing and enforcing limits; Limits for specific areas and activities; Communicating limits
17:   Daily schedules and routines; Transitions

Health, Safety, and Nutrition
17:   Dressing and undressing; Eating, Napping; Toileting; Cleanup

Social-Emotional Development
14:   Promoting a positive self-concept

Part 4 Learning Experiences for Children

Cognitive Development
19: Stages of art skill development; Painting activities; Molding; Collages; Sensory experiences: sand and water play
21: Stages of play; Stages of material use in play
22: Early experiences in writing
23: Mathematical activities
24: Developing the child's understanding of senses
26: Cooking experiences; Setting the table
27: Music activities

Curriculum Development
18: Developing program goals; Responsibility for curriculum; Assessment in curriculum planning; Content and process-centered curriculum; Factors to consider in curriculum planning; Emergent curriculum; Themes; Written plans
21: Scheduling socio-dramatic play
22: Objectives for writing
23: Goals of early math experiences; Assessing math ability
24: Planning science activities
25: Importance of social studies; Develop the curriculum
27: Benefits of music experiences; Scheduling music
28: The importance of field trips; Selecting trips; Planning a field trip

Guidance and Discipline
19: Techniques for guiding art experiences
20: Importance of storytelling; Handling interruptions
21: Teacher's role in guiding socio-dramatic play
23: Assessing math ability
24: Teacher's role in guiding science activities
25: Teacher's role in social studies
27: Teacher's role in music
28: First field trips; Behavioral expectations

Health, Safety, and Nutrition
26: Nutrition concepts; Eating habits

Parent/Teacher and Community Relationships
25: Multicultural concepts; Intergenerational concepts; Community concepts
26: Working with parents
28: Adult-child ratio; Parent preparation

Physical Development

19: Stages of art skill development; Molding; Cutting; Collages; Blockbuilding; Sensory experiences: sand and water play; Woodworking
21: Stages of play; Stages of material use in play
22: Prewriting skills; Building writing skills
24: Developing the child's understanding of the senses
27: Movement experiences and activities

Physical Space and Equipment

19: Art supplies and tools; Displaying children's work
20: Books as a source of stories; Selecting books for children; Displaying books
21: Equipment for socio-dramatic play
22: Manuscript writing systems; Graphic writing tools; Space for writing; Documentation boards
23: Math equipment
24: Science equipment
27: A music center; Rhythm instruments

Social-Emotional Development

20: Selecting stories for children; Reading stories to children; Achieving variety in storytelling
21: Socio-dramatic play; Puppetry
25: Building social studies concepts; Democracy concepts; Ecology, change, geography, community, current events, and holiday concepts; Classroom celebrations
26: Setting the table

Part 5   Other People You Will Meet

Careers and Professionalism

29: Characteristics of infant and toddler caregivers; Record keeping
30: Characteristics of staff
33: Choosing a career; Résumés; Cover letters; Avenues for seeking employment; Preparing for an interview; The interview; Employee rights and responsibilities; Terminating employment; Balancing multiple roles

Curriculum Development

29: Infant-toddler curriculum
30: Planning curriculum; Scheduling; Technology use
31: Individualized Education Plans (IEPs); Integrating children with special needs; Gifted children

Guidance and Discipline
29: Guidelines for infant-toddler care; Caring for infants and toddlers
30: Using positive guidance
31: Teacher's roles in guiding children with special needs

Health, Safety, and Nutrition
29: Handling routines; Toys for infants and toddlers; Maintaining the environment to prevent illness
31: Hearing disorders; Speech and language disorders; Vision disorders; Physical disabilities; Health disorders; Cognitive disabilities; Learning disabilities; Social or emotional impairment

Parent/Teacher and Community Relationships
29: Parent involvement in infant-toddler programs
31: Individualized Education Plans (IEPs)
32: Objectives for parent involvement; Written communication; Class videos; Parent-teacher conferences; Home visits; Discussion groups; Other methods of involvement; Volunteers
33: The hidden job market; Networking

Physical Space and Equipment
29: Infant and toddler environments; Toys; Maintaining the environment to prevent illness
30: The environment; Technology use

Working with Young Children

Dr. Judy Herr
Professor, Early Childhood Education
School of Education
University of Wisconsin-Stout
Menomonie, Wisconsin

Publisher
The Goodheart-Willcox Company, Inc.
Tinley Park, Illinois
www.g-w.com

Copyright © 2008
by
The Goodheart-Willcox Company, Inc.
Previous editions copyright 2004, 2002, 1998, 1994, 1990
All rights reserved. No part of this work may be reproduced, stored, or transmitted in
any form or by any electronic or mechanical means, including information storage and
retrieval systems, without the prior written permission of
The Goodheart-Willcox Company, Inc.

Manufactured in the United States of America.

Library of Congress Catalog Card Number 2007009155
ISBN 978-1-59070-813-2

1 2 3 4 5 6 7 8 9 – 08 – 12 11 10 09 08

Library of Congress Cataloging-in-Publication Data

Herr, Judy.
    Working with young children / Judy Herr.
        p. cm.
    Summary: "Working with Young Children helps students prepare
for a career in early childhood education. It teaches practical
techniques to guide children through a variety of daily experiences
in safe, educational ways. It also includes an overview of physical,
intellectual, social, and emotional characteristics of young children."--
Provided by Publisher.
    Includes index.
    ISBN 978-1-59070-813-2
    1. Child care services--United States. 2. Child care workers--United
States. 3. Early childhood education--United States. I. Title.
    HQ778.63.H47   2007
    362.71'20973--dc22   2007009155

Cover photo: Penny Gentieu/Babystock/Jupiterimages

Introduction

Working with Young Children is designed to help you prepare for a career in early childhood education. It teaches practical techniques to guide children through a variety of daily experiences in safe, educational ways.

Success in working with children begins by understanding children. This book starts with an overview of the physical, intellectual, social, and emotional characteristics of young children. Using this information will help you plan for and react to children with confidence that your actions are developmentally appropriate.

Once you understand children, you are ready to develop and build your guidance skills. This text teaches you practical techniques for guiding children as you establish rules and handle daily routines. It also gives helpful suggestions for dealing with guidance challenges.

An important part of working with young children is creating a safe, healthful learning environment. As you read this text, you will learn techniques for keeping children safe, healthy, and nourished. In addition, you will learn to provide experiences that build children's enthusiasm for learning.

Working with Young Children prepares you for other important aspects of nurturing young children. These include planning developmentally appropriate curriculum and developing strategies for involving parents in child care programs. The book also prepares you to handle special concerns related to infants, toddlers, school-age children, and children with special needs. Finally, the book prepares you to launch a career in child care, helping you explore the types of programs and refine your job hunting skills.

About the Author

The quality of this textbook reflects Judy Herr's intense dedication to early childhood education, with over 30 years of experience in the field. Judy previously supervised and administered seven children's programs at the University of Wisconsin-Stout. She also served as the early childhood program director and Associate Dean of the College of Human Development.

Judy has published numerous books, manuals, and articles on early childhood education. Her articles have been printed in such noted journals as *Young Children*, *Journal of Family and Consumer Sciences*, *Early Childhood News*, and *Texas Child Care Quarterly*. This text, *Working with Young Children*, has been published in Spanish, Chinese, and Arabic.

Judy has been a guest speaker at local, regional, national, and international conferences. She was invited to Pai Chi University in Korea as the Distinguished Invitational International Scholar. She has participated in the prestigious Management Development Program at Harvard University. She is active in professional associations including the National Association for the Education of Young Children. Judy has received many awards, including the Shirley Dean Award for Distinguished Service to the Midwestern Association for the Education of Young Children. She was also named a Dahlgren Professor. In 2006, Judy received the Outstanding Teaching Award at the University of Wisconsin-Stout.

Brief Contents

Contents

Part 4
Learning Experiences for Children

Part 5
Other People You Will Meet

Chapter 33
A Career for You in Early Childhood Education 640

PART
1

The Children and You

Who you are and what you know affects your ability to work with young children. In this part, you will explore current career opportunities in the early childhood field. You will also examine the responsibilities and characteristics of successful early childhood teachers. Various types of early childhood programs will be described.

This part will help you understand the characteristics of children at different ages. It will give you an overview of their physical, cognitive, social, and emotional development. You will learn how to change your teaching skills to fit the developmental needs and interests of children at different ages.

One of the best ways to learn about children is to observe them. Techniques for objectively observing and recording children's behavior will be described in this part.

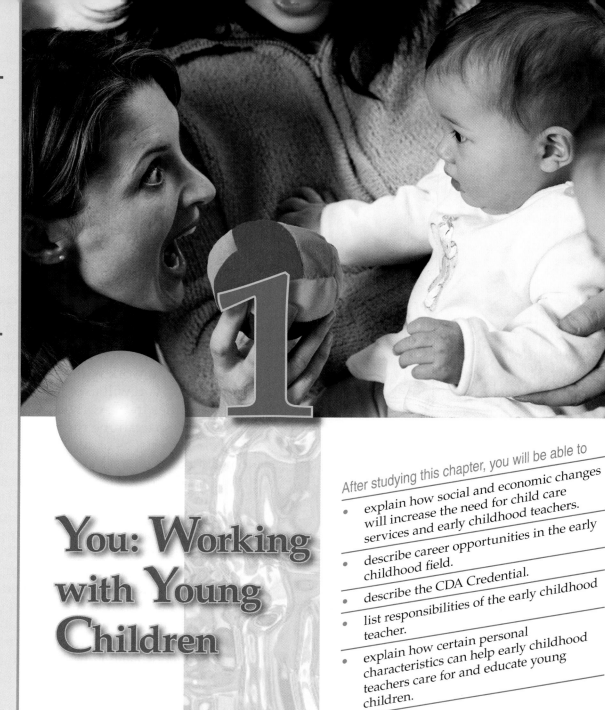

Discuss

Look at the chapter opening photo. What strikes you about the teacher playing with the baby? What words would you use to describe her based just on this photo? How do you think these characteristics would help her in her early childhood career?

Reflect

Look over the objectives for this chapter. What are your feelings about what you are going to learn during this course? How valuable do you think this information will be in your future career search?

You: Working with Young Children

After studying this chapter, you will be able to

- explain how social and economic changes will increase the need for child care services and early childhood teachers.

- describe career opportunities in the early childhood field.

- describe the CDA Credential.

- list responsibilities of the early childhood teacher.

- explain how certain personal characteristics can help early childhood teachers care for and educate young children.

14

Terms to Know

early childhood

prekindergarten (PK)

nanny

au pair

licensing specialist

entrepreneur

Child Development Associate (CDA)
    Credential

developmentally appropriate practice (DAP)

ethics

Mary takes care of toddlers, 1-1. Suzie, who has been a preschool teacher for two years, has taken a position as a center director. Her friend Marko is the parent coordinator in a local Head Start center, while Tom, who was another classmate, is a parent educator. Two other classmates, Sung Jee and Sally, recently opened a children's clothing store. Each of these individuals studied early childhood education. These are just a few of the many challenging and rewarding career opportunities within the early childhood field.

Already you may be asking yourself, "What is early childhood?" **Early childhood** covers the period from birth to nine years of age. During this time, growth is very rapid. The child develops a sense of self as well as language, cognitive, social, emotional, problem-solving, and motor skills. These accomplishments are an important foundation for later learning.

People who are considering careers in the field of early childhood often have at least three main questions. First, they want to know whether there will be a need for people trained in early childhood. They also want to know about the job responsibilities of early childhood educators. In addition, they ask about the personal characteristics needed to be successful in this field.

This chapter reviews social and economic changes that will continue to create a need

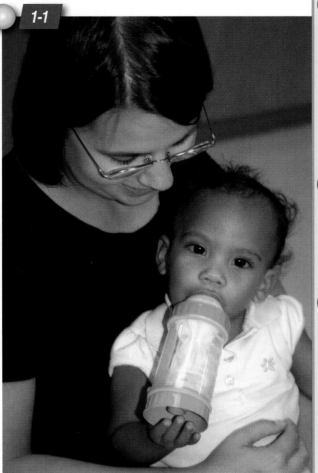

1-1

Taking care of toddlers is one of many job opportunities for people who study early childhood.

for child care teachers. It also gives an overview of teachers' responsibilities and characteristics of successful teachers.

Social and Economic Changes

The social and economic changes in society will continue to create a need for child care services. These changes occur in families, employers' attitudes, education

Vocabulary

Have students review the *Terms to Know* list. Ask students to look up unfamiliar words or terms in the glossary before reading the chapter.

Resource

Is Teaching Really for Me? reproducible master 1-1, TR

Discuss

What is the relationship between your greatest interests and your desire to work in the child care field? What role, if any, would interests play in your choice to work with children?

Meeting Special Needs

Provide an outline of the chapter with all the chapter headings for special learners. Students should fill in each section of the outline as the material is covered in class with a sentence or two about the content. Review the special learners' IEPs to decide if any modifications should be made in presenting the chapter content.

Enrich

Have students explore the Web site for the National Child Care Information Center at **www.nccic.org**. Explain to students this site provides early care and education information links for parents, care providers, policymakers, researchers, and the public. Allow time for volunteers to discuss their findings in class.

Activity

Divide the class into two groups. Ask one group to list the pros and cons of a woman's choice to be a stay-at-home mom. Ask the other group to list the pros and cons of a woman's choice to be a working mother. Have the groups compare their lists.

Note

The Bureau of Labor Statistics reports 40% of mothers with children six years of age or under stay at home. Overall, 13% of the nation's households include a stay-at-home spouse.

attitudes, and studies. Career opportunities change along with these factors.

Changes in Families

A dramatic change has taken place in the early experiences of preschool children during the past 25 years. Most families no longer have a mother as homemaker and a father as wage earner. This traditional family structure exists only in a small percentage of families. An even smaller percentage is expected in the future. Several trends support this prediction.

- Women are becoming more highly educated.

- Married couples are having fewer children.

- More young adults are getting married later in life. When they have children later, they are in a better position financially to afford early childhood programs.

- Smaller family size means families have more money to divide. Therefore, they can spend more on child care.

- Many families need a second paycheck.

- Women are demonstrating increasing commitment to their careers. They work during pregnancy and return to work after birth.

- Sixty-two percent of mothers with preschool children work outside the home. Of those mothers, 70% worked full-time and 30% worked part-time.

- About 5% of preschoolers with employed mothers were cared for by their mothers at work.

- Many working women are widowed, divorced, or single. They do not have the option of a spouse caring for the child.

- Families see the value of having children attend an early childhood program. Three-fourths of young children participate in a preschool program.

In the next decade, the under-five population is expected to rise modestly. Consequently, there will be an increasing need for early childhood teachers, 1-2.

Changes in Employers' Attitudes

Corporate or employer-sponsored child care is one of the fastest growing types of child care. Employers contribute about one percent of the total spent on child care. Some employers provide child care assistance as an optional employee benefit. These trends will present many career opportunities for child care professionals.

By providing some type of child care benefit, companies have reported tangible payoffs. Included are positive effects on recruitment, morale, and productivity. Turnover and absenteeism are reduced. Other positive results are better public relations, tax benefits, ease of scheduling, and improved quality of the workforce.

In addition to on-site child care, employers may offer other means of child care assistance. Included may be a resource and referral service, which helps match the employee's needs with services in the community. Lists

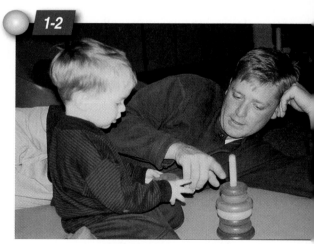

1-2

Young children rely on caring teachers to nurture and protect them while their parents are working.

Portfolio Project

Explain to students they will be creating a portfolio. Ask students to obtain a folder or large manila envelope or use the computer to create the portfolio. Have students brainstorm different items that can be added to a portfolio. Throughout the course designate items students should add to the portfolio such as writing assignments, lesson plans, résumé, certificates, photographs, journal entries, and documentation of service hours.

of child care providers, maps, and brochures may be provided to families. This type of service respects the employee's right to choose a suitable arrangement.

Some corporations may even hire early childhood specialists to provide sick child care. They can provide emergency back-up arrangements for limited time periods. The average child is ill ten days each year. As a result, many parents are forced to stay home from work. This helps reduce the parents' stress, guilt, and worry that occur when their children are ill.

Intergenerational care is another service being provided by some corporations. This model is often called *dependent care*. It provides services for the elderly as well as young children.

Changes in Education Attitudes

Most three-, four-, and five-year-olds are enrolled in early childhood programs. In addition, many younger and older children receive child care while their parents work or attend classes. In the 1970s, only 6 percent of children were cared for in child care centers. The use of center-based care was the least popular form of non-parental care in the 1960s. Only 25 percent of three-, four-, and five-year-old children were enrolled in part- or full-day preschool programs. Today, two out of three children (67 percent) participate in an early childhood program. These children spend an average of 30 hours per week in such care. Moreover, the popularity of center-based care continues to rise.

At the same time, most parents are becoming more aware of their children's developmental needs. As a result, they are seeking quality environments that will promote their children's growth and development. Many working parents search for child care programs that are licensed and accredited.

Ninety-five percent of the nation's five-year-olds attend kindergarten programs for at least half the day. Studies show children who attend full-day versus half-day kindergarten

programs do better academically and socially during the primary years. In addition, most parents prefer full-day kindergarten programs because these programs create fewer transitions for their children. Thus, there is a continuing push toward full-day kindergartens. Some school districts are also introducing prekindergarten programs for four-year-olds, as well as preschool programs for children with special needs.

Early childhood advocates are working toward even greater allocation of public education dollars for the youngest children. Their goal is to remedy current problems in education for young children. The demand for quality child care and other early childhood programs has never been greater.

There is mounting evidence that early childhood professionals should be optimistic. The Bureau of Labor has listed preschool teachers as one of the fastest growing occupations for the next decade. More trained teachers are needed. Recent studies show there are not enough quality programs. The majority of child care is of unacceptably low quality in the first three years of life and does not meet accepted standards of quality. For preschoolers, the majority of programs are mediocre at best. Thus, most children in child care do not receive quality care.

Educational Studies

Studies have confirmed the benefits of high-quality early education. The first five years of life are a critical period in development. The benefits are also long-term. Children who are involved in early learning experiences are more successful in school, as well as later in life. Quality early childhood programs benefit children by nurturing them. The programs also prepare the children to reach school ready to learn.

Children who get a good start are less likely to have behavioral problems. They are also less likely to be referred to special education. One study surveyed the progress of children who attended a high-quality

Activity

Have students check with college-level early childhood programs or local employers for information regarding what they would like to see in a student portfolio for admission or employment opportunities. Ask volunteers to share their findings with the class.

Vocabulary

Note the word *accreditation* indicates a school or child care facility has met a certain set of standards for the program it offers. A school or child care facility accredited by the National Association for the Education of Young Children (NAEYC) has met the high standards of a quality program.

Activity

Invite the school district superintendent to speak to the class about the need for more early intervention programs for young children. Have the speaker include information on programs currently available in the area and how the programs are funded.

Cross-Curricular Activity

Social Studies
Have students investigate child advocacy initiatives currently being sponsored in your state and/or the nation. Arrange for students to contact state or federal representatives for information on the legislative process and any pending legislation affecting early childhood care and education. Have students prepare a written report on the aims of the initiatives, expected results of the initiatives, and what citizens can do to promote child advocacy initiatives.

Vocabulary

Have a student volunteer look up *Prekindergarten (PK)* in the glossary and read the definition aloud. Discuss the different types of prekindergarten programs such as preschool, child care, school- and home-based child care, and Head Start.

Resource

Truths About Early Childhood, Activity A, SAG

Reflect

Imagine you are a parent deciding on in-home child care. Brainstorm advantages of hiring an au pair to care for your child. What would be the disadvantages of this type of care?

preschool program. Over the years, these students fared better than those who did not participate in early education. Fewer of these children committed crimes or required special education. They also earned better grades. More graduated from high school and enjoyed higher earnings. They made less use of welfare and paid higher taxes.

This research has been reinforced by other studies. These studies have shown the importance of brain development and early learning. According to research, early brain development depends on a stimulating environment and nurturing. As a result, the majority of states are introducing prekindergarten programs. **Prekindergarten (PK)** refers to the full range of early childhood programs. These include school-based programs for three- and four-year-olds, preschool, child care, Head Start, and home-based child care.

Benefits to the Economy

Quality early childhood programs do not only affect tomorrow's citizens. They also influence tomorrow's economy. Studies show that preschool education is a sound economic investment. Every dollar invested in early education saves taxpayers future costs. In addition, it is also an investment that pays great returns to children. Therefore, early care and education is cost-effective. Across the nation, states have caught on to the importance of offering early childhood care for all young children.

Career Opportunities in Early Childhood

Never have there been more career opportunities in early childhood. Early childhood programs occur in a variety of settings. Private schools, public schools,

homes, apartment buildings, centers, businesses, parks, and houses of worship are examples. As a result, early childhood specialists may find themselves choosing from many alternatives. Nannies, au pairs, kindergarten teachers, child care teachers and directors, and licensing specialists will be needed. You may find additional possibilities in business settings. See 1-3.

Due to demand, the challenge of maintaining a qualified early childhood workforce will grow more difficult. Workers over 45 years of age will need to be replaced as they retire in the next twenty years. In addition, new teachers will be needed to keep pace with the continued growth of early childhood programs.

Nannies and Au Pairs

There is currently a great demand for trained nannies and au pairs. A **nanny** provides care in a child's home. Depending on the parents' needs, some nannies may live in the child's home. In addition to their wages, they may receive health insurance, paid holidays, room, and board. Other nannies live on their own.

The dual-career family has contributed to the increasing demand for nannies. One employment service reported that it received over 50 requests for nannies per day. Due to a lack of trained personnel, the placement officers were able to place only 50 nannies in an entire year. Since many nannies have come from other countries, tighter immigration laws have decreased the supply of nannies in the United States. This has created new opportunities for nannies who are trained in the United States.

An **au pair** (pronounced *oh pare*) is a person from a foreign country who lives with a family and performs tasks similar to those of a nanny. In exchange for weekly pay, room, board, and transportation, the au pair provides child care and may do housework.

Putting Technology to Use

Using the Internet, have students research training programs for nannies. Note the location, course content, length, cost, and job placement opportunities for the programs. Ask students to compare these to certificate or degree programs in early childhood at a community or area college or university or other training program. Allow time for students to report their findings in class.

1-3

Career Opportunities

Careers in Child Care and Early Childhood Education Programs

- Au pairs
- Curriculum specialists
- Directors of early childhood and school-age child care programs
- Family child care providers
- Nannies
- Teachers: child care centers, early childhood programs, elementary schools, and school-age child care programs
- Assistant and associate teachers: child care centers, early childhood programs, elementary schools, and school-age child care programs

Related Careers in the Early Childhood Industry

- Child care resource and referral specialists
- Early childhood consultants
- Early childhood educators (high school teachers, vocational and technical school instructors, community college instructors, and university professors)
- Early childhood researchers
- Licensing specialists
- Safety specialists
- Sick child care specialist for corporate child care
- Special education specialist
- Staff trainers

Child-Related Careers in...

Business
- Designers of children's products: clothing, computer hardware and software, furniture, school supplies, sports equipment, toys, and more
- Salespeople of children's products
- Playground designers
- Safety testers for children's products

Community Service
- Children's librarians
- Children's art, dance, music, and sports instructors
- Health care: pediatricians, pediatric nurses, pediatric surgeons, pediatric dentists
- Social services: family or children's therapists, counselors, social workers, caseworkers
- Parent educators
- Recreation directors
- Religious education directors or instructors

Publishing and Art
- Authors of books and magazine articles for children and parents
- Editors of books and magazines for children and parents
- Children's artists, illustrators, and photographers

Entertainment
- Entertainers: actors, singers, clowns, magicians, puppeteers
- Writers, producers, and directors for children's TV shows, movies, and theater productions

A variety of career opportunities exist in the field of early childhood.

Kindergarten Teachers

The opportunity to attend kindergarten is now provided in most states. Thus, kindergarten teachers are needed in public as well as private schools. Even many child care centers hire kindergarten teachers. These centers provide full-day kindergarten programs for children of working parents.

Early Childhood Assistant and Associate Teachers

In addition to the lead teacher, state licensing requirements may require an additional staff member. To achieve the required adult-child ratios for a group of young children, an early childhood assistant or associate teacher may be hired. The role of

Activity

Review *Career Opportunities*, Chart 1-3, with the class. Discuss any careers students are not familiar with. Ask students to select and research a career from the list that interests them. Create a bulletin board from all the students' findings.

Enrich

Have students research current early childhood career and employment opportunities in the *Occupational Outlook Handbook* available through your school's guidance department or at **www.bls.gov**. Ask students to write a brief summary of their findings.

Resource

Career Match, reproducible master 1-2, TR

Meeting Special Needs

Modify *Career Match*, reproducible master 1-2, so statements are grouped in sets of six. Pair special learners with volunteer students to complete the activity. Review answers to the statements in class. Spend additional time discussing any statements that are difficult for special learners to understand.

Enrich

Have students investigate the availability of professional development opportunities in early childhood education in their community. Ask students to check the course offerings from a community or technical college. Have students write a brief summary of their results and share their findings with the class.

Note

When students visit child care and early childhood centers, remind them they are bound by the same rules of confidentiality and work ethics as the employees. Ask before taking photographs or identifying children by name in examples, journal articles, and case studies. Make students aware of center rules and regulations before the visit. Secure permission to visit the center from the director well in advance.

Enrich

Invite the director of an early childhood program to class to discuss the training and expectations for the job. Have students prepare a list of questions to ask prior to the visit. If possible, arrange a job shadowing experience for selected students.

the early childhood teacher or associate is to provide support for and assist a lead teacher in providing a developmentally appropriate curriculum.

These positions may not require a degree in many states, although specialized course work or training in child development or early childhood education may be a requirement. For example, the associate teacher may have a CDA credential, or an associate degree from a community or technical college. The assistant teacher is typically an entry-level position. Assistants may have earned a high school degree and participated in a professional development course or training program. This position may help the individual gain experience needed to advance to a lead teacher position. Many students work in these positions while working toward an early childhood education degree at a university.

Child Care Teachers and Directors

With the number of children attending child care centers growing, the need for educated, qualified professionals is also growing. The U.S. Bureau of Labor Statistics predicts an increased number of job openings for early childhood educators. Usually the teacher is responsible for planning curriculum and teaching children. The director's responsibilities are broader. Marketing the program, recruiting children, hiring and supervising staff, and managing the budget are all included. Building maintenance is also the responsibility of the director in some centers.

Family Child Care Home

Family child care homes provide child care for children ranging in age from 6 weeks to 12 years. This type of care allows a child care provider to work from home. Parents may be attracted to this type of program because

of the longer hours of operation and homelike atmosphere. Likewise, child care providers may prefer this arrangement because they can also care for their own children.

Licensing Specialists

Due to the rapid increase in child care centers, the number of licensing positions are expanding. The **licensing specialist** is usually employed by the state. The role of this person is to protect and promote the health, safety, and welfare of children attending centers.

Licensing specialists generally make regularly scheduled on-site visits to assigned centers. During each visit, the licensing specialist observes whether the center is following state licensing guidelines. The number of children in the center, adult-child ratio, size of the facility, food service, and curriculum provided may all be monitored. Building safety, health practices, educational preparation of staff, and physical space are monitored as well.

Other Career Opportunities

Many other career opportunities exist for you in the field of early childhood. With this background, you will be qualified to hold a variety of positions. For example, a career as a parent educator might appeal to you. In this position, you would work with parents to help them learn parenting skills, 1-4. You might work days, evenings, or weekends. You could design educational materials or produce visuals to help parents better understand their roles and the nature of young children. You might even produce materials to be shared on the Internet.

Knowledge of child development is also needed for community recreation leaders and children's art, dance, music, and sports instructors. This knowledge is helpful for those creating television shows, books, toys, music, and magazines for young children, too.

Putting Technology to Use

Have students conduct an Internet search to learn about the job duties of a licensing specialist. What are the educational requirements for this position? How is the job outlook for a

licensing specialist over the next ten years? Ask students to write a brief report or utilize the computer to record their findings. Allow time for students to discuss their findings in class.

1-4

Parent educators present information that will help parents improve their nurturing skills.

Social workers, counselors, and therapists must know about children's development in order to provide appropriate help. This is also true of health care providers who treat children. Indeed, the demand for workers educated in early childhood far exceeds the current supply.

Finally, you might enjoy a career as an **entrepreneur**. This is a person who creates and runs his or her own business. The most common early childhood entrepreneurship is a family child care home. Family child care providers run their business from their homes. They put in all the work, take all the risk, make all the decisions, and earn all the profit associated with their businesses. Consultants, store owners, designers of children's products, and entertainers are other examples of entrepreneurs.

The work available to you as an entrepreneur is limited only by your imagination. If you can shape your ideas into a career that meets a need of children and families, you will likely succeed. For example, you could start a business that specializes in providing substitute staff for child care centers. When a center needs personnel to cover an absent staff member's job, the director could call you. Your responsibility would be to furnish a substitute teacher, cook, janitor, or office assistant.

Education and Training Needed to Work with Young Children

As you can see, there are many opportunities for people who are interested in working with young children. What education and training is required for these jobs?

A few entry-level positions require little training or experience. For instance, some state licensing regulations allow someone with a high school education to work as a teacher's aide or playground supervisor. A teacher's aide would assist the teacher, help the children with their snacks, or supervise play activities.

Most child care jobs require training and education beyond high school. A first step for many is to obtain the **Child Development Associate (CDA) Credential**. Those who have this national credential have taken postsecondary courses in child care education and have demonstrated their ability to work with young children. The six CDA Competency Goals identify the skills

Activity

Ask students to imagine they have decided to turn the family room in their home into a play-room/multi-use space for a family child care business. Have students draw a floor plan for a suitable child-centered space. Indicate what furniture and equipment is needed and record the location on the floor plan. What safety factors need to be considered for a family child care business? What local laws or ordinances apply to home child care in your community?

Note

The Child Development Associate (CDA) National Credentialing Program is designed to evaluate and improve the skills of child care providers in centers, family child care, and home visitor programs. To earn the credential, applicants must take 120 clock hours of coursework and related training, prepare an extensive professional resource file, and meet other requirements including work experience. For further information check The Council for Early Childhood Professional Recognition Web site at **www.cdacouncil.org.**

Resource

CDA Competency Goals and Functional Areas, transparency master 1-3, TR

Putting Technology to Use

Have students conduct an Internet search for information regarding CDA credentialing programs. Are any CDA programs available in your area? What is the cost of the program? How long will it take to earn the credential? What fees are associated with the application and renewal of the credential? Have volunteers share their findings with the class.

Discuss

What is the difference between an associate degree and a bachelor degree with regard to the early childhood education field? What employment opportunities are available to those with a bachelor degree that would not be possible with an associate degree? Are there employment opportunities in child care that do not require a degree?

Reflect

Consider this quote by Rachel Carson: "If children are to keep alive their inborn sense of wonder, they need the companionship of at least one adult who can share it, rediscovering with them the joy, excitement, and mystery of the world we live in." Think about what this quote says to you regarding the importance of the teacher's responsibilities in early childhood.

Resource

The Teacher's Responsibilities, color transparency CT-1, TR

needed by early childhood professionals. These goals are divided into 13 functional areas, which describe major tasks caregivers must accomplish to satisfy the competency goals. To be eligible for this credential, a person must be 18 years of age and have a high school diploma. In addition, the candidate must have a minimum number of hours of child care experience and have taken courses in early childhood education.

Most of the jobs described in this chapter require at least a two-year associate degree in child development or a related area. Some states are requiring that early childhood teachers have a CDA Credential to meet licensing requirements. The credential is not required, however, if the teacher has an associate or bachelor's degree in early childhood education, child development, or a closely related field. A bachelor's degree usually requires a minimum of four years of college. Directors of child care programs generally need a bachelor's degree.

Some jobs require a graduate degree. These include consultants, researchers, and early childhood instructors or professors. Some large early childhood programs require director candidates to have earned a graduate degree.

Each state establishes its own qualifications for staff who work in child care centers. There is no uniform standard established by the federal government. The qualifications will depend on the job you are seeking and the state in which you plan to work. It is important to know the minimum requirements for your state. You can ask the local agency that licenses child care centers what those standards are.

The Teacher's Responsibilities

Many career opportunities exist in early childhood. The majority will be as teachers or teacher's aides. These professionals are

needed for child care centers, preschools, Head Start programs, and in early childhood programs in public and private schools. Because of this need, this book will focus on the knowledge and skills needed to teach young children.

Your responsibilities as an early childhood teacher will be complex and demanding. You will have both direct and indirect influences on children. Directly, you will interact with children. Indirectly, you will influence children through the arrangement of space and activities. As an early childhood teacher, you will serve a dual role. Often you will play both the teacher and parent-educator role. Usually, the younger the child, the more support you need to provide to the parent in the transition from home to center. The parent may also seek advice on such aspects of child development as toilet learning, biting, and thumbsucking.

You will also need to be a friend, colleague, counselor, janitor, nurse, decorator, safety expert, and even a cook on some days. Not all your tasks will be pleasant. Sometimes your work may be unpleasant, such as changing messy diapers and cleaning up after a sick child. Noses have to be wiped and messes, such as spilled milk, dumped paint, or a leaky sensory table, must be cleaned.

Challenging and *rewarding* are two words that can best describe the responsibilities of an early childhood teacher. You will be challenged planning developmentally appropriate curriculum, designing class materials, and coping with behavior problems in the classroom. At times you may become discouraged, particularly when behavioral changes are slow. Once the changes occur, however, the rewards are well worth the time and effort. Early childhood teachers usually feel useful, needed, and important, 1-5. Working with young children is an act of hope for a better future. Most teachers also usually feel loved by the children. For these reasons, most early childhood teachers thoroughly enjoy their profession.

Workplace Connection

Explain to students that early childhood teachers often assume a parent-educator role. Some school districts and youth service agencies provide parent education as part of their early childhood and at-risk programs. Have students research types of parent-education activities available in their community. What role could early childhood educators play in providing parenting education to parents of young children? Ask students to write a brief summary of their findings.

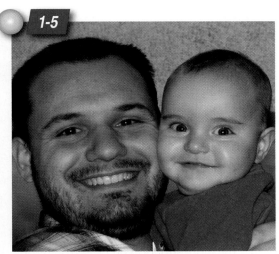

1-5

Love from children helps make teaching in early childhood a rewarding career.

is, what happens to the child after he acts determines whether this behavior will be continued. A child who throws a temper tantrum to get a second turn on a bike (and gets a second turn) will usually repeat this behavior. Thus, you teach children to behave the way they do. Most of what they learn will be learned from other people and you.

As you work with young children, you will notice differences in behavior. Children can learn to be friendly, and they can learn to be aggressive. As a teacher, you will be responsible for teaching children to interact positively. Thus, you will teach them to be cooperative and skillful in getting along with others. To do this, you will need to learn and use developmentally appropriate guidance and group management techniques.

To Know How Children Grow and Develop

Teachers need to know what children are like. Regardless of your position, you will need a thorough understanding of child growth and development. You will need to understand the needs, abilities, and interests of children at particular ages. This understanding will help you prepare inviting and developmentally appropriate environments for young children. Likewise, it will help you design educational experiences that promote children's growth in knowledge, skills, and self-confidence. Moreover, knowing the principles of child development will assist you in developing curriculum that is challenging and interesting without being difficult or discouraging.

Understanding children's behavior will help you work effectively with individuals and groups of children. You will learn that children behave the way they do because their behavior brings them pleasure. That

Health and Safety

Health Policies and Practices

As an early childhood professional, you are responsible for all children's health and safety. Become familiar with your center's policies and practices regarding children's health and safety. This includes *all* forms and documents that should be in every child's file. Forms may include medical checkup and immunization records, accident or injury forms, or medication logs.

Activity

Have students prepare a bulletin board or display depicting the various roles an early childhood teacher assumes. Photos, drawings, magazine pictures, and clipart could be used to represent roles such as teacher, parent-educator, counselor, janitor, nurse, and cook.

Note

Refer students to *Developmentally Appropriate Practice for Young Children* by Susan Bredekamp, a publication by the NAEYC, for comprehensive information on what is and is not good developmental appropriate practice in early childhood education.

Reflect

Think about how knowledge of child growth and development can help you handle the challenge of a temper tantrum thrown by one of your students.

Workplace Connection

Have students review a local child care center's policies and practices regarding children's health and safety. What forms and documents does the center require for every child? Are there any forms not available? What additional forms or policies might be added? Have students discuss their findings in class.

Discuss

Positive interactions with other children and adults are an important step in social development. Brainstorm ideas for setting classroom expectations that would lead to positive social development.

Enrich

Ask students to survey parents of young children about their expectations for early childhood education. What do parents think their children should learn during the preschool years? Discuss the findings and compare them to what is included in a developmentally appropriate curriculum.

Vocabulary

Have a student volunteer define *developmentally appropriate practice (DAP)*. Ask students to research child development theories supported by this idea. Allow time to discuss findings in class.

To Plan a Developmentally Appropriate Curriculum

Teachers are responsible for planning a developmentally appropriate curriculum. **Developmentally appropriate practice (DAP)** is a set of guidelines that focus on the outcomes of learning activities. DAP is based on the idea that children learn from play. This idea is supported by many child development theories. DAP also emphasizes knowing the children well and respecting them.

Using this approach, teachers guide play activities that children choose for themselves. However, the unique differences of each child are stressed. Play activities should be based on the child's

- age
- abilities
- strengths and weaknesses
- cultural and social background
- personal interests

Quality programs focus on the "whole child," matching practice with knowledge of child development and learning. Physical, social, cognitive, and emotional development are all emphasized. Such programs can provide long-term, positive differences in the lives of young children. The knowledge in this book is critical for helping you make developmentally appropriate decisions.

Physical development is stressed in a quality early childhood curriculum. Young children develop a variety of skills through physical experiences that are a foundation for later learning. Coordination, stamina, flexibility, strength, and sensory awareness are all included. See 1-6.

Social development is another important aspect of a quality curriculum. Young children must learn to interact positively with other children and adults. Likewise, they need to learn to adapt to the expectations that are established in the center.

Young children need to acquire information to be able to understand and

1-6

Curriculum should include activities that help improve muscle strength and coordination.

function in the world. As a result, cognitive development is an important area of the child's development. Problem solving through hands-on activities will be an important part of the children's learning.

Emotional development is also an important element of a developmentally appropriate curriculum. Young children need to understand themselves. Feelings need to be understood in order to develop self-awareness and self-knowledge. Children need to become emotionally literate. They need help in learning to recognize, label, and accept their feelings. They need to learn to assert their rights in culturally accepted ways without hurting others.

Your curriculum will need to be designed for the children. A broad knowledge of

Workplace Connection

Have students survey the equipment and materials available in the child care laboratory. Ask students to determine the physical, cognitive, social, and emotional benefits of each. Are any areas in need of more quantity or variety of materials or equipment? What additional items might be added? Have students check catalogs of early childhood education materials for ideas.

all the curriculum areas outlined in this book is important. You will find that an understanding of science, math, music, movement, social studies, art, dramatic play, and storytelling will influence what you do with children.

To Prepare the Environment

A large part of the teaching process involves preparing an inviting and stimulating learning environment. Learning is an active process whereby children gain knowledge and develop new skills. The environment that you provide must encourage children to independently experiment, explore, and manipulate, 1-7. Interaction with materials is an important learning vehicle.

As a teacher, you will need to provide a variety of materials. These materials will encourage children to engage in positive social activities. They also will promote physical, social, cognitive, and emotional development. Lack of variety or quantity can lead to lags in development. For instance, if there are not enough interesting materials, children may fight over the few that they enjoy. Chapters have been included in this book to teach you how to arrange space and select toys, equipment, and supplies.

To Communicate Effectively

To be an effective teacher, you need to have good communication skills. These skills are important for ease in expressing ideas and gaining trust with children, their families, and your peers.

As a teacher, positive communication skills will help you form and maintain a close relationship with the children in your care. Your words will inform, explain, and guide them. Listening actively to what the children share is just as important as speaking.

Effective communication with families is also vital. Most child care teachers have daily contact with the children's parents or

1-7

It is up to you as a teacher to make learning an active process.

guardians. Therefore, information is usually exchanged on a continuous basis.

Early childhood teachers must also be able to form meaningful relationships with their colleagues. To provide a quality educational program for young children, all staff must work cooperatively. This requires open communication.

To Demonstrate Teamwork

An important part of any job is getting along with your coworkers. Staff in early childhood programs need to work as a team, 1-8. To be a team member, you will need to help make your coworkers feel respected and important. Everyone enjoys feeling important and valued.

To work well as a team member, you need to support your coworkers through your actions and words. Empathize with them by recognizing and reflecting their feelings. Share ideas and information with them. Tell them when they have planned interesting activities. Praise them for meaningful interactions with the children. Furthermore, accept their style of caregiving.

Even when team members work well together, conflicts will arise. Knowing how to resolve conflicts effectively is important.

Activity

Have students practice public speaking skills by having them prepare a one-minute introduction of themselves to the class. Ask students to include information about why they chose to study the early childhood field.

Vocabulary

Have a student volunteer define *conflict resolution*. Ask students how knowledge of conflict resolution may assist them in promoting positive workplace experiences.

Discuss

Share experiences you have had in working with a team. Did everyone get along? Did each member of the team feel respected and important? Were all opinions valued? Did any conflicts occur? If so, how were the conflicts handled?

Putting Technology to Use

Ask students to conduct an Internet search for information on active listening techniques. Define *active listening* and explain how it is used in a classroom situation. What are the results when active listening is used effectively? Have students role-play an active listening situation.

Reflect

How do time management skills help you now as a high school student? How will time management skills assist an early childhood teacher?

Note

Have copies of several early childhood journals in class for students to review. Suggestions include: *Early Childhood Research and Practice*; *Early Childhood Education Journal*; and *Young Children*, a publication of NAEYC.

Vocabulary

Define *ethics* and discuss the need for ethics in early childhood education.

When staff members take and give suggestions on curriculum, they are able to give children the best care possible.

Being able to talk through a situation and work together to find a solution can be challenging. With practice, however, you can look at conflict resolution as just a regular part of working on a team.

To Manage Time Wisely

Rarely does an early childhood teacher have time to do everything he or she wants to do. Thus, time management skills are important. Time management skills help teachers work smarter, not harder. They help you organize your time, set priorities, and distinguish between important and urgent matters.

No matter what you accomplish, there is always more that could be done. You might want to make one more bulletin board, write a letter to a parent, or develop new teaching materials. Time management skills will help you make choices and use your time wisely.

To Participate in Professional Organizations

The field of early childhood constantly changes. Joining a professional organization can help you keep up with current developments

in the field. To enjoy the full benefit of membership, you must be an active participant.

Family, Career and Community Leaders of America (FCCLA) is an organization for middle and high school family and consumer sciences students. Members develop skills for life through character development, creative and critical thinking, interpersonal communication, practical knowledge, and career preparation. Participation can be at the local, regional, and national level.

The largest professional organization in early childhood is the *National Association for the Education of Young Children (NAEYC)*. This organization was founded in 1926 to improve professional practice and preparation. With nearly 100,000 members, NAEYC is the primary organization for the early childhood field. This organization has local, state, and national affiliates. Membership services include annual state and national conferences. The organization also publishes a journal and other publications.

You should consider becoming a member of a professional organization. Attending conferences and reading materials are part of being a professional. By participating, you will keep informed of teaching trends, issues, research, legislation, upcoming events, and new publications. Chart 1-9 provides the name and Web sites of major early childhood education professional organizations.

To Follow Ethical Standards

When you work with young children, you will be faced each day with decisions of an ethical nature. You will be called on to choose between conflicting options. To help you make these tough choices, you will rely on your **ethics**, or guiding set of moral principles. Your ethics will help you to choose the option that is most ethical, or conforming to accepted standards of conduct.

People who work with young children should practice ethical behavior at all times. They should maintain the highest standards of professional conduct. For early childhood

Putting Technology to Use

Have students learn more about Family, Career and Community Leaders of America (FCCLA) at **www.fcclainc.org**. What types of programs does this organization offer for middle and high school family and consumer sciences students? What skills can students develop through participation in this program? Ask students to write a brief report of their findings.

1-9

Professional Organizations

American Montessori Association	www.amshq.org
Association for Childhood Education International	www. acei.org
FCCLA: Family, Career and Community Leaders of America	www.fcclainc.org
National Association of Child Care Professionals	www.naccp.org
National Association for the Education of Young Children	www.naeyc.org
National Association for Family Child Care	www.nafcc.org
National Child Care Association	www.nccanet.org
National Head Start Association	www.nhsa.org

Many child care professionals are members of these organizations.

Resource

Teacher Responsibilities, Activity A, OG

Activity

After reviewing Appendix A, *Principles from the Code of Ethical Conduct* from NAEYC, ask students to prepare posters of several key points to be displayed in the classroom. Posters may be rotated throughout the school year.

Resource

Comparing Teaching to Other Careers, Activity B, SAG

professionals, these standards are reflected in the *Code of Ethical Conduct* created by NAEYC. This code establishes guidelines of responsible behavior to follow in relationship to children, families, colleagues, and communities. It is based on a set of core values for the profession set forth by NAEYC. (See the Appendices of this text to learn more about NAEYC's *Code of Ethical Conduct*.)

Professionals who follow the *Code of Ethical Conduct* ensure that programs for young children are based on the most recent knowledge of child development and early childhood education. In their communities, these professionals serve as advocates for children, families, and teachers. They recognize that biases, opinions, and values can alter professional judgment. As a result, these professionals are always open to new ideas and suggestions.

Sometimes choosing ethical behavior is not easy. You might be called upon to make a decision that is unpopular with families, children, or coworkers. A professional who behaves ethically follows the right decision no matter what others do. Being ethically responsible might also mean taking action in some sticky situations. For instance, if you know a coworker is stealing supplies from the center, you may feel a strong pull to report this unethical behavior to the director. You will have to weigh the importance of telling against the consequences of telling. For many professionals, violating their ethics just to avoid conflict is too great a price to pay.

In a sense, much of this text deals with ethics. The chapters of this book will teach you the best practices for working with young children. Following these best practices will bring you into alignment with the *Code of Ethical Conduct*. As you study the chapters that follow, think about ethical dilemmas that might arise and ask yourself how you would handle these situations.

Portfolio Project

Ask students to write an essay explaining their understanding of ethics. How will knowledge of ethical standards affect work performance? Include thoughts on attitude, honesty, teamwork, professionalism, and personal responsibility. Have students refer to any previous ethical dilemmas they have experienced.

Activity

Ask students to research organizations or educational institutions in their area sponsoring meetings, classes, demonstrations, or conferences on early childhood education topics. Find out if there are any upcoming conferences or meetings they may be able to attend.

Reflect

What characteristics of former teachers do you recall as having a positive effect on your learning and on the entire class? What characteristics, if any, had a negative effect on students?

Discuss

What cues do we give children to let them know they are appreciated and understood? How can body language and facial expressions affect a child's emotions?

To Continue to Learn

Professional development is an ongoing process, 1-10. A teacher never finishes learning. In order to keep up with happenings in the field, you need to be a committed, lifelong learner. Conferences, in-service training, course work, journals, study groups, and books all help teachers learn more about their field. In addition, participating in one or more professional organizations is essential to learning new developments in the field.

1-10

Reading is an important part of continuing education for early childhood teachers.

Characteristics of Successful Teachers

Working with young children requires a special kind of person. As an early childhood teacher, you will need to build on your own strengths and develop your own style. Each teacher is different. Some teachers are outgoing and lively. Other teachers may be reserved and naturally quiet. Both styles can be effective. Simply copying the style of another teacher will not necessarily make you a successful teacher. You must develop a style that best suits your personality. When your style suits your personality, you will feel more comfortable working with children and adults. You will also find more enjoyment in your profession.

Although teachers may use very different styles, successful teachers tend to have some common characteristics. See 1-11. These traits help teachers deal effectively with the day-to-day situations that are naturally part of their work.

Fondness for Children

The most important trait of an early childhood teacher is fondness for children. The rapport established with each child determines the program's success. Every child needs to be understood and accepted. Each child's family background, interests, and desires also need to be respected.

As an early childhood teacher, you will need to show love for each child with whom you work. You need to be kind, firm, and understanding with each child. These actions affect how children feel about themselves and show children how to treat each other. As part of their social development, young children need to be taught that people and feelings are important.

Meeting Special Needs

Discuss with gifted students the relevance of Maslow's Hierarchy of Needs, especially the levels of love/belonging and esteem, with regard to a young child's social and intellectual development. What are the positive effects when children's needs are met? What are the consequences if needs are not met? What is the teacher's role in the child's development of positive feelings toward others?

1-11

Characteristics of a Successful Teacher

- Has a positive attitude and a sense of humor
- Is fond of children
- Relates easily and spontaneously to others
- Is patient, confident, and caring
- Is creative and resourceful
- Is dependable and reliable
- Is a keen observer
- Solves problems well and makes sound decisions
- Is flexible and adapts well to the requirements of others
- Is compassionate, accepting children's strong emotions such as anger, love, and wonder
- Enjoys challenges and is willing and able to grow
- Takes initiative in the classroom
- Has knowledge in curriculum, child growth and development, assessment, and child guidance
- Keeps abreast of changes in the field by reading, attending conferences, seminars, and courses
- Desires continuous learning
- Becomes an active member of professional organizations
- Can juggle several activities at once
- Feels rewarded by even minimal progress
- Communicates and resolves conflicts well
- Has a lot of energy
- Has a strong sense of ethical behavior
- Uses reflection to improve practices

Teachers who have these characteristics tend to have high success in teaching and caring for young children.

Feeling loved, safe, and emotionally secure helps children develop intellectually and emotionally, 1-12. As you show children they are important, children have confidence in themselves. They are more willing to try new activities.

Patience

Effective teachers are also patient, allowing children time to explore, solve problems, and create. Young children often need extra time to complete tasks. Children also need the opportunity to repeat tasks. Much of a child's learning occurs as the result of repetition.

Children are naturally curious and may constantly repeat simple questions. Children do not always remember everything they have been told. Repeating information and reminding children of limits may seem tedious at times. When these situations are handled patiently, however, teachers help children grow and learn while building their self-esteem.

Resource

Characteristics of a Successful Teacher, transparency master 1-4, TR

Reflect

Can you think of an example where someone's impatience affected others? Consider situations such as shopping, waiting in a doctor's office, or sitting in a restaurant. What were the negative effects of the impatience on others?

Resource

Pleasures and Problems in Teaching, Activity C, SAG

Putting Technology to Use

Have students conduct an Internet search for any changes in the early childhood field. What reading materials, conferences, seminars, or courses are available to expand knowledge of the changes? Have students share their findings with the class.

Vocabulary

Define *compassion*. How can compassion-ate teachers model respect for all students?

Discuss

Discipline is often necessary at the pre-school level to change and correct behavior. How might punishment negatively impact the behavior of the young child?

Note

Write the following quote by Dwight D. Eisenhower on the board or overhead to spark a discussion on the role of humor: "A sense of humor is part of the art of leadership, of getting along with people, of getting things done."

Discuss

Brainstorm ideas of how to handle common preschool incidents with humor. Examples may include dealing with a child who came to class after cutting his or her own hair, a child who spilled juice at snack time, and a child who mispronounced a word and was laughed at by other children.

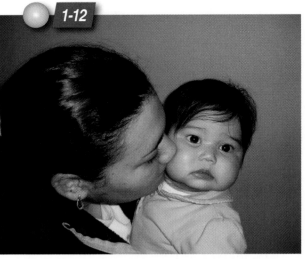

1-12

Children who feel loved are more receptive to learning.

Compassion

Compassionate teachers are able to accept others without prejudice. Being compassionate requires self-knowledge and self-acceptance. It involves accepting any emotion from others such as anger, grief, joy, fear, love, or even hate.

A compassionate teacher does not simply observe a child's feelings. He or she is sensitive to both positive and negative feelings the children express.

Teachers show compassion by complimenting children for their successes. They also avoid actions that make children feel worthless, such as punishment and shaming. Compassionate teachers work to help children understand the feelings of others and motivate children to respect each other.

Confidence

Having confidence in your abilities helps you relax in the classroom. Teachers who are relaxed and natural tend to be more successful with children. Children, especially the younger ones, can become easily excited. By remaining calm and self-assured, you will have a calming effect on the children.

Your confidence is affected by your ability to make sensible decisions. You need to feel sure the choices you make are in the best interest of the children. For instance, when it is raining, children should not be taken outside. Children may not always understand such decisions. If you stand by your choices with confidence, children will accept them.

Sense of Humor

A sense of humor is helpful when working with children. Children enjoy adults who can laugh. Laughter helps children relax and feel content. When children see a teacher with a positive, cheerful attitude, they are more likely to be positive and cheerful. See 1-13.

Keeping a sense of humor also can make your work more enjoyable. Seeing the funny side of children can be a rewarding experience. Seeing the humor in situations can also help you cope with some of the daily stresses of teaching. Of course, you must be careful to laugh with, not at, children.

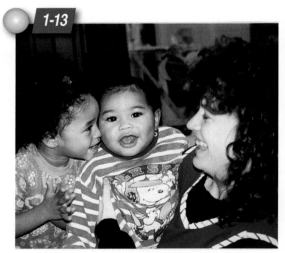

1-13

A teacher who smiles and laughs encourages children to smile and laugh.

Workplace Connection

Discuss with students that successful teachers make sensible decisions. Have students review the steps of decision making to ensure they are confident of the work-place decisions they will make. Provide students with a decision-making model or have students conduct an Internet search for one. Remind students to follow the steps for important decisions they will make this year.

Commitment

In many ways, the job of an early childhood teacher is anything but easy. Demands on your energy will be high. You will be expected to be an expert in child development, child guidance, and curriculum. Parents will ask your advice on such issues as toy selection, toilet learning, and guidance.

You will find that meeting the demands of this field requires a serious commitment. To keep up with current developments in the field, you must constantly study. This can be accomplished through reading books and attending seminars, classes, and conferences. Participating in professional organizations and talking with other teachers are also helpful.

Preparing for daily teaching is also time-consuming. To be a successful teacher, you must be prepared. You, as a teacher, must fully understand the purpose of each activity. You also need to be sure the activities planned for the day address all areas of a child's development. You must balance the pace of activities so children are not constantly active or quiet. Providing a developmentally appropriate curriculum that meets children's needs and is inviting takes time and careful thought, 1-14.

Personal Desire

Knowing that you really want to teach young children is important to your success. Although you may have doubts, you need to feel that working with young children is rewarding for you. Hearing children make comments, such as *I love you* or *you're pretty*, should boost your self-esteem. Otherwise, you will not feel enthusiastic enough about your work to do a good job.

Questioning a career choice is not unusual. You will discover that even experienced teachers have days when they wonder why they chose this career. These questions are healthy. If they help you determine that you belong in early childhood

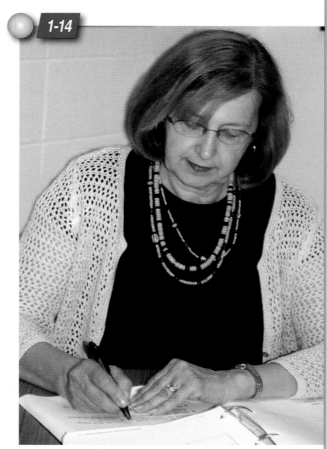

1-14

Spending the time needed to plan a developmentally appropriate curriculum takes a strong commitment from a teacher.

education, you will feel more confident and committed to your career choice.

Only you can decide whether teaching is really for you. You will need to carefully examine your own interests, feelings, and satisfactions. See 1-15. Studying the chapters in this book can help you. Each chapter contains important concepts. Explore possibilities for applying these concepts to a group of young children.

Working with children will increase your insights. However, provide yourself sufficient time. Until you understand how children grow and develop, how to guide them, and how to

Vocabulary

Have a student volunteer define *commitment*. Ask students to reflect on their own commitment to becoming a successful early childhood educator and what they may have to do to achieve that goal.

Activity

Have students survey some of their teachers to discover how much time they spend daily on teaching preparations. What do the preparations involve? Share the information with the class.

Discuss

Have students compare the amount and type of daily preparation needed by secondary teachers with that needed for early childhood educators. How important are meeting learning standards and making individual assessments in planning the daily lessons?

Putting Technology to Use

Staying committed to the job of early childhood educator can cause stress for even the most confident and easygoing individual. Have students conduct an Internet search for strategies on dealing with the daily stress encountered in this field. Have students list "stress builders" and "stress busters." How can knowing how to handle stress affect the student's performance in high school as well as in future employment? Have students write a brief report of their findings.

Discuss

Read aloud *A Letter to a New Teacher*, 1-15. Discuss new challenges teacher's experience and how these challenges can be dealt with. Brainstorm ways in which they can learn more about child guidance and the curriculum process.

Enrich

Ask students how many hours of sleep are recommended daily for teenagers. What are the physical effects of continual lack of enough restful sleep on school performance and personality? Compare these results to adults. Have students list some consequences in work performance that may occur due to lack of sleep.

Resource

Characteristics for Working with Children, Activity D, SAG

1-15

A Letter to a New Teacher

Dear Teacher:

As you begin working with young children, you will meet new challenges and find new answers. This process will continue throughout your teaching career. Like friendship, you will find being a good teacher is a matter of caring for yourself, the children you teach, their families, and your colleagues.

There will be many exciting and fulfilling days. The children will be experiencing many new discoveries. Many times over they may tell you that you are beautiful or you have a pretty voice.

You will also have discouraging days. Teaching is not an easy job. It can be physically, emotionally, and mentally exhausting. At times, the costs may seem to exceed the rewards. Luckily, the majority of the time you will find that teaching is rewarding and personally satisfying.

When you leave the center at night, you will often reflect on the day's happenings. Replaying in your mind something a child said or did is not uncommon. Thinking about your responses is a method of preparing for the next time.

Remember that you will only get out of a career what you invest in it. You must be willing to work overtime if needed and seek new answers. You must also take advantage of opportunities to improve professionally for the benefit of the children and their families.

Try learning as much as you can about child development, child guidance, and the curriculum process. Talking to your colleagues, reading professional journals, joining professional organizations, and attending conferences are several methods. Taking additional course work and obtaining advanced degrees will also strengthen your understanding of young children and improve your competence. Chances are, if you are actively involved, you will never lose your love of teaching.

Deciding whether you want to be an early childhood teacher is an important step in having a successful career.

---

develop appropriate curriculum, you might not feel much self-satisfaction. Given time, however, you are bound to discover the real joys and rewards of working with young children.

Physical and Mental Health

Teaching young children is demanding physically and mentally. It requires you to be constantly alert and handle multiple tasks.

Meeting these demands requires you to take care of yourself. Eating nutritious meals and getting enough sleep is important. You will also need to stay physically active and find ways to reduce stress. Seek counseling or other professional help if you notice problems with your mental health, such as stress, depression, or lasting anxiety. Keeping yourself physically and mentally healthy allows you to meet the challenges of your job.

Meeting Special Needs

Partner volunteer students with special learners to review the chapter together, covering major concepts and vocabulary. Students may work from a teacher-prepared outline of the chapter. Have students quiz each other as they work through the *Review and Reflect* questions on page 33. Ask student volunteers to report areas where reteaching or further understanding is needed.

Chapter 1   You: Working with Young Children   **33**

Summary

Many social and economic changes are creating new opportunities in child care and early education. With fewer traditional families and more dual-career families, the demand for quality child care services is high. Employers are becoming more willing to offer child care benefits for their employees. Child care advocates are working to expand the availability of early childhood programs. Job opportunities are being created and expanded. Most jobs in child care require a CDA Credential, an associate degree, or a bachelor's degree. Qualifications vary from state to state.

Most career opportunities in early childhood are as teachers or assistant teachers. The main focus of this book is to prepare you for a career as an early childhood teacher.

Teachers have many important responsibilities. They must understand principles of child growth and development. Teachers develop curriculum and create classroom environments that meet children's developmental needs. They need to communicate effectively and develop teamwork skills. Teachers must manage time wisely and be lifelong learners. Joining professional organizations and following ethical principles are also important.

A successful teacher develops a style that works well for him or her. However, most successful teachers have many traits in common. If you are interested in becoming an early childhood teacher, you will want to have many of these same qualities. Some may come naturally to you while others may need to be developed.

Review and Reflect

1. _____ covers the period from birth to nine years of age.

2. True or false. Social and economic changes have created a need for more child care services.

3. Why do companies provide child care?

4. _____ or _____ provide care for children in parents' homes.

5. A _____ is responsible for enforcing state child care rules and regulations.

6. Give two job opportunities in which education in early childhood is helpful. Explain how a background in early childhood is helpful in those jobs.

7. Describe the CDA Credential.

8. How does the environment affect a child's development?

9. In teaching, _____ skills are needed to help teachers work smarter, not harder.

10. What is the name of the primary professional organization for teachers of young children?

11. True or false. People who are naturally quiet and reserved cannot be effective early childhood teachers.

12. Give two common characteristics of successful early childhood teachers and explain why these characteristics are helpful.

6. (Student response.)
7. Those who have this national credential have taken postsecondary courses in early care and education and have demonstrated their ability to work with young children.
8. The arrangement of space and selection of materials in a classroom has a direct influence on a child's physical, cognitive, emotional, and social development. A well-designed environment encourages children to experiment, explore, and manipulate objects. It also encourages children to interact with each other in positive ways.
9. time management
10. National Association for the Education of Young Children (NAEYC)
11. false
12. (Student response.)

Review and Reflect **Answer Key**

1. Early childhood
2. true
3. Offering early care and education programs has been found to have positive effects on recruitment, morale, productivity, and absenteeism. Child care services have also had positive influences on turnover, public relations, taxes, scheduling, and the quality of the workforce.
4. Nannies, au pairs
5. licensing specialist

Apply and Explore

1. Take a survey of early childhood teachers. Ask them to share the advantages and disadvantages of teaching. Share your findings with the class.

2. Review the qualities of a successful teacher given in chart 1-11. Make a list of qualities from the chart that you possess.

3. Survey parents of young children to find out what qualities they value in teachers.

Cross-Curricular Link

Reading

1. Look through the want-ad section of a newspaper. Write down jobs listed in which early childhood training would be helpful.

Art

2. Design a bulletin board displaying characteristics of successful teachers.

Writing

3. Write a one-page paper on why you want to teach children.

Technology

4. Visit the Web site for the Council for Professional Recognition (www.cdacouncil.org) to learn more about the CDA Credential. Use a computer to summarize your findings in a brief written report.

5. Explore the National Association for the Education of Young Children Web site (www.naeyc.org) to learn more about the association.

6. Visit the Web site for the National Resource Center for Health and Safety in Child Care at nrc.uchsc.edu. To obtain information regarding licensing in your state, click on *State Licensing and Regulation Information.* Then click on your state on the map.

Workplace Link

Obtain a copy of your state's licensing standards for child care facilities and review curriculum and equipment standards. How would a child care center prepare for an inspection by a licensing specialist in these areas? How often do licensing specialists conduct on-site visits? What could happen if a center fails to meet standards?

Discuss

Look at the chapter opening photo. From the environment, what type of early childhood program do you think this might be?

Reflect

Review the chapter objectives. What do you expect to learn from this chapter? How do you think knowledge of the types of early childhood programs might help you make a career choice in the early childhood field?

Types of Early Childhood Programs

After studying this chapter, you will be able to

- list and describe the various types of early childhood programs available to parents and their children.

- explain the advantages and disadvantages of each type of program.

- name the three types of center sponsorship.

- explain steps families may take in choosing quality child care.

- list indications of quality in early childhood programs.

- list the components of center accreditation.

Vocabulary

List the *Terms to Know* on the board or overhead. Survey the class to see how many of the terms are already known. Ask students to look up unfamiliar words or terms in the glossary before reading the chapter.

Discuss

How does the latest information on brain research affect early childhood programming? Where can you locate this latest research?

Resource

Early Childhood Programs, color transparency CT-2, TR

Terms to Know

family child care home
child care centers
custodial care
Montessori approach
Head Start
school-age child care programs
checking-in services
parent cooperatives
laboratory schools
universal pre-kindergarten (UPK)
accredited

Today, many young children attend early childhood programs. The number of children in these programs continues to grow. Parents place their children in early childhood programs for two main reasons.

First, many parents like the rich learning environment of a high-quality developmentally appropriate early childhood program. Brain research shows that children learn from the earliest moments of life. Their learning is most rapid in the first five years. High-quality programs stimulate learning in this period, 2-1. Studies show that children from high-quality programs did better in primary grades than other children in reading, math, and social skills. They also get along with their peers better and have fewer behavioral problems.

Second, parents who work outside the home must provide for their children's needs during working hours. For this reason, parents may enroll their children in early childhood programs. Parents pay to provide safe and nurturing care in a developmentally appropriate setting. In high-quality programs, learning needs will also be met.

Distinct differences exist among the many types of early childhood programs. These programs may differ in their philosophies, ownership, and program

2-1

A challenging environment can help children develop cognitively, emotionally, socially, and physically.

offerings. Programs also vary in size, staff qualifications, hours of operation, facilities, and fees. Finally, programs may differ greatly in terms of quality, even when they are of the same type.

Some types of programs are more common than others. However, all of them serve a very important purpose by meeting the needs of young children. See Chart 2-2 for child care options parents most often choose.

Family Child Care Homes

A popular form of child care in the United States provided other than by a relative or parent is called **family child care homes**. In this type of program, child care is provided in a private home with a small number of children. Often it is conveniently located in the child's own neighborhood.

Meeting Special Needs

Provide an outline of the chapter with all the chapter headings for special learners. Students should fill in each section of the outline as the material is covered in class with a sentence or two about the content. Review the special learners' IEPs to decide if any modifications should be made in presenting the chapter content.

2-2

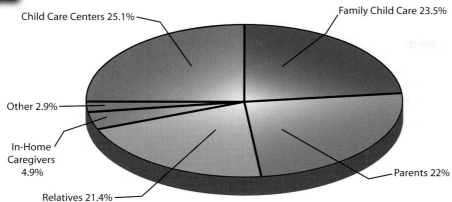

Child Care Centers 25.1%

Family Child Care 23.5%

Other 2.9%

In-Home
Caregivers
4.9%

Relatives 21.4%

Parents 22%

This chart illustrates what percentage of parents chose each type of child care.

Most states require these homes to be licensed. These programs are often popular for infants and toddlers, but children might range from infants to school-age. Moreover, children may attend up to 12 hours per day.

Program

Some states require licensing for family child care homes. Other states may require certification by a community agency. The *National Association for Family Child Care (NAFCC)* is a professional organization for family child care providers. It promotes high-quality early child care and education. NAFCC is committed to improving the awareness and quality of child care. It provides the only national accreditation system for family child care. Training and health assessments are required for accreditation. Other requirements include criminal background checks and an observation to verify that standards are met.

Child Care Centers

Facilities that offer full-day children's programs are often called **child care centers**.

This has become the most popular type of care and education. The focus of most of these centers is to provide care and education. The care is designed to meet the child's basic nutrition, health, and safety needs. The curriculum emphasizes the whole child including his or her social, emotional, cognitive, and physical needs, 2-3.

Most child care centers open early in the morning and remain open until six or seven o'clock in the evening. Some centers provide care for children 24 hours per day. For parents whose children need care during the evening or early morning hours, this service is most convenient.

Program

The program provided by a child care center depends on the educational background and skills of the staff. State licensing rules also influence the program. Some centers simply provide **custodial care**. This type of care focuses primarily on meeting the child's physical needs. The emphasis is on a safe and healthful environment. Meals are usually provided.

Ideally, the program should meet needs in all areas of development. The focus should

Resource

Child Care Program Comparison, reproducible master 2-1, TR

Activity

Obtain a copy of your state's licensing standards for child care facilities. Ask students to compare the ratio of children to caregivers for each type of child care listed in 2-2.

Enrich

Ask students to interview a family child care provider to find out what a typical day involves. How might different age groups affect the daily schedule? Allow time for students to discuss their findings in class.

Discuss

Custodial care focuses primarily on meeting a child's physical needs. Emphasis is placed on a safe and healthful environment. What might be the effect on the intellectual development of a child who received only custodial care?

Putting Technology to Use

Have students learn more about the National Association for Family Child Care (NAFCC) organization at **www.nafcc.org**. What are the goals of NAFCC? What eligibility criteria must providers meet? What is the role of an NAFCC Accreditation Observer? Why do people like being an NAFCC Accreditation Observer? Have students write a short essay of their findings. Ask student volunteers to read their essay in class.

Note

Maria Montessori (1870-1952) influenced our understanding of child-centeredness in early education. Montessori stated "…education is not what the teacher gives; education is a natural process spontane- ously carried out by the human individual as it is acquired not by listening to words, but by experiences upon the environment."

Vocabulary

Have a student volun- teer explain the primary goal of the *Montessori approach*. Discuss how the structured style of this approach provides children with freedom to learn.

Enrich

Ask students to research colleges or universities that offer a Montessori curriculum. How does an early childhood educator become certified to teach in a Montessori school? Have student volunteers share their findings with the class.

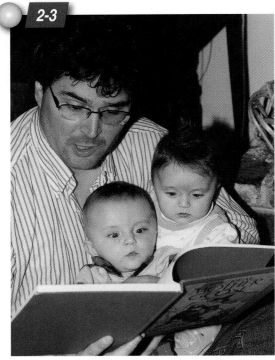

2-3

Many parents rely on the skilled staff of child care centers to provide safe and nurturing care.

be on the whole child and include a balance of engaging activities. Brain development is fostered in an environment that offers a variety of learning experiences.

Montessori Schools

In the early 1900s, Maria Montessori developed her own method of education. She was the first woman in Italy to receive a degree in medicine. Early in her career, she was an assistant doctor at a clinic that served children with mental disabilities.

While working with these children, Montessori developed her theory of education. This theory stated children learn best by being active. Montessori soon learned these methods could also be used with other children. This led to the development of the first Montessori school in Rome.

Montessori's methods became known all over the world. After a short period of popularity, however, interest in this method declined for the next 40 years. In the 1950s, there was a rebirth of the Montessori method. Magazines and television helped make this method known.

Montessori Approach

In her first schools, Montessori stressed proper nutrition, cleanliness, manners, and sensory training. Children also worked with equipment she designed. See 2-4. These materials were self-correcting and required little adult guidance. The materials were organized from simple to complex. By handling and moving the materials, the children's senses were trained and they learned to think. They also learned number concepts as well as motor, language, and writing skills.

Montessori believed in self-education. The primary goal of the **Montessori approach** was for children to "learn how to learn." This approach allowed the child to explore materials that were meant to instruct. Certain materials were given to the child by the teacher in a prescribed sequence. This

2-4

Materials used in a Montessori school are designed to help children learn with little adult guidance.

Cross-Curricular Activity

English
Using Internet or print resources, have students research the biography of Maria Montessori. Ask students to write a one-page report detail- ing how Maria Montessori's early experiences in medicine led her to define a philosophy of early childhood education. Discuss her contribution to the way children are educated today. Allow time to have students read their papers aloud in class.

sequence was related to the child's physical and mental development. Montessori felt that this approach would provide the child freedom within limits.

Independence is stressed in Montessori schools. Children must learn to care for themselves. Teachers provide little help. As a result, children learn to button, zip, tie, and put on coats and boots. These experiences are called *practical life experiences* in the Montessori curriculum.

The purpose of *sensory training* is to help children learn touch, sound, taste, and sight discrimination. One piece of equipment for this training is a set of sandpaper blocks that vary in texture. The children are told to rub their fingers across the blocks. Their goal is to correctly match blocks with like textures. Musical bells with varying tones are used in the same way. Based on tone, children match like tones.

Academics are also stressed in the Montessori program. However, before a child is introduced to these experiences, sensory training must be mastered. Then, to teach letter recognition, sandpaper letters are used. After the teacher introduces a letter, children are encouraged to trace the letter with their fingertips. Numbers are taught in the same manner. When a child demonstrates knowledge of and interest in letters, reading instruction may be started.

Head Start

In the 1960s, the federal government designed the **Head Start** program to overcome the negative effects of poverty on young children. The program mainly provides child care and education for four- and-five-year-olds from low-income families. More recently, it has added some programs for infants and toddlers. Today, Head Start is one of the most successful preschool and family support programs in the country. Head Start programs may be full-time or part-time. The programs may be center based or home based. Head Start provides a variety of medical and social services to promote children's development.

Education

The curriculum in a Head Start program is designed to meet the needs of each child. One goal is to build self-esteem that will lead to future success in school. Staff encourage self-confidence, curiosity, and self-discipline.

A variety of learning experiences are designed to meet the children's needs in all four areas of development. Staff and the child's entire family work as a team to plan curriculum and teach children. Parent involvement is the heart of the program.

On preschool achievement tests, Head Start children perform equal to or better than their peers. Once they enter school, these children are more likely to be successful.

Nutrition

Many children who take part in Head Start do not receive nutritious meals at home. Nutrition then is a vital part of the program, 2-5. Federal rules require the center to provide at least one snack and one hot meal every day. The nutrition program serves foods that reflect the child's ethnic and cultural preferences. The goal is to help children make healthy food choices and develop good eating habits.

Health

All children who attend a Head Start program are given a total health plan. Dental, medical, and mental health services are provided. Prior to enrollment, many of these children have never visited a dentist. Children who have not already received childhood immunizations are given them while they are enrolled.

Note

The Head Start program is administered by the Head Start Bureau; the Administration on Children, Youth, and Families (ACYF); Administration for Children and Families (ACF); and the Department of Health and Human Services (DHHS). Head Start was proposed by President Lyndon Johnson as part of his War on Poverty and began in 1965 with an 8-week summer program. Over 21 million children have been served by Head Start since 1965. The popular children's television show *Sesame Street* was developed as an offshoot of Head Start.

Reflect

Why do you think nutrition plays such an important part in the Head Start program?

Discuss

Parent volunteers are vital to the Head Start program. What role(s) can a volunteer parent play in this and other early childhood education programs?

Cross-Curricular Activity

History/Political Science
Have students research the political platform of Lyndon Johnson and the part the War on Poverty and Head Start may have played in his successful election. Has the United States government been completely supportive of Head Start since its inception? What changes have been made to the Head Start program through the decades, and what is in store for its future?

Reflect

Most states have age requirements for kindergarten attendance. What might be the benefit of having children held back from attending until they are six years of age? Do you know of anyone, including yourself, who was held back from kindergarten for a year? What would be the disadvantage of starting kindergarten before a child was emotionally ready?

Activity

Ask students to research the kindergarten schedules of nearby communities. What types of schedules are favored by parents and by school districts? Have students compare the advantages and disadvantages of a full-versus half-day program.

Enrich

Have students investigate the kind of preparation children need for kindergarten in their school district. What are children expected to know and be able to do before they start school? Are there any types of services available that will help a child transition to the school setting?

2-5

A well-organized, sanitary kitchen is an important link in providing sound nutrition for children.

Parental Involvement

Head Start recognizes the parent as the child's first teacher. Supporting parental involvement is vital to the program's success. Parents are encouraged to help recruit new children, assist in the center, and take part in policy meetings. Thus, Head Start parents are able to influence administrative decisions.

Kindergarten

In 1837, the first kindergarten was opened by Frederick Froebel in Germany. The kindergarten curriculum stressed play. Froebel believed that self-development took place through creative activities such as play. The children in this kindergarten, like many today, engaged in painting, stringing beads, blockbuilding, and clay modeling. The children also cared for pets, sang songs, and gardened.

The first American kindergarten was opened in Watertown, Wisconsin, in 1856. It was held in the home of Margerenthia Schurz. This mother and teacher had studied under Froebel. Mrs. Schurz first opened the kindergarten for her own children and four of their cousins.

Today, kindergartens are part of most public and many private school systems. They are usually restricted to children who are at least four years old.

Schedules

There are three basic scheduling patterns in kindergarten: half-day, full-day, and full-day/alternating day sessions. The half-day session usually runs from two and one-half to three and one-half hours per day. Full-day sessions run from six to eight hours per day. Full-day/alternating day programs vary. Some programs meet every other day. Others require children to attend on Tuesday and Thursday the first week, and on Monday and Friday the next week. Other alternating programs have children attend two full days and one-half day. To illustrate, one group may attend all day on Monday and Wednesday, plus on Friday morning. The other group might attend all day on Tuesday and Thursday, as well as Friday afternoon. For some children, these alternating schedules may be confusing. Studies show that children thrive on predictable schedules.

Goals

Goals for a kindergarten program permit variety. Basic objectives of most kindergarten programs include
- respect for the contributions, property, and rights of other children
- development of positive feelings about school
- development of a positive self-concept
- growth in language, social, and physical, and creative skills
- achievement of problem-solving and cognitive skills
- development of independence, shown by working alone on a task or developing self-help skills

Putting Technology to Use

Have students conduct an Internet search on kindergarten readiness. One source, **www.familyeducation.com**, contains kindergarten checklists and other information for parents concerning their children's kindergarten experience. Ask students to write a brief article directed to prospective kindergarten parents about what to expect.

- development of interpersonal skills
- appreciation of objects of beauty

Similar to preschools, most kindergartens emphasize the growth of the whole child.

Curriculum

Kindergarten curriculum may vary from school to school. Some schools stress certain preacademic skills, such as learning the names and sounds of alphabet letters. Other programs focus more on social development. These programs are less structured than those that stress preacademics.

Kindergarten teachers, unlike most elementary teachers, have more freedom in planning curriculum. Studies show that in most kindergarten programs, about 50 percent of the day is spent on creative activities. Included are art, woodworking, blockbuilding, storytelling, and music. Free play, self-care, and rest fill the remaining time, 2-6. The teacher provides social studies, mathematics, language, and science activities as well.

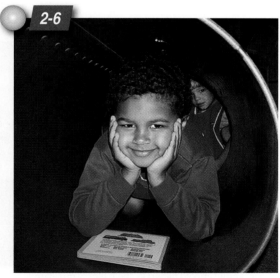
2-6

Free play and creativity are important in kindergarten programs.

School-Age Child Care

School-age child care programs provide care for children before and/or after school. These programs are often sponsored by schools, houses of worship, or child care centers. Children from 5 to 10 years old most often attend. The program supplements regular classes. These children are provided assistance with homework. They also play games and take part in other activities.

As an alternative, some parents use **checking-in services**. These services hire workers who call the home to check whether the child has arrived safely. This is a good option only for children who are mature enough to provide self-care until parents arrive.

Parent Cooperatives

Parent cooperatives are formed and run by parents who wish to take part in their children's preschool experience. Member control allows parents to prepare budgets, hire teachers, set program policies and goals, and assist in the classroom. These programs may offer full-day or half-day programs.

Cooperatives provide developmental experiences for adults as well as children. Specifically, parents

- obtain guidance in their jobs as parents
- learn what children are like at different ages and stages
- gain several free mornings each month
- become familiar with creative activities, materials, and equipment
- gain a more objective picture of their child's development

Due to all of these experiences, many parents have reported feeling a greater sense of self-satisfaction in their parenting roles.

Discuss

What would be the advantages to attending a before- or after-school child care program comprised of a mixed age group? What would be the disadvantages?

Vocabulary

Have a student volunteer look up the term *checking-in services* in the glossary and read the definition aloud. Discuss why this service is not a good option for all children.

Activity

Have students conduct a search for parent cooperative programs in their area. Are full- or half-day programs offered? Do the parents hire the teachers and set program policies and goals? In what ways do the parents assist in the classroom? Allow time for students to report their findings in class.

Workplace Connection

Invite a school-age child care teacher to speak to the class about the challenges of his or her job. What does a typical daily schedule involve including snacks and activities? Have students write additional questions to ask the speaker prior to the visit.

Reflect

What role should a parent volunteer play in the guidance of children attending a parent cooperative child care program? How much authority should the teacher have in setting rules and classroom expectations?

Discuss

Should state licensing requirements for child care facilities be followed for high school vocational child care programs? How might adopting these standards benefit the high school program? What might be the disadvantages?

Vocabulary

Have a student volunteer look up the term *laboratory schools* in the glossary and read the definition aloud. What is the primary purpose of laboratory schools?

Resource

Early Childhood Fill-In, Activity A, SAG

Advantages and Disadvantages

There are many advantages to teaching in a parent cooperative. Since the parents make the administrative decisions, collect fees, and order and repair equipment, the teacher can devote more time to the children and curriculum. Another advantage can be the special relationships that many times develop between parents and teachers.

A major disadvantage of a parent cooperative is the lack of control on the teacher's part. Although the teacher acts as an adviser, parents are usually responsible for making rules. At times, there may be differences of opinion between teacher and parents. For instance, parents may feel that children do not have to help return toys to the storage place. The teacher may feel differently. This can cause problems for many teachers.

Sessions

Parent cooperatives usually operate for two or three hours, two to five days each week. Sometimes these groups are structured by the children's ages. For example, on Tuesday and Thursday mornings, a group of two-year-old children will be scheduled. On Monday, Wednesday, and Friday mornings, three-year-olds may attend. Other centers may prefer to use the "family-type" grouping. In this type of setting, children of mixed ages may all be included in one group.

Fees

Due to the parent's involvement, fees charged at a parent cooperative are often less than at other programs. Costs are reduced by hiring only a head teacher. Parents serve as the classroom aides. Generally, each parent will assist in the classroom several times each month. In addition, parents volunteer to perform many of the service activities.

They may clean and maintain the building, prepare snacks, type newsletters, and do some special jobs, such as painting the classroom.

Laboratory Schools

Laboratory schools, or university- and college-affiliated programs, are located on a postsecondary or college campus, 2-7. Although they provide excellent programs for children, their primary purpose is to support practical experiences for future teachers and to serve as a study group for research. Most of these schools have a highly qualified staff, a well-planned curriculum, up-to-date facilities, and excellent equipment.

High School Child Care Programs

In the last two decades, many high schools have started providing vocational training for child care occupations. Like the laboratory schools, these programs train

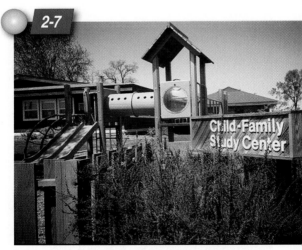

2-7

Laboratory schools generally have highly qualified staffs, well-planned curriculum, and excellent equipment.

Meeting Special Needs

Locate any laboratory schools operating in your area and arrange a visit for the gifted students. These may be found in community colleges, colleges, and universities with a teacher preparation program. Have students observe an early childhood program for as long as possible. Have the students compare the program to other child care centers in the community.

future child care professionals. Many high schools have their own child care laboratory facilities where students can work with preschool children. The preschool program may operate two or three days a week. Preschool children of high school students, faculty, and community members usually attend the program.

The high school students plan and present the curriculum under the supervision of a teacher who has a degree in early childhood education. Some high school students may observe the children while others work directly with the children. The following week, the students who observed the preceding week then work with the preschoolers while the other students observe them.

Sponsorship of Early Childhood Centers

Early childhood centers can be grouped based on sponsorship. Basically, there are three kinds of sponsorship: public, private, and employer-sponsored centers.

Public Sponsorship

Publicly sponsored programs are funded by federal, state, or local governments. Some of these funds come through school districts. Other funds may come through social service agencies.

An example of a publicly sponsored program is Head Start. Most parents pay no fee for their child to attend Head Start. However, a fee is required if their income exceeds the federal guidelines for the program. Most of the expenses for the program are covered through grants received from the federal government. Funding is usually provided on an annual basis.

State funds may help support programs designed for educational purposes. These programs may be housed in a university,

college, secondary school, or vocational school. Examples include child care centers, preschool centers, laboratory schools, and high school child care programs.

Publicly funded child care centers, preschools, and laboratory programs may receive several forms of financial support in addition to parental fees. For instance, a publicly funded child care center may also receive funds from the United Way, community donations, and tuition. Likewise, a laboratory school on a college campus may receive tuition donations or scholarships through alumni groups.

Private Sponsorship

The largest group of privately sponsored programs is the privately owned center. These centers rely on parent fees to cover most of the operating expenses.

A *privately sponsored program* may be operated by a house of worship, hospital, or charitable organization. Many of these child care centers are nonprofit. They may be governed by a voluntary board of community members and operated as a service to the community.

Most private programs are operated by independent owners. Many of these centers are operated by families. Their motivation in operating a center is to provide a service that makes a profit.

Child Care Corporations

Some child care centers are a part of chains operated by large national corporations, although some chains are privately held. Midsize chains typically operate on a regional basis. Often these centers are built and located in large cities and suburban areas. To make a profit in these centers, the enrollment must be high. The chains are managed by a central administration that furnishes the financial backing and sets policy. Curriculum guides may be developed by curriculum specialists

Discuss

How can the type of early childhood program sponsorship affect the delivery of an effective early childhood educational program? For example, a state or federally funded program may have standards and/or restrictions on curriculum content, nutritional guidelines, and eligibility.

Reflect

Should privately sponsored child care programs be subject to local building codes, fire and safety codes, and state licensing standards? Should local and state governments have any authority over a privately owned child care center?

Activity

Have students research national child care chains operating in their area. Ask students to investigate the companies hiring policies. Does the company require specific qualifications for teachers and other staff members? What training, if any, does the company provide? Are tuition costs similar to other child care facilities in the area? Have students write a brief report of their findings.

Cross-Curricular Activity

English
Privately sponsored child care programs operated by a house of worship may include religious education as part of the curriculum. Ask students what their feelings are on this subject.

Should all students enrolled have to take part in the religious curriculum activities the program provides? Ask students to write a short essay detailing the advantages and disadvantages of this type of program.

hired by the organization and provided to the center staff in each of the locations.

Employer Sponsorship

The number of businesses and industries providing their employees with some type of child care assistance is growing. Some employer-sponsored child care providers have extended their services. They may include special activities for school-age children and care for older adults and mildly ill children. The employer may pay part or all of the costs of the services. The center can be located on-site or nearby.

Employers sponsor child care to reduce the conflict between family and work responsibilities. Studies show that there is less employee turnover and absenteeism at companies that provide some form of child care. At such companies, employees have better work attitudes, new employees are attracted, community relations improve, and good publicity is received. Moreover, there are tax incentives for companies who sponsor child care.

Companies can provide child care assistance in several ways, 2-8. The company owned, on-site child care center is one option.

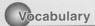

2-8

Types of Employer-Sponsored Child Care Assistance

- Company owned, on-site center
- Off-site center sponsored by one or more companies
- Company sponsored, vendor provided centers
- Vouchers provided by company to subsidize care
- Sick child care
- Referral services

Companies may assist families with child care in many ways.

Such a center may be located at or near the work site. With this type of program, the company may hire a director to run the program. Other companies contract with child care chains or firms specializing in child care to operate the center.

There are advantages and disadvantages to an on-site child care facility. One advantage is that parents can spend breaks and lunch hours with their children. In large cities, however, this model may not work. Employees who commute long distances to work may find it difficult to travel with children on public transportation or in car pools.

The off-site center is another option. This model is often used when several companies form a group. Each company may not have enough need for their own child care center. By sharing a facility, the costs and risks are shared by all the companies in the group.

The off-site location may be closer to the parents' homes. Therefore, transportation times are shorter. If space is available, this type of model may also serve other children from the community.

The vendor model allows companies to purchase space in a child care center or several centers. This model is ideal for small companies. It is not as costly as opening a center. There are no costs for start-up, investment in a building, or center administration.

Companies respect parental choice when the voucher model is provided. Parents receive a voucher or coupon worth a certain amount of money from the company. Some companies will pay for all child care costs, while others pay only a portion. This model may be preferred by parents who do not live close to the work site. Thus, it is a useful model for companies in large cities.

One disadvantage of the voucher model is that the money received must be declared as income on tax returns. However, the employee can deduct the cost of child care from federal taxes (and state taxes where allowed).

Vocabulary

Ask student volunteers to describe the three kinds of childhood center sponsorships: public-, private-, and employer-sponsored.

Reflect

How might on-site employer-sponsored child care affect the work production of employees who enroll their children in the program? Do you think this might cause the parent to be more distracted at work or more focused on his or her job?

Discuss

Why do employers sponsor child care? What types of employer-sponsored child care assistance might be available? What are the advantages and disadvantages to each type?

Putting Technology to Use

Have students conduct an Internet search to discover which large companies in the United States provide some form of employee assistance for child care. What type of assistance is provided? What choices do employees have for child care benefits, if any? What is the percentage of employees who take advantage of these benefits? Ask students to write a brief report of their findings. Allow time for student volunteers to read their reports aloud in class.

Child care for ill children is provided by some companies. This benefit can take two forms. A center may provide services for children who are ill and cannot attend school. When this is done, the health department as well as the state licensing agency must be notified. This works best for children who are recovering from an illness, but are not well enough to return to school. The second form allows for a nurse to be sent to a sick child's home to provide care. This allows the parent to go to work.

Finding a quality child care program near home is a problem for many parents. To assist parents in this process, some companies provide a referral service that matches the parents' needs with centers. The company may hire their own resource specialist or contract a resource and referral agency.

Generally, parents are given a list of community child care centers. Specific information on each center is collected and given to the parents. Included are the center's location, fees, hours of operation, goals, enrollment capacity, policies, curriculum, staff qualifications, and special services. Maps showing the location of the centers are often provided to help the parents in the selection process.

Universal Pre-Kindergarten

Another type of early childhood education program is called **universal pre-kindergarten (UPK)**. UPK is sponsored at the state level. These programs are designed for three- and four-year-old children. A high-quality, literary-rich environment is provided. Children benefit from being involved in this environment before they enter kindergarten. They then start kindergarten eager to learn and ready for success. When children lack quality early learning experiences, they start school at a disadvantage to others.

Selecting a Child Care Program

Selecting an early childhood program is one of the most important decisions that parents make. Comfort with the children's care and education can greatly affect the quality of family life, 2-9. For this reason, parents need to take their time in making this decision.

Parents consider many factors as they search for the right program. Each family makes this choice based on its own needs, priorities, and goals. Many parents do consider some common factors, however. See 2-10 for a list of questions parents can use to compare programs.

First and foremost, parents want their children to be safe and comfortable. They want a program that welcomes their child and promotes all areas of the children's development. Cost and location are important, too. Working parents prefer the convenience of a program near their home or job.

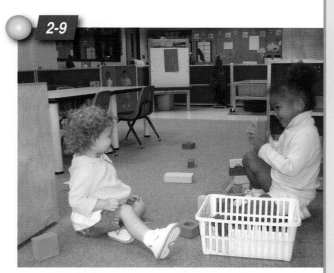

2-9

Parents are greatly comforted when they see their children playing happily in the early childhood program they have chosen.

Vocabulary

Universal prekindergarten (UPK) programs are designed for three- and four-year-old children. Ask students to describe this type of program and list the benefits to children involved in this environment.

Resource

Types of Programs, Activity B, SAG

Reflect

Imagine you are a parent searching for the right childhood program for your child. What needs, priorities, and goals would you consider most important? What factors do you think you would base your decision on?

Workplace Connection

Have students contact the human resource director of a large company in their area. Is child care part of the employee benefits package? What provisions does the company make for parents with ill children? How supportive is the company to its employees who are parents? Allow time for students to share their findings in class.

Reflect

What additional questions might you have to add to the list in Chart 2-10 if you were a parent researching child care facilities for your own child? Why do you think these are important?

Discuss

What are the characteristics of a high-quality child care program? What should be most important to parents?

Resource

Standards of Quality for Early Childhood Programs, transparency master 2-2, TR

2-10

Selecting Quality Child Care

	Yes	No
1. Is the center accredited by the National Academy of Early Childhood Programs?		
2. Do the children appear to be happy, active, and secure?		
3. Are all staff members educationally qualified?		
4. Do staff members attend in-service training, professional meetings, and conferences on a regular basis?		
5. Are staff meetings conducted regularly to plan and evaluate program activities?		
6. Do staff members observe, assess, and record each child's developmental progress?		
7. Does the curriculum support the children's individual rates of development?		
8. Do the staff and curriculum celebrate diversity?		
9. Are the indoor and outdoor environments large enough to support a variety of activities?		
10. Is the environment inviting, warm, and stimulating?		
11. Is equipment provided to promote all four areas of development: physical, cognitive, social, and emotional?		
12. Are safe and sanitary conditions maintained within the building and on the playground?		
13. Are teacher-child interactions positive?		
14. Are teachers using developmentally appropriate teaching strategies?		
15. Are families welcome to observe and participate?		
16. Is sufficient equipment available for the number of children attending?		
17. Does the climate in the center "feel" positive?		
18. Do teachers meet with families regularly to discuss the child's needs, interest, and abilities?		

In order to help ease the burden of choosing child care for their children, you may wish to supply interested families with this questionnaire.

Meeting Special Needs

Discuss the meaning of the following terms appearing in Chart 2-10: *accredited*, *secure*, *in-service training*, *developmental progress*, *diversity*, *stimulating environment*, *interactions*, *developmentally appropriate*, *climate*. Special learners may need further understanding of these terms in the child care context. Ask for student volunteers to explain each of the terms to special learners.

Parents must choose a program they can afford as well. For example, parents with lower incomes may need to use a public program or a private program with low fees.

Quality of the program is a key factor. Parents are interested in the program's goals, activities, and schedule. Variety and balance among activities is desirable. Quality programs offer ample materials, equipment, and space. These programs also offer smaller group sizes and more adults within each group. This allows children to receive more attention and personal care. See 2-11 for the adult-child ratios recommended for various age groups by the National Association for the Education of Young Children (NAEYC).

Many parents ask about the training and experience of the staff. Studies show staff members with early childhood education and experience are often more sensitive to children's needs. They provide more stimulating, developmentally appropriate care and education. Well-trained staff members ensure that learning experiences are meaningful and respectful for child and families. Staff use a variety of teaching strategies to be responsive to the needs of individual children.

Asking about staff turnover rates can help parents in choosing a program. Parents should avoid choosing programs with high staff turnover. First, frequent staff changes may be a sign of low staff wages or poor working conditions and may indicate problems with the quality of the program. High staff turnover also interferes with children's sense of security. To feel secure, young children need to form close relationships with one or two caregivers. They also need a predictable environment. Staff turnover disrupts the environment and prevents children from forming close relationships with caregivers.

Parents want a facility that is safe for their children. For example, many centers have a security system that helps them monitor who enters and leaves the building. The building should also have smoke detectors, fire extinguishers, and evacuation plans. Parents desire a facility that is clean and in good repair.

2-11

Recommended Adult-Child Ratios

Age of Children	Recommended Ratio
6 weeks to 1 year	1 adult to 3 children
1 to 2 years	1 adult to 5 children
2 to 3 years	1 adult to 6 children
3 to 5 years	1 adult to 8 children
5 to 6 years	1 adult to 10 children

These adult-child ratios are recommended by NAEYC for quality child care programs.

Health and Safety

References and Background Checks

In order to keep children safe from abuse, all early childhood providers must submit to reference and background checks before starting employment at a child care facility. This may include fingerprinting and checking state social service records for previous child abuse convictions. People who are known sex offenders or who acknowledge sexual attraction to children will not be allowed to work in child care.

Resource

Selecting Child Care, Activity A, OG

Discuss

What questions about the staff and their qualifications should a parent ask when considering a child care center for his or her child? How does staff turnover affect the quality of a child care program?

Activity

Ask the director or human resource representative from a local child care center to speak to the class about the center's hiring process for obtaining new employees. Is a reference check always completed? Is a background check performed? Are state records checked to determine if someone has a prior conviction? What qualifications are needed for an employee to work in the center? Have students prepare a list of additional questions prior to the visit.

Meeting Special Needs

Have gifted students compare the adult-child ratios recommended by the NAEYC in Chart 2-11 with the ratios required by their state's child care licensing standards. Are the recommended ratios higher or lower than those required by the state? What effect might the ratios have on the delivery of a quality child care program? What effect would higher ratios have on a center's finances? Have students write a one-page report of their findings. Allow time for students to read their report aloud in class.

Reflect

Why do you think many parents start their search for child care by asking other parents about their child care experiences? How can other parents' experiences influence a parent's own choice?

Discuss

What can parents learn about a child care program by viewing the daily and weekly schedules? What questions should parents ask about a center's menus and snack policies?

Note

Parents whose children have special dietary needs should discuss the ability of the center to address the child's needs before enrollment. For example, a child with a peanut allergy may not be able to eat foods containing any form of the nut. The child may not even have his or her food come in contact with utensils that may be contaminated by peanuts. The kitchen and/or food service staff needs to be made aware of any special handling needed to avoid severe medical consequences.

Resource

Choosing a Program, Activity C, SAG

The Selection Process

Most parents follow the same process in selecting a child care program. As a teacher, you need to understand this process and your role in it. Parents need to know much about a program before they can choose it. Your role will be to help parents gain the needed information.

As parents begin a search, they want to identify options. Some parents start by contacting a child care resource and referral agency for a list of licensed programs in their community. Other parents search the telephone book for available programs. Parents also ask people they know about experiences with the available programs. Many parents seek the advice of other parents who use early childhood programs. Parents often trust this more than information given by the program itself.

Next, parents often begin calling available programs. First questions often involve what age groups the program serves, whether openings exist in their child's age group, and what the hours of operation are. Then, parents might ask about fees and location.

Parents who are still interested will ask about the program, staff, and activities. From there, they may arrange a visit to the program. A visit during program hours lets parents inspect the environment, observe the program, and meet the staff. Parents may want to see the whole facility, including the kitchen, restrooms, classrooms, and outdoor play areas. They will often ask to see the daily and weekly schedules as well as the menu for meals and snacks. Parents also want to observe the interactions of staff with children and other adults in the program.

After the visit, parents may have additional questions. They may need to visit a program several times before making a final decision. Parents may also want to bring their child to see how the child responds to the environment. With all of this information, parents can decide which available early childhood program will best meet the needs of the child and family.

Center Accreditation

The best indicator of high-quality early care and education is accreditation. Being **accredited** certifies that a set of standards has been met by an early childhood program. The National Academy of Early Childhood Programs, a division of NAEYC, administers a voluntary accreditation system. This system has been designed for early childhood programs and preschools serving children from birth through age five. It is also designed for programs that serve school-age children in before school and after school care.

The purpose of this voluntary system is to improve the quality of programs for young children in group care. It assists families in their search for high quality programs for their children. In addition, it helps assure parents that their children are receiving quality care. Public recognition is the main benefit of achieving accreditation status.

To be eligible for accreditation status, a center must conduct a self-study. The self-study is an evaluation process designed by the National Academy of Early Childhood Programs. The self-study is a three-step process. It requires from four to eighteen months to complete. First, a self-study on 10 categories of center operations is completed, 2-12. This is done by the directors, teachers, and parents. This process provides valuable professional development experiences. Next, a validation visit is conducted on-site by trained professionals. The final step is a decision by a team of experts representing

Meeting Special Needs

Ask gifted students to research where local parents would go for child care referrals in their area. Contact the county's Health Department, YMCA, state's Department of Children and Families, local school board, and telephone directory to locate sources of child care. What information is available about each program or child care provider? How can a parent use this information to begin the child care selection process? Have students share their findings with the class.

2-12

Categories of Center Operations Covered by the Accreditation Process

- Evaluation processes
- Curriculum
- Administration
- Health and safety
- Physical environment
- Staff qualification and development
- Staff-children interactions
- Staff-parent interactions
- Staffing patterns
- Nutrition and food services

2-12 A quality early childhood program will meet the developmental needs of children. It also fosters positive interactions between families, staff, and administrators involved in the program.

2-13

Standards for Quality Practice

Association	Types of Programs
National Association for the Education of Young Children	Birth through kindergarten programs
National After-School Association	School-age programs
National Association for Family Child Care	Family child care programs
National Association of Child Care Professionals	Child care centers

These organizations have standards for quality practice. Are their names familiar to you?

the National Academy of Early Childhood Programs.

A recent study shows that accreditation has improved program quality. The process has made improvements a smoother and easier process. Center directors reported the greatest gains in the areas of curriculum, followed by administration, health, and safety. Most directors also reported that accreditation had increased the visibility of their programs. Chart 2-13 contains a list of organizations that have accepted standards for quality practice.

Activity

Divide students into small groups and assign each group one of the categories in Chart 2-12, *Categories of Center Operations Covered by the Accreditation Process.* Each group should discuss their understanding of the category and write one sentence to explain its importance to a quality program. Sentences should be shared with the entire class.

Resource

Evaluating Early Childhood Programs, Activity D, SAG

Enrich

Have students research the National Association for the Education of Young Children (**www.naeyc.org**) for information concerning child care center accreditation. This site also has information on locating accredited programs in your area. What is involved in receiving accreditation from NAEYC? What research is available to support the benefit of operating an accredited center?

Portfolio Project

Ask students to write a short essay on their vision of a high-quality child care center. Have students include characteristics of the program they feel would best meet the needs of the children served by the program. These may include facility, curriculum, child-adult ratios, teacher qualifications and training, equipment, and accreditation. (Refer to chart 2-12). What would encourage parents to enroll their children in this program?

Review and Reflect

Review and Reflect Answer Key

1. true
2. family child care homes
3. active
4. instances in which children learn to be independent by doing for themselves
5. to overcome the negative effects of poverty on young children
6. true
7. full-day, half-day, full-day/alternating day
8. (List five:) respect for the contributions, property, and rights of other children; development of positive feelings about school; development of a positive self-concept; growth in language, social, physical, and creative skills; achievement of problem-solving and cognitive skills; development of independence to work alone and develop self-help skills; development of interpersonal skills; appreciation of objects of beauty
9. Caregivers call their assigned children at home to make sure they arrived safely. Children do not go to the caregivers' homes.
10. Parent cooperatives

Summary

Many types of early childhood programs are available. These include family child care homes, child care centers, Montessori schools, Head Start, kindergartens, school-age child care programs, parent cooperatives, laboratory schools, and high school child care programs. Each type of program takes a unique approach to meeting children's developmental needs.

Programs may be sponsored in a variety of ways. The type of sponsorship may affect goals and philosophies. Programs may be publicly or privately funded. Child care corporations can be privately or publicly held. Employer-sponsored programs are designed to reduce some of the burdens of early care and education for working parents. Employers are using a variety of ways to provide these benefits for their employees.

With the variety of child care programs available, families consider many factors in choosing the best program for their child. Some of the factors that families consider include the type of program, quality of program and staff, adult-child ratio, group size, and condition of facilities. As a teacher, you will need to know what families look for in a program. Then you can strive to make your program one that families choose for their children.

Families may look for programs that have been accredited by NAEYC. Accreditation certifies that a program meets a specific set of standards. Obtaining accreditation involves participation in a self-study, which is designed as an evaluation tool. Center directors, staff, and parents participate in this process. Public recognition of a high level of excellence is one of the main benefits of achieving accreditation.

Review and Reflect

1. True or false. Child care centers offer full-day programs for young children.

2. What is the most popular type of child care in the United States?

3. Montessori's theory of education stated that children learn best when they are _____.

4. What are "practical life experiences" according to Montessori?

5. Describe the purpose of Head Start.

6. True or false. Nutrition is a vital part of the Head Start program.

7. Name the three basic kindergarten schedules.

8. List five objectives for a kindergarten program.

9. Describe how a checking-in service works for school-age children.

10. _____ are formed and run by parents who wish to take part in their children's preschool experiences.

11. What is the primary purpose of a laboratory school?

12. Publicly sponsored programs are funded by _____.

13. Describe one way employers can provide child care assistance for their employees.

14. For children ages 3 to 5 years, NAEYC recommends the adult-child ratio of one adult for every _____ children.

15. Why might a high staff turnover be a concern to parents?

16. Why might parents want to select an early care and education program that was accredited?

11. to train future teachers and to serve as a place to conduct research
12. federal, state, or local governments
13. (Student response.)
14. eight
15. A high staff turnover can cause morale problems among teachers. It can also be an indication low staff wages, poor working conditions, and low quality. In order to feel secure, children need consistent, predictable care.
16. Being accredited certifies that a set of standards has been met by a child care center. Parents are assured of a high-quality program for their children

Apply and Explore

1. Visit a family child care home. Ask the provider to outline the daily schedule.

2. Discuss the advantages and disadvantages of teaching in a parent cooperative.

3. Discuss the value of center accreditation.

Cross-Curricular Link

Writing

1. Arrange a visit to a school-age child care program. Ask to review the curriculum. Write a report on what you learn.

Technology

2. Visit the Web site for Effective Parenting (www.parenting-ed.org) to find information for parents on selecting child care.

3. Search the American Montessori Society Web site (www.amshq.org) for a position paper on Montessori schools.

4. Use the Web site www.findcarenow.com to search for licensed and registered child care programs by state, city, and region.

Workplace Link

Contact a local insurance agent. Ask if any additional insurance coverage is needed for a family child care provider beyond a basic homeowner's policy. What additional steps need to be completed to ensure adequate liability coverage? (Consider such areas as fencing, gates, and lighting.) What medical benefits does a typical policy cover if an accident involving a child in the homeowner's care occurs?

Discuss

Study the chapter opening photo. What do you note about the observation taking place in the picture?

Discuss

Look over the objectives for this chapter. How will information about assessments, portfolios, and observations be used by an early childhood professional?

Observing Children: A Tool for Assessment

After studying this chapter, you will be able to

- list purposes of assessment.
- contrast initial and ongoing assessment.
- list the factors to consider in choosing a method of assessment.
- list the advantages and disadvantages of various assessment tools.
- compile a list of contents for a child's portfolio.
- summarize guidelines for observing children.

Terms to Know

assessment
developmental milestones
anecdotal record
checklist
participation chart
rating scale
visual documentation
portfolio

Young children are fascinating to watch. Just ask any new mother, father, or proud grandparent! A young child's awkward attempts to try new skills or early efforts at conversation can be captivating. Observing children is something everyone enjoys doing. Children are charming, creative, active, and emotional.

Observation also serves another purpose. It provides vital information about each child's needs, interest, abilities and learning styles. Observation is one of the oldest and best methods for learning about children. Most of what is known about child growth and development is the result of some form of observation. Many behaviors of children cannot be measured in any other way. A one-year-old, for instance, cannot answer questions orally or in writing, but the child's behavior can be observed, 3-1.

As a student of child development, much of what you will learn about children will come from observing them. You may be asked to observe the children in your program. At times you may be assigned to observe a specific aspect of a child's behavior or development. You will also be encouraged to observe children informally outside of school.

Jafar, a student majoring in child development, was assigned his first observation. He was amazed at the developmental differences he saw within the group of three- and four-year-olds. Jafar

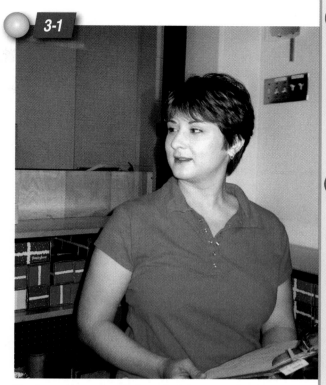

3-1

Teachers observe largely through their eyes and ears.

noticed that Ben was doing an 18-piece puzzle. Sitting next to him was Hunter. He was asking the teacher for help with a puzzle that had only four pieces. Standing at the easel, Wyatt was printing his name across the top of his art project. Next to him was Wendy. She drew a circle in an upper corner of her work and exclaimed with a smile, "That's my name!"

Each of these children is unique. If you were the teacher in this classroom, how would you plan a curriculum that would meet the needs of each of these children? To begin the process, you would need to gather information. This, too, involves observation. You would need to determine each child's developmental stage. With this information, you could then determine the group's developmental status. The data gathered would help you plan a curriculum that

Vocabulary

Have students review the *Terms to Know* list. Ask students to look up unfamiliar words or terms in the glossary before reading the chapter.

Reflect

Write the following quote about observation on the board or overhead: "Observation more than books, experience more than persons, are the prime educators." (Amos Bronson Alcott.) What meaning does this quote have for you as you begin your study of the importance of observation in early childhood education?

Discuss

What is meant by a child's developmental stage and a group's developmental status? How do knowing these affect a teacher's planning of an educational program?

Meeting Special Needs

Provide an outline of the chapter with all the chapter headings for special learners. Have students fill in each section of the outline as the material is covered in class with a sentence or two about the content. Review the special learners' IEPs to decide if any modifications should be made when presenting chapter content.

Resource

Authentic Assessment,
transparency master
3-1, TR

Reflect

How can a poorly
written or incomplete
assessment be
detrimental to a child's
educational progress?
How can teachers
make sure their assess-
ments are accurate?

Activity

Provide actual assess-
ments written by previ-
ous early childhood
students on the children
in their care. Remove
identifying details to
protect confidentiality.
Have students review
examples of the various
types of assessments.
Discuss with the
students when these
assessments might be
made throughout the
school year.

was sensitive to the needs of the individual children and the group.

Assessment

Assessment comes from a Latin word meaning *to sit beside and get to know.* It is the process of observing, recording, and documenting children's growth and behavior. To be an authentic assessment, observations must be done over time in play-based situations. This type of assessment is best because it is the most accurate. It is used to make decisions about children's education. Information is obtained on children's developmental status, growth, and learning styles. Sometimes the terms *assessment* and *evaluation* are used interchangeably, but they are two different processes. Assessment is the process of collecting information or data. Evaluation is the process of reviewing the information and finding value in it.

Purposes of Assessment

Information and data from assessment informs teachers about children's developmental needs. It is important for several reasons. The information collected is used in planning developmentally appropriate curriculum. Assessment keeps the teachers and the curriculum responsive to the needs of the children. An authentic assessment involves gathering information when children are performing tasks in natural settings. Assessment should include all developmental areas—physical, social, emotional, and cognitive. Assessment should provide information on each child's unique needs, strengths, and interests. It also charts progress over time.

During the assessment process, you, as teacher, gain insights into children's learning styles and needs, 3-2. What are their strengths and weaknesses? What does the group know? What are they able to do? What are their interests and dispositions? Finally, what

Each child has unique strengths, needs, and interests.

are their needs? Teachers who have good assessment skills will make better decisions.

Individual and classroom problems can often be identified through the assessment process. When specific examples of a child's behavior are observed and recorded, behavior patterns become more clear. Answers to behavior problems can more easily be found when the specific behavior is observed and noted.

Classroom problems can be identified through assessment. When a problem arises, plans can be made to remedy the problem. To illustrate, perhaps there have been many instances of pushing and shoving in the dramatic play area. By observing and evaluating, you may realize that more classroom space should be provided for this activity. If this is impossible, you may decide to limit the number of children in this area at one time to prevent the undesirable behavior.

Workplace Connection

Invite your school district's early childhood education specialist, school psychologist, or other early childhood professional to speak to the class about preschool screenings. What areas are tested? What recommendations can the school district make about services needed by children who are screened? Have students write additional questions to ask the speaker prior to the visit.

Assessment also allows you to identify children who might have special needs. Perhaps a child has a hearing or vision impairment. Maybe a child has an emotional or behavioral problem that requires counseling. These needs can be identified and specialized services obtained.

Through assessment, you will be able to find out where the children are in their development. Information on each child should be recorded at regular intervals. In this way, you can see how each child is progressing in his or her development. This information will help you make better curriculum planning decisions. It will also help you decide how to set up the environment and stimulate each child's development.

The information gained through assessment can also be useful during parent conferences. Parents want to know how their children are progressing. You will be able to give them concrete evidence on their child's progress. Parents will also be assured you know and understand their child.

A final purpose for assessment is in evaluating your program. Information obtained through assessment can help your staff determine if your program is effective in meeting its goals.

When to Do Assessments

As a teacher beginning a new year, you will need to do an *initial assessment*. This will provide entry data and a baseline to use for each child. You cannot assume all children of a given age are alike. Developmental differences will exist. Culture, economic status, and home background will impact each child's development. Therefore, the purpose of an initial assessment is to get a "snapshot" of each child in the group. Observing children and acquiring information from the families are the most common ways to gather this information.

You will want to learn as much about the children as possible during your initial

assessment. Study the existing folders on each child. Review home background forms. Read the notes from past parent conferences. If possible, visit each child's home. An alliance with families is important. Families can give you useful information on a child's learning needs and interests.

In addition to this initial assessment, you will need to do *ongoing assessments* on individual children as well as the group. A single assessment is not an exact assessment of ability or performance. It is just an indicator.

Ongoing assessment may take more time, but it will also provide more in-depth information. The information gained will be useful in tracking each child's progress and documenting change over time. It should provide evidence of a child's learning and maturation. This information will also be helpful in making decisions for enriching or modifying the curriculum and classroom environment when necessary.

You can gather assessment data during classroom activities. Watch children as they work on art projects and listen to them as they tell stories, 3-3. Observe children as they construct puzzles or build with blocks. Listen in on children's conversations. Discreetly take notes on individual children, especially during free-choice activities. This is when children are most likely to reveal their own personalities and development. These notes will provide important assessment information.

Formal and Informal Observation

Two different methods of observation are used for assessing young children—formal and informal. They differ in how controlled the conditions are for using them. Formal methods include standardized tests and research instruments. As a result of such research, developmental milestones for children have been identified. **Developmental milestones** are characteristics and behaviors

Note

Assessments are used to evaluate the effectiveness of your program in meeting its goals. Refer students to program goals in Chapter 18, *The Curriculum*, to review possible program goals that may be assessed during this process.

Enrich

Family background forms are an important part of initial assessments. Ask students to design a parent questionnaire. Their forms should contain the information they feel is important to know about each child enrolled in the preschool program.

Resource

Assessment Is an Ongoing Process, color transparency CT-3, TR

Activity

Ask the school psychologist to speak to the class about the process used for assessments and evaluations performed in an educational setting. Who is responsible for interpreting the data collected? How is data used to make recommendations for special services? Have the speaker include information on the process of a staffing.

Meeting Special Needs

Ask gifted students to write an article for a preschool parent newsletter or bulletin on the value of assessments. Have students include an explanation of each type of assessment

that may be used during the preschool year. Allow time for students to share their articles with the class.

Vocabulary

Have a student volunteer define the term *developmental milestones*. Refer students to the Appendix to view examples of developmental milestones.

Reflect

Review the fine-motor developmental milestones for two- and three-year-olds. Have students brainstorm activities that could be added to a curriculum to assist children experiencing difficulties in reaching these milestones.

Discuss

Talking with children is a valuable informal assessment tool. Have students discuss guidelines for talking with young children. When should talking with children be avoided?

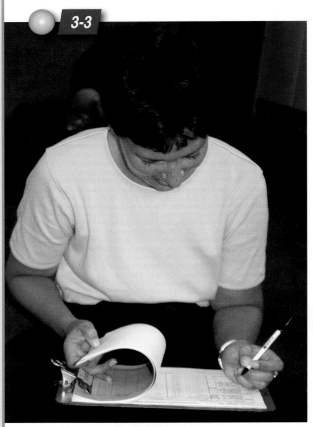

3-3

Teachers can quickly record what they see during classroom activities.

considered normal for children in specific age groups. Some educators refer to these as *emerging competencies*.

Developmental milestones will assist you in comparing and noting changes in the growth and development of children in your care, 3-4. They will also help you as you observe young children in preparation for your career working with young children. Examples of developmental milestones are included in the Appendix of this book. They are useful tools for assessing children's developmental status. They also form the basis for planning developmentally appropriate curriculum.

While formal observation methods provide important information, they require specialized training for recording data on carefully designed forms. Training is also needed for analyzing and interpreting the data.

Preschool teachers usually use informal observation methods to collect data. These methods are easier to use and more appropriate for program planning. They include observing children in the classroom, collecting samples of their work, interviewing parents, and talking with children.

Choosing a Method of Assessment

There are three considerations for choosing a method of assessment. First, the method chosen depends on the type of behavior you want to assess and the amount

3-4

Reviewing developmental milestones will help you assess the progress of children in your care.

Workplace Connection

Have students interview area preschool teachers and other early childhood education professionals to discover how often formal assessment methods, including standardized tests, are used for the preschool child. Have students write a brief report of their findings. Allow time for students to share their reports with the class.

of detail you need. Another consideration is whether the information needs to be collected for one child or the entire group. Finally, the amount of focused attention required by the observer needs to be considered.

Some methods of assessment will require more of your attention. For example, it is difficult interacting with children when you are in the process of writing an anecdotal record. Narratives need to be rich in information with detailed behavioral accounts. Checklists, videotapes, and participation charts are easier to use while working with the children.

Usually teachers use a variety of methods for gathering information about the children. Since no one method is the most effective or reveals everything, several methods are used. More complete information is obtained by using several types of assessment. Multiple sources of information also reduces the possibility of error when making evaluations.

Assessment Tools

There are several types of assessment tools that are used in early childhood programs. These include anecdotal records, checklists, participation charts, rating scales, samples of products, photographs, and tapes. Teachers can also interview families to obtain information.

Anecdotal Records

The simplest form of direct observation is a brief narrative account of a specific incident called an **anecdotal record**. Often an anecdotal record is used to develop an understanding of a child's behavior. Anecdotal records do not require charts or special settings. They can be recorded in any setting and require no special training. All you need is paper and a writing tool to record what happened in a factual, objective manner. The observation is open-ended,

continuing until everything is witnessed. It is like a short story in that it has a beginning, middle, and end.

The process of recording the incident requires a careful eye and quick pencil to capture all of the details. You will need to note who was involved, what happened, when it happened, and where it occurred. It needs to be done promptly and accurately. Figure 3-5 shows the contents of an anecdotal record.

When you use the narrative form of observation, your eyes and ears act like a video camera. You will be recording pictures of children playing, learning, and interacting. During your observations, you will record how children communicate, both verbally and nonverbally. You will record how they look and what they do. Physical gestures and movements should be noted. You will also detail children's interactions with people and materials. Record as many details as possible.

Anecdotal Records Must Be Objective

During the observation process, it is important to record only objective statements. To be objective, a statement must pass two tests. First, it must describe only observable actions. Thus, generalizations about the motives, attitudes, and feelings of the

3-5

Contents of Anecdotal Records
- Identifies the child and gives the child's age
- Includes the date, time of day, and setting
- Identifies the observer
- Provides an accurate account of the child's actions and direct quotes from the child's conversations
- Includes responses of other children and/or adults, if any are involved in the situation

Anecdotal records should include the items listed.

Discuss

What types of assessment tools are used in early childhood programs? Is one form of assessment more effective than another? What is an advantage of using several assessment tools?

Vocabulary

Have a student volunteer look up the term *anecdotal record* in the glossary and read the definition aloud. Discuss Chart 3-5, *Contents of Anecdotal Records*.

Reflect

How might children feel if they notice you watching them and writing during an observation in the classroom? How might you respond to a child's question about what you are doing?

Resource

Writing Anecdotal Records, Activity A, OG

Portfolio Project

Ask students to collect samples of the different types of assessment tools used in early childhood education for their portfolios. Students can design their own forms using those in the book as examples. If your school has a graphic arts department, students may be able to use those facilities for printing the forms. Have students write a brief explanation for each type of assessment tool.

Vocabulary

Have a student volunteer explain *labeling*. Ask students to give examples of labeling that could detract from an objective observation.

Discuss

What is the difference between *objective* and *subjective*? What is the difference between *generalized* and *specific*? Ask students to give examples of statements that reflect their understanding of these terms.

Reflect

How would a thorough understanding of child growth and development help you interpret the example of Tony spilling milk? What additional information would you need to know about Tony to be able to make a factual interpretation?

children are not included. Secondly, the recorded information must be nonevaluative. It should not include an interpretation of why something happened, nor imply that what happened was wrong, right, good, or bad. Labeling should be avoided. No judgments or conclusions should be inferred at this point. The following example is a narrative observation:

Sally arrived at school holding her mother's hand. She slowly walked over to her locker, removed her coat, and hung it on a hook. She turned to her mother and said, "You go to work." Sally's mother hugged her and said, "After work I'll take you to the dentist." Sally looked at her mother and started to cry. She said, "I'm not going to the dentist. I'm staying at school." Sally's mother reached out and hugged Sally. Sally continued crying and hung onto her mother. The teacher walked over to Sally and whispered in her ear. Then the teacher put out her hand and said, "Come and look, Sally. We have a new friend at school today. Jodi brought her new hamster." Sally stopped crying and took the teacher's hand. Together they walked over to see the hamster. Sally's mother watched her for a moment and then left the room.

Notice that only an objective description of the observed behavior is recorded. The statements do not include any of the following: causes, emotions, explanations, feelings, goals, motives, desires, purposes, needs, or wishes.

Interpretation of the Data

Once the narrative data is recorded, a second process begins. This process involves the interpretation of the data. An attempt is made to explain the observed behavior and to give it meaning. Why did the child behave as he or she did? What might have been the child's motives? Did someone or

something cause the child to act in this way? This interpretation takes knowledge and skill. It should not be attempted without a thorough understanding of how children grow and develop. The observation itself serves no purpose without the interpretation of behavior to give meaning to the data.

Though an observation may be factual and unbiased, various interpretations are sometimes made. Since no two people are exactly alike, no two people will interpret facts in the exact same way. Each person who interprets a child's behavior may determine different motives for the behavior based on their own personal experiences. Their personal feelings, values, and attitudes may also influence the interpretation of behavior.

To illustrate, an observer wrote the following about Tony:

Tony picked up the pitcher of milk. He moved the pitcher toward his glass. He hit the glass and tipped it over. The milk spilled.

In reviewing the observation of Tony, his behavior might be interpreted in several ways:

- Tony was careless.
- Tony was inexperienced in handling a pitcher.
- Tony wasn't paying attention to what he was doing.
- Tony lacked the strength needed to lift the pitcher.
- Tony lacked the hand-eye coordination necessary to pour from the pitcher.

To decide which interpretation is most accurate, you will need to observe Tony on several occasions over a period of time. You would also need a thorough understanding of how children grow and develop.

Figure 3-6 shows a form for an anecdotal record, although many teachers just use a file card or plain piece of paper. Teachers who record incidents throughout the year have a means of assessing progress. A series of

Cross-Curricular Activity

English
Stress the importance of good writing skills in this career. Ask students to write anecdotal observations on the same child for a specified time period from different vantage points. Have students trade papers to compare the observations for accuracy. Students should also check grammar, spelling, sentence structure, etc. Final copies may be typed and added to the student's portfolio.

3-6

SUNSHINE CHILD CARE CENTER ANECDOTAL RECORD

Child's Name: _____Carrie_____ Date: __10/9/XX__

Child's Age: ___3___ Years ___9___ Months

Setting: __Dramatic Play__ Time: _8:30_ to _8:45_

Observer: _Geneva Peterson_

Incident:

Carrie went directly to the dramatic play area when she arrived at the center. She placed the cash register on a table. After this, she displayed empty food containers on a table. Tony entered the area. He stepped behind the cash register and said, "I want to play with this." Carrie said, "No, it's mine. I had it first." Then using her arm she hit Tony and began pushing him. Tony looked at Carrie, shrugged his shoulders, and walked away. As Tony walked away, a smile came across Carrie's face.

Interpretation:

You may want to use a form such as this one to record anecdotal events.

records over time can provide rich details. The records can be extremely valuable in noting progress, strengths, needs, and interests.

Advantages and Disadvantages of Anecdotal Records

There are advantages and disadvantages in using the anecdotal record. An important advantage is that it is the easiest method of use since it requires no special setting or time frame. Anecdotal records can provide a running record over time showing evidence of a child's growth and development. Therefore, teachers who record incidents throughout the year have a means of assessing progress.

There are also disadvantages with using anecdotal records. Because the incident observed is based on the observer's interest, a complete picture may not be provided. Records may not always be accurate. If the observer decides to write down the incident at the end of the day and is poor at recalling details, important information may be missed.

Checklists

Another form of assessment is the checklist. **Checklists** are designed to record the presence or absence of specific traits or behaviors. They are easy to use and are especially helpful when many different items need to be observed. They often include lists of specific behaviors to look for while observing. Depending on their function, they can vary in length and complexity. Checklists may be designed for any developmental domain—physical, social, emotional, or cognitive. A checklist that is carefully designed can tell a lot about one child or the entire class.

Checklists may be developed to survey one child or a group of children. The targeted behaviors are listed in logical order with similar items grouped together. Therefore, you can quickly record the presence or absence of a behavior. Typically, a check indicates the presence of a behavior.

Checklists require structuring. You may be able to purchase commercially prepared checklists. Most teachers working in child care centers structure their own. A typical checklist for use in observing an individual child is shown in 3-7. The developmental milestones found in the Appendix of this book may be adapted as checklists for assessing individual children or groups of

Resource

Descriptive or Interpretive? reproducible master 3-2, TR

Note

Commercially prepared checklists are convenient to use, but may give inaccurate information. They may include lists of items that were not part of a particular early childhood program or omit items that should have been included.

Resource

Interpreting the Data, Activity C, SAG

Cross-Curricular Activity

Math
Have students create a Math Readiness Skills Group Assessment checklist for two-year-olds. Students can refer to the chart of math readiness developmental milestones in the Appendix or search the Internet for information. Have students use their checklist to evaluate the math readiness skills of a group of children. How effective was the checklist assessment? Allow time in class for students to share their results.

Discuss

How can reviewing a checklist of skills and abilities based on developmental milestones help preschool educators design a comprehensive curriculum?

Activity

Ask students to write a brief essay comparing the strengths and weaknesses of anecdotal records versus checklist assessments. Which method do they prefer and why? Allow time for students to read and discuss their essays in class.

Resource

Using a Checklist, Activity B, OG

3-7

Name: _____ Wyatt Anderson _____

Program: _____ Sunshine Child Care Center _____

Child's Age: ___3___ Years ___6___ Months

Date of Observation: __2/9/XX__

Observer: Sally Olm _____

Fine-Motor Skills

	Yes	No
Cuts paper	✓	
Pastes with a finger	✓	
Pours from a pitcher	✓	
Copies a circle from a drawing	✓	
Draws a straight line	✓	
Uses finger to pick up smaller objects	✓	
Draws a person with three parts		✓

Checklists are efficient to use and require little effort.

children. Figure 3-8 shows a checklist for assessing the gross-motor skills of a group of children.

Advantages and Disadvantages of Checklists

One of the advantages of a checklist is that there are no time constraints in collecting the data. The information can be quickly recorded anytime during program hours. In addition, checklists are easy to use, efficient, and can be used in many situations. Data from checklists can be easily analyzed.

A disadvantage of using a checklist, however, is the lack of detailed information. Checklists lack the richness of the more descriptive narrative. Because of the format, only particular behaviors are noted. Important aspects of behaviors may be missed, such as how a behavior is performed and for how long. Only the presence or absence of a behavior is noted in a checklist.

3-8

Gross-Motor Skills Group Assessment
Three-Year-Olds

	Henry	Ed	Jo	Vicki	Cari	Deb
Catches ball with arms extended	✓	✓	✓		✓	
Throws ball underhanded		✓			✓	
Completes forward somersault	✓	✓			✓	✓
Rides tricycle skillfully	✓	✓		✓	✓	✓
Throws ball without losing balance		✓	✓	✓	✓	
Hops on one foot		✓				✓

You can evaluate the gross-motor skills of a group of children using a form such as this one.

Putting Technology to Use

Schedule a demonstration of technology tools and equipment with your school's technology coordinator. These may include videotaping, digital photography, sound recording, and computer programs that may be used by students to create electronic portfolios. Students may be able to create slide shows for parent conferences and tape classroom lessons, presentations, and demonstrations. Other uses may include the creation of photo books and public relations material to promote the early childhood program.

Participation Chart

A **participation chart** can be developed to gain information on specific aspects of children's behavior. Participation charts have a variety of uses in the classroom. For instance, children's activity preferences during self-selected play can be determined. See 3-9.

Richard O'Grady, an experienced teacher, uses participation charts to record the time each child falls asleep at nap time. He also charts the length of time each child sleeps. He records this information several times a year. After collecting the data, he decides if a change should be made in the scheduled nap time. Likewise, the length of the nap time can be adjusted to reflect the children's needs.

Sometimes teachers find that children's preferences do not match their needs. To illustrate, Randy has weak hand-eye coordination skills. A participation chart shows he spends most of his time listening to stories and music and watching other children play. To meet Randy's needs, the teacher could introduce him to interesting art activities, puzzles, and other small manipulative learning aids. These materials will help advance Randy's skills in hand-eye coordination, which will be necessary for reading and writing.

Rating Scales

Rating scales, like checklists, are planned to record something specific. They are used to record the degree to which a quality or trait is present. Rating scales require you to make a judgment about the quality of what is being observed. Where a checklist only indicates the presence or absence of a trait, a rating scale tells how much or how little is present. As a result, objectivity could be hampered by the observer's opinion.

Advantages and Disadvantages of Rating Scales

Rating scales are easy to use and require little time to complete. Some scales contain only a numerical range. Others define the behaviors more specifically.

3-9

Activity Preferences During Self-Selected Play

	Bryce	Tina	Saul	Ting	Bergetta	Tanya	Hunter	Shawn	Janus	Vida
9:00 - 9:10	b	dp	a	st	m	dp	a	b	st	s
9:10 - 9:20	b	dp	a	st	m	dp	a	b	st	s
9:20 - 9:30	b	dp	m	m	dp	dp	s	b	st	s
9:30 - 9:40	b	st	m	m	dp	dp	b	b	m	a
9:40 - 9:50	b	m	m	m	dp	dp	b	b	m	a
9:50 - 10:00	b	m	s	m	dp	dp	b	b	m	a

a=art; b=blockbuilding; dp=dramatic play; m=manipulatives; s=sensory; sc=science; st=storytelling

A participation chart is quick and easy to use, but can give you important information.

Discuss

Refer to Chart 3-9. What activities did Saul avoid during the self-selected playtime? What interpretations could be made from this information? What additional information would be needed to make an accurate interpretation?

Reflect

What other areas could be assessed using a participation chart? How useful would these assessments be to you as a preschool instructor?

Resource

Activity Preferences During Self-Selected Play, Activity C, OG

Reflect

A participation chart showed a child spent all of his free time at the puzzle table, yet a checklist and anecdotal records showed he was lacking in social skills. How might you use his preference for puzzles in planning activities to increase his social skills?

Meeting Special Needs

Some special learners may not be able to use a participation chart such as Chart 3-9 because they may not be able to keep track of that many children at the same time. Adapt the chart to cover fewer children at a time, or ask for a student volunteer or the student's aide to work on the chart together. Review the special learner's IEP to decide which modification should be made.

Discuss

Have students review the *Social/Emotional Rating Scale*, 3-10. How could this scale be changed to reflect progress over a longer time period?

Note

Rating scales may be used to assess the high school student's performance in the pre-school laboratory. Refer students to the *Evaluation of Student Teacher Performance* form in the Introduction of the *Teacher's Resources* as an example.

Reflect

What other areas besides the example could be assessed using a rating scale? How useful would these assessments be to you as a preschool instructor and as parents?

Resource

Rating Scale, Activity D, OG

A disadvantage of the rating scale is that only fragments of actions are included. In order to choose a rating, the observer should have a good understanding of the behavior he or she is rating. Figure 3-10 shows a typical rating scale.

Collecting Samples of Children's Products

Collecting samples of children's work systematically over time is another assessment tool. These products can provide valuable information regarding the child's developmental status and growth. Products collected may include artwork, stories dictated or written, photographs, and records of conversations. Over time, these samples can be collected and compared. To illustrate, Chuck could make only random scribbles on paper at the beginning of the year. When Chuck's teacher asked him to tell her about his work, he explained it. She discovered the sample showed more than Chuck's scribbles. He said, "There is my name. That is how to write it. I wrote my mother's name and my sister's." Now he is able to draw a circle. A comparison of the two samples shows the progress Chuck has made in fine-motor and hand-eye coordination skills.

A child's products can be stored in a folder or portfolio. Whenever possible, store materials and items in chronological order. This will save you time when evaluating progress or sharing the materials with families.

3-10

Social/Emotional Rating Scale

Child's Name: _____Jo Ellen_____   Date: _4/6/XX_

Child's Age: ___4___ Years ___1___ Months

Observer: _Mark Zenk_____

Behavior	Never	Sometimes	Usually	Always
Shows increased willingness to cooperate			✓	
Is patient and conscientious		✓		
Expresses anger verbally rather than physically				✓
Has strong desire to please		✓		
Is eager to make friends and develop strong friendships			✓	
Respects property rights of others			✓	

On a rating scale, teachers record the degree to which a quality or trait is present.

Workplace Connection

Students can help children in the preschool record evidence of their progress by creating a "Me" book for each child. Have students choose a blank book and designate pages such as a self-portrait; family drawing; favorite activities, toys, and playmates; samples of writing, cutting, and art skills; etc. Include photographs of the child with written descriptions of his or her activities. Have students add to the book throughout the year.

Records may be kept in different forms. Samples may be preserved by photographing, sketching, or diagramming children's products. These methods are especially useful for large structures such as block displays and three-dimensional artwork that cannot be stored conveniently.

Using Technology for Assessment

Technology is a very useful tool for recording children's development. Making videotapes and audiotapes are excellent ways to preserve information. Tapings may focus on an individual child, a small group of children, or an entire class. Videotapes can preserve both action and speech. Recordings may be made of children telling stories, acting out stories, or explaining their projects.

Health and Safety

Videotaping and Photographing Safety

Be sure to consult parents, families, or caregivers before videotaping or photographing children. Many centers require written consent to be on file before staff can videotape or photograph children for educational purposes. Some families do not want images taken of their children for privacy reasons.

Dramatic play interactions and music experiences can be recorded. By viewing or listening to the tapes, you can note progress in language and speech. The children might also enjoy viewing or listening to the tapes.

Be careful that the presence of the videocamera does not become intrusive. You may want to ask other adults, such as teacher aides or parent volunteers, to assist with the taping. This will allow you to be included in the taping. By reviewing the tape, you can do a self-evaluation of your own interactions with the children.

Visual Documentation

You have probably heard the phrase "seeing is believing." **Visual documentation** refers to collecting or photographing samples of a child's work that portrays learning and development. Visual documentation provides a record that can be studied. Other assessment methods such as rating scales, checklists, anecdotal records all involve on-the-spot interpretation. This can make it difficult to be completely objective when recording the children's behavior.

The digital camera is a convenient way to visually document children's development. The camera can be used to photograph children engaged in creating artwork, participating in dramatic play, or taking part in field trip activities. The camera can also be used to take pictures of a child's accomplishments, such as artwork or building-block structures. In an infant program, the camera may be used to record self-feeding, playing peek-a-boo, sitting up, creeping, or walking. It can be used to record self-help skills such as dressing or brushing teeth. It is important to date all pictures taken on the digital camera for visual documentation. A brief description should also be recorded to show its significance.

The digital camera is also a convenient way to record children's development. Pictures taken by the digital camera are

Resource

Reviewing Assessment Data, transparency master 3-3, TR

Note

The use of photography and video and audio recordings made in class for educational purposes may be regulated by your school district's legal department. Check with the legal department for guidelines concerning use and confidentiality. Ask parents or guardians to sign a permission form allowing their child to be photographed and/or recorded.

Resource

Assessment Tools Summary, Activity B, SAG

Putting Technology to Use

Have students make a videotape or audiotape of a small group of children. Recordings can be of children telling stories, acting out stories, or explaining their projects; dramatic play interactions; or music experiences. Ask other adults to assist students with the taping and be sure permission slips are on file. Have students share their tapes with the class.

Resource

Designing an Assessment Tool, Activity D, SAG

Activity

Have students create a bulletin board or display about children's portfolios. Include examples of items that should be part of the portfolio.

Enrich

Have students write an article for the parent newsletter about the importance of children's portfolios. Explain how they will be used during the school year for assessment.

stored inside the camera as electronic image files that can be downloaded to a computer. Once the files are downloaded, they can be printed or saved onto the hard drive or a CD for later use. Teachers can use a digital camera to take pictures of classroom activities. They can download and print these photos for use in a portfolio. Teachers might want to feature photos on the bulletin board before filing them.

Portfolios

Materials you have collected as a part of ongoing assessment should be placed in each child's portfolio. A **portfolio** is a collection of materials that shows a person's abilities, accomplishments, and progress over time. Portfolios you create for the children in your care summarize each child's abilities. A portfolio includes items that show the child's growth and development over time. Documenting learning is an important skill for teachers to develop.

Depending on the materials collected, the contents of a portfolio can be stored in a variety of forms. Some teachers prefer three-ring binders. Others prefer to use boxes or large folders to store the portfolio contents.

Contents

A child's portfolio needs to be carefully planned and organized. It should be more than a file of anecdotal records, checklists, and questionnaires. Most teachers include work samples as well. Examples include art projects, audiotapes of conversations, and child-dictated stories. Work samples can provide evidence in all developmental areas. In addition, the portfolios include summaries of parent conferences and parent questionnaires. Figure 3-11 shows the contents of a typical portfolio.

Teachers include work samples for each child that reflect unique skills and interests.

3-11

Portfolio Contents

A portfolio may contain…

- teacher observations and other records gathered through assessment
- developmental rating scales or checklists
- parents' comments and completed questionnaires
- a dated series of the child's artwork or writing
- photographs of the child demonstrating skills or engaged in activities
- audiotapes or videotapes of the child speaking, singing, and telling stories
- a list of favorite books, songs, and fingerplays

A portfolio contains a wide variety of materials.

If Thomas built a complex and interesting block structure, his teacher might sketch or photograph it for inclusion in his portfolio. Likewise, teachers may record stories that children dictate to them.

A portfolio should be continually evolving, documenting evidence of a child's progress. Over time, this method provides a vivid picture of each child's development. Visual documentation included in a child's portfolio is a helpful tool when conferring with families. It should be a summary of a child's development. Information gained from evaluating the portfolio can guide teachers in making curriculum decisions, structuring interactions, and setting up the classroom. Families, too, will gain from reviewing the child's portfolio with the teacher.

By reviewing the portfolios of children in a program, you should be able to identify unique characteristics of each child. For instance, according to Mark's portfolio, he remains in the cooking area until the entire snack is prepared every day. Often he provides the teachers with other methods of preparing the foods. Cory develops elaborate and imaginative buildings in the

---

Putting Technology to Use

Have students conduct an Internet research project on the trend toward using student portfolios as an assessment tool. Use the search terms *educational portfolios* or *student portfolios* to find information on using portfolios in the classroom. Why is portfolio use increasing? How can portfolios be fully integrated into the curriculum? What research supports the use of portfolios in education?

blockbuilding area. During self-selected play, Maria always chooses the same theme. She dresses as a ballerina in the dramatic play area. Blake is fascinated with the hamster and rabbit. He wants to learn more about different kinds of animals, their eating habits, and behaviors.

Guidelines for Observing Children

During your study of young children, you will observe them in many situations. Whether in the play yard, in a classroom, or on a field trip, your behavior as an observer is important. Whether you are in an outside child care facility or in your school's own laboratory, certain guidelines must be followed.

Whenever you gather data about children, you must use special care. The information you collect must be kept confidential. This is perhaps the most important guideline for you to follow. Though you can discuss a child's behavior in your own classroom, you must refrain from doing so outside that setting. Whenever you are talking, other people are listening. The information you share could be embarrassing or even damaging to a child, parent, or teacher.

To protect confidentiality, your teacher may request that you avoid using a child's name during classroom discussions. First names only are permitted in other classrooms. Both practices will help protect the real identity of a child. These practices will also prevent information about a particular child from leaving the classroom.

While you are observing, coats, books, and other personal belongings should not be brought into the classroom. Young children are specially curious about purses and bags. Such items may cause an unnecessary distraction. Cosmetics and medications could endanger their safety.

During your observation time, avoid talking to the children, other observers, or the staff. However, it is likely that your presence will spark the curiosity of some of the children. A child may ask you what you are doing. If this happens, answer in a matter-of-fact manner. You might say that you are watching the children play or that you are writing notes on how children play.

One of the best ways to learn about young children is to observe them and to make note of their behavior, 3-12. By sharing your observations with other class members, you will be able to see children as they really are. These records will help you understand children and become a better child care professional.

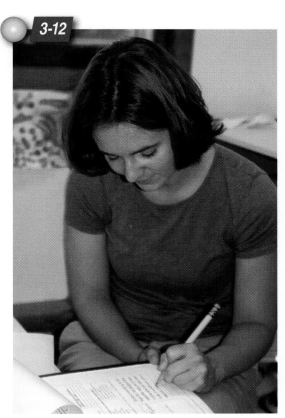
3-12

By observing children and recording their behavior, you will become a better early childhood professional.

Note

Classroom management is always an issue when conducting observations. Limit the number of students in the observation area as much as possible and plan a rotating schedule so all students have equal opportunities to observe.

Resource

Check Your Understanding, Activity A, SAG

Discuss

Ask students to list all the strategies they will practice to protect a child's confidentiality.

Resource

Observation Etiquette, transparency master 3-4, TR

Meeting Special Needs

Review the special learners' chapter outlines to determine if the students have any questions about the concepts or content of this chapter. Review the chapter objectives and ask the students to evaluate their progress in meeting these objectives. Ask the students to summarize, orally or in writing, what they learned from this chapter.

Review and Reflect **Answer Key**

Summary

Assessment is the process of observing, recording, and documenting children's growth and behavior over time in order to make decisions about their education. Assessment has many purposes, but it is primarily used in planning developmentally appropriate curriculum. An initial assessment is made of all children when they enter a program, but ongoing assessment continues as long as a child remains enrolled in a program.

Most assessment methods involve observing children. Formal observation by researchers has led to the creation of developmental milestones. Early childhood teachers usually use informal observation methods to collect data.

There are several types of assessment tools that are used in early childhood programs. These include anecdotal records, checklists, participation charts, rating scales, samples of products, photographs, and tape recordings. All of these methods have advantages and disadvantages. Materials that have been collected during the assessment process should be placed in a portfolio for each child. Portfolios document children's learning and development.

When observing children, it is important to record only objective statements. Once data is recorded, it may be interpreted. This interpretation takes knowledge and skill. It requires a thorough understanding of child development. Information you collect on children must also be kept confidential. This is perhaps the most important guideline to follow.

Review and Reflect

1. List three purposes of assessment.

2. What is meant by the term *authentic assessment*?

3. Which of the following is considered a formal method of assessment?
   A. Checklists.
   B. Standardized tests.
   C. Rating scales.
   D. Anecdotal records.

4. List three considerations for choosing a method of assessment.

5. Which of the following are objective statements?
   A. Pours milk.
   B. Rocks the doll.
   C. Gets even.
   D. Feels lonely.

6. Why is the anecdotal record considered the simplest form of direct observation?

7. Which assessment tool would you use to determine the degree to which a quality or trait was present?

8. List one advantage and one disadvantage in using a checklist.

9. What three methods could you choose to add information on a three-dimensional project to a child's portfolio?

10. Describe how technology can be used as an assessment tool.

11. List five items that might be included in a child's portfolio.

12. Name three guidelines to keep in mind when observing children.

---

1. (List three:) information collected is used in planning developmentally appropriate curriculum; individual and classroom problems can often be identified; allows you to identify those children who might have special needs; can find out where children are in their development; can see how each child is progressing in his or her development; information can be useful during parent conferences; helpful in evaluating your program
2. To be authentic, assessments must be done over time in real-life situations.
3. B
4. the type of behavior you want to assess and the amount of detail you need; whether the information needs to be collected for one child or the entire group; the amount of focused attention required by the observer
5. A, B

6. Anecdotal records do not require charts or special settings. They can be recorded in any setting and require no special training. All you need is paper and a writing tool.
7. rating scale
8. (List one advantage and one disadvantage. Student response.)
9. photographs, sketches, diagrams
10. Videotapes, audiotapes, and digital cameras can be used to record children's behavior or development at a given moment. When used at regular intervals, these methods can be used to assess progress.
11. (List five. Student response.)
12. (Name three. Student response.)

Apply and Explore

1. Prepare a checklist for a group of children to assess color recognition skills.

2. Interview an early childhood teacher about how she or he develops and uses portfolios.

3. Develop a participation checklist for the use of outdoor play equipment.

Cross-Curricular Link

Writing

1. Have each student in the class observe a child for 15 minutes and write an anecdotal record of the observation. Compare and discuss the results. Which records contained the most detail? Which records contained only objective statements? Did any of the records contain interpretive statements? If so, what were they?

2. Videotape a group of children interacting. Show the tape to classmates. Have each class member write a narrative of what he or she sees. Compare the contents of the narratives.

Math

3. Using the Appendix, develop a rating scale to assess the motor skills of four-year-olds.

Technology

4. Use a search engine to find information on the observation of young children.

5. Check NAEYC's position statement in early childhood programs at the following Web site: www.naeyc.org/about/positions/pdf/standlcurrass.pdf

Workplace Link

Survey area preschools, career/technical centers, and community colleges, with observation facilities. What guidelines are used during observation? Can students be seen during observations? Compare findings in class.

Discuss

Look at the three children in the chapter opening photo. What levels of physical, cognitive, and social-emotional development do you think they have reached?

Discuss

Look over the objectives for this chapter. Of what importance might this information be to the future early childhood educator?

Child Development Principles and Theories

After studying this chapter, you will be able to

- describe the areas and principles of development.
- define *windows of opportunity* as related to brain development.
- summarize how theories about development can be used as practical guides to early care and education.
- contrast the developmental theories of Erikson, Piaget, Vygotsky, and Gardner.

Terms to Know

development
infant
toddler
preschooler
physical development
gross-motor development
fine-motor development
cognitive development
social-emotional development
cephalocaudal principle
proximodistal principle
maturation
neurons
synapses
windows of opportunity
theory
schemata
sensorimotor stage
preoperational stage
concrete operations stage
multiple intelligences

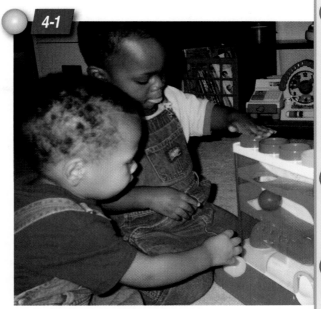

4-1

Knowledge of child development can help you understand how to work with children who have very different personalities.

Studying and understanding child growth and development are important parts of teaching young children. No two children are alike. Children differ in physical, cognitive, social, and emotional growth patterns. Even identical twins, who have the same genetic makeup, are not exactly alike. They may differ in the way they respond to play, affection, objects, and people in their environment.

Think of the children you know. Each is different from the others, 4-1. Some always appear to be happy. Other children's personalities may not seem as pleasant. Some children are active. Still others are typically quiet. You may even find that some children are easier to like.

To help all these children, you need to understand the sequence of their development. Knowledge of the areas of child development is basic to guiding young children. Linked to this is the understanding of healthy brain development.

Healthy brain development results from healthy human contact. Positive stimuli are a major factor in brain development. These stimuli begin at birth. Therefore, it is vital for children to have loving caregivers. Young children need dependable, trusting relationships. They thrive in environments that are predictable and nurturing.

Understanding theories about how people develop helps form your knowledge base in caring for young children. This combined knowledge will help you plan appropriate curriculum.

Vocabulary

Have students review the *Terms to Know* list. Ask students to look up unfamiliar words or terms in the glossary before reading the chapter.

Resource

Understanding Development, Activity A, SAG

Reflect

Ask students to think of a young child they know. Describe the child's personality characteristics and compare them to those of your classmates' experiences with children of the same age.

Discuss

How does being raised in a predictable environment affect a child's development? What might be some negative effects on the development of a child raised in an unpredictable, unstable environment?

Meeting Special Needs

Provide an outline of the chapter with all the chapter headings for special learners. Students should fill in each section of the outline as the material is covered in class with a sentence or two about the content. Review the special learners' IEPs to decide if any modifications should be made in presenting the chapter content.

Vocabulary

Have a student volunteer define the term *development*. Why do we study child development?

Discuss

Explain the following statement: "Development is predictable and consistent for all children." Can you think of any exceptions in which this may not be an accurate statement?

Vocabulary

Have a student volunteer define the term *physical development*. What is the difference between gross-motor and fine-motor development? Give an example of each.

Child Development

Development refers to change or growth that occurs in children. It starts with infancy and continues to adulthood. By studying child development, you will form a profile of what children can do at various ages. For instance, you will learn that two-year-old children like to run. This means you should provide space for them to move freely. Likewise, you will learn that infants explore with their senses, often mouthing objects. Knowing this, you will need to make sure that all toys for infants are clean and safe.

Different names are used to describe young children at different ages. From birth through the first year, children are called **infants**. **Toddlers** are children from age one up to the third birthday. (Because of an awkward style of walking, the name *toddler* describes this age group.) The term **preschooler** is often used to describe children ages three to six years of age.

The basic patterns of child development are a rather recent area of study. Researchers are constantly discovering new information on how children grow, develop, and learn about their world. Studying the basics of child development is just the beginning for you. Throughout your career, you will need to update your knowledge of the latest research and trends in this career field. Seminars, courses, professional articles, and conferences will help you in this goal. Keep in mind that growing as a professional is a lifelong process.

Areas of Development

The study of child development is often divided into three main areas. These include physical, cognitive, and social-emotional development. Dividing development into these areas makes it easier to study.

Physical development refers to physical body changes. It occurs in a relatively stable, predictable sequence. It is orderly, not random. Changes in bone thickness, vision, hearing, and muscle are all included. Changes in size and weight are also part of physical development. See 4-2.

Physical skills, such as crawling, walking, and writing, are the result of physical development. These skills fall into two main categories:

- **Gross-motor development** involves improvement of skills using the large muscles in the legs and arms. Such activities as running, skipping, and bike riding fall into this category.

- **Fine-motor development** involves the small muscles of the hands and fingers. Grasping, holding, cutting, and drawing are some activities that require fine-motor development.

Environmental factors also affect what children can do physically. These factors include proper nutrition and appropriate toys and activities.

Cognitive development, sometimes called *intellectual development*, refers to

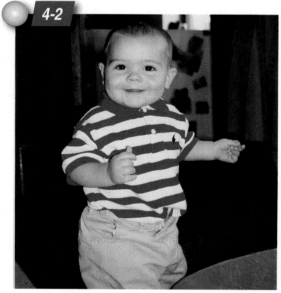

4-2

Changes in height and weight are two of the most obvious signs of physical development.

Putting Technology to Use

Ask students to conduct an Internet search for information concerning conditions in children that might cause development delays. Are these delays the result of genetics, accident, or disease? Are they always permanent? What treatments are available for children with developmental challenges? For genetic conditions, are any prenatal screenings available to detect the presence of the defect before birth? Have students write a brief report of their findings.

The Human Need for Safety

According to psychologist Abraham Maslow, the human need for safety must be met before growth and development occurs in other areas. This is especially true for young children. What does this mean for early childhood teachers? Be alert to what causes children in your care to feel unsafe or have fear. Some children may cling to you for security. Others may act out by hitting or biting. Still others may react negatively to "strangers" in the room. On a continuing basis, look for ways to keep children feeling secure. For example, this may mean standing close to a child who fears strangers when a new person is in the room.

processes people use to gain knowledge. Language, thought, reasoning, and imagination are all included. Identifying colors and knowing the difference between *one* and *many* are examples of cognitive tasks.

Language and thought are a result of cognitive development. These two skills are closely related. Both are needed for planning, remembering, and problem solving. As children mature and gain experience with their world, these skills develop.

The third area of development is called **social-emotional development**. These two areas are grouped together because they are so interrelated. Learning to relate to others is social development. Emotional development, on the other hand, involves feelings and

expression of feelings. Trust, fear, confidence, pride, friendship, and humor are all part of social-emotional development. Other emotional traits include timidity, interest, and pleasure. See 4-3. Learning to express emotions in appropriate ways begins early. Caregivers promote this learning when they positively model these skills. A person's self-concept and self-esteem are also part of this area. As children have success with all skills, confidence flourishes. This leads to a healthy self-concept and sense of worth.

The physical, cognitive, and social-emotional areas of development are linked to one another. Development in one area can strongly influence another area. For instance, writing words requires fine-motor skills. It also requires cognitive development. Language, a part of cognitive development, is needed to communicate with others. It is also necessary for growing socially and emotionally.

Just as research has made known the *areas* of development, it also shows that development follows key patterns, or principles. Think about how these principles might influence how you care for children.

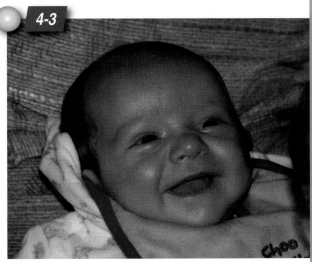

4-3

Learning to trust and show affection for others is a part of social-emotional development.

Discuss

What can parents and caregivers do to promote the development of remembering and problem-solving skills in young children? Give examples of each type of activity.

Vocabulary

Have a student volunteer define the term *social-emotional development*. Why are these two areas linked together?

Discuss

Give examples demonstrating your understanding of how all the areas of development are linked to one another. How can a delay in one area affect development in a different area?

Workplace Connection

Have students visit a local child care center and survey the toys and equipment in each room. Ask students to observe how children use and play with the materials. How does child's play differ with standard equipment such as blocks and dolls as the age of the children increases? What provisions has the staff made for developmental growth in toy and equipment selection for all age ranges? Allow time for students to share their findings in class.

Resource

Characteristics of Development, transparency master 4-1, TR

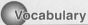

Vocabulary

Have student volunteers define the terms *cephalocaudal principle* and *proximodistal principle.* How are these principles alike? How do they differ?

Discuss

How are thinking abilities and motor skills affected by maturation? Give an example of how cognitive development occurs. What is an example of how physical skills develop?

Reflect

Tanya's mother is concerned her child's development is delayed at four months because she cannot sit up and put shape blocks into a box. How would you reassure Tanya's mother? Students should refer to the principles of development in their explanation. Ask student volunteers to share their responses with the class.

Principles of Development

Although each child is unique, the basic patterns, or *principles*, of growth and development are universal, predictable, and orderly. Through careful observation and interaction with children, researchers and those who work with children understand the characteristics of the principles that follow.

- Development tends to proceed from the head downward. This is called the **cephalocaudal principle.** According to this principle, the child first gains control of the head, then the arms, then the legs. Infants gain control of head and face movements within the first two months after birth. In the next few months, they are able to lift themselves up using their arms. By 6 to 12 months of age, infants start to gain leg control and may be able to crawl, stand, or walk.

- Development also proceeds from the center of the body outward according to the **proximodistal principle**. Accordingly, the spinal cord develops before other parts of the body. The child's arms develop before the hands, and the hands and feet develop before the fingers and toes. Fingers and toes are the last to develop.

- Development also depends on maturation. **Maturation** refers to the sequence of biological changes in children. These orderly changes give children new abilities. Much of the maturation depends on changes in the brain and the nervous system. These changes assist children to improve their thinking abilities and motor skills. A rich learning environment helps children develop to their potential.

Children must mature to a certain point before they can gain some skills, 4-4. For instance, the brain of a four-month-old has not matured enough to allow the child to use words. A four-month-old will babble and coo. However, by two years of age, with the help of others, the child will be able to say and understand many words. This is an example of how cognitive development occurs from simple tasks to more complex tasks. Likewise,

4-4

Improved muscle strength and coordination are needed to walk and push a wheeled toy.

physical skills develop from general to specific movements. For example, think about the way an infant waves its arms and legs. In a young infant, these movements are random. In several months, the infant will likely be able to grab a block with his or her whole hand. In a little more time, the same infant will grasp a block with the thumb and forefinger.

The principles of development help you understand that the order or sequence of development in children is generally the same. However, each child develops at his or her own *rate*. In any classroom, you may find children the same age who have progressed to different levels in each developmental area. Knowing the principles of development will help you observe what abilities each child has gained. It will also help you plan appropriate activities that aid children in successfully developing new skills.

Portfolio Project

Have students create a digital photo file of children at various stages of maturation. Ask students to prepare a slide show of the photos and have class members discuss the stage of development demonstrated in each picture. Contact the public relations personnel of your school and research the legalities concerning taking pictures of children. Have students create a form to use when seeking permission to take and use photographs of children for educational purposes. Have students save the project in their portfolio.

Understanding the areas and principles of development is important. Recognizing how the brain functions in development is equally so. What should caregivers and teachers know about the brain and how it influences development?

Brain Development

Which is more important for the developing brain—nature or nurture? This is one of the oldest debates in the study of human development. Human development depends on the interaction between nature and nurture, often called heredity and environment. Years ago, it was thought that *only* genes contributed to brain development. Today scientists say *both* factors are critical to healthy brain development. However, there are still some questions about which has the greater influence.

Modern technology allows scientists to take pictures of the brain. By comparing pictures, scientists are able to study rates of development. The studies show that young children's brains are highly active. The most rapid development occurs during the first three years of life.

Therefore, hours in infancy may have more impact on development than months in middle age. Figure 4-5 illustrates how different parts of the brain control body functions.

At birth, a child's brain weighs about one pound and is underdeveloped. It contains billions of specialized nerve cells called **neurons**. Although these cells are present at birth, they are not linked. After birth, the links between the neurons develop rapidly. These links, or connections, are called **synapses**. "Brain wiring" occurs as new links form. The larger the number of synapses, the greater the number of messages that can pass through the brain.

These links are a result of the child's interaction with the world. They influence the ability of a child to learn, solve problems, get along with others, and control emotions. For example, the child's growing brain responds each time a caregiver provides *sensory stimulation*. This stimulation could be in the form of holding, talking, reading, or singing. When stimulation occurs, the child's growing brain responds by forming new connections. The ability of an infant's brain to change according to stimulation is known as *plasticity*.

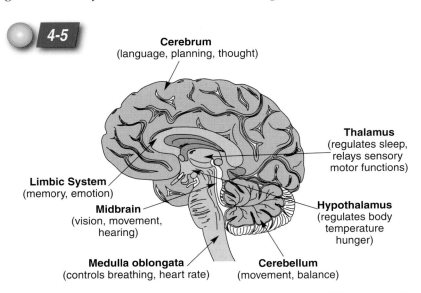

4-5

Cerebrum
(language, planning, thought)

Thalamus
(regulates sleep, relays sensory motor functions)

Limbic System
(memory, emotion)

Midbrain
(vision, movement, hearing)

Hypothalamus
(regulates body temperature hunger)

Medulla oblongata
(controls breathing, heart rate)

Cerebellum
(movement, balance)

This diagram illustrates how different functions are controlled by different parts of the brain. Connections between them are critical to development.

Resource

Brain Research Tells Us…, transparency master 4-2, TR

Vocabulary

Have student volunteers define the terms *neurons* and *synapses*. What role do these play in the development of a child's brain?

Reflect

Two-year-old Joanne is surrounded by age-appropriate toys and play equipment in her child care center and receives care and attention from her teacher and classroom aides. Miranda stays at home with her mother watching television for most of the day. How might the girls' experiences affect their brain wiring and future brain development?

Activity

Ask students to interview parents of infants and toddlers to discover what the parents already know about stimulation, environment, and brain development. Have students prepare a fact sheet on brain development including suggestions for materials and activities parents can use with their children to stimulate brain development.

Service Learning Activity

Have students collect a variety of fabrics and materials to be used to create sensory books for infants and toddlers. Cut fabrics and materials into simple shapes and objects, glue to sturdy paper or cardboard, and bind pages together to create the books. Suggestions include flannel, corduroy, fleece fabric, satin, fleece, and other textured fabrics as well as corrugated paper, sand paper, thin cork, bubble wrap, etc. Ask students to distribute the books to parent support groups, early childhood programs, or other organizations that serve young parents.

Discuss

Describe warm, nurturing, and consistent care. What effect might this kind of care have on the development of a child's temperament and personality?

Vocabulary

Have a student volunteer define the term *cortisol*. What effect does the release of too much cortisol have on the development of a child's brain?

Activity

Refer students to 4-6, *Risk Factors for Healthy Brain Development*. Ask students to give examples for each of the five risk factors listed.

Early care has a long-lasting impact on how children develop. The number of brain connections children form and keep depends on the care they receive. Warm, nurturing, consistent, and responsive care causes positive changes in the brain. Likewise, children need environmental stimulation. A wide variety of visual, auditory, and sensory experiences will help promote brain connections.

On the other hand, a lack of nurturing and interaction can limit a child's potential. Some children are deprived of stimulation either intentionally or unintentionally. These children receive fewer touches. They are spoken to less often. They may also not receive much visual stimulation. This neglect can impair brain development and the child's potential.

The amount of stress created by negative experiences also affects brain development. *Overstimulation*, a flood of sounds and sights, is one factor that can cause harmful stress to infants. When under stress, the body produces a steroid called *cortisol*. High levels of this hormone wash over the brain like an acid. Over a long length of time, cortisol can lead to problems with memory and regulating emotion. A child constantly exposed to stress can develop connections that trigger anxiety, fear, and mistrust. These children may grow up to be unhappy, sad, or even angry. They may also have problems with self-control. Chart 4-6 contains a list of factors that can interfere with healthy brain development.

Windows of Opportunity

The brain has a remarkable capacity to change. However, timing is important. The parts of the brain develop at different times and different rates. Studies show that there are **windows of opportunity**, or a specific span of time, for the normal development of certain types of skills. During these key times, appropriate stimulation is needed

4-6

Risk Factors for Healthy Brain Development

- trauma
- emotional or physical abuse
- poverty
- exposure to environmental toxins such as lead
- parents who suffer from substance abuse, both during the prenatal period and after birth

Any of these factors can interfere with the ability of a child's brain to develop.

for the brain synapses to link easily and efficiently.

After these key periods, chances for creating stable, long-lasting pathways in the brain tend to diminish. Learning will continue to occur for the remainder of the person's life. However, the skill mastery level may not be as high. Chart 4-7 contains a list of brain functions and the approximate windows of opportunity for each. Read the following to further your understanding about windows of opportunity.

Vision: Birth to Six Months

At birth, an infant's brain is not wired for sight. The first six months of life is a key period for developing vision. Covering newborns' eyes or keeping infants in a dark room during this time will affect their vision. Their sight may not develop normally. Once passed, this window of opportunity is impossible to recover. For this reason, newborns' eyes are examined after birth. If a cataract covering the lens of the eye is present, it needs to be removed.

Vision is one area that develops with little stimulation. Infants need interesting objects to look at, including toys and people. As you carry infants, point out interesting objects, pictures, people, and places.

Workplace Connection

Research tells us that physical touching and stimulation is critical to the psychological and emotional development of infants and young children. Have students interview the director of a child care facility to learn how caregivers are encouraged to appropriately touch and stimulate infants. What types of appropriate touching are permissible by caregivers for older children including toddlers and preschoolers? What restrictions, if any, does the center place on touching? What complications could result from these situations? Have students write a brief report of their findings.

4-7

Brain Function	Approximate Window of Opportunity
Vision	Birth to 6 months
Motor development	Prenatal to 8 years
Emotional control	Birth to 3 years
Vocabulary/speech	Birth to 3 years
Math/logic	1 to 4 years

The ages for these windows of opportunity are estimates and can vary according to an individual's development.

Vocabulary/Speech: Birth to Three Years

Infants must hear language to learn it. The speech a child hears during the first three years of life will determine his or her adult vocabulary. Children at this age have an incredible capacity for learning language. On the other hand, infants and toddlers who hear fewer words develop smaller vocabularies.

It is important for caregivers to speak in full sentences. Talk to children often. Tell them what you are doing, what they are doing, and what you will do next. Read them stories and play music. Engage them in social interactions that require language.

Emotional Control: Birth to Three Years

The critical period for emotional control occurs between birth and three years of age. Emotional development includes the abilities to identify feelings, manage strong emotions, and develop empathy. Severe stress or early abuse can damage a child's emotional development.

Infants and toddlers thrive in stable relationships. In early childhood programs, they should be assigned a primary caregiver. Children need caregivers who can read their cues, respond promptly, and meet their needs in a nurturing manner. By using caring words, caregivers reassure children that they are valued. Caregivers can also support emotional understanding by labeling children's feelings. Storybooks are effective in helping to promote this type of development.

Math/Logic Development: One to Four Years

The critical timing for promoting brain connections related to math is from one to four years of age. Young children need chances for working with materials that offer an appropriate level of challenge. Blocks and rhythm instruments are examples of toys that encourage sensory exploration related to math. Caregivers can introduce experiences requiring matching and sorting by size, shape, and color, 4-8. Learning how objects are alike and different is an important skill. When appropriate, caregivers need to introduce words to describe color, size, shape, and texture. They also need to introduce math words, such as *bigger, smaller, more, less,* and *one more.*

Discuss

To develop language, infants must hear it. Discuss the differences in learning language for an infant who hears parents, family, and caregivers speak when compared to an infant who is exposed to language primarily through media.

Reflect

Ask students to think of an early childhood incident they may have experienced that resulted in a significant emotional response. Is the effect still present today or has the individual overcome or handled the response? *(Example: fear of dogs from a bite.)*

Discuss

What may be the effect on future learning potential if a child misses a window of opportunity? What may result if, in an attempt to ensure that a child receives the maximum amount of stimulation, a parent overstimulates or pushes a child to learn before he or she is ready?

Cross-Curricular Activity

Math
Have students search for information regarding the development of mathematical and logic abilities in infants and young children. What do researchers say about this subject? What role if any, do worksheets and flashcards have in the development of these skills? What developmentally appropriate activities can be recommended for the development of these skills during the critical years between one and four years of age? Allow time for students to discuss their findings in class.

Reflect

What is the role of the adult in 4-8? What developmentally appropriate questions could the adult ask to encourage the child to practice problem-solving skills?

Vocabulary

Have a student volunteer define the term *theory*. How are developmental theories used to assist you in working with young children?

Discuss

Compare the personality traits that might develop in a young child raised in a home with many siblings with those of an only child. Consider the positive and negative effects in both situations.

Resource

Erikson's Psychosocial Theory, Activity B, SAG

Blocks of different shapes, sizes, and colors can help promote brain connections related to math and logic.

Motor Development: Prenatal to Eight years

Motor development requires complex brain networking. The window of opportunity begins before children are even born. The window lasts for the first eight years. During this time, stable, long-lasting structures can be created. Young children need a variety of gross- and fine-motor activities to support motor development.

Theories of Development

Psychologists continue to study human development. They are learning more about what people are like and how they develop. Over the past century, many psychologists have provided theories that are considered practical guides. A **theory** is a principle or idea that is proposed, researched, and generally accepted as an explanation. Developmental theories provide insights into how children grow and learn. Theories are helpful for understanding and guiding developmental processes.

Theories can be useful decision-making tools. Since a variety of theories exists, teachers need to understand these different approaches for working with children. Theories will help you form your personal values and beliefs about learning. They will also help you understand strategies for promoting children's development.

Four major theories about how children learn are discussed in this chapter. These include theories of mid-twentieth-century psychologists Erik Erikson, Jean Piaget, and Lev Vygotsky. The final theorist, Howard Gardner, is a twenty-first-century developmental psychologist. These theories are based on observation and experiences with children. Think about the children you know as you read about theories that helped form today's ideas about working with young children.

Erikson's Psychosocial Theory

Erik Erikson proposed a theory of psychosocial development. He believed development occurs throughout the life span. His theory provided new insights into the formation of a healthy personality. It emphasizes the social and emotional aspects of growth. Children's personalities develop in response to their social environment. The same is true of their skills for social interaction.

Erikson's theory includes eight stages. At each stage, a social conflict or crisis occurs. These are not generally tragic situations; however, they require solutions that are satisfying both personally and socially. Erikson believed that each stage must be resolved before children can ascend to the next stage.

Maturity and social forces help in the resolution of the crisis or conflict. Therefore,

Workplace Connection

Have students visit a special education early childhood classroom in their community or school district. Ask them to observe what types of disabilities and challenges are present. What materials and equipment are used to assist children in reaching physical, educational, and social goals? What roles do teachers and aides play in helping children meet their goals? How do theories of child growth and development pertain to children with special needs? Allow time for students to discuss their findings in class.

teachers and parents play a powerful role in recognizing each stage. By providing social opportunity and support, teachers and parents can help children overcome each crisis. Chart 4-9 contains the first four stages of Erikson's theory. These stages occur during the early childhood years. The paragraphs that follow give a brief overview of these early stages.

Stage 1: Trust Versus Mistrust

During the first eighteen months of life, children learn to trust or mistrust their environment. To develop trust, they need to have warm, consistent, predictable, and attentive care. See 4-10. They need caregivers who will accurately read and respond to their signals. When infants are distressed, they need to be comforted. They also need loving physical contact, nourishment, cleanliness, and warmth. Then they will develop a sense of confidence and trust that the world is safe and dependable. Mistrust will occur if an infant experiences an unpredictable world and is handled harshly.

Stage 2: Autonomy Versus Shame and Doubt

This second stage occurs between eighteen months and three years of age. During this stage, toddlers use their new motor and mental skills. They want to be independent and do things for themselves. They are in the process of discovering their own bodies and practicing their developing locomotor (physical movement) and language skills.

The objective of this stage is to gain self-control without a loss of self-esteem. Fostering independence in children is important. At this age, toddlers start to become self-sufficient. They need to learn to choose and decide for themselves. To do this, toddlers need a loving, supportive environment. Positive opportunities for self-feeding, toileting, dressing, and exploration will result in *autonomy*, or independence. On the other hand, overprotection or lack of adequate activities results in self-doubt, poor achievement, and shame.

Stage 3: Initiative Versus Guilt

Between three and five years of age, the third stage occurs. According to Erikson, it emerges as a result of the many skills children have developed. Now children have the capacity and are ready to learn constructive ways of dealing with people and things. They are learning how to take initiative without being hurtful to others. They are also busy discovering how the

4-9

Erikson's Stages of Development During Early Childhood

Stage	Approximate Age	Psychosocial Crisis
I	Birth–18 months	Trust versus mistrust
II	18 months–3 years	Autonomy versus shame and doubt
III	3–5 years	Initiative versus guilt
IV	6–12 years	Industry versus inferiority

The first four stages of Erikson's theory concern children from birth to twelve years.

Activity

Have students interview the director of a child care center with an infant program to learn how the employment of a consistent caregiver affects an infant's development of trust. What is the result in development of trust when staff turnover is high at this age? Have students write a brief report of their findings.

Reflect

In an effort to avoid the loss of self-esteem, do some parents and caregivers avoid disciplining children between 18 months and three years of age? What positive types of discipline would you recommend for children in this age range who lose self-control?

Discuss

Name some typical behaviors and activities of toddlers demonstrating the development of autonomy. How can a loss of self-esteem at this age hinder the toddler's ability to overcome the crisis of autonomy versus shame and doubt?

Resource

Trust Versus Mistrust, Activity A, OG

Workplace Connection

Ask students to observe infant, toddler, and preschool-age children at play in a child care center. Have students try to identify activities or actions a child performs that indicate which of Erikson's stages of development the child is demonstrating. Interview the center's staff to discover how they view Erikson's developmental theories. What role, if any, do Erikson's theories play in the center's daily program? Allow time for students to discuss their findings in class.

Discuss

Why did Erik Erikson believe it is important for children to overcome or handle each of the psychosocial crises or conflicts they face? How can parents, teachers, and caregivers provide support during these stages?

Reflect

Upon entering the preschool classroom, four-year-old Aaron's mom hangs up his tote bag, unzips and hangs up his coat, removes his boots and places them in his cubby, and wipes his nose. What suggestions could you make to her with reference to Erikson's developmental stage of initiative versus guilt?

Resource

Applying Piaget's Theory of Cognitive Development, transparency master 4-3, TR

Discuss

How do the developmental theories of Jean Piaget differ from those of Erikson? How can teachers use Piaget's cognitive development theory to provide successful learning experiences for their students?

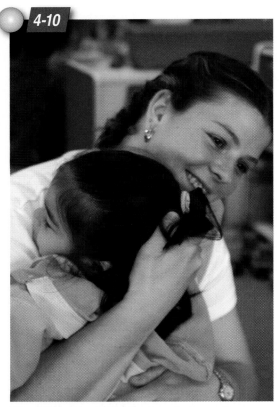

This child builds trust by forming a loving, caring relationship with her teacher.

world works. Children begin to realize that what they do can have an effect on the world, too. Challenged by the environment, children are constantly attempting and mastering new tasks. Aided by strong initiative, they are able to move ahead energetically and quickly forget failures. This gives them a sense of accomplishment.

Children at this stage need to develop a sense of purpose. This happens when adults direct children's urges toward acceptable social practices. If children are discouraged by criticism, feelings of incompetence are likely to emerge. This can also occur if parents demand too much control.

Stage 4: Industry Versus Inferiority

The major crisis of this stage occurs between six and twelve years of age. At this time, children enjoy planning and carrying out projects. This helps them learn society's rules and expectations. During this stage, children gain approval by developing intellectual skills such as reading, writing, and math.

The way family, neighbors, teachers, and friends respond to children affects their future development. Realistic goals and expectations enrich children's sense of self. Children can become frustrated by criticism or discouragement, or if parents demand too much control. Feelings of incompetence and insecurity will emerge.

Piaget's Cognitive Development Theory

Jean Piaget's thinking has challenged teachers to focus on the *ways* children come to know as opposed to *what* they know. His theory of cognitive development focuses on predictable cognitive (thinking) stages. Piaget believed that thinking was different during each stage of development. His theory explained mental operations. This includes how children perceive, think, understand, and learn about their world.

Piaget believed that children naturally attempt to understand what they do not know. Knowledge is gathered gradually during active involvement in real-life experiences. By physically handling objects, young children discover that relationships exist between them, 4-11. Terms Piaget used to describe these processes were *schemata, adaptation, assimilation,* and *accommodation.* These processes occur during each stage of development.

Schemata are mental representations or concepts. As children receive new

Putting Technology to Use

Have students conduct an Internet search for information regarding Piaget's formation of his cognitive development theory. What early professional experiences led Piaget to propose his theory? What are the two major aspects of Piaget's theory? How did Piaget's early training as a biologist influence his beliefs concerning how individuals begin to learn? Ask students to write a short essay based on their research.

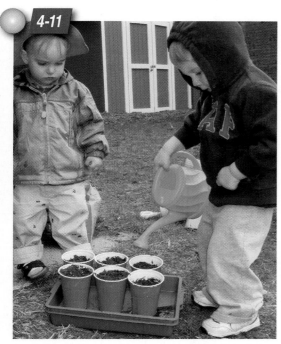

According to Piaget, children construct their knowledge of the world through activities.

Piaget's stages of cognitive development are the same for all children. Most children proceed through the stages in order. Each stage builds on a previous stage. However, the age at which a child progresses through these stages is variable due to differences in maturation.

Although Piaget did not apply his theory directly to education, he did strongly influence children's early education. Many teaching strategies have evolved from his work. Caregivers and teachers now know that learning is an active process. Providing children with stimulating, hands-on activities helps them build knowledge, 4-12. Piaget's theory includes four stages: sensorimotor, preoperational, concrete, and formal operations. The first three stages occur during early childhood and the early school-age years. The following paragraphs describe these stages.

Piaget's Stages of Development

The **sensorimotor stage** takes place between birth and two years of age. Infants use all their senses to explore and learn. In this way, sensory experiences and motor

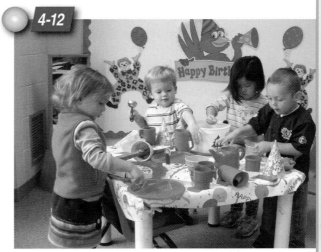

Piaget believed that dramatic play is essential to development.

information, they are constantly creating, modifying, organizing, and reorganizing schemata.

Adaptation is a term Piaget used for children mentally organizing what they perceive in their environment. When new information or experiences occur, children must adapt to include this information in their thinking. If this new information does not fit with what children already know, a state of imbalance occurs. To return to balance, adaptation occurs through either assimilation or accommodation.

- *Assimilation* is the process of taking in new information and adding it to what the child already knows.

- *Accommodation* is adjusting what is already known to fit the new information. This process is how people organize their thoughts and develop intellectual structures.

Vocabulary

Have a student volunteer define the term *schemata*. How does new information affect a child's schemata?

Discuss

Explain Piaget's use of the term *adaptation*. What happens to children when new information or experiences occur? How are assimilation and accommodation related to adaptation?

Activity

Have students interview a parent of three or more children to compare the differences and similarities in the development of learning abilities among siblings. Record the parent's insights on how the older siblings may have influenced the maturation process of the younger children. Allow time for students to discuss their findings in class.

Resource

Dialing for Answers to Piaget's Theory, Activity C, SAG

Putting Technology to Use

Ask students to conduct an Internet search for information regarding the appropriate age for the introduction of technology toys and games for young children. What can young children gain from playing with hi-tech toys? How might growth and development be affected when children engage more often in play with hi-tech toys than in creative and imaginative play with traditional play materials and equipment? Ask students to choose a side and debate the merits of each.

Discuss

In which of Piaget's stages of development are children very egocentric? What is the difference between the egocentricity demonstrated by young children and the selfishness or self-centeredness displayed by some teens and adults?

Vocabulary

Have a student volunteer define the term *concrete operations.* Are children in the concrete operations stage able to think symbolically? Explain your answer.

Resource

Observing for Piaget's Concrete Operations Stage, Activity B, OG

Reflect

The child in 4-13 is using her finger as a symbolic representation of a baby bottle. What other examples of symbolic representation have you observed in young children?

development promote cognitive development. Babies' physical actions, such as sucking, grasping, and hitting, help them learn about their surroundings. Movements are random at first. Gradually they become intentional as behaviors are repeated. Children begin to learn that objects still exist even when they are out of sight. This is known as *object permanence.* Through exploration and exposure to new experiences, new concepts are learned.

The **preoperational stage** takes place between ages two and seven. Children during this stage are very *egocentric.* This means that they assume others see the world the same way they do. Children do not yet have the ability to see others' points of view. During this time, representation skills are learned. These skills include language, symbolic play, and drawing. See 4-13. Children learn to use symbols and internal images, but their thinking is illogical. It is very different from that of adults. Children begin to understand that changing the physical appearance of something does not change the amount of it. They are able to recognize the difference between size and volume. For example, a ball of clay can be stretched into a long rope. Even if the physical appearance changes, the amount of the object does not change. This skill is called *conservation.* At this stage, children can also classify groups of objects and put objects in a series in order.

During the ages of seven to eleven years, **concrete operations** begin. Children develop the capacity to think systematically, but only when they can refer to actual objects and use hands-on activities. Then they begin to internalize some tasks. This means they no longer need to depend on what is seen. They become capable of reversing operations. For example, they understand that 3 + 1 is the same as 1 + 3. When real situations are presented, they are beginning to understand others' points of view.

The fourth stage, *formal operations,* takes place from eleven years of age to adulthood

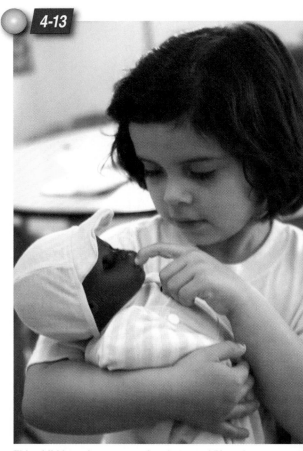

4-13

This child is at the preoperational stage of Piaget's cognitive development. She is using her finger to represent a baby bottle.

(the age range you are in right now). According to Piaget, young people develop the capacity to think in purely abstract ways. They no longer need concrete examples. Problem solving and reasoning are key skills developed during this stage.

Vygotsky's Sociocultural Theory

Both Jean Piaget and Lev Vygotsky believed that children build knowledge through experiences. Piaget believed this

---

Portfolio Project

Using print or Internet sources, ask students to search for information on Piaget's conservation experiments. Have students attempt to duplicate some of the experiments with young children from a local preschool classroom, kindergarten, or early elementary school. What do the results of the experiments convey about a young child's development of conservation abilities? What about a young child's ability to think and reason logically? Have students write an essay of their findings and place a copy in their portfolio.

happened through exploration with hands-on activities. Vygotsky, on the other hand, believed that children learn through social and cultural experiences. Interactions with peers and adults help children in this process. While interacting with others, children learn the customs, values, beliefs, and language of their culture. For this reason, families and teachers should provide plenty of social interaction for young children. See 4-14.

Vygotsky believed language is an important tool for thought and plays a key role in cognitive development. He introduced the term *private speech*, or self-talk. This refers to when children "think out loud." After learning language, children engage in this self-talk to help guide their activity and develop their thinking. Generally, self-talk continues until children reach school age.

One of Vygotsky's most important contributions was the *zone of proximal development* (ZPD). This concept presents learning as a scale. One end of the scale or "zone" includes the tasks that are within the child's current developmental level. The other end of the scale includes tasks too difficult for children to accomplish, even with help.

In the middle are the tasks children cannot accomplish alone. These are achieved with help from another knowledgeable peer or adult. The term used for this assistance is *scaffolding*. Just as a painter needs a structure on which to stand and paint a building, scaffolding provides the structure for learning to occur. For example, a teacher could scaffold a child's learning while constructing a puzzle. The teacher might demonstrate how a piece fits or provide clues regarding color, shape, or size. The "zone" is constantly changing. In contrast to Piaget, Vygotsky believed that learning was not limited by stage or maturation. Children move forward in their cognitive development with the right social interaction and guided learning, 4-15.

Gardner's Multiple Intelligences Theory

Howard Gardner has helped teachers rethink how they work with young children. Traditional intelligence tests mainly focus on language and math/logic skills. In contrast,

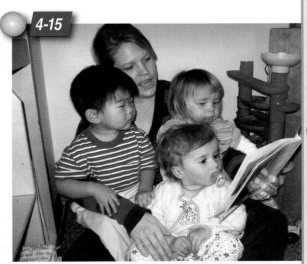

4-14

According to Vygotsky, children learn the rules of social interaction through play.

4-15

Vygotsky believed it is important to support language development. During storytelling, the teacher extends the experience by asking questions.

Discuss

Of what importance, according to Vygotsky, is social interaction in the development of a young child's learning ability? How does this differ from Piaget's theory?

Reflect

What early social interactions do you recall that helped shape your understanding of your family's culture? What examples of early learning directly resulted from specific social interactions?

Vocabulary

Have a student volunteer define the term *scaffolding*. Give an example of how a teacher could scaffold a child's learning while painting on an easel.

Resource

Applying Vygotsky's Zone of Proximal Development (ZPD), Activity C, OG

Meeting Special Needs

Provide special learners with a chart or diagram representing the four major theorists studied in this chapter. Provide a short statement of each theory followed by examples of putting the theory to practice. Ask students to state why each theory is important to consider in the development of learning ability. Have students question each other in small groups to test their understanding of this knowledge. Students may also work in pairs to fill in a blank diagram with the information as a review of the material.

Vocabulary

Have a student volunteer define the term *multiple intelligences*. Of what value is the multiple intelligence theory to teachers?

Resource

Gardner's Multiple Intelligences, reproducible master 4-4, TR

Discuss

What do Vygotsky's and Gardner's theories have in common? How do they differ?

Reflect

How can Gardner's theory help explain why the basketball coach's son is so expert at basketball or why the music instructor's daughter has a beautiful singing voice? How can you account for instances where children do not develop the skills of their parents?

Gardner's theory of **multiple intelligences** emphasizes that there are different kinds of intelligences used by the human brain. Gardner believes intelligence is the result of complex interactions between children's heredity and experiences. This theory focuses on how cultures shape human potential.

Gardner claims that children learn and express themselves in many different ways. In the process, they are using several types of intelligence. Each intelligence functions separately, but all are closely linked. According to Gardner, a potential intelligence will not develop unless it is nurtured. Learning can best be achieved by using a child's strongest intelligence. Gardner claims, however, that all children need opportunities to develop all areas of intelligence.

The multiple intelligence theory allows teachers to see the positive attributes of all children. Teachers also view Gardner's theory as a meaningful guide for making curriculum decisions. It gives them a chance to assess children's learning strengths. From this data, teachers can plan a wide variety of learning experiences. Chart 4-16 lists Gardner's eight intelligences. The paragraphs that follow explain these intelligences in detail.

Bodily-Kinesthetic Intelligence

Bodily-kinesthetic intelligence involves the ability to control body movements. This includes using parts of the body to solve problems, handle objects, and express emotions. People with this type of

4-16

Gardner's Eight Intelligences

Bodily-kinesthetic	• Ability to control one's own body movements and manipulate objects • Use of fingers, hands, arms, and legs to solve problems, express ideas, construct, and repair
Musical-rhythmic	• Ability to recognize, create, and appreciate pitch, rhythm, tone quality • Ability to use different forms of musical expression
Logical-mathematical	• Ability to use logic, reason, mathematics to solve problems • Ability to apply principles of cause-and-effect and prediction • Appreciation of patterns as well as relationships
Verbal-linguistic	• Ability to use well-developed language skills to express self and understand others • Sensitivity to sounds, rhythm, and meaning of words
Interpersonal	• Ability to understand feelings, behaviors, and motives of others • Ability to work effectively with others
Intrapersonal	• Ability to understand personal strengths, weaknesses, talents, and interests • Knowledge of skills, limitations, emotions, desires, and motivations
Visual-spatial	• Ability to form mental images • Ability to visualize the relationship of objects in space
Naturalistic	• Ability to distinguish between living things such as plants and animals

The relationship between multiple intelligences is the foundation of Gardner's theory.

Meeting Special Needs

Assist special learners as well as everyone in the class learn Gardner's eight intelligences by having students create classroom charts for each of the intelligences listed in Chart 4-16. Have students search for pictures, drawings, or photos of children demonstrating each of the intelligences and mount them on poster board under the respective title of the intelligence. Add words or phrases that further explain or indicate understanding of the intelligence. Ask students to assess their own abilities or relate their experiences in each of the intelligences.

intelligence typically enjoy sports, dance, or creative drama. They are able to express themselves with their entire bodies. Children will benefit from creative-movement experiences and role-playing.

Children with this type of intelligence process knowledge through sensation. They enjoy touch and creating with their hands. Therefore, daily opportunities should be provided for hands-on activities. Clay, sand, dough, feely boxes, and other sensory activities help them develop fine-motor skills. Movement is also needed for gross-motor skills and coordination. It is important for caregivers and teachers to provide activities involving physical challenges. These may include playing kickball, jumping rope, and moving to music.

Musical-Rhythmic Intelligence

Musical-rhythmic intelligence involves the ability to recognize musical patterns. It also includes the ability to produce and appreciate music. Since music evokes emotion, this is one of the earliest intelligences to emerge. Composers and musicians are examples of people with this type of intelligence.

Children with this type of intelligence love listening to music. They are drawn to the art of sound and appreciate all forms of musical expression. They have a well-developed auditory sense and can discriminate tone, pitch, and rhythmic patterns. As a result, they often cannot get songs out of their minds. You will hear them repeatedly singing or humming. This helps them understand concepts and remember information.

Activities to support musical intelligence can be included throughout the day. Offer opportunities for sound exploration through listening and singing. Use songs for directions and moving children from one activity to another. Play background music during self-selected play. Include songs during large and small group activities. Record the children creating their own music while singing or chanting. Explore rhythm

by moving to recorded music. Use different instruments and instruments from other cultures to add variety.

Logical-Mathematical Intelligence

Logical-mathematical intelligence is more than just the ability to use math. It is the ability to use logic and reason to solve problems. Math experts have this form of intelligence. Scientists and composers may also have it. This intelligence involves the ability to explore categories, patterns, and other relationships. It includes applying the principle of cause and effect. It also involves the skill to make predictions about patterns, 4-17.

Children with this type of intelligence take pleasure in finding patterns and relationships. They enjoy discovering similarities and differences. Manipulatives for matching, measuring, and counting should be provided. Blocks can encourage the children's problem-solving and reasoning skills. Storybooks that show a sequence of events hold appeal for this type of intelligence. Water and sand activities with different-size containers help teach the concept of volume.

4-17

Children with logical-mathematical intelligence enjoy discovering similarities and differences.

Discuss

Why are hands-on activities so important for children to develop bodily-kinesthetic intelligence? What toys or equipment in the preschool classroom encourage the development of bodily-kinesthetic intelligence?

Activity

Ask students to research songs for young children that give directions or instructions for performing routine classroom tasks. Teach the children one or more of these songs and observe closely for several days to determine if children can remember the songs and perform the activity as a result. Allow time for students to share their findings in class.

Enrich

Have students collect examples of materials that could be used in the preschool classroom to encourage the use and development of logical-mathematical intelligence. Ask students to explain how the items contribute to this development.

Cross-Curricular Activity

All Areas

Ask students to observe specific classes in the high school such as math, science, health, social studies, language, vocational, art, etc. to determine how the teachers in each class apply or interpret Gardner's theory. What opportunities or activities do the teachers use to capitalize on individual students' learning strengths? Ask students to keep a checklist of the eight intelligences and have them record how many times, if any, the teacher makes use of them in the class instruction. Have students repeat the observation in elementary classrooms and compare the findings.

Reflect

How can children best be encouraged to develop verbal-linguistic intelligence? How could following the old adage *"children should be seen and not heard"* have kept older generations of parents from contributing to the development of this intelligence in their children?

Discuss

What is the difference between *interpersonal* and *intrapersonal* intelligence? What is the value in a child's education of developing skills in both of these areas?

Enrich

Ask students to identify materials, toys, or equipment in the preschool laboratory that encourage the development of visual-spatial intelligence. Have students create visual aids for the preschool classroom to assist children in using materials appropriately and to facilitate clean-up and storage.

Resource

Applying Multiple Intelligence Theory, Activity D, SAG

Verbal-Linguistic Intelligence

Verbal-linguistic intelligence involves the ability to use language for expression. People with this type of intelligence have well-developed language skills. They demonstrate sensitivity to the meaning, sound, and rhythm of words. Lawyers, poets, public speakers, and language translators have this type of intelligence.

Young children with this intelligence learn best by talking, listening, reading, and writing. These children quickly learn the words to new stories, songs, and finger plays. They enjoy talking to other people and are able to speak in an interesting and engaging manner. They are also able to learn a second language with ease.

This intelligence can be nurtured by environments rich with language opportunities. Children learn language in settings where it is used. Teachers need to follow the children's interests. They can then use these interests to engage children in meaningful conversations. Children's storybooks, songs, poetry, chants, and rhymes can serve as means for learning new vocabulary words. Listening to and telling stories can also promote language development.

Interpersonal Intelligence

People with *interpersonal intelligence* display excellent communication and social skills. These people have a gift for understanding the feelings, behaviors, moods, and motives of others. They make friends easily. They use language to develop trust and bonds with others. They are also skilled in supporting others and empathizing with them. These skills are important for teachers, politicians, salespeople, and people working in the service industry.

These skills are nurtured in young children when caring behaviors are modeled for them. Teachers should keep this in mind.

They can share experiences and provide the children with chances for verbal interaction. Books focusing on emotions can be acted out.

Intrapersonal Intelligence

Intrapersonal intelligence is the ability to understand the inner self. This is also known as *self-awareness*. It involves knowing your skills, limits, and feelings. It includes understanding your desires and motives. The ability to organize groups of people is part of this strength. Communicating needs clearly is another aspect. Psychologists, social workers, religious leaders, and counselors are examples of people with this type of intelligence.

How can you foster this type of intelligence? In the classroom, share emotions that all children experience. These include joy, sadness, regret, and disappointment. Classroom examples should be shared as well as storybooks that contain emotional concepts.

Visual-Spatial Intelligence

Visual-spatial intelligence allows people to use their vision to develop mental images. People who have this type of intelligence show a preference for pictures and images. Photographers and artists are some examples. Architects, engineers, and surgeons also need this ability. They use it to see the relationship of objects in space.

Teachers can foster this intelligence by providing children with unstructured materials. Building blocks and puzzles strengthen this type of intelligence, 4-18. Make and use visual aids wherever possible. For example, classroom schedules, recipes, and stories can all be displayed on charts. Shelving units can be labeled with pictures cut from equipment catalogs.

Portfolio Project

Have students research the work of Howard Gardner and how he came to develop his theory. For example, why is the work of Dr. Gardner so relevant in light of today's educational crisis? How can applying Dr. Gardner's theory to the classroom encourage greater success in today's students? Have students write a brief essay on how they would incorporate the use of the eight intelligences in education and activities for young children. Ask students to save a copy of the essay in their portfolio.

Visual-spatial intelligence can be promoted through toys such as blocks and puzzles.

Naturalistic Intelligence

Naturalistic intelligence is developed from the need to survive. This is the ability to classify objects in nature such as animals and plants. It depends on a type of pattern recognition. This strength also includes the ability to distinguish among types and brands of objects. Sailors, gardeners, chefs, and farmers are people who have this intelligence.

To build on this intelligence, provide cooking activities and nature walks. These help develop use of the senses to gather information. Planting and growing a garden helps the children observe cycles. Rocks, seashells, flowers, leaves, seeds, and coins can also be collected. In the classroom, they can be sorted and classified. Post picture collections and share books about natural events.

Making the Pieces Fit

You might be thinking, "How will knowing about the areas and principles of development, the brain, and theories help me in my career in working with children?" The answer is both simple and complex. It's much like fitting together the pieces of a puzzle. In order to become a nurturing, responsive teacher, you must have insight into how children grow and develop.

The brain affects all aspects of growth and development. The areas and principles of development are similar for all children. Development generally progresses in a similar way for all children. Although each theory looks at development from a different angle, each offers a wealth of insight into how children develop. On what do the theorists agree? Children learn best in a caring environment rich with opportunity for learning. In addition, caregivers help build the self-confidence and self-worth children need to safely explore the world.

Enrich

Have students compile a list of classroom visitors and guest speakers who could be invited to the preschool classroom to encourage the development of naturalistic intelligence. What objects or materials relating to this area might the visitors bring to class that would interest the children?

Resource

Nurturing Multiple Intelligences, Activity D, OG

Reflect

How does learning about the child development principles and theories affect your view of your own learning and growing experience? If you could go back in time, based on this knowledge, what suggestions would you make to your parents and former child caregivers and educators about how you were raised?

Resource

Check Your Theory IQ, Activity E, SAG

Meeting Special Needs

Review the special learner's chapter outlines to determine if the students have any questions about the concepts or content of this chapter. Review the chapter objectives and ask the students to evaluate their progress in meeting these objectives. Ask the students to summarize, orally or in writing, what they learned from this chapter.

Review and Reflect Answer Key

1. physical development
2. F
3. cephalocaudal principle: the child first gains control of the head, then the arms, and the legs; proximodistal principle: the spinal cord develops before outer parts of the body; maturation: a sequence of biological changes in the brain, nervous system, and other areas of the child's body that must occur before the child can obtain certain skills
4. F
5. When under stress, the body produces cortisol. High levels of this hormone wash over the brain like an acid. Over a long length of time, cortisol can lead to problems with memory and regulating emotion.
6. Windows of opportunity are key times when appropriate stimulation is needed for the brain synapses to link easily and efficiently. After these key periods, chances for creating stable, long-lasting pathways in the brain tend to diminish.
7. Stage 1: trust versus mistrust; Stage 2: autonomy versus shame and doubt; Stage 3: initiative versus guilt; Stage 4: industry versus inferiority
8. Infants need warm, consistent, predictable, and attentive care to develop trust.

Summary

Understanding child development will help make you a successful caregiver or early childhood teacher. The study of child development is divided into three main areas—physical, cognitive, and social-emotional development.

Brain development occurs rapidly during the first three years of life. The connections between nerve cells are created as a child interacts with the environment. The links allow a greater number of messages to pass through the brain. Therefore, infant care and interaction with caregivers is crucial to brain development.

Theories of development can help caregivers understand how to best work with children. Some of the most prominent theories include the eight stages of Erikson's psychosocial theory and the four stages of Piaget's cognitive development theory. Vygotsky claimed that children learn through social and cultural expression. Gardner developed a theory of multiple intelligences used by the human brain. All these theories provide insight into children's development.

Review and Reflect

1. Changes in bone thickness, vision, and hearing are part of _____.

2. True or false. Trust, fear, and pride are part of cognitive development.

3. List and explain three principles of development.

4. True or false. Nurture is more important for the developing brain than nature.

5. Describe how stress created by negative experiences can affect the brain.

6. What are windows of opportunity? Why are they important?

7. List the stages of Erikson's psychosocial theory that take place during the early childhood years.

8. What do infants need to develop trust?

9. List and explain Piaget's stages of development.

10. The term Vygotsky used to describe assistance provided to a child by a knowledgeable peer or adult is_____.

11. _____ believes intelligence is the result of complex interactions between children's heredity and experiences.

12. Which type of intelligence allows people to use their vision to develop mental images?
    A. Bodily-kinesthetic.
    B. Logical-mathematical.
    C. Visual-spatial.
    D. Naturalistic.

9. The sensorimotor stage takes place between birth and two years of age. During this stage, infants use all their sense to explore and learn. The preoperational stage takes place between ages two and seven. During this stage, children are egocentric as they cannot see other's point of view. Representation and conservation skills are being learned. Concrete operations is the third stage. Children develop the capacity to think systematically and become capable of reversing operations. They also are beginning to understand another's point of view. During formal operations, the fourth stage, children develop the capacity to think in abstract ways.
10. scaffolding
11. Howard Gardner
12. C

Apply and Explore

1. Visit an infant or toddler program. Observe and record strategies used by teachers to promote the development of trust.

2. Observe a group of preschool children. Record examples of teachers scaffolding the children's learning.

3. Review Gardner's theory of multiple intelligences. Describe the intelligence area that you believe is your strength.

Cross-Curricular Link

Social Studies

1. Visit the Web site www.pyschology.about.com to review theories of development discussed in this chapter.

Technology

2. Read the information at the Web site Zero to Three (www.zerotothree.org) about stimulating the infant's developing brain through touch, voice, movement, and vision.

Workplace Link

Interview an early childhood teacher. Ask the teacher if his or her teaching methods are based specifically on any particular child development theory or theories. If the teacher mentions any theorists who are not discussed in this chapter, research them and their theories. Does the teacher seem to focus equally on physical, cognitive, or social-emotional development? Write a report on your findings to share with the class.

Discuss

The chapter opening photo shows two children in the age range of birth to two years. How old would you estimate that these children are? How have they changed since they were born? In what other ways will they change before they reach age two?

Discuss

Before beginning the chapter, spend several minutes in class reviewing child development knowledge learned previously about children from birth to age two. Have each student contribute at least one concept.

Understanding Children from Birth to Age Two

After studying this chapter, you will be able to

- chart the physical development of children in the first two years after birth.

- describe how children develop cognitively in the first two years after birth.

- explain how children in the first two years after birth develop socially and emotionally.

Terms to Know

reflex
motor sequence
object permanence
deferred imitation
telegraphic speech
temperament
attachment
separation anxiety

Physical Development in the First Two Years

Growth is rapid during the first two years of life. The child's size, shape, senses, and organs change. Some changes are rapid; others are more gradual. With each change, children gain new abilities. Much of the first year of life is spent coordinating motor skills. Through the repetition of motor actions, infants gain physical strength and motor coordination.

As a caregiver, you need to be aware of physical changes in the first two years. Activities, diets, sleep schedules, and safety policies need to be adjusted as children grow. For instance, infants less than four months old do not have much muscle strength. Typically, these children enjoy being rocked or held for most of the day. They also enjoy sitting in infant seats. However, by twelve months, the infant's large muscles are more developed. At this time, children need time and space for crawling and walking.

Size and Shape

An infant's weight may change almost daily. The average weight at birth is 7½ pounds. Five months later, the infant will have doubled in weight. By one year, the typical child weighs about 22 pounds—about three times the birthweight. By two years of age, most children weigh almost four times their birthweight.

The infant's length also changes rapidly. The average newborn measures 20 inches. Twelve months later, the infant has usually grown 10 to 12 inches. During the second year of life, most children grow 2 to 6 inches more. By 24 months, most children measure 32 to 36 inches in height.

There are weight and height differences between boys and girls by two years of age. At this age, most boys are slightly heavier and taller than girls. Most boys reach about half of their adult height by two years of age. At the same age, girls will have passed their halfway mark by one or two inches.

Health and Safety

Preventing Sudden Infant Death Syndrome (SIDS)

Child care providers who serve infants must be knowledgeable about reducing the risk of Sudden Infant Death Syndrome, or SIDS. Keeping up-to-date with state guidelines and recommendations by groups, such as the *American Academy of Pediatrics*, is essential for care providers. When caring for infants, always

- place infants on their backs for sleep
- provide a firm crib covered by a sheet
- keep soft materials, such as comforters, pillows, and stuffed toys out of the crib
- make sure the sleeping area is a comfortable temperature to keep infants from becoming overheated

Vocabulary

Have students review the *Terms to Know* list. Ask students to look up unfamiliar words or terms in the glossary before reading the chapter.

Enrich

Ask students to research the availability of area infant-parent programs offered by community colleges and family support agencies. What are the benefits of these programs for infants and their parents? Have student volunteers share their findings with the class.

Discuss

What changes can be expected in an infant's sleep habits during the first year? What changes in diet can be expected?

Activity

Arrange a field trip to a local child care center that offers an infant program. Have students survey the infant rooms to discover what types of equipment are needed in this area. Ask the director to speak about the center's daily schedule, feeding and sleeping arrangements, infant-caregiver ratio, and infant activities. How are parents kept aware of their child's development? Have students prepare a list of questions to ask prior to the field trip.

Meeting Special Needs

Provide an outline of the chapter with all the chapter headings for special learners. Students should fill in each section of the outline as the material is covered in class with a sentence or two about the content. Review the special learners' IEPs to decide if any modifications should be made in presenting the chapter content. Prepare a vocabulary matching assignment to assist students with learning the definitions of the *Terms to Know*.

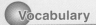

Vocabulary

Have a student volunteer define the term *reflex*. Ask students to name any reflexes they have.

Discuss

What is the difference between survival and primitive reflexes? Which reflexes disappear with age? Why is it so important for doctors to test infants for the reflexes?

Note

Reflexes are important for an infant's development. Using reflexes allows the infant to eventually develop voluntary abilities, such as eating and reaching for objects, as the reflexes disappear.

Reflexes

At birth, the infant's physical abilities are limited to reflexes. A **reflex** is an automatic body response to a stimulus. The person does not control this response. Blinking when something is coming toward your face is an example of a reflex. Some reflexes, such as blinking, continue throughout life. Others appear in infants and disappear after a few months.

Doctors and others who work with children check reflexes to assess brain and nerve development. When normal reflexes are not present in infants, it may be a sign of brain or nerve damage. If these reflexes continue past the time they should disappear, brain or nerve damage may again be suspected. Professionals often test infants for the reflexes listed in Chart 5-1. Infants do not all acquire or lose these reflexes at exactly the same time. The chart shows the age range when each of these reflexes generally disappears.

There are two types of reflexes. *Survival reflexes* are necessary for life. These include breathing, sucking, and swallowing. Unlike survival reflexes, *primitive reflexes* will disappear with age. The Babinski, Moro, Palmar, and stepping reflexes are examples.

Sucking Reflex

The *sucking reflex* helps the infant obtain food for survival. It is a permanent reflex. To test for the sucking reflex, place a finger on the lips or in the mouth. The infant will begin sucking. The course of development for this reflex is from birth to six months.

Rooting Reflex

The infant's reflexes are needed for survival. See 5-2. This reflex causes infants to turn their heads toward anything that brushes their faces. This action helps them find a food source such as a nipple. Once an object is near an infant's lips or cheek, a rooting response will be triggered. The infant's head and mouth will move toward the stimulus. This reflex helps the child search for something to suck. It usually disappears by three to four months of age.

Moro Reflex

The Moro reflex is sometimes referred to as the "startle reflex." It occurs when a newborn is startled by a noise or sudden movement. The infant will react by flinging the arms and legs outward and extending

5-1 Some Newborn Reflexes

Reflex	Age of Disappearance
Rooting	3 to 4 months
Moro	6 months
Palmar Grasp	3 to 12 months
Babinski	8 to 12 months
Stepping	2 to 3 months

Continuation of these reflexes after the time they should disappear may be an indication of nerve or brain damage.

Cross-Curricular Activity

Health
Using print or Internet resources, have students research the reflexes of premature infants in comparison to those of full-term babies. Are there any differences that could have an effect on the premature infant's development? Ask students to write a one-page report of their findings. Allow time for students to read their reports in class.

5-2

The rooting and sucking reflexes help an infant get food.

the head. Then the infant will quickly draw the arms together, crying loudly. This reflex peaks during the first month and usually disappears by six months.

Palmar Grasp Reflex

The grasp reflex is easy to observe. When you touch the infant's palms, the hands will grip tightly. The grip is tight enough that you can lift the infant into a sitting position. However, do not try this. Since the infant has no control over this response, he or she may let go suddenly. This reflex can also be seen if a rattle or another object is placed across the palm. This reflex weakens after the first three or four months after birth. It disappears totally late in the first year.

Babinski Reflex

The Babinski reflex is present at birth in babies who were born at full term. To test for this reflex, stroke the sole of the foot on the outside from the heel to the toe. The toes will fan out and curl and the foot twists in. This reflex usually lasts for the first year after birth.

Stepping or Walking Reflex

A stepping or walking reflex can be observed in full-term babies. When an infant is held so the feet are flat on a surface, the infant will lift one foot after another in a stepping motion. This reflex usually disappears two to three months after birth. Infants learn to step voluntarily late in the first year.

Motor Sequence

Motor sequence refers to the order in which a child is able to perform new movements. Each new movement builds on the previous abilities. Motor sequence depends on the development of the brain and nerves. For this reason, movements tend to develop in areas closest to the brain and spinal cord first.

In the first months after birth, head and trunk control develops. When this occurs, the infant can lift the head from a surface. The infant can also watch a moving object by moving the head from side to side.

By four or five months of age, an infant can roll over. Most infants are first able to turn from the stomach to the back. Soon after, the child will be able to roll from back to stomach.

Most infants can sit upright at four to six months of age. The infant needs to strengthen the neck and back muscles to accomplish this feat.

Gradually, infants are able to pull themselves into sitting positions. After this, crawling is the next skill in the motor sequence. This skill occurs shortly after the child learns to roll onto the stomach. To crawl, the child pulls with the arms and wiggles the stomach. Some infants may even

Note

The Babinski reflex is also known as the *extensor plantar reflex.* If present in a child after age two, it could indicate serious brain or nerve damage.

Resource

Motor Sequence for Infants, transparency master 5-1, TR

Vocabulary

Have a student volunteer define the term *motor sequence.* Point out that movements tend to develop in areas closest to the brain and spinal cord first.

Resource

Reflexes, Activity B, SAG

Meeting Special Needs

Have students who are gifted research Guillain Barre syndrome and its effect on reflexes. Have students write a report that includes information on symptoms, testing, treatment, and recovery. Ask students to give presentations that include visuals on their reports.

Note

Since there is some confusion to the correct meanings of *creeping* and *crawling*, clarify these for the class. Remind students that crawling precedes creeping.

Discuss

What is the normal age range for the development of walking? What influences may affect the age at which a child first begins to walk?

Resource

Progression of Gross-Motor Development, color transparency CT-4, TR

push with their legs. Many people confuse the terms *crawling* and *creeping*. Crawling occurs when the infant's abdomen is on the floor.

Hitching is another movement used by infants. Before they can hitch, infants must be able to sit without support. From this position, they move their arms and legs, sliding their buttocks across the floor.

As the arms and legs strengthen, infants are able to creep. *Creeping* is a movement in which infants support their weight on their hands and knees. See 5-3. They then move their arms and legs to go forward. As arms and legs become stronger, infants are able to stand with help from an adult. Soon after, they are able to stand while supporting themselves with furniture.

With better leg strength and coordination, infants are able to walk when led by an adult. Soon after, they are able to pull themselves up into a standing position. Next, infants are able to stand without any

support. Finally, they become true toddlers—able to walk without support or help.

There are stages of development for each skill that involves movement. To illustrate, when progressing toward mature motor skills, children show changes in movement. Picture the child's first attempts at walking. These actions are awkward. At first, it is difficult to maintain an upright posture. Next, there is an unpredictable loss of balance. Short steps are taken and the toes are pointed outward. The child keeps the legs spread to have a wide base of support.

Gradually the walking pattern appears smoother. The step length increases and the arm swinging decreases. The child also brings the legs closer together, decreasing the base of support. See 5-4.

Earliest hand movements are reflexive. By three to four months, infants enjoy swiping at objects. At this age, they are still unable to grasp objects because they close their hands too early or too late. By nine months,

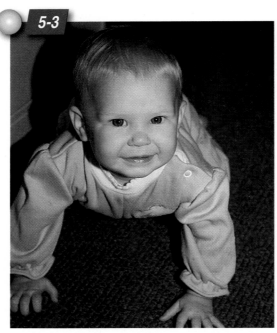

5-3

Creeping requires stronger leg muscles and better leg control than crawling.

5-4

Walking Sequence

Immature Stage
- Upright position difficult to maintain
- Rigid appearance
- Loss of balance occurs frequently
- Short steps taken
- Toes turned outward
- Legs spread wide as base of support
- Arms held above waist

Mature Stage
- Upright position and balance maintained
- Step length increases
- Legs closer together, narrow base of support
- Relaxed appearance
- Arms held at side

Changes in movement cause the walking pattern to gradually become smoother.

Putting Technology to Use

Have students conduct an Internet search for information about Dr. Benjamin Spock (1903-1998), a well-known pediatrician and author of *The Common Sense Book of Baby and Child Care*. What are some of Dr. Spock's beliefs concerning the motor development of infants? How has his work on behalf of children influenced generations of parents? Have students write a report of their findings. Allow time for students to read their reports in class.

Health and Safety

Failure to Thrive (FTT)

Failure to thrive (FTT) happens more often with infants and toddlers. Symptoms include lack of weight gain and height growth as is typical of other infants and toddlers of the same age. The causes can be planned such as malnutrition caused by neglect. Unplanned causes may be low birthweight, poverty, poor social interaction, improper feeding skills, or such diseases as gastric reflux, cystic fibrosis, lead poisoning, and many others.

Diagnosis of FTT is done by a team approach and begins with the child's doctor and parents. Team members may include nurses, dietitians, social workers, and child care providers. As a child care provider, you may be asked to tell about a child's eating patterns and social interactions with staff and family.

The goal in treating FTT is to restore a child's nutritional health. This may help avoid negative effects on brain development and other areas of growth and development. Early intervention may also provide children and families with continuing medical care, counseling, and education about feeding and social interaction.

If FTT is due to abuse or neglect, it must be reported to the proper authorities. Follow the reporting guidelines of your state and the facility in which you work.

hand-eye coordination improves and infants can pick up objects.

Infants can begin scribbling with a crayon by about 16 months of age. Simple figures composed of vertical and horizontal lines can be made by the end of the second year. By two years of age, the child typically is showing a preference for one hand or the other. For some children, hand dominance is not established until age four.

Many other motor skills are gained in the first two years. These skills are listed in the Appendix. The skills listed are milestones for each age group. They are considered milestones because about half of infants at that age can do the skills. For this reason, you should not worry if a child cannot do every skill listed for his or her age. However, you should seek help for a child who is way behind the milestones. For instance, if a 17-month-old cannot roll over, help should be sought.

Cognitive Development in the First Two Years

At birth, most of an infant's movements are the result of reflexes. As infants grow, they begin to learn how to make things happen for themselves. Soon they are able to coordinate the movements needed to grab a bottle and suck milk from it. They also begin to react differently depending on their needs. A baby may spit out a pacifier if he or she is not hungry. However, a hungry baby may be content to suck on the pacifier.

Two main forces—heredity and environment—influence a child's cognitive development. Heredity determines when a child's brain and senses will be mature enough to learn certain skills. Environmental factors also affect learning. Children need opportunities to use their senses and try new things, 5-5. As a caregiver, you need to provide an environment that allows children to develop to their full potential intellectually.

Activity

Ask students to survey toy catalogs, educational equipment catalogs, and parenting magazines to locate appropriate toys to aid in an infant's motor development. What materials are recommended for gross-motor skills? What are the recommendations for developing fine-motor skills? Allow time for students to share their findings in class.

Resource

Observing Motor Development, Activity A, OG

Reflect

What advice would you give to a parent who was concerned her four-month-old son could not hold a cup using two hands? What advice would you give to the parent of a fifteen-month-old girl who was not yet walking?

Resource

Types of Development, Activity A, SAG

Portfolio Project

Remind students that an early childhood teacher is responsible for answering parents' questions about development or directing them to sources for further information. Have students compile a list of resources that might be used to assist in parent communication. These may include books, magazine articles, professional journal articles, newsletters, pamphlets, cooperative extension agency bulletins, and government information. Have students format their list as a bibliography and add to it throughout the year as they learn of additional resources. Have students keep a copy of the list in their portfolio.

Discuss

Give an example of a positive environmental effect on a child's cognitive development. Give an example of a hereditary factor that may negatively impact a child's cognitive development.

Note

Dr. Berry T. Brazelton, M.D. has spent many years on the research of infants' reactions to still-faced mothers. Review of these studies may give students insight into the importance of visual stimulation for infants.

Discuss

What types of normal household sounds may seem disconcerting to a newborn? How can parents use what is known about infants' auditory preferences to soothe a startled newborn?

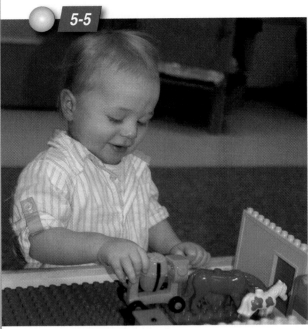

5-5

The activities that you provide infants and young toddlers help them develop cognitively.

Being able to see, hear, feel, taste, and smell are important to learning. Through these senses, children learn about many objects and concepts. All of the senses develop during the first two years of life. Sight and hearing develop especially quickly.

Birth to Three Months

A newborn's vision is blurry at birth. During the first few weeks after birth, infants appear to focus on objects in the center of their visual field. Their near vision is better developed than their far vision. They like to look at objects held 8 to 15 inches in front of them.

As their vision improves, infants show preferences for certain objects. Studies show that infants will gaze longer at patterned disks, such as checks and stripes, than at disks of one solid color. Infants seem to prefer bold colors rather than soft pastels. They also pay more attention to faces than to other objects. In fact, by two months of age, an infant will gaze longer at a smiling face than at a face with no expression.

As infants grow older, they tend to shift their attention on the face. At one month of age, infants appear to focus on the hairline. By two months, infants show more interest in the eyes. The adult's facial expression is most interesting to a three-month-old child. These changes show that children are giving thought to areas of the face that interest them.

Hearing also develops early in life. From birth, infants will turn their heads toward a source of sound. Newborns are startled by loud noises. They often react to these noises by crying. These same newborns are lulled to sleep by rhythmic sounds such as a lullaby or a heartbeat. They also react to human voices while ignoring other sounds. By three weeks, a newborn can distinguish between the voice of the mother or father and that of a stranger.

During the first three months after birth, infants do not distinguish between themselves and the objects around them. If infants see their hands moving, they do not think of themselves as making this movement. In their thinking, it could easily be someone else's hand.

Children this age start to experiment with reflex actions. Newborns suck everything that touches their lips. They even make sucking motions in their sleep. Gradually, children adapt such reflexes to objects in their environment. They learn to suck the breast, bottle, pacifier, and their own fingers in different ways, 5-6.

Three to Six Months

During this time, children start to focus on their surroundings. Before this age, a child would just gaze at objects. The infant now begins to examine objects more closely. By six months of age, the child can distinguish between familiar and unfamiliar faces.

Infants also start to learn that they can touch, shake, and hit objects they see. They notice that toys make sounds.

Putting Technology to Use

Have students research the "Mozart Effect" at **www.mozarteffect.com** as well as other Web sites. How much research is available linking listening to music with an increase in intelligence? How has music been shown to affect infants' moods and emotions? Have students research how the "Mozart Effect" has affected parents' perception of the importance of playing music for their infants. Allow time for students to share their findings in class.

For very young babies, learning to suck a pacifier differently than the breast or bottle is a cognitive skill.

Memory, foresight, and self-awareness are all developing. The child learns that hitting the crib gym makes a noise. The infant also learns that his or her own movement caused the noise.

Infants from three to six months of age also start to show judgment. For instance, they prefer the smell and voice of a parent to that of a stranger. As early as three days after birth, infants will respond to noise. Infants in this stage also try to locate noises by turning toward them. The infant will look around to explore sources of sounds such as a doorbell, a dog barking, or an oven timer. Many times, though, they will turn in the wrong direction.

From birth, an infant makes noises. During this stage, vocalizations begin to increase. You will find that children this age make many noises when you hold and play with them.

Infants in this stage also respond in new ways to touch. If you blow on or kiss the baby's stomach, the child may smile or coo in response. Children this age also respond happily to light touches and tickling.

Infants in this stage think with their senses and movements. By four months, an infant will start using a predictable pattern to learn about objects. If you give a child at this stage an object, you will see this pattern. The child will first look at the object. Then he or she will mouth it and try shaking it, 5-7. The child may also try banging the object on the floor. This is the infant's way of learning what the object can do or how it can be used.

Toward the end of this period, body awareness begins to develop. The infant may bite his or her toe while playing. If the child has a tooth, he or she may be surprised by the hurt this causes. This does not stop the child, however, from making the same mistake with other toes or fingers.

Six to Nine Months

The concept of **object permanence** begins to develop at this stage. This concept is the understanding that objects continue to exist even if the infant cannot see them. Before this time, anything out of sight was out of mind for the infant. For instance, if a rattle was placed under a blanket, the young infant would not search for it. Now, the child begins to understand that the rattle is still there even though it is covered.

Beginning to understand object permanence shows that these infants are

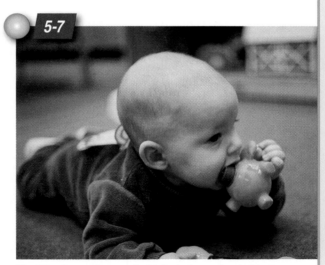

Mouthing is a major way that infants learn about objects.

Reflect

Infants start to learn the concept of *cause and effect* as they manipulate their toys. What popular childhood toys help demonstrate this concept to infants?

Activity

Have students research current studies on the importance of touch to infants. What can parents learn from these studies?

Note

Jean Piaget's studies determined that *object permanence* was present in infants by eight or nine months of age. Infants younger than this are too young to understand the concept, which explains why they do not cry when they cannot see their mothers.

Putting Technology to Use

Jean Piaget conducted many studies to determine how infants learn. Ask students to conduct an Internet search for information about these studies, particularly those involving object permanence. Students may be able to duplicate some experiments in class with infants, such as hiding a toy under a blanket. They might also drop an item off a high chair tray to see if the infant will search for the toy. Discuss what students have learned.

Discuss

Can parents tell by their child's cry what the infant is trying to communicate? How easy is it for others to determine why a child may be crying?

Reflect

Picking up a crying infant used to be seen as spoiling by past generations. What is understood today about the need to respond to an infant's crying?

Discuss

What can infants learn from baby talk? Should baby talk be discouraged when infants start forming their first words?

developing memory and goal-oriented thinking. The child will search under a blanket for a rattle that has been covered. This means that the child remembers that the rattle was there. It also means that the child takes actions with the goal of finding the rattle. At this time though, infants give up within a few seconds if they do not find the rattle.

You can test for object permanence by showing the infant an interesting toy. Then cover the toy with a towel or blanket while the child is looking. If the child attempts to uncover the toy, the child shows an understanding of object permanence. This child also shows goal-oriented behavior.

Part of object permanence involves understanding that other people exist all the time. Before this stage, children would simply cry if uncomfortable and stop crying when needs were met. Now, children begin to understand that they can cry as a call to parents or other caregivers. They know that even if a person is not within sight, the person still exists. Their cry will call the person to them.

Crying to call a person is also a sign that infants are learning to communicate. The child learns that making noises can get an adult to understand the child's needs. At this point, the child starts communicating in other ways. When the infant makes a noise, he or she will often listen for a response. If you make a noise in return, the infant will answer back. Usually the infant will listen when spoken to and look up when his or her name is spoken.

Nine to Twelve Months

During this stage, infants become more intentional about their goals. The child has definite ideas about what he or she wants. If confined to a playpen, the child may cry to be taken out. Once out, the child may crawl across the room to get a forbidden object. At the same time, the child may ignore many interesting objects along the way.

These infants also begin to anticipate certain events. A child at this stage may cry when a parent puts on a coat. The infant has learned that when this happens, the parent will leave. When the child sees the parent enter the child care center, he or she may become excited and happy.

Twelve to Eighteen Months

Between twelve and eighteen months, infants' hearing and speech continues to develop. They enjoy playing pat-a-cake and peekaboo games. Children at this stage like trial-and-error problem solving. They experiment with objects to find new ways to use them, 5-8. These might include rolling, tossing, or bouncing. These children express joy when they find that toys can make noise. They begin to understand that the force they use affects the loudness or softness of noise in a toy.

Relationships between cause and effect fascinate young toddlers. For instance, the child loves to hit water and watch it splash. Children also learn ways to use cause and effect to reach goals at this age. For instance, the child may learn that by pulling on a tablecloth, he or she can reach a plate of cookies.

Language is a change of behavior that occurs as a result of experience and maturation. It is also related to the child's environment. In Spain, for instance, children learn to speak Spanish, while children in Italy learn Italian. Language becomes a bigger part of communication at this stage. Before this time, some children may say a few words, such as *daddy* or *mommy*. Now, children learn to say many new words. Children's first words usually include objects that move and familiar actions. Included are words such as *car, truck, dig, ball, up, down, bye-bye, wet, dirty,* and *hot.* Mostly, children use one or two words to communicate during this stage. They do not yet understand how to combine a series of words to form sentences.

Portfolio Project

Have students write an article suitable for a parent newsletter or child care center bulletin that summarizes cognitive development during the first two years. Have students use their textbooks and other resources as needed.

Students should include what parents should expect with regard to their child's intellectual development during this period. They should also offer suggestions for activities parents can try at home to interact with their child.

5-8

Young toddlers often look for new ways to use objects.

Books become more important to children at this time. A child in this stage will love to sit on your lap and have you read a story. Young toddlers may be able to identify many pictures in simple books. As you point to the pictures, the child may give the names of the objects. Most children at this age can understand even more words than they can say.

Eighteen to Twenty-Four Months

As children near their second birthday, there is a change in how they approach their environment. During this stage, children start to think before taking action. They are able to apply what they know about objects to solve problems without as much trial-and-error. For instance, the child may know that standing on a stool in the bathroom helps the child reach the sink. This same child may apply this knowledge to get a cookie on the kitchen counter. Instead of a stool, the child may use a chair or even an open drawer. Children in this stage still tend to think in terms of actions.

Improved thinking skills and motor skills can make caring for toddlers in this stage exhausting. These children want to actively explore everything. They want to find out as much as they can about new places and objects. However, toddlers are not old enough to understand the dangers that may be involved in exploring. For instance, they may step in an open drawer to reach something without realizing that the drawer may fall. Therefore, you must continually watch toddlers and try to make sure their environment is as safe as possible.

Pretending starts to be part of a child's world at this stage. A young toddler's pretending is often a form of deferred imitation. **Deferred imitation** is watching another person's behavior and then acting out that behavior later. For instance, a father may tuck his child into bed each night and give him or her a kiss on the forehead. At the center the next day, the child may tuck in a doll and give it a kiss on the forehead. Children may also pretend to be animals they have seen, such as dogs.

Children of this age now understand that symbols may represent other real objects. For

Discuss

Describe some of your experiences with children who had just started to communicate using language. What words did the children use to make themselves understood?

Vocabulary

Define *deferred imitation.* Ask students to give examples of actions they have seen toddlers do that could be considered deferred imitation.

Discuss

Why do toddlers continue to do actions such as climbing to get something or handling objects they are not allowed to touch even after parents have discouraged them? Explain in terms of the toddler's thinking skills.

Meeting Special Needs

Have students who are gifted research childhood apraxia of speech (CAS). What is this speech disorder? What early indications of this problem might caregivers notice in children? At what age is the disorder usually diagnosed? Have students write reports summarizing their findings.

Vocabulary

Define *telegrahic speech*. Ask students to give examples of telegrahic speech they have heard from young children.

Discuss

Parents will have the most impact on their infant's social-emotional development. What characteristics of troubled parents may have negative effects on this development? What might be the result?

Resource

Observing Cognitive Development, Activity B, OG

Vocabulary

Have students look up the dictionary definition of *temperament*. Ask students if an infant's temperament can be described as "good" or "bad" and why.

Resource

Social and Emotional Development, reproducible master 5-2, TR

instance, a younger child might play with a doll by swinging it around and hitting things with it. Now, however, the child will hold the doll like a baby and cover it with a blanket, 5-9.

Children are learning more and more words. At first, toddlers only add one to three words to their vocabularies each month. Between 18 to 24 months, however, as many as 10 to 20 new words may be added each month. When their vocabularies reach about 200 words, they begin to combine two words. The term used to describe these two-word phrases is **telegraphic speech**. For instance, the child might say "doggie bark" to let you know that he or she hears a dog barking. Figure 5-10 shows typical two-word phrases used by toddlers during this stage.

Children like to share what they know with you. As you read to them, they may point to objects to tell you what they are. They enjoy pointing to things that you name. For example, you may say to the child "Touch your nose." Children at this age are quick to respond by pointing to parts of their bodies. Later, you may get them to point to other objects in the room.

This child holds her doll like a baby and wraps it in a blanket.

5-10

Toddlers' Typical Two-Word Phrases

Johnny hit.

Big ball.

Give milk.

My bear.

Hi daddy.

No milk.

Toddlers often use two-word phrases.

Social-Emotional Development in the First Two Years

At birth, infants do not show a wide range of emotions. They seem to be basically comfortable or uncomfortable. To communicate this, they use movements, facial expressions, and sounds. By cooing, they show their comfort or delight. By crying, they show discomfort.

In the first few months of life, you will observe a range of emotions. The most reliable clues are infants' facial expressions. Happiness is shown when the corners of the mouth are pulled back and the cheeks are raised, 5-11. Between six and nine months, the infant will begin to show fear, anxiety, and anger. Signs of fear are the mouth opened with the corners pulled back, eyes widened, and eyebrows raised. By the end of the second year, children are expressing their emotions in many more ways.

Socially, young children tend to focus on a few adults who are close to them. This is especially true of infants. After the first birthday, children may take more interest in other toddlers. However, adults are still

Meeting Special Needs

Have special learners check their answers to reproducible master 5-2, *Social and Emotional Development*, using the developmental charts in Appendix B. Reprint the list in the correct order for special learners to use as a study tool.

Seeing items printed in the correct order can help these learners understand the sequence of development. Adding illustrations, photos, or magazine pictures may help serve as a memory tool.

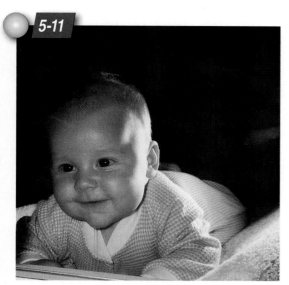

You can tell by his facial expression this young baby is content.

most important to children in this age group. As a caregiver, you need to realize that your actions will have a strong effect on children's social-emotional development. These children are ready for relationships. They need to be able to count on caregivers who will respond immediately to their distress signals. Healthy social-emotional development is a foundation for learning.

Temperament

Even from birth, children differ in temperament or the ways that they react to their environment. **Temperament** refers to the quality and intensity of emotional reactions. Such factors as passivity, irritability, and activity patterns are part of a child's temperament.

Passivity relates to how actively involved a child is with his or her surroundings. A passive infant withdraws from a new person or event. An active infant does something in response to a new person or event.

Children also differ in their level of *irritability* or tendency to feel distressed. Some

infants cry easily. They may be difficult to comfort, even if you hold them and try to soothe them. There are other infants who rarely cry. They do not let changes bother them as much. Caring for these infants is usually easier for adults.

Activity patterns or levels of movement also vary in infants. Some infants can be described as quiet, making few movements. When asleep, they may hardly move. Others are constantly moving their arms and legs. These infants may even sleep restlessly.

If you care for infants, you need to adjust to the temperaments of different children. All infants need loving attention. If given patient, tender care, most children will grow to be happy and well-adjusted. This is even true of very irritable infants.

Attachment

Attachment is the strong emotional connection that develops between people. Most infants become attached to a small group of people early in life, 5-12. They mainly become attached to the people who care for them. Included may be mothers, fathers, caregivers, or older siblings. Young infants learn that when they are hungry,

Attachment between infants and their caregivers begins soon after birth.

Vocabulary

Define *passivity, irritability*, and *activity patterns* when related to an infant's temperament. Are these characteristics constant or could they change?

Reflect

Think of an infant you have worked with recently. How would you categorize this infant's temperament? How did this correspond to the infant's activity level?

Discuss

What are some ways to soothe infants who seem especially irritable?

Note

You may want to remind students when working with irritable infants, they must *never* become angry with the infants. You may also wish to discuss Shaken Baby Syndrome and the effects shaking can have on infants. Remind students that Shaken Baby Syndrome is a form of child abuse.

Resource

Observing Social-Emotional Skills, Activity C, OG

Cross-Curricular Activity

Social Studies
Have students research studies of infants who, for some reason, did not form attachments to others early in life. How did this affect their

behavior as young children and as adults? How did it affect their social-emotional development throughout life? Ask students to give oral reports based on their findings.

Note

The origin of attachment theory can be traced to 1958 with the publishing of John Bowlby's *The Nature of a Child's Tie to His Mother* and Harry Harlow's *The Nature of Love.* These two papers helped define attachment as a tie that binds individuals together and endures over time.

Discuss

What attachment behaviors are shown by infants? What do these behaviors tell us about an infant's emotional development?

Note

Children's fears will be discussed more in Chapter 15, *Guidance Challenges.*

Discuss

When will infants first develop fear? Why might an infant be fearful at the sight of a stranger?

Resource

Development Fill-In, Activity C, SAG

wet, or frightened, they can depend on these people to make them feel better. The quality of attachment depends on the adults.

Several early attachment behaviors are shown by infants. These behaviors show that infants care for and respond to certain people who are important to them. Infants will single these people out for special attention. When approached, the infant may break into a broad, warm smile. Other examples of attachment behaviors are cooing, kicking, gurgling, and laughing. Crying and clinging are also attachment behaviors. These behaviors show that the child is signaling to others.

Attachment begins early in life. Studies show even young babies show signs of anxiety if they are cared for by an unfamiliar person. These distress signs appear as irregular sleeping or eating patterns.

Separation anxiety is another attachment behavior shown by infants. This happens when a child protests because a familiar caregiver is leaving. The child often cries as a sign of distress. The first signs of separation anxiety appear at about six months of age. The reaction becomes clearer by nine months of age. By 15 months of age, separation anxiety is very strong. After this point, this distress gradually weakens.

As a caregiver, you need to be prepared for the attachment behaviors of children in this age group. Children between 9 and 18 months of age will usually have the most difficulty beginning a child care program. To make the transition easier, you should encourage parents to bring the child's favorite toy or blanket.

As children show separation anxiety, you need to remind yourself not to take the reaction personally. These children are simply fearful because their familiar caregivers are leaving them. They do not know what to expect next, and they are in an unfamiliar surrounding with strange people. As children become more familiar with the center, its people, and its routine, they will show less distress.

Changes over Time

During the first two years after birth, you will see many changes in children socially and emotionally. As a caregiver, your actions will affect how these children change. Establishing trust is a key factor in social-emotional development. Trust develops when there is predictability. If you meet childrens' needs and encourage them to interact with others, children will learn to trust and care for others. They will feel safe and happy.

Birth to Three Months

At birth, newborns do not have very refined emotions. General excitement and general distress are the only emotions shown. The child may show excitement by looking alert, smiling, or wiggling. Distress is shown by crying. When observing a child in this stage, you may notice that there are no tears when the child cries.

Three to Six Months

By three months, children respond to people with smiles and laughter. They may make happy sounds as adults play with, hold, or feed them. During this stage, infants start to notice and smile at other babies. Crying is still used to show distress. Early in this stage, tears begin to appear. Later, children start to use different cries to signal different types of distress.

Six to Twelve Months

Infants in this stage become actively involved with their caregivers. As adults play with and care for them, these children express happiness, joy, and surprise. They also make sounds in response to the speech of others. Infants in this stage also begin to develop fear. You should not be surprised if a child this age cries at the sight of a stranger. By this age, children have also developed attachment to their caregivers. They may cry

Workplace Connection

Tell students that as caregivers or early childhood professionals, they may have to deal with separation anxiety when children are left in their care. Have students ask several parents of young children how they have handled this challenge. How did the parents prepare their children for the separation? Did they use any items such as a security object to help make the transition easier? What negative effects could result if threats or bribery are used to control children in this situation?

and even show anger when their caregivers leave them.

This stage may be the most difficult for the child's parents and for you. Separation anxiety starts to show. As a result, a child may start crying and clinging upon entering the center. When you try taking the child from the parent, the child may attempt to push you away. After the parent leaves, the child may continue to cry. Most children, however, will stop crying within a few minutes. This behavior may continue until 14 to 16 months of age.

Twelve to Twenty-Four Months

Early in this stage, children still show separation anxiety. Children in this stage also show anxiety. In other words, they become upset because of something they think will happen in the future. For instance, this child may cling to a parent who will be leaving soon.

These children become more interested in exploring. Although they still fear the unfamiliar, they are curious about new places and objects, 5-13. Children who feel secure are more likely to explore than those who feel unsure of their surroundings. By this age, children start to take more interest in other children. They like to play next to other children, but they do not interact much with them.

Children start to become more aware of their own abilities at this point. This self-awareness is a source of joy and anger for children. Toddlers are proud and happy when they can do things for themselves. However,

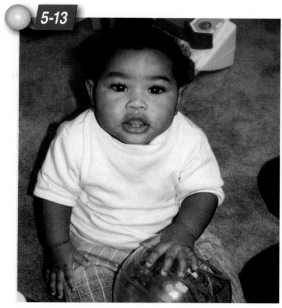

5-13

Curiosity helps toddlers explore new places and objects.

sometimes they insist on doing things for themselves that they can't do yet. This can cause frustration and anger for the child.

Children who are becoming self-aware also like to say *no*. They like to know that they can make things happen, and they do not always want to do what adults want. Sometimes they may say no to you just to see what will happen. You will need to be kind but firm with these children. You must help them understand that there are rules that must be followed. At the same time, you need to reassure the children that their wants and needs are important.

Discuss

How long will separation anxiety last? How might young toddlers demonstrate that they feel secure?

Resource

Developmental Review, reproducible master 5-3, TR

Enrich

Divide students into small groups to debate the pros and cons of having a parent stay with his or her child when the child shows distress at the parent leaving. Ask students to share their viewpoints with the class.

Resource

Encouraging Development, Activity D, SAG

Meeting Special Needs

Review the special learners' chapter outlines to determine if the students have any questions about the concepts or content of this chapter. Review the chapter objectives and ask the students to evaluate their progress in meeting these objectives. Ask the students to summarize, orally or in writing, what they learned from this chapter.

Review and Reflect Answer Key

1. true
2. Crawling
3. true
4. At birth, the newborn's vision is blurry.
5. C
6. Place an object under a blanket; then observe to see if the child searches for it.
7. deferred imitation
8. two-word phrases toddlers often develop between 18–24 months (Example is student response.)
9. passivity—how actively involved a child is with his or her surroundings; irritability—the tendency of a child to feel distressed; activity patterns—levels of movement in children
10. false
11. Three-month-olds respond to people with smiles and laughter. Crying is still used to show distress. By 12 months of age, they show separation anxiety. They start to explore and take more interest in other children.

Summary

Growth in the first two years of life is rapid. Physically, children start with many reflexes that are eventually replaced with voluntary movements. As they become bigger and stronger, infants are able to roll over, crawl, creep, and eventually walk.

Cognitive growth shows in children's reactions to the environment. As infants, children will mouth and hit with objects to learn how they work. With growth, children begin to understand how different objects work. They also begin to understand that objects exist even if they are not seen. Children begin to think about how they can reach goals. They also learn to communicate, first by crying, and later by using words.

Each child is born with a temperament that sets the stage for social-emotional development. Young infants tend to show two main emotions—distress and excitement. As infants grow, they become attached to caregivers. They express joy, happiness, surprise, and fear. They may experience separation anxiety when loved ones leave them. As children grow older, they show interest in other children. They also become interested in their own abilities. Children at this age may often test adults by saying no to rules and suggestions. However, they also take pride in their own achievements. They still look to adults for love and attention.

Review and Reflect

1. True or false. Reflex testing can be used to detect whether an infant has brain or nerve damage.

2. _____ occurs when infants pull with their arms and wiggle their stomachs.

3. True or false. Creeping requires stronger leg muscles and leg control than crawling.

4. Describe the newborn's vision at birth.

5. If you place a toy car near an infant who is three to six months old, what is the child most likely to do?
   A. Ignore the toy.
   B. Cry.
   C. Put the toy in his or her mouth.
   D. Slide the toy along the floor making car noises.

6. Describe how to test a child for an understanding of object permanence.

7. If a toddler sees his or her mother mowing the lawn one day and then pretends to mow the lawn at the child care center, the toddler is practicing _____.

8. Describe telegraphic speech and provide an example.

9. Describe three factors that affect a child's temperament.

10. True or false. Children do not start to show attachment behaviors until after their first birthday.

11. How would the social-emotional development of a three-month-old differ from that of a one-year-old?

Apply and Explore

1. Visit a child care center serving infants. Observe differences among them.

2. Bring to class your baby books or albums in which your parents documented your milestones. Check to see if infant reflexes and other important development such as lifting your head or rolling over were recorded. At what ages did these occur?

Cross-Curricular Link

Writing

1. Observe a parent playing with or caring for an infant. Record the child's age in months. Write an anecdotal record describing the child's interactions with the parent. Share your observation with the class.

Technology

2. Visit the Web site for the National Network for Child Care (www.nncc.org) to review the developmental stages for infants and toddlers and articles on child development.

Workplace Link

Visit your public library or a bookstore to survey books suitable for infants and toddlers. Compile a list of books you might use in an infant or toddler room. Make a display of some of your favorite books for this age group for your class. Explain to the class why these books are age-appropriate.

Discuss

Look at the chapter opening photo. How is the teacher demonstrating that he understands two- and three-year-olds? What guidance do you think he might be giving the child?

Discuss

Ask students to look over the chapter objectives before reading the chapter. How will knowing this information prepare them for a career working with children?

6

Understanding Two- and Three-Year-Olds

After studying this chapter, you will be able to

- describe the physical, cognitive, and social-emotional development of two-year-olds.

- explain how three-year-olds develop physically, cognitively, socially, and emotionally.

- relate how the development of two- and three-year-olds will affect your role as a teacher.

104

Terms to Know

language comprehension
expressive language
egocentric
gender roles
self-concept

To better understand two- and three-year-olds, you need to develop a mental picture. You need to understand how children in these age groups behave. Generally, two-year-olds are active, demanding, and curious. Three-year-old children tend to be more calm. Generally, they try to please and conform. Understanding these differences will help you plan programs that best meet the needs of each child.

Physical Development of Two-Year-Olds

Two-year-old children continue to grow physically, but the rapid growth that occurred during infancy tapers off. A typical two-year-old will grow two to three inches in height and add about five pounds in weight during the year. Organs, such as the eyes, stomach, heart, and lungs, become stronger.

The digestive system matures slowly in children. The appetites of two-year-olds vary from day to day. Some days they may be excited about eating at snack time; other days they may reject their snacks. Likewise, what they eat at mealtimes may vary.

The coordination of two-year-olds' bodies is improving. They are less top-heavy and their center of gravity shifts downward. Provided equipment, space, and support, these children can master a variety of gross-motor skills, 6-1. They can usually run and

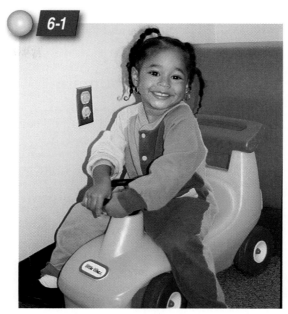

6-1

Two-year-olds have improved muscle strength and coordination.

jump without falling. The fine-motor skills of these children are also improving.

Gross-Motor Development

Improved coordination and body control makes playing with balls great fun for active two-year-olds. They can pick up a ball by bending at the waist. Likewise, they can kick a large ball. They are usually able to throw a ball without falling.

Two-year-olds have more control in leg and foot muscles than before. They can walk up and down stairs placing both feet on each stair. (Most children this age need to hold on to a rail as they step.) They are also able to stand with both feet on a balance beam. These children have the skill to walk on their toes. From a standing position, they can balance on one foot. Jumping is also possible. They can jump several inches off the floor with both feet. Most children this age can do a standing broad jump of about eight and

Vocabulary

Ask students to review the *Terms to Know* list and look up unfamiliar terms in the glossary before reading the chapter.

Discuss

Ask students what they already know about the physical development of a two-year-old. Pass around photos of two-year-old children or refer students to 6-1 and 6-2 to get an idea of what children look like at this age.

Resource

Development of Two-Year-Olds, Activity A, SAG

Discuss

The two-year-old in 6-1 is enjoying the use of a ride-on toy. Would a tricycle be suitable for a child in this age group? Why or why not?

Meeting Special Needs

Provide an outline of the chapter with all the chapter headings for special learners. Students should fill in each section of the outline as the material is covered in class with a sentence or two about the content. Review the special learners' IEPs to decide if any modifications should be made in presenting the chapter content. Prepare a vocabulary matching assignment to assist students with learning the definitions of *Terms to Know*.

one-half inches. In addition, most two-year-olds can sit on a riding toy and move it by pushing with their feet.

Fine-Motor Development

Two-year-old children are rapidly developing finger dexterity and control. They are able to insert keys into a lock and turn pages in a book one at a time. Most children this age can also string large beads or spools and lace cards. They can hold scissors properly. By two years of age, they can open and close scissors.

Hand preference is fairly developed by this age. Many children will use the same hand for most fine-motor activities. However, at this stage of development, children still switch hands for some activities. Alex, for example, draws with his right hand, but eats and throws a ball with his left hand.

You will see children using writing tools at this age, 6-2. At about 24 months of age, children can scribble. At first, these scribbles look like tangles of lines. By 30 months, children can draw horizontal lines, vertical lines, and circles. Most children draw by holding the tool, crayon, or pencil, in their fist.

Two-year-olds become skilled at building with blocks. They can build towers of six to seven blocks. They can also use two or more blocks to make a train and push the blocks along.

Self-Help Skills

With a little help, two-year-olds can accomplish many self-help skills. At this age, they begin to cooperate in dressing. First, they can undress themselves. They are able to remove simple items of clothing such as socks, shoes, and pants. Snaps can be opened successfully. Next, they begin to dress themselves. At first this involves pulling on

Using chalk helps two-year-olds refine their fine-motor skills.

Health and Safety

Activity Plans and Guiding Principles

Part of the service early childhood centers provide is a written plan of daily activities and the principles that guide activity planning. These written plans and principles help parents know that the daily operations of a center support sound practice for children's development and safety. These plans outline activities that support the physical, cognitive, and social-emotional development of children. Along with planning, a facility must ensure proper training of care providers to implement the plan.

Activity

Have students visit an art and crafts store or its Web site to find the kinds of scissors available for toddler use. How safe do students think scissors are for toddlers?

Discuss

What effect will blockbuilding have on the development of a two-year-old's fine-motor skills? How might cognitive development be affected by block play?

Activity

Have students observe toddlers while they are using pencils or crayons. Ask students to note what type of marks the toddlers make and how long do they stay with the task.

Workplace Connection

Have students review your state's licensing standards for equipment required in the two-year-olds' room in centers. For example, what types of blocks are needed? How many of each kind are required? Ask students to survey teachers of two-year-olds to find out how often block play occurs in their program. How popular is blockbuilding with the children in their classroom?

simple garments. Zippers can be zipped and unzipped. By 30 months, most children can unbutton large buttons, close snaps, and put on their socks. However, you will need to help children as they try these skills.

By this age, children can drink from a cup or glass without help. They may spill fairly often, but their drinking skills improve with practice. Two-year-olds are also able to drink using a straw. They can use a spoon to feed themselves, but may revert to eating with their fingers if hurried.

Strides are usually made in toilet learning during this time. At two years of age, most children start to use the toilet or potty chair with reminders. However, accidents are common. Between 24 and 35 months, children seldom have bowel accidents. They may still have problems with wetting for several months. By 33 months, many children can use the toilet without help.

Cognitive Development of Two-Year-Olds

The two-year-old's cognitive development focuses on three main areas. These include language comprehension skills, expressive language skills, and math readiness skills. All of these areas reflect the child's intelligence.

Language Comprehension Skills

A person's understanding of language is called **language comprehension**. Some experts refer to this as *receptive* or *inner language*. This form of language is more advanced than expressive language skills in children. For instance, a 20-month-old child may be able to follow directions. However, this child may not be able to say more than a few words.

Language comprehension grows rapidly in two-year-olds. These children can understand and answer routine questions. While reading a story, you may point to a picture and ask "What is that?" The child may respond by saying "Baby." See 6-3.

By 24 months of age, most children can identify at least six body parts. Children can point to these parts on themselves, others, or dolls. They enjoy playing games in which you state "Find your toes" or ask "Where are your eyes?"

Many other new skills develop around 24 months. Children can comprehend the pronouns *I*, *my*, *mine*, and *me*. They can also provide appropriate answers to yes and no questions.

By 30 months of age, other milestones are reached. When asked, children can give you one cookie. They also can follow two-step commands. For instance, you can tell a child "Take off your coat and put it in your locker."

Children of this age can also give answers to where questions. For instance, you may ask a child "Where is your locker?" or "Where do you wash your hands?"

Understanding the meanings of words continues through the second year. When

6-3

Two-year-olds will answer questions about pictures in the stories you read them.

Discuss

How can parents encourage their two-year-old's self-help skills in dressing? What features of children's clothing contribute to the development of self-dressing skills?

Enrich

Many parents of toddlers continue to use "sippy cups"—infant cups with a secure top and a sipping hole. Ask students to debate the pros and cons of continuing to use these cups throughout toddlerhood.

Discuss

Are most children under two years of age able to use a toilet completely by themselves? What may be the result when toilet learning is attempted too early?

Resource

Physical Skills of Two-Year-Olds, transparency master 6-1, TR

Meeting Special Needs

Using transparency master 6-1, *Physical Skills of Two-Year-Olds*, have special learners indicate which skills on the list are fine-motor and which are gross-motor. Reprinting the list in two columns according to the type of skills may serve as further clarification for the students.

Vocabulary

Have students define *expressive language*. Ask them to describe the type of environment that will stimulate the development of expressive language.

Reflect

Two-year-olds do not yet use or understand grammar. Give some examples of language you have heard from two-year-olds that show they know how to communicate even without this knowledge.

Vocabulary

Have students define *feeding-in* and *expansion*. Ask students to explain why these two language strategies are important when working with two-year-olds.

picking up objects, two-year-olds can tell the difference between *soft* and *heavy*. Size concepts are also developing. Children understand such words as *big* and *tall*. Children also start to understand words related to space. These include such words as *on*, *under*, *out of*, *together*, and *away from*.

Expressive Language Skills

Expressive language is the ability to produce language forms. It is a tool that can be used to express a person's thoughts to others. For most two-year-olds, expressive language develops quickly. Like other aspects of development, it follows a sequence. The child's experiences affect the rate and content of expressive language development. Therefore, it is important you provide an environment that stimulates language development.

Speech usually involves simple sentences by two years of age. In the beginning, only two words may be used. "Johnny hurt" or "Tom dog" are examples. Later, the child will begin to put three-word sentences together. Examples include "Tom go home," "I eat corn," or "See my truck." Sentences follow the word order of the native language.

There are two language strategies that are important when you work with two-year-olds. These are called feeding-in and expansion. *Feeding-in* is a strategy where you provide the child's language. For example, if a child is building with blocks, the teacher might say "You are building with blocks."

Expansion is a strategy used to expand the child's language. Typically this is accomplished by reframing the child's utterance into a sentence. For example, if the child says "car" the teacher might say "This is a blue car." If the child says "wheels" the teacher could say "The car has wheels."

The vocabulary of the average two-year-old is 50 to 200 words. You will notice that children at this age often use words without fully understanding them. You might also observe that girls generally develop language skills faster than boys.

Two-year-olds do not understand how to use grammar to form questions. Instead, they use the tone of their voice. They may ask in a questioning tone "Grandma go?" or "Milk all gone?"

Two-year-olds often make negative sentences. They do this by adding the word no to positive sentences. For instance, a child may say "No milk" meaning that he or she does not want any milk. The child may say "Teacher no here" meaning that he or she cannot find the teacher.

Between 27 and 30 months, children may begin to use prepositions. For instance, children may say "Cookies in jar." Around this age, children also begin using plurals. They may request "cookies" or "candies."

Modifiers are also added to the vocabulary. *Some*, *a lot*, *all*, and *one* are used as quantifiers. *Mine*, *his*, and *hers* are used as possessives. *Pretty*, *new*, and *blue* are some adjectives that might be used as modifiers.

Between 31 and 34 months of age, children may begin adding *-ed* to verbs to show past tense. At about the same time, present tense verb helpers appear. These include such terms as *can*, *are*, *will*, and *am*.

Math Readiness Skills

Math skills are developed as children interact with others and with objects. When you ask, a child can give you "just one" of something. Children also understand size concepts such as *big* and *small*. Awareness of shapes, forms, and colors is also developing during this stage. Children begin to sort objects by shape and color.

Social-Emotional Development of Two-Year-Olds

Two-year-olds continue to grow socially and emotionally. At this age, children tend

---

Putting Technology to Use

Ask students to conduct an Internet search for information on math readiness skills. What math concepts can children understand at the toddler stage? What type of activities can demonstrate and reinforce these concepts? Should two-year-olds be subjected to math worksheets? Have students share their findings with the class.

to show many negative attitudes. Children like instant gratification and find it difficult to wait. These qualities make patience an important quality as you work with two-year-olds.

Social Development

At the beginning of this developmental stage, children play next to each other. However, they do not play cooperatively with each other, 6-4. Children in this stage still tend to be more interested in adults. Therefore, they tend to act out adult experiences as they play. These might include driving a car, making a bed, and talking on the phone.

6-4

Two-year-olds do not interact much as they play.

The average two-year-old tends to be possessive. Usually these children do not want to share. There typically is competition for toys. They tend to use body language to let people know how they feel about their possessions. Two-year-old children can be very physical in their responses. They may push, hit, or shove another child who approaches their toys. Although they have difficulty understanding the concept of sharing, two-year-olds may return a toy that belongs to someone else.

In spite of their negativism and possessiveness, two-year-olds are usually affectionate. They may hug you and hold your hand. Two-year-olds thrive on love and caring from adults. They also enjoy helping you. Whether you are setting the table for lunch or picking up blocks, they are eager to participate.

Emotional Development

These children like to be able to control their surroundings. Because they can't always do that, they tend to get frustrated and angry at times. Trying to do a task that is too hard for them may cause anger, 6-5. Not being allowed to do or have something may stir angry feelings as well. Two-year-olds may have temper tantrums if they do not get their way. They may scream, cry, stamp, or kick. Their anger is not usually at any one person or object; they are simply frustrated. Children this age still have not learned more appropriate ways of expressing anger.

Fears become common at this age. Two-year-olds are often afraid of being hurt or harmed. Many of their fears have to do with their imagination. Two-year-olds can't always separate pretend from reality, so they may be afraid of a monster from a story. A dream may frighten them because they think the characters are real. As a teacher, you need to comfort children when they are afraid. Even imagined fears are real to toddlers.

Love and caring are shown often by these children. They need to receive love and

Discuss

Should two-year-olds be forced to share their toys with other children? What guidance should be used when two-year-olds react with physical aggression when asked to share?

Reflect

Since two-year-olds enjoy acting out adult experiences, what could result when children are exposed to actions such as inappropriate language, gestures, and behaviors? How should caregivers react when children imitate these actions?

Discuss

Why do two-year-olds have temper tantrums? How should adults react during a temper tantrum?

Resource

Behavioral Traits of Two-Year-Olds, transparency master 6-2, TR

Discuss

Why are imagined fears real for toddlers? What is the teacher's role when dealing with a toddler's fears?

Workplace Connection

Most two-year-olds enjoy being helpful to parents and caregivers. Have students interview teachers of two-year-olds about tasks they allow children to perform in the classroom.

How are the children encouraged to participate? What safety concerns should be considered when asking for a two-year-old's help?

Vocabulary

Have students look up *egocentric* in the dictionary. Ask them if egocentric toddlers are selfish. Have them explain their answers.

Resource

Observing Developmental Characteristics of Two-Year-Olds, Activity C, OG

Note

Dr. Berry T. Brazelton, M.D. defines *touchpoints* as moments when children's behavior seems to fall apart but signal an impending rapid spurt of development. In his book *Touchpoints: Your Child's Emotional and Behavioral Development, Birth to Three*, he discusses tantrums and ways parents and caregivers can help children resolve their emotions.

Resource

Studying Two-Year-Olds, Activity B, SAG

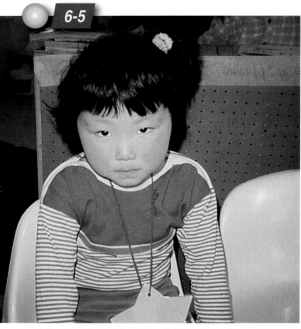

6-5

Being able to meet goals quickly is important to two-year-olds. If they do not get instant results, they often become angry.

caring in return. Two-year-olds need to know that people still care for them even if they get angry. They also need to know that they can depend on others. To build trust and security, children of this age need regular routines. For instance, they may need to sit next to the same person or group of people at every meal or snack time.

Teaching Two-Year-Olds

The development of two-year-olds has a strong effect on the way you teach and work with them. You need to be prepared to handle those situations that are typical with these children.

If you were to observe a group of two-year-olds, your first observation might be that they are negative. Two-year-olds often use the word "no." At times, they may even mean "yes" when they say "no." For instance, you may ask "Do you want more milk?" The child may say "no" while extending his or her glass toward you for more milk.

You may find yourself becoming impatient with two-year-old children at times. They always seem to want their own way. Whether you want to read a story or take the children on a field trip, you are bound to find a two-year-old who refuses. The child may refuse to leave his or her present activity or to put on his or her coat. Working with two-year-olds requires gentle but firm guidance.

Two-year-olds are very **egocentric**. This means that they believe everyone else sees, thinks, and feels like they do. This does not mean they are selfish. They believe that you will think exactly as they do.

Prepare yourself for the dawdling behavior of the typical two-year-old. These children insist on doing things at their own pace. Because of this, routines take longer. When planning a schedule, be aware of this type of behavior. Two-year-olds need plenty of time to move from one activity to the next. Therefore, you will need to be flexible and patient.

Upon entering a classroom of two-year-olds, you will first notice the noise. This is very common. When a child discovers a drum, the child will hit it over and over again. Likewise, they may repeat a new vocal sound many times. If one child starts clapping and stamping his or her feet, the other children may join in. You will need to be prepared for high noise levels and be able to control that noise from time to time.

Curiosity is another trait of two-year-olds. Children of this age enjoy exploring. When new materials are brought into the classroom, the children will carefully inspect them. If you ask them what toy they want, they may have difficulty choosing. Therefore, you should add only a few new items at a time.

Gross-motor activity is a favorite of two-year-old children. They delight in movement

Workplace Connection

When working with young children, students will need to be prepared for a variety of behaviors. No two days will be exactly the same. Ask students what routines could be instituted in the center to help two-year-olds feel secure. What strategies might students use to direct children and keep them together on walks and field trips? What safety measures are needed when considering a two-year-old's curiosity and tendency to explore his or her environment?

and are not afraid to try out new equipment. They love to run and chase others. Therefore, adequate supervision is crucial. On field trips, these children like to run ahead. For this reason, you may want to have extra adults on the trips to help supervise.

Two-year-olds like to act out life experiences. They especially like to imitate the activities of adults, 6-6. Therefore, they need a dramatic play corner. Housekeeping equipment, mirrors, dolls, dress-up clothes, toy telephones, trucks, and cars should all be included.

Two-year-olds need some routine in their day. They like to have things done the same way. These children look forward to certain parts of the day, such as story time. Therefore, you need to be careful to follow a similar schedule from day to day. A few changes add interest, but children need to rely on a predictable schedule.

Two-year-olds may also have temper tantrums, but this is normal behavior. It has nothing to do with your skill as a teacher, although you may be embarrassed by a toddler's outburst. What is important is how you handle the tantrum. It is vital that you remain composed. Use a calm voice when speaking to the child. If the child is kicking, you may have to immobilize the child by holding the legs. If the child is a threat to the other children, move the child to another area of the room.

6-6

Teachers should provide many dramatic play materials so two-year-olds can act out such everyday experiences as shaving.

Physical Development of Three-Year-Olds

For three-year-olds, playing is exploring. They are constantly moving, tasting, smelling, and touching. As a result, their body coordination shows great improvement. You will notice that the arms, hands, legs, and feet are all becoming more coordinated. Likewise, their bodies are becoming less top-heavy and more streamlined. To stay upright, three-year-olds no longer need to keep their legs spread apart. Their walk appears more natural as their toes point forward and their feet move closer together.

Gross-Motor Development

Throwing, jumping, and hopping skills improve as a result of better coordination. The improvement of body coordination is also reflected in the climbing skills of three-year-olds. At this age children can climb and descend stairs easily. In fact, these children can walk up stairs with alternating feet. Their balance is improving.

By 36 months of age, children can catch large balls with their arms. Their catching skill gradually becomes more refined. Eventually, they can catch bouncing balls with their hands. This skill usually emerges toward the end of the third year.

Leg coordination and balancing skills also improve. Three-year-olds can ride and steer tricycles. They can walk heel-to-toe for four steps. They can balance on one foot for

Resource

Development of Three-Year-Olds, Activity C, SAG

Activity

Have students conduct catching and bouncing activities with three-year-olds using a variety of ball sizes, starting with the largest. Ask students to observe how challenging the activity becomes as the balls become smaller. What does this activity show about the appropriate selection of balls for this age group?

Resource

Physical Skills of Three-Year-Olds, color transparency CT-5, TR

Resource

Development of Two- and Three-Year-Olds, Activity B, OG

Cross-Curricular Activity

Math
Refer students to Appendix B. Have them observe the gross-motor skills of a group of three-year-olds in the vocational preschool or local preschool classroom. Then ask students to calculate the percentage of children who are able to perform each of the typical physical traits listed for children between two and three years of age. Ask if all the three-year-olds observed perform at the same level of gross-motor development. Have students explain how knowing these percentages can assist the teacher in planning physical activities for this age group.

Activity

Have students ask several three-year-old children to demonstrate their ability to trace shapes. Tell students to have children trace both around and inside shape stencils. Discuss the children's success with the tasks.

Reflect

What types of cutting activities can encourage three-year-olds to develop scissor skills? What scissor activities may cause frustration and discouragement for this age group?

Discuss

What verbal reminders are needed for three-year-olds as they become increasingly more skillful at performing self-help skills? What visual reminders may be helpful?

Resource

Self-Help Skills, Activity E, SAG

up to eight seconds. They can hop on one foot up to three times.

Fine-Motor Development

The fine-motor skills of three-year-olds continue to develop. Cutting skills become more refined. The two-year-old could only hold and work scissors. However, a three-year-old can use the scissors to cut paper, 6-7. They can cut five-inch squares of paper into two sections. Young three-year-olds can cut across the paper, but they cannot cut along a line. By 42 to 48 months, children can cut along a line straying no more than one-half of an inch away from it.

Three-year-olds have better drawing skills. Making use of their improved fine-motor skills, they often reproduce simple shapes as they draw. If you show these children the shape of a cross, they can copy the shape. They can also trace the shape of a diamond. They enjoy drawing faces. The faces usually include the mouth, eyes, nose, and/or ears. These features are not drawn in proportion, but they are usually placed in the correct position on the face. They lack the fine-motor coordination needed to create complex figures.

Three-year-olds also enjoy manipulating blocks and puzzle pieces. They can build towers with nine to ten cubes. They can also construct simple puzzles.

Self-Help Skills

Three-year-olds become increasingly self-sufficient. Daily care routines now require little adult assistance. These children can turn the water faucet on and off as long as they can reach it, 6-8. As a result, they can attend to routines such as washing and drying their hands and face. They can also brush their own teeth.

Three-year-olds become better at dressing themselves. They can now open buckles and put on shoes that do not tie. Three-year-olds need little adult help when their clothing has elastic waists or large button openings. They still are not able to work small buttons and hooks. Three-year-olds have trouble telling the front from the back on clothing, too. They do better with clothing that has a design on the front or a label in the back.

6-7

This three-year-old can use scissors to cut paper.

6-8

Being able to turn water on and off increases this three-year-old's ability to help himself.

Workplace Connection

Have students survey the dress-up clothes in the dramatic play area. Have them prepare oral reports answering the following questions: What features on these garments promote the development of self-help skills for three-year-olds? What additions or alterations could be made to the clothing to promote self-help skills?

At snack and mealtime, these children are now able to use knives. They can spread butter, jelly, and soft peanut butter on bread. They can also pour liquid from a small pitcher. As a result, the children may enjoy assisting at snack time.

Another step toward independence is mastered at this age. Three-year-olds have almost full control over toilet routines. They are even able to get through a night without wetting. This accomplishment is made possible through improved motor control.

Cognitive Development of Three-Year-Olds

By the third birthday, the ability to think matures. Children move away from thinking only in terms of actions. They are able to solve simple problems. For instance, if you place an object under a cup and place nothing under another cup, the child knows which cup the object is under. If you switch the cups while the child is watching, the child still knows where the object is.

Children at this age still do not think logically. They are still egocentric as they have not yet learned to see things from more than one perspective. For instance, they do not realize that something that seems tall to them might actually seem short to an adult. They get confused about time concepts. These children may also become confused about cause and effect. For instance, if a bell rings before each snack is served, children may think the bell causes the snack to appear.

Even though thinking is still flawed, these children learn quickly. Their language comprehension skills, expressive language skills, and math readiness skills continue to improve.

Language Comprehension Skills

Understanding of language continues to grow in three-year-olds. On request, the child can now give you two objects. These children can also remember and follow three-part instructions. For example, you might say "Go to the sink, wash your hands, and dry them with a towel." See 6-9.

Three-year-olds begin to understand the pronouns *you* and *they*. They also understand such words as *who, whose, why,* and *how.* They are able to provide answers to questions based on these words. For instance, you may ask the child "Who lives at the North Pole?" Another question might be "Whose teddy bear is this?" While reading a story you may ask "Why is the girl crying?" These children

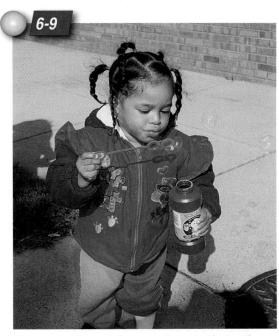

6-9

Three-year-olds can follow your three-part instructions.

Activity

Have students provide three-year-olds with plastic knives and soft play dough to practice using knives. Have students observe how the children hold and use the knives. Ask students to suggest other activities for children to practice knife use.

Reflect

What are some common thinking mistakes three-year-olds may make because they lack the ability to think logically? Think of several examples you have experienced or observed.

Activity

Have students analyze a three-year-old's understanding of the words *you, they, who, whose, why,* and *how* after reading an appropriate story to him or her. Ask students to construct questions about the story using these words and record the child's ability to answer the questions. Have students document the results in the child's portfolio.

Discuss

Refer students to the picture of the child blowing bubbles in 6-9. What three-part instructions might you use during this activity?

Putting Technology to Use

Some three-year-olds, even those with above-average comprehensive and expressive language skills, may stutter when speaking. The Web site of The Stuttering Foundation, **www.stutteringhelp.org**, is a useful resource for information about stuttering. Ask students to review this and other sources of information on stuttering and write a brief report of their findings. Have them include suggestions of ways to help children who stutter.

Example

Explain to students that when children demonstrate incorrect use of negatives, such as "Timmy don't have no show and tell today," they should repeat what was said using correct grammar. "Timmy doesn't have any show and tell today" reinforces correct usage.

Resource

Language Skills, Activity F, SAG

Activity

Ask students to create activities for three-year-olds that teach and reinforce the understanding of the math concepts *full, more, less, smaller, empty, largest, one,* and *many*. Example: present two blocks to a child and ask which one is smaller. Document the results in the child's portfolio.

will be able to answer such questions as "How will your mother bake the pie?"

Space concepts become clearer. While moving objects, children will understand your instructions that include such words as *toward, up, top,* and *apart*. Toward the end of the third year, children master more space concepts. They understand such ideas as *around, in front of, in back of,* and *next to*.

Expressive Language Skills

Children's ability to produce language continues to increase. By now, children may use more than 900 words. Three-year-olds also have improved grammar. They may make sentences of four or five words. They may even join sentences together with a conjunction. For instance, the child may say "The bunny died and we don't have it."

Three-year-olds begin to understand the difference between past and present tense. They like to make verbs past tense by adding *-ed* to them. These children make statements such as "I talked" or "Daddy walked." However, they do not yet understand that there are exceptions to this rule. They may use such past tense verbs as "runned" and "goed." They may even use the correct form, but still add *-ed*. For instance, they may say "ranned" or "wented."

Children start to understand possessive nouns. Three-year-olds may refer to *mommy's car, daddy's hammer,* and *teacher's coat*. Negatives are not fully understood by three-year-olds. They understand that such words as *no, not, can't, don't, nothing,* and *never* are negative. However, they use all negative terms when they form negative statements. For instance, a three-year-old may say "Kelsie can't do nothing" or "Jackson can't never go nowhere."

During this stage, children start to use question words, especially *why* and *when*. These children tend to add on the question word to a regular sentence. For instance, they may ask "When Daddy is coming?" or "Why the cloud is moving?"

As these children play, they frequently talk out loud to themselves. For example, three-year-old Jenny is painting at the easel and saying, "Jenny is painting a picture. I need red. Where is the red? Now I need yellow. I need to paint with yellow."

Math Readiness Skills

Three-year-olds continue to learn concepts basic to math. They start to understand the concepts *full, more, less, smaller,* and *empty*. By 42 months of age, most children understand the concept of *largest*. These children like to constantly compare objects, saying one object is bigger or another is smaller.

Counting skills also begin at this stage. If you ask, a three-year-old can give you two objects. These children can also count to three while pointing to corresponding objects. They may be able to recite numbers in order higher than three, but they are not able to count that number of objects.

Children in this age group can distinguish between *one* and *many*. To check for this skill, place one chip on the table. Nearby, place a pile of chips. Ask the child to point to one chip. Repeat the question asking the child to point to many chips. Children who respond correctly have learned the difference between *one* and *many*.

Social-Emotional Development of Three-Year-Olds

After the third birthday, children start to grow out of the temper tantrums and contrariness of the two-year-old stage. They become cooperative, happy, and agreeable, 6-10. By this time, children start to learn socially acceptable ways of expressing their feelings. They can use language more effectively to communicate with others. Also, they start to form friendships with their peers.

Workplace Connection

Because of the differences in their abilities and behaviors, two-year-olds and three-year-olds are usually separated in a preschool or child care center. However, some settings, such as child care homes, may have mixed-age groups in their programs. Have students interview teachers of mixed-age group programs in your area for their insights on the following: What are the challenges of working with mixed-age groups? What considerations must be made for supervision, activities, and equipment?

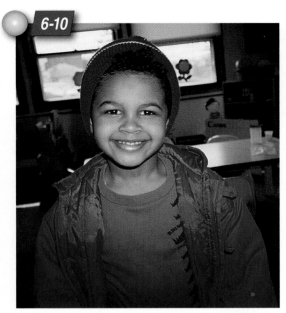

Three-year-olds tend to be more content and agreeable than two-year-olds.

Although their play is not organized, three-year-olds will play with each other.

Social Development

Three-year-olds are eager to help others, especially adults. They like to help with such tasks as passing out crayons and pouring juice. They are learning new ways of showing concern for others. They are learning positive ways to get attention from others. These children are more willing to ac cept attention from adults and children who are not well-known. They adjust to new people more easily than two-year-olds do.

By the third birthday, children begin to play with, rather than next to, other children. See 6-11. Although these children interact with each other, their play is not truly organized. For instance, they may play house and each child playing may be the daddy.

Children this age are not as possessive as two-year-olds. They will share with others, but they do not like to share too much. For this reason, three-year-olds usually play with only one or two main friends. The children use language more to communicate with friends. For instance, they may say to a friend "You play with the baby." To another child, they may say "You can't play with us."

Children this age also begin to learn **gender roles**. These are behaviors that are expected of girls or boys. Gender roles are not as clearly defined as they once were, but they are still an important part of learning. Children this age realize that there are physical differences between boys and girls. With the proper role models, they begin to learn how to treat members of the opposite sex with respect.

Emotional Development

Three-year-olds have strong visible emotions. They get excited. They get angry. They get discouraged. However, they are beginning to understand that there are appropriate ways to express these emotions. They realize that adults do not approve of such actions as temper tantrums. Also, they are eager to act in ways that please others. Therefore, children of this age are developing control over their strong feelings. Instead of striking another child, they may scream "Stop it!"

Unlike two-year-olds, many situations no longer lead to angry outbursts among

Discuss

What behaviors might you observe in three-year-olds that demonstrate concern for others? Give examples of how a teacher could model this ability.

Resource

Behavioral Traits of Three-Year-Olds, transparency master 6-3, TR

Discuss

Give specific examples you have seen of each of the behaviors listed in transparency master 6-3. Are there any three-year-olds you know who do *not* exhibit these typical behaviors? Why might the behaviors be absent or delayed?

Vocabulary

Ask students to define *gender roles*. Have them explain why is it important for three-year-olds to understand gender roles.

Note

Parents and caregivers need to allow three-year-olds to express their emotions, but they should guide children to use appropriate behavior when doing so. Telling a child "you have nothing to cry about" or "you are silly to be afraid" sends the child the message that his or her feelings are not important. This shows lack of respect for the child.

Workplace Connection

Ask students how dramatic play in the preschool can help children understand the concept of *gender identity*. What toys, supplies, and equipment are needed? Have students compare the attitudes or beliefs of parents several generations ago with those of today. Have them especially consider children selecting play materials and activities typically associated with the opposite gender. What are the effects on a child's development when both boys and girls are encouraged to engage in physically active play? in role-playing household activities during dramatic play?

three-year-olds. Because they have improved coordination, three-year-olds are less likely to become frustrated when they cannot do something. They also have improved language skills. When children can understand why something is happening, they are less likely to get angry. For example, a child may want a drink just prior to lunch. You can explain, "It's only a few minutes until lunch. You can have a drink then." When the child understands that he or she will have a drink soon, he or she is less likely to get angry.

Three-year-olds are likely to become angry when things do not go their way. However, they begin to direct their anger at objects. For instance, they may be angry at a pitcher if they spill their milk. Children this age are more likely to express their anger in words. They do not hit, stamp, or cry as much as two-year-olds do.

The three-year-old is beginning to develop a self-concept. Your **self-concept** is the way you see yourself. A child's self-concept includes a set of beliefs about himself or herself. Ask three-year-olds to tell you about themselves. They will likely provide you with their names, possessions, and physical appearance. As a result, you might hear something like this: "I'm Kelly. I have a dog. I have a brother. I have black hair."

By this stage, children are not as likely to be frightened by objects that they know. For instance, they are not frightened by the noise from a car. However, they are quite fearful of imagined dangers. They may be especially afraid of the dark. Children of this age also become more fearful of pain. They may be scared that a dog will bite them or that they will be hurt during a doctor's visit.

Three-year-olds are affectionate, and they tend to seek affection in return. They may follow, cling to, or help an adult in an effort to get attention, approval, or comfort. Three-year-olds still do not think in terms of the feelings of others.

Children learn to express their own feelings by watching the adults around them.

When you express surprise and happiness, they will also show these emotions. Likewise, if you give a hug to comfort someone who is sad, they will imitate your behavior.

Teaching Three-Year-Olds

Three-year-olds are typically happy, sociable, and agreeable. Furthermore, they are very eager to please. As a result, they are likely to accept your suggestions, 6-12. They also adjust easily to new adults, classmates, and situations. For these reasons, you will find that most adults enjoy working with these children.

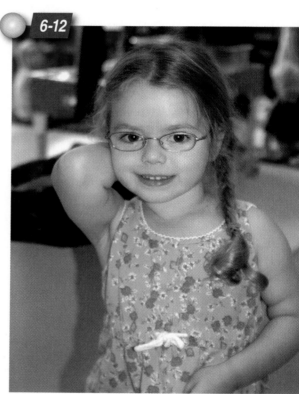

6-12

By the third year, children are more willing to accept and try suggestions from teachers.

Resource

Development Puzzle, reproducible master 6-4, TR.

Vocabulary

Ask students to define *self-concept*. Have them describe how a child's self-concept is influenced by how he or she is treated by parents and significant others.

Resource

Teaching Two- and Three-Year-Olds, transparency master 6-5, TR

Reflect

Most three-year-olds are affectionate and seek attention and approval. As an early childhood professional, how will you handle attention-getting and clinging behavior while still maintaining fairness and refraining from showing favoritism?

Resource

Observing Developmental Characteristics of Three-Year-Olds, Activity D, OG

Meeting Special Needs

Demonstrate how to fill in reproducible master 6-4, *Development Puzzle*, by filling in the first item with the students. Provide a word bank with the answers for students who may need this assistance. Reproduce the puzzle with several answers filled in for students who need a shorter assignment. Ask students to write the word in the blank space in each statement as well as fill in the puzzle.

Three-year-olds enjoy playing. They still like playing alone, but they also enjoy playing in groups of two or three. You can introduce themes to their play. Some themes include treating and healing others. One child will help another who is injured or ill.

The objects that you supply in the classroom will influence a three-year-old's dramatic play. Cooking supplies, tools, phones, and suitcases are popular. These children enjoy pretending to be cooking, making repairs, calling others, and taking trips.

Three-year-old children are becoming increasingly independent. They feel a need to do things for themselves. Signs of independence include such statements as "I can do it" or "Let me do it." These statements are healthy signs that the children are gaining confidence in their abilities.

Some three-year-olds need encouragement to become more independent. They may make such statements as "You do it" or "I can't." When these words are spoken, you need to provide encouragement. These children need to know that you value their independence. They need to feel that they can do things for themselves.

Three-year-olds begin to control their emotions and strive for independence.

Resource

Observing Two- and Three-Year-Olds, Activity A, OG

Activity

Have students photograph children performing tasks by themselves, such as putting away toys, washing hands, flushing a toilet, and hanging up a coat. Have students pass the pictures around in a circle time activity to promote the development of independence in the children. Investigate the possibility of enlarging the photos to use as visual reminders in the classroom.

Resource

Studying Three-Year-Olds, Activity D, SAG

Cooperative Learning Activity

Conduct a chapter review by dividing students into groups and assigning each student in the group one of the following topics: physical development, cognitive development, social-emotional development, and teaching. Assign half of the groups to review two-year-olds and the other half to review three-year-olds. All students in the group should discuss their topics with the group and summarize what they have learned. Randomly select a student from each group to report a one-minute highlight of their discussion to the class.

Summary

Two-year-olds grow and change in many ways. Their motor skills improve so they can run, jump, and balance. They can also scribble, drink, and undress. Children of this age are also learning to control their elimination.

Two-year-olds are able to understand and say many words. They can answer simple questions and follow simple directions. They are beginning to learn basic math concepts related to size, number, shape, and color.

Socially and emotionally, these children are striving to be independent. They want to do things their own way, and when they can't, they may have temper tantrums. These children still need affection and attention from adults.

Three-year-olds grow out of many of the problems of two-year-olds. They have better muscle control and coordination. Children of this age can draw, cut with scissors, and work simple puzzles. They can dress themselves without much help from adults.

The thinking abilities of three-year-olds is improving. These children have a growing understanding and use of language. They have a better understanding of questions and instructions. They are using more complex sentences to communicate. They are beginning to learn grammar rules for past tense. At this age, children are also developing more refined concepts of number and size.

Socially, three-year-olds are beginning to reach out. They seek and favor adults, and they are starting to make friends with other children. These children have strong emotions, but they are learning appropriate ways to express these emotions.

Review and Reflect

1. List three motor skills of two-year-olds.

2. True or false. Most two-year-olds can dress themselves without help from adults.

3. Language comprehension is _____ advanced than expressive language in two-year-olds.

4. Compare the language strategies of expansion and feeding-in.

5. Which sentence is typical of a two-year-old?
   A. "Mommy."
   B. "Mommy go."
   C. "Mommy go and I go too."
   D. "Is Mommy going?"

6. How do most two-year-olds express their anger?

7. When working with two-year-olds, why do you need to allow plenty of time for transitions between activities?

8. True or false. Three-year-olds can climb and descend stairs easily.

9. Describe two self-help skills of three-year-olds.

10. Most three-year-old children can count to _____ while pointing to corresponding objects.

11. Why are three-year-olds less likely to become angry than two-year-olds?

Review and Reflect Answer Key

1. (List three. Student response.)
2. false
3. more
4. Feeding-in is a strategy where you provide the child's language. Expansion is accomplished by reframing the child's utterance into a sentence.
5. B
6. Two-year-olds tend to express their anger physically through temper tantrums that may include screaming, crying, stamping, and kicking.
7. Two-year-olds have a tendency to dawdle, and they insist on doing things at their own pace.
8. true
9. (List two. Student response.)
10. three
11. Three-year-olds have improved coordination, so they are less likely than two-year-olds to become frustrated due to lack of ability. Also, three-year-olds have improved language skills, so they can better understand reasons for what is happening around them.

Apply and Explore

1. Design a toy, activity, or teaching aid to help improve the self-help skills of a two- or three-year-old.

2. Interview a child care teacher about the differences in expression of emotions between two-year-olds and three-year-olds.

3. Visit a children's library and find books designed to help young children express their feelings in positive ways. Write a report on one of these books.

Cross-Curricular Link

Writing

1. Visit a child care center and observe the motor skills of two- and three-year-olds. Write a report comparing the motor skills of the two age groups based on your observations.

Technology

2. Visit the Web site for the National Network for Child Care (www.nncc.org) to review the development of two- and three-year-olds.

3. Review the developmental milestones for preschool children at the Web site for Early Childhood Development (www.ecdgroup.com).

Workplace Link

Construct a book, doll, or activity board that contains buttons and buttonholes, zippers, shoelaces and eyelets, snaps, buckles, and hook-and-loop closures. These can be made using recycled clothing. You might want to look at equipment catalogs for early childhood programs for ideas. Demonstrate the project for three-year-olds and observe how they practice these self-help skills.

Discuss

Study the children in the chapter opening photo. What characteristics do they seem to portray? How is this different from children of younger ages?

Reflect

Review the chapter objectives. What do you expect to learn from this chapter? How can this information prepare you for a career working with children?

Understanding Four- and Five-Year-Olds

After studying this chapter, you will be able to

- describe the physical, cognitive, and social-emotional development of four- and five-year-olds.

- explain how you as a teacher can plan programs and relate to four- and five-year-olds in developmentally appropriate ways.

120

Terms to Know

articulation
stuttering
rote counting

Your days with four- and five-year-olds will be filled with fun and challenges. Preschoolers (as four- and five-year-olds are referred to in this chapter) are capable of handling many basic self-help skills. However, to keep growing and learning, they need new experiences and challenges. Preschoolers have many questions about the world around them. Helping them find answers to these questions can be a rewarding part of teaching.

Physical Development of Four- and Five-Year-Olds

Increased body strength and coordination makes movement great fun for preschoolers, 7-1. Physical skills become easier partly because body proportions are changing. Compared to their total height, toddlers have fairly short legs. But by five and one-half years, most children's legs are about half the length of the body. Their proportions are more similar to adult proportions. This makes running, jumping, and balancing easier for preschoolers.

Preschool children are growing in more than just size. Their bones are becoming harder and stronger. Their permanent teeth are forming beneath their gums. Some children in this age group may begin losing their baby teeth. These children need good nutrition to assure that their bones and permanent teeth form properly. Their diets should include foods that are good sources

7-1

Preschoolers enjoy such gross-motor activities as climbing.

of calcium and vitamin D, such as milk and other dairy products.

Gross-Motor Development

Four- and five-year olds are using previously acquired skills to perform more complex movements. They improve their skills as their bodies becomes stronger and larger. At four years of age, children can hop on one foot. They can also walk down stairs with alternating feet. Four-year-olds can balance on one foot for about 10 seconds. They can walk backwards, toe-to-heel, for four consecutive steps.

Late in the fourth year, many children may begin learning how to skip. Most five-year-olds have developed this skill. Older four-year-olds may also be riding a bike with training wheels. If they have the opportunity, most children have developed this skill by five years of age. Five-year-olds can also walk forward and backward on a balance beam.

Vocabulary

Have students review the *Terms to Know* list. Ask students to look up unfamiliar words or terms in the glossary before reading the chapter.

Resource

Patterns of Physical Development, reproducible master 7-1, TR

Reflect

Do you remember what activities, games, books, and toys were your favorite when you were a preschooler? Do preschoolers still enjoy the same types of materials today?

Discuss

How early should formal training begin in specific sports and other gross-motor activities for children? Are preschoolers capable of developing skills in golf, tennis, soccer, gymnastics, ballet, etc?

Meeting Special Needs

Provide an outline of the chapter with all the chapter headings for special learners. Students should fill in each section of the outline as the material is covered in class with a sentence or two about the content. Review the special learners' IEPs to decide if any modifications should be made in presenting the chapter content.

Activity

Have students contact area parks and recreation departments to find out how many contain playground equipment suitable for preschool-age children. How often is the playground equipment inspected for maintenance and safety? Ask volunteers to share their findings with the class.

Enrich

Invite a physical education teacher to speak to the class about promoting gross-motor skill development for preschoolers. Are the physical education facilities available for the preschoolers' use? Have students prepare a list of questions prior to the visit.

Resource

Development of Four- and Five-Year-Olds, Activity B, OG

See 7-2. They can climb fences and march to music. They can also jump from table height and land on both feet.

Throwing and catching skills also improve during these years. Most four- and five-year-olds are capable of throwing overhand. As they grow, they are becoming better at using their bodies to direct a ball as they throw. When throwing, they rotate their bodies and shift their weight from the back foot to the front foot, using both hands and visually tracking the ball. These children are also able to catch a ball. A five-year-old is able

7-2

Improved balance allows this five-year-old to walk forward and backward on a balance beam.

to keep the hands close to the body until just before catching the ball. As the child's brain matures, there is better coordination of motor and visual systems.

Children this age enjoy working to improve their physical skills. They try to use their skills to the fullest. Sometimes they may even become reckless. For example, they may try to ride scooters as fast as they can.

Fine-Motor Development

Children's fine-motor skills improve rapidly during the preschool years. They find it easier to string beads and work with small game or puzzle pieces. See 7-3. When they build towers from blocks, the towers are straight and tall. By four years, most children can complete 12- to 18-piece puzzles. By five years, children can put together puzzles with 18 to 35 pieces. Five-year-olds are also becoming skilled at working clay. They may sculpt simple forms and figures.

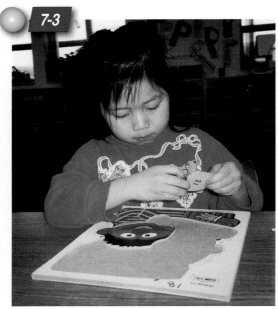

7-3

Four-year-olds have an easier time working puzzle pieces than younger children do.

Putting Technology to Use

Using print or Internet sources, have students research the physical benefits of gross-motor activities and active physical play for preschoolers. How much time do experts recommend preschoolers spend each day in active physical play? Have students use the computer to create a newsletter article encouraging families to promote healthful activities for their children. List suggestions for ways families can interact with their children to model healthful activity habits.

Writing and drawing skills also improve quickly. By four years of age, children's drawing forms are more refined. As a result, you will have an easier time recognizing what they are drawing. Preschoolers are beginning to recognize letters. They can tell writing from nonwriting. They can also copy a square and print a few letters. Often the letters are printed improperly, though. Letters that are mirror images are especially difficult for preschoolers. For instance, the child may print *b* for *d* or even for *p*. The child may place five or six horizontal lines on an *E*.

Five-year-olds show marked improvement in controlling a writing tool. They delight in copying triangles and tracing diamond shapes. They are also fairly skilled at staying within the lines when they color. Most five-year-olds enjoy printing their first names. Preschoolers are capable of copying most letters and printing some simple words, but they may still be having problems printing some letters properly. They are beginning to understand that letters and sounds are linked.

Self-Help Skills

Preschoolers become more and more self-sufficient. They are dressing and undressing themselves with very little help. Most of these children are capable of telling the front from the back of clothing. However, you may need to give them reminders from time to time. By four years of age, most children can buckle belts and close zippers. By five years, many children can even button and unbutton fasteners on the backs of garments. They can also put shoes on the correct feet. Some five-year-olds can even tie their own shoelaces.

Self-feeding is easier for preschoolers, too. They enjoy helping with serving. They can use spoons and forks with ease. By four years of age, children are using their forks to cut some large pieces of food. They may even try cutting foods with a knife. Most five-year-olds are able to cut fairly soft foods with

knives. Preschoolers are also able to clean up their places after they finish eating.

Preschoolers are also better able to take care of their own hygiene. They become more skilled at handling a toothbrush and brushing their teeth. They can also use a washcloth for wiping their hands and faces. Preschoolers become more skilled at brushing and combing their hair as well.

Cognitive Development of Preschoolers

Children in this age group make many gains in understanding the world around them. They become more skilled in thinking without having to act things out. As a result, they have a better understanding of symbols than younger children. Four- and five-year-olds also have increased language comprehension and expressive language skills. Language is a tool that can help children solve problems mentally.

Four- and five-year-olds now have the language skills to describe what they see and remember. You can test a child's recognition and recall skills. Show the child ten small, familiar toys. Then place the toys in a bag or box. Ask the child what items are in the bag. To recall the items requires the child to create a mental image. Although the child can recognize all ten items, she or he probably will only recall four or five. Children have better recognition than recall skills.

Children start creating their own symbols at this age, 7-4. This is reflected in their play. Instead of just imitating the actions of adults, preschoolers add their own ideas. For example, instead of using a bowl for mixing, they may pretend the bowl is a hat. New symbols also appear in art. Before the fourth year, children tend to scribble or just draw simple shapes. Now children make drawings that represent real objects. These drawings

Resource

Development of Four-Year-Olds, color transparency CT-6, TR

Reflect

Imagine you are teaching a class of preschoolers and a child in your class continues to write certain letters backwards or incorrectly. The parents are concerned their child may have a learning disability or vision problem. How would you answer the parent's concerns about the development of their child's writing abilities?

Discuss

Have students brainstorm ideas for encouraging preschoolers to practice printing their names. How much emphasis should you place on skill and accuracy at this age?

Enrich

Have students debate the pros and cons of rewarding preschoolers with stickers or stars on a classroom chart for skills such as writing their names, zipping their jackets, or tying their shoes. What are the possible effects on the children who have not yet mastered these skills?

Portfolio Project

Have students design a photo essay demonstrating the self-help and gross- and fine-motor skills exhibited by four- and five-year-olds. Photos can be obtained from print sources or downloaded to the computer from a digital camera or scanner and formatted into a slide show presentation. Ask the students to write a brief narrative explaining each photo. Have students save the photo essay in their portfolio.

Vocabulary

Have a student volunteer explain how *symbols* are a part of a preschooler's cognitive development.

Discuss

What differences can typically be seen in the drawings of four- and five-year-olds? What do the drawings tell you about their cognitive development?

Reflect

What strategies could you use to promote the development of logical thinking in preschoolers? What role does questioning have in this development?

Activity

Ask students to create an activity for preschoolers that teaches the language comprehension of one of the following words: *beside, bottom, backward, forward, down, low, different, thin, behind, ahead of, first,* or *last.* For example, when setting the table, ask a child to place the spoon *beside* the plate. Allow time for students to share their activities with the class.

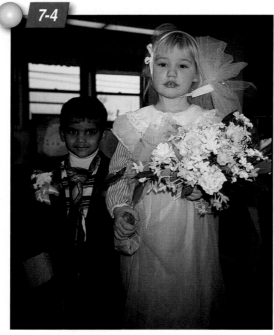

7-4

Four- and five-year-olds enjoy adding their own ideas during cooperative play.

are simple and do not always look like what the child really sees. For instance, a hand may have six or even ten fingers. Four-year-olds often make drawings and then name them. By five years, children decide what they want to draw and then draw it.

Understanding symbols is important for developing more advanced cognitive skills. Symbols are a part of learning in language, math, science, social studies, and many other areas of education. Therefore, cognitive development during the preschool years helps prepare children for future learning during the school years.

Preschoolers are eager to learn about why things happen around them. They may ask "Why do dogs bark?" or "Why do boats float?" With their endless string of questions, they are trying to make sense of their world. They still have flaws in their thinking, as three-year-olds do. Through asking questions again and again, their thinking becomes more and more logical.

Your curriculum should help promote the children's cognitive growth. As you provide new experiences, the children's vocabularies will grow. They will learn new concepts. For instance, you may show the children a live bunny. These children will explore concepts about the bunny, such as size, color, and method of eating. Children may also learn new vocabulary words as you show the animal. For instance, you might explain that the bunny is *timid*. Each new experience helps the children grow intellectually, 7-5.

Language Comprehension Skills

The language comprehension skills of four- and five-year-olds are constantly growing. New words related to space concepts increase their understanding. These include such words as *beside, bottom, backward,* and *forward*. They also understand such words as *down, low, different,* and *thin*. By the fifth year, the words *behind, ahead of, first,* and *last* are added to children's understanding. As you instruct children using these words,

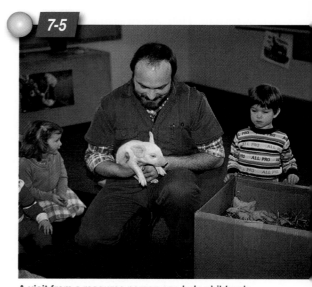

7-5

A visit from a resource person can help children's intellectual growth in many ways.

Putting Technology to Use

Have students conduct an Internet search for preschool vocabulary lists, such as the Dolce Basic Sight Vocabulary. Ask students to compare several lists and print them out. How can knowing the expected basic vocabulary for preschoolers help you design appropriate language learning activities? What ideas have you learned from your research? Have student volunteers share their findings with the class.

children will be able to understand and follow directions. For example, you may tell a child "Place the green block behind the blue block."

Children this age become even better at following three-step commands. These children will be able to follow the directions in the order that they are given. For instance, you may tell a child "Pick up the puzzle, put it on the table, and wash your hands." However, if you do not sequence the directions correctly, the child can become confused.

Children have a better understanding of the difference between plural and singular nouns at this age. For instance, you may tell a child to take a sandwich at lunch time. The child understands that he or she is to take only one sandwich. If you tell the child to take cookies, the child knows that he or she can have more than one.

Children start understanding the passive voice at this time. In a *passive voice* sentence, the object of the sentence is placed before the subject. An example of a passive voice sentence would be "The orange was eaten by Brock." Three-year-olds do not usually understand this word order. They think the sentence means that the orange ate Brock. Four- and five-year-olds understand that Brock ate the orange.

Because many words and phrases have more than one meaning, preschoolers may become confused about some statements. They tend to take literally such comments as "Wanda just flew out the door." See 7-6. You need to be careful about the phrases that you use around children of this age. For instance, a phrase such as "I'm dying of hunger" may frighten children.

Reading

Most four- and five-year-olds cannot read, but they are developing abilities that lead to reading skills. These abilities are made possible as children begin to understand symbolism. Before children learn to read, they need to understand that a group of letters on paper can symbolize any object, from a ball to an airplane.

7-6

> Anne just flew out the door . . . !

Preschoolers may have trouble understanding figurative speech.

Four- and five-year-olds can recognize and name many letters of the alphabet. They can also recognize their own names. Children in this age group enjoy having stories read to them over and over again. As you reread stories, the children may be able to pick out and say words they recognize. The children will also try to guess words they do not recognize. They tend to look at the first letter of a word and name any word that begins with that letter. For example, they may point to the word *ball* and say *baby*.

Expressive Language Skills

Preschoolers become quite talkative. As their vocabularies and grammar skills improve, they enjoy talking to others. See 7-7. At this age, children tend to talk to you rather than converse with you. When you talk about one subject, a child may interrupt to tell you about something entirely unrelated. The child may even make two or three unrelated comments to you in the same conversation. The children can answer your questions.

Vocabulary

Have a student volunteer define the term *passive voice*. Ask students to give examples of passive voice sentences.

Enrich

Ask students to think of everyday phrasing they use that may be confusing to a preschooler. Have students write down several of these phrases. For example, "*John ran up the bill,*" "*The dinner cost a fortune,*" and "*The weather caught me by surprise.*" Have student volunteers share their responses with the class to increase awareness of how their language may confuse a child.

Activity

Remind students that although preschoolers may not be ready for formal alphabet teaching, they can be encouraged to name letters and recognize their printed name. Have students post cards with children's names in the preschool room over their cubbies, on a birthday chart, or on a bulletin board beside a child's picture. Encourage children to find their name and spell it out.

Cross-Curricular Activity

English
Ask students to read *Teaching Our Youngest*, a publication of the Early Childhood—Head Start Task Force, at **www.ed.gov/teachers/how/ early/teachingouryoungest**. After reading the booklet, have students write a one-page summary of their findings. Allow time for students to trade papers in class and check for correct grammar, spelling, and punctuation. Then have students prepare a final draft of their report.

Vocabulary

Have a student volunteer look up the term *articulation* in the glossary and read the definition aloud. Ask students to name common articulation problems of preschoolers.

Discuss

Ask students to explain the term *stuttering*. What may cause stuttering in a preschooler? Does the stuttering problem tend to disappear?

Resource

The Truth About Preschoolers, Activity A, SAG

7-7

Four- year-olds like to talk with you about anything that interests them.

In later years, these children will become better at true two-way communication.

Articulation

Articulation is the ability to speak in clearly pronounced sounds. Articulation improves in many ways at ages four and five. Preschoolers can make most of the sounds needed to form words. Many children still have trouble making the *ch* sound and the *th* sound in words. Others may have trouble with the *S* sound, causing a lisp.

Some preschoolers also have stuttering problems. **Stuttering** includes repeating sounds or words and pausing for unusually long times while speaking. For most preschoolers, stuttering is a result of thinking faster than they can talk. As children's speech ability catches up to their thinking ability, the stuttering problem tends to disappear.

Vocabulary

Vocabulary grows quickly over these two years. Most four-year-olds have about 1500 words in their vocabularies. Five-year-olds have about 2000. Children do not always have clear ideas of the meanings of all the words they use. They may make up their own meanings to some words.

Preschoolers have mainly concrete nouns and action verbs in their vocabularies. They are beginning to add some modifiers and adjectives. However, words related to ideas or thoughts are still not a big part of their vocabularies. For example, children this age would be unlikely to use the words *freedom* or *unfair* unless they were simply imitating the words of adults.

Children of this age do imitate phrases they hear from adults or television. See 7-8. After a meal, a child may say "That was simply delectable!" This child is most likely imitating a statement heard at home or on television. If you ask, the child could not tell you what

7-8

Children may imitate a phrase from television such as "My teeth feel minty fresh and tingly." These children do not always understand the meaning of the phrase.

Meeting Special Needs

Special learners may need some review and clarification of the meanings of parts of speech. Prepare a chart listing the parts of speech (nouns, verbs, pronouns, modifiers, adjectives, and adverbs) in the first column. In the second column, provide several examples of words preschoolers may use corresponding to each part of speech. Leave the third column blank. Reproduce the chart as a handout and ask students to fill in the third column with additional words they have heard preschoolers use. Have students continue to add words to the chart as the year progresses.

delectable means. Children might also use such words as *bionic*, *biodegradable*, and *computer chip*.

Grammar

Children's grammar improves during these years. Children start to learn that there are exceptions to rules for past tense. They use such irregular verbs as *ate*, *ran*, and *went* properly. These children still put *-ed* at the end of these words occasionally.

Children also learn how to properly form questions. The three-year-old would say "Why the sky is blue?" Four- and five-year-olds know to say "Why is the sky blue?"

Some grammar rules still give four- and five-year-olds problems. They especially have trouble using the proper forms of pronouns in sentences. For instance, a child may say "Him and me are going to the zoo." They also have trouble with noun and verb agreement. For example, a child may say "Tommy don't have a crayon."

Math Skills

Number concepts become easier for children in this age group. Rote counting skills increase quickly. **Rote counting** is reciting numbers in their proper order. This skill is gained by most children before they fully understand that each number represents a certain amount. At four years of age, most children can rote count from one to nine. By the end of the fifth year, most children can rote count to 20. Rote counting skills develop at different rates for children in this age group. Therefore, you need to observe children to make sure your curriculum fits their skill levels.

True counting, in which an object is counted for each number named, develops more slowly. For instance, a child may try to count ten objects. The child may touch one object and say "one," another and say "two," and another saying "three." However, the child may then point to another object three times in a row, saying "four, five, six."

Children in this age group may be able to count three or four objects. However, they have trouble counting more objects.

Children start to recognize numerals in this stage. A four-year-old usually recognizes the numerals 1, 2, 3, 4, and 5. Five-year-olds

Health and Safety

Reducing Staff Stress

High stress levels among early childhood workers can negatively impact children. Reducing staff stress is one way that early childhood facilities can protect the health and safety of children. Here are some ways to reduce staff stress:

- Include regular staff breaks in the daily routine in a separate area from child care.

- Reduce noise by using sound-absorbing materials in the facility. Noise can cause hearing damage and psychological stress.

- Provide fair wages and benefits based on staff knowledge and performance.

- Offer training to improve staff skills including hazard recognition.

- Arrange for backup staff to give the early childhood staff members time off when ill or if a staff member needs to have a short break from the children.

Enrich

Ask student volunteers to conduct a search for any bilingual early childhood programs in their school district. Have students investigate the challenges of teaching grammar in these programs to preschoolers. Allow time for students to report their findings in class.

Vocabulary

Have a student volunteer define the term *rote counting*. At what age do children start to exhibit the skill of rote counting?

Resource

Behavioral Traits of Four-Year-Olds, transparency master 7-2, TR

Note

True counting is also known as *rational counting*. This term will be used in Chapter 23, *Guiding Math Experiences*.

Resource

Reading and Math Fun, Activity B, SAG

Cross-Curricular Activity

Math
Ask students to observe a four- or five-year-old while performing rote and true counting activities. How many numbers can the child recite in their proper order? How many objects can the child count for each number named? What difficulties, if any, was the child experiencing? Have students determine the child's skill level and create a math activity that will help the child practice rote or true counting. Have students share their math activities with the rest of the class.

Activity

Have students brainstorm activities for preschoolers that will reinforce the concepts of the following words: *short, fat, tallest, same size, first,* or *last.* For example, "Which is the *tallest* block tower?"

Discuss

As children mature, their emotional reactions change. Compare the reactions you might expect from a three- and five-year-old when they spill a glass of milk, hear a balloon pop, or fall off a chair.

Resource

Behavioral Traits of Five-Year-Olds, transparency master 7-3, TR

Discuss

How is the growing social-emotional development of preschoolers shown in their play? Give examples of behaviors that are more advanced than those of the three-year-old.

learn to recognize 6, 7, 8, 9, and 10 as well. By five years of age, many children can dial their own telephone numbers.

Other math skills develop at this age. Children become better at recognizing shapes. About 80 percent of five-year-olds can recognize the square and rectangle shapes. Four- and five-year-olds also understand more terms related to size and number. These include *short, fat, tallest, same size, first,* and *last.*

Children start to understand money concepts in this stage. Most preschoolers can identify a penny, a nickel, and a dime. Children of this age do not yet understand the true value of money, though. If you ask a preschooler whether a nickel or a dime is worth more, the child is likely to choose the nickel. Since it is bigger, children think that it is worth more. They do not yet realize that a nickel is worth five pennies and a dime is worth ten.

Time concepts become more clear at this age. The children start to understand the difference between *today, tomorrow,* and *yesterday.* However, many time concepts are still confusing for these children. They don't really understand how long an hour or a minute takes. They also get confused because time is described in so many ways. An adult may tell a child that puppet time is at *3:30, at half past three, this afternoon,* or *in a few hours.*

Social-Emotional Development of Preschoolers

Preschoolers continue to be helpful and cooperative, 7-9. With improved language skills, children become more involved with one another. Friendships become more important. They know that a friend is a person who "likes you." Emotions are changing in children at this age. As they learn and grow, the causes of happiness, fear, anger, and sadness change. The ways children react to these emotions change, too.

7-9

Four- and five-year-olds are usually cheerful and cooperative.

Social Development

Companionship is important to preschoolers. Friendships, attention, and approval are important as well. However, preschoolers are also becoming more independent of adults. They like to play on their own or with other children. They may not always want you or other adults to participate in play. They may still need your help to get materials or settle disputes.

Children this age start to value their friendships with others. They tend to have only a few friends. They also prefer friends of the same sex. Children in this age group become more willing to cooperate as they play with others. They are more likely than younger children to offer a favorite toy to

---

Putting Technology to Use

Have students conduct an Internet search for information on the importance of early friendships for preschoolers. What can children learn from such friendships? How can early childhood teachers promote social interactions in the classroom that could encourage friendships? Ask students to write a brief report of their findings. Allow time for students to read their reports in class.

a friend. Many children in this age group choose best friends. They tend to change best friends fairly often, though.

For four-year-olds, over one-third of a child's play is solitary play. However, by age five, play involves more and more interaction and cooperation. Play groups are still small—only two or three children, but children talk to each other more and do more as a group, 7-10.

Children this age accept supervision. They know their own abilities, and they realize that adults have reasons for rules. These children will accept your instructions, and they will ask your permission before doing certain activities.

Emotional Development

Four- and five-year-olds begin to realize new ways of showing love and caring. They still understand hugs and other physical signs of affection. They may hug another child who is sad. However, they are starting to realize that helping others is a way of showing love. These children may show love for others by sharing something or helping with a task. They may also seek this sign of love from others. For example, children may ask for help with a task even if they

don't need it. The children are looking for assurance that you care.

Children in this age group start to develop a sense of humor. See 7-11. Laughter becomes a way of expressing their happiness. These children do not yet understand most verbal jokes, but they laugh at funny faces or actions. They also laugh at things they know are unusual. For instance, they may laugh at a dog that says "meow" in a story. The children also need good role models to learn that harm done to others is not funny.

Fear

Fears are still common, but most only last a few months. Causes of fears change during this stage. These children are still afraid of imagined creatures, such as monsters and ghosts. They may be especially fearful of dreams because they seem so real. However, preschoolers also start to realize that there is a difference between the real and the imagined. This helps children deal with some of these fears. For this reason, you may hear preschoolers state firmly "There's no

7-10

Play becomes more cooperative for four- and five-year-olds.

7-11

Children this age enjoy humor.

Resource

Handling Emotions, Activity C, SAG

Reflect

How would you handle an incident in the classroom when two preschoolers will not let a third child play with them? How could you use this incident as a lesson for the entire class?

Note

Thumbsucking, nail-biting, and tics may be signs a child is suffering from emotional problems. Be sure to keep the lines of communication open with parents to learn about what might be bothering a child and how you can help the child in the preschool classroom.

Discuss

Parents and caregivers may unintentionally increase children's fears when teaching about strangers. How can you teach children about strangers without adding to their fears?

Portfolio Project

Ask students to select one of the preschoolers in the class and write a profile describing the child's physical, cognitive, social, and emotional development. Is the student typical of others in his or her age group according to the characteristics discussed in this chapter? Does the child have any outstanding skills or abilities? Does the child demonstrate any delays in development? Have students keep a copy of the profile in their portfolio.

such thing as dragons." They may ask you repeatedly "Was the story just pretend?"

Other fears may be created by the new knowledge of preschoolers. They are aware of more dangers. However, they do not know enough to fully understand what is and is not dangerous. Their imaginations are vivid. For instance, a child may learn that sharks live in the ocean. This may cause fear of being hurt in the ocean. The child may also become afraid of sharks in rivers, pools, and even bathtubs.

Five-year-olds are also more afraid of being hurt than are younger children. They know of more things that can hurt them. They may be afraid of doctors and dentists. This is because they are aware of pain or injuries associated with these professionals. They may also be afraid of high places and dogs because of prior experiences.

Children this age sometimes work through fears in play. For instance, a child who is afraid of dogs may pretend to be a fierce dog. A child who is afraid of heights may pretend to be a bird. For these children, play is therapeutic. It helps them act out some of their intense feelings and deal with their fears.

Anger

Like three-year-olds, children in this age group do not have as many causes for anger as toddlers do. However, they can become angry if they are unable to reach their goals. Four- and five-year-old children are more likely to use words and yelling rather than hitting or kicking to express anger. If they do express anger physically, they are more likely to take out their anger on objects or other children. They do not usually respond to adults physically because they know this action is not accepted.

Some preschoolers respond more physically to anger than others. They may become angry more easily than others also. They may use pushing, hitting, or kicking to show anger. They may not have learned better ways of expressing anger from adult role models or they may want attention.

Jealousy

Jealousy may be a problem for some children in this age group. These children are most likely to become jealous of a new brother or sister. They may resent the fact that their parents are spending so much time with a new child. They may fear that their parents do not love them as much.

Jealousy may surface in children in many ways, 7-12. The child may regress to earlier behaviors, such as crying or having toileting accidents. The child may also develop physical problems such as stomachaches or nightmares.

These children need to be reassured that they are still loved. Sometimes they may need a little extra attention away from home to make them feel special. Showing children that their sibling needs help from a "big sister" or "big brother" can make them feel better, too.

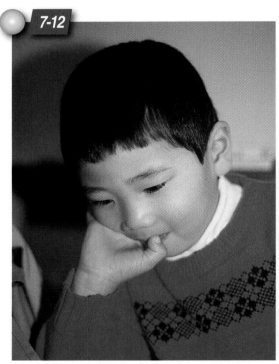

7-12

Children who are jealous of a new sibling may become withdrawn or show regressive behaviors at the center.

Discuss

How do four- and five-year-old children show their anger when they are unable to get their way? How can you encourage them to express their anger in more socially acceptable ways?

Resource

Observing Four- and Five-Year-Olds, Activity A, OG

Discuss

What are some causes of preschool jealousy besides having a new baby at home? What strategies can teachers use to help children deal with their jealousy?

Resource

Developing Activities, Activity D, SAG

Putting Technology to Use

Have students conduct an Internet search for information about using time-outs as a method of handling a preschool child's anger. What are the pros and cons, if any, of using this method in an educational setting? What role will consistency play in helping a child become self-disciplined? What should the ideal time-out area look like in a preschool classroom? Ask students to write a report of their findings. Allow time for student volunteers to share their reports with the class.

Sadness

Four- and five-year-olds start to learn that some situations are sad. They become aware of the concept of death. Their first experiences with death may be the loss of a pet. Preschool children do not understand that death cannot be reversed. As a result, it may take children a while to realize that the pet will not come back to life. However, once they understand this, they often become sad.

Children are not always sure how to express sadness. Children may deal with sadness in play. They may pretend to be the lost pet or to talk to the lost pet. Frequently, they need help from adults to learn that it is okay to cry and talk about their feelings. They also need adults to model appropriate responses to sadness and to provide clear explanations.

Some children must also deal with the death of a close family member. These children need to have as much explained about the situation as they can understand. They also need help from adults in dealing with the loss and sadness.

Teaching Four- and Five-Year-Olds

Like three-year-olds, four- and five-year-olds tend to be cooperative and helpful. These children are eager to please you, 7-13. If you ask a child to help you, the child feels complimented. Children of this age enjoy feeling needed and important. They may even ask "Can I help you?"

Because these children like to help, you need to carefully select helpers. Choosing the same few helpers time after time can make others feel unimportant. Even children who do not volunteer need to be asked from time to time. These children may be too shy to ask, or they may not feel confident in their abilities to help. By choosing them, you can help build their self-esteem.

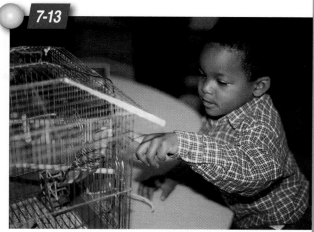

7-13

Preschoolers are eager to help you in such ways as caring for pets.

By this age, children become quite talkative. They still enjoy physical play, but they like to spend more time talking. You will enjoy carrying on conversations with them. These conversations may become a part of learning activities or story time. After you read a story, the children may enjoy retelling the story. They are usually capable of retelling the story in detail and in the proper sequence.

You will notice that children in this age group will imitate your speech. You may hear one child tell another "Christopher, we walk, we don't run, when we are in the hallway." For this reason, you need to be careful of your statements. You should never use words or statements that you would not want the children repeating.

Children are now more content playing with each other. You do not need to function as a playmate as much. However, you will need to handle more disputes among children. At this age, children may have conflicts over group rules. They will look to you for advice on settling these problems. You may also want to add new ideas to play. Preschoolers enjoy playing some simple, organized games that you may lead.

Some children may have imaginary playmates. A child may come to school

Resource

Behavior Review, reproducible master 7-4, TR

Enrich

Ask for two student volunteers to role-play a situation in which a teacher is comforting a child who is very sad at the loss of a beloved pet. Ask students to evaluate the teacher's effectiveness in meeting the child's need.

Discuss

Children may experience an increase in self-esteem when asked to help a teacher in the preschool classroom. Brainstorm additional ways that teachers can help build self-esteem in this age group.

Resource

Observing Developmental Characteristics of Four-Year-Olds, Activity C, OG

Reflect

How will you encourage the development of problem-solving abilities when preschoolers have a dispute over the rules of a group activity? Give examples that contribute to solving the problem and building children's self-esteem.

Resource

Observing Developmental Characteristics of Five-Year-Olds, Activity D, OG

Meeting Special Needs

Have students with special needs fold a piece of notebook paper in half vertically and then horizontally, making four boxes. Ask them to write each of the following emotions in a separate box: fear, anger, jealousy, and sadness. Have students record possible causes of the emotions, typical examples of behavior expressed by a preschooler, and ways teachers could help the child handle his or her emotions. This activity could also be conducted with the entire class on the board or overhead and used as a review of emotional development.

Reflect

Did you have an imaginary playmate during your preschool years? How did your parents and teachers react?

Discuss

What safety and sanitation guidelines need to be followed for woodworking and cooking projects in the preschool? Discuss your opinions on the value of these activities in the preschool curriculum.

Activity

Ask students to write down five new facts they learned about four- and five-year-olds in this chapter. Have students share their list with another student and compare lists.

Discuss

After reviewing this chapter, what do you expect to like about teaching four- and five-year-olds? What will you expect to find challenging?

explaining that Ralph, his playmate, asked to come with him. He may provide space for Ralph on his cot at nap time. He may have conversations with Ralph throughout the day. This kind of play does not necessarily indicate problems. It is simply a way of using the imagination and having fun.

Children in this age group are often proud of their possessions and family members, 7-14. They may like to bring favorite toys to the center. They may also call attention to new shoes or a new jacket. They may beam with pride when their parents visit the center. Children enjoy talking with you and others about their belongings. Asking children questions about something of theirs can help build their self-esteem.

Children of this age also enjoy working on projects. Their attention spans and goal-setting abilities are improving. Children's ideas for projects may come from play with peers or from adult activities. Such projects as woodworking, cooking, and sculpting clay may be fun for these children. As they get older, they will engage for longer periods of time in these activities. The average time spent in most activities at this age is about seven minutes.

7-14

Preschoolers are proud to have their siblings visit the center.

Workplace Connection

Have students work in small groups to design a bulletin board or display for the preschool room showcasing a "student of the week." Solicit photos and appropriate items from parents that could be displayed, such as family and pet photos; souvenirs from trips; favorite toys, colors, foods, and games. Incorporate a circle activity during the week for the child to share information from the display with the rest of the class. Change the display each week until all children have been showcased.

Summary

The growth of four- and five-year-olds helps them become more independent. These preschoolers become stronger and more coordinated. Their changing body proportions help them improve their balance and motor skills. Children of this age also have improved dressing, eating, and hygiene skills.

Four- and five-year-olds' thoughts become more and more adultlike. The children begin to understand and use symbols in play, drawing, and learning. Language skills improve quickly. Preschoolers understand and use more words. Their grammar improves also. Much new knowledge helps prepare children for later math learning. These include rote counting and understanding of size and number concepts.

Children become more social with their peers at this age. Their play becomes more cooperative. Children still seek favor and approval from adults. They like to help and talk to adults. Children are learning acceptable ways of expressing their feelings. They are also experiencing feelings for different reasons.

As a teacher, you will enjoy working with four- and five-year-olds. These children can be independent in terms of self-care. They are eager and able to help you, and they enjoy talking with you and learning about new ideas.

Review and Reflect

1. Why is it important to include foods high in calcium and vitamin D in the diets of four- and five-year-olds?

2. True or false. Four- and five-year-olds stand perfectly still when they throw a ball.

3. Describe the writing skills of four- and five-year-olds.

4. Which of the following dressing skills do most five-year-olds have?
   A. They know the front from the back of garments.
   B. They can buckle belts.
   C. They can put shoes on the right feet.
   D. All of the above.

5. At what age do children make drawings and then decide what they are?

6. Describe the reading abilities of four- and five-year-olds.

7. True or false. A four-year-old who uses the word "imitation" probably does not know what the word means.

8. Why are time concepts confusing for four- and five-year-olds?

9. True or false. Five-year-olds prefer friends of the opposite sex.

10. Describe a situation that is likely to cause fear in a five-year-old. Explain why this situation would cause fear.

11. Typically, what is the teacher's role in the play of four- and five-year-olds?

4. D
5. four
6. Four- and five-year-olds can recognize and name many letters of the alphabet, and they can recognize their own names. As you read stories, these children may be able to pick out and say words that they recognize. They will also try to guess words that they do not recognize by focusing on the first letter of the word.
7. true
8. Four- and five-year-olds don't really understand how long an hour or a minute takes. They also get confused because time is described in many different ways.
9. false
10. (Student response.)
11. The teacher does not function much as a playmate. The teacher does handle disputes and conflicts, and the teacher may add new ideas to play.

Review and Reflect **Answer Key**

1. In these years, bones are becoming harder and permanent teeth are forming. Calcium and vitamin D are important to this growth.
2. false
3. Four- and five-year-olds' writing skills become more refined. Their drawings are more easily recognized. These children can copy a square and print a few letters. (The letters may be flawed, however.) By five years of age, children can copy triangles and trace diamonds. They can also stay within the lines fairly well when they color. Most five-year-olds can print their first names, copy most letters, and print some simple words.

Apply and Explore

1. Play catch with a four- or five-year-old. Make sketches or written descriptions of the movements used by the child to catch and to throw. Report your findings to the class.

2. Interview an early childhood teacher about the artwork of four- and five-year-olds. Ask to see samples that show the types of symbolism these children use.

3. Make a bulletin board based on phrases that might be misinterpreted by four- and five-year-olds. The bulletin board could contain drawings of preschoolers' interpretations of the phrases.

Cross-Curricular Link

Writing

1. Write a research report on recommended ways of helping four- and five-year-olds deal with death.

Technology

2. Visit the Web site for the National Network for Child Care (www.nncc.org) to review the development of four- and five-year-olds.

3. Review the developmental milestones for preschool children at the Web site for Early Childhood Development (www.ecdgroup.com).

Workplace Link

Create file folder activities for preschoolers that will reinforce recognition of numbers, shapes, and coins. Simple drawings, cutouts, or clipart can be used to illustrate the folders. Make sure the activities are hands-on, such as tracing, matching, or puzzles. Use the projects in the preschool classroom or send them home with directions for parents.

Discuss

Look at the chapter opening photo. What characteristics of these children signal that they are in middle childhood? Why might the teacher enjoy working with children of this age as opposed to younger children?

Discuss

Look over the objectives for this chapter. What do these objectives tell you about the differences you can expect in this age group when compared with the age groups studied in previous chapters?

8

Middle Childhood

After studying this chapter, you will be able to

- describe the physical, cognitive, and social-emotional development of school-age children.

- summarize potential health concerns of middle childhood.

- explain moral development during childhood.

135

Vocabulary

Have a student volunteer explain the term *middle childhood*. Why is middle childhood still considered part of early childhood education?

Resource

Understanding Middle Childhood Terms, Activity A, SAG

Vocabulary

Have students review the *Terms to Know* list. Ask students to look up unfamiliar words or terms in the glossary before reading the chapter.

Discuss

Children in this age group begin to care more about what others think of them. What other environmental influences can affect how they feel about themselves?

Terms to Know

middle childhood
visual perception
farsighted
nearsighted
obesity
rehearsal
operation
conservation
seriation
classification
social comparison
self-esteem
empathy
compassion
moral development
morality

Middle childhood refers to the span of years between ages 6 and 12. Since this time period begins with the onset of formal schooling, it is often referred to as the *school-age years*. It is a time of important advances in the child's identity. At this stage of development, children are making strides in becoming self-competent and self-aware.

During middle childhood, children become more self-sufficient and independent. They are interested and involved in many new activities. Peers and adults outside their families play an increasingly important role in their lives. Their circle of friends and acquaintances expands far beyond their own family members. These friendships and school-related activities are taking more and more of their time. As a result, they are learning to adopt new social rules and expectations.

Though developmental changes continue to occur throughout middle childhood, the changes are not as dramatic as they were during infancy and toddlerhood. During the school-age years, the brain undergoes changes that allow more highly developed thinking skills. As a result, the children are becoming better problem solvers. They are also growing in self-knowledge and understanding.

School-age children are beginning the process of entering the adult world and are attending more to their own needs. They are becoming better able to get themselves up in the morning, bathe, dress, and eat without adult assistance. Most families expect more of their school-age children because of their improved skills. Often children this age assist with cooking, dishwashing, and laundry chores. They are also capable of helping with younger siblings.

Physical Development

Physical development during middle childhood is not as rapid as during the first years of life. Between the ages of 6 and 12, children experience steady physical growth, 8-1. There are gradual and consistent increases in weight and height. Heredity and environment account for most differences in physical growth. Health care and nutrition are environmental factors that can affect both weight and height.

During this period, children are interested in their physical growth. They care more about what other people think of them. Thus, their body size, shape, and physical abilities can influence how they feel about themselves.

At the beginning of this stage, children have much better control of their large muscles than their small muscles. During the six-year span, children show continued improvement in skills learned earlier. They show gains in motor skills, agility, and physical strength. These skills are helpful for participation in games and sports.

Workplace Connection

Have students research what programs or facilities are available in their area for the care of school-age children. Ask students to write a description of each program, including program sponsorship, hours of operation, number of children enrolled, fees, program content, eligibility requirements, and number of staff members. What needs are met in the community by these programs? Allow time for students to discuss their findings in class.

Children do not grow as rapidly during middle childhood as they do in the first years of life.

Height

Boys are usually slightly taller than girls at the beginning of this stage. Until age nine, boys retain this edge. Then the reverse occurs as girls begin to grow more rapidly. At 10 years of age, most girls experience a growth spurt. This growth spurt occurs two years later in boys. At ages 11 and 12, most girls have surpassed boys in height. This difference can be a source of embarrassment for some children.

The typical six-year-old is almost four feet tall. During middle childhood, children usually grow about two to three inches per year. By the age of 12, the average child is about five feet tall. By the end of middle childhood, girls may reach 90 percent of their adult height. At the same time, boys may be about 80 percent of their adult height.

Body proportions change during the school-age years. The upper part of the head grew fast during the first six years of life. Now the arms and legs grow more quickly.

Children look less top-heavy now than during the earlier years.

Weight

At age six, the average child weighs about 47 pounds. By age 12, this weight may double. Children gain about five to seven pounds per year during middle childhood.

There are weight differences between girls and boys. From birth through the preschool years, girls usually weigh slightly less than boys. Girls catch up with boys in weight by age 11. By 12 years of age, girls usually weigh about three pounds more than boys.

Gross-Motor Skills

By watching school-age children on the playground, you can see how their motor skills are improving, 8-2. Physical growth

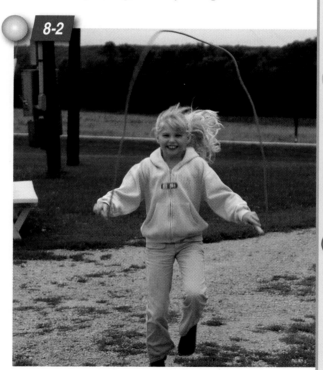

Motor development continues to improve during the school-age years.

Discuss

Ask students to look at 8-1 and notice the ratio of the size of the child's head to the rest of his body. How does this compare to the head-body ratio of toddlers, preschoolers, teens, and adults?

Reflect

Can you recall any instances during your own school-age years when you felt embarrassed because of growth differences from other children? How did you handle these experiences?

Note

Growth charts for boys and girls can be viewed, downloaded, and printed for use at the **keepkidshealthy. com/growthcharts** Web site.

Resource

Check Your Gender IQ, Activity B, SAG

Portfolio Project

Using print and Internet sources, ask students to search for resources on children's growth from ages six through twelve. Have students share their lists in class. After viewing several resources from other students' lists, ask students to select those they feel are most useful. Ask students to compile a list of resources that could be distributed to families. Have students include a copy of their resource list in the school-age section of their portfolio.

Discuss

School-age children are constantly practicing the following skills: jumping, balancing, throwing, catching, running, and sequencing foot movements. What gross-motor activities promote the practice and perfection of these skills?

Reflect

What gross-motor activities did you most enjoy as a school-age child? What fine-motor activities did you find most enjoyable?

Resource

Observing Six- and Seven-Year-Olds, Activity A, OG

Discuss

How does the immune system help protect against disease? Which diseases and illnesses are seen less often in the middle childhood years?

contributes to these changes. Gains in height and weight help with coordination. These children possess greater speed and accuracy of movement, with faster reaction times. Movements are more refined and fluid. Moreover, balance has improved.

Younger school-age children are constantly practicing and perfecting six skills. These are jumping, balancing, throwing, catching, running, and sequencing foot movements. Their running is faster. With practice, they are more accurate in throwing, catching, and kicking. They can throw balls greater distances.

As they grow older, both boys and girls improve their gross-motor skills. Even though girls usually surpass boys in height and weight, boys have more physical strength. They have an advantage in muscle mass. As a result, boys may outperform girls in jumping, catching, throwing, and batting. They can usually run faster and for greater distances.

Girls outperform boys in motor skills that require balance, coordination, flexibility, or rhythmic movement. Some examples include playing hopscotch, dancing, and skipping. Girls also have an edge in skills involving the use of the small muscles.

Fine-Motor Skills

Children show improvement of their fine-motor skills throughout middle childhood. They have better control of the small muscles in their fingers and hands. Their writing is much better since they are using more wrist movement. Letters and words are more uniform and neater. Moreover, the spacing between letters and words has improved. Handwriting involves fine-motor and visual-perception skills. **Visual perception** involves the coordination of the eye and hand. To write, a child must see the differences in size, shape, and slant. Typically, girls set higher standards for themselves in writing. The improvement of fine-motor skills is also reflected in their drawings, 8-3.

8-3

With better control of the small muscles and hands, children's artwork also improves.

Improved finger dexterity allows school-age children to play musical instruments, such as a piano, guitar, or flute. Their hand-eye coordination skills are also improving. While grasping tools, they can control the motion and speed. This allows them to learn such skills as sewing and assembling models with small pieces.

Health Concerns

Middle childhood is often one of the healthiest periods for children. The lowest illness rates are for children between 5 and 12 years of age. Therefore, there are fewer sore throats, upper respiratory diseases, and middle ear infections than during the preschool years. One of the reasons for this reduction is the body's developing immune system, which offers protection against disease. School-age children, however, are not illness-free. Many school-age children still have several upper respiratory illnesses each year.

Several chronic illnesses may surface during middle childhood. Ulcers, asthma, and diabetes are examples. In addition,

---

Putting Technology to Use

Have students conduct an Internet search for the following programs: Action for Healthy Kids; Alliance for a Healthier Generation: Healthy Schools Program; CDC's Healthy Youth! Physical Activity; JumpSTART; and Walking Works for Schools. Have students write a brief summary about each program. Ask students to include information about how the program encourages physical activity in schools. Allow time for students to discuss their findings in class.

many school-age children develop headaches and acne as they approach adolescence. Some children may develop hearing and vision problems. Lack of exercise is another problem. Others exercise too much, placing their bodies under stress. For these children, overuse can cause sprains, tendinitis (inflammation of a tendon), and even broken bones. A variety of other health problems occur even though most children are at their healthiest.

Hearing

Children's hearing is usually well developed by middle childhood. Awareness of midrange sounds develops first, followed by high-range and low-range awareness. By 11 years of age, most children have the auditory awareness of adults.

Ear infections can be a health problem. If left untreated, they can cause permanent hearing loss. For most children, the number of ear infections decreases due to structural changes within the body. The eustachian tube, which connects the middle ear to the throat, has changed position. This change helps prevent bacteria and fluids from moving from the mouth to the ear.

Vision

By age six, most children are ready to read. They can see an object with both eyes at the same time. Their ability to focus improves. Many preschool children are somewhat **farsighted**. This means they can see objects in the distance more clearly than those that are close. During the middle years, their close-up vision improves.

Throughout middle childhood, nearsightedness is the most common vision problem. Being **nearsighted** means being able to see close objects more clearly than those at a distance. The more time children are engaged in reading and close-up work, the greater their chances of becoming nearsighted.

With corrective lenses, nearsightedness can be overcome, 8-4. It is estimated as many as 25 percent of children will need to have their vision corrected by the end of the school years. It is important that children's vision be checked regularly to detect any problems.

Teeth

During middle childhood, children begin losing their primary or "baby" teeth. First and second graders often have toothless smiles! The first teeth to fall out are the central incisors, which are the lower and upper front teeth, 8-5. By the age of 12, all of the 20 primary teeth will be replaced with permanent teeth. At first, these permanent teeth appear to be out of proportion to the child's face. Gradually the facial bones grow, causing the face to lengthen and the mouth to widen. These changes accommodate the larger permanent teeth.

Tooth loss can have a psychological effect on some children. They become

8-4

Corrective lenses can overcome most vision problems.

Vocabulary

Have a student volunteer define the term *eustachian tube*. What effect does growth have on the eustachian tube and the role it plays in middle ear infections?

Enrich

Invite a dentist to speak to the class about children's dental health. What changes in teeth development occur in children during the school-age years? How can good dental health be promoted? Have students prepare a list of additional questions prior to the visit.

Vocabulary

Have a student volunteer define the terms *farsighted* and *nearsighted*. What is the risk to vision health the more time children spend in reading and close-up work?

Workplace Connection

Have students investigate how their school monitors students' vision and hearing. How often are screenings held and what do they involve? Who conducts the screenings? What assistance may be necessary in the classroom for children who have identified hearing and vision difficulties? Allow time for students to discuss their findings in class.

Activity

Ask students to design a creative lesson to reinforce concepts of good dental health for school-age children. Students may work individually or in groups. Lessons may take the form of a commercial, role-playing situation, demonstration, puppet show, power point presentation, or other creative choice. After all presentations are viewed, ask students to evaluate how effective they think the lessons will be for school-age children.

Vocabulary

Have a student volunteer define the term *obesity*. Why is obesity considered a serious problem for school-age children?

Resource

Health Dilemmas, Activity C, SAG

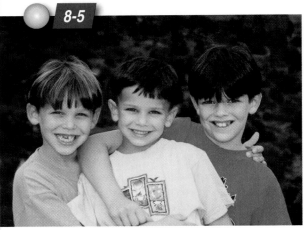

8-5

As you can tell by the missing teeth, two of these three brothers have entered middle childhood.

self-conscious. Calling attention to the change in their appearance may cause them to be uncomfortable.

A common health problem for school-age children is tooth decay. Children with poor dental hygiene habits are most susceptible to cavities. Also at risk are children who are in poor health and who have diets high in sugar.

As a teacher, you should promote good dental health. Begin by modeling proper care of your own teeth. Brush your teeth with the children after each meal. Eat a well-balanced diet and avoid foods high in sugar. Encourage parents to have their children receive regular dental checkups.

Obesity

Obesity is becoming a common problem among school-age children and a national concern. **Obesity** is characterized by excessive bodily fat. A person is considered obese if he or she weighs 20 percent more than other people of the same sex, age, and build. Obesity affects about 25 percent of school-age children. The majority, approximately 80 percent, of obese children will become obese adults.

Being obese can seriously impact a child's emotional health. Obese children are often teased and ridiculed by their peers. Their peers stereotype them as sloppy, ugly, lazy, and stupid. Obese children may have fewer friends, and they are often the last to be selected for group projects and teams. As a result, overweight children may lack self-esteem.

Health and Safety

Healthy Activities for School-Age Children

School-age children are rapidly growing and changing—and so are their activity and relationship needs. With ongoing concerns about childhood obesity and peer relationships, care providers must offer a wide range of healthy activities that promote *all* areas of development. Types of activities for school-age children should include the following:

- vigorous gross-motor activities that increase physical fitness, such as outdoor games, running, biking, or team sports
- healthful food choices to meet energy needs
- time for quiet activities to be creative or to do homework
- opportunities for community involvement that enhance social relationships
- time for developing independent relationships with the guidance and support of parents and care providers

Cross-Curricular Activity

Health
Have students arrange a visit to a local elementary school with a lunch program or a before- and after-school program for children. Ask students to review sample menus and calculate the amount of proteins, carbohydrates, fats, vitamins, minerals, fiber, and calories in a typical meal. Does the meal contribute positively to the recommended daily allowances for children? What changes or modifications could you suggest to make the meal more healthful? Have students write a brief report of their findings.

Several factors contribute to obesity in children. Some obese children have overweight parents. For them, the tendency to be overweight may be inherited. For other children, environment can be a contributing factor. If the parents and other family members overeat, the children will likely do the same. Still other children overeat due to family stress. Children's eating habits can be affected by abuse, the death of a family member, alcoholism, or divorce. Any of these traumatic events can trigger overeating.

Many children are obese as a result of physical inactivity. They may also watch more television than other children. Studies show that those children who spend more time watching television and playing video games get less physical activity. As a result, they are more likely to be overweight.

Research shows that overweight children often are overweight as adults. Adults who are obese may develop high blood pressure, heart disease, or diabetes. Treating childhood obesity, however, is difficult. Obesity is often a family disorder. Behaviors need to be changed that involve both the child and the parents. Obese children need help in making healthier food choices. They need to learn which foods are lower in fat and calories. They need to be shown how to control the portions they eat. They should be encouraged to exercise more. These children may also need help in overcoming emotional problems.

Early childhood programs must set an example. Healthy meals with low-fat foods should be served. Nutrition education needs to be included in the curriculum. The daily schedule should include daily physical activity including vigorous exercise.

Cognitive Development

During middle childhood, children begin to think mentally using logic and symbols. They no longer rely only on what they can see or perceive. They begin to use logical thinking instead of only perception. In addition, their memory improves and their attention span is longer. They can process and recall information more readily. These improved thinking skills allow them to engage in academic tasks. Their reading, writing, science, and math skills develop continually throughout the school-age years, 8-6.

The desire to achieve is an important influence on cognitive development during middle childhood. Achievement is often related to motivation. Some children have an internal desire to work hard and achieve. Others are motivated by the prospect of rewards or recognition. Whether the desire to succeed comes from within the child or externally, the motivation to do well influences performance.

Attention and Memory

Critical to cognitive development is attention and memory. Memory becomes more controlled than during early childhood. The child's age, motivation, health, and attitude determine the effectiveness of memory. Attention also improves. Children now have the ability to ignore unnecessary information. They are able to focus their

8-6

Children learn to read during middle childhood.

Activity

Ask students to bring a snack item to class they consider healthful. Have students taste the snacks and compare ingredient information, suggested serving size, and nutritional content. Ask students to evaluate which snacks are the most healthful for a school-age child.

Discuss

Memory becomes more controlled during middle childhood than early childhood. What factors determine the effectiveness of a child's memory? What improvements are observed during the middle childhood years?

Reflect

As a school-age child, which type of motivation, *intrinsic* (personal desire to achieve) or *extrinsic* (rewards and recognition), played a greater role in your performance on academic tasks? How important is the desire to succeed in the school-age child?

Workplace Connection

The classroom teacher, physical education instructor, school nurse, social worker, and principal may all play a role in parent communications concerning obesity in a child. Have students consult each of these professionals for suggestions on how to approach parents to discuss and find solutions for dealing with a child's obesity. Ask students to write a sample of a tactful, professional, and informative dialog they might have with the parent to address the child's problem. Have students record possible parent reactions and their response to them.

Discuss

What cognitive abilities help children become better problem solvers? How could these abilities be useful during a group project or assignment?

Vocabulary

Have a student volunteer define the term *rehearsal*. How does using the rehearsal technique assist school-age children to remember information?

Resource

Conservation Tasks, color transparency CT-7, TR

Vocabulary

Have a student volunteer define the terms *operation* and *concrete operations*. When do children first begin to use concrete operations?

attention on the important aspects of a task. They can scan detailed tasks and decide what must be done first. These changes allow thinking skills to become more refined. School-age children are better at processing information. As a result, they are better problem solvers.

To remember information, school-age children often use a technique called rehearsal. **Rehearsal** involves the repetition of information after it is used. The following example will illustrate rehearsal. Bobby is a typical six-year-old. He is able to tell you his address and telephone number. In addition, he knows his grandmother's telephone number and those of several of his friends. His neighbor, Alice, cannot understand how Bobby can remember all of this information at his age.

Bobby uses rehearsal. Bobby usually writes the phone numbers down. While recording the numbers, you can see his lips moving. Then he repeats the numbers many times. His memory is improved by this type of organization and process.

Mental Operations

There are changes in reasoning and thinking during middle childhood. Gradually, school-age children change the way they process information. During the preschool years, children relied totally on what they saw or perceived. Sometimes their perceptions were flawed. Now their perceptions are more accurate because they begin to use logical thinking. An **operation** is defined as the manipulation of ideas based on logic rather than perception. Between seven and eight years of age, children enter the stage of *concrete operations*. This means they use logic, but it is based on what they have experienced or seen.

Because they can now use logic in their mental operations, children learn several new concepts during the middle years.

These include the concepts of conservation, seriation, and classification.

Conservation

Children gradually acquire the concept of conservation. **Conservation** means that change in position or shape of substances does not change the quantity. If nothing is added or taken away, the amount stays the same. Such properties as weight, length, mass, and volume do not change. The appearance, however, may change. A child's understanding of the principle of conservation can be tested with liquids, a series of objects, and pliable substances.

To illustrate the conservation of liquids, show a child two identical glasses. Fill each glass with the same amount of liquid. Ask the child if the two glasses have the same amount of liquid, and the child will say that they do. Next, pour the liquid from one glass into a taller, thinner glass. Again ask the child if the two glasses have the same amount of liquid. Until about seven years of age, the child will probably say that the taller glass contains more liquid. Between seven and eight, when children enter the stage of concrete operations, they will say that the amount of liquid has not changed. Their logic has overruled their perception.

You can test a child's understanding of the conservation of length by using a series of identical objects, such as pennies. Place 10 pennies in two rows of 5 each. Place the rows side by side. Ask the child if the number of pennies in each row is the same. The child will agree that the two rows contain the same number of pennies. Next, spread the pennies apart in one of the rows. If the child is at the concrete level of operations, the child will say that the longer row still has the same number of pennies. If the child says that the one row has more pennies, the child is focusing only on the dimension of length. Rather than using logic, the child is relying only on perception.

Meeting Special Needs

Have gifted students conduct research on the work of Jean Piaget, 1896-1980, and his influence on the development of learning theories. Ask students to include information about his studies with children, particularly about conservation. What experiments did he perform to clarify his theory of conservation? How can teachers, parents, and caregivers apply this information to define reasonable expectations for a child's cognitive development? Have students write a one-page report of their findings.

A child's understanding of the concept of mass can also be tested. Show the child two balls of modeling dough that are the same size and shape. Ask the child if the two balls have the same amount of dough. The child will say yes. Then flatten one ball of modeling dough, and repeat your question. The child who understands conservation will note that the amount of dough is still the same.

Figure 8-7 shows several conservation tasks. It lists the questions to ask children to test their understanding of conservation. Those children who have not reached the stage of concrete operations will respond by saying no. If the children respond by saying yes, they have reached the concrete operations stage.

Seriation

Seriation is the ability to arrange items in an increasing or decreasing order based on weight, volume, or size. Like conservation, seriation typically emerges between the ages of six and eight years of age. To illustrate, you may provide a child with a set of sticks of different lengths. Then ask the child to arrange the sticks from the shortest to the longest. Preschool children will lay the sticks haphazardly. Most school-age children will lay the sticks in an orderly fashion from shortest to longest as requested.

Seriation can also involve sequencing the events in a story. After hearing a story, the child should be able to recall the sequence of events. As a result, the child will be able to retell the story. Likewise, following a recipe involves seriation. After preparing a simple recipe, the child should be able to recall the preparation steps.

Classification

Simple **classification** is the ability to group objects by common attributes, such as

8-7

Conservation Task

Present	Change	Ask
liquid		Is there still the same amount of water in each glass?
number		Are there still the same amount of dimes?
substance		Is there still the same amount of play dough?

You can determine a child's understanding of conservation by asking these questions.

Vocabulary

Have student volunteers define the terms *seriation* and *classification*. Ask students to compare the meanings of the two words.

Activity

Ask students to test a school-age child's ability in seriation by reading a comic strip. Then have students cut the strip into individual boxes and ask the child to put them back together in the correct order. Students may vary the activity for older children by not reading the story first.

Note

An advanced understanding of classification is called *class inclusion* or *multiple class membership*. An older school-age child may be able to understand how objects may have several characteristics that put them in more than one classification at the same time.

Resource

Testing Mental Operations, Activity D, SAG

Workplace Connection

High school students in the early childhood education curriculum may have opportunities to work with school children in the before- and after-school programs in their school district or area. Contact your school district office or child care programs to see if they offer internships to vocational students. Arrange a field trip to visit a program with the class. What requirements must students meet before they can be considered for employment?

Activity

Ask students to compare several samples of writing by school-aged children to the writing of high school students. Have students check for differences in grammar, vocabulary selection, sentence structure, spelling, and clarity. Have students share their findings with the class.

Vocabulary

Have a student volunteer define the term *social comparison*. What effect can making social comparisons have on a school-age child?

Discuss

What effect does the increasing time spent with peers have on the development of a school-age child's self-concept? What role does the family still play in the child's social and emotional development at this stage?

size, color, shape, pattern, or function. The typical preschooler can group objects by one attribute only. For instance, if given a group of different-colored shapes, the preschooler could sort by either color or shape. During the early school-age years, children can mentally handle two aspects of the problem, such as color and shape. For instance, they can sort blue squares into one pile and blue circles into another.

Language

The ability to communicate improves gradually throughout middle childhood. Comparing language development to the preschool years, changes are more subtle. The child's vocabulary doubles between the ages of 6 and 12. As they learn to read, they learn many new words each day. Grammar skills improve. They learn sentence structure, using pronouns, plurals, and tense properly. Children during this stage are also moving from using only oral expression to using both oral and written expression.

One form of language play for school-age children is telling riddles and jokes. Cognitive development is linked to humor. Language skills can improve through the use of humor, 8-8.

8-8

School-age children begin to develop a sense of humor.

Social-Emotional Development

School-age children are growing in self-understanding. Their self-concept is forming, which affects their self-esteem. They are experiencing many new emotions and becoming more aware of the feelings of others.

Social relationships become more complex during middle childhood. By choice, children in this stage are spending less time with their parents and more time with peers. Friendships are becoming more important. The family, however, still plays an important role in supporting the child's development.

Self-Concept

As children enter school, they start to take a closer look at the world around them. They begin to make social comparisons. **Social comparison** is a process where people define themselves in terms of the qualities, skills, and attributes they see in others. Personal strengths and weaknesses are identified as a result of this comparison. A self-concept is formed. Self-concept is the view a person has of himself or herself. Though the child's self-concept has been forming since infancy, school-age children are more aware of who they are.

School-age children can describe their strengths and weaknesses in very concrete terms. To illustrate, Luis is seven years old. Recently, his teacher asked him to describe himself. He said, "My name is Luis. I am a boy, and I live in Breckenridge, Colorado. I have brown eyes, black hair, and am tall. My hobbies are biking and skiing. I am good at them. I am not as good using the computer. I swim at the recreation center with my friends. My friends like me. I try to be helpful to them. My teacher says that I am a good speller, so I help my friends with their spelling."

Luis's self-description refers to his sex, physical appearance, and some social

Putting Technology to Use

Have students conduct an Internet search for information about the effect of poverty on a child's social and emotional development. For example, what research is available concerning aggression and depression in a child affected by poverty? What available programs address this problem? What challenges does childhood poverty present to schools and communities? Have students discuss their findings in class.

comparisons. Luis, like other children his age, has extended the number of people he is looking to for information. During the preschool years, his references were primarily his family. Now his reference groups include classmates and teachers. The feedback he receives from these individuals influences his self-concept.

Self-Esteem

Self-esteem is the belief that you are worthwhile as a person. While preschool children usually have very high levels of self-esteem, this sometimes changes in middle childhood. To have healthy self-esteem, school-age children need to believe in themselves. By continually evaluating themselves, some children lose their confidence. Subtle messages echoed by adults and peers can promote or undermine self-esteem. Figure 8-9 shows areas in which children evaluate themselves.

As a teacher, you can play an important role in promoting children's self-esteem. A warm, nurturing attitude is important. Avoid making comparisons among children. By avoiding comparisons, you will be helping children develop confidence in their own abilities. Children feel better about themselves.

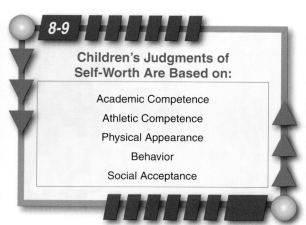

8-9

Children's Judgments of Self-Worth Are Based on:

Academic Competence

Athletic Competence

Physical Appearance

Behavior

Social Acceptance

School-age children judge themselves on these factors.

Accomplishments need to be viewed in relation to a child's efforts and ability. In almost every classroom, at least one child has learned helplessness. These children think, no matter how hard they try, they cannot be successful. You will spot them immediately. When faced with new experiences or challenges, they give up quickly. Before they make an effort to try, they say "I don't know how" or "I can't do that."

Help children during middle childhood avoid feelings of helplessness. Encourage them to persist at difficult tasks. Make them believe that with more effort they can overcome failure. Say "I know you can do this if you try harder." Likewise, celebrate when these children do succeed, even in small ways. Provide them with additional feedback on why they were successful.

Understanding Others

With experience and maturity, school-age children make major advances in understanding others. They are developing **empathy**—the ability to understand the feelings of others. At the same time, they are feeling compassion toward others. **Compassion** is being aware of others' distress and wanting to help them, 8-10.

School-age children can describe another person's feelings and personality traits. Prior to this time, children used only physical descriptions of others. For example, when Ben was a preschooler, his grandmother asked him to describe his teacher. He said, "She has brown hair and brown eyes. She wears glasses and she is pretty." When Ben's grandmother asked him to describe his teacher as an eight-year-old, the description went beyond physical traits. He said, "He is really a happy person. He smiles a lot and says things like 'good job.' Sometimes he gets mad, like when Brian is being a jerk. Then he gets angry with him."

Ben has developed the ability to see another's viewpoint. His ability to imagine what his teacher was feeling or thinking

Vocabulary

Have a student volunteer define the term *self-esteem*. Why does the self-esteem a child possessed as a preschooler often change during middle childhood?

Reflect

Did any of your elementary school teachers ever make comparisons between your work and another student's? Did the comparison motivate you and increase your self-esteem or cause negative feelings and loss of confidence?

Resource

Judgments of Self-Esteem, reproducible master 8-1, TR

Vocabulary

Have student volunteers define the terms *empathy* and *compassion*. Ask students to compare the meanings of these two words.

Workplace Connection

Have students interview a tutor or an educator with a tutoring center or service. How does tutoring help a child achieve academic success? How does the instructor or program help the child overcome feelings of helplessness and failure?

Does the tutor work in cooperation with the classroom teacher in planning a program for the child? Have students prepare a list of additional questions prior to the interview. Ask students to write their findings in a brief report.

Reflect

Has anyone ever asked you if you were in a bad mood? How does the ability to imagine what another person is feeling or thinking help you get along with others?

Resource

Friendships During the School-Age Years, reproducible master 8-2, TR

Discuss

Choosing friends becomes more selective during middle childhood. What factors influence the selection of friends at this age?

Resource

Handling Peer Rejection, reproducible master 8-3, TR

8-10

School-age children are becoming more aware of the feelings of others.

is developing. This is an important developmental milestone. Getting along with others throughout life is dependent on being able to understand another person's point of view. Studies show that children with poor social skills have trouble identifying other people's thoughts and feelings.

Friendships

During the school-age years, friendships take on greater importance. During preschool, a friend was a convenient playmate who shared toys. Now, choosing friends becomes a more selective process.

Gender often influences the selection of a friend. Most school-age children choose close friends of the same sex. Children with common interests usually become friends.

These friendships are important to children. A friend is a person who shares important thoughts and feelings. A friend offers companionship and emotional support. Emotional commitment is learned through these early friendships.

Some children seem to be particularly well liked by other children. These children are friendly to others. They also show sensitivity and have good communication skills. During middle childhood, peer acceptance can be influenced by appearance and behavior.

Other children are rejected and avoided by their peers. They are not included in after-school functions or invited to parties. They also tend to be ignored during recess and lunch. These children often lack self-control and act aggressively toward others. They may be disruptive or hostile.

Without friendships, the child does not receive the important benefits of interacting with peers. This can be traumatic for some children. Lack of self-esteem, the inability to develop social skills, and loneliness are a result. These children often lack confidence in their abilities. They need special help to recognize and overcome their behavior problems.

Peer Group Activities

Peer group activities play an important role in the social development of school-age children. They may join 4-H clubs, religious groups, Girl Scouts, or Boy Scouts. In these groups, they learn how to cooperate with others to achieve goals, and they learn rules of group behavior.

Gender Differences

Informal groups are often single-sex during the early school-age years. See 8-11. The girls cluster with other girls. The boys, too, prefer other boys. Mixed-sex groups may form

Portfolio Project

Ask students to research peer group activities that exist in the area for school-age children. Examples may include 4-H Clubs, Boy Scouts, Girl Scouts, sports activities, dance programs, and gymnastics programs. Have students compile a list of all the activities including a brief statement about each program, cost to participate, membership or participation requirements, location and length of meetings, and adult contact. Distribute the list to families through a newsletter or bulletin. Have students place a copy of the newsletter or bulletin in their portfolio.

Friends tend to be of the same sex.

for talking, eating, or working on projects in the classroom. Boys and girls may enjoy playing kick ball or other games together.

Teasing frequently occurs between boys and girls. Boys love to interrupt the girls' play. When this occurs, the girls respond by chasing them away or tattling to adults.

At school, gender often creates boundary differences in play areas and space. Boys tend to control large fixed spaces that are used for team sports. Studies show they control almost 10 times more space than girls. Space occupied by girls is usually located closer to the school building.

Activity preferences between girls and boys exist. While girls enjoy jumping rope, playing hopscotch, and doing tricks on the jungle gym, boys prefer competitive sports, such as basketball, football, and baseball.

Girls' play involves more taking turns and cooperating with others. Compared to boys, they are often interacting in pairs or small groups. Girls are not as open as boys. They have more select relationships in which they share secrets.

Games with Rules

Can you remember your middle childhood years? Chances are you were enjoying organized games with rules. Rules determine what roles children can play and their standards for conduct. If you were like most children, during recess you were playing hide-and-seek, red rover, and blind man's bluff. You probably played tag, jump rope, and hopscotch. Basketball, soccer, and softball were played during physical education classes.

These games are important for children's development. They are a medium for developing negotiation skills and learning to cooperate. Games also encourage children to take another person's perspective. From this, children learn why rules are important. Children often spend as much time working out the rules for a game as playing the game.

In recent decades, there has been a decrease in the amount of time children spend in child-organized games. More time is being devoted to television, computers, video games, and adult-organized sports. As a result, children are not as physically fit. In addition, they do not have as many opportunities to learn to follow rules.

Team Sports

With improvement in their physical skills, both girls and boys enjoy participating in team sports. Soccer, football, softball, swimming, gymnastics, and basketball are common, 8-12. The most popular team sport is baseball. Through participation in team sports, children often develop lifelong habits that contribute to a healthful lifestyle.

By participating in competitive sports, children benefit in many ways. These include the following:

- They learn teamwork skills.

- They learn to get along with their peers.

- They benefit from the mental and physical exercise.

- The activities bring enjoyment.

- A pattern for a healthful lifestyle begins to form.

Discuss

What do school-age children gain from playing games with rules? What are some social skills children practice while playing games?

Resource

Team Sports, transparency master 8-4, TR

Reflect

Did you ever play a game as a school-age child in which someone interpreted the rules differently from those generally accepted by the rest of the children? How was the situation handled? What was the outcome?

Resource

Observing Eight-and Nine-Year-Olds, Activity B, OG

Cross-Curricular Activity

Health
Using print or Internet sources, ask students to research current statistics on the amount of time school-age children spend on sedentary activities such as playing video games, watching television, or using the computer. What is the recommended amount of time children should spend on active and passive activities to remain healthy and physically fit? Have students write a report of their findings. Allow time for students to read their reports in class.

Enrich

Divide the class into two groups. Have the groups debate the pros and cons of mixed gender competitive sports teams, such as baseball, soccer, and basketball, during middle childhood. Have student s compare the possible viewpoints of the participants, their families, and the coaches.

Discuss

How important are warm-up exercises and stretching prior to physical activity? What strategies are needed to prevent sports injuries at this age?

Resource

Observing Ten- and Eleven-Year-Olds, Activity C, OG

Vocabulary

Have student volunteers define the terms *moral development* and *morality*. What is the most important aspect for children in acquiring morality?

Resource

Beliefs About Middle Childhood, Activity E, SAG

8-12

School-age children enjoy participating in team sports.

There are also drawbacks to participating in team sports. There is no safe sport. School-age children can be injured. Bumps, bruises, and scrapes are common injuries. The most serious injuries are head and neck injuries, which usually result from playing football. To reduce injuries, children need to be instructed on the safe use of equipment. They also need to be taught the importance of conditioning activities, such as stretching and warm-up exercises.

Critics of adult-organized sports teams claim they resemble more work than play for children. As the focus is often on winning, children feel pressure from their peers, parents, and coaches to win at all costs. Since adults often control the game, children may not be developing decision-making and leadership skills.

Moral Development

Moral development is the process of acquiring the standards of behavior considered acceptable by a society. **Morality** involves understanding and using accepted rules of conduct when interacting with others. Standards of behavior become internalized.

Children learn moral behavior by interacting with others, 8-13. Preschoolers begin to learn acceptable behavior through the use of rewards and punishment. Some behaviors bring rewards, such as praise or attention. They learn to repeat these behaviors. Other behaviors bring punishment. They have not yet internalized any standards of behavior, but they learn how to avoid punishment.

Children in middle childhood are more aware of the world around them and more sensitive to the feelings of others. As they become more concerned about others' needs, they want to help them. This desire influences their moral development. They begin to internalize rules of conduct.

8-13

Children during middle childhood internalize standards of behavior they learn from their parents and others.

Service Learning Activity

Ask students to design and carry out community-based service learning activities school-age children would be able to perform. These may include making, collecting, and distributing items to adult care centers, early childhood centers, homeless shelters, and pet shelters. They may also offer services such as lawn raking and community cleanup. Have students record the feelings of the school-age children both before and after their participation to discover their ideas on helping others.

Summary

Middle childhood refers to the span of years between ages 6 and 12. Physical development during middle childhood slows down from the rapid pace of earlier years. Children grow about two to three inches per year during this time period and gain about five to seven pounds per year. Gross-motor skills are improving, including greater speed and accuracy of movement. Fine-motor skills improve the neatness and accuracy of writing.

Though this is often one of the healthiest periods for children, several chronic illnesses may surface during middle childhood. Ulcers, asthma, and diabetes may develop. Vision and hearing need to be checked regularly so that any problems can be corrected. Obesity is becoming more common among school-age children.

Cognitive development continues as children begin to think using logic and symbols. They no longer rely only on what they see or perceive. They can process and recall information more readily. Memory improves and their attention span is longer. Because they can now use logic in their mental operations, children learn several new concepts during the middle years. These include the concepts of conservation, seriation, and classification. Vocabulary and grammar skills also improve dramatically.

Self-esteem develops in important ways for school-aged children. As children take a closer look at the world around them, they begin to make social comparisons. Their strengths and weaknesses become more apparent to them. They also begin to develop feelings of empathy and compassion toward others. Friendships and group activities take on greater importance during the school-age years. Most of these relationships are with friends of the same sex.

Morality begins to develop during middle childhood as standards of behavior become internalized.

Review and Reflect

1. True or false. By 12 years of age, most girls have surpassed boys in height and weight.

2. List the motor skills in which girls generally outperform boys.

3. True or false. A person who is nearsighted can see close objects better than distant objects.

4. List three factors that may lead to obesity in children.

5. Explain how the way children process information changes from the preschool years to the school-age years.

6. Describe a test that you could use to check a child's understanding of the concept of conservation.

7. How does language change during the school-age years?

8. Explain the relationship between self-concept and self-esteem.

9. School-age children begin to develop empathy. What does this mean?

10. Describe the gender differences in play areas and space.

11. Why are team sports important for children's development?

12. True or false. Morality involves the internalizing of accepted rules of behavior.

6. (Student response.)
7. The child's vocabulary doubles between the ages of 6 and 12. Grammar skills improve. They learn to read. They learn sentence structure, using plurals, pronouns, and tense properly. They use both oral and written expression.
8. Self-concept is the view a person has of himself or herself. This affects self-esteem. Self-esteem is the belief that you are a worthwhile person.
9. Empathy is the ability to understand the feelings of others.
10. Boys tend to control large fixed spaces that are used for team sports. They control almost 10 times more space than girls. Space occupied by girls is located closer to the school building.
11. They learn teamwork skills. They learn to get along with their peers. They benefit from exercise. Their activities bring enjoyment. A pattern for a healthful lifestyle begins to form.
12. true

Review and Reflect **Answer Key**

1. true
2. motor skills that require balance, coordination, flexibility, or rhythmic movement (examples include playing hopscotch, dancing, and skipping)
3. true
4. (List three:) overweight parents, environment, family stress, physical inactivity
5. Preschool children rely on what they see or perceive. During middle childhood, children begin to think mentally using logic and symbols. They begin to use logical thinking instead of perception.

Apply and Explore

1. Visit a local elementary school during recess and observe the motor skills of school-age children.

2. Visit an after-school program. Observe the children's social interactions and peer groups.

3. Compile a list of resources for school-age children in your community.

Cross-Curricular Link

Math

1. Visit an after-school program. Bring along 10 pennies and two balls of play dough. With six- and seven-year-olds, assess their ability to conserve number and mass.

Technology

2. Visit the Web site for the National Network for Child Care (www.nncc.org) to review development during middle childhood.

Workplace Link

Investigate the careers of *occupational therapist* and *occupational therapist assistant*. What do professionals in occupational therapy do? What education and training is needed for these careers? If there is an occupational therapy program in your area, interview a professional about his or her work with school-age children.

You will observe many developmental differences as children enter the school-age years.

PART

2

Creating a Safe and Healthful Environment

Your primary goal as an early childhood teacher is to keep children safe and healthy. Creating a safe, healthful environment requires careful planning and preparation.

As you read this part, you will discover how to arrange the space in a center to promote safety as well as learning and fun. You will also learn criteria for choosing toys and equipment that will safely help meet your program goals.

This part gives safety objectives to help you prevent accidents and illness. It also makes you aware of your responsibilities in detecting and reporting child abuse and neglect.

Guidelines for planning and serving nutritious meals and snacks are provided in this part. Also, procedures are given for handling such medical emergencies as wounds, burns, and fevers.

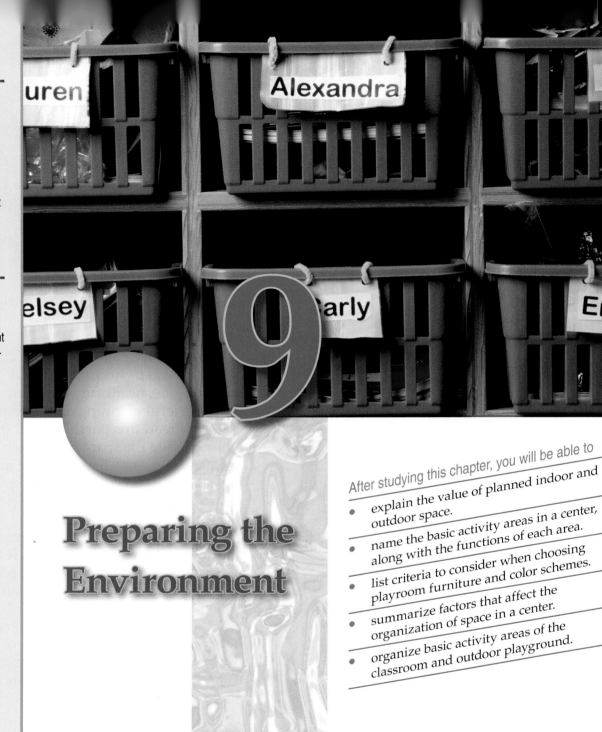

Discuss

In what ways do you think the containers in the chapter opening photo help prepare the environment? How do you think you might identify personal space for children who cannot yet read their names?

Discuss

Review the chapter objectives before reading the chapter. Why is a prepared environment important in early childhood education?

9

Preparing the Environment

After studying this chapter, you will be able to

- explain the value of planned indoor and outdoor space.
- name the basic activity areas in a center, along with the functions of each area.
- list criteria to consider when choosing playroom furniture and color schemes.
- summarize factors that affect the organization of space in a center.
- organize basic activity areas of the classroom and outdoor playground.

154

Terms to Know

isolation area
staff room
audiovisual board
acoustic material
cubbies
cool colors
warm colors
traffic pattern
sensory table
stationary equipment

Michiko is running. Susie is hiding. No one saw Mary take the fish out of the bowl. There is no place for Jose to play with the blocks. The behavior of children in this classroom is affected by the way the space is arranged.

In another classroom, the space is carefully organized. All the children are engaged in constructive play. The layout encourages active exploration, independent learning, and communication. There are few, if any, behavior problems. Heather is smiling. Fred is looking at books in a quiet corner of the classroom. At the same time, Wong and his friends are building a large block structure.

In a developmentally appropriate, well-organized environment, children grow and learn. The teacher is responsible for creating a pleasing environment that is shaped by the needs and interests of the children. It should be designed to promote self-help and independent behavior.

Classroom arrangement reflects program quality. It also provides clues about expected behavior. A well-planned setting usually promotes interesting play, provides children with choices, and reduces behavior problems. It should encourage interaction with other children and adults, as well as active

exploration. Well-planned space is arranged based on the children's temperaments, developmental needs, interests, experiences, and program goals. The classroom should also be attractive and inviting.

A nurturing, safe environment is critical for children's social, emotional, physical, and cognitive development. Children need space to build, move, sort, create, pretend, spread out, work, and interact with friends. They need diverse materials in sufficient quantity to keep them actively involved. They need a place to be quiet, be active, talk, and move. Space affects the activity level of children. The choices children make and the way they carry out their choices are also affected by space. Space can even affect the children's concentration and the length of time they will remain with one activity. Therefore, space should be arranged according to children's needs and interests. However, the space should also be convenient for the staff. See 9-1.

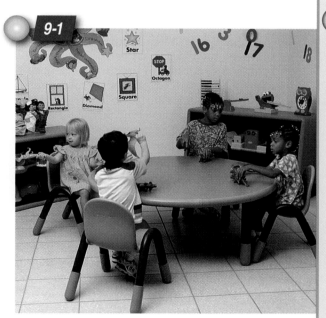

Quality early childhood programs have ample space for children and teachers.

Vocabulary

Have students review the *Terms to Know* list. Ask students to look up unfamiliar terms in the glossary before reading the chapter.

Reflect

Think about what a developmentally appropriate, well-organized environment tells you about a program. What may result when a classroom is not designed to meet children's developmental needs?

Discuss

What are the effects of space on the children in a classroom? What are the effects on the teacher?

Meeting Special Needs

Provide an outline of the chapter with all the chapter headings for special learners. Students should fill in each section of the outline as the material is covered in class with a sentence or two about the content. Review the special learners' IEPs to decide if any modifications should be made in presenting the chapter content.

Discuss

Why is it important to review the developmental objectives of the program before designing the space? Compare the differences that may exist between the rooms planned for two- and four-year-olds in terms of program objectives.

Reflect

The shelving shown in 9-2 allows easy access for children. Think about what skills and tasks may be reinforced in the early childhood classroom when easily accessible shelving is used for children.

Discuss

How does the number of caregivers or teachers in a room affect space planning? How does space affect the teacher's behavior?

Resource

Center Physical Space, Activity A, OG

Value of Planned Space

The early years are crucial for the cognitive development of children. Before arranging a classroom, review the developmental objectives of the program. For example, two-year-old children do not have refined large motor skills. To promote safety and motor development, they need large, open spaces. They need to be able to find adults when they need them. The classroom should be planned with these goals in mind.

An attractive, well-arranged classroom is welcoming and visually pleasing. It conveys a sense of order. It encourages children to use materials and do things for themselves. It respects the children's curiosity and nurtures a desire for exploring. It also molds their behavior. Boundaries found in this type of classroom make the children more responsible. They know where to find classroom materials. They also know where to return them when they are finished.

Safety is an important concern in planning space. When children feel safe, they feel free to learn. Open spaces must be provided so adults can supervise the entire room. The ratio of caregivers to children also affects safety. If the number of caregivers is low, the room arrangement should be simple to make supervision easier.

Studies have shown that the arrangement of space greatly affects teachers' behavior as well as children's. In centers with well-planned space, teachers were more friendly, sensitive, and warm to children. These teachers taught their children to respect others' rights and feelings. In centers with poorly-planned space, teachers were often more insensitive to their students.

The goals for a well-planned space include
- providing a physically safe environment for the children
- providing children with areas that promote cognitive, emotional, social, and physical growth
- providing an abundance of materials so children can make choices
- providing adults with a space that is easy to supervise
- providing space that is pleasing to the eye for both adults and children
- providing easy access to materials when needed so children are able to direct themselves, 9-2
- providing a space with high activity and low stress where children can work and play comfortably

Physical Space

The physical space of a center may be divided into seven main areas. These basic areas include the following:
- entrance
- director's office
- isolation area
- kitchen or kitchenette
- staff room

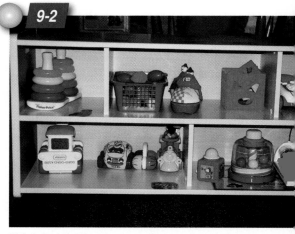

9-2

This infant-toddler classroom features low shelving units that allow children to choose their own activities and clean up after themselves.

Meeting Special Needs

Prepare a chart listing the seven goals for a well-planned space. Give students copies of the chart to use as a study tool. Pair special learners with volunteer students to review each of the goals. Volunteer students may also have special learners review the photos in 9-1 and 9-2 to help reinforce their understanding of the goals. Spend additional time in class discussing any goals that are difficult for special learners to understand.

- bathrooms
- classroom or playroom

Entrance

The entrance to the center should be attractive and appealing to children and adults, 9-3. Plants, the children's artwork attractively displayed, and a bulletin board for families will enhance the appearance. If space permits, chairs and a sofa are welcome additions for families who need to wait.

Director's Office

The director's office should be just inside the center's entrance. School records, children's records, and public relations material can be stored here. This office can also be used for family interviews and conferences. Some directors also have a small table in their offices for teachers' meetings and planning sessions.

9-3

This child care center has an entrance area that helps families feel welcome.

Isolation Area

Most states require centers to provide a special room or space for children who become ill or show signs of a communicable disease. This room, often called an **isolation area**, should contain a cot and a few toys. If the space is not available, a cot may be placed in the director's office when needed.

Kitchen

The size of a center's kitchen depends on the amount of daily food preparation. Even if meals are not served, most centers have a small area with a sink, refrigerator, and stove for preparing snacks. Regardless of the kitchen's use, the local health department personnel should inspect it. They can tell you if all legal requirements are being met.

Floor coverings in the kitchen should be easy to clean. Vinyl coverings and ceramic tile are recommended floor coverings for the kitchen, bathroom, and art area.

Staff Room

Adults need an area for their own use. This **staff room** should contain a locked storage space for personal belongings. A coat rack, sofa, and tables or desks should also be available. Most staff members prefer having a computer, telephone, professional journals, and curriculum guides available, too. Privacy is also important for the staff area. This area may be used for meeting with families or other staff members.

Bathrooms

Most states have laws requiring a certain number of toilets and sinks for a group of young children. Some states require at least one toilet for every 10 children. However, a higher ratio is more convenient. There are many times during the day that several children may have to use the bathroom at the same time.

Vocabulary

Have a student volunteer define the term *isolation area*. Why do many states require an isolation area in a child care center?

Enrich

Invite a representative from the local health department to discuss the rules and regulations for serving food in child care centers. Are any certifications needed to serve food? If so, are any courses available in the area to meet the criteria for certification? Have students prepare a list of additional questions to ask prior to the visit.

Activity

Ask student volunteers to test the water temperature of faucets used by the children in the preschool classroom. What is the recommended temperature of water for hand washing by children? Is the temperature in the classroom adjustable? Have students share their findings with the class.

Portfolio Project

Ask students to brainstorm ideas for bulletin boards located at a child care center's entrance. Topics might include parent information, seasonal or holiday themes, and highlights of children's activities. Have students create the bulletin boards on a rotating basis throughout the year. Conduct teacher and student evaluations on the effectiveness and attractiveness of each bulletin board. Ask students to photograph any bulletin boards they create for inclusion in their portfolio.

Note

Maria Montessori, 1870-1952, is generally recognized as the inventor of child-sized furniture. She felt it encouraged learning in a comfortable environment.

Enrich

Have students research their state's requirements for the amount of space needed per child in licensed child care centers. Ask students to measure the vocational preschool laboratory or a local child care center. Do the measurements meet state requirements? Have students share their findings in class.

Discuss

Compare the advantages and disadvantages of having the entire preschool classroom carpeted. What alternative materials can be used for flooring?

The size of the toilet fixture will vary with the size and age of the children. A group of two-year-old children would be comfortable with toilet fixtures 10 inches from the floor. Five-year-old children would find 13-inch toilet fixtures more comfortable.

If small toilets are unavailable, a sturdy wooden step can be used for smaller children. This same wooden step can be used in front of the sinks that are too high for children to reach.

For safety purposes, the water heater that supplies water to the children's bathroom should be set on low heat.

Bathroom flooring should be easy to clean. Tile is recommended. Also, it should not be slippery. Avoid having wax applied to the flooring in this area.

Indoor Environment

The classroom or playroom should be on the ground floor close to an exit. A rectangular room is the best shape as it allows for optimal supervision. This shape also allows for many more space arrangements than other shapes.

Studies show that aggression increases in programs that lack adequate space. Quality child care centers need to have enough space for children and a variety of materials and equipment. The recommended amount of space varies from state to state. It can range from 35 to 100 square feet of indoor space per child. The National Association for the Education of Young Children (NAEYC) recommends at least 35 square feet of free indoor space per child. This amount should not include hallways or space taken up by equipment, built-in cabinets, closets, or toilets.

Walls

All walls should be painted with lead-free, washable paint. Many teachers like to attach bulletin boards to the walls. This provides space to hang artwork and papers, as well as absorb sound, 9-4.

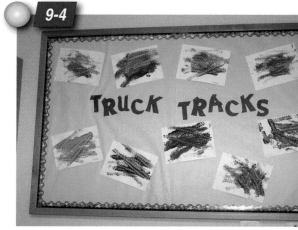

A brightly decorated bulletin board is a welcome addition to any classroom.

Chalkboards can also be attached to walls. They should be installed at the children's eye level.

Instead of bulletin boards and chalkboards, some centers use audiovisual boards. An **audiovisual board** can serve as a bulletin board, chalkboard, and movie screen. It is usually white, off-white, or beige. The disadvantage of the audiovisual board is that magnetic strips must be used to hold up objects when used as a bulletin board. These strips can be costly.

Floors

A recent trend for playroom floor coverings has been carpeting. Carpeting is easy to maintain. It also adds warmth and provides a sound cushion for noise control. Carpeting can also add visual appeal, comfort, warmth, and softness to a room. Use a tightly woven carpet that has a flat, firm surface. This will minimize balance problems for children while stacking blocks.

Windows

Windows in the playroom should be placed so children can see outside. Screens should be installed outside all windows. All windows should open in case of a fire.

Workplace Connection

Have students inspect several child care centers to discover how children's work is displayed on the classroom walls. What types of walls are used? How are bulletin boards and other media boards attached to the walls?

Ask students to research the cost of bulletin boards and bulletin board strips in education equipment catalogs. What other methods are available for display purposes? Ask student volunteers to share their findings in class.

Drapes or blinds may be used to help control light. They also add interest, softness, and color to a room. Drapes or blinds reduce glare, heating bills, and noise. One disadvantage of drapes is that they become soiled easily. This is caused by children brushing by them with dirty hands or art supplies.

For a different effect, you might wish to hang a valance above each window. This can be a nice addition to a classroom if the colors complement the decor. If you use valances instead of drapes, also use miniblinds or pleated shades to reduce glare.

Doors

Doors should be lightweight. To guard against injury, the doors should push out to open. Doorknobs should be low enough so children can reach them.

Acoustics

Studies show that noise affects children's behavior. For this reason, make an effort to use materials that reduce or eliminate noise.

Acoustic material is used to deaden or absorb sounds. Carpets, drapes, bulletin boards, pillows, stuffed toys, and sand are examples. Due to the physical makeup of these materials, noise can be reduced or eliminated. For instance, carpeting will absorb the sound of footsteps.

If the classroom is still noisy after the addition of draperies, carpeting, and bulletin boards, acoustical tile may need to be installed on the classroom ceiling. If possible, the ceiling should be 10 to 12 feet high to reduce noise and provide a feeling of spaciousness.

Temperature

Temperature is important in planning a comfortable environment for young children. They cannot attend to or process information in an uncomfortable environment.

Usually a temperature range of 68 to 70 degrees Fahrenheit will be comfortable.

When vigorous physical activities are planned, the temperature should be decreased. In order for children to be comfortable, adults may have to wear a sweater.

Humidity

Humidity, like temperature, influences the comfort of the environment. Usually a 40 to 60 percent relative humidity range is considered comfortable. To maintain comfort, the relative humidity should be decreased as the temperature rises.

Electrical Outlets

For safety purposes, electrical outlets should be above the children's reach. When outlets are not being used, safety caps should be inserted for protection. Many times a room arrangement will be influenced by the location of electrical outlets. For example, the music area would be located near an outlet so a record, tape, or CD player could be used. For the safety of the children and staff, do not use long electrical cords. These can cause someone to trip or fall. Because of this danger, many states ban the use of long extension cords in the classroom.

Furniture

Classroom or playroom furniture should be durable, washable, and stackable. Tables and easels should be adjustable. Then they can be adjusted to fit each child who may use them. To check if an easel is the proper height, have the child stand next to it. Ask the child to touch the middle of the easel pad. If the child has to bend or reach to touch the middle of the pad, adjust the easel.

Chair and table heights are checked in a different manner. Ask the child to sit on a chair. Then push it under the table. If the table and chair are suited to the child, there will be room between the bottom of the table

Vocabulary

Have a student volunteer explain the term *acoustics*. What types of acoustic material can be used to deaden or absorb sounds?

Discuss

Some child care programs are located in places of worship or community buildings that were not originally designed for use as a child care center. What strategies are necessary to safeguard children against the danger of inappropriately placed electrical outlets in these rooms?

Reflect

Stackable furniture for the child care room is convenient and allows greater use of space. What recommendations do you have for how high furniture should be stacked? How does this depend on the stability of the stack, size, and weight of the furniture? How does it depend on how close the stacked furniture is to where children will be playing?

Putting Technology to Use

Have students conduct an Internet search for information regarding materials used for window coverings that would help reduce the cost of energy to heat or cool a room. Which of these materials or types of coverings are appropriate for a child care center classroom? What are the advantages and disadvantages of each of these materials? Which would you prefer if you were in charge of selection? Have students write a brief summary of their findings.

Discuss

After reviewing pictures of a variety of tables from an educational furniture catalog, ask class members to discuss the advantages and disadvantages of each type or shape of table. Which tables would you choose for a room of two- and three-year-olds? Does your choice differ for a group of four- and-five-year-olds?

Resource

Meeting the Goals of a Well-Planned Space, Activity A, SAG

Discuss

Notice the well-organized shelves in 9-5. How might the colors of the various toy bins contribute to a child's development of classification skills?

Health and Safety

Sanitizing Surfaces

Keeping surfaces free from harmful bacteria and viruses can be a challenge in a child care setting. A simple sanitizing solution of ¼-cup household bleach to one gallon of water can be used for this purpose. You can use this mixture in spray bottles. After spraying the solution on a surface, wait two minutes before drying to kill any infectious agents. You can also allow surfaces to air dry since chlorine evaporates. Commercial sanitizers are also available; however, be sure to check your state and local guidelines regarding products that are safe to use around children, adults, and food.

and the child's knees. The child should be able to place his or her feet flat on the floor.

Chairs

Children's chairs are often used in the art, dramatic play, and dining areas. Chairs should always be the proper height for the children. Plastic, stackable chairs are preferred by most teachers. Plastic chairs have other advantages. They are light enough for the children to move, and they do not require refinishing. An adult-sized rocking chair may be used by children in the library or dramatic play area. The chair may also be used by adults as a special place to hold or comfort a child.

Tables

Classroom tables should be hard, smooth, and washable. The tables should be light enough to move. Most preschool teachers prefer tables that are large enough to seat four to six children. Rectangular tables are often preferred over round tables. The rectangular shape allows children to have their own space. This reduces the chance for aggression. Low, round tables are sometimes used in the library and dramatic play area.

Storage Units

Storage units should be organized for easy access of equipment and supplies. Blocks, books, art supplies, games, and other classroom materials are kept in storage units, 9-5. These units should be arranged to encourage children to independently remove and return materials. For flexibility, all storage units should have casters so they can be moved easily. The casters should be equipped with locks so they do not move accidentally. For units without casters, hardware can be bought and easily installed. Keep in mind that pegboard or corkboard

9-5

Blocks and other toys are well organized on this shelving unit.

Service Learning Activity

Some local nonprofit child care centers may be in need of preschool furniture or furniture repair. Have student volunteers offer to repair, sand, paint, or otherwise refurbish older furniture for the centers. Ask other student volunteers to contact local businesses or a secondhand store to donate equipment that may be in good repair but requires a good cleaning. Have students inspect all furniture for safety before it is used for children.

can be attached to exposed sides and backs of units. These can serve as bulletin boards.

Storage units should match the height of the children. The children must be able to reach the materials. Therefore, choose small, lightweight sections of cabinets.

If doors are needed on the storage units, sliding doors are best. When opened, swinging doors can cause safety hazards.

Lockers and Cubbies

Children can learn responsibility for their own belongings when they are provided personal storage space. Each child enrolled in the program should have a locker, 9-6. The lockers should be labeled with a photograph or other visual clue, depending on the age of

the child. Most lockers for preschool children are 10 to 12 inches wide and 10 to 15 inches deep. Each locker should contain a hook for hanging a coat.

The primary purpose of lockers is to store children's clothing. Finished artwork, library books, parent letters, and other valuable items must also be stored. For storage of these items, many lockers have a top section. These are often called **cubbies**. If the lockers do not have cubbies, containers can be stacked to store the children's belongings. See 9-7.

Lockers and cubbies should have a coat of varnish or paint. This coating will help prevent staining from muddy boots or wet paints. If lockers are painted, use a washable enamel paint.

Lockers should be placed near the entrance. This will save families time when

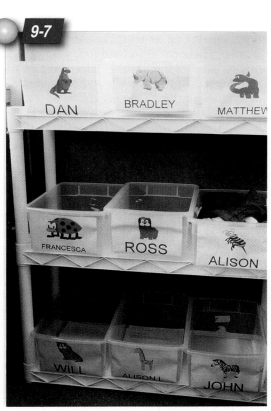

9-6

Use symbols on lockers to help young children identify their space.

9-7

Empty containers can be used to store children's small personal belongings.

Discuss

List advantages and disadvantages of open storage in the classroom. Are there any safety concerns regarding storage with swinging doors? What height should storage units be in the classroom?

Resource

Classroom Physical Space, Activity B, OG

Reflect

What suggestions would you give parents to assist with a child's independence in storing items such as coats, backpacks, and mittens in the child's locker or cubbie? What activities could encourage children to be more independent in storing their belongings?

Resource

Permanent Fixtures and Space, transparency master 9-2, TR

Workplace Connection

Ask students to survey the storage equipment in a child care center. What types of equipment are used? Are any areas in need of more equipment? Is the equipment in good repair? Are there any safety hazards present? What additional items might be added? Have students check equipment and storage catalogs for ideas. Ask students to write a brief summary of their findings. Allow time in class to discuss the findings.

Vocabulary

Ask student volunteers to define the terms *cool colors* and *warm colors*. Have students give examples of each.

Resource

Psychological Impact of Color, transparency master 9-3, TR

Reflect

Various colors are recommended for all the different areas of a pre-school room. However, no one room, especially a multipurpose space, could be painted with all the different colors. How can these colors be incorporated into the room besides being painted on walls?

Discuss

The image in 9-8 shows a colorful wall decoration on which a child's name can be changed weekly. What other suggestions for teacher-produced wall decorations do you have that will add color and interest to the classroom?

Resource

Responses to Color, Activity B, SAG

picking up children. It will save the class from being disrupted when someone must go to his or her locker. It will also save cleanup time during bad weather.

Color Choices for Child Care Centers

An attractive environment contributes to a child's well-being and appeals to the senses. The use of color can affect how teachers and children feel about their classroom. Colors can either calm or stimulate young children. Because of the emotional effects of color, select colors carefully. The goal should be to create a room that looks pleasant and feels spacious. This can be done using **cool colors**, such as blue, green, and purple. Cool colors make a room appear larger. They create a feeling of openness. **Warm colors** make a room seem smaller. These colors include red, yellow, and orange. Studies show that children prefer warm colors until about age six. After the age of six, they start to prefer cool colors.

Other factors affect color selection. These include the amount of available light in the room and the amount of time spent in the room. For example, if the room does not have much light available, a warm color will help the room appear brighter.

Since child care centers are active places and contain a lot of colorful materials, white is often used in classrooms. Children respond well to white. White rooms are perceived as clean and cool. White is an excellent color for the eating, isolation, administration, and reading areas. It is also a good color for the bathroom.

Light blue is often used in child care centers. Children respond to this color by feeling comfortable, soothed, and secure. Therefore, light blue is useful in the nap, reading, eating, and isolation areas.

Light green, like light blue and white, creates a positive response. It makes children feel calm, refreshed, peaceful, and restful. It is

useful for isolation, nap, reading, and eating areas.

Yellow makes people feel happy and cheerful. It is a good color in art and music areas. Playground equipment is often painted yellow.

Orange is a welcoming, forceful, energetic color. Its use should be limited. Clearly, an orange room can be overwhelming. However, orange can be used effectively in small areas, such as an entrance.

As with orange, the use of red should be limited, 9-8. Overuse of red can be too stimulating for children. Children may become overactive. Red is best used on indoor gross-motor equipment, outdoor equipment, and teaching aids designed to stimulate children.

The color purple can have a mournful effect. It is best used only as an accent color on equipment, bulletin boards, and teaching aids. When used as a wall color, limit its use to reading areas.

9-8

The use of red on this decoration creates interest without being overpowering.

Putting Technology to Use

Have students conduct an Internet search to research the impact of color on learning performance. For example, what is the effect of color on eye fatigue, productivity, and accuracy? What is the difference between selecting colors for function rather than for aesthetic appeal? Is there any validity to the effect of color on blood pressure and on instances of aggressiveness by students? Allow time for students to discuss their findings in class.

Factors That Affect Space Organization

An organized classroom can inspire children to take part in the activities of the day. The space should be arranged to define the scope and limits of activities. Space will also affect the children's use of and care of materials. Therefore, the space must provide for proper learning experiences.

When planning classroom space, many factors should be considered. These factors will greatly affect how the classroom is organized. They include licensing requirements, program goals, group size, scale, and traffic patterns.

Licensing Requirements

All states have their own licensing requirements for child care centers. You will need to know your state's requirements before you begin planning classroom space. Requirements vary from state to state. However, some common requirements exist. For example, they all require a minimum number of fire extinguishers. Also, all exits must be clear, and entrance doors must open to the outside. In addition, a minimum number of square feet of space must be available for each child.

Program Goals

A program's goals should be based on the children's abilities, age, and skills. The goals a teacher selects should represent the major stages of development and growth. (These stages were discussed in Chapters 5, 6, 7, and 8.) The environment, as well as planned classroom activities, should stimulate growth and development.

Caregivers concerned with all developmental areas might select the following program goals:

- to promote a positive self-concept
- to promote independence
- to promote problem-solving skills
- to promote fine-motor coordination
- to promote gross-motor coordination
- to promote self-control
- to promote language skills
- to promote prosocial behavior
- to promote an appreciation of cultural diversity

After the goals for the children are listed, review each goal. Decide how each goal will be supported by the classroom environment. For instance, most teachers set a goal to develop independence in children. The arrangement of the room can help children achieve this goal. Materials, locker hooks, and shelving units should all be within easy reach for the children. This will encourage children to act without help from adults in many cases. Chart 9-9 lists a number of ways to meet various program goals.

Program goals should also reflect state licensing requirements. Therefore, if the state requires that children receive one meal and two snacks each day, a program goal might state that children receive nutritious meals and snacks. Some states even state how many toys are needed in the classroom.

Group Size

Group size is an important factor to consider when arranging space. A large number of children crowded into a small area will cause problems. Children are likely to become upset and fight more when crowded.

Reflect

Think about how knowledge of factors affecting space organization can help you organize a classroom that can inspire children to take part in activities and provide for proper learning experiences.

Note

Have current copies of state licensing requirements for child care centers available in the classroom for students to review.

Discuss

After looking over the program goals on this page, explain what is involved in promoting *prosocial behavior*. Why should children learn to appreciate *cultural diversity*?

Workplace Connection

Arrange for students to tour an area child care center. Prior to the visit, ask students to create a checklist to determine if common state licensing requirements are being met. Possible questions on the checklist may include: How many fire extinguishers are present? Where are the fire extinguishers located? Are all of the center exits clear? Do all doors open to the outside? Are space requirements being met? Have students record their responses during the tour. Discuss the findings and compare them to state licensing requirements.

Reflect

Imagine you are organizing a classroom for three-year-olds. Think about ways in which you can arrange the classroom environment to promote independence.

Discuss

What materials might be used in the classroom to promote problem-solving skills? How often should materials be rotated to create interest? Why should a variety of materials be provided?

Resource

Goals and Space, Activity C, OG

9-9

How Goals Are Supported by the Environment

Goal	How Goal Is Supported by Environment
To promote independence	Similar materials are stored together. Drawers, shelves, and containers are labeled with outlines of contents. Materials and equipment are easily accessible to children. Coat hooks are low enough for children to hang their own clothing. Individual storage is provided for each child.
To promote a positive self-concept	Equipment is developmentally appropriate. Children's work is displayed. Unstructured materials are available in each area. A variety of materials are available for children to choose.
To promote problem-solving skills	Equipment is developmentally appropriate. Open-ended materials, such as blocks, are available. A variety of materials are available for children to choose. Materials are rotated to create interest.
To promote fine-motor coordination	A classroom area is devoted to manipulative equipment. Enough material to maintain children's interest is available. Materials are easily accessible to children. Materials are changed frequently to create interest.
To promote gross-motor development	A classroom area is devoted to gross-motor activities. An adequate amount of space is provided to encourage play. The traffic flow does not interfere with the children's use of materials. The area is located away from quiet activities.
To promote self-control	Enough space is provided for children to use materials in each classroom area. The classroom traffic flow permits children to work without interruption. Noisy areas are located away from quiet areas. Sufficient variety and quantity of materials are available in each area.
To promote language skills	A book display space is placed at children's eye level. Classroom materials are labeled. A wide variety of materials, including books, puppets, and tapes, are available.
To promote social skills	Boundaries between areas are defined with low shelving units. A sufficient amount of materials are available to encourage cooperative play. The area is set up for small groups of children.
To promote an appreciation of cultural diversity	Dolls, puppets, puzzles, picture books, posters, and bulletin board figures represent various cultural and ethnic groups. Music and musical instruments reflect various cultural and ethnic groups.

Defining program goals is the first step toward well-organized space.

Meeting Special Needs

Special learners may need some review of program goals and how the classroom environment can support each goal. Create a chart similar to the one in 9-9. List the program goals in the first column. Leave the second column blank. Pair student volunteers with special learners to review the program goals on the chart. Have students fill in the second column with additional ways in which the classroom environment will support each goal. Ask student volunteers to report areas where reteaching or further understanding is needed.

Likewise, a small number of children with too much space will also cause stress. Too much open space encourages children to run. You must strive to create an arrangement that will be the proper size for the group.

The more children, the more empty space is needed. A good rule of thumb is to plan between one-third and one-half of the classroom for open space. Also, the room arrangement needs to be fairly simple. Children will feel safe and secure in this arrangement.

Arrange shelving units and other furniture with group size in mind. A good arrangement allows teachers and children to move easily through the room. It also allows for teachers and children to see and be seen easily. This will promote a relaxed setting.

Scale

The classroom environment must be scaled to the size of its occupants. Child-sized furniture should be purchased or built. Bulletin boards, toilets, water fountains, sinks, pictures, and other items should all be at the children's level. One method to judge if the setting is scaled for children is for an adult to walk on his or her knees through the entire classroom. Anything positioned too high for the children should be noted and adjusted.

Traffic Patterns

The arrangement of a classroom centers around the **traffic pattern**. This is the way children move through the classroom area. Furniture should be arranged to create a useful traffic pattern. For instance, children should be able to walk from the art area to the blockbuilding area without going through the middle of the library area.

Program activities will affect traffic patterns. For example, most child care centers provide breakfast and lunch. These meals may be prepared on site or contracted.

Whichever plan is used, the food will likely be made in or delivered to a kitchen. For this reason, the kitchen should be near a delivery door and near the eating area of the classroom.

Organizing Basic Activity Areas

Classrooms arranged according to activity areas provide an ideal environment for active learning. Each activity area should clearly convey to the children what those choices are. For example, the art area should have an easel and art supplies. By displaying these materials in an inviting manner, the children will be aware of what is available to them. This gives them the chance to make their own choices.

Each activity area is a space of its own, and each area supports the program goals. Each area should be defined, but the space should be flexible. Shelves placed in *U* or *L* shapes can create boundaries for classroom areas. The shelves can be moved when the shape of the space needs to be changed.

Arrange activity areas by function. Think carefully of each area as wet or dry, active or quiet, 9-10. Wet and dry activities should be placed far away from each other. Sensory and science activities are examples of wet/active activities. Art, eating, and cooking are types of wet/quiet activities.

Active activities should take place far from quiet activities. Woodworking, blockbuilding, music, and dramatic play are all active activities. Each of these could disrupt a quiet activity. Sleeping, reading, and small manipulative play are all examples of quiet/dry activities.

Most teachers prefer to map out two or three possible area arrangements. This helps them see what will work best and why. Some room arrangement principles are shown in 9-11.

Remember that rather than being static, room arrangements must be dynamic.

Activity

Have students demonstrate that the preschool room setting is scaled for children by asking student volunteers to walk through the classroom on their knees. The volunteers can paint on the easel, take books from the bookshelves, and wash their hands at the sink. The rest of the class should observe and comment on any difficulties they perceive.

Discuss

Explain the differences among the following types of activity areas: *wet/active; wet/quiet; quiet/dry; active/dry.* Give examples of typical activities for each type.

Vocabulary

Define *traffic pattern.* How can traffic patterns affect safety in the classroom?

Discuss

Explain the difference between a *static* room arrangement and a *dynamic* room arrangement. Which is more appropriate for a preschooler? Why?

Meeting Special Needs

Review the five factors that affect space organization by creating a chart or overhead. List the five headings: licensing requirements, program goals, group size, scale, and traffic patterns. Ask special learners to fill in notes under each heading to be used as a study tool. Ask student volunteers to assist with the chart and the review. Spend additional time discussing any information that is especially difficult for special learners to understand.

Reflect

How could you create separate activity areas when shelves are fixed to the walls and cannot be used for defining space? How can furniture be used to help define activity areas in this case?

Resource

Arranging Basic Activity Areas, transparency master 9-5, TR

Activity

Have students create labels and signs for the preschool classroom. Signs can be decorative, but words and pictures should be clear. Remind students all printing should be done in a consistent style recognizable by preschoolers.

Resource

Organizing Activity Areas, color transparency CT-8, TR

9-10

Basic Activity Areas

Active

Science
Sensory { sand
water

Gross-Motor
Music
Woodworking
Blockbuilding
Dramatic play

Wet ←→ Dry

Art
Eating

Small manipulative
  play
Library
Sleeping
Private space
Writing center
Technology area

Quiet

Planning space requires that you consider each activity as it relates to other activities that take place in the same area.

Rearranging the classroom areas is necessary when the children's interests change. With changing interests, the addition and elimination of equipment and materials needs to be considered.

Introducing Activity Areas

Children require an introduction to the activity areas in the classroom. They need to learn what materials are in each area. They need to learn what activities take place in that area. They also need to learn the safety and cleanup rules of the area. In programs that operate for nine-month sessions, the children can be introduced to the areas at the start of the session. In programs that operate throughout the year, children can be introduced to each area when they first enroll in the program. Children who have been in the program for a time may help the teacher introduce the areas to new students.

Children need to learn the routine for using and replacing materials. Carefully arranging materials will enable the children

9-11

Principles of Room Arrangement

- Whenever possible, arrange areas around the edges of the room. This allows the center of the room to be used for traffic flow.
- Arrange shelving units so that the teacher can clearly view the entire room.
- Store objects together that are used for the same activities.
- Place the art area near a water source.
- Place quiet activities far away from active activities and traffic areas.
- Place dry activities far from wet activities.
- Provide open space for blockbuilding and group activities.
- Define areas by arranging storage units into U- or L-shapes.
- Provide a private space where children can be alone.

Keep these principles in mind when planning space. Would you add any guidelines to this list?

to help maintain the learning environment. To help children feel comfortable in using and moving about the areas, use labels and signs, 9-12. Labels and signs direct children's attention. This then helps children become

9-12

lockers and lunch-room

With the help of labels and signs, children will learn to move around their environment easily.

Workplace Connection

Have students review the *Principles of Room Arrangement* in 9-11. Arrange for students to visit a child care center classroom or survey the vocational preschool classroom. Ask students to determine if the principles are used in the room arrangement. Have students diagram or photograph the room's arrangement. Allow time for students to discuss how effective the arrangement is in meeting the principles. Offer suggestions for any alterations that would provide for more efficiency in the classroom.

self-directed learners. Labels and signs also encourage children to return materials to storage areas. Tape pictures to the storage areas to serve as reminders.

Blockbuilding Area

Blocks give children practice sorting, grouping, comparing, arranging, making decisions, cooperating, and role-playing. Therefore, this area should be well-equipped and well-defined. See 9-13.

The best location for blockbuilding should be on a carpeted area. Carpeting helps by reducing the noise level. Define the area with low cabinets. Allow enough room for building. Children will need room to build structures that go around, up, and out.

To stimulate play, provide items other than blocks in the blockbuilding area. Examples include plastic zoo and farm animals, people representing different cultures, traffic signs, wheeled toys, pulleys, and boxes.

Use the low cabinets that define the area for storage of materials. Make sure there are enough shelves to arrange the blocks according to shape. Place all blockbuilding materials at the children's eye level and within their reach.

Large, heavy blocks (and other heavy materials) should be placed on a bottom shelf or on the floor to avoid accidents. Save higher shelves for lightweight items. Label each shelf with the shape of the block that can be found there. Labels help children return the blocks to the correct shelf. Labels also provide matching practice and reduce cleanup time.

Art Area

Place the art area near a water source. Arrange the space so either groups or individuals can use the area. Use tables, chairs, easels, drying racks, and shelving units that are easy to clean and maintain. See 9-14. Label the shelves with the materials found there.

Dramatic Play Area

The dramatic play area is also known as the home living or housekeeping area. For younger children, this area should be arranged to look like a real home. A stove, refrigerator, table, chairs, sink, and doll bed are basic furniture you may wish to provide. Some centers even include child-sized sofas. Other props may be added. For instance, you

9-13

Blockbuilding areas are very popular. Make sure this area is well equipped and spacious.

9-14

Make efficient use of space by placing a drying rack for artwork overhead.

Discuss

What floor surface materials are available that would promote the encouragement of large blockbuilding play? What are the advantages and disadvantages of using carpeting in the blockbuilding area?

Note

Review your state's licensing standards for the blockbuilding area. Some states require that shelves for blocks be labeled with the shape of the blocks that go there.

Discuss

The art projects in 9-14 are held with clothes-pins on a line strung from overhead. Is this arrangement possible in your school's vocational preschool classroom? What other alternatives are available for display-ing children's artwork?

Meeting Special Needs

Have gifted students research the historical foundations and philosophies associated with block play by preschoolers. What are the viewpoints and contributions of each of the following regarding blockbuilding: Freidrich Froebel, Maria Montessori, Patty Smith Hill, and Carolyn Pratt? How has the Reggio Emilia Approach impacted block play? Have students write a detailed report of their findings.

Discuss

The dramatic play area is typically set up like a home. What additional equipment and props would be needed to outfit the area as a hair salon, bakery, fast-food restaurant, or post office?

Vocabulary

Have a student volunteer define the term *sensory table*. What materials or substances could be used in a sensory table besides water and sand?

Discuss

Where should the woodworking area be located? What items would you want to provide at the woodworking bench? How can you promote independence in the woodworking area?

may wish to provide dolls, kitchen utensils, cleaning tools, and dress-up clothes. For older children, other props may be added to help them extend their understanding of the world. For example, the area could be set up as a hair salon, bakery, fast food restaurant, or post office.

Sensory Area

The key piece of equipment in the sensory area is the **sensory table**. It is also known as a water or sand table, 9-15. The size of the table will depend on the amount of space available and depend on the age of the children. Two- and three-year-old children love the sensory appeal of water and sand. A sensory table can give the children practice interacting with others.

Not all centers have sensory tables. Some centers use plastic wading pools or washtubs. Whatever container is used, it should be placed near a water source. Children and teachers enjoy adding water to the sand to change the feeling.

Other items are often used in the sensory table. Provide rustproof spoons, shovels, sand pails, measuring cups, funnels, strainers, and other kitchen items. Place shelving units near

9-15

This sand table has extra built-in features to increase the children's enjoyment.

or under the table for storage. Items can also be stored in plastic buckets or laundry baskets.

Woodworking Area

After building wood sculptures, many children enjoy decorating them with paint. For that reason, locate the woodworking area near the art area, 9-16. For the children's safety, place this area outside the line of traffic.

Items you may wish to provide at the woodworking bench include safety goggles, tools, wood scraps, and styrofoam pieces. Hang a pegboard next to the wood bench, within children's reach. It can be used to hold tools. To encourage the return of tools, paint outlines of the tools on the pegboard. The children can replace tools by matching them with outlined shapes.

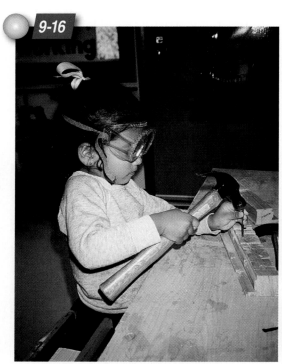

9-16

The woodworking table can hold the attention of children for extended time periods.

Workplace Connection

Directors of preschools and child care centers will expect the teachers and aides to keep the activity areas neat, organized, and supplied with appropriate materials. Assign students the tasks of cleaning and organizing these areas each week in the vocational preschool room. This may include toy sanitation; replacing puzzle pieces and other items from games and toy baskets; washing, repairing, and folding dramatic play clothes and costumes; and washing the easel, paintbrushes, and paint cups. Students will learn the responsibilities involved in the management of a preschool classroom.

Sleeping Area

Most preschool children rest or nap after lunch. In fact, most state's licensing rules and regulations require that children under age five rest or nap. Not all programs, however, have separate sleeping areas. For those that do not, a flexible room arrangement is key. Such an arrangement can be quickly and quietly altered during or immediately after lunchtime into a sleeping area. Allow sufficient space for sleeping. Some states require that two feet of open space exist between cots. Check your state's regulations.

Small Manipulative Area

The small manipulative, or small motor, area should be located in a dry, quiet area of the playroom. Table blocks, puzzles, plastic building pieces, parquetry blocks, stringing beads, lotto boards, sewing cards, and color cubes with pattern cards are some items you may wish to provide. These materials should represent various levels of difficulty. Many teachers also include math materials and equipment in this area. A table, chairs, and shelving unit are also useful in this area.

Language Area

The language area should be located in the quietest part of the classroom. Often this is next to the manipulative area. In addition to providing books and magazines, you will want to promote language arts. For example, paper, pens, pencils, and felt-tip markers encourage writing skills. Shelving units, a table, and chairs are all useful in this area. See 9-17. For comfort, pillows may also be added. Many centers also carpet this area or add an area rug.

Music Area

Rhythm instruments; tapes, records, CDs, and players; puppets; and scarves are

9-17

Display books at the children's eye level in the library area.

found in almost all music areas. When space permits, some centers have a piano. For other centers, an Autoharp® or guitar is an option. Space should be provided in the music area for movements and dancing.

Private Space

Provide a private area in the classroom where children can be alone. Children then have the option of limiting contact with others when they choose. This reduces the pressure of being around others when they wish to be alone. Set a classroom rule stating that children who go to the private space will not be disturbed by others.

A loft is one unique way to provide private space, 9-18. In programs where a wooden loft is not in the budget, large cardboard boxes and wooden crates can serve the same purpose.

The private space should be small, allowing room for only one or two children at a time. The children in the private space

Discuss

Toddlers as well as older preschoolers may share some multipurpose classrooms. What are some suggestions for distinguishing between toys and materials that may be harmful to the younger children, especially in the small manipulative area? Examples may include separating and color-coding.

Reflect

Rhythm instruments, along with all the other manipulatives in the classroom, should be easily accessible for the children's use. However, use of these during certain times may interfere with maintaining a comfortable noise level in the classroom. Would you impose any restrictions on the use of or access to rhythm instruments?

Discuss

What types of shelves or book displays encourage the children's use of the language area? What additions would you recommend to the language area to make it welcoming and comfortable?

Workplace Connection

Ask students to brainstorm ways to create a space in the preschool room that is private and comfortable, yet allows supervision and safety. What student skills in art, woodworking, or sewing could be used to help create the space? Why is a private space recommended for preschool rooms? Have students create a private space in the preschool room if one does not already exist.

Activity

Ask students to locate preschool room lofts by researching in early childhood and school equipment catalogs. Have students note the size and space requirements, costs, and ease of use by preschool children. Have students research the building codes and other standards that might affect the use of lofts. Allow time in class for students to share their findings.

Enrich

Ask students to debate the pros and cons of including technology equipment such as computers in the preschool classroom for the children's use. How much emphasis should be placed on using technology at this age?

Discuss

In what area of the classroom should you place the science area? In what area of the classroom should the technology area be located? If space is limited for an eating area, where can you have children sit?

9-18

Children sometimes like to be alone. This loft provides a perfect setting.

should not be visible to other children in the room. However, the teacher must be able to see into the private space.

Science Area

Place the science area in the wet, active area of the classroom. Most science areas contain at least one table. A shelving unit may be placed here. Small caged pets and project materials would be also found in the science area of the classroom. When possible, place this area near a light and water source for growing plants.

Technology Area

The technology area should be in the quiet, dry part of the classroom. A technology area might be a small area with just one computer and printer or a larger, lab-type section. Electrical outlets are needed for computers and printers. If Internet access is desired, a phone jack will also be needed in this area.

Where you place the computer affects how often children will use it. Keep the monitor visible throughout the classroom. This placement increases children's curiosity about the computer and encourages children to interact. It also helps the teacher supervise from anywhere in the classroom. Store software near the computer. For older children, keep software easy for them to access on their own.

Finally, choose computer furniture designed for young children. Injuries or strains can occur if children must adjust their bodies to reach the mouse or keyboard from adult furniture. Position the top of the work surface two inches below the children's elbows. When seated, children should be able to see the center of the monitor by looking directly ahead. Having a few extra chairs in the area encourages the children to use the computers together.

Eating Area

When space is available, provide a separate eating area. This area could also serve as a special interest area for cooking activities. It should be located near the kitchen. This allows for easy service and cleanup.

If space is limited, have children sit at tables in other areas of the classroom. The daily schedule will have to be arranged to allow for this.

Chart 9-19 summarizes each classroom area and the furniture, materials, and equipment you may wish to supply in each. In each of the activity areas, include ethnic and cultural materials and artifacts whenever possible. Items such as artwork, fabric,

Portfolio Project

It is important to include ethnic and multicultural materials in the classroom to promote understanding of cultural diversity. Many schools ask parents to contribute items that help support this goal. Have students draft a sample letter asking parents to borrow and display items in the classroom. Have students include a request for parents to visit the classroom if they would like to share cultural information with the children. Review the letters for appropriate grammar, clarity, and professionalism. Have students file a copy of the letter in their portfolio under *Parent Communications* and/or *Public Relations*.

9-19

Classroom Area	Furniture	Materials and Equipment
Blockbuilding	labeled shelving units	large hollow blocks; solid unit blocks; wheeled toys: cars, buses, trucks, fire engines, tractors, planes; small toy people of various ethnic backgrounds; small colored wooden blocks; zoo animals; farm animals
Art	adjustable easels shelving unit tables and chairs drying rack	clay, pencils, crayons, colored chalk, ink markers, paper, tempera paint, scrap paper and fabrics, tape, glue, paste, brushes, scissors, painting smocks
Dramatic Play	child-sized refrigerator, stove, sink, cupboard, and doll bed trunk or tree to hold clothes tables and chairs	child-sized cleaning equipment: broom, dustpan, and mops; doll clothes; telephones; mirror; dishes and cooking utensils; empty containers, tubs, buckets, and pans; dress-up clothes, costumes; purses, backpacks, suitcases; dolls of both genders and various ethnicities
Sensory	sensory table shelving unit (optional)	funnels, pitchers, hoses, spoons, sponges, measuring cups, containers, strainers, rotary beaters, water toys, scoops, shovels
Woodworking	woodworking bench	saw, screwdrivers, hammers, vice, nails, screws, scraps of soft wood and foam, glue, protective goggles
Sleeping	cots mats	blankets, pillows, soft music
Small Manipulative	shelving units table (optional depending on space) chairs (optional depending on space)	hand puppets, blocks, puzzles, plastic forms for joining, Lego® plastic building blocks, parquetry blocks, stringing beads, board games, sewing cards, colored cubes with pattern cards, bingo games, rods and blocks of different sizes, flannel board numerals, number puzzles, wooden numbers, magnetic numbers, measuring containers, scale, rulers, Tinkertoy® building blocks
Language Center	table chairs rug soft pillows (optional) bean bag (optional) shelving shelving unit flannel board chalkboard	picture books, children's magazines, child-authored books, charts, games, alphabet letters, pens, pencils, felt-tip markers, chalk, different-colored lined and unlined paper, photographs, word lists, picture dictionary
Music	piano (optional) shelving unit cassette, record, or CD player	rhythm instruments; tapes, records, or CDs; silk scarves or streamers for dancing; puppets for song activities
Private Space	loft TV box wooden crates	pillows
Science and Math	aquarium table shelving unit terrarium	magnets; microscopes; scissors; prism; measuring instruments; jars and other empty containers; collections of related objects such as leaves, nuts, rocks, and insects; magnifying glasses; small pets; scales; mirrors, thermometers

Continued

Providing materials and equipment for activity areas is a thought-provoking process. Many everyday materials can be used for learning.

Resource

Value of Activity Areas, reproducible master 9-1, TR

Discuss

Review Chart 9-19. With so many activity areas recommended for preschool classrooms, how many can be used for more than one activity?

Resource

Activity Area Responsibilities, reproducible master 9-6, TR

Resource

Maintaining the Environment, Activity D, OG

Putting Technology to Use

Have students conduct an Internet search for classroom furniture, materials, and equipment for each of the classroom areas listed in Chart 9-19. Ask students to research at least two items for each classroom area. Have students investigate the price and how functional and safe each item would be for the classroom. Ask students to write a brief description for each item. Allow time for students to discuss their findings in class.

Discuss

What is a suggested
time limit for the display
of children's work in the
preschool classroom?
What methods could be
used to document the
abilities of the children
for referral after their
work goes home?

Activity

Ask students to make a
wall hanging from a 36-
or 52-inch wide piece
of material such as
felt, burlap, or sailcloth.
Have students cut the
material to the desired
length for the wall hang-
ing and hem each end
of the hanging. Insert
a dowel through each
hem. Have students
hang the wall hang-
ing in the preschool
classroom to display
children's work.

Discuss

What factors determine
how much space to
leave empty around
a piece of playground
equipment?

Eating	tables chairs	vases and centerpieces, place mats, plates, eating utensils, cups
Technology Center	child-sized computer workstations or tables and chairs extra chairs computer printer	software, printer paper, manuals for computer and software, typing stand, mouse and wrist pads
Gross-Motor	balance beam steps walking boards jungle gym	balls, ropes, hula hoops, fabric tunnels, tumbling mat

9-19 Continued

jewelry, tools, utensils, toys, and children's
books should be included.

Displaying Children's Work

The work of the children should be
displayed throughout the activity areas.
Bulletin boards, wall hangings, clothesline,
or appliance boxes can be used for display
purposes. Display areas should be placed at
the children's height, allowing them to mount
and view their own work.

A wall hanging can be made from a
36- or 52-inch wide piece of felt, burlap, or
sailcloth. The length of the hanging can vary.
Hem each end of the hanging. Then insert a
dowel through each hem.

Colored yarn or a piece of clothesline
can also be used to display work. Colored
plastic clothespins can be used to clasp work
to the line.

A large appliance box can provide a free-
standing display area. The advantage of this
type of display is that it is portable. It can be
used in any area of the center. Even after it is
assembled, it can be moved.

Recognize the work of all the children
when putting displays together. To keep
displays interesting, set a time limit for each
display. Change the work often.

Outdoor Play Environments

Developmentally appropriate programs
value outdoor as well as indoor play.
Children need to take part in both indoor
and outdoor activities. Many classrooms
do not have the proper amount of space
for large muscle activities. Other activities
such as science, art, and music can also take
place outdoors during pleasant weather. The
outdoor playground can fill these needs, 9-20.

9-20

The playground is an exciting and fun place for children.

Workplace Connection

Have students review their state's requirements
for outdoor space. Arrange for students to visit
their vocational preschool or local early childhood center. Have students compare the amount
of available outdoor space at the center to the
state's requirement for available outdoor space.

Is the playground space rectangular? How is
the playground arranged? Have students draw
a plan of the playground. Discuss with students
the factors and challenges that may affect the
amount of space available.

In outdoor areas, the required number of square feet per child varies from state to state. Usually the requirement ranges from 75 to 200 square feet per child. A rectangular space is most functional. Such a playground can be seen from end to end. U- or L-shaped playgrounds are more difficult to supervise and arrange, 9-21.

Planning the Playground

The playground, like indoor space, needs to be studied in terms of use and then broken into areas. A well-planned playground usually has empty space and a wheeled vehicle path. These two items aid movement through the playground.

The wheeled vehicle path divides the activity areas of the playground. This path creates space between areas and makes moving about easier. Without a path, children may constantly be bumping into each other.

To determine where a path should be laid, the teacher should kneel down to be at the children's eye level. The path should be wide enough and clear enough so children can see all areas of the playground, even when outside school grounds.

Empty space should be located in the center of the playground. Activity areas can be placed around the outside of the playground, around the empty space. You may also need to leave empty space around some pieces of equipment.

When planning playground space, consider the following guidelines:

- Equipment should be far enough apart so a child using one piece of equipment cannot touch a child using another piece of equipment.

- All equipment should be visible to the teacher from any spot in the playground.

- Children should not have to walk through one area to get to another.

- Between one-third and one-half of the playground should be used for play equipment and the remainder should be open space to allow for ease of movement.

9-21

This playground is designed to be completely visible from this angle. This allows for better supervision.

Discuss

What is the value of empty space in the outdoor playground? What proportion of space should be left empty?

Resource

Playground Space, Activity E, OG

Activity

Ask students to investigate a local playground. Have students check the following: Is the playground equipment far enough apart? Is all equipment visible from any spot in the playground? Is there enough open space? Allow time for students to discuss their findings in class.

Portfolio Project

Have students make a scale drawing of a model preschool playground suitable for a toddler or preschool program. Include all pieces of stationary equipment, paths, empty space, storage facilities, and surfacing materials. Ask students to write a brief essay explaining what factors contributed to their choice of equipment and what safety features are included in the plan. Have students consult outdoor play equipment catalogs, building material suppliers, and other sources to estimate the cost of their project.

Activity

Invite your school's head custodian or building and grounds director to speak to the class about proper maintenance of an outdoor facility. What equipment, tools, and supplies are needed? How many of the tasks can be completed by the teachers or aides? Have students prepare a list of additional questions prior to the visit.

Discuss

What factors will need to be considered in the amount of time that should be devoted to outdoor activities? Consider curriculum and program goals, weather or climate of the area, length and time of the program, number of children that must share the space, and number of adults available for supervision.

Enrich

Ask students to research the different types of surfacing materials recommended for playgrounds. Have students debate the advantages and disadvantages of each. After the debate, ask students to select their personal preference and write a brief statement on their selection.

In addition to paths and empty space, there are other factors to consider when planning an outdoor playground. Among items to be considered are fences, the playground surface, landscaping, storage, wheeled toy paths, stationary equipment, a water source, and animal shelters.

Fencing

Most states require that playgrounds be fenced for safety of the children. Fences prevent children from wandering away or strangers from entering the playground area. This makes outdoor supervision easier for teachers.

Selecting the proper fence requires careful thought. The goal is to purchase a fence that can keep children safe. The fence should fasten securely at the gate. There should be no sharp metal pieces or splintered wood to hurt children.

Two types of fences are commonly found in playgrounds: chain link and wood. Each type of fence has its good and bad points. For instance, because chain link is an open design, it is possible for the children to observe activities outside of the playground. This gives the playground an open feeling. However, some children are able to climb chain link fences. This can be dangerous. In addition, many people feel that chain link fences are unattractive.

Wood fences that complement the center design are very pleasing to the eye. However, the fence must also be designed with the children's safety in mind. Children should not be able to climb over or through a well-designed wood fence. The boards should be sanded to prevent children from getting splinters.

Surfaces

A portion of the playground area should have grass. This is best for running and organized games. Under equipment, the best surface for safety is loose material such as bark nuggets, shredded bark, or sand. When children fall on such material, they receive fewer and less severe injuries than when they fall on hard surfaces. A good cushion requires 9 to 12 inches of loose material.

The drawback to loose materials is that they tend to pile up in one spot. They shift under weight placed on them. In high traffic areas, they will thin out and pile up around the edges of the area. Therefore, the material must be raked or shoveled back into position fairly often.

Landscaping

A well-landscaped playground makes for pleasant surroundings. In addition, landscaping can also be used as part of the science program by encouraging the abilities to observe and make discoveries. Trees, shrubs, and flowers in a variety of sizes, colors, and growing cycles will interest children. Trees are also a good source of shade, beauty, and sound control. A well-landscaped playground gives children a place to be alone, as well as corners for play. Hills in the playground can be used to develop large muscle skills.

Before choosing flowers or shrubs, consult a landscape architect. Some plants are poisonous. Any landscape architect can tell you which plants to avoid. The architect can also recommend shrubs and flowers from a number of growing cycles. This will ensure that children will always have a seasonal plant to study and view.

Storage Shed

Tricycles, wagons, scooters, shovels, rakes, balls, plastic wading pools, and gardening tools are just some of the items you may want to keep in a storage shed. See 9-22. The materials stored will vary with the climate of the area.

Storage space should be arranged so children can return materials themselves. Painted lines on the floor of the shed can be used to outline parking spaces for wheeled toys. Large barrels or baskets can be used

Service Learning Activity

Ask students to volunteer in assisting with a landscaping project at the vocational preschool or at another nonprofit program in your community. Students may need permission to participate. They could design a plan or part of a plan, such as planting flowers or bulbs; locate resources for materials, equipment, and supplies; and schedule the work. Students may need to consider fund-raising as part of the project or rely on donations to pay for expenses. Consider a cooperative project with another organization or program such as 4-H, Girl Scouts, Boy Scouts, National FFA Organization, or student council.

9-22

Suggested Contents of a Storage Shed

Water and Sand Play
rakes
shovels
scoop
trucks
cooking utensils
water hoses
empty cans with paintbrushes
funnels
strainers
containers
wading pool
sponges

Wheeled Toys
wagons
doll buggy
wheeled cars and trucks
scooters
tricycles
road signs

Construction
cable spools
packing crates
large wooden blocks
saw horses
wooden boxes
wooden planks

Carpentry
carpentry bench
hammer
saw
vise
clamps
nails
brushes
sandpaper
styrofoam pieces

Science
gardening tools
seeds
worm jars
garden hose
animal feed
butterfly nets
bird feed
binoculars
magnifying glasses

Dramatic Play
dress-up clothes
fabric
tunnel puppet
stage puppets
folding table and chairs
cardboard appliance boxes
blankets

Art
easel(s)
paintbrushes
paper
scissors
paste

The contents of storage sheds varies from center to center.

to store many types of materials. Rakes and shovels can be hung on hooks from the wall.

Wheeled Toy Paths

A path that children can use to push or ride wheeled toys is key for two reasons. The first reason is safety. A path with one-way traffic will prevent children from riding into each other. The second reason is protection of the outdoor play area. A path gives children a place to ride so they do not destroy grassy areas, 9-23. Set limits regarding the use of wheeled toys and paths, and enforce these rules.

The path should be joined to the storage shed. Children can then drive their toys directly into or out of the shed. The path should be designed with curves instead of sharp right angles. This will allow children to make easy turns on curves, keeping them from tipping over on sharp turns.

Stationary Equipment

Jungle gyms, slides, and tree houses are all **stationary equipment** that are set permanently in the ground for stability. For

added appeal, place large pieces of stationary equipment in different corners of the playground. For safety reasons, spacing is also

9-23

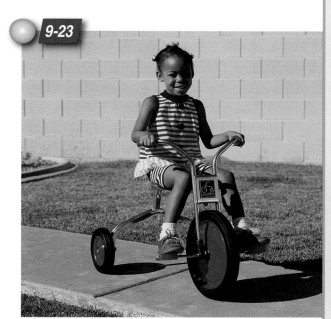

Wheeled toy paths should have a hard surface.

Vocabulary

Have a student volunteer define *stationary equipment*. What guidelines should be followed for anchoring stationary equipment to the ground?

Reflect

Think about what limits you would set regarding the use of wheeled toys and paths. How would you enforce these rules?

Resource

Arranging Space Crossword, reproducible master 9-4, TR

Workplace Connection

Ask students to review 9-22 and document how many of the items your vocational program already owns. Have students make a list of desired additions to the program. Have students investigate the cost of the equipment on the list. Ask students to determine what items should be removed from the list, if any. Have students prioritize the list for future acquisition.

Discuss

Where should sand-
boxes be located in
the playground? What
are the safety risks to
children while playing in
the sandbox?

Activity

Have students consult
their local school guide-
lines or state licensing
standards for including
pets in the classroom
or outdoor play area.
What animals, if any,
could be included in
the vocational program
or the local programs?
Have students write
a brief report of their
findings.

Resource

Activity Areas,
Activity C, SAG

needed for pieces of stationary equipment that
are designed for different age groups.

Sandbox

Children will play in sandboxes for
long periods of time. If the sandbox is in a
sunny area, children are at risk for sunburn.
Therefore, place sandboxes in shady areas. If
there is little or no shade in the playground,
build a roof over the sandbox for protection.
Also, place the sandbox near a water source.
By adding water to dry sand, children can
build more detailed structures.

To prevent cats from using the sandbox
as a litter box, build a cover for the sandbox.
When the sandbox is not being used, place
the cover over it, 9-24.

Water

Water play is a pleasant activity for
children during warm weather. For this
reason, some centers have built-in wading
pools. Other centers use plastic, aboveground
wading pools when licensing permits.
Regardless of the type of pool, constant
supervision is necessary. For reasons of
safety, pools need to be emptied at the end of
each day.

A garden hose is also useful in the
playground. Attach it to a sprinkler so the
children can play in the water during hot
weather. The hose can also be used to water
gardens and other plants.

Animal Shelter

Playgrounds for young children often
have a number of animals. The type of

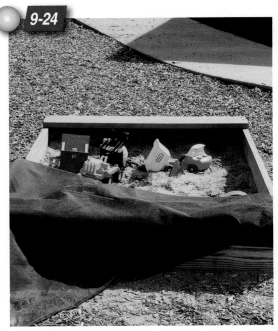

9-24

This sandbox can be covered with a tarp when not in use.

animals may be determined by city zoning
laws or state child care licensing rules. Some
states are beginning to exclude animals in
early care and education programs. Therefore,
it is important to check your licensing
requirements before purchasing animals.

To shelter animals, use cages. These
should be large enough for the animal, have
a mesh floor to keep the cage tidy between
thorough cleanings, and have a quality
padlock to protect against vandals. Place
the cages where animals will be protected
from wind, sun, and rain. Provide adequate
protection from extreme heat and cold, too.

Meeting Special Needs

Review the special learners' chapter outlines
to ensure that all areas have been filled in.
Then review the chapter objectives and ask
the students to evaluate their progress in
meeting these objectives. Ask the students to
summarize, orally or in writing, what they have
learned from this chapter.

Summary

Properly organized space is a key to promoting children's learning. It provides children with the option of working alone or cooperatively. It defines expected behavior for children. Properly organized space frees the children to play without interruption. They will stay with activities for longer periods of time, increasing their attention spans. Properly organized space also provides children with choices.

Space should reflect children's developmental needs, interests, and experiences as well as program goals. In such a space, children are more relaxed and positive. They feel good about themselves. As a direct result, teachers can spend more time nurturing and less time redirecting children's behavior.

Review and Reflect

1. Properly planned space is arranged based on _____.
   A. children's developmental needs
   B. children's interests
   C. program goals
   D. All the above.

2. True or false. Teachers are affected by the arrangement of their classrooms.

3. List four goals for well-planned space.

4. What is the purpose of an isolation area?

5. A _____ room is the best shape for a classroom.

6. Name three uses for an audiovisual board.

7. List four examples of acoustic materials.

8. Storage units should be selected based on the _____ of the children.

9. The top part of a locker is often called a _____.

10. Until about age six, children prefer _____.
    A. warm colors
    B. cool colors
    C. plaid

11. Organized space should define the scope and _____ of activities.

12. List two ways to promote
    A. self-control through the classroom environment
    B. social skills through the classroom environment

13. Are problems created when a small group of children have too much space? Why or why not?

14. _____ are the paths people follow through an area.

15. Activity areas are best defined by arranging storage units into _____ or _____ shapes.

4. An isolation area is a room or space for children who become ill or show signs of a communicable disease.
5. rectangular
6. chalkboard, movie screen, and bulletin board
7. (List four:) carpet, drapes, bulletin boards, stuffed toys, pillows, sand, acoustic tile
8. height
9. cubbie
10. A
11. limits
12. (Student response.)
13. Yes. Too much open space encourages children to run. This can be the cause of many problems.
14. Traffic patterns
15. U, L
16. music, woodworking, blockbuilding, dramatic play
17. false
18. (List two. Student response.)
19. Empty space, wheeled vehicle path
20. loose material, such as bark nuggets, shredded bark, or sand

---

Review and Reflect **Answer Key**

1. D
2. true
3. (List four:) providing a physically safe environment for children; providing children with areas for cognitive, emotional, social, and physical growth; providing an abundance of materials so children can make choices; providing adults with a space that is easy to supervise; providing space that is pleasing to the eye for both adults and children; providing easy access to materials when needed so children are able to direct themselves; providing space with high activity and low stress where children can work and play comfortably

16. What activities should be placed in the active/dry area of the classroom?

17. True or false. Children do *not* need to spend time alone.

18. Give two guidelines for a technology area in the classroom.

19. _____ and a _____ in the playground divide activity areas and make moving about easier.

20. What is the safest surface to use under playground equipment?

Apply and Explore

1. Draw a room arrangement that includes each of the basic activity areas. Include a center of interest for each area.

2. Plan a color scheme for a classroom. Be prepared to explain the reasons you chose the colors you did.

3. Interview child care teachers about space arrangement. Ask them what they like best about their classroom space. Ask them what they would like to change.

Cross-Curricular Link

Reading

1. Read your state's licensing requirements as they apply to classroom space. For instance, how many square feet of space is required per child? How many toilets are required for a group of 40 children?

Technology

2. Check your state's child care licensing requirements by using the Web site for the National Resource Center for Health and Safety in Child Care (nrc.uchsc.edu).

3. Design a classroom at the Childcraft Web site (www.childcraft.com) by clicking on Classroom Designer.

Workplace Link

What types of sandboxes are available from early childhood and preschool equipment sources? Research the cost to purchase and install an outdoor playground sandbox at your school. What factors affect the location of the sandbox in the playground? What school safety guidelines and policies must be considered when installing a sandbox?

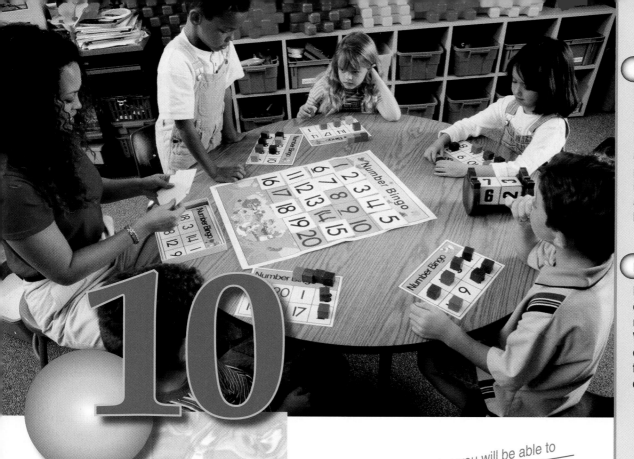

Discuss

Look at the chapter opening photo. Why do you think the teacher might have selected the activity shown in the picture? Do you think it might be a game, a learning activity, or both?

Discuss

Review the chapter objectives before reading the chapter. Why will meeting these objectives be important for the future early childhood educator?

10

Selecting Toys, Equipment, and Educational Materials

After studying this chapter, you will be able to

- explain guidelines for selecting developmentally appropriate toys, equipment, and educational materials.

- describe safety factors to consider when purchasing toys and playground equipment.

- explain how to report unsafe toys and equipment to the appropriate agencies.

- list sources and methods for purchasing toys and equipment.

- identify toys and educational materials that teach children appreciation for people of all cultures.

Vocabulary

Have students review the *Terms to Know* list. Ask students to look up unfamiliar words or terms in the glossary before reading the chapter.

Reflect

What is your philosophy about using toys in an educational setting? How does playing with toys relate to learning?

Discuss

Ask students to look at the photo in 10-1 and discuss the social skills these children might be practicing. What cognitive skills are they using?

Terms to Know

spectator toys
physical age
chronological age
developmental age
multicultural
co-op (cooperative)
consumable supplies

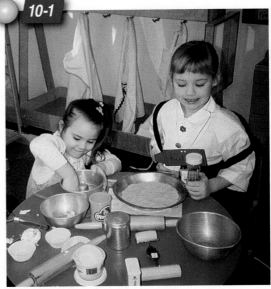

10-1

Toys help children build many skills. By playing together, these children learn important social skills.

Children learn about their world by playing with toys, exploring materials, and interacting with other people. They learn best when provided with a wide range of toys and educational materials that match their abilities and interests. This allows them to make choices. Toys play an important role in facilitating the learning process. For instance, children can learn speech and dressing skills while playing with toys. Children can learn about other people and cultures through the use of toys. When playing with toys, children often interact with others. They make choices, solve problems, and apply some control over their environment, 10-1.

Developmentally appropriate toys motivate and engage children as active learners. Simple toys like building blocks can promote cognitive growth. For example, if children do not build a strong foundation under their block building, the building will topple. Thus, they learn physics concepts. If they join two semicircular pieces, they make a circle. In this way, they learn math concepts.

Selection Criteria

In early childhood programs, selecting toys and equipment for children is often the teacher's responsibility. In preparation, you will need to determine what the children's needs, interests, and abilities are. You will then need to choose the materials that would best meet those needs. As you can see, this is an important job. Careful planning is required.

Safety is a concern when selecting toys. Choking and improper use cause the majority of injuries in childhood. Developmentally appropriate toys can help reduce the number of injuries. Age warnings on packaged products are not always reliable.

The program goals, budget, and curriculum will influence which materials you buy for the classroom. The number of children in the program and the available space and storage should also be considered. You will want to choose toys that are safe, appropriate, and interesting for the children. Guidelines for choosing educational toys are described in the sections that follow.

Meeting Special Needs

Provide an outline of the chapter with all the chapter headings for special learners. Students should fill in each section of the outline as the material is covered in class with a sentence or two about the content. Review the special learners' IEPs to decide if any modifications should be made in presenting the chapter content.

Health and Safety

Shopping for Safe Toys

Although your daily routine at a child care center may involve checking toys for broken parts and other hazards, you also need to think about these factors when you buy toys. The *Consumer Product Safety Commission (CPSC)* offers tips on toy-shopping safety as well as information on toy recalls. Before you shop, check out their Web site at www.cpsc.gov.

Program Goals

- To develop a positive self-concept and view self as worthwhile
- To develop a curiosity about the world
- To develop sensory exploration skills
- To develop prosocial behavior skills
- To value own rights as well as those of others
- To develop language skills, both listening and speaking
- To develop fine-motor skills
- To develop gross-motor skills
- To develop problem-solving skills

Listing your program goals can help clarify the program areas you need to develop.

Program Goals

Classroom toys and equipment should reflect program goals. If a program goal is to have the children develop language skills, then language materials should be placed in the classroom. Books, pictures, cassettes, CDs, alphabet cards, puppets, pencils, and paper can all be used to promote language skills.

Write your program goals on paper, 10-2. Then make a list of items that promote each goal. Review the goals and lists. Take count of items you already have in the classroom. Then decide in which areas more toys and equipment are required. You may find a planning sheet helpful for this task, 10-3.

Budget

When purchasing items for your class, you will need to stay within your budget. To do this, first purchase the basics, such as tables, chairs, and shelving units. You can continue adding items as your funds permit.

Teachers are often surprised at the cost of toys, equipment, and materials. The major portion of the budget for a new program will go toward furniture.

Balance

Examining program goals helps you decide what toys and equipment might be purchased. Before buying, however, review each item to decide if it will add balance to the items already available. Ask yourself the following questions: Can the item be used with other toys? Will it help children reach program goals that are not being met sufficiently with current toys? Will it promote interaction with peers? Will it help balance toys for all areas of development—physical, cognitive, emotional, and social?

Space

Keep in mind the space and storage needed for any new items you are thinking

Activity

Ask students to review the program goals for the vocational preschool program. Have students compare the program goals to the toy and equipment selection in the classroom. Ask students to locate any items that do not meet the program goals and remove them from the classroom.

Resource

Toys Meeting Goals, Activity A, SAG

Note

State licensing requirements for child care centers may include lists of equipment needed for a provisional license with additional equipment needed for the regular license. In some cases, centers may have between six months to a year to acquire the additional equipment.

Putting Technology to Use

Ask students to record or watch a video of a group of preschoolers at play. Have students evaluate the video to identify the types of play children engaged in, the amount of time children spent on a particular toy or activity, and the social skills children used in play. Ask students to prepare a brief summary of their evaluation to share with the class. Allow additional time for students to discuss the similarities and differences seen in the way children play.

Discuss

How will the number of staff available for supervision affect the possibility of offering a woodworking table with easy access to the tools and materials? What modifications may have to be made in this activity area, or to the rules for using it, when proper supervision is not available?

Reflect

Students or volunteers with sewing skills could construct handmade cloth items such as puppets and dolls. This may save cost when considering the budget. What standards would you follow to judge the durability of hand-sewn cloth toys and equipment?

Resource

Equipment Construction: Advantages and Disadvantages, transparency master 10-1, TR

10-3

Toy Selection Planning Sheet

Program Goals	Available Toys	Toys Needed
To encourage sensory exploration To promote gross-motor skills	water table, shovel, cups, pitchers, scoops, clay, egg beaters, feely box, harmonica, kazoo, guitar low climber, wagon cart, large rubber balls, planks, boxes, jungle gym	bells, drum, texture matching games, pumps, funnels low slide, balance boards, bicycle

Committing program goals to paper can make the selection of proper toys an easier task.

about buying or building. This is especially true for large pieces of equipment. For instance, an indoor jungle gym is a useful item in many centers. However, if the space for storing it is not available, it is a poor investment. It may end up being stored in another part of the building. If the location is inconvenient, the jungle gym will not be used very often.

Supervision

Quality supervision is vital to safety. Consider the number of staff available for supervision when selecting toys and equipment. Think about how each item will affect your ability to properly watch over children. You will have to consider each item individually, balancing safety and developmental needs. Safety is a primary concern. For example, you may want to buy swings for the playground. The state may require one adult supervisor for every 10 children. You can comply with state guidelines for ratios, but you might feel that more supervision is needed for safety. You may decide, in this case, that the swings would be an unwise purchase.

The developmental stages of children also need to be considered when choosing toys and equipment. This will affect the amount

of supervision required. For instance, many five-year-old children can use blunt-nosed scissors with some guidance. However, four-year-old children require much more supervision for the same task.

Maintenance

All toys and equipment require maintenance. The care required varies with the type of toy or equipment and the amount of use. For example, a plastic jungle gym needs less upkeep than a wooden or metal one. Upkeep of equipment can become costly.

Durability

Children's toys need to be durable. Children bang, drop, stand on, sit on, and lie on toys. When angry, they may even throw toys. Broken toys can pose a danger to children. For instance, a broken toy can have sharp edges that cut. It is usually best to buy toys and equipment that are well built. You want to buy quality toys that will last through much use.

Wood and cloth are two materials that are durable, warm, and pleasurable to touch, 10-4. Wood toys can withstand many years of use by many children. When buying wood toys, look for those made of hardwoods

Workplace Connection

Ask students to visit a preschool classroom and observe how the amount of storage space available affects the quantity and type of play materials and equipment in the classroom. What strategies do the teachers employ to get the most use from their play space and storage space? Have students write a brief report of their observation findings. Allow time for students to discuss their findings in class.

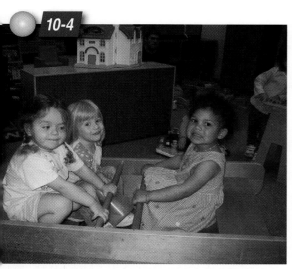

10-4

Wooden equipment is durable and can withstand rough play from children.

such as maple. The toys should also be split-resistant. The corners of the toy should be rounded.

Quantity

The quantity of toys can be as important when purchasing materials as the quality. In most classrooms, it is common to find two or more children playing with the same toys. To promote this type of cooperation, supply an ample amount of toys and materials for children. If there is a shortage of play materials, undesirable behavior can result. Therefore, be certain that any toys you wish to add to the classroom can be purchased in the needed amounts.

Variety should also be considered along with quantity. Is the item you wish to add to the classroom similar to existing items? Studies show that children who have been exposed to a wide variety of toys are more imaginative and creative. In order to provide variety, rotate toys and equipment regularly.

When choosing toys, keep them simple. Children do not have freedom to express themselves if there is too much detail. Unstructured toys, such as blocks and paints, encourage the children to use their imagination.

The chart in 10-5 lists suggested toys and equipment for a class of 15 children. These items represent a varied group of toys and equipment.

Child Involvement

Choose toys that will actively involve children. Toys should move children to explore, manipulate, invent, and problem solve. In this way, children learn for themselves. They learn to use their imaginations.

Reflect

Unstructured toys, such as blocks and paints, can encourage children to use their imagination. What other simple toys might allow children the freedom to express themselves?

Discuss

Why is it as important to consider the quantity and variety of toys purchased as the quality? What social skills can children learn from waiting and taking turns with a particular toy?

Resource

Evaluating a Toy, Activity A, OG

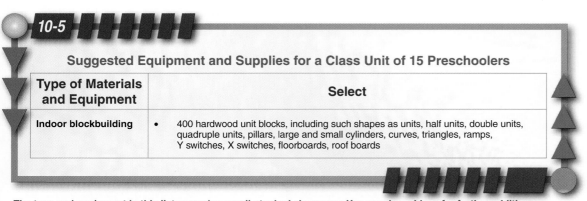

10-5

Suggested Equipment and Supplies for a Class Unit of 15 Preschoolers

Type of Materials and Equipment	Select
Indoor blockbuilding	• 400 hardwood unit blocks, including such shapes as units, half units, double units, quadruple units, pillars, large and small cylinders, curves, triangles, ramps, Y switches, X switches, floorboards, roof boards

The toys and equipment in this list comprise a well-stocked classroom. You may have ideas for further additions.

(continued)

Putting Technology to Use

Have students conduct an Internet search for five new toys and equipment that can be added to a preschool classroom. Ask students to choose items that will actively involve children. Do the items encourage children to explore, manipulate, invent, and problem solve? Are the items affordable when purchasing in quantity? Do the items represent a variety of toys and equipment? Allow time for students to discuss their findings in class.

Discuss

Ask students to review the list of family living and dramatic play supplies in Chart 10-5, *Suggested Equipment and Supplies for a Class Unit of 15 Preschoolers*. Have students brainstorm additional equipment and supplies that could be added to the list.

Activity

Ask students to review the list of art equipment and supplies in Chart 10-5. Have students compare the list to the equipment selection in the vocational preschool classroom. Have students make a list of any items missing from the classroom.

Enrich

Invite a preschool teacher to speak to the class about purchasing equipment and supplies for the classroom. How is the classroom budget determined? How many of the supplies and equipment in the classroom were donated? Where can items be purchased? Have students prepare a list of additional questions prior to the visit.

Suggested Equipment and Supplies for a Class Unit of 15 Preschoolers

Floor play materials	• 24 cars, airplanes, boats, fire engines, wagons, tractors, trains of assorted sizes • 30 rubber, plastic, or wooden figures of farm and zoo animals; community workers: police officers, firefighters, and doctors; family members: mother, father, boy, girl, baby, grandparents • 1 rocking boat
Family living and dramatic play	• 8-10 rubber dolls representing all cultures and both genders; doll clothes; chest for doll clothes; baby bottles • 2 doll carriages • 1 doll bed, big and sturdy enough for a child to crawl into • 1 smaller doll bed or crib • Blankets, mattresses, pillows for doll beds • Furniture for household play: wooden stove, cupboard for dishes, sink, small table and chairs • Kitchenware: plastic dishes, tea set, small cooking utensils, silverware • Housekeeping equipment: broom, mop, dustpan, brush, iron, ironing board, clothesline, clothespins • Full-length mirror • Dress-up clothes: men's and women's shoes, handbags, jewelry, hats, belts • Supplies for other dramatic play: office equipment, telephones, cash registers, firefighters' hats, badges, play money, stethoscope, doctors' bags and white coats, nurses' hats
Table and perceptual activities	• Bingo and lotto games • 12 wooden inlay puzzles of varying degrees of difficulty • 1 puzzle rack • Pegs and Pegboards • Matching games • Sets of small blocks (cubes, parquetry, interlocking, snap-in, number) • Large table dominoes: picture sets, number sets • Nested blocks • Color cone • Pounding peg board • Cuisenaire rods, counting frames; abacus • Cards: geometric shapes
Art activities	• 2 easels • Drying rack for art materials • 24 easel paintbrushes with ½ in. and ¾ in. handles • 75-100 quarts liquid tempera paint of various colors* • 8000 sheets white manila paper, 4000 sheets newsprint 24 in. by 36 in. • Paste and paste brushes • 20 packages finger paint paper or glazed shelf paper • 24 packages construction paper of various colors* • 4 clay boards, 2 plastic covered pails for storing clay, and clay • 100 lb. flour and 40 lb. salt for dough • 18 blunt scissors, including some left-handed and training • 5 aprons or smocks • Miscellaneous supplies: orange juice cans, baby food jars, drying rack, florist wire, pipe cleaners, armature wire, colored toothpicks, macaroni pieces, transparent colored paper • 5 dozen crayons* • Rolling pins • Transparent tape • Stapler and staples

10-5 Continued *Include colors and hues of art materieal and supplies to reflect skin tones.   *(continued)*

Cross-Curricular Activity

Math

Divide students into groups and assign specific sections of Chart 10-5 on page 184. Ask students to determine the cost of all the equipment if purchased new. Have students search equipment catalogs and the Internet for prices. Have students add the prices to total their section. Once all students are finished, have student volunteer's share their groups total with the class. Ask a student volunteer to add all the group totals together.

Suggested Equipment and Supplies for a Class Unit of 15 Preschoolers

Music	• CD/cassette player, CDs, cassette tapes • Autoharp® • Xylophone • Scarves, streamers • Rhythm instruments: kazoos, shakers, maracas, sticks • Drums, triangles, tambourines, cymbals, tom-toms • Sleighbells for hands and feet • Balls, hoops
Woodworking	• 1 sturdy, low workbench with 2 vises • Tools: four 7 oz. claw hammers, two 12 in. crosscut saws, 1 hand drill, 1 rasp, 1 file, 2 screwdrivers, assorted nails with large heads, screws, 2 large C clamps • Soft wood scraps, doweling • Sandpaper • Miscellaneous: buttons, washers, corks, wire, nuts, hooks and eyes, spools, bottle caps
Furniture	• 15 chairs, 8 in. to 12 in. in height • 3 tables, 18 in. to 22 in. in height, for snacks, meals, and tablework activities • 2 room dividers • 15 cots for resting • 15 lockers for hanging coats, hats, boots, extra change of clothes
Science and special projects	• Bar and horseshoe magnets • Children's cookbook • Magnifying glass • Large indoor and outdoor thermometers • Tubes • Seeds • Animals: hamsters, mice, rabbits, fish, ducks, and gerbils (where permitted by law) • Magnets • Picture collection: machines, animals, plants, and geography • Books with science concepts • Tape measure, yardstick, rulers • Scales • Measuring cups and spoons • Dry cell batteries, flashlight bulbs, electric wire • Pulleys and gears • Hand mirrors • Hot plate and electric frying pan • Aquarium and terrarium • Cages for pets
Water play (indoor and outdoor)	• Small pitchers, watering cans, measuring cups, bowls of various sizes, plastic bottles, medicine droppers • Funnels, strainers, egg beaters, ladles, straws, lengths of hose, brushes • Soap and soap flakes • Sponges

10-5 Continued

(continued)

Resource

Toy and Equipment Worksheet, reproducible master 10-2, TR

Discuss

Ask students to review the list of woodworking supplies in Chart 10-5, *Suggested Equipment and Supplies for a Class Unit of 15 Preschoolers.* Have students brainstorm additional equipment and supplies that could be added to the list.

Activity

Ask students to review the list of music equipment and supplies in Chart 10-5. Have students compare the list to the equipment selection in the vocational preschool classroom. Have students make a list of any items missing from the classroom.

Cross-Curricular Activity

Math

Divide students into groups and assign specific sections of the Chart 10-5 on page 185. Ask students to determine the cost of all the equipment if purchased new. Have students search equipment catalogs and the Internet for prices. Have students add the prices to total their section. Once all students are finished, have student volunteer's share their groups total with the class. Add all totals from pages 184-185 together.

Discuss

Ask students to review the list of language arts supplies in Chart 10-5, *Suggested Equipment and Supplies for a Class Unit of 15 Preschoolers*. Have students brainstorm additional equipment and supplies that could be added to the list.

Vocabulary

Have a student volunteer define the term *spectator toys*. What is their role, if any, in the preschool classroom?

Discuss

What is the role of open-ended materials in the preschool classroom? Have students give examples of open-ended materials besides those listed in the text.

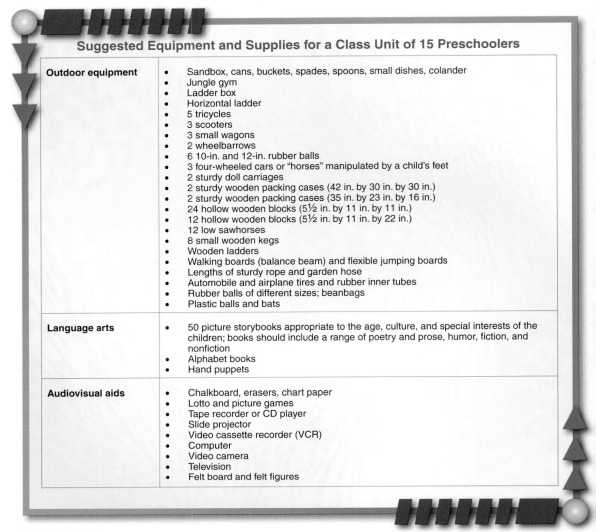

Suggested Equipment and Supplies for a Class Unit of 15 Preschoolers

Outdoor equipment	• Sandbox, cans, buckets, spades, spoons, small dishes, colander • Jungle gym • Ladder box • Horizontal ladder • 5 tricycles • 3 scooters • 3 small wagons • 2 wheelbarrows • 6 10-in. and 12-in. rubber balls • 3 four-wheeled cars or "horses" manipulated by a child's feet • 2 sturdy doll carriages • 2 sturdy wooden packing cases (42 in. by 30 in. by 30 in.) • 2 sturdy wooden packing cases (35 in. by 23 in. by 16 in.) • 24 hollow wooden blocks (5½ in. by 11 in. by 11 in.) • 12 hollow wooden blocks (5½ in. by 11 in. by 22 in.) • 12 low sawhorses • 8 small wooden kegs • Wooden ladders • Walking boards (balance beam) and flexible jumping boards • Lengths of sturdy rope and garden hose • Automobile and airplane tires and rubber inner tubes • Rubber balls of different sizes; beanbags • Plastic balls and bats
Language arts	• 50 picture storybooks appropriate to the age, culture, and special interests of the children; books should include a range of poetry and prose, humor, fiction, and nonfiction • Alphabet books • Hand puppets
Audiovisual aids	• Chalkboard, erasers, chart paper • Lotto and picture games • Tape recorder or CD player • Slide projector • Video cassette recorder (VCR) • Computer • Video camera • Television • Felt board and felt figures

10-5 Continued

Spectator toys such as battery-powered cars and talking dolls require little action on the child's part. Avoid purchasing these types of toys. Besides being costly, their appeal with children is quite often brief. Children will leave these toys for others that involve more imagination.

Choose simple toys, 10-6. Too much detail limits imagination. Open-ended materials free children to use their minds and express their creativity.

Blocks, play dough, paint, sand, and construction sets are open-ended toys. Using these items, children build structures, make designs, and play games. Children find endless ways to use such toys.

Use the checklist in 10-7 to define what skills can be learned from a specific toy. This

Cross-Curricular Activity

Math

Divide students into groups and assign specific sections of Chart 10-5 on page 186. Ask students to determine the cost of all the equipment if purchased new. Have students search equipment catalogs and the Internet for prices.

Have students add the prices to total their section. Once all students are finished, have student volunteers share their groups total with the class. Add all totals from pages 184-186 together. Allow time for students to discuss how this amount could affect a classroom budget.

10-6

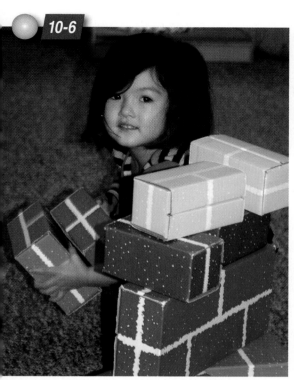

Cardboard blocks can be the source for a variety of unstructured play. What is built with them is limited only by a child's imagination.

10-7

Checklist for Skills Learned from Toys

Will the children learn or improve:	Yes	No
auditory discrimination?		
balance?		
color concepts?		
counting?		
fine-motor skills?		
gross-motor skills?		
hand-eye coordination?		
hearing-doing skills?		
language concepts?		
matching?		
number concepts?		
patterning?		
seeing-doing skills?		
self-esteem?		
sensory discrimination?		
sequencing?		
social skills?		
space perception?		
strength?		
throwing-catching skills?		
visual discrimination?		

What other skills might you add to this list?

task will help you see in what ways a toy will affect children. This knowledge can then be used when deciding on a purchase.

Developmentally Appropriate Toys

Children's physical age and developmental age are often quite different. **Physical age** is an age determined by a birth date. It is also known as **chronological age**. **Developmental age** refers to a child's skill and growth level compared to typical skills for that physical age group. For example, Kathy may be four years old physically, but only functions as an eighteen-month-old child. A child who functions as a four-year-old would be able to string beads. However, Kathy would only be able to do those tasks

that an eighteen-month-old child can do. She lacks the hand-eye coordination needed to string beads. As you choose toys, remember the difference between physical and developmental age, 10-8.

Toys are teaching tools. Those that suit children's developmental ages help them build self-esteem. For instance, Leon will feel powerful as he learns to ride a scooter, or as he pushes a wagon up a hill. As he masters this skill, he gains a sense of control and builds an "I can do it" feeling.

Vocabulary

Have a student volunteer define the term *chronological age*. What are the differences among *physical age*, *chronological age*, and *developmental age*?

Discuss

How is developmental age determined? Why is it so important to remember the difference between physical and developmental age when choosing toys?

Resource

Learning Skills and Toys, Activity C, OG

Portfolio Project

Have students write a preschool parent newsletter article that demonstrates their understanding of the skills children will develop from using toys. The article can explain developmental appropriateness and developmental age. It should also suggest toys that provide opportunities for learning and creativity. Have students refer to the *Checklist for Skills Learned from Toys* in 10-7 to explain how they would analyze a toy for its potential as a learning tool. Ask students to keep a copy of their article in their portfolio.

Reflect

When you were a preschooler, did a toy or piece of equipment ever cause you frustration or a sense of failure? How did you handle this challenge? What intervention, if any, was needed from an adult or parent to help deal with the problem?

Discuss

How many students were exposed to weapon-style toys such as guns, swords, and laser weapons? How many were exposed to toys such as superhero figures and war toys? Did more boys than girls play with these types of toys? Do the students feel they experienced any negative effects as a result of playing with these toys?

Vocabulary

Have a student volunteer define the term *multicultural*. What is the primary reason to include multicultural materials in the preschool classroom?

Resource

Choosing Age Appropriate Puzzles, transparency master 10-3, TR

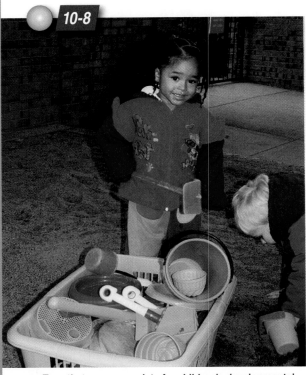

10-8

Toys that are appropriate for children's developmental ages are challenging for those children.

Toys that do not match the child's development can cause frustration. This does little for a child's self-esteem. Lack of success with a toy can have a negative effect on a child. For instance, it is not likely that a two-year-old child would be able to put together an 18-piece puzzle. The child may make a number of attempts at the puzzle. Soon the child will become frustrated and move on to a toy that is more rewarding.

Chart 10-9 lists a number of toys and equipment pieces that are appropriate for various age groups. The ages on the chart refer to developmental ages.

Violence and Toys

Children should not be taught to handle conflict with aggression or violence. Instead, they need to find positive ways to vent their feelings. One way to prevent aggressive behavior is to avoid giving children superhero or monster toys, toy guns, and war games. Children learn very little from these toys. The play that revolves around such toys is most often aggressive and destructive. For instance, when a child plays with a toy gun, he or she does little more than pull the trigger. Research shows that violent behavior increases when children play with action toys and replicas of weapons. Children who played with toy guns were more likely to destroy other children's work.

Many parents and teachers are opposed to the presence of these toys in the classroom. Therefore, it is best to simply avoid buying these toys.

Nonsexist Toys and Materials

Nonsexist toys and materials provide children with the opportunity to explore nontraditional roles. Children are not locked into play that is common of their sex. For instance, boys can be nurses, preschool teachers, and stay-at-home fathers. Girls can be airplane pilots, truck drivers, and plumbers. This type of play will also help children form early ideas about careers.

As a teacher, it is important to set up an environment that is free of gender bias. Your attitude about toys will affect what children learn about sex roles. Make a conscious effort to use or suggest a variety of toys to all children. At the same time, however, be matter-of-fact. For instance, you might suggest for Omar to try playing in the kitchen. You can explain to him that there are many fun things to do in the kitchen.

Multicultural Toys and Materials

Toys and materials that are **multicultural** represent a variety of cultural and ethnic groups. These items are an essential part of a multicultural curriculum that teaches respect

---

Putting Technology to Use

Have students conduct an Internet search for information and research regarding the effects of gender bias on preschoolers. For example, how can nonsexist toys and materials affect children's perceptions of their gender identity? What is the teacher's role in breaking traditionally held stereotypes? What questions might parents have concerning your program's attempt to remain unbiased while still offering traditional play activities? Allow time for students to discuss their findings in class.

10-9
Developmentally Appropriate Toys and Equipment
(Ages 6 months to 5 years)

Age Group	Block and Dramatic Play	Gross-Motor Equipment	Housekeeping	Sensory and Science	Creative Art and Books	Classroom Furnishings	Miscellaneous
Six months to one year	grasping toys foam blocks soft animals bucket and blocks	beach balls push/pull toys activity gym	soft dolls stuffed animals puppets acrylic plastic mirrors	tub tub toys sensory mat	wall hangings mobiles	infant seat crib changing counter adult rocking chair cubbie high chair	soft balls stroller standard crib and mattress music boxes mirrors rattles
One-year-old	Add: large trucks interlocking blocks	Add: toddler stairs driving bench large foam blocks toddler barrel tire swing	Add: doll bed doll blankets doll mattress unbreakable doll wooden telephone	Add: sponges buckets funnels pitchers measuring cups scoops	Add: large crayons hard books cloth books tapes or CDs tape or CD player	Add: clothing lockers storage shelves book display cots	Add: stacking and nesting toys pull toys simple puzzles pop beads stacking cones Pegboards
Two-year-old	Add: unit blocks wooden figures people zoo animals farm animals	Add: doll wagon hollow blocks rocking boat small jungle gym simple climber and slide tricycle	Add: simple doll clothes doll carriage child-sized sink, stove, pots, pans, aprons	Add: sand table water table	Add: picture books blunt scissors paste finger paints play dough	Add: bookcase block cart play table and chairs	Add: more complex puzzles large wooden threading beads small cots rest mat and cover sheet
Three-year-old	Add: dollhouse small dolls furniture	Add: walking board large wooden nesting boxes scooter wheelbarrow	Add: ironing board iron rocking chair broom, dustpan	Add: balance scales magnets ant farm prisms water pumps spray bottles sand molds	Add: easels paints brushes glue scissors	Add: work and library tables and chairs	Add: increasingly complex puzzles portable screens (room dividers) cots plants
Four-year-old	Add: puppets puppet theater more unit blocks	Add: planks swings slide shovel, pail, and rake triangle set coaster wagon large climber and slide	Add: chest of drawers washbasin clothesline and pins basket child-sized bed/cradle, carriage, wardrobe	Add: thermometer incubator plastic tubing	Add: clay modeling wax	Add: storage cart chalk/peg and bulletin boards	Add: aquarium pets
Five-year-old	Add: derrick	Add: balls roller skates	Add: tepee balance scale microphone	Add: microscopes tape measures motors	Add: sewing machine camera video camera	Add: woodworking bench tool cabinet tools	Add: giant dominoes construction sets

Plan toy selection well. In this case, the toys from one age group blend into the next age group.

Resource

Selecting Toys and Equipment, reproducible master 10-4, TR

Activity

Have students observe a preschooler playing. What type of play is the child engaging in? What toys is the child playing with? Does the child become frustrated with any toys? Are the toys developmentally appropriate for the child? Have students write a brief report of their findings. Allow time for students to share their reports in class.

Resource

Age-Appropriate Equipment, Activity B, SAG

Meeting Special Needs

Ask student volunteers to modify Chart 10-9, *Developmentally Appropriate Toys and Equipment (Ages 6 months to 5 years)*, so it can be viewed one or two sections at a time. Pair special learners with volunteer students to review the chart. What other toys and equipment could be added to the list? Spend additional time discussing any information that is difficult for special learners to understand.

Reflect

Think about children's books you have read in the past. Did any of the books *not* reflect cultural diversity? How would you feel if you were members of a culture that was never represented in any educational materials?

Activity

Ask students to design a bulletin board promoting the concept of cultural diversity that is appropriate for the preschool classroom. Have students use the bulletin board to encourage discussion with the children during a circle time activity.

Resource

Multicultural Checklist, Activity D, OG

for people of all cultures. Multicultural toys and materials encourage children to explore the world's diversity, 10-10. This helps them learn to appreciate others.

In addition, the early childhood environment needs to help each child develop a sense of identity. The child needs help to understand and appreciate his or her cultural and ethnic heritage. Each child needs to feel welcome and supported in the classroom. Thus, children need to see their heritage reflected among the program's toys and materials.

By choosing multicultural toys and materials, you communicate respect and appreciation for all cultures. A checklist for evaluating a classroom for multicultural toys and materials is given in Figure 10-11.

Puppets, dolls, and people figures should reflect cultural diversity. Puzzles, books, and other toys should also be chosen with multiculturalism in mind. Pick items that

10-10

Include multicultural toys and materials in all areas of the classroom.

10-11

Multicultural Checklist

Does your classroom provide the following multicultural items?	Yes	No
• A variety of books containing accurate information about many cultures		
• A culturally diverse collection of puppets, dolls, and people figures		
• Puzzles and small manipulatives representing people from around the world		
• Musical instruments from various cultures, such as maracas, drums, and flutes		
• Musical recordings in various cultural styles and languages		
• Art materials and supplies that reflect various skin tones		
• Multicultural posters, pictures, and decorations		
• Culturally relevant dress-up clothes, food, kitchen items, and furnishings for the dramatic play area		

Use this checklist to choose multicultural toys that reflect diversity.

show people of various cultures in positive and accurate ways. Art supplies should reflect a range of skin tones. Classroom decorations and bulletin boards should show people of all cultural and ethnic groups. Recorded music and musical instruments should represent various cultures, too.

Cross-Curricular Activity

Social Studies
Have students research the history of multicultural education in the United States. Ask a social studies teacher to share information about the struggle for equality in education during the last half of the twentieth century. Have students find changes in textbooks, audiovisual materials, and curriculum that demonstrate positive attitudes toward multicultural education today. What challenges still exist? How does this information affect a developmentally appropriate preschool program? Have students share information with the class in a poster presentation.

Using Technology in the Classroom

A critical issue teachers face is the use of technology in the early childhood classroom. Computer use should foster the children's learning, imagination, and creativity. It should complement other activities and social interaction. Computer use cannot replace physical activity or play with puzzles, blocks, and other materials.

For the most part, computers are considered inappropriate for children younger than three years. Very young children need to focus on learning fine- and gross-motor skills through body movements. They also need one-to-one interaction to develop language and cognitive skills. Most software programs require cognitive skills these children have not yet developed.

Studies have shown benefits for children older than three years who use the computer, however. These benefits are greatest when developmentally appropriate software is used with supporting activities. In studies, children who used the computer had gains in nonverbal, verbal, problem-solving, and conceptual skills as compared to other children.

Adults should use discretion in choosing children's software. Many programs exist, but not all are equal in terms of benefits for children. For instance, programs that model aggression are not appropriate for early childhood programs. Software that promotes learning is often preferred over programs that merely entertain. Two factors are vital—the program must be age-appropriate and easy to operate. Other qualities to look for include

- clear, user-friendly directions that children can follow without adult help
- colorful, animated, realistic graphics to hold children's attention
- logical sequences

- interactions with the child, including feedback
- promotion of problem-solving skills by offering choices
- investigation of concepts, such as numbers, colors, shapes, letters, or counting

By six years of age, most children can operate simple programs and follow instructions from a picture menu. They like showing others how to use the computer.

Selecting Safe Toys

To promote safety, choose toys carefully. Serious injuries can result from poor toy selection. Many hazards cannot be seen at a glance or with normal use. For this reason, you must study each toy thoroughly before buying it. The safest toys are not always those that appeal most to adults. Rather, the safest toys are those that meet the standards outlined in this chapter.

There are thousands of toys to choose from, and hundreds of new ones are available each year. Toys are supposed to be safe. However, over 200,000 children were treated in hospital emergency rooms in one year for playground-related injuries. Brain injury is one of the top diagnoses for playground-related injuries. There are over 190,000 reported toy-related injuries each year. The National SAFE-KIDS Campaign has reported the following:

- Falls and choking cause most toy-related deaths and injuries in children. Choking alone causes one third of all toy-related deaths—most often from balloons.
- Children 4 years old and younger account for almost half of all toy-related injuries and almost all deaths.
- Children under 3 years of age are at the greatest risk of choking because they tend to put objects—especially toys—in their mouths.

Resource

Selecting Computer Software, color transparency CT-9, TR

Discuss

Why might computers be considered inappropriate for children younger than three years? How can children over three years of age benefit from using the computer?

Resource

Criteria for Selecting Materials and Equipment, transparency master 10-5, TR

Reflect

Why does it benefit toy manufacturers to follow voluntary safety standards? Would the fact that a toy manufacturer voluntarily follows safety standards influence your purchase of one of their toys?

Putting Technology to Use

Have students conduct an Internet search for information regarding toy safety resources that could be distributed to teachers and families of preschoolers. Some examples include: PIRG (Public Interest Research Groups) Toy Safety Hotline; W.A.T.C.H. (World Against Toys Causing Harm) 10 Worst Toys list; The American Red Cross, as well as many other resources. Have students make a bibliography or resource list that could be handed out to families containing sources of information. Have students include Web sites of online sources.

Note

Occasionally children may bring toys from home to play with or for show and tell. Be sure to have guidelines in place for toys brought from home. Ask families to follow these guidelines so you will not have to deal with removing a toy that is inappropriate or unsafe.

Activity

Have students visit a craft fair or a store where handmade dolls and toys are sold. Ask them to compare the safety of the handmade items to those commercially manufactured. Have students identify any areas that may concern them regarding safety. Be sure students notice the difference between handmade products purely for show or decoration and those made for play by a preschooler.

Discuss

What is a *product recall* or *ban*? Do you know of any toys or childhood equipment that have been recalled in recent years? Share your information with the class.

- Riding toys—including bicycles and scooters—cause many injuries in children.

Several federal laws regulate the manufacture and labeling of children's toys. Two of these laws are the Child Protection and Toy Safety Act and the U.S. Child Safety Protection Act. The Child Protection and Toy Safety Act sets basic standards for toy manufacturers. The U.S. Child Safety Protection Act mandates warning labels on toys that indicate whether the toy poses choking hazards to children younger than three years. Manufacturers must make sure toys and other children's products comply with all federal laws. Always check these labels carefully for warning recommendations.

The government agency that issues and enforces these laws is the U.S. Consumer Product Safety Commission (CPSC). Its mission is to reduce the risk of injuries and deaths associated with consumer products. The CPSC is heavily involved in the safety of children's products. The CPSC also recalls or bans unsafe products, conducts product research, and informs and educates consumers about product safety.

As a result of laws and standards, most new toys are developed with safety in mind. When used by children of an appropriate developmental age, these toys are generally safe. For example, small stringing beads are safe and useful for many four-year-old children. In the hands of a two-year-old, however, they present a risk of choking. Keeping inappropriate toys away from younger children is important.

Older toys are much more likely than newer toys to present safety hazards. This is because the toys were made prior to the most recent standards. They may contain the hazards addressed by these standards. Check older toys (or toys of an unknown age) very carefully for potential risks. Discard any items you find that contain any of the following safety hazards:

- *Breakable pieces.* For children under three years of age, toys must be unbreakable and able to withstand use and abuse.

- *Sharp edges or points.* Toys made with sharp edges or points are dangerous. Also hazardous are older toys that break and expose internal sharp edges or points. An example is a stuffed toy with sharp wires inside to stiffen its ears, legs, paws, and tail. Dolls that have hair or clothing held in place by straight pins are also dangerous.

- *Small parts.* For children under three years of age, toys and all parts of toys smaller than 1⅝ inches in diameter or 1½ inches long present a choking hazard, 10-12. Check product labeling to verify whether a toy is appropriate for children under three years of age. For toys with no label attached, use a plastic form or empty cardboard tube (from a roll of toilet tissue) to test the size. Any toy that fits inside the form or tube presents a choking risk for children under three years of age. Of particular risk are balls

10-12

Toy Part Measurements

1⅝-inch diameter

1½-inch length

The safest toys for children under age three years have small parts that meet these size standards.

Cross-Curricular Activity

Language Arts

Ask students to write, perform, and videotape thirty-second and sixty-second television public safety announcements regarding toy safety. Your school's technology or television department may be able to offer assistance in shooting and editing the video. Videos should contain needed information in a concise and visual method. Show the videos to preschool parents at conferences or to high school parents during parent nights.

with a diameter or 1¾ inches or less and rattles that are small enough to be lodged in the throat or with pieces that can separate.

- *Toxic materials in or on toys.* For example, older toys may be painted with lead paint, which can be poisonous if ingested. Older art materials may contain toxic materials.

- *Electrically operated toys with heating elements.* These toys can cause burns, fires, or electrocution. Any electrical equipment should have a seal from a safety testing organization, such as Underwriters Laboratories, Inc. (UL).

- *Battery covers with no locking mechanism.* Children can remove these covers, which exposes the batteries. Batteries present a choking risk and are poisonous if placed in the mouth or swallowed. Also dangerous are battery covers with removable screws. If these tiny screws are lost during battery changes, a child might later find and swallow them. Instead, look for covers that incorporate the screws or other locking mechanisms as part of a single-piece. Even safer is a single-piece cover that is attached to the toy. An attached battery cover eliminates the risk of choking on the cover itself.

- *Fabric products or toys that are not flame retardant or flame resistant.* The label will indicate whether a product is made to resist or slow the rate of burning.

- *Balloons.* Many children each year die from choking on uninflated balloons or balloon pieces. Inflated balloons can also be hazardous if they pop and are swallowed.

- *Toys with small beadlike objects inside them.* If these toys are broken, the objects can fall out and pose a choking risk.

- *Pull toys with long cords or strings.* Cords and strings on toys should be too short to wrap around a child's neck, preventing the chance of strangulation. Strings should be no longer than 12 inches.

- *Plastic climbing equipment used indoors without proper surfacing.* Carpeting does not provide adequate protection from falls from indoor climbing equipment. The CPSC reports these falls are the leading cause for significant injuries in child care settings. For indoor climbing equipment, approved rubber flooring or tile is needed.

If you have a safety problem with a product, you have an ethical obligation to report it. Your report can help protect other children from the same danger. Call the CPSC or visit the CPSC Web site to report an unsafe product. The CPSC investigates the reports it receives from consumers. If the CPSC finds the product to be unsafe, it may issue a product recall or ban. The CPSC can also set new standards in response to reports of consumer safety problems.

Safe Playgrounds

The National Program for Playground Safety (NPPS) has identified four components that contribute to safe playgrounds.

Supervision

Supervision is the first component. This begins with designing the playground into zones to promote safety. Each zone should reflect the type of activity occurring in the area. Zones may include gross-motor, quiet undisturbed play, sand-water, planting and digging, and wheeled-toy.

Discuss

Falls from indoor climbing equipment are the leading cause for significant injuries in child care settings. What safety precautions can be taken to avoid this type of fall?

Activity

Have students investigate the Consumer Products Safety Commission (CPSC) Web site at **www.cpsc.gov**. What toys are on the recently recalled list? What safety hazards caused these toys to be recalled? What other information can be found on the Web site? Allow time for students to share their findings in class.

Discuss

What are the four components that contribute to safe playgrounds? List the five zones that may be included in the playground area.

Putting Technology to Use

Have students search the Internet for information on the standards for playground safety and the relation of standards to the Consumer Products Safety Commission (CPSC). Sources to consider include: the National Playground Contractor's Association (NPCA), the International Playground Equipment Manufacturer's Associations (IPEMA), the National Program for Playground Safety (NPPS), and the National Playground Safety Institute (NPSI). Have students write a brief summary of their findings. Allow time for students to share their findings in class.

Discuss

Why do playgrounds need to be age-appropriate? What playground developmental design features should be considered for preschoolers?

Vocabulary

Have student volunteers explain the difference between *unitary surfacing materials* and *loose fill impact absorbing materials.* Ask students to provide examples of each type of material.

Activity

Have students perform a safety check of a local playground. Ask students to inspect the equipment for loose screws or bolts, sharp edges, and broken and missing parts. What types of surfacing materials are used in the playground? Is the playground age-appropriate? Allow time for students to discuss their findings in class.

Health and Safety

Playgrounds for Children with Special Needs

Children with special needs may require a variety of playground modifications for accessibility and safety. For example, children with mobility problems may need wheelchair ramps or transfer systems. Consult the *Americans with Disabilities Act* (ADA) Web site at ada.gov for more information on accessibility for play areas.

Proper Developmental Design

Proper developmental design is the second component. Playgrounds should be age-appropriate. Preschool children need equipment designed closer to the ground. Ramps on this equipment should have railings for grasping. Platforms should be low with only a few access points. When over 3 feet high, decks need a railing to prevent falls. The sand table or area should have a cover to protect the children from sun.

Protective Surfacing

Protective surfacing or shock absorbers are the third component. All equipment other than sandboxes and playhouses that have no elevated space needs *protective surfacing.* Suitable shock-absorbing surfacing materials are energy absorbing and resilient. Concrete and asphalt are unsuitable under or around equipment of any height. They have poor shock-absorbing properties.

Hard-packed dirt and earth surfaces are poor shock absorbers, so they are not recommended. Likewise, grass and turf are not on the recommended list. Wear and tear can reduce their effectiveness in absorbing a shock.

There are two types of acceptable playground surfacing materials: unitary or loose fill. *Unitary surfacing materials* are rubber mats or a blend of rubber-like materials. A shock-absorbing surface is formed when the loose fill materials are poured in place at the playground site and cured.

Loose fill impact absorbing materials should be soft and resilient. Examples include gravel, wood chips or mulch, rubber mats or tile systems, and sand. Ten or more inches are required under and around equipment on preschool playgrounds. This should reduce the chances of serious injury for falls up to eight or ten feet. See Chart 10-13 for a comparison of surfacing materials.

Equipment Maintenance

Equipment maintenance is the fourth component of safe playgrounds. Well-maintained playgrounds provide greater protection and help minimize risk. Conduct general inspections and look for loose screws or bolts, sharp edges, and broken and missing parts. Cap open pipes and remove tripping hazards. When using loose fill under equipment, monitor the depth. If needed, add more fill. Inspections should also include checks for rotten lumber.

Putting Technology to Use

Have students conduct an Internet search for information about designing playgrounds for use by children with disabilities. For example, how has the Americans with Disabilities Act affected the development of playgrounds? Who helps decide how to design the playgrounds, and what types of experiences should be offered? How have communities and schools funded the building of accessible playgrounds? Have students present an oral report of their findings to the class.

10-13

Surfacing Materials: Advantages and Disadvantages

Material	Advantages	Disadvantages
Gravel	• Readily available • Inexpensive • Drains easily • Easy to install	• Needs barriers to contain • Pea gravel not recommended for children under five years of age • Medium-sized gravel causes more superficial scrapes • Occasionally needs replacement • Becomes compact when wet
Bark Mulch	• Readily available • Inexpensive • Drains easily • Easy to install	• Needs barriers to contain • Compacts easily • Decomposes quickly so needs replacement periodically
Shredded tires	• Inexpensive • More wheelchair accessible than loose fill	• Requires a good drainage system • May stain clothing if not treated • Is flammable
Mat systems or rubber matting	• Easy to clean and maintain • Accessible for wheelchairs • Does not absorb water • Prohibits mold and fungus growth • Foreign objects are easy to see • Annual replacement requirements are lower	• The most expensive to install • Needs to be installed on a flat surface
Sand	• Inexpensive • Does not deteriorate • Easy to install	• Attractive to cats • Must be raked • Undesirable or harmful objects may become embedded

When choosing a playground surfacing material, weigh the advantages and disadvantages carefully.

Note

A playground surfaced with a hard material such as asphalt or concrete can cause serious head injuries if a child falls. Make sure preschoolers are supervised constantly while on the playground.

Reflect

Think about the surfacing material in your local playground. Would you have selected these materials or would some other type of material be more effective?

Discuss

What types of materials are accessible for wheelchairs? What are the advantages and disadvantages of using these materials?

Putting Technology to Use

Have students conduct an Internet search for more information about surfacing materials. Ask students to compare cost and ease of installation. Have students prioritize their selection of appropriate playground surfacing materials based on recommendations from reputable online sources. Have students write a brief report explaining their choice. Allow time for students to discuss their selections in class.

Resource

Playground Equipment Dangers, transparency masters 10-6A and 10-6B, TR

Note

Have students review Chapter 9 for information on planning for an outdoor playground.

Resource

Evaluating a Swing Set, Activity B, OG

Selecting Playground Equipment

In Chapter 9, you learned about planning for an outdoor playground. In this chapter, you will learn about selecting the equipment that will be used on the playground. This equipment may consist of stationary equipment, wheeled toys, wading pools or sprinklers, a shaded resting area, and animal shelters. Stationary equipment is the most costly and difficult to choose.

Selecting playground equipment may be the job of the director. Teachers are often asked for suggestions to help in this process. In other programs, a committee of parents, teachers, and directors choose the playground equipment. Everyone involved in the decision needs to know key points to consider.

Safety

When it comes to playground equipment, safety should always be the main concern. Many children are injured each year on outdoor playgrounds. Choosing equipment with safety in mind can reduce the number of serious injuries. Visit the CPSC Web site for detailed information about specific kinds of equipment.

Avoid choosing new equipment that is unsafe and check existing equipment for dangers. Repair or remove any dangerous equipment at once. General hazards to avoid include the following:

- *Exposed pinch-crush parts on seesaws or gliders.* Children's skin or clothing can be caught in these areas. In addition, a child might lose a finger or toe if pinched here. Remove equipment with exposed pinch-crust parts from the playground at once.

- *Head entrapment openings.* Measure the exercise rings or space between parts of equipment, such as rungs in a ladder. Openings should be smaller than 3.5 inches or larger than 10 inches.

Children can get their heads caught in openings between these sizes. Remove any rings or close in any risers on ladders of unsafe sizes.

- *Open-end S-rings on swing sets.* These rings can pinch skin or catch clothing. You can close the S-ring by pinching the ring shut with a pair of pliers.

- *Hard swing seats.* Children can be injured if hit by a hard swing seat, such as those made of wood, metal, or hard plastic. Replace any hard swing seats with those made of rubber or canvas, 10-14.

- *Exposed screws, bolts, or sharp edges.* Cuts and scrapes can result from these hazards. Use your hands to feel all the equipment. Cover bolts, screws, or sharp edges with layers of duct tape. Recheck the area often and reapply tape as needed. In addition, exposed screws and bolts are a danger because a child's hair or clothes can catch on them.

- *Hot metal playground equipment.* The U.S. Consumer Product Safety Commission (CPSC) advises adults to check for hot metal surfaces before allowing children to play on them. Solid steel slides, decks, steps, and railings in

10-14

The safest swings have closed S-rings, rubber or canvas seats, steady anchoring, and adequate surfacing.

Meeting Special Needs

Pair student volunteers with special learners to review the playground equipment hazards listed in the text. Have students visit the Consumer Product Safety Commission (CPSC)

Web site at **www.cpsc.gov** for further information about playground safety hazards. Spend additional time discussing any information that is difficult for special learners to understand.

direct sunlight may reach temperatures high enough to cause serious burns. Unlike adults or older children, young children are at major risk since they do not react quickly. They may remain in place when in contact with a hot surface. The result could be second or third degree burns to the buttocks, hands, and legs.

Even if a piece of equipment is free from safety hazards, it still may not be safe for use by children in a particular program. Adults should consider each piece of equipment in terms of the following:

- Is the equipment safe for the children's ages and level of development? Some pieces of stationary equipment are designed for older children. Others are made for younger children. Programs with children of mixed ages need separate equipment for each age group.

- Is there enough room for the equipment on the existing playground? This includes room required around the equipment for safety. Pieces of play equipment should be spaced at least 6 feet apart. Equipment should not be placed too close to sandboxes, wheeled toy paths, fences, or sidewalks.

- Can the equipment be anchored properly? Equipment must be stable to avoid overturning, tipping, sliding, or moving in any way. The equipment needs to be anchored in concrete below ground level before it is used. The anchoring process needs to comply with manufacturer's specifications.

Appeal

If the equipment does not appeal to children, they will not use it. Before choosing equipment, teachers might ask children what they want to do on the playground (such as climb, swing, run). Then equipment can be chosen to allow children to meet their goals.

Equipment needs to be able to accommodate several children at once, 10-15. It should also be accessible for children with special needs. Colorful and interesting design attracts children's interest. Children prefer having a variety of equipment. They enjoy being able to push, pull, balance, swing, and slide. Children also like equipment on which they can climb or crawl in, out, under, and around. What they seem to like least is equipment with just one use.

Maintenance

When shopping for playground equipment, keep maintenance in mind. The program's staff will be responsible for repairing or replacing broken equipment. For safety reasons, children must not use or play near broken equipment.

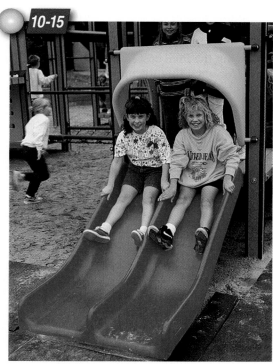
10-15

Playing together on the equipment enhances children's social skills and enjoyment of active play.

Enrich

Have students compare children's appeal of playground equipment that seems to have just one use (such as a stationary horse) with equipment that may have many uses. Which type of equipment helps encourage children to play and practice social skills with other children? Allow time for students to discuss in class.

Reflect

What might either of the children using the double slide in the photo in 10-15 be feeling as they play together? What childhood memories of playground play with a friend or friends do you recall? What effect did playing with others have on your use of the playground?

Resource

Actions to Take, Activity C, SAG

Workplace Connection

Have students survey local playgrounds in the community that might be accessed for field trips by preschool children. What features of the playgrounds make them a good location for a field trip? How can you justify taking a field trip to another playground if your program already has outdoor equipment and play space? What additional program goals can be met by taking preschool children on field trips? Have students write a brief report of their findings.

Vocabulary

Have a student volunteer define the term *co-op*. How can co-ops help manage costs in a preschool program?

Activity

Have students locate co-ops, warehouse stores, or wholesale suppliers of toys or equipment that could be used in an early childhood program. Ask students to research membership costs, limits or special requirements for ordering, return and refund privileges, and recommendations by other child care facilities that have used these sources. Allow time for students to discuss their findings in class.

Vocabulary

Have a student volunteer define the term *consumable supplies*. Why do preschool programs need consumable supplies?

Choose equipment that is durable. This equipment will withstand many years of heavy use. It will be less likely to break and need repair, which lowers maintenance costs.

For durability and safety, many of the newer playgrounds are constructed from plastic with metal and wood supports. This type of equipment combines the best features of each type of material. All-metal equipment is too hot in summer and too cold in winter. Over time, this equipment will also rust. All-wood equipment will weaken, splinter, and rot.

Cost

Of course, programs must follow their budget when making playground purchases. Some programs plan a fundraiser to help meet the cost of expensive items. Staff should search catalogs and Web sites of several companies to learn what is available. Programs should receive cost estimates from each company. They should ask about costs for delivery, assembly, and installation. Knowing the final cost helps the program set goals for obtaining the money needed.

Sources for Toys and Equipment

Before you begin selecting new toys and equipment, take an inventory of materials that are on hand. After this is done, compare the inventory with program goals. For example, you may note that there are too few manipulative toys. These then should be at the top of the list for purchase. See 10-16.

Using your list, browse through catalogs to find items you need. Take time to look through all the catalogs at the center. Catalog prices can vary a great deal. Consider all costs before ordering. For instance, does the shipping cost for an item make the purchase price too high? Some companies will not charge a shipping fee if the order is large.

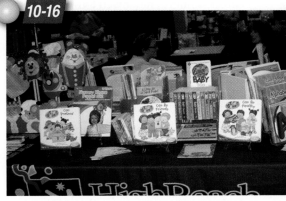

10-16

The exhibit area at an early childhood conference is a good source for toys and equipment.

Equipment can also be bought through a co-op. A **co-op (cooperative)** is a group of people or organizations who join together for the mutual benefit of more buying power. Co-ops are sometimes formed by directors of several small centers. One of the goals of the co-op is to purchase toys and equipment at the lowest cost. Companies will often give a discount on large orders. The directors share the savings with all those who are making purchases.

If time is available, you may wish to visit flea markets, garage sales, and discount stores. Materials can often be purchased at reduced prices. When buying used items be extra cautious regarding safety. Check for product recalls and know the safety standards for the objects you seek.

Toys can also be designed and built at the center. Senior citizens, Girl Scout and Boy Scout troops, and others may volunteer to help. Many of these people are skilled in making puppets, doll clothes, dramatic play clothes, and wooden toys.

Buying Consumable Supplies

Clay, paper, paint, paste, glue, and other art materials are called **consumable supplies**. Once a consumable supply is used, it cannot be used again. In order to save money, some

---

Cross-Curricular Activity

Math
Give students a specific amount of money to be budgeted for toy and equipment acquisition for the coming school year. Predetermine the percentages of the amount to be spent on each area. Ask students to select the materials to be purchased without going over budget. Have students create a spreadsheet to keep track of selections and amount of money spent. Have students figure out the percentages of their expenditures for each activity type after they have selected the materials for that area. Remind students they are to consider consumable supplies as part of the total. Students should be able to justify their selections.

centers order these materials only once or twice a year. There are many ways to purchase these supplies.

If the order is large, the center may ask vendors to make bids on the sale. *Vendors* are the people who sell the supplies. Their bid is the price at which they will sell the items.

The center might also contact a vendor when placing a large order and ask for a 10 percent discount, plus free shipping. Many directors are surprised to learn that this can be done. This is very useful for stretching the center budget.

Another approach is to make a list of the supplies needed. Mark those items that could be donated, 10-17. Note who is in charge of securing what items. For example, the head teacher may be in charge of getting newsprint. Another teacher would be in charge of getting wallpaper. In some centers, the director is solely responsible for securing all donations.

10-17

Consumable Supplies

Quantity	Item	Purchase	Solicit Donation	Source	Person Responsible
1 roll	Newsprint		X	Dunn County News	Anna
10 cans	Red tempera paint	X		ABC School Supply	Jodi
10 cans	Yellow tempera paint	X		ABC School Supply	Jodi
5 rolls	Wallpaper		X	Menomonie Paint Store	Anna
2 buckets	Sawdust		X	Peterson Lumber Co.	Anna
4 gallons	Dried corn		X	Hardy's Elevator	Jodi
4 yards	Fabric scraps		X	Northwest Fabrics	Anna
2 gallons	Paste	X		ABC School Supply	Jodi
1 box	Foam packing pieces		X	James Jewelers	Anna
24 boxes	Crayons	X		ABC School Supply	Jodi

Many groups are often eager to donate materials to worthy programs such as child care centers.

Note

Several programs exist to help schools obtain play equipment and other items by collecting and turning in labels. Other activities include hosting a show or party, shopping with a fundraising coupon, or using a credit card with a designated nonprofit group as the beneficiary. Discuss the advantages and disadvantages of using these programs to help augment your budget.

Discuss

Ask students what local sources may be available for the donation of consumable supplies. What may be some drawbacks to depending on locally donated items on a regular basis?

Resource

Comparing Prices, Activity D, SAG

Meeting Special Needs

Review the special learners' chapter outlines to determine if the students have any questions about the concepts or content of this chapter. Review the chapter objectives and ask the students to evaluate their progress in meeting these objectives. Ask the students to summarize, orally or in writing, what they learned from this chapter.

Review and Reflect Answer Key

1. true
2. program goals
3. (Student response.)
4. Space must be available for the item purchased. If space is not available, the item may end up in an inconvenient location and seldom used.
5. false
6. D
7. If there is a shortage of play materials, undesirable behavior can result.
8. Spectator
9. Physical age is determined by a birth date. Developmental age refers to a child's skill and growth level compared to what is thought of as normal for that physical age.
10. Suitable toys help build self-esteem. Unsuitable toys can cause frustration.
11. B
12. Multicultural toys represent a variety of cultural and ethnic groups.
13. (List two. Student response.)
14. (List two. Student response.)
15. six
16. (List three. Student response.)

Summary

Selecting toys and equipment is an important task. There are several guidelines that should be followed before purchases are made. Key factors to be considered are program goals, budget, balance, space, supervision, maintenance, durability, quantity, child involvement, and developmental age. Toys should also be nonviolent, nonsexist, multicultural, and safe.

Safety is a key consideration when buying toys and playground equipment. Laws and guidelines have been developed to help you choose safe products for the children in your care. Report any defective or unsafe products to the U.S. Consumer Product Safety Commission.

Once guidelines are reviewed, purchases can be made. The teacher must know where and how to make these purchases. In this way, the teacher will be able to use the center budget wisely.

Review and Reflect

1. True or false. Toys can promote the development of specific skills.

2. Classroom toys and equipment should reflect the _____ the center has developed.

3. Why is budget an important consideration when buying items for the classroom?

4. How does available space affect toy and equipment selection?

5. True or false. Maintenance is *not* an important factor in choosing equipment.

6. Toys must be durable because _____.
   A. children will sit on, stand on, and drop them
   B. broken toys can be dangerous
   C. it is expensive to replace broken toys
   D. All the above.

7. Why is the quantity of toys an important consideration in toy selection?

8. _____ toys require little action on the part of children.

9. Explain the difference between physical age and developmental age.

10. Why is it important to choose toys that are appropriate for a child's developmental age?

11. Play that revolves around violent toys is often _____.
    A. constructive
    B. aggressive and destructive
    C. a good learning experience

12. What are multicultural toys?

13. Give two guidelines for setting up a technology area in the early childhood classroom.

14. List two characteristics that are vital in selecting developmentally appropriate software programs.

17. A. Rings that are between 3.5 and 10 inches in diameter can trap a child's head.
    B. Wooden swing seats can injure a child who might walk in the path of them.
    C. Screws and bolts can scratch and cut children.
18. supervision, proper developmental design, protective surfacing, and equipment maintenance
19. (List three:) resilient tiles, wood chips, wood mulch, fine sand, fine gravel, bark nuggets, shredded bark, shredded tires, rubber matting or mat systems
20. A consumable supply is an item that, once used, cannot be used again.

15. The age at which most children can comfortably operate simple computer programs is _____ years.

16. List three safety guidelines to follow when purchasing toys.

17. Describe the dangers of each of the following:
    A. Rings.
    B. Wooden swing seats.
    C. Screws and bolts.

18. According to the National Program for Playground Safety, what four components contribute to playground safety?

19. Name three impact-absorbing materials that are acceptable playground surfacing materials.

20. What is a consumable supply?

Apply and Explore

1. In small groups, make a basic list of equipment for a classroom.

2. Ask an early childhood program director about toy and equipment selection criteria.

3. Cut pictures of toys from equipment catalogs that would be safe and appropriate for most two-year-old children.

Cross-Curricular Link

Language Arts

1. Discuss favorite childhood toys and the value of each.

Technology

2. Check the age-by-age toy guidelines as well as tips for choosing toys for children with disabilities at the Web site of the Toy Industry Association, Inc. (www.toy-tma.org).

3. Search the Web site for the U.S. Consumer Product Safety Commission (www.cpsc.gov). Check the warning related to playground hazards that can endanger children.

4. Check the Web sites for online catalogs for the following vendors: www.eichild.com; www.kaplanco.com; and www.lakeshorelearning.com. Prepare a brief written report describing offerings from each of these vendors.

5. Visit the Web site www.childrenandcomputers.com to review software recommendations for young children.

Workplace Link

Compare the durability of classroom equipment and toys that have been purchased recently with those that have been in use for many years. You may need to locate area schools and programs that have both new and older items. What materials have stood up over time and are functioning as well as the newer items? What recommendations do you have for future purchases based on this research?

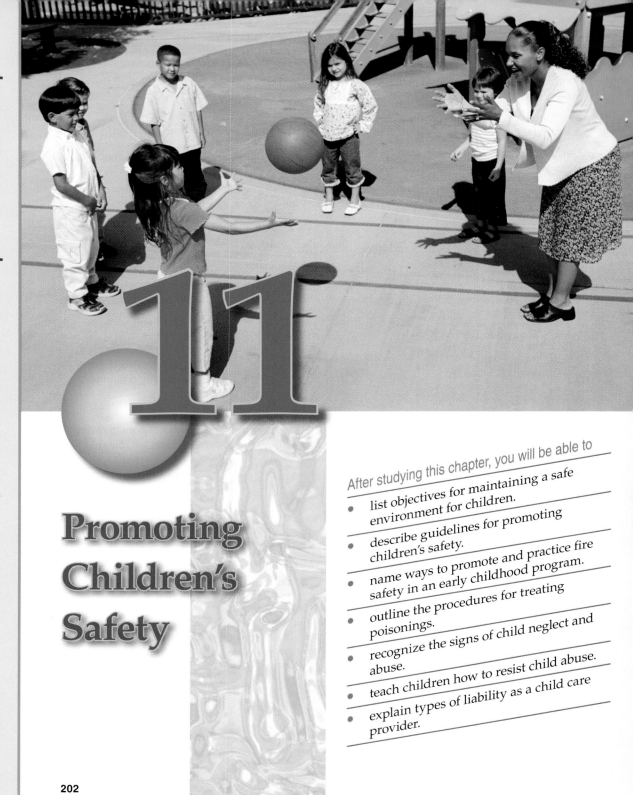

Discuss

Look at the chapter opening photo. How do you think the teacher is promoting children's safety? Do you think she should be doing anything more to keep the children safe?

Discuss

Review the chapter objectives before reading the chapter. Remember that the teacher in an early childhood classroom is ultimately responsible for the children's safety and well-being. How does this affect your attitude toward approaching the chapter content?

11

Promoting Children's Safety

After studying this chapter, you will be able to

- list objectives for maintaining a safe environment for children.
- describe guidelines for promoting children's safety.
- name ways to promote and practice fire safety in an early childhood program.
- outline the procedures for treating poisonings.
- recognize the signs of child neglect and abuse.
- teach children how to resist child abuse.
- explain types of liability as a child care provider.

Terms to Know

limits
emetic
nonaccidental physical injury
neglect
emotional abuse
sexual abuse
incest
molestation
statute
privacy law

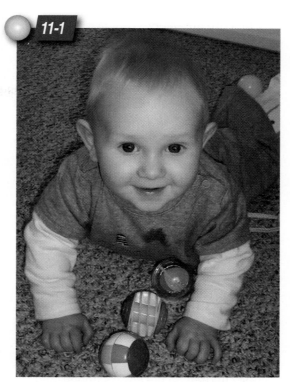

11-1

Young children are active and adventurous. They can get themselves into dangerous situations in seconds. Supervision is necessary at all times.

"Please give me that broken toy," teacher Tina Goldstein said to the child. She immediately saw the danger of the unsafe toy. At the same time, Gloria Hernandez, the center director, was checking the art supplies. In the kitchen, the cook was filling out the monthly safety and sanitation checklist. All these staff members were showing their concern for the children's safety by checking the safety of their surroundings.

Dangers can be found everywhere in a child care center, 11-1. Electrical outlets, cleaning supplies, woodworking tools, outdoor climbing equipment, and cooking tools can all cause injuries. Staff members must closely watch for and remove these dangers. Failure to do so may result in accidents. Most of these accidents can be avoided.

Accidents are more likely to occur when the children's routine is disrupted. Accidents also occur more frequently when staff are absent, busy, or tired.

Children can also be put in danger through abuse. Teachers must be aware of the signs of physical and emotional abuse. By law, teachers must report known or suspected child abuse.

As an early childhood teacher, you will need to be alert to any dangers that threaten the safety of your children. In addition,
your program must have safety limits and procedures. The staff must also be aware of their legal responsibilities for protecting the children in their care. Because safety standards vary from state to state, consult your licensing standards.

Safety Objectives

The staff is responsible for providing a safe environment for children. The following are basic objectives toward this goal:

- Supervise the children at all times.

- Maintain at least the minimum adult-child ratio as required in your state.

- Develop safety limits.

- Provide a safe environment.

Vocabulary

Review the *Terms to Know* list with students. Ask students to look up unfamiliar words or terms in the glossary before reading the chapter.

Reflect

Did you ever experience an incident where a child was hurt even though adults were present and supervision seemed adequate? What does this tell you about the need for anticipation of any possible accidents or injuries that may occur where children are concerned?

Discuss

Go around the room and have students quickly mention items they spot that could be dangerous to children. Ask if they can think of ways to childproof these items.

Meeting Special Needs

Provide a chapter outline with all the headings for special learners. Emphasize that this is one of the most important chapters they will study this year. Prepare a vocabulary list or matching assignment to assist in learning the meanings of the new vocabulary words in this chapter. Review the special learners' IEPs to decide if any modifications should be made in presenting the chapter content.

Note

Impress on students the idea that children cannot *ever* be left alone. Child care teachers are responsible for children's safety. If an accident or incident should occur in the moment children are left alone, the teacher is liable.

Discuss

Why can't young children always recognize that their behaviors or actions can cause injuries? Explain how the lack of logical thinking abilities at this age may contribute to reckless or dangerous behavior.

Enrich

Have students research the adult-child ratios required for your state according to licensing rules. Have them also research the liability issues related to not meeting these ratios.

- Practice fire safety.
- Develop plans for weather emergencies.
- Know emergency procedures for accidental poisoning.
- Recognize signs of child abuse and report any known or suspected cases.
- Teach children how to protect themselves from sexual assault.

The following sections will summarize procedures for meeting each of these objectives.

Supervise the Children at All Times

"It happened so fast—I just left them for a moment or two," said the child care teacher. This teacher did not understand that children cannot be left alone for even a moment. A teacher who is responsible for a group of children should supervise constantly. Young children do not always understand the concept of danger. As a result, child care teachers must protect the children until they can protect themselves.

Young children are unpredictable, quick, and fearless. They lack sound judgment because they lack experience and cannot see from another's viewpoint. They may bite, throw, push, or shove. All these actions can endanger others as well as themselves. Young children may not recognize behaviors or actions that can cause injuries.

To properly supervise a group of children, keep your back to the classroom wall. Focus on the interior of the classroom. The entire room should be visible. Move closer to an area if you observe children who need assistance or redirection. Likewise, constantly observe children who are not involved in an activity. Be especially protective of younger children. Usually, younger children require more staff supervision than older children.

Health and Safety

Reducing the Risk of Abuse—Facility Layout

In order to protect children from abuse, early childhood facilities should be arranged so all areas of the center are visible by at least one other adult in addition to the care provider. An arrangement that provides high visibility eliminates isolation of children and the child care staff. To enhance visibility and safety, child care facilities may also use video surveillance equipment or other such devices.

Bumps and bruises can occur in overcrowded classrooms. Make sure there is enough space for furniture and equipment. Observe children as they play. Can they move from area to area without bumping into furniture or other children? If sufficient space does not exist, remove some furniture or rearrange the classroom.

Maintain Minimum Adult-Child Ratios

Adult-child ratio relates directly to safety. A classroom should never have fewer adults than required by state law for its age level and group size. Having more adults than the minimum is even safer. These extra adults can step in quickly to protect children when unsafe situations arise.

Meeting Special Needs

Have students who are gifted read the *Child Care Center Design Guide,* published by the U.S. General Services Administration, which can be found at **www.gsa.gov**. (Students may wish to start with Chapter 3, "Adults and Children in the Center.") Have students note how many of the guidelines listed relate to child safety and report on their findings.

At least the minimum number of staff members set by your state's licensing rules must be present at all times. Failure to comply may result in the center's license being revoked or a citation indicating the center was not in compliance. Remember, too, if a child is injured and staff/child ratios are not being met, center staff may be held liable.

Develop Safety Limits

Limits are guides to actions and behaviors that reflect the goals of a program. Limits have also been called *rules*. The most important limits set by early childhood teachers involve safety issues. These limits protect the children in the classroom. Make safety limits clear, simple, and easy for children to understand, 11-2.

Some typical safety limits include:

- Walk indoors. Do not run.

- Use blocks for building, not for hitting.

- Wipe up spills right away.

- Tell the teacher when equipment breaks.

- Always fasten your seat belt when riding in the center van.

- Always use safety straps on equipment when available, 11-3.

11-2

Use bulletin boards to teach children about safety.

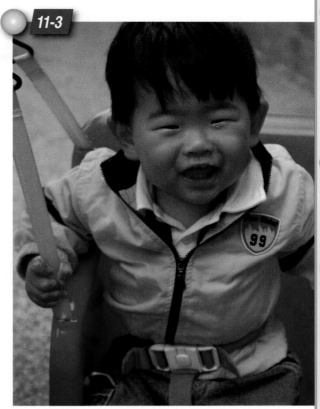

11-3

Child care teachers should use safety straps when available on outside equipment.

- Climb the ladder to go up the slide. Do not walk up the slide from the bottom.

- Wear a helmet when riding bikes.

Remind children about the limits. Otherwise, they may forget or ignore them. For example, Eino may walk in front of moving swings. When this happens, say, "Eino, walk around the swings, not in front of them." Usually, this reminder will redirect a child. If Eino still fails to comply, you may have to say, "Eino, you need to stay away from moving swings." Do not allow anyone to continue swinging until Eino moves a safe distance away from the swings.

Teach children to wipe up spills promptly. Always keep paper towels within

Vocabulary

Have a student volunteer define *limits*. Ask students to explain how limits are used to protect children in the preschool program.

Discuss

Look at the photo in 11-3. What safety features do you see?

Activity

Ask students to design a lesson plan for a circle time activity to teach the classroom limits and rules to the preschoolers. Remind students to be creative and keep the lesson child-centered.

Workplace Connection

Ask students to write a letter to parents explaining the preschool classroom limits and rules. Students should ask for parental support and encouragement in going over the limits with children at home. Some suggestions include asking the child why he or she thinks there needs to be a particular rule. Ask parents to compare the limits and rules that might be in effect at home with the ones followed in the classroom. Review sample student letters in class and decide which one will actually be sent home with the children.

Enrich

Ask students to research the role of children's independence in cleaning up after themselves in the Montessori Method. What can children gain from the act of following the rule to wipe up spills promptly?

Activity

Many items in the preschool room are inherently safe if used appropriately. In an effort to anticipate and deal with accidents or injuries that could result from inappropriate use, ask students to brainstorm the possible misuse of center materials besides those already listed in the text.

Enrich

The photo in 11-4 shows a playground with impact-absorbing surfaces of rubber tiles. This provides a smooth surface for wheelchair accessibility and a loose material surface made of wood chips. Have students research the recommendations for the depth of the loose material required for the best impact-absorbing qualities. Have them also discover how often impacted surfaces need to be refilled.

the children's reach. When children forget to wipe up a spill, remind them. Likewise, it's important to praise children who remember. Say, "Gerald, thank you for wiping up that spill. Now no one will slip and fall." Praise will encourage all the children to remember the limits. In time, you may hear the children remind each other of the limits.

Provide a Safe Environment

Closely observing children and setting safety rules for them to obey helps create a safe center. This is only part of the process. You must also keep watch for hazardous situations. Toys, equipment, electrical appliances, hot water, and cleaning supplies can pose danger to children. Center vehicles and the building itself can also be hazardous to children.

Toys and Materials

A teacher's first job regarding toy safety is to choose items wisely. Picking safe toys and materials greatly reduces the risk of serious injury. (Refer to Chapter 10 to review toy selection safety.)

Selection is just the start, however. As a teacher, you must supervise children using the toys. Children often use toys in ways for which they were not designed. While most times this play is harmless, sometimes you must step in for safety reasons. For instance, a wooden mallet for use with a pegboard might be dangerous if children use it to hit each other. A metal toy car can be used safely for driving on the floor. This same car poses a safety risk if thrown, however. You must teach children about safe toy use and repeat safety limits often. Be firm but pleasant when enforcing the limits.

Remember, a toy can be safe for one child, but dangerous for another. Accidents can occur when children use toys that are too advanced for them. For instance, five-year-old children love to play with large marbles. These same marbles are a choking hazard for younger children.

Check toys frequently for safety. To illustrate, check the seams of cloth toys for tearing and weak threads. Tug at the different parts of the toy to test its strength. If the toy lacks durability, remove it from the classroom. Depending on the condition and value, it can either be repaired or discarded.

Toys should also be examined for sharp or splintered edges. Observe to see if any small pieces have broken off or splintered. If a toy needs repairs, immediately remove it from the classroom.

As a teacher, you must also stay informed about changes in safety standards. When new standards are issued, check current toys to be sure they conform. Discard items that do not meet the new standards.

Playground Equipment

Staff members have several duties when it comes to playground safety. First, they must be sure to plan the play yard with safety in mind. (Refer to Chapter 9 for guidelines about planning play yards.) For example, proper surfacing is a key safety concern, 11-4.

Second, staff members must select safe play yard equipment. Safer equipment

11-4

An impact-absorbing surface was installed under this playground equipment to prevent serious injuries related to falls.

Workplace Connection

Ask students to survey the areas in the school that children access and then document any possible hazards they could encounter. This may include slippery walkways, loose flooring materials, equipment meant for older children, dangers in the parking areas, landscape plants, and weed treatments. What changes could be made to make the areas safe or reduce the hazards? Would child care centers not associated with a high school program be subject to the same types of hazards?

eliminates many preventable accidents. (Refer to Chapter 10 for more on this topic.) Many products are available today to help children enjoy safe outdoor play.

Third, staff must evaluate existing equipment for safety. Older equipment may not meet current safety standards. This equipment often contains hazards not found on newer equipment. These hazards include head entrapments, sharp edges, hard swing seats, and all-metal slides. Staff should research laws on play yard equipment safety. They must be sure their program complies with these requirements. Next, staff can seek tips from professional organizations regarding play yard safety. These tips can offer extra protection by exceeding legal requirements.

As equipment ages, it is likely to need upkeep and repair. For this reason, all play yard equipment must be checked often for dangers. Many programs devise a safety checklist to guide teachers in inspecting the play yard. Teachers conduct weekly checks, fill out the checklist, and give it to the director. The director must then arrange for needed repairs or maintenance.

Finally, and perhaps most importantly, staff are responsible for supervising children on the play yard. Even the safest equipment can cause accidents when it is not used properly. Limits must be set and enforced regarding equipment use. Children can be involved in setting these limits, if developmentally appropriate. Teachers must closely watch children using the equipment and step in when needed. Staff should praise children who are practicing safety.

Transportation

Motor vehicle accidents pose the greatest threats to children's lives. Vans, buses, and other vehicles owned by the center should have safety door locks and safety restraints installed according to manufacturers' specifications.

- Infants weighing up to 22 pounds should be placed in an infant carrier. The carrier

should be installed facing the rear of the vehicle.

- Safety seats should be installed facing forward for children capable of sitting up by themselves and weighing 20-40 pounds.

- Children under 54 inches in height who have outgrown car seats need a booster seat, lap belt, and shoulder harness.

- Children who are 55-58 inches and above need a lap belt and shoulder harness.

Train all staff and parent volunteers on the proper use of safety seats. While riding in any center vehicles, children should be fastened in a properly adjusted seat belt or safety seat. Do not allow children to put their arms or heads out of the vehicle's windows. When a number of children are riding in a vehicle, extra adult supervision may be required.

Center vehicles should be equipped for emergency situations. A first aid kit for treating minor injuries should be located in each vehicle. Moreover, a fire extinguisher and tools for changing tires should also be present in each vehicle. Vehicle drivers should be informed how to use these items.

Building Security

Safety measures must be taken to control unauthorized access to the building. Some centers issue keypads or card keys such as those used in hotels to parents and staff. Outside gates should have locks installed and be locked. Some centers also install observation cameras to monitor entrances and exits.

Many accidents that occur in centers involve the building and building fixtures. Windows, doors, floors, and stairs all may cause injuries. Doors should have rubber gaskets to prevent finger pinching. They should be designed to open to the outside and have see-through panes. This will help prevent injuries by making the children visible to anyone opening the door.

Discuss

Playgrounds located on public school property may be accessible for community use during nonschool hours. What problems may occur with playground equipment and the playground environment as a result of this accessibility? How will this affect the selection of equipment for the playground?

Note

High school students will not be allowed to operate motor vehicles for the transport of preschoolers during the vocational preschool experience. However, future employment may require students to drive. (Check the state's age restrictions for drivers.) Remind students to maintain a safe driving record. Driving violations and accidents may affect the student's ability to secure employment where driving children is required.

Resource

Equipment Dangers, color transparency CT-10, TR

Service Learning Activity

Some community groups, service organizations, and police departments conduct periodic safety checks of infant and child seats installed in motor vehicles. Child care students may have an opportunity for community service during the safety checks.

They can assist in public relations, encourage parent participation, and hand out literature and safety information to parents. Ask students to research the possibility of participating in a project like this or starting their own car seat safety checkup.

Enrich

Have students investigate licensing standards in your state for the use of safety glass in preschool and child care centers. Have them determine if the preschool classroom in your school meets the requirements for safety glass.

Discuss

What might happen if a preschooler was able to access and activate a fire alarm? What precautions, if any, exist in your school to prevent this from happening?

Resource

Outdoor Safety Checklist, Activity B, OG

Keep windows closed at all times unless gates or sturdy screens are in place. Keep floors dry. If wax is used, use a nonslip type. Cover stairways with carpet or rubber treads. Make sure stairways are well-lighted and free of clutter. Install railings at the children's level on both sides of the stairs.

Sliding patio doors, doors with glass panels, and storm doors can all be dangerous. To protect the children, use only safety glass. Decals applied to sliding glass doors at their eye level warn children of glass they might not otherwise see.

Cover all unused electrical outlets in the building. Avoid using extension cords, particularly if they are placed under carpets or rugs. If the cord becomes worn, a fire may occur.

Practice Fire Safety

To promote fire safety, check the center regularly for fire hazards. The best protection against fires is prevention. For instance, store matches where children cannot reach them and accidentally start fires. As a teacher, you need to find and correct fire hazards. A fire safety checklist is shown in 11-5. Study this list so you will be able to spot hazards and take action quickly.

Check smoke alarms at least once each month to make sure they are working. If smoke detectors are battery powered, change batteries when indicated.

Fire Extinguishers

Each child care center needs several fire extinguishers. One fire extinguisher should be placed in or next to the kitchen. Place an extinguisher in or near each classroom. Another extinguisher is needed in the laundry area. Check your state's licensing regulations for the placement of fire extinguishers.

The director is often in charge of buying fire extinguishers for the center. Before buying an extinguisher, contact your local

fire department. The fire chief can tell you which type of extinguisher is best suited for your center's unique needs. You will want one that fights the types of fires your center is most likely to have. In addition, ask the fire chief how to maintain the extinguisher and recharge it after use.

Schedule an in-service on fire extinguisher use prior to the opening of the center. Some directors prefer to have a local firefighter conduct this in-service. After this orientation, update all staff members yearly (and newly hired members) on fire extinguisher use.

Check the condition of each fire extinguisher monthly. Note any problems you find. Replace immediately any extinguisher with any of the following conditions:

- pressure gauge indicating the higher or lower pressure than recommended
- blocked nozzle or other parts
- missing pin or tamper seal
- dents, leaks, rust, or other signs of damage

Fire Drills and Evacuation Procedures

Most state licensing rules and regulations require fire and disaster drills. Most states also recommend drills be scheduled on a regular basis, such as once a month. Vary the time of day and day of week. These drills will prepare staff and children for a real fire or other emergency. During drills, use the daily class roster to take roll. It is an important tool for checking on the evacuation of all children and their safe return indoors.

Every center needs to have well-planned evacuation procedures. The procedures should include escape routes, staff assignments, and location of alarms. The evacuation procedures should be posted in every room where they can be easily seen. Emergency phone numbers should also be posted. In case of blocked routes, alternative evacuation routes should be planned. An

Portfolio Project

Many states require a specific number of in-service continuing education credits be earned each year by child care professionals. A fire extinguisher demonstration would qualify for an in-service training activity. Ask a representative of the extinguisher company or your school's head custodian to give

a demonstration. Prepare a certificate for each student in the class to document their attendance. The certificate can be filed in the students' portfolios as a representation of attending a professional educational activity. (The fire extinguisher will need to be recharged after the demonstration.)

11-5

Fire Safety Checklist

	Yes	No
1. Exit passageways and exits are free from furniture and equipment.		
2. Locks on bathroom and toilet stall doors can be opened from the outside and can be opened easily by center staff.		
3. Protective covers are on all electrical outlets.		
4. Permanent wiring is used instead of lengthy extension cords.		
5. Each wall outlet contains no more than two electrical appliances.		
6. A fire evacuation plan is posted.		
7. Fire drills are conducted at least monthly, some of which are unannounced.		
8. Flammable, combustible, and other dangerous materials are marked and stored in areas accessible only to staff.		
9. Children are restricted to floors with grade level exits (no stairs).		
10. The basement door is kept closed.		
11. There is no storage under stairs.		
12. Smoke and carbon monoxide detectors are in place and checked regularly.		
13. Smoke alarms and fire alarms are checked at least once a month.		
14. Matches are kept out of the reach of children.		
15. Toys, chairs, tables, and other equipment are made of flame-retardant materials.		
16. Carpets and rugs are treated with a flame-retardant material.		
17. Emergency procedures and numbers are posted by each telephone.		
18. Fire drill cribs fit easily through the doors.		

A fire safety checklist may include many items. Would you add any items to this checklist?

example of procedures to be used is shown in 11-6.

If a fire is discovered in the center, sound the alarm immediately. Stay calm. If you panic, the children will panic as well. Evacuate children from the building at once, even if you do not see flames. Smoke, not fire, is responsible for more deaths. Leave the classroom lights on and close the doors. Do not lock the doors, however. Lights allow firefighters to see better in a smoke-filled structure.

Take roll as soon as the children and staff have cleared the building. When firefighters arrive, inform the chief whether anyone is still in the building.

When making evacuation plans, remember that infants are more difficult to remove than older children. This is because infants cannot walk. Most adults cannot carry

Enrich

Ask a firefighter to come to class and discuss fire safety for children. Ask students to prepare questions ahead of time.

Activity

Have students plan a field trip for preschoolers to a local fire department. Some fire departments offer fire safety training in a specially designed "burning house." This helps children learn how to safely get out without panicking. Ask students to investigate the availability of a program in your area.

Resource

Fire Safety Evaluation, Activity B, SAG

Meeting Special Needs

Review the *Fire Safety Checklist* in 11-5 and ask students with special needs to provide reasons why each item in the list is important. Assist students with the meanings of the words *evacuation, flammable, combustible,* and *flame-retardant*. Ask for student volunteers to pair up with the special needs students to conduct the fire safety evaluation of the classroom. Ask each student to explain his or her understanding of fire safety in the child care center.

Discuss

What role can parents play in the fire and burn prevention curriculum in your program?

Enrich

Have the class divide into two teams and debate the following question: Will talking to preschoolers about the dangers of fires make them to be more curious and more apt to want to explore and play with fire?

Note

Consult with the school principal for advance notice of weather, fire, or disaster drills whenever possible. Ask for special consideration if a lockdown or drug search has been scheduled for a time when the preschool children are present.

11-6

Evacuation Procedures

1.	Sound fire alarm.
2.	Evacuate the building.
3.	When leaving the building, leave lights on and close doors. Do not lock doors.
4.	Call the fire department after leaving the building.
5.	Take roll as soon as the children are together in a safe place.
6.	When the firefighters arrive, report whether all children and staff are out of the building.

Review evacuation procedures with children. Post the procedures in a noticeable place.

more than two infants at one time. Therefore, when ratios are higher than one caregiver to two infants, a careful plan needs to be made. Some centers practice by placing several babies in a crib and rolling it out of the building. Wagons can be used for evacuating older children.

Plan and introduce fire and burn prevention into the curriculum, if developmentally appropriate. Remind the children to tell staff right away if they smell smoke. Explain that in a fire, clean air is near the floor. By crawling close to the ground it will be easier to breathe. Teach the children what to do if their clothing catches fire. Chart 11-7 shows the stop, drop, and roll technique. Also, share books about fire safety and firefighters.

Sun Safety

The sun's ultraviolet (UV) rays cause harm. The result can be skin damage, eye damage, and even cancer. The sun's rays are the strongest between 10:00 a.m. and 4:00 p.m. During these hours, the children's exposure should be limited as it is the most damaging. Before going outside, always check the UV index. Daily newspapers often provide this information on the weather page. Otherwise, check the U.S. Environmental Protection Agency's Web site at www.epa.gov.

Early childhood teachers need to teach children sun safety precautions. Always apply a broad-spectrum sunscreen 30 minutes before going outdoors. The sunscreen should provide a sun protection factor (SPF) of at least 15 or higher. Apply wherever the skin is showing. Reapply every two hours if the children remain outdoors. Also reapply sunscreen after water play for maximum protection.

While outdoors, promote sun safety by teaching the shadow rule. If the children cannot see their shadows, they should seek shade or go indoors. The children should also be encouraged to wear hats and sunglasses designed to block UV radiation. Protecting the eyes is important since too much sun can cause cataracts. Wearing a hat with a brim will help protect the eyes, face, ears, and back of the neck.

Weather or Disaster Emergencies

Blizzards, hurricanes, floods, electrical storms, tornadoes, and earthquakes are examples of weather or disaster emergencies. All these conditions pose safety threats for the children and staff. Therefore, it is important to have an emergency plan for possible weather or disaster emergencies. The plans you formulate will depend on the geographical area in which you are located.

In areas where natural disasters occur more often, evacuation drills should be practiced with the children on a monthly basis. Evacuation procedures need to become routine for the children.

In some weather emergencies, you may decide to close the school. You need to have a plan in place for notifying parents of such an emergency. Special arrangements may need to be made for transporting the children.

Be prepared for weather emergencies. Always keep a battery-operated radio and

Workplace Connection

If children in the vocational preschool classroom will be in session during a regularly scheduled weather, fire, or disaster drill in your school, have students prepare the children ahead of time. Expose children to the type of alarm signal they will hear and have students practice escorting children to the proper location with student teachers. This will help children feel comfortable when the actual drill takes place.

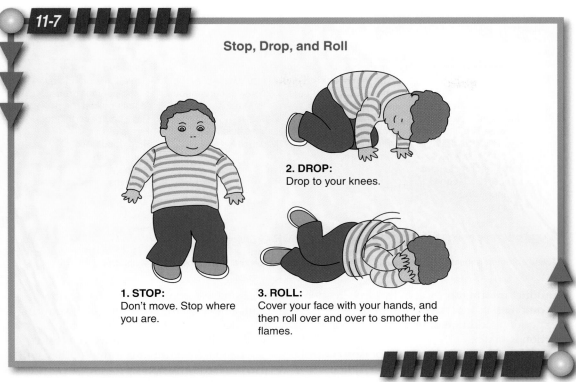

11-7

Stop, Drop, and Roll

1. STOP:
Don't move. Stop where you are.

2. DROP:
Drop to your knees.

3. ROLL:
Cover your face with your hands, and then roll over and over to smother the flames.

If clothing catches fire, the stop, drop, and roll technique should be used.

Activity

Referring to 11-7, ask students to design a lesson plan about safety that incorporates the *stop, drop, and roll* technique. How can student participation make this a more effective lesson?

Discuss

What items can you see in the classroom that could be poisonous if ingested?

Activity

Randomly select one of the preschoolers in the vocational preschool and ask students to tell you the child's exact age, height, and weight. Remind students that not knowing this information can cause a delay in the proper treatment for poisonings.

flashlights in a convenient spot. For some weather emergencies, blankets, water, food, and a first aid kit should also be available.

Poisonings

Studies show that children under five years of age account for almost two-thirds of poisonings that occur each year. Nearly any substance can, under certain conditions, be poisonous. The National Safety Council claims that the average residence contains over 40 poisonous products. Chart 11-8 lists many of these poisonous products.

Children eat many things adults would not think of placing in their mouths. There may be times when you are not sure whether a child has eaten something. For instance, you see a child playing with an empty aspirin bottle. The child has powder around the mouth. When in doubt, always assume the worst. If the child has eaten the aspirin, failing to act may result in great harm.

If you suspect that a child in your classroom has eaten something poisonous, remain calm. Telephone the nearest poison control center. If your area does not have a poison control center, call the nearest emergency room. Ask for instructions on treating the child.

Emergency Procedures for Poisonings

Poisoning emergencies often involve swallowing toxic substances. Other types of poisoning emergencies can occur. These include breathing toxic fumes and chemical injuries to the eyes or skin.

If any type of poisoning emergency occurs, follow these procedures. Do not rely on first aid information, antidote charts, or

---

Putting Technology to Use

Ask students to research *pica*, an eating disorder associated with eating nonfood items, on the Internet. (One suggested Web site with information is **www.kidshealth.org**.) How might preschool children be affected by pica? What is the possibility that children in your program will exhibit pica?

Note

The American Academy of Pediatrics no longer recommends using syrup of ipecac to treat accidental poisoning. It is safer to allow doctors and poison control centers to treat poisonings, and induced vomiting is usually not recommended.

Enrich

Have students locate a list of poisonous plants that are harmful to children if ingested or that cause skin rashes or reactions. Have students also locate a list of nonpoisonous plants that are recommended for classroom use. The Cincinnati Drug and Poison Information Center is one source for this information.

Resource

Indoor Safety Checklist, Activity A, OG

11-8

Poisonous Substances

Batteries/battery acid Candle wax Cleaners: ammonia, bleach, dishwasher detergent, dishwashing liquid, disinfectants, drain cleaner, dusting spray, lemon oil, spot remover, toilet bowl cleaner, window cleaner	Cosmetics and personal care items: after-shave lotion, hair care products, makeup, mouthwash, nail polish and nail polish remover, perfume, sunscreen	Flowers and plants: many varieties—consult a greenhouse for names Glue Lighter fluid Matches	Medications: many prescription and over-the-counter drugs Mouse poison Paint and paint thinners Pesticides Plant food Shoe polish Soap Vitamins

These common household items are all poisonous and should be kept out of the reach of children.

product information. Often this information is outdated or incorrect. The child may experience additional injury if the wrong action is taken.

Always contact your local poison control center for all cases of poisonings. When you call the center, be prepared to provide specific information. You will be asked to describe the child's symptoms. You will also be asked to identify any first aid procedures you have already administered. Report the time at which the substance was taken and the child's age and weight. Then provide the name of the poisonous substance. If the child removed the substance from a container, have the container with you when you call. Report the amount of substance the child consumed. Unless the exact amount is known, overestimating the amount consumed is better than underestimating it.

All first aid stations at child care centers should have an emetic available for poisoning emergencies. An **emetic** is a substance that induces vomiting when swallowed. Syrup of ipecac is an example of an emetic. Use extreme caution before giving a child syrup of ipecac. *Never give a child syrup of ipecac unless the physician at the poison control center advises this treatment.* Some poisons, such

as drain cleaner or lye, can cause serious damage to the child's esophagus if vomiting is induced. These substances are called *caustics.* They burn going down the child's esophagus. If vomiting is induced, they will also burn coming up.

One of the leading causes of poisoning in young children is plants. When eaten, many popular house and garden plants can produce toxicity ranging from minor to severe. They can cause skin rashes, upset stomachs, or even death. Many common household plants are poisonous. To prevent poisoning, check with your florist before purchasing a plant for the classroom. Finally, teach children never to put any leaves, flowers, or berries into their mouths.

Neglect and Abuse

During the past twenty-five years, the number of reported abused or neglected children has almost tripled. Ninety percent of the abusers are family members. Neglect and abuse can happen in any family type or socio-economic group. Certain situations increase the risk. The three leading factors are financial problems, substance abuse, and the

Putting Technology to Use

Have students use the computer to make a handy reference chart of all the preschoolers in the class. This list should include important information you would need to locate quickly in the event of an emergency. Suggested headings include child's name, birth date, age, height, and weight; and parents' or guardians' names, address, and phone numbers. Students should keep a copy of the chart in a readily accessible, private location.

stress of handling parental responsibilities. Single parenthood, isolation from others, and teen parenthood are other factors. Violence between parents can also lead to abuse of their child.

As a child care professional, you are very concerned about the health and safety of the children in your care. You do everything you can to see that the center is a safe place for them to be. However, the children are not in your care all the time. When they are away from the center, some children are abused. Because you are with the children for several hours a day, you may be the one to notice signs that a child is being abused or neglected. State law requires you to report known or suspected cases of child abuse. Follow your center's procedures for reporting.

Studies show that abused children often become troubled adults. Abused and neglected children are more likely to drop out of school, be unemployed, and commit violent crimes. When they are parents, they are also at high risk for becoming child abusers.

There are four types of child abuse: nonaccidental physical injury, neglect, emotional abuse, and sexual abuse. Be aware of the signs of each type of abuse.

Nonaccidental Physical Injury

The most visible type of child abuse is **nonaccidental physical injury**, 11-9. This is physical abuse inflicted on purpose. Children being abused in this way often come to school with bruises, bites, burns, or other injuries. They may have frequent complaints of pain.

Physically abused children often refuse to discuss their injuries. This may be because their abusers threaten them with further harm if they tell someone. Other children may talk about harsh punishment they have received.

Often these children come to the center wearing clothing to hide their injuries. Their clothing may be unsuitable for the weather.

Signs of Possible Physical Abuse

Child has unexplained or repeated injuries (bruises, bites, cuts, burns, fractures)

Child and parent provide illogical or conflicting explanations for injuries

Child complains frequently of pain

Child lacks ability to give or seek affection

Child avoids giving or receiving affection

Child displays fear of adults, including parents

Child wears clothing that can hide injuries, even when unsuitable for the weather

Child can be withdrawn or aggressive

Child appears anxious about routine activities such as toileting, eating, and sleeping

These signs may indicate a child is being physically abused.

As a result of being physically abused, some children may show an unusual fear of adults. Kelly is one example. She was abused by her father for two years. A teacher at Kelly's child care contacted authorities with her suspicions. Kelly had an unusual fear of adults, especially her father. Whenever he came to pick her up, she backed away and avoided eye contact with him.

Child abuse was suspected for other reasons as well. Kelly often arrived at the center with visible bruises. She also wore long-sleeve turtleneck tops in warm weather. One hot summer day, her teacher was concerned that Kelly might be too warm. When she was changing Kelly's top, the teacher found many bruises. Kelly could not explain the injuries.

Neglect

When children are not given the basic needs of life, they suffer from **neglect**. Neglect takes many forms. A neglected child may be deprived of proper food, medical

Note

Be aware when the subject of child abuse is covered in class that some students may have been abused themselves. Take special care to treat the topic with sensitivity and professionalism.

Vocabulary

Have a student volunteer define *nonaccidental physical injury*. Ask students to name the signs of this type of abuse.

Discuss

What excuses might parents give if a children shows signs of nonaccidental physical injury? (Examples include: "She's just clumsy" or "He only said it hurts because he didn't want to go to school today.") What is the teacher's responsibility regardless of the explanation?

Meeting Special Needs

Ask gifted students to interview an employee of a shelter for abused children or a hotline that provides support and intervention. Students should ask the employee questions such as the following: What motivated you to choose this job? What difference do you feel your work has made to individuals? What is the most difficult part of your job? Ask students to prepare other questions of interest to them ahead of time. Have students summarize the findings of their interviews in oral reports to the class.

Vocabulary

Have students define *neglect* and *emotional abuse*. Ask them to name the signs of these types of abuse.

Note

Statistics on abuse can be found online at Web sites such as the Child Welfare Information Gateway, **www.childwelfare.gov**.

Vocabulary

Ask student volunteers to define *sexual abuse, incest,* and *molestation*. Have students name some signs or symptoms that might make them consider that a child may be suffering from sexual abuse.

and dental care, shelter, and/or clothing. Children who have been unsupervised may also be neglected. Neglect may or may not be intentional on the part of the abuser. However, the potential for harm is possible.

Children who wear clothing that is too small or dirty may be neglected. Neglected children may also wear clothes that are inappropriate for the weather. They may lack warm coats, gloves, or hats for the winter. Children who are poorly groomed may also be neglected.

Other signs of neglect may appear in a child's health. Neglect may result in children who are too thin or malnourished. These children may ask to take food home. Constant fatigue, illness, or poor dental care may be other signs of neglect. These children may have a bad odor. This may be due to a lack of bathing. Wearing dirty clothes could also contribute to bad odor.

Alert teachers should observe for signs of neglect. They must be sensitive to different child-rearing practices as well as cultural expectations and priorities. Signs of possible neglect include the following:

- the child often arrives early or is picked up late
- the child wears inappropriate or unclean clothing
- the child seems always hungry
- medical needs are unmet
- poor hygiene often results in odor
- the child appears fatigued or falls asleep

Derek is a neglected child. He often arrives early or is picked up late. His teacher observed that he appeared small for his age. After observing him for several more months, she noted developmental lags. He appeared to be lagging behind many of his same-age peers. Often he would ask when snack or lunch would be served. During cooking activities, he would try to eat or take food. He also complained of being hungry. Derek lacked proper nutrition. As a result, he was constantly fatigued and sometimes fell asleep.

Observing these signs, Derek's teachers suspected neglect. They compared information and shared their concerns. As child care teachers, they knew they were required to report suspected child abuse. They knew Derek would never reach his full potential without proper nutrition.

Emotional Abuse

Emotional abuse is abuse of a child's self-concept through words or actions. Children lose self-esteem due to emotional abuse. Excessive or inappropriate demands may be made on the children by parents or guardians. This can cause emotional harm to children. Emotional abuse is the result of insufficient love, guidance, and/or support from parents or guardians.

Children who are emotionally abused may repeat certain behavior over several months. Look for the following signs:

- refusal to talk
- unusual or unpredictable behavior
- rare smiling or laughter
- excessive clinging or crying
- withdrawn behavior
- destructive behavior
- poor motor coordination for age
- fear of adults

Sexual Abuse

Sexual abuse is forcing a child to observe or engage in sexual activities with an adult. Rape, fondling, and indecent exposure are all forms of sexual abuse. Each of these acts involve adults using children for their own pleasure. **Incest** is sexual abuse by a relative. **Molestation** is sexual contact made by someone outside the family with a child.

There are many signs of sexual abuse. A child may have problems when walking or sitting. The child may complain of itching, pain, or swelling in the genital area. Some

---

Cross-Curricular Activity

Health
Consult the health or psychology teacher at your school for information on the effects of emotional abuse on children. Explain the following types of abuse: belittling, corrupting, isolating, rejecting, and terrorizing. Why is the loss of self-esteem from emotional abuse so devastating to young children? What is the effect on the child's emotional development and potential for positive social interactions in the future?

sexually abused children have bruises in the genital or anal areas. They may also have bruises in their mouths and throats. Some may complain of pain when urinating.

Sexually abused children commonly have poor peer behaviors. They may show extremely disruptive or aggressive behaviors. Often they will regress to infantile behaviors, such as baby-talking, thumbsucking, or bed-wetting. Some will show a lack of appetite. These children often express affection in improper ways. See 11-10.

Reporting Child Abuse

Health care workers, social workers, school administrators, and teachers are *mandated reporters* of child abuse. This means they are required by law to report any known or suspected cases of child abuse or neglect. As a mandated reporter, you should read your state's **statute**, a formal document drawn up by elected officials. The statute will explain your legal responsibilities and the penalties for failing to make a report. To receive a copy of the statute, contact your local law enforcement office.

Follow your center's procedure for reporting child abuse and neglect to the proper authorities. Your program must

11-10

Case Study

Annabelle is a sexually abused child. She refused help with clothing and toileting needs. She would not allow teachers to help her remove her outdoor clothing. Her teachers thought Annabelle's behavior was unusual. After observing another incident, they suspected she was sexually abused. Annabelle liked Richard, one of the children in her group. They saw her rubbing his crotch with her hand during group time.

After observing Annabelle's behavior, the teachers reported their suspicions of abuse. They realized if they continued waiting for more proof, there could be greater risk to the child.

In caes such as these, the teacher's priority is the children's safety.

comply with the law, but may also have other guidelines in making a report. For instance, you might need to complete certain paperwork and report the abuse to the director or health consultant. Some programs designate one employee to make all reports of child abuse for the program. In other programs, each staff member reports these cases himself or herself.

If you must make a child abuse report, do so immediately by telephone. Include the name, age, and address of the child and his or her parents or guardian. Report the facts that led to your suspicion. After the telephone conversation, confirm the report in writing. Make a copy of the written report for the program and one for yourself. As long as you make the report in good faith, you will not be subject to legal action if your suspicions are found not to be child abuse or neglect.

Should a child abuse case result in a trial, you may be required to testify in court. This may make you feel nervous, but focus on telling the truth. Your legal and ethical responsibility is to tell the court what you know about the case that will help the court protect the child.

Background Checks

Early childhood programs need to protect themselves from potential child abuse accusations. This is a licensing requirement of many states. A background check needs to be conducted on every new employee, student teacher, and volunteer. This check will determine if they have had any felony or child abuse convictions.

Protection Education

Planning for children's safety goes beyond the classroom. Children need to learn how to deal with dangers outside the classroom. They must learn about sexual abuse and how to protect themselves from it.

Warning children about strangers has been a common practice for some time. However, only 10 to 15 percent of child abusers are strangers to the children they abuse. The other 85 to 90 percent are people

Activity

Have students investigate what happens after a report of suspected child abuse is filed. Where is the report filed? How long is the time of response or action from the time the report is made?

Resource

Understanding Child Abuse, Activity C, SAG

Activity

Have students request a copy of your state's statute on mandated reporters and become familiar with the legal responsibilities of reporting child abuse and neglect.

Workplace Connection

Invite a case worker or social worker from your state's Department of Children and Family Services to class to discuss child abuse. (Some states may have a different title for the agency responsible for child abuse reports and child welfare.) Ask the official how child abuse cases are handled, what strategies are used to investigate abuse claims, and what happens to children in this situation. The official may also be asked to share some cases to give students an increased awareness of the impact of this problem.

Discuss

What is *protection education*? Why is protection information so important for young children?

Enrich

Have students locate a copy of the book *It's My Body* by Lory Freeman. Review the book and determine how it can be used in the preschool classroom to help children learn how to stay safe.

Resource

Protection Education Questions, transparency master 11-1, TR

known to the children. These people may be neighbors, relatives, friends of the family, scout leaders, siblings, or parents. Most offenders are men. However, women are also reported.

Before age eight, 3.0 to 4.6 percent of all children are sexually assaulted. About 10 percent of these children are assaulted by the time they are five years old. Girls are reported as victims far more often than boys. Studies show that race, intelligence, family income, and social class do not appear to affect the occurrence of sexual assault.

Teach children to resist sexual attacks. They must first resist the offender by saying no. Then they must tell a trusted friend or relative about the attack. Role-play this process with the children. Give them phrases to use if they find themselves in trouble. For example:

- If someone tries to give you a wet kiss, shake hands instead.

- If someone tries to get you to sit on his or her lap and you do not want to, say "No, not now."

- If someone wants to give you a hug and you do not want it, say "No thanks."

- If someone tries to touch your genitals, say "Stop. That is not okay."

- If someone rubs or pats your bottom, say "Do not do that."

Children may have trouble identifying sexual abuse. This is especially true with people they know. To combat this problem, explain to the children the difference between good touch and bad touch. A *bad touch* is any of the following: a touch the child does not want or like, a touch that hurts or makes the child uncomfortable, a secret touch, or any touch to a child's private parts (genitals). A *good touch* is wanted and appropriate. It does not make the child uncomfortable.

Suggest various scenarios and ask the children whether these are good or bad touches. In the classroom, encourage children to tell the other person when they don't want to be touched or don't like how a touch feels. Help them put these feelings in words. Intervene if a child persists with a touch after being asked to stop.

Children also need to learn how and who to tell if someone assaults them. Use puppets, charts, movies, or other materials to teach children this lesson.

Helping Families

Early childhood teachers are in a position to help families. Daily face-to-face contacts provide opportunities for recognizing families in crisis. Teachers can share parenting information on child development and management of behavior problems. They can also guide them in seeking community programs and services. These may include

- parenting classes

- self-help or support groups

- financial planning

- family counseling

- help lines

- preventive health care programs for children

- nutrition for healthy living

Promoting Resiliency

Neglect and abuse causes children to feel vulnerable. Teachers can play an important role in helping these children become resilient. The children benefit from developing a secure relationship with a trusting and supportive teacher. Knowing that someone cares can help them develop faith in themselves. They also learn that they are important. Over time, resiliency can be fostered when the teacher provides

- consistency and predictability

- developmentally appropriate limits

- responsive and stimulating care

Putting Technology to Use

Have students conduct an Internet search for information on the national Court Appointed Special Advocates (CASA) program and answer the following questions: What are the goals and mission of this organization? How does this program help abused and neglected children? How can an individual become a CASA? Have students present oral and visual reports to the class on their findings.

- encouragement for persisting and exploring new opportunities
- positive expectations
- problem-solving skills
- praise for efforts and accomplishments
- verbal expressions of caring
- labels for feelings

Liability

By law, young children are not expected to care for themselves. This is the primary role of the staff at the center. The staff must ensure the children's safety and health. Education is a secondary function.

Center directors are liable for the acts of their employees. *Liable* means having a responsibility that is upheld by the law. Having liability means you can be punished for failing to uphold your legal responsibility. The extent of liability may vary, however. As a result, only individuals who are safety- and health-conscious should be hired, 11-11.

Safety-conscious staff members watch for danger in all situations.

The director needs to observe newly hired people to ensure they use good supervision techniques.

Types of Liability

Child care staff can be punished by law for failing to follow state licensing rules and regulations. Center staff can be liable for not doing the following:
- obtaining a signed health form from a licensed physician for each child
- requiring a staff member to have an approved physical and background check before working with children
- providing safe indoor and outdoor equipment
- operating a center with the required adult-child ratios
- providing proper supervision
- providing proper food storage
- maintaining fence and door locks in proper condition
- providing staff with information about children's special needs
- refraining from corporal (physical) punishment
- providing a safe building
- removing children who lack self-control and are a hazard to themselves as well as others
- covering electrical outlets

Center directors and staff must keep constant watch over the center environment. They must ensure that it is safe as well as healthy. New teachers will need constant support from the staff and director.

Forms

Every center should develop a number of forms related to the health and safety of

Vocabulary

Define the words *liable* and *liability*. How does liability affect a director's choice when hiring an employee?

Note

Review the list of liabilities with students. Add any liabilities that you know of that apply to your state and answer any questions students may have about them.

Resource

You Are Liable, transparency master 11-2, TR

Workplace Connection

Have students interview the director of a child care center or preschool to discover what type of liability insurance coverage is needed for programs for children. Do the individual teachers and aides need to have their own liability coverage? What are the insurance limits for accidents, injuries, and other harm to children? How much does yearly insurance coverage cost?

Enrich

Have students collect various forms related to safety from area programs. Review the forms with the class, pointing out similarities and differences between them.

Activity

Ask students to design a standard accident or injury report form that could be used in your preschool. What specific information needs to be on the report? Why is it important that the parent signs the report?

Discuss

What types of information are kept in a child's file? Why should parents have access to this information?

the children. Many of these forms direct the staff in the care of the children and protect staff members from possible liability. Two forms commonly used by centers are injury report forms and various types of release or permission forms.

Every center should have a standard injury report form. Any information recorded on this form is useful if legal action is brought against the center. Parents also need to be informed about the details of a child's accident. A sample form is shown in 11-12.

Various permission forms should also be on file. These forms should be filled out at the time of the child's enrollment. Permission is usually required for such items as special screening tests or walks around the neighborhood. To protect children from being picked up from the center by a stranger, unauthorized person, or even a noncustodial parent, a transportation form should be used. This form should contain the names, relationship, telephone numbers, and driver's license numbers of people who have permission to transport the child to and from the center. Staff should check the identification of anyone other than the parents who comes to pick up the child from the program. In the event a parent wants to add or remove an individual from the list, a new form needs to be completed.

11-12

Injury Report Form
Child and Family Study Center

Child's Name _____

Date of injury _____ Time of injury _____ a.m./p.m.

Type of injury: bite, broken bone, bruise, burn, choking, cut, ear, eye, head, poisoning, scrape, sliver, sprain,
other _____

Staff members present: _____

Witness(es): _____

Description of the incident: (Include specific information, such as where the child was playing, with whom, and with what.)

Description of injury: (Include specific information, such as type, location, size, and severity of injury and symptoms noted following injury.)

Action taken by staff: (Include all actions, such as treating injury, seeking medical advice or care, comforting child, and notifying director and parents.)

_____
(staff signature)

_____
(parent signature)

The information in an accident report form is useful for parents and teachers.

Portfolio Project

Ask students to write a brief essay explaining how they will keep children safe under their supervision and care. Students should be able to explain their understanding of the various factors that are part of this responsibility. These may include: building, room, and equipment safety; proper supervision and management of disruptive and aggressive children; reporting suspected abuse situations; and fire safety. The essay should be printed and filed in the student's portfolio.

Privacy Law

The **privacy law** is designed to protect children. It states that a child's records cannot be given to anyone other than parents without the parents' permission. Give a child's records only if the parents have made the request in writing. After receiving the request, the materials must be released within 45 days. A form that can be included in each child's file is shown in 11-13.

Parents are given unlimited access to all their child's records kept by the center. Included may be screening information, developmental evaluations, and parent meeting planning sheets and summaries. Many teachers share all this information during parent meetings. These meetings will be discussed more in Chapter 32, *Involving Parents and Families.*

11-13

The information contained in this file is confidential and is not to be circulated outside the center without the prior written consent of the child's parents.

Under Public Law 93-380: Parents have access to all educational records. According to this law:

(1) You are not allowed to provide the information contained in this file to anyone without the written consent of the child's parent or guardian.
(2) You must advise parents of their rights concerning their child's file.
(3) Parents have the right to read and review the file. Moreover, they may request a revision of information in their child's file.
(4) Within forty-five (45) days, you are required to respond to a parent's request.

File reviewed by:

Name and Title	Address	Reason	Date
_____	_____	_____	_____
_____	_____	_____	_____
_____	_____	_____	_____
_____	_____	_____	_____
_____	_____	_____	_____

Use a form such as this to record reviews of children's files.

Vocabulary

Have students define *privacy law.* Ask them to explain how the privacy law protects children.

Note

If you do not plan to cover Chapter 32 during the course, you may wish to combine information about parent meetings with this chapter.

Resource

Safety Procedures, Activity A, SAG

Meeting Special Needs

Review the special learners' chapter outlines to determine if the students have any questions about the concepts or content of this chapter. Review the chapter objectives and ask the students to evaluate their progress in meeting these objectives. Ask the students to summarize, orally or in writing, what they learned from this chapter.

Review and Reflect Answer Key

1. true

2. (List four:) Supervise the children at all times. Maintain at least the minimum adult-child ratio as required in your state. Develop safety limits. Provide a safe environment. Practice fire safety. Develop plans for weather emergencies. Know emergency procedures for accidental poisoning. Recognize signs of child abuse and report any known or suspected cases. Teach children how to protect themselves from sexual assault.

3. more

4. decals

5. Keep fire extinguishers in the kitchen, in or just outside the classroom, and in the laundry area.

6. true

7. true

8. An emetic is a substance that, when swallowed, will cause vomiting.

9. The four types of child abuse are nonaccidental physical injury, neglect, emotional abuse, and sexual abuse.

10. (List three. Student response.)

Summary

Providing a safe environment for children requires a great deal of time and attention to details. Danger can be found in every corner of the center. These dangers can threaten both the physical and mental well-being of children. Protecting children from these dangers is the most important job of a teacher.

Child care professionals need to be prepared for any emergency. You should know how to use fire extinguishers and how to safely evacuate the children in case of a fire or other disaster. You should know how to handle accidental poisonings. Child care workers also need to recognize signs of possible child abuse and know how to report suspected cases.

Child care staff can be held responsible for failing to follow state licensing rules and regulations. It is important to know what those rules are and to know the extent of any possible liability.

Review and Reflect

1. True or false. Most accidents in a child care center can be avoided.

2. Name four basic safety objectives.

3. Usually, younger children require _____ staff supervision than older children.

4. Applying _____ at eye level to glass doors makes glass visible to children.

5. Name three ideal places to keep fire extinguishers in a child care center.

6. True or false. Smoke claims more lives than fire does.

7. True or false. Nearly any substance, under certain conditions, can be poisonous.

8. What is an emetic?

9. Name the four types of child abuse.

10. List three behavior patterns exhibited by emotionally abused children.

11. Explain what is meant by a *bad touch*.

12. What is the primary role of the staff at a center?

13. List three unsafe situations for which a center is liable.

14. True or false. Parents are allowed only limited access to records kept by the center concerning their child.

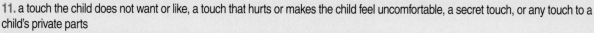

11. a touch the child does not want or like, a touch that hurts or makes the child feel uncomfortable, a secret touch, or any touch to a child's private parts

12. The primary role of the staff is to ensure the safety and health of the children in their care.

13. (List three. Student response.)

14. false

Apply and Explore

1. Design an evacuation chart for the classroom.

2. Using the poisonous substances chart in this chapter, conduct a safety check of your home. List the poisonous substances you found.

3. Arrange a visit to a center to learn about their safety objectives. Ask to view any safety checklists they might use.

4. Explain sun safety precautions for an early childhood center.

5. Create a puppet play using phrases that children may use if ever faced with sexual abuse.

Workplace Link

Invite a preschool director to speak to the class concerning the use of cleaners and other chemicals in the preschool classroom. Find out what type of cleaners are recommended and are safe to use in environments used by young children. Find out if your school is restricted to using certain cleaners. What procedures are used to disinfect the surfaces used by children and students at your school? Does the staff have information on file for use in the event of accidental poisoning or ingestion?

Cross-Curricular Link

Language Arts

1. Interview the local fire chief concerning the proper use of fire extinguishers.

Science

2. Arrange a visit to the emergency room of a local hospital. Ask the doctor on duty to discuss emergency procedures used for poisonings.

Technology

3. Check the Web site of the National Resource Center for Health and Safety in Child Care (nrc.uschsc.edu) for safety tips for child care centers.

4. Review the Web site for the National Program for Playground Safety (www.uni.edu/playground) to learn more about planning a safe playground.

Discuss

Look at the chapter opening photo. Does it look like the children are enjoying a meal or a snack? What do you notice about the food? the dishes and cups? the environment?

Discuss

Look over the objectives for this chapter. How important is a healthful diet to you? What are some nutritional problems that can result from a poor diet?

Planning Nutritious Meals and Snacks

After studying this chapter, you will be able to

- list goals for a good nutrition program.
- explain the importance of a healthful diet.
- describe nutritional problems that can result from a poor diet.
- name the food groups in MyPyramid and the main nutrients they supply.
- plan nutritious and appealing meals and snacks for children.

Terms to Know

nutrition
nutrients
undernutrition
malnutrition
diabetes
MyPyramid
insulin
allergy
allergen
anaphylactic shock

It was lunchtime at the New Horizons Child Care Center. Nidda asked for a second serving of spinach, a food being served for the first time. Maria said the potatoes were yummy. Geneva said her mother was sending oranges for her birthday treat. Throughout the meal, the teacher talked with the children and ate portions of the foods served.

The lunchroom was decorated with 12 large paper ice cream cones. Each cone represented one month of the year. The children's names and birthdays were written on paper scoops of ice cream. These scoops were placed in the cone that matched their birthday month.

On the other side of the lunchroom was a large carrot cut out of tagboard. A cloth measuring tape was pasted down the center. Each child's height was marked next to the tape.

In this classroom, children learn about nutrition both directly and indirectly. For instance, the variety of foods served and the teacher's comments about the food are direct learning experiences. Children learn about many types of food and that mealtime is a pleasant time. The positive attitudes and pleasing surroundings of the lunchroom are indirect learning experiences. By watching friends and teachers, children develop habits and attitudes about food. Many of their food attitudes and behaviors will last into adulthood. Hopefully, they will establish a lifelong pattern of eating a nutritious diet.

Teaching children about nutrition will be an important responsibility for you as a teacher. Proper nutrition is needed for children's health, growth, and development. Behavior and learning ability is related to nutrition. Some studies suggest that young children who have learned healthful food choices may experience lifelong health benefits.

Teaching nutrition concepts requires a good nutrition program. A good program centers on the needs of the children, including their ethnic backgrounds. Nutrition concepts should be integrated into all subject areas. Program goals should include the following:

- providing nutritious meals and snacks
- introducing new healthful foods
- encouraging healthful eating habits
- involving children in meal activities
- providing nutrition information to parents

To meet these goals, you will need to understand how food is used by the body. In addition, you must know the various nutrients and their sources. Meal plans and food experiences for the children are also needed to meet program goals.

Nutrition

Nutrition is the science of food and how the body uses the foods taken in, 12-1. **Nutrients** are the chemical substances in food that help build and maintain the body. Certain nutrients are needed to build a strong body and mind. There are six groups of nutrients needed for growth and maintenance of health. These are proteins, carbohydrates, fats, vitamins, minerals, and water. Chart 12-2 lists some of the most important nutrients, their functions, and sources.

Reflect

Have you ever decided not to try an interesting food because you heard someone make a negative comment about the food? Do you have any negative food attitudes you know developed in your childhood?

Resource

Nutrition Program Goals, transparency master 12-1, TR

Discuss

Why is providing nutrition information to parents an important program goal? What type of information would you provide?

Vocabulary

Have student volunteers define the terms *nutrition* and *nutrients*. What are the six groups of nutrients needed by the human body?

Meeting Special Needs

Provide an outline of the chapter with all the chapter headings for special learners. Students should fill in each section outline as the material is covered in class with a sentence or two about the content. Review the special learners' IEPs to decide if any modifications should be made in presenting the chapter content.

Discuss

Jason's fifth birthday is next week. His mother would like to bring frosted cupcakes from the bakery and red fruit punch to class to share with the other children. What is your reaction? What is your response to Jason's mother?

Vocabulary

Have a student volunteer define the terms *undernutrition* and *malnutrition*. What are the effects of both of these on a child's growth and development?

Reflect

You've told four-year-old Serena's mother that Serena cannot keep up with the other children during a running activity. Her face gets red and she breathes heavily. You are concerned about her health because she appears to be overweight for her age. Her mother tells you that Serena is not overweight; it is just baby fat and she will probably lose it without any trouble. How do you respond to this?

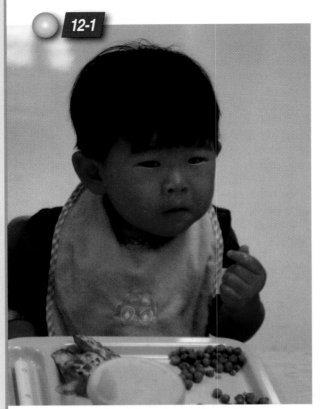

12-1

Knowledge of nutrition is needed for planning healthy meals and snacks.

Food also provides the body with energy. Each food has its own energy value. This value is measured in calories. Energy from food supports body processes, such as breathing and blood circulation. All your organs and body systems need energy to function. Your body's physical and mental activities require energy, too.

The amount of calories a person needs depends on age and activity level. Children need more energy than adults, in relation to body weight. For instance, a very active four-year-old boy weighing 42 pounds needs about 1,600 calories per day. A somewhat active 45-year-old man weighing 160 pounds needs about 2,600 calories per day. Thus, the child needs about 38 calories per pound while the man needs about 16 calories per

pound. Children's physical growth is greater than adults' growth. Children are also very active. All their physical activities use a great deal of energy.

Nutritional Problems

Undernutrition, malnutrition, and overeating are problems that affect children's health and development. The effects of poor nutrition on cognitive abilities have been proven in several studies. In order to plan nutritious meals and snacks, you need to know the effects of these problems.

Undernutrition means not eating enough food to keep a healthful body weight and activity level. The person gets too few nutrients because not enough food is eaten. This often results from poverty. **Malnutrition** is a lack of proper nutrients in the diet. It happens when a nutrient is absent or lacking from the diet. An unbalanced diet, poor food choices, or the body's inability to use the nutrients properly can be the cause.

Children with these problems often are shorter than their peers. Long-term deficiencies can slow, or even stop, growth. Other signs of poor nutrition include irritability, bowed legs, sunken eyes, decaying teeth, and fatigue.

Overeating is the intake of more food than is needed by the body to function properly. Many factors contribute to overeating. There is a larger and more available supply of food. There also is a trend toward more snacking. Unfortunately, overeating can cause many health and emotional problems. A major health problem caused by overeating is obesity.

Obesity can lead to many other health problems in adult life. These include hypertension (high blood pressure and related problems), diabetes, heart disease, hardening of the arteries, and many other diseases. **Diabetes** is a condition in which the body cannot properly control the level of sugar in the blood.

Putting Technology to Use

Have students conduct an Internet search for information on childhood obesity. What has caused this growing problem in the United States? What are the physical and emotional effects on children? What is being done to help educate children and parents about childhood obesity prevention and treatment? Have students write a one-page report of their findings. Allow time for students to read their reports in class.

12-2

Nutrient	Functions	Sources
Proteins	Build and repair tissues, antibodies, enzymes, and hormones Regulate fluid balance in the cells Regulate many body processes Supply energy when needed	Meat, poultry, fish, eggs, milk and other dairy products, peanut butter, lentils
Carbohydrates	Supply energy Help the body efficiently digest fats	Sugar: Honey, jam, jelly, sugar, molasses Fiber: Fresh fruits and vegetables, whole-grain cereals and breads Starch: Breads, cereals, corn, peas, beans, potatoes, pasta, rice
Fats	Supply energy and carry fat-soluble vitamins Protect vital organs and body from shock and temperature changes	Butter, margarine, cream, cheese, marbling in meat, fish, nuts, whole milk, olives, chocolate, egg yolks, lunchmeats, salad oils and dressings
Vitamins *Vitamin A*	Helps promote growth Helps keep skin and mucus membranes healthy Helps prevent night blindness	Liver, egg yolk, dark green and yellow fruits and vegetables, butter, whole milk, cream, fortified margarine, cheddar cheese
Thiamin (Vitamin B-1)	Promotes normal appetite and digestion Helps keep nervous system healthy Helps body release energy from food	Pork, other meats, poultry, fish, eggs, enriched or whole-grain breads and cereals, dried beans
Riboflavin (Vitamin B-2)	Helps cells use oxygen Helps keep skin, tongue, and lips healthy Aids digestion	Milk, cheese, yogurt, liver, meats, fish, poultry, eggs, dark leafy green vegetables, enriched breads and cereals
Niacin (B-vitamin)	Helps keep nervous system, skin, mouth, tongue, and digestive tract healthy Helps cells use other nutrients	Meat, fish, poultry, milk, enriched or whole-grain breads and cereals, peanut butter, dried beans and peas
Vitamin C	Helps keep gums and tissues healthy Helps heal wounds and broken bones Helps body fight infection	Citrus fruits, strawberries, cantaloupe, broccoli, green peppers, raw cabbage, tomatoes, green leafy vegetables, brussels sprouts, cauliflower

Each nutrient performs a specific function and can be found in several sources.   *(continued)*

Resource

Nutrients and Their Functions, Activity A, SAG

Note

Your body breaks down the protein in food into amino acids. There are 20 different types of amino acids and they are commonly referred to as the building blocks of protein. Nine of the essential amino acids can be obtained from protein found in animal sources such as meat and milk. These proteins are called *complete proteins*. Most vegetable protein is considered incomplete because it lacks one or more of the essential amino acids.

Resource

Identifying the Sources, Activity D, SAG

Putting Technology to Use

Have students conduct an Internet search for information about the effects of food sources on the brain. Ask students to research one food from each of the nutrient sources listed in Chart 12-2. How does this food affect the brain? For example, kidney beans promote a steady energy supply to the brain; improve alertness; and increase attention and memory. Have students prepare a chart of their findings. Allow time for students to share their findings with the class.

Note

The calcium you take in from your diet protects the calcium stored in your bones. If you lack calcium in your diet, your body takes what it needs from your bones. If your body continues to take more from your bones than it replaces, over a period of years your bones become weak and brittle, causing them to break easily. This calcium deficiency can lead to a bone disease called *osteoporosis*.

Activity

Obtain copies of *Tips for Families* on the two-sided MyPyramid for Kids mini poster available at **www.MyPyramid.gov**. Have students prepare a bulletin or newsletter asking parents to help encourage their children to eat nutritious foods and get plenty of physical activity as recommended on the poster.

Resource

Serving Adequate Meals, Activity A, OG

Vitamin D	Helps build strong bones and teeth in children Helps keep adult bones healthy	Fortified milk, butter and margarine, fish liver oils, liver, sardines, tuna, egg yolk, sunshine
Vitamin E	Acts as an antioxidant	Liver and other variety meats, eggs, leafy green vegetables, whole-grain cereals, legumes, salad oils, shortenings, other fats and oils
Vitamin K	Aids in blood clotting	Organ meats, pork, leafy green vegetables, cauliflower, other vegetables, egg yolk
Minerals *Calcium*	Helps build bones and teeth Helps blood clot Helps muscles and nerves function properly Helps regulate the use of minerals in body	Milk, cheese, other dairy products, leafy green vegetables, fish without bones
Phosphorus	Helps build strong bones and teeth Helps regulate many body processes	Protein and calcium food sources
Iron	Combines with protein to make hemoglobin Helps cells use oxygen	Liver, meats, egg yolk, dried beans and peas, leafy green vegetables, dried fruits, enriched and whole-grain breads and cereals
Water	A basic part of blood and tissue fluid Helps transport nutrients and waste Helps control body temperature	Water, beverages, soups, and most foods

12-2 Continued

Obesity can also cause emotional problems. Many obese children lack self-esteem. They may be treated poorly by classmates and lack friends.

Obesity is easier to prevent than to treat. First, note the activity level of any heavy children. Encourage them to join in gross-motor play. Second, discuss your concerns about a child's nutrition with staff and parents.

MyPyramid

To ensure good nutrition, children need to eat a variety of foods. Their specific nutritional needs differ from those of adults, however. The U.S. Department of Agriculture (USDA) developed **MyPyramid**, a set of online tools to help plan nutritious diets to fit individual needs. You can access it at the

---

Putting Technology to Use

Team Nutrition is an initiative of the USDA Food and Nutrition Service. It supports the Child Nutrition Programs through training and technical assistance for foodservice, nutrition education for children and their caregivers, and school and community support for healthful eating and physical activity. Have students research this program at **www.fns.usda.gov/tn**. Ask students to write a brief summary of their findings. Allow time for students to share their findings with the class.

www.MyPyramid.gov Web site. Use MyPyramid as a guide for planning meals and snacks.

A special version of MyPyramid, called *MyPyramid For Kids*, is designed specifically for children, 12-3. The figure climbing the steps of MyPyramid is a reminder to stay active and avoid eating too many calories. Notice the first line that runs across the full page. It tells you the recommendations are based on an 1,800-calorie diet. This calorie level is appropriate for very active children ages 4 to 8 as well as older, less-active

Resource

MyPyramid for Kids, color transparency CT-11, TR

Note

Keep a copy of the Dietary Guidelines in the classroom for reference. A copy can be printed at the Web site **www.mypyramid.gov**. You can also learn more information about each part of MyPyramid by visiting the *Inside the Pyramid* link located on the Web site.

Resource

MyPyramid, Activity C, SAG

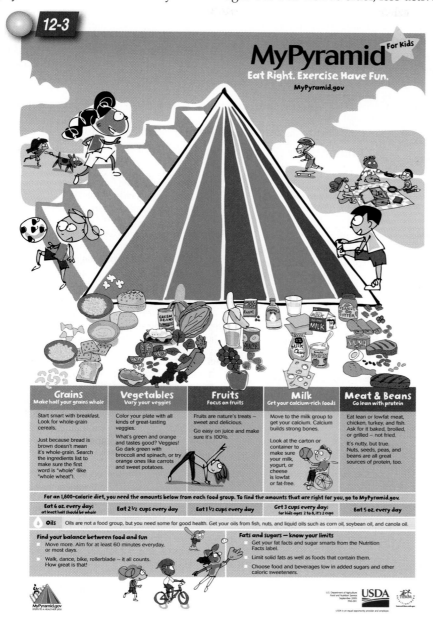

12-3

MyPyramid for Kids can help you see how the different food groups work together to form a nutritious diet.

Cross-Curricular Activity

Health and Nutrition
Ask students to use the *MyPyramid Plan* link located on the Web site **www.mypyramid.gov** to find out how many calories they need each day based on their height, weight, and physical activity level.

Have students use this information to track their daily caloric intake and physical activity for one week using the *MyPyramid Tracker* link. Ask students to write a brief summary of their results and what they learned about their nutritious habits from this activity.

Resource

Fruit and Vegetable Sources of Vitamin A, Vitamin C, and Iron, reproducible master 12-2, TR

Enrich

Using print or Internet sources, ask students to research the difference between a *dairy allergy* and a *dairy intolerance.* What alternatives can you suggest for dairy foods for children who are affected by either of these conditions? Have students write a brief report of their findings. Allow time for students to share their findings with the class.

Resource

Nutrition Crossword, Activity B, SAG

children ages 9 to 12. By accessing "MyPyramid Plan" on MyPyramid's Web site, you can find similar information for children as young as age 2.

MyPyramid's six colorful triangles stand for the five major food groups (grains, vegetables, fruits, milk, and meat and beans) plus oils. The foods from these six sources are vital to good health. The triangles are different sizes to remind you that more food is needed of some types than others.

For example, the orange triangle (grains) is thickest, while the yellow triangle (oils) is thinnest. Chart 12-4 lists foods that are included in the food groups and the amounts to plan for an 1,800-calorie diet.

Milk Group

Children need at least two cups of milk products daily. The most important nutrient provided by this group is calcium, 12-5.

12-4

Food Groups, Sources, and Daily Needs

Food Group	Amounts for Young Children	Sources
Grain	6 ounce-equivalents, at least half from whole-grain sources	Enriched or whole-grain breads, buns, bagels, muffins, rolls, cornbread, tortillas, biscuits, pita bread, pancakes, waffles, cereals, crackers, rice, macaroni, noodles, rolled
Vegetable	2½ cups Serve several vegetables rich in vitamin C and vitamin A each week.	**Rich in vitamin C:** tomatoes, sweet red peppers, green peppers, broccoli, brussels sprouts, sweet potatoes; tomato and mixed vegetable juices **Rich in vitamin A:** carrots, asparagus, greens, broccoli, brussels sprouts, cabbage, collards, green and black-eyed peas, red and green peppers, pumpkin, spinach, squash, and sweet potatoes; vegetable juices **Other vegetables:** potatoes, onions, mushrooms, eggplant, corn, cucumbers, beets, green beans
Fruit	1½ cups Serve one fruit rich in vitamin C daily and several fruits rich in vitamin A weekly.	**Rich in vitamin C:** strawberries, papayas, oranges, tangerines, grapefruit, cantaloupe, kiwifruit; orange, grapefruit, and other fortified juices **Rich in vitamin A:** apricots, avocado, cantaloupe, nectarines, papayas, peaches, prunes, tangerines **Other fruits:** apple, banana, blackberries, blueberries, cherries, dates, figs, grapes, pears, pineapple, plums, raspberries, watermelon
Meat and Beans	5 ounce-equivalents	Beef; pork; turkey; chicken; eggs; fish; shellfish; tuna; lamb; frankfurters (hot dogs); veal; variety meats such as heart, kidney, and liver; lima, navy, pinto, great northern, kidney, and garbanzo beans; lentils; peanut butter
Milk	2 cups; 3 cups for children over 8	Milk: whole, reduced fat, low-fat, fat-free, buttermilk, evaporated, and nonfat dry; yogurt; cheese; cottage cheese; pudding

Nutritious meals can be planned using MyPyramid for Kids.

Portfolio Project

Ask students to review the *MyPyramid for Kids* and Chart 12-4, *Food Groups, Sources, and Daily Needs.* Have students prepare a daily meal plan for a physically active four-year-old within a normal weight range. Make sure the meal includes variety. Have students record the serving amounts on the meal plan along with a choice of substitutions for each food item. Ask students to write a brief summary on the importance of nutritious meal planning. Have students put a copy of the completed project in their portfolio.

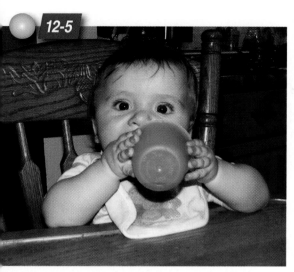

12-5

The calcium found in milk helps build strong bones. This is very important for the body of a growing child.

Riboflavin, protein, and phosphorous are also provided. Fortified milk and milk products also contain vitamins A and D.

Milk is considered the best source of calcium in this group. Milk products such as cheese, pudding, and yogurt are also good sources. Children ages two years and younger need the fat that whole milk contains. For children over two, low-fat or fat-free milk and other dairy products are better choices. They have all the nutrients found in milk, but much less fat and, therefore, fewer calories.

Grain Group

A child's diet should include six ounce-equivalents of grains daily. An *ounce-equivalent* is the amount of some foods that are counted as an ounce. For example, a one-ounce slice of bread equals one cup of dry cereal.

Foods in the grain group include whole-grain and enriched breads. Also included are pancakes, pastas, crackers, and hot and cold cereals. Carbohydrates, iron, and B-vitamins are the chief nutrients in these foods. Only

whole-grain and enriched products should be served to children. Check labels on products to be sure. Also, if you make bread products at the center, be sure to use whole-grain or enriched flour.

Meat and Beans Group

Like grain foods, the foods in this group are counted in ounce-equivalents. Protein is the most important nutrient supplied by foods in this group. Meats are also good sources of B-vitamins, iron, and phosphorous.

Animal products in this group provide the highest quality of protein. These include beef, pork, veal, lamb, eggs, seafood, and poultry. Dried beans, dried peas, lentils, nuts, and seeds are also included in this group. (Nuts and seeds should not be given to young children, however, since they pose a choking hazard.) The proteins in these foods are not as high-quality as the proteins in animal products. However, they are good sources, especially if they are served with milk, milk products, breads, or cereals.

Vegetables

Children at the 1,800-calorie level should eat 2½ cups from this group daily. Foods in this group are major sources of vitamins C and A, 12-6.

Rich sources of vitamin C include green peppers, brussels sprouts, broccoli, and tomatoes. Rich sources of vitamin A are found in deep yellow and dark green vegetables. Carrots, pumpkin, and winter squash are examples of deep yellow vegetables. Spinach, broccoli, and asparagus are deep green vegetables.

When planning meals for children, be sure to include several sources of vitamin C and vitamin A weekly. Other vegetables are important as well. Vegetables should be served raw if children are able to chew and swallow them without choking. Otherwise, cook them as little as possible. This is because cooking in water can lower the vitamin content of foods.

Discuss

Why do you think children ages two years and younger need the fat whole milk contains? Besides milk, what other foods provide a good source of calcium?

Activity

Ask students to conduct a taste testing of various whole-grain products in class. Have students rate the foods on taste and visual appeal, nutrition content, ease of preparation, and appropriateness for a preschool food program. Have students discuss their reactions to the taste of any of the foods.

Discuss

Have students survey a group of preschool children to discover what vegetables they like to eat raw as opposed to cooked. Do raw or cooked vegetables provide more nutrients?

Putting Technology to Use

Ask students to conduct an Internet search to find out about protein in the vegan diet. How easy is it to meet protein needs without the use of animal products? What foods provide a source of protein for vegans?

What is the recommended daily allowance of protein for vegans? Have students prepare a sample menu plan based on their findings. Allow time for students to share their menus in class.

Note

Some children are unable or unwilling to eat the skin on whole or sliced fruit such as apples, peaches, and pears. Try cutting the unpeeled fruit into small pieces and serve in a fruit salad so children will not lose the valuable nutrients and fiber present in the skin.

Discuss

After reviewing reproducible master 12-2, ask students to list any of the fruits or vegetables that are unusual or unfamiliar to them. Could any of these foods be incorporated into a preschool snack?

Resource

Fruit and Vegetable Sources of Vitamin A, Vitamin C, and Iron, reproducible master 12-2, TR

Discuss

Why are some foods containing oils essential for good health while other foods containing oils can be harmful? Give examples of each type of oil source.

Serving a fruit or vegetable at snack time gives children one of the servings they require.

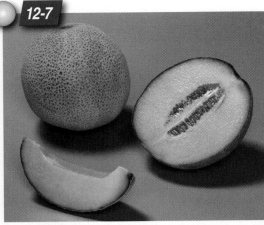

Cantaloupe provides a good source of vitamin A.

Fruit Group

Like vegetables, fruits are measured in cups. They are major sources of vitamins C and A. Serve fruits raw, slightly cooked, or in the form of 100% juice.

Rich sources of vitamin C include citrus fruits such as lemons, limes, oranges, and grapefruits. Strawberries and kiwifruit are other sources. Deep yellow fruits, such as apricots, peaches, and cantaloupe, are rich sources of vitamin A. See 12-7. Serve several sources of vitamin C and vitamin A several times weekly. Other fruits are important, too.

Oils

Oils are found in nourishing foods like fish, peanut butter, olives, and avocados. In fact, the oils they contain are essential for good health. Oils also are present in margarine, salad dressings, and cooking oils. All oils are rich in calories, and so is the solid form of oil, fat. Limiting oil and fat intake to just the oils that provide good health is highly recommended.

Eating foods high in fats or oils is an easy way to gain weight. High-calorie pastries, candies, doughnuts, and other snack items provide the types of fats and oils that may actually cause harm in later years. These foods often are also high in sugar. While children are growing, a diet high in fats and sweets can deprive them of the nutrients they need for forming healthy muscles, organs, and bones. That is why it is important to limit these foods.

For snacks, offer such items as fresh fruit or crackers with cheese. Of course, it is okay for children to have a few extra calories from time to time. However, be sure you also offer enough nutrient-rich food each day.

Workplace Connection

Have students conduct an Internet search to learn about the job duties of a nutritionist or a dietitian. What are the educational requirements for this position? How is the job outlook for a nutritionist or a dietitian over the next ten years? Ask students to write a brief report or utilize the computer to record their findings. Allow time for students to discuss their findings in class.

Meeting Special Nutritional Needs

As a teacher, one of your tasks is helping each child in your care meet his or her nutritional needs. Most children of a certain age share similar nutritional needs, but some children have unique needs. These special needs are often created by a health condition, such as diabetes or allergies. When you understand the special nutritional needs of the children in your care, you can plan appropriate meals and snacks for them.

People with diabetes do not produce **insulin**, the hormone that regulates blood sugar level. Many children with diabetes take insulin injections to keep their blood sugar level within a healthy range. When blood sugar is too high or too low, the child will feel sick.

According to the American Diabetes Association, there is not a specific "diabetic diet." People with diabetes need to follow the same basic eating guidelines as other people. They need a varied diet with plenty of fruits, vegetables, and grains. Keeping the diet low in saturated fat and cholesterol is important. Moderating sugars and salt is advised.

Blood sugar fluctuates with food intake and physical activity. For this reason, the foods chosen and portion sizes eaten should reflect balance. Eating at regular intervals also helps the blood sugar remain steady.

Managing the planning and scheduling of snacks and meals for a child with diabetes can be challenging for a teacher. The child's parents can provide specific instructions. Chances are they have worked with a registered dietitian (RD) to develop a personalized meal plan for the child. Parents also need to tell you about the best spacing of meals and snacks for their child. With practice and communication, you can work together with parents to meet the special food needs of a child with diabetes.

Special nutritional needs may also exist among children with allergies. An **allergy** is the body's negative reaction to a particular substance. The offending substance is called an **allergen**. Sometimes the allergen is a substance in the environment, such as pollen, dust, or mold. Other times the allergen is a food. Food allergies are more common among children than adults. Children often outgrow food allergies by six years of age.

Wheat, soy, peanuts, tree nuts, fish, shellfish, eggs, and milk cause 90 percent of food allergies. Corn, beans, and berries are other foods that can produce an allergic response. Most allergic reactions to foods occur within hours after contact with the allergen. Some occur within minutes.

An allergic reaction can range from mild to severe. Symptoms might include sniffles; abdominal pain; diarrhea, nausea, and vomiting; and swelling of the lips, face, tongue, throat, or eyes. Hives and nasal or respiratory congestion may also occur.

The most severe allergic reaction, called **anaphylactic shock**, is potentially fatal. Shock symptoms develop quickly. These symptoms include weakness and collapse. Other signs include problems breathing, a drop in blood pressure, and severe itching and swelling. Abdominal cramping can also occur accompanied by diarrhea and vomiting. Seek immediate medical help for anyone with signs of anaphylactic shock.

A child with food allergies needs to have a restricted diet. The child must not eat even a trace amount of the food that is an allergen. You should offer a safe substitute that provides similar nutrients. In some cases, just the smell of the offending food can cause a severe allergic reaction. This child cannot even be in the same room with the allergen, which means you must eliminate this food from the classroom. Food allergens can make meal and snack planning difficult for teachers.

Again, parents are your best resource for meeting a child's special nutritional needs. Include a question on your enrollment forms regarding food allergies. This will remind parents to share the information with you. If a child has food allergies, get detailed notes from the parents about what foods to exclude from the diet, which foods to offer as substitutes, and what steps to take

Vocabulary

Have a student volunteer define the terms *diabetes* and *insulin*. What factors need to be considered in the diet of a child with diabetes?

Enrich

Ask students to explore the Web site for the American Diabetes Association at **www.diabetes.org**. Students will be able to gather information on diabetes, treatment plans, prevention, recipe tips, exercise, and more. Have students share their findings with the class.

Vocabulary

Have student volunteers define the terms *allergy*, *allergen*, and *anaphylactic shock*. What are some of the symptoms of food allergies?

Cross-Curricular Activity

Health

Have students prepare a list of questions concerning diabetes, blood sugar regulation, insulin production, and the body's response to allergens for the biology or health teacher. Ask the teacher to review the questions and prepare a presentation to the class to further explain the body's digestive system. Ask the teacher to answer any questions students may have on these subjects. Have students create a list of recommendations for healthful living based on what they have learned.

Discuss

Ask students to describe a recent meal they ate that was very enjoyable. Did the meal meet all the characteristics recommended for food appeal?

Reflect

How important is food color, texture, and shape to you? What characteristics of foods make them appealing to children?

Enrich

Have students conduct an interview with a child care center director or food service personnel. Compare the usual size servings of food they offer to children with the serving sizes recommended in 12-8. Are the serving sizes similar? What foods seem to give children trouble and may often be discarded? What foods are most popular and asked for more frequently? Have students write a summary of their findings.

if an allergic reaction occurs. Always check enrollment records of a newly enrolled child before serving the child any food or drink. Read product labels to check the ingredients of foods. Be mindful of children's food allergies as you plan menus for meals and snacks.

In addition to diabetes and allergies, the children in your care may have other special food needs. Your menu must meet the nutritional needs of every child. Talk with parents about any special needs their children might have. Find out what, if any, modifications are needed. Make sure all staff members who will feed the children are aware of these needs.

Planning Meals and Snacks

Nutrition is the most important part of a well-planned menu. However, many other factors also contribute to a well-planned menu. For instance, scale serving sizes to the children's appetites. Children manage best with small servings. Their appetites often vary from day to day. Suggested serving sizes for specific age groups are listed in 12-8. These are recommended by the USDA Child and Adult Care Food Program (CACFP).

Food Appeal

Children will eat more if the food appeals to them. Variety, texture, flavor, color, form, temperature, and food preferences all affect how much a child enjoys a meal.

Variety

Children like variety in the foods served to them. A meal with all the same texture or color could be boring for children. They also enjoy trying new foods. A new food should be added

12-8

Food	Ages		
	1-2	3-5	6-12
Milk	½ cup	¾ cup	1 cup
Bread	½ slice	½ slice	1 slice
Biscuit, roll, or muffin	½	½	1
Cereal, cold	¼ cup	⅓ cup	¾ cup
Cereal, hot cooked, or pasta or noodles	¼ cup	¼ cup	½ cup
Vegetable	¼ cup	½ cup	½ cup
Fruit	¼ cup	½ cup	½ cup
Meat, lean cooked without bone	1 ounce	1½ ounces	2 ounces
Egg	½	¾	1
Dried peas or beans, cooked	¼ cup	⅜ cup	½ cup
Peanut butter	2 tablespoons	3 tablespoons	4 tablespoons
Cheddar cheese	1 ounce	1½ ounces	2 ounces
Yogurt	4 ounces	6 ounces	8 ounces

Consider the age of children as you plan meals and snacks.

Portfolio Project

Ask students to prepare a meal plan for one week for a child care center that serves breakfast, lunch, and two snacks daily. Make sure meals are appealing, meet the nutrition guidelines for young children, and promote the use of fresh fruits and vegetables whenever possible. Have students share their menu with a food service director to determine if the menu is nutritionally adequate. Have students save a copy of the meal plan in their portfolio.

with a meal of familiar and well-liked foods. This is because children may be overwhelmed if given too many new foods at once.

Texture

Soft, hard, chewy, mashed, chopped, crisp, creamy, and *rough* are all textures. It is wise to combine textures when planning meals and snacks for young children. This makes the meal more interesting for the children. For instance, at mealtime, serve one soft food, one crisp food, and one chewy food. See 12-9. Combine contrasting textures for a pleasing effect. This also provides you with an opportunity to include language concepts during meals and snacks.

Dry foods are hard for children to eat. Serve dry food only in combination with two or more moist foods.

Some meats are difficult for young children to chew. Their teeth cannot grind meat as easily as adults' teeth. Because of this, children usually prefer hamburgers. Chili, spaghetti, and casseroles are other ways of serving meat with varied textures.

Flavor

In general, children prefer mildly seasoned foods. One rule of thumb is to use only half as much salt as noted in a recipe. Whenever possible, enhance the natural flavor of the food. This means that only small amounts of sugar and spices should be added.

Color

Children enjoy color in their meals. If the foods you are serving are not very colorful, add color to one or more of the foods. For example, tint the applesauce pink. For St. Patrick's Day, you might color vanilla pudding green.

Food Forms

Serve most foods in bite-sized pieces. Children have poorly developed fine-motor coordination skills. They find it difficult

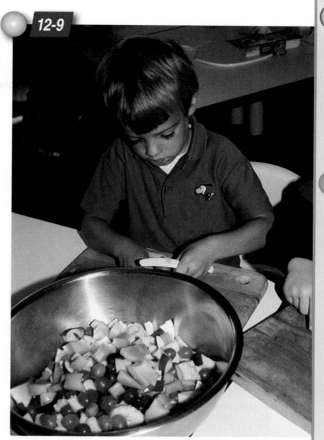
12-9

The crisp apples, soft pears, and squishy grapes in this fruit salad provide an appealing texture combination.

to use spoons and forks well. Therefore, slice cooked carrots and other vegetables in large pieces rather than dicing them. Try adding diced vegetables to another food. For instance, add diced carrots to mashed potatoes.

Soup is also difficult for many young children to eat. They become tired from spooning. Children may get frustrated if they spill on clothing or the table.

Two methods can be used to make soup easier to eat. One method is to thicken the soup. This can be done by adding solid ingredients or a thickener, such as flour. The second method is to let the children drink the soup from a cup.

Discuss

Why are dry foods difficult for children to eat? Give some examples of combining dry foods with moist foods to make mealtimes more enjoyable for children.

Activity

Demonstrate to students that food can be appetizing and flavorful without additional salt, sugar, and strong spices. Obtain samples of foods such as unsweetened applesauce, salt-free pretzels, natural fruit spreads, unsalted butter, and low-sodium crackers. Have students conduct a taste test of each item in class.

Reflect

Would you eat blue mashed potatoes? brown peas? How does color affect your appetite? How might this also be true of children? Give some examples of unusually colored foods you may have experienced.

Workplace Connection

To reinforce the concept that children will eat more if the food appeals to them, have students create a poster on *Food Appeal for Children.* Ask students to select pictures of various types of foods from magazines, pamphlets, and clip art and arrange them under the headings *Variety, Texture, Flavor, Color, Food Forms,* and *Temperature.* Pictures should appropriately represent each of the headings. Ask students to use the posters in conjunction with a preschool lesson on food and nutrition for children.

Activity

Have students plan and present a lesson to introduce an interesting cultural food item or recipe in the preschool. Present opportunities for children to help prepare and serve the food and include parental involvement if appropriate. For example, an Asian American parent may be able to demonstrate making egg rolls.

Discuss

How can serving food from children's cultures promote cultural identity and self-esteem? Why should children be exposed to multicultural food experiences even when their group is not diverse?

Activity

Have students conduct a survey of young children to discover their preferences for combination foods such as casseroles and mixed salads. Also ask children about foods that include several food items such as tacos or wraps. Do the children prefer eating foods separately, or do they enjoy combination foods? Allow time for students to share their findings with the class.

Resource

Nutrition Crossword, Activity B, SAG

Whenever possible, prepare foods so they can be eaten with the fingers, 12-10. For example, serve chopped raw vegetables instead of a tossed salad.

Temperature

Variety in the temperature of foods served can be appealing, too. For a snack, offer a cold glass of milk with a room-temperature food, such as crackers. At mealtime, serve a cold fruit or pudding with a warm casserole. For safety reasons, be sure to serve each food at its proper temperature (hot foods hot and cold foods cold). Keep in mind, however, children are more sensitive to temperature extremes than adults.

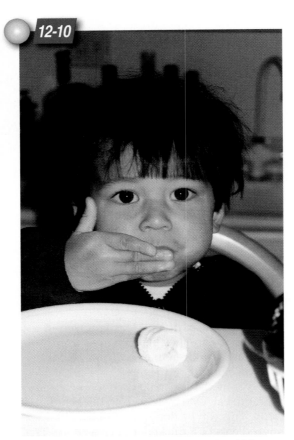

12-10

These large slices of banana will be easy for children to pick up with their fingers.

Food Preferences

Children differ in their individual food preferences. For example, while some children enjoy spicy foods, others prefer milder flavors. Most children have at least a few foods they strongly like and some they strongly dislike. Although food preferences are personal, they are also influenced by home life. One family may eat many vegetables, while another family might eat them less often.

As a teacher, you will learn quickly about the children's likes and dislikes. When possible, honor the child's preferences unless they are unhealthful. Suppose Courtney likes her sandwiches cut diagonally. Accommodating this food preference when possible will help mealtimes run more smoothly.

Multicultural Experiences

Children need to be exposed to healthful foods from various cultures. This will help create community among a diverse group of children. Through repeated experiences, children will learn how food relates to social and cultural customs. Including foods from the children's cultures helps promote cultural identity and self-esteem. Foods from other cultures help children learn to taste new dishes and respect cultural differences.

Family members can help you promote a multicultural approach to the food program. Encourage them to share recipes for snacks, meals, and holiday celebrations. Invite parents to prepare for the class special foods from their culture. Some parents may enjoy teaching children to help prepare the foods.

Serving Meals

Licensing requirements outline how often and how much food must be provided for young children in child care centers. These requirements vary from state to state. As a rule, the number of hours a child spends at

---

Meeting Special Needs

After assigning *Nutrition Crossword,* Activity B, SAG, demonstrate how to fill in the puzzle by doing the first item with the students. Provide a word bank with the answers for students who may need this assistance. Reproduce the puzzle with several answers filled in for those students who need a shorter assignment. Ask students to write the word in the blank space in each statement as well as fill in the puzzle for further clarification.

a center governs the number of snacks and meals served. In most states, children who attend less than four hours a day must be served a fruit juice or milk and a snack item. Children who attend five or more hours must be served both a meal and a snack.

The decision to serve breakfast is often based on two factors. These are the length of the program day and the distance the child travels to reach the center. Centers with full-day programs or children who travel long distances often serve breakfast.

Breakfast

The purpose of breakfast is to break the 10- to 14-hour overnight fast. Breakfast provides energy for morning activities. Studies show that children who eat a nutritious breakfast perform better mentally and physically.

A good breakfast should include a variety of foods in the amounts recommended for the child's age. The minimum recommendations of the CACFP are

- 1 milk
- 1 fruit, vegetable, or 100% juice
- 1 grain source, such as bread, hot or cold cereal, or pasta or noodles

Fruit drinks or punches are not juice substitutes, even when fortified with vitamin C.

Self-Serve Breakfasts

Self-serve breakfasts are popular with center staffs. This is because children can eat their breakfasts as they arrive. They can choose what and how much to eat, based on their own appetites. The self-serve breakfast gives children the chance to prepare their own breakfasts.

Many prepackaged breakfast foods come in child-sized servings. These include dry cereals, yogurt packs, and muffins. Juice and milk are also available in child-sized servings.

Snacks

Most children eat small amounts of food at one sitting. They may not be properly nourished by just eating three meals a day. Therefore, provide snacks between meals. Snacks satisfy hunger and help meet daily food requirements.

In most centers, snacks are served mid-morning and again in mid-afternoon. Snacks should not interfere with a child's appetite for meals. Because of this, it is best to schedule snacks at least 1½ hours before meals.

Plan a snack based on the menu for the day. Consider the nutrients, colors, and textures of the meals. Then choose snacks that complement the meals. Avoid fats, sweets, and highly salted foods such as potato chips, pretzels, and corn chips. Children usually enjoy simple snacks they can eat with their fingers. Suggestions for snack ideas are shown in Figure 12-11.

Lunch

To ensure that children receive the proper nutrients, be sure to include the minimum recommendations of the CACFP:

- 1 milk
- 2 fruits, vegetables, 100% juice, or any combination
- 1 grain source, such as bread, hot or cold cereal, or pasta or noodles
- 1 meat or alternate, such as poultry, fish, soy product, cheese, egg, cooked dry beans or peas, peanut butter (or similar nut or seed butter), or yogurt

Grains, protein-rich foods, and vegetables are often served together as one dish. They might be used in a casserole or soup, for instance. Combining food groups can make mealtimes more interesting than always serving each of these groups separately.

Try including foods from various cultures. This will help the children develop

Enrich
Have students research the connection between eating a nutritious breakfast and mental and physical performance. Compare the effects of school performance between children who ate a nutritious breakfast and those who ate very little or not at all. Allow time for students to share their findings with the class.

Resource
Serving Breakfast and Lunch, transparency master 12-3, TR

Discuss
Do children really need snacks if they are eating three nutritious meals a day? Why should children be offered snacks?

Resource
Breakfast Foods Children Can Easily Make, reproducible master 12-4, TR

Workplace Connection

Using print or Internet sources, ask students to investigate their state's licensing requirements or restrictions, if any, for serving snacks during the preschool or child care center day. What foods, besides those listed in the text, are inappropriate to serve as snacks to young children? Have students compare their findings to the preschool or child care center snack menu. Allow time for students to discuss their findings in class.

12-11

Snack Ideas

Grain Group

Granola
Rice cakes
Dry cereal mixes (not presweetened)
Roasted wheat berries, wheat germ, bran as
   roll-ins, toppers, or as finger food mix
Variety of breads (tortillas, pita breads, crepes,
   scones, pancakes, English muffins, biscuits,
   bagels, cornbread, popovers) and grains (whole
   wheat, cracked wheat, rye, oatmeal, buckwheat,
   rolled wheat, wheat germ, bran, grits)
Toast (plain, buttered, with spreads, cinnamon)
Homemade yeast and quick breads
Waffle sandwiches
Whole-grain and spinach pastas
Pasta with butter and poppy seeds
Cold pasta salad
Rice (brown or white)

Vegetable Group

Vegetables (with or without dips): sweet and
   white potatoes, broccoli, cauliflower, radishes,
   peppers, mushrooms, zucchini, squashes,
   rutabagas, avocados, eggplant, okra, pea pods,
   turnips, pumpkin, sprouts, spinach, carrot sticks
Kabobs and salads
Vegetable juices and juice blends
Vegetable soups
Stuffed celery, cucumbers, zucchini, spinach,
   lettuce, cabbage
Vegetable spreads

Fruit Group

Fruits (use variety): pomegranates, cranberries,
   apricots, pineapples, tangerines, kiwifruit,
   apples, strawberries, cantaloupe, banana, cut
   grapes
Kabobs and salads
Fruit juices
Fruit in muffins, yogurts, and breads
Stuffed dates or prunes

Meat and Beans Group

Meat strips, chunks, cubes
Meatballs, small kabobs
Meat roll-ups (cheese spread, mashed potatoes,
   spinach as stuffing)
Meat salads (tuna, chicken, turkey)
Sardines
Fish sticks and chicken nuggets
Hard boiled eggs
Deviled eggs
Egg salad spread
Beans and peas mashed as dips or spreads
Bean, pea, or lentil soup
3-bean salad
Chopped nut spreads
Nut breads
Peanut butter on, in, around, over, or with anything

Milk Group

Dips (yogurt, cottage cheese)
Cheese (balls, wedges, cutouts, faces, strips,
   slices)
Milk punches made with fruits or juices
Yogurt or pudding
Cottage cheese with vegetables or pancakes
Cheese fondue (preheated, no open flame in
   classroom)

Plan snacks to coordinate with MyPyramid for Kids.

Reflect

Ask students to review 12-11, *Snack Ideas*. Do you see any snack ideas you had not previously considered for preschoolers? What snacks from the list would you be willing to try? Do you think children would like to try them?

Note

The Web site **www.kidshealth. org** is a good source of recipes for children. Recipes can be found for children with diabetes, cystic fibrosis, and celiac disease. The Web site also contains recipes for children who are lactose intolerant or vegetarian.

Reflect

"You can't have your broccoli unless you eat all your chocolate cake!" How might you think of vegetables if you had heard a statement like this when you were growing up? Do you feel too much emphasis is placed on dessert and not enough on eating the rest of the meal?

an appreciation of other foods. The children will learn that people have different food preferences. Where rice is an important staple in some cultures, bread is in others.

When included, desserts should be part of the meal, like the vegetable or bread. They should not be treated as a special part of

the meal. Never tell children they must eat everything on their plates in order to get dessert. This will only make desserts appear special.

Those desserts high in fat and sugar and low in other nutrients should be avoided. For example, plain cookies and cakes have little nutritional value, but are high in calories.

Portfolio Project

Have students create a healthful choices snack recipe booklet for use in a preschool classroom. Ask students to collect at least ten recipes that are low in sugar, fat, and sodium. Recipes should also contain nutritious ingredients such as fruit, vegetables, and dairy products. Have students assemble the recipes into a booklet with an appropriate cover and write an explanation about why each recipe is a nutritious choice. Have students file the completed booklet in their portfolio, allowing room for additional recipes to be added later.

Instead, plan to use carrots or pumpkin in recipes to provide vitamin A. Custards and puddings are considered good desserts since they contain calcium and protein.

Chart 12-12 contains sample daily food plans for one meal and a snack. Note how each meal-snack pair complement one another.

Serving Safe Meals and Snacks

When planning nutritious meals and snacks, keep safety in mind. Remember that young children are learning how to chew and swallow. When they are in a hurry, they may gulp their food. This can create a risk of choking. To prevent choking, avoid serving foods that, if swallowed whole, could block children's windpipes. Foods to be avoided include cherries with pits, hard or sticky candies, marshmallows, nuts, peanut butter by the spoonful, gum, raisins, popcorn, pretzels, raw celery, whole raw carrots, whole grapes, and hot dogs (unless sliced lengthwise, then crosswise into bite-sized pieces).

12-12

Sample Menus for Lunch and Snack

Pattern	I	II	III	IV	V	VI
Snack	Orange juice Whole-wheat bread Butter	Apple wedge Cheese	Banana Milk	Hard cooked egg Tomato juice	Apple juice Celery stuffed with peanut butter	Milk Peanut butter and cracker
Lunch	Ground beef patty Peas Carrot strips Enriched roll Milk	Roast turkey Broccoli Mashed potatoes Whole-wheat bread Milk	Fish sticks Scalloped potatoes Stewed tomato Whole-wheat bread Milk	Black-eyed peas with ham Mustard greens Purple plums Corn bread Milk	Scrambled eggs Spinach Fried apples Biscuit Milk	Oven-fried drumsticks Corn-on-the-cob Sliced tomato/green pepper rings Whole-wheat bread Milk

Pattern	VII	VIII	IX	X	XI	XII
Snack	Apple juice Cheese toast	Milk Pineapple Cottage cheese	Grapefruit juice Finger-size pieces of leftover meat	Milk Raw carrot strips, green pepper with dip	Tomato juice Flour tortilla with melted cheese	Fresh fruit in season (strawberries, melons, tangerines)
Lunch	Meatloaf Green beans Baked potato Carrot strips Enriched bread Milk	Tuna sandwich on whole-wheat bread Tomato juice Raw cabbage (small pieces) Apricots Milk	Pinto beans with melted cheese Chili peppers, chopped Tomato, onion, lettuce Flour tortilla Milk	Meatballs in tomato sauce over spaghetti Zucchini Peaches French bread Milk	Lunchmeat roll-ups Sweet potato Apple, banana, and orange salad Rye bread Milk	Swiss steak cubes Cauliflower Cooked carrots Whole-wheat roll Milk

Planning menus is the first step toward teaching nutrition concepts.

Discuss

Look over the snack and meal pairings in 12-12, *Sample Menus for Lunch and Snack.* Are there any selections you would change? What nutritious alternatives can you suggest for these foods?

Resource

Choosing Nutritious Snacks, reproducible master 12-5, TR

Enrich

Ask students to design displays featuring nutritious snacks, nutrition information, food samples, manipulatives, games, puzzles, puppet shows, videos, or research projects to share what they have learned in this chapter. Have students present their display in class.

Meeting Special Needs

Review the special learners' chapter outlines to determine if the students have any questions about the concepts or content of this chapter. Review the chapter objectives and ask the students to evaluate their progress in meeting these objectives. Ask the students to summarize, orally or in writing, what they learned from this chapter.

Review and Reflect **Answer Key**

1. true
2. (List four:) provide nutritious meals and snacks; introduce new foods that are nutritious; encourage healthful eating habits; involve children in meal activities; provide information to parents on nutrition
3. Nutrition is the science of food and how the body uses the food taken in.
4. Nutrients are the chemical substances in food that help build and maintain the body.
5. proteins, carbohydrates, fats, vitamins, minerals, and water
6. calories
7. Undernutrition means not eating enough food to keep a healthful body weight and activity level. Malnutrition is a lack of proper nutrients in the diet.
8. grains; vegetables; fruits; milk; meat and beans
9. D
10. carbohydrates, iron, B-vitamins
11. A, C
12. oils

Summary

Teaching children about nutrition is an important responsibility. Children who learn healthful food choices can use the information their entire lives. Good nutrition promotes children's growth and development.

In order to teach about nutrition, you must first understand how food is used by the body. You must also understand how nutrients fuel the body. You can then use this information to plan nutritious meals and snacks. MyPyramid is a useful tool for planning menus. Food will appeal more to children if you consider the texture, flavor, color, form, and temperature of the foods you plan to serve.

Review and Reflect

1. True or false. Children who have learned healthful food choices may also experience lifelong good health.
2. List four goals of a good nutrition program.
3. Define nutrition.
4. What are nutrients?
5. Name the six groups of nutrients.
6. The energy value of food is measured in _____.
7. Describe the difference between undernutrition and malnutrition.
8. What are the five food groups in MyPyramid?
9. Milk is a good source of _____.
   A. calcium
   B. riboflavin
   C. phosphorus
   D. All the above.
10. What are the chief nutrients found in breads and cereals?
11. A good source of vitamins _____ and _____ should be served several times a week.
12. Good sources of _____ include fish, olives, and avocados.
13. Describe the eating guidelines for children with diabetes.
14. True or false. Ninety percent of food allergies result from wheat, soy, peanuts, tree nuts, fish, shellfish, eggs, and milk.
15. Why should food be served to children in bite-size pieces?
16. List the recommended foods for a nutritious breakfast outlined by the USDA Child and Adult Care Food Program.
17. True or false. It is a good idea to tell children to eat everything on their plates in order to get dessert.
18. Name four foods that should not be served to young children because they might cause choking.

13. Children with diabetes should eat at regular intervals. They should balance food choices and portion sizes. Physical activity and medications should be considered when planning meals and snacks. Keeping the diet low in saturated fat and cholesterol is important. Moderating sugars and salt is advised.
14. true
15. Children have poorly developed fine motor skills. This makes handling forks and spoons difficult.
16. 1 milk; 1 fruit, vegetable, or 100% juice; 1 grain source, such as bread, hot or cold cereal, or pasta or noodles
17. false
18. (Name four:) cherries with pits, hard or sticky candies, marshmallows, nuts, peanut butter by the spoonful, gum, raisins, popcorn, pretzels, raw celery, whole raw carrots, whole grapes, and whole hot dogs

Apply and Explore

1. Plan a breakfast, lunch, and snack menu for one week for a group of three-year-old children.

2. Observe a group of children at lunchtime. Describe their food preferences. Note what is or is not lacking in their lunch menu based on the recommendations given in this chapter.

3. Prepare a list of desserts. List the nutritional information for each of these desserts. Are they nutritious? Why or why not?

4. Discuss why obesity is easier to prevent than treat.

5. Discuss why MyPyramid for Kids contains pictures of young children being active and playing sports.

Cross-Curricular Link

Language Arts

1. Interview a dietitian about the importance of a nutritious diet for children.

Technology

2. Use a search engine to find information on snack ideas for toddlers and preschoolers.

3. Connect to the Web site for the American Diabetes Association (www.diabetes.org) and search for Diabetes Food Pyramid. Compare this with MyPyramid. How are they alike and different?

Workplace Link

Interview a child care center or preschool director to discover how food allergies and food intolerances are handled. Are special foods and meals supplied by the center? Do parents have to supply foods and snacks that will keep their child free from reactions? What precautions does the center take to ensure that a child is not accidentally exposed to a food that can cause a severe reaction? What foods generally cause the most severe reactions?

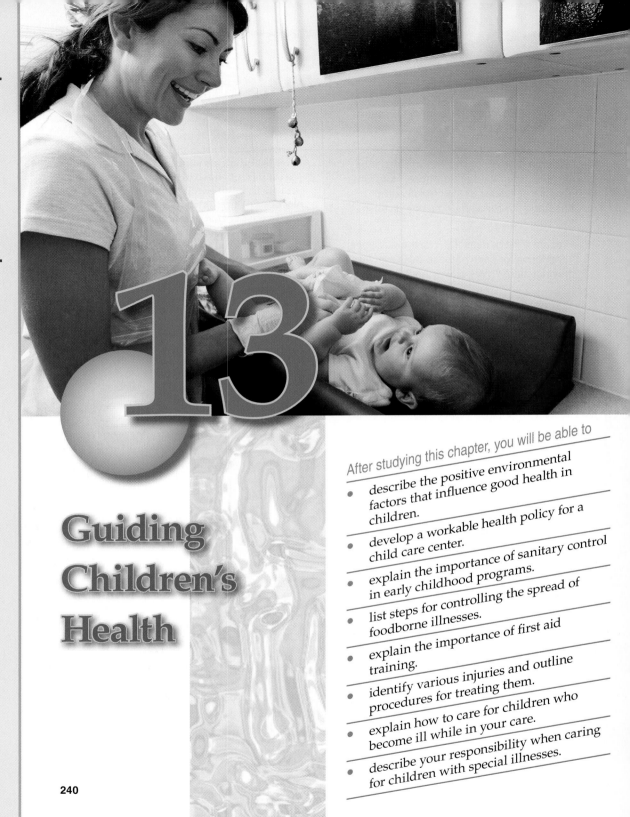

Discuss

How is the teacher in the chapter opening photo protecting this child's health? What other steps might she take to protect the health of other children in the class?

Discuss

Look over the objectives for this chapter. Why is children's health a responsibility of the early childhood professional?

13

Guiding Children's Health

After studying this chapter, you will be able to

- describe the positive environmental factors that influence good health in children.
- develop a workable health policy for a child care center.
- explain the importance of sanitary control in early childhood programs.
- list steps for controlling the spread of foodborne illnesses.
- explain the importance of first aid training.
- identify various injuries and outline procedures for treating them.
- explain how to care for children who become ill while in your care.
- describe your responsibility when caring for children with special illnesses.

Terms to Know

policy

communicable diseases

sanitizing

disinfecting

universal infection and control precautions

foodborne illness

first aid

wound

abrasion

rabies

burn

first-degree burn

second-degree burn

third-degree burn

head lice

asthma

epilepsy

human immunodeficiency virus (HIV)

acquired immunodeficiency syndrome (AIDS)

Tu-Ling's health affects his performance, ability to learn, and behavior. Tu-Ling has a constant inner ear infection, and he is having trouble hearing. This hearing loss may affect his development of language skills, contact with peers, and general behavior.

A child's health is a key concern when planning, preparing, and maintaining a classroom environment, 13-1.

A healthful environment for young children starts with sound health policies. To avoid the transmission of disease, stress personal hygiene and safe food handling practices. Plan for emergencies such as control of head lice. Also plan for sudden illnesses. In addition, obtain the knowledge and skill to provide first aid treatment.

13-1

Contact parents on health issues when appropriate.

Healthy Children

There are many different definitions of *healthy*. Today the concept of health extends beyond the absence of illness and disease. The broader emphasis of health focuses on physical, mental, and social well-being. Factors that affect one area of health also influence another. For example, a child living in an abusive home environment may experience frequent illnesses.

A child's heredity sets the limits for his or her health potential. However, environment plays an equally important role. The child's environment consists of cultural, social, physical, and economic factors. These factors influence a child's diet, opportunities for exercise, and stress levels. These are all issues that influence health. Positive environmental factors that influence good health include

- good nutrition and dietary habits

- daily physical activity

- personal hygiene

- regular medical and dental care

Vocabulary

Have students review the *Terms to Know* list. Ask students to look up unfamiliar words or terms in the glossary before reading the chapter.

Resource

Health Match, Activity A, SAG

Reflect

Did you ever suffer from an illness or sustain an injury at school when you were a young child? What was done to keep you comfortable or treat your injury until you could go home?

Meeting Special Needs

Provide an outline of the chapter with all the chapter headings for special learners. Students should fill in each section of the outline as the material is covered in class with a sentence or two about the content. Review the special learners' IEPs to decide if any modifications should be made in presenting the chapter content.

Discuss

What health-related policies already exist in your school? What additional policies exist in the child care program in your school?

Vocabulary

Have a student volunteer define the term *communicable diseases*. Do immunizations exist for every communicable disease?

Activity

Why do you think child care centers require new employees to have an up-to-date physical examination prior to the start of employment? Have students contact a child care center or review the state's licensing standards to determine if any additional tests, such as a TB test or chest X-ray, may be required. Who is responsible for paying for the physical examination? Have students discuss their findings in class.

- exposure to clean and safe environments at home and school
- respectful and stable relationships that provide predictability and consistency

On the other hand, factors such as poor nutrition and inactivity can lead to obesity. This affects children's health negatively. Child abuse, violence, and poverty also have a negative impact. Exposure to lead paint and chemicals can be harmful to a child's health. A lack of medical attention can interfere with optimal health.

Objectives for Guiding Health

It is your responsibility to protect, maintain, and improve children's health. Thus, you will need to create a healthful environment. The following objectives should be considered:

- Develop center health policies.
- Review the children's health records to ensure that they receive immunizations.
- Recognize ill children when making daily health observations.
- Isolate from the group any children who may have an illness.
- Contact parents on health issues when appropriate.
- Plan a safe environment to prevent accidents.
- Provide first aid treatment.
- Take part in health-related in-service training.
- Include health in the curriculum.

Health Policies

A **policy** is a course of action that controls future decisions. It is important for your center to have health policies. These policies will help you make consistent decisions regarding the health of the children in your care.

In most states, the health of children in child care is regulated by state licensing rules and regulations. Their purpose is to protect young children. These rules and regulations address only the basic health requirements. Your center may have additional health policies that are more specific.

Medical Examination

All children enrolled in your program should have a preadmission medical examination. This exam will help you learn

- whether the child is free from **communicable diseases**. (These are illnesses that can be passed on to other people.)
- if immunizations are up-to-date.
- if the child has any health problems that need special attention.

To provide the best environment for children, the staff must also be in excellent physical, mental, and emotional health. They should have an examination prior to their first day of work. A record of these examinations should be maintained in the employees' files.

Immunizations

To protect all children, each child attending the center must have the proper

---

Cross-Curricular Activity

Social Studies
Ask students to research epidemics and pandemics such as influenza, typhus, and tuberculosis that have affected the United States over the last century. What was the nation's response to these incidents? What medical and public health policies or agencies were developed to avoid similar epidemics in the future? How has education been affected by public policies designed to avoid the spread of disease? Have students write a one-page report of their findings. Allow time for students to read their reports in class.

Doctor and Dental Visits

At times, you may be called on to assist parents in preparing their children for doctor or dental visits. Note that it is not recommended that families and caregivers talk a lot about these visits in advance. Take your cue from the children.

- Provide age-appropriate information and be positive.

- Answer children's questions directly and honestly.

- Always provide comfort and assurance.

- Encourage family members to plan a fun activity (not a bribe) after doctor and dental visits are over.

immunizations. The only exception to this policy is when a child is exempted by state laws for religious or medical reasons. Children who are not properly immunized or exempted must be excluded from the center. Partial immunizations do not provide protection against many diseases. The American Academy of Pediatrics suggests the following immunizations: hepatitis B; diptheria, tetanus, and pertussis (DTaP); measles, mumps, and rubella (MMR); inactivated polio vaccine (IPV); Haemophilus influenzae type b (Hib) vaccine; varicella

(chicken pox) vaccine; and pneumococcal conjugate vaccine. See 13-2. Find out which immunizations are required by law in the state where you live.

Exclusion Policy

For the safety of all the children, centers need a policy stating when an ill child should be kept at home. For example, your policy might state that a child should be kept at home if he or she has shown any of

13-2

Immunizations for Young Children

Immunization	Range of Recommended Ages
Hepatitis B vaccine	Birth; 1 to 4 months; 6 to 18 months
Diptheria, tetanus, and pertussis (DTaP)	2 months; 4 months; 6 months; 15 to 18 months; 4 to 6 years
Tetanus (td)	After 4 to 6 years, every 10 years
Polio vaccine (IPV)	2 months; 4 months; 6 to 18 months; 4 to 6 years
Haemophilus influenzae type b vaccine (Hib)	2 months; 4 months; 6 months; 12 to 15 months
Measles, mumps, and rubella vaccine (MMR)	12 to 15 months; 4 to 6 years
Varicella (chicken pox) vaccine	12 to 18 months
Pneumococcal vaccine	2 months; 4 months; 6 months; 12 to 15 months

Proper immunization is a health policy required by most state licensing agencies.

Reflect

Were you ever afraid to go to the doctor or dentist as a child? Did your family talk to you before the visit? Did you engage in a fun activity after the visit? Ask student volunteers to share their experiences.

Note

A child may have a chronic condition that is not contagious and may not affect a child's ability to participate in preschool activities. This may include symptoms such as a runny nose due to allergies, red eyes due to chlorine exposure, or dry and scaly patches on the skin from eczema. Share this information with student teachers or other staff because they may think the child should be sent home.

Resource

Immunizations for Young Children, transparency master 13-1, TR

Cross-Curricular Activity

Health
Invite the school nurse or other health professional to speak to the class about each of the immunizations listed in 13-2. What are the symptoms of each disease that the immunizations prevent? What may result if children contract these diseases? Have students prepare a list of additional questions to ask prior to the visit.

Discuss

What might result if the exclusion policy is not followed in a school setting? Why is it important for parents to report all sicknesses of their child even if the child is no longer symptomatic?

Reflect

Tanya's mother does not want to bother with dropping off and picking up her child's medicine each day. She wants to know if she can divide up the medicine and put it in another container to be kept at school. Knowing that prescription medicine can only be dispensed from the original pharmacy container, what suggestion do you have for Tanya's mother?

Discuss

What should you do if a child is given the wrong medication dosage? What if a medication is given to the wrong child? What other medication errors may occur in a child care center?

the following symptoms within the past 24 hours:

- an oral temperature over 101°F or rectal temperature of 102°F, unless the child's normal temperature is above the average

- intestinal upset along with diarrhea or vomiting

- severe, persistent cough or cold

- drainage from open sores, eyes, nose, or ears

- rashes, excluding diaper rash

- lice

Parents should be advised to keep a child home for 24 hours after a fever subsides, 13-3. Likewise, children should remain at home until they have been free from diarrhea

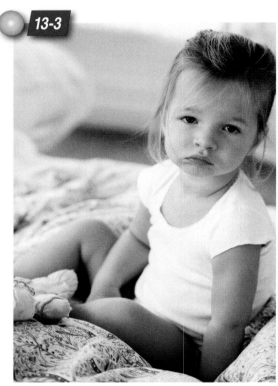

13-3

Even after a fever subsides, it can take up to 24 hours for children to feel well enough to attend child care.

for twenty-four hours. Instruct parents to report all sickness to center personnel.

Administering Medications

Mildly ill children may need to be provided medications. To protect staff and children in their care against lawsuits, most centers have policies for medication. These policies must adhere to, but can exceed, your state's licensing requirements. For instance, your state may require that only a doctor-prescribed medication may be given to a child. You must follow this rule. Some states, however, prohibit administering medications.

Medicines should also be stored appropriately. Refrigerated medications should be stored in a secure, labeled plastic bag. The bags should then be stored in a locked container in the refrigerator. Nonrefrigerated medicines should be stored in a locked place out of the children's reach. It is important that medications contain a label specifying the child's name, physician's name, name of medication, dosage, and how often to administer.

Always use caution when giving medications. Give the correct medication and exact amount prescribed at the prescribed time. If you do not know the child well, verify his or her name before giving the medicine. This is especially true in programs where one person, such as the director, administers all medications. Always read the label on the medication at least three times. First read the label as you remove the medication from storage to be sure you have the right medication for the right child. Read it again as you dispense the medicine into the measuring device. Look at the label one last time before giving the medicine to double check it is the right amount of the right medicine for the right child. If you have any questions about the medication, call the parents or the prescribing doctor before giving the medicine.

Workplace Connection

Ask students to review their state's licensing requirements for administering medications. Do the regulations allow doctor-prescribed medications to be administered? Does the state prohibit the administering of any medications?

Have students contact a local child care center to learn about their policy for administering medications. Does the policy exceed the state's licensing requirements? Have students discuss their findings in class.

Keeping a Medication Log

At times, child care teachers or center directors may need to administer medicine to children in their care. For each child, keep a special log that includes signed parental consent, copy of the health care provider's documentation for the child's need of medicine, the medication, name, dosage, time(s) it should be given, and other requirements, such as "with a glass of water." The log should also list signs of negative reactions and instructions for handling them. In addition, you may be asked to keep a checklist of medication brought to the facility by the parents.

Napping

One health policy that is needed to help prevent the spread of illness is related to napping. Children should not share cots or beds. Rather, each child should be provided with a washable cot or bed and clean sheets. Clean sheets should be provided on a weekly basis. At times, it may be necessary to change sheets more frequently, such as when a child is ill, has perspired a great deal, or has soiled the sheets.

Daily Health Inspection

To protect children's health, conduct an informal health inspection each day. This inspection is best conducted as soon as each child arrives at school. Observe for rashes, sores, swelling or bruising, changes in appearance of eyes, runny noses, flushing of skin, coughing, sneezing, and a sweaty appearance.

Even after the health inspection at arrival time, observe the children throughout the day for symptoms of illness, 13-4. If a child appears sick, contact the parents.

13-4

Symptoms of Illness

- atypical behavior: more quiet, tired, fussy, or aggressive than usual
- excessive crying
- breathing difficulties
- complaint of stomachache or cramping
- diarrhea
- fever
- frequent scratching of body or scalp
- change in color of urine or stools
- urine with a strong odor
- headache or stiff neck
- infected skin lesions
- loss of appetite or refusal to eat
- neck pain or stiff neck
- redness or discharge from eyes
- severe coughing
- congestion
- runny nose (a yellow or green discharge indicates infection; a clear discharge indicates allergies)
- sores
- sore throat or difficulty swallowing
- achiness
- seizure for the first time
- spots on throat
- rashes or spots
- vomiting

Watch the children for these signs of illness.

Discuss

How often should a medication log be reviewed? What types of notations should staff record in the medication log?

Note

As children arrive each day at the center, parents may share their children's minor health symptoms or incidents that may affect the child's health or participation during the class. Remind students to write these down to share with the rest of the class.

Resource

Infection Symptoms, transparency master 13-2, TR

Activity

Invite the school nurse to class to explain transparency master 13-2. Ask the nurse to explain what each symptom indicates is happening in the body. Have students prepare a list of questions to ask prior to the visit.

Workplace Connection

Have students investigate how child care centers in the area manage sleeping arrangements for babies and young children. Do state licensing standards exist pertaining to required naps or rest periods? Are they based on the number of hours a child is in attendance? What types of cribs, cots, or sleeping mats are used at the center depending on the child's age? How easy are these items to clean and disinfect? How often is the bedding changed? Have students compare their findings to those of other students in the class.

Preschool children are prone to communicable diseases. These include chicken pox, conjunctivitis (pink eye), influenza, and measles among others. Observe for symptoms of each of these diseases. Make this information known to all staff. Post a communicable diseases chart in the staff room, 13-5.

Contacting Parents

Children may arrive at the center in good health, but later show symptoms of illness or infection. When do you decide to contact a parent to pick up a sick child? The answer to this question depends on the illness and the center's policies. Most states require centers to

Discuss

Why is it so important to be aware of the symptoms and treatment for communicable diseases and illnesses? How often should preschool children be observed for symptoms of communicable diseases?

Note

All staff should be aware of the signs and symptoms of communicable diseases. Make sure a communicable diseases chart is posted in the staff room. Information regarding communicable diseases may be obtained from your local health department.

Discuss

Did you ever have chicken pox as a child? Why may some parents try to expose their children to this disease when someone else is infected?

13-5

Communicable Diseases

Disease	Incubation Period (Time from Exposure to First Signs)	Signs and Symptoms	Period of Communicability Precautions and Restrictions	General Information
Chicken pox (varicella)	2 to 3 weeks, commonly 13 to 17 days	Sudden onset, slight fever, lesions often appear first on scalp, then on face and body. Successive crop of lesions remain 3 to 4 days, leaving crusts.	Keep patient home until all lesions are crusted over, usually 5 to 6 days after onset of rash.	Mild disease in children. May be more severe in adults and in children with cancer, leukemia, and other high risk conditions. Vaccine is available.
Conjunctivitis (pink eye)	24 to 72 hours	Redness in the white of the eye. May or may not have pus discharge. Eye irritation.	The communicable period depends on the cause, but is usually while inflammation or drainage is present. Keep patient home during communicable period, and refer for medical diagnosis and treatment.	Most infections are viral by cause; some are bacterial. May spread person to person through hand to eye contact. Also an early symptom for measles. Some symptoms may be an allergy and are noncommunicable.
Herpes simplex (cold sores)	Up to 2 weeks	Blisters develop on face, lips, and other places.	Following recovery, the virus can remain in the saliva for up to seven weeks.	Child does not need to be excluded from the center.
Viral hepatitis type A (formerly infectious)	15 to 50 days Average 25 days	Usually abrupt onset with fever, fatigue, loss of appetite, nausea, and abdominal pain. Jaundice is less common in children than in adults.	Most communicable during first week of illness and up to 1 week after jaundice. Keep patient home and no food handling or patient care while communicable.	Vaccine not available in all areas. May be confused with Hepatitis B. Differential diagnosis is important for prevention and control. Household contacts should be given immune serum globulin as soon as possible.
Influenza	2 to 4 days	Rapid onset with fever, chills, headache, lack of energy, muscle ache, sore throat, cough.	Communicable for 3 to 7 days after clinical onset. Keep home until symptoms disappear. Non-communicable 36-48 hours after treatment.	Vaccine is available and should be given to all children or persons with greatest risk of serious complications from the disease: the chronically ill and older adults.
Measles (rubeola)	8 to 13 days	High fever (101°F or more), with cough, runny nose and/or conjunctivitis. Blotchy rash appears 3 to 5 days after early signs, beginning on face and becoming generalized, lasting 4 or more days.	Communicable from onset or respiratory illness until 4 days after appearance of the rash. Keep patient home until 5 days after the appearance of rash.	A very serious, highly contagious but vaccine-preventable disease.
Mononucleosis, infectious	2 to 6 weeks	Characterized by fever, sore throat, fatigue, and inflamed posterior lymph nodes. May be accompanied by a headache.	Keep patient home at the discretion of physician. Length of communicability is unknown.	In children the disease is usually mild and difficult to recognize. Use frequent hand washing.

Awareness of the symptoms and treatment for communicable diseases and illnesses is important in order to control the spread of sickness through the center.

(continued)

Portfolio Project

Invite the school nurse or a public health nurse to class to present an in-service opportunity on children's health. Topics should cover symptoms of illness, treatment, responsibilities, policies, illness prevention, abuse, sanitation, reporting, and forms. The nurse could cover basic first aid and CPR, but students should take a formal class in these subjects and become certified by the Red Cross or American Heart Association. Design a certificate for each student who attended the in-service to be signed by the nurse and filed in their student portfolio.

Discuss

Have students review the diseases listed on this page. Are there any diseases that do not have a vaccine available? Which disease is the most dangerous to preschool children?

Resource

Communicable Diseases, Activity B, SAG

Discuss

Which disease is spread directly by contact with articles and surfaces contaminated by infected persons or animals? What are the signs and symptoms of this disease? How long is this disease communicable?

Disease	Incubation Period (Time from Exposure to First Signs)	Signs and Symptoms	Period of Communicability Precautions and Restrictions	General Information
Mumps	12 to 26 days, commonly 18 days	Fever, pain and swelling about the jaws involving one or more salivary glands. Many infections occur without symptoms.	Keep patient home until salivary gland swelling has subsided, or other symptoms have cleared.	Infectious early. May cause complications in adults. Vaccine available. Children should be excluded from the center until all symptoms have disappeared.
Pediculosis (lice)	Eggs hatch in a week; reach maturity in about 2 weeks	Excessive scratching on head or other parts of body. Light gray insects lay eggs in the hair, especially at the nape of the neck and around the ears. Lice are seldom visible to the naked eye.	Keep patient home until treated and nits have been destroyed (should not need to miss more than 1 day of school).	Hair needs to be washed with a special medicated shampoo. Then it needs to be rinsed with a solution of vinegar and water. Avoid sharing personal belongings such as clothing, head gear, combs, brushes, and bedding.
Ringworm (scalp, skin, feet)	Variable, 4 to 10 days	Scalp: Scaly patches of temporary baldness. Infected hairs are brittle and break easily. Skin: Flat, inflamed, ringlike sores that may itch or burn. Feet: Scaling or cracking of the skin, especially between the toes or blisters containing a thin watery fluid.	Communicable as long as active lesions are present. Keep patient home until adequate treatment is begun.	Preventive measures are largely hygienic. All household contacts, pets, and farm animals should be examined and treated if infected. Ringworm is spread directly by contact with articles and surfaces contaminated by such infected persons or animals.
Rubella (German measles)	4 to 21 days	Mild symptoms, slight fever, rash lasting about 3 days, enlarged head and neck glands common (particularly in back part of neck, behind ears.)	Keep patient home until 4 days after appearance of rash.	Highly communicable but vaccine-preventable disease. Complications are mild except in pregnancy when fetal infection or damage may occur. If contacts include a pregnant woman, she should consult her physician immediately.
Pertussis (whooping cough)	5 to 10 days	Begins with upper respiratory symptoms. An increasingly irritating cough develops with a characteristic "whoop" and frequently occurs in spasms accompanied by vomiting.	Keep patient home for 21 days from beginning of "whoop," or 5 to 7 days after onset of appropriate therapy.	Most dangerous to preschool children. Immunization is not recommended for children over 6 years of age. Susceptible contacts should be treated and observed for respiratory disease.
Scabies	4 to 6 weeks with first infections, several days with reinfection	Small raised reddened areas or lesions with connecting grayish-white lines. Marked itching. Most commonly found in the folds of the skin, finger webs, wrists, elbows, thighs, beltline, abdomen, nipples, buttocks.	Keep patient home until under adequate treatment and no open lesions can be observed.	All cases, family members, and other physically close contacts should be treated for scabies simultaneously.
Streptococcal Infections including scarlet fever (strep throat)	1 to 4 days	Sudden onset with high fever, sore throat; tender swollen glands with a fine, red rash present in Scarlet Fever. May also have headache, vomiting and white patches on tonsils.	Keep patient home for 7 days from onset if untreated; with adequate medical treatment, 24 hours.	Medication for symptomatic patients is recommended because of possibility of complications, including rheumatic fever. Culture survey rarely recommended.

13-5 Continued

Meeting Special Needs

Have student volunteers partner with special learners to review Chart 13-5, *Communicable Diseases*, together. Make sure students are covering all of the major concepts and any terms that are unclear. Have students quiz each other as they work through the information in the chart. Ask student volunteers to report areas where reteaching or further understanding is needed.

Reflect

Imagine you are a parent deciding on a child care program. How would a center's policies on illness affect your decision to enroll your child in a program?

Discuss

When should you contact a parent about a child's illness? What should you do if the child becomes very ill and the parent and other emergency contacts cannot be reached?

Enrich

Invite the director of a child care center to class to discuss the center's illness policies and procedures. Ask the director to bring a sample of the child care center's emergency information form for students to review. Have students prepare a list of questions to ask prior to the visit.

have an isolation area for sick children. A sick child should be removed from the classroom and wait with an adult in the isolation area until a parent arrives.

Always contact parents when a child shows signs of illness. Describe the symptoms to the parent. If the child is very ill, the parents should be responsible for picking the child up within a reasonable amount of time. Programs need to have this clearly stated in their policies.

Each child's folder should contain emergency information. Record parents' or guardians' home, cell, and work telephone numbers. Also note phone numbers of the family doctor and dentist. An example of an emergency information sheet is shown in 13-6.

13-6

Emergency Information

Child and Family Study Center

Child's Name _____ Birthdate _____

Home Address _____ Home Phone _____

Mother's Name
(wife or guardian)
Home Address _____ Home Phone _____

_____ Cell Phone _____

Place of Employment _____ Business Phone _____

E-mail Address _____

Father's Name
(husband or guardian)
Home Address _____ Home Phone _____

_____ Cell Phone _____

Place of Employment _____ Business Phone _____

E-mail Address _____

In Case of Emergency
(Person to be called if the parent or guardian cannot be reached.)

Name _____ Phone _____

Relationship _____

Name _____ Phone _____

Relationship _____

Family Doctor _____ Phone _____

Address _____

Family Dentist _____ Phone _____

Address _____

Parent or Guardian Signature _____ Date _____

Always have the information needed to contact parents in an emergency.

Workplace Connection

Ask students to review 13-6, the *Emergency Information* form, and compare it to the form used at the vocational preschool. Does the vocational preschool form contain all the necessary information? Should any information be added to the form? Does the school district require parents to sign a waiver of liability in the event that emergency treatment is needed when parents cannot be reached? Allow time for students to discuss their findings in class.

Parents should also be notified if their children have been exposed to a communicable disease. Send notices home to all parents if even one child has been infected with head lice. An example of a notice is shown in 13-7. Provide space to include the child's name, illness exposed to, and the date. Report any cases of communicable diseases to the local health authorities.

Personal Hygiene

Personal hygiene is an important component of a healthful environment. When cleanliness is stressed, fewer children and staff become ill.

Stress the importance of cleanliness to all new employees, as well as volunteers. This can be done through an in-service

13-7

Date: _____

Dear Parents:

It is important that we work together to promote a healthful environment for young children by minimizing communicable diseases. Therefore, I want to inform you that today your child was exposed to *conjuncitivitis*, sometimes referred to as *pink eye*. Since conjunctivitis spreads easily and quickly, please observe your child carefully. Signs and symptoms include the following:

- redness in the eye
- itching of the eye
- blurred vision and sensitivity to light
- discharge in the eye that forms a crust at night

If your child has any of the symptoms, please call your physician immediately. Moreover, if you have questions, please call the center.

Thank you for your cooperation

Moe Hendricks

Director

It is important to inform parents when children are exposed to a communicable disease.

training, employee handbook, or orientation. Each person should follow basic habits of cleanliness. They should bathe or shower daily and keep their hair clean. A hairnet should be worn while working in the kitchen. Use disposable tissues and discard them after use. Cover the mouth when coughing or sneezing.

Environmental Control

Early childhood centers need sanitary practices to keep the environment clean. Studies show that children in group settings have more upper respiratory infections. Germs are everywhere. Young children have not learned good hygiene practices. They drool everywhere, sneeze in their hands, and mouth toys. They forget to wash their hands after using the bathroom or blowing their noses. They may share cups and food. These practices spread communicable diseases. Everyone is at risk—the children, teachers, support staff, and parents.

Environmental control is important to prevent the transmission of diseases. Sanitary practices can remove bacteria and dirt. These are practical measures to help keep the center as germ free and clean as possible.

Every center needs written health policies. Cleaning, sanitation, and disinfection procedures should be included. To coordinate home and center practices, these policies should be shared with families. Procedures should address hand washing, diapering, toileting, cleaning, and disinfecting. Hand washing is one of the most important sanitary practices.

Hand Washing

Emphasize to all staff members the importance of proper hand washing while working with children. Hand washing helps prevent the spread of contagious diseases in early childhood centers. Studies show that when proper hand washing practices are followed, many illnesses, such as diarrhea,

Note

Obtain copies from your school nurse of forms similar to the one in 13-7 that are used to report communicable illness or conditions such as lice to parents and display them for the class.

Reflect

Imagine a child in your class has been infected with head lice and you have sent notices home to all parents informing them their child has been exposed. How should you respond if a parent asks which child or children were affected?

Discuss

What are the basic habits of cleanliness all employees should follow? In what ways can the importance of cleanliness be stressed to employees and volunteers in the child care center?

Workplace Connection

Have students review a local child care center's written health policies regarding sanitary practices. What health information, forms, and documents does the center require for every child? Are policies in place for cleaning, sanitation, and disinfection procedures? Are there any policies that are not available? What additional policies might be added? Have students discuss their findings in class.

Resource

Six Steps for Hand Washing, color transparencies CT-12A and CT-12B, TR

Activity

Ask students to design small posters to remind high school students and staff about hand washing practices. Have students laminate or mount the posters for placement on the walls in all the school's restrooms. (Hand washing reminders are also available commercially from school, food, and health suppliers.)

Resource

When Is Hand Washing Needed? transparency master 13-3, TR

can be greatly reduced. Modeling hand washing teaches children the techniques and importance. Chart 13-8 shows when children should wash their hands. Teachers need to follow the same guidelines. However, they also need to wash their hands before and after administering medications.

Use liquid soap for hand washing since germs can grow on bar soap. Wet the hands and lower your arms under the running water. Using friction, lather the hands to loosen bacteria and dirt. Rub the hands together vigorously. Continue rubbing between the fingers, on the backs of the hand, and under the nails for 30 seconds. Rinse thoroughly under running water. Keep the hands lower than the wrists to prevent recontamination. Using a paper towel, turn off the faucet. By touching the faucet, hands can become recontaminated.

- *Mobile infants.* Mobile infants' hands are in constant use, handling toys, crawling, and eating. Hand washing is the most effective method of controlling the spread of communicable diseases. Water alone will not kill germs. To wash an infant's hands, moisten a damp paper towel with child-safe liquid soap solution. Wipe the infant's hands with the moistened paper towel. Then moisten another paper towel with water and rinse each hand.

- *Toddlers.* Chances are you are going to need to teach and assist toddlers with the hand washing process. Begin by squirting a drop or two of liquid soap on one of the child's hands. Help them, if needed, to wash and rinse their hands under warm, running water for at least ten seconds. The water should flow down from the wrists to the fingertips. After they have finished rinsing, hand them a paper towel to dry their hands. If needed, provide assistance.

- *Preschool children.* Preschool children may need to be reminded to wash their hands. They may also need supervision. After applying liquid soap, encourage them to rub their hands together to create a soapy lather. Then they need to wash both the fronts and backs of each hand. After this, the area between their fingers needs to be washed before rinsing under warm, running water.

Sanitizing and Disinfecting

The transmission of diseases in a childcare center occurs from the contamination of hands, toys, diapering table, high chair trays, kitchen counters, and food preparation equipment. Just as care must be taken in hand washing, care must also be taken in wiping up spills and cleaning surfaces. After each use, toys in an infant and toddler room must be cleaned and disinfected. Wash stuffed toys at least once a week or when soiled. Toys for non-diapered toddlers must be cleaned weekly when soiled.

13-8

When to Wash Hands

- Upon arriving at the center
- After handling classroom pets
- After playing outdoors
- After coughing, sneezing, rubbing the nose, or handling a handkerchief or tissue
- Before handling food or eating
- After changing a diaper
- After using the toilet
- Before and after playing in the water table or sandbox
- After handling clay, play dough, paint, and other art materials

Hands should be washed after each of these activities with warm water and soap.

Putting Technology to Use

Have students conduct an Internet search to locate DVDs, videos, posters, and programs that can assist in teaching hand washing skills to young children. Have students design a hand washing lesson plan and present it to the children. Ask students to observe the children closely following the lesson to determine the effectiveness of the lesson. Allow time for students to share their findings in class.

Begin the cleaning process by washing the toys in warm water with a liquid detergent. **Sanitizing** is designed to remove dirt or soil and a small amount of bacteria. All surfaces that food touches need to be sanitized. After rinsing, the toys will need to be disinfected.

Disinfecting is the process of eliminating germs from surfaces. A bleach solution for disinfecting surfaces can be prepared by adding ¼ cup of bleach with hypochlorite to a gallon of water. To prepare a small amount, add 1 tablespoon to a quart of water. Mix a fresh solution daily. Since a poisonous gas can result, never mix bleach with anything but water. If desired, pour the bleach solution into labeled spray bottles.

Toys should be disinfected after every use. Cots and cribs can be disinfected weekly or when changing soiled linen. Disinfect bathroom, kitchen surfaces, and kitchen sinks one or more times daily. Vacuum play areas daily. Any spilled food should be removed immediately. Hard surfaces need to be washed, rinsed, and then sanitized.

Prevention of Exposure to Blood

The U.S. Department of Labor's Occupational Safety and Health Administration (OSHA) is responsible for protecting workers' safety. Federal laws have been passed to protect staff from accidental exposure to *bloodborne pathogens*. These include any microorganism that can cause infection, such as HIV or Hepatitis B. The law requires programs to develop and practice **universal infection and control precautions**. Otherwise, children could be unknowingly infected with HIV, Hepatitis B, or some other infection. The Hepatitis B virus can survive for at least a week or longer in a dried state.

Consider all bodily fluids to be potentially infectious and contaminated. Wear either disposable latex or utility gloves only once. Remove them without touching the outside with your hand and discard. If using utility gloves, wash them with warm

soapy water. Then dip them into a bleach solution up to the wrist to disinfect and hang to dry.

Separately wash blankets, sheets, pillows, stuffed toys, towels, and other center materials containing any child's bodily fluids. If the fluids are on a child's clothing, remove the clothing and seal it in a plastic bag marked with the child's name. Send the soiled clothing items home for laundering.

Controlling Foodborne Illness

Foodborne illness is caused by eating food that contains harmful bacteria, toxins, parasites, or viruses. People who eat these foods can become very ill. They can have painful symptoms, including stomach pain and cramps, diarrhea, bloody stools, nausea, vomiting, severe headaches, or fever.

Young children and pregnant women are at high risk if they get these diseases. As a teacher or center director, you should take precautions to prevent these illnesses among your staff and the children. Foodborne illness often results from improper food preparation, handling, or storage. Using safe food handling techniques will prevent many of these illnesses.

When preparing foods, keep your work area clean. Avoid transferring harmful bacteria from one food to another. This can occur when you or your utensils touch a contaminated food and then touch another food. It can also occur when foods touch a contaminated counter, appliance, or towel. Keeping these items clean will prevent spreading contaminants, 13-9.

Cook all meat, poultry, seafood, and egg dishes thoroughly. This will kill any harmful bacteria in these foods. Learn federal recommendations and your state's requirements for institutional food preparation. Other policies may be set by your center or the agencies that fund your center.

Resource

Universal Precautions to Prevent Transmission of Bloodborne Diseases, reproducible master 13-6, TR

Vocabulary

Have a student volunteer define the term *foodborne illness*. What factors may lead to a foodborne illness?

Activity

Have students observe workers in a fast-food restaurant to determine if they follow standards for safe food handling. Do workers who handle money also touch or serve food? Do workers have their hair restrained and wear plastic gloves? Do the workers wash their hands after using the rest room? The purpose of this activity is to develop an awareness of the risks you could be facing from improper food handling. Have students report their findings to the class.

Workplace Connection

Have students visit their school's cafeteria to observe the strategies practiced to cut down on the incidence of foodborne illness. What training is provided to foodservice workers to teach them these important strategies? What clothing or hair requirements do you see? How are food preparation surfaces treated or cleaned and what precautions do foodservice workers take when serving the food to students? Have students volunteer, if possible, to spend an hour or a half-day in the kitchen to assist with food preparation and sanitation to get a better idea of what is involved in food safety.

Resource

Safety Rules for Avoiding Food Contamination, transparency master 13-4, TR

Activity

Have students explore how food is served at a local child care center. Are individual meals plated or is the meal served family style on platters and in bowls? Can leftover food that was served family style be returned to the kitchen and reused? What are the regulations on reusing or serving previously served food? Allow time for students to discuss their findings in class.

Resource

Staff Health Practices, Activity A, OG

Enrich

Have students investigate the first aid courses offered by the Red Cross at **www.redcross.org** and the American Heart Association at **www.americanheart. org**. Why do child care workers need to be certified in first aid and CPR? What is AED training? Allow time for students to discuss their findings in class.

13-9

A refrigerator that is clean and kept at 40°F helps control transmission of foodborne illness.

Store foods at safe temperatures, too. Foods that are cold (below 40°F) or hot (above 140°F) are safest. According to the USDA, temperatures between 40°F and 140°F promote bacteria growth. Never leave perishable foods out at room temperature for more than two hours. Discard foods left out longer than this. This applies to plates of food, baby food, formula, and breast milk as well.

If foodborne illness should occur at your center, seek medical help for those affected. Alert any parents whose children may have eaten the contaminated food.

Health and Safety

Keeping Food Areas Clean

Preventing outbreaks of foodborne illness is a challenge for the child care staff. They must follow established state and federal guidelines for cleaning and sanitizing food preparation areas, food serving areas, and dining areas. This must be done before and after meals and snacks.

First Aid

In every preschool, injuries and illness occur. Sometimes, it may just be a scratch or bumped knee. At other times, it may be a sudden high temperature.

First aid is immediate treatment given for injuries and illness, including those that are life-threatening. First aid training provides the knowledge and skill needed to handle emergency medical care. With the proper training, you will know how and when to treat illnesses and injuries. You will also know when professional medical help is required.

All employees in child care should be certified by the American Red Cross. This certification may have been acquired through prior course work or past employment. If an employee is not certified, he or she should be required to obtain certification in order to be employed.

Conduct a first aid in-service training session for all center personnel each year. Include secretaries, janitors, cooks, and bus

---

Workplace Connection

Have students investigate the possibility of becoming certified in First Aid and CPR through their school's Physical Education or Health departments. The instructors may be certified through Red Cross or the American Heart Association to train and certify the student teachers. Ask students to interview area child care directors to find out if they provide training and/or recertification each year for their employees. How much does a certification class cost? Who pays for the classes? Ask students to share their findings in class.

drivers in the training session. Training should focus on updating personnel on first aid procedures of the American Red Cross.

First Aid Supplies

In order to administer first aid, you will need some basic supplies. Most drugstores, department stores, and school supply catalogs sell first aid kits that would include these basic supplies. You may also purchase your supplies separately and put them together in a kit.

Store all first aid items in one area. Keep them out of children's reach. However, do not keep first aid supplies in a locked cabinet. During an emergency you may not have time to search for a key.

Each month, check the contents of the first aid kit. Make sure all first aid kits have the necessary supplies, 13-10. To do this, check the contents against a list. Many programs have one person responsible for this duty. Replace any supplies that have run out.

If some children have special health needs, you will need additional supplies. An antihistamine or bee sting kit may have to be added for children with allergies. Children with diabetes may need sugar or honey. For emergency preparedness, always take a first aid kit on field trips.

Wounds and Their Treatment

A **wound** is damage to the surface of the skin or body tissue. Basically, there are two types of wounds. A *closed wound* is an injury to the tissue directly under the skin surface. It does not involve a break in the skin. An *open wound* is a break in the skin.

Closed Wounds

Children usually get closed wounds from falling, being struck, or running into some object. Most closed wounds involve the soft

13-10

Basic First Aid Supplies

Emergency medcial numbers	Safety pins
Quick reference first aid manual	Hydrocortisone cream for insect bites
Individual adhesive bandages in ½-inch, ¾-inch, and round sizes	Flashlight
	Synthetic ice pack
2 by 2 inch sterile first aid dressings, individually packaged for burns and open wounds	Box of temperature strip thermometers for use on the child's forehead or digital thermometer
4 by 4 inch sterile first aid dressings	Alcohol wipes
Gauze bandage, 2 inches by 5 yards	Cotton swabs
Adhesive tape or surgical tape, 1 inch wide	Absorbent cotton balls
Disposable paper tissues	Antibacterial skin cleaner
Antibacterial soap or cleanser	Jar of petroleum jelly
Tweezers for removing splinters	Disposable nonporous gloves
Blanket	Plastic bags
Blunt-tipped scissors for cutting tape and bandages	

Make sure basic first aid supplies are available.

Activity

Make a list of all the items in the school or preschool program's first aid kit. Assign students to take inventory at least once a month and replace items such as bandages, zipper bags, and disposable gloves that have been used.

Resource

First Aid Kit, Activity B, OG

Vocabulary

Have a student volunteer define the term *wound.* Do all wounds need first aid treatment?

Resource

First Aid Scramble, Activity C, SAG

Meeting Special Needs

Create a word bank of possible answers for *First Aid Scramble*, Activity C, SAG, for those students whose IEP requires this modification. Break down the assignment into two groups of words for those students who may benefit from a shorter assignment. Ask student volunteers or the special learner to create a visual teaching aid of a first aid kit with labeled drawings of all the needed supplies. The visual learner may benefit from actually seeing the first aid kit or the drawing and be able to effectively remember the required items.

Discuss

What are the major dangers of open wounds? How can wounds become contaminated or infected?

Vocabulary

Have a student volunteer define the term *abrasion.* What preschool activities may result in children suffering from abrasions?

Reflect

Did you ever have an injury that left a scar? What treatments are needed to prevent scarring and the spread of infection?

tissues under the skin. The most common type of closed wound is a bruise.

Common signs of a closed wound are discoloration, tenderness, and pain in the damaged area. To help control the pain, apply a cold cloth or pack to the injured area, 13-11.

Open Wounds

Cuts and scrapes that break the skin are called open wounds. Two first aid problems are caused by open wounds. First, there may be rapid blood loss. If this is the case, the injured child may go into shock. Second, exposed body tissue may become contaminated and infected.

Some open wounds bleed freely. This reduces the danger of infection. Other wounds bleed very little. These are more likely to become infected.

Open wounds on the top skin layer require simple treatment. To clean the wound, wash it with soap and water. If the wound is deep or does not stop bleeding in a short amount of time, seek medical attention.

13-11

Cold packs help reduce swelling in closed wounds.

Abrasions

An **abrasion** is a scrape that damages a portion of the skin. Children usually get abrasions from falling and handling rough objects. It is common to have several children in a classroom with skinned knees, scratched arms, or rope burns.

Bleeding from an abrasion is often limited to blood flow from broken capillaries (small veins). However, bacteria or dirt may still enter the wound and infection can still occur. Dirt particles may actually slow down the healing process. Sometimes abrasions heal around the particles, forming a permanent scar.

Cuts

Cuts, or incised wounds, on body tissues are often caused by broken glass, metal, or sharp edges. Bleeding can be heavy if a blood vessel has been cut. Nerves, muscles, or tendons can also be damaged if the cut is deep enough.

Puncture Wounds

Puncture wounds are made by sharp objects such as nails, splinters, thumbtacks, and even sticks. In order to puncture the skin, the force at which the object meets the skin must be strong. Bleeding is often light. As a result, the wound is not flushed out. Infection may set in. Harmful bacteria such as tetanus may grow in the presence of moisture and warmth. This can then be carried within the body.

Bites

Bites are a type of puncture wound. They can be inflicted by humans and animals. In the case of a mild human bite, you may need only to thoroughly wash the injured areas. However, if the skin is broken, consult a doctor at once. This is especially important if the bite

Workplace Connection

Ask students to research various careers in the health field that relate to the care of children. What are the educational requirements for each career? How much background in child growth, development, and education is needed for each career? How is the job outlook over the next 10 years for each career? Information on careers can be located in the school's guidance or career center. Another source is the *Occupational Outlook Handbook* published by the United States Bureau of Labor Statistics at **www.bls.gov/oco**.

was from an animal. This is because there is a danger of an infection such as rabies.

Rabies is a disease caused by a viral infection of the nervous system and brain. Humans who are infected are not able to swallow. This is a result of the tightening of throat muscles.

Rabies is transmitted through the saliva of a rabid animal. It can be contracted by a human when animal saliva enters an open cut. The infection is most often spread to humans when the rabid animal bites and breaks the skin.

Call a doctor at once if a child is bitten by an animal. Report the animal's size and color to the police. If the animal cannot be caught and tested for rabies, the child will need to undergo rabies immunization. This is a very painful series of shots. Without the immunization, the child can die.

All animal bites are dangerous. They carry great risk of infection. Most animals carry a wide variety of bacteria in their mouths, not the least of which is rabies. For that reason, take immediate action when a child is bitten by an animal.

Open Wound Care

Some open wounds require medical attention. See 13-12. As the teacher, you can usually treat minor wounds such as abrasions and small cuts. First, wash the area with antibacterial soap and warm water. Then, as you apply a bandage, bring the wound edges together. This will help prevent scarring.

Assume that any loss of blood is harmful. To control severe bleeding, place a sterile gauze over the wound. Press on the wound with the palm of one hand. The object is to control the bleeding by pressing the blood vessels against something solid such as a bone or muscle.

If there is no sign of a fracture, elevate open wounds of the leg, arm, neck, or head.

13-12

Open Wounds That Require Medical Attention

- An animal or human bite that has broken the skin
- Bleeding that cannot be stopped in five minutes despite all effort to control it
- Deep cuts on the face, neck, hand, head, or some other part of the body where scar tissue will be noticeable
- A wound that goes deeper than the outer layer of skin
- Wounds with foreign objects such as dirt deep inside the tissue
- A wound with foreign matter that cannot be removed
- Puncture wounds if child is not current on tetanus immunizations

Recognizing the severity of wounds can help you determine if medical care is needed.

To elevate, raise the injured area above the level of the child's heart. The force of gravity will help reduce blood pressure in the injured area, thereby slowing blood loss.

Burns and Their Treatment

A **burn** is an injury caused by heat, radiation, or chemical agents. Burns vary in size, depth, and severity. Burns are generally classified by degree or depth. There are three classes: first-degree burns, second-degree burns, and third-degree burns. A person can have more than one type of burn from a single accident.

Children are commonly burned by hot liquids, cooking and electrical equipment,

Discuss

What is the purpose of elevating an open wound of the leg, arm, neck, or head? What else can you do to cut down on blood loss from an open wound?

Vocabulary

Have a student volunteer define the term *rabies.* How is rabies transmitted? What type of treatment is needed for someone who is infected with rabies?

Discuss

How are burns generally classified? Can a person have more than one type of burn from a single accident? What are children commonly burned by? What should children be taught in case their clothes catch fire? How can you teach children about burn hazards?

Cross-Curricular Activity

Health
Invite the school nurse to speak to the class about open wound care and burn treatment. What is the difference between an electrical and chemical burn? How can you recognize the severity of a wound? When is medical attention required for a wound or burn? Ask the nurse to demonstrate how to stop an open wound from bleeding. Have students prepare a list of additional questions to ask prior to the visit.

Vocabulary

Have student volunteers define the terms *first-degree burn* and *second-degree burn*. Give examples of each type of burn.

Discuss

How likely is it that burns might happen in the preschool classroom? What type of activities might expose children to potential burns?

Vocabulary

Have a student volunteer define the term *third-degree burn*. Why are third-degree burns so serious?

Resource

Burns, Activity D, SAG

open fires, matches, chemicals such as strong detergents and acids, and overexposure to the sun. See 13-13. When developmentally appropriate, you should teach children to stop, drop, and roll in case their clothes catch fire.

First-Degree Burns

First-degree burns are burns to the top layer of skin. They are the least severe of all burns. They may result from brief contact with hot objects, overexposure to the sun, or scalding by hot water or steam. Common signs include redness or mild discoloration, pain, and mild swelling. Healing is normally rapid because the burn does not go deep.

Special medical treatment is not needed for first-degree burns. Applying cold water to the burn will often help relieve some pain.

13-13

Care must be taken to keep children safe around items that cause burns.

Second-Degree Burns

Second-degree burns cause damage to underlying layers of skin. These burns are more serious than first-degree burns. They are caused by extreme overexposure to the sun, contact with hot liquids, and contact with flash fires from gasoline, kerosene, and other products.

Second-degree burns are marked by pain, blistering, swelling, and discoloration. Over several days, the burn is likely to swell a great deal. Due to the severity of these burns, they require medical treatment. Do not treat the burn by breaking blisters or by placing an ointment on the burn. This may cause infection. If infection arises in the wound, a second-degree burn can quickly become a third-degree burn.

Third-Degree Burns

Third-degree burns destroy the skin layer and nerve endings. They can be caused by open flames, burning clothing, immersion in hot water, contact with hot objects, and contact with live electrical wires.

Third-degree burns are very serious. They require prompt medical attention. An ambulance should be called at once.

Sunburn

Children can get first- or second-degree burns from exposure to the sun's ultraviolet rays. There is usually a 3- to 12-hour lapse in time between exposure and development of sunburn. Sunburn does not usually require a hospital stay. However, sunburn can cause a child to be out several days due to swelling, pain, headache, and fever. Sunburn also raises the risk of skin cancer later in life.

Protect the children in your care from sunburn. Babies younger than 6 months

---

Service Learning Activity

Have students conduct an Internet search for information on burn camps for children. Are any burn camps operating in the area and, if so, what are the qualifications needed for camp counselors or volunteers in the programs including age requirements? Have students design a fund-raising activity to increase awareness of the need for children to attend burn camps or to supply needed equipment. Consider the possibility of coordinating a fund-raiser with local service organizations or other school-sponsored service groups.

should not be exposed to direct sunlight. Their skin burns easily since it is thinner. Keep these babies in the shade. For children older than 6 months, apply a children's sunscreen with a sun protection factor (SPF) of 15 or higher. Sunscreen should be applied to all exposed areas of skin 30 minutes prior to sun exposure. Reapply sunscreen after swimming, heavy sweating, or 2 hours of sun exposure. Hats and sunglasses also protect children from the damaging rays of the sun. Schedule outdoor play periods to avoid sun exposure from 10 a.m. to 4 p.m.—the time when the sun's rays are most intense and particularly harmful.

Splinters

Children often get splinters. It will be your job to remove them. A pair of sterilized tweezers is the best tool for this process. To sterilize tweezers, store them in a jar of rubbing alcohol. You can also soak them in alcohol or boil them for 10 minutes. A third option is to hold the tip of the tweezers in a flame and wipe the carbon away with a clean cloth before using.

First wash the area with soap and water. Then remove splinters at the same angle they entered the skin. Do not put any ointment or antiseptic on the wound. Cover with a sterile bandage until a doctor can see it. If you cannot remove a splinter, consult a doctor.

Insect Stings

Wasps, bees, hornets, yellow jackets, and fire ants are all stinging insects. The stings are painful to all children. For children who are allergic to insect stings, a sting can be fatal. React quickly when a child has been stung. Most deaths from insect stings occur within two hours of the incident.

If a child is stung, scrape the stinger away with your fingernail. Avoid using tweezers to pull the stinger out. This might squeeze the stinger and release more toxins into the skin. After removing the stinger, watch for signs of an allergic reaction.

A rash or swelling usually indicates a mild allergic reaction. Anaphylactic shock can result from an extremely allergic reaction. Watch the child closely for signs of anaphylactic shock. If you notice any of these signs, get prompt medical help.

Children who are allergic to stings and have been stung before may have their own medication and injection equipment. Make sure it is available for emergencies. When you leave the classroom, take the equipment.

Choking

While choking can occur among people of all ages, children are at highest risk. Young children are more likely than adults to put small objects, such as toys, buttons, and coins, in their mouths. Children younger than four years are more likely to choke on hard or round foods. They are less likely to chew food well or sit still while eating. Children are also more likely to stuff their mouths with too much food. All these actions increase the risk of choking. Chart 13-14 contains a list of choking hazards.

The best way to prevent choking is to protect children from choking hazards. Infants should have their heads elevated when being bottle-fed. Keep small toys and other objects that pose a choking hazard out of the reach of children younger than four years. Avoid offering foods that are known choking hazards. (Refer to Chapter 12 for more information.) Have children sit while eating and eat only a small amount at a time.

When the brain goes without oxygen for more than four minutes, a result can be brain damage or even death. Therefore, when choking occurs, program staff must respond quickly. All staff members need to know what techniques to use to treat choking and how to perform them. If the child can speak,

Reflect

Did you ever need to have a splinter removed when you were a young child? If so, what methods were used to calm or distract you from focusing on the splinter removal?

Note

Review Chapter 12 for more information about foods that are known choking hazards.

Discuss

Why should children eat only small amounts at a time? What children's actions increase the risk of choking? How can you prevent children from accessing choking hazards?

Putting Technology to Use

Ask students to conduct an Internet search for information on the reactions a child may display when stung by an insect. For example, what are the signs a child may be going into anaphylactic shock? What is an *epinephrine* pen and how is it used for children who suffer from severe reactions to insect stings? How does epinephrine treat the symptoms of anaphylactic shock? Have students write a brief report of their findings

Discuss

Why should the abdominal thrust not be used on a child who is choking when the child can speak, breathe, or cough? Explain how the abdominal thrust dislodges the item that causes the choking.

Activity

Have students interview a dentist to find out the treatment for broken, chipped, or knocked-out teeth. Knowing the procedures can help you inform and calm a parent if you ever have to report an injury of this type. Have students prepare a list of questions to ask prior to the interview.

Discuss

What might be some causes of toothache in a young child? What health policies should be in place to help you deal with a child's dental problems?

13-14

Choking Hazards	
Foods	**Toys and Objects**
• Carrots	• Batteries
• Celery	• Dice
• Cough drops	• Game pieces
• Grapes	• Jacks
• Gum	• Jewelry
• Hard candy	• Nails
• Hot dogs	• Paper clips
• Olives	• Pen or marker caps
• Peanuts	• Safety pins
• Popcorn	• Vending machine toys

These foods and objects are choking hazards for children. Be especially careful with children younger than four years.

13-15

When given by a trained person, the abdominal thrust can save the life of a choking child.

cough, and breathe, encourage the child to cough. The child should be able to cough up the object. If, however, you see that the child is not able to breathe or speak, take immediate emergency steps.

The emergency procedures used to relieve choking are taught by the American Red Cross and the American Heart Association. Their recommended techniques differ slightly. The American Red Cross recommends a "five-and-five" response. This means delivering five back blows between the shoulder blades, followed by five abdominal thrusts, 13-15. For simplicity in training, the American Heart Association recommends use of the abdominal thrust. According to both organizations, these procedures should be followed for children one year of age or older. The procedures differ slightly for infants under one year of age.

Most choking incidents are relieved by back blows and/or abdominal thrusts, but sometimes cardiopulmonary resuscitation

(CPR) is needed. Newly hired staff should be required to attend pediatric first aid training, which focuses on techniques for choking relief and CPR for infants and children. Staff members who successfully complete the course will be certified by the American Red Cross or American Heart Association. All staff must complete refresher courses for these techniques yearly to keep their certifications current. The director can arrange to have these trainings offered as a yearly in-service.

Oral Hygiene

Good oral hygiene begins with regular toothbrushing. After each snack or meal, children over the age of two should brush their teeth with fluoride toothpaste. All toothbrushes should be labeled. For younger children, use symbols they can easily identify. The child's name can be placed on older children's brushes. After use, the brushes should be stored to allow air to circulate. To prevent contamination, the brushes should not touch one another or contact any surface.

Putting Technology to Use

Have students conduct an Internet search to learn about the job duties of a pediatric dentist. What are the educational requirements for this position? How is the job outlook for a pediatric dentist over the next ten years? Ask students to write a brief report or utilize the computer to record their findings. Allow time for students to discuss their findings in class.

Dental Emergencies

Dental emergencies include cut or bitten tongues, lips, or cheeks; knocked out permanent teeth; and broken teeth. With any of these problems, take quick action and remain calm.

If a child complains of a toothache, help the child rinse the affected area with water. Apply cold compresses if the face is swollen. Urge the parents to take the child to a dentist.

If a child has a cut or bitten lip, tongue, or cheek, apply ice to the injured area. If you see blood, hold a clean gauze or cloth over the area. Gently apply pressure. Contact the child's parents if the bleeding does not stop in 15 minutes. If the cut is severe, take the child to an emergency room.

To provide emergency care for a knocked out permanent tooth, first find the tooth. Pick it up by the crown, not the roots. If the tooth is dirty, rinse it gently with milk. Do not use water. However, avoid unnecessary handling. Keep the tooth moist. If the tooth is not broken, put it back in its socket and gently hold it in place. If you cannot put it back, place the tooth in a container of cool, clean milk. Call the child's dentist and parents immediately. In order to save the tooth, the child must see a dentist at once.

If a child breaks or chips a tooth, report it to the parents. They can decide whether a dentist should be consulted. Gently clean the injured area with warm water. Use a cold compress to reduce swelling.

Head Lice

To maintain a healthy environment, you will need to recognize head lice. **Head lice** are small insects that live on people's hair and scalp. They are about one-tenth to one-eighth of an inch in length. They have no wings and do not fly. They have six pairs of hooks in their mouths. With these hooks, they attach themselves to the hair shaft. Short legs and large claws help them keep their grip on hair. They produce small round eggs, called *nits*. Nits look like grains of sand.

It is difficult to see head lice with the naked eye. However, there are several signs you can recognize. Look for the following:

- A constant itch of the scalp, especially behind the ears and at the base of the scalp. Often the child will have infected scratches or a rash on the scalp.

- Small, silvery eggs attached to individual hairs. Usually a magnifying glass will help reveal these.

- In severe cases, lymph glands may swell in the neck or under the arm.

Head lice can spread through direct contact with the hair. Combs, brushes, hats, and bedding are key sources of transportation. Head lice can also crawl from person to person.

If one child in your classroom has head lice, other children and staff members may get it, too. Send notices home to all parents if even one child has been infected with head lice. In some areas, a county or city nurse will conduct daily inspections at a center that has had an outbreak.

The best way to get rid of head lice is to seek medical help. Most physicians prescribe a medical shampoo or lotion. All family members should be treated. Doctors also suggest boiling or dry-cleaning all hats, combs, brushes, clothing, bedding, and furry toys. Items that cannot be washed or dry-cleaned should be sealed in a plastic bag for 30 days, which is the life cycle of a louse. Rugs, upholstered furniture, and mattresses should be vacuumed. Combs and brushes should be boiled for 10 minutes or soaked for one hour in a bleach solution.

Vocabulary

Have a student volunteer define the term *head lice*. What is your school's policy on attendance and notification if head lice are found on any children in the class?

Discuss

Ask students to describe the procedures that must be followed to clean the classroom in the event head lice or nits are found on one of the students. Who must be checked besides all the children in the class?

Resource

Emergency Medical Care, reproducible master 13-5, TR

Workplace Connection

Research the possibility of a job-shadowing activity in children's health for the students in your class. Possible jobs to shadow might include school nurse; home or school health-care aide; pediatric nurse or physician assistant; physical or occupational therapist working with children; child life specialist; and vision and hearing screener. Ask students to report to the class what they learned about the job they shadowed. Have students create informational posters about the various jobs or write articles showcasing the jobs for the school's career and guidance newsletter.

Discuss

What are the challenges in caring for children who are ill? How can you meet these challenges in the child care setting?

Note

The use of *oral electrolyte solutions* is one effective treatment for dehydration caused by diarrhea or vomiting. Electrolyte solutions are a mixture of salts and sugars. The solution may be prescribed by a physician or purchased over-the-counter. As with all medications, make sure you follow the dosage instructions on the package.

Discuss

What effect might excessive vomiting, fever, and diarrhea have on the child's body? Should child care personnel attempt to replace the fluids lost from the body by encouraging children to drink liquids?

Caring for Children Who Become Ill

Whenever a child becomes ill, he or she should be moved into a separate area at once, 13-16. An isolation area or room is needed in every early childhood center. Some states require that centers have isolation rooms.

Due to a lack of space, some centers do not have a special room for this purpose. Instead, a cot in the director's office is used for these emergencies.

When children become ill, they may vomit, develop diarrhea, or develop a fever. Child care workers need to know how to handle these signs of illness.

Children often vomit when ill. After the child has vomited, he or she will need to rest and keep warm. Remove the child from the group and contact the parents.

The child may request food or drink. However, only provide sips of water. Any

13-16

Children who show signs of illness should be isolated from other children promptly.

other foods may prompt more vomiting. Record the number of times the child vomits and the amount thrown up. Report this information to parents when they arrive.

Diarrhea may be caused by a virus, foodborne illness, or allergies. Many illnesses cause diarrhea that lasts for two or three days. Chronic diarrhea may be a symptom of infection, inflammation of the intestines, or allergies. Chronic diarrhea may last for up to 10 days.

With diarrhea, a child will have an increased number of stools compared to the child's normal pattern. The stool may be loose, watery, and unformed.

Children who have diarrhea need to be isolated. Remove them from the classroom and contact their parents. They should be diarrhea-free for 24 hours before returning to the center.

Temperature Emergency

The human body normally maintains an average internal temperature of 98.6°F. Normal temperatures range from 97°F to just under 100°F. For this reason, it is important to have each child's normal temperature recorded on a health form.

A slight change in a child's temperature is a signal that the body is preparing against illness. A temperature at least two degrees above normal is significant. Most, but not all, young children will run a higher fever than adults.

A child may have a slight rise in temperature for several reasons. For example, the presence of infection raises a child's temperature. Too much physical activity will raise a temperature. Temperature may also vary depending on the time of the day. Temperatures are somewhat lower in the morning than the evening.

Workplace Connection

Ask students to review the state licensing requirements to learn about regulations regarding isolation rooms. Does the state require a center to have an isolation room? Ask students to contact local child care centers to find out their policy on isolating children who become ill. Have students write a brief report of their findings. Allow time for students to discuss their findings in class.

To take a child's temperature, you have a few options, including

- traditional mercury thermometers
- digital thermometers
- single-use temperature strips (for forehead)

Experts now advise against using mercury thermometers, especially with children. If this type of thermometer breaks, mercury can spill or evaporate into the air. Inhaling, touching, or swallowing mercury can damage the brain, spinal cord, kidneys, and liver. For this reason, it is best to keep these thermometers out of early childhood programs.

Although they are more expensive than other types of thermometers, digital thermometers are preferred. They are easy to use and give a quick and accurate reading. Some digital thermometers are designed for the ear, 13-17. Others can be used orally, rectally, and under the arm. Read the directions for proper use of any

13-17

At many centers, digital ear thermometers are used to get an accurate temperature reading quickly and easily.

digital thermometer. Temperature strips are easy to use but less accurate than a digital thermometer.

Call the parents right away if a child has a fever. Report any other unusual behavior.

Special Health Concerns

If a child with a special physical condition is enrolled in the program, you will need to make plans for this child's health and well-being. Begin by discussing the child's condition with the parents. Be certain you understand what the condition is and what type of emergencies may arise. Find out what approach the center needs to take. Does the child require a special diet, medications, or specific exercises? Also ask the parents how to help the child feel comfortable.

You will likely encounter several common health concerns among the children in your class. Some of the most common of these include the following:

- *Allergies.* An allergy is the body's reaction to a substance in the environment, which is called an *allergen*. Smoke, dust, mold, mildew, pet dander, pollen, and certain foods are common allergens. Reactions to an allergen include sneezing, runny nose, coughing, itchy or watery eyes, headache, skin rashes, hives, diarrhea, and vomiting. Some allergies are seasonal, while others are continuous. Ask parents what the allergens are and try to avoid exposing the child to these. Medications may be needed to treat the symptoms of allergies.

Discuss

What type of thermometer provides the most accurate reading when taking a child's temperature? Why do experts now advise against using mercury thermometers? What type of thermometer is used in the school's child care program?

Activity

Using print or Internet sources, ask students to research the health effects on the body when exposed to mercury. What factors determine how severe the health effects are? How are people primarily exposed to mercury? Have students write a brief summary of their findings. Allow time for students to discuss their findings in class.

Discuss

What substances might cause a child to have an allergic reaction? Are there any steps that a child care center could take to lessen the child's exposure to allergens?

Meeting Special Needs

Review the special learners' chapter outlines to determine if the students have any questions about the concepts or content of this chapter. Review the chapter objectives and ask the students to evaluate their progress in meeting these objectives. Ask the students to summarize, orally or in writing, what they learned from this chapter.

Vocabulary

Have a student volunteer define the terms *epilepsy, seizure,* and *convulsion.* What response is needed by child care personnel during a child's seizure?

Note

If a child with diabetes enrolls in your program, you will have to monitor the child's exercise and food intake. After very vigorous exercise, the child may need to drink fruit juice or take a sugar tablet. Consult with the parent for information on the particular child's needs.

Vocabulary

Have a student volunteer explain the difference between the terms *human immunodeficiency virus (HIV)* and *acquired immunodeficiency syndrome (AIDS).* Are children with either of these conditions allowed to attend school?

Discuss

What precautions may need to be taken when a child with HIV or AIDS is enrolled in a child care program? Why is it important to alert parents when any children in the program are diagnosed with communicable diseases?

- *Asthma.* **Asthma** is a chronic inflammatory disorder of the airways. Symptoms include coughing, wheezing, rapid or labored breathing, shortness of breath, and chest tightness. Ask parents what conditions trigger their child's attacks and try to prevent these conditions. Examples include smoke, cold air, exposure to an allergen, and overexertion. Find out what medications should be given and when. For older children, ask the child to tell you right away when an asthma attack is starting so you can administer medications. For younger children, you will need to observe carefully for signs of an attack.

- *Diabetes.* For a child with diabetes, the body cannot properly control the level of sugar in the blood. Having too much or too little sugar in the blood can cause serious health problems. Children with diabetes cannot regulate blood sugar because they do not produce insulin. They must balance their food choices, intake, and activity levels. Many children with diabetes must also monitor their blood sugar throughout the day and take insulin injections as needed. You will likely need to help with these procedures. Ask the child's parents about your role in managing the disease. Learn the signs of an *insulin reaction,* the body's response to an imbalance of insulin. If a reaction occurs, offer juice, sugar, or candy to help adjust the blood sugar level quickly. Keep these items handy at all times just in case. In severe cases, a child may pass out. Take the child to an emergency room or call an ambulance at once.

- *Epilepsy.* **Epilepsy** is a condition in which a person has periodic seizures. There are two types of seizures. *Grand mal seizures* consist of repeated convulsions or jerking over the entire body. *Petit mal seizures* are milder than grand mal seizures. They consist of a few brief muscle twitches and a sense of confusion. Ask the child's parents what medical treatment should be given to prevent seizures. Have them describe the seizures and how they can be prevented. In the case of a grand mal seizure, protect the child from injuring himself or herself. Help the child lie down and monitor the child's breathing. Contact the child's parents and doctor after every seizure. Describe what occurred before, during, and after the seizure.

- *Human immunodeficiency virus (HIV).* **HIV** breaks down the body's immune system. This virus eventually leads to the disease **acquired immunodeficiency syndrome (AIDS)**. AIDS further destroys the immune system and over time can be fatal. Most children with HIV got the virus from their mothers during pregnancy, birth, or breast-feeding. It can also be acquired through contact with the blood of an infected person. Hugging, touching, or being near someone with HIV does not spread the disease. Children with HIV can attend child care unless they have open sores, uncontrollable nosebleeds, bloody diarrhea, or are at high risk for exposing others to blood-contaminated bodily fluids. Ask parents about the treatment, diet, and activity level recommended for children with HIV. These children have a weakened immune system and have trouble fighting even common illnesses. Alert the parents about communicable diseases of other children in your class right away.

More information about most of these illnesses is given in Chapter 31, *Guiding Children with Special Needs.* Children may have other special health concerns, too. Have all parents complete a health questionnaire upon admitting their children to the center. Talk to parents about how to manage these concerns. Follow parents' instructions and keep careful records about diet, medications, physical activity, and rest. These records give the child's parents and doctor a more complete picture about how the child is doing or what changes should be made.

Putting Technology to Use

Have students conduct an Internet search for information on asthma, one of the leading causes of school absenteeism today. What typically triggers asthma and what can school personnel do to help a child who has an asthma attack? What symptoms can be expected and what medications are used? Have students find out if their school has an action plan for asthma management that includes in-service training on asthma for all school personnel. Allow time for students to discuss their findings in class.

Summary

Children's health can be protected, maintained, and improved in many ways during each day at the center. This is a very important part of the job of a teacher.

The best way to begin guiding children's health is by setting health policies. Policies might include requiring all children enrolled to have medical exams and immunizations. Contacting parents about health-related issues might also be addressed in your health policy.

The second step in guiding health is having knowledge of various illnesses and diseases. You will need to know how to control transmittable illnesses and diseases. Keeping the center sanitary is one important aspect of controlling the spread of disease. You will also need to know what steps you should take in caring for children who are injured or become ill while at the center.

Protecting, maintaining, and even improving health is a major responsibility of a teacher. The teacher is trusted with the well-being of many children.

Review and Reflect

1. List three environmental factors that influence good health in young children.
2. What will a preadmission medical exam help you learn about a child being enrolled?
3. List the immunization(s) needed for children at the following ages:
   A. 0 to 4 months
   B. 12 to 18 months
   C. 4 to 6 years
4. True or false. Each child should be provided with a washable cot or bed and clean sheets for napping.
5. Name four signs of illness you should watch for daily.
6. True or false. Parents should be contacted whenever a child shows symptoms of illness.
7. What is the difference between sanitizing and disinfecting?
8. Why should center staff take precautions when handling bodily fluids?
9. What is foodborne illness?
10. A _____ is damage to the surface of the skin or body tissue.
11. The most common type of closed wound is a _____.
12. Skinned knees, scratched arms, and rope burns are examples of _____.
13. Why should a doctor be contacted immediately if a child is bitten by an animal?
14. Which is the most serious burn, a first-degree burn or a third-degree burn?
15. How should you treat a burn caused by a child touching a hot object?
16. Most deaths from insect stings occur within how long of the incident?
17. What is the best way for a child to get rid of blockage in the windpipe?
18. List two symptoms of head lice.
19. _____ is a hormone that keeps sugar in the blood at a proper level.
20. What is epilepsy?

5. (List four:) rashes, sores, swelling or bruising, changes in appearance of eyes, runny noses, flushing of skin, coughing, sneezing, a sweaty appearance
6. true
7. Sanitizing is designed to remove dirt or soil and a small amount of bacteria. Disinfecting is a process of eliminating germs from surfaces.
8. Bodily fluids could carry bloodborne pathogens. These include any microorganism that can cause infection, such as HIV or Hepatitis B.
9. Foodborne illness is an illness caused by eating food that contains bacteria, parasites, viruses, toxins, or chemical contaminants.
10. wound
11. bruise
12. abrasions
13. The animal may have rabies.
14. The most serious burn is the third-degree burn.
15. Apply cold water to the burn.
16. two hours
17. The best way for a child to get rid of blockage in the windpipe is for the child to cough up the object causing the blockage.
18. (List two:) constant itch of the scalp, often including infected scratches or a rash; small, silvery eggs attached to individual hairs; swollen lymph glands in the neck or under the arms
19. Insulin
20. Epilepsy is a condition in which a person has periodic seizures.

Review and Reflect Answer Key

1. (List three:) good nutrition and dietary habits; daily physical activity; personal hygiene; regular medical and dental care; exposure to clean and safe environments at home and school; respectful and stable relationships that provide predictability and consistency
2. A preadmission medical exam will tell you if a child has communicable diseases, has had all needed immunizations, has any allergies, or has any health problems that affect enrollment.
3. A. two doses each of: hepatitis B, DTaP, Hib, IPV, and pnemococcal vaccine
   B. one dose each of: hepatitis B, DTaP, Hib, IPV, MMR, varicella, and pneumococcal vaccine
   C. one dose each of: DTaP, IPV, and MMR
4. true

Apply and Explore

1. Prepare a handout listing the health policies of a center for preschool children.

2. Interview a child care center director about food safety requirements and policies followed by the center. Ask if the center has ever had an outbreak of foodborne illness and if so, how this was handled.

Cross-Curricular Link

Reading/Writing

1. Write a research paper on a serious illness that can affect children. Explain the illness itself and dispel any commonly believed untruths about the illness. Explain various treatments for the illness.

Technology

2. Check online at the National Resource Center for Health and Safety in Child Care Web site (nrc.uchsc.edu) for health tips suggested for child care centers.

3. Visit the Web site www.kidshealth.org to learn more about allergies and asthma. Use the computer to write a brief paper on your findings.

4. Use the Web site of the American Red Cross (www.redcross.org) to search for the chapter nearest you. Contact this chapter to learn what resources are available near you for first aid training.

Workplace Link

Research the cost of commercially prepared first aid kits available in local stores, at medical supply companies, and on the Internet. What supplies are included? Compare the cost of the commercial kits with the cost of obtaining all the supplies and creating your own first aid kit for use in a child care center. Do any of the items, such as anti-itch cream for insect bites and antibiotic treatments for wounds, have expiration dates?

Keeping the center clean is an important factor in protecting children's health.

P A R T

3

Guiding Children

As you work in child care, guidance will be a routine part of your experiences with children. Children need positive guidance to learn how to get along with others and to stay safe.

In this part, you will study and practice techniques for guiding children throughout the day. You will gain insight into methods for handling such guidance problems as negativism and fear.

You will learn guidelines for establishing and enforcing limits throughout the classroom. This part will also teach you ways to guide children through such daily routines as dressing, eating, and napping.

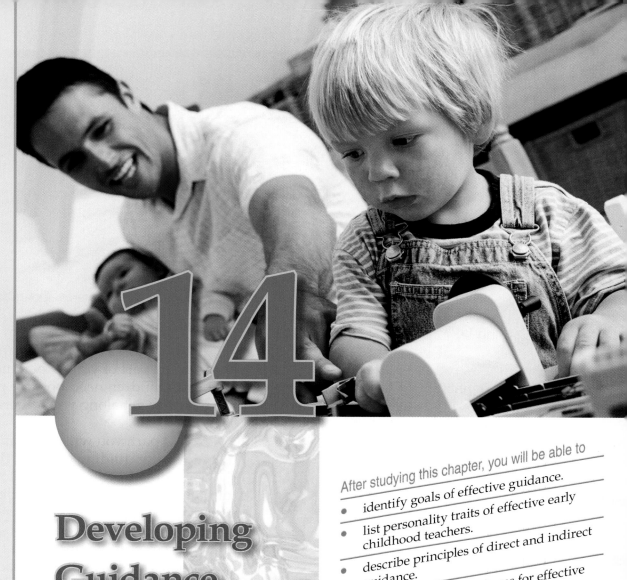

Discuss

Look at the chapter opening photo. How do you think the teacher might be providing guidance to this child? What do you notice about the teacher's demeanor? What does this say about how teachers should guide children in their care?

Discuss

Look over the objectives for this chapter. Discuss the role guidance plays in helping children become self-controlled.

Developing Guidance Skills

After studying this chapter, you will be able to

- identify goals of effective guidance.
- list personality traits of effective early childhood teachers.
- describe principles of direct and indirect guidance.
- explain various techniques for effective guidance.
- summarize ways to promote a positive self-concept in each child.

Terms to Know

guidance
prosocial behaviors
nonverbal behavior
indirect guidance
direct guidance
verbal environment
positive reinforcement
consequence
natural consequences
logical consequences
time-out
I-message
prompting
redirecting
modeling
active listening

Alicia sat in the corner looking at a library book. Slowly she ripped a page from the book. On the other side of the room, Wyatt knocked Hunter's block tower over. Then she sped to the art table and grabbed Ryder's play dough. At the same time, May entered the room, greeted another child, and threw her coat on the floor.

How will you, as a teacher, guide each of these children? How will you empower them to solve their own problems? Guiding children is a complex process. Understanding and guiding children's behavior requires knowledge of child growth and development. It also requires the ability to understand each child's behavior. This is a constant process that never ends. As a teacher, you will continually learn more about your role in guiding young children.

Goals of Guidance

Guidance consists of direct and indirect actions used by an adult to help children develop appropriate behavior patterns, 14-1. Effective guidance should maintain children's self-esteem and produce a desired change in behavior. Self-regulation and self-control are the long-term goals of guidance. That is, the children should learn to direct their own behavior without outside control.

Another goal of guidance is to promote prosocial behaviors among the children. **Prosocial behaviors** are acts of kindness that benefit others. They are behaviors that demonstrate cooperation and helpfulness. The following are examples of prosocial behaviors:

- accepting and respecting others' feelings
- verbally and physically comforting others
- expressing strong emotions in acceptable ways
- helping others

14-1

Younger children often require more guidance than older children.

Vocabulary

Have students review the *Terms to Know* list. Ask students to look up unfamiliar words or terms in the glossary before reading the chapter.

Resource

Guidance on the Spot, reproducible master 14-1, TR

Vocabulary

Have a student volunteer define the term *guidance.* What is the long-term goal of guidance?

Discuss

Why is it important for children to develop prosocial behaviors? Give examples of prosocial behaviors. How can prosocial behaviors be promoted among children?

Resource

Observing Prosocial Behaviors, Activity A, OG

Meeting Special Needs

Provide an outline of the chapter with all the chapter headings for special learners. Students should fill in each section of the outline as the material is covered in class with a sentence or two about the content. Review the special learners' IEPs to decide if any modifications should be made in presenting the chapter content.

Discuss

How does a teacher's personality affect the behavior of children? Why might children in a class with a talkative teacher exhibit shyness? How do the students react when their teacher acts negatively or seems unwilling to nurture children?

Reflect

Did you ever have a "bad day?" How do you respond to people around you when you are not feeling your best?

Resource

Open-Ended Questions, color transparency CT-13, TR

Discuss

What is the effect on children when a teacher uses open-ended questions? What characteristics will children show in this kind of environment?

Resource

Comparing Closed- and Open-Ended Questions, reproducible master 14-2, TR

- cooperating with others in play and cleanup time
- sharing toys and materials
- sharing affection
- showing concern

Guidance and You

As a teacher, your personality will affect the behavior of the children in your care. Many studies have been conducted to determine the effect that specific personality traits have on children's behavior. These studies show that effective early childhood teachers encourage and show interest in children. These teachers use more suggestions than commands. Children respond faster to suggestions than commands.

According to research, teachers should interact often with their children and ask open-ended questions. These questions require more than one-word answers. Children in this type of environment will show certain positive characteristics. These include independence, verbalization, cooperation, task persistence, and high self-esteem. See 14-2.

Model prosocial behaviors. Children will imitate your example, so let it be a positive one. Studies also note that uncooperative teachers have more hyperactive, disruptive, and bored children. On the other hand, children in the classes of talkative teachers tend to be more shy. Nurturing teachers have children in their classes who interact easily with others.

Aggressive and attention-seeking behavior on the part of the children is also influenced by the teacher. This behavior occurs most often with permissive teachers. Such teachers often fail to get involved with or stop aggressive and attention-seeking behavior. The children who behave this way may see the teacher's lack of involvement as permission to engage in such behavior.

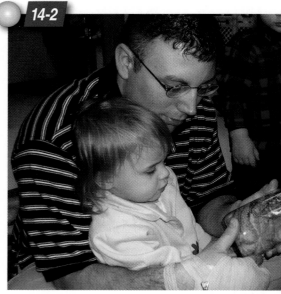
14-2

This child will learn a great deal through interaction with the teacher.

Preparing for Guidance

There are some general guidelines for developing effective guidance skills. Study these guidelines. They will help you become an effective teacher.

One of the first steps toward effective guidance is observation of the children. Watch and note how individual children behave in certain situations. This will help you understand the children in your class. Review the observation techniques described in Chapter 3.

Ask yourself how you respond to each of the children in your class. Do you have any biases? Are you expecting certain behaviors from children based on culture, gender, personality, or appearance? The stereotypes you hold may affect your perception of a child. For example, do you expect Clarice to be better behaved because both of her parents are doctors? Being honest about your own attitudes and how they may influence

---

Workplace Connection

Invite your school's guidance counselor or one of your school district's elementary guidance counselors to speak to the class about his or her job and answer the following questions: What prompted or encouraged you to enter this field of work? What are the challenges in guiding children successfully today? How important is parental support to your effectiveness? Have students prepare a list of additional questions to ask prior to the visit.

your interactions will allow you to be more objective.

Cultural Variations

It is important to learn about family and cultural variations in children's nonverbal behavior. **Nonverbal behavior** consists of actions rather than words. These can include facial expressions, eye contact, touch, gestures, and position in space. For example, it is common for people in some cultures to look down to show respect. In these cultures, a child who speaks in a soft voice and maintains less eye contact is reflecting respect and courtesy.

Sharing Observations

Another important guideline is to plan with other teachers. Sharing observations, feelings, and suggestions will help you fully understand the children. One teacher may be able to add to your observations, 14-3. As a result, you will better understand why a child refuses to take part in art activities.

Avoid talking to other staff when you are teaching unless it is important. The children's needs should always come first. Being alert

14-3

With the help of other teachers, you can learn more about the children in your center.

to these needs requires your full attention. Make a practice of talking with other teachers only if necessary. Save other comments for after program hours.

Finally, sit with the children whenever possible. You will be closer to the children's level. As a result, they will find it easier to approach you and gain your attention. Do not interrupt an activity unless you can add to knowledge or safety. Let the children begin interaction with you. Remember that to develop independence and self-confidence, never do for the children what they can do for themselves.

Direct Guidance

Child guidance may be direct or indirect. **Indirect guidance** involves outside factors that influence behavior. The layout of the center is a form of indirect guidance. Indirect guidance will be discussed later in the chapter.

Direct guidance involves nonverbal (physical) and verbal actions. Nonverbal actions include facial gestures such as eye contact, a smile, or even a surprised look. Your words are also a form of direct guidance.

Facial expressions can communicate a variety of messages ranging from disapproval and sadness to approval and reassurance. Body gestures are another type of direct guidance. Putting your arm around a child is one form of direct guidance.

Young children gain much information from nonverbal actions. They might learn the caregiver's mood and expectations. Infants and toddlers focus most of their attention on what they see and feel rather than on verbal clues. Even as children begin to pay more attention to words, they still rely on nonverbal actions to help them understand messages.

Your nonverbal actions need to reinforce what you are communicating verbally. Watch that your words match your nonverbal signals. For example, if you are asking a child to stop a behavior, your facial expression

Enrich

Have students role-play a situation in which three teachers are having a conversation while children are misbehaving or trying to get the teachers' attention. Ask students to reflect on the teachers' roles in the behavior of children.

Vocabulary

Have a student volunteer define the terms *direct guidance* and *indirect guidance*. How are these two types of guidance similar?

Resource

Direct and Indirect Guidance, Activity A, SAG

Reflect

Why do you think preparing for guidance is as important as actively guiding children's behavior? How can your preparation make you more effective in guidance?

Resource

Child Guidance Principles, Activity B, OG

Cross-Curricular Activity

Social Studies
Ask your school's psychology instructor to help locate examples of case studies involving children with severe guidance issues and the resulting effects on their family. Ask the instructor to discuss the cases and add his or her observations and ideas for helping families deal with these issues. Have student volunteers offer suggestions for effective behavior management and ideas to make sure all family members' needs are met while dealing with the guidance issue. Investigate the possibility of a joint research project on this topic involving students from both classes.

should also convey disapproval. Children become confused when adults' words give one message and their actions another.

Direct guidance principles are shown in 14-4. Following these principles will help you develop direct guidance skills.

Use Simple Language

Using simple language is important. Young children have limited vocabularies. To communicate clearly, use language they can understand. Consider the ages of the children. Adjust your vocabulary to fit those ages. For instance, two-year-olds usually learn the word *big* before they learn *large*. Therefore, use the word *big* with these children. When working with three-year-olds, you might use the word *large*. This depends, however, on their level of development. With four- and five-year-olds, again adjust the level of your vocabulary. With these children, you might say *huge*.

14-4

Direct Guidance Principles

- Use simple language.
- Speak in a relaxed voice.
- Be positive.
- Offer choices with care.
- Encourage independence and cooperation.
- Be firm.
- Be consistent.
- Provide time for change.
- Consider feelings.
- Intervene when necessary.

These direct guidance principles outline the verbal and nonverbal skills you will need for effective guidance.

Speak in a Relaxed Voice

Speak in a calm, quiet, relaxed tone of voice. Children will listen to this type of voice. Save loud, high-pitched voices for emergencies. Since loud, high-pitched voices are associated with strong emotion, you will gain the children's attention. If you raise your voice during the normal course of the day, children will become used to this level. When an emergency occurs, you may not be able to gain their attention. In addition, when you raise your voice, the children will also raise their voices. The classroom will become a very noisy place.

Be Positive

Guide the children by telling them what to do as opposed to what not to do. Children will feel more comfortable with a positive comment. For example, instead of saying "Don't put that puzzle on the floor," say "Put the puzzle on the table." See 14-5. This will remind the children of the rule that puzzles are used on a table.

Offer Choices with Care

New, unskilled teachers sometimes confuse offering a choice with giving a direction. For example, when it is lunchtime, the teacher may say "Do you want to go in for lunch?" By asking this question, the child is given a choice. If the child is not interested in eating lunch then, he or she may answer by saying no.

Children should be offered a choice only when you want them to have a choice. In this case, a better direction would be "It is time for lunch now," or "We need to go inside for lunch now." Make sure that once you offer a choice you allow the child to carry through with his or her choice. For example, you might ask a child if she or he prefers watering the plants or feeding the fish. If the child chooses feeding the fish, accept the choice. Do not try to get children to change their minds.

Resource

A Teacher's Speech and Voice Should:, transparency master 14-3, TR

Reflect

Try to keep track of any negative comments you may make in one day. Did the fact that you were tracking your negatives cause you to change what you were going to say? Share some examples with the class.

Discuss

When should you offer a child the opportunity of making choices? What should you do when a child does not make the choice you wanted them to make?

Resource

Suggestions for Talking with a Child, reproducible master 14-4, TR

Meeting Special Needs

Partner volunteer students with special learners to review 14-4, *Direct Guidance Principles*, to be sure they understand all ten principles. Have students quiz each other by explaining the purpose and giving an example of each principle. Then have students review the meaning of *direct guidance*. Ask student volunteers to report areas where reteaching or further understanding is needed.

14-5

Using Positive Guidance

Negative	Positive
"Do not put the puzzle on the floor."	"Put the puzzle on the table."
"Do not touch anything!"	"Place your hands in your pockets."
"Do not run."	"Please walk."
"Quit screaming."	"Use your indoor voice."
"Do not drip paint."	"Wipe your brush on the container."
"Do not get paint on your clothes."	"Put on a painting smock."
"Do not rip the pages."	"Turn the pages carefully."
"Do not walk in front of the swing."	"Walk around the swing, please."
"Do not use your fingers."	"Use your fork."

Be aware of negative comments you make and try to replace them with positive comments.

When you do this, you are telling them that there really was not a choice.

Encourage Independence and Cooperation

Give children the least amount of help they need. In this way, they will have opportunities to learn independence. For instance, encourage children to dress and feed themselves. Encourage them to share responsibility for keeping the classroom clean and orderly.

Some children begin school dependent on others. At home, these children have an adult or sibling to attend to their needs. As a result, they come to school expecting the teacher to dress them, pick up after them, and intercede for them. Encourage independence from the start in order to change this behavior. For instance, when Eugene reports that Tommy is teasing him, ask Eugene how he feels when this happens. If he says he does not like it, tell him to share his feelings with

Tommy. Likewise, if Talia does not want to share her clay, Eugene needs to tell Talia he is mad because she will not share.

Children only become independent if allowed the opportunity. Many people are surprised at the competence of three-, four-, and five-year-old children who are provided the chance to do for themselves. See 14-6.

These children must also learn to help each other. Encourage children to work with each other. When Toby tells you he cannot zip his coat, say "Ask Joanne if she can help you." If Marlene cannot tie her shoe, say "Ask Luis to help you tie it." These experiences help the children to learn prosocial behaviors.

Be Firm

Be firm when disciplining children. At the same time, speak in a quiet voice. Some children are very demanding. When you tell them that they cannot do something, they may cry. Some may even throw temper

Reflect

Think about a negative comment you have made recently. How could you have changed the negative comment into a positive comment?

Resource

Positive Guidance, Activity B, SAG

Discuss

What can children gain when another child is asked to help them with a task such as tying shoes or zipping up a jacket? What can the child who is the helper gain?

Resource

Building Positive Skills, transparency master 14-5, TR

Cross-Curricular Activity

Language Arts
Ask students to locate books written for children to help them deal with guidance problems. Suggested authors may include: Roger Hargreaves's *Little Miss* and *Mr. Men* books; Barbara Hazen's *Hello Gnu, How Do You Do*, a book about polite behavior; books by Janine Amos such as *Jealous, Moody, Sad*; and books by Aliki such as *Manners* and *Feelings*. Have students review copies of the books in class. Discuss how reading a story about another child with problems may be an effective tool for helping children recognize their own difficulties.

Discuss

What are some examples of positive guidance techniques? Give examples of appropriate ways for dealing with negative behavior.

Reflect

Have you seen a child throw a temper tantrum in a public place such as a store or restaurant? How did the parents handle the child's behavior? What was the child's response? Would you have tried to handle the situation differently?

Discuss

What does it mean to be consistent? Why is it frustrating for children when their teacher is not consistent in discipline or approval?

Written Discipline Policies

Written discipline policies are a requirement for child care facilities. The policies are to be available to all staff and to families. They outline strategies for positive, non-abusive ways to guide children's behavior. Staff members sign an agreement saying they will follow and implement the policies. A written policy should include the following:

- age-appropriate expectations for behavior

- positive guidance techniques such as redirection, specific limits, consistent rules, planning to prevent problems, and encouraging positive behavior

- examples of appropriate ways for dealing with negative behavior, such as time-out for preschoolers or denying privileges for school-age children

For additional information about written discipline policies, contact your state licensing agency. You might also check out resources on staff-child interactions published by NAEYC.

14-6

Young children are good at doing tasks for themselves, if given a chance.

tantrums. If it is behavior that you cannot allow to continue, you must stand firm.

When a child throws a temper tantrum, you may feel like giving in. If you do, the child will likely use the same method again when he or she wants his or her own way. Effective guidance requires firmness.

Be Consistent

Children are good at testing adults. If they feel an adult is not firm in disciplining, they will repeat their unacceptable behavior. In fact, they may want to find out what will happen if they continue to repeat their unacceptable behavior. For this reason, discipline and approval should be given consistently. For instance, do not discipline children one day and praise them the next for running to the door at playtime.

Make sure that you are also consistent from child to child. Children quickly develop

---

Workplace Connection

Have students review their state licensing agencies information about written discipline policies. Then ask students to review a local child care center's written discipline policies. What strategies are outlined in the center's policies for guiding children's behavior? Are age-appropriate expectations for behavior included in the policies? What examples of appropriate ways for dealing with negative behavior are provided? Should any other information be included? Allow time for students to discuss their findings in class.

a sense of fairness. If you tell one child to pick up the toys at cleanup time, all children should have to clean up. When you are not consistent, children will challenge your requests.

Provide Time for Change

Young children need time to change activities. It is important to provide them with ample time for change. Without this time, children can become confused. By allowing time, you will provide children with an adjustment period. For instance, when children are preparing to go outside during cold weather, allow them time to put on their coats, hats, and mittens. This time will allow them to prepare themselves for new activities and new surroundings.

Consider Feelings

Although it is not always included in daily lesson plans, learning about feelings and emotions is an important part of any early childhood program. Children need to recognize, understand, and learn to express their feelings.

Young children can have strong feelings. These feelings often center around control of their environment. The feelings may relate to their bodies, siblings, eating, friendship, and toileting.

Feelings are best discussed in small group settings or alone with a child. For some children, talking about feelings and emotions is difficult. It is your responsibility to help them understand and express their feelings. See 14-7.

Facing someone else's pain is also difficult for young children. You will observe that children do not know how to deal with the pain of others. When a new child begins school and cries over separation from parents, the other children do not

14-7

Many children do not know how to handle their feelings. They may require your help in order to feel good about themselves.

usually get involved. Some may pretend to not see or hear the child. Others may have a pained look on their faces. This shows sensitivity. Although they may feel sympathy, they tend not to get involved. Usually, if a child is bleeding, only then will they get involved. They will bring the child to you for a bandage. However, they will not usually console the child.

Reflect

Do you think preschool children understand fairness? Give an example of how you would demonstrate fairness to children.

Discuss

Why are feelings best discussed in small group settings or alone with a child? How can you help children express and understand their feelings?

Enrich

Ask students to write and illustrate a children's storybook or write a puppet play that demonstrates how preschoolers can deal with their feelings. The characters in the story or play should portray situations and feelings a typical preschooler may encounter such as nervousness or anxiety on the first day of school. Allow time for students to share their projects in class.

Portfolio Project

Ask students to select one of the children in the child care lab and write a brief profile of the child focusing on the child's usual behavior and use of social skills in relationships with other children. Have students identify any guidance issues they have seen displayed by the child and describe any intervention used to handle these guidance issues. If possible, interview the child's family to get additional insights into the child's behavior. Have students file the writing example in their portfolio.

Discuss

Why might a child who makes a mistake such as spilling milk or breaking a toy be fearful? Discuss situations you may have observed where children might have lied or hidden what happened because they feared the consequences.

Reflect

How would you intervene when children are smearing finger paint all over the table instead of on their papers? What intervention would you make when one child refuses to get off the slide so no other children can use it?

Enrich

Invite a child care center teacher or director to speak to the class about strategies used to deal with children who exhibit consistent guidance problems. What strategies are the most effective in guiding children's behavior? What staff training is provided to deal with guidance problems? Have students write a list of questions to ask prior to the visit.

You can show children how to help others. For instance, if Patrick is crying, put your arm around him. By doing this, you will teach the children a way to comfort each other. They will learn that crying can be mended with a hug.

Young children also need to learn how to handle mistakes. When a child spills milk or breaks a toy, do not overreact. Instead, show the child how to handle the mistake. The child will then know not to fear mistakes. See 14-8. For example, remind the child who spilled the milk that the milk must be cleaned up. Show the child how to do this. Depending on the situation, you may wish to help clean up.

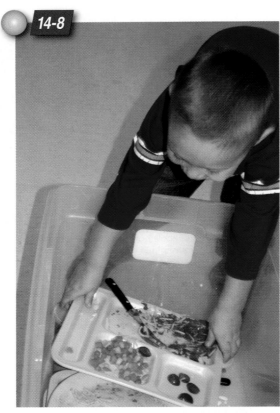

14-8

Children need to be encouraged to help with cleanup.

Intervene When Necessary

To be an effective teacher, you will need to know when to intervene. Observe children carefully before saying anything. Allow them to explore on their own. Interrupt only when you can add to their knowledge or promote their safety. For example, if a four-year-old says "Cows give eggnog at Christmas," clarify this statement. Unless you intervene, children who are listening may believe this comment.

Safety intervention will often require words and action. If James is not careful climbing up the slide, you will need to walk over and review the limits with him. Make clear the dangers of falling. Intervention would also be required if you were observing a group of children and noticed that a child was in danger of being hurt. It is important to intervene before this happens by redirecting the play or providing assistance.

You may also need to intervene for health purposes. Remind children to dress properly for outdoor play in the winter. Encourage children to cover their mouths with their arms when they cough. When cooking, remind children not to use the cooking utensils to taste the food.

Children need to learn to be friends with all the children. Thus, do not allow children to be excluded from play because of age, culture, or gender. When Erica says, "Only girls can come into the playhouse," it is important for you to intervene. One way to handle this is to say "This school is for everyone." By doing so, you will give the children the words they need to defend their right to participate.

You must also intervene when children are impolite. Sometimes you will hear a child say "I do not like you," or "You are ugly." When this happens, you need to intervene. Point out to the child that such words can

Putting Technology to Use

Have students conduct an Internet search for professional articles dealing with the positive guidance of young children. Suggested Web sites may include the following: The National Association for the Education of Young Children at **www.naeyc.org** and the National Child Care Information Center at **www.nccic.org**. Ask students to write a brief summary of the articles. Allow time for students to share their findings with the class.

hurt another's feelings. With young children, that may be sufficient to end the behavior.

Property arguments may also require intervention. Classroom property does not belong to the children, but to the center. Therefore, the children must share it. During a property argument, remind the children to share. If this does not work, give the equipment to one child for a set time period. Then give it to the other child for another time period. For instance, tell Mandy that she may play with the truck in the morning and Mark may play with it in the afternoon. Then make sure each child has a turn.

It is important for children to learn that they cannot grab materials from others. No matter how strong the child's feelings, others have rights, too. Children need to take turns painting at the easel, participating in cooking activities, and watering plants, 14-9. While children learn and develop, you will need to intervene. That is why in many early childhood classrooms, you will hear a teacher saying many times a day "You can have a turn next," or "After she is finished, you can paint."

14-9

These children have learned that they must take turns as they participate in activities.

Indirect Guidance

You will recall that indirect guidance involves outside factors that influence behavior. The physical setup of a center is a form of indirect guidance. It can indirectly influence both the children's and teacher's behavior.

For example, a well-planned facility makes supervision easier. If you can supervise properly, it will help you feel relaxed and in control. The children will feel safer knowing they are being protected.

In order to carefully supervise young children, an open classroom is best. Stand with your back toward the classroom wall. You should be able to view the entire room. Such an arrangement will allow you to observe and give help when needed. It will also reduce your own fatigue, since you will have to run back and forth between areas less often.

A healthy, safe environment can be promoted through the physical setup of the facility. In one large room, you will be able to see everything that happens, 14-10. Therefore, you can step in when dangerous situations arise. For instance, the behavior of two-year-old children needs close monitoring. Many two-year-olds will hit another child instead of saying "I do not like that." With the proper physical arrangement, you can see such situations occurring and step in immediately.

Young children, and especially two-year-olds, often do not have well-developed gross-motor skills. They often stumble, trip, or fall. To reduce the number of these accidents, large, open areas are best. Shelving units should be placed around the outside walls of the room.

Children's independence can also be encouraged through the physical setup of the facility. Independence should be a learning objective of every early childhood program, no matter the ages or abilities of children

Discuss

Brainstorm ideas for making sure that all children get opportunities to use play equipment when they have to wait for a turn. How can you handle this in a way that is fair to all the children?

Discuss

Four chairs at the science table are all being used and Zachary wants to sit down, too. When he sees that there is no room, he starts getting distressed. How would you use direct guidance principles to handle this incident?

Vocabulary

Have a student volunteer define the term *indirect guidance*. Give an example of how indirect guidance affects behavior.

Discuss

What is an open classroom? What are the benefits of an open classroom?

Cross-Curricular Activity

Social Studies
Have students research the educational trend favoring open classrooms in the 1960s and 1970s. Ask students to write a report about the events or situations that led to encouraging this trend. Explain what an open classroom is and what it is not. Describe how this trend fell out of favor, but include an explanation of how some of the philosophies followed at the time still remain in education today. Allow time for students to share their reports in class.

Reflect

Why do you think shelving units should be placed around the outside walls of a classroom? Why should you consider children's gross-motor skills as a factor in placing the shelves?

Activity

Many preschool programs use a "Helping Hands" chart to encourage children to participate in classroom tasks and duties. What tasks need to be on the chart? Have students draw an example or make an actual "Helping Hands" chart if your program does not already have one.

Discuss

What is the difference between guidance principles and guidance techniques? How do guidance principles relate to techniques for effective guidance?

14-10

This teacher has positioned herself so she can see all the children.

in the program. For example, you should encourage toddlers to use the washroom if they have developed control of their bowels and bladders. For this reason, the washrooms should be easy to find and use. Sinks, toilets, and hand dryers should be set at the children's level.

Children can also be encouraged to hang up their own coats and assist with cleanup. To encourage this, provide low hooks for hanging coats and hats. Low shelf units and sinks will encourage children to help with cleanup. All toys and materials should have a designated place in the classroom. Placing a picture of the item on a shelf or container is one way of assisting the children. When containers are marked, teachers are usually more successful in having the children replace toys and equipment to the proper storage place.

Through these arrangements, you will save time and energy assisting the children. This will allow you more time to observe and work with the children and plan meaningful activities.

Techniques for Effective Guidance

As an early childhood teacher, you will teach children acceptable behaviors. Likewise, the children in your classroom will also teach each other. Whatever effect you have on the children's behavior, the children, in turn, will affect others.

There are specific guidance techniques that can be useful in guiding children's behavior. These techniques include creating a positive verbal environment, using positive reinforcement, and using consequences. In addition, you will want to include warning, time-out, I-messages, praising, affirming, suggesting, prompting, persuading, redirecting, modeling, listening, ignoring, and encouraging.

Positive Verbal Environment

The **verbal environment** includes all the communication that occurs within the setting. These exchanges may be made by an adult or child. In addition, it includes the nonverbal communication of actions rather than words. Eye contact, facial expressions, gestures, and touch are examples. What is said and how it is said determines whether the environment is positive or negative.

Teachers can help create a positive verbal environment by using active listening skills. They can start by having the environment set up before the children arrive at the center. This would allow them to give the children their full attention when the children enter the classroom. When engaging in a conversation, caregivers should use the children's names and words to indicate their interest. Words such as *thank you, please,* and *excuse me* should be modeled throughout the

---

Workplace Connection

Have students observe the verbal environment at a local child care center. Are active listening skills being used in the classroom? What nonverbal communications such as eye contact and facial expressions do you notice? Are caregivers using the children's names and words to indicate their interest in conversation? What is the tone of the conversation? Is this a positive verbal environment for children? Why or why not? Have students discuss their findings in class.

day. Likewise, these adults should be sincere and constructive when praising children.

Positive Reinforcement

Children's behavior can often be molded by rewarding positive behavior. This technique is called **positive reinforcement**. For instance, if you thank a child for holding the door, the child will most likely hold the door again. You have provided a positive reinforcement of the child's behavior. Positive messages will encourage the child to repeat the behavior. Repeated positive reinforcement will result in repeated behavior.

You must be careful when using positive reinforcement that you are rewarding behaviors you want the child to repeat. Teachers sometimes do not realize they are rewarding children for unacceptable behavior. For instance, laughing at a child who is acting silly at group time is reinforcing the child's behavior. This reaction is seen by the child as a reward. It encourages the child to repeat the behavior.

Using Consequences

Consequences are important in molding children's behavior. A **consequence** is a result that follows an action or behavior. Consequences can be very effective in shaping behavior. There are two types of consequences: natural consequences and logical consequences.

Natural consequences are those experiences that follow naturally as a result of a behavior. They do not require anyone's intervention. For example, the natural consequence of forgetting to put away an art project is that it might be thrown away during cleanup time. The natural consequence of forgetting to put on your

gloves is that your hands will get cold. See 14-11. Natural consequences can be very effective in guiding children's behavior, but they cannot be used if a child's safety is at risk. For instance, if a child runs into the street without stopping to look for cars, the child could be hit by a car. In this case, an adult must intervene to make sure the child stops and looks before crossing a street.

14-11

This girl may learn that a natural consequence of sitting on a ball can be a fall.

Vocabulary

Have a student volunteer define the term *positive reinforcement*. What is the goal of positive reinforcement?

Discuss

When a teacher offers positive reinforcement, it encourages a child to repeat a behavior. What are some examples of children's behavior that should *not* be rewarded with positive reinforcement?

Vocabulary

Have student volunteers define the terms *consequence* and *natural consequences*. When are each used? Give examples.

Putting Technology to Use

Ask students to conduct an Internet search for information on teacher burnout. Have students define the term *burnout* and list the major causes. What role do unruly and unmotivated students play in a teacher's decision to leave the teaching field? Explain how early attention to the promotion of positive guidance techniques might have an impact on student behavior that would affect the rate of teacher burnout.

Vocabulary

Have student volunteers define the terms *warning* and *time-out*. How many warnings should a child receive? What is the purpose of a time-out?

Discuss

Do you think time-outs are effective in helping children become self-disciplined? Ask students to compare their viewpoints.

Reflect

Have you ever been put in a time-out to calm down? How did it make you feel? Have student volunteers share their experiences with the class.

When natural consequences cannot be used to guide behavior, logical consequences may be established. **Logical consequences** are those that are deliberately set up by an adult to show what will happen if a limit is not followed. The consequences should be related to the behavior as much as possible.

When using logical consequences, the children must first be made aware of the limits. Then they need to know the consequences of choosing not to follow the limits. For example, if Brad drives his scooter into Lawrence, tell him to stop. Remind him of the consequence if he does not stop. The consequence might be that he will have to give up his turn on the scooter. If Brad runs into Lawrence again, enforce the consequence. Thus, Brad will learn that driving into others is not acceptable behavior.

Warning

When children fail to follow a limit, you must remind them that they are misbehaving and their behavior will have consequences. You are *warning* the children. Warn only once. If the behavior continues, proceed with the consequences. Effective warnings contain only two parts. First, state the misbehavior. Then state the consequences. Examples include:

- "Joel, sand needs to be kept in the sandbox. If you throw it again, you will lose your turn."

- "Tunde, either choose a place in the circle, or I will choose one for you."

- "Mandy, blocks are not to be used like guns. If you use the block as a gun again, you will need to leave the block area."

These warnings provide children an opportunity to change their behavior. After giving the warning, provide time for the child to comply. If the child does not comply, follow through with the consequences.

Time-Out

Time-out is a guidance technique that involves moving a child away from others for a short period of time. Time-out is used when a child's disruptive behavior cannot be ignored. The child needs time to calm down. In some classrooms, this technique is used when a child is out of control with anger. To protect the other children, the teacher moves the angry child to a quiet place away from the group. This is one way of allowing the child to gain self-control. However, time-out should never be used as a form of punishment.

Time-out can be an effective guidance tool for some children. Four- and five-year-olds usually understand the purpose better than younger children. By this age, most children have the ability to understand their behavior can have negative consequences. Time-out is an example of a logical consequence.

To be effective, tell children in advance what behaviors will result in time-out. If you decide to use time-out, carry it out in an unemotional, direct way. Simply state the limit that has been broken and say "Time-out." Promptly remove the child to an area away from the group, but within your vision. Nothing further should be said. You do not want to reward the child with added attention. Limit the time to a few minutes. If the child returns to the group and the behavior continues, add another minute to the original time.

Not all teachers agree with the use of time-out. Some teachers feel the technique should seldom be used, if at all. Others feel that time-out provides time for children to think about the skills they need to function more appropriately in the classroom.

I-Messages

When a child misbehaves, use an I-message to communicate your perceptions and feelings. An **I-message** tells the child

---

Meeting Special Needs

Ask gifted students to arrange to interview a clinical psychologist or licensed social worker to discuss a career in child guidance. What background, motivation, or interest led the professional to his or her chosen career? What education, training, certification, and licensing is needed to practice in this field? Ask the professional to describe some challenging cases and explain the philosophies or psychological concepts that were used to determine the most effective treatment for the children.

how you feel about his or her behavior in a respectful manner. It does not place blame with the child, which would cause the child to feel he or she was a bad person. Rather, it helps the child learn how others view his or her actions.

Your I-message statement should include three parts: (1) the child's behavior, (2) your feelings about the behavior, and (3) the effects of the behavior. After you state the I-message, you should then say what you want done. For instance, you may say "When I see you hitting Yasser, I am unhappy because you are hurting him. I want you to stop hitting Yasser." Note that in this example, the behavior is hitting, it makes you feel unhappy, and the effects cause another child to be hurt. An I-message shows the child how his actions are perceived by others.

Effective Praise

Studies show that not all praise is equally successful. *Effective praise* is sincere and constructive. It is specific and individualized to fit the situation and child. It acknowledges the child's actions or progress. It is thoughtful and does not interrupt the child's activities. Effective praise recognizes the child's positive behaviors and encourages the child to persist at a task. This type of praise may compare a child's progress to past performance. The goal is to make the child feel competent and valued. Young children thrive on effective praise. When you say "I like the way you helped, Cedric," you tell the child he is important. This is a form of verbal praise. See 14-12. Nonverbal praise can also be used successfully. A smile, wink, or pat on the back are all types of nonverbal praise. Displaying a child's work on a bulletin board is also a form of praise. Some teachers paste a star or sticker on paperwork or artwork that a child has done. This is also nonverbal praise.

When praising young children, remember the following:
- Make praise age appropriate.
- Give praise immediately. It is most effective to praise children while they are still in the act.

Ineffective Praise	Effective Praise
"Good job!"	"I like the way you picked up the puzzle and returned it to the puzzle rack."
"Beautiful work!"	"You used the chalk to make bright and dark green colors."
"Wonderful!"	"I like the way you shared your blocks with Tommy. He is enjoying using them."
"I'm proud of you!"	"You put on your coat and fastened the zipper all by yourself."
"Terrific!"	"You are using your hands to hold tightly onto the climber. Your muscles are working hard."

Effective praise is specific and acknowledges the child's actions or progress.

Vocabulary

Have a student volunteer define the term *I-message*. What three parts are needed in an I-message?

Enrich

Have students change the following statements into I-messages: *"You lied to me." "You better do it this way or else!" "You are always late." "Why didn't you pick me?"* Do the statements show how you feel about the behavior without placing blame?

Discuss

What is the difference between effective praise and ineffective or empty praise? Have students give examples of each.

Putting Technology to Use

Have students utilize the school's video recording equipment or their own video recorders to create a short educational movie to promote the use of effective guidance techniques. Ask interested students to write a script that includes an explanation of all the techniques listed in the text. Record children and student teachers in the child care lab interacting and demonstrating the various techniques. Students will use editing, writing, interviewing, and organizational skills as well as other skills in creating the movie.

Enrich

Have students compare the following statements: *"Your room is so messy. I don't know why I buy toys for you when you leave them all over the floor."* and *"You need to pick up your toys and put them back on the shelves. I'm always proud that you know how to keep your room neat."* Which statement will probably produce the desired effect? Why?

Vocabulary

Have a student volunteer define the term *prompting.* How does prompting differ from *suggesting?*

Discuss

Why should you always make positive suggestions to children? What could be the result of making negative suggestions? Give examples of when you might be able to use suggestions to mold behavior in the preschool classroom.

- When praising, always establish eye contact.

- Do not overuse praise. If you do, it will not be as effective.

Affirming helps the children by identifying and labeling positive behavior. Like adults, children love to be acknowledged, and they repeat behaviors that are acknowledged. A teacher might use such affirmations as "You enjoy helping others" or "Raul likes having you share the toys with him." When behaviors are affirmed, they are likely to be repeated, 14-13.

Ineffective praise may be more damaging than helpful. This type of praise is often called *empty praise* because it is repetitive and not genuine. Frequent use of ineffective praise can lead children to base their feelings of self-worth on adults' opinions of them. Examples of ineffective praise include sayings such as *good job, super, terrific,* and *fantastic.*

Suggesting

Suggesting means placing thoughts for consideration into children's minds. This, in turn, often leads to action. For instance, after Candy spills her milk at the table, you may have to suggest she clean it up. To do this, say "Candy, here is a sponge." This will likely be enough to encourage Candy to wipe the spill. If not, you may have to add, "You need to wipe up the milk." During snack time, you may suggest to the children that they try a new fruit. This can be done directly or indirectly. Simply stating "This fruit is delicious," is enough to encourage some children to try the food. A more direct approach may work for other children. For example, you may say "Tammy, try this fruit today. It is delicious."

Always make suggestions positive. Lead children's thoughts and feelings in a desirable direction. If you tell the children to listen carefully to the story, they will probably follow your advice. However, if you tell the children that they are noisy and behaving poorly, they will probably continue to act this way. Negative suggestions usually produce negative behavior.

Effective teachers use suggestions many times each day. You will have many daily opportunities to mold behavior through suggestion. For example, Darlene may forget to put the blocks back on the shelf. A suggestion may work here. Corinna may drop her coat on the floor as she enters the room. A suggestion may work here, also.

Prompting

Children often need **prompting** either to stop an unacceptable action or start an

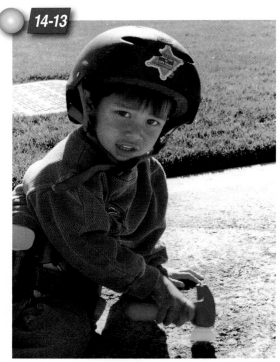

14-13

By saying, "It looks like you enjoy pretending to build," a teacher could encourage this boy to continue this play.

Portfolio Project

Write a short essay on your understanding of the role of guidance principles and techniques in managing student behavior. Explain the concept of *positive guidance.* Describe your beliefs on the role it plays in helping children become self-disciplined. Include examples of incidents where you observed an effective use of positive guidance techniques, especially detailing those situations that occurred while you were teaching. Summarize your feelings about how learning these techniques will help you in your future career.

acceptable one. Prompting can also be used to prepare children for transitions. Prompting differs from suggesting because a response is required of a prompt. Examples of verbal prompting include the following:

- "Moses, do you remember where we keep the play dough?"

- "Glenda, what must we remember when riding bikes?"

- "Michelle, do you remember where you put your painting?"

Prompting can also be nonverbal. You may place a finger over your lip at group time to signal "Quiet, please!" Limits printed on a poster board (if age appropriate) are nonverbal prompts. Frowning can show your disapproval. Even turning a child around to attend to group activities is a form of prompting.

Generally, make prompting simple and noncritical. Prompt in a calm, impersonal manner. You may ask a child "What are you supposed to be doing?" or "What should we be doing before we have a snack?"

Prompting may need to be repeated often before acceptable behavior is developed. A child who is new to the center may need to be prompted for several days to hang his or her coat on the hook before this behavior is developed. Once the child complies, praise this behavior.

Persuading

By *persuading*, you encourage children to act or behave in a certain way by appealing to their basic wants and needs. Seeing things from their point of view will give you an idea on the best way to approach a situation.

Link behavior with the children's feelings. For instance, a child who hangs back from an activity might be persuaded to join by appealing to his or her need to belong. You might say, "We are having such fun, Elizabeth. Will you join us?"

A child who interferes with another child's activities also needs to be persuaded. You can persuade the interfering child by helping him or her understand the other child's feelings. For instance, you may say, "Kenny, Joanie is afraid that if you keep jumping, you will knock her building down."

Redirecting

Children often need redirecting to a substitute activity. When **redirecting**, you divert, or turn, their attention in a different direction. One way to redirect is through distraction. A child who cries when his or her parent leaves may need to be distracted. Choose an interesting toy or book to distract the child's interest away from the parent.

Redirection encourages children to express themselves in more socially acceptable ways. For example, an active child may constantly push other children. To help this child release energy, provide activities that are physically demanding. Playing with a punching bag, carpentry tools, or play dough will provide an outlet for extra energy. The key to redirecting is providing an appealing substitute.

Modeling

Children learn by imitating others. When they see others helping, sharing, and cooperating, they are likely to act in these ways. Whenever you speak or move, you are **modeling** behavior. Modeling involves both verbal and nonverbal actions. It is a powerful tool when working with young children. At an early age, children become aware of the actions of the adults around them. Thus, it is important to set a good example. Social-emotional development is an important part of the early childhood curriculum. Much of what children learn is the result of watching others and imitating their behavior. Set an example by modeling prosocial behavior, 14-14.

Vocabulary

Have a student volunteer define the term *persuading*. Why do you need to see things from a child's point of view when you use persuading?

Reflect

What response could you make to someone who thinks that a teacher who uses guidance is not really disciplining children? This person believes that using discipline or punishments for misbehavior is the only way children can learn to behave.

Vocabulary

Have student volunteers define the terms *redirecting* and *modeling*. How do these techniques help children learn to control their behavior?

Cross-Curricular Activity

Language Arts
Ask students to write their own guidance policy. Students may want to contact local child care centers to view their guidance policies before beginning the assignment. Make sure the policies include the qualities and behaviors that students are trying to establish; guidance techniques that will be used to model prosocial behaviors; and strategies that will be used to handle inappropriate behaviors. Have students prepare a rough draft and exchange papers with other students to review for grammatical and spelling errors before finalizing their policy.

Reflect

Think about the last conversation you had. Were you a good listener? Did you give your full attention to the conversation? How can you become a better listener?

Discuss

How can you model appropriate behavior to children to help them learn how to acknowledge their feelings? What if a child is sad? What if a child is angry? Give examples.

Reflect

How do you feel when a family member, teacher, or another adult recognizes your accomplishments? What happens when your accomplishments are ignored? In what ways can you recognize children's accomplishments?

Modeling can be used in many situations at the center.

Workplace Connection

Have students visit a local child care center or preschool classroom to observe how manners are modeled and taught. Were children learning good manners by imitating the teacher's behavior? What instances of verbal and nonverbal modeling were observed? Were active listening techniques being used? What other guidance techniques were being used in the classroom? Have students write a brief report of their findings. Allow time for students to discuss their observations in class.

Listening

Listening involves giving children your full attention. It is more effective when you are at eye level with the child. Nodding and letting the children talk without interruption convey your attention. One type of listening is called active listening. Through **active listening**, you first listen to what the child is saying to you. Then you respond to the child by repeating what was just said. This lets the child know you have heard what he or she said and you accept it. It does not mean, however, that you solve the problem. See 14-15.

For instance, Jerome was playing in the housekeeping area. He wanted to use the broom that Sherry was using. He asked Sherry, "May I have the broom?" Sherry responded, "No, I am using it. Besides, I had it first." Jerome got angry. He ran over and shared the incident with the teacher's aide. The aide listened carefully to what Jerome was saying. Then the aide repeated what Jerome had just said to make certain she heard correctly. The aide said, "You are angry because Sherry will not let you use the broom." Jerome learned that people will listen to him and his feelings will be accepted. However, he will have to solve the problem himself.

14-15

Active listening is a nonverbal skill that helps children develop self-esteem.

Ignoring

Do not encourage inappropriate behavior. When a child is able to gain your attention by whining, crying, or throwing a temper tantrum, you have reinforced the child's behavior. The child will likely continue this behavior rather than control it.

If a child's inappropriate behavior is not dangerous, avoid giving the child attention. Do not look directly at the child. Avoid acknowledging the behavior. This is called *ignoring*. On the other hand, praise the child when he or she models acceptable behavior.

Ignoring is inappropriate when the child's behavior is harmful, either verbally or physically, to the child or others. Likewise, it is inappropriate to ignore a child who is damaging property. If you choose to ignore the behavior, you should tell the child what the behavior is that you are ignoring. Also, tell the child the behavior you desire. Then, do not look at the child. Be sure you do not acknowledge the behavior in any way through your actions or words. When the child models acceptable behavior, praise him or her.

For example, Mrs. Garcia has noticed that whenever Miranda wants something she whines and uses baby talk. Mrs. Garcia tells Miranda that she will not pay attention

Vocabulary

Have a student volunteer define the guidance technique of *ignoring*. How often do you have to use ignoring before a child is ready to change inappropriate behavior?

Discuss

When should you *not* ignore a child's inappropriate behavior? What message should you give the child when you notice an improvement in behavior?

Resource

Techniques for Effective Guidance, Activity C, OG

Putting Technology to Use

Ask students to conduct an Internet search for information on the process of active listening. What are the major benefits and outcomes of engaging in active listening? How does active listening help an educator's effectiveness in the classroom? How can active listening help improve students' motivation and communication skills? Have students explain the steps involved in active listening and give examples of each step.

Vocabulary

Have a student volunteer define the term *encouraging.* How is encouraging different from persuading?

Resource

Evaluating Self-Concept, Activity D, OG

Discuss

Which children in the vocational preschool exhibit positive self-concepts? Which children exhibit signs of inadequacy or lack of confidence? Give examples of a child's actions and behavior that leads you to this conclusion.

to her until she uses her "big girl" voice. Mrs. Garcia also demonstrates for Miranda what she means. Miranda continues to whine and use baby talk, so Mrs. Garcia ignores Miranda's requests. Eventually Miranda uses the appropriate words, and Mrs. Garcia answers Miranda's request.

Changing a young child's behavior is usually not a quick process. In fact, the behavior may actually become worse before it improves! It is important to be patient. Unless you ignore unpleasant behavior 100 percent of the time, it is likely to reoccur.

Encouraging

Encouraging is a guidance technique that helps children believe in themselves. By *encouraging* children, you are recognizing their efforts and improvements. You may observe that successful teachers often use this technique. They want children to feel good about themselves. Examples of encouraging phrases you may use include:

- You can do it all by yourself!
- You know how it works.
- I know you can fix it.
- You were able to do it last week.
- You must be pleased.

Promoting a Positive Self-Concept

When guiding children's behavior, your actions should always promote a positive self-concept in each child. A child's self-concept includes the qualities the child believes he or she possesses. It is a result of beliefs, feelings, and perceptions a child has of himself or herself, 14-16. Children's self-concepts reflect the feelings others have for them and the confidence they have in themselves. A child's self-concept develops gradually and continues into adulthood.

14-16

A child with a healthy self-esteem is not afraid to explore new and different types of play.

During early childhood, another part of the self-concept emerges. This is *self-esteem.* Self-esteem involves making judgments about your own worth and feelings. It answers the question "How worthy am I?" It is the belief that you are a worthwhile person.

Children's self-esteem is mirrored in their behavior. A child who lacks confidence may reveal feelings of inadequacy. For instance, the child may not be willing to try new activities, may withdraw from an experience, show little curiosity, or appear overly anxious or overly dependent. This child may also be hostile, seek attention, or perform poorly.

Children with positive self-esteem perceive themselves as able and important. They accept and respect themselves as well as others. These children are often able to judge their own skills and cope with problems they confront. Typically, they are more objective and understand other people's behaviors.

You can promote or undermine a child's self-esteem by your words and actions. In

Workplace Connection

Have students write a lesson plan for preschoolers to teach them the skill of encouraging. Students may have children create an art project or engage in gross-motor activities. Follow the activities with a circle activity to demonstrate encouraging and discuss how this might have motivated the children who participated. Students may also choose to model encouraging and observe to see if children begin to use the technique themselves. Refer students to lesson plan design in Chapter 18 to include all eight steps in their lesson plan.

many subtle ways, a teacher affects how children feel about themselves. Your reactions may give children the feeling they are bad or annoying. For instance, you may need to ask children to be quiet. Consider the message the children will receive. If you ask them to be quiet because they are too noisy, they may feel they are bad people because they make too much noise. If you ask them to make less noise because it is disturbing you, the children see they can help you by being quiet. They do not feel they are bad, noisy people.

If a child spills juice, do you call the child clumsy or react negatively by scowling? Instead, do you accept this as common behavior for a young child and help wipe up the spill? Caring adults are able to separate children's needs from their own. Clearly, they are able to see the difference between adult's needs and children's.

Every day you provide subtle messages in the form of verbal and nonverbal feedback. These signals can either promote or decrease children's sense of self-esteem. You can make children feel appreciated, worthy, loved, and secure by being accepting, concerned, and respectful. Helping young children grow to respect themselves, as well as others, is not easy. Listen carefully to what you say and how you say it. Consider the impact your words have on the children. Watch the subtle ways you interact with them. Your message should always convey that they are important. Review the checklist shown in 14-17 to see if you are promoting positive self-esteem.

A child's self-concept is reflected in his or her stress-coping abilities. Children who spend time with nurturing and supportive adults develop more effective coping skills. Gradually they learn that their lives are influenced by the choices they make. Moreover, they learn that all choices have consequences.

There are many ways you as a teacher can promote the development of positive self-esteem. You can plan activities that focus on making children feel good about themselves

14-17

Teacher Checklist for Promoting Positive Self-Esteem

- ✓ Do I observe children carefully before speaking?
- ✓ Am I an open-minded person?
- ✓ Do I recognize and value differences in children?
- ✓ Do I constantly strive to gain more knowledge about the world and share it with the children?
- ✓ Do I provide the children with choices so they may become independent decision makers?
- ✓ Am I constantly trying to increase my human relations skills?
- ✓ Do I state directions in a positive manner?
- ✓ Do I encourage parents to share their attitudes with me?
- ✓ Do I avoid showing favoritism?
- ✓ Do I listen to the children?
- ✓ Do I help children sort out their mixed emotions?
- ✓ Do I plan developmentally appropriate activities?
- ✓ Do I respect cultural differences in young children?
- ✓ Do I permit enough time to complete activities?
- ✓ Do I call attention to positive interactions between and among children?
- ✓ Do I make expectations clear?
- ✓ Do I acknowledge the child's attempts at tasks as well as accomplishments?
- ✓ Do I encourage children to use self-statements of confidence?
- ✓ Do I use praise effectively?

The teacher's behavior can promote or hinder development of positive self-esteem.

and their abilities. Several are described in 14-18. You can also provide children with experiences with which they will have success.

Reflect

Did you ever experience a situation as a young child in which a teacher or other adult reacted negatively to your ideas, suggestions, or behavior? How did the incident affect your self-esteem? Ask student volunteers to share their experiences with the class.

Discuss

In the situation where a child spills juice, what are the child's needs that should be considered? What are the adult's needs in this situation?

Resource

Putting Effective Guidance into Practice, Activity C, SAG

Putting Technology to Use

Ask students to conduct an Internet search for information on teacher burnout. Have students define the term *burnout* and list the major causes. What role do unruly and unmotivated students play in a teacher's decision to leave the teaching field? Explain how early attention to the promotion of positive guidance techniques might have an impact on student behavior that would affect the rate of teacher burnout. Have students write a report of their findings. Allow time for students to share their reports in class.

14-18

Building Positive Self-Esteem

After an outing, make an experience chart. Include children's names and their exact words.

Provide a special chair and crown for each child on his or her birthday. Take an instant photo of the child.

Make a slide show of the children in action: on a field trip, at a party, at a play, or at the end of an ongoing project. Present the slide show to the children.

Record children's stories from sharing and telling time on a large piece of posterboard titled *Our News*.

Make charts of children's likes. For instance, you might chart children's favorite colors or animals.

Make charts of hair and eye color to reinforce concepts of similarities and differences among people.

Tape-record children telling their own stories.

Make height and weight charts.

Add a full-length mirror to the room.

Label children's lockers and artwork with their names.

Make a mobile or bulletin board with the children's pictures or names.

Provide children with family face puppets of various cultures. Encourage children to act out imaginary family situations using the puppets.

Outline children's bodies on large sheets of paper for them to decorate and display.

Provide dramatic play kits to encourage children to try new roles and roles they find interesting. For example, a carpenter kit could include a hat, an apron, a hammer, nails, and boxes or scraps of wood.

Display children's pictures at their eye level.

Use children's names frequently in songs and games.

These activities are quite useful for helping children build positive self-esteem.

Discuss

After reviewing the list of ideas in 14-18, *Building Positive Self-Esteem*, brainstorm any additional ideas that students may have to add to the list. How many of the activities listed can be incorporated in the vocational child care lab?

Activity

Assign students tasks from the list of suggested activities in 14-18, *Building Positive Self-Esteem*, that include displays with the children's names. Make sure students use a consistent printing style on all projects and only the first letter of each name is written in a capital letter. Have students display their projects in class.

Resource

Guidance Techniques, Activity D, SAG

Meeting Special Needs

Review the special learners' chapter outlines to determine if the students have any questions about the concepts or content of this chapter. Review the chapter objectives and ask the students to evaluate their progress in meeting these objectives. Ask the students to summarize, orally or in writing, what they learned from this chapter.

Summary

Effective guidance skills are necessary for effective teaching. Effective guidance should maintain children's self-esteem and produce a desired change in behavior. Self-regulation and self-control are the long-term goals of guidance. That is, the children should learn to direct their own behavior without outside control. Another goal of guidance is to promote prosocial behaviors among the children.

Child guidance may be direct or indirect. Direct guidance involves physical and verbal actions. The direct guidance principles described in this chapter will help you to more effectively guide children's behavior. Indirect guidance involves outside factors that influence behavior. One important factor that indirectly affects guidance is the physical setup of the classroom.

You may wish to develop some specific guidance techniques to help in creating a positive environment. These include positive reinforcement, natural and logical consequences, warning, time-out, I-messages, praising, affirming, suggesting, prompting, persuading, redirecting, modeling, listening, ignoring, and encouraging.

When guiding children's behavior, your actions should always promote a positive self-esteem in each child. A child's self-esteem includes the qualities the child believes he or she possesses.

Review and Reflect

1. What are prosocial behaviors?
2. Studies show that _____ teachers have more hyperactive, disruptive, and bored students.
3. Why do children of permissive teachers often exhibit aggressive and attention-seeking behavior?
4. Describe one of the general guidelines you should follow for effective guidance to occur.
5. Give three examples of actions useful in direct guidance.
6. Use positive guidance statements to rewrite the following:
   A. Do not scream!
   B. Do not get paint on your dress.
   C. Do not spill the milk.
   D. Quit running!
7. Name the direct guidance principle being used in each of the following examples.
   A. Penny was disciplined yesterday for running through the cooking area. When she ran through the cooking area today, she was again disciplined.
   B. The children are playing in the art area. It will be lunchtime in 10 minutes. Their teacher says to them, "Children, it is almost time for lunch. Please start cleaning up the area."
   C. Henry is running from one end of the teeter-totter to the other. His teacher comes over to him and says, "Henry, stop that. You might hurt yourself."
   D. A teacher says to her children, "On Friday, we will be eating lunch outdoors. You can choose to have either a hot dog or a hamburger for lunch."
8. Give an example of how the physical setup of the classroom can be used to encourage independence in the children.
9. Why would a teacher want to use positive reinforcement?
10. Explain the difference between natural consequences and logical consequences.

6. A. Talk quietly.
   B. Wear a smock.
   C. Pour the milk carefully.
   D. Walk in the classroom.
7. A. Be consistent.
   B. Provide time for change.
   C. Intervene when necessary.
   D. Offer choices with care.
8. (Student response.)
9. Positive messages will encourage the child to repeat positive behavior.
10. Natural consequences are those experiences that follow naturally as a result of a behavior. Logical consequences are those that are set up by an adult to show what will happen if a limit is violated.
11. false
12. A prompt requires a response; a suggestion does not.
13. redirecting
14. Through active listening, you first listen to what the child is saying to you. Then you respond to the child by repeating what was just said.
15. false
16. (List three. Student response.)

Review and Reflect **Answer Key**

1. acts of kindness that benefit others; behaviors that demonstrate cooperation and helpfulness
2. uncooperative
3. It is thought that failure of permissive teachers to become involved is seen by children as permission to engage in aggressive and attention-seeking behavior.
4. (Describe one.)
5. (List three. Student response.)

11. True or false. Praise should be given at the end of the day for any positive behaviors observed during the day.

12. How does a prompt differ from a suggestion?

13. The key to _____ is supplying an appealing substitute.

14. Explain the process of active listening.

15. True or false. Ignoring is an appropriate guidance technique when the child's behavior is verbally harmful to other children.

16. List three ways that you can encourage the development of children's positive self-esteem.

Cross-Curricular Link

Language Arts

1. Practice verbal guidance techniques by showing a friend how to use a puzzle.

Technology

2. Search the online catalog for the National Association for the Education of Young Children (www.naeyc.org) for resources on guidance and discipline of young children. Use the computer to create a bibliography listing these resources.

Workplace Link

Write an article for a parent newsletter explaining the strategies you will use in the classroom to help children become independent. Explain in your article why developing independence skills is important for preschoolers. Offer suggestions on how parents can encourage children to practice these skills at home. Give examples of the tasks that three-, four-, and five-year-old children can perform by themselves. File a copy of the article in your portfolio.

Apply and Explore

1. Observe a teacher interacting with children for one hour. Record all incidences of verbal guidance.

2. Discuss situations in which a teacher may have to intervene in the classroom.

3. Conduct a self-observation. Using a tape recorder, record your interactions with children. Listen to your interactions. Were they positive? Did you help the children in identifying and labeling positive behavior? How would you change some of your interactions with the children to make them more positive?

4. Make a list of children's activities that promote a positive self-esteem.

5. Observe in a classroom setting for half an hour. List all examples of praise you hear. After your observation, identify each example as effective or ineffective praise.

15

Guidance Challenges

Discuss

What guidance challenges do you think the teacher might be facing in the chapter opening photo? What do you observe about the children's behavior? What does this say about guidance?

Discuss

Look over the chapter objectives. How can studying guidance challenges help you handle or avoid these problems in your early childhood classroom?

After studying this chapter, you will be able to

- identify situations and feelings that cause tension in children.
- describe behavior problems that result from tension.
- guide children as they learn appropriate social-emotional skills.
- describe the effect of family stressors on children and families.

Vocabulary

Review the *Terms to Know* list. Ask students to look up unfamiliar words in the glossary before reading the chapter.

Reflect

What stressors during a typical school day cause you to experience tension? How similar are these stressors to those typically experienced by a preschooler?

Vocabulary

Have a student volunteer define *overstimulated*. Have students explain the effects of overstimulation on the preschool child.

Terms to Know

overstimulated

frustration

stress

All behavior is goal directed and purposeful. Four-year-old Missy is an example. She is tattling on the other children. After arriving at the center, she told the teacher that Toby had pushed her the day before. During snacktime, she announced loudly that Hunter did not take the muffin he touched. Later, during clean-up time, she told the teacher that Jafar did not put away his puzzle.

Hoa does not like to take a nap during naptime. He begins crying every day after lunch as naptime approaches. Yolanda, who is normally very cooperative, has been less so in the weeks following the birth of her new brother. Rather than taking turns, she has become bossy on the playground. The teacher has also seen her hitting other children.

During your teaching career, you will likely have several children in your classes who will model behavior similar to that of Missy, Hoa, and Yolanda. Many times, behavior problems will be disruptive to the class. The behavior may be harmful or it might infringe on the rights of others. Mishandling of classroom pets, equipment, and materials may also occur.

Disruptive behavior often is caused by tension. Overstimulation, changes in routine, and loud noise are just a few causes of tension in children. Because children do not know how to handle tension, they often react with disruptive behavior such as pushing and disturbing other children, running, and yelling, 15-1. They lack the skills in masking their feelings and expressing them in words.

Helping children deal positively with tension-causing events is an important role of the teacher. You will need to understand situations and feelings that cause tension in children. Recognizing behavior patterns that

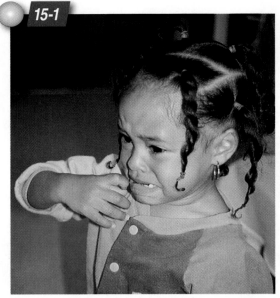

15-1

Some children cry and withdraw from the group when they feel tension.

result from tension is also important. Then you will need to be able to help children deal with this tension. With this information, you will be able to effectively guide and help children.

Causes of Behavioral Problems

There are many causes of behavioral problems in children. These include certain stressors and frustrations children do not know how to handle. In addition, there are physical problems that can cause tension in children. Being aware of situations and emotions that produce tension is important. This knowledge will allow you to avoid these causes, or at least reduce the effects of them.

Overstimulation

Children can become overexcited, or **overstimulated**, by many things. For instance, simply playing with other children

Meeting Special Needs

Provide an outline of the chapter with all the chapter headings for special learners. Students should fill in each section of the outline as the material is covered in class with a sentence or two about the content. Review the special learners' IEPs to decide if any modifications should be made in presenting the chapter content.

can overstimulate some children, 15-2. Usually, the larger the group of children, the greater the likelihood that overstimulation will occur. You may want to limit the number of children that can be in a certain classroom area at any time. This will help prevent the chaos created when a large group of children play together. For example, post a sign in the blockbuilding area limiting the space to four children at any given time. For younger children who do not read, make a simple sign showing four stick people. It will serve the same purpose. Similar signs can be posted in other areas of the classroom.

Some children become overstimulated when there are program changes. Holidays, such as Halloween and Valentine's Day, can be overstimulating times for children. Avoid making holiday plans too early. When this

happens, the children may get keyed up long before the event occurs.

Overstimulation can also result from having too many activities planned. When this happens, some children have a hard time making choices. Instead of staying with one activity, they run back and forth between several. Their activity and excitement, in turn, can affect others.

Breaks in Routines

Routines are important to children. They let children know what to expect and when. If routines are not followed, children become confused. Behavior problems can arise. For instance, Jimmy takes a nap at 12:30 p.m. everyday. If this schedule is not followed, he may become overtired. This may result in disruptive behavior. If a child's family follows a different routine at home from that of the center, this can affect the child's behavior. Family members may notice behavior problems at home because the child does not know what to expect next. In addition, you may see more behavior problems after weekends and holidays when the child readjusts after being away from the center for a few days. Talking with the family members about these problems may help them adjust their schedule to more closely match the child's routine at the center.

All children need consistent daily schedules. Quiet activities need to be followed by active activities, 15-3. If children sit still too long, they may lose interest in the activity and become disruptive. Likewise, if children remain active too long, they may become overstimulated and disruptive. When changes in routine are necessary, such as a planned field trip, prepare the children ahead of time. Talk to them about what will happen. Also, explain to the children what your expectations are before, during, and after the trip.

15-2

The combination of being outside and climbing on a jungle gym can cause overstimulation in some children.

Discuss

What can be the major benefit to children in preschool programs that avoid celebrating holidays such as Halloween and Valentine's Day? Do any programs like this exist in your area?

Activity

Ask students to determine the maximum number of children that should be allowed at a time in each of the activity centers in the child care lab. What factors did they use to help determine these numbers?

Discuss

What situations in the child care lab schedule may contribute to changes in routine? How might these changes be minimized so children are less stressed?

Workplace Connection

Have students conduct a survey of area child care programs to discover how they handle the period between Thanksgiving and New Year's Day. Have students ask the following questions: Are special activities, guests, or entertainments planned that differ from the regular schedule?

Do children display more energetic or atypical behavior during this period even if holiday events are not part of the program? Do parochial and secular programs differ in their programs' focus during this holiday period? Have students share their findings with the class.

Reflect

Waiting time can definitely be a stressor in the preschool. Have you been responsible for any situations in the child care lab where a lengthy waiting time caused any children to be disruptive? What should you have done differently to avoid this problem?

Vocabulary

Have a student volunteer define *frustration*. Ask students what activities they have observed that may cause children to become frustrated.

Resource

Guidance Advice, reproducible master 15-2, TR

15-3

After a quiet activity, such as storytime, children need periods of active free play.

Noise

Noise affects children differently. Children with very sensitive ears are particularly upset by noise. For example, these children will cover their ears or cry when a smoke alarm goes off. Likewise, if an ambulance drives by with its siren wailing, some children will cringe. While some children may try only to escape the noise, others may react by pushing or hitting others.

To avoid the problems caused by noise, control the volume of tapes and CDs. Also pay attention to the volume of your own voice. In frustration, you may raise your voice or yell. Unfortunately, this causes a chain reaction. As the volume of your voice increases, the children's voices also become louder. This, in turn, will affect children sensitive to noise. The result will be chaos.

Waiting Time

Children often begin leaving the group or behave poorly when they have to wait for long periods of time. By nature, they are usually in motion. Therefore, if they are kept

waiting too long for a story, they may start pushing or hitting. This behavior is not the children's fault. However, it may gain the teacher's disapproval. If this occurs, it may damage the children's self-concepts.

Manage your time wisely. Cut down on waiting time by being prepared. If you are going to read a book for a large group, choose it in advance. Place it where it will be convenient. Likewise, prepare materials for all group activities in advance. If the children are actively involved in self-selected activities, it will reduce waiting time and resulting behavior problems.

Frustration

Children sometimes feel they are not in control. They feel defeated or discouraged. These feelings are called **frustration**. They cause tension in children, 15-4. In order to

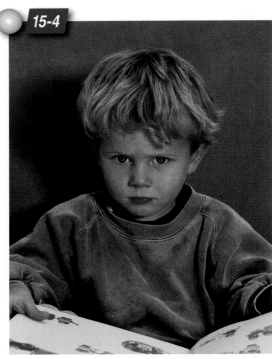

15-4

Being in control is important for young children. When they are not in control, they may become frustrated.

Workplace Connection

Conduct an experiment in the child care lab to determine the optimum time that children should spend on specific activities to avoid behavior challenges. An example may be to spend twenty, fifteen, and ten minutes respectively on different days on gross-motor, fine-motor, and circle time activities. How long should free play or discovery time activities be conducted? Ask students to discuss their observations with the class and make suggestions for future scheduling.

control frustration, carefully plan each day's activities. The activities you choose should be developmentally appropriate. They should reflect the needs, interests, abilities, and experiences of the children in the center.

Some children arrive at the center full of energy. These children need to be active. Provide wheeled toys, blockbuilding materials, and woodworking activities for these children. Other children prefer quiet activities, such as books, puzzles, stringing beads, or play dough. By observing the children in your program, you can provide the proper activities, materials, supplies, and equipment.

Forcing children into activities they are not prepared to join can result in frustration. A better approach is to allow the children to decide what is best.

Conflicts often arise over toys, which creates frustration. Therefore, make certain that several kinds of toys are available to children at all times. Whenever possible, you should purchase several toys of the same kind. To prevent conflict, always buy more than one telephone, wagon, scooter, or car.

Select materials and equipment to match children's developmental level. This allows the children to feel success and develop an "I can do it" attitude. Working with mixed-aged groups presents special problems. Include open-ended materials such as blocks, play dough, and sand. Children of all ages will play with these, but in different ways. See 15-5. Provide puzzles, small manipulatives, and books for a range of abilities.

When necessary, redirect children to materials that match their abilities. Repeated failures will cause frustration, which may lead to anger. An angry child may pinch, hit, push, kick, or bite.

As an adult, you may become frustrated. When this happens, try to relax. Carefully watch your words and actions. If the children sense you are upset, they, in turn, will become more upset. They need to feel you are calm and in control.

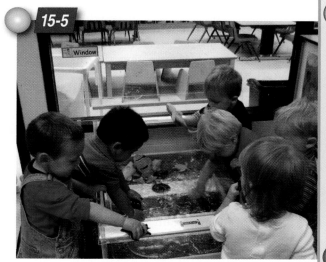

15-5

A sensory table and paints are materials that appeal to children of many ages.

Physical Problems

Poor health or other physical problems can cause tension and behavioral problems in children. One teacher, Mr. Peterson, had such a problem in his center. During Ethan's first day at the center, Mr. Peterson and several other teachers observed Ethan. They feared he would be a behavior problem. He ignored all directions and suggestions made by Mr. Peterson. Ethan also seemed to have a high anxiety level.

Ethan's behavior became a source of frustration for Mr. Peterson. More than once, he wondered whether Ethan should even be in the center. He feared that other children would copy Ethan's behavior. Mr. Peterson was also concerned about his ability to handle Ethan's behavior. This concern continued for several weeks.

Mr. Peterson finally decided to ask the center director to observe Ethan's behavior. After observing Ethan, the director determined a possible cause for Ethan's problem. First, the director noted that Ethan did not respond to many of the verbal requests made by Mr. Peterson or other children. The director also noted that

Discuss

Should the energetic and very active children in the class *have* to participate in a quiet time activity such as story time? If not, how can you meet the child's needs while still managing the classroom and providing a well-rounded and developmentally appropriate program?

Reflect

Have you ever become angry and frustrated when children do not behave when you are teaching in the child care lab? Were children aware of your feelings? How did you handle the situation? What was the effect on the children?

Activity

As an experiment, display negative or frustrating behavior to your students when they arrive for class and keep up the behavior for five to ten minutes. Afterwards, explain to your students that you were just testing them. Survey the class to find out what effect your behavior had on each of them.

Meeting Special Needs

Arrange for gifted students to visit your local early childhood special education program. Have these students observe children with behavior disorders and answer the following questions: What techniques are used to help children gain self-control and handle challenging behaviors? What successes do the special education teachers have with these techniques? What strategies observed might be adapted for use in the child care lab? Ask students to prepare a report on their observations to share with the class.

Activity

Review the physical health records of all the children in the child care lab with the class. Determine if any of the children have health concerns that could lead to guidance challenges. Discuss how the students may have to modify any activities as a result.

Discuss

What is the difference between an *onlooker* and an *aggressive* child? What strategies should preschool teachers use with children who display these characteristics?

Activity

Have students find out what health restrictions, if any, exist in your school district that might prevent a child from participating in the child care lab. Have students determine if additional training may be necessary to avoid guidance challenges when children with health concerns are enrolled in the program.

while interacting with others, Ethan closely watched their faces when they spoke. The director suspected that Ethan had hearing loss. For added information, the director then picked up two wooden blocks, stood behind Ethan, and clapped them together as hard as she could. While several other children either jumped or turned to see what was happening, Ethan did not respond.

Before sharing these observations with Ethan's father, Mr. Peterson repeated the clapping incident. Ethan failed to respond. In addition, other staff members tried speaking to him when they were out of his field of vision. Again, each time he failed to respond. At this point, the center director shared these observations with Ethan's father. She encouraged Ethan's father to have his hearing tested.

Luckily for Ethan, his father, the staff, and other children in the center, the cause of Ethan's behavioral problems was pinpointed. After having his hearing tested, Ethan received a hearing aid. His behavior improved dramatically. At the same time, his speech also improved.

Children may be overly active or tense due to other health problems, 15-6. A child who is in constant pain due to lack of dental or medical care may act inappropriately.

Medications can affect some children's behavior. Observe for symptoms such as dilated pupils, drowsiness, slurred speech, poor coordination, and general irritability. In many states, parents are required to report to the staff when their children are on medication.

Prolonged or recurring illness or hospitalization can cause frequent absences from the center. When this occurs, some children are not able to maintain their friendships. Coming back to the center is difficult for them. Some of these children may become *onlookers*. This means they watch others, but do not get involved. Other children may become aggressive. By acting out, they hope to gain the other children's attention. Onlookers and aggressive children

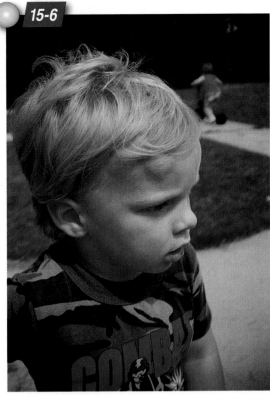

15-6

Pain from this child's head injury may cause him to be tense and uncooperative.

need your help. Carefully observe them. Focus on their needs.

An onlooker needs to get involved. Encourage this child by suggesting activities he or she might try. If the child does not respond, gently take the child by the hand and walk him or her to an appealing activity. You may have to play with the child for awhile or involve other children in the activity.

Aggressive children need a calming influence. Direct these children to activities in which they can release energy. For instance, direct the aggressive child to woodworking, sculpting, or water play activities.

Poor or inadequate nutrition can also affect behavior. Studies show that between one-fourth and one-third of preschool

---

Cross-Curricular Activity

Health

Have students interview the health instructor to discover how the subject of students' health challenges is treated. What strategies or precautions are taught to students to help them avoid health risks? How is the subject of bloodborne pathogens approached? Ask all the students in the class who have already taken Health to anything from the course that could be applied to the child care lab.

children do not receive the caloric intake recommended for them. Children who do not have the proper caloric intake or nutrients may be inattentive and sluggish. Motor skills and motivation are also affected.

Stress

Stress is the body's reaction to physical or emotional danger signals. This reaction often takes the form of tension. Mild or occasional stress is not a problem. However, constant stress, prolonged stress, or the piling up of many stressors can threaten a child's ability to cope.

The foundations for life are laid during childhood. Early in life, children watch how adults cope with stress. Children learn their responses to stress from these adults. As a result, children vary widely in how they handle stress. Children who learn negative coping skills may become more prone to stress. They may become illness-prone, withdrawn, nervous, aggressive, or angry. On the other hand, some children learn positive coping strategies. These children are resilient—they bounce back quickly from stress.

Stress can be caused by both negative and positive events. One negative event that can cause stress in children is the breakup of a family. Even the most amicable divorce is a major stressor for young children because it disrupts the family stability. Other negative stressors include abuse, neglect, rejection, separation, and fights. Positive events that cause stress may include parties, vacations, overnight visits with friends or relatives, the birth of a sibling, or getting a new pet.

Starting child care or changing to a new early childhood program can be stressful for some children. In many centers, children also move from one classroom to another as they get older. Adjusting to new teachers, playmates, and surroundings can take time. Learning a new routine can also cause tension. This stress should subside as the child adjusts to the new center or classroom.

Helping children feel safe and welcome is the most helpful way to ease this discomfort.

In poor-quality programs, however, the stress continues. Programs with insufficient adult-child ratios and large group sizes cannot adequately meet children's needs. Adults in these programs often lack the necessary time to nurture each child's development. These programs often lack enough toys and materials for the number of children enrolled. The facilities may be inadequate in other ways, too.

Family Stressors

As the primary social unit, the family can serve as a buffer from stress. It can also be a source of many stressors in a child's life. The influences of family can be positive or negative, depending on how the family operates. Family harmony is important for the health of all the members. Stress within the family disrupts this harmony. All family members, including young children, can be affected. Stress can also strain family relationships. Children can sense this tension.

Family crises cause major stress within a family. See 15-7 for a list of family stressors. What others can you identify? In any of these situations, daily family life will be disrupted, at least for a time. Resulting changes in routine can upset infants as well as older children. These children lose a sense of predictability and security when they do not know what to expect next. This can cause children to become irritable, have problems eating and sleeping, and become clingy or demanding. These are normal responses to stress.

In some families, the stressor is a temporary condition. For example, the loss of a parent's job may be short-lived as the parent seeks a new job. With other stressors, family life is permanently changed, such as with a death or divorce. Extra support from friends, extended family, and the community may be needed to cope with a permanent stressor.

Discuss

Have you eaten a nutritious breakfast or lunch today? If not, have you had any difficulties paying attention in school? Did the lack of attention cause any behavior or guidance challenges?

Vocabulary

Have student volunteer define *stress* and *stressors*. Ask students what might be some results of constant stress on children.

Reflect

What family stressors affect your participation and behavior in school? How can you use this knowledge to help children who may also be experiencing family stressors?

Resource

Family Stressors, transparency master 15-1, TR

Putting Technology to Use

Have students conduct an Internet search for information on the effects of family stress on preschoolers. Students should research answers to the following questions: What stressful life events in a family most affect children? How do children typically manage these events? What are the effects of family stress on a child's behavior and on academic performance? How can a preschool teacher use this information to help a child deal with stress?

Discuss

What is the effect on a child when caregivers offer consistent, predictable, and responsive care? What is likely to happen if the child does not receive this type of care?

Note

Review with students the term *window of opportunity* in relation to the development of a child's brain. This term first appeared in Chapter 4, *Child Development Principles and Theories*. Ask students what is critical about the window of opportunity in handling stress.

Resource

Family Stressors Affect Guidance, Activity C, SAG

15-7

Possible Family Stressors

Birth or adoption of a sibling

Marriage, separation, or divorce of parent(s)

Custody, visitation, or child support issues

Marriage of a parent

Stay-at-home parent entering the workforce

Family member moving into or out of home

Serious illness of self or family member

Death of a friend, family member, or pet

Moving to a new home

Friend moving away

Parent's loss of employment

Financial or legal problems in the family

Substance abuse or addiction of family member

Exposure to violence (unsafe neighborhood)

Incarceration of family member

Becoming homeless

Arguing, fighting, or violence among family members

Abuse or neglect of self or family member

Crisis and changes within the family account for much of the stress children feel.

Being constantly active from morning to night causes another, less intense type of stress. In a family with this schedule, a young child's needs may be overlooked as parents and older siblings rush to meet their obligations. Both children and adults need time to unwind and be together as a family. Family time and relaxation help people ward off the harmful effects of stress.

Handling family stressors of any type is difficult for young children. The intensity of a child's reaction will depend on how threatening the stressor is. Children feel worse if they believe they have caused a divorce, separation, death, or other family crisis. Feeling their behavior caused the crisis leads children to feel guilty. Explaining that a crisis is not a child's fault can be helpful.

Effects of Stress

Prolonged stress in early childhood can undermine healthy brain development. A child depends on his or her environment for experiences that will promote optimal brain development. Stimulation from caregivers also influences the wiring of the brain. That is why consistent, predictable, and responsive care is needed.

Good beginnings can last a lifetime. Healthy relationships promote brain growth and healthy social attachment. A strong, secure attachment to a nurturing caregiver appears to provide a protective biological structure. It buffers children from the effects of stress. Studies show children with strong, secure attachments have fewer behavioral problems when confronted with stress throughout life.

Neuroscientists describe *windows of opportunity* in the development of a child's brain. These are periods when experiences or the lack of experiences will have the greatest impact. The window of opportunity for learning to control emotions and cope with stress is limited. This period extends only from birth to three years of age.

In addition, abuse, neglect, or constant stress can cause the body to release chemicals that impact the brain's complex wiring. The effects are lasting; they include smaller brain size and diminished ability to control emotions and behavior. Children with these problems find it harder to form lasting relationships with others.

Service Learning Activity

Have students contact a local youth services agency, welfare agency, board of health, or state department of children and families to discover what programs may be available to young mothers. What services are provided to help reduce stress for young mothers? Have students find out what other volunteer opportunities exist at these agencies and publicize the need for helpers. Students may also volunteer for babysitting and other child care tasks that may help a young mother to cope with the stresses of parenthood.

Signs of Stress

When family stability is disrupted, this can often be observed in the children's behavior. A frequent sign of stress is regression. *Regression* means showing behaviors that were typical at earlier stages of development. Toileting accidents and thumbsucking are examples. A child who has used the toilet successfully for some time may begin to have accidents. Likewise, a child who had given up thumbsucking might revert to soothing himself or herself with this habit.

In addition to regression, many other behavior changes can indicate children are stressed. Being aware of the common signs of stress listed in Figure 15-8 is also helpful. Sometimes, however, these behaviors can be unrelated to stress. How then can you determine which signs are caused by stress? Knowing the typical behavior of each child in your class helps you note these behavior changes.

15-8

Possible Signs of Stress in Young Children

- Accident-proneness
- Anger
- Anxiety
- Baby talk
- Bed wetting
- Biting
- Crying spells
- Detachment
- Eating problems
- Excessive aggressiveness
- Excessive laziness
- Fingernail biting
- Headaches
- Hitting
- Indigestion
- Insomnia
- Irritability
- Kicking
- Nightmares
- Pounding heart
- Respiratory tract illness
- Stuttering
- Tattling
- Teeth grinding
- Temper tantrums
- Thumbsucking

The problems shown in this list may signal stress.

Health and Safety

Policy on Aggressive Behavior

Aggressive behavior in children can happen in the early childhood setting. Even with the most careful planning, children may sometimes act out. As an extension of the written discipline policy, a facility should include procedures to follow when an act of aggression occurs. The policy procedures may include the following:

- training staff in guidance techniques in caring for victims of aggressive acts

- training staff in discipline techniques to avoid rewarding children who act aggressively

- separating children who act out

- notifying parents of all children involved, especially if another child or staff member was hurt or bitten

- completing an incident report if the act caused an injury requiring first aid or other medical attention

- reviewing staff-to-child ratios to determine if enough staff was present to prevent the act

- examining facility layout and activity plans to avoid potential sources of conflict

Vocabulary

Have students define *regression*. Ask how likely is it that regression could be caused by a disruption in family stability.

Reflect

Have you ever noticed a behavior change in yourself, a family member, or friend? How many times was this behavior change related to stress? How often were these changes *not* related to stress?

Resource

Possible Signs of Stress, Activity A, OG

Workplace Connection

Have students locate storybooks for young children that deal with typical situations that may cause a child stress. After reading the story to the children, students should ask children how they would feel in a similar situation. Some suggested books are: *A Boy and a Bear*; *When I Feel Angry*; *The Very Angry Day That Amy Didn't Have*; *The Ugly Duckling*; and *The Berenstain Bears and Mama's New Job*, among others.

Reflect

What would you say to a child who has suddenly started sucking his or her thumb during preschool? How would you make sure the child's self-esteem was not affected negatively?

Discuss

What are some skills that adults use to handle the pressure of stress? When are children likely to develop these skills?

Enrich

Have students research community resources that can help families in crisis. Have them create a booklet of different types of resources available, including each resource's address, phone number, Web site, e-mail address, or any other contact information.

Communicating with Families About Stress

A partnership with families is important to support children's development. Two-way communication between teachers and families is vital. Teachers should realize the important role families play in children's lives and vice versa.

Families have a responsibility to support children through times of stress and crisis. Children depend on and turn to family members (especially parents) to protect them from the effects of stress. Parents can often provide the comfort children need to overcome stress. By their example, parents teach children how to cope with stress and handle problems.

As a teacher, you can help children handle stress when you are aware of family situations that could affect the child's behavior. Ask parents to keep you informed of any major family events, such as births and deaths. Events that change the structure of the family are also important, such as marriage, separation, or divorce. Children need the loving support of family and teachers through these times of adjustment.

If a child's behavior changes suddenly, share with the family the signs of stress you have noticed. Ask what they think might be causing the stress. Work with family members to plan ways to help the child and address the troubling behavior. As with other guidance issues, children benefit the most when there is consistency of guidance between parents and teachers.

Recognize, however, that crises in the family will affect parents, too. During a divorce, for example, children are not the only ones hurting—parents suffer the loss as well. While your main focus is helping the children, you want to approach this task in the most sensitive and relevant way. Listen to the parents and offer kind words to let them know you understand they must be hurting, too. If family members seem open to suggestions, you may be able to refer them to community resources that can help.

Helping Children Cope

Stress affects children as much or more than it affects adults. Unlike adults, however, children lack the skills to understand and handle the pressures. As a teacher, you can help children develop positive responses to stress.

When you note that a child's behavior has changed, observe the child more carefully. Calmly accept the child's behavior, if possible. (Of course, hurtful or unsafe behavior would be an exception to this. You must gently but firmly stop these behaviors.) Criticizing a child for his or her response to stress only leads the child to feel more stress. For example, scolding a child for thumbsucking in response to stress may make the child feel badly about himself or herself. Talk to the child about his or her feelings. Reassure the child you care about him or her. Offer comfort, closeness, and encouragement.

Provide a supportive, affectionate environment. Children exhibit less stress when teachers are attentive, 15-9. Observe carefully and really listen to the children. Talk with children about their feelings. Help them recognize, label, and clarify their feelings. Teach them coping behaviors. Use

15-9

Children are better able to handle stress when their teachers care about them enough to listen attentively.

Cross-Curricular Activity

Language Arts
Pair up students to write a possible dialogue between a teacher and a parent to show how they would handle communicating with parents about a child's stressful behavior. Assign students specific scenarios, such as aggressive behavior related to a divorce; regressive behavior related to a new baby; or anxiety and fearfulness related to a family member's serious illness and hospitalization. Have students role-play the dialogue for the rest of the class.

effective praise and acknowledge the child's actions, feelings, and progress. Correct any misconceptions children have about themselves or their feelings to help children see themselves as positive, worthwhile people.

Specific Problem Behaviors

Young children often behave in a socially unacceptable way when they are tense. Negativism, theft, anger, biting, exploration of the body, thumbsucking, and fear are all possible reactions to tension. These reactions remind us children are people, too. You must deal with and guide their behavior, just as you would an adult.

Negativism

Preschool children can be negative, particularly between two and three years of age. See 15-10. It is not unusual for a child of this age to oppose every request you make. Children at this age are wanting to become more independent. A "no" in many cases is a child's attempt at independence. For instance, you may say "Pick up the block." The child might look at you and say "No."

Handling Negative Behavior

Accept a young child's negative behavior. However, keep in mind all health and safety regulations. For example, children must wash their hands before eating. If a child refuses to do this, take the child's hands and walk him or her to the sink. Tell the child "You need to wash your hands." Let the child know, through your voice and body language, that you expect cooperation.

A negative child cannot be hurried. If he or she is hurried, opposition will be stronger. Given time, most children outgrow this stage of development.

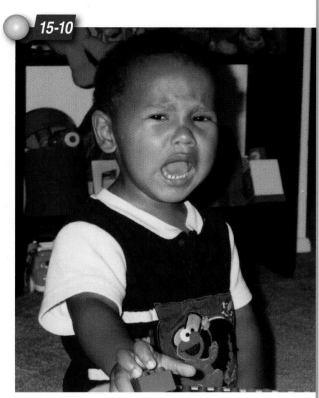
15-10

Young children may resist your requests to end their free play.

Stealing

Preschool children do not understand the difference between *mine* and *yours*. When children under three years of age take something, they are not stealing. At this age, children do not understand the concept of stealing. Before considering the needs of others, preschoolers attempt to meet their own needs. The desire for something appealing may combine with a young child's natural impulsiveness. As a result, they may take items that do not belong to them.

Small objects, such as toy cars and puzzle pieces, may vanish from the classroom. When you notice these items missing, warn the other teachers. Ask them to closely observe the children.

Reflect

Have you ever witnessed a young child and a parent in a store when the parent refuses to buy something for the child or the child refuses to cooperate with the parent? How did the parent handle the situation? Would you agree or disagree with the parent's methods?

Discuss

Why don't children under three years of age understand the concept of stealing? Should these children be disciplined for taking items that do not belong to them?

Enrich

Ask the parent of a young child who exhibits negative behavior to talk to the class. Have the class prepare questions ahead of time regarding the child's behavior and the parent's handling of the behavior.

Workplace Connection

Have students imagine the following scenario: Tony arrives at class sullen and withdrawn. He refuses to hang up his coat and join other children in a parachute activity, and he won't come to the circle for story time. He responds with "no" to any suggestions made by the teachers. He won't even participate in snack time. Ask students to list the steps they would take in analyzing Tony's behavior and determining a solution to the problem.

Discuss

A teacher observes Amanda taking crayons from Sean's cubby and putting them in her own backpack. The teacher draws Amanda aside and asks her why she took Sean's crayons. When Amanda doesn't answer, the teacher tells her that stealing is wrong. How should the teacher have handled this incident? What advice can you give her if this situation occurs again in the future?

Enrich

Have students debate the pros and cons in each choice of the following situation: Juan is angry and needs an outlet for his feelings. Should he be allowed outside to run on the playground, or should he sit in the time-out corner for five minutes until he calms down?

Activity

Have students survey the child care lab and make a list of toys and equipment that could be used to help children relieve aggressive behavior. What safety precautions, if any, are needed when children use these items to "let off steam"?

Handling Stealing

Help children learn to respect the possessions of others. If you see a child take something, do not ask the reason he or she stole it. Likewise, do not lecture about stealing. Instead, make the child return it. Otherwise, the child may keep taking things from others. Remember that preschoolers do not understand ownership.

A useful way to teach children about ownership is to respect their property rights. That is, before trying Jodi's new puzzle, ask her permission to use it. If you see another child looking at Jodi's toy, say "Why don't you ask Jodi if you can use it?"

You should also try to minimize opportunities for stealing. When children bring toys or other items from home, problems can occur. If toys are allowed to be brought to the center, there need to be clear rules. Toys are best left in the child's cubby and only taken out for naptime or show-and-tell. To avoid potential problems, many centers have a policy stating that toys should not be brought from home.

Anger

A child's anger can serve a useful purpose. Anger draws attention to something that annoys the child. You can then help that child learn to deal with anger. The greatest number of tantrums typically occur at about 18 months of age. After this age, there is a sharp decline. Age also affects how a child will project anger. Young children often use their whole bodies to express anger. By age two, children may hold their breath for as long as they can. Screaming, kicking, hitting, pounding, and hitting one's head against a wall are other ways these children express anger. By the time children turn three, verbal abuse is more common, while four-year-olds often engage in name-calling.

Handling Anger

Discourage hurting behavior. Young children should not be allowed to hit each other. However, they will try. When they do, stop them immediately. Say "I am sorry, but Jeff does not like that." At the same time, you might have to hold the child's hand. The child may try to hit you. Stop that action also. For older preschoolers, you may also use comments. For example, you may say, "You are usually kind. We cannot treat our friends this way." When young children are upset, they need calming down.

Ignoring outbursts is also a successful technique when dealing with an angry child. Of course, ignore this behavior only if there is no threat to the health and safety of the children. If children are able to get attention or gain control through outbursts, they will keep using this behavior. For example, if Carrie cries and yells for another cookie and then receives one, she will cry and yell again. On the other hand, if she does not receive the cookie, she will learn that her outburst is unacceptable.

The children need to express their feelings and assert their rights in socially acceptable ways. You can redirect anger through activities such as finger painting, modeling with clay, punching a punching bag, hammering, and playing at the sensory table, 15-11. All these activities involve use of children's hands, arms, and legs. Their anger will be redirected into physical movements. Remember to have enough supplies and equipment for these activities. Use a minimum of rules.

Surprisingly, noise can also help relieve aggression. Yelling, beating drums, dancing to loud music, crying, and making animal noises can all relieve anger. Remember, however, that noise can be catching. If several children make too much noise, the rest of the group may also become noisy.

Putting Technology to Use

Have students conduct an Internet search for information on the value of martial arts training for young children as it relates to behavior. Have them answer the following questions: What research is available that supports the idea that children exposed to martial arts training are better behaved, are more respectful, and practice good manners? What other positive effects are reported? What is the youngest age recommended for martial arts training? What styles, such as aikido, karate, or judo, are the best choices for the youngest children?

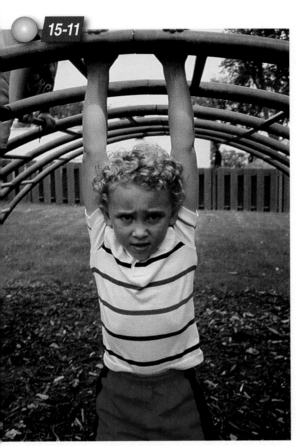

15-11

Children can release energy through physical activity.

they cannot express themselves using words. For them, biting is a form of body language. Typically, property is the main source of conflicts that result in biting.

Biting can be a reason for a class meeting. For instance, Molly Crown called a class meeting in her classroom at group time. She said, "We have a problem in our classroom. We cannot bite our friends. When you think someone is going to bite, hold up your hands and say *stop*."

Molly's meeting was successful. Whenever a child held up his or her hands and said "Stop," the impulse of the child to bite was broken. It also signaled to the teacher that there was a potential problem.

Handling Biting

You need to help children who bite. Start by keeping playtime simple for these children. Limit the number of playmates they may have at any time. Large groups often create stressful situations. Therefore, biters become nervous and then bite.

You need to respond quickly to prevent children from hurting each other. Isolation of a biter sometimes helps to curb this habit. When the child bites another, say, "Paula does not like that." Then say, "I am sorry, but you must sit down over here." Make the child sit for a few minutes, but no longer than five. Then, allow the child to return to the play area.

Do not forget the child who has been bitten. This child also needs to feel secure. To provide security, observe constantly. Never allow a child to bite back. Biting back does not prevent biting. It only creates more aggressive behavior.

Whenever possible, catch children before they react angrily. For instance, if you see that Mattie is going to kick over Tommy's blocks, stop her. Then say, "Mattie, would you like Tommy to knock over your blocks?" Mattie will be forced to think about what she was going to do.

Biting

Young children often bite when they are upset. This is not unusual behavior, particularly with two-year-olds. For many children, biting is only a temporary problem. Biting usually peaks just before children are able to use words. Children may bite because

Tattling

Tattling seems to occur in many classrooms and is a typical behavior for many young children. Frequently, the child who tattles is insecure and tattles to get your attention. As a teacher, you may find tattling irritating, but you need to listen to the

---

Note

Check your school district's policy for handling biting episodes and make students aware of their responsibility to follow the policy. A school district nurse can be consulted for accurate information. Be sure the policy is included in the child care lab parent handbook.

Discuss

Why should biting a child back never be used as a consequence or means of discipline? What messages does biting back send to the child?

Resource

Guidance Tips, Activity B, SAG

Meeting Special Needs

Modify Activity B, *Guidance Tips*, by dividing the statements into two groups for students who have difficulty handling the longer assignment. Ask students to rewrite each false statement so it is true to demonstrate their understanding. Students could also verbally restate the statements instead of writing them out.

Activity

Ask students to create a puppet play suitable for preschoolers that deals with the problem of tattling. Make sure the characters in the play use positive methods to teach children to avoid tattling behavior.

Note

Excessive exploration or touching of the body might be a sign that a child has been sexually abused. Remind students to carefully observe children for additional signs of abuse before coming to an incorrect conclusion.

Resource

Guidance Match, Activity A, SAG

children. You want the children to be aware that classroom limits are important. You do not need to be told, however, each time a child misbehaves.

Handling Tattling

To prevent tattling, try to build children's self-esteem. This, in turn, will make them feel more secure. For a child who is insecure, stay close while supervising. Knowing that a caring adult is nearby is helpful.

Try to have a daily one-to-one time for listening and talking with each child. This may be during free play or small group time. During this time, provide the child feedback by recognizing his or her positive qualities. To illustrate, you may say, "Sharice, I like the way you help Marco" or "Eileen, Brian enjoys having you help him with the puzzle." Positive reinforcement will help prevent a child's need to tattle.

Try ignoring tattling behavior. If Jared tattles to you that Ronnie has taken his scissors, comment by saying "You need to tell Ronnie to return your scissors." This encourages Jared to speak to the child who has misbehaved. Likewise, if Christopher tattles that Julia has taken his bicycle, encourage problem solving. Say "Christopher has taken your bike. What should you do?" See 15-12. If Kelsi always talks about other children, set a limit by saying "I enjoy talking with you, but we shouldn't talk about others."

Exploring the Body

Children begin to explore their bodies early in life. It is common for one-year-olds to explore their genitals during diaper changing. As children begin to gain control of their body functions, interest in the genital area grows. By three years of age, children are aware of sex differences. Boys may, in fact, become concerned because girls do not have penises. By age four, children who have to use the bathroom may hold the

15-12

To help prevent tattling, encourage children to problem-solve with each other.

genital area. When this occurs, remind the child to use the bathroom. By five years of age, children may begin to manipulate their genitals. They may do this by rubbing pillows between their legs or squeezing their thighs together tightly. Some children may rub their genitals in an effort to reduce irritation caused by tight clothing.

Handling Body Exploration

Exploration of the body is normal behavior in development. However, it is not considered proper to engage in such behavior in public. Therefore, it is important to guide children away from public display of body exploration.

During naptime, you might see children touching themselves. Children sometimes rub their genitals while trying to get to sleep. When this occurs, never shame or threaten the child. Remember, whenever possible, use a positive approach when guiding young children. This can be done by firmly telling a child privately that this behavior is impolite in public.

Thumbsucking

Like adults, children feel certain tensions. To relieve the tension, some children may suck their thumbs. Studies show that almost half

Portfolio Project

Ask students to write a brief article for the child care parent newsletter for a guidance advice column. Assign students different topics such as *handling fears*, *thumbsucking*, or *tattling*.

Select the best examples and print a different article in each issue. Students should file a copy of their printed articles in their portfolios.

of all infants suck their fingers or thumbs. By 18 months, thumbsucking usually reaches its peak. Then the behavior becomes less frequent, especially during the day. By four or five years of age, children who suck their thumbs usually only do so before they go to bed. Children of this age will sometimes engage in thumbsucking if they are tired.

Many parents are concerned about thumbsucking. Reassure them that usually there is no need to worry about this behavior. Encourage them to accept this behavior as a normal stage of growth. Most children outgrow thumbsucking by six or seven years of age.

Parents may be concerned that thumbsucking will affect children's facial appearance or damage teeth. Dentists state that there is no cause to worry if thumbsucking stops before permanent teeth erupt.

Handling Thumbsucking

Children's urge to suck may be satisfied by supplying a pacifier. One advantage of a pacifier is that it does not place pressure on the roof of the mouth or the jaw. When they're ready, most children give up their pacifiers. In fact, some children may have an intense sucking need for only the first few months of life. When these children stop using their pacifiers, they can be taken away permanently. If, however, a child reverts to sucking fingers or thumbs, return the pacifier.

If you notice thumbsucking, do not pull the thumb out of the child's mouth. This guidance may not be successful. In some cases, it might cause the child to increase thumbsucking. During the first three years, the harder you try to stop thumbsucking, the stronger it becomes. Instead, accept and ignore the behavior. In this way, children will usually stop thumbsucking between four and five years of age.

Attending a child care program may help curb thumbsucking for some children. At the center, the child will find many new interests and friends. As a result, you may not notice thumbsucking. Many times children will only suck their thumbs when they lie down for naps or are tired.

Fear

Every child experiences fear. By three years of age, most children have many kinds of fear. Some fears will be real while others will be imaginary. As the child grows, real fears will be kept. Imaginary fears will be outgrown.

Common childhood fears include falling from high places, putting faces in water, thunder, the dark, people in uniforms, fire engines, ambulances, and animals. Fear of the unknown is also common in young children. You may see this fear on the first day of school. Children may cry, cling, and refuse to leave their parents. As the teacher, be prepared for this fear. Inform parents in advance that this is a common fear.

Handling Fear

Understanding children's fear is important in guiding young children, 15-13. For example, fear of the dark is quite common among young children. You may notice this fear at naptime or when a video is being shown. Understand that this behavior is due to unfamiliar surroundings. These children cannot sleep or concentrate on videos. Instead, the children may focus on scary images formed by the shadows in the darkened room. Help these children by keeping a small light turned on during these times. Then the room will not be totally dark. Also, allow children to keep a familiar stuffed toy or blanket near them.

Accept children's fears. For young children, even the silliest fear is real. When a fire engine passes the playground and a child cries, give the child immediate attention. You may wish to hold the child's hand, kneel down and put your arms around the child, or hold the child on your lap. When you do this, you are meeting the child's immediate needs. After the crisis, talk to the child about the fear.

Enrich

Have students research products used to deter children from thumbsucking and list the ingredients these contain.

Resource

Handling Guidance Problems, Activity B, OG

Reflect

What fears did you have during your preschool years? What do you remember about how you conquered or dealt with these fears?

Resource

Dialing for Answers, Activity D, SAG

Putting Technology to Use

Have students conduct an Internet search for information on thumbsucking and answer the following: What are the dangers of thumbsucking after age five? What do the experts recommend for effectively handling a child's thumbsucking habit? What are the pros and cons of using devices such as bandages, gloves, and bitter-tasting solutions to deter a child from thumbsucking? Have students share their findings with the class in an oral report.

Enrich

Imagine a notice was sent home to the pre-school parents letting them know a volunteer from the pet rescue center was bringing some dogs to class. One child's mother decided to stay in class that day because her daughter was afraid of dogs. Ask students to debate the pros and cons of allowing parents to attend class with their child when the child has fears.

Discuss

When having uniformed professionals visit the preschool class, ask them to explain their gear piece by piece as they put it on. For example, ask firefighters to explain each item until they are fully covered with helmets, breathing tanks, gloves, and boots. How might seeing a fire-fighter before and after putting on gear may help a child deal with fear that could prevent his or her rescue during an actual fire?

Activity

Have students arrange a field trip for the preschoolers to the local police station. Ask children to volunteer to be fingerprinted and photographed. Have the officers explain how they could use this information. Check to see if the officer can demonstrate the police radio and siren and give children safety information.

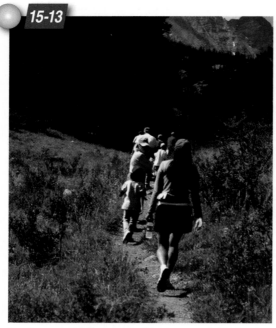

Teachers need to be prepared for fears on field trips that may be caused by unfamiliar sights or sounds.

Playing hospital helps many children deal with their fears of hospitals and doctors.

Children may need to act out situations in order to conquer their fears. See 15-14. For instance, Toby's grandmother died in the hospital. When Toby came back to the center, he asked two other children to play hospital with him. Toby played the role of a doctor while one of his friends played the nurse. This was Toby's way of handling the fear he felt when his grandmother died at the hospital.

Talking with children can also help them control fear. For example, Mark visited his cousin Chris. When he returned to school, Mark told his teachers that the house had ghosts. As a result, Mark said that he was never returning. Mark's teacher was observant. He talked to Mark about his visit with Chris. He explained that sleeping in strange places is often frightening because it is new.

Jennifer was afraid of the new bunny. Fortunately for Jennifer, her teacher was understanding. She helped Jennifer face her fear by introducing her to the bunny in gradual steps. First, she asked Jennifer to place a carrot in the cage. Then she encouraged Jennifer to watch the bunny eat. The next day she encouraged Jennifer to touch the bunny's fur. Jennifer continued this for about one week. Her teacher did not rush Jennifer. Finally, she asked Jennifer if she wanted to hold the bunny. Jennifer said yes. Jennifer's teacher carefully and slowly took the rabbit from the cage and placed it on Jennifer's lap.

When children feel unsafe or strange, they may reject a person or situation. For example, a child may greet a new aide with "Go away, I hate you." If this happens, do not scold the child. Telling the child that he or she likes the aide will not help either. Instead, accept the child's feelings. You may say "Miss Brown is our new teacher. When you get to know her, you will learn to like her."

Children will sometimes hit others when they are afraid. For instance, a resource person visited a group of four-year-olds. This person brought a large snake to show the children. When Janice saw the snake, she began to act aggressively. She hit Susan and Peggy. The teacher then stepped in. She explained to Janice that her friends might be frightened, too. She then explained to Janice that this type of snake was not dangerous. There was no need to fear it.

Meeting Special Needs

Review the special learners' chapter outlines to determine if the students have any questions about the concepts or content of this chapter. Review the chapter objectives and ask the students to evaluate their progress in meeting these objectives. Ask the students to summarize, orally or in writing, what they learned from this chapter.

Summary

As a teacher of young children, at times you will experience problems guiding the children in your care. Common causes of guidance problems include overstimulation, changes in routine, and loud noise. Frustration and physical problems can also cause guidance problems. Your goal is to guide children as they learn appropriate social-emotional skills.

Knowing how stress affects young children is also important. Stress can have many causes. Changes or problems within the family can cause stress among children and families. Young children do not know how to handle this stress very well. As a result, they most often express stress through their behavior. If adults note that a child shows signs of stress, they can offer the child the help he or she needs. Although family events can be a source of stress, families can also serve as a buffer for children during times of stress.

Your role as a teacher will be to help children and families deal positively with tension-causing events. Knowing more about common family stressors and signs of stress will help. You can help by communicating with families, modeling coping skills, and providing an extra measure of comfort and reassurance for the child.

In addition, you will face other problem behaviors in the classroom. These include negativism, stealing, anger, biting, exploring the body, tattling, thumbsucking, and fear. Handling each of these problem behaviors takes guidance skills and techniques that are unique to the situation.

Review and Reflect

1. Why do children react disruptively when they experience tension?

2. Name four events that can cause tension in a child.

3. True or false. Usually, the larger the group of children, the greater the likelihood that overstimulation will occur.

4. _____ let children know what to expect and when to expect it.

5. True or false. Noise affects all children in the same way.

6. Name two ways to cut down on waiting time.

7. Describe frustration and list two causes of frustration in children.

8. Frustration can be prevented by _____.
   A. supplying the same materials to all children
   B. letting children choose which play activities they would like to do
   C. forcing children to play with certain materials, regardless of their abilities
   D. planning only one or two activities a day

9. Name four ways that medications can affect children's behavior.

10. _____ are children who watch others participate, but do not participate themselves.

11. What is stress?

12. Name two steps you can take to help a child deal with stress.

13. List four possible family stressors for children.

14. What will happen if you hurry a negative child?

8. B
9. (Name four:) dilated pupils, drowsiness, slurred speech, poor coordination, irritability
10. Onlookers
11. the body's reaction to physical or emotional factors
12. Accept the child's behavior; promote a positive environment.
13. (List four. Student response. See Figure 15-7 in the text.)
14. The child will resist your requests even more strongly.
15. (Student response.)
16. true

***Review and Reflect* Answer Key**

1. because they do not know how to handle tension
2. (List four. Student response.)
3. true
4. Routines
5. false
6. be prepared and manage time wisely
7. feelings of discouragement, defeat, and lack of control (Student response for causes.)

15. Explain how you would effectively guide the children in the following situations.
    A. Philip gets angry whenever you announce cleanup time.
    B. Joanne bites George whenever he takes a toy from her.
    C. Amber runs to tell you every time another child misbehaves.
    D. Martin cries and clings to you when a clown visits the class.

16. True or false. Exploration of the body is a natural stage in development.

Apply and Explore

1. Prepare a checklist of ways to avoid overstimulation of children.

2. Discuss teacher strategies for reducing waiting time.

3. Visit a child care center. Observe children for any signs of stress. Note what signs you see. Discuss your findings when you return to class.

4. Discuss the advantages of thumbsucking from the child's point of view.

Cross-Curricular Link

Language Arts

1. Interview four parents to learn what problems they have guiding children.

Writing

2. Research common fears among children and compose a report that summarizes your findings.

Technology

3. Search the Web site www.daycare.about.com for guidance tips and resources related to the problems described in this chapter.

4. Check the Web site www.parenting-ed.org handouts related to guidance problems.

Workplace Link

Imagine a child in your care refuses to pick up blocks or put away toys. What are some possible solutions for handling this problem? Would you allow the blocks or toys to remain out on the floor or table? Would you encourage other children to clean up for this child? Would there be any consequences for the child's negative behavior?

16

Establishing Classroom Limits

Discuss

Look at the children in the chapter opening photo. What limit do you think they are demonstrating? What do you think is the purpose of this limit?

Discuss

Look over the objectives for this chapter. How do limits help children become self-controlled?

After studying this chapter, you will be able to

- explain the reasons for having classroom limits.
- list guidelines for establishing classroom limits.
- describe methods for enforcing limits.
- list useful limits for various classroom areas and activities.

Resource

Classroom Limits, reproducible master 16-1, TR

Discuss

Explain the difference in the following two limits: "Be nice to everyone" and "Keep your hands to yourself during circle time." What may be the result if a limit is stated in broad and general terms rather than in specific and easily understood language?

Reflect

How would you explain the reasons to a child for the following limits? "Blocks can be built only as high as the shoulders of the shortest child participating in the activity." "Children sit only on chairs or on the floor."

Resource

Stating the Positive, Activity A, SAG

Term to Know

flexible limits

Limits are necessary to help children effectively work in groups. They promote safety, respect, and responsibility. In child care centers, effective limits serve as a kind of shorthand to state the goals of the center. Limits should focus on actions and behaviors that reflect goals. As a teacher, your input in suggesting limits for the center is important.

Every area of the classroom will need to have limits. As the classroom teacher, it is your responsibility to explain and enforce limits. Limits need to be explained at the children's level of understanding. The staff and children should also know the reasons for the limits. In addition, you should make sure that each adult working in the classroom understands the limits. The limits should also be posted in the teachers' lounge and in the classrooms.

Establishing Limits

There are three reasons for establishing classroom limits. First, according to the law, children's health and safety must be protected. Limits help make the classroom a safe place for the children. Second, children feel free to explore when they know their teacher will stop them if they go too far, 16-1. Thus, they feel protected from mistakes. Finally, limits help children develop self-control. As children learn to accept and obey limits, they gradually come to learn that limits are part of life. One of the center's goals should be to develop socially responsible behavior in young children. Establishing limits will help the center reach this goal.

Guidelines for Setting Limits

When setting limits for children, make the limits short and positive. Focus on one

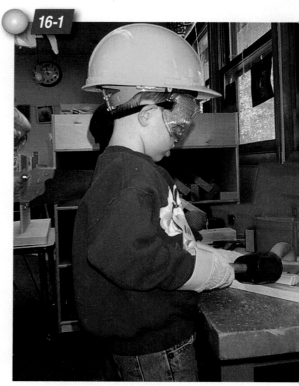

Enforcing limits about the use of safety equipment allow this boy to explore his woodworking project more freely.

main point. Use familiar language and short, simple sentences the children can understand. You and the children need to have the same understanding of what the limit means. Be sure the words you use describe the exact behavior you desire. Children are often confused by such general words as *be nice, stop it,* or *behave.* These words can have many meanings and do not say precisely what you want. State the limits in terms of the positive behavior you expect.

Set limits that are reasonable. This means that children have the ability to carry out the action. Limits should serve a useful purpose. Give children specific reasons for each limit. If you cannot think of a reason for having a limit, rethink the limit. Try to determine whether your expectations really are that important. Unreasonable limits can cause young children to feel angry.

Meeting Special Needs

Provide an outline of the chapter with all the chapter headings for special learners. Students should fill in each section of the outline as the material is covered in class with a sentence or two about the content. Review the special learners' IEPs to decide if any modifications should be made in presenting the chapter content.

Avoid making too many limits. Having a few well-established limits is better for the children and for you. If you have too many limits, the children will forget them. You, too, may have trouble remembering and enforcing them.

Define both acceptable and unacceptable behavior. Decide how to deal with unacceptable behavior. Normally, the best approach is to stop such action firmly and quickly. You may find, however, the child will become angry, 16-2. This anger may show in several ways. The child may resist the set limit, cry, yell, or simply stare at you.

Limits need to be reexamined by the entire staff on a regular basis. Children's behavior will change as they grow and develop. Therefore, limits should change as the children change. Any limit changes must be discussed with the entire staff. Discuss what changes need to be made and why. If

Undesirable behavior should be stopped, even if the child becomes upset.

you determine that a limit no longer fits the group's needs, discard it.

Limit changes also need to be discussed with the children. When an issue arises, invite the children to discuss the problem. Begin by stating the issue. Then ask the children to think of ways of solving it. During the discussion, encourage the children to state the limits in a positive way. Write out each new limit, calling attention to the printed words.

Enforcing Limits

Children follow limits best when the limits are consistently enforced. Children need to know what is expected of them. However, children will often test these well-established limits. You should feel comfortable with this testing process. At the same time you should also maintain your position. Do not be afraid or back down. For example, if you said each child may do only one painting, make sure no child paints two. Friendly reminders may also be helpful, such as "When you are finished, Tommy wants a turn to paint a picture."

Enforcing limits also requires that limits be flexible at times. **Flexible limits** allow you to adapt to the needs of an individual or situation. For instance, your limit states that children are expected to wear smocks in the art area. If an art activity is not messy, you might be flexible about this limit and allow the children to work without a smock. Your limits must be flexible enough to handle such situations, 16-3.

The way you react to children who break limits affects children's feelings of security. Children feel secure knowing the limits protect them. However, when one child violates a limit, another child's security may be threatened. For instance, a child may express his or her anger in a violent way, such as hitting. That child is violating a limit. You must tell the child that hitting is wrong. The child who was hit is also affected. He or she has lost some security. You need to reassure

Activity

Have students review the child care lab's limits and ask students to list possible consequences for children who do not follow them. Will the consequences differ for children of different ages?

Discuss

Why do children test limits? What can you infer if a child continuously tests the same limit?

Vocabulary

Have a student volunteer define the term *flexible limits*. Give an example of a flexible limit and explain why it is flexible.

Reflect

How would you feel if a classroom limit was enforced for you, but an exception was made for another student in your class? Can you relate how you would feel to a similar situation with a preschooler in the child care lab?

Portfolio Project

Ask students to create a list of the ten limits they feel are most important in an early childhood setting. Ask students to explain why they included each item on the list and give an example of the type of behavior they are trying to control with each limit. Have students write a brief reflection on their understanding of the need for limits and how they contribute to the ultimate goal of helping a child become self-disciplined. Have students file the list in their portfolio.

Resource

Setting Limits Throughout the Classroom, reproducible master 16-2, TR

Discuss

Brainstorm ideas for handling a child who continuously refuses to wear a smock during art activities and whose mother had told him that he does not have to wear one. How would you incorporate dialogue with the mother into finding a solution to this problem?

Resource

Observing Classroom Limits, Activity A, OG

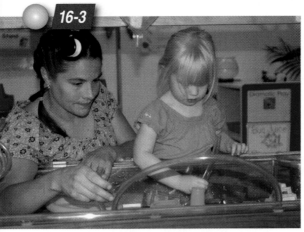
Limits may need to be adapted to the needs of an individual child or situation.

and pay attention to this child. In fact, giving attention to the injured child shows that hitting is not a good way to gain attention.

Limits for Specific Areas and Activities

The limits you set may be very different from the limits set at another center. This is because no two centers are alike. Equipment, facilities, and staff vary among centers. However, similar activities take place at many centers, regardless of location. For instance, cooking, blockbuilding, and reading occur at most centers. General limits for some of these areas and activities can be used as guidelines for all centers.

Sensory Play

In some classrooms, sensory activity is provided each day. A water or sand table is often used for this activity. During a typical week, shaving cream, ice cubes, snow, colored water, or soapy water may be used in the water table. Dried beans, seed corn, oats, rice, or pebbles may be used in the sand table.

Depending on the material being used, the limits may change somewhat. For instance, a child would not need to wear a smock for protection when playing with dried seed corn. With shaving cream, however, the smock may be required.

Limits for sensory play might include the following:

- Wear smocks for all wet or messy activities, 16-4.

- Wipe up splashes and spills immediately.

- Keep sensory materials inside the table.

Eating or throwing sensory materials is not allowed, but this should be stated in a positive manner as shown above. If a child does not follow the limit, he or she must face the consequences. For example, you might say, "Jacques, I cannot let you throw sand. It could get in someone's eyes and hurt them. If you choose to throw sand, you will have to stop playing here." If Jacques keeps throwing sand, stop his play immediately and offer him a choice between more acceptable activities.

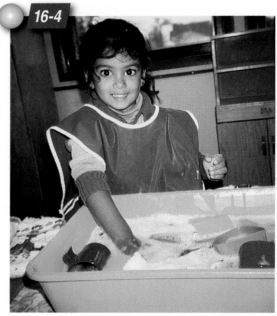
Wearing smocks during messy activities will keep children clean and dry.

Meeting Special Needs

Have gifted students survey the list of limits or rules that guide student behavior at their school. Then interview the school personnel responsible for the enforcement of these limits. Are there sound reasons for all the limits? Are there consequences in place that encourage students to follow the rules? What limits are required because of school codes and legal guidelines? How does the process of determining the limits for the high school compare to designing limits for child care centers? Ask students to share their findings with the class.

Dramatic Play

The dramatic play area might be called the home living or housekeeping area in some centers. Materials should be provided to help the children gain a better understanding of themselves and others around them. Dramatic play also allows children to work out their own feelings. Thus, to provide the children with the least restrictive environment, limits can include the following:

- Wipe up all spilled water.
- Put materials away after use.
- Respect the participation of others.

Small Manipulative Activities

This area of the classroom contains games and small objects. With these materials, children learn to build, compare, sort, arrange, and match. Also, color, number, size, and shape concepts can be mastered. As children use small manipulatives, they also develop fine-motor and hand-eye coordination.

Usually, there are few limits in this area. Suggested limits include the following:

- Return toys to the shelf after use.
- Keep games and puzzle pieces in this area of the classroom, 16-5.
- Take turns with materials.

Cooking

Children learn about food by participating in cooking activities. Cooking allows children to feel a sense of accomplishment. Tasting, smelling, touching, listening, and seeing help build language, number, sequence, and physics concepts.

Health and safety precautions must be addressed in the limits. Therefore, the following limits are needed:

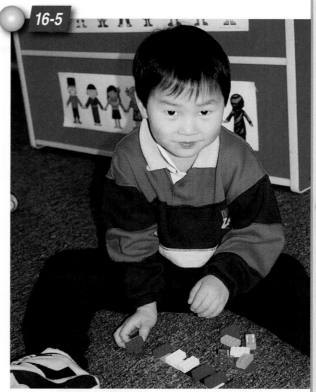

16-5

The limit that small manipulatives cannot leave the designated classroom area makes cleanup much simpler.

- Wash hands before cooking.
- Wear an apron or smock.
- Wipe up spills immediately.
- Only teachers pick up hot items.
- Eat prepared foods only during lunch or snack time.
- Everyone assists with cleanup.

Supervision is required during all cooking activities. Whenever electrical appliances are being used, never leave the activity area! If more supplies are needed, signal for another teacher to get them for you. Always use pot holders and hot pads with cooking appliances.

Discuss

Dramatic play may include instances where children are acting out roles as superheroes or villains. What limits would you enforce to prevent overly aggressive play by the preschoolers in these roles?

Reflect

What indirect guidance techniques would you use in the small manipulative area to help children follow limits? What types of materials and equipment in this area may make enforcing the limits particularly challenging?

Resource

Limit Pyramid, Activity B, SAG

Discuss

Ask students to create a list of possible cooking activities that would require minimal limits for preschoolers. What general limits should always be followed when children are working with food and cooking utensils?

Resource

Know the Limits, Activity C, SAG

Meeting Special Needs

Provide a word bank of possible answers for *Limit Pyramid,* Activity B, SAG. After students complete the activity, assign *Know the Limits,* Activity C, SAG. Assist special learners to rewrite each of the false statements to make them true. Ask students to explain why the true statements are correct. Student volunteers may partner with special learners to work on the assignments together.

Blockbuilding

Blockbuilding encourages children to be productive and creative. Blockbuilding also provides children with a way to release energy. The children's safety is important in this area. Limits must stress safety. Close supervision is always required in this area. Because of this need, building activities should be allowed only during a set time period.

Limits for blockbuilding activities might include the following:

- Use blocks for building only, 16-6.
- Keep blocks in the blockbuilding area.
- Return blocks to the storage shelves after use.
- Touch only your own building project unless you ask permission.

Discuss

Why is safety such a big concern when establishing limits in the blockbuilding area? What limits, besides those listed in the text, do you think might be needed to maintain children's safety in this area?

Reflect

What would you do if a preschooler throws blocks at another child or uses blocks as pretend weapons during blockbuilding activity time? Remember that your response must be positive.

Discuss

What limits can you suggest to prevent the noise level from becoming excessive and still allow children freedom of expression during music play? Give examples of limits for music play that may differ depending whether individual or group activities are taking place in this area.

Music

All children enjoy music, 16-7. It is a universal language. By participating in music activities, children can develop self-expression, listening, language, and coordination skills. Music, like other activities, needs specific limits that promote safety, respect, and responsibility:

- Children select the instruments they want to use.
- Return instruments to their assigned places on the shelves after use.
- Use musical instruments only for creating sounds.

Art

For children, art is usually a pleasing activity. Therefore, they usually spend a lot of time playing in this area. Art is offered

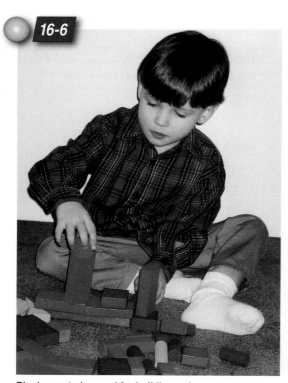

16-6

Blocks are to be used for building only.

16-7

Children enjoy creating music.

Workplace Connection

Have students survey area preschool and child care teachers to discover how often music activities are conducted in the classroom. Do children have daily access to musical and rhythm band instruments, or are they used only on special occasions? What limits have been established for music activities? Ask student volunteers to observe a preschool class during music time. Are children following the established limits? Allow time for students to discuss their findings in class.

daily in most centers during the self-selected activity period.

Children in this area should be encouraged to explore materials. They should not be told what to make, nor should their artwork be compared. Most centers use only the following limits:

- Cover tables.
- Wear smocks for messy activities.
- Wipe up spills immediately.
- Work only with your own materials.

Book Corner

In the book corner, children can develop language and pre-reading skills. Children should be encouraged to explore the books in this area, 16-8. In doing so, they will learn about their own family and community. They will also learn about other cultures. Limits for the book corner might be the following:

- Turn one page at a time.
- Give torn books to the teacher.
- Return books to the shelf after use.
- Handle books gently.

16-8

Children can learn valuable pre-reading and language skills in the book corner.

In order to encourage the children to explore, change books on a regular basis. Some teachers change books on a weekly basis, leaving several favorites to carry over. Control the number of books available at any given time. When too many books are in the area, it can become cluttered. Likewise, a child may have difficulty locating a favorite storybook.

Science

All children need science activities. These activities encourage them to discover their own environment. As they observe and question, they will see relationships and draw conclusions.

Teachers need to carefully plan science activities. Include a variety of classroom and outdoor activities. Emphasize hands-on activities that allow children time to explore their surroundings, 16-9. During these activities, encourage the children to participate by observing, touching, holding, and questioning.

As a teacher, you will need to demonstrate some of the limits in this area. For example, you will need to show the children how to hold a bunny, water a plant, or feed classroom pets. Equipment use will also need to be demonstrated for the children. You may even choose to have children assist with cleaning the animal housing.

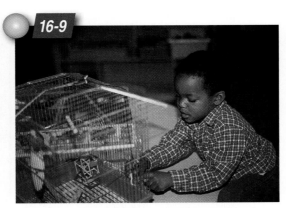

16-9

Hands-on activities encourage children to become involved in the world around them.

Discuss

What indirect guidance strategies are necessary when art activities are available to children during the self-selected or free-play activity period? What limits may be needed to ensure that all children have equal access to equipment such as painting easels and chalk or white boards?

Reflect

What science activities do you remember as most interesting when you were a preschooler? What limits might discourage a child from participating in the science activity center?

Discuss

What furniture arrangements in the book corner encourage children to follow limits for this area? How can reducing the number of books available at a time help children to develop self-control in this area?

Cross-Curricular Activity

Art
Consult with the art instructor to partner students to create signs or posters to remind children of limits for the various centers of the classroom. Students can use drawings, symbols, and photos to portray the limits. If words are part of the posters or signs, remind students to use a consistent manuscript printing style. Have students show the finished posters to the preschoolers to determine if they understand the limit expressed by each one.

Enrich

Ask students to observe children at a neighborhood park or playground to see how they play. What limits would be necessary at the park or playground that would differ from those at the child care lab? What limits would be similar?

Activity

Locate catalogs with a variety of styles of jungle gym equipment. Ask students to determine the number of children that could safely play on each type and indicate the number of supervisors that would be necessary to ensure that safety rules and limits could be followed.

Reflect

Did you ever have an accident or suffer an injury while playing outdoors on the playground or on playground equipment? What limit or limits might have prevented the injury?

Limits for the science area might include the following:

- Feed pets and water plants only with a teacher's supervision.
- Keep science equipment in the area.
- Handle pets with care.
- Wash your hands after touching pets.

Playground Activity

On the playground, children can express themselves in creative ways. They can build ships, houses, forts, and other objects with wooden crates and other materials. Through play, children develop motor coordination skills, social play skills, and a sense of cooperation.

The primary concern of the teacher is the children's safety. Limits must be set and enforced if children are to play happily and safely on the playground. These limits will vary, depending on the equipment being used and the children's abilities.

Swings

Swings are not found on all playgrounds because they require constant teacher supervision. If swings are available, specific limits must be set, such as the following:

- Only one child on a swing at a time.
- Sit in the center of the swing.
- Use both hands for holding on.
- Stay on the swing until it has stopped.
- Only teachers push children on swings.
- Keep clear of moving swings.

Slides

Slides are a source of hazard for young children. Accidents happen when children bump into each other. Some children are injured when they stand up as they go down the slide, or when they slide head first. As a result, set these limits:

- Use both hands when climbing up the steps.
- Wait until the person in front of you is off the slide before you slide down.
- Slide down feet first and sitting up.
- Get off the slide as soon as you get to the bottom.

Jungle Gyms

Jungle gyms are very appealing to young children. Since children are adventurous, any activity on this piece of equipment has to be carefully supervised. Children must also be taught the correct and safe way to use the jungle gym. Include the following limits for jungle gym use:

- Only four or five children may use the jungle gym at one time.
- Use both hands to hold on.
- Make sure you do not step on another child when climbing.

Seesaws

Seesaws are another piece of equipment that require constant supervision when being used. Therefore, the limits you establish should stress safety. Include the following:

- Hang on to the handle with both hands.
- Keep feet out from under the board as it goes down.
- Tell your partner when you want to get off the seesaw.

Wheeled Toys

Tricycles, bicycles, and other wheeled toys can pose dangers when not used properly. For this reason, safety limits are

---

Service Learning Activity

Ask student volunteers to visit and survey the parks and playgrounds in the area. Have them determine if safety precautions are being met to protect children from injury. Have students list any problem areas such as splintered wood, sharp areas, rust, broken glass or other trash, and missing bolts or other parts. Report the problems to the local parks department or other agency responsible for park maintenance. Students can also suggest any signage they think would enhance the park's use and volunteer to conduct any cleanup that may be necessary.

needed regarding the use of these toys. These limits include the following:

- Each wheeled toy can have only one rider at a time.

- Always wear proper safety gear when riding, 16-10.

- Sit on the seat to ride.

- Ride only on the wheeled toy path.

- Watch for other riders or walkers.

16-10

When riding wheeled toys, helmets are a must.

Communicating Limits

What method can you use to clearly communicate limits to young children? As you have already read, limits need to be short, simple, and reasonable. Some teachers make this task easier by first dividing their limits into three categories. These categories include (1) be safe, (2) be kind and respectful, and (3) be neat and responsible. When reminding children about certain limits, the teachers begin by using one of the three categories. Figure 16-11 shows examples of this method.

16-11

Category	Examples
Be safe!	Use both hands to hang on to the swing. Sit at the table while using scissors.
Be kind and respectful!	Say thank you when someone helps you. Hold the door for others.
Be neat and responsible!	Hang your jacket in the locker. Wear your smock while painting.

Use clear, concise language when communicating limits to children.

Resource

Setting Limits,
Activity D, SAG

Activity

Ask students to conduct an Internet search for information on safety for children concerning helmet use when riding wheeled toys. Students can access information from the following sites: Pedestrian and Bicycle Information Center at **www.bicyclinginfo.org**; National Safety Council at **www.nsc.org**; National Highway Traffic Safety Administration at **www.nhtsa.gov**. Allow time for students to discuss their findings in class.

Resource

Enforcing Limits,
Activity B, OG

Meeting Special Needs

Review the special learners' chapter outlines to determine if the students have any questions about the concepts or content of this chapter. Review the chapter objectives and ask the students to evaluate their progress in meeting these objectives. Ask the students to summarize, orally or in writing, what they learned from this chapter.

Review and Reflect Answer Key

1. Limits are necessary for people to effectively work together in groups. Limits state the goals of the center. As such, the limits of the center stress actions and behaviors that reflect these goals. They promote safety, respect, and responsibility.

2. to protect children's health and safety; to allow children freedom to explore, knowing their teacher will stop them if they go too far; to help children develop self-control

3. (List three:) Make limits short. Write the limits in language that children can understand. State the limits in terms of positive behavior you expect. Set limits that are reasonable and serve a useful purpose. Define both acceptable and unacceptable behavior. Avoid making too many limits.

4. (Student response.)

5. Yes. Limits should change as the children grow and develop.

6. When limits are enforced consistently, children know what is expected of them. Limits that are inconsistently enforced may confuse children as to what is acceptable behavior.

Summary

Limits focus on actions and behaviors that reflect the goals of the center. Limits must be made for all classroom areas and for all activities. As the classroom teacher, it is your responsibility to explain and enforce limits. Limits need to be explained at the children's level of understanding. The staff and children should also know the reasons for the limits.

Limits that are consistently enforced and fair help create a relaxed atmosphere at the center. Limits may need to be flexible to adapt to the needs of an individual or situation. Limits will be different from one center to another. It is important that all staff members have input into setting limits. These limits should be reviewed on a regular basis and revised as needed.

Having limits teaches good citizenship. Children know what is expected of them. Adults know what to expect. Both groups find the center a pleasant place to be.

Review and Reflect

1. Explain the importance of having limits in a child care center.

2. List three reasons for establishing classroom limits.

3. Name three guidelines for setting limits for children.

4. Give an example of a limit that is stated negatively. Rewrite the limit so it is stated positively.

5. Should limits ever change? Explain your answer.

6. Why is it important that limits be enforced consistently?

7. _____ limits allow you to adapt to the needs of an individual or situation.

8. Why should children be expected to wipe up any spills they make in various areas of the classroom?

9. List two ways teachers can encourage children to look at the books in the book corner.

10. Name one limit for each of the following pieces of playground equipment: swings, slides, jungle gyms, seesaws, and wheeled toys.

7. Flexible
8. Spills are messy and can lead to slips and falls.
9. Change books on a regular basis. Control the number of books available at any given time.
10. (List one limit for each. Student response.)

Apply and Explore

1. Discuss ways in which limits may change as children grow. Give some specific examples.

2. Collect classroom limits from two centers. Discuss the similarities and differences between the two sets of limits.

3. Role-play the following scenes that might occur in early childhood programs. How should caregivers respond?

   A. Toby is in the book corner. While looking at a book, she accidentally tears a page.
   B. Tommy goes down the slide. When he reaches the bottom, he continues to sit there.
   C. Sarah and Frank are on the seesaw. Suddenly, Sarah jumps off.
   D. During a cooking activity, Mark accidentally spills his milk.

Cross-Curricular Link

Writing

1. Cut pictures of two pieces of outdoor play equipment from a catalog. Write limits for each piece.

Technology

2. Check the Web site of the National Network for Child Care (nncc.org) for information on guidance, discipline, and appropriate limits for children of various ages.

Workplace Link

Brainstorm ways to communicate to parents the limits their child will have to follow while attending the child care lab preschool. How can parents become part of the process in communicating and enforcing limits with their preschool children? Plan a parent meeting or orientation session that deals with limits. Should children be exposed to the limits all at once or gradually? Share your ideas with the class.

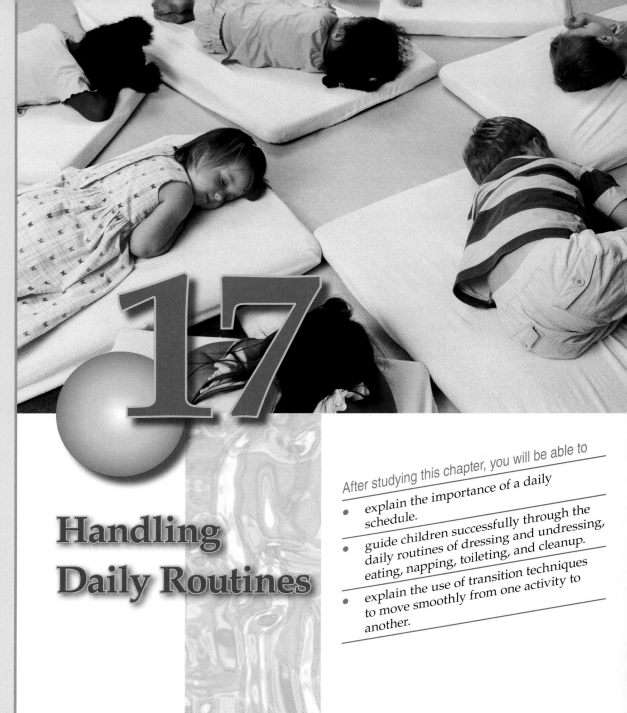

Discuss

Look at the chapter opening photo. Did you know that naps should be part of the daily routine? What other activities might this chapter's opening photo have portrayed?

Discuss

Look over the objectives for this chapter. What role do routines play in the guidance of children?

17

Handling Daily Routines

After studying this chapter, you will be able to

- explain the importance of a daily schedule.
- guide children successfully through the daily routines of dressing and undressing, eating, napping, toileting, and cleanup.
- explain the use of transition techniques to move smoothly from one activity to another.

Terms to Know

routines
pica
dawdling
transitions
auditory signals

Routines, such as dressing, undressing, eating, napping, and toileting, are everyday experiences. They promote the children's social, self-help, and learning skills. Routines at child care centers reassure children by providing a predictable pattern. By following a schedule, children know the order of daily events. They also know what to expect with each event. This offers them emotional security.

Daily routines provide opportunities for children to develop independence. Young children feel great satisfaction in doing things for themselves. See 17-1.

Daily routines will need your guidance. The children will need to learn the classroom schedule and daily routines. Before understanding time, children learn to understand a sequence of events. For

17-1

Teaching children how to put on outerwear allows them to be more independent.

instance, Vivian and Merena, twin three-year-olds, began attending a local preschool. When their older sister asked what they do at preschool, Vivian responded in this way: "First we play; then we hear a story; then we have a snack; then we go outside; and then mama comes to get us."

The Daily Schedule

A well-planned schedule provides the framework for the day's activities. Schedules for early childhood programs vary by type of program. For instance, the sequence of events in an all-day program will not be the same as that for a half-day program. Factors such as the length of the program's day and the time children arrive will need to be considered.

A well-planned schedule should help prevent conflicts. It must also be planned to meet the children's needs. Health and safety are important considerations. To feel comfortable and secure, children need to have consistency and predictable routines.

The daily schedule should be designed to include basic routines. Figure 17-2 shows the segments of a typical schedule. Include time for both indoor and outdoor play. Consider the weather when deciding how much time to allow for outdoor play. Remember to plan time for eating and napping, too.

When planning the daily schedule, include large blocks of open time. At least half of the day should be set aside for self-selected activities. Young children enjoy selecting activities and deciding how long to remain with each activity. Many preschool children have short attention spans. Differences also exist in the speed at which they complete projects. By providing larger blocks of time, you will be meeting these children's individual needs.

There will be differences in each child's response to the schedule. For some children, the pace may be too fast, and they may feel stressed. Other children may become bored if the pace is too slow. Children's reactions often

Vocabulary

Have students review the *Terms to Know* list. Ask students to look up unfamiliar words or terms in the glossary before reading the chapter.

Discuss

Why do changes in weather affect the daily preschool schedule? Give some examples of changes you would make in the daily schedule to account for changes in temperature and weather.

Vocabulary

Have a student volunteer define the term *routines*. How do routines help children grow in independence?

Meeting Special Needs

Provide an outline of the chapter with all the chapter headings for special learners. Students should fill in each section of the outline as the material is covered in class with a sentence or two about the content. Review the special learners' IEPs to decide if any modifications should be made in presenting the chapter content.

Reflect

What changes would you make in the sample schedule in 17-2, *Scheduling Segments for a Full-Day Program*, for a program that operated for only a half day or less? What important components in the schedule should always be included regardless of the time period the class is operating?

Resource

Planning a Daily Schedule, Activity B, SAG

Enrich

Ask student volunteers to role-play a situation where a preschooler is reluctant to leave his or her parent or guardian and is resistant to separation attempts. How will this situation affect the child and the rest of the children in the classroom if this happens every time the child arrives at school?

Discuss

What props or equipment might be used to get children's attention and call them to group time? What effect will using a consistent signal for group time have on the children in the class?

Resource

Tips for Successful Group Times, transparency master 17-1, TR

17-2

Scheduling Segments for a Full-Day Program

I. Arrival, greetings, and self-selected indoor activities
II. Cleanup, toileting, and hand washing
III. Snack, cleanup, and hand washing
IV. Self-selected activities and cleanup
V. Teacher-structured large group activity
VI. Outdoor self-selected activities
VII. Cleanup, toileting, and hand washing
VIII. Lunch, cleanup, hand washing, and toothbrushing
IX. Transitioning for nap time: quiet music or story time
X. Toileting, hand washing, nap
XI. Self-selected activities, indoor or outdoor
XII. Cleanup, toileting, and hand washing
XIII. Snack, cleanup, and hand washing
XIV. Outdoor free time
XV. Departure

A daily routine may give children a feeling of security.

depend on the number of hours they spend at the center. Children attending full time may feel differently than those attending part time.

Arrival Routines

The arrival of children should follow a regular routine so children know what to expect. The children's arrival requires the teacher's full attention.

A typical arrival routine begins with the greeting of each child. Kneel down to the child's level, make eye contact, and make each child feel welcome. Acknowledge any item the child might have brought from home. The children should then be directed to store their outer garments and other belongings in their cubbies. They then can move to a self-selected activity until all the children have arrived.

Children react differently to separation from their parents or guardian. Some will

remain silent while others cry. Some will refuse to enter the room, and others will bring favorite toys from home. Children vary in the duration of their separation anxieties. Some children will feel comfortable in a day or two. For other children, this may take a week or even several weeks. As a teacher, recognizing and responding to these anxieties is important. Your caring and understanding will be a key in helping the children make this transition.

Large Group Activities

In most programs, time is included in the schedule for large group activities. Teachers may refer to this segment as group time, story time, or circle time. Often this time is used for stories, songs, fingerplays, and discussions. If developmentally appropriate, teachers also use it for discussions about the weather and calendar.

Schedule large group activities when the children are well-rested and nourished, such as mid-morning. Since not all children arrive at one time, avoid scheduling group time at the beginning of the day. Problems can also occur when large group time is scheduled just before lunch. Usually the children are under the most stress at this time of day. They are becoming tired and hungry, which could impact their behavior.

Group time should take place in an area where there are few distractions. The children should be seated away from books, puzzles, and other materials that they could pick up. Many programs have a carpeted area for group time. Some teachers prefer using individual carpet squares. A teacher or aide may prearrange the squares prior to large group activity to make sure the children are not sitting too close together. It will also ensure that the children are sitting near the teacher and not blocking other children's views.

A key to the success of group time is being organized and ready. Immediately capture the children's attention with a fingerplay, puppet, or song. This will

Workplace Connection

Ask students to obtain samples of schedules used in several area preschools and child care centers. Compare the schedules for similarities and differences. Do the students notice consistent routines and transitions in the schedules? Ask students to interview the teachers to discover how scheduling is accomplished by individual teachers, group planning, or the director or administrator. Allow time for students to discuss their findings in class.

encourage stragglers to pick up their pace and join the group. Always end group time before the children lose interest.

Small Group Activities

Small group activity periods may be scheduled for 10 to 15 minutes. Typically, the four to six children in the group have similar interests or abilities. During this time, the children work with a teacher or aide. The purpose may be to teach specific concepts such as colors, numbers, shapes, or sizes.

Self-Selected Activities

The largest block of time in the schedule is for self-selected activities. This may also be referred to as center time or free play. The activities may be scheduled for indoors or outdoors. A variety of developmentally appropriate activities should be available.

When longer play periods are available, children engage in more involved activities. Larger blocks of time help develop the children's attention spans. These longer time periods are also valuable to you. As a teacher, you can engage in conversations with the children, asking questions and assessing learning.

Meals and Snacks

A half-day or two-hour preschool program usually provides a 15-minute snack period. Lunch is usually provided in centers that operate full-day programs. Typically a half hour is allowed for lunch. The amount of time needed for snack or lunch will vary depending on the age of the children and the number in the group.

Nap Time

Check your state's regulations on rest or nap time. Most states require children enrolled in a full-day program to have a nap time.

Usually this is scheduled after lunch. Allow one to two hours for this activity. Nap time routines will be discussed later in this chapter.

Daily Routines

Throughout the day, many routines take place in the center. As a teacher, you will need to know how to handle basic routines. These include dressing and undressing, eating, napping, toileting, and cleanup. Encourage the children to become as independent as possible in carrying out basic routines.

Dressing and Undressing

As a teacher, you will want to encourage the children to dress and undress themselves as much as possible. Begin by telling the children what you expect of them. This is important. When four-year-old Frankie hands you his coat, refuse to help him put it on. Instead, tell Frankie he is able to dress himself. If needed, prompt him by providing verbal instruction. Once his coat is on, do not forget to praise him for his accomplishment. This will help him enjoy becoming independent. See 17-3.

17-3

Letting children know they are capable of dressing and undressing themselves helps children build independence.

Activity

Ask students to determine the best size group for small group activities by changing the size of the group for several classes and documenting the results. Numbers may differ depending on the specific activity, the equipment available, and the number of teachers needed to work with the children during the activity.

Reflect

Do you feel that self-selected activities should always be part of the daily routines in an early childhood program? Can you think of any situations when self-selected or free play activities should be limited or removed from the daily schedule?

Resource

The Daily Schedule, Activity B, OG

Discuss

Daniel's mother always escorts him into the classroom, removes his coat, and hangs up the coat and his tote bag for him. How can you encourage her to allow Daniel to be more independent in performing these tasks for himself?

Resource

Your Style of Managing Daily Routines, Activity A, SAG

Putting Technology to Use

Ask students to conduct an Internet search on the value of free play activities in an early childhood program. What types of activities are encouraged during free play or self-selected activities? What routines are incorporated into free play? What is the philosophy behind encouraging children to engage in activities that interest them during the daily preschool or child care center schedule? Have students write a brief report of their findings.

Activity

Ask students to design a sample label for an individual child's locker or cubby. The label should include the child's name written in a consistent manuscript style and a recognizable picture, symbol, or design that will help the child remember which locker is his or hers. Ask a committee of students to select the labels that will be used in the child care lab during the year.

Discuss

What clothing suggestions could you make to parents regarding the type of activities that may be conducted during the preschool day? What type of clothing, if any, would you ask parents to avoid?

Enrich

Ask students to share their feelings on the policy many kindergartens follow—children must be able to tie their shoes before they enter the program. What are the pros and cons of such a policy?

Children should also be responsible for hanging up their coats. You may notice that many of the children simply lay their coats in their lockers. Do not allow this. For instance, if you see Eileen lay her coat in the locker, say "Eileen, you need to hang your coat on the hook." If she does not understand, show her how to hang it on the hook. Then take the coat off the hook and let Eileen hang it herself.

Label lockers so children can find their own spaces. The labeling method you use will vary with the ages of the children. Names are usually written on the lockers for infants. This helps both teachers and families. For two-year-olds, use a picture of the child. Names and symbols are helpful to three-year-olds. If children cannot recognize their names, they can find their symbols. Give each child a different symbol. Most four- and five-year-olds can recognize their names.

Suggestions for Families

Dressing can be time-consuming and frustrating for teachers and children. For this reason, some centers provide families with a list of clothing suggestions for the children. The list usually includes the following:

- Send an extra set of clothing for your child to keep at school. These can be used in case of an emergency. For instance, a child might fall in mud, rip a pair of pants, or have a toileting accident.

- Attach labels to the inside of your child's clothing. It is common for several children to have the same style and size of clothes. Labeling helps prevent confusion.

- Select clothing for your child with large zippers, buttons, or snaps. This makes dressing easier for children who do not have well-developed fine-motor skills.

- Boots and shoes should fit properly and slide on and off easily.

- Shoelaces should not be too long because they can be a tripping hazard and are hard for children to tie. You may want to choose shoes with Velcro® closings, which are easier for younger children to manage independently.

- Consider buying elastic-waist slacks and shorts instead of snap or button types. They are easier for children to handle during toileting.

Demonstrating

Buttoning, zipping, pulling on boots, tying shoes, and putting fingers in gloves are all actions that can be demonstrated. Demonstrating at the child's eye level is the most effective. Sometimes verbal guidance is all a child needs. At other times, you may need to start an action. Allow the child to finish the process. He or she will feel a sense of accomplishment. For example, Siri can put on his coat but cannot get the zipper started. Start the zipper and have Siri finish zipping it by himself.

Tying Shoes. Tying is a skill that requires advanced coordination. As a result, most children do not learn this task until five years of age.

There are several methods for teaching children how to tie shoes. One method is to place the child on your lap. From this angle, the child can observe the process. For most children, the easiest technique to learn is to loop each string like a bunny ear. Tie these loops into a double knot. Encourage the child to repeat this process.

Some children will have shoes that clasp with Velcro instead of tie with laces. Bring shoes with ties to the center to teach these children how to tie. Let them use these shoes to practice. This will help them learn tying skills, or you can let them practice on a shoelace box, 17-4.

Boots. Boots that are too small can be hard to put on. When this happens, place a plastic bag over the child's shoes or feet. This will help the boot slip on and off more easily.

Some centers keep a box of surplus boots. When a child is wearing boots that are too

---

Service Learning Activity

Research the possibility of conducting a coat and jacket drive to assist those in need. Have students search for programs in need of assistance such as The Salvation Army, Veteran's organizations, homeless and displaced persons' shelters, and women and children's shelters. Find out what requirements need to be met to donate and deliver the coats and jackets. Include the preschool children and their families in your donation requests. Ask students to use this opportunity to present a lesson on sharing to the children when they bring in their donations.

17-4

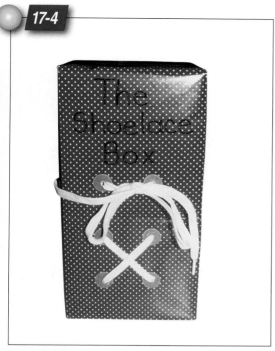

A shoelace box is useful for teaching tying to children.

small, the teacher can make an exchange. Boots from this box are also handy if a child forgets to bring boots from home.

Children can practice putting on and taking off their own boots, or they may practice using the extras in the box.

Coats. To demonstrate putting on a coat, lay the child's coat, button or zipper side up, on the floor. Have the child kneel at the collar end. Tell the child to place his or her hands and arms into the sleeves. Then tell the child to put it over his or her head. Use your own sweater or jacket to demonstrate this for the children. See 17-5.

Eating

Nutritional services provided by centers vary. Some centers serve only lunch, while others may also serve breakfast. Snacks may be the only food served in centers that do not operate all day. Some centers require that children bring their own bag lunches. While most centers p rovide older children with meals, they require parents to provide infant formulas, breast milk, or baby foods.

As a teacher, you will have many concerns during mealtime. A main concern is serving nutritious meals that children will like. This concern is addressed in Chapter 12, "Planning Nutritious Meals and Snacks."

You will also want the children to enjoy eating and practice their table manners. Making mealtime pleasant and orderly is another concern of teachers, 17-6. This means making meals appropriate for the ages, abilities, and interests of children. It also

17-5

1. The child kneels at the collar end of the coat.

2. The child puts his or her hands in the coat sleeves.

3. The child flips the coat over his or her head.

4. The child puts his or her arms all the way into the sleeves.

This technique can be used by children to help them learn how to put on a coat.

Activity

If your school is located in a part of the country where boots will be needed as the weather changes, schedule a "Boot Day" or "Boot Camp." Children can practice putting on and taking off their boots and putting on their shoes after the boots have been removed. Ask students to create additional activities tied into the theme. Plan for the special day well in advance of weather changes.

Resource

Tips for Oral Health, color transparency CT-14, TR

Enrich

Ask students to design a preschool activity encouraging children to practice self-dressing skills. For example, children may enjoy a clothing relay using dress-up clothes from the dramatic play area, a zipper challenge, a shoe race, or a coat race.

Putting Technology to Use

Have students obtain permission from parents or guardians to photograph children as they master self-dressing skills such as zipping, tying, and buttoning. Ask students to create a photo booklet for each child to document their growing skills.

Leave some pages blank so additional pictures can be added in later. Students could also use the photos to prepare a slide show for a parent night or conferences. Allow time for students to share their books in class.

Discuss

What are some potential guidance issues when children bring food from home to the child care center? What guidelines would you suggest parents follow when their children bring snacks and meals from home?

Reflect

How early in your life were you made aware of table manners? What table manners and other eating procedures did your parents teach and expect you to follow when you were young?

Discuss

What routines will be necessary to follow when infants and toddlers attempt self-feeding with finger foods? What expectations should the caregiver have when children begin self-feeding?

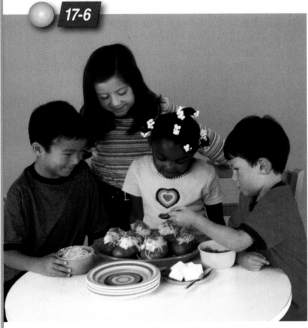

17-6

Proper manners and order contribute to a pleasant snack.

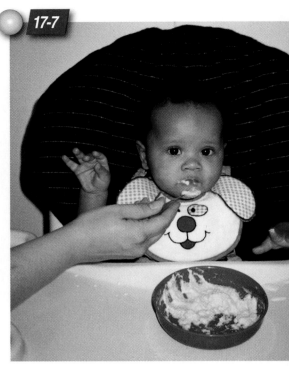

17-7

Infants can use facial expressions to communicate their food preferences.

means teaching rules of etiquette during meals.

You will notice that children's appetites change. Children's appetites are influenced by illness, stage of development, physical activity, and a body's individual nutrient needs. Emotions can also affect appetite. For example, if Lila has cried since her parents dropped her off this morning, she may not be hungry at lunchtime. Appetite changes will require you to be flexible regarding the children during meals.

Infants and Toddlers

Infants and toddlers have definite food likes and dislikes, 17-7. It is not unusual for them to spit out or refuse foods they do not like. On the other hand, they will eagerly eat foods they enjoy.

A cup can be introduced as early as six to seven months of age. At first, children may take only a few swallows. Spilling will occur for several months. Later, children will enjoy using cups by themselves. To help these children, provide spill-proof cups.

Once children become mobile, their interest in food may decrease. During this stage, some children are too interested in moving to sit still very long. Even if placed in a high chair or feeding table, they may try to get out and continue with their play.

Provide finger foods to infants and toddlers whenever possible. By picking up small bits of food, the child will develop fine-motor skills and hand-eye coordination skills. It also gives them a sense of accomplishment and helps them in developing independence.

Interest in self-feeding using spoons may occur between 15 and 18 months of age. You will need to be patient with children who are learning to feed themselves. You may have to help them fill their spoons. Since spilling occurs often, the children should wear bibs.

Workplace Connection

Toddlers and preschoolers are not too young to begin learning table and eating rules commonly known as *etiquette*. Ask students to brainstorm possible etiquette rules and determine those that are appropriate for the child care lab. Have students work in small groups to design posters or signs that depict each of the rules. Each group should then take turns introducing their specific rule and poster to the children over several classes.

Also expect food to be spilled on the feeding tray, high chair, and floor. Wipe up the spills immediately so others do not slip on them.

Two-Year-Olds

Two-year-old children become increasingly skilled at handling cups and spoons. Provide these children with child-sized spoons and small, unbreakable cups. Fill the cups only halfway. Then if a drink is spilled, there is less to clean up.

Use small milk or juice pitchers (16 ounces) with two-year-olds. Encourage the children to fill their own cups. Watch carefully and provide support. See 17-8.

Three-Year-Olds

By the age of three, children have distinct food preferences. They may refuse to eat certain foods because of their color, shape, or texture. Your attitude will help children accept these foods. In addition, family food attitudes and preferences can influence what children may eat. Other children can also influence food preferences. Some children who flatly refuse to eat vegetables at home may enjoy eating them with their peers.

Three-year-olds are old enough to assist with mealtime. Ask them to set the table. Make place mats containing outlines of the plate, glass, fork, and spoon. These patterns will help children set the table properly with minimal adult assistance. Provide forks and spoons to help the children develop handling skills. Use glasses with weighted bottoms to help prevent spills. Use pitchers with lids and pour spouts. Shallow bowls allow the children to see what is in the bowls.

Have children serve themselves. As a rule, tell children to fill their milk glasses only halfway. Keep portions small. If children want more food, they may ask for second portions.

Keep a wet sponge on the table for spills. When children spill, accept this as a normal occurrence. Avoid scolding the child. Rather, guide the child in wiping up the spill.

Four- and Five-Year-Olds

Four- and five-year-olds like to help at mealtime. They may ask to set the table, serve, and assist with after-meal cleanup. They may also enjoy helping to prepare the meal. Encourage them to do so. For a classroom activity, have them prepare pudding, rolls, or other simple foods, 17-9. Later, serve these foods for snack or lunch.

Older children enjoy talking at the table. You may wish to help them begin conversations. Mention activities they have seen, heard, or done. They will begin talking with each other and naturally move on to other subjects.

Limits

Limits for eating depend on the ages of the children. However, general limits might include the following:
- Taste all foods before asking for seconds of food or milk.

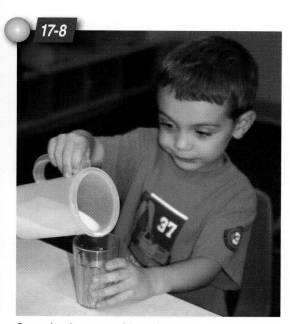

17-8

Supervise three-year-olds as they pour their own drinks. They may need help handling the pitcher.

Enrich

Ask students to debate the pros and cons of allowing two-year-olds to pour their own milk and juice from small pitchers. How can children be encouraged to perform this task for themselves?

Resource

Limits for Eating, Activity C, OG

Reflect

What foods do you avoid because of their color, shape, or texture? Can these foods be prepared so you will eat them? Can you relate your experiences to those that may be shared by a three-year-old?

Resource

Daily Routines Puzzle, reproducible master 17-2, TR

Meeting Special Needs

Distribute the *Daily Routines Puzzle,* reproducible master 17-2, TR. Students with visual processing challenges may find it easier to fill in the blanks in each statement instead of filling in the puzzle. Provide a word bank of possible words to be used for special learners. Special learners may benefit from creating a word search puzzle that includes important words and terms from the chapter. Provide a grid for the puzzle or use graph paper to create the grid for the letters.

Discuss

What routines will be important to follow for four- and five-year-olds when they assist with snack and meal preparations? What guidance challenges can you anticipate when children help prepare and serve food?

Vocabulary

Have student volunteers define the terms *food refusal* and *pica*. What routines may be affected when children exhibit these problems in school?

Discuss

What might be the effects of forcing a child to eat the food he or she has been served? What strategies would you use to encourage the reluctant eater to try some of the food?

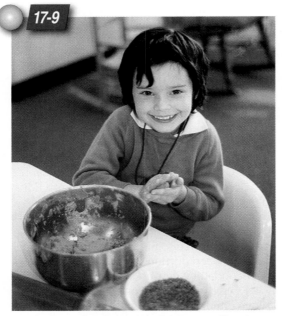

17-9

Children enjoy helping prepare foods they will eat later.

- Remain at the table until everyone has finished.

- Wipe up your own spills.

- Eat food only from your own plate.

- Say thank you after someone has served or passed you food.

- Say please when asking to have food passed or served to you.

Eating Problems

Eating problems are common during the preschool years. These problems usually peak at three years of age. Eating will remain a problem for 25 percent of four- and five-year-olds. In most cases, problems will end somewhere around the sixth birthday. Food refusal, dawdling, pica, and vomiting are all eating problems that can become serious.

Food Refusal. Food refusal problems are related to a lack of interest in food. Food refusal often begins between one and two years of age, 17-10. At this time, children's need for food decreases. Some children may need only one meal a day. Refusing food because it is not needed is not a problem. However, children who do not eat even when they need food have food refusal problems.

Lack of exercise or energy, excess energy (hyperactivity), and illness can all cause a lack of interest in food. These fairly common problems sometimes cure themselves. There are steps you can take, however, to help children with food refusal problems.

To encourage children to eat, serve small portions. Avoid pushing the children to eat. Instead, talk with the families of children having problems. Find out what these children eat at home. Despite mealtime refusal at the center, these children may be getting proper nourishment at home.

Do not provide extra snacks to children who refuse to eat breakfast and lunch. If you do, they will not be hungry at mealtime.

Pica. **Pica** is a craving for nonfood items. Cravings include paper, soap, rags, and even toys. This condition is fairly uncommon in most preschool children.

If you think that a child may have this problem, ask other staff members to observe the child. Compare your observations. Discuss the problem with the center director. You may want to schedule a conference with the family to discuss the problem. A combined effort between parents, medical professionals, and teachers may solve the problem.

17-10

Toddlers are especially known for their strong responses to foods they dislike.

Portfolio Project

Using print or Internet sources, ask students to search for information on teaching good manners to young children. How early should manners and etiquette training begin in a child's life? After a review of the information, ask students to create lists of the most important basic manners and basic table manners for preschoolers. Have students reproduce the lists as a handout or pamphlet for families. Encourage students to use desktop publishing programs or software, if available. Have students file a copy of the handout or pamphlet in their portfolio.

Dawdling. While one child eats only one or two bites, the other children may have finished an entire meal. It is common to have several children who eat slowly in a group of preschoolers. This is called **dawdling**. Some may hold food in their mouth for a long time, failing to chew or swallow it. Others are so busy talking at the table they forget to eat. Still others may push the food around their plates or play with it. These children lack interest in food.

Many times dawdling is an attempt to gain attention. Therefore, do not urge or threaten dawdling children. Instead, provide these children with small portions of food. After being given a reasonable amount of time to eat, clear the table without comment. Children will learn that if they want to eat, they must do so in a timely fashion.

Vomiting. Young children are able to *induce* (to produce on purpose) vomiting. If a child in your class vomits often without other signs of illness, he or she is possibly inducing it.

If you are sure a child is not sick, ignore repeated vomiting. Clean up the mess quickly, without emotion. If the child notices any concern, he or she may begin vomiting to get your attention.

You should, however, share the child's behavior with the family. Find out if this behavior also occurs at home during or right after a meal. If it does, you will need to work with the center director and parents to solve the problem.

Napping

"Will my child be required to take a nap?" This question is often asked by parents who are thinking of enrolling their child in a center. Some children may have outgrown napping at home. Your response will depend on your state's child care licensing regulations and center policies.

Most states require that preschool children nap at least one hour, 17-11. A center can expand that requirement if they

17-11

Naps are required in many states.

wish. For instance, if a state requires all children under the age of five to have naps, a center may expand that rule to require all enrolled children to have naps. In any case, you should check your state's guidelines for requirements.

Most child care centers have a set nap time. At the end of this time, most children are awake. If not, they are gently woken. You may note that a certain child needs to be woken every day. If this happens, the child may not be getting enough rest at home. This needs to be discussed with the family. Check with your center director to find out who is responsible for talking to the family. If you are asked to contact the family, use a positive approach. Share your observations with the family. Try to arrive at a solution together.

Nap Time Rituals

Schedule quiet activities prior to nap time. Children often enjoy hearing a story at this time. Select stories that will soothe the children. Four-year-olds may like to look at books until they fall asleep. You may want to play soft music.

Lack of rest can cause irritability in young children. Most preschool children,

Vocabulary

Have student volunteers define the terms *dawdling* and *vomiting*. What should you do when a child is inducing vomiting or refusing to chew or swallow their food?

Enrich

Have students review the suggested general limits for eating. Ask students to brainstorm additional limits that may be appropriate for a child care program. Remind students to state the limits positively.

Reflect

Did your parents or caregivers ever resort to bribes or threats to get you to eat? What were the results?

Putting Technology to Use

Ask students to conduct an Internet search for information that ties eating problems in young children to the development of other problems such as eating disorders and stress. What triggers may exist that result in a young child's food refusal behavior? Does anorexia exist in young children? What effect can stress have on the eating habits of the young? What is the significance of this information for teachers and parents of the young child? Allow time for students to share their findings in class.

Discuss

Why are routines and rituals especially important to follow at nap time? Why might some children be reluctant to take a nap while at the center?

Enrich

A child in your child care class expresses the need for a backrub every time she is ready to take a nap. Ask students to debate the pros and cons of giving in to the child's request on a regular basis.

Vocabulary

Have a student volunteer define the term *elimination*. Explain why elimination is a reflex action for infants.

tired or not, can postpone sleep at nap time. Younger children may simply cry. Older children, however, may make repeated demands for your attention. They may request to go to the washroom or have a drink of water. In most cases, these are only pleas for attention.

Plan ahead to prevent children from making too many demands at nap time. First, have the children use the toilet, brush their teeth, wash their hands, and have a drink of water before they lie down. Ask if anyone needs a tissue or wants to look quietly at a book. Make sure they have their blankets and stuffed toys. After this, begin to cover them. Do not be surprised, however, if a child still asks for another drink of water or trip to the bathroom. These rituals seem natural to most two- and three-year-old children. They sincerely believe their needs are real. However, if you allow these children to meet these needs before nap time, they will have an easier time getting and staying settled. See 17-12.

Not all children will fall asleep at nap time. Their need for sleep varies. It is common for some of the five-year-olds to remain awake. Five-year-olds will cooperate, however, if nap time limits are stated clearly and enforced.

Children who do fall asleep may tell you they had bad dreams while sleeping. Others may cry out in their sleep. When this happens, calmly approach the child. Let the child know you are near. One way to do this is to hold the child's hand or straighten the covers.

As a teacher, it is important to respect the children's need for sleep. Because it is difficult for some children to fall asleep, try to remain as quiet as possible. Avoid talking to other teachers during nap time.

Toileting

The toileting needs of infants are met through the use of diapers. Infants cannot control *elimination*, bowel and bladder release. For them, elimination is a reflex action. The

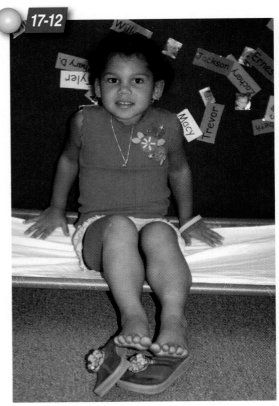

17-12

Allow children to remove shoes and socks at nap time. They will be more comfortable and relaxed.

first few weeks after birth, infants eliminate many times each day. They may cry when it happens. The number of eliminations will decrease as the infant gets older. However, the volume increases. By 28 weeks, a child may remain dry from one to two hours. When they do eliminate, however, the diaper is usually soaking wet. It may leak unless it is changed immediately. Diapers need to be checked often and changed when wet to prevent diaper rash.

Children differ in their toilet learning needs and schedule. Some children use the toilet as early as two years. Others may not have full bladder and bowel control until three years or later. For some children, toilet learning will take just a few days. Other children may require several months.

Workplace Connection

Have students locate storybooks that will promote a calming atmosphere for nap time. Ask the students to practice reading the stories aloud using voice inflections that will soothe and comfort children as they begin to fall asleep. Ask student volunteers to contact local preschool classrooms or child care center's to read their story before nap time. Was the story calming to the children? Allow time for students to share the results of their experience in class.

Using Potty Chairs

Because non-flushing toilets, or potty chairs, can pose a significant sanitation risk, take special care when you use them. Keep the following guidelines in mind when using potty chairs:

- Empty, clean, and sanitize the potty chairs after each use.

- Clean and sanitize potty chairs in a sink that is used only for this purpose.

- Use potty chairs *only* in the bathroom area.

- Keep potty chairs out of children's reach when not in use.

- Wash your hands thoroughly according to accepted standards when assisting children with toileting or cleaning and sanitizing potty chairs. If desired, wear disposable vinyl gloves when cleaning and sanitizing potty chairs. Remove the gloves when finished and follow-up with the proper hand-washing technique.

Toilet Learning Timetable

Children cannot be taught to perform toilet functions until their central nervous systems are ready. As a rule, this does not occur until after two years of age. At this age, most children will express their need to use the toilet. Some may pull down their pants and sit on the toilet. Others will tell you they have to use the bathroom.

Each child in the center will have his or her own toilet learning timetable. Never force children to develop self-regulation. When they are ready, they will master control of their bodily functions. Instead praise them as they become better at keeping themselves dry. Controlling elimination is one step toward independence. It is a real accomplishment for young children.

Certain factors may affect a child's toilet learning timetable. Illness, a new baby in the home, or weather changes are common factors. Remember, too, that toileting accidents are common during a child's first few weeks at the child care center. These accidents may indicate the emotional stress the child is feeling in a new environment. Another factor is the toilet learning attitudes and practices at home. In some homes, adults may overreact to children's toileting accidents by showing their disapproval. These children may feel ashamed by their failure to control elimination. In the center, you need to be sensitive to children's feelings following an accident. Quietly help them change into clean clothes.

Guidance

As a teacher, keep a matter-of-fact attitude in toilet teaching. Shaming and scolding have no place in helping a child develop control. Instead, provide children with the facilities and encouragement to stay dry.

Have toilet seats or potty chairs available. If you provide a seat for the toilet, also provide a step stool to help the children reach the toilet. Not all children like to sit on the toilet. Some are afraid they will fall in the toilet and be flushed down. These children will prefer the potty chair.

During toilet learning, the child's clothing should be easy to manage. Pants that pull down easily work better than those that are hard to unfasten. Also during this time, it is a good idea to keep several extra pairs of underwear and clothing at the center.

Discuss

What is necessary before children are able to perform toilet functions? At what age does this generally occur?

Reflect

Should rewards be offered for toilet learning? If so, what types of rewards can you think of to offer a child who is toilet learning?

Discuss

What factors affect a child's toilet learning timetable? How might new situations affect a child's toilet learning?

Putting Technology to Use

Have students conduct an Internet search for information on toilet learning aids available commercially. What types of products can help parents and teachers have success with toilet learning? Compare the costs of dolls, diaper alternatives, potty seats and chairs, storybooks, pictures, and posters designed to promote toilet learning. Which of these products, if any, would be useful for teachers to use in a child care program? Allow time for students to share their findings in class.

Children often provide clues when they have to use the toilet. Some start wiggling. Others cross their legs. When you notice these signs, provide reminders to the child. You can remind the child by saying, "It is toilet time again," or "Louis, do you need to use the toilet?" After children use the toilet, remind them to flush the toilet and wash their hands. At the same time, be sure to wash your own hands. See 17-13.

Cleanup

Cleanup is an important routine in early childhood classrooms. Children learn to be responsible for themselves, their belongings, and classroom materials and equipment. Cleanup time can be stressful for a new teacher. Consider Carlos, who recently began teaching in a preschool. He frequently finds himself raising his voice and scolding or nagging the children to help in cleanup. Carlos's frustration is not uncommon. The following suggestions may be helpful.

Guidance

Try to maintain a positive attitude toward cleanup. Scolding or nagging the children usually is ineffective. You will discover that some children are unresponsive and do not want to participate.

Begin by setting firm ground rules and then follow through. All children should be expected to participate in cleanup. You must deal on an individual basis with the child who refuses to participate. You may say "Tanya, you need to put the puzzle away." Observe Tanya closely. If she walks away from the table, take her hand. Then say "Tanya, come. You need to return the puzzle to the tray." If Tanya still refuses to put the puzzle away, she needs help in understanding the consequences. Explain that if she fails to put the puzzle away, she will not be able to play with the puzzles.

You will find that some children need encouragement or reminders. You might try saying the following:

- Help me put the blocks away.
- Show me where the puzzles are stored.
- Where do we hang these dress-up clothes?
- Timmy, you worked hard making your block structure. Now show Malcolm how to put the blocks away.

Foster independence by visually assisting the children in seeing where materials and equipment belong. For instance, in the woodworking area, paint a silhouette of each tool on a piece of poster board. Hooks in the dramatic play area should be available for hanging dress-up clothes. To assist the children, attach an eight-inch loop of string to each item of clothing. On the block shelves, provide separate sections for each shape and size of blocks. The manipulative area needs to have separate, transparent containers for different types of pieces.

Young children enjoy pleasing others. They will work hard to win your approval. Thus, it is important that children's efforts at cleanup be praised. Praise their efforts by saying "Sally, I like the way you are helping Frankie put the blocks away" or "Ampario, I like the way you picked up all of the pieces of your puzzle."

Resource

Children, Teachers, and Routines, Activity A, OG

Discuss

What additional strategies or techniques might be used to encourage a child who continually refuses to participate in cleanup? How can the child's parents be included in helping to solve this problem?

Resource

Managing Conflicts, Activity C, SAG

17-13

Tips for Guiding Toilet Learning

- Each child has his or her own toilet learning timetable. Never force children to learn before they are ready.
- Maintain a matter-of-fact attitude.
- Praise children as they become better at keeping dry.
- Do not shame or scold.
- Make toilet seats or potty chairs available.
- Watch for clues that children provide when they need to use the toilet.

Remember these rules for effective toileting guidance.

Workplace Connection

Ask students to survey the child care lab, identifying any areas that need to be rearranged to foster more independence in cleanup by the children. What is already being done in the child care lab that encourages children to participate in cleanup? Have students write a report of their findings to share with the child care teacher. Ask students to obtain permission to make any adjustments in the child care lab, if needed. Allow time for students to discuss their findings in class.

Transitions

Transitions are changes from one activity to another or moves from one place to another. They occur many times during the day. Children may go from self-selected activities to using the bathroom to snack time to outdoor play in just a few hours. Transitions must be carefully planned to help children get through the daily routine without a fuss.

Tell the children in advance that a transition will occur. Many teachers provide a five-minute warning prior to making the transition to the next activity. This will allow children time to finish what they are doing. You might play the piano for five minutes or use an egg timer.

There are four basic methods for making successful transitions. You may use concrete objects, visual signals, novelty, or auditory signals. You may use several types of transitions in one day. Remember to be consistent. Young children respond better if they know what to expect. Therefore, it is best to use the same transition for individual activities. For instance, play the same cleanup song every day to let the children know it is cleanup time.

Concrete Objects

Using concrete objects as a form of transition involves children moving items from one place to another. This technique directs a child's attention from one activity to another, 17-14. Examples include the following:

- "Leon, please put your picture in your cubby." This will direct Leon from an art activity to a new activity.
- "Rose, hang up your coat." Rose will move from an outdoor activity to an indoor activity.
- "Ting, here is some play dough. Take it to the art table." Ting is directed toward starting an art activity.
- "Shilpa, put these washcloths on the bathroom hook." This signals the end of cleanup.

17-14

Putting away toys helps prepare children for the next activity.

Visual Signals

Using visual signals is another transition method. This method involves informing children of a change through signals they can see. For instance, when you show the children a picture of lunchtime, the children move to the lunch table. After story time, you might hold up a picture of outdoor play. This will serve as a signal to the children that it is time to put on outdoor clothing and wait at the door for you. See 17-15 for other examples of visual transitions.

The first few times you use visual signals, you will need to explain them to the children. After you use them several times, the children will know what to expect.

Novelty

Novelty transitions involve the use of unusual, new actions or devices to move the children from one activity to another.

Vocabulary

Have a student volunteer define the term *transitions*. Why is it necessary to anticipate and plan for transitions?

Discuss

What methods of warning are used in the child care lab to alert children that an activity is about to end? Are students consistent in using the same method for transitions for specific individual activities? Why is this important?

Reflect

Did you ever have to abruptly stop what you were doing because a parent or other authority figure told you, without a warning, that it was time to do something else? How did this make you feel? Can you relate this feeling to what a preschooler may feel when the same thing happens to him or her?

Resource

Not-So-Smooth Transitions, reproducible master 17-3, TR

Cross-Curricular Activity

Music
Collaborate with the vocal or instrumental music instructors in your school for this activity. Divide students into small groups to collaborate on creating a simple song to serve as a transition for cleanup time. Students may write a simple rhyme and add it to the tune of a popular song or compose their own melody for the transition. Have each group of students demonstrate their song for the class so students can choose one or two songs to teach the children in the child care lab.

Discuss

After reviewing 17-15, *Using Visual Transition*, ask students to brainstorm any additional visual transition ideas that may be incorporated into the child care lab. How could visual and auditory transitions be combined to be effective for children who may have a disability in either area?

Reflect

What identification games, if any, were used as a means of transition in your own preschool or early childhood classes? Which did you recall liking the best and found worked successfully to keep children controlled until being dismissed by the teacher?

Vocabulary

Have a student volunteer define the term *individual transition*. When might an individual transition be needed or used?

Locomotion is one type of transition. The children use motion to make their transition. For instance, ask the children to pretend they are elephants. Have them walk like heavy elephants to the snack table, or ask them to tiptoe lightly like tiny monkeys.

Using locomotion is limited only by imagination. Children can march, skip, or walk backwards. Before introducing a transition, however, consider the abilities of the children. For instance, do not ask a group of two- or three-year-olds to skip. They may not have developed this skill yet.

Transportation is another type of novelty transition. The children can move like freight trains, jets, buses, or cars. Each time you introduce a locomotion or transportation transition, get involved with the children. Model the movement you want them to make.

Identification games are also used for novelty transition. For instance, you may direct the children from one activity to another by asking "Who is wearing red today? You may go into the bathroom and wash your hands before we have our snacks." Continue using other colors that the children are wearing until every child has departed from the group.

Novelty transitions can also be made using single alphabet letters. Direct the

children to another activity by asking "Whose name starts with the letter *T*? You may go outside." Continue calling out letters until all of the children are outdoors.

Auditory Signals

Auditory signals inform the children of a change through the use of sound. A bell, timer, Autoharp®, tambourine, or piano can all inform children of a transition. Some teachers use a simple song or chord of music as a transition signal. For example, when Mr. Andrews plays "Mary Had a Little Lamb" on the piano, the children know it is time to clean up.

Auditory signals also need to be developed for individuals. There will be times when you may wish to signal only one child. For instance, you may quietly tell a child that he or she needs to clean up or go to the snack table. This is called an *individual transition*.

Auditory signals are quite useful for providing warnings. For instance, a ringing bell tells the children that playtime will end in five minutes. At the end of the five minutes, they know it is time to clean up.

17-15

Using Visual Transition

Visual Transition Method	Application of Method
Construction paper	Use to break children into small groups. Place a piece of blue, red, green, or yellow construction paper at each table. Divide children into four groups and assign each group one of these colors. Have groups find their tables.
Hand motions	Use on playground to motion children indoors or to a specific area.
Blinking lights	Use to gain children's attention or to warn children to complete an activity.
Clock	Use with older children by telling them "When the big hand is on the 12, it will be lunchtime."
Words	Use to dismiss children from a group. Make a name card for each child. Hold cards up one at a time. Children are dismissed when they see their names.

Visual signals can be used many ways for transition.

Meeting Special Needs

Review the special learners' chapter outlines to determine if the students have any questions about the concepts or content of this chapter. Review the chapter objectives and ask the students to evaluate their progress in meeting these objectives. Ask the students to summarize, orally or in writing, what they learned from this chapter.

Summary

A daily schedule and routines provide structure to each day. Within this structure, children have the opportunity to develop independence. Having a predictable schedule and helping children handle daily routines allow the center to run smoothly. This also offers the children emotional security.

A well-planned schedule provides the framework for the day's activities. Schedules for early childhood programs vary by type of program. Factors such as the length of the program's day and the time children arrive will need to be considered.

The daily schedule must also be planned to meet the children's physical and psychological needs. Health and safety are important considerations. For comfort and security, children need to have consistency and predictable routines.

Dressing, undressing, eating, napping, toileting, and cleanup are all daily routines. Each of these presents its own particular challenges and problems during the course of a day. For instance, asking children to participate with cleanup seems like a predictable activity. However, without the proper guidance, this task may become frustrating for both the children and the teacher. Therefore, it is important for you to learn positive guidance strategies to help children learn responsibility.

Review and Reflect

1. How do routines and daily schedules benefit young children?

2. Why is it important to provide large blocks of open time in the daily schedule?

3. Describe a typical arrival routine.

4. Why do many programs ask families to send a second set of clothing for children to keep at school?

5. Name five factors that may influence a child's appetite.

6. List three limits for eating that might be used with young children.

7. Give two suggestions for handling a child who refuses to eat.

8. What is pica?

9. Do child care centers have the right to decide if nap time should be included in the daily schedule? Explain your answer.

10. At what age are most children ready to begin toilet learning?

11. Describe one way you could encourage children to participate in cleanup.

12. List four types of transitions and give an example of each.

5. illness, stage of development, amount of physical activity, body's nutrient needs, emotions
6. (List three:) Taste all foods before asking for seconds of food or milk. Remain at the table until everyone has finished. Wipe up your own spills. Eat food only from your own plate. Say thank you after someone has served or passed you food. Say please when asking to have food passed or served to you.
7. (List two. Student response.)
8. Pica is a craving for nonfood items.
9. No. You must follow your state's child care licensing regulations.
10. after two years of age
11. (Student response.)
12. concrete objects, visual signals, novelty, auditory signals (Student response for examples.)

Review and Reflect Answer Key

1. Routines promote the children's social, self-help, and learning skills. Routines at child care centers reassure children by providing a predictable pattern. They know the order of daily events and what to expect with each event. This offers them emotional security. Daily routines provide opportunities for children to develop independence.
2. Young children thrive on making choices. They enjoy selecting activities and deciding how long to play. Many children have short attention spans. Differences also exist in the speed at which they enjoy complete projects.
3. (Student response.)
4. A second set of clothes can be used if a child soils or rips his or her clothes.

Apply and Explore

1. Practice putting on your sweater or jacket using the technique outlined in the chapter.

2. From a sitting position, practice teaching tying, buttoning, and zipping to one of your peers.

3. Observe children at cleanup. Record the techniques the teacher uses with the children to encourage them to participate. Discuss your findings with your classmates.

4. Ask parents what clues their children use when they need to use the toilet. Compare these to the clues you observe.

Cross-Curricular Link

Language Arts

1. Ask experienced teachers for their successful nap time techniques. Present this information as a report.

Technology

2. Explore the Web site www.smallfolk.com to learn more about how to handle feeding problems for children under five years of age.

Workplace Link

Select music that would provide a soothing environment for naptime. You may be able to access musical sources on the Internet or check out CDs and tapes from the public library. Create a mix of songs for a CD to be used during naptime. (Be aware of copyright infringement laws and use only music that is free from restrictions.)

Transitions help children understand when to clean up and move on to another activity.

PART

4

Learning Experiences for Children

Good learning experiences for children are based on careful planning. This begins with the establishment of program goals for your early childhood program. Quality programs reflect children's developmental needs, interests, and experiences. In this part, you will learn how to plan curriculum that is based on the development of the whole child. You will learn appropriate methods of developing and writing program curriculum.

Providing a variety of learning experiences helps children learn and grow in many ways. As you read this part, you will learn techniques for guiding the following types of experiences: art, storytelling, puppetry, manuscript writing, math, science, social studies, food and nutrition, music and movement, and field trips.

Each chapter will give you guidelines for planning and supervising activities. You will read many ideas for specific activities to try with children. You will also discover what types of supplies and resources you will need to conduct these activities.

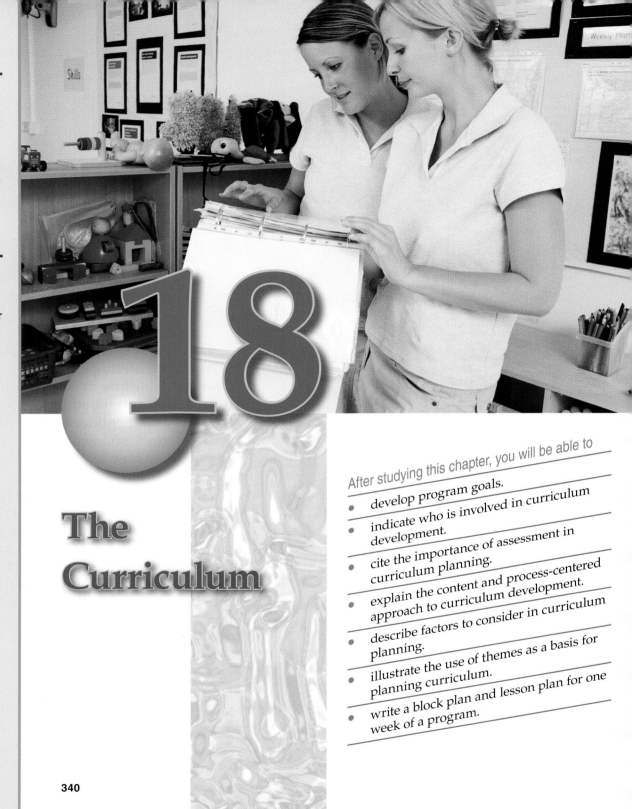

Discuss

Look at the chapter opening photo. Do you think it is a good idea to review the day's plans with coworkers every morning or evening? What might this accomplish?

Discuss

Look over the objectives for this chapter. How will learning this material prepare you for a career in early childhood education?

18

The Curriculum

After studying this chapter, you will be able to

- develop program goals.
- indicate who is involved in curriculum development.
- cite the importance of assessment in curriculum planning.
- explain the content and process-centered approach to curriculum development.
- describe factors to consider in curriculum planning.
- illustrate the use of themes as a basis for planning curriculum.
- write a block plan and lesson plan for one week of a program.

340

Terms to Know

program goals
content and process-centered approach
direct learning experience
indirect learning experience
teachable moment
field-sensitive
field-independent
visual learner
auditory learner
emergent curriculum
theme
spiral curriculum
web
concept
block plan
lesson plan
learning objective
motivation
closure

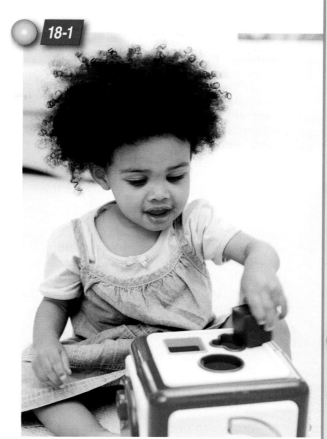

18-1

Age-appropriate play materials should be part of the curriculum.

Vocabulary

Have students review the *Terms to Know* list. Ask students to look up unfamiliar words or terms in the glossary before reading the chapter.

Reflect

Why do you think room arrangements reflect or are part of the curriculum? Give an example to show you understand this concept.

Resource

Planning the Curriculum, color transparency CT-15, TR

Reading a story, feeding a bunny, singing songs, and playing outdoors are all parts of the curriculum. Cooking, scribbling on paper, building with blocks, and playing in the dramatic play corner are also considered the curriculum. The curriculum includes all the activities, materials, and equipment used, 18-1. Even room arrangements reflect the curriculum.

A developmentally appropriate early childhood curriculum is based on how children develop and learn. It consists of a wide range of concepts, experiences, and materials designed to meet the developmental needs of a group of children. These needs include their social, emotional, physical, and cognitive needs. The curriculum also considers and respects families' cultural background. Curriculum should develop, support, and encourage positive relationships with the children's family. It involves determining what children need to be able to do and what they need to know. A good curriculum also focuses on children's learning styles and characteristics. It is based on the premise that play is an important part of the curriculum. It often organizes important concepts into themes.

A developmentally appropriate curriculum tailors learning experiences to children's ages, stages of development, interests, needs, abilities, and experiences. The curriculum should provide the children an opportunity to make meaningful choices. It also requires detailed planning. This chapter will describe the factors to consider when planning a curriculum.

Meeting Special Needs

Provide an outline of the chapter with all the chapter headings for special learners. Students should fill in each section of the outline as the material is covered in class with a sentence or two about the content. Review the special learners' IEPs to decide if any modifications should be made in presenting the chapter content. Prepare a vocabulary matching assignment to assist the special learners in understanding the *Terms to Know*.

Vocabulary

Have a student volunteer define the term *program goals*. How are program goals tied to effective and successful teaching?

Discuss

What are some possible learning activities that would meet the program goal of developing a positive self-concept? What possible learning activities might promote the goal of developing positive social skills and cooperation?

Activity

Ask students to keep program goals in mind as they survey the child care lab. Have students list examples of how the lab's environment contributes to meeting the program's goals. Allow time for students to discuss their findings in class.

Developing Program Goals

Before the curriculum can be planned, the goals of the program need to be determined. In an early childhood program, the program goals outline the philosophy of the center. **Program goals** are broad statements of purpose that state the desired end results—what is to be achieved. Some people describe goals as the "why" of the curriculum.

Program goals based on child development focus on the whole child. Goals for children in an early childhood setting might include the following:

- to develop a positive self-concept and attitude toward learning
- to develop independence
- to develop problem-solving skills, 18-2
- to respect and understand cultural diversity
- to develop effective language skills, both listening and speaking
- to develop fine-motor coordination
- to develop gross-motor coordination

18-2

Bulletin board activities are a good method to teach problem-solving skills.

- to develop personal initiative
- to develop a curiosity about the world
- to develop positive social skills, including cooperation and interdependence
- to develop respect for one's own rights as well as the rights of others
- to develop an understanding of the relationship between people, events, and objects

Each of these goals is broad. The goals relate to all four areas of development since a developmentally appropriate curriculum considers the whole child.

Meeting Goals

Teachers, available resources, activities, and the environment all influence whether goals will be met. For example, if one of the goals is to create independence, provide children with a minimum of help. This gives children many opportunities to grow in independence. Classroom activities should be designed to require little involvement on the part of the teacher. Children should be able to make choices and participate in most activities without an adult's help. The activities, then, will need to match children's skill levels.

The classroom environment, including room arrangement, can also foster the development of independence. Placing coat hooks, paper towels, tables, chairs, and equipment within children's reach is helpful. This allows the children to act on their own. They do not have to depend on teachers for help at all times.

Who Plans the Curriculum?

Curriculum development can involve one person or several staff members. In small

Workplace Connection

Many schools, organizations, and companies have mission statements to let others know their ideals and what they represent. Survey local groups for examples of mission statements or search for examples on the Internet. In addition to program goals, create a mission statement for the child care lab program. Be sure to include who you are, what you do, what you stand for, and why you do what you do. Mission statements should be written as a collaborative activity with all students participating.

centers, the head teacher is often the person in charge of planning the curriculum, 18-3. Teachers have firsthand knowledge of their children's interests, needs, learning styles, and prior experiences. In some centers, a wide range of additional people are involved in the process. Directors, teachers, aides, parents, and in some cases even the center cook may all be included at some time. Each of these people can provide helpful information in planning the curriculum. In large organizations, a curriculum specialist may be hired to help plan the curriculum.

18-3

Using a self-planned curriculum allows teachers to create their own games for the children.

The child care director usually plays a key role in curriculum development. In most centers, the director is in charge of supervising all center activities. Therefore, the director's position usually includes curriculum supervision.

Some child care corporations provide the directors of their centers with preplanned curriculum units. Each director is responsible for introducing the curriculum to the teaching staff. After modifying it to fit the children's needs, the teachers are expected to use the curriculum.

A preplanned curriculum has both advantages and disadvantages. For a staff with little training or experience, a preplanned curriculum can be helpful. Activities, procedures, and suggestions are often outlined in detail. Having these curriculum ideas at their fingertips saves teachers time and energy.

A preplanned curriculum has some disadvantages. It may not factor in the individual differences and learning styles of the children in your program. The curriculum needs to be based on the learners' abilities so it can build on what the children already know. It needs to be relevant, interesting, and challenging. Experienced teachers may feel stifled or limited by a preplanned curriculum. Because of their experience, they are more likely to observe a mismatch between children's needs and the curriculum. If this happens, experienced teachers are likely to feel frustrated.

Assessment: An Important Step in Curriculum Planning

Every child is unique, even though there are many similarities within age groups. For this reason, assessment is necessary in order to plan a curriculum that is both individualized and age appropriate for all areas of learning.

Discuss

Why might a curriculum specialist be hired to help plan a child care center's curriculum? What role does the director have in curriculum planning?

Activity

Have students locate an example of a preplanned curriculum from a local child care center that uses one. Ask students to review the curriculum to see if the goals you have set for the child care lab could be met by following the planned curriculum.

Discuss

Refer students to Chapter 3 to review information on assessments. Ask students to explain why assessments are an important part of the curriculum-planning process.

Workplace Connection

Have students interview a curriculum director (or other school administrator in charge of curriculum) to discover what this job entails. What background training and experience is needed? What are the challenges of designing and selecting a curriculum? How difficult is it to meet the needs of school administration, teachers, parents, and state learning requirements? What advice or suggestions does the curriculum director have for a child care center director or instructor in designing and choosing an effective curriculum? Have students prepare a list of additional questions to ask prior to the interview.

Vocabulary

Have a student volunteer explain the *content and process-centered approach* to curriculum planning. What is stressed in this type of curriculum plan?

Discuss

What items are the key parts of a content and process-centered curriculum? What does the physical environment of the child care center have to do with this approach?

Vocabulary

Have a student volunteer define the terms *direct learning experiences* and *indirect learning experiences.* Is it possible to plan indirect learning experiences?

The assessment process should provide you with useful information on all developmental levels for planning a curriculum. The first assessment supplies data on what the children already know and what skills they have achieved. It should also identify their needs and interests. This data can help you fit curriculum to individual children. It can also be helpful for informing parents of their children's progress over a period of time.

Assessment should be based on the children's activities at the center. It should occur as part of the ongoing life of the classroom. It should rely on multiple sources. Assessment should also highlight the children's strengths and capabilities. It should highlight what the children know and what they can do. It should include collections of the children's work, such as artwork, stories, and projects. Teachers' observations and summaries may also be included.

The Content and Process-Centered Curriculum

Though there are a number of approaches to curriculum planning, the most popular method is the **content and process-centered approach**. Learning is seen as a constant process of exploring and questioning the environment. A hands-on curriculum is stressed. All four areas of child development—social, emotional, physical, and cognitive—are included. A wide range of age-appropriate materials, supplies, and experiences are used to enrich the environment, 18-4. Materials and equipment are matched to the children's abilities, cultural background, and development.

Basic learning materials are a key part of the content and process-centered curriculum. These materials are chosen and structured

In this process-centered environment, a child learns more about firefighters by trying on a firefighter's outfit.

by the teacher. They may include puzzles, games, blocks, sand, water, books, records, and supplies for dramatic play and science study.

The physical environment is carefully planned and prepared with the content for learning. It should be based on an assessment of children's developmental needs, interests, abilities, and experiences. Once established, the children assume responsibility by choosing most of their own activities. As a result, the use of time, space, and equipment is largely determined by the children.

A good curriculum includes direct and indirect learning experiences. **Direct learning experiences** are planned with a specific goal in mind. For instance, a carpentry learning activity may be planned to develop fine-motor skills and to teach the use of safety goggles. The room arrangement may be planned to foster the independence needed for this task and call attention to the activity.

Indirect learning experiences occur on the spur of the moment. For example, while watching Reina, Dwayne may learn how

---

Portfolio Project

Have students write an essay explaining their understanding of direct and indirect learning experiences. Ask students to plan a direct learning experience to teach preschoolers self-help skills. Students may choose to teach preschoolers how to tie their shoes, button their coats, wash their hands, etc. Have students include in their essay examples of indirect learning experiences and teachable moments that could be used as a learning opportunity for teaching the self-help skill. Have students file a copy of the essay in their portfolio.

to button his coat. Shelly may learn how to paint by watching Mark. While mixing paint, Kelsie may learn that adding red paint to blue paint makes purple paint.

In teaching, timing is important. A **teachable moment** is an unexpected event the teacher can use as a learning opportunity. It occurs when the children are curious and responsive to being taught. These occasions are not planned. However, good teachers are able to take advantage of them by observing and listening. They can make the most of the moment by capturing the children's attention. They can then share important skills, concepts, and ideas. These opportunities happen every day.

Some teachable moments start with a new discovery. Others start with mistakes. A teachable moment is an opportunity for children to learn why something happens. Examples may include the following:

- Without advance notice, Huda's mother brought in a basket of baby bunnies.

- Mai tripped on some blocks.

- Amparo had a bike accident and wasn't wearing her helmet.

- Sonia said that play dough feels "sticky."

- The class gerbil gave birth to babies.

- The tulips bloomed in the flower garden.

Factors to Consider in Curriculum Planning

As you begin planning a curriculum, there are a number of important factors to keep in mind. You must first decide what skills and content should be covered. There are three important questions to ask as the content of the curriculum is determined. The learning activities selected need to be balanced. In addition, various learning styles and learning characteristics need to be considered.

Choose the Skills and Content to Cover

As you begin planning the curriculum, you must decide what skills and content to cover. Three basic questions can help you with this process. First, consider the question: Is the information worth knowing? In order to answer this question, think about the cultural context. In some societies a certain learning outcome may be important. Ask yourself if the outcome will help the child better cope with his or her surroundings.

Children in the United States at some point must learn to read. Our culture places great importance on reading. As a result, children are read many stories in child care centers. Through listening, children learn to enjoy and appreciate literature. In some societies, these skills would not be needed. Other skills important to that culture would be stressed.

A second question needs to be answered: Is the information testable? In other words, the child should be able to see firsthand that the information is true, 18-5. Many times,

18-5

Information on bubbles is testable if children can blow and catch bubbles.

Reflect

In your childhood, what learning outcome besides the ability to read helped you cope with a specific task you were required to perform? What learning outcome helped you develop a specific attitude important in coping with your surroundings?

Discuss

If an activity or topic includes information that is testable, must the testing be done during the preschool class? What effect on the child's learning might result if the information is not tested in class?

Reflect

How are you affected when a long lesson is being taught to you without a change in teaching style? What variations of teaching style might help you to stay on task and pay more attention to the teacher?

Cross-Curricular Activity

Social Studies
Have students research other countries and cultures of the world to discover how their educational systems are based on cultural factors. What countries or cultures have little or no emphasis on education due to cultural expectations for their children? Which have developed requirements based on high expectations for education and learning? Students can report to the class through a poster session on their chosen country. The teacher may be able to coordinate this activity with a social studies class and include an opportunity for collaboration with social studies students.

Enrich

Information about dinosaurs is not testable by preschoolers, yet many early childhood programs include learning activities related to dinosaurs. Ask students to debate the advantages and disadvantages of including dinosaurs in the preschool curriculum based on the factors to consider in curriculum planning.

Reflect

Shawna spends all her time alone during unstructured play drawing or coloring in the art area. As a result, she lacks the social skills to play with other children. Should the art materials be put away for a time to encourage her to try other activities? How might this affect other children in the class?

Discuss

How do *structured* or *close-ended* learning activities contribute to a balance in curriculum? How much of the schedule should be devoted to structured activities?

teachers choose activities based on personal appeal. They like the activity. For instance, activities related to dinosaurs have long been included in the curriculum of many early childhood programs. Think about the activity based on this question. Will children ever see a live dinosaur? This activity is not testable. Another activity might be more appropriate. Instead of reading a book about dinosaurs, choose one about an animal children know about or may have a chance to see at the zoo.

Here is another example. If you were going to do a unit on foods, making butter would be a testable activity. To begin this activity, tell the children that cream can be made into butter. Then show the children the consistency of cream. After this, give each child an unbreakable container filled with whipping cream. Show them how to shake the container. Tell the children to keep shaking until the mixture becomes thick. After the cream has turned to butter, let each child taste the butter. This will help them test their knowledge.

The third basic question remains: Is the information developmentally appropriate? A learning activity that requires giving scissors and paper to three- and four-year-olds is appropriate. Children this age can use scissors properly. This activity would be inappropriate for children 18 to 24 months old.

Balance Learning Activities

An appropriate curriculum contains a balance of learning activities supporting all developmental domains. These activities must be chosen with care. Activities designed to keep children busy are not always the best activities. Likewise, just because children prefer a certain activity does not mean it must be kept included in the curriculum. You must evaluate each activity to be sure it is developmentally appropriate for the children.

A good curriculum includes a balance of structured as well as unstructured learning activities. Examples of unstructured activities include blockbuilding, collages, water play, and sand play. Children should spend most of their time in self-initiated play with unstructured activities. This type of play allows them opportunities to practice newly developed skills.

Structured, or close-ended, learning activities also need to be included. These activities indirectly prescribe children's actions. Stringing beads, working puzzles, and cooking are all examples.

Whenever possible, also plan a balance of indoor and outdoor learning activities, 18-6. The climate in your area will determine whether this is possible. During extremely hot and cold weather, the children should remain indoors. When this happens, provide children with gross-motor activities appropriate for indoors.

In warmer climates, weather permitting, many indoor learning activities can be moved outdoors. Painting, water play, and story and music time can all be done outdoors.

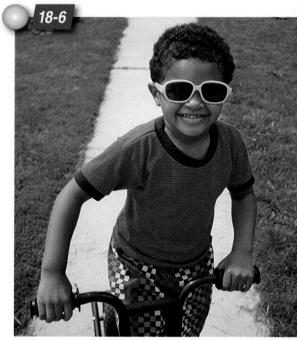

18-6

Outdoor activities allow children to get fresh air and work off excess energy.

Workplace Connection

Divide students into groups and ask them to brainstorm a list of typical preschool activities. Have them write the results on large sheets of paper. After five minutes, have students take turns in determining which activities on their lists are developmentally appropriate for four- and five-year-olds. Students must be able to support their choices or give reasons why an activity might be inappropriate. Have students repeat the activity for two- and three-year-olds. Display the lists around the classroom.

Active and quiet learning activities must be balanced. Planning too many active learning activities in a row may overstimulate some children. The result can be chaotic. To prevent this, follow active learning activities with quiet ones. For example, outdoor activity followed by a story and small group would be a good balance.

Too many quiet learning activities in a row also have a drawback. Children will get restless. The results can be just as chaotic as too many active learning activities. Children may lose interest in the activities and begin to wiggle and talk out of turn.

Consider Learning Styles

When planning activities for young children, consider the diversity of individual learning styles. Basic learning styles include field-sensitive, field-independent, visual learner, and auditory learner.

Field-Sensitive

Field-sensitive children like to work with others, 18-7. In a group setting, they are helpful. They will volunteer and assist others in picking up blocks, setting the table, and finding a place for a puzzle piece. Field-sensitive children will also try to gain your attention.

When introduced to a new activity, field-sensitive children want a model to follow. They may ask to be shown how to do the activity. If there is not a model or demonstration, they may wait. When someone else begins, they will observe. After this observation, they will begin their work.

Field-Independent

Field-independent children like to try new activities. They enjoy discovery. These children do not have to be urged to try new activities. In most cases, they will be the first to try new activities. Children who are field-independent will rarely contact the teacher

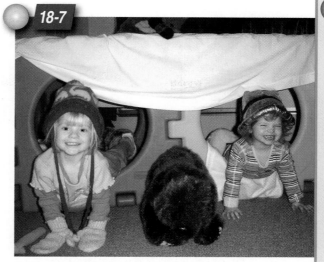

18-7

Field-sensitive children enjoy playing with others.

for help. They enjoy engaging in new tasks without directions or assistance from the teacher.

Field-independent children prefer to work on their own, 18-8. However, they enjoy competition as well as individual recognition. Field-independent children are also task orientated. When engaged in an activity, they generally do not notice what is going on around them.

Visual Learners

Visual learners depend a great deal on the sense of sight. These children notice small changes in the environment. When a plant is added to the science table, they are the first to notice. Visual learners enjoy looking at books and other objects.

Auditory Learners

Auditory learners are those who learn best through hearing. These children are the first to hear a fly in the classroom or a snowplow outdoors. You will find that auditory learners enjoy listening. To meet their needs, music, stories, and poems need to be included in the curriculum.

Vocabulary

Have student volunteers define the terms *field-sensitive*, *field-independent*, *visual learners*, and *auditory learners*. Why is it important to identify the preschoolers' learning styles when planning the curriculum? Why might teachers tend to favor field-sensitive children? What might result from this favoritism?

Discuss

What may be a challenge in dealing with a field-independent child when it is cleanup time? How can the teacher plan ahead for this challenge?

Reflect

What strategies do you notice your high school teachers using to account for various learning styles of their students? Which strategy or strategies do you think best suit your own learning style or preference?

Resource

Learning Styles, Activity B, OG

Portfolio Project

Ask students to select a preschooler to profile for an anecdotal observation of the child's learning style and preferences. Students should observe the child while he or she is engaged in different types of play as well as when the child is playing alone or with others. Examples of the child's behaviors during structured and unstructured time can be written to document characteristics of the child's learning styles. Using the observation notes, have students write a professional profile that could be filed in both the child's and the student's portfolios.

Discuss

How are your personal learning characteristics related to how you will teach? Give examples of ways you may need to alter your teaching style to meet the needs of the children.

Activity

Have students brainstorm ways to keep children's attention during a group story time when several of the children are easily distracted and need to move around more frequently. Consider adopting the most popular ideas during the next story time and ask students to document their effectiveness.

Note

"A child is a work in progress, constantly honing new skills and making developmental leaps, so expect her learning style to change as she grows." This is a quote by Kurt Fischer, director of the Mind, Brain, and Education program at Harvard University's Graduate School of Education.

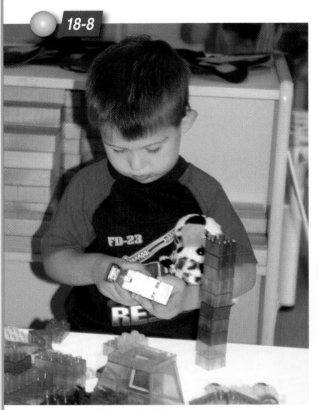

18-8

Field-independent children enjoy working alone.

Consider Learning Characteristics

The children in each classroom have a wide range of learning characteristics. Some work slowly and others quickly. Some children are attentive, and others bore easily. Some are quick decision makers, while others take more time.

Evaluate children's learning characteristics in relation to your own. If you work quickly, keep this in mind as you plan the curriculum. When demonstrating for children, slow down so they can understand concepts. Avoid reading or talking too fast.

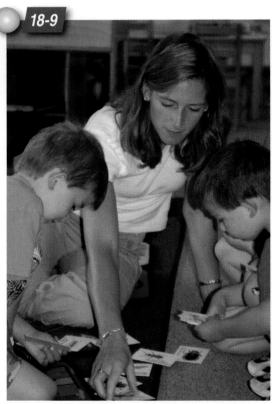

18-9

Showing and talking about a new activity appeals to a child's visual and auditory senses.

You may find that learning styles vary from program to program. That is, last year more children might have been field-independent, while this year more children are field-sensitive. The number of children who are primarily visual learners may also vary from year to year. This information is important for planning a program that relates to the children's learning styles.

Most children use a combination of senses. That is, they use both visual and auditory input to learn. To provide for these children's needs, plan activities that involve several senses, 18-9. For example, while reading a book, also show the pictures. Using this method, children should retain more knowledge. They will also find activities more satisfying.

Putting Technology to Use

Have students conduct an Internet search for additional information on children and their learning styles and characteristics. What additional learning styles such as simultaneous/sequential learner, connecting/compartmentalizing learner, inventing/reproducing learner, kinesthetic learner, and two- or three-dimensional learner have been identified? What are the benefits for parents and teachers of knowing a child's learning style? What could result if a child was allowed to learn using only his or her preferred style? Allow time for students to discuss their findings in class.

Use caution when planning group learning activities. If Joey works extremely slow and Tommy works quickly, being in the same group may be frustrating for both. It is better to place children with others who work at the same pace.

Some children have long attention spans. They are able to pay attention and sit still for long periods of time. Other children, however, are easily distracted. To hold their interests, plan novel and interesting group activities. For instance, during story time use a variety of teaching methods. During one week, use at least three types of media. Flannel board figures, flipcharts, puppets, draw and tell charts, and videotapes could all be used to tell a story.

Children also make decisions in different ways. Some children are quick to make decisions. This type of decision making is called *impulsive*. When given the chance, impulsive decision makers act immediately.

Other children are slower to make decisions. This type of decision making is called *cautious*. These children approach a new activity carefully. They study the environment before they begin.

Remember that not all children complete activities in the same amount of time. Children move and learn at different rates. As a teacher, you will need to be aware of individual learning styles and characteristics when planning the curriculum.

Emergent Curriculum

The **emergent curriculum** is child-centered. It "emerges" from the children's interest and experiences. This type of curriculum is an alternative to the teacher's selection of themes in advance. It involves both the participation of teachers and children in decision making. Initially, the teacher carefully listens and observes to take clues from the children. These observations help identify the themes of children's interest. It also helps the teacher plan themes that

are personally meaningful to children. The intent is to provide an appealing, play-rich environment. This environment will stimulate the children to become involved with the materials. From this experience, children will construct their own knowledge.

The curriculum might emerge from events, things, and people in the environment. The teachers follow the direction of the children's interests in planning the curriculum. For example, a group of children may notice a fire truck across the street from the center. They may become curious about fire trucks and the role of firefighters. As a result, the teacher might select a theme of firefighters. He or she may even sit down with the children and find out exactly what they wanted to learn.

The emergent curriculum is always responsive to the children's changing interests. Teachers observe the children carefully. This is so they can see what the children are playing with, as well as what they are avoiding. For example, children may be avoiding the small manipulative area of the classroom. The teacher will think about how to make the environment more appealing. New or more stimulating small manipulative materials may be set out on the tables to capture the children's attention.

Appropriate themes have a meaningful connection to the children's lives. There is no time frame for the length of a theme. The word *emergent* implies spontaneity. The length depends on the children's interests and the teacher's planning. Children learn through repetition, and repetition reinforces understanding.

Themes

As teachers plan their curriculum, they often use themes. A **theme** is one main topic or idea around which the classroom activities are planned. Connecting activities through the use of a theme allows children to build on previous learning. It helps them

Vocabulary

Have a student volunteer define the term *emergent curriculum*. What does a teacher take into consideration when planning an emergent curriculum?

Discuss

What is the difference between an impulsive decision maker and a cautious decision maker? Give examples of how children with these characteristics may behave in your class.

Vocabulary

Have a student volunteer define the term *theme*. Explain how themes provide for the connection of preschool activities.

Workplace Connection

Have students observe a group of preschoolers at a local child care center to identify themes that might interest the children. What events, things, or people in the environment are the children interested in? Has the teacher followed the direction of the children's interests in planning the current curriculum? What themes do you think the children will respond to? Ask students to write a brief report of their findings. Allow time for students to discuss their findings in class.

Enrich

Ask students to review 18-10, *Activities for a Puppet Theme*. Have students brainstorm additional activities that could be added to the list.

Activity

Have students give examples for developmentally appropriate hands-on activities they could teach that would support a theme on each of the following: the Olympic games, bread, horses, sports, and whales. What storybooks could be used with any of these themes?

Discuss

Besides the activities in the text, what other activities do you think could be included in an apple theme? What math activities could be incorporated around an apple theme?

build connections and reinforce what they've learned. Successful themes take the children's age, abilities, interests, and experiences into consideration. Also consider the time of the year and the availability of supportive resources. Be sure the theme includes some hands-on activities.

Once a theme is chosen, the activities can be developed, 18-10. The number and types of activities will vary with the theme. For example, a theme on apples may include a trip to an orchard. A bulletin board might show the three colors of apples. Books such as Johnny Appleseed could be read at group time.

An apple theme also lends itself to cooking. Applesauce, baked apples, apple muffins, and apple butter could be made. An art activity might be making apple prints from sponges cut in the shape of apples. Lotto games could be made using the three colors of apples. Apples of various sizes and colors could be placed on the science table.

18-10

Activities for a Puppet Theme

Fine-Motor Development

Handling puppets

Making puppets

- Paper bag puppets
- Peanut puppets
- Sock puppets
- Paper plate puppets
- Stick puppets
- Milk carton puppets
- Spoon puppets

Art

Designing and making puppets

Social Studies

Attending a marionette show

Language, Storytelling, and Dramatic Play

Telling a story using a puppet

Putting on a puppet show

Telling a shadow puppet story

Learning new vocabulary related to puppets

Looking at pictures of puppets at group time

Setting up a puppet stage with a variety of puppets

Sensory Table

Provide a variety of puppets made from different materials

A brainstorming session among several teachers yielded this list of activities for a puppet theme.

Putting Technology to Use

Ask students to conduct an Internet search for sites devoted to preschool themes. Students should review possible sites that contain developmentally appropriate themes and activities. Compile a resource list for all students in the class. Ask students to select one of the themes and conduct research to determine if there are enough activities such as art, music, storytelling, science, and math that would be possible to use with the selected theme. Allow time for students to discuss their findings in class.

These can be cut apart and studied under a microscope. Chart 18-11 lists other examples of themes.

Very seldom do the majority of the activities that are planned relate to the theme. Some themes will have more related resources than others. Stories and bulletin board displays are the only two activities that nearly always relate to the theme.

Theme Ideas

Themes should have a meaningful connection to the children's lives. As a rule, certain themes appeal to certain age groups, 18-12. Very young children's interests center on their immediate surroundings. As children grow, their circle of interests

becomes larger, like a spiral. A curriculum based on this concept is called a **spiral curriculum**.

Two-year-old children are interested in their immediate world. Themes such as sight, sound, touch, taste, and smell are appealing to them. Families, colors, shapes, pets, farm animals, and foods are also good themes for two-year-olds. For each classroom area, plan a variety of activities that relate to the theme you choose. This will keep the young children interested.

Three-year-old children are interested in their families. However, they are becoming interested in their neighbors and their community. Themes based on the supermarket, bakery, library, post office, fire station, and police station are of special interest to children of this age. Their interests

Discuss

Give some examples of themes that might interest two-year-olds. What themes might interest three-year-olds? What are the two activities that nearly always relate to the theme?

Vocabulary

Have a student volunteer define the term *spiral curriculum*. How does a spiral curriculum meet the growing needs of children?

Resource

Themes in the Classroom, Activity A, OG

18-11

Examples of Themes

Alphabet Letters	Directions	Friends	Seasons
Animals	Exercise	The Garden	Fall
Farm Animals	Fairy Tales	Flowers	Spring
Flying Animals	The Family	Plants	Summer
Pets	Mother	Trees	Winter
Water Animals	Father	Gestures	Shadows
Zoo Animals	Sisters	Hats	Shapes and Sizes
Books	Brothers	Health	Signs and Pictures
Boxes and Containers	Grandparents	Holidays and	Telephones
Brushes and Brooms	Aunts	Celebrations	Toys
Bugs	Uncles	Homes	Transportation and Travel
Camping	Cousins	Hospitals	Land
The Circus	Fantasy and Reality	How I Care for Myself	Water
Clothes	The Five Senses	The Library	Air
Colors	Feelings	Machines	Watches and Clocks
Community Helpers	Foods	Measuring	Water
Doctors	Fruit Group	Money	We Act
Firefighters	Grain Group	Music	Weather and
Nurses	Meat & Beans	The Newspaper	Temperature
Police Officers	Group	Numbers and Counting	We Create
Postal Workers	Milk Group	Our Town	We Dance
Computers	Vegetable Group	Puppets	We Sing
Cooking and Baking	Oils Group	Safety	Wheels
Costumes			

Themes can come from all segments of children's environments.

Portfolio Project

Ask students to select a theme or choose one from 18-11, *Examples of Themes*. Have students create a bulletin board display based on the theme. Using print or Internet sources, ask students to compile a list of stories that could be used as teaching activities to relate to the

theme. Conduct teacher and student evaluations on the effectiveness and attractiveness of each bulletin board display. Ask students to photograph any bulletin boards they create and copy the story list for inclusion in their portfolio.

Discuss

Why might an outer space theme be considered inappropriate for two- and three-year-olds? Why might the same theme be appropriate for four- and five-year-olds?

Reflect

Review the list of themes for two- and three-year-olds in 18-12. What types of themes do you think six-year-olds would find interesting?

Activity

Brainstorm lists of themes that could be used for one day or part of a day on a monthly basis throughout the school year such as weather, celebrations, seasons, or community helpers. Have students suggest activities to fit these themes.

18-12

A Spiral Curriculum

Themes for Two- and Three-Year-Olds

All About Me
I'm Me, I'm Special
My Family
My Friends
My Home
My Senses
My Toys
Foods I Eat
Colors in My World
Shapes I See
  Circles
  Squares
  Triangles
  Rectangles
  Hearts

Concepts I'm Learning
  Big/Little
  Up/Down
  Soft/Hard
  Wet/Dry
Things That Go
  Cars and Trucks
  Trains
  Boats
  Airplanes
Animals in My World
  Dogs
  Cats
  Farm Animals
  Zoo Animals

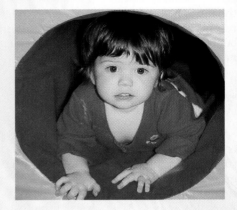

Themes for Three- and Four-Year-Olds

People in My World
  My Family
  My Friends
  Police Officers
  Firefighters
  Bakers
  Meat Cutters
  Librarians
  Printers
  Medical Doctors
  Nurses
  Pharmacists
  Ambulance Attendants
  Bankers
  Chefs
  Waiters and Waitresses
  Musicians
  Hair Stylists
  Photographers
  Artist

  House Painter
  Zookeeper
  Postal Worker
  Office Workers
  Computer Programmers
  Clerks
  Sanitary Engineers
  Pilots and Flight Attendants
  Gas Station Attendants
  Auto Mechanics
  Painters
  Carpenters
  Plumbers
  Farmers
  Florists
All About Me
  My Senses
  My Feelings
  My Home
  My School

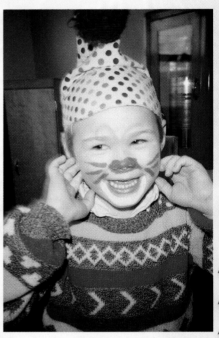

Children's interests widen as they get older. Study this chart for evidence of the spiral curriculum concept.   *(continued)*

Workplace Connection

Using the lists of themes from 18-12, *A Spiral Curriculum*, ask students to survey area early childhood educators to determine which of the themes they have used with the children in their care. Which themes provided opportunities for interesting activities and good participation by the children? What challenges, if any, did using any of the themes present to the teachers? What themes have they personally found successful and would they recommend adding to the lists? Allow time for students to share their findings in class.

Reflect

Review the list of themes for four- and five-year-olds in 18-12. What other themes could you add to the list?

Discuss

What sub-themes could be contained in the broad theme of *Transportation?* What sub-themes could be incorporated in the theme of *Things I Like to Do?*

Note

Remind students of the guidance challenges caused by overstimulation when incorporating holiday themes into the curriculum as studied in Chapter 15. When planning the program, consider the stress associated with overstimulation when holidays are used as a prolonged theme.

Themes for Four- and Five-Year-Olds

My Body
  Good Health
  Exercise
  Nutrition
Communication
  Speaking
  Listening
  Reading
  Puppets
  Acting
  Writing
  Radio
  Television
  Computers
  Fairy Tales
My World
  Pets

Plants
  Flowers
  Insects and Spiders
  Seeds
Safety
Transportation
  Air
  Land
  Water
Tools at Work
  Gardening
  Carpentry
  Mechanics
  Cosmetology
  Dentistry
  Art

18-12 Continued

are growing in the spiral outside of their immediate surroundings.

Themes related to animals are also enjoyed by three- and four-year-olds. These themes can focus on groups of animals. Groups might include farm, forest, water, and zoo animals. Bugs, birds, dogs, and cats can also have appeal for young children.

Four- and five-year-old children enjoy themes related to a wider variety of topics. Themes can be grouped into a few broad categories. For instance, broad themes might include *My World, Things I Like to Do, Things That Move,* and *Transportation.*

These categories could be broken down to contain a few sub-themes. *My School, My Home, My Feelings,* and *My Family* are just a few examples of sub-themes in *My World.*

Holiday Themes

Use caution when planning holiday themes for children. Think about the children in your group. Is the theme appropriate to every family in the group? Some families can be offended by the celebration of some holidays. Only holidays that are celebrated by all the children in the class should be introduced.

Caution must also be exercised since preschool children lack a clear concept of time. If a holiday theme is introduced too early, children may become too excited. For instance, if Halloween is introduced the first week of October but does not actually happen until four weeks later, children will become confused. They will not know when to expect Halloween.

Workplace Connection

Have students interview area preschool teachers and other early childhood education professionals to discover how often holiday themes are used in the classroom. What holidays are celebrated? Are the themes appropriate to everyone in the group? How far in advance is the holiday theme introduced? Have students write a brief report of their findings. Allow time for students to share their reports with the class.

Vocabulary

Have student volunteers define the terms *web* and *concept*. What is the major benefit of using a web when planning preschool curriculum? What role do concepts have in a child's learning?

Resource

Web Example, transparency master 18-1, TR

Discuss

Why is writing objectives an important part of designing a web? How should the objectives relate to the overall program goals?

Resource

Dogs Web, Activity A, SAG

The activities planned around holiday themes are also often quite stimulating for children. If this excitement goes on for weeks, behavior problems could arise. More guidance will be needed. Some teachers prefer to integrate holidays into broader themes. They may include Thanksgiving in a celebration theme, Valentine's Day in a friends theme, or Halloween in a costumes theme.

A theme can last any amount of time. Some themes may last a couple of days or a week. Other themes can be carried out for a month or longer. A community helpers theme could go on for months by featuring many different community helpers. Children's attention spans, needs, interests, experiences, and available resources are major factors affecting theme length.

Developing Themes Using Webbing

An effective method for developing themes is to use resource books. To make this possible, many centers have a set of encyclopedias to use as references for background information. After using this resource, a web can be drawn. A **web** is a planning tool or map that outlines major concepts and ideas related to a theme.

Drawing a web is a simple method for listing concepts related to a theme. For example, when developing a theme on puppets, consult a resource. List all concepts you might include, 18-13. The major headings in a puppet web could be *vocabulary, movement, types, stages, materials,* and *characterization*.

After drawing up a web, writing objectives is the next step. Study the web for objectives that can be developed. For instance, based on the web in Chart 18-13, children might be expected to

- identify the types of puppets

- develop skill in moving puppets with rods, wires, strings, and hands

- enjoy a puppet show

- learn new vocabulary words: *marionette, shadow,* and *dummy*

- construct puppets from a variety of materials

- express their own thoughts and feelings using puppets

- practice using a puppet behind a puppet stage

Concepts Based on the Theme

Curriculum themes are an important medium for helping children form concepts. A **concept** is a generalized idea or notion. Learning basic concepts helps the children to understand their world. By forming concepts, children learn to group experiences in a meaningful way.

Concepts can be developed around a theme. To do this, review your web, then write the concepts. For instance, if your theme is birds, concepts might include the following:

- There are many kinds of birds.

- Some birds are pets.

- Birds hatch from eggs.

- Most birds fly.

- Birds live in nests, trees, houses, and cages.

- Birds have a head, body, wings, a beak, and feathers.

Written Plans

After considering your curriculum approach, theme, concepts, and activities, written plans need to be developed. Many centers require two types of written plans.

Service Learning Activity

Ask the librarian at your local public library to allow students to present a monthly learning activity at the library to the young children in the community. Students would be responsible for selecting a theme consistent with current library programming and designing a story time and related activities. Lesson plans need to be approved by both the child care instructor and the librarian. Scheduling will need to be discussed with the school principal and library staff to select appropriate times for the presentations.

18-13

Webbing of Puppet Curriculum Theme

Stages
tables
bookcases
cardboard TV box
blanket
sheet

Vocabulary
marionette
shadow
dummy

Types
finger
hand
rod
paper bag
paper plate
marionette
dummy
stick
sock

Puppets

Materials
wood
mittens
sticks
paper plates
paper bags
gloves
socks
cloth
milk cartons
wooden spoons

Movement
hand
string
wire
rods

Characterization
figure
person
plant
object

Webs can be developed using resources such as encyclopedias.

A **block plan** is an overall view of the curriculum. It outlines the general plans. A **lesson plan** is more detailed than a block plan. It outlines specific actions and activities that will be used to meet goals and objectives.

Block Plan

A block plan is key to planning a balanced curriculum. Without this written block plan, curriculum areas may be overlooked. You may think these areas were covered, but without a written record, you cannot be sure.

A block plan usually includes days of the week, time periods, and scheduled activities. Figure 18-14 shows a sample block plan.

Block plans should be kept on file. They can be used as a reference to review what has happened during the year. The plans also contain a variety of activities that may be used in future years, if appropriate.

Resource

Apple Web, reproducible master 18-2, TR

Vocabulary

Have a student volunteer define the terms *block plan* and *lesson plan*. What is the major purpose of each?

Resource

Objectives for Apple Theme, transparency master 18-3, TR

Resource

Apple Theme: Concepts for the Children to Learn, transparency master 18-4, TR

Meeting Special Needs

Ask students to review *Apple Web*, reproducible master 18-2, *Objectives for Apple Theme*, transparency master 18-3, and *Apple Theme: Concepts for the Children to Learn*, transparency master 18-4. Pair special learners with volunteer students to complete the activities. Allow time for students to share their activities in class. Spend additional time discussing any topics that are difficult for special learners to understand.

Resource

Learning Activities Related to a Theme on Apples, reproducible master 18-5, TR

Resource

Learning Activities Related to a Theme on Dogs, Activity B, SAG

Resource

Sample Block Plan, transparency master 18-6, TR

Resource

Evaluating a Block Plan, Activity C, OG

18-14

Morning Session: 2-Year-Olds

Week: August 27-31 Theme: My School

	9:00-10:10 Free Play/Centers	10:10-10:25 Large Group	10:25-10:40 Snack	10:40-11:00 Small Groups #1	#2	#3	11:00-11:30 Outdoors
Monday	• watercolors • water & toys in sensory table • tunnel • tennis shoes color match game	My Nursery School story cards / If You're Happy & You Know It	crackers tomato juice	stringing beads	table blocks	stringing beads	• sand toys
Tuesday	• crayons and markers • goop in sensory table • driving wheel • tuff blocks	Short walk around the neighborhood	banana milk	table blocks	stringing beads	table blocks	• balls
Wednesday	• play dough • styrofoam pieces in sensory table • balance beam • color clowns	Little Red Wagon song / My Nursery School	apple & cheese milk	book: *Where Is It?* by Tana Hoban	puzzles	feely box	• painting with water
Thursday	• soap flake finger painting • water in sensory table • rocking boat	Tour of school	veggies & dip milk	feely box	*Where Is It?*	puzzles	• bubbles
Friday	• roller painting • sand in sensory table • crawling cubes	"Little Red Wagon" / If You're Happy & You Know It / Tour of school	peanut butter & crackers milk	puzzles	feely box	*Where Is It?*	• rocking boat

This block plan is for a group of two-year-olds. Notice the theme and the large group activities related to it.

Portfolio Project

Have students select a theme for three-year-olds from the list on page 352. Ask students to create a block plan for a morning session following the example provided. Make sure students add a variety of large group activities that directly relate to the theme. Have students trade papers to check the block plans for accuracy, grammar, spelling, etc. Final copies may be typed and added to the student's portfolio.

Teaching About Health Through Daily Routines

As you plan lessons on various themes, look for ways to include developmentally appropriate health topics and healthful behaviors. For example, you might teach preschool children about hand washing after a lesson on handling small animals or before a lesson that involves food. What are some other ways that you can incorporate health education into the daily program?

To write a block plan, follow these steps:

1. Review your program goals.
2. Review your observations and assessment of the children.
3. Note the children's interests.
4. Consider the availability of your resources.
5. Select a theme.
6. Develop concepts.
7. Select activities and record them on the block plan.

Lesson Plans

Lesson plans are more detailed than block plans. While a block plan gives just the title of a book, a lesson plan provides step-by-step directions for sharing the book. Figure 18-15 contains a sample lesson plan. Lesson plans contain the following:

- developmental goals
- learning objective
- concepts
- materials needed
- motivation
- procedures
- closure/transition
- evaluation

Lesson plans help teachers organize their teaching. Many centers only require lesson plans for large or small group activities. Writing good lesson plans is a skill that is learned much like other skills. With practice, you will gradually increase your skill.

Developmental Goals

Developmental goals are statements that tell the "why" of the activity. They are more specific than program goals. Examples of goals for cooking applesauce with a group of four-year-olds are shown in the sample lesson plan in 18-15. To write developmental goals for a lesson plan, think carefully about each activity. Ask yourself, "What can the children learn from this experience?" Then write the lesson plan, as outlined above, including all the learning involved.

Learning Objective

A **learning objective** describes the expected outcome of an activity. Objectives are used to plan teaching strategies. There are three parts to learning objectives. These parts are the conditions of performance, the behavior, and the level of performance. Figure 18-16 includes examples of each part of the behavioral objective.

The *conditions of performance* list what materials, equipment, or tools the child will use. Included could be puzzles, paper, scissors, beads, or any other materials and equipment found in early childhood settings. The conditions of performance can also

Vocabulary

Have a student volunteer define the term *learning objective*. Why are learning objectives important in curriculum planning?

Resource

Learning Objectives, transparency master 18-7, TR

Reflect

Have you ever observed a preschool activity without knowing what was expected of children as a result of their participation in the activity? What is your opinion on including activities in which the only goal is to entertain children?

Workplace Connection

Ask students to survey the lesson plans from several preschool classrooms. Do the plans have all eight steps of lesson design? Are lesson plans only required for large and small group activities? Are the lesson plans well written and easy to follow? Ask students to write a brief summary of their findings. If possible, include copies of the lesson plans to share with the class.

Resource

Writing a Lesson Plan,
reproducible master
18-8, TR

Enrich

Have students ask several of their high school teachers to share how they plan their daily lessons. What steps of lesson design do they incorporate into their plans? How are these similar to the steps suggested in the text?

Resource

A Sample Lesson,
Activity E, SAG

18-15

A Sample Lesson Plan

Date: 9/21 **Time:** 10:00 A.M.
Group: 4-year-olds
Activity: Cooking Experience—Applesauce

Developmental Goals:

- To practice following directions.
- To develop cooking safety habits.
- To practice using a knife as a tool.
- To practice personal hygiene by washing hands before and after cooking experience.
- To observe the beauty of an apple.
- To learn the parts of an apple: seed, core, flesh, skin, and stem.
- To taste the ingredients in applesauce.
- To taste cooked apples.
- To observe the changes in texture and color when heat is applied to the apples.

Learning objective:

Given apples, knives, measuring cup and spoons, a bowl, a mixing spoon, a microwave oven, sugar, cinnamon, and a recipe chart, the children will help peel apples, measure the ingredients, and prepare applesauce.

Materials needed:

6	peelers	measuring cup and spoon
12	apples	kettle
	recipe chart	bowl
	water	mixing spoon
2	cups of sugar	microwave oven
3	tablespoons of cinnamon	

Motivation/introduction:

Set up the housekeeping area with recipe chart, cooking utensils, and tray with food. Ask "What can we make from apples?" Listen to responses. Tell the children "Today we are going to make applesauce."

Procedure:

1. Tell the children to wash their hands.
2. Review the recipe chart step-by-step.
3. Cut an apple in half. Show the children the parts of an apple: seed, core, flesh, skin, and stem.
4. Demonstrate how to use a peeler as a tool, stressing safety.
5. Pass out apples and peelers, again explaining safety.
6. Encourage children to observe and feel the apples.
7. Peel apples.
8. When apples are peeled, focus children's attention back to recipe chart. Proceed by following directions step-by-step until the mixture is ready for a heat source.
9. Discuss each of the ingredients, allowing children to taste them if they wish.
10. Ask individuals to measure the sugar, cinnamon, and water.
11. Direct children's attention to the applesauce as it cooks. Clarify the process by asking questions such as *How are apples different?*
12. Serve the applesauce as a snack.

Closure/transition:

Assign cleanup tasks to the children. Have the children wash their hands. Tell the children the applesauce will be eaten at snack time. Then prepare the children for outdoor play.

Evaluation:

Lesson plans contain much more detail than block plans. Notice all the details needed to write a lesson plan for cooking applesauce.

Portfolio Project

Ask students to select several of their own lesson plans to add to their portfolio. Selected plans should have all eight steps of lesson design. Plans should be developmentally appropriate for the age of the children for which the lessons were designed. Students may wish to document the presentation of a lesson by including photographs of the student teaching as well as the children participating. A self-evaluation of the lesson should also be included along with a teacher evaluation, if available.

18-16

Learning Objectives

Conditions of Performance: States the conditions under which the child will perform.
   Given a three-piece puzzle…
   Given crayons and a pencil…
   Given a set of blocks…
   Without the aid of a teacher…
   Given farm animals…
   After listening to the story…

Behavior: States what the child will be able to do.
   …the child will cut…
   …the child will draw…
   …the child will construct…
   …the child will sing…
   …the child will match…
   …the child will climb…
   …the child will jump…
   …the child will skip…
   …the child will stack……
   …the child will retell…

Level of Performance: States the minimum level of achievement.
   …four inches…
   …all…
   …at least three feet…
   …two out of three times…
   …within a five minute period…

Studying these parts of learning objectives will help you write effective objectives.

include what the child will be denied. For example, they may need to construct a puzzle without the aid of a teacher.

Behaviors are any visible activities done by the child. It tells what the child will be doing. When choosing behaviors, avoid words that are open to many interpretations. *To know, understand, enjoy, believe,* and *appreciate* are all words that can mean many things. For instance, how will you judge if a child understands? Useful words for writing learning objectives are listed in 18-17.

The *level of performance* states the minimum standard of achievement. It

should note how well you want the child to do. The level of performance many times is understood. Therefore, it is not always included as part of the objective.

Materials

Under the materials section of the lesson plan, list everything that is needed for the activity. For example, if you are going to make instant pudding, include *milk, pudding mix, bowl, wire whisk, spoon, scraper,* and *measuring cup.* If you are going to do a finger painting activity, list *paint, paper, aprons,* and *wet sponge.*

Motivation

Motivation describes how you will gain the children's attention. The best devices are items that interest the children. A picture of a cat may be used as motivation before reading a story about cats. Motivation devices include pictures, puppets, alphabet letters, tapes, resource people, cards, artwork, photographs, animals, stuffed toys, clothing, and masks.

Procedures

The procedures section resembles a cookbook. Simple step-by-step directions should be provided. The directions should be in order. If needed, number each step to remember the order. Each of the developmental goals should be included in the procedures. For example, if a goal is to have each child taste the ingredients, this should be a step in the procedures. An example of procedures for an activity is shown in 18-18. The sample lesson plan also contains procedures.

Closure/Transition

Closure refers to how an activity will end. It might include clean-up tasks or sampling of food items at snack time. *Transition* refers to the movement from one activity to another. In some cases, closure and

Vocabulary

Have a student volunteer define the term *motivation.* Why is motivation an important step in lesson planning?

Discuss

Why are the words *to know, understand, enjoy, believe,* and *appreciate* not appropriate to include as behaviors in writing a learning objective? Why should learning objectives include only concrete terms?

Vocabulary

Have a student volunteer define the term *closure.* How are closure and transition related?

Putting Technology to Use

Have students conduct an Internet search for information on mentoring new teachers. What is the purpose of mentoring? How might mentoring affect teacher retention rates? Does your school or school district have a mentoring program? Consult local child care programs to find out if mentoring is used in these programs as well. Have students write a brief summary of their results and share their findings with the class.

Resource

Behaviors, Activity C, SAG

Reflect

Have you ever been unprepared or unorganized for an activity that you were responsible for presenting? What happened as a result? What effect did this have on future activity planning?

Resource

Assessing Curriculum, transparency master 18-9, TR

18-17

Behaviors for Objectives

answer	dry	measure	remove	take
arrange	feed	mix	replace	tap
ask	find	move	return	taste
brush	finish	name	roll	tell
button	follow	open	run	throw
catch	follow directions	organize	say	tie
choose	group	paint	select	touch
clap	hit	paste	separate	turn
climb	hold	peel	sequence	use
close	jump	pick	show	use two hands
collect	label	place	sing	wait
color	list	point to	sit	wash
construct	locate	pour	skip	weigh
count	look at	print	solve	wipe
cut	make motions	put hand on	sort	write
describe	mark	put in order	stack	zip
draw	match	recall	stand	

Learn to use concrete terms such as these when stating learning objectives.

transition are the same task. For example, at the end of a creative drama activity, you may ask the children to walk like heavy elephants to the snack table.

Evaluation

A staff who provides a quality early childhood program is continually evaluating the curriculum. In some centers, time is set aside every day for this purpose. Many child care centers, however, do not have the resources to do this with the entire staff. Instead, staff members will evaluate the activities they conducted on their own. This process involves three steps: (1) evaluating the learning experience, (2) evaluating the children and their responses, and (3) evaluating your own teaching strategies.

When evaluating the learning experiences, ask yourself whether the activity was proper for the age group. If, for example, children had trouble cutting paper there could be several reasons for the trouble. Were the scissors in good repair? Scissors with dried glue on the cutting edge will not

18-18

Procedure Chart

Activity: Visual perception (This type of activity encourages children to see fine differences between and among objects.)

1. Place individual cards face down on the table.
2. Provide each child with one game board.
3. Demonstrate how to play the game, stressing the importance of taking turns.
4. Ask one child to begin by choosing a card from the middle of the table.
5. After the child has drawn the card, ask "Do you have an object like that on your board?"
6. If the object does not match, instruct the child to return the card to the center of the table, face down.
7. Continue with the next player until one child has filled all of the game board spaces.

Using a procedure chart, you should cover each step of an activity.

Meeting Special Needs

Make copies of *Assessing Curriculum*, transparency master 18-9, for use by special learners as a study tool. Go over any words from the master that the student might find difficult to understand such as *sequenced, competence, linguistic,* *integration,* or *pursue.* Pair special learners with volunteer students to go over each statement so the meaning is clear. Be sure to include special needs students in the discussion when presenting this material to the class.

cut properly. Left-handed children need left-handed scissors. Paper thickness could also be a problem. Children who are learning to cut need lightweight paper and proper tools.

Successful learning activities give children the chance to test their knowledge. For example, children will learn more about making applesauce by taking part in the activity than if they only watched an adult make it.

Your teaching skills only have meaning if the children learn. Therefore, it is important to study the children and their responses to activities and to you. First, see that the children reach the objective. If they do not, think through the activity. Ask yourself what you could have done differently. Likewise, if there were behavior problems, try to find the cause.

Lack of organization, you will find, can affect the outcome of an activity. If you forget some of the ingredients for a cooking activity, leaving the group to gather them could affect outcomes. During your absence, some child may start to mix the ingredients. The product may not turn out if the ingredients were not measured properly.

Chart 18-19 includes a sample evaluation form for an activity. Your center may have a similar evaluation form, or you can create one using these questions. Completing this form can help you reflect on an activity and evaluate it. After using the form a few times, you may find that you can remember the three parts of the form, including the specific questions. At this point, you may want to start writing your evaluations on index cards. In time, you will be able to go through this process mentally.

At first, you may find the evaluation process time-consuming. You will learn, however, that it is useful. With constant evaluation, you will improve your teaching skills as well as the curriculum.

Resource

Lesson Plans,
Activity D, OG

Discuss

Why should self-evaluation always be included in the evaluation of a learning activity? What can you learn from professionally evaluating your effectiveness as a teacher?

Activity

Ask students to collect samples of the different types of evaluation forms for an activity used in early childhood education. How many child care centers use an evaluation form? Allow time for students to share their findings in class.

Workplace Connection

Ask students to design their own evaluation form using 18-19, *A Sample Evaluation of an Activity*, in the book as an example. Have students use their form to evaluate an activity in a local child care center. Was the activity interesting to the children? Was the teacher well organized? How effective was the evaluation form? Allow time for students to share their findings in class.

Reflect

Think about a time when you were not organized in presenting an activity. Did you evaluate your performance? What questions did you ask yourself? What did you learn from the experience?

Discuss

Does your school require or suggest that teachers ask their students to evaluate the teacher's performance at the end of the semester or end of the class? Should child care students be responsible for evaluating the teaching performance of their classmates?

Resource

Curriculum Building, Activity D, SAG

18-19

A Sample Evaluation of an Activity

Activity: Story—"Never Talk to Strangers"
Group: Five-year-olds

I.   **The Activity: Selection and Development**

  A. **Was the content (concept) worth knowing?**
     The content is valuable for five-year-old children since it deals with personal safety. With the increased incidence of child abuse, this is an important topic.

  B. **Was it developmentally appropriate?**
     Although fantasy was involved in the story, almost all the children were able to understand the content.

  C. **Was it interesting to the children?**
     All the children but Don listened and responded. During the repetitive sentences, the children repeated, "Never talk to strangers."

  D. **Did the activity include opportunities for the children to use or "test" their knowledge?**
     After the story, the children were asked questions. These included:
     - Is your grandmother a stranger?
     - Is your neighbor a stranger?
     - Is a man you never saw before a stranger?
     - Who is a stranger?

  E. **What would you suggest as a follow-up experience?**
     Children's books related to child abuse will be read tomorrow. The game "Good Touch and Bad Touch" will also be introduced.

II. **The Children: Responses**

  A. **Did all the children reach the objective(s)? If not, why?**
     With the exception of Don, all the children reached the objective.

  B. **Were there behavior problems? If so, do you have any insight as to what caused them?**
     If Don and Ben were separated during the story, Don may have paid attention. Likewise, Ben found Don's behavior disturbing. He tried to move away from him, but another teacher made him sit down.

III. **The Teacher: Strategies**

  A. **Were you well organized?**
     Yes, the book was placed so I could easily find it. During the outdoor play period, an individual carpet square was laid out for each child. Approximately ten inches were left between each square. This spacing probably helped maintain group control.

  B. **Were you satisfied with the effectiveness of your teaching strategies in reaching the learning objective? If not, why?**
     I should have practiced the story beforehand. In addition, I should have held the book so all the children could view the pictures.

  C. **Did you effectively guide or manage the group?**
     Yes, with the exception of Don, I managed the group effectively.

  D. **Did you introduce the concepts in a stimulating manner?**
     The cover of the book appealed to the children. After the story, two children asked to have it read again.

  E. **Did you involve the children in the closure of the activity?**
     Yes, I did. The children were involved through a series of questions. Concepts of strangers and safety were both discussed.

  F. **What strategies would you change if you were to repeat this activity?**
     First, I would separate Don and Ben. I would also practice reading the book to myself several times before sharing it. This would make me less dependent on the words in the book. As a result, I would feel confident enough to share the pictures with the children.

Evaluation is the final step in the curriculum development process. It can be used to determine how well your curriculum worked.

Meeting Special Needs

Review the special learners' chapter outlines to determine if the students have any questions about the concepts or content of this chapter. Review the chapter objectives and ask the students to evaluate their progress in meeting these objectives. Ask the students to summarize, orally or in writing, what they learned from this chapter.

Summary

A developmentally appropriate early childhood curriculum is based on how children develop and learn. It consists of a wide range of concepts, experiences, and materials designed to meet the developmental needs of a group of children. Before the curriculum can be planned, the goals of the center's program need to be determined. Program goals focus on the whole child. Assessment is also an important part of curriculum planning. It should rely on multiple sources and occur as part of the ongoing life of the classroom. Assessment will identify children's needs, interests, strengths, and capabilities.

The content and process-centered approach to curriculum planning is the method most often used. Learning is seen as a constant process of exploring and questioning the environment. As the curriculum is planned, several factors need to be considered. You first must decide what information you will cover in the curriculum. You will also want to balance the learning activities and consider individual learning styles and characteristics.

Activities are often selected based on a theme. Webs may be used to develop ideas related to the theme. Concepts are formulated for the theme as well. Finally, written plans are developed that include activities for all the classroom activity areas. Both block plans and lesson plans are developed. The final step is evaluation. A staff who provides a quality early childhood program is continually evaluating the curriculum and finding ways to improve their teaching plans.

Review and Reflect

1. What are program goals?
2. True or false. Curriculum development involves only the teacher who is responsible for the group.
3. List two advantages of a preplanned curriculum.
4. Describe a content and process-centered approach to curriculum development. Explain how materials and environment relate to this approach.
5. How do direct and indirect learning experiences differ?
6. List three questions to ask when choosing the information to cover.
7. _____ children like to work with others and often volunteer to help.
8. _____ children like to try new activities and work on their own.
9. _____ learners enjoy looking at books and other objects.
10. _____ learners enjoy activities involving music, stories, and poems.
11. Explain what is meant by an emergent curriculum.
12. Explain the meaning of spiral curriculum.
13. What is a web?
14. How does a block plan differ from a lesson plan?
15. How do developmental goals and program goals differ?
16. Name the three parts of learning objectives. Explain each of these parts.
17. The _____ section of the lesson plan gives step-by-step directions.
18. When evaluating the success of a specific learning activity, what three steps should you follow?

7. Field-sensitive
8. Field-independent
9. Visual
10. Auditory
11. Emergent curriculum is child-centered. It "emerges" from the children's interest and experiences. This type of curriculum is an alternative to the teacher's selection of themes in advance. It involves both the participation of teachers and children in decision making.
12. Spiral curriculum is a concept that explains the growth of children's interests from the immediate surroundings to a wider variety of topics.
13. A web is a planning tool or map that outlines major concepts and ideas related to a theme.
14. A block plan is an overall view of the curriculum. It outlines the general plans. A lesson plan is more detailed than a block plan. It outlines specific actions and activities that will be used to meet goals and objectives.
15. Developmental goals state the expected outcome of a specific activity. Program goals state the expected outcome of an entire program.
16. the conditions of performance, the behavior, and the level of performance. (Student response for explanations.)
17. procedures
18. First, evaluate the learning experience. Then evaluate the children and their responses. Finally, evaluate your own teaching strategies.

Review and Reflect **Answer Key**

1. Program goals are broad statements of purpose that state the desired end result—what is to be achieved.
2. false
3. A preplanned curriculum is helpful to a staff with little training or experience and it saves teachers time and energy.
4. (Student response.)
5. Direct learning experiences are planned with a specific goal in mind. Indirect experiences occur on the spur of the moment.
6. Is the information gained worth knowing? Is the information testable by the children? Is the information developmentally appropriate for the children?

Apply and Explore

1. Review the web for the puppet theme in Figure 18-13. How would you adapt this web for a group of two-year-olds?

2. Write five learning objectives. Exchange papers with classmates and evaluate the learning objectives.

3. Discuss strategies for meeting the program goals given in the chapter.

Cross-Curricular Link

Writing

1. Interview a child care teacher about curriculum planning. Write a report based on what you learn.

Language Arts

2. Write a lesson plan for preparing pancakes.

Technology

3. Check the Web site www.perpetualpreschool.com for a variety of resources related to curriculum planning, teaching tips, and professional development activities.

Workplace Link

What learning activities might be moved to the outdoors in the child care lab program? What additional equipment would be needed to conduct the activities outdoors? Do you anticipate any supervision challenges as a result of moving activities outdoors? What are the benefits of this strategy? What are the major disadvantages?

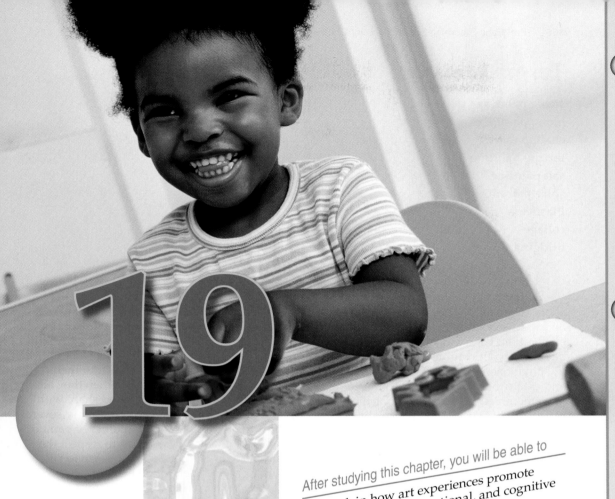

Discuss

Look at the chapter opening photo. In what kind of art or sensory experience is this child participating? What other activities might be involved in sensory experiences? What might be the connection between art, block-building, and sensory experiences?

Discuss

Look over the objectives for this chapter. How do art, block-building, and sensory activities relate to the program goals for our child care lab?

19

Guiding Art, Blockbuilding, and Sensory Experiences

After studying this chapter, you will be able to

- explain how art experiences promote physical, social, emotional, and cognitive growth.
- describe techniques for guiding art experiences.
- list the stages of art skill development.
- compile a list of art supplies needed for a well-stocked classroom.
- plan a variety of art, blockbuilding, sensory, and woodworking activities suitable for young children.

365

Vocabulary

Have students review the *Terms to Know* list. Ask students to look up unfamiliar words or terms in the glossary before reading the chapter.

Reflect

Ask students to give examples of how they feel art activities promote social growth among preschoolers. How could sharing be promoted through art activities?

Resource

Value of Art Experiences, transparency master 19-1, TR

Discuss

Should angry or frustrated children be allowed to express their emotions physically through art activities? What precautions should you take if you allow children to express themselves in this way?

Resource

Learning Through Art Experiences, Activity A, OG

Terms to Know

string painting
mono painting
chalk painting
texture painting
salt painting
spice painting
Plasticene®
collage
bridging

Preschool children are curious about their world. They thrive on hands-on experiences that encourage creative exploration. For them, art activities can be learning opportunities. Using their imaginations, young children can think, plan, and create their own ideas. Their need for movement, self-expression, and achievement is fulfilled by working with modeling materials. Like physical development, there is a sequence to developing drawing skills. While developing basic skills using art media, young children are expressing feelings and ideas.

The Importance of Art Experiences

Art promotes physical, social, emotional, and cognitive growth in children. Physical growth is promoted through the movements involved in painting, coloring, drawing, scribbling, and playing with clay, 19-1. All these motions improve fine-motor skills. Art activities foster motor and hand-eye coordination. In turn, these skills promote growth in other areas.

Social growth is promoted by art. Art experiences help children learn responsibility. For example, the children learn that they must put on their smocks before painting.

19-1

Children improve hand-eye coordination during art activities that use small muscles.

They also learn that they must put their work in a safe storage space when they are finished. Learning to work and share with others is stressed. In many programs, several children will share one container of paint or a box of crayons. They learn to respect the property of others. They also learn to value the work and ideas of others.

Art experiences also promote emotional growth. Through a creative activity, children are allowed to express emotions. For example, pounding at the woodworking bench, hitting play dough, or scribbling with crayons allows angry children to express their frustrations in an acceptable way. Children also have the chance to choose their own activity. For instance, during a painting session children decide what they will paint. Their choices—a pet, a friend, or a flower—are often expressions of their feelings. Through art, they learn to communicate feelings nonverbally.

Finally, the children's cognitive growth is promoted by exploring, experimenting, and problem solving with many materials and tools. Through this process they use the skills of an investigative scientist. They learn important concepts such as color, size,

Meeting Special Needs

Provide an outline of the chapter with all the chapter headings for special learners. Students should fill in each section of the outline as the material is covered in class with a sentence or two about the content. Review the special learners' IEPs to decide if any modifications should be made in presenting the chapter content. Prepare a vocabulary matching assignment to assist special learners in understanding the *Terms to Know*.

texture, and shape. By manipulating and controlling tools, skills such as drawing and cutting are learned. They learn that cutting takes things apart while taping and stringing helps put materials together. Visual and tactile skills (skills related to sight and touch) are also developed. For example, rolling, rubbing, pounding, and tearing can change how an object looks and feels.

Techniques for Guiding Art Experiences

As a caregiver, you must be creative in your approach to art. You must observe in order to find new ways to expand children's learning experiences. Creative growth is promoted through the careful choice of *open-ended art materials* (those that can be used in many ways). A good art program allows children to express their ideas. It also provides them with time to experiment and explore new materials and techniques. These experiences should involve all five senses: sight, smell, taste, touch, and hearing.

Helping children during art sessions is an important task. If done properly, children will accept your help. If done improperly, however, children will come to think of you as an intruder. Tasks done for or forced on children often cause tension and displeasure.

To foster independence, start each session by telling the children what supplies and tools are available that day. Encourage them to use the supplies, 19-2. For instance, if they have never worked with cotton balls, tell them "I think you will enjoy painting with cotton balls. They are very soft."

As you walk through the class, observe what the children are doing. However, it is best not to ask them what they are making. They might just be experimenting with different tools and supplies. In this case, they do not know what they are making. Keep in

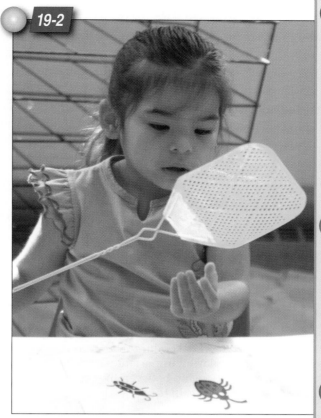

19-2

Devise new supplies to use during sessions and show children how to use them.

mind that some children lack the language skills needed to explain their artwork. Asking questions may make them uneasy. Always focus on the process when commenting on the children's art experiences. Your goal is to make the children feel successful and confident. Make comments such as those listed in 19-3.

Let children decide when their work is finished. Take them at their word. Do not urge them to fill up space or add to their work. This decreases their pride and confidence.

Model art appreciation by offering feedback to the children about their work. However, avoid singling out one child's work as being the best. Instead, use praise that

Discuss

What is more important when considering the artwork of children: the process of making the artwork or the finished product? What effects might too much attention to the finished product have on the preschool child?

Enrich

What concepts related to math can children learn through participation in art and blockbuilding activities? Ask students to give some specific examples.

Reflect

Why should you refrain from asking children what they are making during art activities? How can questions such as *"What are you making?"* or *"Why did you glue that there?"* cause children to feel uneasy or less enthusiastic about their artwork?

Workplace Connection

Have students contact area child care centers to survey the importance placed on art activities. How much emphasis is placed on creative art? Do children have the freedom to create and invent their own original projects?

Are art activities presented as a large group activity or can children choose art as individuals during the free-choice period? Are art activities offered every day? Allow time for students to share their findings in class.

Reflect

If a three-year-old child colored pictures using mostly a black crayon, would you assume the child was depressed or moody? If a child colored a tree blue, would you assume that he or she is lacking in visual or cognitive skills? Explain your answers.

Resource

Art Stages, color transparency CT-16, TR

Discuss

Children between 18 months and three years of age do not make connections between the marks they make on paper and their own movements using a crayon. Why should they be given the opportunity to make the marks in the first place? Include reference to the stages of art as you explain your answer.

Resource

Stages of Artwork, Activity A, SAG

19-3

Commenting on Children's Art

"You're using a purple crayon."

"Your work has interesting lines."

"What a nice yellow star you're making."

"You must really like green."

"That type of brush stroke feels smooth, doesn't it?"

"These colors look happy."

Children have deep emotions about their artwork; choose your comments carefully.

19-4

Children prefer painting with bright colors such as yellow and green.

invites everyone to respect everyone else's work. For instance, you might say "Mary loves red and blue," or "Mark's colors are happy colors." Hanging the children's work tells them that their work is valued.

In preschool children's artwork, color does not play an important part. Often there is no relationship between the colors chosen and the objects in the artwork. Children choose colors they like as opposed to colors that mirror real life. An apple may be painted bright pink or an elephant red. Studies show children do have color preferences. Beautiful colors, according to young children, include yellow, blue, orange, and green, 19-4. Brown, white, and black are labeled ugly. You may wish to keep a large supply of preferred colors on hand.

Talking About Art

Conversations about art are important learning experiences for young children. These are a great way to promote literacy and language development. Young children love to share and talk about their art. When talking with them, use descriptive terms that include the language of art—color, line, size, and shape. Instead of making comments such as "Beautiful!" or "Nice!" in reference to their

work, share what you like or find interesting. You might comment about how the colors make you feel, or introduce comparison words like *lighter* or *darker*.

Stages of Art Skill Development

Children move through three distinct stages as they build art skills. These stages are scribble, basic form, and pictorial drawing, which is sometimes referred to as first drawings. Knowing these stages helps child care workers plan activities that reflect children's skill level. See Figure 19-5 to learn how a child's drawing movements' progress from simple to more complex.

Scribble Stage

The first stage is called the *scribble stage*. This usually occurs between 18 months and three years of age. Children's motor control and hand-eye coordination are not well developed yet. However, they can make dots, lines, multiple lines, and zigzags. Often they hold the drawing tool with their fist. They

---

Cross-Curricular Activity

Art
Ask your school's art instructor to present a lesson to the child care class on early childhood art. The instructor could include information about basic art activities and expectations for preschoolers. The art instructor could also demonstrate

unfamiliar techniques that would be suitable for preschool children. The art classroom may serve as resource for an in-school field trip so children can see how the students create art and view any items that may be currently on display.

19-5

Progression of Drawing Movements

- Dots
- Horizontal lines
- Vertical lines
- Diagonal lines
- Curved lines
- Multiple lines
- Loops
- Zigzags
- Circles
- Crosses
- Stars
- Closed shapes
- Sun faces
- Human figures with limbs
- Human figures with a torso

A child learns the simple dot movement long before learning to draw crosses.

may also appear to be drawing with every moving part of their body. In the scribble stage, children do not connect the marks on the paper with their movements. Their scribbles are by-products of the experience. They enjoy the physical sensation of moving a marking tool across the page.

To help children in this stage, make them aware of their movements. Comment on how hard they press their pencils, how fast they move their arms back and forth, or how large they make their movements. Such remarks help children make the connection between their actions and the art they create.

Comments about the look of children's artwork are also helpful. For example, you may say "This is a long line," or "This line has a curve." As you speak, trace some of the lines with your finger. The children's attention will focus on the form they have created.

Basic Forms Stage

The second stage in art skill development of children is basic forms. This often occurs between ages three and four. In this stage of development, children learn and recognize basic forms such as circles, rectangles, and squares. They now have more control over their movements and better hand-eye coordination. As a result, they can control the size and shape of a line. During this stage, they are beginning to enjoy their ability to create forms by combining scribbles.

At this stage, children also begin to see the connection between their movements and the marks they make. Before this time, children's scribbles were the result of the sheer pleasure of moving their arms and hands. Now children connect those motions to their artwork. Children may even begin to name their drawings at this stage. They also start to feel pride in their work.

As in the scribble stage, you can help the children understand and talk about their work by commenting on their movements. For example, say "You are moving your arm in big circles." You might describe the end product. Say "You have drawn a big picture."

Pictorial Drawing Stage

The third stage of art development occurs during the fourth and fifth years, 19-6. During the pictorial drawing stage, children are able to draw marks that are representational of pictures. They attempt to mimic their view of the world. Using their increasing skill with basic forms, they begin to combine shapes to represent objects or people. The drawings are often large. Objects are randomly placed. Color is unrealistic. First the humans are drawn with a circle for a head and lines for limbs. Then, crudely drawn human figures include a torso with straight lines for arms and limbs. Later, children often add animals, trees, houses, cars, boats, and airplanes to their artwork.

Reflect

Can you remember any comments made to you by parents or former teachers about artwork you produced when you were young? Were the comments encouraging or discouraging? How did the comments affect your future art experiences?

Activity

Have students observe a group of three- and four-year-olds as they draw or paint basic forms. What do you notice about the forms and the way children draw them? Allow time for students to discuss their findings in class.

Discuss

What characteristics would you expect to see in four-year-olds' drawings of themselves or family members? Will all body features be represented in such a drawing?

Resource

Characteristics of Children's Art, Activity B, SAG

Portfolio Project

Write the following statements about art on the board or overhead: "Possibilities and discoveries are deeply involved in the concept of 'art.' Art is not 'crafts.' Creative art must be open-ended no matter how messy it might be. Art is more than drawing, painting, cutting, and gluing. It's an attitude expressed from your emotions and your surroundings." Ask students to write a one-page paper about the advantages or disadvantages of creative art occurring in the preschool program. Have students file the completed paper in their portfolios.

Vocabulary

Have a student volunteer define the term *bentonite*. What is its purpose? Where can it be obtained?

Note

A product called Media Mixer may be purchased to add to tempera paint to extend it and make it suitable for use as finger paint. Media Mixer is a clear gel-like product that has many uses, including papier mâché and collage work. It is available at art suppliers.

Resource

Sources of Free Art Materials, Activity C, SAG

Activity

After assigning *Sources of Free Art Materials*, Activity C, SAG, ask students to brainstorm possible free items from four additional sources: landscape or garden center, hardware store, furniture or appliance store, and photography studio.

19-6

First drawings represent a child's view of the world. Colors are often unrealistic. Notice that the sun is blue.

Art Supplies and Tools

You have the option of buying or making many of your own art supplies and equipment. Most teachers need to purchase the basic tools: scissors, paintbrushes, cookie cutters, easels, and paper punches. Many of these items can be purchased at school supply stores, catalogs, Web sites, or large discount stores.

Tempera Paint

Tempera paint is used in many child care centers. It has a slight odor and tastes chalky. When dry, painted surfaces tend to crack and peel. Tempera can be purchased in both liquid and powdered form. Many teachers prefer liquid over powdered tempera because it does not need to be mixed. Since liquid tempera is much more expensive, however, many teachers still use powdered tempera. Powdered tempera paint is water soluble (dissolves in water). Thickness of the mixed paint varies from a sticky paste to runny fluid. To avoid drips and runs, mix the paint to the consistency of thick cream. Consistency will also affect color. The colors should be bright and rich.

To reduce costs, many teachers add *bentonite*, a thickening agent, to powdered tempera paint. Bentonite can be purchased through landscape and gardening stores. Adding bentonite to powdered paint extends the paint much further.

Some teachers mix enough paint to last for a week or two. Usually teachers only mix a small amount of paint daily to eliminate waste due to drying. Whichever you prefer, remember to put the powdered paint in the container before you add the liquid. To avoid paint that is too thin, add only a small amount of liquid to the tempera while stirring constantly. This will make a very thick paste. Then slowly add more liquid until you get the desired thickness.

To prepare a large quantity of tempera paint, use the recipe in 19-7. Some teachers prepare paint daily because they are unable to store it. Instead, they make a basic bentonite mixture that can be mixed with any color. The recipe for this mixture is given in 19-8. You will notice that in this recipe, the powdered paint is added to the liquid. This method differs from mixing tempera with a plain liquid (either water or pure bentonite). Other teachers might prefer to add a powdered detergent as a thickening agent.

19-7

Tempera Paint

7 to 10	tablespoons bentonite
	A large bowl or jar
	One-pound can powdered tempera
2	tablespoons soap flakes or detergent
3	cups liquid starch
	Water

Place bentonite into large bowl or jar. Add entire can of powdered tempera. Stir in soap flakes/detergent and liquid starch. Add water until desired consistency is obtained.

This recipe will yield a large amount of one color of tempera paint.

Putting Technology to Use

Ask students to create a library of art supply resources by contacting businesses that offer art supplies and materials used in art activities. Students can begin by conducting an Internet search for suppliers and contacting them for copies of their current catalogs.

Family and consumer sciences catalogs may also contain materials suitable for art. Some suggested resources are: **www.saxarts.com, www.dickblick.com, www.ssww.com, www.enasco.com, www.abcschoolsupply.com**, and **www.elmers.com**.

Health and Safety

Buying Nonhazardous Art Supplies

The *Labeling of Hazardous Art Materials Act* requires labeling of all art materials that pose a chronic hazard to children and others. The law applies to such children's art supplies as paint, crayons, chalk, modeling clay, pencils, and other art products.

When buying art materials for children, look for the statement "Conforms to ASTM D-4236" on the product label. This ensures that the products meet the *American Society for Testing Materials Standards* (ASTM). For more information about art supplies, consult the Consumer Product Safety Commission Web site.

19-8

Basic Bentonite Mixture

¾   cup powdered detergent
1   cup powdered bentonite
2   quarts water

Mix all ingredients using a beater or wire whisk. Place mixture into crock or plastic container. Let stand for two or three days. When you are ready to mix paint, remove some basic bentonite mixture from container and add enough tempera to make desired color.

Use this recipe to make bentonite, a paint extender.

Brushes

Provide children with a number of paintbrushes. They should range in size from ½ to 1 inch wide. The youngest children should use the widest brushes. As their small muscle coordination improves, they can be given smaller brushes. Pieces of string, cotton swabs, sponges, and feathers may be used as tools for applying paint by older children.

Easels

Sturdy, adjustable easels should be provided as a place to paint. Brushes and paint should be placed in an attached tray. Clamps or hooks at the top of the easels should be used to hold the paper in place, 19-9. Adjust the height of the easel so children do not need to stretch or stoop to paint. The easel should also be adjusted so the painting surface is angled or slanted outward. This reduces the dripping and running of paint. Cleanup time is also reduced.

19-9

Easels are useful tools. They can be used to hold paper for painting or drawing activities.

Resource

Tips for Buying Art Supplies, Activity D, SAG

Discuss

What size paintbrushes should young children use? What items can older children use as tools for applying paint?

Enrich

Ask student volunteers to make a basic bentonite mixture by using the recipe provided in the text. When you are ready to mix paint, have students add enough of the mixture to tempera to make the desired color.

Putting Technology to Use

Ask students to explore the Consumer Product Safety Commission Web site at **www.cpsc.gov.** Have students locate information about art product safety standards and voluntary standards for art materials, paints, paper, etc. What information is available on the Web site regarding the *American Society for Testing Materials Standards (ASTM)*? Ask students to evaluate the safety information for several products and write a brief report of their findings.

Discuss

Why might children prefer using felt-tip markers over crayons when drawing and coloring? What different effects are possible with water-based felt markers children would find unusual and interesting?

Note

Some art papers are designated by weight, such as 60 lb., 70 lb., 80 lb., etc. The weight usually indicates the thickness and quality of the paper. For example, an 80 lb.-weight construction paper will usually fold without cracking. It is easier for children to hold while cutting than a 60 lb.-weight paper.

Enrich

Ask students to research the different types of art papers available for use by pre-school children. Survey art and school supply catalogs or visit local art supply businesses. Determine the types of paper that are suitable for use with various media and tools including pencils, crayons, tempera paint, finger paint, chalk, watercolors, and scissors.

Crayons, Chalk, and Felt-Tip Markers

Children enjoy using crayons, chalk, and felt-tip markers. However, these items are harder to use than paint. As a rule, these tools need to be pushed hard with small muscles that are not well-developed in young children. Paint, however, flows easily.

Crayons come in regular and kindergarten sizes. Kindergarten-size crayons are round and large. These crayons do not break easily, nor do they roll easily off tables or other surfaces. Crayons can be stored in bowls, baskets, or boxes.

Chalk is available in both an art and chalkboard form. Art chalk comes in a variety of sizes. As with crayons, chalk can be purchased in large, fat sticks. Choose basic colors that are clear and brilliant. Be careful that children do not use art chalk on a chalkboard. Marks from art chalk cannot be erased from a chalkboard. Store chalk in baskets, boxes, trays, or bowls.

Felt-tip markers come with washable or waterproof inks. Always buy washable felt-tip markers for use in child care centers. Be sure that any markers you buy have tight caps. This prevents the markers from drying out. Remind children to replace the caps after use.

Paper and Painting Surfaces

There are many types of paper and painting surfaces that can be used successfully for art activities. Included are newsprint, manila paper, construction paper, wallpaper, cardboard, and old newspaper. Other alternatives are listed in 19-10.

The least costly paper is newsprint. It is durable and easy to use. Roll ends of newsprint can be bought at little or no cost from local newspaper printers. Cut the large sheets into the size sheets you want. To determine the size of the paper, remember younger children have poorer muscle control. As a result, they need large surfaces on

19-10

Paper Alternatives for Art Activities

sandpaper
waxed paper
foil
shelf paper
butcher paper
magazines

egg cartons

paper bags
tissue paper
crepe paper
wallpaper
wrapping paper
boxes and tubes

Paper for use in art activities comes in many forms. Some of these types of paper can be obtained for little or no cost.

Workplace Connection

Have students investigate the types of pencil and crayon grips available to help young children hold writing and drawing tools. School supply and art supply catalogs are possible resources. Ask students to locate examples of triangular and six-sided pencils and crayons. Then have students interview an occupational therapist to find out the recommendations for using these with preschool children.

which to paint or draw. A good size for easel painting is 18- by 24-inch sheets.

Coloring Books

Coloring books contain images created by adults. Studies show that coloring books have a negative effect on children's creativity by blocking their creative impulses. For this reason, avoid relying heavily on coloring books for children under six years old. The value of art as a form of expression is lost when children are limited to designs in a coloring book. Children become self-conscious and doubtful about their art talents.

For example, Sara colors in the outline of a kitten in a coloring book. The next time she is asked to draw something, she recalls the perfect kitten from the coloring book page. She knows she could not draw that perfect kitten. She becomes frustrated and says, "I cannot draw very well." The frustration occurred because she knew her work looks like a child's opposed to an adult's. As a result, Sara may lose interest in the creative process of drawing.

Some teachers see no harm in using coloring books and feel that their children enjoy working in them. Coloring books are also easy to buy and keep on hand. However, for more enriching art experiences, rely on activities that allow children to explore interesting materials and experience cause and effect.

Paste

Library paste works well for adhering lightweight paper. Paste can be prepared or purchased. Many teachers prefer to buy paste by the gallon, which is more economical. Other teachers prefer to prepare their own paste, 19-11. To improve bonding strength, you can add small quantities of glue to your paste. For young children, water-soluble

19-11

Paste

1	cup cold water
1	cup flour
2¼	cups boiling water
1	teaspoon powdered alum
¾	teaspoon oil of wintergreen (optional)

Mix the cold water with the flour, stirring until smooth. Continue stirring while adding boiling water. Cook mixture on low heat in a double boiler until smooth. Add the alum and stir. At this time, the mixture should look slightly bluish-gray and shiny. Remove from heat and add oil of wintergreen for an interesting smell. Store in a cool place.

Making paste is easy and can be a source of budget savings.

adhesives are the best. They are inexpensive and easy to handle.

Glue

The best all-purpose adhesive is a white liquid glue. It can be used on heavyweight paper, cardboard, fabric, plastic, and wood. Glue is more permanent than paste and often more costly. If purchased by the gallon, it is a better bargain. Many building supply stores carry glue in gallon containers.

Take precautions when using white glue. Glue is difficult to remove from clothes, carpeting, and art tables. Therefore, wipe up spills immediately. Children should wear smocks. Table surfaces should be covered with newspapers. If used, you can provide small squeeze bottles of glue or pour small quantities into shallow pans or jar lids. Wipe the glue bottles immediately after the children are finished using them. Glue cleans up easily while it's still moist. Once it has dried, cleanup is difficult. Use with older preschoolers who are less likely to spill the glue.

Resource

Planning an Art Activity, Activity D, OG

Activity

Have students design a preschool art activity in which children can use either paste or glue. Observe children to determine which product is more effective and which is easier for children to use. Allow time for students to discuss their findings in class.

Resource

Paste Recipes, reproducible master 19-2, TR

Putting Technology to Use

Ask students to conduct an Internet search for information about the pros and cons on the use of coloring books or coloring pages in a developmentally appropriate curriculum. What is the position of NAEYC on using coloring books? What other fine-motor skill tasks might children be exposed to that would help them develop skills without affecting creativity and self-esteem? Findings can be shared with the class using a debate format.

Discuss

What general preparations are needed before art activities begin to cut down on cleanup time? What preparations are needed for really messy activities to ensure children can enjoy the activity while cleanup remains organized and efficient?

Activity

Have students look through the art supply cabinets and shelves in the child care lab to inventory the materials available. Have them make suggestions for adding supplies. Ask students if they have any ideas for improving the storage and accessibility of materials or to explain why the current arrangement is efficient and accessible.

Resource

Approaches to Painting, Activity B, OG

Cleanup Tools

Keep cleanup tools in the art area so they are available when spills occur. Small buckets, sponge mops, and various sizes of sponges are useful. Keep supplies within children's reach. Cut mop handles down so they are child sized. This will encourage children to be responsible for cleaning up.

Space and Storage

Well-planned space is needed to encourage children to use art areas. Storage and display areas for artwork are part of a well-planned space. Bookshelves can be used to store staple supplies. These supplies include paper, scissors, paste, glue, collage materials, crayons, markers, chalk, tape, and paint.

Containers are needed to store paint, paste, scissors, and collage materials, 19-12. Baby food jars, plastic cups, and plastic bowls are often used to store tempera paint. Shallow dishes, including empty frozen food containers, can be used to hold paint during painting activities. After use, the paint can be covered for storage.

Paste containers may be small enough for one child or large enough for a group to use.

19-12

Store materials in individual containers.

The size will depend on the activity. Empty squeeze bottles and baby food jars are useful for individual activities. Foil or small plastic dishes are useful for several children to use together at one time.

Scissors should be stored within easy reach. Special scissor holders may be bought. Scissor holders can also be made by the staff. Egg cartons, turned upside down, are often used to hold scissors.

Collage materials need to be well-organized to appeal to children. They should be sorted and placed in clear plastic boxes, shoe boxes, plastic dishpans, or baskets. Place these containers on a shelf within eye level of the children.

Painting Activities

To learn what painting means to young children, listen and watch. You will note that most children find their work pleasing. The artwork of a two-year-old is different from that of a four-year-old. Children's paintings change from simple dots and strokes to crude figures as they move through art development. Some children enjoy moving the tools, 19-13. Other children enjoy the feelings and visual aspects.

Consider some of the children you might meet. Noah, a two-year-old, seems to be fascinated by the painting process. He dips his brush and paints, making large circles over his entire paper. His friend, Renee, delights in moving her brush back and forth. When she dips her brush into different colors, she ignores the cleaning process.

Mark, an active three-year-old, makes large dots and zigzags all over his paper. He pays little attention to the paint color but carefully watches his strokes. Heidi, another three-year-old, paints different colors on top of each other. As a result, her paper becomes soaked. At this point, she uses her hand to feel the paint. Then she proceeds to remove her painting from the easel. During this process, it tears. This does not bother Heidi.

Cross-Curricular Activity

Math
Obtain geometric models of shapes and multidimensional figures such as cubes and cylinders from a math instructor. Have students arrange a display for the preschoolers, allowing them to handle the shapes and models. Have children engage in drawing and painting activities and observe them to see if they incorporate the models into their artwork. Ask the math instructor to speak to the students and share any knowledge he or she may have related to early childhood math awareness.

Many children enjoy using different painting tools.

Like most three-year-olds, she is interested in the process, not the product. She paints one color on top of another and enjoys observing the changes in the layers of colors.

Jon, a highly verbal five-year-old, is comfortable handling the brush. He paints a man by making a circle face. Then he paints straight lines to represent legs. He uses a smaller circle for a mouth, two large round dots for eyes, and a V-shaped figure for a nose. As he paints, he keeps renaming his figure and inventing related stories. First, he tells the child standing next to him that the figure is a police officer. Later, he claims the same figure is a firefighter.

Children like Jon are not unusual. Some comment to themselves as they paint. They appear to be carrying on a conversation with their painting. These comments are useful. They tell you what the child feels and thinks. Sometimes children are eager to discuss their artwork; other times they are not.

There are many types of painting activities that children will be eager to do. Included are easel, finger, string, texture, salt, mono, spice, and chalk painting. From these experiences, children learn to apply the correct amounts of paint and to recognize color and shapes.

Easel Painting

Easel painting should be a daily activity in all early childhood programs. Provide an easel, paper, brushes, and paint. Easels should be adjusted to the correct height for the children. Brushes with long handles (about twelve inches) in a variety of sizes should be provided on the easel tray. The size of the paper you give the children will depend on the activity and age of the children. For young children, provide large sheets of newsprint. Sheets of this size will encourage the use of large muscles. On special occasions, you may wish to provide colored paper and white tempera.

To ensure success in easel painting, plan the session ahead of time. Provide only a small amount of paint since children often spill. Pour only enough paint to cover the bottom of the container. This will save cleanup time. Make only one color of paint available for early experiences. When a second color is added, provide a brush for each container.

Permit only one child to use each easel. Encourage children to wear smocks. Push long sleeves above their elbows to prevent paint from getting on their clothing.

Teach young children how to use the paintbrush. Gently dip the brush into the paint container, 19-14. Then wipe the brush on the side of the container. This will rid the brush of extra paint. As children gain skill, give them smaller brushes and pieces of paper with which to work. Wash brushes after use. Until they are used again, place them with handles down in a storage container. This allows the bristles to dry.

Reflect

How would you handle the problem of space for only one double-sided easel in your classroom and a class full of fifteen eager painters? How can limiting the time a child is allowed to work at the easel affect the child's creativity and enjoyment of easel time?

Enrich

Have students explore the possibility of constructing simple table top easels for the child care program. What materials, tools, and equipment are needed? What is the potential cost? How does this compare to the cost to purchase the easels ready-made? Allow time for students to discuss their findings in class.

Resource

Painting Activities, reproducible master 19-3, TR

Workplace Connection

Have students observe two- through five-year-olds during painting activities. What activities are the children performing? Ask students to record the characteristics they notice in the processes used in creating the art. Have students photograph the finished artwork and label the photos by age of child. Allow time for students to compare their photos with those of other students in the class. Have students discuss the differences in art activities based on the child's age.

Discuss

Shavonne enjoys the sensation of finger painting so much that she usually rubs the paint right through the paper then complains that she needs more paper. Discuss ideas for giving Shavonne the sensory experience she enjoys while conserving the paper supply.

Note

The company that made Ivory® Soap Flakes discontinued them in 1993. Many craft recipes, including those for finger paints, still call for soap flakes. You can substitute your own flakes made from grated pure soap (such as Ivory soap or Castile soap).

Reflect

During a finger painting activity, you notice that Jeremy refuses to touch his paint. When questioned, he tells you that his mother said he is not allowed to get his hands dirty. How would you handle this situation?

Resource

Finger Paint Recipes, reproducible master 19-4, TR

19-14

Recycle plastic food containers by using them as paint containers.

Finger Painting

Finger painting is a sensory experience. It promotes expression and release of feelings. It is one of the most satisfying experiences for young children. Some may resist their first experience because they fear getting dirty. These same children, after having the chance to observe, may begin painting with one finger. Later, when they become comfortable, they will use their hands and arms as brushes.

Since finger painting can require a lot of cleanup, cover the tables if they are not washable. Otherwise, provide a plastic cover. The children should always wear aprons during this activity. Provide wet sponges and rags to facilitate the clean up process.

Finger painting requires more supervision than most other painting activities. For this reason, work with no more than four children at a time. Children need to stay at the table until they are finished painting. Hands must be washed immediately after painting.

Finger paint recipes are given in 19-15. Finger paint may also be made from instant pudding, soap flakes whipped with water, partially-set flavored gelatin, and shaving cream. Children enjoy using a variety of paints.

Provide children with paper that has a shiny surface. This can be finger-painting paper, butcher paper, shelf paper, or freezer wrap.

19-15

Finger Paints

Speedy finger paint
1   cup laundry starch
3   cups soap flakes
1   cup cold water

Mix all ingredients together. If colored finger paint is desired, add food coloring or colored tempera.

Blender finger paint
1   pound powdered tempera paint
¼   cup liquid starch
1/3   cup water
1   tablespoon powdered laundry detergent

Place in blender. Mix until finger paint is blended well.

Cornstarch finger paint
1   cup dry starch
½   cup water
1½   cups boiling water
¾   cup powdered laundry detergent

Mix starch and ½ cup water in heat-resistant bowl. Add 1½ cups boiling water while stirring rapidly. Blend in ¾ cup powdered laundry detergent until smooth. Add food coloring if color is desired.

Using recipes allows you to make the type and color of finger paint you need.

Workplace Connection

Have students individually or with partners select an art activity and demonstrate it to the class. Students must include learning objectives, materials needed, process, and suggested age or stage of development. Suggested activities might include: mirror image painting; texture painting; object printing and stamping; coffee filter and tissue paper art; cutting and weaving; nature art; noodle, bean, or seed art; art created from recycled objects; yarn and fiber art; marble painting; crayon art and resist techniques; or sculpture art.

String Painting

To prepare for **string painting**, cut several pieces of heavy yarn or string. Place a tray, or trays, of colored tempera paint and paper on the table. Show the children how to slide the yarn through the paint and across the piece of paper. Another technique is to place the string in a folded piece of paper and pull it out.

Mono Painting

A **mono painting** starts with a regular finger painting. After this, an 8×12 inch piece of paper is placed over the finger painting. The papers are patted together, then pulled apart.

Chalk Painting

To make a **chalk painting**, dip chalk into water and draw on construction paper. Use chalk at least one inch thick. Choose paper color based on the color of chalk being used. Add vinegar to the water to deepen the color of the chalk.

Texture Painting

Make paint for **texture painting** using liquid tempera or mixing powdered tempera with liquid starch. To this mixture, add sand, sawdust, or coffee grounds. For best results, the paint should be thick.

Salt Painting

Materials needed for **salt painting** include construction paper or cardboard, paste or glue, cotton swabs or tongue depressors, and salt mixed with colored tempera in shakers. Have the children spread paste or glue on the paper. Then have them shake the salt mixture onto the glue or paste. Shake off excess paint and set aside to dry.

Spice Painting

Spice painting results in a scented painting. Prepare the mixture by adding a small amount of water to liquid glue. Give each child enough glue to spread over their piece of paper. They can use their fingers to do this. Then have them shake spices onto the paper. When it dries it will look as interesting as it smells.

Cinnamon, onion powder, garlic powder, and oregano all make aromatic paintings. For texture, use bay leaves, cloves, or coffee grounds. The center's budget may dictate which and how many spices you can use. In addition, consideration must be given to any policies toward the use of food. Some directors tend to discourage this type of food use.

Molding

Play dough, Plasticene®, and clay are open-ended materials that can be molded and formed. Children enjoy the tactile appeal of these responsive materials. Because they can be reshaped, they stimulate the imagination and allow children the freedom to change their minds. You will observe them poking, rolling, stretching, pounding, squeezing, coiling, flattening, tearing, and attaching pieces to the clay or play dough. It can be turned into a ball, snowman, cat, pancake, or snake. Often the children will use accessories such as pans, cookie cutters, and rolling pins to make pies, cookies, and other "baked goods" from these materials.

Children's play with molding materials reflects their level of development. Two-year-old children pull, beat, push, and squeeze. When children are about three years of age, they make balls and snake-like shapes. By age four, children can make complex forms, some of which they name. By age five, children will often announce what they are going to make before they begin.

Vocabulary

Have student volunteers define the terms *string painting* and *mono painting*. How do these activities contribute to the development of fine-motor skills?

Discuss

Have students explain the following painting techniques: chalk, texture, salt, and spice painting. Why might these techniques be interesting to children?

Note

Glitter is very difficult to use with small children as they lack the motor control needed to use this art material correctly. Glitter can be transferred to a child's eye and cause irritation and possible scratching of the cornea. To get a glittery effect, try salt or use metallic paper confetti, which is larger, easier to use, and requires less cleanup.

Service Learning Activity

Have students conduct an "art expo" babysitting service in the child care lab during parent/teacher conferences. Provide care for small children during this time so their parents can attend the school activity. Ask students to coordinate the donation or acquisition of art supplies and determine what activities can be offered. Students will need to publicize the service, secure permission from the school administration, and schedule the child care.

Vocabulary

Have a student volunteer define the term *Plasticene*®. What is the major benefit of using this material?

Activity

Have students explore using an air-dried modeling medium such as Crayola® Model Magic®. What are the advantages and disadvantages of using this type of art material with preschoolers?

Resource

Rating Play Dough, Activity E, SAG

Regardless of age, children have fun developing their small and large motor coordination skills. Clay provides an emotional outlet for the children to express and explore their feelings. Working with clay also helps them make important math and science discoveries.

Clay may be purchased at local art-supply stores and through school catalogs. It is available in two colors, white or red. When wet, the white clay appears grayish in color. Since red clay can stain clothing, most teachers prefer the white. Mixed properly, it should be stored in a plastic bag, diaper pail, or garbage pail to prevent drying. Clay can be used on a vinyl tablecloth or tile to save on cleanup time.

Play dough is soft and pliable, and it has a softer texture than clay. It offers little resistance to pressure and responds easily when touched. Each type of play dough has different features. Provide the children with a number of types by using the recipes in 19-16. You can vary these play doughs even further by adding rice, cornmeal, pebbles, sand, oats, and coffee grounds. Scented oils such as peppermint and wintergreen add a fragrant smell.

Many teachers use Plasticene® for modeling. **Plasticene**® is an oil-based, commercially manufactured modeling compound. It is available in many bright colors including blue, green, orange, red, and yellow.

Unlike play dough and clay, Plasticene® does not dry out. It can be rolled up and used over and over again. It needs little care, even when used daily. However, one disadvantage of Plasticene® is that it can leave an oily residue on the children's hands and table surfaces. For this reason, some teachers do not make it available to the children.

19-16

Play Doughs

Refrigerator play dough

1	cup salt
2	cups flour
1	tablespoon alum (optional, a preservative)
1	cup water
3	tablespoons oil
	Food coloring or tempera (optional)

Mix salt, flour, and alum. Add oil, water, food coloring, and mix. Check the consistency. If sticky, add more flour. Store in a tightly covered container in the refrigerator.

Sawdust play dough

3	cups flour
3	cups sawdust
1	cup salt

Mix the three ingredients together. Add water as needed to form a soft dough.

Cooked play dough

1	cup salt
½	cup flour
1	cup water

Mix ingredients together in a pan. Cook over medium heat, stirring constantly. Remove the mixture from the heat when it becomes thick and rubbery. After cooling, the mixture will not be as sticky. Store in an airtight container.

Drink Mix Play Dough

2	packages sugar free drink mix
2½	cups flour
2½	cup salt
½	teaspoon alum
2	cups boiling water

Mix the drink mix, flour, salt, oil, alum, and boiling water. Knead until dough is the proper consistency.

Varying the types of play dough you make helps give children a variety of sensory experiences.

Cutting

Children need time, supplies, and space each day for cutting. Young children learn to cut because they enjoy using scissors. At first, children just snip in a straight line. Provide strips of construction paper or wrapping paper. The paper should be long enough so the children may hold fast to one end of it. Avoid heavy wrapping paper, corrugated paper, or vinyl paper. These materials are

---

Portfolio Project

Ask students to collect recipes for making homemade play doughs. Have students contact area child care centers for their favorite recipes. Students may also find recipes in resource books or through an Internet search. Peanut butter and pumpkin pie play doughs are just two examples of unusual types. Ask students to compare the qualities of cooked versus uncooked recipes of play doughs and determine which type they most prefer for preschool use. Have students compile favorite recipes and file them in their portfolio.

developmentally inappropriate for young children. Children do not have enough small muscle strength to cut through these materials. As children progress, they may wish to cut in curves. This requires good hand-eye coordination skills.

Have children work with one type of paper. This allows them to master handling one type of material and tool. To avoid failure, give children quality scissors. Provide left-handed children with proper scissors. Mark these scissors with colored tape. All scissors should have blunt, rounded tips.

Collages

The term **collage** means a selection of materials mounted on a flat surface. Collages are two-dimensional arrangements of many materials. Making collages gives children the chance to make choices. They can decide what material will be placed where. Two-year-olds may paste layers of materials on top of each other. Collages also introduce many materials of contrasting colors and textures to children. Materials that can be used in collages are listed in 19-17. Consider the children's ages when choosing collage materials. For instance, buttons, beads, or other small objects would be inappropriate for children younger than three. These tiny items can present a choking hazard.

The base for a collage should be a heavyweight material. Construction paper or cardboard is ideal.

Arrange collage materials in attractive shallow containers. These may be baskets,

Activity

Have students collect examples of various types of children's scissors and observe children using them. Which types cut well, are easy for children to use, and are safe? Allow time for students to discuss their findings in class.

Vocabulary

Have a student volunteer define the term *collage*. What skills can children learn and practice while making a collage?

Discuss

Have students review the list of objects for collages in 19-17. What items would be appropriate for a three-year-old to use? What about a five-year-old?

19-17

Objects for Collages

aluminum foil	feathers	rubber bands
aluminum pans	felt	sandpaper
baking cups	flower petals	scrap yarn, string, & ribbon
bark	frozen food trays	seashells
beads	gift wrap	seeds
bottle lids	greeting cards	sequins
burlap	juice cans	shoeboxes
buttons	lace	shoelaces
candy wrappers	leather	small tiles
can labels	leaves	sponges
cartons	magazine pictures	straws
cellophane	netting	styrofoam packing pieces
cereal boxes	newspaper	suede
chalk	paper cups	tape
clear plastic trays	paper plates	tin foil
cloth scraps	paper ribbons	tissue paper
confetti	paper towel or toilet paper tubes	tongue depressors
construction paper pieces	pebbles	twigs
corks	pinecones	used gift boxes
cotton balls	plastic or foam packing material	wallpaper samples
doilies	plastic milk jugs	wooden clothespins
egg cartons	plastic or wooden spools	wood shavings
fabrics	plastic pieces	yarn

The types of items used in collages are nearly limitless. Many types of items are listed here. What other interesting items could be used?

Portfolio Project

Make copies of reproducible masters 19-2, 19-3, and 19-4, TR, for the students to file in their portfolios. Have students research additional art recipes and directions for art activities to include in their portfolio. Many Web sites are dedicated to preschool and home child care activity ideas that are copyright-free. Have students create a resource list of Web sites that carry preschool and early school-age art activity ideas. An example is **www.preschoolrainbow.org**.

Reflect

Why should information on blockbuilding be included in a chapter that focuses mainly on art? How do blockbuilding activities relate to the program goals for the child care lab?

Discuss

Should children who prefer solitary play with blocks be discouraged from playing alone? What social skills might children develop and practice during block-building activities with others?

Resource

Evaluating an Art Activity, Activity C, OG

paper, or clear plastic trays. This will allow the children to view the materials. The children can browse through the containers choosing items for their collages. Some children will use the pieces as they are. Others will prefer cutting them into different size pieces.

Remember to provide adhesives. Library paste is a good medium for younger children to use. As children gain skills in making collages, liquid starch, rubber cement, and white glue can be used. Liquid starch works well on tissue paper. Rubber cement or white glue is a better choice for heavier materials, such as buttons. To add interest, tint white glue with tempera paint.

Young children enjoy exploring paste. They often apply an excessive amount of paste to paper. Then they will pick the paste up and spread it over their fingers. They enjoy the feeling of rubbing this medium over their fingers. When children apply paste to paper, their approach is much like finger painting. They will use sweeping motions. Gradually they will develop wrist action.

Blockbuilding

Blocks are important learning tools for young children. They are probably the most popular materials in child care centers. While playing with blocks, children are in constant motion, reaching, stretching, and changing body positions. As they build with the blocks, they are improving their eye-hand coordination and strengthening their muscles. Through block play, children also learn many new concepts and skills. Figure 19-18 lists the many ways that block play promotes learning in the four developmental domains.

19-18

Learning Through Block Play

Domain	Learnings
Physical Development	• Developing fine- and gross-motor skills • Building hand-eye coordination skills • Understanding object-space relationships • Increasing motor coordination by lifting, carrying, stretching, and stacking
Cognitive Development	• Understanding balance, weight, and measurement concepts • Exploring shapes, sizes, and proportions • Understanding mathematical concepts, such as *larger than* or *smaller than* • Understanding language concepts related to location, such as *over*, *under*, *same different*, and *beside* • Experimenting with gravity, balance, and cause and effect • Developing skills in predicting, comparing, sorting, and classifying • Developing creative expression
Emotional Development	• Gaining self-confidence • Finding a sense of accomplishment and success • Developing patience and tolerance • Expressing feelings through role-playing
Social Development	• Improving cooperation skills by learning to compromise and negotiate • Practicing turn-taking and sharing skills • Learning to respect the work of others

Children benefit in many ways from blockbuilding experiences.

Meeting Special Needs

Pair special learners with volunteer students to review Chart 19-18, *Learning Through Block Play*. Have students quiz each other and give examples of how blockbuilding provides each of the bulleted "Learnings" in the chart. Allow time for students to share their examples with the entire class. Spend additional time discussing any areas that are difficult for special learners to understand.

Stages of Blockbuilding

Children play with blocks in different ways as they grow older. The following stages of blockbuilding have been identified:

- **Stage One.** At one to two years of age, children carry the blocks around and do not engage in construction. They enjoy filling containers with blocks and dumping them out.

- **Stage Two.** From two to three years of age, building begins. The children will either stack the blocks vertically or lay them in horizontal rows. They strive to build towers higher until they fall down, and their "roads" become longer and longer. They usually keep building until they run out of blocks or space. They may also combine horizontal rows of blocks.

- **Stage Three.** Simple bridging occurs. **Bridging** is a process of placing two blocks vertically a space apart. Then a third block is added. Children build these bridges and tunnels over and over again.

- **Stage Four.** Children begin to construct square enclosures. They enjoy building houses, apartments, barns, stores, caves for animals, and other types of buildings. Naming begins at this stage.

- **Stage Five.** By three to four years of age, children begin to build more intricate buildings. These buildings are now higher, wider, and more elaborate. They are beginning to choose blocks carefully in order to carry out their designs.

- **Stage Six.** The children begin naming their structures and include dramatic play. They may build an airport for toy airplanes.

- **Stage Seven.** By five years of age, children are engaged in representational play. They decide what they want to build prior to construction. Their structures becoming more symbolic and are used in dramatic play. They will build stores, garages, houses, and barns. Once built, their play becomes more creative by adding props and accessories. Often the children like to play with the same structure for several days.

Types of Blocks and Accessories

Blocks come in a variety of materials including wood, cardboard, plastic, rubber, and foam. Square and rectangular blocks made from lightweight materials are best for younger children. Children from three to six years of age prefer unit blocks made from wood in a variety of shapes and sizes. Use blocks for counting, patterning, arithmetic, and building geometric shapes. See 19-19.

The children enjoy having accessories to use with block play. Usually they prefer simple figures such as animals and multicultural people. Often they will want to recreate a setting they have experienced. After a field trip to the farm, they may build a barn. Other settings may include airports, firehouses, parking garages, a zoo, racetracks, train stations, and bus stations. To maintain the children's interests, rotate the materials occasionally. To facilitate sharing and cooperative efforts, always purchase two of each item.

Stimulate block-building play by being present in the classroom area and calling attention to the children's work. Begin by labeling the children's constructions using their words. For example, Marena was building a boat and said, "This is Grandpa Jose's new boat." Four- and five-year-old children often enjoy dictating a story for you. If your classroom does not have the space to save constructions for several days, take photos of the structures. Then you can place the photos on a bulletin board with the dictations.

Vocabulary

Have a student volunteer define the term *bridging*. Where does bridging occur in the stages of blockbuilding?

Discuss

Review the seven stages of blockbuilding. In which stage do children usually keep building until they run out of blocks? In which stage do children decide what they want to build prior to construction?

Reflect

Think about math skills you can teach with the use of blocks such as counting, addition, or subtraction. What other skills can be taught by using block-building play?

Workplace Connection

Have students contact area child care centers to arrange a visit to observe children during blockbuilding activities. What ages are the children? What types of blocks are the children using? Do the children have accessories to use with block play? Does the teacher call attention to the children's work? Are any children naming their structures or creating stories about them? Allow time for students to compare the blockbuilding activities and stages they observed with those observed by other students in the class.

19-19

Discuss

Review the limits for blockbuilding in Chapter 16. What additional limits for blockbuilding might be needed for our child care lab?

Resource

Blockbuilding Evaluation, Activity E, OG

Activity

Ask student volunteers to inventory the child care lab's block collection. Are all of the common shapes of blocks shown in 19-19 found in the child care lab? If not, which blocks are missing? Allow time for students to share their findings with the class.

Common Blocks

Units

Buttresses

Intersection

Side road

Pillars

Ellipse, curve, and quarter circle

Switches

Cylinders

Arches

Triangles

Half circle

These are the most common shapes of blocks.

Service Learning Activity

Ask student volunteers to perform the following block repair tasks as a service project. Sand and finish wooden blocks; tape or cover large cardboard or brick-style blocks with brick- or wood-patterned self-stick paper to renew their appearance; clean small plastic interlocking blocks and check for broken or cracked pieces; construct new blocks by using scrap wood and woodworking tools in the school's industrial or technical arts department. Students may also want to perform these activities for area child care centers.

Displaying Children's Work

Children need to know that their artwork is valued. Displaying children's work shows respect for them and their development. However, children should always have a choice in whether they want to save their work.

Print the children's name and the date on their work for identification purposes. Provide drying racks in the classroom away from traffic areas. Then, if the children want to take their work home, their clothing or the family vehicle will not be soiled.

Bulletin boards are a way that centers can share and display the children's work. To be effective, position bulletin boards low enough for the children to benefit from seeing their work. Often teachers will print a title that represents the collective work. For example, titles could be *Easel Paintings*, *Finger Paintings*, and any other type of painting. Teachers might also take pictures of children working with an art medium. These pictures can then be posted on the bulletin board.

Bulletin boards also are an important way of conveying information to families. They can be used to share the children's work and teach families about the curriculum. For example, a bulletin board could be titled *Developmental Stages of Children's Art*. An example of each of the stages could be posted. Likewise, you could make a bulletin board titled *The Value of Children's Art*. Then you could list all the skills children can learn or develop by participating in the artistic process.

Sensory Experiences: Sand and Water Play

Sand and water play are often referred to as sensory experiences. These are developmentally appropriate for children of all ages, cultures, and ability levels. Like paint and play dough, water and sand are basic materials for young children. Fortunately, these materials are almost always available at little expense.

Most preschool programs offer water and sand play. Both activities can occur indoors and outdoors. Children find pleasure in these unstructured and fluid materials. Working with sand or water is relaxing and relieves tension. This type of play fosters a child's imagination, creativity, and experimentation. A list of sensory table accessories for fantasy, floating, pouring, and squirting or dribbling are listed in 19-20. Water and sand play also encourage social interaction as children play side-by-side or with others.

19-20

Sensory Table Accessories

Floating	Boats, corks, foam, jar lids, meat trays, paintbrushes, rubber balls, sponges, wood pieces
Pouring	Bottles, buckets, cardboard tubes, funnel cups, ice cube trays, ladles, measuring cups, measuring spoons, pitchers, pots, pans, scoops, sifters
Squirting and Dribbling	Hoses, margarine tubs, meat basters, medicine or eye droppers, plastic tubing, spray bottles, sifters, spoons, water pumps, whisks, rotary egg beaters
Fantasy	Airplanes, trucks, cars, motorcycles, toy boats, plastic people, plastic animals, dolls, muffin tins, bread tins, cookie cutters, rubber or plastic people

These items can be used to promote exploration in sand and water play.

Discuss

How should children's artwork be marked for display? Should children have a choice in whether they want to save their work?

Reflect

What other materials besides sand and water can also provide sensory experiences for preschoolers? How does providing sensory experiences to preschoolers help meet the child care lab's program goals?

Discuss

What is the relationship between sensory play and the development of thinking skills in preschoolers? How do preschoolers use sand, water, and other sensory materials to test their thinking?

Putting Technology to Use

Have students conduct an Internet search for information about the role of sensory education in Maria Montessori's method. Why did Montessori believe that educating the senses was an important part of a child's education?

What types of activities did Montessori design for sensory exploration? What equipment or materials are used for sensory experiences in the Montessori method? Have students write a brief report to share with the class.

Discuss

In what area of the playground should a sandbox be located? Why is the use of moist sand preferable to dry sand?

Note

In rooms where having a water and sand table year round is not possible due to space constraints, offer children the opportunity to play with individual containers filled with sand, rice or beans, water, shaving cream, gel, and soap mixtures. Use large, shallow plastic containers such as underbed storage containers, sweater boxes, and food storage containers. Make sure they have tightly fitting lids or covers.

Reflect

Besides the ones in the text, can you think of additional safety guidelines that should be followed during water play activities? What about during sand play activities?

Sand Play

An outdoor sandbox should have an 8- to 12-inch ledge around it. This gives the children a place to display their molded sand forms. It will also provide seating for the children.

Outdoors, the sandbox should be placed in a quiet area of the play yard, 19-21. If possible, it should be placed near a water source so the sand can be moistened. Moist sand can be used to pack molds and cans and to create castles. Moist sand is preferable to dry sand because it does not get into the eyes, shoes, or hair as easily. By placing the sandbox far from the building entrance, less sand will be brought into the center. As the children walk across the play yard, some of the sand should fall off.

An indoor sensory table should also be placed near a water source. It is usually located in or near the art area on flooring that is easily cleaned. Ceramic tile and linoleum are good choices. Sensory tables come in different sizes to meet the needs of each group of children and the space available.

Water Play

With careful supervision, water play is another activity that is developmentally appropriate for all children. Water play can

This canopied sandbox helps protect children from the sun when they are playing outdoors.

take place indoors using a water table, plastic bins, laundry tubs, or wading pools. For variety, you can fill the tub with snow. Food coloring and soap can also be added for interest. Occasionally you may want to use shaving

Water-Table Safety

Water tables give children much enjoyment. As a child care teacher, make sure you use the following safety guidelines:

- Fill the water table with fresh water before children begin to play.

- Permit only children without cuts, scratches, or sores to play in the water table with others. In addition, if children are sick they should not play in the water table to avoid spreading illness.

- Require children to wash their hands before and after using the water table.

- Supervise children at all times at the water table.

- Make sure that children do not drink water from the table.

- Clean and sanitize the water table and all toys that are used in it before the next water-play activity.

Workplace Connection

Ask students to prepare individual bags of "Rainbow Stew" for each child using the following recipe: Mix together 1/3 cup granulated sugar, 1 cup cornstarch, and 4 cups cold water. Cook this mixture until thick, then divide into individual bowls and add food coloring.

After cooling, carefully spoon some of each color side by side into a zip-type plastic bag and seal. The children can squeeze the bags to mix colors and enjoy the sensory experience while creating their own rainbow.

cream in the water table. The cream can be colored to correspond with different holidays.

A sensory or water table should have a splash control. For safety, the edges of the frame should be rounded and the table should have casters. Whenever possible, it is wise to purchase a table with a drain and valve. This will assist you in filling and draining the table if you need to move to a water source. For safety purposes, the tables and accessories need to be disinfected daily when used with water.

Children should wear plastic aprons during water play to protect their clothing. The floor should be covered with a plastic mat or covering to protect any carpeting. Only unbreakable accessories should be used in a sensory table.

A sensory table can promote important learning in the classroom. As children pour water, their physical skills are promoted. They also learn mathematical concepts, social skills, and problem-solving skills. Figure 19-22 shows the concepts that children can learn from sand and water play.

There are many vocabulary words that can be learned through water play. For instance, you could place a chunk of ice into the water table. From this experience, children could learn that ice is frozen water; ice can melt; melted ice is water, ice can be picked up; ice is cold; and ice melts in warm places. When ice is held in hands, it melts. Other concepts children can learn about water includes opposites such as *fast* and *slow*; the difference between *drip* and *drop*; and objects can *float* and *sink*. In addition, the children can learn the following words:
- leak
- measure
- mopping
- pour
- scoop
- shower

Concepts Developed Through Sand and Water Play

Sand Play	Water Play
• Sand can be dry or wet. • Sand absorbs water. • Wet sand is heavier. • Sand can be used in many ways. • Objects can be buried in the sand.	• Water flows when poured. • Water takes many forms. • Water dissolves some foods. • Water can be held in a container. • Some items float on water. • Some materials absorb water.

These are just some of the basic concepts children can learn from sand and water play.

- splash
- spray
- swish
- sprinkle
- squeeze
- squish
- stir
- trickle

Woodworking

Children enjoy woodworking activities. Hammering is usually their first interest. When provided the proper tools, they may pound nails for 20 minutes. Developmentally, woodworking can be a valuable experience. It promotes hand-eye coordination, fine- and gross-motor development, and creative expression. Woodworking provides the

Reflect

What water play activities did you enjoy as a child? Can you think of some vocabulary words that can be learned from water play?

Discuss

Ask students to review 19-22, *Concepts Developed Through Sand and Water Play*. What other concepts can children learn from sand play? What concepts could be added to the list for water play?

Activity

Have students research the cost of different types of sand and water tables. Students can search through supply catalogs or conduct an Internet search. Have students compile a resource list of their findings.

Portfolio Project

Ask students to write a one-paragraph description of their favorite art activity to teach. They should explain why it is their favorite and why they think children would enjoy participating in the activity. Students should then write a complete lesson plan for teaching the activity. They should include a sample of the project and/or photographs of the steps involved in the art activity. Have students file the project in their portfolio.

Discuss

What are some examples of woodworking tools that could be used by children? What safety precautions should be observed when using these tools?

Enrich

Ask students to debate the pros and cons of allowing preschool children to use saws, hammers, and nails at the woodworking table. Students must be able to explain their viewpoint.

Activity

Contact area preschools that have a woodworking table and tools and arrange to have students observe children working in this area. Have students make special note of the precautions taken to ensure the children's safety.

children with an emotional release. It also encourages children to experiment and develop problem-solving skills.

If properly used, carpentry tools are safe for children to use, 19-23. Teachers need to demonstrate how to use the tools safely. In some classrooms, teachers demonstrate hammering using golf tees and styrofoam. Some teachers have a large tree stump cut for their classroom. They place a can of large roofing nails and a hammer near the stump to encourage participation. Children using a hammer for the first time may want you to start the nail.

Tools for the woodworking bench need to be carefully chosen. They should be lightweight and have handles that are easy for the children to grip. Examples of woodworking tools include claw hammers, screwdrivers, hand drills, pliers, sandpaper blocks, a vise, and saws. Mount tools the children use frequently on the wall next to the woodworking bench. Thin nails with large heads are easiest for children to use. Wood glue should also be available.

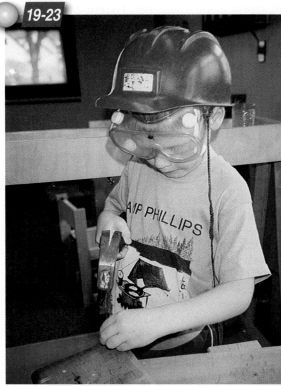

19-23

Proper safety equipment should be provided for woodworking activities.

Meeting Special Needs

Review the special learners' chapter outlines to determine if the students have any questions about the concepts or content of this chapter. Review the chapter objectives and ask the students to evaluate their progress in meeting these objectives. Ask the students to summarize, orally or in writing, what they learned from this chapter.

Summary

For young children, art activities are important open-ended learning experiences. Through their own creativity, children express their ideas, as well as their emotions. Art promotes physical, social, emotional, and cognitive growth in children.

A good art program fosters independence. Let children decide when their work is finished. Model art appreciation by offering feedback to the children about their work. Use praise that invites children to respect the value of each person's work.

Children move through three distinct stages as they build art skills. Knowing these stages helps child care workers plan activities that reflect children's skills level.

The teacher has an important job in guiding art, blockbuilding, and sensory experiences. The teacher will decide what types of activities will be introduced. A variety of materials and techniques should be used. Knowing how to carry out this task so children benefit from the experience is important for the teacher.

Review and Reflect

1. How do art experiences promote social growth?
2. Why is it best not to ask children what they are making?
3. True or false. Children are careful to choose colors that mirror real life instead of choosing colors they like.
4. Name the stages of art skill development. Explain one stage in detail.
5. Explain how to mix tempera paint to get the desired consistency.
6. True or false. As children progress in art skills, paintbrushes should become more narrow.
7. Why are chalk, felt-tip markers, and crayons more difficult for children to use than paint?
8. Summarize the controversy concerning the use of coloring books.
9. _____ painting is a sensory experience that promotes the release of feelings and is very satisfying for children.
10. How does a two-year-old's play with clay differ from a five-year-old's?
11. Which molding material would you choose for children to use? Give the reasons for your selection.
12. Name three ways children benefit from blockbuilding experiences.
13. Name three concepts children can learn by playing in sand.
14. Name three woodworking tools that children might enjoy using.

5. Add only a small amount of liquid to the tempera while stirring constantly. This will make a very thick paste. Then slowly add more liquid until you get the desired consistency.
6. true
7. These tools need to be pushed hard with small muscles that are not well-developed in small children. Paint, however, flows easily.
8. (Student response.)
9. Finger
10. Two-year-old children pull, beat, push, and squeeze. By age five, children will often announce what they are going to make before they begin.
11. (Student response.)
12. (List three. See Figure 19-18.)
13. (List three:) imagination, creativity, experimentation, fantasy, pouring
14. (List three:) claw hammers, hand drills, pliers, sandpaper, blocks, vise, saws

Review and Reflect Answer Key

1. Children learn responsibility. They learn to work and share with others. They learn to respect the property of others. They also learn to value the work and ideas of others.
2. They might just be experimenting with different tools and supplies and might not know what they are making. Some children lack the language skills needed to explain their artwork. Asking questions may make them uneasy.
3. false
4. scribbles, basic forms, pictorial drawings (Student response for one explanation.)

Apply and Explore

1. Collect children's drawings. Determine what stage of development each drawing represents. Give reasons for your conclusions.

2. Prepare and use each of the finger paint recipes given in the chapter. Discuss which has the best texture. Suggest methods for storing the paint.

3. Use the recipe in this chapter to prepare play dough and match scents to colors. Add strawberry gelatin to red play dough; add lemon flavoring to yellow play dough; add mint flavoring to green play dough.

4. Review equipment catalogs and prepare a list of the different types of blocks and accessories for this area of the classroom.

Cross-Curricular Link

Math

1. Prepare each of the play dough recipes given in the chapter. Compute the cost to make each recipe. Compare these costs to the cost of purchasing commercial play dough products.

Technology

2. Explore the Web site for Crayola (www.crayola.com) to learn more about using art to stimulate creativity in young children.

Workplace Link

Practice composing letters that both request and thank businesses for free and donated items. Write a sample letter asking for the donation of items that are overstocked or damaged but still useful for an arts program. Include examples of possible items and projects for which they would be used. Businesses may have materials they do not realize could be utilized for creative art. Write a sample business letter thanking the business for their donations. Letters could also be sent to preschool parents who may have items to donate.

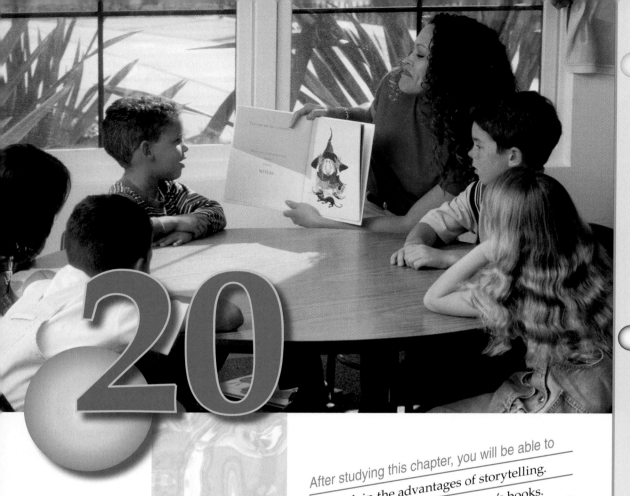

Before starting the chapter, obtain examples of each of the following: picture books, storybooks, family life stories, animal stories, fairy tales, draw and tell stories, flipchart stories, flannel board stories, children's book reviews, and story props. Display these items in class and refer to them throughout the chapter.

Discuss

What types of stories do you think the children in this photo are interested in? How can children benefit from storytelling experiences?

20

Guiding Storytelling Experiences

After studying this chapter, you will be able to

- explain the advantages of storytelling.
- list the four types of children's books.
- discuss the process of choosing children's books.
- outline the steps to follow when reading aloud to children.
- explain a variety of storytelling methods.

Vocabulary

Have students review the *Terms to Know* list. Ask students to look up unfamiliar words or terms in the glossary before reading the chapter.

Resource

Why Use Stories and Books, transparency master 20-1, TR

Activity

Have students write a lesson plan for specific stories using one or more of the objectives listed on transparency master 20-1, *Why Use Stories and Books*. How can deciding on an objective in advance help a teacher present a more effective storytelling experience? Allow time for students to share their lesson plan with the class.

Terms to Know

storytelling
picture books
storybooks
family life stories
animal stories
fairy tales
reviews
props
draw and tell
flipcharts
flannel boards

The words *once upon a time* contain magic for young children. The art of storytelling has delighted millions of children throughout the ages. By inviting children to share in a make-believe world of adventure, the storyteller provides a strong educational tool.

Storytelling is an important task for child care teachers. It involves reciting a story or reading from a book. In most centers, storytelling is routine. It is included in the daily schedule, 20-1. Storytelling is a valuable experience for children. They develop a love

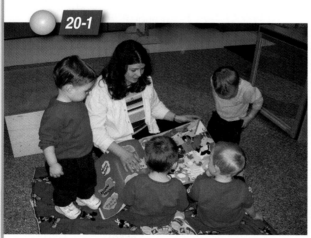

20-1

Storytelling is an enjoyable time for teachers and children.

for both stories and books as a result of daily storytelling sessions. This in turn enhances their language development. Moreover, children develop an understanding of customs and culture through traditional stories.

The Importance of Storytelling

Regular storytelling promotes children's cognitive, social, and emotional development. Storytelling helps young children

- understand the world in which they live
- understand other people
- develop a positive attitude toward books
- develop listening skills
- build correct concepts of objects and form new ideas
- increase their vocabulary
- associate written and spoken words
- understand that print carries meaning
- develop an appreciation of printed words
- learn the difference between everyday conversation and written language
- understand that letters can be capital or small
- develop a desire to read, 20-2
- learn that people read from left to right across a page

Carefully chosen stories are a key part of the storytelling experience. Stories that draw on the children's backgrounds help them understand themselves better. Children learn the words that describe feelings and experiences they have. They learn to think about familiar situations in new ways. Stories invite children to explore and wonder about their world.

Stories also provide models of acceptable behavior and positive relationships. When exposed to a variety of characters, children

Meeting Special Needs

Provide an outline of the chapter with all the chapter headings for special learners. Students should fill in each section of the outline as the material is covered in class with a sentence or two about the content. Review the special learners' IEPs to decide if any modifications should be made in presenting the chapter content.

20-2

Children's desire to read is often rooted in early storytelling experience.

learn that other people often feel the same way they do. They learn how people express their feelings. They become more understanding of others' needs.

Storytelling helps children learn reading skills. As a teacher reads aloud from a book, children learn to follow the pages from left to right and top to bottom. By watching the storyteller read, children learn the relationship between spoken and printed words. They also learn to listen. Books help children learn alphabet letters, numerals, and language.

Storytelling is also a good form of relaxation. Listening to a story is a quiet

activity. Children are not moving about or interacting with other children.

Books as a Source of Stories

Children's books are an important source of stories. Most can be divided into two main groups: picture books and storybooks. **Picture books** have single words or simple sentences and simple plots. These are usually the first books shared with young children. Some picture books are wordless. These books allow the teacher or children to tell the story.

After picture books, storybooks are introduced. **Storybooks** are often categorized as family life stories, animal stories, and fairy tales. These books also contain pictures, but they have more words and more complex plots than picture books. They help children understand how others feel, act, and think. Most of these books are built around themes of achievement, love, and reassurance. A book that uses all three themes is *Peter Rabbit*. In the story, Peter has an adventure but safely returns home (achievement). His mother tucks him into bed and gives him tea (love and reassurance). Examples of other such stories include *Little Bear*, *Mike Mulligan and His Steam Shovel*, and *Little Tim*.

Family life stories contain the theme of social understanding. The children in these stories usually have problems. Some problems may be funny; some are serious. However, all problems are resolved with love and concern. The purpose of these stories is to help children develop social understanding by sharing the problems, troubles, and feelings of others. Examples include *Johnny Crow's Garden*, *My Dog Is Lost*, *My Grandpa*, *Timid Timothy*, and *Will I Have a Friend?*

Young children also enjoy **animal stories**. In these stories, animals have some human qualities. Usually, the animal hero has some unusual success or ability.

Resource

Language Arts, color transparency CT-17A, TR

Reflect

What factors may make children dislike storytelling experiences? What might be the effect of unsatisfactory experiences on a child's later reading progress?

Activity

Ask students to review several children's alphabet and number books and then answer the following questions. Are the letters printed in a simple, block style children can recognize? Are lowercase and uppercase letters represented? Are the numerals printed in a simple style without additional seraphs or lines? Allow time for students to discuss their answers in class.

Vocabulary

Have a student volunteer explain how *family life stories* may affect children. Give an example of a positive effect.

Workplace Connection

Ask students to survey local child care centers to find out how often storytelling activities are scheduled. What is the average length of a story session? What does the teacher do to prepare for storytelling? What classroom setup (location of children and teacher) provides the most effective story time experience? Have students write a brief report of their findings. Allow time for students to share their reports with the class.

Discuss

Most fairy tales end happily ever after. However, sinister or disturbing elements such as wicked step-mothers, greedy trolls, and hungry wolves may affect sensitive children. What fairy tales do you think are suitable for older children? How can the teacher prepare children for storytelling when using fairy tales?

Resource

Storytelling, Activity A, SAG

Reflect

What factors may cause new teachers to avoid planning storytell-ing activities in their classes? What steps can a new teacher take to gain confidence in his or her storytelling skills?

Resource

Illustrations and Story-telling, Activity A, OG

Examples include *Little Brown Bear*; *All About Dogs, Dogs, Dogs*; *Nothing But Cats, Cats, Cats*; and *Angus and the Cat*.

Fairy tales are another type of book enjoyed by older children. **Fairy tales** have a theme of achievement. The characters or heroes perform difficult tasks in order to succeed. They must confront giants, witches, or other obstacles. Kindness and goodness win out over evil. *Three Billy Goats Gruff*, *Three Little Pigs*, and *Cinderella* are popular examples of fairy tales. These books are predictable. To help children make sense of the stories, obvious clues, pictures, and repeated phrases are included.

Selecting Books for Children

Storytelling is an art that requires study and practice. The key to a good story is selection. Choose books that have dramatic elements. Children will enjoy "seeing" and "feeling" the events. Stories that mirror the children's emotional experiences will engage their hearts and minds. A story is only good if children enjoy it. If the story is to be an effective classroom activity, the teacher should also enjoy and value it. Otherwise, sharing it in an interesting way will be difficult.

Selecting storybooks is often hard for new child care teachers. Public libraries have many useful lists and descriptions of books. These are called **reviews**. Reviews will help you find titles, authors, and publishers of books. Reviews can also be ordered from the American Library Association Children's Service.

Fictional Content

Stories should reflect the children's developmental level, backgrounds, and experiences. When choosing books for children, consider the content, illustrations,

vocabulary, durability, and length of the book. Familiar objects, people, and situations make stories more interesting to children. Stories about children with backgrounds and activities similar to their own are special favorites.

Most preschool children cannot separate fact from fiction. Therefore, it is important to look for realistic stories. Until children are about five years old, they are often not ready for fantasy, 20-3. Books in which animals or inanimate objects, such as trees and flowers, behave as humans should be avoided for very young children.

Illustrations

A children's book should have illustrations and text that are integrated. The illustrations should create interest and arouse children's imagination. The pictures in a book for young children should almost tell the story by themselves. Children will be more

20-3

. . . And the tree grabbed Dorothy . . .

Younger children may become confused or even frightened by fantasy stories.

Cross-Curricular Activity

Science
Ask students to prepare a list of questions children might ask about animals they may encounter through storytelling. (Examples: bears, caterpillars, fish, snakes, etc.) These questions may involve environment, food,

and physical characteristics. Invite the school science teacher to speak to the class and provide information about the questions they formulated. Obtain photos or other artifacts from the science teacher to share with the children during animal stories.

interested if they can "read" the story by looking at the pictures.

Pictures should be easy to recognize and help the children make sense of the story. Good pictures also help the children anticipate what happens next in the story. Too much detail and shading or lack of color will confuse young children. Instead, children respond best to brightly colored pictures with large, clearly defined objects. Illustrations should

- be large, colorful, and plentiful
- represent the written word
- reflect actions
- avoid unneeded detail
- be realistically and attractively colored

Vocabulary

Writing a children's book is difficult. In an entire book, the author introduces only a limited number of words. A good book creates a sense of wonder. It uses words that can be understood by most children of a certain age. Only a few new words should be introduced in a story. Repetition of some words will increase the children's enjoyment. This rhythm of word sounds is one major reason children enjoy stories such as Mother Goose tales.

Durability

Children should be allowed to hold and carry books as well as turn pages. Therefore, covers and pages must be sturdy. Covers made of strong, washable material are best. Pages should be easy to handle. The page surface should be dull to prevent glare. The book's binding should lay flat when the book is open.

Length

Appropriate book length varies with children's age. Infants and toddlers may stay with a book for just a few minutes. Their books are often only a few pages long. Two-year-olds will remain interested in a book for 5 to 8 minutes; three-year-olds from 6 to 10 minutes; four-year-olds from 8 to 12 minutes; five-year-olds from 10 to 15 minutes. This interest is reflected in the number of pages in the book.

Selecting Books Based on Age

Age plays an important part in choosing books for children. Chart 20-4 outlines some factors to consider for different ages.

Infants and toddlers need durable picture books. These books may be made of washable cloth or firm cardboard. Thick pages allow for easier handling. Pictures should be large and clearly defined. Simple items in children's surroundings should be represented in the pictures. Toddlers may enjoy pointing at and touching objects in the pictures.

Two-year-olds prefer books about things they know, do, and enjoy. They respond enthusiastically when favorite activities, such as running, eating, and dressing, are mentioned. Animals and small children are the favored subjects. Books for two-year-olds should still be quite durable with plenty of large, clearly defined drawings. Actions and sounds represented in the pictures should be familiar. The colors should be realistic.

Three-year-old children may request stories by title. They show preference for stories about familiar subjects. They also enjoy learning about people outside the home. They enjoy stories about community helpers such as police officers, mail carriers,

Enrich

Illustrations in children's books should generally be brightly colored. However, black and white drawings and photographs may also be effective in children's literature. Ask students to locate children's books containing black and white illustrations and share them with the class. Have students discuss the merits of the illustrations and compare them to ones that have more color.

Activity

Have students examine books written for toddlers and preschoolers. Look for unfamiliar words for these age groups. Have students decide how they will explain the definition of each word to a child. Allow time for students to share their definitions with the class.

Discuss

Why is it important to consider the length of a book when making reading selections for young children? How can you keep younger children interested in a book when reading to a mixed-age group of preschoolers?

Putting Technology to Use

Ask students to conduct an Internet search for information about popular children's book illustrators such as Tomi di Paola, Jack Kent, Patricia Polacco, Eric Carle, and Arnold Lobel. What influenced the artist to become an illustrator? How does the artist's work contribute to the enjoyment and understanding of the story? Have students obtain examples of their illustrations. Allow time for students to discuss their findings and share their illustrations with the class.

20-4

Considerations for Children's Books

Toddlers	2-year-olds	3-year-olds	4-year-olds	5-year-olds
Thick pages Large, clearly defined pictures Brightly colored pictures of simple, familiar objects and routines	Imitate familiar sounds Repeat children's own experiences Contain large pages with big pictures Include the familiar Simple plots	Include things and people outside of the home Explain the *who* and *why* Interpret the child's own experiences Contain repetitive sound words	Include humor in reality Contain new words Explain the *how* and *why* Include exaggeration	Add something to their knowledge Take them beyond the here and now Contain new information and relate it to familiar facts

Children of different ages each have their story preferences.

Resource

Age and Children's Books, transparency master 20-2, TR

Discuss

Have students review Chart 20-4, *Considerations for Children's Books*. What stories do you think children in each of these age groups would enjoy? Give examples.

Resource

Choosing Books for Children, Activity B, SAG

and garbage collectors. Three-year-olds want to know what these people do and why, 20-5. Pictures should be realistic, simple, and clear. The number of sentences on each page should be limited.

Four-year-old children are less self-centered than the younger group. These children are becoming more curious about the world around them. They want to know how and why things work. At this age, children enjoy short, simple stories that use exaggeration. Four-year-olds often enjoy pranks in books. Looking at the pictures can help them experience the story.

Five-year-old children like stories that give them added knowledge. They will frequently memorize favorite stories word for word. They prefer stories that take them beyond here and now. These children want new information and relationships along with familiar facts. Fantasy trips beyond the confines of their world are now appreciated. Examples of these books include *Little Red Riding Hood*, *Peter Rabbit*, and *Goldilocks and the Three Bears*. Children of this age will clearly tell you their likes and dislikes.

Health and Safety

Choosing Stories Wisely

As an early childhood teacher, you will select books and stories for a variety of children. Books and stories can have a strong emotional impact on young children. Always consider the age and developmental level of the children to whom you will be telling a story. Although a classic tale such as *Little Red Riding Hood* may be fun for four- and five-year-olds, it may be truly frightening for two- or three-year-olds.

Meeting Special Needs

Ask gifted students to locate and review computer software suitable for promoting literacy in young children. (Example: *Reader Rabbit*.) Have students demonstrate the use of the software to the class, if possible, and list advantages and disadvantages of the program. Ask students to research current thought of the early childhood community toward using computer software in the early childhood classroom. Have students write a brief report of their findings.

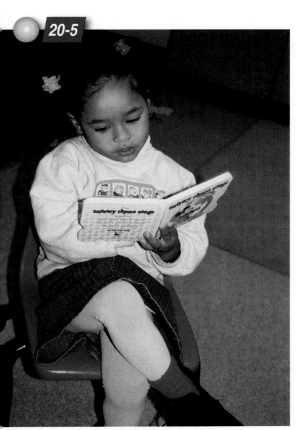

20-5

Children enjoy looking at books that contain familiar subjects.

Avoiding Stories That Reinforce Stereotypes

It is important to choose age-appropriate stories. Selecting anti-bias stories that are free from stereotypes is essential, too. *Stereotypes* are preset ideas about people based on one characteristic, such as sex, culture, nationality, religion, or age. Stereotypes are unfair and should be avoided. Read stories and study illustrations carefully before using them. Stereotyping is often easiest to spot in pictures. Pictures should be examined closely since they have more impact on children than words.

Children's stories need to be free of sexism. *Sexism* is any action, attitude, or

outlook used to judge a person based only on the sex of that person. In the past, many books did not show women who possess a full range of interests and skills. Most children's books showed women wearing aprons and doing housework. Girls were passive and helped their mothers around the house. Boys, on the other hand, were active and adventurous. Doctors, lawyers, and police tended to be men. Also, few men were shown in roles of teachers and nurses.

Study the ratio of men to women in the illustrations. As a rule, there should be as many men as women or girls as boys. Notice how characters are described and what kinds of activities the pictures show them doing, 20-6. Books that avoid sexism will describe women and girls as lively people who do interesting things. Likewise, men and boys will be shown as caring people who are interested in homes, families, and friends.

Through books, children can also gain an understanding of people who have different skin coloring, food preferences, and languages. Knowledge of the differences among people can promote acceptance. Both illustrations and text should depict people of all ethnic and cultural groups in a positive way.

Finally, search stories for stereotyping of older people. Children must be given a realistic and positive picture of seniors. Stories

20-6

Books that show men involved with their families and women in interesting jobs do not promote sexism.

Vocabulary

Have a student volunteer explain the meaning of the term *anti-bias* as it relates to the selection of children's literature.

Enrich

Ask students to locate an appropriate story for a multicultural curriculum. Does the story teach about a particular culture without stereotyping? How can the story be used to teach about acceptance of diversity? Have students write a brief report of their findings.

Discuss

Why is it important to study the pictures as well as the storyline in a child's book when examining the book for evidence of stereotyping?

Meeting Special Needs

According to Piaget, preschool children are in the preoperational stage of cognitive development. Have gifted students write a one-page report answering the following questions: How can stories about community helpers and workers help the preschooler develop concepts about the world outside the home? How can these stories affect the development of a child's ability to think logically? Allow time for students to share their reports with the class.

Reflect

Using volunteer older adults for story time may portray them in a positive way to children. What questions would you ask of an older volunteer before he or she participated in story time? What requirements would you expect of older volunteers?

Discuss

How can preparation for storytelling affect the flow of the story? How might the teacher's enthusiasm for reading the story benefit the children listening to the story?

Activity

Have students select a popular child's story that would be effective when told with a variety of voice expressions. Ask student volunteers to tape record themselves reading the story. Play the tapes back to the class and have students identify the voice characteristics most interesting and enjoyable.

should describe warm, pleasing relationships between older people and children. In this way, children can learn to know and admire older members of their community.

Reading Stories to Children

Good oral reading takes time and effort. Three steps need to be taken before reading stories to young children. First, choose stories that both children and you will enjoy. Then become familiar with the story. Finally, decide how you will present the story. The success of the story lies in your ability to be interesting and enthusiastic.

Preparing to Read

Read the story several times so you know it well. Then a quick glance at the page will remind you of the text. This leaves your eyes free for contact with the children. No one way is best for learning stories. Each person has his or her own method.

Oral reading skills are important when storytelling. One way to build these skills is to practice reading in front of a mirror. Another method is to record yourself as you read. Using these methods, you can correct any problems you notice. For example, tape yourself and then ask the following:

- Did I convey enthusiasm about the story?
- Did I keep the tempo lively?
- Did I suggest different voices for different characters?

After you are familiar with the book, decide whether you want to read or tell the story. Reading the story has its advantages when working with young children. They can look at the drawings as they listen to the story. Reading stories may also get some children interested in reading. As they watch you, the children will learn the link between

printed and spoken words. The advantage to telling a story is you are able to better dramatize action and characters.

A comfortable setting is required for a successful reading time. Children must be free from distractions as well as feel safe and secure. They should sit in a group to listen. Some teachers like to have children sit on carpet squares or pillows. A colorful quilt may also be used. Such seating arrangements prevent children from moving around and help them focus more on listening.

Story groups should be small, 20-7. You may wish to divide children into two or more groups, based on age and interest. This also allows the children more interaction.

Most children need a settling down time. To help children get ready to listen, some teachers recite a fingerplay. Another technique is to talk to the children using a puppet. Other teachers simply discuss the events of the day.

Introducing the Story

Begin stories by setting the mood. Ask questions, make personal comments, or show the book cover to get children involved in the story. Ask children to predict what the story

20-7

In small groups, children are free to interact with the teacher.

Cross-Curricular Activity

Creative Writing and Art
Enlist the cooperation of a creative writing teacher and an art teacher for a joint children's book writing project. Partner students in groups with each curriculum area represented. Have students interview a preschooler to help them come up with a story

idea. The art students are responsible for creating the illustrations for the story. The child care students are responsible for age-appropriate content and for ensuring that the illustrations represent what is happening on each page. The writing students are responsible for story and plot development.

is about. Setting the mood should be brief. A few sentences are often enough.

A personal comment is one way to introduce a story. You may share where you learned about the story. For example, "This is a story that my grandmother told me as a child." You can set a humorous mood by asking "How many of you like to laugh?" You might hold the book up and show the cover. The picture on the cover should suggest the story content.

Props are also good for introducing stories. **Props** are any items that relate to the story and would attract children's attention. To introduce *Peter Rabbit*, for example, you may bring in a live rabbit, a stuffed rabbit, or a picture of a rabbit. See 20-8.

Store props in a storytelling apron. As you introduce a story, pull props out of the apron pocket one at a time. A storytelling bag can be used in the same way. The bag is also useful for storing books in the reading area.

Explain any words the children do not know before you begin the story. For example, before reading *The Gigantic Elephant*, define the new word *gigantic*.

Before you start, create a feeling that something special is about to be shared. This feeling can be produced by the enthusiasm in your voice as you introduce the book. Your facial expression can also create excitement.

Reading the Story

Read stories with pleasure and feeling to show children you value and enjoy reading. Maintain eye contact with the children. Pause before introducing a new character or idea.

Read the story in a normal speaking voice. Speaking too softly or at a high pitch may cause the children to lose interest. Think of your voice as a tool. To add interest, you can whisper or shout when appropriate. By lengthening your dramatic pause, you can

20-8

Props for Introducing Stories

🎈	A red balloon	"The Red Balloon"
🍎	A red apple	"The Apple Is Red"
🪆	A doll	"William's Doll"
🐈	A black cat	"The Tale of the Black Cat"
🖍️	A purple crayon	"Harold and the Purple Crayon"

Well-chosen props will grab children's attention.

Vocabulary

Have a student volunteer explain how *props* are used during storytelling activities. Give examples of several props besides the ones listed in Chart 20-8.

Discuss

Why is a storytelling apron or bag an effective tool when used during story time?

Reflect

How can asking questions during story time affect a child's self-esteem, behavior, memory, and attention? Give examples of questions you would use for a specific story you select.

Discuss

What effect will lack of eye contact or a too-soft voice have on your ability to keep the children's attention while reading to them during story time? What effect will whispering have?

Resource

Story Comparisons, Activity C, SAG

Portfolio Project

How can preschool teachers encourage parents to include storytelling activities at home? Ask students to write a short letter to a preschool parent citing the benefits of reading to their child on a regular basis. Students should include suggestions of the types of books appropriate for the age of the child. Have students file a copy of the letter in their portfolio.

Resource

Effective Storytelling Techniques, color transparency CT-17B, TR

Discuss

What rules should be followed during story time? List a few simple rules that will help the teacher maintain behavior, encourage attention, and ensure that all children have an equal opportunity to see the pictures, hear the story, and benefit from the storytelling experience.

Enrich

Ask students to locate examples of comic books and review them for appropriate themes, plots, conflicts, characters, and illustrations. Have students debate the pros and cons of comic books as a literary tool for promoting skill in reading.

Resource

Book Evaluation Form, reproducible master 20-3, TR

let the children savor the words. You may mimic a sound or adjust your pace to reflect the story. The pitch of your voice can also be changed. An example would be the story of *Goldilocks and the Three Bears*. Project yourself into the characters. Use a high pitch for the baby bear and a low pitch for the papa bear.

Occasionally point out the illustrations. Encourage child participation by predicting outcomes, such as "What will happen next?" Another technique is to ask opinions, such as "What is your favorite vegetable?" Ask about previous parts of the story. For example, you might say "What did Tim Mouse say to his mother?"

Handling Interruptions

Interruptions happen often when telling stories to young children, 20-9. The children will ask such questions as "Why is baby bear brown?" Accept these interruptions and answer questions patiently. There may be children who continue to ask many questions. If this happens, say "Mark, please save your questions until after the story."

Wiggling children can distract other children. Do not make an issue of this. It is best to ignore the wiggling and keep reading. A positive response is to praise children who

20-9

Do not be annoyed by interruptions. Young children like to ask questions and make comments on stories they are hearing.

sit still. For example, you may say "Joellen, I like how quietly you are sitting." This will strengthen Joellen's actions. It will also encourage wigglers to sit still.

Maintaining Interest

Children's interest in a story can be seen in their laughter, stillness, and expressions. If children do not appear to like a story, talk faster. You might use more emphasis or skip over some details. You can also restore interest by asking the children simple questions about the story. To quiet a bored or disruptive child, ask "Louis, what color is baby bear?" Sometimes, no matter what you do, a book does not have holding power. If this should happen, end the story. You may say, "Boys and girls, this is not the right story for today."

Ending Stories

Ending a story is as important as introducing it. The children need to know when you are finished. Therefore, the ending should be clear. You may ask a question about the story such as "What did you like best about the story?" You also may ask a question about the characters, the plot, or the setting.

At times, a simple "Thank you for listening" may be enough. You may also wish to give the children something to take home after some stories. This is done most often for special occasions. For example, when reading *Winnie the Pooh*, you may wish to give the children balloons.

Be prepared to read the same story over and over again. You will be pleased to hear "Please tell us that story again." This request tells you the children enjoyed the book.

Evaluating Your Performance

After reading a story, you will need to evaluate your methods. Children's reactions are good feedback. As a rule, the more

Workplace Connection

Invite the drama or theater teacher or advisor to demonstrate to the class dramatic storytelling styles. Have students select a favorite child's book and ask the teacher to suggest various ways to enhance the story using vocal and physical expression techniques. Have students write a list of questions to ask prior to the visit.

children respond to a story, the better your methods. If children lose interest, you may have talked too fast or too slow. In other cases, you may have spoken so carefully that you forgot to add expression and vary tone.

Note your strengths as well as your weaknesses. When children smile, laugh, and watch closely, you have used methods that hold their interest. Build on your strengths as you read stories in the future. In addition, review the tips for effective storytelling listed in 20-10.

Teaching About Books

Books enthrall young children. As you read, you are teaching children about books. They learn that a book has front and back covers. On the front cover, there is a title. An author is the person who has written the book, and the author's name is also on the cover. The illustrator prepares the drawings. Books have a beginning and an end. Inside the book, there

are pages. Each page has a top and bottom. People read books from left to right.

Children watch how you handle a book. From this, they learn how to handle a book. During the story, be sure to turn the pages one at a time.

Achieving Variety in Storytelling

In addition to reading stories aloud, there are other creative methods that help storytelling come alive. Guidelines for these methods are like those for reading aloud. First, decide whether you will read from a book or make up your own story. Next, practice the story in front of a mirror using a tape recorder until you know it well. This will help you prepare to perform as a storyteller.

Younger children in particular will stay interested longer when several methods are used during storytime. As a child care teacher, you will need to learn a number of storytelling methods.

New research shows that infants and young children seem able to process only one stimulus at a time. Sounds appeal to them more than visuals. The younger the child, the more dominant his or her auditory preference. In fact, infants prefer sounds almost totally to visuals. Four-year-olds prefer sounds to visuals except for familiar objects. When familiar objects were associated with unfamiliar sounds, they paid more attention to the objects.

Adults are capable of processing both sounds and visual together. However, they prefer visual information. Why do children pay more attention to sounds? The research claims that visual stimulation is somewhat stable, but sounds disappear. Perhaps for this reason, infants will look at pictures longer when they are paired with new sounds.

20-10

Tips for Effective Storytelling

- Choose a book that is developmentally appropriate for the children.
- Use a good introduction to establish the mood of the story.
- Explain unfamiliar words.
- Encourage child participation.
- Tell the story with a conversational tone.
- Use eye contact.
- Convey enthusiasm.
- Demonstrate good posture.
- Use different voices for particular characters to create interest.
- Pronounce words clearly.
- Use a lively tempo.
- Allow comments to be added to story.

Determining your strengths and weaknesses will help you improve your storytelling skills.

Resource

Evaluation of a Storyteller, Activity B, OG

Activity

Have students write each of the tips for effective storytelling listed in Chart 20-10 on separate sheets of paper. Post these around the classroom. Ask students to describe how each tip contributes to an effective storytelling experience. Leave the tips up for several days to reinforce student knowledge.

Resource

Types of Storytelling, transparency master 20-4, TR

Reflect

Do you stay more interested in a class when a teacher uses a variety of teaching methods? What strategies might a teacher use to keep and increase student interest?

Resource

Evaluating a Storytelling Activity, Activity C, OG

Putting Technology to Use

Have students conduct an Internet search for information on how to incorporate the National Education Association's program, Read Across America, into local child care programs. Information can be found at **www.nea.org/readacross**. The program celebrates the birth of Theodor

Seuss Geisel, better known as Dr. Seuss and the author of many popular children's books. Students will be able to download resources such as posters, bookmarks, certificates, book lists, press releases, and suggestions for starting a program.

Discuss

One advantage of draw and tell stories is that the large size of illustrations can be seen and enjoyed by all children as the story is being told. How else can children be encouraged to take part in this type of storytelling method? (Examples: suggest what colors to use; answer questions about what is being drawn; predict what will happen next; and assist in turning the page for the next sheet of paper.)

Resource

Practice Reading a Story, Activity D, OG

Activity

Ask students to survey all the puppets in the child care classroom and determine if any could be used to help tell a story or teach a rhyme. Have students suggest suitable stories for the puppets that are available.

Resource

Evaluate Your Storytelling Technique, Activity D, SAG

Draw and Tell

Draw and tell, or *chalk talk*, is one storytelling method. Drawings are made on chalkboard, poster board, or an 18- by 24-inch newsprint pad as the story is told. Textbooks containing draw and tell stories can be purchased from school supply stores or catalogs. Some child care workers prefer to find a storybook and adapt it. Illustrations may be deleted, combined, and added. As a general rule, no more than five sheets of paper should be used.

If you do not have good drawing skills, you may want to use an opaque projector to prepare the stories. Find a draw and tell book that gives copyright permission to enlarge the illustrations and place it on the projector. Tape a piece of cardboard or paper on the wall. Project a few select pictures from the book onto this paper or cardboard. Lightly trace the drawings with a pencil. Then as you tell the story, use brightly colored felt-tip markers to retrace the lines.

Draw and tell stories may be prepared so they can be used more than once. Cover original light tracings with clear laminate. Use grease pencils to draw in the outline and fill in the color. After the story is done, clean the clear laminate by wiping it with a piece of felt. Window cleaner may also be used for cleaning.

Tapes

Audio story tapes have appeal for young children. They contain sound effects and music. Story tape sets often include an illustrated booklet that children can use to follow along with the story. Tapes of many popular stories are available.

Videotapes can hold the interest of most children. One disadvantage is that children may already have seen them on television. Commercially purchased or teacher-made tapes may be used for storytelling. Audio- and videotapes may be purchased through school supply stores, catalogs, or in the exhibit area at early childhood conferences.

To save money, some child care teachers prefer to make their own tapes. To do so, you will need a tape recorder, cassette tape, and story. As you make the tape, read the story clearly. Pause after each two-page spread. At this point, insert a signal. You may want to hit a spoon against a glass or play a piano key. This signal will tell children listening to the tape to turn the page in their book, 20-11.

Puppets

Puppets have always appealed to young children. Having puppets tell a story is a useful change of pace. Use a puppet as a listener who remarks and asks questions about the story. Puppets can be made from

20-11

Even young children who do not yet read can follow along in a book while listening to a tape.

Putting Technology to Use

Ask students to conduct an Internet search to find sources for children's books on audiotape cassettes, videotapes, CDs, and DVDs. Have students list the advantages and disadvantages for using this technology in a child care program for the children and adults. Compare the costs to those for traditional printed books. Find prices for the equipment needed to play audio and video stories. Allow time for students to discuss their findings in class.

tin cans, tongue depressors, socks, and other inexpensive materials. A mitten also makes a good puppet. Cut eyes, a nose, and a mouth from construction paper and paste them onto the mitten. Use the mitten puppet with the story *The Lost Mitten*. Stuffed animals can be used in the same manner. For example, a brown teddy bear could be used to tell the story of *Little Brown Bear*.

After you tell the story, place the puppet in the library area. Puppets help children in constructing and expressing their understanding of stories, 20-12. (Refer to Chapter 21, *Guiding Play and Puppetry Experiences*, for more information.)

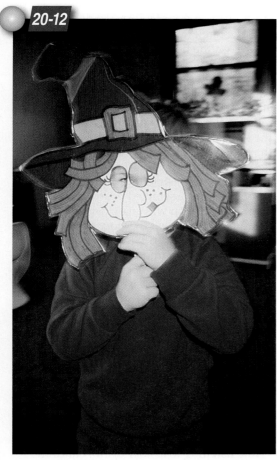

20-12

Puppets help children express their understanding of stories.

Individual or Group Stories

Given the chance, children can be clever storytellers. After a field trip, guest visit, or other special event, ask children to record a story about that special time. You might have the children work together in small groups. Write down the children's ideas as they tell you their story. Seeing their own words helps children understand the link between spoken and written words. You could write the ideas on a piece of poster board, paper, or on the board. You can also record these stories with a camcorder and play them later for the children to enjoy.

Flipcharts

Flipcharts are stories drawn on large poster board cards. If you lack drawing skills, you will find the opaque projector helpful. After you finish drawing, tracing, and coloring the cards, number the back of each card. This will help you keep the cards in correct order for storytelling. You may also wish to print the story for each drawing on the back of each flipchart. To protect the flipchart, cover it with a plastic film.

After telling the story, you may wish to place the flipchart in the book area. Then the children have an opportunity to use the flipchart themselves and retell the story. Some children also enjoy arranging the cards in order of the story.

Slide Stories

Slide stories usually center around pictures taken on field trips or during classroom events like holiday parties. You might start a slide story at the beginning of the year. Then at the end of the year the slide story can be told. Slide stories involving the children are also enjoyed by families at special events.

Note

Group story activities provide opportunities for teachers to model and for children to practice social skills such as taking turns, speaking in front of a group, sharing ideas, and making decisions. All children will see their input is valued, especially if the teacher refers to children by name when they contribute to the story.

Enrich

Writing an individual story with a shy child may help the child develop more confidence in verbal expression. Have students ask the child what he or she would like to write about. Write down what the child says. Encourage the story development with questions and comments about the characters or timeline. Have the child draw illustrations for the story and read it to the class when complete.

Discuss

Flipchart stories are large books that may be difficult to display and store. Suggest classroom solutions for making flipcharts visible and easily available for teachers and children to use.

Putting Technology to Use

Many schools have access to digital cameras. Explain ways a digital camera can be used to present a slide story in a child care classroom. Have students take pictures and put together a slideshow about the child care program. The slideshow can be demonstrated at parent-teacher conferences, school board presentations, middle school recruitment, and preschool program functions and events. Have students investigate ways to include visual or audible captions for each picture.

Activity

Have students investigate the possibility of making a flannel board and creating a flannel board story with the use of recycled materials. Corkboard can be covered with felt to create the board. Solicit felt scraps, scraps of wood, masonite, foam core, cardboard or heavy poster board for making patterns. Also look for leftover craft supplies such as fabric paint tubes, buttons, beads, trims, and ribbons from students, parents, and local businesses.

Enrich

Ask students to survey the child care book collection and make suggestions on several books suitable for use in a flannel board story. Divide students into small groups and, after assigning a suggested book to each group, have students rewrite the story to make it suitable for use in a flannel board presentation.

Resource

Planning a Storytelling Activity, Activity E, OG

Flannel Boards

A flannel board story is one of the most popular listening activities for young children. **Flannel board**, or *felt board*, storytelling uses characters and props cut out of felt and placed on a felt background, 20-13. Flannel boards may be purchased from school supply stores and catalogs or made by the teacher. To make a board, you will need a piece of foam insulation board, 27 by 17½ inches. This material can be bought at a lumber supply company. To prepare the board, cover it with two contrasting pieces of felt, 29 by 19½ inches. The two pieces provide different-colored backgrounds for felt figures.

Pieces of paper, cardboard, or felt are used to show major characters or objects. These may be hand drawn, bought, or cut out of storybooks. Flannel board books contain many stories. They also often contain patterns for characters and props. These can be bought from school supply stores.

A quick way to make figures is to use a nonwoven interfacing fabric. Hold the fabric in place and trace over the patterns with a black felt pen. Fill in the areas you wish to brighten.

These felt figures can be placed on the flannel board as the story is told.

Felt figures may also be made from a storybook pattern. Place a piece of carbon paper behind the paper and on top of a piece of cardboard. Trace over the drawing with a paper clip. This transfers the image onto the cardboard. Cut out the cardboard figures to use as patterns. The patterns can be placed on felt and traced. If you need larger figures, use the opaque projector to enlarge the drawings.

Presenting a Flannel Board Story

Before you present a flannel board story, you will need to do some advance preparation. Practice reading the story script several times. Check your flannel board figures and place them in order of use. Keep the figures on your lap in a flat box or basket when you tell the story. Avoid placing the figures on the floor as a curious child may pick them up. This could interfere with the success of the story.

Place the figures on the flannel board one at a time. Like writing, the figures should follow a left-to-right sequence. Practice telling the story and placing the flannel figures on the board. For emphasis, look directly at the figure as you place it on the board.

After you finish telling a flannel board story, leave the assembled board in the book area. The children will enjoy using the flannel board figures to retell the story or create new tales. By observing and listening, you will be able to assess their understanding of the story. You may even want to encourage the children to create their own stories by providing them figures from a variety of stories.

Retelling Stories

Retelling stories to young children is important for their language development. It relates to their ability to both receive and express information.

Through listening, children develop vocabulary and a sense of the story structure. While listening to a story again, children

Portfolio Project

Quality children's magazines are another source to consider when selecting children's literature. Have students visit the local library or bookstore and survey the magazines available. Ask students to select one magazine and write a review including typical content, recommended ages, quality of illustrations, variety of activities and stories, related activities such as arts and crafts, cost of a subscription, and amount of commercial content. Suggested magazines to review may include: *Highlights for Children, Ladybug, Cricket, Preschool Playroom, Click,* and *Your Big Backyard.* Have students file a copy of the review in their portfolio.

often reflect on and share their own life experiences. You might have to prompt them. For example, you might ask

- "How did the story begin?"
- "What was the story about?"
- "What happened in the story?"
- "What did the monkey do?"

You can use children's responses to assess their comprehension skills. Consider what the children say about the story details, sequences, and characters. Include these comments in your evaluation.

Displaying Books

An important area of a classroom is the library area. Books, flannel boards, tapes, and other storytelling equipment are located in this area. The books should be arranged in an appealing manner. The book covers should be visible to attract the children's interest, 20-14. Books should be arranged so they will not fall after one is removed.

The library area should be located away from traffic. It should also be separated from the rest of the classroom by dividers. This provides a quiet atmosphere. Scissors, crayons, and painting should not be allowed here. These limits should prevent the books from being misused.

The books for the library area should be carefully chosen. Each child's developmental needs should be considered. You may wish to include books on topics children in the group are facing, such as divorce, illness, and death. Some books, such as the children's favorites, can remain in the area continually. Other books can be rotated frequently. Fun books should always be available. Add new books often to stimulate children's interest and enthusiasm. You may want to borrow books from the public library, friends, and parents.

20-14

Displays that show book covers encourage children to look at books on their own.

Activity

Have students periodically change and arrange a book display in the child care classroom. Students should consider books of seasonal interest, stories related to current curriculum, books suggested by children or parents, and literature selected to teach a specific concept or idea.

Discuss

In addition to all the types of books and stories mentioned in this chapter, what other types of reading material may be used in a preschool classroom? (Examples: pop-up books, books with electronic or computer components, big books, children's dictionaries and encyclopedias, hands-on books that teach or reinforce a task such as lacing and tying shoes, and computer software.)

Activity

Invite a child's librarian or early childhood professional to speak to the class about reading readiness. How can parents encourage reading readiness at home? When should they start? Have students prepare a list of additional questions to ask prior to the visit.

Meeting Special Needs

Review the special learners' chapter outlines to determine if the students have any questions about the concepts or content of this chapter. Review the chapter objectives and ask the students to evaluate their progress in meeting these objectives. Ask the students to summarize, orally or in writing, what they learned from this chapter.

Review and Reflect Answer Key

1. backgrounds
2. true
3. A
4. social understanding
5. fairy tales
6. false
7. to create interest and arouse children's imaginations
8. age
9. Sexism is any action, attitude, or outlook used to judge a person based only on the sex of that person.
10. true
11. practice reading in front of a mirror; make a recording as you read
12. (List three:) ask a question, make a personal comment, show the book cover, use a prop
13. ending
14. (Student response.)
15. false

Summary

Storytelling can be a useful learning tool for children. Through storytelling, children can develop an enjoyment of books and learn many skills. Some of these skills include learning to form new ideas and increasing vocabulary.

Stories must be selected with care. Content must match the developmental levels and experiences of the audience. In addition, content must be free of stereotypes.

Illustrations should spark interest and be pleasant. The vocabulary and story length must match children's skills. Finally, the books must be durable.

Before reading to children, it is important to prepare ahead of time. There are several ways to present a story. Draw and tell, story tapes, and flannel boards are a few options.

Review and Reflect

1. Stories that draw on children's _____ help them understand themselves better.
2. True or false. Storytelling is a good form of relaxation.
3. Which types of books are usually the first books shared with young children?
   A. Picture.
   B. Fairy tales.
   C. Animal.
   D. Family life.
4. What theme is used in family life stories?
5. In _____, kindness and goodness win over evil.
6. True or false. It is not important if a teacher likes a story as long as the children enjoy it.
7. What are the functions of illustrations?
8. The appropriate length of a book will vary with the _____ of the child.
9. What is sexism?
10. True or false. Teachers should choose books that show people from all ethnic and cultural groups in a positive way.
11. Name two ways to build oral reading skills.
12. Name three ways to introduce a story.
13. The _____ of a story must be clear.
14. Explain one storytelling method.
15. True or false. Infants and young children prefer visuals to sounds.

Apply and Explore

1. Prepare a bibliography of children's books you might use in storytelling. Divide the books into groups based on age: toddlers, two-, three-, four-, and five-year-olds.

2. Create an introduction for a story. Use props when reading your introduction.

3. Listen to a children's story on CD or audiotape. List the strategies used to hold the children's attention.

Workplace Link

Contact local child care programs, libraries, after-school programs, or home child care providers to find opportunities for volunteering your services during story time. Your service may be in the form of making or preparing props or other materials; setting up the story area; greeting parents and children; managing children during story time; or actually reading a story. Discuss the expectations with the head of the program beforehand. Document your service for inclusion in your portfolio.

Cross-Curricular Link

Language Arts

1. Using one of the storytelling methods explained in the chapter, prepare a children's story. Share it with the class.

Reading

2. Select several multicultural children's books to add to the book area.

Technology

3. Videotape yourself reading a book to a group of children. Evaluate your presentation.

4. Visit the following Web site sponsored by the U.S. Department of Education especially for teachers of young children: www.ed.gov/teachers. Explore the Web site for tips about the importance of reading and storytelling. You might also want to read the document *Teaching Our Youngest—A Guide for Preschool Teachers*.

Discuss

What type of puppet is shown in this photo? What other types of puppets can you name? How might children benefit from puppetry experiences?

Reflect

Look over the objectives for this chapter. How do socio-dramatic play and puppetry activities relate to the program goals for our child care lab?

21

Guiding Play and Puppetry Experiences

After studying this chapter, you will be able to

- describe the stages of play.
- explain the stages of material use in play.
- summarize the benefits of socio-dramatic play.
- prepare the classroom environment and guide socio-dramatic play activities.
- summarize the benefits of puppetry experiences.
- make and use three types of puppets.
- write and tell a puppet story.

Terms to Know

dramatic play

socio-dramatic play

projection

solitary play

parallel play

cooperative play

personification

manipulative stage of play

functional stage of play

imaginative stage of play

role-playing

coaching

modeling

prop box

puppetry

conflict

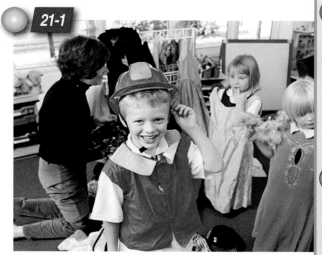

21-1

This child is imitating a firefighter.

Play is an important part of a young child's day. Young children love to pretend and play make-believe. Such fantasy play provides opportunities for growth and development. Play also encourages experimentation and discovery. Young children are actors without stage fright. They say what they feel and feel what they say. By observing children at play, you will gain insight into their cognitive, physical, social, and emotional development. Play is a window into their minds.

Dramatic play is a form of play in which a single child imitates another person or acts out a situation, 21-1. **Socio-dramatic play** involves several children imitating others and acting out situations together. It is the most complex form of play seen in early childhood settings. However, it is seldom observed before age three.

Puppetry is another type of play that allows a child to imitate others. A child's puppet may become a wolf, a police officer, or even a witch. Through this play, a child may

share his or her inner world. The child places feelings and emotions he or she feels onto the puppet. This is known as **projection**.

Stages of Play

Children go through several stages of play before they are able to take part in socio-dramatic play. First is solitary play, followed by parallel play. Finally, children learn to engage in cooperative play.

Infants most often play by themselves. This play is called **solitary play** or *independent play*. Their play is basically exploratory in nature. Solitary explorations involve the child gathering information. Until about nine months of age, infants explore single objects. After this, they can examine multiple objects at once.

Parallel play is typical of two-year-olds. In **parallel play**, children play beside each other, but not with each other. All the children may be involved in similar activities, but there is little interaction among the children. Children in this age group focus more on using play materials on their own.

Cooperative play is play between two or more children. As children grow socially and

Vocabulary

Have students review the *Terms to Know* list. Ask students to look up unfamiliar words or terms in the glossary before reading the chapter.

Discuss

What are the stages of play children go through before taking part in socio-dramatic play? Which type of play is typical of two-year-olds? What do children learn through cooperative play?

Vocabulary

Have a student volunteer define the terms *dramatic play* and *socio-dramatic play*. Which type is the most complex form of play seen in early childhood settings?

Meeting Special Needs

Provide an outline of the chapter with all the chapter headings for special learners. Students should fill in each section of the outline as the material is covered in class with a sentence or two about the content. Review the special learners' IEPs to decide if any modifications should be made in presenting the chapter content.

Discuss

In which stage of play do children begin to learn to share play materials? When do children become more interested in social relationships? How does this interest affect their play?

Resource

Playtime Match, Activity A, SAG

Discuss

What characteristics do children need to be able to participate in cooperative play successfully? What characteristics will prevent children from being able to join in this type of play?

emotionally, they begin playing with their peers for short time periods. Gradually they learn to respect the property rights of others. This is a clue they are gaining social skills, 21-2. At the same time, they are learning that permission is needed to use some materials. They are more willing to share with others.

It is at this stage that socio-dramatic play begins. As children take part in cooperative play, they become more interested in social relationships. As this occurs, they learn how to develop and maintain peer relationships. From this grows socio-dramatic play.

Children who are aggressive and uncooperative may have problems with cooperative play. To be successful in cooperative play, they need to give affection, be friendly, and consider other children's wishes. They also need to understand the viewpoint of others.

As you observe children in these three stages of play, you will notice that many engage in personification. **Personification**

Children learn social skills such as cooperation in socio-dramatic play.

Health and Safety

Wearing Shoes in Infant Play Areas

Infants may spend much of their playtime on the floor. Teachers, care providers, and other children should remove or cover their shoes when in the infant room. Wearing "street" shoes in infant play areas may introduce disease-causing agents. When infants touch these surfaces and then put their hands in their mouths, they may become ill. As an alternative to removing or covering shoes, teachers and care providers might keep a special pair of shoes or slippers just for use in the infant play area.

means giving human traits to nonliving objects. For instance, children may talk to dolls or puppets. They act as if the toys can hear what they say. Many everyday situations are acted out. A child may say "Mommy is going to feed you now." While speaking to a puppet, a child may say "You're going to go for a walk now." They will use exaggerated movements and voices. This is typical behavior for most young children.

Stages of Material Use in Play

Children move through three stages of material use in their play. Not all young children, however, will reach the second or third stages.

Meeting Special Needs

Before assigning *Playtime Match,* Activity A, SAG, divide the list of terms in half and prepare two separate matching assignments instead of the one longer assignment. Special learners may find it easier to concentrate when there are fewer choices and may be more successful in completing the assignment correctly. Allow students to use their textbooks so they can refer to the Glossary to help them complete the assignment.

The first stage of material use is called the **manipulative stage**. A child at this stage handles props. For instance, when given a baby bottle, children in the manipulative stage will screw and unscrew the cap.

The second stage is called the **functional stage**. During this stage, the child will use the prop as intended while playing with other children. Using a doll bottle, the child will pretend to feed a doll.

The third stage is called the **imaginative stage**. Children in this stage do not need real props, 21-3. They are able to think of substitutes. Instead of feeding the doll with a bottle, they may use their finger, a stick, a clothespin, or a pencil. Likewise, if a broom is needed to sweep the floor, a yardstick may be used.

Many times children at the imaginative level come up with unique ideas for their socio-dramatic play. They may use a toy to represent a dinosaur, a doll carriage for a grocery cart, or a paper bag as a chef's hat. When dramatizing a restaurant theme, they may make paper money to buy food.

Some children find it difficult to get involved in a role if there are no real props. In a restaurant scene, for instance, some children will play the role of servers. Children at the manipulative or functional stage will say they cannot play the role without paper and pencil. Children who have reached the imaginative stage might use their hand for the paper and use a finger as a pencil. Not all young children are able to reach the imaginative level.

Socio-Dramatic Play

As children engage in socio-dramatic play, they mimic adult roles. They may play at being a wife, husband, mommy, daddy, doctor, or police officer. This is called role-playing. **Role-playing** allows children to try out a variety of roles, 21-4. As one child plays the role of a hairstylist, another plays the role of the customer. Each role follows social rules determined by the group of children. Children engaged in role-playing often give specific instructions for roles. A child might say "You be the doctor, and I'll be the little girl." Conditions are also common. For

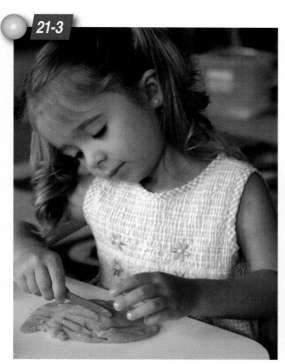

21-3

Cutting a pie made of play dough is a sign of imaginative play.

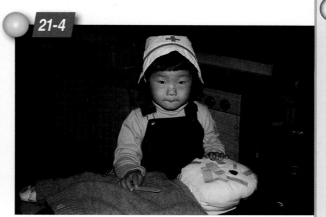

21-4

This child is role-playing a nurse.

Vocabulary

Have students discuss the meanings of the following terms: *manipulative stage*, *functional stage*, *imaginative stage*, and *role-playing*. Why might some children never reach the functional and imaginative stages of material use in play?

Reflect

Can you recall any instances from your childhood when you used objects as props during imaginative play? Share your experiences with the class. Add additional examples of materials children may use to represent objects while they play in the imaginative stage of material use.

Discuss

What types of roles do children engage in during socio-dramatic play? How are rules determined for role-play? Give examples.

Putting Technology to Use

Ask students to conduct an Internet search for information about preschoolers and role-playing. Have students relate what experts and research say about gender-based role-playing. What are the positive effects of children exploring gender identity through role-playing? Are there any negative effects? Have students write a brief report of their findings. Allow time for students to share their reports with the class.

Discuss

Why does socio-dramatic play promote cognitive development? Give examples of instances when you have observed children using decision-making and problem-solving skills during this type of play.

Reflect

LaRhonda, Libby, and Renee are all playing house. Jonathan wants to join them. How will you handle the situation when Libby tells him that only girls can play house and he should go play with the boys?

Resource

Encouraging Socio-Dramatic Play, Activity B, SAG

example, a child may say "I'll play, but I have to be the bus driver."

Benefits of Socio-Dramatic Play

Children benefit in many ways from participating in socio-dramatic play. From this type of play, children grow cognitively, physically, socially, and emotionally.

Studies have revealed a strong connection between play and cognitive development. Children's roles range from babies to parents to bears to astronauts. Their imaginations allow them to act out what they cannot yet be in real life. During this type of play, children make decisions and choices. By doing so, they learn problem-solving skills, 21-5. Language concepts are also developed as children engage in play. They learn new names for equipment and gain new ideas

21-5

Cognitive development occurs as this child uses a mixer in the dramatic play area.

from other children. As they generate plots and storylines, language skills, creativity, and imagination are fostered.

Physical development is promoted through the play actions of children: sweeping floors, dressing dolls, and pretending to paint furniture. Building structures that enhance socio-dramatic scenes also helps develop physical skills.

Social and emotional development are promoted through socio-dramatic play. Children try out different social roles. Sometimes negative feelings and situations that disturb children are acted out. Through these experiences, children learn about human relationships. They learn what kind of behavior upsets another child. They learn how to get along with others and discover important social skills. As a result, they gradually learn how to balance their play to satisfy and please others.

Play Themes

Themes for socio-dramatic play vary. The themes of play often focus on everyday situations children experience, 21-6. Children may imitate auto mechanics fixing cars, cooks making dinner, or painters working on a house. Teachers will often provide props that complement a unit of study, as well as the children's interests.

Themes change with age. The emphasis in three-year-old children's play is on process. There is no preplanned plot or theme. Real and pretend are still not firmly separated, so the child becomes what he or she imitates. Routines are important. Many three-year-old children always begin their day with the same activity.

Four-year-old children are more likely to take part in socio-dramatic play. Their play no longer centers primarily around the home. Play now involves more aggressive behaviors. Four-year-olds like to imitate ghosts, monsters, or TV action heroes. As you watch their socio-dramatic play, you will often notice feminine and masculine

---

Workplace Connection

Have students observe a group of preschoolers during socio-dramatic play to discover gender-based differences in role-playing. Do girls and boys display "typical" sex roles in their play such as girls playing house and boys playing as superheroes? Do you observe some situations in which girls and boys are playing together and portraying nontypical roles? Allow time for students to share their observations in class.

21-6

Themes for Dramatic Play

Occupational Roles

Artist
Baker
Barber
Builder
Bus driver
Computer operator
Cook
Dentist
Disc jockey
Doctor
Farmer
Fish catcher
Florist
Firefighter
Garbage collector
Gas station attendant
Grocer
Hairstylist
Librarian
Mail carrier
Mechanic
Office worker
Pharmacist
Pilot
Photographer
Police officer
Post office clerk

Sailor
Scientist
Shoe salesperson
Teacher
Truck driver
Waiter/waitress
Veterinarian

Other Themes

Airport
Beach
Camping
Circus
Costume shop
Farm/ranch
Gardening
Hat shop
Hospital
Pet show
Post office
Radio station
Restaurant
Spa
Store
Television station
Theater
Zoo

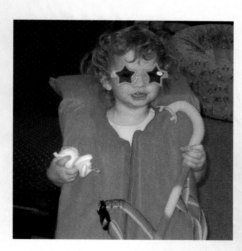

Many roles and situations can become the theme of play.

traits exaggerated. For example, to role-play a mother, children need all the props: gloves, hats, purses, high heels, and scarves.

Children's roles change frequently. One moment a child may be a career woman, and the next she may be a helpless baby. Children are included in or excluded from play based on sameness and difference.

The socio-dramatic play of five-year-olds reflects games with rules, as well as fears and hostile feelings. At this age, the child usually can tell the difference between reality and fantasy. As a result, you may hear the child say "This is just pretend."

Real-life roles as well as folk heroes are part of five-year-olds' socio-dramatic play,

21-7. Queens, kings, nurses, teachers, brides, and characters such as Big Bird and Batman are all frequent themes. At the same time, children are quite interested in romance. Thus, they like to act out fairy tales such as Cinderella.

The Teacher's Role

The first role of the teacher is to act as a resource person who provides materials and space. Studies show that in classrooms where theme-related props were provided, children spent more time in socio-dramatic play. The quality of toys and activities in the classroom will also affect the time spent

Resource

Dramatic Play Themes and Props, transparency master 21-1, TR

Enrich

Review the list of possible themes in 21-6, *Themes for Dramatic Play.* What themes might be appropriate for participation by the whole class for the entire day? Which might be appropriate themes for an entire week? What props and other materials would be needed to carry out the themes?

Reflect

Richard and Sam are acting out a scene in which the boys are role-playing being a policeman and a robber. Rhythm sticks are being substituted for guns. What intervention, if any, should you as the teacher make in this situation?

Discuss

Should children be allowed to act out aggressive behaviors that are part of a role or theme they are interpreting as part of their socio-dramatic play? What reasons do you believe support your viewpoint?

Workplace Connection

Ask students to observe children at a local child care center during socio-dramatic play. Have students look for and write down instances when children are using rules they have made up during play, such as "only the mommy can wear an apron." What is the role of rules in this type of play? Allow time for students to share their observations in class.

Vocabulary

Have a student volunteer define the terms *coaching* and *modeling*. How do these teacher behaviors contribute to a child's successful experiences during socio-dramatic play?

Discuss

What everyday roles might children enjoy imitating? What other roles may be enjoyable but require additional coaching by the teacher because the children may not be as familiar with the role?

Enrich

Ask several students to role-play an example of socio-dramatic play with one student acting as a teacher and the others as children. The student acting as the teacher should demonstrate examples of coaching, modeling, and reinforcing, and have the rest of the class identify which of the behaviors the teacher is using.

Resource

Dramatic Play, color transparency CT-18, TR

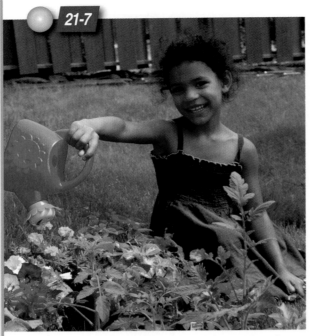

21-7

Five-year-olds enjoy playing roles they see every day.

in socio-dramatic play. Provide interesting materials, 21-8. Real materials will also enhance play. That is, instead of supplying small plastic firefighter hats, provide real hats from a local fire station. Change materials often to maintain interest.

The teacher's role also includes coaching, modeling, and reinforcing. **Coaching** requires that you provide children with ideas for difficult situations. For instance, a child may not want to be a baker because there is no baker's hat. You may then suggest that the child use a paper bag as a hat. Another child may be hitting a classmate. In this case, you should tell the child to stop because the other child does not like to be hit. You might also remind the child that others will stop playing if the experience is not pleasant.

In **modeling**, you show the children the appropriate behavior to use during their socio-dramatic play. In a shoe store scene, a

child may not know how to sell shoes. You may say "Would you like to buy some shoes today?" Watching you, the child has a chance to model this behavior for the other children.

Verbal guidance is helpful. Remaining outside of the play, you may offer comments and suggestions. For example, you may see a child unable to get involved in play. You may say to the child "Your son looks hungry. Shouldn't you go to the store and buy some food?" This statement may encourage the child to take the role of the parent. It should also get the child involved in dramatization with the children who have set up the grocery store.

Children's positive behaviors during socio-dramatic play should be reinforced. Comments may be made directly to the children who are using the desired behavior. If Sally just gave Sam a turn to use the cash register in their restaurant, say "Sally, I like the way you are giving Sam a turn."

Scheduling

Dramatic play is best scheduled during self-selected play periods. These periods must be long enough for the children to carry out their ideas. Many child care programs allow the first hour in the morning for this type of play.

21-8

Teachers need to provide realistic props to encourage socio-dramatic play.

Portfolio Project

Have students create photographic essays of children engaged in socio-dramatic play using a regular or digital camera. Students should identify the age and stage of development of the children and any theme they are using. Ask students to write a short anecdotal observation to explain what is going on during the play period, how long the session lasted, and what props or equipment were used. Students should creatively mount their photo essay with captions. Have students file a copy of the essay in their portfolio.

Avoid scheduling too many activities. This affects the number of children who take part in and remain with socio-dramatic play. If few children are playing, too many activities may be scheduled. Reduce the number of activities. Schedule only activities that complement each other. Blocks, woodworking, puppets, and art activities all encourage dramatic play.

Equipment and Setup for Socio-Dramatic Play

The first decision in arranging for socio-dramatic play is to decide on the location of the play area. Children spend more time in socio-dramatic play when the area is in the center of the classroom. Small areas tend to promote quiet, solitary play. Large, open areas promote more socio-dramatic play.

The quality of socio-dramatic play is promoted through age-appropriate materials. To promote harmonious play, provide plenty of these materials and store them in accessible play areas.

Prop Boxes

Extend children's play by providing prop boxes. A **prop box** contains materials and equipment that encourage children to explore various roles. Boxes that are the same size, clearly marked, and made of lightweight cardboard can be stored and carried with ease.

Prop box themes might include an office worker, shoe shop owner, painter, hairstylist, post office clerk, baker, grocer, florist, gas station worker, librarian, chef, fast-food worker, bride/groom, chef, doctor, painter, prince/princess, or carpenter. Each prop box should contain materials for one role, 21-9. Whenever possible, integrate books that can be used to reinforce the theme. In addition, the materials should be nonsexist and multicultural. To illustrate, a prop box for a hairstylist should include styling tools and products for men as well as women. It should

21-9

Beauty Salon Props

brushes	towels
cordless curling iron	aprons
cordless hair dryer	emery boards
combs	newspapers and
empty hair care	magazines
product containers	cosmetics
mirrors	play money
rollers	cash register

A prop box for a beauty salon might contain some of these items.

also include hair care items for people of various ethnic groups.

Costume Corner

Every dramatic play area should have a costume corner. Rotate costumes to complement current studies. For instance, if the theme of the week is community service, provide clothing to reflect this. Clothing for firefighters, nurses, doctors, and post office clerks can all be included. If Halloween is the theme, provide a variety of Halloween costumes. Make sure the costume corner contains clothing from a variety of cultures. For example, you might try to include wooden shoes, grass skirts, and kimonos.

Store these costumes after use. Lightweight cardboard boxes are good for storage. Mark each box clearly so it is easy to locate.

Housekeeping Area

Every early childhood classroom should have a housekeeping area. Dramatic and socio-dramatic play often occurs in this area. Supply child-sized furniture and equipment. Kitchen utensils, furniture, and other household items that complement current themes should be included. To keep interest, rotate equipment often.

Resource

Socio-Dramatic Play, Activity A, OG

Vocabulary

Have a student volunteer define the term *prop box.* How do prop boxes enhance socio-dramatic play?

Resource

Evaluating a Socio-Dramatic Play Activity, Activity B, OG

Workplace Connection

Ask students to inventory the clothing and accessories in the child care lab's costume corner. What items are in need of cleaning or repairing? Can any items be discarded? What additional costume items may be needed in the classroom? Have students write a list of their findings to present to the child care teacher. If possible, have student volunteers clean, repair, or discard items based on their findings.

Activity

Have students design activities revolving around a camping theme. Set up a free-standing tent outdoors (or indoors if space permits) and allow children to bring sleeping bags, canteens, and flashlights to school to play out the theme.

Vocabulary

Have student volunteers define the terms *puppetry, puppet, hand puppet,* and *mascot puppet.* Of what value are puppets to a self-conscious child?

Reflect

Did you ever have a childhood experience related to a puppet? How did the experience affect your view of puppets?

Outdoor Play Area

The outdoor play area needs equipment that promotes socio-dramatic play. Include a jungle gym, sandbox, housekeeping items, toy cars and trucks, sawhorses, wooden boxes, planks, and boards. Accessories such as tents, large blankets, and hats are also useful. With these materials, children can build forts, houses, and ships.

Puppetry

Puppetry involves the use of puppets in play. A *puppet* is a figure designed in likeness to an animal or human. Puppets come in a number of sizes and shapes. People make puppets move by using their fingers, hands, and wrists. Puppets can appear to express emotions if they have movable mouths, legs, and arms.

Puppets are powerful learning tools for young children. With a puppet, a self-conscious child can act out feelings such as anger and love. While using the puppet, the child often becomes the character and loses himself or herself. All children can learn how to communicate feelings and thoughts using puppets, 21-10. They may say things to a puppet that they will not say to a person. By listening, teachers may learn what makes children angry, sad, or happy.

For the teacher, a puppet can be a teaching aid. Puppets can be used effectively in almost every area of the curriculum. Chart 21-11 points out some of the values of puppets. Often, puppets are used to motivate children, to encourage them to share their thoughts, and to spark ideas. Group time can begin with a puppet. The appearance of a puppet may be changed for special occasions. For instance, green can be worn for St. Patrick's Day.

Puppets can be used to help children solve problems. When children fail to cooperate in cleanup, the puppet can say "I feel bad when all the boys and girls do

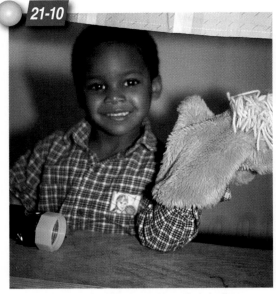

Children can use puppets to express their feelings.

not help pick up the toys." Puppets can also be used to give suggestions, such as "Tell Ricardo you want a turn."

Types of Puppets

Puppet types include hand, mascot, and "me" puppets. The value of each type depends on the needs and interests of the children.

Hand Puppets

Hand puppets are the easiest to use since no strings or rods need to be worked. A hand puppet is worked by placing the second and third fingers in the puppet's head. In this position, the hand is more relaxed and the puppet's entire body can be spread open. The thumb should be placed in one of the puppet's arms and the fourth and fifth finger in the other arm.

Hand puppets can be held in front of the face or over the head. This allows the puppeteer to work the puppet from a sitting, standing, or kneeling position.

Putting Technology to Use

Have students conduct an Internet search for information on the use of puppets and puppetry to help traumatized children handle their emotions. Why do therapists find puppets useful in situations where children have been abused or victims of catastrophes? Why might children respond better to a puppet than to a human voice? What programs currently use puppets and puppetry routinely when working with children? (UNICEF'S Return to Happiness is one example.) Allow time for students to discuss their findings in class.

21-11

Puppets and Curriculum

Curriculum Area	Value of Puppets
Art	• Offers emotional release • Provides sensory stimulation • Promotes fine- and gross-motor development • Encourages problem solving and decision making • Provides for exploration of materials
Math	• Encourages thinking through problems • Introduces concepts • Promotes the development of classification skills • Encourages measuring, ordering, and counting skills
Social studies	• Promotes communication skills • Models sharing and cooperation with others • Models critical thinking skills • Demonstrates concepts, such as friendship and self-esteem
Language arts	• Encourages development of language skills • Encourages listening and speaking skills • Promotes the development of concepts such as *above*, *below*, *under*, *over*, *in front of*, and *behind*
Dramatic play	• Offers emotional release • Promotes listening skills • Encourages problem-solving skills • Promotes decision-making skills • Promotes self-expression and creativity • Provides opportunities to gain self-confidence as group members • Provides opportunities to express feelings
Science	• Introduces concepts • Promotes classification of foods, animals, and objects • Explores the value of the five senses • Demonstrates differences and changes in texture, shape, and size • Provides for exploration of animal and nature themes

Puppets can be used as a learning tool in many areas of the classroom.

Reflect

Review the value of puppets in each of the curriculum areas listed in Chart 21-11. What concepts have you learned through puppetry experiences?

Resource

Value of Puppets, reproducible master 21-2, TR

Activity

Ask students to choose one of the curriculum areas listed in the *Value of Puppets*, reproducible master 21-2, TR. Have students discuss the use of puppets in their curriculum area and give one or more examples for each bulleted item. Allow time for students to share their examples with the class.

Cross-Curricular Activity

Family and Consumer Sciences
Enlist the cooperation of the clothing/fashion instructor for a joint class project. Have the clothing students demonstrate the use of sewing machines and sewing equipment to the child care students. Partner students from each class to use sewing skills to design and sew a simple hand puppet. Displays of finished puppets and photos of the students working together may be useful for publicizing both programs in school and in the local community.

Vocabulary

Have a student volunteer define the term *"me" puppet*. How can "me" puppets help children develop and practice language skills?

Activity

Provide to students various glue and bonding agents along with wooden spoons, plastic flyswatters, sponge dish mops, knit gloves, wiggle eyes, and felt. Have students construct various puppets with the different glues and bonding agents to see which products have the greatest success in permanently attaching materials to the puppets.

Note

A puppet stage or theater can be easily constructed from a three-sided poster or display board available at office and school supply stores. Boards are made from sturdy cardboard or foam core board, can be painted or decorated, and fold easily for storage.

Mascot Puppets

Some teachers choose to have a mascot puppet in their classroom. A mascot puppet is typically large. It usually remains in the classroom all year. Therefore, it should be well made to withstand handling from the teacher and children.

Mascot puppets can be used in many classroom routines. It can help introduce new activities and class members. The puppet can also be used as a teaching tool. It can model proper classroom manners. For this reason, the puppet should be given an expressive face and a strong personality. The mascot puppet can also be used to teach classroom rules. If a child neglects a rule, the teacher may have the mascot puppet provide a reminder.

Mary Arntson, a teacher of three- and four-year-old children, created a mascot for her classroom. She called him Mr. Dosendorf. Each day she used him for opening the morning meeting during larger group time, and again for transitions. She kept him on a shelving unit where he could "observe" the entire room. Throughout the day, he provided the children with reminders. For example, when El Rang started running across the room, Mary used Mr. Dosendorf to provide a friendly reminder. She picked up Mr. Doesendorf and walked over to El Rang. Then Mr. Dosendorf said, "We walk in the classroom."

"Me" Puppets

Children can also be taught how to make puppets using their own hands. These are sometimes called "me" puppets. To make "me" puppets, you will need nontoxic, washable markers; felt pieces; fake fur; construction paper; and double-stick tape. Demonstrate how to make a "me" puppet using your own hand. Line the inside opening between your index finger and thumb with a red marker. This line will be the puppet's lips. Using another colored marker, add the puppet's eyes. Use a piece of construction paper or fleece fabric for the hair.

With double-stick tape, attach the hair to the top of your knuckle.

Show the children how the puppet can open and close its mouth and talk when you move your thumb. Urge the children to make a variety of puppets, including people and animals. School-age children may enjoy making "me" puppets on the first day of school. After making their puppets, each child can share something about himself or herself. This might include age, hobby, grade in school, or favorite stories.

Making Puppets

Many teachers make their own hand and mascot puppets using store-bought or self-designed patterns. Chart 21-12 contains a list of materials for making puppets. After cutting the fabric, the mouth, eyes, ears, nose, and other parts should be sewn on. It is quicker to attach these parts with glue. However, this method is not durable. In fact, many times the parts will fall off once the glue has dried. All seams should be sewn with a ¼-inch seam allowance. The seams on a hand puppet should be on the outside of the puppet.

Puppet Stage

A puppet stage is not always needed, 21-13. However, most classrooms have a lightweight, portable stage. The puppet stage should be easy to fold and store. In fact, a cardboard cutting board is an excellent puppet stage. These can be bought at fabric shops. If the board is too tall for children, it can be cut to the correct height. To make the stage more interesting, the cutting board can be painted or wallpapered. It can also be covered with contact paper or fabric.

A tension rod can also be used in creating a puppet stage. When covered with a gathered curtain, the rod can be placed across a door as a temporary stage. Use a simple curtain in a solid color that will not be distracting.

Portfolio Project

After researching various materials and techniques of puppet construction, have students create their own mascot puppet by selecting a method of construction suitable to their skills. Have students write a "biography" of the new puppet including the puppet's name, characteristics, likes, and dislikes. Each student should demonstrate their puppet by introducing it to the class. Students should critique one another's creations. Have students file the puppet or photographs of it in their portfolio.

21-12

Materials for Making Puppets

terry cloth	tongue depressors	drinking straws
velvet	mittens	pictures
felt	foam packing materials	paper towel or toilet paper tubes
flyswatters	coat hangers	plastic bottles
dishmops	plastic packing materials	envelopes
pliers	construction paper	boxes
brooms	aluminum foil	fake fur
wooden spoons	egg cartons	ribbons
velour	paper bags	buttons
suede	paper plates and cups	foam balls
gloves		
socks		
hats		

Items that can be used to make puppets are limited only by imagination.

Puppet stages can be ordered through most equipment catalogs. Generally, they are made of wood. As a result, they are often quite heavy. Teacher-made puppet stages have the advantage of being more portable and less expensive.

Writing Puppet Stories

Not all puppet stories are found in books. In fact, most puppet stories are written by teachers. These stories are often contemporary and designed to fit the children's needs and interests.

To begin writing a puppet story, select a theme. Using a theme will help you decide the order of the events in the story. Themes can be based on friends, relatives, or other people. Personal experiences are another useful theme, as are manners, safety, friendships, vacations, holidays, and center

experiences. Some other theme ideas for puppet stories are listed in 21-14.

Developing a plot is the most challenging aspect of writing a puppet story. The children

21-13

A low shelf can be used as a puppet stage.

Enrich

Ask students to locate examples of puppet stages that can be ordered from school supply catalogs. Have students debate the pros and cons of purchased and hand-made stages based on cost, ease of use, and ease of storage.

Discuss

Have students explain theme and plot as they apply to writing a puppet story. Why is the plot usually the most challenging factor in writing a puppet story?

Resource

Materials to Make Puppets, reproducible master 21-3, TR

Cross-Curricular Activity

Speech and Drama
Ask the speech or drama instructor to teach students a variety of voice techniques suitable for puppets. Partner child care students with speech and drama students to practice the

voice techniques. Make recordings of the students so they can hear what they sound like. After listening to the recordings, students can critique their own style and alter or add modifications for a more effective puppet voice.

Vocabulary

Have a student volunteer define the term *conflict* as it applies to a story. Why is solving the conflict the most important part of the puppet story?

Discuss

What limits or rules are necessary for children and teachers to follow during a puppet presentation to the entire preschool class? What limits are necessary for children using puppets during free-play or individual time?

Activity

Have students view animated movies or cartoons in class to get ideas of how professional actors use their voices to add interest to the characters. Ask student volunteers to imitate and demonstrate some of the voices from the movies or cartoons.

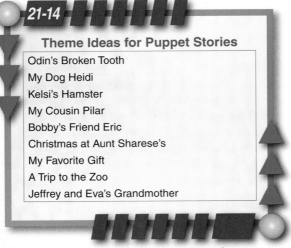

21-14

Theme Ideas for Puppet Stories

Odin's Broken Tooth

My Dog Heidi

Kelsi's Hamster

My Cousin Pilar

Bobby's Friend Eric

Christmas at Aunt Sharese's

My Favorite Gift

A Trip to the Zoo

Jeffrey and Eva's Grandmother

Children do not require complex themes for stories. Simple, familiar experiences are more interesting to them.

must be able to follow the action of the story. The events should occur in a logical manner. Begin with the theme and include the story events and problems. Remember, it is the problems that add interest and tension to the story.

End the story by resolving the conflict. In a story, **conflict** can be described as two or more forces that oppose each other. Conflict adds interest. When developing scenes of conflict, think in terms of synonyms and antonyms. Make a list of opposites. For example, opposite pairs might include: ugly-beautiful; poor-rich; weak-strong; soft-hard; kind-mean.

The ending of a puppet story finishes the picture for the children. The ending should make clear that the story is over. It should leave children with the story's most important point.

Working Puppets

When using a puppet in the classroom, the puppet should always model proper communication skills for the children. When the puppet speaks, it should move and face the children. When children or you speak, the puppet should be held still, facing the speaker.

Three basic types of movements can be modeled with hand puppets. The fingers, wrists, and arms may be moved. The fingers can create small movements in the puppet's arms and head. Waist movements can be made using the wrist. Arm movements can be used for locomotion movements. Chart 21-15 explains the various finger, wrist, and arm movements that can be used in puppetry.

Telling a Puppet Story

At this point, you have practiced the story and are comfortable working the puppets. You are now ready to tell the children a puppet story. Begin by creating the story setting and preparing the children.

The room should set the mood for a story. For a circus theme, you might place colorful balloons next to the storyteller. A Valentine's Day event might include a valentine box set next to the storyteller. Likewise, a Halloween story could be enhanced with dimmed lights. The purpose of this preparation is to put the children in the proper frame of mind for enjoying the presentation.

The first few minutes of a puppet story set the tone of the story. Make a special effort to gain the children's attention. This may be done using recorded music, slamming doors, or having the children sing a song. However, keep some surprises for later in the story.

Puppet Voices

To develop your puppet's character, use a special voice. Since puppets are not people, their voices should not be similar to human voices. Pitch is important. If there are two puppets being used, one should have a low-pitched voice and the other a high-pitched voice.

The children should be able to hear the puppet voices clearly. Voices should also be constant. The puppet should have the same voice throughout the story. If the puppet begins with a high-pitched voice, it should finish with one.

The voice should also match the puppet's size and character. A huge tiger should have a booming voice. On the other hand, a spider should have a tiny voice. A puppet of an older person may have a slower voice than that of a child.

Meeting Special Needs

Review the special learners' chapter outlines to determine if the students have any questions about the concepts or content of this chapter. Review the chapter objectives and ask the students to evaluate their progress in meeting these objectives. Ask the students to summarize, orally or in writing, what they learned from this chapter.

Resource

Design a Puppet,
Activity C, SAG

Resource

Writing Puppet Stories,
Activity D, SAG

Resource

*Planning a Play or
Puppetry Activity,*
Activity C, OG

21-15

Movements for Puppetry

Finger Movements

- The puppet's head can nod *yes* by moving the fingers up and down inside the puppet's head. This movement can also mean *I understand* or *I can do it*.
- The idea of *me* or *mine* can be expressed by pointing the fingers inside the puppet's hands toward the puppet.
- The puppet can gesture for someone to *come here* by waving one hand toward the body.
- Clapping and jumping up and down can express joy or enthusiasm.
- Pointing can convey such ideas as *you* or *over there*.
- Waving can be used to say *good-bye* or *hello*.
- Rubbing the puppet's hands together can mean the puppet is cold or thinking of doing something sneaky.
- Thinking can be expressed in a number of ways. The puppet can cross its hands or tap its head lightly.
- The fingers can be used to mimic sneezing, crying, and snoring (move the puppet's head up and down slightly).

Wrist Movements

- To show a *no* movement, rotate the puppet back and forth.
- To show a seated puppet, pivot the wrist, changing from a front to a side view. After this, the wrist needs to be bent, allowing the puppet to rest on a seat.
- To show a bow from the waist, bend the wrist down. At the same time, use the finger to make the puppet point toward itself.
- To show a puppet reading a book, model left to right progression skills by pivoting the wrist to mimic this action. At the same time, slowly move the fingers in the puppet's head to show reading action.
- To make a puppet appear to be looking for something, move the wrist back and forth. Using some arm movement, the puppeteer can make the puppet look to the sides of the stage and above and below it.

- To show a lifting movement, bend the wrist down as in bowing and grasp objects with the hands using hand and finger movements.

Arm Movements

- To mimic running, move the wrist up and down in a rapid, choppy motion. At the same time, move the puppet quickly across the stage.
- To mimic walking, hold the puppet upright and straight. As the puppet is moved across the stage, move its arms up and down.
- To mimic hopping, each hop needs to be deliberate. For variety, have the puppet hop in circles, returning to the ground as the last motion for each hop.
- To mimic flying, use broad arm movements. The puppet should always face the direction that it is flying.
- To mimic fainting or falling, use a broad arm movement and have the puppet land on its back. The speed at which the puppet lands depends on the desired effect. The best effect is acquired by freezing the puppet's movements for a few seconds before falling.

Simple finger, wrist, and arm movements can be used with puppets.

Service Learning Activity

After students have completed *Writing Puppet Stories,* Activity D, SAG, have them construct simple puppets for the story or use suitable classroom puppets. Contact area preschools and child care programs to arrange for students to visit and present their puppet shows. Students should practice their puppet show for the child care class and child care lab before "going on the road." Have students investigate additional opportunities for presenting puppet shows at area libraries; the YMCA and other organizational programs; playgroups; and local recreation department or park district early childhood programs.

Review and Reflect Answer Key

1. Socio-dramatic play involves several children imitating others and acting out situations together.
2. C
3. false
4. manipulative
5. false
6. A. four-year-old children
   B. three-year-old children
   C. five-year-old children
7. modeling
8. Coaching
9. (List two:) Schedule during self-selected play periods. These must be long enough for the children to carry out their ideas. The first hour of the morning is good. Avoid scheduling too many activities. This affects the number of children who take part in and remain in socio-dramatic play. Schedule only activities that complement one another.
10. materials and equipment that encourage children to explore various roles
11. (Student response.)
12. "Me"
13. Conflict adds interest. It should be resolved in the end.
14. (Student response.)

Summary

Play is an important part of a young child's day. Children go through several stages of play before they begin to take part in socio-dramatic play. These stages are solitary play, parallel play, and cooperative play. Children also move through three stages of material use in their play. These are the manipulative stage, the functional stage, and the imaginative stage. Socio-dramatic play and puppetry experiences are two types of make-believe in which children like to take part. Each offers its own benefits to children's growth.

Socio-dramatic play allows children the chance to try out many roles. Through this play, children grow physically, socially, emotionally, and cognitively. Themes for socio-dramatic play vary. With proper teacher guidance and age-appropriate materials, socio-dramatic play can be an excellent form of play for children.

Puppetry experiences provide children the chance to explore emotions, thoughts, and situations. Children can project their feelings onto puppets. Teachers can help children learn how to handle difficult emotions and situations in a constructive way through puppetry experiences.

Several types of puppets can be used with children, depending on their needs. Puppets can be purchased or handmade. Most puppet stories are written by teachers.

Review and Reflect

1. Define *socio-dramatic play*.

2. Play in which children play by themselves but stay close by other children is called _____ play.
   A. cooperative
   B. solitary
   C. parallel
   D. dramatic

3. True or false. Socio-dramatic play is the simplest and first type of play used by children.

4. Children in the _____ stage of material use will screw and unscrew the cap on a baby bottle.

5. True or false. All children reach the imaginative stage of material use.

6. Indicate what age groups use the following play themes:
   A. Imitation of ghosts and monsters.
   B. No preplanned themes.
   C. Real life roles as well as folk heroes.

7. In _____, the teacher shows correct behavior for children during their socio-dramatic play.

8. _____ requires that teachers provide children with ideas for difficult situations during socio-dramatic play.

9. State two recommendations for scheduling socio-dramatic play.

10. What is included in a prop box?

11. How can puppets help teachers to better understand children?

12. _____ puppets are made using the puppeteer's hand.

13. Why is conflict an effective element in a puppet story?

14. Explain how you would match a puppet's size and character with your voice for the puppet.

Apply and Explore

1. Brainstorm a list of prop box materials for a zookeeper, painter, baker, and carpenter.

2. Visit a local child care center and observe the socio-dramatic play area. What types of play did you notice? What stages were the children in?

3. Observe and compare a group of two-year-old and four-year-old children. Describe the differences in their play.

Cross-Curricular Link

Art

1. Design a hand puppet.

Writing

2. Write a puppet story.

Technology

3. Search the Web site for the National Network for Child Care (www.nncc.org) for information on children's play.

4. At the Web site www.perpetualpreschool.com, review the information on dramatic play.

Workplace Link

Survey early childhood equipment catalogs for furniture and materials to use in a preschool housekeeping area. What types of materials are available? What is the price range for each type? List the minimum equipment and materials needed for a functional housekeeping area and calculate the total cost. What are the pros and cons of having volunteers construct the equipment or furniture needed in this area?

Discuss

Look at the children in this photo. At what age can children informally begin to learn writing? What types of activities can help preschoolers learn writing skills? Give examples.

Discuss

Look over the objectives for this chapter. Why is it important for teachers to use a consistent writing style?

Guiding Manuscript Writing Experiences

After studying this chapter, you will be able to

- define *manuscript writing*.
- list reasons for encouraging the development of writing skills in preschool settings.
- explain activities that help children develop writing skills.
- make letters following the Zaner-Bloser writing system.
- outline the sequence children follow in learning alphabet letters.
- discuss guidelines for helping children develop writing skills.

Terms to Know

manuscript writing
hand-eye coordination
conventions of print
skywriting

"Writing before kindergarten?" asked a concerned visitor. "Preschool children can't even read yet." This person was unaware that children can informally begin to learn writing at this age. Correct spelling, form, and style are given only minor attention during the preschool years. Instead, the emphasis is on a readiness to develop needed skills and attitudes for writing. As children explore, they learn how symbols and meaning combine. Art and play activities are critical in children's growth as symbol makers. Learning to write is a result of maturation, exploration, and practice.

When children use symbols or drawings to represent ideas or words, they are beginning to write. When observing children at this stage, you will note that they use a combination of "sticks" and "circles" in their scribbling. Although writing is a complex and lengthy process, eventually this scribbling becomes writing.

For preschool children, learning to write is similar to learning to speak. Children must first observe others in the process and then imitate what they have seen. Children should be immersed in a print-rich environment. Children who are not ready for writing must be introduced to activities that will help them prepare. Activities that promote fine-motor and hand-eye coordination are needed. Eventually children will become interested in writing.

Manuscript writing, or print script, is a simple form of calligraphy. These simple strokes look like the printed words seen every day in the children's world in books, in newspapers, on street signs, and on computer screens. Print script does not require the sustained muscle control needed for cursive writing. It involves unconnected letters that are made of simple, separate strokes. Vertical lines (|), horizontal lines (—), diagonal lines (/), and circles (O) are used to compose the strokes. These basic strokes can be made easily by children who lack well-developed fine-motor skills. Because of the separate strokes, this process is also slower to complete than cursive writing. However, manuscript writing is more legible. Children can learn their letters at a faster rate.

Manuscript writing is not taught formally in the preschool setting. Most young children are not developmentally ready for this task. It is included in this book only to introduce readiness activities and the sequence by which children should learn manuscript. It is also included to teach caregivers of young children correct letter formations. All teacher-made materials should be prepared using proper manuscript format, whether they are hand printed or computer generated. See 22-1. Your work will then serve as a model for children. It may also stimulate older children to identify individual letters of the alphabet and to write.

22-1

Teacher-made materials must be carefully prepared to serve as models for children. All letters must be accurately reproduced as shown on this game board.

Vocabulary

Have students review the *Terms to Know* list. Ask students to look up unfamiliar words or terms in the glossary before reading the chapter.

Discuss

Ask students to explain the following statement from the textbook: *Learning to write is a result of maturation, exploration, and practice.*

Vocabulary

Have a student volunteer define the term *manuscript writing*. What is the difference between *print script* and *cursive writing*?

Discuss

Why is manuscript writing not formally taught in the preschool setting? Why do preschool teachers need information on manuscript writing if they are not going to formally teach this process?

Meeting Special Needs

Provide an outline of the chapter with all the chapter headings for special learners. Students should fill in each section of the outline as the material is covered in class with a sentence or two about the content. Review the special learners' IEPs to decide if any modifications should be made in presenting the chapter content.

Discuss

What does it mean when we say that manuscript writing is mainly a *perceptual skill?* How can the environment help support or encourage the development of this skill?

Vocabulary

Have a student volunteer define the term *hand-eye coordination.* How often should activities that encourage and promote hand-eye coordination be scheduled in the preschool classroom?

Activity

Ask several left-handed students to demonstrate printing with their right hand and repeat the process with several right-handed students using their left hands to write. Ask the students to share how difficult they found the exercise. Relate the experiences to the difficulties a young child may face in learning to write.

Objectives for Writing

There are many reasons to encourage writing in preschool, especially with children who are ready for the task. Children need to learn

- to note the differences in the formation of letters
- to write the alphabet letters and numerals
- that words are made of groups of letters
- that letters represent sounds
- that letters in the English language go from left to right and top to bottom
- letter/sound associations
- that the spelling of words is related to their sound
- that there are spaces between words
- that print carries a message

Four elements are needed if children are to meet these objectives. Included are interest, enthusiasm, clear instructions, and support given by you to each child.

Prewriting Skills

Manuscript writing is mainly a perceptual and motor skill. Two skills are needed before children are able to use manuscript writing. These include fine-motor and hand-eye coordination skills. Children need enough fine-motor coordination to hold a writing tool and make basic strokes. They also need their hands and eyes to work together. Early childhood teachers need to include activities that promote these skills in the daily routine. This will ensure that children learn the basic skills needed to learn manuscript writing.

Fine-Motor Activities

Fine-motor activities are those that encourage children to use the small muscles in their hands and fingers. Materials used in these activities are listed in 22-2. Observe the children's interest and success with these materials. Provide interesting developmental materials. Practice should provide the children with the fine-motor coordination skills needed for manuscript writing.

Hand-Eye Coordination Activities

Hand-eye coordination is muscle control that allows the hand to do a task in the way the eye sees it done. Activities that promote this type of coordination are listed in 22-3. These activities will promote the

22-2

Materials Used in Fine-Motor Activities

play dough
clay
sand
building blocks
puzzles
finger paints
table blocks
small, wheeled toys
snap beads
threading beads
buttons and
    buttonholes
easel paints
rubber stamps
wooden letters

Using these materials will require use of small muscles, thus promoting their growth.

Putting Technology to Use

Ask students to conduct an Internet search for information about the philosophies involved in teaching young children to write. For example, what is NAEYC's position on this subject? What are some of the challenges teachers face in teaching young children to write? How can teachers enhance children's experience with print concepts? Have students write a brief report of their findings. Allow time for students to discuss their findings in class.

22-3

Activities That Improve Hand-Eye Coordination

painting	drawing
pasting	tracing
finger painting	copying
stringing beads	stapling
weaving	cutting
tying	constructing puzzles
building with blocks	fastening zippers,
placing pegs in	snaps, and buttons
Peg-Boards	lacing
hammering	

Hand-eye coordination activities help train the eye and hand to work together to accomplish a task.

development of writing skills. Therefore, they should be available for use at all times.

Manuscript Writing Systems

There are a number of manuscript writing systems available for teachers to use. The differences in these systems are minor. Included are the directions in which strokes are made and the shapes of the letters. Research does not support one system over another. Whatever system you use, be a skilled and consistent model.

Zaner-Bloser is perhaps the most widely used system in preschools and kindergartens. It is the system introduced in this book, 22-4. It was selected because of its common use and the ease by which children can learn to print using it. D'Nealian is another manuscript system that is used in some kindergartens. Since the letter formation is more difficult, it is not popular for preschool children.

Graphic Writing Tools

Provide a variety of graphic writing tools for young children. Chalk, crayons, washable felt-tip markers, and colored and lead pencils are examples. Until three years of age, children are interested in making something happen with a writing tool. They enjoy scribbling and may hold a writing tool in each hand. They often use colored felt-tip markers and soft lead pencils. These very young children hold the writing tool in the fist and use their shoulder and arm muscles to produce a marking. With time and practice, they will gain better control of the writing tool.

In addition to moving the shoulder and arm muscles, three- and four-year-old children start to use their wrists to move the writing tools. These children enjoy writing tools including chalk, crayons, felt-tipped markers, and colored lead pencils. Children's controlled scribbling begins emerging into letter-like forms. Circles, crosses, horizontal lines, and vertical lines are produced. Gradually children will use the tools to write the letters of their names. At this stage, children do not use correct spacing or position. They may also invent their own spellings for words.

Between four and five years of age, children begin to use a mature tripod grip on the writing tool. They enjoy writing their names and drawing simple stick figures, suns, and snowmen. Five- and six-year-olds exhibit good control of writing tools and can form both upper- and lowercase letters. They like

Enrich

Ask students to review 22-3, *Activities That Improve Hand-Eye Coordination.* What additional activities can students suggest adding to this list to improve the hand-eye coordination of young children? Examples: using squeeze bottles for paint and glue; using large-eyed sewing needles for sewing yarn; using spray bottles.

Discuss

What is the connection between drawing and scribbling and the development of handwriting skills? Why are crayons, pencils, markers, and chalk considered *tools*?

Note

Post charts of both the Zaner-Bloser and the D'Nealian writing systems in the child care classroom so students can see the differences in these two writing styles. Charts can be obtained commercially or prepared by hand. They should be duplicated in notebook size so all students can file copies in their portfolios.

Portfolio Project

Depending on the size of the class, divide students into groups to create letter cards from a variety of textural materials. Suggestions include sandpaper; foam craft sheets; textural fabric such as corduroy, burlap, or fleece; small bubble wrap; plastic perforated shelf liner; and corrugated cardboard. Each group should create the entire alphabet and numbers 1 through 10. Allow the child care lab children to handle and use the cards throughout the year for tracing and sensory experiences. Divide the cards up at the end of the year so each child care student will have a variety of examples to file in his or her portfolio.

Resource

Zaner-Bloser's Six Simple Strokes, color transparency CT-19, TR

Discuss

Why is using lined paper discouraged for preschool-aged learners? How will children learn to write straight without some guidelines?

Resource

Practicing the Zaner-Bloser Writing System, reproducible master 22-1, TR

Discuss

Should the process of learning to write the letters of the alphabet follow the same order as learning the alphabet? Why or why not?

22-4

The Zaner-Bloser writing system is easy for children to use and for teachers to teach.

to draw more complex objects, such as flowers and houses. At this age, children are just beginning to learn the **conventions of print**. This includes standardized spelling, word spacing, and upper- and lowercase letters.

Paper

Provide a variety of paper to encourage children to write. Young children enjoy making choices, so offer colored paper as well as white. Most preschool children lack the muscle control and hand-eye coordination to use lined paper. Use large, unlined pieces of paper such as newsprint instead.

Manuscript Sequence

There is a sequence in how children usually learn alphabet letters. First children recognize whether a line is curved or straight. Next they learn to distinguish round letters (*O*, *C*) and curved letters (*S*, *D*). Then they learn to recognize curved letters that have intersections, such as *B* and *R*. Finally, letters with diagonal lines (*K*, *X*) and horizontal lines (*L*, *H*) are recognized.

Certain letters are easiest for children to form. The sequence recommended in the Zaner-Bloser method follows the similarities in lowercase letters. This is because lowercase

---

Workplace Connection

Invite an occupational therapist to speak to the class about the development of handwriting skills. What psychological and physical reasons may affect children who have difficulty in handwriting? What techniques are used with children who have visual, learning, or sensory challenges to help them learn to compensate for their disabilities? How can therapists, teachers, and parents collaborate to support and encourage children with writing difficulties? Have students write a list of additional questions to ask prior to the visit.

letters are used more often. Zaner-Bloser's recommended sequence is as follows:

litoadcefgjqusbhprnmvywkxz
1, 2, 3, 4, 5, 6, 7, 8, 9, 10
LITOADCEFGJQUSBHPRNMVYWKXZ

The easiest letters are those made of straight lines or circles. You can follow this sequence as you design written materials.

Building Writing Skills

Proper writing skills are based on a few basic guidelines. With practice and maturity, children learn the importance of letter size, proportion, spacing, and line quality. You must be able to guide them through common problems, such as letter reversals. Also, you must be able to work through unique situations faced by left-handed children.

Size and Proportion

To provide useful models for children to imitate, perfect your own writing skills. You must use the correct letter size and proportion. Lowercase letters are always half the size of uppercase, or capital, letters. This rule holds true no matter how small or how large the writing, and no matter where the writing appears (name tags, charts, board, or games).

The size of the children's writing reflects development of their fine-motor and hand-eye coordination. First writings are typically large. The letters vary in size and proportion. As the children's coordination skills mature, their writing decreases in size. Within any given classroom, there will usually be a wide range of skill. Look at the writings in 22-5. Kathryn's writing is mature for a four-year-old child. Her letters are similar in size and proportion. Amy's writing shows some variation in both size and proportion. Given time, she will develop the skill to make letters of proper proportion and size. Jena's writing almost looks like a scribble. Even though she

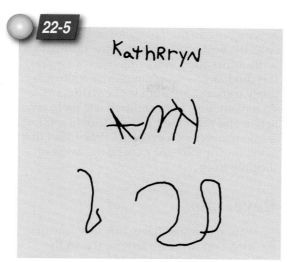

22-5

These writings show three levels of writing skill. Jena requires extra practice to bring her skills up to a higher level.

is the same age as Kathryn and Amy, she still lacks the skills needed to write her name legibly. Jena needs many more hand-eye and fine-motor activities.

Spacing

Achieving proper spacing between letters and words is difficult for many beginning writers. Proper spacing requires more fine-motor control than most preschool children have. To help children gain control, have them write the letter *O* between words. However, this may still be too difficult for some preschool children. If so, direct them to place their index finger on the paper after the word. Then have them write the first letter of the next word to the right of their finger. Unless a child's fingers are unusually large, this should produce proper spacing.

Line Quality

Observe the line quality of children's writings. If a line wavers, this usually means immature coordination. Wavering lines

Reflect

Braden's mother is concerned her four-year-old son is dyslexic because he writes the *d* in his name backwards and the *e* upside down. What advice do you have for Braden's mother?

Resource

Children's Writing Skills, Activity A, OG

Reflect

How did you first become aware of the need for proper spacing between letters and words in writing? What techniques for proper spacing worked for you when you learned to write?

Workplace Connection

Have students collect several samples of young children's manuscript writing. Identify the age of the child who wrote each sample and compare the characteristics of writing seen at each age. How does the letter size differ with each sample?

Do letters vary in proportion and size? Is the writing legible? Is proper spacing used? What types of fine-motor skills could children do to improve their writing skills? Allow time for students to discuss their findings in class.

Discuss

What is a *reversal*? What letters are usually reversed? What techniques can you use to help children correct their reversals?

Reflect

Was any special attention focused on left-handed children during your early school years? Do you recall any techniques teachers used or statements made to assist left-handed children in writing correctly?

Discuss

Why is *drill* as a means of perfecting a writing technique to be avoided during the preschool years? What activities can substitute for drill and still encourage proper letter formation?

Note

Ask left-handed students to share any challenges they faced growing up left-handed. What challenges still exist today? How do the students deal with them?

can also result from writing too slowly or moving fingers but not the pencil. In this case, the writer is trying to draw rather than write. Most often, wavering lines are a sign the child lacks enough muscular control to apply constant pressure to the writing tool. To remedy this, have children use more arm action and relax their grips. Illegible writing is another common problem. Pencil lead that is too fine or too hard may be the cause of illegible work.

Reversals

Young children have difficulty learning the direction in which letters face. In the early stages of writing, children often reverse letters. For instance, one letter becomes another letter. Children will print *b* when they intend to write *d*. Some letters are written backwards. A *J* may have the tail reversed. Children may also write the letters of a word in the reversed order. For instance, Mark may write his name *kraM*.

You can guide children with reversal problems by pointing out differences in direction. If the child confuses the letters *b* and *d*, say "*b*, line, then circle." This tells the child that b contains a straight line first and then a circle. If the child is having a problem writing *d* correctly, say "*d*, circle, then line." After being given these directions, some children will repeat them aloud when writing *d* or *b*.

Practice

Children need many opportunities to practice their writing. Be selective in what activities you provide to promote this skill. Be careful these practices do not become meaningless drills. For instance, when children are required to write a line of ten letters, they can become bored and tired. Their fingers become tense. The result can be the last letter is not formed as well as the first. The lines will waver. Children usually use

the last letter they wrote as a model, so any errors will be repeated.

During practice with writing tools, show children how to hold the writing tool properly. First, ask children to watch the way you pick up a pencil. Place the pencil between your first finger and thumb. Lightly rest your index finger on the top of the pencil. Show the children how the index finger controls the heaviness of the letter. See 22-6.

Left-Handed Children

About 10 percent of all children are left-handed, 22-7. A series of activities can assist you in learning a child's preferred writing hand. Ask children to pick up a piece of paper, throw a ball, pick up a fork or spoon, or place pegs in a pegboard. To avoid stressing the use of one hand over the other, center objects in front of children. If a child repeatedly uses his or her left hand, he or she has shown a preference for that hand. Left-handed children should be placed so the left arm is at the left end of a table for eating and

22-6

By holding this pencil properly, this child is successful in the practice activity.

Workplace Connection

Have students collect crayons, pencils, chalk, and colored markers of various thicknesses and set them out for children to use during group art time at the child care lab. Have students observe how children handle these tools. Which tools are preferred and are easiest for children to use?

Does the thickness of the writing tool relate to a child's ability to use the tool effectively? Put out only the thick or thin utensils at a time. Compare the line quality produced by the children when offered these types of tools. Have students write a brief report of their findings.

Work with left-handed children to make sure they are in a comfortable position for writing. This child has been correctly seated with her left arm toward the left end of the table.

work. Such placement prevents the problem of bumping arms with a right-handed child.

Early Experiences in Writing

Early experiences often determine whether children like or dislike an activity. For this reason, start slowly and provide activities children will not find frustrating. Since most children have an interest in the letters of their own names, begin by encouraging children to copy their first names. Most children have had experience writing or watching adults write their names. Early childhood teachers should stress that children learn the proper letter forms. Do not capitalize all the letters. Children can become

confused if they see their name written in different ways at school and at home. For instance, the name *Tom* should be written using an uppercase *T* followed by lowercase *o* and *m*.

Techniques for Encouraging Writing

Your major role is to carefully prepare an environment that will encourage children to scribble and write. Children experience more success in developing print awareness in a print-rich environment. Some children will learn to recognize names and other words in their environment. To encourage this skill, you will need to use many teaching tools, 22-8.

Provide children with copies of their names. Then make a bulletin board containing the children's pictures. Under each picture, place the correct name.

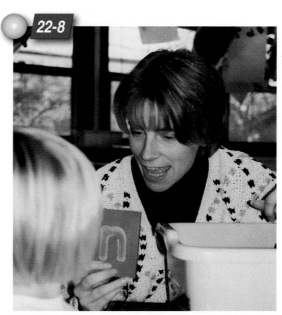

Letter blocks provide an opportunity to trace and match letters. This helps children become familiar with all letters.

Resource

Evaluating a Handwriting Activity, Activity B, OG

Discuss

Why is it important not to write a child's name in all capital letters? How can students promote the recognition of lowercase letters by the preschoolers?

Resource

Planning a Handwriting Activity, Activity C, OG

Workplace Connection

Have students survey the children in the child care lab to discover if they recognize lowercase letters. Using individual flash cards or a lowercase alphabet chart, point out a letter and ask the child to name it. Then ask the child to point to a specific letter that the student has named. Have students keep records for individual children of the letters they need to learn and make opportunities available daily to include recognition activities for those letters not yet learned.

Vocabulary

Have a student volunteer define the term *skywriting*. How does this process encourage children to practice writing skills?

Activity

Encourage children to learn to write the names of their classmates by addressing their own holiday cards. If holidays are not celebrated in the preschool, have students design an activity that includes sending children mail to their individual mailboxes or cubbies.

Enrich

To promote a print-rich environment, have students create individual name mobiles for each child in the child care lab. Make sure students use a consistent handwriting style and letter size. Hang the mobiles in the preschool classroom so all children can see and recognize their names and the names of their classmates.

Resource

Practice Your Writing, Activity A, SAG

Other practices to provide a print-rich environment and encourage writing include using place mats at mealtime. Print the child's first name on the place mat. In addition, print names in the upper-left corner of all papers. Writing can also be encouraged by printing labels for classroom materials and furniture. Label cots, toothbrushes, cubbies, tables, windows, doors, clocks, sinks, shelves, and curtains, as well as other items.

Make children aware of printed names other than their own. Do this by printing all the children's names on poster board cards. At transition times, place all the cards in a small basket. Then draw one name at a time, allowing the children to identify the name.

Encourage children who are ready to print their name on their artwork. To prepare them for the left to right progression required in reading, tell children to print their names in the upper left corner of their artwork. Gradually the children will learn that letters must be kept in a certain order. They will follow the left-to-right, top-to-bottom patterns of written English.

When working with children who are having trouble in writing a particular letter, try **skywriting**. Stand beside the child. Demonstrate the correct way to make the letter by writing it in the air in front of you. Have the child observe your motion, hold up his or her writing hand, and follow the strokes. Observe the child to be sure that he or she is making the correct letter.

Always use the correct terminology. For example, when writing capital letters call them capital or uppercase letters. Do the same for lowercase letters.

Provide children with letters cut out of sandpaper and mounted on poster board. By feeling a letter, the children learn its form and shape. Another technique is to print the manuscript letters on paper and cover the paper with clear acetate sheets. Give children grease or china marking pencils to trace the letters. Remove their markings with a piece of felt or window cleaner. The acetate sheets are reusable. You might also develop puzzles that require children to match corresponding uppercase and lowercase letters.

Think of every way possible to create a print-rich environment. Create and place signs around the room, post travel posters in the block area, and have the children dictate stories as well as thank-you notes to you. Post them in the classroom. Dramatic play could be made into a literacy event. To illustrate, an office or grocery store could be set up for four- and five-year-olds. The children could be encouraged to print labels and signs. You could also add message pads and pencils in this area to encourage writing.

Group Experiences

There are many group situations in which writing can be encouraged, 22-9. Write in the children's presence. Have children dictate an invitation, letter, or thank-you note to you. As they dictate, record their message in print. It is important for the children to watch as you write. Make sure to point out the letters and read the message back to them. Follow the correct manuscript format. Call attention to the use of an uppercase letter at the beginning of a sentence, a question mark or a period

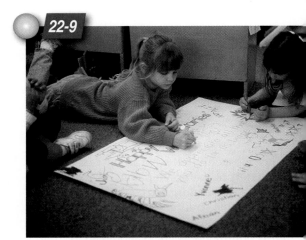

22-9

An oversized thank-you card from the entire class encourages these children to practice their writing skills.

Service Learning Activity

Have students create file folder activities relating to the recognition and writing of alphabet letters and numbers. Activities may include matching, tracing, sensory experiences, and actual writing. File folders should be designed with pockets to keep items such as letter cards or cutouts, pictures, or writing utensils. They may also include the use of wipe-off surfaces, magnets, or hook-and-loop tape or other materials. File folders can be donated to local Head Start or other early childhood programs that encourage early literacy.

Apply and Explore

1. Collect, compare, and discuss writing samples from a group of five-year-olds.

2. Practice making the letters following the Zaner-Bloser writing system.

3. Prepare two sets of tracing alphabet cards that children can use. Make one set using uppercase letters. Use lowercase letters for the second set.

4. Brainstorm a list of all equipment and fixtures in the classroom that could have labels attached. Prepare the labels.

5. Create a writing suitcase. Include a variety of graphic writing tools and paper. Show your suitcase to the class.

Cross-Curricular Link

Writing

1. Practice writing a letter using manuscript writing. When you finish, check your letter for line quality, spacing, and letter formation.

Technology

2. The Web site school.discovery.com/clipart offers teachers an array of powerful tools to create their own materials. Explore the site to find appropriate clip art for use in a writing center for four- and five-year-old children.

Workplace Link

Write an article for the preschool newsletter about the development of handwriting skills in preschoolers. Include an explanation of the progression of development. Offer suggestions for activities parents can do at home with their child to promote and encourage writing abilities. Include information on the role of letter recognition and the awareness of symbols and print in the learning process. Articles should include a request for parent feedback on the activities and progress they see in their child's handwriting skills.

Discuss

Study the chapter opening photo. What math concepts can this child learn from the apples? How can math concepts be included in the daily routine of the child care lab? Give examples.

Discuss

Look over the objectives for this chapter. Are math concepts really appropriate for preschool learners?

23

Guiding Math Experiences

After studying this chapter, you will be able to

- list objectives of early math experiences.
- use two basic assessments to determine math skills of children.
- recognize a variety of three-dimensional objects that can be used to promote math experiences.
- identify math experiences that promote the development of key math concepts.
- design math experiences that stress specific math concepts.

Terms to Know

specific task assessment
parquetry blocks
classification
matching
sorting
sequencing
recognizing
set
empty set
one-to-one correspondence
cardinality
rational counting
numerals
spatial relationships

"One, three, five, two" and similar phrases can often be heard from young children. They are searching for meaning as they echo these words. Reciting numbers is a key step in learning math concepts. Math is sometimes defined as the science of shapes and numbers. For young children, math is an active process of thinking about and organizing experiences to make sense of their world. This process involves reasoning, problem solving, and communication.

Children construct math concepts by relating new experiences and information to what they already know. Meaningful learning requires the ability to see patterns. Classroom equipment, materials, and activities must provide opportunities for the children to understand patterns through play.

Early math experiences for children should focus on exploration, discovery, and understanding. Concepts are developed by the exploration of hands-on materials, three-dimensional objects, and the discovery of their relationships. Math concepts are usually taught informally in day-to-day activities in early childhood classrooms. These include art, cooking, games, dramatic play, music, sensory play, and storytelling, 23-1. Almost every activity area in the classroom promotes math exploration.

The teacher's role is offering opportunities for the children to develop mathematical thinking. Children may learn shapes, color, and order (logic) concepts through art activities or by playing with blocks. Cooking activities teach how quantities are related and ordered. For instance, you might tell a child "Beat the eggs first, add the sugar second, and add the vanilla last." Classroom games can teach the concepts of first and last, as well as high and low numbers. If dice are used in games, addition concepts can be taught to the older children. Dramatic play offers many teaching opportunities. For example, as children play store, they can learn about money, 23-2. Songs, stories, and fingerplays can contain numbers and math words.

Other ways to include math concepts in the daily routine include asking "Are there enough chairs?" "Is everybody here today?" or "Is there a cookie for each child?" Math concepts can be used in any appropriate situation. For example, you may introduce counting concepts by remarking "Kelsie brought three kittens to school."

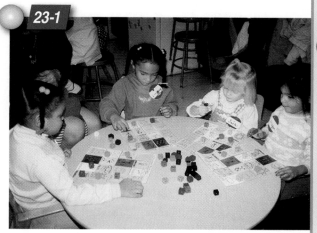

23-1

Games help children learn many math concepts.

Vocabulary

Have students review the *Terms to Know* list. Ask students to look up unfamiliar words or terms in the glossary before reading the chapter.

Resource

Math Match, Activity A, SAG

Note

Copy the following statement from the textbook and post it in the classroom during this unit to remind students of the reasons for learning this material: "For young children, math is an active process of thinking about and organizing experiences to make sense of their world."

Enrich

Divide students into small groups to brainstorm lists of preschool activities related to math concepts. Post the lists in the classroom and ask students to discuss which activities children are most likely to enjoy.

Meeting Special Needs

Provide an outline of the chapter with all the chapter headings for special learners. Students should fill in each section of the outline as the material is covered in class with a sentence or two about the content. Review the special learners' IEPs to decide if any modifications should be made in presenting the chapter content.

Discuss

Ask students to look over the eleven goals of early math experiences and discuss those they have already met this year in the child care lab. Discuss ideas for incorporating those goals that have not yet been achieved.

Reflect

Why is it important for children to understand patterns? What examples of patterns are already in place in the child care lab?

Enrich

Ask students to design an observation form to be used during preschool activities. The form should involve math concepts with specific questions to be answered during the observation period. Students should also include areas to describe what they have observed. Compare students' forms to decide which would produce the most effective observation tool.

Resource

Classroom Areas and Math Concepts, Activity A, OG

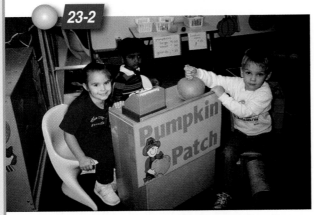

23-2

As children play store, they start to form concepts about money.

Transitions (time between scheduled activities) are a good opportunity to present new math concepts. For example, while pointing at the clock, you might say "It's two o'clock and time to go to the library." At clean-up time, one-to-one relationships can be taught if there is one puzzle for Juan and one for Nikki to put back on the shelf. After group time, you may have the group of children wearing red use the bathroom first. See 23-3 for a list of general activities that help promote math concepts.

Goals of Early Math Experiences

Well-planned settings provide developmentally appropriate play experiences that also help promote math skills. These math experiences should help form concepts such as color and shape recognition, classification, measurement, counting, time, temperature, space, and volume concepts. The math experiences should stress the following:

- observing and describing concrete objects
- recognizing colors, patterns, and attributes
- classifying sets of objects
- comparing objects and using terms that describe quantity, such as *more than* and *lighter than*
- copying patterns
- recognizing shape concepts
- recognizing and writing numerals
- using logical words such as *all*, *none*, and *some*
- using one-to-one correspondence
- estimating quantity and measurement
- developing problem-solving skills

Assessing Math Ability

Before planning math activities for children, first determine the children's skill levels. In order to do this properly, children need to be assessed individually. There are two common forms of assessment: observation and specific task assessment. The information obtained from these processes will help you plan developmentally appropriate math activities.

Assessment by Observation

Observation involves informal viewing of a child during self-selected activities. Specific behaviors to watch for include the following:

- identifying colors and shapes
- sorting and classifying objects, 23-4
- counting objects
- setting a table correctly
- pouring liquids and carefully watching the amount poured
- constructing patterns
- writing numerals

Through observation, you will be able to determine a child's needs. If you notice that a child cannot sort objects, you will need to

Putting Technology to Use

Have students conduct an Internet search for information on kindergarten readiness with regard to math knowledge. What should a child know and be able to do mathematically before entering kindergarten? What are the major benefits of entering kindergarten with the knowledge of basic math concepts? Are the recommended concepts and skills already part of the child care lab curriculum?

23-3

Strategies for Teaching Mathematical Concepts

- Refer to times when you will eat lunch, take a nap, and play outdoors.
- Use teaspoons and cups to measure ingredients for cooking and feeding pets.
- Divide portions using language such as "This half of the sandwich is for Raul, the other half is for Ali."
- Count the children at group and snack time.
- Give children an order of events for the day, such as "First we will have group time and then playtime. Then we will have snacks and go outdoors."
- Keep score when children are playing games such as beanbag toss. Begin by using small blocks, tees, or other small objects to represent points. Later, use numbers.
- Place a cash register with money in the dramatic play area.
- Place books with math content on the bookshelves.
- Read counting picture books. Encourage participation by allowing the children to practice counting and identifying numerals.
- Introduce finger plays and poems that encourage counting such as "Five Little Monkeys."
- Provide children with three-dimensional objects to group according to their likenesses and differences.
- Review the calendar during large group time.
- Hang a large thermometer outside your classroom door where the children can view it.
- Discuss the temperature of foods at snack and lunch times.
- Prepare and introduce lotto games with different colored, shaped, and sized figures.
- Make obstacle courses outdoors that require *under*, *over*, *around*, and *across*.
- Cut sponges into circles, squares, triangles, and rectangles. Let children use them to apply paint.
- Measure the children and record heights on a chart.
- Provide puzzles that prompt children to identify shapes and match colors as they complete the picture.

These daily activities can all help teach children basic math concepts.

provide sorting activities. Specific activities are outlined later in this chapter.

Specific Task Assessment

Specific task assessment involves giving children set activities to determine skill and/or needs. Examples include the following:

- Present a child with crayons and say "Tell me the colors." After the child has replied, say "Now count these for me."
- Show a child one group of four pennies and one group of seven pennies. Then ask the child "What group has more pennies?"

- Present a child with circle, diamond, square, and rectangle shapes. Say "Find the square." Then have the child identify each of the remaining shapes.
- Show a child four different-sized balls. Ask "Which is the smallest ball?" and "Which is the largest ball?"
- Lay 10 blocks in front of the child. Ask "How many blocks do I have here?"

As with observation, the information provides information for use in planning math activities.

Reflect

Fingerplays such as *Five Little Monkeys Jumping on the Bed* and *One, Two, Buckle My Shoe* can promote number knowledge and awareness in young children. What other examples of rhymes, poems, and songs can you suggest?

Activity

Have students identify shapes in the child care lab such as square or rectangular windows and cabinet doors, round light fixtures and drains in sinks, triangular patterns in floor tile, in carpeting, etc. Encourage students to regularly point these out to children and quiz them to see if they can name the shapes.

Discuss

Sal and Vito, four-year-olds in your class, are playing with various colored foam shapes and trying to sort them into groups by shape. Why might this be a difficult task for them to perform?

Cross-Curricular Activity

Art

Ask the art instructor at your school to demonstrate color values to students by creating shades and tints of a specific color. Have students adapt the demonstration for the preschoolers and allow them to experiment with paint in their favorite color by creating shades and tints on several small cards. Ask children to identify the lightest color they painted and the darkest. Ask children to put the rest of the color samples they created into the proper sequence from light to dark and observe the results. Allow time for students to discuss their observations in class.

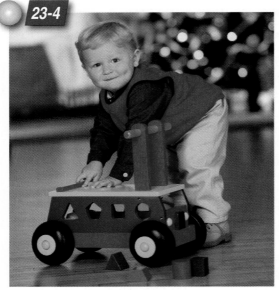

23-4

A teacher can observe this toddler playing with a shape sorter as a way to assess his math readiness skills.

Resource

Mathematical Language in the Classroom, Activity B, OG

Activity

Have students design a lesson titled *My Favorite Color*. Include opportunities for preschoolers to wear clothing to class and bring in show-and-tell items of their favorite color. Design a collage art project for children to complete with their parents. Send home a sturdy paper or cardboard cutout shape for the child and parent to decorate together using materials in the child's chosen color. Hang the collages up in the classroom when they are returned to school.

Resource

Math Materials and Equipment, Activity C, OG

Health and Safety

Math Equipment

Math equipment such as puzzles, matching games, nesting items, interlocking plastic shapes, stringing beads, and pegboards with large pegs can all be used to teach preschool children about math. Take care to store these small manipulatives out of reach of children less than two years of age. A five-year-old is not likely to swallow smaller pieces, but a two-year-old might.

Math Equipment

Encourage the children by providing an active, stimulating environment to foster mathematical thinking. Provide the children with a variety of three dimensional objects that promote physical and mental activity. Collections of items for counting, observing, creating, sorting, discussing, construction and comparing should be included. From these experiences, children can construct math concepts. Chart 23-5 lists numerous materials for learning math concepts. If these materials are available in the classroom, children can explore and discover many math concepts.

Mathematical Activities

A quality curriculum provides a rich environment. It also provides developmentally appropriate activities to help children explore key concepts. Math activities for preschool children should promote the development of many skills. For example, children should learn to identify, classify, and understand the concept of a set. Children should also learn to count and recognize numbers and understand the concepts of space, size, volume, and time. The art of curriculum design is matching children's needs to their interests. This requires keen observation skills, listening skills, and thorough understanding of child development.

Color Concepts

Color is considered a math concept since it helps children learn to discriminate among objects. Using color, children can classify, pattern, and sequence, 23-6. Identifying colors also seems to help language development. It requires the skill to recall a name and

---

Putting Technology to Use

Have students conduct an Internet search to locate sources for math equipment and manipulatives for preschool and child care programs. Ask students to select several items that would meet the child care lab program goals for math.

Then write a brief description of the concepts children would learn from using the items and explain how the goals will be met. Have students create a "wish list" of items they propose be added to the child care lab.

23-5

Supplies for Math Activities

flannel boards
felt-covered numerals
felt cutouts of various sizes,
  colors, and shapes
scraps of cloth
pegboards
magnetic shapes
calendars
lines numbered 0 through 20
rules, yardsticks, and tape
  measures

thermometers: indoor, outdoor,
  play
alarm clock
egg timer
giant wooden dominoes
giant counting rods
scales: bathroom and balance
light and heavy objects; rocks,
  pennies, corks
measuring containers of various
  sizes and types

buttons for counting and sorting
empty spools
puzzles with geometric inserts
jigsaw puzzles
sequencing puzzles
tactile numbers
counting frame
pattern blocks

Many items can be used to stress math experiences.

23-6

The color in this bulletin board helps children see differences between the circles, crayons, boy, and girl.

associate it with a visual image. Then, as the children's language skills grow, their skill at naming colors improves.

According to studies, children learn to identify colors before shapes. However, it is not uncommon for a preschool child to confuse color and shape. For example, you may ask a child to name a shape, and the child will answer with the name of a color.

By age two, many children can match a color to a sample. However, some three-, four-, or five-year-old children may not be able to match colors. This problem may be caused by color blindness. Color blindness can be discovered through careful observation of children as they try to learn colors. Children who are color-blind see shades of green and red as grayish brown. They may even see all colors as gray. If you notice that a child has a problem, report it to the center director. Often

Activity

Look over 23-5, *Supplies for Math Activities.* Have students survey the child care lab to determine which materials are already available. Make a list of the missing items and find out if any can be added through student and parent donations.

Resource

Mathematical Classroom Materials, reproducible master 23-1, TR

Enrich

Locate willing students or faculty who are color-blind and invite them to participate in a class activity to demonstrate this deficiency. Have the volunteers name the colors of selected items, especially those that are red and green, and observe the results.

Portfolio Project

Have each student create a file folder activity or game that incorporates color concepts suitable for a preschooler. Examples are: color matching of items; sorting of colored items; sequencing of colored shapes in varying sizes; and games in which the child advances to a certain color. Folders may be laminated or plastic coated for durability. They may contain pockets for items used in the activity such as shapes, buttons, magnets, cards, or pictures. Have students try out their project with a child in the child care lab and evaluate the results.

the director can discuss the problem with the child's parents. The parents can then decide if their child should be tested for color blindness.

Color concepts can be taught formally or informally. You can teach children to name colors using different-colored blocks. Hold up a blue block and ask for the name of the color. Continue by asking the children to point out other red objects around the room. Repeat these steps using the rest of the blocks.

Color recognition can also be taught at transition times. For instance, at the end of story time you may say, "All the children who are wearing blue may go to the bathroom." Repeat this, using different colors, until all the children have been excused.

Sorting objects by color can also be used to teach color concepts. Provide each child with a small bag containing several colors and shapes cut from poster board. The children can be directed to sort by color and then by shape.

Charts are another way to teach color concepts. Charts also teach children the usefulness of graphing. An example would be a chart labeled *Eye Colors*. Divide a piece of poster board into four even, vertical sections. Then divide the poster board into enough horizontal sections for every child in the class. Have each child in the class look at the chart and determine their eye color. If the children are able, encourage them to write their name under the color that matches their own eyes. See 23-7. If the children cannot write, give them pictures of themselves or round faces cut out of poster board. After all the children are done, ask "Which eye color is the least common?" Then ask "What eye color is the most common?"

Colored shapes can also be graphed on charts. For example, cut basic shapes from colored poster board. Using a felt-tip marker or pencil, divide the poster board into four equal horizontal sections. Next, divide the poster board vertically into five or six sections. Glue different shapes in each box in the first vertical column. See 23-8. Then give the children shapes to match.

Activity

Assign groups of students to design color day activities for preschoolers. An example of "Red Day" might include wearing red clothing to class; fingerpainting and play clay activities with red materials; reading *Clifford The Big Red Dog;* serving red apple slices, red peppers, and radishes with vegetable dip; and serving cherry juice for snack.

Resource

Color, Shape, and Counting Concepts, Activity B, SAG

Discuss

Why should color and shape concepts not be taught at the same time? How many attributes of items are young preschoolers able to recognize at a time?

23-7

Eye Colors

Brown	Blue	Green	Hazel
Pablo	Mark	Sandy	Cory
Sally	Chris	Reina	Rose
Shawnna	Pouneh		Ingrid
Tom			
Sung Jee			
Pedro			

This chart can be used to help children understand the concept of eye color.

A feely box or bag is useful for teaching color. Place colored buttons, paper, felt strips, or blocks into the box or bag. Have children draw an object from the bag and identify its color.

Color hunts in the classroom are a fun way to teach color concepts. To conduct a color hunt, ask a child to choose a color. Then

23-8

Draw the shape

This chart helps children learn to identify shapes. Children need to focus on the outlines before they can identify the shape.

Portfolio Project

Ask students to write an article for the preschool newsletter to describe the math curriculum of the child care lab. Even if math is not formally taught in the program, what activities contain elements that promote the understanding of math concepts? How do these activities relate to the overall program goals? What suggestions do students have for activities parents can do at home to promote their child's math knowledge? Select an article to print in the newsletter and make copies of all the articles for students to file in their portfolios.

have other children point out objects of the same color found in the classroom.

Discussion helps children learn to recognize colors. Have a child choose a color. Then ask the child what thoughts the color brings to mind. One child may choose red and say, "Red makes me think of fire trucks and valentines." Another child may choose blue and say, "Blue makes me think of the sky."

Other activities you can conduct to teach color concepts include the following:

- Hold up a piece of green construction paper. Ask children wearing green to stand up. Repeat using different colors each time. To add interest for four- and five-year-old children, give more complex directions. For instance, say "If you are wearing blue, stand on one foot."

- Pour all your crayons into a basket or box. Then set out several empty baskets or boxes—one for each color of crayon. Encourage the children to sort the crayons by color.

- Display several identically colored shapes on a flannel board. Then add one that is the same shape, but a different color. Ask the children "Which one does not belong?" This activity can also be done using different shapes.

- Play "I Spy" with a group of children. First, note a brightly colored classroom object. Then say "I spy something yellow." Encourage the children to take turns guessing what object you are thinking about. If they cannot guess it, give them more clues. The next game is started by the child who guesses correctly.

Shape Concepts

Children are often confused by shape. At first they will say circles and squares are the same figures because both have closed boundaries. Over time they will become aware of the features of the boundaries

themselves. Typically, roundness is the first shape-related concept that children learn.

The skills needed to identify and draw shapes do not develop at the same time. Children can most often name shapes before they can draw them. When copying shapes, circles are easiest for children, followed by squares, then rectangles and triangles. Most children cannot copy shapes other than circles until they are about four years of age. Before this, their copies have round corners and distances of uneven length.

To learn basic shape concepts, use a variety of activities that stress touching, holding, and matching of shapes. *Shape* is defined by what "goes around the outside," or the outline of the object, 23-9. To help the child grasp this concept of shape, have them trace around the outside of the shape.

Some teachers prefer to use **parquetry blocks** to teach shape concepts. These blocks are geometric pieces that vary in color and shape. When the children are familiar with the blocks, hold up a block and ask the children to find a block with a similar shape.

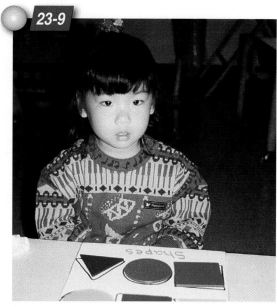

23-9

Children need to focus on the outlines of these shapes before they can identify them.

Discuss

How can long pieces of rope, string, yarn, or ribbon tied together at the ends be used to teach shape concepts to preschoolers? For what age of child would this be a safe learning activity?

Activity

Have students collect several 6-inch or larger plastic lids from food containers such as margarine tubs, whipped topping containers, and resealable ice cream containers. Use a sharp craft knife to cut out shapes in the lids. Children can use the lids with markers, crayons, and pencils to practice tracing skills and shape identification. These can also be used with paint as stencils.

Vocabulary

Have a student volunteer define the term *parquetry blocks*. What role can parquetry blocks play in teaching children shape concepts?

Workplace Connection

Have students design a snack or food preparation activity that incorporates shape recognition and identification. Investigate food items and recipes that might be used in this activity, such as crackers, cheese, bread, pancakes, muffins, French toast, thin-sliced meats, fruits, and vegetables. What utensils can children use safely for the activity? Which steps need to be completed by the teachers? How effective is a lesson that includes hands-on opportunities and a chance to eat the finished product? Have students write a brief report of their findings.

Vocabulary

Have a student volunteer define the terms *matching* and *sorting*. Why are both of these considered math activities?

Activity

Have students design an activity to promote understanding of the classification of magnetic and nonmagnetic. Collect several strong magnets and classroom items such as small plastic and wooden blocks, crayons, puzzle pieces, paper clips, scissors, and nails. Have students predict which items are magnetic or not before they test their predictions. Collect enough items so every child can have a turn.

Reflect

What early classification activities do you remember from your early years? Did they involve colors, shapes, animals, taste, temperature, and size?

Next, build a simple design with three or four blocks. Ask the children to copy it.

Other activities to encourage the identification of shape include the following:

- Cut geometric shapes out of one color of poster board. Ask the children to name and sort the shapes.

- Place a circle on a flannel board. Ask the children to name an object in the classroom of that shape. Repeat this activity using squares, rectangles, and triangles.

- Use jump ropes, masking tape, or chalk to make shapes on the floor. Ask children to name the shapes as they walk, march, or walk backwards over the figure.

- Give each child a shape cut out of poster board. Then have the children move around the classroom to find another child with the identical shape. This activity is most useful with four- and five-year-old children.

- Introduce a game called "It's in the Bag." The objective of this game is to help children name shapes by touch. Begin by placing a variety of poster board shapes or blocks in a paper bag. Hold up one shape and ask a child to find its match by feeling in the bag.

- Plan a treasure hunt. Instruct children to find shapes around the room. For example, a round clock can be pointed out as a circle.

Do not teach shape and color concepts at the same time. Wait until color concepts are well understood. Otherwise, some children may confuse color names with shape names.

Shape concepts are harder to teach than color concepts. Since color descriptions are used more often in everyday conversation, they may be easier for children to understand. For example, children often hear phrases such as a black puppy, yellow socks, red shirt, and green room.

Classification

Classification is the process of mentally sorting and grouping objects or ideas by a common attribute. Attribute examples include size, color, shape, pattern or function. This is one of the first skills displayed by young children. If the object belongs to a class, it has one or more features in common with another object. Classification allows people to cope with large numbers of objects.

Matching is a form of classification. It involves putting like objects together, 23-10. **Sorting** also involves classification. It is the process of physically separating objects based on unique features. **Sequencing** is the process of ordering real-life objects from shortest to tallest or tallest to shortest.

Children begin to learn classification skills in their first few weeks of life. By two months, children begin to classify experiences as pleasant or unpleasant. Eating applesauce may be pleasant. Sitting in an infant seat may be unpleasant.

Infants gather information to make classifications by using their senses through repeated experiences. This gives them the ability to relate past and present experiences.

23-10

The simplest matching activities involve putting two objects that are exactly alike together.

Workplace Connection

Have students interview high school, middle school, and elementary school math teachers for information on their jobs. What background and education is needed to be successful in this field? What are the state teacher certification requirements for math? What do they find most enjoyable and most challenging about their jobs? What is the effect of early childhood math experiences on the attitudes and motivation of students? How does this relate to the child's future success in math? Allow time for students to discuss their findings in class.

This process is known as **recognizing**. Recognizing is a simple form of classification.

First classroom experiences with classification should involve only one feature. Often this feature is color, size, or shape, 23-11. Provide items with obvious differences. For young children, this might include size, length, height, shape, color, or thickness.

Some useful classification tasks for young children include the following:

- Provide children with a set of black and red buttons. Have them sort the buttons into piles by color.

- Give children toys with and without wheels. Have them sort the toys into two piles based on whether or not they have wheels.

- Give children pictures of known and unknown objects cut from old magazines. Ask them to sort the pictures into "I don't know the name of" and "I know the name of" piles.

- Provide children with a bucket of household items. Fill the water table. Have them put the items in the water, then sort them into "float" and "sink" piles.

- Give children kitchen and bathroom items. Have them sort the items based on use.

As children build classification skills, increase the number of common features in the activities, 23-12. This can be done in two ways. Either increase the number of items to be classified, or increase the number of groups into which items can be sorted.

Advanced activities include classifying classroom items according to function. For example, some items are used for listening, some for talking, and some for writing. As another activity, give children a set of fabric squares. Ask the children to sort the materials into piles of striped, plaid, polka-dotted, and solid fabrics.

Notice that after children learn classification skills, they begin to watch and describe features of objects. First a child may say an apple is round and red. Later the child may classify it as good food. Finally the child may say the apple belongs to a group of foods known as "fruit."

Sets

Before children learn to add and subtract in elementary school, they need to understand sets. A **set** is a group of objects that are alike in some way and, therefore,

These blocks are designed to be classified by shape or color.

This child followed her teacher's pattern when placing the plastic shapes on the cord.

Vocabulary

Have a student volunteer define the term *recognizing*. Is recognizing the same as identifying?

Enrich

Have students work one-on-one with a preschool child in the child care lab to determine how many attributes they can name to describe a specific item in the classroom. As an example, ask the child to tell you one thing about a selected item, such as color. Then ask the child to name two things about another object, then three things, etc., until the child is no longer able to identify any more characteristics. Compare the results of each student's experience with the entire class.

Vocabulary

Have a student volunteer define the terms *set* and *empty set*. Why do children need to be able to understand the concept of sets before they can learn to add and subtract?

Putting Technology to Use/Meeting Special Needs

Ask gifted students to search for information on the teaching of math concepts to preschoolers. Some sources for information include: Constance Kamii, renowned professor of early childhood education; Jean Piaget, learning theorist; The High Scope Educational Research Foundation; and the National Council of Teachers of Mathematics among other sources. What is the NAEYC's position on this subject? What research-based studies are available? How can you apply what you have learned from this research to the child care lab program? Have students write an essay of their findings.

Vocabulary

Have student volunteers define the terms *one-to-one correspondence and rational counting.* How do these differ from rote counting?

Resource

Graphing, color transparency CT-20, TR

Activity

If snacks are served to the entire class at one time, have children practice a one-to-one correspondence by asking for help in setting the table. Ask a child to put one napkin on the table in front of each chair and count the napkins as he or she sets the table. Continue with spoons, cups, plates, etc.

Resource

Math Terms and Techniques, reproducible master 23-2, TR

belong together. Common features of a set may be color, shape, size, material, pattern, texture, name, or use.

A key objective of early math activities is to have children learn to organize objects. Objects belonging to a set are its members. A set can have a few or many members. A set of glasses is often a certain number, such as four or twelve. A set with no members is called an **empty set**.

In order to understand the concept of a set, children first need to learn about sets that have like members. This is best taught in small groups. Items needed are sets of objects having like members, such as puzzle pieces, blocks, crayons, and squares of colored paper. See 23-13. Introduce one set of objects at a time. Say "What are these? These are all blocks. We call them a set of blocks." Then introduce the remaining sets. Repeat the process. Stress the concept of set. To conclude the activity, ask "What are some other sets in the room?"

The concept of set can be strengthened by asking a small group of children to divide themselves into a set. First divide the children into sets of light- and dark-haired children. Encourage them to regroup themselves into different sets. They might divide by sex, age, color of eyes, or color of clothing.

23-13

Many common items can be used to teach the concept of *set.*

Teach the concept of an empty set during snack time. Provide each child with a plate holding a banana sliced into five pieces. Tell the children to eat one piece of banana. Explain that they now have a set of four banana pieces. Tell the children to eat another piece. Ask the children how many pieces remain. Tell them that is the number of members still in the set. Keep going until all the pieces are eaten. Then explain that a set without any members is called an empty set. To strengthen this lesson, ask the children to name other empty sets in the room. For example, the set of tables without legs or the set of children with beards are empty sets.

Counting

Counting is a basic math skill. It needs to be included in the curriculum because it is a key problem-solving tool. The foundation for understanding counting is called one-to-one correspondence. **One-to-one correspondence** is the understanding that one group has the same number as another. It is the most basic part of the concept of numbers.

Studies show that finger counting helps children develop mathematical understanding. Children love to count. They may start developing oral counting skills as early as two years of age. Two- and three-year-olds learn to count at least up to their ages. They count objects by pointing to them as they say the numbers one by one. Four- and five-year-olds can often count higher. These children touch an item each time they say a number. Sometimes they forget which items they have counted. They might skip several items or touch (count) an item more than once. Gradually they will learn the concept of **cardinality**. This means that the last number of the counting sequence tells how many objects exist in a set. This number will not change regardless of the order in which the objects are counted.

Children are often first exposed to counting by listening to adults count objects. In time, children repeat these counting words.

Meeting Special Needs

Special learners may benefit from a revised *Math Terms and Techniques,* reproducible master 23-2. Although a word bank has been provided, break down the assignment into two or three smaller groups of statements for the student who cannot handle the longer assignment all at once. Ask student volunteers to work with special learners to complete the activity. Spend additional time discussing any statements that are difficult for special learners to understand.

After they know the names of the numbers, they can later learn to identify written number words (two) and numerals (2).

The ability to count occurs in two stages: rote and rational counting. Rote counting is learned before rational. *Rote counting* is recitation of numbers in order. This skill involves memory, not understanding. **Rational counting** involves attaching a number to a series of grouped objects, 23-14. For example, a child has a box of crayons sitting on the table. If you ask the child for some crayons, he or she may place them on the table one at a time. As the child places each crayon, he or she assigns it a number in sequence.

Many children you teach will be able to recite numbers in their correct order. However, they will often not understand the meaning the numbers represent.

Three-year-old Tammy has typical number skills. The following activities illustrate her understanding:

- The teacher places seven pennies on the floor and asks Tammy to count them. She counts from one to nine before she touches the last penny.

- The teacher then arranges the pennies in a circle. Again she asks Tammy to count

them. She becomes confused several times and has to begin again.

- Next, the teacher places seven pennies in a pile and spreads out seven pennies more. When asked which pile has more pennies, Tammy points to the pennies that are spread out.

Children should always be exposed to rational counting using concrete objects. The simplest way to do this is through physical guidance. Use buttons, books, disks, table blocks, and crayons. Lay the objects in a straight line. Then model counting the objects for the child. After this, guide the child by taking his or her hand and touching each object as it is counted. At first, you may have to help the child count aloud.

After children have had many counting experiences, test their understanding. Send a child to get four crayons, two pieces of paper, or three blocks.

Identifying Numerals

In order to read and write, children must be able to recognize written numbers and their symbols. **Numerals** are the symbols that represent numbers. Each numeral represents a quantity. Numerals serve as shorthand for this quantity.

Children gain these recognition skills as they are continually exposed to numerals. Children see numerals at home, at school, and in the community. Numerals can be found in the grocery store, on signs, and on TV programs and commercials. They can also be seen on calculators, clocks, and watches.

A good activity for teaching number symbols is to have the children take part in a number walk. To do this, collect 10 sheets of 9-by-12-inch paper. Number the sheets from 1 to 10. (To increase the durability of these sheets, cover them with clear adhesive sheets.) Then place the papers in a circle on the floor at random. Play some familiar music and ask the children to walk through the path of numbered pieces. When you stop the

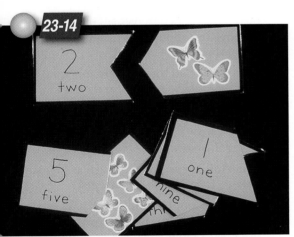

23-14

Rational counting involves attaching a number to a series of objects.

Reflect

Pamela's mother tells you her three-and-a-half-year-old child is quite advanced because she already knows her numbers and can count to twelve. However, when you ask Pamela to tell you how many blocks are on the table or to point out the number 8 on the class calendar, she is unable to answer correctly. How do you explain this to Pamela's mother?

Vocabulary

Have students define the term *numerals*. What examples of numerals can you see in this classroom?

Resource

Evaluating a Math Activity, Activity D, OG

Portfolio Project

Ask students to refer to 23-14 and construct a set of number cards similar to those pictured. What items, especially textural items, might be used to represent the numbers besides the stickers shown in the photo? Allow the child

care lab children to handle and use the cards throughout the year for math experiences. Divide the cards up at the end of the year so each child care student will have a variety of examples to file in his or her portfolio.

music, ask the children to tell the name of the number on which they are standing.

Another way to teach symbols is to set up a grocery store in a dramatic play area. Collect empty food containers and attach stickers with price tags from one to five cents. This activity can also include a toy store or drugstore. Look for numbers on measuring tools, calendars, books and puzzles.

A number line is yet another way to teach numbers. This teaching aid is based on units of length instead of objects. Make a calendar using a number line and refer to it daily during group time.

Children should have the opportunity to write numerals in their symbol form. Since children often find numerals hard to form, you may see many reversals. These problems are common and usually are self-correcting in time. You may be surprised to learn that children often prefer to write numbers over alphabet letters. Have children practice by writing in numerals on calendars or charts.

Space Concepts

Spatial relationships refers to the position of people and objects in space relative to each other. Describing the positions of objects in space is an important part of early math experiences. Space concepts that should be introduced are listed in 23-15. You should be aware that prepositions are abstract—they represent a location in space. To best learn the meanings of prepositions, children should be shown concrete examples. Since children's awareness of location and space grows out of their own bodies, have them move physically.

Space concepts can be taught during cleanup time, art time, blockbuilding, and other activities. Some experiences for teaching space concepts include the following:
- Play the game "Simon Says" using the words listed in 23-15. Give directions to the children, such as "Place your finger

23-15

Space Concepts

before, after
high, low
up, down
here, there
far, near
above, below
in front of, in back of, between, beside
inside, outside
top, center, bottom
first, middle, last

These word groups stress space concepts.

on top of your nose" and "Raise your right hand above your head." Using simple concepts often works well, even with two-and-a-half and three-year-old children. When using a new concept, you may have to model it for the children. You can also use an animal puppet, stuffed toy, or doll to lead the game. To get the children more involved, allow them to take turns using the puppet and giving directions.

- Place several pictures of fruit on a flannel board. Then ask, "Which piece of fruit is below the orange?" "Which piece of fruit is above the apple?" "Which piece of fruit is beside the grapes?"

- Give each child three different items, such as a block, a penny, and a button. Then give the children verbal directions using space words: "Place the penny on top of the block." "Place the button under the block."

- Use familiar circle games such as "Hokey Pokey" to teach space concepts.

- Stack five familiar items, such as a penny, stick, rock, clothespin, and puzzle piece, on a table. Then ask the children questions about the items: "What item

Reflect

How do you know that you have enough room to park your car when you see a parking space? How do you know if the leftovers from a meal will fit in the storage container you have selected?

Resource

Teaching Space, Size, Volume, and Time, Activity C, SAG

Discuss

Why is the teacher's enthusiasm and support important when conducting repetitious activities with the children? How could a teacher's attitude affect the success of the activity?

Resource

Planning a Math Activity, Activity E, OG

Service Learning Activity

Conduct a canned food drive for the local food pantry. Have students compose a letter to the preschool parents asking for cooperation and explaining how the drive will give children a chance to learn math concepts. As the canned foods arrive, have children count and sort them according to size or type of food. Students should create charts to indicate the progress of the drive. Place all the cans in a line and have children measure the length of the line. Have students brainstorm additional ways the food drive can be used to teach math concepts.

is at the top?" "What item is at the bottom?" "What item is in the middle?" A stack of colored blocks or puzzle pieces can also be used to teach the concepts of top, bottom, and center.

Remember that children need frequent review to maintain any skill. Unlike adults, children do not tire easily from repetitive experiences. Your enthusiasm and support is important.

Size Concepts

Children develop size concepts only through experience. Introduce and stress the words listed in 23-16 to teach children about size. These words can be used throughout the day.

Volume Concepts

An early childhood program should offer many opportunities to explore volume. Sand tables and water tables are useful for this task. Provide many containers of varying volumes and shapes for measuring. During the children's play with these materials, introduce volume concepts such as empty, full, little, much, a lot, and some. When children use these concepts, they think about their world in terms of quantity.

Time Concepts

"Is yesterday Christmas?" Molly, a four-year-old, asked one of the other children. Molly's question is common of a young child. Time is a difficult concept for children to understand, partly because *time* can stand for so many situations. Past, present, future, and soon are all examples of time concepts. Others include hours, days, tomorrow, yesterday, and today.

Studies suggest that young children have only a vague concept of time. In fact, the average five-year-old child knows only the difference between afternoon and morning, and night and day. Children usually cannot read the time on a watch or clock until about age seven.

23-16

Size Concepts

big, little
large, small
long/tall, short
wide, thin
big, bigger, biggest
small, smaller, smallest
inches, feet, pounds
smaller than, bigger than
thick, thin
high, low
large, larger
longer, taller, shorter

Use of proper terms, along with visual aids, will help children grasp the size concepts.

Activity

Have students provide children with clear containers and liquids or dry materials to pour into the containers. Ask children to show their understanding of *empty, full, little, much, a lot,* and *some* by using these materials while the child care students observe and document which students successfully complete the tasks.

Enrich

Ask students to debate the pros and cons of teaching children to tell time using a standard clock with numerals and hands versus using a digital clock with only numerals. How can children understand a sense of time passing if they cannot see the number of minutes between numbers as they would on a standard clock?

Activity

Ask students to survey the preschoolers in the child care lab program to determine their understanding of time concepts. Have students work with a child one-on-one as they ask questions using time concepts and document the results in the child's portfolio.

Workplace Connection

Divide students into small groups to create posters to decorate the child care lab while teaching the size concepts listed in 23-16. Students should use simple drawings or graphics to illustrate each concept. Posters may be laminated for durability. Ask students to brainstorm ideas to depict concepts that may be difficult to show in a concrete method such as a poster.

Activity

Have students design an activity using a kitchen timer to help children understand the time concept of minutes. Find examples of songs or music that lasts only a minute or two and play them for the children. Have the children decide which song was longer. These songs could also be used for transition time. If used consistently, the children will eventually learn how much time they have left before the next activity.

Enrich

Ask students to locate rhymes or songs that incorporate concepts such as *night and day*, *hot and cold*, and *summer or fall*, or have students compose suitable songs or poems using math concepts. Have students teach these to the preschoolers.

Resource

Using Recipes to Teach Math Concepts, Activity D, SAG

You can use routines to teach time concepts to young children. For example, you might say the following: "After lunch, we take naps." "Your mother will come to pick you up after outdoor playtime." "Before large group time, we need to put our toys away." You can offer time experiences to children by using the correct time words. Include the words such as those listed in 23-17.

Children should also learn about the passing of time. For example, you may ask "Do you remember the clown that came to school?" or "How did we make the play dough last time?"

There are many activities for teaching children time concepts. Included are the following:

- Provide children with a large, month-long calendar. Use the calendar each day during a large group activity. Review the days of the week and use such words as *yesterday*, *tomorrow*, *last week*, and *next week*.

- Encourage children to play with a toy alarm clock.

- Hang a large classroom clock at the children's eye level.

- Use a cooking timer during cooking experiences. Some teachers also use a cooking timer to give children a warning before they change activities. For example, the teacher may set the timer and say "In five minutes, it will be time to clean up."

- Provide time-recording equipment, such as a stopwatch, an alarm clock, a wristwatch, and an hourglass. Place these items on a table where children will feel free to explore them.

Temperature Concepts

Cooking and outdoor activities help introduce temperature concepts. (Ideas for cooking activities are given in Chapter 25.) To teach these concepts, include such words as *thermometer*, *hot*, *cold*, *warm*, and *cool*.

Using Math Books

Children's literature has gradually become an important strategy for teaching math concepts to young children. Books enhance children's natural interest and curiosity about math. Books also help children see numbers in many contexts. They are a meaningful tool for exploring, thinking, and exchanging math concepts. Chart 23-18 lists books that can be used in the classroom for teaching math concepts.

23-17

Time Concepts

day, night
before, after
minute, second
now, later
morning, afternoon, evening
yesterday, today, tomorrow
early, late
spring, summer, autumn, winter
new, old

Use terms such as these to describe time. This reinforcement will help children understand time concepts.

23-18

Books for Teaching Math

Corduroy by Don Freeman
I Know an Old Lady Who Swallowed a Pie by Allison Jackson
Inch by Inch by Leo Lionni
Make Way for Ducklings by Robert McCloskey
Peter's Chair by Ezra Jack Keats

These books can help teach children math concepts as well as entertain them.

Meeting Special Needs

Review the special learners' chapter outlines to determine if the students have any questions about the concepts or content of this chapter. Review the chapter objectives and ask the students to evaluate their progress in meeting these objectives. Ask the students to summarize, orally or in writing, what they learned from this chapter.

Summary

With high-quality opportunities to play, explore, and learn, children's understanding of math concepts will grow. The teacher's role is to provide a rich environment that fosters learning. Teachers also need to provide the children with time for demonstrations, explanations, support, and open-ended questioning.

Math experiences in the early childhood setting should stress exploration, discovery, and understanding and encourage a life-long interest. Young children require these broad, basic experiences. With such a foundation, they can build more advanced mathematical thinking skills as they get older.

Teachers can find many ways to integrate math learnings in the classroom. For younger children, math experiences can be informal in nature. Many daily events and routines lend themselves to informal math experiences. Play experiences can also be a setting for promoting mathematical thinking in young children.

Review and Reflect

1. List four objectives of early math experiences.

2. Name and describe the two common forms of assessment used to determine math abilities.

3. True or false. Math materials and equipment should consist of only traditional items such as an abacus and flash cards.

4. Why is color considered a math concept?

5. What is the first shape-related concept that children recognize?

6. _____ defines "what goes around the outside."

7. Is it a good idea to teach shape and color concepts at the same time? Why or why not?

8. _____ is the process of mentally sorting and grouping objects or ideas by a common attribute.

9. What is the difference between sorting and matching?

10. A _____ is a group of objects that are alike in some way, and, therefore, belong together.

11. _____ is a difficult concept for children to develop because the word represents the past, present, and future.

12. List three vocabulary words that can be used to teach temperature concepts.

5. roundness
6. Shape
7. No, because children may confuse color names with shape names.
8. Classification
9. Matching involves putting objects together that are the same. Sorting is the process of separating objects into categories based on a unique feature.
10. set
11. Time
12. (Answers will vary but may include *thermometer, hot, cold, warm, cool.*)

Review and Reflect **Answer Key**

1. (List four:) observing and describing concrete objects; recognizing colors, patterns, and attributes; comparing objects and using terms that describe quantity; classifying sets of objects; copying patterns; recognizing shape concepts; recognizing and writing numerals; using logical words; using one-to-one correspondence; estimating quantity and measurement; developing problem-solving skills

2. observation, specific task assessment (Student response for descriptions.)

3. false

4. because color helps children learn to discriminate between objects

Apply and Explore

1. Review a school equipment catalog and list any equipment that can be used to teach space concepts.

2. Discuss methods to use to help young children understand size concepts.

3. Make a list of activities parents or guardians can use to teach counting.

4. Discuss activities that could be used to teach children the concept of a set.

Cross-Curricular Link

Science

1. Find a recipe that could be used for a cooking activity to teach temperature concepts.

Reading

2. Research and compile a bibliography of children's storybooks that include mathematics.

Technology

3. Use the Web site for Super Kids Educational Software Review, www.superkids.com, to read reviews of educational software for teaching math to young children.

Workplace Link

Look for examples of numerals that already exist in the child care lab, such as room numbers, clocks, thermometers, number charts, puzzles, and birthday or height charts. Are the numerals consistent in style on both commercial and student- or teacher-prepared items? Do you notice any differences, particularly in the numbers one, two, and four? What effect will the different styles or types have on children who are attempting to learn to recognize numerals?

24

Guiding Science Experiences

Discuss

Look at the chapter opening photo. What science concepts can these children learn from water activities? What is the teacher's role in guiding these activities?

Discuss

Look over the objectives for this chapter. Why do you feel teaching science concepts is important in early childhood education?

After studying this chapter, you will be able to

- explain what is meant by the term *science*.
- discuss reasons for studying science.
- outline the procedure for planning science activities.
- list a variety of science activities and sources for supplies.
- explain the role of the teacher in guiding science experiences.
- identify methods for developing children's understanding of their senses.
- name and explain various ways to teach science concepts.

451

Vocabulary

Have students review the *Terms to Know* list. Ask students to look up unfamiliar words or terms in the glossary before reading the chapter.

Discuss

How are each of the following terms related to the study of science: *observing, exploring, measuring, comparing, classifying, predicting,* and *discovering*? Give an example of a preschool science activity for each term.

Vocabulary

Have a student volunteer define the term *science*. Why should early childhood science experiences involve a hands-on approach?

Resource

Science Processing Skills, color transparency CT-21, TR

Terms to Know

science
science table
open-ended questions
closed-ended questions
feely box

Two-year-old Ricardo's first contact with a butterfly was accidental. His study of the bug was brief but intense. It involved mainly his senses of sight and touch. Quickly he picked the butterfly up and said, "What's dat?" His mother replied, "It's a butterfly." This experience opened the world of natural science to Ricardo. Later, whenever he saw a butterfly or a moth, he repeated his new word, "butterfly."

Science is everywhere. Much of what children learn relates to science concepts. Their first learnings are often simple but meaningful. You can help form children's science concepts through science experiences. Encouraging children's curiosity about science during normal classroom routines will help them develop respect for their environment, too.

What Is Science?

Science is the study of natural processes and their products. It is a way of viewing the universe. In order for children to understand their world, they must explore and question. As children explore, they actively learn. For this reason, early childhood experiences should use the hands-on approach for both process and products. This approach allows children to be involved in and think about the sights, sounds, and smells of their environment. Your role as a teacher is to provide a rich, inviting and supportive environment filled with

hands-on activities. Children need experiences with materials, ideas, and events.

Science is a creative field of study. It requires the development of curiosity and imagination. As children watch, study, wonder, or question, they learn about science.

Science is a way to gain understanding of why events happen the way they do. Studying science inspires children to be aware of, and involved with, their surroundings. The answers to such questions as *How will it change?* and *What will happen if…?* can be found. As children try to make sense of what is happening, they are building theories.

Science involves observing, exploring, measuring, comparing, classifying, predicting, and making thrilling discoveries. The focus for young children should be on observing and exploring, 24-1. Young children are good at those tasks because they see the world from a fresh point of view. They have no preset ideas of how the world and nature work.

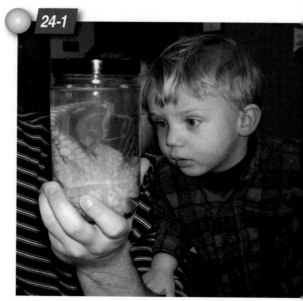

24-1

This child is learning to observe and explore as he views the octopus in the jar.

Meeting Special Needs

Provide an outline of the chapter with all the chapter headings for special learners. Students should fill in each section of the outline as the material is covered in class with a sentence or two about the content. Review the special learners' IEPs to decide if any modifications should be made in presenting the chapter content.

All attempts to gain information about our surroundings begin with observation. By using their senses, children begin to observe relationships between events. They start to group information and make generalizations.

Why Study Science?

Studies show science activities enhance the curiosity of children, 24-2. Children also build skill in picking out similarities and differences. Vocabulary growth is supported. Children improve their language skills and general knowledge as concepts such as *round*, *triangular*, *big*, and *small* are discussed. This promotes reading readiness skills.

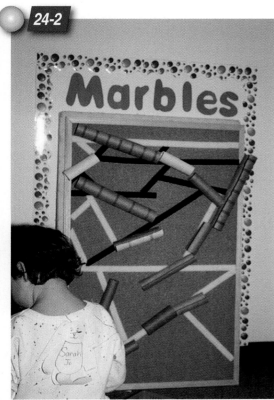

24-2

Developing a marble bulletin board that illustrates the concept of gravity enhances the curiosity of young children.

Fine-motor and hand-eye coordination improve as children measure items, collect samples, and handle objects. By weighing and counting items, math skills are also enhanced.

Planning Science Activities

Some of the most successful science experiences will be unplanned. For instance, you might bring in a flower you found on the way to the center. This can be the starting point to a discussion of flowers. As an ant moves across the floor, you can watch, study, and discuss it. If the wind rises suddenly, blowing debris around the play yard, you can discuss the wind.

Science can be found in every area of the curriculum. However, most science experiences need to be planned. Focusing on a theme helps children learn about their world by structuring and organizing information. You will need to schedule events, prepare materials, and arrange the science area. You will find that science activities mesh well with an integrated curriculum. You may plan a food or sensory activity that teaches a science concept. Fingerplays, stories, field trips, math activities, physical activity, and art projects can all teach science concepts.

Give children time to play with, examine, and try the science materials and equipment, 24-3. Science activities should offer children the chance to

- observe and explore
- note differences and likenesses
- make predictions and solve problems
- build theories to explain what they see
- collect samples
- develop new interests and skills
- listen to sounds
- view videos

Discuss

What is the relationship between science and the development of language skills? How might science experiences improve a child's fine-motor skills and hand-eye coordination? How are science and the development of math skills related?

Reflect

What early childhood science experiences did you most enjoy? Were the science experiences planned or unplanned? Have student volunteers share their experiences with the class.

Resource

Science Activities, transparency master 24-1, TR

Cross-Curricular Activity

Science
Have students conduct an Internet search for information on the science curriculum used in the Montessori Approach. What areas of science are studied in Montessori schools? What materials or equipment are used in the classroom to promote and encourage scientific thought? What suggestions do you have for the child care lab science center as a result of your research on the Montessori science curriculum? Have students write a one-page report of their findings.

Discuss

Why is the science area best located near a kitchen? What are some ways in which an outdoor science area may be used? Give some examples of science concepts children might learn from using the outdoor science area.

Vocabulary

Have a student volunteer define the term *science table*. What types of seasonal items would you suggest be placed on the science table during the month of September? April?

Reflect

How can playground equipment be used to teach science concepts? What science concepts did you learn as a child from using playground equipment?

24-3

Having the chance to play with, examine, and use science equipment will promote children's growth in science knowledge.

- look at books
- collect pictures

Science Area

The science area is often set apart from other classroom areas. Tables, shelves, and/or storage cabinets can be used. The science area is best located near a kitchen. This allows access to both heat and water sources, which are quite important for many science projects.

An outdoor science area may also be used. This area may contain a garden space and an area for conducting weather tests. Small animals, such as rabbits and birds, may be raised. Store garden tools, insect nets, and water tubes in an outdoor shed to encourage children to use the outdoor area.

Equipment and Materials

Equipment and materials for a science area need not be costly. Most items can be obtained at little or no cost. Two factors must be given some thought during the selection process. First consider the safety of the item.

Then decide whether the children have the skills needed to use it. See Chart 24-4.

Many child care centers have a **science table**, 24-5. This table is used to display science-related items. The teacher often obtains the items to be placed on the table. Whenever possible, the science table should have a focus. The collection of items should provide direction for advancing the children's learning. A group of plastic reptiles may be placed on the science table. Resource books showing pictures of the reptiles should also be placed on the table next to the reptile. This will allow the children to compare the model reptiles with those in the book. Finally, concept-related literature books should be included on the table. Children can also be encouraged to bring their own items for the table. Collections children often enjoy adding include leaves, nuts, rocks, insects, nests, cocoons, and seeds.

Children should feel motivated to explore the science table on their own. Therefore, the material on the science table should be changed often. If collections remain on the table too long, children become bored and lose interest. It also helps to house collections in an appealing way. You might display items in a tent, store setting, cave setting, booth, trailer, push cart, or wagon.

The science table should sit away from walls. This allows children to move about the table freely. They will feel comfortable touching, smelling, hearing, and observing as they explore.

Centerpieces at the snack or lunch table also promote children's interest in nature. A bowl of pinecones or gourds or a bouquet of flowers brings the world of science indoors. They also promote discussion during mealtime.

Playground equipment can be used to teach science concepts. For example, pedaling a bike makes the energy needed to move a bike. Using a teeter-totter demonstrates the laws of balance.

Putting Technology to Use

Ask students to conduct an Internet search to locate sources for science equipment and supplies for preschool and child care programs. Select several items that would meet the child care lab program goals for science. Have students write a brief description of the concepts children would learn from using the items. Explain how the goals will be met. Ask students to create a "wish list" of items they propose be added to the child care lab. Allow time for students to share their findings with the class.

24-4

Science Supplies

School supplies		
	globes	construction paper
	paints	chart paper
	clay	scissors
	chalk	paste or glue
	markers	string
	straws	blocks
	colored paper	

Scrap items		
	pocket mirrors	flashlights
	large spoons	watering cans
	clocks and watches	airplane and automobile parts
	sawdust	funnels
	locks and keys	wood scraps
	metal scraps	cameras

Classroom pets		
	hamsters	aquariums
	harmless snakes	spiders
	frogs	fish
	birds	mice
	rabbits	guinea pigs
	animal homes	gerbils
	cages	

Nature items		
	stones	pinecones
	snails	leaves
	rocks	plant bulbs
	shells	seeds
	soil	birdfeeders
	sand	windsocks
	logs	flowers

Tools		
	hammers	vice
	nails	pliers
	rulers	levers
	saws	ramps
	screwdriver	pulleys
	screws	wheels
	bolts	magnets
	air pumps	magnifying glass
	trowels	thermometer

Household items		
	jars	cloth pieces
	strainers	cardboard tubes
	food coloring	flashlights
	salt	scales
	sugar	measuring cups and spoons
	spoons	pots and pans
	corks	empty containers and trays
	tongs	

Materials and equipment that can be used in science experiences are nearly endless.

Resource

Science Equipment and Supplies, Activity A, OG

Enrich

Ask students to design a lesson plan for a circle activity involving science-related items children may bring from home for show and tell. What guidelines should be followed? What suggestions should be made to parents to help their child present his or her items?

Resource

Sources of Science Supplies and Equipment, reproducible master 24-2, TR

Workplace Connection

Ask students to review Chart 24-4, *Science Supplies.* Have students survey the child care lab to determine what equipment and materials are already available. Ask each child care student to bring a small item from home to be donated to the science center in the child care lab. Have students design a science activity for the children using one of the items. How effective was the activity? What did the children learn from the activity? Compare the results of each student's experience with the entire class.

Reflect

How many of the five basic process skills did you already use today? What typical daily activities might a preschooler experience using the same process skills?

Vocabulary

Have a student volunteer define the terms *open-ended* and *closed-ended questions*. What is the role of questioning in developing cognitive skills? Ask student volunteers to give examples of open-ended and closed-ended questions.

Resource

Science Overview, Activity A, SAG

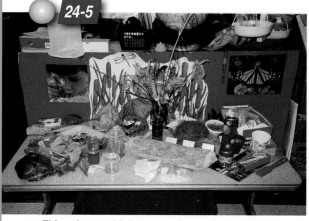

24-5

This science table has many interesting items for children to explore.

Role of the Teacher

As a teacher, your role is to offer space, materials, and activities that encourage discovery. For safety reasons, you must provide constant supervision. You also want to learn when to let children work alone and when to step in, 24-6. At times, a simple suggestion can help a child who is frustrated. On the other hand, unneeded input can sometimes stifle curiosity. This can destroy the desire to keep experimenting.

The activities you plan should include materials for all children. Children should have ample hands-on activities in which they work with materials. This process allows children to discuss relationships and concepts among themselves.

Activities should promote development of the following five basic process skills:

- observing objects using the five senses

- drawing conclusions from observations based on past experience

- classifying objects into sets based on one or more observable properties

- comparing sets of objects by measuring and counting

- communicating by describing objects, relationships, and occurrences

Provide many chances for children to practice observing. Children enjoy watching and wondering. Going on field trips, viewing filmstrips, looking at pictures, and viewing objects on the science table are all good ways to help children build on powers of observation.

To encourage children to explore, use effective questioning techniques. Asking numerous questions is not always a useful technique. Instead, ask fewer questions that require more thought. **Open-ended questions** promote discussion and require decision-making skills. **Closed-ended questions** (sometimes called *single-answer questions*) demand few decision-making skills and are most often answered with *yes* or *no*. See 24-7. Poor questioning techniques encourage children to guess.

Children need time to answer open-ended questions. Positive response should be

24-6

Teachers direct science experiences, but they must also know when to step back and let children do for themselves.

Meeting Special Needs

Special learners may benefit from a revised *Science Overview*, Activity A, SAG. Break down the assignment into two or three smaller groups of questions for the student who cannot handle the longer assignment all at once. Ask student volunteers to work with special learners to complete the activity. Spend additional time reviewing and discussing any areas that are difficult for special learners to understand.

24-7

Open-Ended and Closed-Ended Questions

Open-Ended	Closed-Ended
What are you observing?	What color is it?
How could you classify these?	Can you classify these by shape?
What happens to hamburger when it is fried?	Has the hamburger changed color?

Can you think of other pairs of open-ended and close-ended questions?

given to all answers. When a better answer is offered, explain how it adds to other answers. Children also need to be heard. Being listened to strengthens a child's wish to participate.

The teacher generally sets the tone for learning science in the classroom. A simple rule is to base activities on children's questioning. Do not give answers to questions children have not asked. Let the children use process skills as well as listen, watch, or read about science. Teachers who control the activity do little to promote questions. To create the right climate, provide material for all children, study their interaction with the materials, and listen to them talk to each other. Finally, ask only those questions that add to the child's knowledge. Chart 24-8 includes questions to ask to encourage children's thinking.

Developing the Child's Understanding of Senses

As children learn more about their senses, they become aware of how to explain their surroundings. Help children learn to focus on how they use their senses by peeling an orange. During the experience, children can see and smell the orange. After it is peeled, they can feel it and taste it. By peeling an orange, children can learn the following concepts: we see with our eyes; we smell with our noses; we feel with our skin; and we taste with our tongues.

Feeling

Feeling is a fun and important sense to explore through science activities. Whenever time permits, provide opportunities to feel a number of objects in the classroom. A **feely box** can be made by cutting a circle in a box large enough for the children to put their hands in.

24-8

Questions to Encourage Thought

What will happen if…?
What can you tell me?
What is happening?
How do you know?
How can we find out?
How are these alike?
How are these different?
Why isn't this working?
How can it be put together?

Why do you think these questions would be stimulating for children?

Discuss

Ramon asks a question of the preschoolers while presenting a science lesson. When no one answers the question, Ramon gives the answer. What suggestions do you have for Ramon to encourage the children to use their thinking skills?

Resource

Forming Open-Ended Questions, Activity B, SAG

Discuss

What factors might contribute to an unsuccessful science lesson or activity? What factors should students consider to ensure a successful activity? How do you know if the science activity was a success?

Cross-Curricular Activity

Science

Contact the biology, chemistry, physics, earth science, or other science teachers in your school. Determine the possibility of creating mini science lessons suitable for the preschoolers. Determine if students in any of the science classes would be willing to work with the child care students to present the lessons. Enlist the advice of the teachers to adapt the lessons to the correct level. Discover the possibility of using science lab equipment or resources if available and appropriate. Make sure students include hands-on opportunities when presenting the lessons to the preschoolers.

Discuss

How is the recognition of smells related to memory skills? Have students give examples of smells associated with specific memories from their childhood as well as from today.

Activity

Ask students to collect five small jars with tight-fitting lids and fill each with one of the following: water, vegetable oil, liquid dish detergent or shampoo, corn syrup, thick hair gel. Have children in the child care lab observe the viscosity or density of each and ask them to arrange the jars in order from thinnest to thickest viscosity. Have students number the jars on the bottom so children can check after they arrange the jars.

Enrich

Ask students to brainstorm a list of sounds associated with safety, and those related to keeping individuals organized and aware of their surroundings. Would preschoolers be aware of the meanings of all the sounds on the list? Examples: car horns, railroad signals, sirens, alarm clocks, and planes flying overhead.

(A feely bag can also be used. It should be opaque and easy to reach into without exposing the contents.) Put different objects and materials inside the box. Let each child reach in the box and try to identify an object. If they are unable to respond, provide clues. For example, if the item is a spoon, you may say "It is something we use to eat cereal with in the morning."

Children can also build the sense of touch using fabric samples of varying textures. These may include velvet, leather, flannel, knit, burlap, felt, and cotton. Encourage the children to explain what each piece feels like. You might add other materials such as pinecones, bark, leaves, fake fur, sandpaper, glazed paper, sponge, pebbles, and cork. To add variety, place the materials on the science table where the children can sort them based on like textures.

Smelling

Preschool children need to learn that objects can be named by their smells. One method for teaching this is to collect items in the classroom that have distinct odors, such as tempera paint, markers, crayons, play dough, bar soap, sawdust, and gerbil food. Place a small amount of each item in a container such as a small paper cup. Explain to the children that the game you will be playing involves naming items by smell.

Food can also be used in the smelling activity. For example, place ketchup, mustard, applesauce, chocolate syrup, orange juice, and other common foods in containers and repeat the same steps.

Seeing

Experience using sight is just as important as smelling. One game to use is "I Spy." For example, you may say "I spy something green. It is small and round. It is in the art area." After you speak, pause to allow the children to guess. If the children are not able to guess, provide more clues.

An activity that helps children build visual memory skills is naming what is missing from a group. Use this activity for one child or small groups of children. Collect common classroom objects such as crayons, blocks, puzzle pieces, paintbrushes, and toy cans. Gather the children, show them the objects, and explain that you will remove one object. Instruct the children to close or cover their eyes. Remove one object, then have them open their eyes and tell you what object is missing.

There are many variations to this game. You may increase the number of objects. You might place three or four objects in a sequence and ask which objects are out of sequence. You may remove two or three objects from the group and have the children name what is missing.

Hearing

Hearing is another sense that helps children understand and explain their environment. To help children become more aware of this sense, use a tape recorder.

Teach the concept that each person's voice sounds different from any other. Record the voice of each child. To encourage the children to talk, ask each child to tell you about a family member, a favorite person, or a story. After you have taped all the children in the classroom, play the tape to the group. Ask the children to identify each child's voice by name.

Tasting

Tasting skills can be built through the use of food. Plan a tasting party using a number of common foods. Blindfold a child and give him or her a small sample of some food. Ask the child to name the food. Repeat the activity with all the children in the group. Some teachers prefer to do this as a group activity, providing a sample of each food for all the children at the same time.

Portfolio Project

Ask students to use a digital camera to take photos of familiar items such as flowers, leaves, trees, pine cones, houses, and cars. Have students upload the photos to the computer. Select areas of the pictures to enlarge, and crop the picture to print only the enlarged area. Make a booklet of the enlarged pictures, placing an overlay sheet with a small cutout on top of each picture. Ask children to identify the picture by looking at only the area of the small cutout, and then turn the page to see if they are correct. Students may want to incorporate the original photos into the booklet for reference.

Using Color to Teach Science Concepts

Color is a part of science that children observe daily. Naming colors is one way children describe their world. Color also serves as a basis for grouping. The primary colors, red, blue, and yellow, can be introduced to the children in the science area. Encourage the children to match red, blue, and yellow toys, such as beads or blocks, with similarly colored boxes. The secondary colors, purple, green, and orange, can be introduced next. Again, using toys, have the children match the color of the toy to the container.

Some teachers have special color days. For example, Monday may be orange day. To prepare for this day, send a note or letter to parents or guardians. Ask that children wear the color of the day. This may be in the form of a hair ribbon, pin, barrette, or any article of clothing. You may also use a nature walk to observe colors, 24-9. Snacks may be coordinated with the color of the day. For example, orange slices, carrots, or cantaloupe may be served on an orange day.

Mixing colors is another way to teach color concepts. By mixing primary colors to make secondary colors, the children learn how colors are made. Thus, as children learn color concepts, they become aware of their surroundings. One way to show mixing of colors is to overlap colored cellophane. Another way is to set up jars or clear plastic glasses in the science area. Have the children fill the jars with water. Using food coloring, place drops in each container. Stress color comparisons by using terms such as *lighter than*, *darker than*, or *same color as*.

Using Water to Teach Science Concepts

Water delights almost all children. As young children play with water and accessories, they learn about science concepts by trying to make sense of what happens. Some concepts taught with water include the following:

- Water flows when poured.
- Water dissolves some foods.
- Water takes many forms.
- Water makes objects wet.
- Water can be held in a container.
- Some items float on water.
- Some materials absorb water.
- Frozen water is called ice.

Equipment and Accessories

In programs without water tables, large washtubs, sinks, photographic developing trays, or plastic swimming pools can be used. A table can also be made, 24-10. Supply water table accessories. Include funnels, spoons, sprinkling cans, nesting cups, plastic containers, egg beaters, measuring cups, strainers, corks, sponges, plastic tubing, soap, and food coloring.

24-9

Nature walks are a good time to observe colors, such as the many colors of leaves.

Reflect

How is color a concept in art, math, and science? Have students suggest several examples of lessons or activities that incorporate these three areas.

Note

Whenever children will be using food coloring, have them rub a small amount of mineral or baby oil on their hands first to keep the food coloring from being absorbed in their skin and make cleanup easier.

Discuss

If a child care program does not have a water table, what items could be used instead? (Examples: sinks, washtubs, or plastic swimming pools.) What accessories should be included with a water table?

Workplace Connection

Ask students to make red, yellow, and green play dough using the recipes in Chapter 19 on page 378. Have students use the play dough in the child care lab for a color activity that also incorporates science concepts. Have students observe children as they add strawberry gelatin to red play dough, lemon flavoring to yellow play dough, and mint flavoring to green play dough. Can children match the scents to the color? Allow time for students to discuss their observations in class.

Activity

Collect empty plastic water bottles and have students brainstorm ways to use them to teach water concepts. Suggestions may include filling them with colored water and oil to shake and observe separation; filling with liquids and other objects that may sink or float in the liquid; making "ecology bottles;" etc.

Enrich

Invite a science teacher to speak to the class about different types of water activities and the science concepts that are taught through them. If possible, ask the teacher to give demonstrations. Have students write a list of questions to ask prior to the visit.

Resource

Science Literature, Activity B, OG

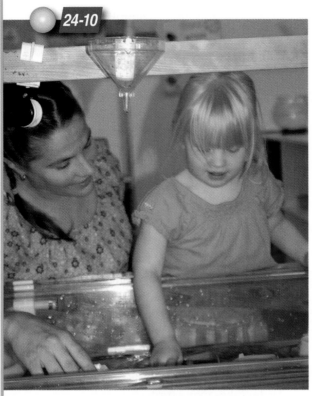

This water table is transparent allowing children to observe the contents.

To avoid excessive cleanup, put down a shower curtain or plastic tablecloth to protect the floor. Plastic aprons may be used to protect the children's clothes.

Fill the container with water based on the children's experience and age. (Younger children only need two or three inches.) Provide the children with accessories and allow them to experiment freely.

Activities

Freeze water for the children. From this, the children will learn that
- ice is frozen water
- ice can melt

- melted ice is water
- ice can be picked up
- ice melts in warm places

Teach the children that some materials absorb water. Use sponges, terry cloth, tissues, paper towels, cardboard, plastic wrap, waxed paper, newsprint, finger paint, and plastic. You may wish to make a chart listing the materials and noting whether they absorb water. From using these materials, children should learn that some materials soak up water.

Water can teach children about floating. Fill the water table half full. Provide items such as wooden blocks, pencils, paper, plastic alphabet letters, metal spoons, and aluminum foil. Record each item that floats on a chart. Children will learn that some items float on water.

Through observation and participation, children can also learn what materials dissolve in water. Fill several small pitchers with water. Then have each child fill several baby food jars or plastic glasses. Give each child a material that dissolves in water, such as salt, sugar cubes, or baking soda. Also supply items that will not dissolve, such as cooking oil, rice, or margarine. Then let each child stir the mixture. Ask the children "What happens when you add (salt, rice, etc.) to water?" Encourage the children to discuss the results as each item is added to the water.

Painting with water is an activity best suited to the outdoors. Provide the children with cans of water and wide paintbrushes. Select a cement area that will not be used for walking to avoid accidents. Have the children paint surfaces such as a cement sidewalk. Then ask them what happens to the water. Try this in different types of weather. Children will see that on hot days the water evaporates and on cold days it freezes.

Workplace Connection

Ask students to conduct the following experiment in the child care lab. Provide children with Styrofoam, plastic, metal, and paper cups; ice cubes; and a variety of wraps and paper such as wax paper, aluminum foil, bubble wrap, freezer paper, or plastic wrap. Let each child wrap an ice cube in selected material(s) and place it in the cup of their choice. Have children describe the results of their choices 30 minutes later as they examine the condition of their ice cube. Allow time for students to discuss their observations in class.

Using Foods to Teach Science Concepts

Science experiments that can be eaten are both fun and educational. By watching foods as they cook, children learn how solid materials can change. Some foods become softer and some firmer as they are heated. Heat may also change the color and blend the flavors of foods. Many guidelines for using foods in classroom experiences are given in Chapter 26.

Baking bread is a science project that involves both a process and a product. In order to have baked bread, a process must be followed. This process involves

- reading the recipe
- collecting all the ingredients, pans, and utensils
- mixing the correct amounts of ingredients

Cooking Safety

When cooking foods with children, keep their safety and developmental levels in mind. If cooking activities take place in the kitchen, preschool and school-age children *must* be supervised at all times according to federal guidelines. Infants and toddlers are never allowed in the child care kitchen. Limit cooking experiences for these children to things that can be made in the dining area.

- setting the correct oven temperature
- observing the change in matter
- checking when the bread should be removed

A number of other cooking projects can be used. Some teachers prefer to tie these experiences to weekly themes or units. For example, they may have a unit on fall, Halloween, or Thanksgiving. Cooking experiences can focus on pumpkins, squash, apples, or cranberries. Activities should include

- preparing food in different ways (boiling, baking, broiling)
- using many kitchen tools (mixers, food processors, blenders)
- examining the insides of foods (peeling a potato, slicing an apple)
- observing the way foods change during preparation

Foods that can be prepared easily in the center are listed in 24-11.

Children can learn that food varies in size, shape, and color. Some foods are heavier than others. One way to teach these concepts is to supply children with carrots,

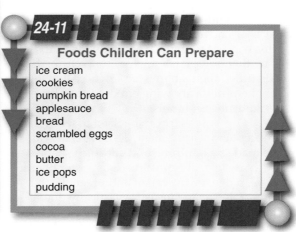

24-11

Foods Children Can Prepare

ice cream
cookies
pumpkin bread
applesauce
bread
scrambled eggs
cocoa
butter
ice pops
pudding

Making food items such as these will give children the chance to both proceed through a recipe and see the finished product.

Discuss

What factors need consideration when selecting a recipe for use with preschoolers during a science activity? What suggestions do you have when children begin to lose interest in a cooking activity because the item takes too long to cook?

Reflect

What early childhood cooking experiences do you remember? Were you allowed to participate in the actual food preparation or did you just watch?

Resource

Learning Science Through Cooking Experiences, reproducible master 24-3, TR

Portfolio Project

Have students write a brief essay to explain their understanding of the value of teaching science concepts through the use of food. How can food activities help children meet the overall goals of a program? How can food activities be used to teach children good nutrition principles? What general and specific science concepts can children experience through their hands-on participation in food activities? Allow time for students to share their essays with the class.

Enrich

Ask the parents of the child care lab children to send in a sample of baby clothes worn by their child and a similar item of the child's normal size. Ask the children to discuss the changes in size they notice as they compare the two clothing items. Encourage them to talk about their growth processes.

Note

Be sure to take photographs of the child care lab preschoolers at the beginning of the session and near the end, especially for year-long programs. As children view the photographs, ask them to describe any changes they notice in their physical growth. File both pictures of each child in his or her personal portfolio.

Activity

Have children trace around their hands and the hands of their teachers on colored construction paper or card stock. Cut out the hands. Have children compare their hand size to their teachers' hands; group hands according to size; classify hands by color; and measure length of hands and fingers.

celery, apples, bananas, oranges, and pears for snacks. Have them discuss the differences among these foods.

Using the Child's Own Body to Teach Science Concepts

Children go through rapid physical changes during the preschool years. These changes are more obvious to parents and teachers than to the children themselves. One way to help children understand their own bodies is through science experiences. Using photographs and drawings of the children is quite effective.

One science concept to introduce is that people can be recognized by the way they look. To teach this, take pictures of each child using a digital or instant camera. After the picture is taken, show it to the child. Encourage the child to tell you about the picture. If he or she does not respond, ask specific questions about the photo, such as "What are you wearing in the picture? What color eyes do you have? What color hair do you have?"

Some children may find it hard to link a photo with themselves. For instance, one teacher had a very difficult time teaching this concept to twins. Each time the twins saw themselves in a mirror or a picture, they identified their sibling. Experiences like these are helpful for showing children they have unique physical traits.

A growth chart can be used to teach the concept of measurement, 24-12. A chart can be made by outlining and cutting a shape such as a carrot from a piece of poster board. Use orange for the carrot and green for the stem. Glue a tape measure vertically down the center of the carrot. Hang the carrot to a door, wall, or bulletin board. Have each child stand next to the tape. Record the children's heights on the poster board.

Colorful growth charts are a fun way to teach children about measurement.

The concept of weight can be taught in the same way. Create a chart to record each child's weight. You may want to record weight at the start of the year and again at midyear to show this concept to the children.

Measurements and the concept of growth can also be taught using body shapes. Have each child lie down on two large pieces of paper. Trace around the child's body and cut the shape from each piece of paper. Choose one piece for the front and one for the back. On the front piece, have the child draw his or her facial features, hair, and clothing. Color clothing and hair on the back piece. Place the two shapes back to back and staple together on one side. Stuff the figure with newspaper and staple the entire figure closed. Hang each child's figure in the room and use it as a frame of reference for the child's growth.

Putting Technology to Use

Have students conduct an Internet search for information on science magazines suitable for young children. Descriptions of the magazines' content usually give a recommended age range, so students can make a listing of educational magazines according to age. Some magazines are available online and can be made available to children right in the classroom. Have students select several magazines to review and discuss in class. Suggested titles are: *Ask: Arts and Sciences for Kids*; *Chickadee*; *Your Big Backyard*; *Click*; *Kids Discover*; and *Wild Animal Baby*.

Using Gardening to Teach Science Concepts

The study of gardening and seeds helps children build an interest in growing things. By five or six years of age, most children can identify common seeds such as watermelon, apple, and peach seeds. However, not many children know they are eating seeds when they eat bananas. Not many children know walnuts, pecans, rice, and peas are also seeds.

Seeds and Food

Science experiments using seeds can be introduced during snack or lunchtime. Talk about only one type of seed at a time. For example, ask the children "What color is the orange? What is inside the orange?" Then give each child an orange that you have begun to peel. Show them how to peel the rest of the fruit. Show them how to pull the orange apart. Encourage the children to look for seeds. Ask questions about the orange seeds, such as "How many seeds are there in your orange? Are the seeds the same size? How do the seeds look? How do the seeds feel?" When children are through, have them place their seeds on the science table.

Introduce new seeds at snack times or lunchtimes. Use the same steps. Compare the seeds from different fruits in terms of size, color, and texture. Again, collect the seeds. Place them on the science table. Collect seeds from a number of fruits to display on the science table.

Seed Party

Have a seed party to teach children that some seeds must be shelled before they are eaten. Collect a number of nuts that can be eaten: peanuts, walnuts, pecans, and a coconut. Ask the children to help you crack the seeds and remove the meat. As they

Health and Safety

Nut and Seed Allergies

Some children have severe allergies to peanuts, tree nuts, and some seeds. Be sure that you know about all children's health records before you introduce nuts. Some children cannot even sit at a table at which nuts are being served without having an allergic reaction.

sample the meat from each seed, discuss the flavors and talk about which seeds are grown underground.

Pumpkin, sunflower, soybean seeds, and mixed nuts may also be used. You may want to roast or sauté some of the seeds. During the roasting period, ask questions such as "Which seeds are labeled *nuts*? How does cooking change the taste? How does cooking change the texture?"

Observing Seeds

A nature or seed walk is another way to teach children that seeds come from fruits of plants. Before leaving on the walk, give each child a paper bag with the child's name on it. You may prefer to wrap a piece of packing tape with the sticky side out on each child's wrist. The children can stick the seeds to the sticky tape as they are discovered. Walk to a park or other area where seeds are plentiful and encourage the children to collect seeds. When the group returns to the classroom, ask each child to choose three seeds to add to the

Reflect

How would you teach or explain the purpose of seeds to children? What safety precautions need to be observed when using seeds in preschool science activities?

Note

Contact local garden suppliers for donations of the previous season's leftover seed packets. Although some of the seeds may not germinate, many of them will. You may find this an economical resource for preschool seed experiences.

Activity

Have students assist children in the child care lab by cracking and removing walnut, pecan, almond, and peanut shells. Then allow the children to create their own art collages while saving the nuts for snack or food projects. *(If children in the program have allergies to certain nuts, do not use this project.)*

Workplace Connection

Many child care programs rely on donations from local businesses and companies of materials that are incorporated into projects and activities. To ensure continued cooperation and support from these businesses, plan to express appreciation and acknowledgment of their contributions. Have students create written and illustrated thank-you notes. Students can design and print certificates of appreciation and decorate frames for the certificates. If possible, take photos of children using donated materials and/or include a sample of a finished product to include with the thank-you notes.

Discuss

What science concepts can you teach children from planting seeds? What is the best mixture for seed growth? Why?

Activity

Have children collect samples of leaves and small flowers (or obtain them from a local florist) to make pressed flower place mats. Ask students to put specimens between two sheets of waxed paper and press in a telephone book for several weeks. Place flowers and leaves on sturdy paper and cover with clear adhesive plastic.

Enrich

Have students make a dish garden using pineapple, turnip, carrot, or beet tops by following the instructions in the text. Display the dish garden in the child care lab where children can observe it.

science table. Save the rest of the seeds for an art display.

Place magnifying glasses on the science table next to the seeds. Encourage the children to use the glasses to view the shapes, sizes, colors, and textures of the seeds. This activity should help the children become aware of the seeds' differences and similarities, 24-13.

Planting Seeds

Planting seeds indoors and outdoors is another way to teach children concepts about plants and their growth. Have children plant bean, corn, carrot, and radish seeds in individual containers. Use paper cups, tuna

24-13

This child is using a magnifying glass to study the shape, size, color, and texture of seeds and flowers.

cans, milk cartons, or clay pots. If possible, use transparent recycled containers so the children can observe root growth below the surface. Write the children's names on the containers. Provide soil for the children to use for planting. The best mixture for growth is garden soil, or loam. It supplies nutrients for the plant and provides good moisture and drainage control. Have children fill the containers with soil. Then let the children choose seeds to plant. Show them how to use their fingers to make holes in the soil. Add the seeds and cover with soil. Label each container with the seed name. Then show the children how to lightly dampen the soil using a watering can.

Most seeds will grow when given proper moisture and temperature. When the seedlings emerge from the surface of the soil, place the containers where they will receive sunlight. Encourage the children to check the containers daily. Ask questions such as "What seeds sprouted first? Do all plants have similar leaves? How many leaves does each plant have?" From this experience the children should learn the following:

- Seeds planted in soil and given water, warmth, and sunshine grow.

- Some seeds germinate earlier than others.

- As plants grow, their size changes.

- Plants droop or die if they do not get enough water.

Dish Garden

Make a dish garden using pineapple, turnip, carrot, or beet tops. First, cut the tops off about one and one-quarter inch below the leaves. Then place the tops in clear, shallow dishes with water and sand. Put the dish on the science table where the children can observe the growth.

Workplace Connection

Ask students to obtain seedlings from a local garden supplier or plant their own. Have students select locations for the seedlings in the child care lab, including placing some in cabinets or closets with very little or no light. Work with children in the child care lab to maintain regular watering of the seedlings. Have children examine the plants after several weeks and discuss the differences they see in growth and color. Have students write a brief summary of their experiences.

Vase Garden

Collect an onion, potato, sweet potato, or avocado pit and a jar large enough to hold the vegetable. Suspend the vegetable on toothpicks, 24-14. You may have to add small amounts of water from time to time. As the vegetable sprouts and evaporation takes place, the water level will decrease. Students can observe the roots and stems as they grow.

Bulletin Board Garden

Plants can also be grown in resealable plastic bags. Hang one bag for each child on a bulletin board that is decorated like a garden. With help, each child can plant a seed in a bag. Start by folding a paper towel and soaking it. Put the wet towel inside the bag. Place a bean seed between the side of the bag and the paper towel. In time, the seed will sprout and its roots will fill the bag.

You can also grow flowers in these bags. Fill the bags with potting soil instead of a paper towel. Add flower seeds. After the seeds sprout, move the plants to indoor pots or an outdoor garden (if the weather permits).

24-14

Many vegetables grow with little care if suspended in this way.

Outdoor Garden

When space allows, grow an outdoor garden. The available space as well as the children's ages and interests may influence what you grow. It might be a flower garden, a simple vegetable garden, or both. Let the children take part in caring for the garden and enjoying its end results.

Chart 24-15 is an example of what children may learn by observing the seeds they planted in a flower garden. You may wish to print the children's comments on a large sheet of paper to document their learning.

Using Air to Teach Science Concepts

Every day children have experiences with air. They watch airplanes and birds, fly kites, and blow up balloons. They feel the wind blow against their bodies and clothing.

24-15

Our Flower Garden: What We Learned from Observing

Raul: Seeds grow in the ground.

Tonya: Seeds need water.

Cha: Seeds can grow into pretty flowers.

Jose: Plants come from seeds.

Vivian: Big and little flowers come from seeds.

Other things the children learned:
- Flowers smell.
- Flowers can be many colors.
- Flowers can be short or tall.
- Flowers can die without water.

From a garden, children may learn very basic facts or more complex ideas.

Reflect

How does the following quote relate to the study of science in the preschool? "It must be remembered that the purpose of education is not to fill the minds of students with facts… it is to teach them to think." (Robert Hutchins)

Enrich

Ask students to investigate the growth processes of flower bulbs such as tulips and daffodils. Have students prepare a flannel board or draw and tell story on the topic for the preschoolers. Depending on the season and region, plant the bulbs outdoors or learn how to force them indoors to serve as examples for the children.

Reflect

Have students review Chart 24-15. What did the children from the child care lab learn from planting experiences? Did they learn basic facts or more complex ideas? What were some of the children's comments while observing plants?

Service Learning Activity

Enlist the help of the preschool parents to help acquire pots, soil, and flower seeds to provide spring flowers for an area nursing home or care facility. Have student volunteers plan the activity ahead so the flowers are ready to be delivered in the spring. Ask children from the child care lab to assist students by placing soil in the pots, planting the seeds, and keeping them watered throughout the growing period. Children may also enjoy decorating the pots for the recipients. Check with local garden suppliers for seeds that have the most success in growing under classroom conditions.

Activity

Have students give each child in the child care lab a piece of painting paper with several blobs of paint on it and a drinking straw. Ask the children to create an air painting by aiming the straw at the paint and blowing air through it to move the paint around. This works best when children have plenty of room to move around and when the paint is not too thick or thin.

Enrich

Have students research the use of windmills and wind farms to produce environmentally conscious energy. Find pictures of modern and traditional windmills and adapt the information to a lesson on wind power that is suitable for preschoolers.

Discuss

What limits or guidelines do you suggest children follow when working with bubbles? How would you positively state your limits to achieve the desired results?

Teaching About Air

To help children understand the concept that air takes up space, inflate some balloons. Do this activity in a group. Start by showing the children a deflated balloon. Then tell them to watch closely as you blow up the balloon. After the balloon is inflated, ask "What is inside the balloon?" Pass out balloons to all the children. Encourage them to fill the balloons with air. After the activity, collect the balloons.

Bubble solutions are another way to teach children that air takes up space. You can buy a prepared solution or use the recipe in 24-16. Give each child a straw and a paper cup. Using a pencil point, make a hole about one inch from the bottom of the cup. Have the children place a straw in the hole. Then have them dip the open end of the cup in the bubble solution. Finally, ask them to remove the cup from the solution and, with the cup in an upside down position, blow into the straw.

Encourage the children to blow bubbles. Ask them "What is inside of the bubbles? How did you get air inside of the bubble? How can you make the bubble larger? How can you make the bubble smaller?"

Use clear containers, such as aquariums or glass mixing bowls, to conduct another experiment. Fill the containers with water. Assign containers and pass straws to each child. Tell the children to place their straws in the containers and blow, 24-17. Ask "What happens when you blow air through the straw into the water?" (Be sure to caution the children against drinking soapy water.)

Teaching About Wind

To teach the concept that the wind makes things move, use thin strips of newsprint or crepe paper streamers. For this activity to work, you need to introduce it on a windy day. Take the children outside and hand out the streamers. Show them how to hold the streamers. Ask "What happens to the streamer when the wind blows? What direction is the wind moving? What happens when you run fast?"

Using Weather

Develop environmental awareness by focusing on the weather—snow, wind, rain, thunderstorms, and rainbows all appeal to young children. Develop a weather felt board to use at group time. Include figures of children, clothing for all seasons, clouds, sun, snow, and raindrops. Each day a child can select the clothing and symbols to represent the weather.

24-16

Bubble Solution

½ cup glycerin (purchase from drug store)
2 cups water
3 tablespoons liquid detergent

Bubble solutions are very easy to make.

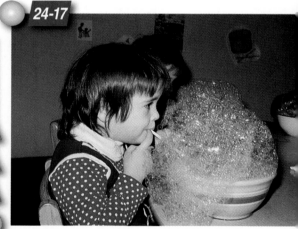

24-17

As children blow bubbles they become aware that the bubbles, and therefore air, take up space.

Putting Technology to Use

Ask students to show children from the child care lab how to locate current weather information on the Internet if computers are available for classroom use. Check out local weather conditions by accessing **www.nws.noaa.gov, www.weather.com,** or **www.weatherbug.com.** Students should help children click on their area on the map or type in their zip code. Have students keep track of weather predictions and observe how accurate the predictions are for the area. Ask students to chart the results for children to view during circle time or weather and calendar activities.

Using Magnets to Teach Science Concepts

Children are intrigued by magnets. Concepts about magnets are best learned through a combination of teacher guidance and hands-on activities, 24-18. Therefore, teachers need to buy quality magnets. These can be bought through science equipment or school supply stores. Buy a variety of magnets, including horseshoe, ceramic, bar, disk, and rod-shaped magnets.

As children work and play with magnets, they will observe the following:

- Magnets pull some things, but not others.

- Some magnets are big; others are small.

- Some magnets are stronger than others.

- Magnets pick up objects made of iron.

To aid in building these concepts, place several magnets on a table. Collect objects that magnets will pick up and others they will not. Types of objects magnets attract include metal screws, staples, nails, paper clips, and other small metal objects. A magnet will not pick up objects that do not have an iron content. Such objects include

paper, cloth, wooden pencils, crayons, shoelaces, and aluminum dishes.

Place a variety of horseshoe and bar magnets in a small box. In a second box, place chalk, toothpicks, paper, nails, paper clips, plastic spoons, and other objects. Have the children name each object and tell whether the magnets can lift it.

Careful supervision is required when children are working with magnets. Small magnets can be choking hazards. In addition, if two or more magnets are swallowed, they can stick together and form a blockage in the intestines. Surgery may be required to remove the blockage. Also be cautious when allowing children to play with toys that contain magnets because the magnets could be detached. Finally, carefully monitor any of the small metal objects used when working with magnets. Screws, paper clips, and nails could all be choking hazards.

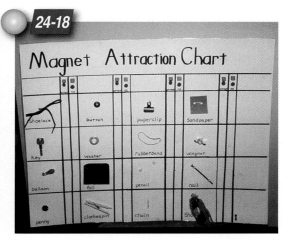

24-18

Charts are also useful for learning magnet concepts.

Using Wheels to Teach Science Concepts

Children see wheels every day. They may travel by car, truck, bus, or train to the child care center or preschool. There they see wagons, tricycles, scooters, and other toys with wheels. At home they might see machines with wheels, such as vacuum cleaners and lawnmowers. Perhaps on a trip to the airport they have seen people pulling suitcases with wheels. All these experiences should help them learn about the uses of wheels.

Children can learn the following concepts about wheels:

- Wheels are round.

- Wheels roll.

- Wheels usually turn on an axis.

- Wheels make work easier for people.

To learn these concepts, children need to be exposed to many types of wheels. You might demonstrate these concepts using wagons and wheelbarrows.

Activity

Have students help children in the child care lab complete a magnetic art project. Place a Masonite® or Plexiglas® board across two boxes on top of a table and tape a piece of painting paper to the top. Allow children to use a magnetic wand underneath the board to move metal objects, such as large washers that have been dipped in paint, around on the paper to create magnetic art designs.

Discuss

Why is careful supervision required when children are working with magnets? What safety hazards do you need to be aware of when teaching with small magnets?

Activity

Have students help children in the child care lab complete a wheel art project. Spread out large sheets of painting paper on the floor and collect several small toy cars. Dip the cars in tempera paint poured into pie tins and "drive" the cars all over the paper. Discuss the results when colors cross each other or when they notice an interesting tire tread pattern.

Cross-Curricular Activity

Science/Physics
Contact the physics instructor at your school to determine the possibility of adapting a lesson using wheels for the child care lab program. Many physics classes test movement theories with wheeled projects such as a Mousetrap

Car. The preschoolers may be interested in seeing these wheeled projects work. Allow time for questions from the children to be answered by the physics students. Remind the students of the challenge of phrasing the answers in terms that preschoolers can understand.

Reflect

What will children observe on a short walk around the outside of the child care lab? What questions will you ask to encourage awareness of the environment as the children participate in the walk?

Activity

Divide the child care class into groups and assign each group one of the bulleted items listed under *Value of Animals*. Each group should use pictures or drawings to create a poster to use with the preschoolers to illustrate the assigned value. Example: show pictures of animals with various numbers of legs, or show examples of the different body coverings such as feathers and fur.

Resource

Evaluating a Science Activity, Activity C, OG

To help children learn to identify a wheel, use a feely box or bag. Place cubes, balls, wooden blocks, and rubber wheels in the box. Ask one child at a time to feel in the box and find the wheel.

Another way to teach children about wheels is to cut out and hang pictures of wheels from magazines. Include fire engines, cars, trucks, tractors, wagons, airplanes, golf carts, scooters, and roller skates. Then cut out and hang pictures of other types of transportation. These might include motorboats, sailboats, skis, rafts, sleds, ice skates, donkeys, elephants, and horses. When you have finished, ask the children to point out the pictures with wheels.

Using Field Trips and Walks to Teach Science Concepts

Field trips promote curiosity, supply opportunities for discovery, and encourage interaction with the environment. During field trips, children can observe how machines make work more precise, easy, and orderly. For example, on a trip to the fire station, point out the fire alarm system, ladder, ax, hose, and fire extinguisher.

Short walks with a focus can also help the children learn about science. Topics for these walks could include colors, seeds, rocks, footprints, animals, insects, plants, or leaves. On rainy days, it might be interesting to take a walk to study earthworms, puddles, or rainbows. Chart 24-19 lists field trip locations and things to observe there.

Using Animals to Teach Science Concepts

Some animals can be used as classroom pets. Science concepts can be taught to young children using these pets. For example, children can learn how different animals look and feel, what they eat, how they should be handled, and how they respond to their environment. Pets can help teach responsibility, empathy, and respect for all kinds of life. After having the opportunity to observe and compare animals, children can draw conclusions from their experiences, 24-20.

Care of Animals

All animals brought into the classroom should receive humane care and treatment. Children should always see animals being handled and cared for properly. Make every effort to provide for the basic needs of classroom animals. These needs include food, water, light, air, proper space for movement, and exercise.

Before purchasing pets for your classroom, check your state's licensing rules and regulations. Some states do not allow pets in the classroom. Health is the primary reason since some children are allergic to pet dander.

Value of Animals

Experiences with animals should teach children the following concepts:
- There are many kinds of animals.
- Animals are fun to watch.
- Animals, especially pets, require care.
- Pets depend on humans for proper care.
- There are many kinds of animals; some are small and some are large.
- Animals need water, proper food, shelter, and exercise.
- Animals have different kinds of body coverings, such as feathers, scales, hair, and smooth skin.
- Animals move in different ways. They may fly, swim, walk, run, crawl, creep, or hop.

Workplace Connection

Have students research the rules or restrictions relating to having animals in the classroom in their school. What type, if any, are allowed? What type would provide learning experiences for preschool children in the child care lab? Have students contact area preschools and child care centers to discover their use of classroom pets. How are pets cared for during weekends and vacation periods? Allow time for students to discuss their findings in class.

24-19

Science Field Trips

Location	Science Concepts Studied
Lumber company	Nature of wood and sawdust
Automobile and bike shops	Workings of motors, gears, chains, wheels; use of tools
Grocery stores	Forms of foods
Vacant land	Insects, plant life, animal shelters
Print shop	Mechanics of the printing process
Commercial laundry	Effects of cleaners, heat, starch
Produce market	Nature of fresh fruits and vegetables
Interior decorating shop	Nature of fabrics, use of colors
Television and radio studios	Production and transmission of images and sounds
Fire department	Mechanics of trucks, engines, ladders
Animal hospital	Care of pets
Toy shop	Nature of toy materials, such as plastic, wood
Excavation site	Nature of soil, rocks, building materials
Zoo	Birds, insects, animals
Botanical gardens	Plant life
Museum	Rocks, geological formations, other science concepts

Field trips can be used to teach a variety of science concepts. For instance, a trip to a fruit market can teach children about plants and seeds.

24-20

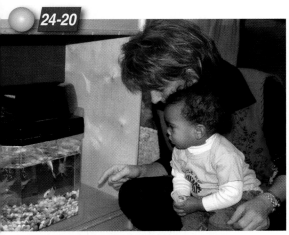

Having classroom pets gives children a chance to observe, care for, and learn about pets as a part of their daily routine.

- Animals have different numbers and kinds of legs. Some have two legs, some four, some six, some eight, and some have none.
- Animals can be identified by the different sounds they make.

Animals as Classroom Pets

Many animals can be used as classroom pets. Hamsters, snakes, toads, frogs, fish, rabbits, and guinea pigs have all been used in early childhood programs. Other classroom pets might be a gerbil, mouse, or bird. Chart 24-21 lists the average life span of some common classroom pets.

Discuss

Look over the suggested locations in 24-19, *Science Field Trips*. How many of these locations are available in your area? What additional locations can you suggest that would incorporate science concepts?

Reflect

What positive effects do you believe animals have had on your life? What is your attitude toward pets in the pre-school classroom?

Enrich

Have students debate the pros and cons of having pets in the pre-school classroom. Students may cite personal experiences as well as research to support their viewpoints.

Cross-Curricular Activity

Science
Ask students to survey the science labs in the school to discover any possibilities for in-school field trips. Have students make a list of the objects and equipment children might observe in the labs. What science concepts can be taught? Enlist the support of science instructors in demonstrating or showing materials to the children. After the field trip, be sure to discuss with the children what they learned.

Reflect

Review Chart 24-21, *Average Life Span of Classroom Pets*. Based on the life spans listed, which animal do you think would make the best classroom pet? Why?

Discuss

What can classroom pets such as hamsters or gerbils provide for a shy child? What effect might a snake have on a preschooler?

Enrich

Have students visit a local pet store and make a list of possible classroom pets available for purchase. Research the cost of the animal, housing, supplies, equipment, food, and medicines the animal may need.

24-21

Average Life Span of Classroom Pets

Mouse	1 to 2 years
Hamster	1½ to 2½ years
Gerbil	4 years or more
Guinea pig	6 years
Rabbit	6 to 7 years
Canary	10 to 15 years

When cared for properly, classroom pets have long life spans.

Hamsters

A healthy hamster is chubby and has a shiny coat and bright eyes. The average life expectancy of a hamster is one to two years. Buy hamsters only from pet stores that handle healthy animals. (One strain of hamster spreads a form of meningitis.)

Each hamster needs a wire, rustproof cage. The cage should have an exercise wheel. Since hamsters are able to chew through many materials and escape through small holes, a wire cage prevents escape. Wood shavings should be spread on the floor for cage litter. This litter should be replaced daily. Uneaten food and soiled bedding should be removed. Newspaper should also be placed in the cage for the hamster to shred for nesting. Provide hamsters with nutritious food. You can buy a hamster mix at a pet store. This contains cracked corn, seeds, grain, and pellets.

Because hamsters have two pair of gnawing teeth, they enjoy chewing a piece of soft wood or dog biscuit. Gnawing helps keep the hamsters' teeth at a healthy length. Hamsters also need to be provided fresh water in a special bottle purchased at a pet store. The bottle prevents spilling and ensures that the animal has a constant supply of water. See 24-22.

24-22

Note the water bottle in this gerbil's cage. It is the type used for hamsters and rabbits, too.

Hamsters are nocturnal by nature. This means they usually sleep during the day and are awake at night. When awakened and picked up, they tend to nip. As a result, children under the age of six should only be allowed to observe the hamster. They should not be allowed to handle the animal. Furthermore, children over six years of age need to be supervised by their teacher when handling a hamster.

Snakes

Harmless snakes make good classroom pets. They require little care and, when handled properly, rarely bite. Having a snake in the classroom can also prevent or dispel any fear the children might feel.

Aquariums are good housing for snakes. Spread newspaper on the bottom of the aquarium. Then cover the newspaper with gravel and a small piece of wood. For privacy, build a cave in one corner with small rocks. Add a small dish of water. To prevent the

---

Putting Technology to Use

Ask students to conduct an Internet search for information about therapy dogs. What is the difference between a therapy dog and a service dog? How are therapy dogs trained and certified? How might therapy dogs be used in a school or child care center setting? Have students write a brief report of their findings. Allow time for students to discuss their findings in class.

snake from escaping, cover the top with a secure screen.

Different types of snakes require different foods. Your local pet shop salesperson or conservation authority worker can help you determine the snake's dietary needs. As a rule, small snakes can exist on insects, worms, and meat. Frogs and mice are required by the larger species. Some teachers prefer to arrange for their local pet store to feed large snakes.

Toads and Frogs

Toads and frogs are common classroom pets. They can be housed in an aquarium. To avoid odors, clean the housing often. Water should be changed at least twice a week. You will notice that frogs often sit in their water. They do this to moisten their bodies, which is necessary for their survival.

Toads and frogs enjoy eating small earthworms or insects. They will accept raw or chopped beef or canned dog food. Children enjoy watching these animals use their sticky tongues to catch food such as bugs.

Fish

Fish are an ideal pet for some teachers because they require less attention than most other pets. If you would like fish as classroom pets, you will need to decide whether to buy tropical or freshwater fish. Freshwater fish are less costly and have easier care requirements. They can be kept in a fishbowl rather than in an aquarium.

Tropical fish require an aquarium. Most teachers prefer 20-gallon aquariums. They are easier to maintain than smaller tanks. Also, children can see the fish more easily. Maintain a water temperature between 70°F and 80°F at all times. To ensure this range, purchase a thermometer and a self-regulating aquarium heater.

The pH balance of the water is important. It should be kept close to neutral. This is especially important if you wish to breed tropical fish. If the pH is acidic, it can be corrected by adding sodium biphosphate or sodium bicarbonate. These products can be purchased at a pet store. You might also buy a kit to test the water.

Set the tank on a sturdy table away from sunlight. Then fill the tank with water and allow it to settle. There should be a half gallon of water for every inch of fish in the aquarium. Wait one week for the water to reach the correct temperature and pH balance. Then add the fish.

Talk to the salesperson at your pet store to find out exactly what, how much, and how often to feed your freshwater or tropical fish. Chances are a prepared fish food and/or shrimp brine will be recommended.

Rabbits

Rabbits have always been a favorite pet of young children and their teachers. They are sociable, intelligent, and affectionate. Rabbits come when called and can be trained to use a litter box. However, not all teachers enjoy having a rabbit indoors. This is because rabbits are messy and must be cleaned quite often.

Rabbits are often kept in large wire cages that allow plenty of room for movement. For shelter, place a wooden box at one end of the cage. Wood shavings or straw should also be placed in the bottom of the cage for bedding.

A rabbit cage should always be placed indoors. Traditionally, some early childhood programs have introduced an outdoor hutch for their pet rabbit. This forces the animal into social isolation. Moreover, a predator or vandal can cause the rabbit to have a heart attack.

Because rabbits are hearty eaters, they require large amounts of food and water. You can buy rabbit feed at a pet store. Green or leafy vegetables, including lettuce, cabbage, and celery tops, are also enjoyed. You may wish to omit cabbage and other strong-smelling vegetables from their diet. This will

Activity

Arrange for a local animal control or wildlife specialist to visit the child care lab to discuss the role of wildlife in the area. The specialist may be able to bring an animal to class that has been rescued and is being treated before being returned to the wild.

Resource

Pet Care, Activity C, SAG

Activity

Have students collect pictures of various types of fish, including shellfish, and mammals that live in the water, such as whales and dolphins. Using the pictures for sorting and classification, ask students to plan a lesson to teach the difference between fish and mammals.

Resource

Science, reproducible master 24-4, TR

Meeting Special Needs

Before assigning *Pet Care*, Activity C, SAG, divide the assignment into two parts for students who may benefit from a shorter assignment. Have student volunteers partner with special learners to complete the activity. Have students explain the false answers. Divide

Science, reproducible master 24-4, TR, in the same manner. Both activities can be used for reviewing the chapter content. Spend additional time discussing any statements that are difficult for special learners to understand.

Resource

Methods of Teaching Science, Activity D, SAG

Activity

Have students design a lesson plan to teach the 3 *R*s: the concepts of recycle, reuse, and reduce. Students should include examples of each in their lesson and provide hands-on opportunities for children to experience these concepts.

Resource

Planning a Science Activity, Activity D, OG

help control the unpleasant odor of strong-smelling urine.

Exercise caution when handling a rabbit. Rabbits have sharp toenails and may scratch to protect themselves if they are afraid. Dropping a rabbit accidentally may result in a broken back and legs. Therefore, it is important that you teach the children how to handle a rabbit.

Guinea Pigs

Most early childhood teachers agree that guinea pigs make good pets for young children. They are easy to handle and they do not bite. Also, guinea pigs are very gentle. They enjoy being held and cuddled by children. In addition, even very young children can easily observe, care for, and handle them. These pets have heavy bodies and tight skins. They can be picked up easily by placing a hand under the pig's body.

Wire cages provide good housing for these animals. Recommended cage sizes are about two and one-half to three feet in length, one and one-half feet deep, and one and one-half feet wide. Doors on cages need to fit tightly to prevent the animals from escaping. Spaces to hide, exercise, and sleep should be included. A small cardboard box can be placed inside the cage for sleeping.

Food for a guinea pig is similar to that of rabbits. They enjoy pellets or grains including corn, wheat, and oats. Grass, alfalfa, clover, and carrots can be added to their diets for variety. Most teachers who have guinea pigs for classroom pets recommend pellets as the most convenient type of food.

Care of the Earth

The children need to learn to preserve the earth by keeping it clean, 24-23. Set the stage by recycling in your classroom. To do this, place four bins labeled *paper, glass, metal,* and *plastic* in a classroom area. Encourage the children to sort items.

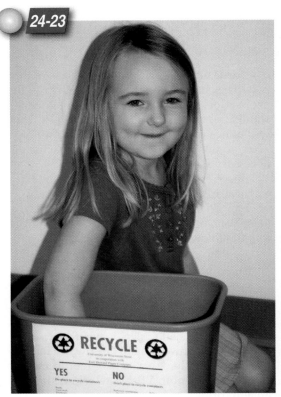

24-23

Children should be encouraged to recycle whenever possible.

Meeting Special Needs

Review the special learners' chapter outlines to determine if the students have any questions about the concepts or content of this chapter. Review the chapter objectives and ask the students to evaluate their progress in meeting these objectives. Ask the students to summarize, orally or in writing, what they learned from this chapter.

Summary

The nature of modern life makes studying science important. Young children can be introduced to science at the center through simple experiences.

In order to guide these experiences, teachers must know the objectives of studying science. They must also know how to help children reach these goals. This will require planning.

With a solid plan, teachers can then design a variety of activities to teach science concepts. Many methods and items can be used to teach these concepts, including colors, water, food, bodies, gardens, air, magnets, wheels, field trips, and pets.

Review and Reflect

1. What is the definition of *science*?

2. Because science is creative, it requires the development of children's _____ and _____.

3. List three reasons why science should be studied.

4. True or false. All science projects need to be planned in detail.

5. During their science experiences, children should have many opportunities to _____.
   A. observe
   B. solve problems
   C. collect samples and pictures
   D. All the above.

6. Why should the science area be located near the kitchen?

7. What is a science table?

8. True or false. Unneeded teacher input can sometimes stifle children's curiosity, thereby limiting their desire to continue experimenting.

9. List the five basic process skills.

10. _____-ended questions promote discussion, but _____-ended questions tend to require only one word answers.

11. Name four ways to teach science concepts. Of these four methods, explain one in detail.

6. Kitchens have sources of heat and water, two sources that are needed in many science experiences.
7. A science table is used to display items related to the science area.
8. true
9. observing objects using the five senses; drawing conclusions from observations based on knowledge gained in past experiences; classifying objects into sets based on one or more observable properties; comparing sets of objects by measuring and counting; communicating by describing objects, relationships, and occurrences
10. Open, closed
11. (List four:) color, water, food, bodies, gardens (plants), air, magnets, wheels, field trips and walks, animals (Student response for explanation.)

Review and Reflect **Answer Key**

1. the study of natural processes and their products
2. curiosity, imagination
3. (List three. Answers will vary, but may include:) enhances curiosity, builds vocabulary and language skills, enhances reading readiness, improves hand-eye coordination, develops fine-motor skills, enhances math skills
4. false
5. D

Apply and Explore

1. Develop a collection of items that could be placed on the science table. Explain how the collection would contribute to the science experiences of young children.

2. Brainstorm a list of centerpieces for the snack or lunch table that would help develop science concepts.

3. Draw a sketch of a science area as you would design it. Include placement of equipment.

4. Develop a recipe file of foods that can be prepared by the children in an early childhood setting.

5. Make a dish garden using a pineapple, turnip, carrot, and beet top. Document the amount of time it takes for each to sprout.

Cross-Curricular Link

Reading

1. Review a recipe book. List examples of cooking activities that would involve a process and product.

Technology

2. Explore the Web site of the National Wildlife Federation (www.nwf.org) for information related to science learnings for children.

3. Search the Kids section of the Kids Health Web site (www.kidshealth.org) for rules for staying safe around animals.

Workplace Link

Visit local child care centers to observe each center's setup of the science area. Interview the teachers to discover the role of science in their programs. Draw a simple diagram of the center's science area and list some of the equipment and supplies that are available to children. Discuss your findings with the class. Discuss any changes or additions that would enhance the child care lab science center.

25

Guiding Social Studies Experiences

Discuss

Look at the chapter opening photo. What social studies concepts do you think these children are learning by playing together? How can social studies help children understand and appreciate how other people live?

Discuss

Look over the objectives for this chapter. How might the social studies curriculum for a young child be similar to that studied by a high school student? What are the major differences?

After studying this chapter, you will be able to

- explain the importance of social studies experiences.

- outline the role of the teacher in designing and guiding social studies experiences.

- describe ways to include multicultural, intergenerational, democracy, ecology, geography, community living, current events, and holiday concepts in the curriculum.

- explain the importance of morning meetings.

475

Vocabulary

Have students review the *Terms to Know* list. Ask students to look up unfamiliar words or terms in the glossary before reading the chapter.

Discuss

Why should social studies experiences be part of the early childhood curriculum? How might social studies activities contribute to meeting the overall program goals?

Reflect

What early memories do you have of being asked for your opinion about something and having your viewpoint considered by adults? What effect did the adult's response have on your self-concept?

Terms to Know

incidental learnings
perceptions
culture
omission
morning meetings
ecology

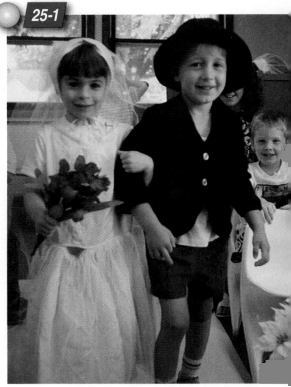

25-1

Through social studies experiences, children learn to accept themselves and get along with others.

Young children approach classroom life eagerly and positively. They are interested in everything that goes on and are always full of questions. For instance, they might ask

- Where is Iraq?

- How does the police officer help me?

- Why doesn't she have a daddy?

- What is Passover?

Many of these questions arise naturally during daily classroom activities. Children's questions might relate to social skills, cultures, families, careers, holidays, current events, history, or geography. These questions all revolve around social studies as a curriculum area.

The field of social studies includes many subjects that help children learn about themselves, as well as other people. Children learn about families, peers, and people in the community. In addition, they learn positive group living skills, such as cooperation and responsibility, 25-1.

Young children build social studies concepts as they move through the world around them. For example, children learn key social studies concepts when they walk around the neighborhood. Social studies concepts can also be developed by looking at many types of housing. Role-playing doctors, mail carriers, grocers, or parents also promotes an understanding of social studies. So does the process of making and eating ethnic foods or hearing a story about community helpers. By taking part in tasks for maintaining the classroom, children learn social studies concepts. Watering flowers, feeding classroom pets, and putting blocks away teach children about getting along in their world.

Importance of Social Studies

Children need to understand and appreciate how other people live—their lifestyles, languages, and viewpoints. Social studies helps children acquire skills for living. By including social studies concepts in the curriculum, children will

- develop self-respect and a healthy self-concept

- develop respect for others

Meeting Special Needs

Provide an outline of the chapter with all the chapter headings for special learners. Students should fill in each section of the outline as the material is covered in class with a sentence or two about the content. Review the special learners' IEPs to decide if any modifications should be made in presenting the chapter content.

- develop self-control and independence
- learn to share ideas and materials, 25-2
- develop healthy ways of relating to and working with others
- gain the attitudes, knowledge, and skills needed for living in a democracy
- develop respect for other people's feelings, ideas, and property
- learn about the roles people have in life
- learn to appreciate the past and its relationship to the present
- learn the need for and purpose of rules

The value of the social studies curriculum, then, is that it makes children better able to understand their world and their place in it.

The Teacher's Role in Social Studies

The key to a good social studies program is your skill as a teacher and the knowledge you bring to the classroom, 25-3. Your interests will determine the degree to which social

Learning to share ideas helps children build communication skills.

Teachers play a crucial role in quality social studies programs.

studies will be included in the curriculum. Through your training, you will understand the need to use community resources, chance learnings, themes, group participation, observation, and evaluation to enrich the social studies program.

To provide quality learning experiences, you need to make daily observations. These routine checks should provide data related to the children's interests, abilities, developmental levels, attitudes, and knowledge. From this data, you can determine what children need to know and what behaviors need to be changed.

Determine the Children's Needs, Interests, Abilities, and Experiences

Every group of children brings a wide variety of interests to the classroom. Some children may be interested in airplanes, trains, or geography. Other children may

Note

Write the following quote from the textbook on the board or overhead to inspire students as they study this chapter: "The value of the social studies curriculum is that it makes children better able to understand their world and their place in it."

Discuss

Why is it important for children to learn about or experience the various roles an individual may have in life? What social skills might children practice as they participate in role-playing?

Resource

Social Studies Activities, Activity A, SAG

Meeting Special Needs

Special learners may benefit from a revised *Social Studies Activities*, Activity A, SAG. Break down the assignment into two or three smaller groups of questions for the student who cannot handle the assignment all at once. Ask student volunteers to work with special learners to complete the activity. Spend additional time reviewing and discussing any areas that are difficult for special learners to understand.

Enrich

Have students debate the pros and cons of the practice of grouping children according to their ability levels. Should this be done at the preschool level? What might be the effects on the children?

Note

Remind students to review the material on assessments and observations already covered in Chapter 3 while observing children. Have students refer to their observations as they plan developmentally appropriate social studies activities.

Resource

Social Studies Themes, transparency master 25-1, TR

prefer to study community helpers. To determine children's interests, you can

- observe them during play, noting the type of play and their use of materials and equipment, 25-4

- interact with them in a casual way, asking them what they enjoy

- ask the children's parents to share their children's interests with you

- observe the children's choice of books

Like interests, the skills of every group of children should influence the social studies program. In any given classroom, there will be many levels in cognitive, physical, social, and emotional development. As a teacher of young children, you will need to match materials and equipment with each child's ability level.

Determine children's ability levels by

- observing the children's social skills as they play with other children

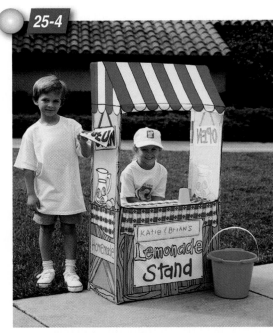

25-4

Children have many interests. To determine individuals' interests, playtime is an excellent time to observe.

- reviewing the children's physical growth and health records

- structuring a variety of tasks for each child to complete, noting their success

There is no shortcut for gathering data to determine the children's skill levels. Gathering takes time. The information, however, is essential for planning a developmentally appropriate social studies curriculum.

Developmental experiences are key to designing a social studies program. These traits can be observed and used as a starting point for planning social studies activities. Characteristics and their implementations are listed in 25-5.

Develop the Curriculum

Once the children's needs, interests, abilities, and experiences have been determined, you are ready to plan the curriculum. Encourage children to take part in the planning. This process will help them organize their thoughts, express their ideas, and experience the results.

During the planning process, allow children to make important choices. Involve all children in the group. You may find that some may be quite shy. These children may feel better if given a chance to plan individually in a small group.

Young children are able to plan the following aspects of their activities:

- Whom to play with

- Materials needed for a project

- Places to visit

- People to invite to the classroom

- How to celebrate birthdays and holidays

Themes

Many teachers use themes when planning a social studies program, 25-6. One theme can be used to integrate the learning opportunities

---

Portfolio Project

Assign students to interview individual children in the child care lab for information on interests and abilities. Observe the children during play and interact with them in a casual way to learn more about them. Have students use the information to design a page for the child's portfolio. Ask small groups of children to take turns sharing their pages and comparing their information.

25-5

Activities Related to Children's Characteristics

Characteristics	Implementations
Interest centered on immediate environment	Provide opportunities to explore the school, home, and neighborhood.
Enjoys opportunities for self-expression	Provide small group opportunities whenever possible.
Shows interest in people with whom he or she is acquainted	Share resource people with whom the children have indicated an interest.
Learns best through direct experiences	Provide concrete materials and hands-on activities.
Enjoys pretending	Provide opportunities and props for dramatic play.
Tends to be egocentric (self-centered: *I* or *me*)	Provide consistent guidance in respecting other's rights and following rules.

Watch for children to show these characteristics. Social studies activities can be implemented to either enhance or discourage such traits.

25-6

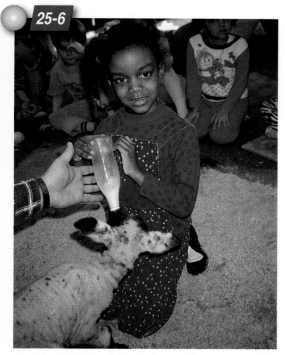

A pet theme can be the basis for teaching many social studies concepts.

of many different concepts. Social studies is not introduced at a particular time each day. Therefore, a variety of daily experiences help children learn concepts. (See Chapter 18 for additional information on themes.)

Use Community Resources

Look closely at your community resources for a variety of learning opportunities. Record the names of stores, museums, art galleries, community services, community workers, and housing groups that may be of interest. The people providing these services might also have suggestions for curriculum objectives and goals.

Incidental Learnings

You should structure the classroom to promote **incidental learnings**. These are learning experiences that happen during the course of a normal day. Watch for everyday happenings that can teach children something. For example, point out the paint

Discuss

What are the benefits of allowing each child in the class an opportunity to select a theme to be followed for a day's activities? What are some drawbacks to this approach?

Enrich

Have students brainstorm a list of guidelines for speakers and other classroom guests to assist them in planning a presentation appropriate for young children. Consider items such as length of presentation, opportunities for hands-on experiences, visual aids, appropriate vocabulary, and time for a question-and-answer period.

Vocabulary

Have a student volunteer define the term *incidental learnings*. Ask students to observe and keep track of the opportunities for incidental learnings that occur in a single class.

Resource

Using a Theme in Planning, Activity B, SAG

Putting Technology to Use

Discussions of current events may bring up questions about war, terrorism, or natural disasters. This can cause stress in young children. Have students conduct an Internet search for information on handling these questions to help children feel safe and secure. What materials or programs exist to help children who are victims of stressful situations? How can these topics be addressed in an early childhood program at a level children can understand without causing further anxiety? Have students write a brief report of their findings.

Reflect

Imagine you planned a field trip to the local city hall and had the children meet the mayor or city administrator, view offices, and sit in the council chamber. The children were not interested and several were uncooperative. How can your evaluation help plan a more successful outing in the future?

Resource

Evaluating a Social Studies Activity, Activity A, OG

Vocabulary

Have student volunteers define the terms *perceptions* and *culture.* How are perceptions related to concept formation? What is the effect of culture on a young child's behavior?

that dried out when the lid was left off or the plant whose leaves yellowed when not watered. These situations cause children to question and learn on their own.

Every classroom has unique incidental learning experiences. The following are examples:

- Classroom and playground repairs
- Classroom rules
- Roles of center workers such as the janitor, bus driver, or office worker
- Handling an argument
- Happenings in the local community

Evaluation

Evaluation is a key part of planning the social studies curriculum. The evaluation process will help you see if goals have been met, what new goals are needed, and whether any current goals need modification. This process can be done with the children. For example, you may ask the children the following questions:

- What did you like best?
- Why did you like it?
- What did you learn?
- What do you want to learn more about?
- What would you like to do again?

Building Social Studies Concepts

Young children want to find out about their world. They touch, taste, smell, see, and hear in an attempt to learn. They form perceptions from such activities. **Perceptions** are ideas formed about a relationship or object as a result of what a child learns through the senses. Repeated experiences form a set of perceptions. This gives rise to concept formation. For instance, a young child sees a black and white cow. Later, the

child sees a black and white dog and calls it a cow. Given proper feedback, the child will learn the difference between a dog and cow.

Concepts help children to organize, group, and order experiences. Concepts help them make sense out of the world. Once learned, they help children communicate with each other.

Personality, experiences, language skills, health, emotions, and social relationships all affect the formation of accurate concepts. Many varied experiences help form more concepts. Experiences are affected by feelings and emotions. Therefore, by having contact with others, children learn to view other ways of thinking. Children with well-formed language skills form useful concepts. Good physical and mental health help children form proper sensory concepts.

A number of concepts are formed through social studies activities. These include multicultural, intergenerational, democracy, ecology, change, geography, community living, current events, and holiday concepts.

Multicultural Concepts

Social scientists use the word *culture* to describe all the aspects of people's lives. This includes a group's ideas and ways of doing things. It includes traditions, language, beliefs, and customs. **Culture**, then, is learned patterns of social behavior. Studies show children typically are aware of their own racial identity around four years of age.

A child's culture is a lens by which the child judges the world. Culture influences feelings, thoughts, and behavior. It imposes order and meaning on all experiences. Culture provides children with a lifestyle that often defines what foods are eaten and when. Culture becomes a vital part of people. As a result, they do not realize that their behavior might be different from behaviors learned in other cultures.

A multicultural perspective is very important in planning a social studies curriculum. Studies show that children's

---

Cross-Curricular Activity

Social Studies
Ask students to research various cultures and gather information that will help them understand, appreciate, and teach about cultures other than their own. Each student should be responsible for learning aspects of the particular culture including traditions, language, beliefs, customs, clothing, foods, family structure, and roles of family members. Have students share what they have learned through a poster display and suggest ways to adapt the information for young children.

attitudes toward their own identities and other cultural groups begin to form during preschool years. They are aware of skin color as early as three years of age.

When planning the *multicultural curriculum,* you will want to keep the following goals in mind. You will want each child to develop

- respect for oneself as a worthwhile and competent human being

- acceptance and respect for others' similarities and differences

- an appreciation of the child's own cultural and ethnic background

- the skill to interact positively with all people

- an understanding that there are many ways to do things

You can meet these goals by involving parents and choosing appropriate learning materials and activities. Your behavior will also influence the success of your social studies curriculum. Chart 25-7 contains a list of multicultural books for promoting social studies concepts.

Parent Involvement

Parents can play a key role in meeting multicultural goals for children. As a teacher, study the cultural background of each child. Parents or other family members are the best resources for this task. They can provide you information on their culture's parenting beliefs and practices. Meeting and talking with parents can provide knowledge of the family and their needs, customs, concerns, and hopes. Parents can also share their heritage by taking part in classroom activities, 25-8. They can share stories, games, songs, dances, foods, and holiday observances related to their culture.

Selecting and Preparing Materials

Select materials that reflect the ethnic heritage and background of all children.

25-7

Multicultural Books for Promoting Social Studies Concepts

Animal Friends: A Global Celebration of Children and Animals by Maya Ajmera and John D. Ivanko

The Story of Little Babaji by Helen Bannerman

Honey…Honey…Lion! A Story from Africa by Jan Brett

The Camel's Lament by Charles Edward Carryl

Mama Panya's Pancakes: Village Tale from Kenya by Mary and Rich Chamberlin

Fiesta! by Ginger Foglesong Guy

Pino and the Signora's Pasta by Janet Pedersen

The Human Alphabet by Pilobolus

All Kinds of Friends, Even Green! by Ellen B. Senisi

The Librarian of Basra by Jeanette Winter

Visiting Day by Jacqueline Woodson

These children's books help promote awareness and appreciation of diversity.

The following are items useful for reaching this goal: cooking utensils; flags; weavings; traditional games; and ethnically diverse children's books, musical tapes and CDs, pictures, and videos.

Teachers should examine materials for their appropriateness in teaching social science concepts. If biases exist in any materials, they should be noted. Then teaching methods must be developed to overcome the bias.

Be sure to watch for stereotyping when selecting materials for classroom use. Stereotyping ignores individual differences. Take care when choosing games, books, puzzles, videos, classroom decorations, and visual aids.

Omission is another bias found in some teaching materials. **Omission** implies that

Resource

Goals for a Multicultural Perspective, transparency master 25-4, TR

Activity

Have students plan a show-and-tell day for children in the child care lab to share their family's cultural heritage. Determine guidelines for items brought from home. Encourage parents to share interesting cultural information with their children.

Vocabulary

Have a student volunteer define the term *omission* as it applies to bias in teaching materials. How are omission and stereotyping examples of disrespect for individuals?

Putting Technology to Use

Have students conduct an Internet search for information about children's books with a multicultural perspective and criteria for evaluating these materials. What guides are available for evaluating books for multicultural content? How can books be evaluated for authenticity? Have students locate lists or sources of books that celebrate diversity and multicultural content and are suitable for young children. Allow time for students to share their findings in class.

Resource

Planning a Social Studies Activity, Activity B, OG

Reflect

Why are children more likely to focus on people's differences than on similarities? What activities would you include in the curriculum that show all people have similar ways of living within a family or other social group?

Enrich

Ask students to investigate the Multi-Cultural Educational Services Web site at **www. mcedservices.com.** This Web site provides language translations of child care forms, online activities, and other educational materials. Allow time for students to share their findings in class.

25-8

Encourage parents to become involved in promoting multicultural perspectives in their child's classroom.

some groups have less value than other groups in our society. This is done by omitting a group's presence in the material. All groups must be included and respected in teaching materials, 25-9. To build self-esteem in children, show them positive role models from all cultural backgrounds.

Activities to Encourage a Multicultural Perspective

Studies show children are more likely to focus on differences than on similarities

25-9

Dolls should represent the racial makeup of society.

Health and Safety

Communicating with Native Language

Oftentimes children or their parents speak a language other than English. The early childhood facility should have at least one staff member who can communicate with children and their parents in their native language. This helps parents and their children feel included and can avoid miscommunication about issues such as children's health needs. If no staff members speak this language, work with the parents to find a translator to help express their needs.

among people. As a result, you need to focus on people's similarities whenever possible. In the curriculum, include activities that show all people have similar ways of living within a family or other social group. Emphasize that all people have similar needs including food, clothing, and shelter. Language, art, and music are ways of expressing various attitudes, feelings, ideas, and knowledge.

Special activities can be planned to focus on similarities. For example, schedule a "special day" for a particular child. During group time, the child may share his or her favorite toy, food, or color. Ask each child to bring in family photographs. They can use these photos to observe similarities. Cooking and eating a variety of cultural foods is another way of stressing multicultural concepts.

Workplace Connection

Ask students to search school supply catalogs or the Internet for sources of multicultural materials. Examples of materials include dolls, children's books, food replicas, posters or pictures representing individuals of various cultures, etc. What items are needed for the child care lab to avoid bias caused by omission? Have students write a "wish" list of items for the child care lab. Allow time for students to discuss their findings in class.

Intergenerational Concepts

Young children's concepts of older adults are not always positive. When a group of preschool children were asked about older adults and growing older, their comments included:

"Well, they sure have a lot of extra skin."

"My grandpa fixes my bike."

"They walk slow and have to sit a lot."

"They're sick."

"You get bald if you are old."

"They help you make cookies."

Such responses show the need to include intergenerational concepts in the early childhood program.

The number of older adults in American society is steadily increasing. With this growth, there is a need to inform all people about the benefits of aging, as well as the problems older adults face. For many children today, their only contact with older adults is with their grandparents. This may lead to one-sided views and ideas. Therefore, young children need to learn from and about older adults.

Negative stereotyping is one of the greatest problems faced by older adults. These views about growing older have also been noted in children. Studies have found that some young children have already formed some stereotypes of older adults.

Studies show attitudes are formed early in life. These feelings and thoughts remain a strong force in a person's life. Children's attitudes toward older adults are generally based on their families' views. Negative stereotypes of older adults may be caused by lack of knowledge. Another reason may be little or no contact with older people. These attitudes can be changed through contact with older adults. Early childhood teachers can invite older adults to take part in the classroom. Intergenerational contacts can benefit both the young and old. Contact with older adults will affect the formation of positive concepts of older persons. Education and information from the radio, television, and newspaper can also change these attitudes.

Include intergenerational concepts in the program to encourage children to view older adults more positively. The goals for such a program are listed in 25-10. Interaction with older people should be included. Books, videos, and pictures used in the classroom should all portray older people without bias. These materials should show the varied

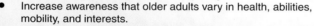

25-10

Goals for an Intergenerational Curriculum

- Encourage social integration of the young and old.
- Increase awareness that older adults vary in health, abilities, mobility, and interests.
- Challenge the stereotypes of older adults as being inactive, unhappy, incapable, or immobile.
- View the actions and traits of older adults in a wide variety of roles.
- Develop an appreciation of others' points of view.
- Promote growth of healthy, positive attitudes toward aging.
- Promote healthy development of their self-concepts to reduce the fear of growing older.
- Provide opportunities to learn how all people, including themselves, change as they move through the life cycle.

The goals of an intergenerational program should include these items.

Discuss

How do the goals of an intergenerational curriculum relate to the overall early childhood education program goals? What does the increasing number of older adults in our population have to do with promoting positive attitudes among young children toward this group?

Reflect

What beliefs or attitudes do you hold about older adults? What challenges have you had in relationships with older people?

Discuss

How can older adults contribute to the child care lab? How would you prepare the children for a visit to the preschool by any guest, including older adults?

Portfolio Project

Have each student interview an older adult about what school was like when they were young. What instructional methods did teachers use to present information to students? How much homework was required? What discipline methods were used? Ask students to write a short essay to compare and contrast educational methods of the past with those used today. Have students file the writing sample in their portfolio.

Vocabulary

Have a student volunteer define the term *gerontology*. What resources already exist in the child care classroom that can be used for activities involving gerontology and intergenerational concepts?

Reflect

What older adults have had an impact on your life? How would you share this information with others, including young children?

Activity

Have preschool children invite their grandparents or other older adults to class to celebrate Grandparent's Day or Senior Citizens Day. Help the children plan activities, snacks, and presentations for the celebration.

interests, abilities, mobility, and health of older adults.

Selecting and Preparing Materials

There are increasing numbers of resources for teaching gerontology to young children. (*Gerontology* is the study of older adults.) Use care when choosing them. Books and other materials should depict older adults positively. Pleasing relationships between the children and older adults should be shown.

If materials are limited, use your imagination to design your own. Cut pictures from magazines or take photographs of active older adults. Then combine several pictures and use them to tell stories.

Activities for Developing Intergenerational Concepts

The curriculum needs to contain concepts of older adults that will foster positive ideas of them. There are many themes where these concepts can be shared, 25-11. For instance, using the theme "Me, Myself," children could focus on their own aging. Pictures of the children as babies could be brought to school. These could serve as a basis for a talk about growth and development. You might also

discuss other changes to come. Height and weight records could be compared. Children could then guess what other changes will occur as they continue to grow. If developmentally appropriate, the children could also make booklets telling of things they liked to do when they were younger, things they enjoy doing now, and the things they think they might like to do when they are older.

If daily contact is not possible, arrange opportunities for contact with older adults. Arrange field trips to visit older neighbors or a retirement home. You might arrange to do seasonal activities, such as singing Christmas carols or making May Day baskets. Other classroom activities include having the children use drawings or pictures cut from magazines to form a large collage or mural depicting older adults in positive, active roles (swimming, jogging, skiing, nurturing). A caption such as "It can be fun to be older" can be added to the collage.

Older Adults in the Classroom

Older adults can contribute to the classroom. For example, they may help with projects, work with children who need special attention, or direct small groups of children. The roles taken by older adults depend on the needs of the teacher, children, and the older person.

Intergenerational programs that focus on developing positive concepts of older adults need to consider the needs of the older person. Like other programs using volunteers, careful planning is required for a successful program. Consider the following guidelines:

- Ensure that each older adult has a definite role to play in the classroom.

- View each older person as an individual, using his or her special talents, interests, and training.

- Maintain close communications between the administration, teachers, and the older volunteer.

25-11

Themes That Can Contain Concepts of Older Adults

- Families
- Friends
- Helpers
- Crafts
- Games
- My Favorite Older Person
- Clothes
- Nursery Rhymes
- Grandparents
- Neighbors
- Hobbies
- Holidays
- Homes
- Grandparents' Jobs
- Music
- Our Town
- Me, Myself

Can you think of activities that would revolve around these themes?

Service Learning Activity

Many schools and service organizations and groups involving youth have an "Adopt a Grandparent" program they carry out with local nursing homes or senior centers. Investigate the possibility of working with one of these organizations and including the preschool children in the activities. The child care students could "adopt" older adults and share activities with the preschoolers. Have students debate the pros and cons of participating in this kind of program, as well as the goals and objectives they would expect to meet as a result of their participation.

- Design and provide training and sharing opportunities for the older person.

Intergenerational programs benefit adults as well as children. Both often enjoy the growth of caring relationships. Adults have the chance to observe children's interest as they share their special talents with them. The children gain understanding of and appreciation for older adults.

Democracy Concepts

Before age five, children's concepts of living in a democratic society are based on the information they receive from the media, home, and center. By this age, children can usually point out the flag and pictures of the president. They may also recognize the national anthem and the Pledge of Allegiance.

To help children learn governmental concepts, design group activities based on the function of a democracy. Such activities will help children understand the purpose of rules and laws. The following list contains sample activities that help build governmental concepts:

- When your class gets a new pet, let the children vote on its name.

- During cooking, let the children vote on what type of food to make.

- When a new toy arrives, let the children outline rules for its use.

- Encourage the children to suggest field trips they would like to take.

- Let children plan the type of sandwiches they will have on a picnic.

- Let the children vote on plans for classroom celebrations, 25-12.

Morning Meetings

Morning meetings promote a caring community at toddler, preschool, kindergarten, and school-age levels. They are

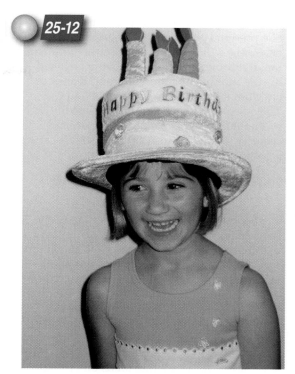

25-12

One way to celebrate birthdays is to use a special birthday hat to make the birthday child feel special.

also sometimes referred to as *class meetings*. These meetings help create and model a democratic environment. Class meetings can be either unscheduled or scheduled.

The purpose of morning meetings is to address concerns of the learning community. This includes children and staff. During these meetings, children are held accountable for their behavior and work. They participate in discussion and problem solving. This helps them develop an understanding of the democratic process. They also develop important life skills in citizenship.

Some teachers use the morning meeting to provide structure for the day. Heidi Weber, a teacher of four-year-old children, holds a daily morning meeting. She begins with a greeting to make each child gain a sense of belonging. After this, she reviews the schedule, additions to the classroom environment, and special events. She also

Activity

Ask students to plan a lesson on their country or state flag. Obtain samples of the flags for the children in the child care lab to see up close. Allow the children to create their own flags using paper or fabric and appropriate art media such as crayons or paint.

Discuss

What can children gain from participating in a classroom voting activity? How can the results of the vote be displayed for all children to observe?

Vocabulary

Have a student volunteer define the term *morning meetings*. What is the purpose of morning meetings?

Cross-Curricular Activity

Social Studies
Contact the social studies teachers in your school. Determine the possibility of creating mini democracy lessons or activities suitable for the preschoolers. Determine if students in any of the social studies classes would be willing to

collaborate with the child care students to present the lessons. Enlist the advice of the teachers to adapt the lessons to the correct level. Make sure students include hands-on opportunities when presenting the lessons to the preschoolers. Allow time for students to compare their experiences.

Vocabulary

Have a student volunteer define the term *ecology*. How can activities related to ecology contribute to meeting the overall goals for the preschool program?

Activity

Ask children from the child care lab to bring a baby picture and a current photo of themselves to class for use in a matching game. Have students observe the children and record what they say as they try to match up the pictures.

Discuss

Why are geography concepts included in a preschool social studies curriculum? How can the area surrounding your school be used to help children become aware of geography concepts?

reviews expectations and promotes rules. She presents problems to the group and encourages the children to discuss them and make recommendations. By being engaged in rule-making and simple group decisions, children learn to solve social problems. They also develop communication skills and promote feelings of belonging, trust, and security. This all leads to the sense of a caring community.

Ecology Concepts

Ecology is the study of the chain of life. It focuses on water, land, air, grass, trees, birds, and insects. In order to develop ecology concepts, children need good observation skills. Using these skills, they can build an appreciation of their environment. They can also learn about the interdependency of all life on the planet. As a result of these activities, children will develop a social concern for the environment.

Sample activities that focus on ecology include the following:

- Take children on a trip around the block. As you walk, point out plants, trees, flowers, shrubs, and birds.

- Keep plants and animals in the classroom or the play yard, 25-13.

- Provide magazines that children may use to cut out pictures they feel are beautiful. Let each child explain the beauty of a picture.

- Give each child a paper bag and take a "trash hike" around the play yard. Encourage children to pick up trash and place it in their bags.

Change Concepts

Children need to learn that change affects their lives in many ways. Change is constant. To help the children learn this concept, use nature and the family. Taking part in these experiences will help children learn to accept change.

25-13

Giving children their own plants helps children learn the importance of caring for the environment.

By observing nature, children learn to understand the concept of change. Plan a nature walk. During the walk, point out the cherry trees budding, the leaves turning colors, flowers blossoming, and fruit ripening. Each of these experiences should help the child understand that all things change.

People are always changing. To help children understand how they have changed, include concepts about changes they have experienced. You might try the following:

- Show a videotape on babies.

- Record children's height and weight at the beginning of the year, at mid-year, and at the end of the year. Discuss with the children how they have changed.

- Collect a variety of baby clothes and toys. Place these items on a table where the children can explore them.

Geography Concepts

Young children are geographers as soon as they become mobile. They explore space, play in water and snow, and dig in dirt. They note differences in wet and dry sand and begin to form some concepts about the earth.

The earth is home to many people. The relationship of humans to the earth is important for children to understand. They need to learn that man's food, shelter, and raw

---

Putting Technology to Use

Explore the possibility of creating a worm farm in the child care lab. Ask students to conduct an Internet search for sites that give directions for making the farms in quart-size clear jars by layering soil, sand, and food or compost medium. Have students collect the food/compost from school cafeteria lunch waste. What ecological principles can be taught through this project? Allow time for students to share their findings in class.

materials are provided by the earth. Since these concepts are quite complex, formal lessons are most often first introduced in elementary school. There are, however, some informal activities to use with younger children. For instance, allow children to dig in a sandbox or a garden area and play in a sandbox with cars, trucks, pails, and shovels. You might also play readiness games that use symbols that can prepare children to read maps. Finally, design a bulletin board that maps out the neighborhood surrounding the center. Children can study this board and then help "navigate" a field trip through the neighborhood.

Community Living Concepts

During the preschool years, children are becoming more and more aware of the world outside their homes and families. They are ready to explore their communities and to learn about the people they will meet there. Explore with the children the neighborhood around the center. What buildings and businesses will they find? Who are the people they will meet? What do these people do? How can they help you? Answering these questions with the children will help them develop community living concepts.

Plan field trips to some of the places in your community that provide services for people. These might include the library, museum, police station, fire station, bus depot, post office, train station, radio or television station, or newspaper. Introduce the children to the people who work at these places. These people should be introduced as community helpers because they help people live together in the community. Police officers, firefighters, postal workers, and librarians are some of the community helpers that might speak with the children.

Also plan visits to various workplaces in the community so the children can see how people work. There are probably many businesses in the local neighborhood that would interest the children. You might plan to have them visit a grocery store, restaurant, farm, pet store, beauty salon, or doctor's office.

You can also invite people in various careers to visit your class and tell about the work they do. They can bring samples of the materials or tools they use in their work. You might invite a dentist, doctor, nurse, teacher, secretary, banker, chef, or other worker to visit. These activities will develop career awareness concepts.

Current Events

Preschool children are usually unaware of events outside their own environment. Therefore, they need to be encouraged to share events affecting their own lives. Show-and-tell is one activity that helps children understand current events. Some of the events children may share include personal achievements, family events, and special celebrations.

Some classrooms develop a current events bulletin board titled *News*. Children can display cards, pictures, invitations, newspaper pictures, drawings, and paintings. You may want to add items such as pictures of the children's classroom activities or field trips.

Holiday Concepts

Almost every culture celebrates holidays throughout the year. Holidays and families are a natural combination. During these times, families and friends share excitement and fun as they join together to eat, sing, and interact in other meaningful ways. Holiday celebrations teach children about their own culture and other cultures. They provide opportunities for meaningful learning about similarities and differences. These learnings will help children form a sense of cultural identity. For these reasons, holiday celebrations are a key part of your social studies curriculum.

Carefully choose and prepare for the holidays that will be celebrated. Classroom celebrations need to be connected to and support a child's home experiences. Holidays are personal and highly valued events. Talk with parents. Let them know

Resource

Know Your Resources, Activity C, SAG

Reflect

What community helper do you first remember from your childhood? How was the individual's job explained to you?

Resource

Current Events Calendar, color transparency CT-22A, TR

Resource

Holiday Concepts Calendar, color transparency CT-22B, TR

Portfolio Project

Have students rotate writing a current events article for the preschool newsletter. The article may contain information about what activities and lessons have taken place in the classroom. It may also contain interviews with individual children who answer a "question of the week/month." Children may contribute information to the article by dictating family news or sharing their impressions of a classroom guest. Have students file a copy of the article in their student portfolio.

Enrich

Have students debate the pros and cons of including holiday celebrations in the preschool curriculum. What factors should be considered in celebrating holidays that some of the children's families do not celebrate?

Activity

Have each student select a specific holiday and write one related lesson activity idea appropriate for each of the following age groups: two-year-olds, three-year-olds, four-year-olds, and five-year-olds.

Resource

Social Studies Terms, reproducible master 25-5, TR

you welcome their involvement. Prepare a parent questionnaire to learn what holidays that parents would like to have celebrated (or not celebrated) at the center. Ask parents how they would like to be involved. Family members may have time to share a family recipe, song, dance, tradition, or story from their culture. Be aware that some families may be hesitant to share personal information. Chart 25-14 shows an example of a family celebration survey.

For each celebration, provide age-appropriate experiences and activities. They should be culturally sensitive and non-stereotyped. Hands-on activities should be provided so the children can control the process. Teach children the social importance of the holiday. Children will also begin to learn concepts about the continuity of life.

Remember that children differ in their ability to understand holiday concepts. It is difficult to make holidays meaningful and developmentally appropriate for young children. Holidays are based on complex concepts. Two-year-olds do not grasp the concept of holiday, but do catch the excitement from their caregivers and families. Three-year-olds view holidays in terms of their families' own experiences. They need holiday activities that are accurate, concrete, and related to their home experiences. Four-year-olds begin to understand simple information related to holidays. They can recall celebrations from the previous year. Four-year-olds can also note similarities and differences in celebrations. By five years of age, children understand that people celebrate holidays in different ways. They enjoy decorating, preparing food, and celebrating holidays with family and friends.

When introducing holiday concepts, observe some precautions. Avoid introducing a holiday more than one week before it occurs, otherwise the children may get confused. They do not have a well-developed concept of time. Choose celebrations that represent many cultural groups. For instance, you may want to celebrate more than one Jewish holiday. Consider celebrating Passover in the spring and Yom Kippur or Rosh Hashanah in the fall. Cinco de Mayo, Three Kings' Day, Juneteenth, and Kwanzaa are other cultural holidays you might want to celebrate. If you have children in your classroom who have come from other countries, ask what holidays and celebrations they enjoy. Learn to include these in your curriculum, too. Also, consider including a "Special People's Day." Invite parents, grandparents, uncles, aunts, neighbors, and volunteers to join the celebration.

Family diversity needs to be considered when planning mother's day and father's day. Not all children have a father and mother. As a result, some programs prefer to celebrate family's day instead. Mothers, fathers, grandparents or even an aunt or uncle could be invited to participate in classroom activities. Likewise, the child could make a picture, card, or gift for any of these people.

Involve the children in your planning for holidays and special events. You will be pleased by their input. They may suggest special foods, songs, books, or games. They may even suggest inviting special people. You may expand upon their ideas by introducing new foods, fingerplays, songs, and stories.

Classroom Celebrations

Holidays are sometimes difficult to plan and implement for young children. Therefore, some teachers plan classroom celebrations. These observe any milestone a child has mastered. For instance, a bulletin board with the title *Classroom Celebrations* can be placed in the classroom. When a child ties his or her shoes for the first time, a digital photo can be taken and printed. It can then be posted on the bulletin board with a caption such as "Hao tied her shoes." Other examples include sitting up alone, walking, printing, riding a tricycle, cutting paper, walking a balance beam, zipping a coat, or even helping a friend. Other occasions to celebrate might include birthdays, the birth of a new sibling, and the arrival of a new child in the program.

Workplace Connection

Have students review a local child care center's policies and practices regarding children's holiday celebrations. What holidays are celebrated (or not celebrated)? How early is a holiday introduced to the children? Do celebrations represent different cultural groups? Are children involved in the planning for holidays and special events? Have students write a brief report of their findings.

25-14

Family Celebration Survey

Dear Parents:

When planning holiday celebrations, it is important that we connect them to and support the child's home environment. We want to honor the holidays of all children and encourage your participation. Therefore, it would be helpful if you could respond to the following questions.

  A. What celebrations does your family celebrate and who is involved?

  B. How would you feel if the center introduced celebrations that are not part of your family's traditions?

  C. What celebrations do you feel the center should include?

  D. Would you be willing to contribute to the classroom holiday celebrations? If so, how? (Check those that apply.)

_____ share artifacts

_____ play an instrument

_____ dance

_____ sing

_____ share records

_____ share photographs

_____ share folk art

_____ cook and share recipes with the children

_____ play games

_____ Other: _____

_____

_____

Parent Name _____ Date _____

Thank you for your participation.

Involving families can help ensure that all cultures are represented.

Resource

Halloween Theme, reproducible master 25-2, TR

Reflect

What holiday celebrations in school do you remember from your childhood? What family participation was involved in classroom celebrations?

Resource

Valentine Theme, transparency master 25-3, TR

Meeting Special Needs

Review the special learners' chapter outlines to determine if the students have any questions about the concepts or content of this chapter. Review the chapter objectives and ask the students to evaluate their progress in meeting these objectives. Ask the students to summarize, orally or in writing, what they learned from this chapter.

Review and Reflect Answer Key

1. (List three:) develop self-respect and healthy self-concept; develop respect for others; develop self-control and independence; learn to share ideas and materials; develop healthy ways of relating to and working with others; gain the attitudes, knowledge, and skills needed for living in a democracy; develop respect for others' feelings, ideas, and property; learn about the roles people have in life; learn to appreciate the past and its relationship to the present; learn the need for and purpose of rules

2. Observe children during play, interact with them in a casual way, ask the children's parents to share their children's interests with you, and observe the children's choice of books.

3. Young children are able to plan whom to play with, materials needed for a project, places to visit, people to invite to the classroom, and how to celebrate birthdays and holidays.

4. Learning experiences that happen during the course of a normal day. (Example is student response.)

5. evaluation

6. perceptions

Summary

Social studies concepts help young children understand the world in which they live. They gain skills, attitudes, and knowledge for living in a democratic society. A well-planned social studies program teaches children about people and customs with differences and similarities from those in their own families. Children learn to accept and appreciate these differences.

When planning the social studies curriculum, teachers need to determine the children's interests, abilities, and experiences. Connecting with parents to obtain information about the children's families is important. This information can be used to develop the curriculum using various themes and taking advantage of community resources. Incidental learnings also provide an opportunity to teach social studies concepts.

Effective social studies programs introduce children to different cultures and generations of people. They learn basic principles of a democracy. Children also learn about ecology and geography. These are just some of the many social studies themes that can be included in early childhood programs.

Review and Reflect

1. List three social studies skills that children can learn in an early childhood program.

2. Describe four ways to determine children's interests.

3. What aspects of their activities are children capable of planning?

4. Define *incidental learnings* and give an example.

5. The _____ process will help you see if goals have been met, what new goals are needed, and whether any current goals need modification.

6. Ideas formed about a relationship or object as a result of experiences are called _____.

7. List the goals of a multicultural curriculum.

8. Explain how omission is a bias that should be avoided when selecting teaching materials.

9. True or false. Children are more likely to focus on similarities than on differences among people.

10. True or false. Young children have not yet developed stereotypes concerning older adults.

11. Give your own example of how you could teach a democracy concept to young children.

12. Explain the purpose of morning meetings.

13. Explain this statement: "Change is constant."

14. How do show-and-tell activities relate to the social studies curriculum?

15. True or false. Five-year-old children enjoy decorating, preparing food, and celebrating holidays with family and friends.

7. Respect for oneself as a worthwhile and competent human being; acceptance and respect for others' similarities and differences; an appreciation of one's own cultural and ethnic background; the skill to interact positively with all people; an understanding that there are many ways to do things.

8. Omission implies that some groups have less value than other groups in our society. This is done by omitting a group's presence in teaching materials.

9. false

10. false

11. (Student response.)

Apply and Explore

1. As a class, choose a theme and brainstorm a list of activities that could be used in various social studies areas.

2. Visit a toy store and prepare a list of toys that reflect cultural diversity.

3. Ask a group of preschoolers what they think about older people. Are their comments similar to those listed in this chapter, or are they different? Do they reveal any stereotypes?

4. Plan a lesson for preschoolers on recycling as a way to protect the environment.

Cross-Curricular Link

Social Studies

1. Brainstorm a list of community resources. Include museums, art galleries, stores, and services that are available.

Reading

2. Select a social studies topic and find three children's books related to the topic.

Technology

3. Check the information provided on the Web site www.celebrateexpress.com for easy party games and a party-planning checklist.

4. Explore the Web site school.discovery.com to find links for holidays and seasons.

Workplace Link

Contact local preschools and child care centers to discover the role that social studies plays in their curriculums. Is social studies formally taught as a separate activity, or is it integrated with daily activities? What materials or equipment are used to promote the understanding of social studies concepts? What are the most popular and most successful social studies themes used at the various programs?

12. The purpose of the morning meeting is to address the concerns of the children and staff. Often teachers may also use the meeting to provide structure for the day. The process helps children develop communication skills and promote feelings of belonging, trust, and security. It also promotes important skills in citizenship.

13. (Student response.)

14. Preschool children are usually unaware of events outside their own environment. Therefore, they need to be encouraged to share events affecting their own lives. Show-and-tell is one activity that helps children understand current events. Some of the events children may share include personal achievements, family events, and special celebrations.

15. true

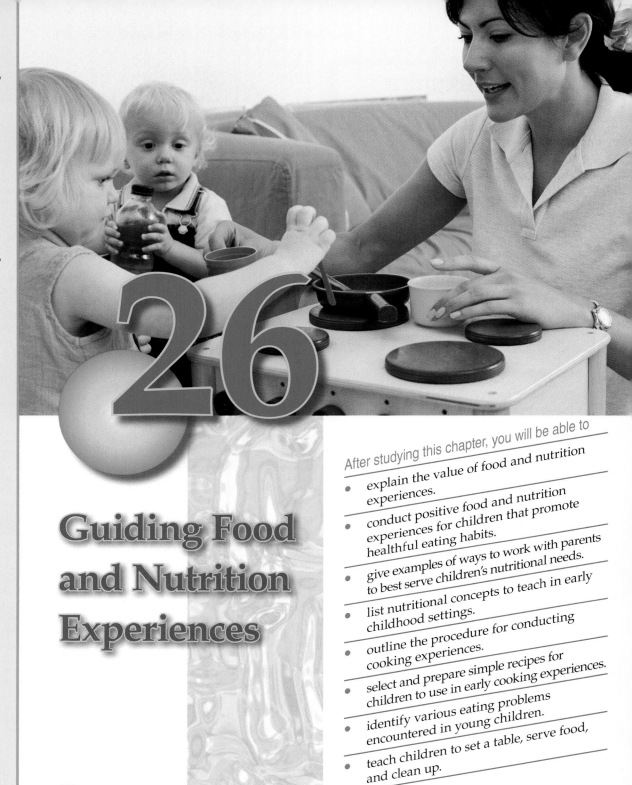

Discuss

Look at the chapter opening photo. How might food and nutrition experiences benefit this child? What nutritional concepts do you think should be taught in an early childhood setting?

Discuss

Look over the objectives for this chapter to get a sense of the material to be covered. What questions do you have about food and nutrition for young children you hope will be answered in this chapter?

26

Guiding Food and Nutrition Experiences

After studying this chapter, you will be able to

- explain the value of food and nutrition experiences.
- conduct positive food and nutrition experiences for children that promote healthful eating habits.
- give examples of ways to work with parents to best serve children's nutritional needs.
- list nutritional concepts to teach in early childhood settings.
- outline the procedure for conducting cooking experiences.
- select and prepare simple recipes for children to use in early cooking experiences.
- identify various eating problems encountered in young children.
- teach children to set a table, serve food, and clean up.

Terms to Know

nutrition concepts
portable kitchen

Food and nutrition experiences involve many activities: preparing foods, setting the table, eating snacks and meals, and cleaning up. These activities help provide learning experiences that prepare children for an independent lifetime. Participating in food and nutrition experiences also builds feelings of independence, responsibility, and worthiness. These activities provide opportunities for teaching nutrition concepts. **Nutrition concepts** are basic concepts that will help children develop good lifetime healthful eating habits.

Experiences with food and nutrition promote the development of the whole child. Cognitive, physical, social, and emotional development are all impacted. Studies show that feeding practices can be a stronger factor in the growth of young children than genetics or ethnic background.

Cognitively, children learn observation and critical thinking skills by participating in food and nutrition experiences. By measuring, comparing, analyzing, observing the change in ingredients and predicting outcomes, children learn science and math concepts. By learning cooking vocabulary and the names of food preparation tools, children develop language skills. By following a sequence of visual illustrations and directions provided on recipe charts, children develop left-to-right progression skills that are necessary for reading and writing.

Physically, cooking experiences promote the development of large and small muscles. Young children develop muscular control by rolling, pounding, peeling, and stirring. They also develop hand-eye coordination skills by measuring, spooning, and cutting.

Socially and emotionally, food and nutrition experiences promote self-esteem. Children take pride in being able to take part in an "adult" activity, 26-1. By taking turns and sharing utensils and ingredients, young children learn cooperation skills. By participating in food and nutrition experiences with their peers, they also learn about foods from their own and other cultures. Finally, by taking part in cooking activities, children learn independent living skills they can use throughout their lives.

The key to an effective food and nutrition program is presenting cooking activities in a positive way. It is quite easy for food experiences to become tense and unproductive. There may be children who refuse to eat. Other children refuse to help with the tasks. Still other children may eat too much or help to a point where others cannot take part. Set several simple limits to promote happy, relaxed food and nutrition experiences:

- Schedule quiet, relaxing activities just before mealtimes.
- Provide child-sized tables, chairs, and serving tools.
- Eat with the children.

26-1

Preparing their own nutritious snacks is fun and promotes feelings of competence for these children.

Vocabulary

Have a student volunteer define the term *nutrition concepts.* What skills will children use as they become familiar with nutrition concepts?

Activity

Have students collaborate to create a picture file of food items. Provide magazines for cutting out pictures of typical as well as unusual foods and mount them on card stock. Food items may also be available through clip art. Pictures may be used as needed for the food activities children will participate in throughout the year.

Reflect

Do you recall any food preparation activities from your childhood? How did your participation affect your sense of self-esteem or sense of accomplishment?

Meeting Special Needs

Provide an outline of the chapter with all the chapter headings for special learners. Students should fill in each section of the outline as the material is covered in class with a sentence or two about the content. Review the special learners' IEPs to decide if any modifications should be made in presenting the chapter content.

Discuss

How do parents influence their child's eating habits? What role does the media or peer group have on a child's food preferences?

Activity

Locate examples of preschool meal and snack menus and cafeteria menus from your school district. Have students compare the menus for types of foods offered. Discuss the probability of the foods on the menus being eaten by the respective students.

Reflect

Do you find the study of nutrition to be an interesting and enjoyable task? If not, what could make it more enjoyable and interesting and how will you use this insight when preparing lessons on nutrition for young children?

Resource

Teaching Nutrition,
Activity A, SAG

- Encourage children to serve themselves.

- Expect some accidents. Children will spill drinks and drop food. Be prepared by keeping damp sponges handy in all food areas. Encourage children to clean up their own messes.

Working with Parents

Parents need to be aware of how they can and do influence their children's eating habits. These influences can be direct or indirect. For instance, the snacks they provide their children are a direct influence. The atmosphere of the home at mealtime is an indirect influence. Several methods are useful for working with parents in this key area of child development.

Many centers have lending libraries. These libraries are a good way to share nutrition information with adults. Parents and guardians may check out pamphlets, magazines, and books to learn or update their nutrition knowledge. Recipes may also be shared in such a setting.

Parents' meetings, workshops, and discussion groups are also useful methods for interacting with parents. Here, parents, guardians, and teachers can discuss reliable information on nutritional needs of children, suggestions for dealing with common mealtime problems, and resources in the community for food.

Some centers find that a weekly or monthly newsletter is a good way to keep parents and guardians informed and involved. Such a newsletter can contain a great deal of useful information: home food activities that reinforce concepts learned at the center, suggestions for menu planning, serving, and stressing good nutrition. A center menu is also a useful addition. Parents can use this to coordinate home meals with those served in the center.

Health and Safety

Foods from Home

As a child care provider, it is your responsibility to talk with parents about safe foods to bring from home. At times, parents may want to contribute food and baked goods for a special class project. Inform parents that they should only bring whole or packaged foods and commercially made foods and baked goods. Talk with parents about proper storage temperatures and safe transportation of foods that require refrigeration.

Nutrition Concepts

Nutrition knowledge is useful throughout life. Teaching nutrition, then, is an important part of guiding food experiences. For instance, children learn that a wide variety of foods are available to meet the needs of their bodies. This concept can be taught by introducing children to many foods during snack and mealtime. These experiences can also teach children that foods can be eaten in a number of ways. For example, apples can be eaten raw or cooked. They can be made into applesauce, apple bread, apple pancakes, apple pie, apple juice, and apple dumplings. Chart 26-2 highlights other nutrition concepts to include in an early childhood setting.

Workplace Connection

Ask a registered dietitian to speak to the class about the nutritional needs of young children and how they are met through proper meal and snack planning. How can having accurate information about nutrient needs for specific age and growth stages help students plan appropriate food activities for the children? Have students prepare a list of additional questions to ask prior to the visit, especially about nutrition myths or misinformation.

26-2

Nutrition Concepts for Young Children

- Nutrition is how our bodies use the foods we eat to produce energy, growth, and health.

- There is a wide variety of food available. Foods come from both plants and animals. In addition, the same food can be used to make many different dishes.

- Foods vary in color, flavor, texture, odor, size, and shape.

- Foods are classified into basic food groups:
  ✓ grain group
  ✓ vegetable group
  ✓ fruit group
  ✓ milk group
  ✓ meat and beans group
  ✓ oils

- A good diet includes foods from each of the food groups.

- There are many factors that enhance the eating experience:
  ✓ aesthetics of food
  ✓ method of preparation
  ✓ cleanliness, manners
  ✓ environment/atmosphere
  ✓ celebrations

- We choose foods we eat for many reasons:
  ✓ availability
  ✓ family and personal habit
  ✓ aesthetics of food
  ✓ social and cultural customs
  ✓ mass media

Young children need to learn simple nutrition concepts.

Cooking Experiences

Children enjoy cooking experiences, which also help them learn about healthful eating. These experiences promote language, math, and science concepts and skills. Children learn the vocabulary of cooking.

Words such as *stirring*, *measuring*, and *pouring* extend their vocabularies. Basic math concepts such as shape, size, number, and temperature change are learned. By "reading" recipe charts, children learn to follow directions. By exploring similarities and differences in food they develop critical thinking skills. By finding new ways to combine ingredients, they also learn creative thinking skills.

By taking part in food and nutrition experiences, children learn how to use cooking utensils and work as a team. They learn how to use can openers, vegetable peelers, and egg beaters. Children learn left-to-right progression skills as the teacher helps them read recipes. Cooking is also a natural way to learn how to follow directions, 26-3.

The "Cook's Corner"

Most teachers know the value of cooking experiences. To increase learning and decrease safety and health hazards, follow these actions:

- Have all cooks wash their hands in warm, soapy water and wear aprons.

26-3

Even young children can follow recipe charts that are written using picture symbols.

Resource

Nutrition Concepts for Young Children, transparency master 26-1, TR

Enrich

Have small groups of students brainstorm ways to teach young children about the basic food groups. Have each group select and demonstrate one of their ideas for the rest of the class.

Discuss

How do cooking experiences promote language, math, and science concepts and skills? Give examples.

Resource

Important Food Learnings, Activity A, OG

Putting Technology to Use

Have students conduct an Internet search for sources of cooking activities for young children. Students should evaluate each Web site by looking through the suggested activities and then rating them based on age-appropriateness; availability of ingredients and equipment; nutritional content; amount of adult help needed; relationship to program goals; and length of time. Each student should print out a list of the sites they recommend and any ideas they find particularly interesting or useful to save for future reference.

Resource

Collecting Recipes,
Activity B, SAG

Enrich

Ask students to watch
two television cooking
shows or food demon-
stration videos. Have
students observe for
pointers on food dem-
onstration and the pre-
preparation involved in
the cooking activities.
What information from
these shows can be
adapted to the early
childhood classroom?

Resource

*Sensory Experiences
with Food,* reproducible
master 26-2, TR

- Clean and disinfect all work surfaces.

- When using recipe cards, print short, clear, sequential instructions. Food labels, picture symbols, numerals, short phrases, and single words make recipes easy for young children to "read."

- Place the recipe, ingredients, clean-up supplies, and utensils on a tray before the activity begins, 26-4.

- Use large, stable, unbreakable bowls for mixing ingredients.

- Have the children sit when using sharp utensils such as knives and peelers.

Preparing needed items on a tray beforehand makes cooking experiences go more smoothly.

First Experiences

First food experiences should be developmentally appropriate. They should revolve around simple recipes that can be served at snack time. Choose activities that require no cooking, 26-5. Have the children shake cream to make butter or prepare instant pudding. Measure the ingredients before the experience. This will help ensure a successful experience. Success is important. Then children will want to take part in future activities.

Planning

Plan a series of cooking experiences that gradually become more complex. Prepare the same food in a number of different forms. Each time, add something new. For example, add berries to instant vanilla pudding. Later you can add other types of fruit.

As you select recipes, be aware of any food allergies children may have. Common culprits include milk, milk products, plant

No cooking is needed for young children to make this fun snack with fresh carrots, cherry tomatoes, broccoli, and vegetable dip.

Cross-Curricular Activity

Math
Contact your school's foodservice director or cafeteria manager for several nutrition-conscious recipes that might be appealing to young children. Have students determine the serving sizes appropriate for children and calculate the ingredient measurements needed

for a much smaller yield. What modifications will need to be taken into account? Examples include baking or cooking times for smaller pan sizes and how to figure out accurate amounts when many food service recipes are written in pounds of ingredients rather than in cups.

and tree nuts, and orange juice. You must also observe the children's family beliefs about food. Some families avoid certain foods in their diet.

Limit the number of children who will take part in any activity. Usually no more than four to six children should be involved. Therefore, children may have to take turns. Some teachers schedule cooking during small group activity times. In that way, the number of children is naturally limited and the children can be encouraged to take turns.

Collect enough tools and unbreakable equipment for all children involved. Plastic bowls and blunt tools are best. Each child should have a tool when activities such as peeling apples are scheduled. For cutting, provide strong plastic knives.

Cooking

Some teachers create a portable kitchen in their classrooms. Create a **portable kitchen** by placing the ingredients, tools, and other equipment on a low table so all children can watch. Find an area near an electrical outlet so you can use portable appliances such as an electric skillet or a hot plate rather than a stove. To prevent accidents, turn pan handles away from children. Remind children of safety rules.

Start the activity by telling the children what you are going to make. Then have all cooks (including you) wash their hands with soapy water. After this, explain the sequence of steps you will use. Discuss the different sizes of measuring cups and spoons. Ask simple questions such as which holds the most. If you have not prepared a recipe chart, write the steps on a board or large piece of paper. The children will enjoy following directions.

As the children move through the preparation steps, encourage them to talk about what is happening. Point out the changes in food form(s) due to blending, cooking, or freezing. Ask them to predict what will happen. Whenever possible, science, math, language arts, and social studies concepts should all be included if they mesh with the lesson. Name any new foods, processes, and equipment.

Cleanup is an important part of the experience. Children should be involved in the process. Dishes and ingredients will have to be returned to the kitchen. The table and dishes will have to be washed.

Tasting Experiences

After cooking, tasting helps children learn about new foods. New foods can be compared with familiar foods. For example, a lime can be compared with a lemon, or a sweet potato can be compared with a white potato. Food temperature and texture can be discussed. Many teachers use these activities as part of an interest center. This limits the number of children who can be involved at any given time. For safety reasons, an adult should be part of any tasting activities, 26-6.

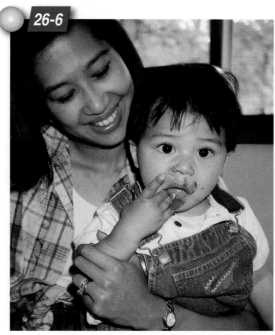

26-6

This young boy did a tasting experience with different colors of frosting on his birthday cake. Having an adult nearby is comforting as well as a good safety practice.

Vocabulary

Have a student volunteer define the term *portable kitchen*. What is the benefit of having a portable kitchen in the preschool classroom?

Resource

Chocolate Chip Cookies, color transparency CT-23, TR

Note

Some recipes may not have enough steps for each student to have a chance to participate, so they may lose attention. Consider dividing the recipe portions among all the children so each child can prepare his or her own recipe or product. A source for individual recipes is *Cup Cooking* by Barbara Johnson Foote.

Resource

Recipes for Young Children, reproducible master 26-3, TR

Portfolio Project

Print *Recipes for Young Children*, reproducible master 26-3, TR, on card stock and make enough copies for each student. Recipes can be added to the student's own recipe booklet made as a portfolio project from Chapter 12. Have students enhance their booklets by selecting additional recipes representing food products children can prepare by themselves or with very little assistance. Ask students to determine suggested age groups for each recipe added.

Resource

Promoting Good Eating Habits, transparency master 26-4, TR

Discuss

What effect might family or friend's negative comments about food have on a child's attitudes toward trying the food? How can teachers encourage a reluctant child to try a new food?

Reflect

What eating habits or food preferences did you have as a young child that you have outgrown? What foods would you refuse as a child that you really enjoy eating now? How did you get over your distaste or reluctance to eat these foods?

Eating Habits

No doubt you will find that some children have poor eating habits. Often, these habits are learned from others. If parents, relatives, and peers have poor eating habits, chances are that the young children will have them, too.

You can use food and nutrition experiences to model and encourage good eating habits. By tasting all foods in front of children, you will encourage them to do the same. You also can model appropriate attitudes toward eating. Offering constructive comments is another way to improve eating habits. For instance, you might say, "Seth, I'm glad you tried the peas today. You probably found out how good they taste."

Changing Appetites

Children do not always eat the same amount of food every day, 26-7. If a child is

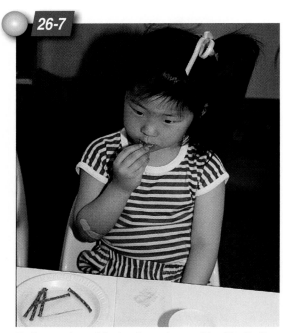

26-7

Earlier meals, activity level, weather, and health all affect a child's appetite.

Health and Safety

Nutrition Policies and Resources

According to federal guidelines, early childhood facilities must have a written nutrition plan. This plan should be shared with *all* staff members, including the foodservice staff, and parents. The plan should link food and feeding experiences to those for the home. Early childhood teachers work with the foodservice staff and parents to ensure that meal plans and food-related activities fulfill the nutritional requirements of children. Resources for planning meals and food-related activities may include

- nutritionists at local and state health departments or hospitals
- cooperative extension nutritionists and WIC
- USDA Child and Adult Care Food Program
- USDA Child Care Nutrition Resource System (part of the Food and Nutrition Information System)
- organizations such as the Dairy Council, American Heart Association, American Dietetic Association, and many more

very active on a certain day or has a light breakfast, the child will likely have a big appetite. If the weather is hot or a child has just eaten before coming to the center, he or she probably will not be very hungry. Fatigue and illness can also cause a change in children's appetites.

Workplace Connection

Have students conduct an in-school field trip to the school's cafeteria so the child care lab children can observe the sanitary procedures followed in food service. Ask the cafeteria manager to explain what the employees do to keep the foods they are preparing and serving safe. Allow time for children to ask questions during the field trip. After the field trip, be sure to discuss with the children what they learned.

If a child's lack of appetite at mealtime continues for a length of time, observe the child. Ask these questions:

- Is the child getting enough nutrients?
- Is the child eating too much at snack time?
- Is the child paying attention at mealtime?
- Is the child being properly reinforced at mealtime?
- Is the child always tired at mealtime?

After observing the child, you may notice one of these problem areas. For instance, if the child is always tired at mealtime, provide him or her with a quiet period before eating. If the problem continues, contact the child's parents.

Refusing Foods

Young children may refuse to eat at times for a number of reasons. Consuming too many liquids is a leading cause. Too much liquid can make a child feel full and displace other foods in the diet. To avoid this problem, limit milk and juice to snack and mealtimes. Offer water between meals to quench thirst.

Children may dislike a food they have tried. They may also reject a food that is prepared in an unfamiliar manner. More often, however, children are copying the actions of others they have seen refuse to eat a certain food. Children need you to be a positive model for healthful eating.

Improper portion size can be another problem. Adults often overestimate how much food children can eat. This is one reason children should serve their own food. Young children have internal signals that tell them when they are full. Pushing children to eat may cause them to ignore their internal cues. This could lead to overeating and childhood obesity.

Pushing children to eat has another consequence—children may refuse the food just to see your reaction. In this way, eating can quickly become a power struggle. To avoid this situation, take a matter-of-fact approach to mealtimes. Provide nutritious foods and let the children choose which foods and how much of each food they will eat. Avoid becoming emotionally involved in their food choices.

Setting the Table

Children should be expected to set the table. This routine provides experiences in counting and in space relationships. Have children take turns performing this routine. Teachers often list this task on a chart, along with other tasks to be done around the classroom.

Begin teaching children to set the table by explaining rules. Before the table is set, the children must wash their hands. Then they must wash the table with a sponge or cloth and soapy water. After this, they may participate in setting the table.

Place mats that show the positions of eating utensils, plates, and glasses are quite helpful for beginners, 26-8. These mats also help children learn the space relationships of eating utensils.

26-8

Young children enjoy setting the table using outlined placemats.

Discuss

How is portion size linked to childhood obesity? How might parents and caregivers unwittingly contribute to overeating by a child in their care?

Reflect

Sandy, a four-year-old child in your child care center, consistently refuses to eat the cooked vegetables served at lunch. Her teacher has told her she may not have dessert. What is your opinion of the teacher's actions?

Discuss

What math concepts can children experience when helping to set a table with a place mat such as the one in 26-8? At what age can children begin to help with setting the table?

Putting Technology to Use

Ask students to conduct an Internet search to find out more about childhood eating disorders. How can you determine a young child has an eating disorder? What treatments are available for children diagnosed with an eating disorder? What can you do to prevent a child from developing an eating disorder? Have students write a one-page report of their findings. Allow time for students to share their reports with the class.

Resource

Setting the Table,
Activity C, SAG

Activity

Prepare children for
pouring their own milk,
juice, or water from
small pitchers at the
table by allowing them
to practice using the
pitchers at the water
table. Provide a variety
of substances such as
beans, sand, and salt
as well as liquids for
pouring practice.

Resource

*Evaluating a Cooking
Activity,* Activity B, OG

Resource

*Evaluating Children's
Learnings,* Activity C,
OG

Teach children to place the plate on the middle of the place mat. Then have them place the fork to the left of the plate. Place the napkin next to the fork. After this, the knife is placed to the right of the plate (if you are using knives). The spoon is placed next to the knife. Finally, the glass is placed at the tip of the knife.

Small centerpieces are a nice addition to the dining table. Those made of unusual materials can become the focal point of conversations. Centerpieces may be something a child has brought from home or something the class has made.

Seating

Teachers should always sit face-to-face with the children at the children's eye level during snack and mealtime. This position provides an opportunity for the "teachable moment." Positive social interactions and manners can be modeled. Words such as *please* and *thank you* can be reinforced. To illustrate, the teacher can use effective praise after hearing one child thanking another. The teacher's response might be, "It pleases me to hear you say thank you."

Children can be encouraged to respect and care for others while sitting at the table. For example, the teacher may say, "Eva, will you please ask Jeffrey if he wants more pizza?" If Eva asks Jeffrey and passes the pizza plate to him, the teacher can comment, "It was very kind of you to pass the pizza to Jeffrey." Likewise, the teacher can encourage children to use expressive language skills at mealtimes with comments such as, "Nicole, if you would like another taco, ask Devan to pass them to you."

Health and Safety

Avoiding Choking Hazards

When creating developmentally appropriate food plans for children, avoid foods that can cause children (especially those under four years) to choke. Examples of high-risk foods include: hot dogs; raw carrots, sliced or in strips; nuts and seeds; large amounts of peanut butter; chunks of meat and other foods that cannot be swallowed whole; whole grapes; or hard candy. These foods are high risk because they can partially or totally block a child's airway.

Serving and Eating

To foster independence, children should serve themselves and others. Place serving dishes on each table. They should be the proper weight and size for young children to handle. To encourage independence, provide small pitchers, allowing the children to pour their own milk, juice, or water.

Begin a meal encouraging children to try a small amount of each food. This will be about one or two serving spoons. If a child tastes all the food on his or her plate, allow the child to have another serving.

Workplace Connection

Ask student volunteers to role-play appropriate and positive table behavior for preschoolers to the class. Have the students demonstrate the role-playing activity to the preschoolers after students have had an opportunity to critique the presentation and offer their suggestions. Arrange time after the presentation for preschoolers to practice appropriate and positive table behavior. Allow time for students to discuss their observations.

Milk should be served with the meal. Some children prefer liquids to solid food. They will often drink their milk right away and then ask for more. Remind these children that more milk will not be provided until all other foods are tasted.

Cleaning Up

Cleaning up is also part of the eating routine. Children one year and older can begin to learn how to clean up after themselves.

Place a utility cart and garbage can next to the eating area. After the main meal is completed, have the children take their plates to the cart. Ask them to throw napkins and other disposable items in the trash. You may wish to have children scrape the food scraps from their plates directly into the trash, too. If dessert is being served, they may keep their eating utensils and glasses. When they have finished dessert, the children should then take all their dinnerware and eating utensils to the cart.

Resource

Mealtime Tips Puzzle, reproducible master 26-5, TR

Resource

Planning a Food Activity, Activity D, OG

Resource

Observing Snack Time, Activity E, OG

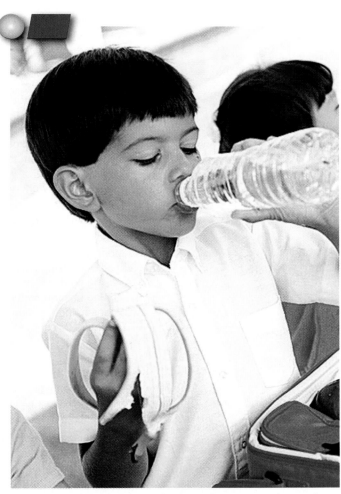

Some basic guidance can make food experiences more pleasant for children and teachers.

Meeting Special Needs

Review the special learners' chapter outlines to determine if the students have any questions about the concepts or content of this chapter. Review the chapter objectives and ask the students to evaluate their progress in meeting these objectives. Ask the students to summarize, orally or in writing, what they learned from this chapter.

Review and Reflect Answer Key

1. (List three:) preparing foods, setting the table, eating snacks and meals, cleaning up
2. true
3. (List four:) schedule quiet, relaxing activities just before mealtimes; provide child-sized tables, chairs, and serving tools; eat with the children; encourage children to serve themselves; expect some accidents
4. lending libraries, meetings/workshops/ discussion groups, newsletters (Student response for explanations.)
5. recipe cards
6. false
7. B
8. Children learn poor eating habits from people with whom they have contact, such as parents, relatives, and peers.
9. C
10. C
11. true
12. true

Summary

Food and nutrition experiences are of great value to children. Food and nutrition experiences promote cognitive, physical, social, and emotional development in children.

Guiding food and nutrition experiences includes many tasks. It requires planning cooking experiences, teaching basic nutrition concepts, setting tables, and eating. The skills children learn in this area will be used throughout their lives.

Food and nutrition experiences also involve movement and activity. The children may become excited and require extra supervision. For this reason, the experiences must be well planned and limited to small groups of children.

Guiding food and nutrition experiences will require extra effort from you as a teacher. Carefully structured and supervised, these experiences can be very useful and enjoyable for you and the children.

Review and Reflect

1. List three activities involved in food and nutrition experiences.

2. True or false. Experiences with food promote the development of the whole child.

3. List four limits that promote relaxed food and nutrition experiences.

4. Name three methods for working with parents regarding their children's nutrition. Explain one method.

5. When using _____, write short, clear instructions using food labels, picture symbols, and simple phrases.

6. True or false. Allowing 10 to 12 children to participate in a cooking experience at one time is a good idea.

7. As children move through the food preparation steps, _____.
   A. plan the next activity
   B. remain with the experience, encouraging them to talk about what is happening
   C. clean up the work area
   D. None of the above.

8. Where do many children learn poor eating habits?

9. Among young children, _____ is a leading cause of refusing food.
   A. being tired
   B. being uninterested in food
   C. consuming too many liquids
   D. None of the above.

10. If a child constantly refuses to eat a certain food, _____.
    A. ignore the behavior
    B. scold the child
    C. give the child small portions of the food
    D. force the child to eat the food

11. True or false. Teachers should always be seated with the children during snack and mealtimes.

12. True or false. To promote independence, children should serve themselves and others.

Apply and Explore

1. Writing. Design a nutrition newsletter to be sent out to parents. Determine columns and special features you would include.

2. Choose one nutrition concept. Design a brief lesson for teaching this concept.

3. Choose a simple recipe to use with young children. Write the recipe out in chart form, making it understandable to the users.

Cross-Curricular Link

Writing

1. Watch a Saturday morning television program designed for young children. Compile a list of the food advertisements shown during the program. Determine whether the ads conveyed positive messages about good nutrition. In a written report, summarize your findings. Briefly describe how these ads may affect young children's food choices.

Social Studies

2. Prepare a list of foods from various cultures you could have children prepare in a classroom setting. List other ethnic foods you could have parents bring in for the children to taste.

Technology

3. Explore Dole's fun food and nutrition activities and curriculum ideas under *Kids* at www.dole.com.

Workplace Link

Survey area programs that serve meals and snacks to young children. Investigate the ways they handle food refusals and picky eaters. What strategies are successful in getting children to eat a suitable portion of nutritious foods? Which methods do not work? How often are parents involved in the process? What effect does a picky eater's behavior have on the other children at the table?

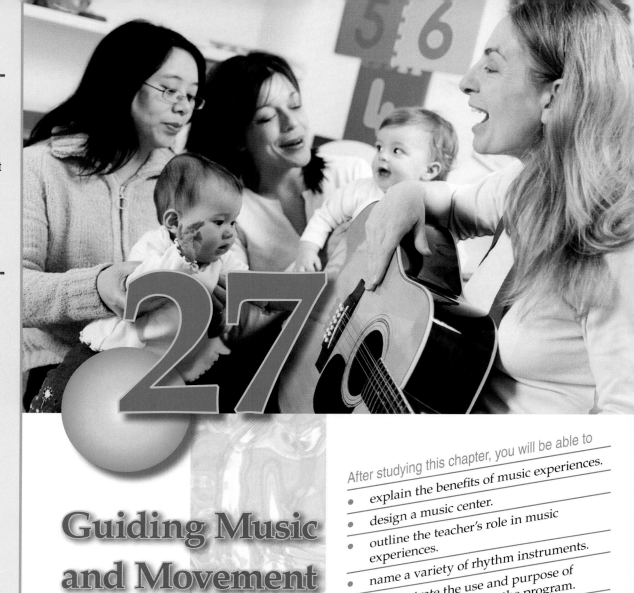

Discuss

Look at the chapter opening photo. What message do you think the adults are trying to convey to the children through music? In what ways might children benefit from music experiences?

Discuss

Look over the objectives for this chapter to get a sense of the material to be covered. What knowledge, information, or skills do you think will be needed to effectively teach music experiences to young children?

27

Guiding Music and Movement Experiences

After studying this chapter, you will be able to

- explain the benefits of music experiences.
- design a music center.
- outline the teacher's role in music experiences.
- name a variety of rhythm instruments.
- demonstrate the use and purpose of rhythm instruments in the program.
- list considerations for scheduling music activities.
- plan a variety of music activities.
- explain how to teach various movement activities.
- describe movement activities that promote children's development.

504

Terms to Know

phrase method
whole song method
phrase/whole combination method
Autoharp®
chant
body percussion
auditory discrimination skills
pantomiming

27-1

Music can be used many ways as a form of communication.

On a rainy afternoon, Mrs. Kohler noticed that the children in her classroom were restless. They needed some activity. She decided to guide them in a movement activity using a piece of music designed to promote movement.

The children were told to listen closely. Then Mrs. Kohler told them to move the way the music made them feel. Watching the children, she saw that fast music made them quickly hop up and down. Slow music made them tiptoe, taking tiny steps.

After the activity, Mrs. Kohler felt she had met her goal. The children gained practice in listening. They also released pent-up energy and played cooperatively with each other. The activity Mrs. Kohler planned included both music and movement.

Music is a powerful form of communication through which every culture speaks, 27-1. It is an important form of communication between adults and children. Adults often rock babies to sleep with lullabies. Adults play musical games with children, such as *Ring-Around-the-Rosy*, *London Bridge*, and *Pat-a-Cake*. As adults play with children, adults convey messages. They communicate feelings to children. They pass on culture. They teach an appreciation for music. They also teach language skills and music basics.

Teachers use music of all cultures and styles with young children for many reasons. Music

- builds a sense of community
- provides an opportunity to learn and use language concepts and vocabulary
- provides an opportunity to practice counting skills
- provides a pleasant background for playing, eating, and sleeping
- calms angry feelings and releases tension and energy
- can be used to express feelings through movement and dance
- can be used to manage behavior
- makes learning fun
- teaches listening skills
- helps build an understanding of musical concepts, including loud/soft, high/low, fast/slow, up/down
- helps build an appreciation of different cultural backgrounds (Encourage the children and their families to share their songs.)
- helps build community

Vocabulary

Have students review the *Terms to Know* list. Ask students to look up unfamiliar words or terms in the glossary before reading the chapter.

Discuss

How is music a form of communication? Give examples of how music communicates feelings to others.

Resource

Value of Music Activities, transparency master 27-1, TR

Discuss

Can child care students who have no musical background, other than the enjoyment of listening, teach music and movement activities to young children? Can those who think they do not have good singing voices teach music to children?

Meeting Special Needs

Provide an outline of the chapter with all the chapter headings for special learners. Students should fill in each section of the outline as the material is covered in class with a sentence or two about the content. Review the special learners' IEPs to decide if any modifications should be made in presenting the chapter content.

Benefits of Music Experiences

Note

Write the following quote on the board or overhead to stimulate a discussion on the value and role of music in education: "Music, like math, physics and poetry, is an essential part of our culture. Children improve their future lives immeasurably by gaining a deep understanding of its structure and its beauty. This is justification enough for music in our schools." (Project Zero, an arts program at Harvard Graduate School of Education)

Discuss

What is the relationship between music and a child's expression of thoughts and feelings? How can music help children express their creativity and contribute to the development of thinking skills? Give examples.

Reflect

What early musical experiences in your life affected your attitudes toward music today? What skills and attitudes can children develop from singing and creating music and rhythm that may not be developed from just listening to music?

Music experiences can build creativity when children are urged to experiment, explore, and express themselves. Music can enhance the expression of feelings and thoughts. The music can be happy, soothing, sad, boisterous, or relaxing. Also, music helps children build an awareness of the feelings of others. For young children, music can be a natural form of expression.

Language skills build as children take part in music activities. As children listen and sing, they learn new words and sounds and develop new concepts. The children also experiment with the volume, tempo, and sound quality of the music.

Music activities help children grow cognitively. They memorize words to songs. They learn to sing musical notes. They also learn to compare musical concepts, such as loud/soft and fast/slow.

Music appears to strengthen pathways in the brain. Researchers have found a link between music and the development of spatial intelligence. This type of mental ability helps children form math and science concepts.

Children grow physically as they move in rhythmic activities and play instruments. Music experiences can also help children build positive self-concepts. As children learn about their culture and learn new skills, they learn to like themselves. Children also learn to respond to moods expressed by music. They become more at ease with their emotions.

Children respond to and enjoy many forms of music experiences. They delight in listening to music and stories about music. They enjoy singing and moving to music. They enjoy making simple rhythm instruments. With their instruments, children enjoy making sounds, 27-2. Four- and five-year-old children might even create their own songs. If they do, record their songs and play them back for listening enjoyment.

Health and Safety

Music and Brain Development

Most early childhood teachers will tell you that children enjoy music because it is fun. Recent research shows that the benefits of music for brain development go far beyond just being fun. Music helps young children build brain connections that lead to improved abilities in reading and math, language and vocabulary, motor skills, and spatial relationships.

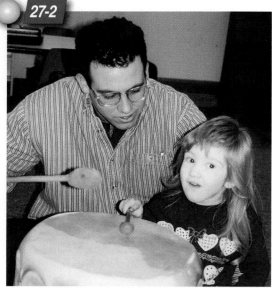

27-2

Children enjoy listening to the sounds of a drum.

Putting Technology to Use

Ask students to conduct an Internet search for information about music and its effect on brain development. What is the relationship between musical training and the development of higher brain functions? What is the role of music in promoting emotional intelligence? What research can you find to support the view that educators who use more movement, singing, and music will improve their students' learning efficiency and retention? Have students write a brief report of their findings.

A Music Center

Design and decorate a music center to encourage use by children. Place it in an open section of the classroom to allow room for freedom of movement. The active section of the room is best. Creative play will be encouraged if housekeeping and block-building areas are nearby. Provide beanbag chairs and pillows so children can sit and listen to music.

Display instruments on a table or open shelf, 27-3. The children should feel free to use these. Include drums, kazoos, melody bells, clackers, maracas, rhythm sticks, guitars, tambourines, cymbals, and recorders on the shelf or table.

When buying instruments, look for quality. Quality instruments produce the best sounds. Instruments and other supplies can be bought through local music stores, school supply stores, or catalogs. Music of all cultures and styles should be purchased. Consult the Yellow Pages for names, addresses, and telephone numbers. These businesses are listed under such headings as *school supplies, music instruments, music, piano,* or *music dealers.*

Parents are a good source for instruments. Often they are happy to lend or give instruments to the program. Instruments from various cultures help promote multicultural awareness. Many times these instruments are supplied or shared by parents.

The music center should also contain pictures of dancers, instruments, and singers. Choose pictures that represent many cultures. Local music stores may be happy to supply you with these. See 27-4.

The Teacher's Role

The teacher's role is to encourage musical expression. To do this, children need surroundings in which they feel free to explore, sing, and move to music. The extent of their participation and time they will spend in musical activities will vary. Children may be nonparticipants, distant observers, close observers, limited participants, or eager participants. The time they spend in musical activities will depend upon their age, interest, ability, and experiences.

27-3

This inviting display of instruments encourages the involvement of children.

27-4

Contents of a Music Center

Autoharp®
CD player
Variety of CDs
Tape recorder and cassettes
Pictures of dancers, instruments, and singers
Rhythm instruments
Sound-producing objects (clocks, containers filled with pebbles)
Songbooks
Scarves, crepe paper streamers
Piano, guitar (optional)

The contents listed here are part of a useful music center. What other items might you add?

Activity

Have students create a picture file of musical instruments from computer clip art programs or Internet clip art sites. Print pictures on 8½ by 11 inch paper or card stock, laminate, and use to introduce children to the variety of instruments available.

Resource

Music Experiences, Activity A, OG

Enrich

Ask students to attend a concert, music performance, or musical play and observe the reactions of the people listening in the audience. What were people's physical and emotional responses to the music? What responses did you personally exhibit?

Resource

Musical Truths, Activity A, SAG

Meeting Special Needs

Divide *Musical Truths,* Activity A, SAG, into two sets of ten statements each for those students who may benefit from shorter assignments. Pair special learners with volunteer students to complete the activity. Review answers to the statements in class and have students explain why the false statements are incorrect. Spend additional time discussing any statements that are difficult for special learners to understand.

Discuss

Why should young or new teachers not be shy when singing and/or directing singing activities for young children? What characteristic is more important than vocal talent when teaching songs to young children?

Reflect

Marcy wants to teach the *Hokey Pokey* song to the children but doesn't want to sing in front of them. She decides to play a recording of the song and just have the children follow the directions. What possible outcomes do you predict as a result of this approach?

Activity

What type of musical activities can you locate for routine tasks such as cleanup time, washing hands, and transition times? Have students review classroom resource materials and Internet sites such as **www. preschoolrainbow.org** for possible ideas.

Singing with young children is fun. However, you will find that it is not uncommon for novice teachers to be shy about singing before a group of children. This fear is needless. Young children are not critics. They enjoy hearing their teachers sing.

Enthusiasm is the key factor in conducting a positive experience, 27-5. Your delight in music will be catching. Share an expressive face. Remember to smile and enjoy yourself. If you do, you will see children smiling and enjoying themselves, too.

When singing with or to children, use a light, pleasant singing voice. Children find it easier to match the tones of human voices rather than pianos or instruments. Therefore, with children through age three, use instruments as little as possible.

Avoid forcing children to participate. Singing is a learned behavior, and whether singing alone or in a group, it takes some courage. Generally, preschool children will participate in group singing. By age five, most children will be comfortable singing alone. When children feel ready to take part, they will. Meanwhile, try to make music an enjoyable experience for them. As a result, the children's natural creativity will blossom.

Music does not have to be introduced at a set time and place. It should occur throughout the day. For instance, children respond better to musical directions than spoken directions. For this reason, many teachers use music to make announcements, provide transitions, and direct cleanup activities. Teachers also may use music to welcome and say good-bye to the children. It is also important that the surroundings promote and support music. Cassette recorders, cassettes, CDs, rhythm instruments, and singing all invite children to share music.

Encouraging Discovery

Another role of the teacher is to promote children's interest in instruments and their sounds. This helps children grow in awareness. To promote children's interest, you must also show interest. For example, during a group play activity, you may ask one of these questions:

- How can you make a different sound?
- How was this sound different?
- Can you make a faster sound?
- Can you make a slower sound?
- Can you make a louder sound?
- Can you make a softer sound?

You may also increase music awareness by asking children to listen to each other play instruments. Place four or five instruments on a table during free choice play periods. Otherwise, introduce the instruments at group time. A comment like "Here are some instruments that you may wish to play," may be all that is needed to arouse children's curiosity.

To encourage the children, comment on their efforts. Such statements as "You are making some interesting sounds," "Your sounds are beautiful," or "You found a new way" build positive self-concepts. You may also encourage children by prompting. For example, you may say "Show me how you did that."

Encouraging Nonparticipants

In every group of young children there are some children who prefer to observe. These

27-5

This teacher's enthusiasm is more important to the children than the instrument she is playing.

Cross-Curricular Activity

Music

Contact the music instructor at your school. Cooperate to design an activity to introduce children to various musical instruments. One example might be an in-school field trip to see and touch the instruments and listen to students play. Another example might be having music students bring their instruments to the child care lab to demonstrate for the children. Allow children to hold some instruments to see how heavy they are. Have students play some music samples for children to determine the types of sounds produced by the instruments.

children prefer to listen and watch the group. Nonparticipating children generally need more time to take part in music activities. Such children should be handled with patience, 27-6. Try to stand next to such children during movement activities. With a smile on your face, slowly take their hands and swing to the rhythm. Then continue to encourage participation by nodding and smiling at them, showing your approval and enthusiasm. A skilled aide can also help encourage children who do not want to take part.

Selecting Songs

When choosing songs for young children, respect the children's age, abilities, experiences, and interests. Simplicity is the key. The best songs for young children

- tell a story
- have repetitive easy-to-learn phrases
- have a developmentally appropriate vocabulary
- have a strongly defined and attractive mood or rhythm
- have a range of no more than one octave. Most children are comfortable with the range from C to A or D to B

27-6

Children who avoid taking part in music activities can be helped through individual contact with the teacher.

- encourage active involvement
- relate to children's level of development

Selecting success-oriented songs is the key to involving the children. Begin by choosing songs that you enjoy. To arouse children's interest, you must convey enthusiasm for a song. Have an expressive face and know the song well. Encourage the children to clap the words of their favorite songs. Children will not tire of a well-loved song. They will repeat it over and over again once they know it.

Most children enjoy many types of songs. Songs about familiar objects, families, lullabies, holiday songs, and songs with actions are all enjoyed by children. Songs are rich stories about the world. Some songs are best for older children. Others, because of their content, are best for younger children, such as *Twinkle, Twinkle, Little Star*.

Children's songbooks are available at music stores, professional conference exhibits, and from early childhood catalogs. These books can be used to find new songs. The books also may be used along with the piano, guitar, or Autoharp®. If possible, keep several of these books on hand.

Creating Songs

The best way to create a song is to use a known melody with new words. For example, *Baa, Baa, Black Sheep; Twinkle, Twinkle, Little Star;* and *The Alphabet Song* are all tunes that can be used for other songs. You will find that changing words to these tunes is a good way to teach language skills. You can translate some of the children's favorite songs from English into other languages.

Teaching Songs

The teacher's attitude about music influences children's responses. If you, as a teacher, are thrilled by and enjoy music, the children will likely also enjoy music. Know the song well. Try to sing clearly,

Discuss

Mrs. Lyon is embarrassed and apologetic because her son Mark would not sing with the other preschoolers at the winter program. What response would you make to Mrs. Lyon's concerns? What information could you share to help explain Mark's behavior?

Resource

Selecting Songs, transparency master 27-2, TR

Reflect

What were some of your favorite repetitive songs from your early childhood? What is the role of repetitive songs in developing language skills?

Resource

Creating a Song, Activity B, OG

Portfolio Project

Have students create lists of songs suitable for teaching toddlers, preschoolers, and young school-age children. Students should review children's songbooks and recordings for song ideas and interview early childhood educators for their favorites. Lyrics for many songs are available online. Students should write down the words to songs they don't already know. Ask students to design a music section in their portfolio to file song lists and words, as well as suggested music and movement activity ideas and sample lesson plans.

Vocabulary

Ask students to define the following methods of teaching songs to children: *phrase method*, *whole song method*, and *phrase/whole combination method*. What method do you find most effective?

Enrich

Demonstrate how to play an *Autoharp*® if one is available in your classroom. Allow the students a chance to practice their skills on this instrument. If an *Autoharp*® is not available, attempt to borrow one so students can see how easy it is to play.

Activity

If a piano is available in your child care lab or school, open the top (or front on uprights) and show children how the instrument produces sound. Allow the children to take turns hitting a key while the other children see what is happening and experiment with the pedals to see what effect they make on the sound.

using expression, proper pitch, and rhythm. If necessary, use a cassette or CD to learn it. Sing with vitality and zest. When you do, the children will learn by imitating your voice. There are three methods for teaching songs; the phrase method, the whole song method, and the phrase/whole combination method.

The **phrase method** of teaching is used with longer songs and younger children. First, prepare the children by telling them what to listen for. For example, say "I'm going to sing you a song about a dog named Wags. I want you to listen carefully and tell me what Wags does."

After this introduction, sing the entire song. Then stop and talk about the song. Next, sing short sections and have the children repeat these sections after you. Keep singing, increasing the length of the sections until the children know the song. After the children appear comfortable, drop out. This will prevent them from depending on you to lead songs.

The **whole song method** is used to teach songs that are short and simple with a repetitive theme. Tell the children to listen to you. After they have listened to you sing the song once, ask them to sing with you. Repeat the song a few times to be sure the children know the words.

The **phrase/whole combination method** is done by teaching key phrases. Sing a key phrase and have the children repeat it. Continue until you have introduced a few key phrases in the song. Then sing the whole song and have children join in when they can. Repeat the song until children have learned all of the words. Stress key phrases with rhythmic movement or visual props to make them more meaningful, 27-7. An example would be "Johnny Pounds with One Hammer." As the song is sung, both you and the children can mimic a pounding action.

Accompanying Singing

Many early childhood teachers like to play the piano, Autoharp®, or guitar while children sing. Instruments' availability and your playing skills will affect the choice. Remember,

This prop for *Five Green Speckled Frogs* helps children learn and remember the song.

though, your enjoyment of the music is much more important than flawless playing.

Some teachers do not use instruments even if they are skilled. They believe that playing instruments detracts from the total experience. Children's attention tends to wander. To avoid this pitfall, use the Autoharp® or guitar. With these instruments, facial expressions and lip movements can be seen by the children. They will feel your involvement in the activity.

Piano

A piano has a clear sound and can be used to play melodies as well as to accompany singing. Advanced playing skills are not needed for successful music experiences. Children seldom notice missed chords or bad notes. Instead, they notice enthusiasm and delight.

Autoharp®

An **Autoharp**® is a simple chording instrument that can be used to accompany singing. The Autoharp® is more useful than a piano for several reasons. It is not as costly as a piano, and it is portable. It can be taken to class picnics, on field trips, and out on the playground.

Putting Technology to Use

Ask students to conduct an Internet search for information about popular children's music composers and performers. Students should include information about Raffi, Ella Jenkins, and Hap Palmer among others. What philosophies did these music educators follow in their work? What topics do they address in their songs for children? Why should teachers interested in promoting a music program for children be interested in their work? Have students share examples they have found of the composers' works with the class.

Learning to play an Autoharp® is quite simple. Begin by positioning the instrument so you can read the identification bars. Use your left hand to press the chord bars. Strum the strings with your right hand. For each beat, strum one cord. Many teachers have learned to play within a few hours by using a self-instruction book.

Guitar

The guitar is a string instrument. It is more difficult to learn to play than the Autoharp®. Like the Autoharp®, it is portable. It can be moved to the playground or taken on a field trip. For this reason, it is often a favorite of many early childhood teachers.

Rhythm Instruments

Rhythm instruments can be used by children participating in music activities. By playing rhythm instruments, children can express their feelings. Children who have expressed little interest or skill in singing may respond to musical instruments, 27-8.

Rhythm instruments can be used to
- build listening skills
- accompany the beat of a sound or recording
- classify sounds
- discriminate between sounds
- project music or mood
- experiment with sounds
- organize sound to communicate feelings and ideas
- develop classification skills by learning the difference between *quiet* and *loud*, *hard* and *soft*, and other sounds

Your role should be to purchase instruments and create objects that can be used for music. Rhythm instruments can be store-bought or made by teachers, parents,

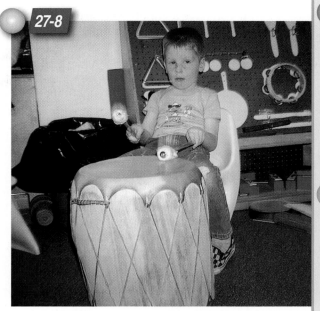
27-8

Children can have fun with rhythm instruments without worrying about their musical talents.

volunteers, and sometimes even children. Handmade instruments often will not have the same quality as store-bought instruments. However, handmade instruments serve a purpose by exposing children to many sounds.

Introducing Rhythm Instruments

Rhythm instruments can be used during individual or group experiences. Before giving children instruments to play, set rules. The following guidelines are suggested for using rhythm instruments in a group:
- Quietly hand out the instruments. This prevents children from getting too excited and becoming disruptive. One method that works well is to choose one child to hand out the instruments. This prevents children from struggling with each other in an attempt to get their favorite instruments. Some teachers prefer setting the instruments in a circle to prevent crowding.

Enrich

Survey class members to discover if any students have experience and skill in playing the guitar. Have the class brainstorm ways to incorporate use of the guitar in the preschool program.

Activity

Select a variety of music types to play in class while students experiment with rhythm sticks. What music types are more appropriate for use with rhythm stick activities with young children? Which types might not be as successful or effective?

Discuss

Have students brainstorm ideas for using rhythm band instruments in the child care lab. How can rhythm band activities be spontaneous, creative, and child-centered? How do you keep children from becoming so carried away with excitement and energy that the noise level is so high the directions cannot be heard?

Resource

Purpose of Rhythm Instruments, transparency master 27-3, TR

Workplace Connection

Randomly hand out rhythm band instruments to the students. If you have more students than instruments, partner the students for this project. Have students create a music lesson plan based on their assigned instrument. The plans should include goals and objectives for the activity and a description of how students would introduce and explain the activity. Ask each student or group to present their lesson to the class for evaluation and suggestions.

Discuss

What are the major benefits of making rhythm instruments for the early childhood classroom? What safety factors need to be considered when constructing the hand-made instruments?

Note

Large cans for making drums can probably be obtained from the school cafeteria. Ask the foodservice director to save appropriate cans for the child care lab. Large cans may also be used to construct can stilts for movement activities. Directions are available at **www.kidsdomain. com/craft/canstilts. html**.

Resource

Rhythm Instruments, Activity B, SAG

- If you have a variety of instruments, introduce only one at a time. The number of different instrument types should be limited to two, three, or four to keep the volume lower.

- Explain to the children that the instruments must be handled with respect and care. The instruments will be taken away from children who abuse them.

- After the children have instruments in their hands, allow them a few minutes to experiment. Most children will want to play their instrument right away. Use a signal such as beating a drum, raising your hand, or playing the Autoharp® to have the children stop.

- Rotate instruments after children have had time to experiment. This gives each child a chance to play all the instruments.

- After the activity, have the children return their instruments to the box, table, or shelf where they belong.

Building Rhythm Instruments

Some teachers have the time and resources to make rhythm instruments. Directions are included for making sandpaper blocks and sticks, bongo and tom-tom drums, rattlers and shakers, rhythm sticks and bells, and coconut cymbals.

Sandpaper Blocks

Sandpaper blocks can be used by children of all ages. For this reason, they are often the first rhythm instruments used in the classroom. Some classrooms contain one pair of sandpaper blocks for each child.

Sandpaper blocks can be used for sound effects. They make a soft swishing sound and are played by rubbing the two sandpaper blocks together. See 27-9 for instructions on making sandpaper blocks.

27-9

Sandpaper Blocks

Materials
2 blocks of soft pine, 4 by 3 by 1 inches in size
Several sheets of coarse sandpaper
Colored enamel paint
Thumbtacks or staples
Strong glue (epoxy based)
2 straps of leather or flexible plastic, 4 to 4½ inches long
Scissors
Hammer

Procedure
1. Sand the wood to remove all rough edges.
2. Paint the blocks a bright color to make them attractive and to prevent the wood from becoming soiled.
3. Glue the straps to each block to form handles:

4. Cut the sandpaper to fit the bottom and sides of each block:

5. Attach the sandpaper to the blocks with thumbtacks or staples. (As sand is rubbed off the paper, replace with new sandpaper.)

It takes just a little effort to make these inexpensive sandpaper blocks.

Sandpaper Sticks

Purchase rough sandpaper and wooden doweling 1 inch wide and 12 inches long for each stick. To construct the sticks, wrap and glue sandpaper around each of the dowels. Leave a small section for use as a handle. Then sand the end of the sticks smooth. Direct the children to scrape the dowels back and forth across each other to make a sound. These sticks, like the sandpaper blocks, will

---

Cross-Curricular Activity

Social Studies
Ask students to research the historical as well as current role of drums in world cultures. What kinds of drums, such as conga, steel, or bodhran, are unique to specific cultures? How were drums used in historical cultures for communications, ceremony, war, entertainment, or other purposes? How has our current culture adapted the use of drums for energizing and team-building purposes? Have students locate and display pictures or actual samples of the drums they encountered in their research.

need to have the sandpaper replaced from time to time.

Bongo Drums

Bongo drums are a favorite of many preschool children. With a drum, they can create many tones by hitting the drumhead near the rim, in the center, and elsewhere.

To construct bongo drums, collect a pair of scissors, string, a piece of rubber, an empty coffee can with both ends removed, a hammer, and a large nail.

Use the plastic lid from the coffee can to trace two circles on the rubber. Allow an extra inch to pull over the edges. Cut the circles out. Take the hammer and large nail and punch holes around the outside edge of the circle. After the holes have been punched, place each of the rubber circles over an end of the can. Then lace the rubber circles to each other using string.

Tom-Tom Drums

Making tom-toms can be a group project for the children. You will need oatmeal boxes (with lids) and tempera paint, watercolor markers, or construction paper. One way to get all the empty oatmeal boxes needed is to ask parents to send them from home. To make the tom-toms, tell the children to tape the lid on the box. After this, give them tempera paint, watercolor markers, or colored construction paper and paste to decorate their tom-toms. A rhythm stick can be used for a drum stick.

Tin can tom-toms can be made with large empty coffee cans. Use the plastic top to cut three sheets of wrapping paper 2 inches larger than the top of the tin for each tom-tom. Glue the three sheets together. Stretch the glued paper over one end of the coffee can. Secure the paper with a large rubber band or string.

Rattlers

Making rattlers is a simple activity in which the children can take part. To collect supplies

for making instruments, ask parents to send a round salt box to school with their children.

To make the rattlers, give each child a handful of dry beans, corn kernels, or rice. Show the children how to pour them into the box. Then give each child a strip of tape to seal off the pour spout on the box.

After the box has been filled and the spout taped closed, the children can decorate their rattlers. Give the children tempera paint, washable markers, crayons, colored construction paper, and paste. After the rattlers have been decorated, put them on display. Encourage the children to explore the variety of sounds made by the different materials.

Shakers

Collect empty paper towel tubes. Tape one end of the tube shut with paper fastened by masking tape. Pour small pebbles, dried corn, dried beans, or rice into each tube. Tape the open end shut. If desired, cover each shaker with construction paper, gift wrap paper, or enamel paint.

Shakers are most useful with light, fast music. Show the children how to hold the shakers at face level. Then demonstrate how to shake them briskly. You will discover that children delight in using shakers.

Rhythm Sticks

Rhythm sticks are always made in matching pairs. Wooden doweling from ¾ to 1 inch in diameter is needed. Cut the doweling into 12-inch lengths. Sand each end of the doweling. Add a protective coat of shellac or enamel paint.

Rhythm sticks can also be made from bamboo. This type of wood will produce a hollow sound. A good source for bamboo is a local carpet dealer. To make the rhythm sticks, cut the bamboo into 10- to 12-inch pieces. Tape each end of the stick with tape to prevent splinters.

Teach the children to play rhythm sticks holding one stick in each hand. One stick

Reflect

What early childhood rhythm activities do you remember? How did the teacher or adult in charge manage to control behavior during the activities?

Discuss

What other containers besides paper towel tubes could be used to construct shakers? What methods could be used to decorate the shakers that would be more durable than paper?

Note

Avoid using empty toilet paper tubes for any art or craft project in the preschool because of their potential to spread rotavirus, which is the most common cause of severe diarrhea among children.

Putting Technology to Use

Ask students to conduct an Internet search for information about programs that take advantage of early childhood as a prime time to begin formal music lessons. How do methods, such as the Suzuki method, manage to teach children as young as three or four to play the piano and violin? What starting age is recommended by music educators to begin traditional music lessons? How can you tell if a child is ready to begin music lessons? Allow time for students to discuss their findings in class.

Activity

Many small electronic keyboards have a variety of rhythms, voices, and sound effects programmed into them. If a keyboard is available, allow children in the child care lab to experiment with different sound effects. Students may also choose a sound effect and ask the children if they can identify the sound.

Discuss

What concerns do you have with children using instruments that are played by mouth, such as in the photo in 27-11? What challenges do these types of instruments present? What actions or precautions are needed?

Enrich

Ask student volunteers to collaborate with a sign language teacher to learn how to sign a simple child's song. Have students design a lesson to teach the children how to sign the song.

should be held steady while it is struck near the top with a second stick. See 27-10.

Jingle sticks are rhythm sticks with bells attached to each end. The bells can be attached with a small cup hook. After placing the bell on the hook, use pliers to force the cup hook closed. You may wish to paint the sticks bright colors. This may make them appealing to children.

Rhythm Bells

Materials needed to make rhythm bells include strips of elastic, ½ to ¾ of an inch wide and 5 inches in length. Five to six bells are needed for each strip of elastic. A needle and thread are needed to sew the bells to the elastic.

Sew the ends of the elastic together by overlapping the ends. This can be done by hand or on a machine. On one side of the loop, sew on five or six small bells. Vary the size of the bells on the loops for a variety of sound. The children will then learn that the sounds made by bells of different sizes vary.

Coconut Cymbals

Cymbals made of coconut halves offer many sounds. They can sound like horses galloping when clapped together. They can also be hit with a rhythm stick to make fast, light music.

To make coconut cymbals, buy several large coconuts at the supermarket. Each coconut will make a pair of cymbals. Cut each coconut in half with a sharp saw. Drain the milk and remove all the meat. Sand the outside and inside edges of the shell until smooth. After this, shellac or paint both sides of the shell.

Buying Rhythm Instruments

Many teachers do not have time to make all the instruments needed for their programs. As a result, some instruments will have to be bought.

Buy instruments that are sturdy, 27-11. For instance, buy maracas that are constructed in one piece. Otherwise the handles may come loose. Triangles should hang from sturdy holders. If the holder is not strong, the instrument may twirl around when a child is trying to strike it. Jingle bells should always be

27-11

Center instruments get much use, so they need to be durable.

27-10

Children quickly learn to play rhythm sticks properly.

Workplace Connection

Have students research the cost of rhythm band instruments for a child care lab. Are instruments priced more economically when buying a complete set versus buying separate instruments? Which instruments are more costly and should be purchased in smaller quantities? What materials are used to construct the instruments? How can you check for quality? Compare the choices available from different music supply companies or vendors. Allow time for students to discuss their findings in class.

attached to elastic. This makes them flexible enough to use as either wrist or ankle bracelets. Check drum and tambourine heads to make sure they are durable and fastened firmly. The skins should be free from cuts or holes.

Try to buy instruments in a number of sizes. This allows for a good mix of tones. Usually, smaller instruments have higher tones. Larger instruments have deeper tones.

Scheduling Music

Music should be scheduled throughout the day. It fits in well after a story, at the start of the day, after a snack, and during free playtime. It can be used during waiting times, such as the end of the day, a bus ride on a field trip, or before and after lunch. Music can be used to remind children of rules they may have forgotten. For instance, if Sam and Gail did not hang up their coats, you may sing "At school we hang up our coats, hang up our coats."

In addition to these impromptu uses, music should also be scheduled as a group activity for four- and five-year-old children. This should occur at the same time every day since children thrive on consistent schedules.

Using Group Music

Group music activities are useful in building group feelings and pride. A group setting is a good way to introduce new songs and new instruments. These activities should focus on the group, not the individual.

Group time should be fairly brief. Schedule seven to ten minutes for two- and three-year-olds. You may later extend the period up to 15 minutes for four- and five-year-old children. Some centers schedule two short music periods. Early childhood programs may have to adjust their music time to meet the attention spans and developmental levels of the children.

Suggestions for Group Music

You will need to be well-organized for a successful music experience. The following suggestions may help:

- Always be prepared. Make sure you have collected all the instruments, music, and other accessories needed.

- Use the same signal for calling the children together for group music time. This signal may be a song, an Autoharp® chord, a beat on a drum, or a piano tune.

- Have the children sit in a circle or semicircle. Then the children can see you and you can see them. To help children sit in the proper places, mark the floor with chalk, tape, or carpet squares.

- Require all adults in the classroom to take part. Their support encourages children to join in, too. These adults can also sit on the floor by the children and help them learn words and responses to the music.

- Switch between active and quiet music activities. Children may become bored if they are always required to listen to music. Likewise, they may tire quickly from, or become too excited by, activities that involve a great deal of movement.

- Reward children for positive behavior. Tell them what type of behavior you expect: sitting quietly, waiting for their turns, holding instruments correctly, singing clearly at the proper volume. Ignore disruptive behavior if it is being used by only one child. If the child continues despite being ignored, ask another adult in the group to remove the child. Children who act up when they sit together should also be separated during group time.

- Use familiar songs that include fingerplays every day. Such songs are favorites because children find it easy to take part.

Discuss

How can large group music activities benefit the child who is confident and proud of his or her skills? How can individual or small group music activities benefit the child who is unsure or shy in front of a large group?

Activity

Have students make visual aids that may help children remember the words to a song. For example, draw or print pictures of a bus, wheels, horn, windshield wipers, and babies for *The Wheels on the Bus.*

Resource

Evaluating a Music Activity, Activity C, OG

Service Learning Activity

Many special education facilities, adult living centers for people with disabilities, and senior-assisted homes and programs conduct special music activities. Have volunteer students assist local facilities in planning and presenting these activities or have students design and present an activity themselves. Students will need to work with the facilities to determine the type of music activities that are possible and acceptable, taking into consideration those with physical disabilities may need adapted activities. Students will also need to consider the cost of the program and seek sources for the funding.

Resource

Educational Value of Fingerplays, transparency master 27-4, TR

Activity

Ask students to locate fingerplay resources in the child care classroom, public library, or on the Internet. Choose several developmentally appropriate fingerplays for toddlers and preschoolers. Have students make a file for the fingerplays or create a file on the computer and save it to a disc.

Resource

Fingerplays, Activity C, SAG

Using Individual Music

Group music activities tend to stress conformity. Children are not as free during these times to express their creativity. For this reason, individual music activities are also an important part of the music experience.

During self-selected play, encourage children to interact with the music. Play music during this period. Make rhythm instruments, the piano, and a tape recorder available throughout the day, 27-12. It is also a good idea to station a teacher or other adult in the music area. An adult's presence will encourage children to enter the area and engage in musical experiences.

Music Activities

Listening, singing, playing rhythm instruments, and moving to rhythm are all music activities. A good program contains all of these activities.

Listening

All music activities involve listening. The ability to listen is important for learning.

27-12

Many children love to spend time listening to taped music.

Good listening skills help children build proper speech habits, an extended attention span, and reading readiness skills.

Listening to music can enrich the imaginations of young children. It also can help them relax and release pent-up feelings. Listening can take place when singing or when playing rhythm instruments, the piano, the CD player, or a tape player.

Children need to be taught how to listen. You, as a teacher, need to give them reasons for listening. For example, you may say "Listen to this music and tell me how it makes you feel." After playing the music, let the children express their feelings. The games in 27-13 can help young children develop listening skills.

Fingerplays

Fingerplays are another useful method for teaching listening skills. Choose fingerplays based on developmental levels. For example, a fingerplay for two-year-olds should be short and contain simple words.

Teachers who enjoy fingerplays may wish to order their own fingerplay books. These books can be ordered through a local bookstore. Also, they can be bought in the exhibit area at a professional conference or from a local school supply store.

The words of a fingerplay reinforce movements. Likewise, the movements reinforce words. Using body movements, the children learn how to express emotion.

Some teachers prefer to file fingerplays under certain themes. For example, "Two Little Apples" could be filed with units on apples, fall, or nutrition. "Roll Them" could be filed under transitions, movements, or body concepts. Size concepts or numbers would be good themes for using "Here's a Ball." "Lickety-Lick," a childhood favorite, is often filed under science concepts. It is used for teaching these concepts during cooking experiences. See 27-14.

Workplace Connection

Have students design a classroom chart with the four categories of music activities, *listening*, *singing*, *rhythm instruments*, and *moving to rhythm*, listed at the top of each of four columns. Have students keep track of the lessons and activities presented to the preschoolers during the class by listing each activity under the specific area. Ask students to determine which areas may need more emphasis by reviewing the chart. Have students design lessons for the preschoolers based on their findings.

27-13

Listening Games

What's the Sound?
Tape sounds from different parts of the home. These may include running water, flushing toilets, ringing telephones, closing doors, or sounds made by scissors, doorbells, washing machines, radios, and electric garage door openers. Play each sound back to the children and ask them to name the object making the noise.

Body Sounds
Tell the children that you are going to play a body sound game. Tell them to close their eyes or cover them with their hands and listen carefully. Then stomp your feet, snap your fingers, slap your thigh, smack your lips, and clap your hands. Have the children guess how you are making the sounds.

Instrument Sounds
Provide the children with a box or basket of rhythm instruments to explore. Then ask the following questions:
- What instrument sounds like jingle bells?
- What instrument sounds like a church bell?
- What instrument sounds like the tick of a clock?
- What instrument sounds like thunder?
- What instrument has a loud sound?
- What instrument has a quiet sound?

Guess the Instruments
Let the children become familiar with the classroom instruments. Then, based on developmental level or age of the child, choose a few instruments to use in a game called "Guess the Instrument." With two-year-old children, choose only two instruments. These should have very different sounds. As the children progress, add more instruments. To play the game, tell the children to cover their eyes and listen to the sound made by the instrument you are playing. Then they can guess what instrument you are playing. After children are familiar with the game, older children may want to play the teacher's role. In this event, you, too, should cover your eyes and take part.

Children have fun and develop their listening skills while playing these games.

Singing

Children's best musical instruments are their voices. Their voices are always with them. Even very young children make musical cooing and crying sounds. These tones vary in strength and pitch. Singing is a learned behavior. Voice control is learned as children participate in singing experiences.

After children babble, tonal patterns emerge. By age two most children can sing. They often sing as they dress, eat, and play. By this time, singing is a meaningful activity.

Children's singing skills vary a great deal. In a group of two-year-olds, there may be children able to sing in tune and make up tunes. Other children may not be able to master these skills until they are three or four years old.

You may notice that children who stutter often sing clearly. Speech skills can be improved through singing, 27-15.

Mouthing

Children's mouths can be used to make coughing, gurgling, sipping, kissing, and hissing sounds. Animal, train, plane, machinery, and traffic sounds can also be made with the mouth. As children compare these sounds, they will learn that some are fast, others are slow, some are loud, and some are quiet. Thus, exploring mouth sounds can add to knowledge. As children explore these sounds, they learn others. Joining a variety of sounds can produce unique music.

To encourage children to make sounds, bring pictures to a group activity. For

Reflect
Review Chart 27-13. What other examples of listening games can you think of to help children develop good listening skills?

Discuss
Should you be concerned if a child cannot sing in tune? At what age can a child be expected to develop this skill?

Vocabulary
Have a student volunteer explain *mouthing*. Demonstrate several sounds children can make by mouthing.

Workplace Connection
Have students survey area preschool and child care teachers to discover the role music education plays in their curriculums. How often are music activities conducted in the classroom? Do children have daily access to musical and rhythm band instruments, or are they used only on special occasions? Do children participate in listening, singing, creating music, and moving to music, or are some of these areas neglected? Allow time for students to discuss their findings in class.

Resource

Favorite Fingerplays, reproducible master 27-5, TR

Vocabulary

Have a student volunteer define *chant.* What makes a chant different from a song or poem? What do singing, performing fingerplays, and performing chants all have in common?

Activity

Have students collect several examples of chants. Ask students to experiment with adding an accompanying beat to the chant with a drum or other percussion instrument and demonstrate the result to the class.

24-14

Fingerplays

Two Little Apples

Two little apples hanging high in the tree. (Place arms above head.)
Two little apples smiling at me. (Look up at hands and smile.)
I shook that tree as hard as I could. (Make a shaking motion.)
Down came the apples. Mmmmmmm, so good. (Make a falling motion with arms. Hold hands to mouth pretending to eat.)

Roll Them

Roll them and roll them. (Roll hands.)
And give your hands a clap. (Clap hands.)
Roll them and roll them. (Roll hands.)
And place them in your lap. (Place hands in lap.)

Here's a Ball

Here's a ball (Make a small circle with thumb and index finger.)
And here's a ball (Make a large circle by using both thumbs and index fingers.)
A great big ball I see. (Make a huge circle with arms.)
Shall we count them? Are you ready? One, two, three.

Lickety-Lick

Lickety-lick, lickety-lick. (Make a big circle with the left arm by placing hand on hip. Place the right hand inside the circle.)
The batter is getting all thickety-thick. (Stir with the right hand.)
What should we bake? What shall we bake? (Gesture by opening hands.)
A great big beautiful cake. (Extend arms to show a big cake.)

How would you file these fingerplays?

instance, collect pictures of large, medium, and small dogs in a number of poses. The dogs might be barking, showing their teeth, or playing with their owners. Show the children each picture. Ask them to mimic the sounds a dog would make in each instance. You can use pictures of other animals, people,

24-15

Singing along to music helps many children correct speech problems.

machines, cars, trucks, and other objects. These activities will help children become sensitive to sounds.

Chants

A **chant** is a group of words spoken with a lively beat. It is a song that has word patterns, rhymes, and nonsense syllables in one to three tones repeated in a sequence. "Teddy Bear, Teddy Bear, Turn Around" is a chant. Mother Goose rhymes are also chants. Chants are an important form of early childhood song. Children learn to speak together in unison by chanting.

Chanting is a beneficial activity for all children. They learn to share the joy of language. They also learn to cooperate. The rhythmic response to chants are useful for children who are learning English as a second language. Chanting is also good for children who speak nonstandard English. Shy children can develop self-confidence and self-expression by chanting.

Like singing, you will need to model chanting for the children. Begin by repeating

---

Workplace Connection

Ask students to design a program in which children sing songs, perform fingerplays, and participate in a movement activity. Students should choose a theme for the program, pick out suitable activities for the age group of the children, and suggest room decorations that might enhance the theme. Students should also determine a timeline for teaching and practicing the songs, fingerplays, and movement activities. Ask students to design and print invitations for families, obtain suitable refreshments, and set up the classroom or other location for the program.

it aloud several times. When the children feel comfortable, encourage them to join you.

Movement Experiences

For learning, movement is an important nonverbal tool that often includes math concepts. Movements provide opportunities for children to pretend and make comparisons. They can walk like elephants, crawl like worms, or pilot an airplane. Children almost always enjoy these experiences.

Movement activities should provide children with the chance to

- explore the many ways their bodies can move

- practice combining movement with rhythm

- discover that many ideas can be expressed through movement

- learn how movement is related to space, 27-16

Some children will take naturally to movement activities. Other children may feel more self-conscious or embarrassed. To help these children, begin with some short, simple movement activities. Knowing what type of responses to expect can help you prepare.

Children's Responses

Studies show that two- and three-year-old children's responses to movement vary. Most two-year-old children actively respond to rhythm, but at their own tempo. Their response may be to repeat the same basic movement through the entire activity. For example, a two-year-old may simply jump up and down during an entire song.

By age three, children have gained greater motor coordination. As a result, they have more control of rhythmic responses. Three-year-old children will likely use many

27-16

Children like to discover what their bodies can do through movement activities.

responses. That is, they may circle with their arms, run, and jump during the same recording.

Between ages four and six, muscular coordination keeps improving. At the same time, their interest in movement and space increases. If you watch children at this stage, you will notice they skip, run, climb, and dance to music. These movements are now done to the beat of the music. If the beat is fast, their movements are fast. They move more slowly to slow beats.

Teacher Preparation

To prepare for movement activities, first select your activity. Chart 27-17 lists many movements. Then stand in front of a full-length mirror and practice the movements. Do each movement in the activity. If possible, repeat the movements several times.

In the classroom, children learn best when they can see and hear. Rather than

Discuss

When do most children first begin to actively respond to rhythm? At what age do children usually begin to have more control of their rhythmic responses? Give examples of some rhythmic responses you might observe.

Activity

Have students visit area child care programs to observe children at various ages engaging in music and movement activities. What characteristics do you notice in two- and three-year-olds? How do they compare to four- and five-year-olds? Allow time for students to discuss their findings in class.

Resource

Expression of Feelings Through Movement, Activity D, OG

Portfolio Project

Have students write an observation of a preschool lesson using music and movement. What were the goals and objectives of the lesson? What did children do during the activity? Were teacher directions clearly stated? Were children able to follow them and participate in the activity? If possible, take a photograph while children are participating to help document the activity. Have students file the observation in their portfolio.

Reflect

What music and movement activities do you remember from physical education classes in elementary, middle school, and high school? Can you remember any feelings or emotions you experienced during these activities? Compare these feelings to what preschoolers may be experiencing during similar activities.

Resource

Planning a Music or Movement Activity, Activity E, OG

Discuss

How can beanbags, ribbons, scarves, and balls be used to enhance music and movement activities? What movement activities can you design that incorporate items such as these?

Resource

Teaching Movement, Activity D, SAG

27-17

Body Movements

Finger Movements	Hand and Arm Movements	Whole Body Movements
Cutting	Carrying	Bending
Folding	Circling	Bouncing
Holding	Clapping	Climbing
Patting	Dropping	Crawling
Petting	Grabbing	Creeping
Pinching	Lifting	Dancing
Pointing	Punching	Galloping
Poking	Pulling	Hopping
Pulling	Reaching	Jumping
Rolling	Shaking	Rocking
Rubbing	Slapping	Rolling Over
Smoothing	Stretching	Running
Snapping	Sweeping	Scooting
Tickling	Swinging	Shaking
Touching	Twisting	Shuffling
Typing	Waving	Skipping
Wiggling		Sliding
		Swaying
		Walking

These movements can be included in a variety of movement activities.

simply explain, you may have to act out certain movements. In the fingerplay "Two Little Apples," for instance, during the line "way up high in the sky," place your hands high above your head. Reinforcing the words with actions also adds interest.

Teaching Movements

In most movement activities, children should be encouraged to explore and express their own way of moving. A tambourine can be used to capture children's interest before and during the activities. Tambourines are very useful. They can be played loud or soft, slow or fast. They can represent a galloping horse or a frightened kitten.

For successful movement activities, you will need to follow certain guidelines:

- Choose a time when the children are calm and well rested.
- Define space limits. There needs to be enough open, clear space. If space is limited, move chairs and furniture to the side.
- Tell children they need to stop when the music stops.
- For variety in movement experiences, provide props such as paper streamers, balloons, balls, and scarves, 27-18.
- Use movement activities involving cassette tapes or CDs, rhythm instruments, and verbal instructions.
- Allow children to get to know activities by repeating many of the experiences.
- Stop before signs of fatigue appear.

You may want children to be involved in planning some movement activities. Ask the children to suggest movement activities and to bring in their favorite cassette tapes or CDs. After the group experience, cassettes can

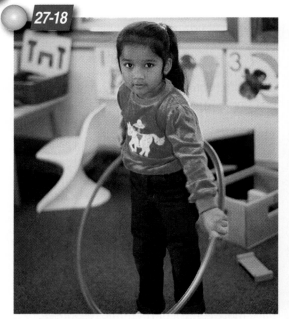

27-18

Using props adds a new dimension to movement activities.

Meeting Special Needs

Have gifted students research the role ballet and dance plays in helping individuals develop and use coordinated and rhythmic body movements. Interview ballet and dance instructors for their insight on early dance training and recommendations for starting ages. Observe several dance classes with students of different ages. Notice the different techniques of teaching and variety of skills demonstrated. Have students learn several dance movements to teach the children in the child care lab. Allow time for students to share their findings with the class.

be placed in the music center. This will give children the chance to listen to the music again.

Body Percussion Activities

Early movement activities should be simple. Stomping feet, clapping hands, patting thighs, and snapping fingers are all simple movements. These are called **body percussion**. All of these movements involve using the body to make rhythm. Body percussion can be used to learn to do more than one movement at a time. Body percussion also helps children build **auditory discrimination skills**—the ability to detect different sounds by listening.

Stomping feet to music has always been a favorite action of young children. To stomp correctly, children should bring their legs back and stomp down and forward.

Children should be taught to clap with one palm held up steadily. You should refer to this palm as the instrument. The other hand serves as the mallet. Children should clap with arms and wrists relaxed and elbows out.

The thigh slap is easy to teach. Relax your wrist for modeling the thigh slap. With arms relaxed, move your hands to slap your thigh.

When teaching children to snap their fingers, hold your hands high. Tell the children to follow you. Snap once. Have the children repeat this action. After they have mimicked your action, have them do two snaps, and then three snaps. Keep this up as long as they are able to repeat your action.

After children have learned to stomp, clap, slap, and snap, you can have them combine two actions. They might "snap, snap, snap," and then "clap, clap, clap." Depending on the skills of the children, you may gradually introduce all four levels of body percussion during one experience.

Movement Activities

Children learn to explore and express their imaginations through movement activities.

One of the first movement activities should focus on listening to a drum beat. A drum is the only instrument needed for the activity. First, tell the children to listen to the drum and see how it makes them feel. For two-year-old children, provide one steady beat. With older children you may vary the rhythm: fast, slow, heavy, soft, big, small. Then ask them to respond. Encourage them to run, crawl, roll, walk, hop, skip, and gallop. After experiences using the drum, many more movement activities can be used with or without music. The key is to encourage the children to use their bodies to express themselves.

Partners

This activity is best for four- or five-year-olds. Instruct the children to choose partners. You will also need a partner to demonstrate. With your partner, move under, over, and around each other. Then have the other children mimic your movements.

Time Awareness

Use a drum to provide a beat that tells the children to run very fast. After they have done this well, tell them to run very slowly. Then tell them to jump on the floor quickly. Again, follow this request by having them jump slowly.

Space Awareness

Have the children stand in front of you. Make sure there is enough space between each child so movements can be made freely. Stress your instructions with actions as you tell them to do the following:

- Lift your leg in front of you.
- Lift your leg backward.
- Lift your leg sideways.
- Lift your leg and step forward.
- Lift your leg and step backward.

Vocabulary

Have student volunteers define *body percussion* and *auditory discrimination skills*. How are these terms related to movement and music activities?

Resource

Movement Activities, reproducible master 27-6, TR

Discuss

How can body percussion movements help children discriminate between right and left? Give some examples.

Activity

Many children gallop when asked to skip. To teach skipping, take an individual child to a large open area such as a hallway or a gym. Have the child imitate your movements as you *right foot step-hop, left foot step-hop*. Continue in slow motion until the child catches on and can skip faster.

Putting Technology to Use

Many schools use parachute play as part of music and movement activities. Have students locate sources for quality parachutes, musical accompaniment, and lesson plan ideas. Consider parachutes from S&S Worldwide at **www.ssww.com**, *Parachute Play—Revised* by Liz and Dick Wilmes at **www.ghbooks.com**, and *Playtime Parachute Fun* CD from Kimbo Educational Music and Movement at **www.kimboed.com**. Have students practice parachute activities with fellow students before introducing them to the children. Remind children of the type of grip you want them to use and any rules or limits appropriate for parachute play.

- Lift your leg and step sideways.
- Reach up to the ceiling.
- Reach down to the floor.
- Stretch to touch the walls, 27-19.
- Move your arm in front of you.
- Move your arm behind you.

- Lift your arms slowly into the air.
- Lift your arms quickly into the air.
- Walk on your tiptoes.
- Stomp on the floor with your feet.
- Kick your leg as slowly as you can.
- Kick your leg as hard as you can.

Weight Awareness

Children can learn differences between *light* and *heavy* using their own body force. To begin this activity, give verbal directions and demonstrate the actions. Tell the children to focus on the weight of their bodies as they make the movements. Give the following instructions:
- Push down hard on the floor with your hands.
- Push down softly on the floor with your hands.

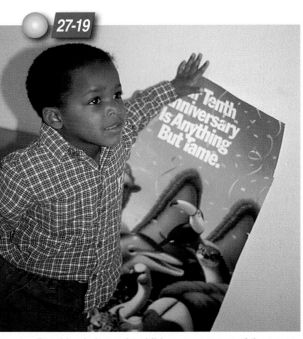

27-19

Reaching helps make children more aware of the space around them.

Organizing Movement into Dance

Combining time, space, and weight movements, children can learn to form movements into dance. To teach this concept, have the children do the following:
- Walk around quickly in a circle on the floor.
- Walk around slowly in a circle on the floor.
- Tiptoe slowly around the circle.
- Tiptoe quickly around the circle.
- Jump hard around the circle.
- Move your arms in a circle above your head.
- Move your arms in circles everywhere.

Word Games

Word games can help children move in ways that express feelings. To play word games, tell the children to move the way the words you say might feel. Use such words as *happy, sad, angry, sleepy,* and *lazy.* After they have moved to these words, remind them to use their bodies and faces. Keep repeating the words. See 27-20.

Moving Shapes

Four- and five-year-old children enjoy the moving shapes game. As with other movement activities, children will need

Discuss

What partner activities can you suggest for music and movement experiences? At what age can children easily work with a partner?

Reflect

Donna always shows up to class wearing dresses and shoes suitable for special occasions. Then she doesn't usually participate in active play because she is not suitably dressed. What suggestions do you have for Donna's parents? How can you tactfully and professionally inform them of the need for active playwear and sneakers?

Discuss

Should the teacher assign partners for music and movement activities or should children be allowed to select their own partner? What are the advantages and disadvantages of each?

Workplace Connection

Have students visit special education classes to observe how music and movement activities are adapted for the students with disabilities. Assign students to observe techniques and strategies for teaching children with varied ages and needs. Are students with severe physical and mental disabilities given opportunities that include music? Interview the teachers to discover the role music plays in special education classes. Allow time for students to discuss all their observations in class.

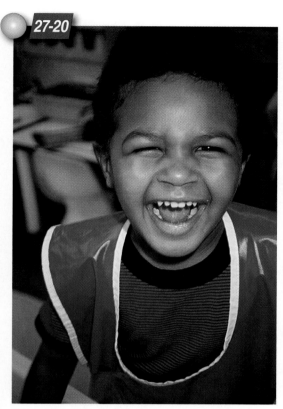
27-20

Older children can laugh to show how they move when they're happy.

is best for use with four-, five-, and six-year-olds. Begin by telling the children they are going to get imaginary presents. Tell them to show you the size of their box. The children should show you a shape made by outlining with their hands and arms. Continue with the following statements:

- Feel the box.
- Hold the box.
- Unwrap the present.
- Take it out of the box.
- Put it back into the box.
- Rewrap the present.

Another pantomime children enjoy is acting out an occupation. Tell the children to think about an occupation. Then have them show how the worker acts. Sometimes this is fun to do one by one. Have one child act out his or her occupation while the rest of the class tries to guess it.

Pretending

Pretending is an activity best used with older children. Tell the children to pretend they are crying, singing, boxing, driving, cooking, laughing, typing, scrubbing, painting, playing an instrument, flying, playing cards, or building a house. There are many songs that children can act out as they sing. Classics include *Here We Go Around the Mulberry Bush* or *This is What I Can Do*. The music to *Peter and the Wolf* provides the same opportunity for drama.

Another pretending activity involves telling the children to imagine there is a box in front of them. Then tell them they are outside the box and they should crawl into it. After they have crawled into the box, tell the children to crawl out of it. Continue by telling them to crawl under and beside the box.

ample space. Give children the following instructions:

- Try to move like something big and heavy: an elephant, tugboat, bulldozer, airplane.
- Try to move like something small and heavy: a fat frog, bowling ball, brick.
- Try to move like something big and light: a cloud, beach ball, parachute.
- Try to move like something small and light: a snowflake, flea, feather, butterfly, bumblebee.

Pantomiming

Pantomiming involves telling a story with body movements rather than words. It

Activity

Have students adapt the song and activity *If You're Happy and You Know It, Clap Your Hands* to include other actions besides clapping hands, stomping feet, and shouting "Hooray!" Add additional activities such as jumping, turning around, flapping arms, etc. Depending on the age of the children, lengthen the song to make greater use of their physical and memory skills.

Vocabulary

Have a student volunteer define *pantomiming*. How are pantomiming and pretending related?

Activity

Divide students into groups to discuss and write down the most important points they learned about the role of music and movement in early childhood education. When lists are complete, ask students to condense their understanding of this topic by writing a joint sentence of exactly 20 words. Have students share the 20-word review sentences with the class.

Meeting Special Needs

Review the special learners' chapter outlines to determine if the students have any questions about the concepts or content of this chapter. Review the chapter objectives and ask the students to evaluate their progress in meeting these objectives. Ask the students to summarize, orally or in writing, what they learned from this chapter.

Review and Reflect Answer Key

1. (List four:) builds a sense of community; provides an opportunity to learn and use language concepts and vocabulary; provides an opportunity to practice counting; provides a pleasant background for playing, eating, and sleeping; calms angry feelings; releases tension and energy; can be used to express feelings through movement and dance; can be used to manage behavior; makes learning fun; teaches listening skills; helps build an understanding of musical concepts, including loud/soft, high/low, fast/slow, up/down; helps build an appreciation of different cultural backgrounds; helps build community
2. true
3. C
4. Your delight in music will be catching.
5. false
6. B
7. phrase method, whole song method, phrase/whole combination method (Student response for explanations.)

Summary

Music is a powerful form of communication for every culture. It can be used to teach many skills. Through music experiences, children develop listening and math skills. They also learn about emotions and feelings, their culture, and sound. For these reasons, teaching music is an important part of an early childhood program. It nurtures the development of their minds, bodies, and emotions.

The music center in the classroom should be designed to encourage participation in music and movement activities. A variety of multicultural instruments can be made or purchased.

Music and movement activities should be planned considering the ages, abilities, interests, and experiences of the children in mind. Enthusiasm is the key factor in constructing a positive experience.

Movement provides children with opportunities to pretend and exercise. Movement activities can be easily combined with music activities for meaningful experiences.

Review and Reflect

1. List four reasons teachers use music with young children.
2. True or false. Music experiences help children grow cognitively.
3. A music center should _____.
   A. be in a congested section of the classroom
   B. have instruments stored on high shelves or in a closet
   C. contain pictures of dancers, instruments, and singers
   D. None of the above.
4. Why is enthusiasm a key factor in conducting useful music experiences?
5. True or false. Nonparticipants should be pushed into taking part in music activities.
6. The best songs for young children should _____.
   A. have little or no repetition
   B. tell a story
   C. have a vocal range of two or three octaves
   D. All the above.
7. Name three methods for teaching songs. Explain one method.
8. Why are the Autoharp® or guitar good instruments to use to accompany singing?
9. List four uses of rhythm instruments.
10. True or false. Music should be scheduled throughout the day.
11. _____ music activities are useful in building feelings of togetherness.
12. State five useful suggestions for conducting group music experiences.
13. True or false. All music activities involve singing.
14. _____ are songs that have word patterns, rhymes, and nonsense syllables used in sequence with one to three repeated tones.
15. List four objectives for movement experiences.

8. With these instruments, facial expressions and lip movements can be seen by the children. They will feel your involvement in the activity.
9. (List four:) build listening skills; accompany the beat of a sound or recording; classify sounds; discriminate between sounds; project music or mood; experiment with sounds; organize sound to communicate feelings and ideas; develop classification skills by learning the difference between *quiet* and *loud*, *hard* and *soft*, and other sounds
10. true
11. Group

16. List three guidelines for successful movement activities.

17. _____ activities involve stomping feet and clapping hands.

18. What are auditory discrimination skills?

19. Combining time, space, and weight movements, children can learn to form their movements into _____.

20. _____ involves having children act out a story as it is told.

Apply and Explore

1. Observe a teacher during a music experience. Note the methods used to teach songs. Share these methods with the class.

2. Select a movement activity and demonstrate it to your class.

3. Construct two or three types of rhythm instruments. Plan a music activity using these instruments.

4. Create two songs that could be used for daily transitions in the classroom.

Cross-Curricular Link

Math

1. Design a music center. Start by reviewing equipment catalogs. Develop a budget for this center. Make a list of multicultural instruments and equipment to include.

Social Studies

2. Select a simple song and translate it into Spanish or another language.

Language Arts

3. Select a song and teach it to your class.

Technology

4. Search the Web site www.kaplanco.com for items early childhood teachers could include in a multicultural music curriculum.

Workplace Link

Contact area early childhood educators for suggestions on handling children who are reluctant to participate in music activities. What methods or strategies have they tried with success? What does not work? Have educators contacted parents to request support and encouragement? What were the results? Do the teachers have more success with large-group, small-group, or individual music activities?

16. (List three:) Choose a time when the children are calm and well rested. Define space limits. Tell children they need to stop when the music stops. For variety in movement experiences, provide props such as paper streamers, balloons, balls, and scarves. Use movement activities involving cassette tapes or CDs, rhythm instruments, and verbal instructions. Allow children to get to know activities by repeating many of the experiences. Stop before signs of fatigue appear.
17. Body percussion
18. Auditory discrimination skill includes the ability to detect different sounds by listening.
19. dance
20. Pantomiming

12. (List five:) Always be prepared. Use the same signal for calling the children together for group music time. Have the children sit in a circle or semicircle. Require all adults in the classroom to take part. Switch between active and quiet music activities. Reward children for positive behavior. Use familiar songs that include fingerplays every day.
13. false
14. Chants
15. Movement experiences should provide children with the opportunity to explore the many ways the body moves; practice combining movement and rhythm; discover that many concepts and ideas can be expressed to others through movement; learn how movement is related to space.

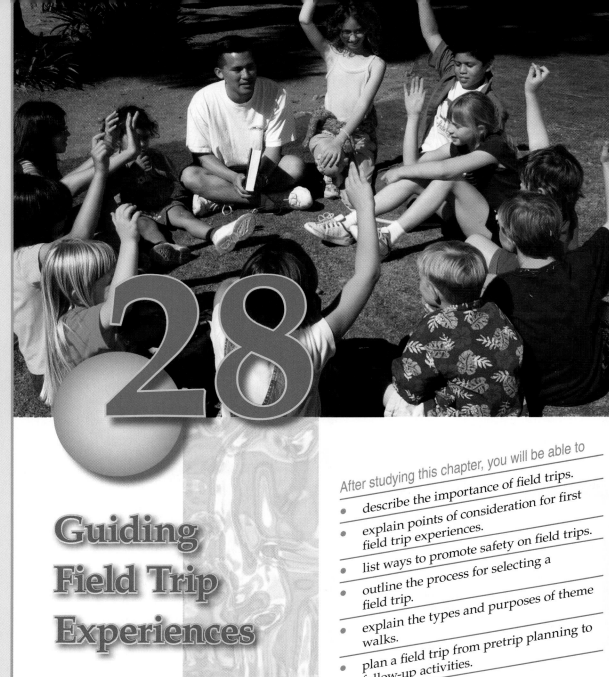

Discuss

Look at the chapter opening photo. Why is media alone not enough experience for young children to learn about their world? What do you know about how young children learn that would encourage you to plan meaningful field trips as part of an early childhood curriculum?

Discuss

Look over the chapter objectives before reading the chapter to get a sense of the material to be covered. Why do you think field trips enhance an early childhood program?

28

Guiding Field Trip Experiences

After studying this chapter, you will be able to

- describe the importance of field trips.
- explain points of consideration for first field trip experiences.
- list ways to promote safety on field trips.
- outline the process for selecting a field trip.
- explain the types and purposes of theme walks.
- plan a field trip from pretrip planning to follow-up activities.

Terms to Know

theme walks
resource people
behavioral expectations

"Apples grow on trees," announced Karla after a recent field trip. Alberto replied, "I know that, and I know something else. Apples are grown in special places called orchards." Hearing the conversation, Robbie added, "Orchards can have red, green, or yellow apples." By going on a field trip, these children have expanded their concept of an apple.

Mr. Smith, after hearing the children's comments, promoted further learning by saying, "It sounds like you know a lot about apples." All the children agreed. Mr. Smith then suggested they write a story about the trip.

From the field trip, the children learned many concepts related to apples. They learned about color, size, shape, and plant growth. When planning the field trip for the children, Mr. Smith had two main goals. The first was to expand the children's concepts of apples. The second was to introduce *orchard* as a new vocabulary word.

The Importance of Field Trips

Young children have limited experience in understanding their world. Much of what they understand comes from books, pictures, television, and movies. Although these media help children learn about their world, they do not replace real experiences. To fully understand their world, young children need concrete experiences to connect them with their community. They need to see, hear, feel, taste, and smell, 28-1. The more senses children use, the more they are likely to learn.

28-1

While children often learn about animals through books and videos, contact with live animals further enhances their learning.

Children gain firsthand experiences during field trips. They are able to look at, listen to, smell, touch, and feel their world. As children connect words and concepts with real objects, people, and places, vague concepts become clearer to them. Field trips also help children

- build keener observation skills
- build vocabularies
- clarify concepts as new information is learned
- learn about their community
- take part in multisensory experiences
- gain new insights for dramatic play
- learn about their environment
- practice following directions in a group

First Field Trips

For young children, field trips can be a very new experience. They may be unfamiliar with such activity. As a result, they may

Vocabulary

Have students review the *Terms to Know* list. Ask students to look up unfamiliar words or terms in the glossary before reading the chapter.

Resource

Value of Field Trips, transparency master 28-1, TR

Discuss

Give examples of field trips with opportunities for multisensory experiences. Give examples of field trips that would give children new insights for dramatic play.

Meeting Special Needs

Provide an outline of the chapter with all the chapter headings for special learners. Students should fill in each section of the outline as the material is covered in class with a sentence or two about the content. Review the special learners' IEPs to decide if any modifications should be made in presenting the chapter content.

Enrich

Have students walk around the neighborhood of the school to determine a list of vocabulary words children can learn and use while on a short field trip in the area. Have students plan an activity that would familiarize the children with the words before the trip.

Activity

Have students practice for an outdoor field trip experience by first designing an in-school trip to a location such as the gym, library, or cafeteria. Students should determine what children will be seeing and doing on the field trip. Observe as children practice the limits set for the trip.

Vocabulary

Have a student volunteer explain *theme walks*. Why is it a good idea for children to focus on only one theme during a theme walk?

Resource

Community Field Trips, Activity A, SAG

be anxious about what will occur. For this reason, first field trips should be short, nonthreatening, neighborhood events. For instance, a first trip could be a simple walk around the block, 28-2. Some children may be hesitant to leave the building. They may fear their parents will come for them while they are gone. Relieve them of their fears by reassuring them that this will not happen.

To provide security, remind children of their daily routine. Say, "First we are going to walk around the block. When we return, we will have a story. Then it will be snack time. After that we will play outside, and then it will be time to go home." Knowing a familiar routine will help prevent some fears.

After taking a few trips around the neighborhood, field trips may be taken to familiar places. A visit to a local grocery store is often a rewarding trip. Here, children can see and talk about things that are well known to them.

First field trips can build or hinder children's confidence. Therefore, first trips need to match children's developmental needs. Generally, two-year-olds do best with short mini-trips. Three-year-olds can take longer trips that may extend to an hour or so in duration. With longer field trips, allow plenty of time for walking slower and resting. Trips for four- and five-year-olds may be

First field trips should involve familiar surroundings.

lengthened in time. Often these children can take trips that last several hours. Plan trips in which children will meet with success.

Selecting Trips

The trips you select will depend on the ages of the children, location of the site, and the budget available. Centers located within walking distance of many potential sites will take more trips than those centers located in more isolated areas. Centers located in large cities have the option of using public transportation. Other centers may have their own vans to provide transportation.

Field trips are sometimes selected based on the season or weather. A trip to a pumpkin patch or an orchard can be taken in the fall. Trips that require walking, such as a trip to a zoo, should be taken during warm weather. Substitute days should be scheduled in case of bad weather.

Field trips are sometimes chosen based on the curriculum themes being studied. For instance, a trip to a farm may be chosen while children are studying about farms, food, or machinery. While learning about health, a trip to a dentist's office, doctor's office, or hospital may be chosen. Chart 28-3 lists many field trip suggestions based on themes.

Theme Walks

Simple field trips involving walks near the center based on a theme are called **theme walks**. The center neighborhood contains many interesting and meaningful opportunities for children to learn about the world. Most children enjoy walking, and the exercise is good for their bodies. Theme walks also provide an opportunity to sharpen their observation skills.

Theme walks may center on many topics: numbers, colors, people, occupations, buildings, flowers, trees, or cars. For best results, focus on only one theme during each walk.

Workplace Connection

Contact your school principal and/or director of school transportation services to determine the feasibility for using school buses or vans for child care lab field trips. Arrange for a school bus driver to speak with the children before a practice outing to explain the guidelines and limits they must follow. On the day of the practice outing, have students line up children in pairs and assist them in getting on the bus. After the short trip, have the children discuss their feelings about riding on the bus. Give them opportunities to ask questions.

28-3

Field Trip Suggestions

Field Trip	Related Themes
Airport	Air transportation or airplanes
Animal shelter	Pets, dogs, cats
Apple orchard	Apples, fruits
Aquarium	Fish, water, water animals
Artist's studio	Careers, art
Bakery	Foods, community helpers
Bird sanctuary	Birds
Bookstore	Reading, books
Butcher shop	Foods, careers, tools
Cafeteria	Nutrition
Car dealer	Transportation, car, truck, wheels
Car wash	Cars, trucks, water
Carpenter's shop	Careers, construction
Circus	Animals, careers
Construction site	Buildings, construction, tools
Dairy farm	Food, farm animals, machinery
Dance studio	Movement, communication, careers
Dentist's office	Health, careers, teeth
Doctor's office	Health, careers, "My Body"
Family garden	Plants, vegetables, food
Fire station	Community helper, fire safety
Garage	Tools, careers, machines
Greenhouse	Plants, spring, flowers, food
Grocery store	Food, community helpers
Hair salon	Health, "I'm Me—I'm Special"
Hatchery	Animals
Hospital	Health, careers, people and places
Laundry	Health, careers, clothing
Library	Community helper, books
Newspaper office	Books, careers, communication
Orchard	Nature
Park	Nature, My community
Pet shop	Pets, animals, careers
Photography studio	Communication, careers, art
Planetarium	The universe, planets
Police station	Community helper, safety
Post office	Community helpers, communication
Potter's studio	Art, careers
Poultry farm	Food, farm animals, eggs
Print shop	Books, careers, communication
Radio or TV station	Communication, careers, listening
Retail store	Clothing, careers
Train station	Transportation, careers
Veterinarian's clinic	Pets, animals, health, careers
Zoo	Animals, homes

In your community, there are probably even more field trip sites that can be related to a theme.

Before starting a theme walk, talk about what children might observe. If the theme is buildings, tell the children to observe types of buildings they see. They may see houses, apartments, offices, stores, and service stations.

Color is a good concept for a theme walk. Choose one or more colors the children should watch for throughout the walk. Two- and three-year-old children should be asked to look for only one color. Older children, especially five-year-olds, may enjoy looking for many colors. In fact, a fun walk for these children would be to record as many colors as they observe.

A shape walk is a way to teach children about shapes. Before leaving the classroom, review with the children what shape(s) they are to observe. As with colors, the number of shapes children are to observe depends on their ages.

Shapes are everywhere. Tires are round; most sidewalk slabs are square; doorknobs may be oval or round. Children encouraged to use their eyes to recognize shapes will also be busy using their minds.

Theme walks based on numbers and letters may also be useful learning experiences. As children walk, they will see numbers and/or letters everywhere. Numbers are seen on license plates, street signs, store windows, billboards, passing trucks, and houses. Determine the number of numbers or letters to observe based on children's ages, skills, and abilities.

People walks can teach many social concepts. The children will see that people may be tall or short and have different-colored hair and eyes. Children will also notice some people wear glasses or have beards or long hair.

Two-year-olds may be able to identify a baby, man, woman, boy, or girl. Three-year-olds may be able to distinguish differences among people based on dress, hair color, and height. Four- and five-year-olds may be able to describe the actions of people they have observed.

During occupational walks, children observe what people are doing. They may see

Activity

Have students look over Chart 28-3, *Field Trip Suggestions*, and select five of the suggestions for field trips they would be interested in planning. Students should then write the educational goals and the learning objectives to be achieved for each suggested trip.

Enrich

Imagine you are working as a counselor for your town's park department summer playground program in charge of a group of six- to ten-year-olds. You must come up with a weekly field trip for the eight weeks of the program. What suggestions for eight field trips do you have that are suitable for this age group?

Discuss

Explain the concept of a people walk. How can you prepare children in a positive way before a people walk to ensure they will not say uncomplimentary remarks to or about the people they will meet or see on the walk?

Putting Technology to Use

Have a student volunteer take photographs with a digital camera during a preschool field trip and upload the pictures to the classroom computer. Make sure each child appears in at least one of the pictures. Select those pictures that are most representative of the trip and prepare a computer slide show for the children to see and discuss. Have students create a book, either printed or using presentation software, for the child care lab with the pictures.

Activity

Have students conduct an *I See It* or *Treasure Hunt* walk in which children are assigned a specific shape, color, letter, or other item to find on the walk. Teach children to say *Eureka*, Greek for *I have found it!*, when they have located their item and point it out to the others.

Resource

Community Resource People, color transparency CT-24, TR

Vocabulary

Have a student volunteer define the term *resource people*. What program goals could be met by including resource people in the early childhood program?

Resource

Resource People, transparency master 28-2, TR

a bus driver, truck driver, bank teller, street sweeper, or house painter.

A building or architectural walk may be of special interest to older children. As you approach buildings, note their purposes. When children see a gas station-garage combination, discuss why large windows and large doors are part of the architecture. (Large windows are needed to see customers; large doors are needed for cars and trucks.) You may also encourage children to imagine what is inside the building.

To gain the most on these theme walks, carry a notepad and pencil, camera, or even a video recorder. Record observations that can be discussed when the children return to the classroom. These observations make good discussion topics for lunch, snack, or group time. Listening to the children's discussions, you will be able to note their interests.

Resource People

To promote further learning, invite interesting people to class. Another option is to take the children on field trips to visit the people. These guests or field trip hosts are called **resource people**, 28-4.

Parents, grandparents, great grandparents, aunts, uncles, neighbors, siblings, and friends are some of the best resource people. Ask them what interests and hobbies, photos, crafts, clothing, and foods they would be willing to share. This can be done personally or through a questionnaire. Select only people who enjoy children. They should represent many cultural groups, both sexes, and people of different ages. Compile a list of these people along with their interests and hobbies. During the year, select people from the list who complement your curriculum.

To be the most useful, resource people need an orientation before meeting the children. This is a necessary step for making the experience a success for both the children and resource people. Tell the resource people the number of children in your group, their interests, ages, and length of their

Firefighters are nearly always at the top of the list of interesting resource people.

attention spans. Suggest questions that they may ask the children. Let them know their presentation and words must be kept simple.

Warn the resource people that children often become very excited when they visit. They are proud of their guests, their classroom, and their classroom friends. Because of the stimulation, they may exhibit overly active behavior.

If possible, suggest to resource people that the children be allowed to have a "hands-on activity," 28-5. For example, if a grandmother is willing to demonstrate how she paints, encourage her to let the children try painting, too. If a person demonstrates playing the drums, ask that each child have the chance to hit the drum.

After a resource person has visited the classroom or hosted a field trip, always send a thank-you note or some other form of appreciation, 28-6. You may write a personal note, or children who can write may wish to express their own thanks. Younger children

Portfolio Project

Have students design a questionnaire to be filled out by potential resource people. The questionnaire should include spaces for information about the person's interests, career, or work he or she would share with the children. It should also include the person's experience with children and contact information. Finally, include any special notes about the field trip location or special needs when visiting the classroom, such as a table for displaying items. Students should file a copy of the questionnaire in their portfolio.

28-5

Hands-on experiences help make vague concepts more concrete for children. After holding this goat, the children will have a real experience to remember when they see goats in a book or hear about them in the classroom.

28-6

Dear Firefighter:

Thank you for showing us your fire truck. We enjoyed sitting in the truck. Thank you for showing us the truck's parts. Thank you for sounding the siren. Thank you for showing us a firefighter's clothing. We enjoyed trying it on, too.

Love,

Ron Smith's Class

Build a positive image of the center in your community with a thank-you note to resource people.

may choose to dictate thank-you notes to you. Other forms of thanking people include sending children's artwork or freshly baked cookies.

Appreciation may also take other forms. For instance, in February, handmade valentines may be mailed to all resource people who took part in the program during the year. Taped thank-you notes, songs on a cassette, and videotapes or photographs of the children at the site are other thoughtful ways to thank resource people.

Planning a Field Trip

Successful field trips for young children need to be carefully planned. Consideration should be given to appropriateness, costs, scheduling, adult-child ratio, behavioral expectations, educational goals, and the children's preparation. As a teacher, you need to think about all of these factors. A good way to do this is to take a pretrip to the site to prepare for the field trip.

Pretrip

The success of any trip depends upon preparation, 28-7. After setting goals, always make a pretrip if you have never been to the site. This visit will give you a chance to
- describe the purpose of the trip to the tour guide
- explain the children's interests and their need to use a number of senses
- prepare the tour guide for the types of questions the children may ask
- locate bathrooms
- check for any potential dangers
- ask about parking (if necessary)
- observe for teaching opportunities
- revise trip goals, if necessary
- determine how many adults or chaperones you will need to provide maximum security

Note

After a field trip, have the children decorate a large thank-you poster with their individual drawings. Then take a photograph of all the children holding the sign and deliver the photo along with the poster. The business or store can display the photo longer and more easily than a large poster.

Discuss

Dwayne, Jennifer, and Blanca are the lead teachers for next Monday's child care lab. Their teacher expects well-written lesson plans by the end of the class. It's Friday afternoon, and Dwayne suggests a field trip to the local sporting goods store. What concerns would you have about the potential success of this plan?

Resource

The Pretrip,
Activity A, OG

Putting Technology to Use

With the field trip resource person's permission, have students video record the presentations to create a mini-movie of the experience. Students will have the option of inserting an introduction, voice-overs for explanations and additional information, interviews with the speakers and the children attending the presentation, and conclusion. Students may need to contact the school's technology department for assistance with this project. Show the movie to the children to refresh their memories. You may also show it to parents at open house and parent programs.

Discuss

What is the advantage of keeping the file for resource people and field trips on a computer database instead of or in addition to keeping the file in a notebook or index card box? How else can computer technology, including e-mailing, be used to facilitate the arrangements for a field trip?

Reflect

What are some of the safety risks you would think about when planning a field trip? How would you prepare children for these risks?

Enrich

Have students make replicas of signs children may encounter on a field trip such as street signs, stop signs, crosswalk signs, restroom signs, and building signs such as enter, exit, push, and pull. Have students design a learning activity to teach awareness of and meanings of the signs.

28-7

The best field trips will be those the teacher has planned well.

Keep a field trip file. In some centers, teachers maintain their own files. In other centers, the director maintains a file for use by all personnel. This file may be a notebook, a folder, or an index card file box. As a rule, information to note for each trip includes

* name of site
* telephone number
* address
* contact person (tour guide)
* costs
* distance from center in blocks or miles
* dangers
* special learning opportunities
* location of bathrooms and water sources

Permission slips signed by parents or guardians must be on file for each child before a trip, 28-8. For convenience, many center directors use one form for all trips and walks. This form is filled in and signed at enrollment time. This saves the staff's time in obtaining permission slips for each trip. Busy parents will also benefit from this timesaving method.

Before the trip, plan your "trip bag." It should include the essential supplies that you will need to take along. Paper tissues; a first-aid kit; premoistened towelettes; a garbage bag; emergency telephone numbers; and a cell phone, calling card, or coins for a pay phone are a must. Many centers also require that you take a folder with copies of emergency forms and signed permission slips. Depending on the length of the trip and the weather, you may want to take snacks and refreshments for the children. For young children, diapers, bottles, and extra clothing might be a consideration.

In hot weather, children often become thirsty. Make sure water or some other nutritious drink is on hand. Insulated jugs are a good way to transport liquids.

Field trips involve added safety risks and responsibilities for child care centers. Before taking field trips, teach the children pedestrian safety. Practice taking short walks near the center. Before leaving the center, explain the rules the children must follow when crossing streets. When approaching a crosswalk, review these rules with the children. Be sure to observe traffic signals when crossing intersections. Make sure you consistently enforce and follow the rules. This is important since children learn by experience and imitation.

Suitability

Before choosing a trip, ask yourself "How appropriate is this trip for the children?" Consider the developmental level of the children. For five-year-olds, a trip to a television studio may be both fun and educational. This same trip would not be appropriate for two-year-olds. Two-year-olds are more interested in those things closer to their immediate

Workplace Connection

Ask students to interview a child care center director for information about liability and accidents that may occur when a child is on a field trip. Does the center's permission slip absolve the center or individual teachers from a lawsuit for damages? What is covered if an accident occurs in a center's vehicle? What situations may cause special concern on field trips? What suggestions does the director have for addressing these concerns? Have students write a brief report of their findings.

28-8

Brown's Child Care
Field Trip Permission Form

Child's Name _____   Date _____

Parents' Name(s) _____   Business Phone _____

_____   Cell Phone _____

_____   Business Phone _____

Cell Phone _____

Home Address _____   Home Phone _____

Home E-Mail _____

In consideration of _____ 's
(child's name)

acceptance as an enrollee in Brown's Child Care Center, I hereby give permission for my child to participate in any walks or field trips planned and supervised by the staff. I understand that various modes of transportation may be used for these trips, and I will be informed of each trip before it occurs.

_____   _____
(Parent Signature)   (Date)

_____   _____
(Parent Signature)   (Date)

Permission slips from parents, such as this one, are a necessity when planning a field trip.

surroundings. For example, pets, animals, babies, mothers, fathers, and grandparents are topics that capture their interest.

Field trips for children under 24 months are often simple walks around the neighborhood. For safety purposes, use strollers for these children. Many centers purchase special strollers that hold up to six children. This allows one teacher to handle several children at one time, 28-9.

When planning field trips for young children, avoid crowds. Crowds may be overwhelming to some children. It is also difficult to watch children in a crowded setting. Trips to the zoo and the circus

28-9

Strollers such as this one make it possible for one adult to take several young children on a walk near the center.

Discuss

Ask students to review the permission form used by the child care lab. Is any information missing from the form? What changes, if any, would you make to the form?

Reflect

Look over the sample field trip permission form in 28-8. Is there any more information you would suggest that needs to be listed on the form?

Discuss

What is the youngest age of a child who would benefit from and enjoy a trip to the following places: a newspaper printing plant, a pet store, a bank, the police department, and a playground?

Putting Technology to Use

Have students look over the Americans with Disabilities Act of 1990 to learn what is required for accessibility to businesses you may be visiting for field trips. As part of pre-trip preparations for a field trip, visit the site and check to see the business or location complies with ADA guidelines so all the trip participants can be accommodated. Make sure parking, building access, hallways, aisles, viewing areas, and restrooms are all in compliance. Information on the Act can be found at **www.usdoj.gov/crt/ada.**

Discuss

How important are hands-on activities as part of a field trip for young children? What examples of hands-on participation would you suggest for field trips to each of the following: a bakery; a pet store or pet rescue facility; the fire department; a garden center?

Enrich

Some home-based or small child care programs may not be able to support the cost of owning their own van or other transportation for children. Have students debate the pros and cons of using private vehicles for child care programs such as these.

Resource

Planning the Trip, Activity B, SAG

Health and Safety

Accessible Field Trips

When planning field trips, consider the special needs of children in your care. Visit the field trip site before you schedule the trip to ensure it is accessible and safe for all children. Is it accessible for students who use wheelchairs or have vision impairments? Will the site accommodate strollers if toddlers take part in the trip? Evaluate these issues before confirming field trip plans.

usually involve large groups of people. In these cases, during your pretrip ask what days are least crowded. When crowds cannot be avoided, ask for help from parents and other volunteers.

Choose trips that provide learning through participation. Children enjoy touching and doing things. When planning a trip to a farm, ask if the children can pet the animals, assist in milking the cows, and help collect the eggs. Likewise, a trip to an apple orchard could provide children with opportunities to pick and taste apples.

Cost

When planning a field trip, always figure the costs. This helps you decide if the trip is the best use of your resources. You may feel that the cost of chartering a bus to the zoo is more than your budget allows. You may decide that the money needed

for chartering a bus could be more wisely spent on classroom materials. If most of the children have already had this experience, you may want to use the money for some less costly trips. This would give the children new experiences.

Most field trips involve little or no expense, particularly if the site is within walking distance. In some cases, the only costs are admission and/or transportation. If there is an admission fee, call in advance and ask if group rates are available for child care centers. At times, you may get a generous discount or free admission.

Transportation

Costs for transportation vary greatly, depending on the type used. For centers that own their own vans, the costs of most field trips are minimal. To cut costs, some centers ask parents and teachers to drive their own cars. This type of arrangement is not recommended. In case of an accident, legal problems could arise, and the driver and/or center could be sued for damages.

Public transportation, such as the city bus or subway, is often less costly than a chartered bus. However, there are disadvantages to public transportation. Trains can be crowded and noisy. This can be stressful for children. There is also the danger of children being hurt or lost during the course of the trip. Accidents often happen as children enter or exit buses or trains. This is why some teachers elect not to use public transportation for their children.

If you decide to use a chartered bus, call several reputable companies. Check to see that the company meets any state safety inspection guidelines. Explain where you intend to go, the length of your stay, the number of passengers, and request prices. Ask them to send you the price quote in writing. After you receive all the quotes, compare to find the company that will provide the best service for the least amount of money. By thoroughly checking costs for a field trip, you can get the most for your resources.

Cross-Curricular Activity

Math

Have students calculate the total cost for a field trip for 20 four-year-olds and their adult chaperones to a museum 35 miles from the school. The admission charges are $7.00 for children and $10.00 for adults. Determine the number of chaperones needed and include their admission in the calculations. Include transportation costs. Students should plan on stopping for lunch at a fast-food restaurant that serves child meals and include the adult meals, including the bus driver's, in the total.

Scheduling

Midmornings are the best time to schedule field trips. This time of day works best for several reasons. First, children are usually well rested. They often find it easier to listen, observe, and follow instructions. Second, children arrive at different times during the morning. Some parents may bring their children to the center at 7 a.m. Others may not bring their children until 8 or 9 a.m. If you schedule the trip too early, some children would be deprived of the experience. Also in colder climates, early morning temperatures can be too cool for children. This is a key consideration for trips that require walking, 28-10.

Afternoon field trips are also difficult to plan. Most preschool children need to take a nap at this time. Also, children may be deprived of the trip if their parents pick them up early in the afternoon.

28-10

Petting farm animals is most enjoyable in the warmth of late morning sunshine.

Health and Safety

Vehicle Safety for Field Trips

When transporting children in a vehicle other than a bus or school bus, make sure the children are properly secured in a developmentally appropriate car seat, seat belt, or harness. The child's height and weight will determine the type of restraint. Check local, state, and federal rules about transporting children of various ages in different types of vehicles.

Field trips should begin after a quiet activity. This helps children avoid excess excitement or overstimulation during the trip. Overstimulated children are very active and difficult to manage.

One question often asked is, "What is the best day for a field trip?" The answer to this question depends on the group and attendance. First, study the behavior and routine of the group. Some groups are always tired and restless by Friday. You may want to choose a day early in the week for such a group. Monday may not be a good day, depending on the program. The children may be tired as a result of weekend activities. Second, consider the days children attend. Some children may be deprived of trips if they are always scheduled for a day they do not attend.

The right day for a field trip may also depend on the site. If formal arrangements must be made, ask the contact person to suggest a day. Many resource people prefer midweek. This allows time to prepare for the visit.

Carefully plan around the children's needs, children's schedules, and resource person's schedule. This takes time. However, a well-planned field trip produces the greatest amount of learning and pleasure for the children.

Discuss

What are the primary concerns for scheduling field trips for the child care lab preschoolers? Would the same concerns apply to scheduling trips for children who attend private or organization-run programs?

Resource

Evaluating a Field Trip, Activity B, OG

Discuss

Give some reasons why scheduling mid-week field trips may be best for the children. Why might mid-week be best for the field trip location?

Workplace Connection

Have students develop a field trip proposal for the children in the child care lab. Students should review schedules for the children and determine the best time for a field trip. Students should also take into consideration what form of transportation will be most appropriate. Have students write a formal proposal for their suggested field trip. Allow time for students to review the plans in class. Select the best proposal and arrange to take the child care lab children on the field trip.

Discuss

How many adult chaperones would you suggest accompany a field trip for a group of 16 four- and five-year-olds? How many adults for a group of 12 three-year-olds? What else should you consider in determining the amount of adults needed for chaperones?

Vocabulary

Have a student volunteer define *behavioral expectations*. Why are behavioral expectations needed for field trips if classroom expectations are already in place?

Resource

Field Trip Checklist, reproducible master 28-5, TR

Health and Safety

Training Staff for Transporting Children

In order to safely transport children, the driver or other care provider must be trained in developmentally appropriate procedures. According to state and federal guidelines, at least one staff member on the vehicle should have a valid pediatric first aid certificate and training in rescue breathing and managing blocked airways. In addition, mandated staff-to-child ratios must be followed to properly supervise children during transportation.

Field trips can have many hidden dangers. For this reason, extra adult supervision is required.

Adult-Child Ratio

To ensure safety and the success of the trip, provide enough chaperones. The most desirable adult-child ratio is based on the number of children in the group, the nature of the field trip, and the dangers involved, 28-11. Walks around the neighborhood can often be handled by the center staff. More adults may be needed for trips using public transportation or for visits to places with potential dangers.

Provide as many adults as possible to promote safety. For two-year-olds, it is recommended that there be one adult for every two children. An adult should be assigned to every four three-year-olds, five four-year-olds, and six five-year-olds for optimal safety. However, if some children need to be closely watched, this ratio should be adjusted. Many times, children are grouped based on their temperaments. For

instance, if Sam and Frank behave badly when together, they should be separated. Place them in different groups. If there is a child who has a difficult time following rules, you may assign the child to one adult. Often, an "extra" adult is recruited who is not assigned any specific children. This adult can relieve a teacher to handle emergencies or give children one-to-one contact as needed.

When more adults are needed for field trips, invite parents. Many programs maintain lists of parents and other volunteers interested in helping on field trips. When the need arises, give these people from one to several week's notice. Parent volunteers may have to make special arrangements at work. Prior to the trip, provide the volunteers with information regarding the trip. Time of departure, arrival at the site, length of stay at the site, planned events at the site, and arrival time back at the center should be included. In addition, volunteers should be told the behavioral expectations.

Behavioral Expectations

Behavioral expectations need to be planned and discussed with children before the trip. Expectations for the children to follow will vary with the children and nature of the trip. Some expectations may apply

---

Meeting Special Needs

Pair student volunteers with special learners to write a list of expectations or limits for your adult chaperones. Be sure to use a professional style. Example: Instead of "You can't use your cell phone on the trip," consider "We request you avoid personal or non-emergency use of your cell phone to give the children in your care your full attention." Have students share their lists with the class.

to all trips. Regardless of the type of trip, expectations are most often the same in most early childhood programs.

For best results, state all expectations in a positive way. Tell the children exactly what they must do, 28-12. For example, tell the children to place their hands at their sides when they are in a store.

The first expectation for field trips is that all children must wear an identification tag at all times. These tags should be durable so they can be reused. They should be worn on all field trips. The tag should include the program name, address, and telephone number. This information is helpful in case a child wanders from the group.

The second expectation for field trips is that children should speak softly. To ensure this, teachers need to set a good example. Speak in a low-key voice to avoid overstimulation.

The third expectation is that children must remain with their assigned group and adult supervisor on field trips. Then each adult will know the names of the children they are responsible for supervising.

Many teachers prefer to have children follow the "hold-your-partner's-hand" rule. However, this is not always useful. It is unfair to interested children to have partners whose attention is not focused on the learning

28-12

This child can quietly watch the birds and listen to the speaker because his teacher shared these behavioral expectations with him ahead of time.

experience. Also, constant physical contact can result in stress for some children.

Instead of holding hands children can hold on to a rope to keep them together as a group. To make this rope, purchase several 20-foot pieces of rope. With each piece of rope, loop and tie handles at 2-foot intervals. Show the children how to hold on to the handles and explain expectations during the trip.

Educational Goals

For the most benefit on a field trip, educational goals must be carefully planned. For example, a trip to a local service station may have a number of goals:

- to observe mechanics at work
- to learn about the care of cars
- to see how machinery works
- to learn vocabulary words: *technicians, gas pump, nozzle,* and *hoist*

During the pretrip visit, these goals need to be discussed with the resource person.

Children's Preparation

Preparation for children may begin a few days before the trip. Introduce the trip by putting up displays, reading a book, sharing a video, looking at the pictures, or simply talking about the trip.

On the day of the trip, tell children what to observe (educational goals) and how to behave (behavioral expectations). Give an identification tag to each child. Assign children to their adult guides. After this, encourage children to use the bathroom. Explain that a bathroom is not always available on walks or some field trips.

Parent Preparation

Parents should always be informed in advance of field trips. A newsletter, calendar, or notice posted on a bulletin board or classroom door are all useful methods, 28-13.

Enrich

Have students debate the pros and cons of children wearing a name tag on a field trip when they will be in a public area with many people. Include opinions on wearing the groups' official T-shirt or hat.

Resource

Educational Goals, reproducible master 28-3, TR

Discuss

Why is it important to determine education goals for a field trip when planning the trip? Why should these goals be discussed with the resource persons or guides at the field trip location?

Activity

Consider using suggesting, prompting, and questioning (guidance techniques from Chapter 14) to prepare children for field trip expectations instead of just telling children what you expect. Have students write a list of suggested questions to ask preschoolers to remind them of the limits. Example: "What do we do when Officer Burns is speaking?"

Workplace Connection

Have students design a pretrip activity to help children become aware of what to expect on a field trip. Example: Seat the children in a circle and start the game by saying, "I'm going on a trip to _____ and I'm taking _____." Insert examples such as *bakery* and *coat.* Let the children add their items. Provide magazines for children to cut out their selected items, then "pack" them in a shirt-sized gift box decorated to look like a suitcase. "Unpack" the items one-by-one to see if children can remember who selected each item.

Resource

Pretrip and Posttrip Activities, transparency master 28-4, TR

Activity

Have students design a page for a child's portfolio to document a field trip experience. Include an area for a photo of the child on the trip or a drawing by the child and some information about the trip such as *Where I Went, What I Did, What I Learned, What I Liked*, etc.

Resource

Before and After the Field Trip, Activity C, SAG

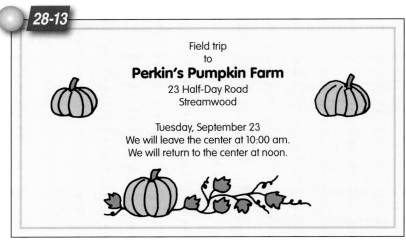

Field trip
to
Perkin's Pumpkin Farm
23 Half-Day Road
Streamwood

Tuesday, September 23
We will leave the center at 10:00 am.
We will return to the center at noon.

Placing this notice on a center bulletin board helps remind parents of an upcoming field trip.

E-mail can be used, too. Inform the parents of the date, location, address, and exact times you will be leaving and returning. In case of emergency, you should also provide them with the name and telephone number of the person at the site. This will help parents plan their schedules for dropping off and picking up the children.

You should also notify parents in advance if they are expected to pay any costs of the trip. Let parents know if you will need them to provide any special items, such as sack lunches or car safety seats.

Before leaving, post a sign on the classroom door. Note where you have gone and when you will return. This will also serve as a trip reminder for the parents and center staff.

Share trip goals with children's parents. This information may help them plan related home experiences such as discussions and books that complement the trip.

Follow-Up Activities

To help children clarify their learning, plan follow-up activities. Once you return to the center, talk about what they saw,

heard, and experienced. Plan an activity that reinforces the learning that occurred on the trip. A class thank-you note could be a follow-up activity, 28-14.

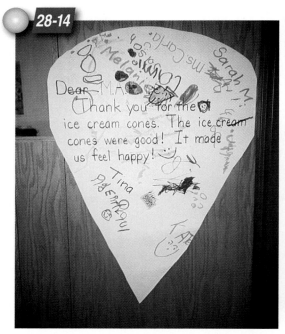

After a trip to an ice cream parlor, the children signed this thank-you note.

Portfolio Project

Have students write an article describing a field trip experience for the parent newsletter. Include the goals of the activity, the names of resource people and chaperones, and what the children learned from the trip. Include a few quotes by the children to personalize the article. Include a photo of the trip, if possible, and file a copy of the printed article in the student's portfolio.

Recall the classroom scene after the trip to the apple orchard described at the beginning of the chapter. Apples were discussed at lunch. Then the experience was used as a basis for writing a story. After a trip to a bakery, children could bake bread or cookies. Ice cream or butter could be made after a trip to a local dairy. See 28-15.

28-15

Follow-Up Activities

Trip	Activities
Apple orchard	• Taste a variety of apples. • Make applesauce or apple muffins. • Read stories about apple orchards. • Serve apple butter, baked apples, or some other form of apple.
Fire station	• Place puzzles and stories related to the role of firefighters in the classroom. • Read stories about firefighters. • Place firefighters' clothing in the dramatic play area. • Act out fire safety procedures.
Print shop	• Provide rubber stamps, ink pads, and paper on which to print. • Place a typewriter or computer in the classroom. • Make games using alphabet letters.
Hair salon	• Provide a prop box containing hair rollers, combs, brushes, towels, and a hair dryer with the cord removed. • Place dolls with hair and combs in the dramatic play area. • Hang up a mirror and have children compare the ways they wear their hair.

Follow-up activities based on field trips can be simple or complex.

Resource

Planning a Field Trip,
Activity C, OG

Discuss

What follow-up activities can you suggest for each of the following field trips: grocery store, post office, florist or garden center, police department, pet store?

Resource

Completing the Trip,
Activity D, SAG

Meeting Special Needs

Review the special learners' chapter outlines to determine if the students have any questions about the concepts or content of this chapter. Review the chapter objectives and ask the students to evaluate their progress in meeting these objectives. Ask the students to summarize, orally or in writing, what they learned from this chapter.

Summary

Field trips can be a concrete learning experience for children. Through field trips, children gain firsthand knowledge of the world around them. This learning can involve new experiences or enhance previous knowledge.

Field trips require planning. Children must be prepared for the experience. Their preparation includes pretrip talks and activities, rules to follow, and discussions.

The teacher must also be prepared. This preparation includes selecting a trip, taking a pretrip, setting goals, obtaining permission from parents, and arranging transportation. After the trip, thank-you notes should be sent to helpful individuals. Follow-up activities will also reinforce the value of the experience.

Review and Reflect

1. List four benefits children experience from field trips.

2. For young children, first field trips should be _____.
    A. long and unique
    B. short and nonthreatening
    C. at unfamiliar places
    D. None of the above.

3. True or false. The location of the site and the budget are two factors that affect what field trips you will select.

4. True or false. For best results, focus on many topics during a theme walk.

5. How should resource people be selected?

6. List four opportunities a teacher is given by conducting a pretrip.

7. When planning field trips for young children, avoid _____.
    A. crowds
    B. hands-on activities
    C. age-appropriate activities
    D. All the above.

8. What are the disadvantages of using public transportation to reach your field trip site?

9. Explain how to determine what the best day for a field trip would be.

10. True or false. More adults may be needed for field trips using public transportation or for visits to places with potential dangers.

11. List three basic rules for field trips involving young children.

12. What is the purpose of follow-up activities?

Review and Reflect Answer Key

1. (List four:) children build keener observation skills, build vocabularies, clarify concepts as new information is learned, learn about their community, take part in multisensory experiences, gain new insight for dramatic play, learn about their environment, practice following directions in a group.
2. B
3. true
4. false
5. Select only people who enjoy children. They should represent many cultural groups, both sexes, and people of different ages. Select people who complement your curriculum.
6. (List four:) Teachers have the opportunity to: describe the purpose of the trip to the tour guide; explain the children's interests and their need to use a number of senses; prepare the tour guide for the types of questions the children may ask; locate bathrooms; check for any potential dangers; ask about parking (if necessary); observe for teaching opportunities; revise trip goals, if necessary.
7. A
8. Public transportation is often crowded and noisy, which can be stressful for children. There is a danger of children being hurt or lost during the course of the trip.

9. The best day for a field trip depends on several factors. First, the behavior and routine of the group is a factor. Some groups are always tired and restless by Friday. For such a group, earlier in the week might be better. Monday may not be a good day, depending on the program. Children may be tired as a result of weekend activities. Second, the attendance schedule of the children is a factor. All children will not attend the center on the same days. The specific trip being planned is also a factor for choosing the right day.
10. true
11. Children must wear an identification tag at all times. Children must speak softly. Children must remain with their assigned group and adult supervisor.
12. Follow-up activities help children clarify their learning.

Apply and Explore

1. Compile a list of safety guidelines that should be followed on all field trips.

2. Make a list of follow-up activities for a field trip to a grocery store.

3. Plan a field trip for your class. Go through the same steps you would when planning a field trip for a group of young children.

Cross-Curricular Link

Social Studies

1. Start a file of ideas for field trips that could be taken by young children in your community.

Language Arts

2. Interview a center director about successful field trips he or she has conducted.

Technology

3. Brainstorm 10 possible local field trip sites. For each site listed, find out the address, phone number, Web page address, contact person's name, and price information. Use a computer's word-processing program to compile your information into a chart.

Workplace Link

Contact local child care program teachers to get suggestions for their most successful field trips. Interview the teachers to find out what they suggest for each of the age groups between two and six years old. How much preparation and cost were involved in the planning for the field trips? Discuss with teachers the reasons they felt the trips were successful. Ask for pointers on expectations for the children and chaperones.

PART

5

Other People You Will Meet

Most early childhood programs are geared toward preschoolers. However, you may choose to work with younger children (infants and toddlers), school-age children, or children with special needs. In this part, you will discover what special qualities are needed by teachers in infant-toddler programs and school-age programs. You will learn special techniques for providing care and learning experiences for these children. This part also introduces you to the concerns of children with special needs. You will understand how such needs as speech disorders, health disorders, and giftedness may affect your role as a teacher.

Parents and family members are very much involved with the care and guidance of their young children. You will want to keep them informed of everything that is happening at the center. Family involvement can be the key factor in the success of a program.

A world of career possibilities is open to early childhood teachers. It's up to you to choose a career path that fits your goals and to find a job that will start you on your path. This part will help prepare you for your job hunt. You will read about how to prepare a résumé and find available positions. You will also discover ways to make the best impression possible in an interview and land the job you really want.

Discuss

What characteristics do you think the caregiver in the chapter opening photo needs in order to work with infants and toddlers? How might her behavior influence the behavior of the children? Give examples.

Discuss

Look over the chapter objectives before reading the chapter to get a sense of the material to be covered. Why are more centers offering programs to care for very young children?

29

Programs for Infants and Toddlers

After studying this chapter, you will be able to

- list the characteristics of a nurturing infant-toddler caregiver.
- state guidelines for proper infant-toddler care.
- design functional and developmentally appropriate infant and toddler environments.
- handle the routines of infants and toddlers.
- select toys that are safe and developmentally appropriate for infants and toddlers.
- plan the curriculum for infants and toddlers.
- maintain the environment to prevent illness.

544

Terms to Know

stranger anxiety
sudden infant death syndrome (SIDS)
overfamiliarity

Ian is learning to walk. Hector has just said his first words and Pouneh has just begun exploring books. Working with infants and toddlers can be exciting and rewarding, 29-1. This is a unique and challenging stage in the life cycle.

Recent studies show brain development is more rapid from birth to age three than at any other period in life. As an infant-toddler caregiver, your nurturing and support play

29-1

Infants and toddlers grow and change rapidly. They are constantly learning new skills, such as standing on their own.

an important role in influencing brain growth during this most critical time. Providing a safe, stimulating, and nurturing environment promotes optimal brain development. Offering developmentally appropriate activities can form and strengthen the connections in the brain, which increase lifelong learning power. As you watch a child learn and develop, you will feel satisfied knowing your efforts have made a difference. You can share in and enjoy each new accomplishment the child exhibits.

Characteristics of Infant and Toddler Caregivers

As an infant-toddler caregiver, your behavior will influence the behavior of the children. Children will react based on the ways you treat them. If you are warm and loving, the children will be warm and loving. Touch, smile, make eye contact, and speak affectionately to the children. Cuddle them, rock them, talk and sing to them, and play with them. Likewise, be patient and accepting while working with them. Infants and toddlers need responsive caregivers. Trust, confidence, and self-esteem are promoted through caregiver responsiveness. See 29-2.

Young children are dependent on consistent and predictable relationships with their caregivers. You must have a high energy level, be healthy, and enjoy children. You must always be readily available to comfort and protect the children. You must also be able to handle many situations and understand feelings. Part of your responsibility includes helping children express feelings such as joy, love, anger, pleasure, satisfaction, and sadness.

Infants and toddlers need caregivers who provide consistent guidance. To provide this consistent environment, all center staff must agree on what is acceptable behavior. In most

Note

Have students review their notes from Chapters 5 and 6 to remind them of the development of children from birth through age three.

Discuss

What is the effect of touch on the brain development of infants? How does visual and auditory stimulation affect the brain development of infants and toddlers?

Reflect

How do you see yourself as a nurturer? What behaviors do you exhibit that demonstrate your ability to nurture children, especially infants and toddlers?

Resource

Caregiver Traits, Activity A, SAG

Meeting Special Needs

Provide an outline of the chapter with all the chapter headings for special learners. Students should fill in each section of the outline as the material is covered in class with a sentence or two about the content. Review the special learners' IEPs to decide if any modifications should be made in presenting the chapter content.

Enrich

Ask student volunteers to role-play the arrival and greeting of a parent and their child at the start of the day and again when the parent comes to pick the child up at the end of the day. What questions and information from both parent and caregiver should be a part of the daily dialogue?

Resource

Infant Equipment Checklist, reproducible master 29-1, TR

Discuss

Describe an ideal environment for an infant room. How does the environment support nurturing care and proper stimulation?

Resource

Environment Needs, Activity B, SAG

29-2

All areas of this young child's development are nurtured by her affectionate, responsive caregiver.

- Care for each child affectionately.
- Respond to children's distress or discomfort signals immediately.
- Follow a consistent and predictable routine in providing for children's needs.
- Encourage curiosity by providing opportunities for the children to explore.
- Help children develop trust, respect, and a positive regard for their world.
- Avoid overstimulation. Too many new experiences at one time can overwhelm young children, particularly infants.
- Plan opportunities for infants and toddlers to master new skills.

cases, having only a few limits for children increases the chances that limits will be consistently followed.

Finally, you need to be aware of new research in the infant-toddler field. Read professional journals, books, and articles. Attend professional workshops and conferences. Another way to stay informed is to discuss your observations and needs with other infant-toddler caregivers.

Guidelines for Infant-Toddler Care

In order to provide a quality infant-toddler program, consider the following general guidelines:
- Provide the children with a safe and healthful environment.
- Develop trusting relationships with the children and their families.
- Respect the cultures represented by the children and their families.
- Design a curriculum to meet the unique needs of each child.

Infant Environments

Providing a quality infant environment cannot be left to chance. Such an environment should be attractive and comfortable for infants as well as caregivers. Environments for infants should address their daily routines. Areas for feeding, diapering, cuddling with a caregiver, sleeping, and playing should all be included.

The most convenient feeding area is near the entrance to the center. Parents arriving with baby food and bottles can place these items in the refrigerator at once. This area should be equipped with high chairs, feeding tables, a heat source, and comfortable, adult-sized chairs.

The diapering area should be located next to a sink. As in the feeding area, the floor surface needs to be washable. This allows for easy cleaning and disinfecting. To prevent back strain for adults, changing surfaces and storage areas should be waist high. Place a mirror on the wall next to the changing surface so children can look at themselves.

The sleeping area usually uses the most space because cribs take a large amount of

Workplace Connection

If students have not already had the opportunity to visit an area child care center's infant program, arrange for a visit now. Have students observe a typical day in the infant room and document the activities that take place throughout the day. What challenges in caregiving do infant room teachers face? How does the infant-caregiver ratio provide for adequate supervision? Have students write a brief report of their observation findings.

floor space. The ideal location for this area is joining the diapering area. Do not worry about light. Infants do not need a dark room in which to sleep. However, a dimmer switch can be installed in this area to control lights used in the diapering area.

Infants also need their own play area, 29-3. They need to be safely out of the way of older children. To ensure safety, use low dividers to make a crawling area. Short pile carpeting should be on the floor for comfort and warmth.

Toddler Environments

Balancing safety and health concerns is important in designing spaces for toddlers.

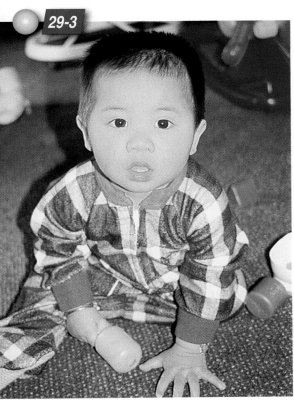

29-3

Infants need a safe place to play and explore their toys.

Toddlers need more open areas than infants. When they are not sleeping, they are usually moving. Toddlers' needs can be met in several areas. Included are receiving, playing, napping, diapering, and eating areas. (Napping, diapering, and eating areas for infants can be shared by toddlers.)

The receiving area should be located near the main entrance. This area should contain a bulletin board for parent information and lockers or hooks to hold children's clothing. When standing in the receiving area, you should be able to have a clear view of all other areas, especially the play area. Provide interesting equipment in the room to encourage children to play and help ease separation anxiety.

Toddlers need a play area that allows them to move freely. To provide this, leave one-third to one-half of the total space open. In crowded areas, some children may find it hard to play. As a result, they are more inclined to cry and grab. If adequate space is not provided, the children will bump into each other.

Although a tile floor is easier to maintain, some teachers prefer a carpeted floor in the play area. Carpeting has two advantages. First, it provides a cushion for falls. Second, it is warmer for crawling children. If carpeting is used, it should have a tight weave and be washable.

In a section of the play area, there should be equipment that encourages toddlers' rapidly changing physical skills. Open areas and equipment for crawling, walking, and climbing should be available. Scaled slides and tunnels are two types of equipment that invite exploration and climbing, as well as carpeted platforms and low shelves. Cardboard boxes can also be fun for toddlers. Equipment should be arranged so all areas can be seen by the caregiver.

The outdoor play area should connect to the indoor play area. This outdoor area should have a large, grassy area for running and crawling. Grass, like carpeting, helps cushion falls.

Activity

Have students visit an infant program and measure the size of the room to determine the square footage. How much area is taken up with cribs? How much area is available for crawling and play activities? Allow time for students to discuss their findings in class.

Discuss

Compare the environment for toddlers with one suitable for infants. How are the areas similar? How are they different?

Resource

Toddler Environment, Activity A, OG

Workplace Connection

Invite a home child care provider for infants and toddlers to speak to the class about his or her program. What licensing is recommended or required for home child care providers? What is the procedure for becoming licensed? How many children are they able to care for at a time? Have students prepare a list of additional questions to ask prior to the visit. If a home child care provider is unable to visit the class, try to arrange for a small group of students to visit the program.

Discuss

What is the role of consistent care in developing trust? How do caregivers show young children they are special?

Reflect

What challenges in infant care do you remember from early experiences in babysitting or family child care? How did you handle crying infants?

Discuss

Review Chart 29-4, *Appropriate and Inappropriate Teaching Practices.* What are some appropriate and inappropriate caregiver practices that are not listed in the chart? Give examples.

Caring for Infants and Toddlers

As you work with infants and toddlers, you will notice each child has his or her own rhythm. Some will go about their routines quickly. Others move slowly. As a caregiver, you must adjust your own rhythm to each child's rhythm.

All infants and toddlers, regardless of their differences, require their needs to be met promptly if they are to learn trust. A child who has been promptly and properly cared for is likely to be happy. To provide this attention to needs, you must provide consistent care. Through this care, children learn that they are special persons and develop trust. Chart 29-4 contains a list of appropriate and inappropriate caregiver practices.

Crying as a Means of Communication

Infants often communicate by crying. They may cry to express needs, cope with frustration, or get attention. They may also cry when they feel lonely, uncomfortable, neglected or over-stimulated. Regardless of the reason, you should never ignore crying. Always remember that the crying has some meaning for the child.

Studies support the theory that an infant's crying should always be given prompt attention. According to these studies, when cries are answered promptly, the frequency of the crying will be reduced.

You will observe that babies have individual differences in their crying behaviors. Some babies cry more often and with greater strength. Other babies may

29-4

Appropriate and Inappropriate Teaching Practices

Appropriate	Inappropriate
Caregivers interact frequently face-to-face with individual infants.	Infants are left unattended for long periods of time without adult attention.
Toys are picked up immediately after discarded to be sanitized. After being sanitized, they are reintroduced into the environment.	Toys that were mouthed by one child are left on the floor.
Caregivers are constantly talking, singing, and using nonverbal language with the children.	Infants are left to entertain themselves.
Caregivers recognize and provide for individual differences in children's sleeping and eating needs.	All children must conform to a rigid schedule for sleeping and eating.
Caregivers interact verbally and nonverbally while diapering.	Diapering is a hurried nonverbal routine.
Each child is assigned a primary caregiver to receive predictable care.	Children are passed from one caregiver to another providing little consistency or predictability.
Adults model warm, sensitive, nurturing behavior.	Adults often display unfeeling and chilly behavior.

The actions listed in the left column promote healthful development in infants.

Portfolio Project

Have students visit the library and locate parenting and family advice magazines. Students should select a sample issue of each publication and write a brief review of the types of articles the magazine contains. Also check newsstands, magazine sections in bookstores, department stores, and grocery stores for additional titles the library may not have. Have students compile a list of the parenting resources and file it in their portfolio.

seldom cry. All babies have various reasons for crying.

As a caregiver, you will have to learn the meaning of each child's cries. By listening to how a baby cries, you will soon learn his or her needs. A short and low-pitched cry usually means the baby is hungry. A loud and sudden high-pitched shriek followed by a flat wail is a distress cry. Sometimes the types of cries overlap. For instance, a baby may wake up hungry and will cry for food. If you do not quickly respond to this need, the baby may then cry with rage. You will also learn which cries indicate fussiness, soiled diapers, boredom, or discomfort related to being too cool or warm.

Always respond to a child's crying by first trying to solve the problem. If the baby is wet, change him or her. Likewise, if the child is hungry, feed him or her. If you cannot find an obvious reason for the child's crying, check the baby's daily care record. (This record is described later in the chapter.) Perhaps the baby is sleepy, teething, reacting to medication, or catching a cold. A baby may also cry out of a feeling of loneliness or wanting to play or be cuddled.

Tired, crying babies can be comforted in a number of ways. Some enjoy being held; others love to be rocked. Often a child can be quieted simply by speaking or singing softly to him or her.

Stranger Anxiety

Usually between seven to nine months of age, infants will begin showing fears of strangers, or **stranger anxiety**. Ricardo is an example. He was a very friendly and happy child no matter whom he encountered. Then at about seven months of age, he began to react to strangers. He often would frown, cry, turn his head away, and display wariness.

Ricardo's behavior is typical of a child experiencing stranger anxiety. His behavior shows increased cognitive functioning. Ricardo is trying to make sense of his world by distinguishing between strangers and people he knows. When he sees an unfamiliar person, he experiences fear.

Working with young children, you will observe that not all children react like Ricardo. Great differences exist. Some infants who have had experience with strangers will react less intensely. Other infants will show more anxiety with males than females.

In addition to strangers, you will notice that some children react strongly to sudden movements, noise, or strange objects. To help support children, let them explore at their own pace. Allow them to stay near you until their upset feelings have subsided. Meanwhile, gradually expose them to new objects in the center, 29-5.

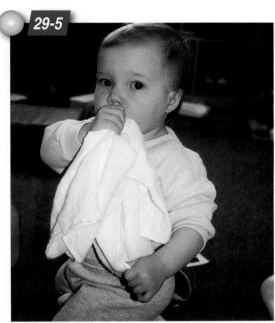

29-5

When a child shows stranger anxiety, it's important to introduce new people and objects gradually.

Discuss

How can you determine what a crying baby needs when the types of cries overlap? What can you do to comfort a tired, crying baby? Give examples.

Vocabulary

Have a student volunteer define the term *stranger anxiety*. At what age do infants usually begin showing fears of strangers?

Reflect

Think about a child you have seen experiencing stranger anxiety. What were some of the behaviors you observed? How did the parent or caregiver respond to the child? Have student volunteers share their experiences with the class.

Putting Technology to Use

Using the Internet, have students search for information about stranger anxiety. What are some steps a parent can take to minimize a child's distress during this developmental period? How should new caretakers be introduced to a child that is experiencing stranger anxiety? How can a parent help their child avoid the development of extreme stranger anxiety? Ask students to write a brief report or utilize the computer to record their findings. Allow time for students to discuss their findings in class.

Vocabulary

Have a student volunteer explain the term *separation anxiety*. Why do infant caregivers need to be particularly aware of handling separation anxiety?

Enrich

Ask student volunteers to role-play a situation involving a parent, caregiver, and crying child who seems to be experiencing separation anxiety. What should the caregiver say and do to relieve the parent's feelings of sadness and guilt for leaving a crying child? How can the child be comforted?

Note

While most adults enjoy a change of pace now and then, young children thrive on consistent routines. The sameness in daily infant care may negatively affect those caregivers who do not have the temperament for this type of work. They may decide to transfer to a class for older children.

Separation Anxiety

Between 9 and 18 months of age, some children will start experiencing *separation anxiety*. This is a feeling of fear and distress at being separated from a parent. It can include crying, protesting, clinging to the parent, withdrawing, or begging the parent not to leave. Many children experience separation anxiety. It is a sign they are learning and developing close relationships with their parents.

Separation anxiety is often strongest among children of this age who begin a child care situation for the first time. Children who start child care earlier can experience separation anxiety at this age, too. Their anxiety may be somewhat less severe, however, because they are already familiar with the surroundings and people at the center.

Feelings of separation anxiety are difficult for young children to handle. They need your acceptance and emotional support. Accept the child's feelings and describe them for him or her. Reassure the child the parent will return for him or her. Offer alternate activities, but be prepared for the child to refuse at first. In his or her own time, the child will join in. You might say, "You're sad because Mommy is leaving. She went to work, but she will come back for you this afternoon. Would you like to play blocks with me?"

It can take several weeks or months for separation anxiety to fade. Throughout this time, continue to show support and understanding. You may find yourself feeling frustrated by the child's crying or other behavior at these times. Remind yourself that it will pass in time and your support is vital. It will help the child learn to depend on you and feel secure in the child care environment.

When children experience separation anxiety, it's difficult for their parents, too. Parents do not enjoy seeing their child in distress. They may feel upset, sad, or guilty for having to leave their crying children. When their child begs them to stay, this can tug at their emotions. Remind parents that separation anxiety is normal and it will fade in time. Share with the parents any signs of progress you see. For example, if the child cries for less time or joins in with the others more quickly, let the parents know. This will help ease their minds.

Handling Routines

With infants and toddlers, routines make up much more of the day than routines do with preschoolers. It is important that daily routines be predictable. This will help the children gain a sense of security. It will also help them know what to expect and the sequence of activities. Much of your day will be spent on routines such as feeding, taking care of diapering and toileting needs, and preparing for nap time. See 29-6.

29-6

Routines such as diapering are an important part of caregiving curriculum for infants.

Putting Technology to Use

Have students conduct an Internet search for information comparing home child care with center child care for infants and children under two years of age. What are the advantages and disadvantages of each type of care? What are parent's opinions on each type of care? Have students prepare a graph, poster, or diagram to present their comparisons. Allow time for students to share their comparisons with the class.

It is important to coordinate home and center schedules for infants. To do this, parents need to provide you with information daily. One effective method is to provide parents with a daily record to complete when they arrive each morning with their infants. Likewise, the caregiver also needs to record the infants' eating and elimination patterns during the day. Nap information and activities for the day can also be included. See 29-7 for an example of an infant daily record.

Feeding Infants

Nutrition is very important for infants. At no time do children grow faster than during their first year of life. If they don't get the nutrients they need, their growth and development can be hindered. This makes your task of infant feeding a high priority. It is a task you will handle several times each day.

Throughout infancy, babies rely mainly on either breast milk or iron-fortified infant formula. The majority of feedings will be by bottle. However, some mothers may come to the center to breast-feed their infants. If so, provide them a quiet, comfortable place to do this.

It's important to immediately label and refrigerate all bottles containing breast milk or formula. Bottles left at room temperature for more than two hours can start to grow bacteria. These bacteria multiply rapidly and can cause illness. Discard any bottle that has been out of the refrigerator two hours or more. Once a child has put his or her mouth on the bottle, bacteria from the mouth and saliva can enter the milk or formula. This causes it to spoil even more quickly. After one hour, discard any milk or formula remaining in a used bottle.

Many infants prefer their bottles at room temperature. When taking a bottle from the refrigerator, place it under a stream of warm running water. This will quickly bring the bottle to room temperature. Never place a bottle in the microwave. This is dangerous because the microwave heats unevenly. When part of the milk or formula is warm, another part might be hot enough to scald the baby's mouth. With breast milk, the excessive heat can also destroy the living substances and nutritional content of the milk. If you need to warm a bottle, use a pan of hot water or bottle warmer.

Starting at four to six months, infant cereals are often introduced as the first "solid foods." Be sure to feed cereals with a spoon rather than in a bottle. Putting cereal in the bottle does not give an infant the needed practice of eating from a spoon. It can also create a choking hazard.

Baby foods, such as pureed fruits, vegetables, and meats, will soon follow. While most parents use store-bought jars of baby food, others make their infants' foods at home. Your task will be serving the children the breast milk, formula, and foods provided by the parents. When serving baby foods, use a clean spoon to remove the desired portion from the jar or container. Put this into a small serving dish. Replace the lid and refrigerate the jar. Use within two to three days. Discard any uneaten food in the serving dish at the end of the feeding. This will keep the food from growing bacteria from the baby's saliva.

Talk with parents about feeding practices, preferences, and habits. Ask the parents which foods to offer as well as when to offer them. Try to follow the parents' wishes regarding feeding, unless safety is a concern. In this case, discuss with your center director how to proceed. The director can inform you of center policies and advise you how to handle the situation. It's often best to inform parents of the risks involved and suggest a more appropriate option. For instance, propping an infant's bottle is an inappropriate practice. It creates a choking risk and deprives the infant of the personal attention and social contact needed when eating. It also promotes ear infections. If parents ask you to prop their child's bottle, the director might advise you to gently explain your concern and tell the parents that center policy is to hold infants during feedings.

Discuss

Why should you discard partially consumed bottles of formula or breast milk that have been out of the refrigerator after one hour? What suggestions might you make to a parent to cut down on waste from discarding half-empty bottles?

Reflect

To save time and clean-up, Andrea decided to feed Rowan baby food peaches right from the jar. Rowan only ate half the jar, so Andrea replaced the cap and returned it to the refrigerator for the next day. What concerns do you have about Andrea's actions?

Discuss

Ten-month-old Manny is at the day care center from 6:30 a.m. to 5:30 p.m. each day. His parents send only bottles with milk and juice, and baby cereal and pureed fruit in jars. What other foods does Manny need? How can you professionally discuss this information with his parents?

Workplace Connection

Invite a pediatrician, pediatric nurse, or dietitian to speak to the class about the nutritional needs of infants and toddlers. What are the recommendations for types of milk to be served? What is the timeline for adding solid foods, meats, and eggs? What should parents and caregivers know about food allergies, food sensitivities, and digestive disorders in young children? Have students write a list of additional questions to ask prior to the visit.

Resource

Infant Feeding Guide-lines, color transparency CT-25A, TR

Discuss

What information should parents record on an infant daily record when they arrive to the child care center each morning with their infant? What information do caregivers need to record throughout the day?

Reflect

Think about how recording an infant's eating and elimination patterns, nap information, and activities for the day can help you when trying to maintain a predictable routine for the infant.

29-7

Infant Daily Record

Infant's name: _____   Parent's name:_____

Day/Date:_____   Time of arrival:_____

Parent's signature:_____   Time of departure: _____
          (filled in by parent)   (filled in by staff member)

Baby seems: ❑ Normal, typical
            ❑ Bit fussy
            ❑ Not acting as usual

Baby slept: ❑ Soundly
            ❑ Woke up several times
            ❑ Did not sleep well

Baby ate:

Food/Drink	Amount	Time
_____	_____	_____
_____	_____	_____
_____	_____	_____

❑ Nothing this morning

Bowel movement number:_____

❑ Regular   ❑ Irregular

Number of wet diapers: _____

Diet change for today: _____

_____

Special instructions:_____

Medicine taken today: _____

Time_____ Amount _____

Time_____ Amount _____

Medicine to be given today:_____

Time_____ Amount _____

Time_____ Amount _____

(See medication form for details)

Bottles:	Time	Food/Drink	Amount
	_____	_____	_____
	_____	_____	_____
	_____	_____	_____
	_____	_____	_____
	_____	_____	_____
Foods:	_____	_____	_____
	_____	_____	_____
	_____	_____	_____
	_____	_____	_____
	_____	_____	_____

Diaper checks and changes	Time	Description
	_____	_____
	_____	_____

Medication given: _____   _____
                      (Time)   (Caregiver)

_____   _____
   (Time)   (Caregiver)

Activities, accomplishments, skills shown today:

_____

_____

_____

Caregivers' initials _____

An infant daily record can help to coordinate home and center schedules.

Portfolio Project

Ask students to review 29-6, *Infant Daily Record*, for an example of how to keep track of the infant's day. Have students contact area child care centers to discover if they use a similar form for toddlers. Ask students to design a toddler daily record form making sure there are areas for communicating the daily activities, new words, new skills, playmates, and behavior. Students should ask area toddler caregivers for suggestions on making the form easy to fill out when most of their time is spent with the children. Have students file a copy of the record in their portfolio.

Meeting infants' nutritional needs will be an important part of your job as a caregiver. Very young infants express their hunger by moving their mouths, rooting, or crying. Older infants may cry for food, grunt and point at the food they want, or respond positively to a caregiver's offer of food. It's important to feed infants on demand rather than on a set schedule. Feed each child when he or she is hungry, not when it is convenient.

By the same token, do not force an infant to eat. Watch for cues that the baby is full or doesn't want more. These include crying in response to the bottle or spoon, turning the head away, closing the mouth tightly, and stopping sucking from the bottle. If you see these or other signs of refusal, respect the baby's cues and end the feeding.

Feeding Toddlers

Children's hand washing is important before and after eating. Many toddlers crawl on the floor and later use their hands to feed themselves. Before eating, always wash toddlers' hands. If child-sized sinks are not available, use a small pan of water at the table. In the beginning, you may have to assist the children in swishing their hands as well as wiping them on a paper towel or cloth. You may want to apply a small amount of liquid soap to a dampened towel and wipe the child's hands. Rinse the hands with a clean towel moistened with water. Finally, wipe the child's hands with a dry paper towel.

Whenever possible, toddlers should be served finger foods. These are easy for children to handle. Always provide many sizes and shapes so children can practice picking them up. Examples include cubes of pear, cooked green peas, chopped cooked eggs, banana pieces, and cheese.

For feeding, toddlers can be seated in high chairs, at eating tables, or on low chairs placed in front of a low table, 29-8. They will need some table space on which to move their food. Children of this age love to explore their food. Before eating, toddlers may smell, touch, and push around their food. This behavior should be encouraged. Exploring food can give children important sensory experiences that foster cognitive growth.

Diapering and Toileting

Changing diapers is a routine that a caregiver will repeat many times each day. For this reason, it should be a pleasant experience. Give the child all your attention.

Health and Safety

Sanitary Diaper-Disposal Containers

Containers for sanitary diaper disposal follow specific guidelines for the early childhood classroom. Note these guidelines:

- Use disposal containers with tight-fitting covers that can be released without touching them with your hands. Step cans are one type. Simply step on the release to open the can.

- Use washable containers. Line them with plastic liners or garbage bags.

- Store soiled diapers in disposal containers away from other waste receptacles.

- Keep disposal containers out of children's reach.

- Empty containers into the outdoor trash daily or as often as necessary throughout the day.

Discuss

How do young infants express their hunger? How might older infants express their hunger? Should infants be fed on demand or on a set schedule? What cues should you watch for to indicate the infant is full or doesn't want more?

Enrich

Have students demonstrate how to help toddlers wash their hands. Why are paper towels preferred over cloth towels for drying hands?

Activity

Provide several foods that would be suitable finger foods for toddlers. Have students take turns demonstrating how they would cut them up so toddlers could easily grab them. What safety factors need to be considered when deciding what size to cut the food?

Workplace Connection

Ask students to survey area infant and toddler care centers to discover what type of disinfectant cleaners are used to treat the changing table and potty seats after each use. Are spray cleaners made by mixing chlorine bleach and water? Are commercial products used? What precautions do the caregivers need to take when using spray products around children? What additional janitorial services are completed each day to keep the infant and toddler room clean and safe? Allow time for students to discuss their findings in class.

Discuss

What is the advantage to parents of providing their own disposable diapers to the child care center for their child's use? What is the advantage to the child care center to provide the diapers?

Resource

Diaper Check Chart, reproducible master 29-2, TR

Activity

Have students conduct an unofficial poll the next time they visit the rest room to observe how long most students wash their hands after using the facilities. Ask students to count to twenty while they simulate washing their hands in the classroom to get an idea of how long proper hand washing should take.

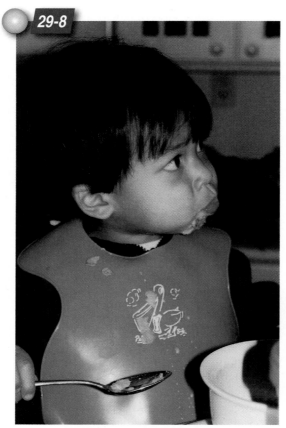

29-8

Toddlers can feed themselves with a spoon, but expect a mess. Use bibs to protect their clothing.

Look into his or her eyes. Smile, sing, and talk softly to the child. Stroke the child's hair. Diapering can be a wonderful time for personal interaction.

A diaper-checking routine is a useful policy to follow. Infants need frequent diaper changes because they eliminate often. For the infants' health and comfort, you need to change soiled diapers promptly. This prevents chafing, diaper rashes, infections, and discomfort. Your center should have a specific diaper check routine. This might be checking each child's diaper once every hour or half-hour except when the child is sleeping. In addition to scheduled checks, diapers should be checked before each feeding and after each nap.

Most center policies state only disposable diapers may be used. Cloth diapers leak more often, causing more mess and the possible transmission of infection to others. Diaper pails for cloth diapers have a strong unpleasant odor and may present a drowning risk. Disposable diapers are more convenient and sanitary. In most centers, parents are responsible for supplying diapers. A few centers provide diapers for the children in their care.

When diapering, you may come into contact with many disease-causing germs. Thorough hand washing will greatly reduce the spread of these germs. Therefore, all staff should follow proper hand washing procedures before and after each diaper change. See 29-9.

29-9

Hand Washing Procedures for Diapering

1. Dispense enough liquid soap into the hand to provide a good lather.
2. Turn on the faucet. Add a small amount of warm water to the soap. Rub hands back and forth to produce lather. Lather over your wrists and clean under your fingernails. Scrub your hands for 20 seconds.
3. Rinse well with warm water, keeping your hands pointed down.
4. Turn off the faucet using your elbow or paper towels. (Do not touch the faucet controls with clean hands).
5. Dry hands thoroughly using paper towels. Discard used paper towels.
6. Apply latex disposable gloves, if needed.
7. Change diaper and place the soiled diaper in a special container.
8. Wash the infant's hands.
9. Disinfect changing area.
10. Remove gloves, if worn. Wash hands again, using steps 1 through 5.
11. Apply lotion to hands to prevent chapping.

Proper hand washing is vital to preventing the spread of disease from diapering.

Workplace Connection

Have students investigate a local child care center's policies and practices regarding diapering. Does the center have a specific diaper check routine? Are diapers checked before feedings and naps? Are only disposable diapers used? Who is responsible for supplying the diapers? Does the staff follow proper hand washing procedures? Have students write a brief report of their findings. Allow time for students to discuss their findings in class.

It is important to wash with warm water and use liquid soap. Liquid soap should be used because bar soaps, when wet and jellylike, harbor microorganisms. You will probably find that a soap dispenser is most convenient. Remember, though, that microorganisms may also grow in liquid soap. Therefore, clean the dispenser each time it is refilled.

In many centers, it is policy to use lightweight, disposable gloves for all diaper changes. Other centers require these gloves only when there is a crack or cut in the skin of the hands. Rubber gloves will reduce the spread of infection from germs entering an open wound on the hand. Medical experts agree it is nearly impossible to prevent microorganisms from growing in an open wound in the skin.

Remove the soiled diaper and discard it. Clean the diaper area from front to back with a baby wipe or wet washcloth. Place a clean diaper under the baby. Avoid applying baby powder during a diaper change. If inhaled, the fine powder can harm the lungs of an infant or caregiver.

Next, check for signs of *diaper rash*. This is a skin rash that occurs in the baby's diaper area. It may result when the diaper is changed too infrequently. The wet, damp diaper promotes the growth of bacteria that can irritate and infect the skin in the diaper area. Itching, redness, and discomfort are common. If you notice any signs of diaper rash, notify the parents that same day.

Keeping the baby clean and dry will prevent many cases of diaper rash. Check infants' diapers often and change them promptly. If diaper rash does occur, the rash can be treated with a diaper rash ointment at every change. The parents would supply this ointment. To prevent diaper rash, some parents prefer to apply ointment with every change when no rash is present. Follow the parent's instructions on this matter. If a rash worsens or won't clear up, advise the parents to seek their doctor's advice.

After each change, spray the diapering table or changing mat with a disinfectant solution. Wash your hands. Then record

diapering information on the daily record. The time of the check or change and whether the child urinated and/or had a bowel movement all need to be noted. If the child had diarrhea, this should be noted along with the amount, color, and consistency.

Do not be shocked if, as a child grows older, he or she objects to having a diaper changed. Many times this objection occurs because the child is having fun playing and does not want to be interrupted. When this occurs, there is no harm in waiting a few minutes. Wait until the child finishes with an activity, and then gently guide him or her to the changing area. Many times this transition is easier if the child is allowed to carry a toy into the changing area.

Some toddlers may be in the process of or showing an interest in toilet learning. For these children, it is important that the home and center coordinate their efforts. Discuss with the parents the toilet-learning process. Explain that it will be easier for the child if the home and center routines are consistent.

Like diapering, toileting policies must be used for health purposes. Children need to wash their hands after using the potty chair, 29-10. After each use, the seat of the potty

29-10

Young toddlers may need help washing their hands correctly.

Enrich

Have student volunteers use a product such as Germ Juice™ or Germ Powder™ to demonstrate how germs and bacteria are spread from improper hand washing. Some residue of the material stays on the hands if not washed properly and can be seen under a UV bulb.

Vocabulary

Have a student volunteer explain *diaper rash*. What are some of the signs of diaper rash and how can it be prevented?

Discuss

Why might toilet learning go faster and with more success for a toddler who attends a child care center in comparison to one who is cared for at home? What techniques might a child care provider use to encourage toilet learning?

Putting Technology to Use

Have students conduct an Internet search for information on the causes and types of diaper rashes and other rashes that may affect infants and toddlers. What else besides not changing diapers often enough contributes to the formation of an irritating rash? What can parents and caregivers do to treat a diaper rash? What over-the-counter medicines or products can help? When is professional medical care suggested for the treatment of severe diaper rash? Have students write a brief report of their findings.

Discuss

Why might some parents prefer their child take short naps while at the child care center? What situations may make longer naps preferable?

Vocabulary

Have a student volunteer define the term *sudden infant death syndrome (SIDS)*. What precautions can be taken to help prevent SIDS?

Reflect

Why do infants need toys? How can caregivers make sure toys and objects providing visual stimulation for infants are effective?

chair needs to be sprayed with a disinfectant solution and wiped. The container under the chair must be emptied and rinsed with the solution. Finally, you will need to wash your hands with warm water and soap.

Nap Time

All children need a certain amount of sleep. This amount varies from one child to another. Newborns sleep 16 to 20 hours a day, 29-11. Most infants need at least two naps a day ranging from one to three hours. Without adequate sleep, a child can become cranky and difficult to handle. When this happens, it can have a negative influence on other children and staff in the center.

One consideration for planning a nap time schedule is to check parents' preferences. Some parents keep their infants up late and wake them early in the morning. They want their child to sleep at the center so he or she is awake and alert at the end of the day. Other parents, who may have to travel some distance to get home, prefer to have a sleepy baby at the end of the day. Their goal is to have the baby sleep on the way home.

Nap times may have to be staggered to meet the individual needs of the children.

29-11

Provide a safe, quiet, and comfortable sleeping area for infants and toddlers.

This type of scheduling will allow you time to feed and rock each child to sleep. Often this will require meshing individual needs with group needs. Once a schedule has been developed that fits individual needs, it is necessary to be consistent.

When putting infants down for naps, certain precautions will help reduce the risk of **sudden infant death syndrome (SIDS)**. SIDS is the death of a healthy infant due to unexplained causes. To help prevent SIDS, napping infants should always be placed on their backs on a firm mattress. Soft items, such as quilts, pillows, and stuffed toys, should never be placed in a crib with an infant. Infants should be covered with light blankets only up to their chests. Sleeping babies should be checked visually every two to five minutes by a caregiver.

Toys for Infants and Toddlers

To meet the special needs of infants and toddlers, appropriate equipment is needed. Toys serve as sensory stimuli for young children. For instance, by positioning an infant's toys, you can create an incentive for the child to use his or her memory or locomotive abilities, 29-12. Even during the first few weeks of life, an infant can touch, see, and hear. As the child exercises these abilities, physical and mental development are fostered.

Toddlers need a range of equipment from soft blocks to puzzles. To promote language skills, include picture books, story books, audiotapes, CDs, dramatic play props, and puppets. The audiotapes and CDs can be used to promote music and movement. Sensory materials, including nontoxic crayons, markers, and play dough, should also be available.

When planning environments for toddlers, balance is important. You need to provide a sufficient quantity and variety of

Workplace Connection

Ask students to locate catalogs or Internet sources for suppliers of furniture, equipment, and supplies for infant and toddler child care centers. What differences, if any, do students notice in products for child care centers from those used at home? What products do you find interesting and suitable for a program for young children? Have students select five products available through different suppliers and compare them in quality, materials, and cost. Allow time for students to discuss their findings in class.

Crawling babies need a safe, appealing play area.

toys to encourage exploration. However, you must guard against overstimulation. Too many choices can overwhelm the children.

Many infant-toddler centers maintain a toy inventory that lists all the equipment available in the center. The inventory is subdivided into developmental sequences. See 29-13 for a sample toy inventory. This list is quite helpful when planning activities for children. Since it is important to frequently change toys, the list will help you keep a record of the toys already used and toys that are available. Another advantage of keeping a toy inventory is that it is helpful when ordering new toys.

Safety Issues

When choosing toys for the infant or toddler, safety is the number one consideration. Check each piece carefully for sharp edges or points. To avoid splinters, all wooden toys should be smoothly sanded. Small toys or toys with small parts should be avoided. Objects smaller than 1½ inches

across and 1⅝ inches in diameter could be swallowed or cause choking.

To check whether an object is a choking risk, buy a plastic safety tube for measuring small toys. Try to fit the object inside this tube. If it fits, it's too small to be safe for an infant or toddler.

Each year many infants and toddlers accidentally swallow small toys or parts. This can cause suffocation from choking on the object. Also, a child may develop intestinal or respiratory problems as a result of swallowing a small toy. Unfortunately, most plastic toys do not show up on X-rays. Toy companies, therefore, are now adding a special plastic to children's toys. This plastic is known as *nontoxic radiopaque plastic*. Toys made with this material will show up clearly on an X-ray. When you choose toys, check the label or package to see if this material is included.

Reflect

Why do toys have to be frequently changed in an infant or toddler room? How can an inventory be used to keep track of how often a toy is changed?

Resource

Toy Inventory, Activity B, OG

Health and Safety

Safety Covers for Electrical Outlets

According to state and federal standards, all electrical outlets accessible to children need to be covered. Attach safety covers to the outlets with a screw or other fastener to prevent easy removal of the covers. These covers keep children from placing their fingers into the electrical outlets, preventing injury from electrical shock.

Service Learning Activity

Ask students to make simple play mats for crawling infants and young toddlers similar to the one pictured in 29-12. Determine the dimensions of the mat and coordinate donations of fabric, batting or foam filler, and thread. Students can design patchwork square patterns or large motifs depending on the materials donated. Sew the layers together, bind, and add carry handles. Donate the mats to local agencies or facilities that work with young mothers and their babies.

Resource

Types of Infant-Toddler Toys, color transparency CT-25B, TR

Activity

Invite several mothers of infants between six weeks and six months old to visit the class with their infants for an observation. Have students rotate among the babies and write down the characteristics of play they notice and compare them to those listed in the textbook.

Discuss

When do infants usually begin touching objects within their reach? What safe toys could be provided for the child to touch? Give examples.

29-13

Infant-Toddler Center Toy Inventory

Looking
- dog mobile
- farm animal mobile
- shape mobile
- plastic mirror
- cloth and cardboard books

Reaching and Grasping
- ring activity gym
- musical activity gym
- colored activity gym
- colored rattles

Cuddling Toys
- monkey
- black bear
- baby lamb (with chime)
- pink pig
- brown pony
- black puppy
- dolls

Kicking and Hitting
- large rubber beach balls
- colored foam balls
- bouncing clowns

Squeezing/Manipulation
- fish squeaker
- pretzel squeaker
- mouse squeaker
- bunny squeaker
- busy box
- plastic rings
- plastic rattles (various colors)
- snap beads
- chain of plastic discs
- activity mats

Pull/Push
- wooden train (makes a noise)
- wooden dog
- lawnmower
- wooden car
- wooden wagon

Sound
- music box
- drum
- jingle bells
- CD or tape player and music
- xylophone
- squeaky animals

Gross-Motor
- rubber balls
- push toys
- pull toys
- small, light wagon
- wheeled train
- wheeled lamb
- climbing tunnel
- small gym
- toy trucks big enough to ride
- activity saucer

Fine-Motor
- geometric form board
- snap beads
- small cards
- nesting cups and boxes
- shape sorting box
- strings of large beads
- sand or water toys
- stacking rings
- puzzles with large pieces
- plastic or foam blocks
- large crayons
- activity center

A toy inventory is useful for planning and buying.

Appropriate Toys for Infants

Mobiles make excellent first toys for infants. They provide visual appeal and require a minimum of physical interaction. Select mobiles carefully. Avoid mobiles that are not sturdy. If your center has such mobiles, hang them out of reach. For the young infant, place toys 7 to 24 inches from the eyes.

Between 1½ and 3½ months of age, infants will discover their hands. The hands then become a toy for the child. Infants will study their hands as they move them back and forth. Infants between three and six months of age will continue to watch their

hands. Even when infants move objects to their mouths, they will continue watching.

Smiles begin to appear at about two months of age. Infants at this age also want to touch what they see. To provide stimulation for the child, place a mirror over the changing table. You will find it fun to watch the child smile at his or her reflection in the mirror.

Soon, infants begin touching objects within their reach. This behavior usually occurs between three and six months of age. As they do this, they gain information about the world and develop intelligence. Provide a variety of toys for the children to touch. These may include soft rattles and stuffed, furry animals.

Workplace Connection

Have students make a list of the toys available in the child care lab. Ask students to compare this list to Chart 29-13, *Infant-Toddler Center Toy Inventory*. Are any areas in need of more quantity or variety of materials or equipment? What additional items might be added? Have students check catalogs or the Internet for ideas.

To provide grasping exercise, infants need a variety of toys within reach, whether in the crib or on the floor. Since the child is likely to place these toys in his or her mouth, choose only safe toys. By placing objects in the mouth, babies learn about objects. Studies show that between 6 and 10 months of age, nerve endings in an infant's mouth are very sensitive.

Rattles are important for the infant's development. When a rattle is handed to an infant, he or she goes through a specific process. The first step is to locate the toy with the eyes. After this is done, the child will move his or her hand toward the rattle. Just before contact, the infant's hand will open. In this process the child will be persistent. He or she will repeatedly try to pick up a small toy.

Observations have shown that infants follow a progression of hand movement skills. First, there are raking motions which appear to be somewhat random. Next, scissor motions are made. The child uses the whole hand to pick up an object. Finally, the child develops the pincer grasp. Using this method, the infant is able to pick up objects using only the forefinger and thumb. A child using this method will usually shape the hand into the grasp before reaching for the intended object.

Toys will encourage the development of all these hand movement skills. A variety of toys such as cradle gyms can be used to encourage raking motions. Scissor motions can be encouraged by providing small balls or figures that will fit into the hand. Finger foods, such as dry, ready-to-eat cereal, can be used to practice the pincer grasp.

As the child develops, he or she begins to experiment with cause and effect. Up to this time, the infant has been more interested in watching the hands than the objects that were touched. By five to eight months, the child is more intent on watching the effects of his or her actions, 29-14.

Around this age, the child will enjoy dropping objects. He or she will often drop objects, including utensils and toys, from the high chair or feeding table. As the child does this, he or she will watch for the consequences

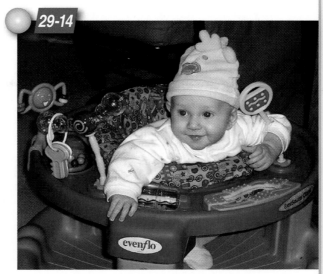

29-14

By using the toys on this activity saucer, this child can learn the effects of her actions.

of the actions. As the toy hits the floor, the infant may wince at the sound it makes.

At about the same time the child begins to enjoy dropping objects, he or she will become interested in simple gadgets in the environment. Electrical outlets appear to be appealing. For safety purposes, it is important that these all be capped. Other appealing objects include light switches, cupboard knobs, doorknobs, fringe on rugs, and locks. The manipulation of these objects gives the child a sense of magic.

Appropriate Toys for Toddlers

Once the child begins to crawl or walk, he or she will want to continually explore the environment. To encourage this curiosity, make the environment safe. Maintain large, open areas where the child can pull or push toys, straddle large trucks, or roll large balls.

Toddlers love to climb. To meet their large muscle needs, provide them with small slides, jungle gyms, and sets of stairs. Make sure that you closely watch toddlers when

Discuss

Why are rattles important for an infant's development? What process does an infant go through when he or she is handed a rattle?

Reflect

Nine-month-old Danny is constantly throwing items off his high chair tray. His mother attached long ribbons to the items and tied them to the high chair so she wouldn't have to keep getting up to pick up the items. What is your opinion of the mother's actions?

Activity

Have students conduct an Internet search to find out about child-proofing a home. What kinds of accidents happen at home? What safety devices are recommended for doors, windows, and stairs? How can you prepare for accidents? Allow time for students to discuss their findings.

Putting Technology to Use

Have students explore the American Academy of Pediatrics Web site at **www.aap.org** to find information concerning the use of infant walkers. What are the dangers of using walkers? What is the effect of using a walker on the physical development of the child? Have students write a brief report of their findings. Allow time for students to share their reports with the class.

Discuss

What precautions are needed for toddlers engaged in water play? What toys and objects are safe for toddlers to use for water play?

Reflect

Two young children in the toddler room have just discovered some fuzzy hand puppets and are examining them. Is any intervention needed by the teacher to encourage the children to play with the puppets properly?

Vocabulary

Have a student volunteer define *overfamiliarity*. What is the effect of overfamiliarity with certain toys on the development of new skills?

they use the large muscle equipment. Some children may try to walk up the slide. When this happens, you need to take their hand and direct them back to the stairs. Once they learn how to use the equipment, it is not uncommon for children of this age to use the equipment over and over again. As they explore, they are growing physically and cognitively.

Small wagons, wheelbarrows, doll buggies, and strollers also appeal to toddlers. If you lack indoor space, limit the use of these toys to an outdoor area.

Toddlers love to play with water. Encourage this play by providing floating toys, spoons, sponges, and unbreakable cups in a water-play area. Demonstrate how to pour water, sail a floating toy, and squeeze a sponge. For interest, add color to the water.

Books are also of interest to toddlers, 29-15. They enjoy stories about families, people, animals, and objects. Objects in the books should be recognizable. Toddlers love the surprise of flipping the pages in a book. Since they enjoy turning pages, select books with large pictures, thick pages that are easy to turn, and contain only a few words. Book bindings should be strong and sturdy.

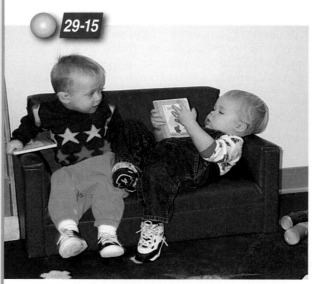

29-15

Since toddlers enjoy looking at books, provide a variety of age-appropriate and appealing books for them.

Puppets also appeal to young children. Children enjoy puppets that are soft and recognizable. Puppets made of fabric, instead of plastic or rubber, are the easiest for the children to work. Before buying puppets, ask if they are washable.

The most time-consuming activity of toddlers is staring. Approximately one-fifth of their time is spent either sitting or standing and staring. They may stare at a picture, another child, a toy, or even at you. Therefore, keep the room visually stimulating.

Some children will lack interest in a particular toy. This is a sign of **overfamiliarity**. Children who are given the same toy day after day may become bored. Once they are comfortable with a particular toy, they repeat the same actions over and over again. When this happens, new skills do not develop. It is time to provide a different toy that offers new challenges.

Young children like to have a variety of toys and need opportunities to make choices. Care must be taken, however, not to include too many choices. Toddlers need to feel a sense of control. As the teacher, you should change some toys every other day.

Curriculum

A balanced curriculum is based on the needs of the children attending the center. It is also based on child growth and development principles.

Curriculum for infants or toddlers differs from that planned for older preschool children. Babies set their own goals. As the teacher, you support this growth. The curriculum consists of simple, basic activities. It includes physical activities: being fed, cuddled, held, bathed, rocked, diapered, and taken on walks. It involves both verbal and nonverbal communication: being sung to, talked to, and listened to. Curriculum for infants should include lots of materials, activities, and time for exploring and building fine- and gross-motor skills.

Cross-Curricular Activity

Art

Ask students to design visually stimulating posters to be displayed in an infant or toddler room. Students may choose to work with each other. You may also partner students with interested students from an art class who could assist with drawing or creating images. As students produce their projects, they should keep in mind that young children enjoy patterns, color contrasts, primary colors, simple shapes, and familiar objects. Posters may be donated to an infant-toddler program or to parents of young children.

Curriculum for toddlers requires more planning. Much of their day will involve activities that promote physical, emotional, cognitive, and social growth. Most of these activities can take place in various activity areas within the center.

Activity Areas for Toddlers

A developmentally appropriate environment promotes child-directed, age-appropriate learning. It supports the children's emotional well-being and challenges their motor skills. It also stimulates their social development. Toddlers need opportunities for seeing, touching, tasting, moving, and hearing.

The layout of the classroom needs to encourage play. The middle of the room should be open since motor development is critical to toddlers' development. This area can contain portable equipment such as tunnels, bolsters, and gyms. Toddlers also need some private space where they can rest and observe. This space may be included by introducing a small loft, a tunnel, a cabinet with a door removed, or even an enclosed corner of the room. The activity areas should be placed around the outer walls of the room.

Similar activities can be grouped into centers around the room. Each center should contain equipment and materials that offer the child a choice of activities. An interesting, well-equipped room invites children to take part. Areas that can be included in a toddler program include art, sensory, small muscle, large muscle, music, and language.

When planning the activity centers, ask yourself the following questions:
- Does the center encourage active exploration?
- Are the toys developmentally appropriate?
- Is there enough room for the children to play?
- Are the materials at the children's eye level and within their reach?

- Are the heavy toys stored on the bottom shelves?
- Are the children provided choices so they can pursue their own interests?
- Are a variety of toys presented including those for solitary play and those that support cooperative play?
- Are the toys safe and checked frequently for sharp edges, loose pieces, and small parts that could be swallowed?
- Are toys rotated so the children are exposed to new toys from time to time?

Art

A center for art activities can be fun for toddlers. Plan the area to encourage freedom and creativity. Art activities provide good opportunities for promoting small muscle development. Chart 29-16 lists tips for art activities.

Finger-painting experiences are quite appealing and soothing to young toddlers. Tempera paint, shaving cream, and colored

29-16

Tips for Art Activities

- Provide only nontoxic materials. Young children tend to put materials in their mouths.
- Allow plenty of space to prevent children from putting paint, chalk, or markers on one another.
- Cover the table and/or floor with a plastic cloth or newspapers to catch spills.
- Provide art smocks or large plastic bibs.
- Keep cloth or paper towels handy to clean children's hands as soon as they finish activities.
- Wipe spills as they occur to prevent children from slipping or getting soiled.

Plan safe, healthful art activities. Then toddlers will not need to remember a large number of rules.

Discuss

What are the major differences between curriculum for babies and toddlers and curriculum for older children? Can a childcare classroom meet the needs for a mixed group of toddlers and preschoolers at the same time?

Reflect

It is Jamie's first day helping in the toddler room. She suggests an art activity involving cutting out flower shapes and stems and pasting them onto construction paper. What concerns do you have about Jamie's suggestion?

Resource

Evaluating Activity Areas for Toddlers, Activity C, OG

Workplace Connection

Have students survey an area child care center to observe the preschoolers classroom. Does the center encourage active exploration? Are materials within children's reach? Are children provided choices in activities? Are a variety of toys present? Ask students to record their observations in a brief report. Allow time for students to discuss their findings in class.

liquid soap can all be used for finger painting. As the children use these materials, they enjoy squeezing them through their fingers. During the process, they learn to sense the different feel of each one.

Older toddlers also enjoy painting. Provide a variety of brushes for this type of experience. Regular art brushes, toothbrushes, small household brushes, and sponge staining brushes may all be used. You will need to mix paint with a thickener to help prevent dripping. Bentonite, starch, or a powdered laundry detergent usually work very well.

Toddlers also enjoy scribbling. At this age, they now make simple, random marks. Provide a variety of marking tools. Large crayons, chalk, and nontoxic markers can be used. To help children feel some control over their movements, give younger children larger tools. As their control improves, smaller tools can be used.

According to developmental principles, large muscle development precedes small muscle development. To accommodate large muscle movements, provide large sheets of paper for children to scribble or paint on. If paper is too small, drawings or paintings will run off the paper and onto the table or floor. This will require additional cleanup for you.

Sensory

Sensory activities should stimulate many of the children's senses. Most activities involve at least seeing, hearing, and touching. Many teachers often add the sense of smell. Food flavorings and extracts with unique scents may be added to some activities at the sensory table.

Chart 29-17 lists sensory materials that can be used with toddlers. Small objects that can be inhaled or swallowed should be avoided. Likewise, discourage toddlers from chewing or eating any of the sensory materials.

Fine-Motor

Most fine-motor activities will revolve around toys. Stacking toys, building blocks,

29-17

Sensory Materials

- Colored and/or scented water
- Soap bubbles
- Small plastic boats
- Shaving cream, plain or with drops of food coloring
- Dry or wet sand
- Shovels, strainers, and/or small wheeled trucks
- Wet or dry oatmeal
- Snow
- Ice cubes
- Musical instruments such as drums, tambourines, bells on wristbands, and cymbals
- Common foods with strong smells such as peanut butter, oranges, or lemons

You will find that toddlers are most interested in simple, everyday objects.

sorting boxes, puzzles, stringing beads, and play dough are all safe toys that promote fine-motor development in toddlers. Most of these toys will also provide toddlers with problem-solving opportunities. These toys may also provide for hand-eye coordination and visual-discrimination opportunities.

Gross-Motor

Gross-motor activities can take many forms. These may involve indoor equipment, outdoor equipment, or simple movement. As children crawl, walk, and run, they are developing their gross-motor skills.

Much space is needed for gross-motor equipment, both indoors and outdoors. Plenty of free space is needed around it. Allow enough space for active use by several children.

Balls, slides, tumbling mats, pull toys, small wagons, and large blocks can all be used to promote gross-motor development. The development of the children's large

Discuss

What items besides those listed in 29-17 would you add to the list of sensory materials? What precautions would you need to take with any of the items on the list when used by toddlers?

Activity

Have students experiment with various additions to tempera paint to give it a thicker texture more suitable for artwork by toddlers. Use the textbook suggestions as well as other ideas and demonstrate each product. Decide which mixtures produced the best results.

Discuss

Explain how toys such as stacking toys and puzzles encourage the development of problem-solving skills. What other typical toddler toys can you suggest for practicing and building problem-solving skills?

Portfolio Project

Observe a toddler at play and write an observation describing the fine- and gross-motor skills the child uses. How does the child use his or her hands to pick up, move, or otherwise manipulate items? What fine-motor tasks does the toddler consistently perform with skill? What gross-motor skills does the child use? What equipment or materials does he or she enjoy while using movements? Be sure to indicate the exact age in months of the child and file the observation in their portfolio.

muscles can also be promoted by having them run, crawl, or even chase bubbles outdoors.

Music

Young children love music. Background music from a tape or CD player is quite enjoyable and soothing for many toddlers. Some toddlers will even move to the music. If they do not, you may want to dance with them. The toddlers may also enjoy hitting drums with their hands, shaking bells, or clapping their hands.

Language

Although planned activities are not required, you should be encouraging language growth at all times. During play, speak to the children. Encourage them to respond. Avoid using baby talk with toddlers. Young children will often mimic your speech patterns. If they hear baby talk, chances are they will imitate it. It is also important to use complete sentences and introduce new words. Use adverbs and adjectives to create colorful descriptions.

Puppets, unbreakable mirrors, books, pictures, posters, and dolls can all be placed on shelves in the language area. These materials should be placed so the children can safely remove them from the shelves. See 29-18.

Activity Files and Picture Collections

Many teachers maintain a file listing activities that have met with success. This will help you remember the best activities. Ask other infant-toddler caregivers to share their favorite activities. Observe other caregivers in your center. Make notes of useful interactions and activities.

You will also want to start your own picture collection. The best source for obtaining pictures is from calendars, children's books, magazines, and travel

29-18

Encouraging children to play with dolls is one way to promote language development.

posters. Infants and toddlers enjoy large, simple pictures. People, animals, vehicles, and toys have the most appeal.

Before displaying a picture, mount it on a piece of colorful poster board. To frame each picture, leave at least a ½-inch border around the entire picture. Since young children enjoy touching pictures, protect the pictures by covering with clear contact paper or laminate.

Parent Involvement

Communication with the families of infants and toddlers is very important. Keep the parents informed of how their child's day went. Also, encourage parents to provide you with the significant happenings in their home. When children are first enrolled, always find out their routines at home, food preferences, and favorite toys. You can use a form at enrollment time to record the information, 29-19. This information will help coordinate center and home activities.

To help you provide a quality experience for children, parents' goals and concerns need to be shared. It will also be helpful if any change in the home environment is shared.

Discuss

Compare the toys suitable for infants with those designed for toddlers. What are the major differences, especially in toys promoting gross-motor skill development?

Activity

Have students write a lesson plan for a music activity for toddlers. What are some realistic expectations for participation by this age group?

Resource

Toys for Development, Activity C, SAG

Activity

Locate several books for toddlers and ask students to review them for colorful and descriptive language. Have students list new words toddlers may learn from these books.

Portfolio Project

Have students research educational topics of interest to toddler parents. These may include toilet learning, language development, and toy selection. Students should write a short article suitable for a parent newsletter on their chosen topic. Remind students to document the sources for the information they use in their articles. Have students file a copy of the article in their portfolio.

Reflect

The form shown in 29-19 gives parents opportunities to share information about their child with the child care center staff. How might this information be helpful in planning activities and protecting the child's health and safety?

Discuss

How can information about a child's family background help the teacher provide a quality experience while meeting the child's needs? Give examples of specific types of information and explain how you would use the information in planning for the class.

Resource

Child Care Procedures, Activity D, SAG

29-19

Infant-Toddler Center Parent Information Sheet

Child's Name _____   Birth Date _____

Home Phone _____   Home Address _____

_____

Mother's Name _____   Father's Name _____

Address _____   Address _____

_____   _____

Place of Employment_____   Place of Employment _____

Work Phone_____   Work Phone _____

Cell Phone_____   Cell Phone _____

E-mail _____   E-mail_____

If there are any special family circumstances such as divorce, separation, remarriage, parental death, or adoption, please indicate them._____

_____

In case of emergency, who should be notified?

Name_____   Phone _____

Name_____   Phone _____

Doctor or Clinic _____   Phone _____

Environment and Experiences

Names of others living in the home   Relationship

_____   _____

_____   _____

_____   _____

How does your child react when you leave him or her with someone other than a parent? _____

_____

List the name(s) of any previous child care center that your child attended._____

_____

What was your child's response? _____

_____

Stress to parents the importance of the information on this form.   *(continued)*

Meeting Special Needs

Pair special learners with volunteer students to complete *Child Care Procedures*, Activity D, SAG. You may want to modify the activity by assigning paragraphs to different groups of students. Review responses to the activity in class. Spend additional time discussing any material that is difficult for special learners to understand.

Physical Development

Are there any special characteristics or problems which the school should know about in order to best help your child and your family? Include any vision, hearing, physical difficulties, and unusual abilities or disabilities of which you are aware.

Toilet Learning

Has your child completed toilet learning yet? _____

Does he/she usually stay dry all day? _____

Eating Habits

In general, describe your child's attitude toward eating.

What are his/her special food likes?

What are his/her special food dislikes?

Does your child have any food allergies, sensitivities, or foods that are excluded from the diet?

Favorite Toys

Describe your child's favorite toys.

Favorite Activities

Describe your child's favorite activities.

29-19 Continued

Note

Have samples of information sheets from several child care centers in class for students to review.

Reflect

Review 29-19, *Infant-Toddler Center Parent Information Sheet*. Is there any additional information you would provide about a child? How useful is this information to a caregiver?

Discuss

Have students compare the form in 29-19 with the information sheets the child care lab uses. Is there information requested on one form that is not on the other? How often are updates made to the form?

Putting Technology to Use

Have students conduct an Internet search for viewpoints on the need for regular activity for infants and toddlers. How much physical activity should young children get? How can good habits of physical activity started as toddlers help reduce the rate of childhood obesity?

The following Web site for the National Association for Sport & Physical Education contains valuable advice: **www.aahperd. org/naspe/template.cfm**. Have students write a brief report of their findings.

Enrich

Have students brainstorm topics of information parents of toddlers might like to receive from the child care center. For example, parents may like to receive information on toilet learning or language development. Create a list of the topics for students to include in their portfolio.

Activity

Ask students to role-play a caregiver reporting a child's daily routines to the parents. What information should be included in the report? How should the information be presented? Was the information objective and factual?

Discuss

What steps can you take to prevent illness in the child care center? How often should toys in the child care center be cleaned? How often should cribs and strollers be cleaned?

These changes, such as a death in the extended family, can cause stress for children. Other changes may cause pleasure. Examples include a new family pet or a grandparent visiting. Parents should also let the teacher know about such home routines as toilet learning.

From time to time, you may wish to share reading materials with parents. Information on topics such as toilet learning, separation anxiety, language development, and toy selection can be quite useful for parents. Parents also enjoy receiving information on developmental stages. Knowing and watching for stages of normal development can be reassuring to parents.

Record Keeping

Record keeping is an important part of an infant-toddler program. Such records should track children's eating, sleeping, and eliminating routines. Also, keep track of new behaviors and skills as they occur and change over time.

Good records provide valuable information. Parents will be especially interested in their child's daily eating, sleeping, and eliminating patterns. Unusual patterns may signal illness or a need to change the child's diet.

By maintaining a record of the child's skills and behaviors, you will be able to note the child's progress and the start of any problems. Early detection is important for the child's development.

When reporting the child's daily routines to the parents, be objective and factual. Do not be negative or judgmental. Try to state comments in a positive manner. For instance, avoid remarks such as "Mark was very crabby and difficult to be with today." Rather, say "Mark's new tooth was causing him some pain today." Whenever possible, provide the parent with comments in writing.

Maintaining the Environment to Prevent Illness

As a staff member in a child care center, you will need to take steps to prevent illness. Disease-causing microorganisms grow in a damp, dirty environment. Play equipment, cribs, changing tables, strollers, floors, tables, high chairs, and feeding tables—as well as the children's hands—all need to be cleaned.

Since infants and toddlers explore with their mouths, it is important that all toys be routinely cleaned. Saliva forms a film on the surface of toys. Microorganisms grow on this film. As a result, any toys such as rattles and teething rings that go into the infant's mouth must be cleaned on a daily basis or when used by a child. If your center has a dishwasher, use it. Most small toys are dishwasher safe.

Clean by hand the toys that cannot be washed in the dishwasher. First, wash the toys in a hot, sudsy detergent and rinse well. Then mix a disinfecting solution of one gallon of water with one tablespoon of chlorine bleach. Wipe or spray each piece of equipment with the solution. Air dry.

Depending on the frequency of use, cribs and strollers need to be cleaned daily or twice weekly. Likewise, floors, tables, high chairs, and feeding tables also need cleaning each day. Food left on any of these can grow microorganisms. This process should be similar to cleaning toys. Begin by washing each piece with warm, sudsy water. Rinse well. Wipe or spray with a solution of disinfectant. Air or sun dry.

Contaminated hands are a common cause of the spread of illness in child care centers. To prevent illnesses, it is most important that you follow proper hand washing procedures to keep your hands and the children's hands

Workplace Connection

Ask students to survey area infant and toddler programs to discover the role of the teacher and aides in classroom cleaning and sanitation. What cleaning and sanitation tasks do they regularly perform? Does a custodian complete any of the tasks? How are waste products such as soiled diapers treated? Have students write a brief report of their findings.

clean. Some centers also spray a disinfectant on the door knobs several times a day to kill viruses and bacteria.

Illness Policies

Sick children cannot be cared for in a center without endangering the health of other children. An environment for infants and toddlers needs to be healthful. As the teacher, it is your responsibility to maintain the best health conditions. In order to do this properly, it is important to have a center illness policy. This policy will help staff and parents decide whether a child is too sick to be brought to or remain in the center.

Prior to enrollment, every parent should be given a copy of the center's illness policy. At this time, it should be stressed that a primary objective of the program is to protect the children's health. Thus, center illness policy is always adhered to. An example of a center illness policy is shown in 29-20.

29-20

Infant-Toddler Center Illness Policy

To protect all the children's health, you must keep your child home when he/she has

- an oral temperature of 101°F or above or a rectal temperature of 102°F or above
- diarrhea
- vomiting that extends beyond the usual spitting up
- bronchitis symptoms, including hoarseness and/or cough
- a severe cold that is accompanied with a fever and nose drainage
- a rash that has not been diagnosed by a doctor
- impetigo, chicken pox, mumps, measles, scarlet fever, or whooping cough

An illness policy helps avoid misunderstandings when infants and toddlers are ill.

Enrich

Ask students to compare 29-20, *Infant-Toddler Center Illness Policy*, to the child care lab's illness policy. Have students point out any similarities and differences between the policies. Is there anything missing from the child care lab's policy that should be included?

Reflect

What could you do to make an environment for infants and toddlers healthful? What would happen if a child care center's illness policy was not adhered to?

Activity

Ask students to find out if any area child care programs have a "sick room" or allow children who are ill to attend. Have students discuss the pros and cons of allowing children who are ill to attend child care centers.

Meeting Special Needs

Review the special learners' chapter outlines to determine if the students have any questions about the concepts or content of this chapter. Review the chapter objectives and ask the students to evaluate their progress in meeting these objectives. Ask the students to summarize, orally or in writing, what they have learned from this chapter.

Review and Reflect **Answer Key**

1. (List three: Student response.)
2. Parents arriving with baby food and bottles can place these items in the refrigerator at once.
3. receiving, playing, napping, diapering, eating
4. one-third to one-half
5. trust
6. C
7. Separation anxiety is a feeling of fear and distress that occurs in children 9 to 18 months of age who have difficulty at being separated from a parent.
8. Student response.
9. Yes. Exploring their food gives toddlers important sensory experiences that foster cognitive growth.
10. Bar soaps, when wet and jellylike, harbor microorganisms.
11. The inventory is useful for planning activities and for knowing what toys have been used recently and what toys are available. The inventory is also helpful when ordering new toys.
12. They like to see the consequences of their actions.
13. goals
14. (List five: Student response.)
15. Be objective and factual. Do not be negative or judgmental. State comments in a positive manner.
16. An illness policy helps staff and parents decide whether a child is too sick to be brought to or remain in the center.

Summary

Infants and toddlers are at a special stage in their lives. They are just learning about their world and yet they learn and grow quickly. The care they receive at this stage is very important for brain development.

Caring for infants and toddlers requires skill in areas unique to the age group. Emphasis is shifted toward care of daily routines such as eating, diapering, and sleeping. However, infants and toddlers also require a developmentally supportive environment. The environment should balance safety and health concerns with developmental needs.

Infants often communicate by crying. As a caregiver, you will have to learn the meaning of each child's cries and respond promptly. Stranger anxiety typically emerges between 7 and 9 months of age. Separation anxiety is common between 9 and 18 months of age.

To meet the special needs of infants and toddlers, appropriate equipment is needed. Safety is again the number one consideration. Curriculum for infants and toddlers differs from that planned for older preschool children. Though the curriculum for infants consists of simple, basic activities, the curriculum for toddlers requires more planning. Activity areas should be designed to meet toddlers' needs.

Review and Reflect

1. List three characteristics of a successful infant-toddler teacher.

2. What is the reasoning behind locating the feeding area near the entrance to the center?

3. Name the five major areas in the toddler space.

4. What portion of the play area should be left open for toddlers to move about freely?

5. All infants and toddlers require their needs to be met promptly if they are to learn to _____.

6. Always respond to a baby's crying by _____.
   A. ignoring the baby
   B. feeding the baby
   C. trying to solve the problem
   D. None of the above.

7. What is separation anxiety?

8. Describe how to feed an infant.

9. Should toddlers be encouraged to smell, touch, and push around their food before eating? Why or why not?

10. Why should liquid soap be used in the diapering area?

11. Name two advantages of keeping a toy inventory.

12. Why do infants seem to enjoy dropping objects from their high chairs?

13. In terms of curriculum, babies set their own _____.

14. List five questions to ask yourself when planning activity centers for toddlers.

15. What should be your attitude when reporting the child's daily routines to his or her parents?

16. What is the purpose of a center illness policy?

Apply and Explore

1. Collect and compare illness policies from three child care centers.

2. Design an infant space on a large piece of poster board.

3. Collect daily care records from several centers. Discuss the contents of each.

4. For a toddler environment, design three private spaces.

Cross-Curricular Link

Writing

1. Design a pamphlet for infant caregivers regarding infant feeding using the information given in the chapter.

Language Arts

2. Interview several parents. Ask them the type of characteristics they desire in an infant or toddler caregiver. Share your findings with the class.

Technology

3. Use the Zero to Three Web site (www.zerotothree.org/brainwonders) to look up activities for infants and toddlers that stimulate brain development.

Workplace Link

Locate a copy of the licensing standards for child care centers in your state. Compare the amount and type of equipment and supplies needed for infant-toddler programs with those required for preschool programs. What are the major differences in requirements between the two types of programs? What items are similar for both? Locate catalogs of early childhood equipment and find examples of the types of furniture, equipment, and supplies needed.

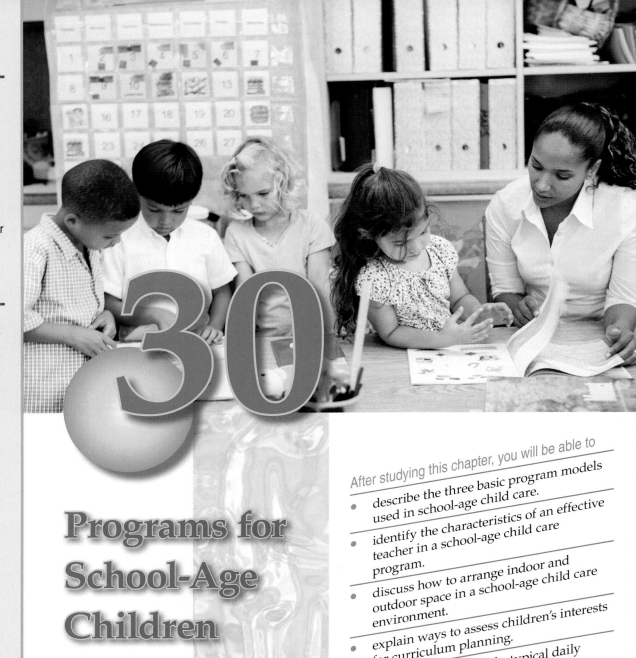

Discuss

Look at the chapter opening photo. What positive outcomes might you expect from enrolling a child in a school-age program? What are some negative effects of leaving school-age children on their own before or after the school day?

Discuss

Look over the objectives for this chapter. What do you expect to be the major focus in programming for school-age children?

30

Programs for School-Age Children

After studying this chapter, you will be able to

- describe the three basic program models used in school-age child care.

- identify the characteristics of an effective teacher in a school-age child care program.

- discuss how to arrange indoor and outdoor space in a school-age child care environment.

- explain ways to assess children's interests for curriculum planning.

- list the components of a typical daily schedule in a school-age child care program.

Terms to Know

child-centered program model
adult-centered program model
unit-based program model

There is a critical need for school-age child care. Two main factors account for this trend. First, the number of working parents with children between the ages of 6 and 12 has grown. Second, there are more single-parent families.

Due to cost or lack of quality programs, many school-age children are left to care for themselves. Felix, an eight-year-old, is an example. He returns home from school at about 3:40 in the afternoon. Felix carries a house key. When he arrives home, he unlocks the front door. Then he enters and locks the door behind him. Felix watches television until 6:00 p.m., when his mother returns home from work.

Felix's mother, like many others, cannot find affordable after-school care. Children like Felix are sometimes called *latchkey children*. This term refers to children left in self-care or in the care of a sibling under age 15. Many children are left in self-care for several hours each day.

Yolanda is another eight-year-old child. Unlike Felix who goes home to an empty apartment, Yolanda is fortunate. She attends a school-age child care program after school. Ricardo, her cousin who lives in the same community, also attends the program.

Parents need to decide on an individual basis about how old children should be before leaving them in self-care. State laws regarding self-care are an important consideration. In some states, it is illegal for a child under a set age (often 12) to stay home alone. If no such law exists in their state, parents can use age 12 as a good general guideline. However, parents may not feel comfortable leaving some immature 13- or 14-year-old children in self-care.

Even mature children can benefit from attending a school-age child care program. Studies show children who lack adult supervision tend to have a variety of problems. They are more likely to experience loneliness and unhealthy fears. They are also more likely to lack physical exercise and have poor nutritional habits. Attending a quality school-age program can help children avoid these problems.

Parents want more than custodial care for their school-age children. They want their children to do some of the following while in child care:

- broaden their education
- develop caring relationships with adults and other children
- acquire new skills
- receive tutoring
- study art and music
- perform community service

Studies have shown positive outcomes for children attending high-quality school-age child care programs. These children tend to earn better grades and demonstrate higher academic achievement. They turn in higher-quality homework assignments and spend more time in the learning process. They have an increased interest and ability in reading. These children also have better school attendance records and lower dropout rates.

Quality School-Age Programs

School-age children are developing a sense of who they are and what they can do. These children need challenges. They need to be independent. They need others to accept them for who they are. A quality school-age program will meet these needs. It will also provide companionship, supervision, a safe environment, and activities to promote

Vocabulary

Have students review the *Terms to Know* list. Ask students to look up unfamiliar words or terms in the glossary before reading the chapter.

Discuss

Have a student volunteer explain the term *latchkey children.* How can school-age child care programs benefit latchkey children?

Enrich

Have students search the Internet or contact your state office of the Department of Children and Families to discover if your state has a law about leaving young children unattended. If so, at what age can children be left alone at home?

Meeting Special Needs

Provide an outline of the chapter with all the chapter headings for special learners. Students should fill in each section of the outline as the material is covered in class with a sentence or two about the content. Review the special learners' IEPs to decide if any modifications should be made in presenting the chapter content.

Activity

Have students survey the local area to discover what school-age child care programs exist. Does your school district offer a program at the local elementary schools? Allow time for students to discuss their findings in class.

Reflect

When you were a school-age child, what was the first thing you wanted to do after school got out? Would an after-school program for school-age children be able to meet this need?

Resource

Quality School-Age Programs, Activity A, SAG

children's development. A good school-age program has

- low adult-child ratios
- caring, well-trained staff members
- well-organized space with room for active play, quiet play, and interest centers
- curriculum based on the children's ages, abilities, interests, needs, and experiences
- parent involvement to achieve shared goals for the children
- flexible scheduling to allow a balance of individual, small group, and large group activities

Studies show that high-quality programs have common characteristics. These programs set goals and have strong leadership. They hire skilled staff and provide them with ongoing training. Quality programs also reach out to families.

Accreditation and Standards

The *National AfterSchool Association* (NAA) has developed standards. The standards have been carefully designed to reflect best practices for children from five to fourteen years of age. They have been divided into six sections:

- Human relationships
- Indoor environment
- Outdoor environment
- Activities
- Safety, health and nutrition
- Administration

You can learn more about these standards at NAA's Web site, www.naaweb.org.

Types of Programs

Parents have a variety of options when choosing after-school child care. See 30-1.

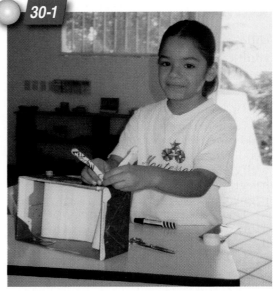

A variety of child care options is available for school-age children.

A nanny, an au pair, or a housekeeper can provide care in a child's home. Family child care homes and child care centers provide care outside the child's home.

Many for-profit child care centers provide school-age child care and transportation. These centers offer programs during the school year. Many have special summer programs, too. Parents who can afford the tuition often select this type of program. Often, children participating in these programs have attended preschool in the same facility.

Nonprofit organizations such as United Way, YMCA, and the Salvation Army offer school-age child care programs in some communities. Houses of worship may also provide school-age child care for their members.

Program Models

There are three program models used as curriculum formats in school-age child care programs. These are the child-centered,

Workplace Connection

Ask students to research the role of volunteers in school-age programs in the area. Do the programs allow volunteers to work in their programs? If so, what are the requirements to participate as a volunteer? What training is required? What supervision should a volunteer expect? How do the school-age children in the programs respond to the volunteers? Have students write a brief report of their findings.

adult-centered, and unit-based models. A good program uses all three models to complement children's school and home experiences.

Several factors may influence the program model chosen. These include the ages, interests, abilities, and experiences of the children. Staff preferences and the amount of time children spend in the program can have an influence, too.

Child-Centered Program Model

The **child-centered program model** is a curriculum format that allows children an opportunity to do self-selected activities. Staff members encourage children's involvement by serving as facilitators and resource persons. Together the staff and children plan the daily activities. Available resources and the children's interests help determine the activities. See 30-2.

Adult-Centered Program Model

The **adult-centered program model** is a more structured curriculum format that includes a high level of adult direction. The curriculum includes recreation and tutoring programs. Children may also have

30-2

Children in a child-centered program model may select activities that interest them.

opportunities to take music and dance lessons.

Unit-Based Program Model

The **unit-based program model** is a curriculum format that revolves around curriculum themes that reflect the children's interests. Frequently, these themes focus on special events and holidays. Staff members offer a variety of cooking, science, music, and art activities that relate to the theme. They choose children's literature and plan field trips, creative dramatics, and games to support the theme, too. Children can then choose many of the specific theme-related activities in which they will participate.

Regardless of the model used, school-age programs should focus on developing competence and self-confidence. Self-confidence contributes to an "I-can-do-it" attitude. It will help children master reading and writing skills. Self-confidence will also help children develop positive social relationships with their peers.

Adult-Child Ratios

Program quality is enhanced when there are enough staff to meet the individual needs of children. Studies show that appropriate adult-child ratios and small group size improve program quality.

Children in school-age child care programs must be able to get adult help when they need it. Children will need assistance with homework, 30-3. They will also need adults to serve as role models and provide emotional support and encouragement.

Having more adults available benefits staff as well as children. In this case, adults can provide the constant supervision needed to create a safe environment. While supervising, adults can use observation to gain information about the interests, needs, abilities, and experiences of each child.

Most states have laws addressing adult-child ratios for children's programs. These

Resource

School-Age Program Models, color transparency CT-26, TR

Vocabulary

Have a student volunteer explain what is meant by *program model*. Ask volunteer students to define the three program models: *child-centered, adult-centered*, and *unit-based program model*.

Discuss

Why might school-age programs that involve student input and are based on student interest be successful? What type of student might benefit more from an adult-centered program?

Workplace Connection

Have students discover their state's requirements for child-to-adult ratio for licensed school-age programs and compare them to the local programs in the area. What is your opinion on the minimum number of adults required? Would you add any more teachers or aides to this number? Allow time for students to discuss their findings in class.

Discuss

What differences in characteristics, if any, might you expect to find in teachers of young children as compared to teachers in a school-age program? What characteristics would you expect of teachers in both programs?

Enrich

The staff of school-age programs must be familiar with a wide range of teaching techniques to help students learn. Ask students to conduct an Internet search for new teaching techniques. Have students write a one-page report of their findings. Allow time for students to share what they have learned with the class.

Resource

Quality School-Age Programs, Activity A, OG

30-3

School-age children may need staff to help them with homework and other tasks.

ratios vary from state to state. However, for children through six years of age, a minimum 1:10 ratio is usually recommended. For children seven years and older, a minimum 1:12 ratio is usually recommended.

Characteristics of Staff

Who should care for school-age children? High-quality programs are staffed by well-trained personnel. These individuals understand child growth and development. They like school-age children and enjoy conversations with them. Personnel should have age-appropriate expectations of the children's behavior and abilities. They are continuously seeking new ideas and learning new teaching techniques. These teachers also respect the cultural diversity of the children they teach.

Staff in school-age programs need to be understanding, honest, patient, fair, trustworthy, and warm. They need to model standards for behavior. Moreover, they need to respond positively to each child's uniqueness and changing needs. They need to encourage the children to be independent.

Act as Facilitators

Staff in school-age programs act as facilitators. They need good communication skills. This includes being able to listen in order to convey messages. Teachers of school-age children need to ask the children to share thoughts and listen to the view of others.

Children at this stage of development are striving for autonomy. They want the opportunity to solve their own problems. Staff assist the children in developing skills and abilities and guide children in social problem solving. They help by offering suggestions, providing encouragement, and recommending activities. They use demonstrations, explanations, and coaching to help children learn. Staff also ask thought-provoking questions that require children to use mental reasoning skills.

Use Positive Guidance

School-age children are learning social expectations. They are learning to recognize the impact of their behavior on others. They need to learn to make their own decisions. Often they test their place in the group. By experiencing consequences, children begin to understand what is acceptable and unacceptable behavior.

Workplace Connection

School-age programs that are an extension of a licensed child care center will probably be operated under the standards set by your state's Department of Children and Families. After-school programs run by your local school district in school facilities will probably be operated under the standards set by your state's Board of Education. Have students investigate the possible differences in requirements. Allow time for students to discuss their findings in class.

Skilled staff use positive guidance to help children achieve self-control. They encourage prosocial behaviors, such as taking turns, helping, cooperating, negotiating, and talking through interpersonal problems. Staff work with children to develop clear and firm limits. When needed, staff remind children of the limits. After this, they redirect the children to more acceptable behavior.

Working with school-age children can be challenging. Some children will constantly test you. They are trying to see how far they can go before you intervene. Often these children do not understand the balance between individual and group rights. Edwardo is an example of a child who is constantly testing his teacher. While a group of children were listening to a story, he kept pounding on a drum. Several times his teacher reminded him to play the drum softly. She told him that the other children were listening to a story and he was distracting them. Finally, Edwardo had to experience the consequences. His teacher took the drum away from him and suggested alternative activities.

After school, teachers need to know how to cultivate children's friendships with one another. Although some children make friends easily, others find it challenging. Developing friendships involves the capacity to recognize that others have separate identities. Children also have feelings of their own, which include a characteristic way of reacting.

School-age children need to see the importance of their behavior. For example, Ian wanted the basketball Brett was using. Ian hit Brett hard on the back and then quickly grabbed the ball out of his hands. His teacher observed this happening and used the incident as the teachable moment. She knew that Ian would need to control certain behaviors in order to have friends. She approached him and asked, "How do you think it feels to be hit and have your ball taken away?" Then she talked with Ian about what makes a good friend, including alternative ways of behaving.

Involve Children

School-age children are learning to be independent. They want to solve problems. Staff of school-age child care programs need to involve children in daily problem-solving activities. While developing limits, staff should involve the children in a discussion of expectations. This will help children make decisions related to their actions. Staff should also involve children by allowing them to help plan curriculum and make choices about activities, 30-4.

30-4

Allowing children to help plan their own activities promotes self-esteem and enjoyment of the program.

Discuss

How can staff help school-age children achieve self-control? In what ways can staff involve the children in daily problem-solving activities? Give examples.

Reflect

When four-year-old Douglas has a behavior problem in preschool, his teacher removes him from the group and assigns him to a time-out for several minutes. What consequences could you suggest for an eight-year-old who experiences behavior challenges in the after-school program?

Resource

School-Age Child Care Advice, reproducible master 30-2, TR

Meeting Special Needs

Pair special learners with volunteer students to complete *School-Age Child Care Advice*, reproducible master 30-2, TR. You may want to modify the activity by assigning each of the letters to different groups of students. Review responses to the activity in class. Spend additional time discussing any material that is difficult for special learners to understand.

Enrich

Consult with the elementary teachers in your school district to discover what multicultural activities they already include in their curriculums. Have students determine additional activities that would interest school-age children without duplicating the classroom programs.

Discuss

What is the benefit to children from participating in after-school activities that include opportunities for active physical play? Is it necessary for teachers to participate in the active play with the children?

Reflect

Imagine a local house of worship wants to start an after-school program in a room that is also used for choir practice, Boy and Girl Scout meetings, the women's club, and a nursery during worship services. What suggestions would you have for making the space "user-friendly" for school-age children?

Promote Respect for Cultural Diversity

As school-age children become more aware of the world around them, they begin to make social comparisons. Through this process, children not only define themselves, they also identify qualities in others.

Conscientious teachers help children learn about and appreciate cultures other than their own. They help children appreciate cultural diversity. Children need to learn how others express beauty through art, literature, and music, 30-5. Teachers use toys, games, foods, and special celebrations to teach children about different cultures. They use storybooks, videos, posters, and puzzles to show people from all cultures in a variety of positive roles.

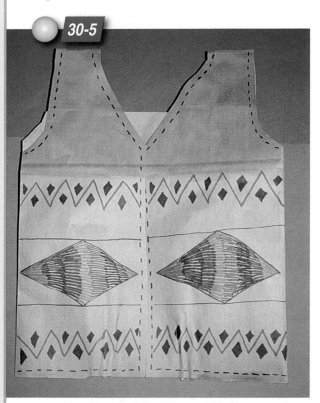

30-5

Teachers can plan activities to help children appreciate cultural diversity.

Seeing images of people who look like them helps children develop a sense of pride in their culture. Seeing images of people from other cultures helps children respect and value people's differences and similarities.

Enjoy Physical Activities

School-age children thrive on physical activity. During a typical school day, they spend much time sitting in classrooms. When they arrive at after-school programs, they have pent-up energy to release. They want to move around, play games, run, and jump.

Teachers who are well suited for school-age programs enjoy physical activity. They do not have to be athletic. However, they need the energy and desire to join children in active play.

The Environment

Throughout middle childhood, children need room to practice their emerging skills. A quality school-age child care environment should provide appropriate space, materials, and equipment. The environment needs to be developmentally appropriate, reflecting the children's interests, ages, abilities, needs and experiences. This environment will allow children to have fun, learn, and thrive as they move at their own pace.

The ideal environment is designed specifically for school-age programs. However, any facility with a large activity room and an outdoor play area can serve as a school-age program environment. Many programs are housed in libraries, cafeterias, gyms, and church basements.

When facilities are designed for other purposes, restrictions may apply. Providing an appropriate environment may be difficult. Teachers in these spaces often have only a limited time to prepare the environment. They must develop creative strategies for getting the room ready each day. They may use movable

---

Putting Technology to Use

Have students research the possibility of implementing a computer-based pen pal program with students in foreign countries for the children in a school-age program. What sources exist online for setting up a program? What guidelines are suggested? How can teachers in a school-age program locate suitable pen pals? What precautions are necessary to ensure the children's safety? What can students gain from participating in a pen pal program with children in another country? Allow time for students to discuss their findings in class.

carts to store games, art supplies, books, and other program materials, 30-6. They may have the children help by including setup and cleanup in the children's daily schedule.

Indoor Space

The indoor space for a school-age program should be adequate for the number of children enrolled. Children need room for individual, small group, and large group activities. At least 35 square feet of space should be available for each child.

Children need a secure and safe environment. For them, a child care center is a home away from home. A quality school-age child care environment is informal and provides a homelike atmosphere. In this setting, the children can explore interests and develop one-on-one relationships.

Indoor space should be well designed and pleasing to the eye. Provide storage units for children's personal belongings that are separate from those used to hold classroom materials and supplies. Children are likely to bring some clothing and backpacks. Use pillows, pictures, posters, bean bag chairs, carpeting, couches, and curtains to help create a warm and inviting environment.

As a teacher in a school-age program, you will need to carefully plan how to use the space in your room. As in programs for preschool children, the room needs to include interest centers. You will also need to provide space for quiet activities. Create some open areas for group activities, too. This will provide a space where the entire group can be together as needed.

Interest Centers

Interest centers are a focus of quality school-age child care programs. Whenever possible, set up centers for hobbies, blocks, cooking, science, math, games, music, dramatic play, and arts and crafts. Try to provide bulletin boards or display areas near each center to show children's work.

Arrange interest centers to encourage independent use by the children. Place labeled open shelving units in the centers. These units will help children know where to acquire and return materials and equipment.

30-6

In a shared environment, staff can use wagons to store and transport art supplies.

Health and Safety

Height Limitations for Outdoor Equipment

Outdoor play equipment has a height restriction to ensure children's safety. Generally, this is one foot per year of age. The height restriction is 6.5 feet for school-age children who are six to twelve years old. Check with your local and state licensing agencies to see if there are further requirements.

Discuss

How many square feet of space is needed in the classroom for each child? What is the height restriction for outdoor equipment for school-age children six to twelve years old?

Activity

Write one of each of the following headings for school-age interest centers on a separate sheet of large paper: *Hobbies, Blocks, Cooking, Science, Math, Games, Music, Dramatic Play, Arts and Crafts*, and *Language*. Ask students to write down at least one suggestion for an activity and equipment and supplies for each area.

Enrich

Ask students to make a list of retired adults they know who might be willing to share information about their former career, job, hobby, or personal interest with children in a school-age program. Contact the individuals for their permission before you put their names on the list.

Service Learning Activity

Consider starting a mentor program with the students in the child care class and children in a school-age program. Students will need to discuss the program with their school principal and investigate what type of mentor training, if any, is available to them. Students will need to design questionnaires to match up child care children with school-age children. Students will also need to consult with the director of the school-age program; set parameters for the program such as requirements for attendance, duties, and issues of confidentiality; and sign up interested children.

Discuss

What furniture, equipment, and supplies should be available in the quiet area of a school-age program? What suggestions do you have for separating this area from the more active spaces in the classroom?

Resource

My Ideal Environment, Activity B, SAG

Discuss

What characteristics do you suggest for the outdoor play area of a school-age child program? How might the outdoor play area for an after-school program differ from that used for a summer school-age program?

Quiet Areas

Your room needs to include quiet areas. Children should be able to do homework, use computers, read, and relax in these areas. See 30-7. They should feel protected from the intrusion of others. Children often enjoy flexible quiet spaces they can rearrange with movable furniture and privacy screens. Often there is a child or children who need their own space to work alone.

Open Areas

Your room needs to include large, open areas. Children can use these areas for group planning times and special projects. They can enjoy movement activities, creative dramatics, and indoor games in open areas, too.

Outdoor Space

Outdoor space is just as important in a school-age program environment as indoor space. The design should be based on the development of school-age children, as they need room for physical activity. At the end of the day, they need to make noise, play, and enjoy their friends, 30-8.

These activities require at least 75 square feet of outdoor space per child. Make sure this space is protected from unwanted visitors and traffic. Create separate areas for running, climbing, swinging, and organized sports. School-age children want to be competent at physical skills. Also provide quiet outdoor play space where children can be with their friends, either in a group or one-to-one.

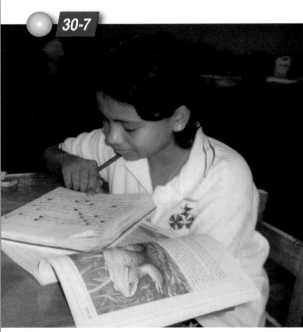

In a quiet area of the classroom, children can focus on their reading.

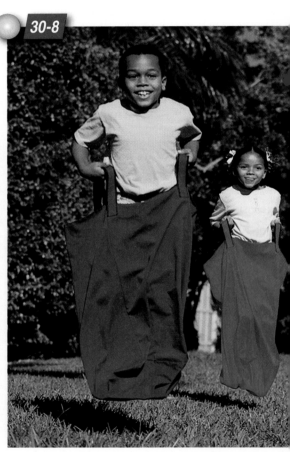

Children need plenty of safe outdoor space for physical activities, such as sack races.

Cross-Curricular Activity

Math/Geometry

Have students measure the classroom they are sitting in right now and determine how many square feet of space is available. If the room was used for an after-school program with a minimum requirement of 35 square feet per child, how many children could participate? Locate an after-school program and measure the outdoor space available. Does the play area allow for 75 square feet of space for each child that would be using the outdoor facility at a time?

Planning Curriculum

Good planning allows you to offer an inviting and challenging school-age program. When you provide an appealing curriculum, everybody wins. You win because the children will enjoy participating. The children win because they have choices as well as opportunities to develop new skills and interests.

The question is, "Who should plan?" The answer is everybody—children, parents, and staff. Begin by finding out what is important to each of these groups.

Parents and staff are likely to have general goals for your program. They want you to provide a safe environment for school-age children during nonschool hours. They expect you to offer a variety of developmentally appropriate activities that allow children to develop new skills, 30-9.

These goals will help guide your overall planning. However, your specific day-by-day activity plans will be guided more by the interests of the children.

Assessing Interests

No two school-age children are exactly alike. As a teacher in a school-age program, you must consider children's individual abilities and needs. You must also be aware of family backgrounds and special situations. This will help you plan personally meaningful curriculum built on what the children already know.

To plan a developmentally appropriate school-age program, you need to begin by assessing the children's interests, energy levels, and temperaments. Children's interests are always changing. Therefore, you need to conduct assessment exercises on a continuing basis to improve teaching and learning.

Informally, you can assess children by observing their play and interacting with them individually and in small groups. You can also assess interests through get-acquainted interviews, group discussions, self-reports, and surveys.

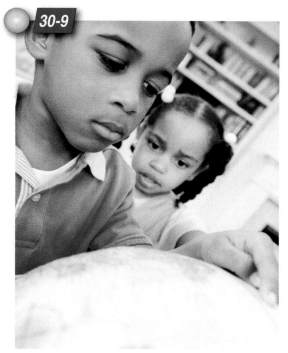
30-9

Activities should interest the children while encouraging their development.

Get-Acquainted Interviews

Get-acquainted interviews can help you assess interests at the beginning of the year or when new children enroll. This assessment technique involves having a child ask a peer questions about himself or herself. Questions can focus on favorite hobbies, sports, foods, holidays, music, books, television programs, and vacation activities.

Because school-age children enjoy using technology, you may want to record the interviews on videotape or an audio cassette. You can share the tapes during group time to help all the children learn more about their classmates.

Group Discussions

Group discussion is a useful method of determining individual interests of school-age children. Using this method on a regular

Activity

Ask students to consult the children's librarian at the local public library to find out what fiction and nonfiction topics are most popular for the school-aged audience. How does the library promote interest in various topics for school-age children?

Enrich

Have students make a list of the special interest clubs and activities available to school-age children in the area. Examples may include 4-H, scouts, gymnastics, dance, computer groups, martial arts, drama, and sports. Investigate the possibility of using the resources of any of these groups to enhance a school-age child care program.

Reflect

Gerald has just moved to your city and is new to the school-age program. He has told you he would rather go home after school, watch TV and play video games, and not have to participate in your "dumb" activities. What can you do to make Gerald feel welcome? How can you make him want to join the other children in play and learning activities?

Putting Technology to Use

Have students conduct an Internet search for curriculum resources for after-school and summer school-age child care programming. What sources for curriculum can you locate that will enhance a student's interests and abilities in science and math? What sources are available for enrichment in the arts and drama field? How can school-age program directors make sure that curriculum planning coordinates with or enhances the school district's curriculum? Allow time for students to discuss their findings in class.

Resource

Design a Survey,
Activity C, SAG

Enrich

Have students survey
the school-age pro-
grams in the area to
compare the fees for
their programs. Make
a chart showing the
costs for before- and
after-school care,
school holidays, and
summer programs. Is
transportation to and
from school included,
extra, or unavailable?
Do families receive a
discount for more than
one child attending? Are
reduced rates available
for families in need?

Activity

Have students investi-
gate what the policies of
child care centers in the
area are when parents
arrive late to pick up
their children. Are extra
charges assessed, and
if so, how much? Do
the charges deter the
parents from consis-
tently arriving late?

basis can also help you keep up with changes in children's interests.

Group discussions are particularly effective with nonreaders. Begin the process by asking the following questions:

- What are your hobbies?
- What new hobbies would you like to learn?
- What are your favorite sports?
- Are there any new sports you would like to learn?
- What are your favorite activities at school?
- What are your favorite program activities?
- What do you like least about the program?
- What else would you like to do in the program?

Self-Reports

Another way to learn about children is through self-reports. These reports can take the form of either stories or pictures. Ask children to focus on a theme as they write or draw. Possible themes include "All About Me," "My Family," and "When I Grow Up." Invite children to share their stories and pictures with the class. Celebrate the children's diversity. Then display stories and pictures on a bulletin board or wall.

Surveys

You can design a survey to assess children's interests. Children who are readers can complete the survey on their own. A staff member can ask questions and record the responses of nonreaders. When designing the survey, keep it brief.

Group Planning Sessions

After you have gathered information about children's interests, you are ready to begin making some specific plans. Group planning sessions are especially effective for planning themes, celebrations, special events,

and field trips. Begin by asking the children to brainstorm a list of ideas. Be sure to acknowledge each suggestion. You may want to record the ideas on a board or flipchart.

After children have presented all their suggestions, discuss each one. Explain your reasons for eliminating any ideas due to expense, location, safety, or lack of staff. When you have reviewed all the ideas, encourage the children to prioritize them as a group.

Scheduling

Most school-age child care programs are open before and after school hours. Children may participate in these programs for up to five hours a day while attending kindergarten or elementary school. Some programs are available all day during vacation periods, holidays, and summer months.

As a school-age program teacher, you must carefully plan a daily schedule that meets children's needs for predictability. At the same time, your schedule should be flexible enough to allow for children's individual differences.

You will set up your daily program schedule between arrival and departure times. Your schedule will include times for children to eat and rest. It will include periods for children to participate in a variety of activities. It will also allow time for children to clean up. Figure 30-10 shows a typical schedule for a school-age child care program.

Arrival and Departure Times

Arrival and departure times represent more than just the beginning and end of the daily schedule in a school-age program. These are valuable times to share information with children and parents. They serve as a bridge between home and the program. Use these moments to update parents about their children and to solicit parents' support for

Portfolio Project

Have students select a school-age program director, curriculum specialist, teacher, or aide and interview the individual about his or her job. What is most enjoyable about working with school-age children in this program? What presents more challenges? How important is parent communication to your position? Do you favor a child-centered, adult-centered, or unit-based program? What resources do you regularly use in your work? Have students write a brief review of the job and file in their portfolio.

30-10

School-Age Child Care Program Daily Schedule

6:00-8:30 a.m.
- Arrival of children (Children will arrive at different times dependent on their parents' work schedules)
- Breakfast
- Self-selected indoor activities, such as games, blocks, sewing, crafts, pegboards, art materials, books, stories, discussions, hobbies, conversation, computers, card games, puzzles, and homework

8:30-12:00 p.m.
- Children attend morning kindergarten and area elementary schools

12:00-12:30 p.m.
- Lunch (morning kindergarten children return and afternoon kindergarten children go to school)

12:30-1:00 p.m.
- Group Time: Story, discussion, show-and-tell

1:00-2:00 p.m.
- Rest time

2:00-3:00 p.m.
- Self-selected activities, such as dramatic play, crafts, sand, water, checkers, card games, cooking, science, books, tapes, computers, and hobbies

3:15-3:30 p.m.
- Group Snack (afternoon kindergarten and elementary children return to program)

3:30-5:30 p.m.
- Outdoor Play: Field trips; organized sports; team games; mud, water, and sand play; gardening; jumping, skipping, hopping, climbing and other physical activities involving balls and jump ropes; music and dance lessons

5:30-6:00 p.m.
- Group Time: Discussion, program planning

6:00-6:30 p.m.
- Indoor individual and small group activities, outside and indoor cleanup in preparation for going home

A comprehensive school-age child care program provides care 12 hours a day.

program activities. Also use these interaction times to gain insight about family values, roles, and events that may be affecting children.

When the children enter and leave your room, be available. Identify children by name. Give them warm greetings. Listen to their parting comments. Be sincere. Remember that the tone of your voice and the expression on your face tells children how you feel about seeing them.

Mealtimes

As you begin to plan your program schedule, think of your childhood. How did you feel when you arrived home from school? Chances are you were hungry. Like you, the children in your program will probably want something to eat when they arrive.

Mealtimes should be a learning experience. Mealtimes should also provide children with a sense of responsibility and community. Children can learn how to measure and prepare foods. They can assist with planning the menus, setting and decorating the tables, serving, and cleaning up. They can use the time when they are gathered around the table to share the events of their day, too.

You can use mealtime as an opportunity to introduce multicultural foods. Invite children to share favorite family recipes. Ask them to help plan special meals for holidays, birthdays, and other events. For special

Discuss

Ask students to review 30-10, *School-Age Child Care Program Daily Schedule.* Why is there more leeway in the school-age program schedule and longer activity time blocks when compared to a schedule for preschoolers?

Activity

Have students develop a daily schedule for a school-age child care program. Be sure to include activity ideas for each area. Have student volunteers share their schedules with the rest of the class.

Reflect

What are the advantages of working for a before- and after-school program for only a few hours in the morning and a few in the afternoon? What are the disadvantages of this schedule from a personal viewpoint?

Workplace Connection

Have students contact the local public library to discover what summer reading group or special summer programming is available for school-age children. How long are special sessions, how often are they held, and what types of topics are typically scheduled?

Are the topics tied into literature or other materials on the subject that are available at the library? What suggestions do you have for topics for summer school-age programs? Have students write a brief report of their findings.

Enrich

Have students debate the pros and cons of doing homework right after school or doing it later in the evening so they can have a break from schoolwork. Why might doing homework at an after-school program be advantageous to the child? Why might it be a poor idea?

Discuss

Why should school-age programs focus on recreational rather than academic activities? Give examples of activities that use academic skills but are recreational in nature. Example: counting money when playing Monopoly.

Resource

Scheduling School-Age Programs, Activity B, OG

events, you may want to have children invite a guest, such as a parent or grandparent.

Rest Time

School-age programs sometimes include a daily rest time. The amount of time you schedule for rest will depend on the children in your program. Age, health, and activity level will affect a child's need for rest.

Some children, especially those who are younger, may want to sleep during rest time. Other, older children may simply enjoy low-key activities. You might encourage these children to play quiet games, listen to music, or read books. The activities they choose should not disturb children who are resting.

Soft music may help some children relax during rest time. Other children find pleasure in having a teacher read to them.

Activity Time

You are likely to devote the largest part of your daily school-age program schedule to activity time. You will notice fewer conflicts among children when they are all engaged in meaningful activity. Providing a variety of familiar and unfamiliar activities will ensure that all children can find something interesting to do. The specific types of activities you offer will depend on the length and time of your program.

Before-school programs should focus on quiet activities. Some children may need to spend the time before school finishing their homework. Other children may enjoy looking at books, constructing puzzles, or playing quiet games. They may also enjoy talking with friends.

After-school programs are generally longer than before-school programs, and they offer a wider variety of activities. After sitting in a classroom all day, many children enjoy physical activities that help release energy. They enjoy outdoor play, competitive sports, preparing snacks, and working on projects.

They may want to participate in clubs, such as Cub Scouts, Boy Scouts, Brownies, and Girl Scouts. They may want to join book clubs and special interest clubs.

Other children need to find space to be by themselves after school to recharge their energy. For them, being with a group of people, following directions, and completing tasks all day may be stressful. They may simply want to listen to music, page through a book, enjoy quiet games, do homework, or rest.

Balance of Activities

A good school-age program does not duplicate activities that take place during the school day. Rather, it complements the child's home and school experiences. The emphasis should be on recreational activities as opposed to academic ones, 30-11. The activities should

30-11

Recreational activities, such as music, provide good balance for a full day of schoolwork.

Workplace Connection

Ask students to arrange a visit to observe a local school-age program. Does the teacher use arrival or departure times to share information with the parents? Are both indoor and outdoor activities provided? Are there times for children to choose their own activities? Is a rest time provided? Are children given the responsibility of helping maintain the environment? Is there a balance between child-directed and teacher-directed activities? Have children write a brief report of their findings.

be developmentally appropriate and provide opportunities for skill development.

The schedule for a school-age child care program needs to include a balance of activities. Schedule separate times for child-directed and teacher-directed activities. Allow time for small group, large group, and individual activities. Plan for gross-motor activities, such as team sports and outdoor play. Also plan for fine-motor activities, such as writing and drawing. Chart 30-12 shows a list of indoor activities for school-age children.

30-12

Indoor Activities

- Board games
- Card games
- Checkers
- Chess
- Clay modeling
- Collages
- Collections: stamps, shells, rocks, baseball cards
- Cooking
- Gardening
- Map construction
- Needlework
- Painting
- Papier-mâché
- Photography
- Puppet constructions and plays
- Model building
- Musical instruments
- Sewing
- Solitaire
- Tie-dying
- Tic-tac-toe

Many school-age children find these indoor leisure activities enjoyable.

Group Activities

Some school-age program activities will involve all the children. However, children in the middle childhood years also need opportunities to participate in small, self-selected peer group activities. Listening to a story, taking a field trip, and planning a project can all be group activities. Such activities help children communicate, develop friendships, and learn social skills.

Use different ways of dividing children into groups. You may group children according to age, interests, and needs. However, you may also group children according to such factors as favorite sports, recording artists, cars, foods, pets, and hobbies.

Mixed groups representing different developmental stages benefit children at all levels. Such groups reduce competition. These groups give older children an opportunity to develop leadership skills. Older children can help younger children with such activities as board games and crafts. The younger children learn by observing and interacting with the older children.

Groups may undertake special activities. For example, publishing a newsletter is a special activity for a group of children. The children can write, edit, and print it using a computer. They can decide who will be the editors, reporters, and production staff. Once the newsletter is published, children can share it with parents. Other groups might want to start a science or math club. Some after school programs feature a chef's club.

Outdoor Games

Outdoor games are especially important for allowing children time for physical activity. Physical activity is necessary not only to development, but also to good health. Children who get plenty of activity are less likely to grow up disliking exercise.

School-age children particularly like to play group games. At this stage of development they understand rules.

Discuss

Ask gifted or high-achieving students in your class to share experiences in which they were asked to help other children instead of moving through material at a faster pace. Did they resent having to help others, or were they pleased with the opportunity to share what they knew?

Activity

Have students collect unused board games, unfinished or unopened craft kits, books, and other materials suitable for school-age children. Locate a school-age child program that could make good use of the donations.

Resource

Games for Fostering Development, Activity D, SAG

Portfolio Project

Have students contact a local community college or training program for early childhood educators and review the curriculum offerings in school-age programming. Are courses in school-age programming included in degree or certificate requirements or are they an option?

What are the differences in course content between school-age and infant/toddler/preschool classes? Are internships in school-age programming offered at this institution? Have students write a brief report of their findings and file the information in their portfolio.

Discuss

What types of computer software programs would be developmentally appropriate for six- and nine-year-olds? Give examples.

Activity

Have students conduct an Internet search to find out more information about filtering software and other technologies that keep children from accessing certain information on the Internet. Allow time for students to discuss their findings in class.

Discuss

Why should children be included in cleanup activities? Should children be expected to do cleanup tasks that involve using cleaning fluids or preparations other than water?

Health and Safety

Ergonomics and Computer Use

Recent studies show an increase in repetitive-stress injuries in children under twelve who engage in excessive computer use. These injuries can be due to poor posture at the computer and furniture that doesn't fit. For example, neck injuries may result when children must strain or hunch forward to see the computer screen. Wrist and hand injuries may occur when children overextend their reach. Mouse pads can be easily out of reach for young children.

Computer furniture that is ergonomically designed for children age six to twelve can help prevent injuries. Make sure that children sit at the computer properly with their feet flat on the floor and backs straight against the chair backs. Arms and hands should be at a 90-degree angle and parallel with the keyboard and mouse pad.

Moreover, they understand that you must abide by the rules to be part of the group. Outdoor games include basketball, volleyball, gymnastics, and jumping rope. Other games enjoyed outdoors include hide-and-seek, hopscotch, kick ball, marbles, obstacle courses, ping-pong, tug-of-war, and shuffleboard.

Technology Use

Computers offer special learning opportunities for school-age children. As a result, school-age programs need to provide computers and developmentally appropriate software. Children of this age can use the computer for a variety of tasks. They can compose letters, practice keyboarding skills, complete homework, play games, or search for information on the Internet. Through these experiences, children improve their thinking skills by seeking information, making decisions, and solving problems.

Children need age-appropriate freedom to use the computers on their own, 30-13. This helps them develop self-confidence. Children must be protected from inappropriate content when using the computers, however. Programs must develop and enforce online safety limits. They should also investigate the use of filtering software and other technologies that keep children from accessing certain information. Supervision is also needed.

Cleanup

Your school-age program needs to include scheduled time for cleanup. All children need to participate in cleanup activities. They have a responsibility for maintaining their environment.

Let children know your expectations for cleanup time. Tell them that they should return games and equipment to the proper storage units. Instruct them to place their personal belongings, projects, and art work in their lockers. Completing these tasks will help children develop a sense of pride.

Meeting Special Needs

Review the special learners' chapter outlines to determine if the students have any questions about the concepts or content of this chapter. Review the chapter objectives and ask the students to evaluate their progress in meeting these objectives. Ask the students to summarize, orally or in writing, what they learned from this chapter.

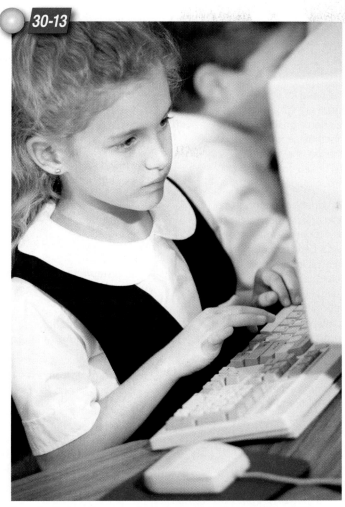

30-13

Learning to use the computer independently is a valuable skill for school-age children.

Discuss

Look at the photo in 30-13. What learning opportunities can computers provide for school-age children? Give examples.

Reflect

Think about the types of tasks for which you use a computer. How much easier are these tasks with the use of a computer?

Resource

Online Safety Agreement, transparency master 30-1, TR

Cross-Curricular Activity

Review the student use and parent permission form used by your school district for computer and Internet use. Show the form and the *Online Safety Agreement*, transparency master 30-1, to the director or staff of a local after-school program. Compare it to any forms used by their program. How important are agreements such as these in making sure students follow the rules and are protected?

Review and Reflect Answer Key

1. loneliness, unhealthy fears, lack of physical exercise, poor nutritional habits

2. (List four:) earn better grades, demonstrate higher academic achievement, turn in higher-quality homework assignments, spend more time in the learning process, have an increased interest and ability in reading, have better school attendance records, lower dropout rates

3. child-centered program model, adult-centered program model, unit-based program model (Descriptions are student response.)

4. Children can get adult help when they need it. Adults can provide the constant supervision needed to create a safe environment. While supervising, adults can use observation to gain information about the interests, needs, abilities, and experiences of each child.

5. act as facilitators, use positive guidance, involve children, promote respect for cultural diversity, enjoy physical activities

Summary

There is a critical need for school-age child care. Too many children are left alone to care for themselves. Parents should observe state laws regarding self-care for their school-age children. Within the limits of the law, they should decide about using self-care based on the child's age and maturity. A common guideline is 12 years old.

Parents have a variety of options when choosing before- and after-school child care. These include in-home care, family child care homes, and child care centers. School-age child care programs follow any of three models: child-centered, adult-centered, or unit-based. High-quality programs are staffed by well-trained personnel. These individuals understand child growth and development. They have age-appropriate expectations of the children's behavior and abilities.

A quality school-age child care environment should provide appropriate space, materials, and equipment. The environment needs to reflect the children's interests, ages, abilities, needs, and experiences. This environment will allow children to have fun, learn, and thrive as they move at their own pace.

Parents and staff are likely to have general goals for the school-age program. They expect a variety of developmentally appropriate activities that allow children to develop new skills. Specific day-by-day activity plans will be guided more by the interests of the children.

Most school-age child care programs are open before and after school hours. Children may participate in these programs for up to five hours a day while attending kindergarten, primary, or elementary school. Some programs also operate all day during vacation periods and summer months.

Review and Reflect

1. List four common problems of children who lack adult supervision.

2. List four positive outcomes for children who attend a school-age child care program.

3. Name and describe the three program models for school-age child care programs.

4. How do appropriate adult-child ratios benefit both the children and the adults?

5. Name five characteristics of staff members in high-quality school-age programs.

6. Describe a quality school-age child care environment.

7. In order to plan a developmentally appropriate school-age program, what must you do first?

8. Name four techniques you can use to assess children's interests.

9. In planning activities for school-age programs, the emphasis should be on _____ activities as opposed to _____ ones.

10. How do mixed groups representing different developmental stages benefit children at all levels?

6. A quality school-age child care environment provides appropriate space, materials, and equipment. The environment reflects the children's interests, ages, abilities, needs, and experiences. The environment also allows children to have fun, learn, and thrive as they move at their own pace.

7. You need to begin by assessing the children's interests, energy levels, and temperaments.

8. get-acquainted interviews, group discussions, self-reports, surveys

9. recreational, academic

10. Mixed groups reduce competition. These groups give older children an opportunity to develop leadership skills. Older children can help younger children with such activities as board games and crafts. The younger children learn by observing and interacting with the older children.

Apply and Explore

1. Visit two school-age child care programs that use different models. Write a report explaining how the programs are alike and different.

2. Interview a school-age child care provider about the characteristics that are important in his or her work. Share your findings in a brief oral report.

3. Discuss methods for including school-age children in curriculum planning.

Cross-Curricular Link

Math

1. Measure the indoor and outdoor square footage at a school-age child care facility. Calculate how much space is available for each child enrolled in the program.

Technology

2. Check the Web site www.gameskidsplay.net for an extensive list of children's game ideas.

3. Visit www.yahooligans.com, the Web site Yahoo! developed for school-age children. Which parts of the site do you think school-age children would find most interesting?

4. Visit the Web site of the National AfterSchool Association (NAA) at www.naaweb.org. Read the full text of their standards.

Workplace Link

What type of after-school tutoring programs are available in your area? Are the programs part of established school-age child care programs or are they stand-alone businesses? Are private tutors available through your school district or through classified advertising? Compare the types of tutoring available in the following areas: subjects; length and number of sessions per week; cost; staff requirements and qualifications; location; and guarantees of success.

Discuss

Look at the chapter opening photo. What special needs does this child appear to have? How do you think the teacher may meet this child's needs? How do you think the teacher may work to make the child comfortable in the classroom?

Discuss

Look over the objectives for this chapter. What attitudes are important when considering working with children with special needs?

31

Guiding Children with Special Needs

After studying this chapter, you will be able to

- contribute to the development of an Individualized Education Plan for a child with special needs.
- develop individualized learning objectives and teaching strategies for a child.
- explain the role of the teacher in working with children who have special needs.
- describe methods for identifying and working with special needs that may be encountered in the early childhood program: hearing, speech, language, vision, physical, health, cognitive, and behavioral disorders.
- describe methods of integrating children with special needs into a typical program.
- explain the special needs of children who are gifted and how these needs can be met.

Terms to Know

Individuals with Disabilities Education Act (IDEA)

inclusion

Individualized Education Plan (IEP)

Individualized Family Service Plan (IFSP)

referral

hearing impairment

articulation problems

visual impairment

chronic health needs

asthma

hemophilia

learning disability

behavior disorder

autism

giftedness

acceleration

enrichment

Miguel, a lively four-year-old, has a hearing impairment. He can speak and understand only a few simple words. Rosie, an active five-year-old, is color deficient. She cannot identify the primary colors. Stephen has cerebral palsy. He needs special help to develop fine-motor skills. Toby is a two-year-old who has taught herself to read. These are children who have special needs.

By federal law, children with disabilities must be provided with free, appropriate public education when they reach three years of age. The **Individuals with Disabilities Education Act (IDEA)**, passed by Congress, requires that all states provide education for children who are developmentally delayed. Under this law, all three- to five-year-old children with disabilities that require special educational services must be provided with individual education programs. The same programs are available for children from birth to three years of age who are high risk or have significant developmental problems. Infants, toddlers, and preschoolers who might have a physical, sensory, cognitive, or emotional disability are guaranteed the right to a professional assessment under the Federal Education of Handicapped Children Act.

Inclusion, previously referred to as *mainstreaming*, means placing children with special needs in regular classrooms. This process allows children to learn in the least restrictive environment. All children gain skills by interacting with one another. In this type of environment, children with disabilities have children who are nondisabled as role models. This interaction can lead to imitation. Inclusionary classrooms are frequently team-taught by regular and special education teachers.

There are many types of special needs. Communication needs are the most common. These usually fall into three categories: hearing, speech, and language problems. Visual, physical, and learning disabilities and chronic health problems are other types of special needs. Gifted children also have special needs, 31-1.

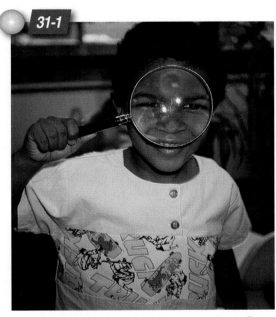

31-1

Children who are constantly curious and trying to figure out how objects work may be gifted.

Vocabulary

Have students review the *Terms to Know* list. Ask students to look up unfamiliar words or terms in the glossary before reading the chapter.

Discuss

What is the significance of the *Individuals with Disabilities Education Act*? Why should parents of children with special needs become familiar with this law?

Vocabulary

Have a student volunteer define *inclusion*. What is the benefit of inclusion for children with special needs?

Meeting Special Needs

Provide an outline of the chapter with all the chapter headings for special learners. Students should fill in each section of the outline as the material is covered in class with a sentence or two about the content. Review the special learners' IEPs to decide if any modifications should be made in presenting the chapter content.

Discuss

How do nondisabled children benefit from having a child with disabilities in their classroom? What reminders do nondisabled children need about helping their classmates with disabilities?

Vocabulary

Have a student volunteer define the term *Individualized Education Plan (IEP)*. Why are IEPs required for children with a diagnosed disability?

Discuss

How do IEPs help teachers and parents meet a child's needs? How do IEPs ensure that children receive any special services they need?

Assistants and volunteers can be most useful in inclusion. Instruct all staff members on the nature of the child's condition and how they are to help. Encourage adults to meet the special needs of the children in group settings, if possible. To do this, the staff may have to modify or adapt classroom materials, change expectations, or give extra help when needed.

Nondisabled children can also assist in inclusion by helping a child with a disability adjust to the environment. The nondisabled child might introduce the other child to the classroom setting. At times, the nondisabled child can help the child organize his or her materials or practice a new skill. Nondisabled children also benefit from inclusionary classrooms. Children with disabilities frequently model unique adaptive skills and problem-solving abilities.

A word of caution is necessary when working with children with disabilities. Sometimes other children in the classroom will want to do too much for these children. They try to "help" by doing the disabled children's work for them or by helping them with self-help skills. Remind the children that assistance should be provided only when needed. Encourage staff, volunteers, and the other children to be patient and give extra encouragement to children with special needs.

Individualized Education Plans

Federal law requires that an **Individualized Education Plan (IEP)** be written for each child with a diagnosed disability. The purpose of an Individualized Education Plan is to ensure that each child receives an appropriate education. By law, parents are allowed to take part in designing their child's program. This plan is jointly developed by the teacher, the parents or guardians, and experts on the particular disability. A copy of the plan is given to

the parent(s). Some children with special needs will come to your center already identified. These children will already have an IEP. Usually an IEP is written for a 12-month period extending from October 1 to September 30. Children with a correctable disability or one that requires no special accommodations will not need an Individualized Education Plan.

Each IEP requires six components. These components are

- a description containing an assessment of the child's current level of performance and skill development

- annual goals for the child

- short-term educational objectives

- a statement outlining the involvement of the child in the regular educational program

- specific services that will be provided with a time line noting the dates services will begin and end

- evaluation criteria that will be used to decide if educational objectives are met

When a preschool age child is diagnosed as having a disability, an **Individualized Family Service Plan (IFSP)** is developed. The IFSP includes

- the family's needs in regard to enhancing the child's development

- goals for the child and resources to increase the child's ability to learn

- services to be provided to the child and/or family, by whom and when

- how the child is learning

- a plan for transitioning the child to other services and regular education

Teachers' Roles

Teachers' roles have expanded since federal law first mandated including children

---

Cross-Curricular Activity

Social Studies
Have students research the history of special education from its beginnings in the 1700s through today. What major events in special education history are notable? What legislative action mandated special education services? How have the laws

kept up with the needs of children and adults with disabilities today? How have schools responded to special education mandates? How have special education teacher preparation programs changed and improved over the years? Present information to the class as an oral report or a poster display.

with special needs in classrooms. Now teachers need to

- take part in identifying children with special needs.

- work with speech clinicians, school psychologists, health professionals, and other resource persons to design individual programs.

- teach children who have special needs and nondisabled children in the same classroom.

- share information with parents and make suggestions for referrals.

- base program decisions on input from several resources including parents, other professionals, and personal observations.

- encourage parents to participate in their child's education. This is their right. Find out what they are feeling as well as thinking. Be an equal partner with parents; keep them informed.

First, as a teacher, you will need to learn how to identify children with special needs. Then you will need to develop a basic understanding of the learning needs of children with hearing, visual, speech, physical, learning, behavioral, and health disabilities. With this knowledge, you can then adapt the curriculum and classroom environment to meet their special needs.

Identification

Early identification of special needs is the key to promoting the child's successful development, 31-2. Children who are not identified early may go through years of failure. This failure, in turn, can create a poor self-concept that can compound the disability.

Many young children's special needs are identified after they enter an early childhood program. Often, identification is made by an adult who is not part of the family. As a teacher, you may be the first to detect a speech, visual, or hearing problem. You may

31-2

Annual hearing tests are a vital tool for identifying hearing problems early.

also be the first to note a cognitive, emotional, or physical disability.

To learn to identify special needs, you will need a strong child development background. It is important to recognize when a child is lagging in reaching a milestone. When a problem is suspected, observe the child closely and make careful notes. Informal observation may be used for assessing a child's needs. These observations may be noted on cards or paper. When recording observations, mention those signs of behaviors that suggest a special need. Any unusual social, cognitive, emotional, or physical development could signal a possible special need.

For instance, you may suspect a certain child has a special need. Development appears to be far above or below average. In this case, you observe the child closely. Make notes about any unusual behavior. If Terry cannot identify primary colors after studying color concepts a number of times, observe him closely. Ask yourself "Could Terry be

Discuss

What educational background and experience will teachers need to be able to identify special learning needs of students? What are teachers required to do for students with special needs to promote and encourage their learning?

Vocabulary

Have a student volunteer define the term *Individualized Family Service Plan (IFSP)*. How can an IFSP help in transitioning a child when he or she is no longer a preschooler?

Discuss

Why is it important that a child's disability be identified as early as possible? Why do you think that teachers may be the first to identify a problem and not a family member?

Putting Technology to Use

Have students conduct an Internet search to discover if college or university programs in early childhood education require students to take coursework in special education. Students should select one or two colleges in your state that they may be interested in attending for research. What courses are available to education students who are not special education majors? Does your state require special education coursework as a condition for issuing a teaching license? What are the requirements for teachers and child caregivers in child care centers and preschools?

Activity

Have students role-play a situation in which an early childhood teacher is sharing concerns in a parent conference about a child's lack of attention in class and difficulty in speech. Have the rest of the class observe the role-play and offer their suggestions on handling the conference in a professional manner.

Reflect

How might you handle a situation in which a parent does not want to admit his or her child has a developmental delay or disability?

Vocabulary

Have a student volunteer define *referral*. What professionals may be involved in a referral?

color deficient?" Consider a child's behavior in comparison to his or her usual behavior and in comparison to his or her peers.

A number of techniques can be used to collect data. You might study a child's work, 31-3. Photographs and videos are also useful. Scales or checklists that name skills children of certain ages should be able to perform can be helpful.

After you have made and confirmed your findings, alert the center director. The director may wish to confirm your observations. He or she may give other tests to measure the child's abilities. After this, a conference will likely be scheduled with the child's family. The conference can be a delicate situation that you will need to handle with care and respect.

Begin the conference by introducing the suspected problem. Share your observations. Provide family members with examples from your observations. Ask family members if they have noticed any of these behaviors at home. If their observations confirm yours, suggest a formal diagnosis.

For some parents, coming to terms with their child's developmental delay or disability takes time. They may not share your concern. If this is the case, keep making your observations and schedule more conferences. It sometimes helps to ask the family to take part in structured observations in the home and school. Remember, any delay in diagnosis can hinder the child's development. However, remember it's the family's choice to have their child evaluated. This must be respected. Chart 31-4 shows the disabilities that qualify a child for services.

Referrals

When the parent(s) agree a problem may exist, direct them to the needed service. Your role as a teacher is to help them see a need for their child's treatment. Once this has been done, obtain a diagnosis. Public schools are responsible for planning and paying the costs associated with the diagnosis of a disability unless parents choose to have their own assessment conducted. In that case, school staff are obligated to consider the results. You may be able to suggest a professional parents can take their child to see. This is called a **referral**. Vision or physical problems may first be referred to a county or school health nurse. Hearing, language, or speech problems may

31-3

Closely observing children's skills allows teachers to note behavior that might indicate a special need.

31-4

Disabilities That Qualify a Child for Services

- Autism
- Blindness
- Developmental delay
- Emotional disturbance
- Hearing impairments including deafness
- Mental retardation
- Multiple disabilities
- Orthopedic impairments
- Speech or language impairments

A child with one of these disabilities may be qualified for a special needs program.

Workplace Connection

Invite a school psychologist to speak to the child care class about the policies and procedures followed in identifying, assessing, and placing students in special programs. What tests are given to children? What form do the tests take? What is the difference between a test and an assessment? What assessment tools are generally used by school psychologists? What options do parents have for ensuring that their child receives all the services he or she is entitled to by law?

be referred to a speech clinician. Learning and behavioral problems are most often referred to a school psychologist or local agency. Depending on the state, a referral may be made to the Department of Social Services.

Hearing Disorders

Hearing impairment refers to a problem in one or more parts of the ear. This prevents the child from hearing adequately. A hearing impairment is one of the most common *congenital disabilities* (present since birth, but not necessarily hereditary). A child who is hearing impaired can often be identified by his or her lack of vocabulary and overall delays in language development. This child may only speak a few simple words. Before you begin to alter your program, learn the extent of the child's hearing loss. This information can only be learned through a professional. Typically infants with a hearing impairment can babble and make noises for about five months after birth.

The child's hearing loss may range from mild to profound. With a mild hearing loss, the child's vocabulary will not be as large as that of his or her peers who have normal hearing. This child might also have difficulty during large group activities, stories, and field trips. He or she may appear inattentive and distracted. The child may miss as much as half of what is being communicated.

A child with a moderate hearing loss will also have trouble responding to a teacher in large group situations. This child often fails to turn his head or eyes in the direction of sound. He or she has a limited vocabulary. To understand the child's speech, you should stand face-to-face. This will allow you to read the child's lips.

Children with severe, or *profound*, hearing loss often have little understandable speech. These children must rely largely on their vision, body language, and contextual clues to communicate.

To make up for or alleviate hearing losses, many children will wear either a hearing aid in their ear or a Y-shaped hearing aid over their chests. The advantage of the ear hearing aid is that it can be adjusted to compensate for the hearing loss in each ear. The Y-shaped aid is the most popular. It has one hearing aid with tubes going to both ears.

It is important that you understand the type of hearing aid used by a child. Ask the parents to tell you about it. If it falls out of the child's ear during program hours, you will need to replace it. You should also know how to check the batteries. Keep a ready supply on hand.

The purpose of the hearing aid is to amplify and magnify all sounds. It will not perfect a child's hearing. In fact, most hearing aids are only useful within a 10-foot radius. Seat children who use hearing aids away from distracting noises. Hearing aids amplify close sounds.

Teaching Suggestions

When approaching a child who is hearing impaired, get down to the child's eye level, 31-5. Then get the child's attention before speaking. Sometimes this can be done by lightly touching the child's hand or arm. With practice, you will learn how close you must stand in order to be understood. You should also follow these suggestions:

- Speak in a normal volume and speed.

- Speak clearly and distinctly while looking into the child's eyes.

- Use the same sentence structure as you would for other children.

- Pause and wait for a response after you speak.

- If the child does not understand you, repeat, rephrase, or demonstrate.

- Encourage other children to imitate you when they communicate with the child. That is, when they need to get the child's attention, look into his or her eyes, and speak at a normal volume and speed.

Vocabulary

Have a student volunteer define the term *hearing impaired*. Have students explain what behavior exhibited by a child may lead them to consider suggesting a hearing evaluation.

Discuss

What are the benefits of a hearing aid for a child? What are some of the disadvantages?

Enrich

Invite the parent of a child who was diagnosed with a hearing impairment to class. Discuss the child's behavior before and after diagnosis and treatment or services were received. How did the child respond to the treatment or services? How has the behavior and learning ability been affected?

Cross-Curricular Activity

Science
Have students research the ear and its hearing mechanisms. Have students locate or draw a diagram of the structure. Students should explain how the process of hearing works and the factors that cause hearing loss or disability.

What situations may cause temporary or permanent hearing loss? What products or techniques can help those with hearing losses hear better? What surgical interventions are available that may improve an individual's hearing? How can nondisabled people protect their hearing ability?

Discuss

Why do you think most professionals recommend that children with hearing losses learn both sign language and lipreading? What are the major benefits of this approach?

Reflect

The preschool teacher tells the mother of four-year-old Cory, Mrs. Green, that she cannot understand what Cory is saying most of the time. Mrs. Green doesn't share this concern because she understands exactly what Cory wants. What would you reply?

Activity

Have students find out how vision and hearing screenings are conducted in their school. Have them discover if parental permission is needed for routine screenings.

31-5

The key to working with hearing impaired children is to modify your teaching methods to meet the needs of the child.

- Whenever needed, use gestures and facial expressions to reinforce the spoken word.

- In a group situation, let the child sit in front of you. This will encourage him or her to watch your body language and lips as you speak.

In addition to using these teaching strategies, adapt the curriculum for the hearing impaired child. Before you begin making these changes, however, you may wish to consult a language and speech clinician. This person will likely offer you suggestions for working with the child.

Visual skills are important for children who are hearing impaired. Finely tuned visual skills help compensate for their lack of hearing. However, children who are hearing impaired do not automatically acquire acute visual skills. To provide for their needs, stress visual activities.

- Use concrete materials to demonstrate abstract concepts. For example, if you are talking about pumpkins, use a real pumpkin or a picture of a pumpkin. (Avoid drawing on the board as you are talking. These children need to see your face as you communicate with them.)

- Provide a variety of classification games and puzzles for the children to practice visual perception skills.

- Label classroom furniture and materials.

- Select books with simple, large, and uncluttered illustrations. These children will rely more on vision than hearing during story time.

- Teach safety by using traffic signals with the wheeled toys in the playground.

- Teach daily routines and transitions using a light switch. Flash the light to get the children's attention.

- Use a picture poster to point to the upcoming activity.

Some children with hearing impairments are taught to communicate manually through finger spelling and sign language. An oral approach, emphasizing lip reading and speaking, is used with other children. Some parents feel very strongly about using one approach over the other even though most professionals today recommend a combined or eclectic approach with children who have hearing impairments.

Speech and Language Disorders

Communication impacts all areas of child development. You may find a child in your center may refuse to talk. Another child may speak but may be *inarticulate* (cannot be understood by teachers or peers). Still another child may not be able to recall sentences correctly. These children have speech and language disorders.

Identification

Speech impairments are interference with specific sounds or sound blends. This results

Putting Technology to Use

Have students conduct an Internet search for information about learning American sign language and lipreading or speech-reading. What resources exist online to learn these communication techniques? What sources can you find for DVDs, books, and online courses? Find out if your local community college offers courses on these subjects.

in sounds that are missing, inappropriate, or irregular. You must identify the problem causing the speech impairment before you can alter a program. Informal observations are the most common method used to identify speech and language problems. Chart 31-6 contains a checklist to use when observing for these problems. You will need to listen carefully as the child speaks. Listen to both sounds and content.

When a child is having trouble pronouncing words, record those sounds causing the difficulty. Young children find the consonants *p, b, m, w,* and vowels the easiest to pronounce. *Cr, bl, sh, ch, th, j, r, 1,* and *z* are more difficult sounds to pronounce and take longer to learn. Chart 31-7 contains the approximate ages at which most children use certain sounds.

Observe and listen to children in a variety of settings: on the playground, in the housekeeping area, during lunchtime, and as they converse with others. As you identify the problem, make notes and continue observing to collect information.

A child's speech is generally impaired when it is so different from the other children's that it calls attention to itself. It can also interfere with conversation and

31-7

Developmental Order for Speech Sounds

Age	Sounds					
1½ to 3½ yr.	p	m	h	n	w	b
2 to 4 yr.	k	d	t	n	g	
2½ to 5½ yr.	f	y				
3 to 6 yr.	r	l	s			
3½ to 7 yr.	ch	sh	z			
4½ to 8 yr.	j	r				

Keep these parameters in mind when observing a child you believe may have a speech disorder.

cause the child to be self-conscious. Based on repeated observations, you may conclude a child likely has a speech problem. Share your observations with your director. The director will determine whether a parent conference should be scheduled. The child may then be referred to a speech therapist for assessment.

Articulation Problems

The terms *lazy tongue* and *baby talk* are frequently used to describe articulation problems. **Articulation problems** are most often omissions, distortions, or substitutions of vowels or consonants or both. Articulation problems include slow, labored speech as well as rapid and slurred speech. An articulation problem can be a result from hearing loss or lack of tongue and mouth control.

Certain speech sounds are left out in an omission error. This results in only a part of a word being said. For example, a child may say "oat" for "boat." The child may say "had" for the name "Thad."

A child with a distortion problem sometimes has trouble identifying and producing the intended sound. For example, instead of pronouncing an *s*, a child may suck air in between his or her teeth.

31-6

Speech Observation Checklist

- Do the sounds the child makes match those listed for his or her age group on a developmental chart?
- Is the rate and fluency of the child's speech appropriate for his or her age group?
- Is the child's speech understandable?
- Does the amount of talking done appear to be average?
- Does the child recall and repeat sentences correctly?

If you suspect a speech disorder, observe the child, paying close attention to the items listed.

Reflect

Have you ever had a conversation with an adult with a speech disorder? What was the most difficult part of the conversation? How might this insight prompt you to handle a conversation with a child with a speech disorder?

Discuss

How can Figure 31-7, *Developmental Order for Speech Sounds*, help you decide if the young child in your preschool class has a speech disorder? Does a four-year-old who cannot pronounce *r* correctly have a speech disorder?

Vocabulary

Have a student volunteer define *articulation problems*. Why are the terms *lazy tongue* and *baby talk* incorrect when referring to articulation problems?

Putting Technology to Use

Have students conduct an Internet search for information on careers in the speech-language-hearing sciences. Have students define the jobs of speech-language pathologist, speech therapist, speech clinician, and audiologist. Have students answer the following questions: What education and degrees are required to be certified and practice in this field? What does the coursework cover? Where are individuals in this field typically employed? What salaries and job outlook can they expect?

Vocabulary

Have students explain the difference between a speech *distortion* and a *substitution*. What is a *lisp*? What is *phonation*?

Discuss

What is the role of the speech clinician in speech disorders? What is the teacher's role in working with a child after he or she has been diagnosed with a speech disorder?

Vocabulary

Have students define the following terms and explain how they are related to voice disorders: *pitch, loudness, voice flexibility, voice-quality disorders*.

Substitutions involve speech patterns such as "thome" for "some" or "tate" for "cake." The most common sound substitutions include *f* for *th*, *t* for *k*, *b* for *v*, *th* for *s*, *k* for *t*, and *w* for *i* or *r*. One common substitution problem is referred to as a *lisp*. It involves substituting *th* sound for the letter *s*.

After a child has been diagnosed as having an articulation problem, a speech clinician should be consulted. This professional will provide direct therapy and/or advise you. Ask for advice on how to help the child.

As a teacher, your reaction to the child with articulation problems has a great effect. To help a child feel secure, always react positively. Ensure that the other children do, too. If the child does not respond verbally, do not demand a response. Instead, provide the correct answer for him or her.

Model good listening skills and speaking skills with all the children. Use slow, deliberate speech. Give the children your total attention. Look directly into their faces as they speak, 31-8. Verbally respond with

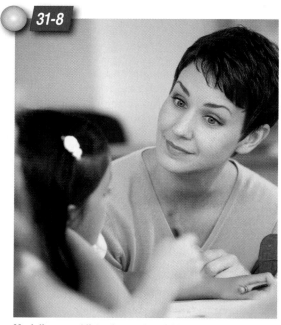

31-8

Modeling good listening and speaking skills can help children who have articulation problems.

interest to what the children are saying. If you do not understand, ask the children to repeat what they have said.

Children with articulation problems need to be encouraged to talk. Set an example by feeding in language as they take part in activities. To illustrate, you may say to a child "You are placing a large red block in the square hole" as he or she plays with a sorting box.

Use language that is proper for the child's developmental level. For example, the child may point to a large red car and say "far." You should then say "That is a large red car." This technique is called *expansion*. It involves taking the child's mispronounced words and correctly expanding them into sentences.

Some children are more comfortable talking about things that are special to them. One technique you can use is to have the child bring something special from home. Then have him or her tell everyone about the item.

Always provide a variety of activities in your classroom. The wider the variety, the more the children will have to talk about. Try to relate classroom activities to children's home experiences and cultural backgrounds.

Demand communication from all children, including those with articulation problems. Do this by asking open-ended questions. Instead of asking "Did you like the book?" ask "What did you like about the book?"

Voice (Phonation) Disorders

Voice characteristics include pitch, loudness, flexibility, and quality. The lowness or highness of the voice is the *pitch*. It is not uncommon for some children to use a pitch that is too low or too high. These disorders occur less frequently than speech impairments.

Loudness is related to the amount of energy or volume used when speaking. The voice may be strong or weak. A strong voice will be loud and can be disturbing. A weak voice may be hard to hear and can also hinder communication.

A good speaking voice during routine conversation uses a variety of pitches and

Putting Technology to Use

Have students search the Internet for information on the role of the tongue in speech. Have students explain how parts of the tongue and tongue mobility relate to the ability to make sounds. What problems with the tongue can hinder speech? What types of surgeries can be performed on the tongue? Have students prepare written reports.

loudness levels. This is referred to as *voice flexibility*. Changes in pitch and loudness often reflect the emotions of the speaker.

Harshness, hoarseness, breathiness, and nasality are all *voice-quality disorders*. The harsh voice is often louder than normal. Hoarseness may indicate a problem in the throat. A breathy voice sounds like a whisper. It is weak and not clearly phonated. Nasality is a condition in which sound passes through the nasal cavities instead of the throat.

With speech therapy and possible medical assistance, most voice disorders are treatable. To help prevent or correct voice disorders, promote voice control:

- Encourage children to use the correct voice volume during indoor play. You may need to say "Teddy, you need to use your indoor voice in the building."

- Discourage children from screaming or yelling too much during outdoor play.

- Model good voice characteristics. Your own voice should be the proper pitch, loudness, quality, and flexibility.

Stuttering

Stuttering in young children is often characterized by repetition, hesitation, and prolongation. Few young children stutter all the time. It is often only under certain conditions that some children stutter.

In the early stages of language development, many children experience stuttering. This most often occurs when they feel pressured, 31-9.

Children function best in a warm, noncritical classroom. This type of environment helps all children speak with confidence.

If you have a stuttering child in your classroom, focus on creating good speaking conditions.

- Plan activities so all children will experience success. Praise the children.

- Provide children with enough time to say what they have to say.

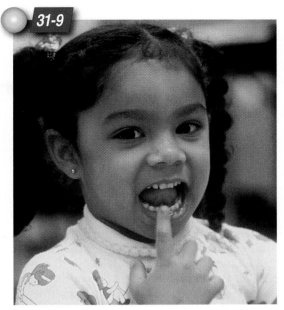
31-9

Children who feel pressured are more likely to stutter than children who are relaxed.

- Listen closely to what the children are saying as opposed to focusing on the stuttering.

- Avoid rushing children through a task. Do not complete a word or sentence for them.

Unfortunately, many well-meaning people try to provide directions to a child who stutters. "Stop and think," "Start over," and "Speak slower" are common examples. These suggestions often make the child feel even more fearful. A child's difficulty could continue as a result of this fear. An environment free of pressure is important. When stuttering is severe, speech therapy may be necessary.

Vision Disorders

One of the smallest groups of children with special needs is the visually impaired. The term **visual impairment** refers to any eye

Discuss

What is *nasality*? What can teachers do to help prevent or correct voice disorders and promote voice control?

Reflect

Have you ever heard a person who stutters frequently speak without stuttering at times? Why may this person be able to control his or her disability during these times?

Discuss

What conditions may cause some young children to stutter? Why are remarks such as "slow down" or "speak slower" usually nonproductive when interacting with a child who stutters?

Putting Technology to Use

Have students conduct an Internet search for information on famous individuals such as singers, actors, athletes, newscasters, and politicians who stuttered. How did stuttering affect their lives? What did they do to overcome or deal with their stuttering? What advice do they have for people who stutter? Have students summarize their findings in an oral report.

Discuss

Describe the process of how the eye "sees." What is the effect on vision if the optic nerve is damaged?

Resource

Special Communication Needs, Activity B, SAG

Reflect

Do you wear glasses or contacts? At what age were you diagnosed with a vision problem? How were you diagnosed? Was the vision problem affecting your schoolwork or hobbies?

or nerve problem that prevents people from seeing normally. Common vision problems include amblyopia, nearsightedness, farsightedness, and/or a color deficiency. Physically, children with visual impairments are similar to children with normal vision. However, this disability can limit their motor abilities as they take part in some physical activities. See 31-10.

To understand visual impairments, you need to understand how a healthy visual system works. Despite young children's thinking, the eye does not actually see. The purpose of the eye is to take in light. After it has taken in light, the eye transmits impulses to the brain through the optic nerve. The brain then decodes the visual stimuli, and "seeing" takes place. Most defects of the eye itself are correctable. If the brain or the optic nerve is damaged, however, the impairment is not correctable.

Early Identification

Early identification of a visual impairment is important. Many child care centers have a volunteer from the National Society for the Prevention of Blindness, a county health nurse, or some other

professional conduct a visual screening each year. See 31-11. Children who appear to have problems are given a referral for a complete exam by an eye specialist.

Classroom staff need to observe children closely to identify vision problems. Certain symptoms may suggest problems:

- excessive rubbing of the eyes
- clumsiness and trouble moving around the classroom
- adjusting the head in an awkward position to view materials
- moving materials so they are close to the eyes
- squinting
- crossed eyes
- crust on eye
- iris on one or both eyes appearing cloudy
- crossed eyes or an eye that turns inward

Children with visual impairments often lack small muscle coordination. They need to experiment with an art medium to build these skills.

Annual eye exams can mean early detection of visual impairments.

Service Learning Activity

Have students conduct a drive to collect used prescription eyeglasses, reading glasses, and sunglasses for distribution to the needy. Contact a local Lions Club at **www.lionsclubs.org** or Glasses for Humanity at **www.glassesforhumanity.org** for information on how used eyewear is collected and how distribution is handled. How do these organizations promote eye health in the United States and internationally? Place collection boxes in prominent locations in your school and community.

- red, encrusted, or swollen eyelids
- excessive blinking

Types of Visual Disabilities

There are several common visual impairments that young children may have. Amblyopia is a disorder you might note in your classroom. You may also find children with glaucoma, nearsightedness, farsightedness, a color deficiency, and some uncorrectable conditions.

Amblyopia

Amblyopia is often called *lazy eye*. This disorder is the result of a muscle imbalance caused by disuse of an eye. It is one of several visual conditions that can be corrected if found during early childhood. To force the use of the weaker eye, a patch is placed over the stronger eye. If this does not work, surgery may be required. If treatment of amblyopia is not done by age six or seven, the child's vision may always be poor.

Glaucoma

Glaucoma is a condition caused by failure of the eye fluid to circulate in the proper way. This results in increased pressure on the eye. Over time, this pressure can destroy the optic nerve. This problem can be treated with medicated eyedrops if diagnosed early. This can prevent loss of vision.

Nearsightedness

Some children may be unable to see things that are far away. These children are *nearsighted*. The medical term for this visual disorder is *myopia*. It results when the eye focuses in front of the retina.

Farsightedness

Children who have a difficult time seeing objects that are close to them are *farsighted*.

The medical term for this visual disorder is *hyperopia*. It is caused by having the visual image focus behind the retina.

Color Deficiency

Color deficiency, or *color blindness*, as it is sometimes called, is the inability to see a color. This problem is hereditary. It mostly affects males and is caused by a recessive gene. You should be able to quickly identify children with color deficiencies. They are not able to recognize one or more primary colors.

Uncorrectable Conditions

There are several visual disorders that cannot be corrected by glasses, surgery, or other means of treatment. Any damage to the optic nerve by disease or trauma is an example. After damage, signals do not get to the brain to provide the child with sight.

Teaching Suggestions

You may need to make changes in your classroom depending on the visual needs of the children. The following teaching suggestions may be helpful:

- Always create a need to see. For instance, if farsighted children refuse to wear their glasses, provide them with materials that have fine detail and print. The children will then realize the importance of wearing their glasses, 31-12.

- Include a study unit on sight to help all the children understand vision.

- When ordering chalkboards, purchase those with a dull finish. Use yellow chalk on chalkboards. Use colored, rather than black, markers on white boards. Glare can be very tiring for partially-sighted children.

- Hang children's work at their eye level.

- Safety is always important. To ensure a safe environment, blocks, cars, and other items should be picked up right after play.

Discuss

What can result from untreated glaucoma? What are the usual treatments for nearsightedness and farsightedness?

Vocabulary

Define the following terms and explain how they are related to vision disorders: *amblyopia, glaucoma, nearsighted (myopia), farsighted,* and *color deficiency.*

Discuss

What safety precautions in the classroom are needed for children with vision disorders? How can you make other children in the class sensitive to the needs of children who are visually impaired?

Portfolio Project

Children who must wear glasses at a young age may feel different from the other children in the class. Have students write a short story about a young girl or boy with vision difficulties. Include references to how the child feels before and after getting glasses. Promote wearing glasses in a positive way so a child hearing the story will feel good about wearing glasses. Illustrate the story and keep a copy in the student's portfolio.

Discuss

Should the teacher make it difficult for the farsighted child to see when the child refuses to wear his or her glasses? How can parental communication assist in the process of getting the child to wear glasses regularly?

Activity

Have students determine if the child care lab meets the needs of children who are visually impaired. What characteristics of the lab are already in place? What changes or additions need to be made so children with vision disorders can safely and freely use the room?

Reflect

How many people have you known with physical disabilities? How did the disability affect the person's mobility? What special arrangements were made for this person? How did the person's disability affect him or her socially and emotionally?

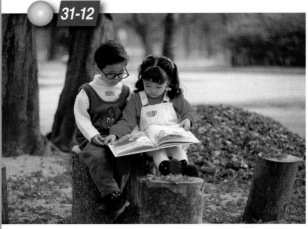
31-12

Make sure children who need glasses understand the importance of wearing them at all times.

- Auditory clues are important for children with visual impairments. Provide a comfortable environment by keeping the noise level low.

- In the reading area, always have a number of large print books with clear, simple pictures.

- Provide many tactile (touch), olfactory (smell), and auditory (sound) clues to structure the environment for the child. For instance, use a piece of shag carpeting in the story area and a bubbling aquarium or fragrant flowers in the science area.

- Use auditory reminders for transition times. These may include singing a song, beating a drum, playing a piano, or hitting tone bells.

- During activities, always encourage children to describe what they remember using their senses.

Remember that children with visual impairments may need to learn some skills children with normal vision already have. For instance, children with normal vision acquire eating, toileting, and dressing skills by watching others. A visually impaired child, however, may not possess these skills when he or she comes to the center. You will need to teach these skills. You will also need to teach the child the classroom areas. Do this by repeatedly guiding the child from one area to another.

Physical Disabilities

Most preschool children can crawl, walk, run, climb, and move their bodies in different ways. A child with a physical impairment may have a limited range of motion. Due to this limitation, his or her experiences may vary from those of his or her peers.

Types of Physical Disabilities

Children who are physically impaired are grouped based on their ability to function. Disabilities are classified as severe, moderate, or mild. Children with severe impairments usually cannot move independently. Typically, they have to be carried, pushed, or moved about using a wheelchair. Children with moderate impairments can do more for themselves, but they still require much help from staff members. Due to their need for accessible facilities and adaptations, children with severe or moderate physical impairment are not often enrolled in nonadapted child care centers.

Children with mild physical impairments can often do what most other children do, 31-13. These children may need to use walking aids or other devices to help them move about. As can be expected, they will need more time to move about or to do tasks.

The children you will meet in the typical child care center will be *ambulatory*. They will be able to move from place to place. You may elect, however, to work in a center that caters to children with special needs. In these centers, you will observe a higher staff-to-child ratio. This is necessary to meet the special needs of these children.

Workplace Connection

Have students research changes a child care center must make to become wheelchair accessible. Have students note such factors as carpeting or rugs; doorways, ramps, and doorknobs; space between furniture; height of furniture; and nonslip flooring, grab bars, and height of bathroom fixtures. Have students check the child care center for these factors. What problems might need to be addressed?

31-13

Children who use a wheelchair can often use the playground equipment with a little help from teachers.

Cerebral Palsy

Cerebral palsy is a neurological disorder that results from damage to the brain. This damage can be caused by an infection or improper nutrition during pregnancy, physical injury to the brain during birth, or lack of oxygen during birth. It can also be acquired during the developmental years as a result of a tumor, head injury, or brain infection. Cerebral palsy is characterized by lack of control of voluntary movements.

Speech or expressive communication problems are often found in children with cerebral palsy. These problems are caused by the inability to control the muscles used to make speech sounds. Speech is a motor function in which hundreds of small muscles are involved.

If a child in your group has a speech disorder, consult with the parents and a speech clinician. A child with severe cerebral palsy may benefit from use of an *augmentative communication device* such as a board containing pictures of commonly referred to objects. Thus, the child can point to a picture of a glass of milk when he or she is thirsty.

Children with cerebral palsy also often lack fine-motor skills. Many of their self-help skills are impaired. Eating utensils and other equipment may be difficult for them to use. An occupational therapist and the child's parents can best advise what type of eating utensils, crayons, and other items are most useful. Modifications may be needed on equipment. For example, you may want to glue large wooden knobs on puzzles so the child with cerebral palsy can remove and insert the pieces. A wide range of adapted toys and personal care devices are available. Consult your nearest rehabilitation technology center for suggested adaptive aids.

Spina Bifida

Spina bifida is a condition in which the bones of the spine fail to grow together. The nerves are left exposed. This results in paralysis. This is a congenital problem. The cause of spina bifida is unknown. Children with this problem often lack bowel and bladder control. They often cannot tell when they have eliminated because of lower body paralysis.

In order for a child with spina bifida to focus on learning activities, he or she needs to feel comfortable. You may need to ask such questions as "Are you comfortable?" or "Do you want to sit another way?" To provide the best environment for this child, discuss positions with the parents and physical therapist. They may suggest positions that will provide the child with a sense of balance. Specific questions you may want to ask them include "Should learning activities be on the floor or table?" and "Should the classroom tables be modified?"

Muscular Dystrophy

Muscular Dystrophy is a genetic condition characterized by weakness in the muscles. This results in a progressive loss of muscle tissue. In time, the muscles of the legs, chest, and arms progressively weaken as fatty tissue replaces muscle tissue. Some children with muscular dystrophy are able to control

Vocabulary

Have a student volunteer define *cerebral palsy*. How is a child with cerebral palsy helped by using an *augmentative communication device?*

Activity

Have students research school supply catalogs and online sources for information about products designed especially for classrooms that serve children with physical disabilities. What products are available for body control and gross-motor skills? What products are available for promoting the use of fine-motor skills?

Enrich

Invite a health care professional to class to answer students' questions about cerebral palsy, spina bifida, and muscular dystrophy.

Putting Technology to Use

Have students conduct an Internet search on the latest research on spina bifida. What possible causes or risk factors have been associated with spina bifida? What is the role of folic acid and fetal alcohol syndrome as possible factors in the condition? How does spina bifida affect the body? Locate statistics on the disease and describe the treatment possible.

Vocabulary

Have a student volunteer define *prosthesis*. What is the teacher's role in caring for a child who uses a prosthesis?

Activity

Ask students to visit a program or class that serves the needs of children with disabilities. Observe the modifications that have been made in the classroom. What type of equipment is used to help children participate as much as possible in the class activities?

Enrich

Ask a volunteer from a center or school that transports children to visit your class. Ask them to demonstrate to students how a wheelchair is secured in the vehicle.

their finger and hand muscles. Their fine-motor muscles are more easily retained and exercised than gross-motor muscles.

When working with a child with this disability, it is important to interact closely with the agency working with the family. There are certain therapeutic techniques that can be taught to families and caregivers. Exercises for stretching the child's weakened muscles might help delay some of the progression.

Amputation

At some point, you may have a child in your classroom who is missing a hand, arm, or leg. Perhaps the severed limb resulted from an accident or cancer. Sometimes the limb is missing from birth. A child who is missing a limb is often fitted with an artificial limb called a *prosthesis*. Research has shown that young children adjust to an artificial limb quite easily.

In order to use a prosthesis, it must fit and be cared for properly. To avoid frustrating the child, you, as a teacher, will need to know how the artificial limb works. Parents usually welcome a teacher's questions related to the device. In fact, these questions assure them of your interest in providing the best care for their child. Other children will model their teacher's matter-of-fact acceptance of a prosthesis.

Teaching Suggestions

Although it is difficult for some, movement is important for all children. Children with physical disabilities may have to crawl or move with special equipment such as wheelchairs and walking aids. As a result, they need more time and energy to do fine- and gross-motor tasks. It takes them longer to use the bathroom or finish a project. To allow for this, you will need to provide time in your schedule. You may also have to make some adjustments in the facility.

Health and Safety

Accommodating Wheelchairs in Vehicles

Early childhood facilities that transport children must make sure the vehicles are ready to accommodate wheelchairs. Children in wheelchairs must be placed in the face-forward position in the vehicle. The wheels must be secured with four tie-downs that are installed according to the manufacturer's instructions. In addition, children in wheelchairs must be secured with a three-point tie restraint during transportation.

- Modify chairs to accommodate the child.
- Provide space for a child's wheelchair, crutches, cane, walker, or cart.
- Provide ramps so the child has access to the classroom.
- Raise tables so wheelchairs fit under them.
- Glue knobs on puzzle pieces so the pieces are easy to remove and replace.
- Secure all carpeting or area rugs to the floor so the child does not slip or trip on them.
- Provide two-handled mugs and deep-sided bowls rather than plates.
- Serve finger foods as often as possible at snack time.

Putting Technology to Use

Have students conduct an Internet search on prosthetics. Have students view at least three companies that make prosthetics and discover if they also offer counseling services. Have students discuss why someone may need counseling before being fitted with an artificial limb.

Health Disorders

Some children have more illness than others. These are often the children with chronic health needs. A **chronic health need** can be defined as an illness that persists over a period of time. For some children, a problem may last a lifetime, while for others, it may last a few months.

Children with health problems often have cycles of good and poor health. Since health needs are the most common type of special needs, it is vital that you be aware of a variety of these disorders.

Allergies

The most common health problem of young children is allergies. Studies note that up to 50 percent of all people have mild or severe allergies. An allergy may begin at any age. Studies also note that only a small percentage of children with allergies have been diagnosed.

An *allergy* is a reaction of the body to a substance in the environment. The offending substance is called an *allergen*. Exposure to the allergen may cause rashes, swelling, sneezing, or other reactions, 31-14. There

are four categories of allergenic substances: inhalants, ingestants, contactants, and injectables. *Inhalants* are airborne substances that are inhaled. *Ingestants* are foods, drugs, or anything taken through the mouth. *Contactants* are things that make contact with the body through touch. *Injectables* are chemicals or drugs injected into the body.

Animal dandruff, dust, feathers, fungi spores, molds, and plant pollens are all types of airborne allergenic substances. If a child in your classroom has a severe allergy to animal dandruff, you may have to remove any hamsters, gerbils, guinea pigs, or rabbits.

Beans, berries, chocolate, cinnamon, citrus fruits, corn products, cola drinks, eggs, fish, shellfish, milk, tomatoes, nuts, and wheat are typical foods to which the body reacts. Fabric dyes and fragrances or colorings added to soaps and shampoos are contactants that may also cause reactions. Aspirin, penicillin, and sulfa drugs are common drugs that are offenders. It is important that you ask parents at the time of enrollment whether their children have any known allergies.

If a child has food allergies, you will need to plan accordingly. Try to plan menus that avoid foods to which the child is allergic. At times, you may have to offer the allergic child food substitutes. For instance, if a child has an allergy to milk, you will have to supply a substitute beverage. Many times parents will provide the substitute to make sure their child is not tempted to have cow's milk.

Cosmetics, some detergents, wool, and starch are all substances that may cause an allergic reaction when they come in contact with the skin. Common reactions include a red rash and itching. These symptoms are a warning for the child to avoid contact with whatever substance caused the problem.

Some substances cause a reaction when they enter the body through the skin. Examples include the drug penicillin and the venom from bee or wasp stings. You need to be keenly aware of insect bites. For some children, these bites can be fatal.

31-14

An allergic reaction to insect bites on this child's face has caused swelling and skin irritation.

Vocabulary

Have a student volunteer define the term *chronic health need*. What do teachers of early childhood programs need to know about chronic health needs to be able to meet the needs of their students?

Discuss

What is an allergen? Have students explain the biologic mechanism that produces an allergic reaction.

Enrich

Have students debate the teacher's role in reducing a child's exposure to inhalants, ingestants, contactants, and injectables. Should a teacher be liable if a student is exposed to an allergen? Do circumstances make a difference?

Workplace Connection

Have students interview the head custodian of your school or a custodian at a local child care center. Are the products used for cleaning and sanitizing in the school safe for children who have allergies and breathing disorders? Do the cleaning techniques leave residue or fragrances in the air that might cause an allergic reaction? How is cleaning scheduled to avoid the least possible reactions by sensitive students? Have any products been recalled or dropped from use because of possible problems such as these?

Enrich

Ask the school nurse to visit the child care class to discuss the problems associated with bee and wasp stings. In a severe reaction, what treatment is needed? How is the treatment delivered?

Discuss

What program changes need to be made to safeguard the health and comfort of a child who suffers from seasonal pollen reactions? Should the child be banned from taking part in outdoor activities during periods of high pollen activity?

Reflect

Do you or any close friend or family member suffer from allergic reactions? Think of the physical effects and resulting effects on the ability to stay focused, work, and participate in activities. Why is it important for teachers of students with these reactions and feelings to be aware of how the students feel?

Bee or wasp stings usually result in redness and swelling around the wound. This indicates only a mild allergy. With a severe allergy, the child may swell all over the body and have trouble breathing. If this should occur, promptly seek medical attention. Death can result if treatment is not received immediately.

Some symptoms of allergies may be related to the season. For example, a child who is allergic to tree pollens may sneeze often in the spring. There are three major pollen seasons: early spring with tree pollens, late spring or early summer with grass pollens, and late summer and fall with weed pollens.

You may be the first to suspect allergies in a young child. Allergy symptoms are listed in 31-15. If you suspect that a child has an allergy, discuss it with his or her parent(s).

You may be responsible for some aspects of treatment for children with allergies.

There are three basic treatment methods for people with allergies. The sensitive person may avoid the offending item. For instance, if a child is allergic to chocolate, foods with chocolate should be taken out of the diet.

If the person cannot avoid the irritant, he or she may be desensitized. In this process, a doctor injects small amounts of the allergen into the body over a period of time. This builds immunities so the person is eventually able to withstand the irritant.

Finally, medication may be used to treat the symptom. For example, a person who has nasal congestion and blockage could use a medication to control this symptom.

Arthritis

Arthritis is a condition brought on by inflammation that produces painful swelling of the joints and surrounding tissues. The

31-15

Allergy Symptoms

Eyes
- pink and puffy
- red from being constantly rubbed
- dark circles underneath
- burning feeling and much tearing
- lids may appear glued together by dry mucus

Skin
- frequent rashes
- lesions
- redness and swelling
- itching and hives

Mouth
- constant dry hacking cough
- mouth breathing more common than nose breathing
- wheezing
- canker sores

Throat
- tickling
- enlargement of lymph nodes

Nose
- inability to smell
- nasal discharge
- frequent sneezing
- itchy nose

Body
- chills
- fever
- sweating
- abdominal cramps
- vomiting
- headache

Allergies are quite common in young children. As a result it is vital that you recognize symptoms of more common allergies.

Cross-Curricular Activity

Science
Have students do detailed research reports on the body's response during allergic reactions. Have students create visuals to go with their reports, such as models, posters, or slides in presentation software. Have students present their reports orally to the class.

most common form of juvenile arthritis is called *rheumatoid arthritis*. General fatigue, loss of appetite, fever, aching joints, and a stiffness of joints as they become tender from swelling are the first signs of the disease.

After 10 years, 60 to 70 percent of affected children are free from juvenile arthritis. Adults who acquire the condition have a much smaller chance of recovery.

Children with arthritis often find it difficult to remain in one position for long periods of time. They may also require more space and time to move freely from one place to another. They may need adapted toys, utensils, and clothing. Activities requiring fine-motor dexterity, such as cutting paper or stringing beads, are particularly troublesome. Rheumatoid arthritis is typically most acute in the morning and subsides somewhat during the day. Regular but moderate activity is best. When the disease is in its active stage, the child will need more rest.

Asthma

Asthma is a chronic inflammatory disorder of the airways. Symptoms include coughing, wheezing, rapid or labored breathing, shortness of breath, and chest tightness. When symptoms occur, this is called an *asthma attack*. It may last minutes, hours, or even weeks. Some children outgrow asthma as they get older, but others never do.

An asthma attack occurs when the airways are inflamed, or swollen and irritated. This is most commonly caused by exposure to an allergen. Attacks can also be caused by exposure to extremely cold or hot weather. Overexertion or excessive exercise can cause attacks, too. Asthma attacks are treated with medication. This is usually given in a fast-acting inhaler or nebulizer machine, 31-16. If the inhaled medicine does not provide relief or the child stops breathing, this is a medical emergency. You must call 911 or rush the child to the nearest emergency room.

Depending on the severity of the disease, some children also take daily medications to

31-16

A nebulizer is a machine that turns liquid medicine into a fine mist. A person with asthma can inhale the mist through the tube and mask.

reduce inflammation of the airways. These medications might be a pill or an inhaler. Their purpose is to prevent attacks. Once an attack has begun, these medications provide little or no relief.

As the teacher, your role might be to administer medications and to monitor the child's breathing. Try to teach the child to let you know when symptoms occur. If the child doesn't seem to be breathing well, take action immediately. Keep calm during the attack, and help the child stay calm, too.

Ask the parents what triggers their child's asthma and try to prevent these conditions. For example, if exposure to dust is a big trigger, be sure to keep your classroom as dust-free as possible.

Cystic Fibrosis

Cystic fibrosis is a hereditary disease that occurs almost from birth. This chronic condition involves persistent and serious lung infections; failure to gain weight; and loose,

Vocabulary

Have a student volunteer explain *arthritis* and *rheumatoid arthritis*. What are the challenges for children who have these conditions?

Note

You may have students view the Sesame Street® special "A is for Asthma" and discuss how it can help children understand this condition. The program is available on video and may also be available for download.

Activity

Ask students to name changes or modifications to the early childhood curriculum that might help prevent asthmatic children from having an attack while attending the program. What substitutions can students suggest to the changes or modifications?

Workplace Connection

Have students contact an area hospital that employs a child life specialist and arrange for an interview. What chronic health disorders affect the majority of the specialist's patients? What services does the child life specialist provide to patients and their families? What roles does the specialist play in therapeutic medical play, support during medical procedures, activities to promote normal growth and development, and supervision and education of students in the child life program?

foul-smelling stools. Some of these symptoms are caused by thick mucus produced by the sweat glands. This mucus interferes with the digestive and respiratory systems.

Seldom do children with cystic fibrosis enroll in early childhood programs. This is because they cannot risk developing lung infections, such as pneumonia. Moreover, these children must be treated under the close supervision of a doctor. If children with cystic fibrosis are enrolled, they need frequent rest and a lot of fluids. They may also need to urinate frequently. The teacher should consult with the child's doctor and parents for specific care plans.

Diabetes

Juvenile diabetes is a hereditary disease. Common symptoms of diabetes include frequent urination, loss of weight, constant hunger, itching (especially around the groin), and slow healing cuts and bruises. However, it is also possible that some affected children will not show any obvious symptoms.

With juvenile diabetes, insulin is not produced by the pancreas to burn or store foods as energy. This causes the body's sugar content to increase which, in turn, increases the sugar level of the blood. When the blood passes through the kidneys, the sugar is excreted in urine. This loss of carbohydrates is damaging to the body over time. If diabetes is not controlled, it can be fatal.

A careful diet is extremely important. A balance of proteins, fats, carbohydrates, vitamins, and minerals is necessary.

In most cases of juvenile diabetes, children need insulin injections. These are prescribed by a doctor and are usually given by the parents. Blood sugar levels may need to be checked with special medical equipment. This keeps the parents informed so they can better control the child's health.

To maintain blood sugar levels, it is necessary to balance physical activity, insulin, and diet. The child's parents and doctor can

devise a plan for this. Follow this plan as closely as possible. If an imbalance occurs, this is called an *insulin reaction*. It may include trembling, dizziness, headache, confusion, sweating, fatigue, and weakness.

In an insulin reaction, the body needs sugar right away to keep it from slipping into shock or a coma. For this reason, keep fast sources of sugar, such as orange juice or candy, with you at all times in case an insulin reaction occurs. If the child passes out as the result of an insulin reaction, call 911 or rush the child to the emergency room. This is a medical emergency.

Several teaching suggestions are important when diabetic children are enrolled in the program. These are given in 31-17.

Epilepsy

Epilepsy is a convulsive disorder caused by damage to the brain. It affects about one percent of the population. As a result of this disorder, the electrical rhythms of the central

31-17

Suggestions for Teaching Diabetic Children

- Ask the parents how to handle emergencies. Have them put these recommendations in writing. Place this information in the child's file.
- Schedule snack and lunch at the same time each day.
- Make sure diabetic children follow eating, medication, and activity plans each day.
- Keep quick sugar sources, such as candy bars, soda, or orange juice, on hand in case an insulin reaction occurs.
- Take the child immediately to a hospital emergency room if she/he becomes unconscious.

Follow these suggestions to assure that a diabetic child receives proper care in your program.

Note

Have students review their notes from Chapter 12 to remind them of the dietary information and modifications they may need to make for children with diabetes enrolled in a child care program.

Enrich

Invite the parent of a young child who has diabetes to discuss the management of this condition. What information is needed daily from the parent? What information needs to be sent home after a preschool or child care session?

Vocabulary

Have students define *epilepsy*. Why might some parents be afraid that epilepsy is contagious? How should these fears be addressed?

Putting Technology to Use

Have students conduct an Internet search for information about triggers or conditions that may cause epileptic seizures. What does current research show about the connection between video and computer games and photosensitive seizures? Can video games, rapid pattern changes on television, flashing lights, and rapid movement such as that experienced on amusement rides cause epilepsy? What are the guidelines proposed to prevent video game-induced seizures in children by the Epilepsy Foundation (**www.epilepsyfoundation.org**)?

nervous system are disturbed. Epilepsy is not a disease.

Epilepsy can cause varying degrees of reactions or seizures. Two major types are petit mal and grand mal. Petit mal seizures result in reactions that many times go unnoticed. Often, the only visible signs are the fluttering of the eyelids, frozen postures, staring, and a temporary stop in activity. This type of seizure may only last five to ten seconds.

As a teacher, you may not always notice a petit mal seizure. You may notice the child's behavior is strange or he or she may not be paying attention. During the seizure, the child may have only a brief lapse of consciousness. Most of these seizures do not require medical attention.

Grand mal seizures are much more pronounced. During a grand mal seizure, a child will lose consciousness. He or she may also jerk, thrash, or become stiff. The child may also be injured by hitting objects or biting the tongue.

When the child regains consciousness, he or she may be confused. In fact, the seizure will not be remembered. Instead, the child may get up and continue with classroom activities.

Epilepsy is treated primarily with drugs. These drugs will either prevent or reduce the frequency of the seizures. Unfortunately, many drugs for epilepsy cause serious side effects, such as restlessness and lethargic behavior.

There may be times when you, as a teacher, may have to control a seizure. If a child falls, you should do the following:

1. Let the child remain on the floor, clearing the area to provide him or her with ample room to thrash.

2. Remain calm.

3. Cradle the child's head in your lap. Avoid restraining movement. If possible, turn the child's body to the side, allowing saliva to drain from the mouth. This should help keep the child from choking. Never place your finger or other object in the child's mouth.

4. If the convulsion does not stop within two minutes, call for emergency medical help.

5. After the child has regained consciousness, allow him or her to remain lying down. Place a blanket over the child and allow him or her to sleep.

6. Call the child's doctor and family to inform them of the seizure and ask for advice regarding further actions.

Hemophilia

Hemophilia is a genetic blood disease in which the blood cannot clot normally. Extreme internal (under the skin) bleeding and deep bruising may result from simply bumping against something. This causes joint problems and extreme pain that may require a stay in the hospital. The real threat, however, is death caused by internal bleeding of vital organs or by blood flowing into air passages.

With the help of the parent(s), decide what equipment is safe for the child to use. You should also

- tag the outdoor and indoor equipment the child can use

- ask the parent(s) what to do if the child is injured

- carefully watch the child's play to prevent accidents

Leukemia

Leukemia is a form of cancer that affects the blood-forming organs and the blood. There is a sharp increase in the number of white blood cells in the bloodstream. This destroys bone marrow. Moreover, the number of healthy white blood cells decreases. Other signs and symptoms include bleeding, bruising, fever, infection, and weight loss.

Leukemia can be fatal. Children with leukemia are generally treated with chemotherapy to increase their life expectancy. These children are encouraged to

Discuss

What response should the teacher have when a child experiences an epileptic seizure during class? When is emergency medical help needed?

Vocabulary

Define *hemophilia*. What dangers does a child care or preschool classroom present for a child with hemophilia?

Discuss

Why might it be more feasible today for children with leukemia to enroll in an early childhood program? Why is focusing on these children's quality of life the most important factor?

Cross-Curricular Activity

Social Studies
Have students do research the role hemophilia played in the downfall of Imperial Russia. Why was it so devastating for the heir to the throne, Tsarevich Alexei, to be born with hemophilia? In what multiple ways was this seen as the fault of his mother, Tsarina Alexandra? What was the role of Rasputin in treating Alexei? How was Rasputin related to the eventual downfall of the Romanovs? What other European royal families at this time were affected by hemophilia? What was the source of this connection?

participate in the classroom. The focus should be on the quality of their life.

Cognitive Disabilities

The term *cognitive disability* describes a child whose intellectual functioning is significantly below the developmental milestones for his or her age. It is difficult to cite a specific cause of an intellectual disability. It can be caused by a genetic or chromosomal disorder. Other causes may include prenatal or postnatal injuries or environmental conditions.

Mental retardation is a form of cognitive impairment. This term is used when a child's intellectual functioning is significantly lower than average. Mental retardation has varying degrees of severity, as well as many potential causes. Down syndrome is the most common.

Down Syndrome

Down Syndrome, a chromosome disorder, is the most identifiable form of mental retardation. People with Down Syndrome usually have very distinct physical features. These include a small round head with a flattened mid-face, slightly pugged nose, and large tongue. In addition, individuals with Down Syndrome typically have slightly slanted eyes, small ears, and short fingers. People with this condition may also have other physical health problems. See 31-18.

Learning Disabilities

Although children who have learning disabilities are in almost every classroom, their disabilities can be hard to define. Generally, a **learning disability** means having a problem with one or more basic skills of learning.

Children with learning disabilities model some common traits. They may have trouble

31-18

Most children with Down Syndrome have distinct physical features and happy, loving personalities.

following directions or have poor memory skills. After listening to a story, some children cannot remember it. They may have problems storing, processing, and producing information. Others have problems identifying or reproducing numbers and letters. Poor hand-eye coordination skills may be another trait.

These learning disability traits may occur in varying patterns. As a teacher, you will need to carefully observe all children for signs of possible learning disabilities. Remember, there are marked differences in young children.

Likewise, there are marked differences within a normal range of development. You may find that children who have disabilities in one area of development are developing normally in other areas.

Attention Deficit Disorder

Five to ten percent of school-age children have trouble focusing and staying on task. They are easily distracted. These children have an *attention deficit disorder (ADD)*. Many children with this disorder are also overactive, restless, and impulsive. This condition is called *attention deficit hyperactivity*

Discuss

What behavior can early childhood teachers expect from children who have attention deficit disorder and attention deficit hyperactivity disorder?

Vocabulary

Have a student volunteer define *learning disability*. Why shouldn't child care students conclude that a child has a learning disability if he or she exhibits a few of the traits listed on *Identifying Children with Learning Disabilities*, transparency master 31-1?

Discuss

The teacher has just introduced a new student, Charlie, to the preschool class. She told the children that Charlie has ADHD; has trouble listening and following directions; and will need a lot of help from everyone in the class to help him fit in. What is wrong with this introduction in timing and content? What would you improve?

Workplace Connection

Have students contact the special education department in your school for information on learning disabilities. What is the percentage of students with learning disabilities serviced in your school district? What are the most typical learning disabilities represented? What types of teachers or specialists assist children with these needs? What are the roles of the special education teachers, classroom teachers and aides, specialists, parents, and student advocates in meeting the needs of students with learning disabilities?

disorder (ADHD). Often such children become hostile and fail to follow classroom limits.

Attention deficit hyperactivity disorder affects more boys than girls. For every girl, there are five boys affected. The cause of ADHD is not known. However, children identified as having ADHD are usually treated with drugs that have a calming effect. Many of these children also receive behavior therapy.

Social or Emotional Impairment

A **behavioral disorder** is a condition that affects an individual's social and emotional functions. These challenges can include attention deficit disorder, hyperactivity, or conduct disorder. The most commonly known condition is autism.

Autism

Children with **autism** are unable to interact with others socially. Their language development is atypical. They also display ritualistic and compulsive behavior, although behaviors vary from child to child. Typically this disorder first becomes noticeable at about 2½ years of age. Usually there are more boys than girls with this impairment. Some children with autism may also have mental retardation.

One of the first signs of early infantile autism is the resistance to being hugged or cuddled. When held, these children typically will not mold to the caregiver's body. Likewise, they fail to make eye contact or use nonverbal communication. Self-stimulating behaviors such as rocking and head flapping are characteristic. These children often treat others like lifeless objects. Simple changes in routines, such as providing a different type of spoon, may bring about a violent temper tantrum. See Chart 31-19 for a list of behaviors children with autism may display.

Working with these children is challenging. Consistency is needed in both

31-19

Possible Behavioral Symptoms of Children with Autism

- Resist hugging and cuddling
- Lack social gestures such as waving and smiling
- Fail to respond to name
- Exhibit unreadable facial expressions
- Upset by changes in routines
- Throw temper tantrums without apparent reason
- Preoccupied with repetitive behaviors
- Unaware of dangers

Children with autism commonly demonstrate these traits

classroom routines and environment. When interacting with children with autism, use simple and direct speech. The classroom focus should be on promoting language, appropriate behaviors, and interactions with others. Forming a partnership with the child's family and other professionals is important.

Integrating Children with Special Needs

The number of children with special needs who can be accommodated in a center classroom varies. Several factors must be considered: the teachers' training and experience, the ratio of adults to children, and the specific needs of the children.

Regardless of a child's needs, he or she should be grouped with others based on developmental level, not age. This requires careful observation of the child before grouping.

It is important for children with special needs to enjoy the center, 31-20. Some of these children have not had a full range of home and neighborhood experiences. Others

Resource

Identifying Children with Learning Disabilities, transparency master 31-1, TR

Reflect

Which is more important: grouping children according to developmental level or according to age? Why?

Resource

Physical and Health Disorders, Activity C, SAG

Putting Technology to Use

Have students conduct an Internet search for the latest research on ADD, ADHD, and Oppositional Defiant Disorder. What drug therapies are recommended in handling these disorders?

How do they work? What are the roles of diet, counseling, family therapy, and biofeedback in treating the symptoms of these disorders? Have students report their findings to the class.

Resource

Helping Children Who Have Special Needs, Activity D, SAG

Discuss

When a child with special needs makes a short visit to the class before his or her first day, what are the benefits to the teacher, child, parents, and students? What teacher preparation is needed before the visit?

Resource

A Child with Special Needs, reproducible master 31-3

Encouraging a child with special needs to try new experiences may help the child enjoy being at the center.

receive painful medical treatment. For these children, the center will provide a chance for companionship and education.

At times, to meet the individual needs of the children properly, you must ask for help from a specialist. For example, if a child has a speech problem, a speech therapist can be most valuable. The therapist can also help you plan activities for the child.

If the parent does not remain with a child on a first visit, provide the parent(s) with feedback on the progress of that time. Parents will be most interested in their child's adjustment to the school setting. Some teachers make a habit of either verbally sharing some positive experiences or writing a short note each day during the child's first week or two.

The children in your classroom should be prepared for a child with special needs. Explain any changes that will need to be made in the classroom. As you talk to the children, be positive and focus on strengths. This will help your group of children focus on positive expectations.

Inform the other children about this child. Some children are afraid of children with special needs. They fear the disorder

or illness is contagious. Create an open climate in which children are free to ask questions and discuss differences, 31-21. The older preschooler should be encouraged to educate classmates about his or her disability. Sometimes children's parents influence their attitude toward a classmate who has a disability. Respond to parent's concerns or fears while maintaining the right to privacy of the child with special needs.

Develop a few simple rules for classroom behavior. Stress to the children that the child with special needs should be encouraged to be independent. Young children may want to be overly helpful. This type of behavior can cause dependence and prevent a child from developing to his or her fullest potential. As children become more independent, they feel better about themselves.

Puppets that represent people with disabilities may help prepare children for classmates with special needs.

Meeting Special Needs

Ask the gifted students in your class who may have been assigned to an accelerated program to share their experiences by answering the following questions: How did you feel being the youngest student in the class? Did the teacher have higher expectations for you than for the rest of the class? Was the term *gifted* ever used inappropriately when the teacher or other students referred to you? What changes or additions would you suggest for the program for gifted students in your school district?

As a teacher, your attitude toward the child with special needs will set the classroom tone. To make yourself feel comfortable, study the disorder or illness before the child begins at the center, 31-22. If the child is already enrolled and the condition has just become known, learn as much as you can about it. This will help lessen any fears that you may have.

After you have learned about the disorder, arrange to have the child visit the classroom for a short period of time. This visit will reduce the fears of the child, the other children in the classroom, and perhaps the parents

Parents of the child with special needs may wish to remain with the child for the first, brief visit. This practice usually reduces the separation anxiety the child and parents may feel.

Remember that parents are the primary teachers of their children. Therefore, it is vital that parents take part in planning useful, proper learning experiences. Parents should always be involved in planning for the child's

31-22

You will feel more comfortable working with a child with special needs if you study the need in advance.

individual needs, as well as planning for complementary opportunities in the home.

Gifted Children

No one had prepared Yvonne Libby, an early childhood teacher, for all the children she would meet in her first teaching position. Thad, a two-year-old child enrolled in the program, had taught himself to read. By 10 months of age, this same child had spoken in complete sentences. Thad is a minority in Ms. Libby's classroom. He is a child who is gifted, and he needs help.

Often, gifted children's unique educational needs are neglected in traditional education. They often spend time doing things they already know. Only a small number receive instruction at the appropriate level for their needs or abilities. These children need programs and services different from those provided in the average classroom. This is vital since gifted children's skills vary more than other groups with special needs.

Giftedness

Giftedness can be defined in many ways. Traditionally, giftedness was based only on intelligence quotient scores (IQ). Today scholars argue that there are many forms of giftedness.

People who are gifted can be defined as having exceptional skill in one or more of six areas:

- creative or productive thinking
- general intellectual ability
- leadership ability
- psychomotor ability
- specific academic aptitude
- visual or performing arts

About three to five percent of young children could be gifted. These children

Vocabulary

Have students define *giftedness*. In what areas may a child be considered gifted?

Discuss

Why is *giftedness* considered a special need? Why might a child who is gifted be neglected in traditional education?

Resource

Identifying the Gifted Child, transparency master 31-2, TR

Portfolio Project

Ask students to look over some of the lesson plans they have written this year for the children in the child care lab preschool. Are the lessons suitable for working with a child who is gifted? What additional information, activities, or enrichment would students add to make lessons appropriate for a gifted child? Could they manage to do this without making lessons that would be too difficult for other children?

Vocabulary

Ask a student volunteer to define *acceleration* and *enrichment*. How do these strategies attempt to meet the needs of a gifted child in the regular education system?

Activity

Have students consult your school superintendent or gifted coordinator for information on how your school district meets the needs of children who are gifted. What factors need consideration in placing a child in a class with older children?

Resource

The Child Who Is Gifted, Activity E, SAG

need to be identified so they can receive the education they require.

Identification

Identifying children who are gifted is difficult. No single test, checklist, or observation will point out all types of giftedness. During the preschool years, observations are commonly made by parents and teachers.

A child's parents are often most familiar with his or her development, interests, and abilities. Because of this, they may be better able to identify their children as gifted.

Teachers are more aware of how the child's behavior compares with that of his or her peers. However, identification of children who are gifted by the teacher is not always the best method. Studies found that teachers who identified giftedness chose about one-third of the children incorrectly. In addition, over half the children who are actually gifted were not identified by their teachers.

There are certain characteristics that can be used to identify the gifted. Many children who are gifted have a constant curiosity about many subjects. Their social and emotional behavior equals or exceeds that of children the same age. They are also more independent and motivated. Chart 31-23 lists other characteristics of children who are gifted.

Teaching Suggestions

The needs of a preschool child who is gifted can be met by including acceleration and enrichment in the program. **Acceleration** is a process in which a gifted child is assigned to a class with older children. The objective is to move the child through activities at a faster pace than children with average ability. After spending a year with older children, the child who is gifted may be ready for even older children.

In **enrichment** the range and depth of experiences is broadened to provide the child

Characteristics of Children Who Are Gifted

- Early speech
- Advanced vocabulary for age
- Keen observation skills: see more on field trips, in films, or pictures than other children
- Unusually long attention span for age
- Inquisitive nature: constantly asking questions
- Flexibility: adapt easily to new situations
- Persistence
- Strong sense of responsibility for age
- Self-criticism
- Tendency to strive toward perfection
- Good memory
- Awareness of others' feelings

Early identification of children who are gifted will promote further growth.

with a special curriculum. This process will help the child identify areas of interests.

Children who are gifted often receive enrichment through individual or small group instruction. You or a volunteer may use audiovisual materials, games, and field trips to promote learning. The key to a useful program for these children is to build educational experiences around student interests.

Provide open-ended learning activities for creative children. They prefer loosely structured activities that give them the chance to express ideas and inquire and discover on their own, 31-24.

Children who are gifted in a certain area, such as reading, should have instruction designed to match their skills. They should be provided a variety of books related to their special interests. It also helps to have an adult who will take the time to listen to the child read and tell the child about the story.

Many small group activities should be planned to build leadership skills. These

---

Workplace Connection

Invite an early childhood teacher who has taught a child who is gifted to discuss the challenges in working with gifted children. Ask the teacher to describe the special skills and behavior of the child and how he or she adapted to the rest of the classmates. How important was parental communication in determining how to meet the child's needs and provide an enriching environment? What examples can the teacher give of situations, activities, and interesting anecdotes about the experience? What insight do these give the child care students about working with gifted children?

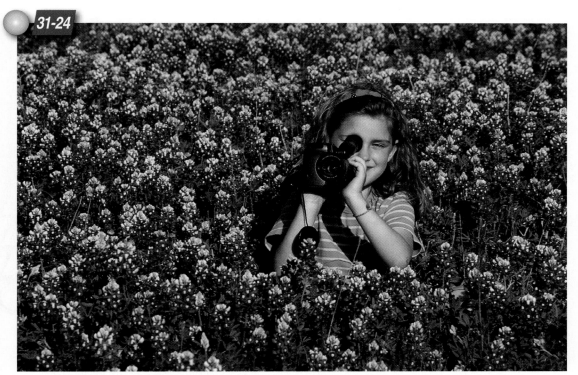

31-24

During the science theme *Plants and Flowers*, a teacher could extend learning for a gifted child by asking her to videotape plants and flowers around the building during outdoor play time.

activities provide children with opportunities to learn to plan, organize, and make decisions.

As a teacher of children who are gifted, you need to understand the problems these children face. Children who are gifted tend to be self-critical. As a result, they tend to be too hard on themselves. To help them, you will need to provide guidance so they learn to accept failure.

Sometimes, because of a critical nature, a child who is gifted will not involve himself or herself with other children. You will need to help the child learn to be considerate of others. This will help improve his or her social skills.

Resource

Special Needs Match, Activity A, SAG

Discuss

A child who is gifted may have special talents and the intellectual abilities of an older child. However, he or she may not have the social skills and behavior expected of older students. What false assumptions might teachers make when gifted children are enrolled in their class?

Resource

Observing a Child with Special Needs, Activity A, OG

Meeting Special Needs

Review the special learners' chapter outlines to determine if the students have any questions about the concepts or content of this chapter. Review the chapter objectives and ask the students to evaluate their progress in meeting these objectives. Ask the student to summarize, orally or in writing, what they have learned from this chapter.

Review and Reflect Answer Key

1. Communication
2. Inclusion
3. (1) A description containing an assessment of the child's current level of performance and skill development.
(2) Annual goals for the child. (3) Short-term educational objectives.
(4) A statement outlining the involvement of the child in the regular educational program.
(5) Specific services that will be provided with a time line noting the dates services will begin and end. (6) Evaluation criteria that will be used to decide if educational goals are met.
4. hearing
5. p, b, m, w
6. omissions, distortions, substitutions
7. Amblyopia
8. Nearsightedness is an inability to see things that are far away. Farsightedness is an inability to see objects that are close by.
9. Consult with the child's parents, a speech clinician, and possibly an occupational therapist. Supply eating utensils and play items that can be used even with poor fine-motor skills. Possibly adapt some toys such as putting large wooden knobs on puzzle pieces.
10. Spina bifida

Summary

All children, including those with special needs, are entitled by law to an appropriate education. As a result, you may have children with special needs in your center.

Children with special needs require Individualized Education Plans. As a teacher, you will need to know how to identify a child with special needs. You must then work to provide the child the most effective education possible. Teachers must be able to accommodate special needs of children with hearing, speaking, language, vision, physical, health, cognitive, and behavioral disorders. These children must be integrated into a typical program. Teachers must also be able to identify and meet the needs of children who are gifted.

Review and Reflect

1. _____ needs are the most common special needs.

2. _____ is the term used to refer to a regular educational setting in which children with and without special needs are integrated.

3. Each Individualized Education Plan needs six components. Name them.

4. A child who is _____ impaired can often be identified by his or her lack of vocabulary and overall delays in language development compared to nondisabled children.

5. What four consonants are easiest for children to pronounce?

6. Articulation problems usually take the form of _____, _____, and _____ of vowels or consonants or both.

7. _____ is the result of a muscle imbalance caused by disuse of an eye.

8. What is the difference between nearsightedness and farsightedness?

9. What actions might you need to take if a child with cerebral palsy is enrolled in your program?

10. _____ is a condition in which the bones of the spine fail to grow together.

11. List four teaching suggestions for working with children who are physically disabled.

12. The most common health problem of young children is _____.

13. _____ is a genetic blood disease.

14. Describe the physical characteristics of children with Down Syndrome.

15. List four signs of a possible learning disability.

16. List six characteristics of a child with autism.

17. List six characteristics of a child who is gifted.

11. (Student response.)
12. allergies
13. Hemophilia
14. Physical characteristics of children with Down Syndrome may include a small round head with a flattened mid-face, slightly pugged nose, large tongue, slightly slanted eyes, small ears, and short fingers.
15. (List four:) trouble following directions or poor memory skills; problems storing, processing, and producing information; problems identifying or reproducing numbers and letters; poor hand-eye coordination

Apply and Explore

1. Discuss the disadvantages of labeling children's special needs.

2. List items found in a child care center that may cause an allergic reaction in children.

3. Contact your state's Department of Education. Request information on early childhood programs for children with special needs.

Cross-Curricular Link

Language Arts

1. Interview a speech therapist about stuttering.

Technology

2. Go to the Web site for the National Dissemination Center for Children and Youth with Disabilities at www.nichcy.org. Click on your state to obtain the State Resource Sheets.

3. Check the Web site for the National Association for Gifted Children (www.nagc.org) for information on teaching gifted children.

Workplace Link

Investigate the health policies for licensed child care facilities in your state. Are facilities required to have a health form signed by a physician for each child in their care? Locate a sample of the health form to review. Have students note what types of important health information are required. After admittance, are any other follow-up physicals required for children? Compare this to the required physicals for children attending school in your state.

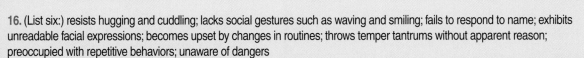

16. (List six:) resists hugging and cuddling; lacks social gestures such as waving and smiling; fails to respond to name; exhibits unreadable facial expressions; becomes upset by changes in routines; throws temper tantrums without apparent reason; preoccupied with repetitive behaviors; unaware of dangers

17. (List six:) early speech, advanced vocabulary for age, keen observation skills, attention span is unusually long for age, inquisitive nature, flexible, persistent, responsible for age, self-critical, strive toward perfection, good memory, awareness of others' feelings

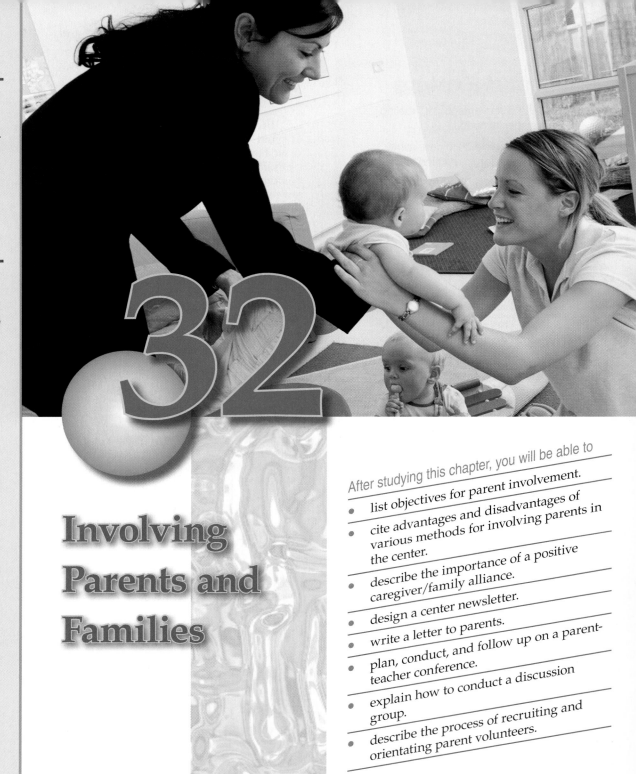

Discuss

Look at the chapter opening photo. What type of environment is this teacher creating for children and families? How can this teacher build positive relationships with parents?

Discuss

Look over the chapter objectives before reading the chapter to get a sense of the material to be covered. What new skills do you expect to develop as a result of studying this chapter?

32

Involving Parents and Families

After studying this chapter, you will be able to

- list objectives for parent involvement.
- cite advantages and disadvantages of various methods for involving parents in the center.
- describe the importance of a positive caregiver/family alliance.
- design a center newsletter.
- write a letter to parents.
- plan, conduct, and follow up on a parent-teacher conference.
- explain how to conduct a discussion group.
- describe the process of recruiting and orientating parent volunteers.

Terms to Know

parent involvement
newsletters
letters
daily news flash
home visits
traveling backpack
problem-solving file
sunshine calls
theme bags

Frequent, two-way communication between teachers and parents creates an environment that welcomes families. The teacher-parent relationship is vital. Parents need caregivers for reassurance and emotional support. Caregivers need to learn from family members to create an environment that reflects the children's home experience. To do this, they need to learn the parenting beliefs and culture of the family. This can only occur by building partnerships between child care teachers and parents.

Parent involvement refers to patterns of participation in educational programs by parents. There is no one model of parent-program interaction. Parent involvement activities may include assisting in the classroom, helping with fund-raising activities, home teaching, supplying classroom resources, and attending parent education classes. Parent involvement can be the key factor in the success of a program, 32-1.

It is unfortunate, then, that little information has been written about the parent-teacher relationship. At times, staff and parents fail to view each other positively. Historically, teachers have neglected to contact parents to praise the child's efforts and accomplishments. Likewise, parents have neglected to express their appreciation of the teachers' roles.

32-1

A parent's involvement in a child's school program reaps many benefits for both child and parent.

The relationship between parents and teachers needs to be one of mutual support and learning. Often, teachers are surprised to learn that parents want unhurried time to experience relating with them. Parents want to learn more about their children's experiences, interests, and development. They may also want advice on how to work with their children at home. To provide this support, teachers and parents need to become partners in teaching young children.

As a teacher, you will need to build positive relationships with parents. To do this, set aside time to communicate with parents, particularly at the beginning or end of the day. During these casual conversations, share your observations and knowledge of early development behaviors. Parents also enjoy learning of their children's preferences and ways of responding to people and things. Communicate a child's strengths to the parents. Parents will then be more accepting when you have to share a child's weaknesses.

Always welcome parents to the center. Whenever possible, include them in program functions. Parents may be observers, resource people, volunteers, or guests at special celebrations. They can share a hobby or

Vocabulary

Have students review the *Terms to Know* list. Ask students to look up unfamiliar words or terms in the glossary before reading the chapter.

Discuss

How can daily casual conversations with parents before and after the program encourage mutual support in reaching the center's goals for the children? What are some other benefits you may experience through this daily communication?

Vocabulary

Have a student volunteer define the term *parent involvement*. Why is parent involvement important to the success of the early childhood program?

Meeting Special Needs

Provide an outline of the chapter with all the chapter headings for special learners. Students should fill in each section of the outline as the material is covered in class with a sentence or two about the content. Review the special learners' IEPs to decide if any modifications should be made in presenting the chapter content.

Resource

Family Relationships, reproducible master 32-1, TR

Discuss

How can information about community resources be useful to parents? Give some examples of resources in your community that might be of interest to the parents of the child care lab preschoolers.

Vocabulary

Ask students to define *newsletters, letters,* and *daily news flash* as means of parent communications. When is each of these used in the communication process?

interest as well as ethnic traditions. Studies show that teachers who are confident of their skills and abilities are more inclined to include parents in program functions. Likewise, studies show that good relationships with parents affect a teacher's feelings of self-esteem and competence as a teacher.

Studies also indicate that parental involvement affects a child's later school success. Children have better attendance and homework habits. Their attitude toward school is more positive, and they show gains in reading skills.

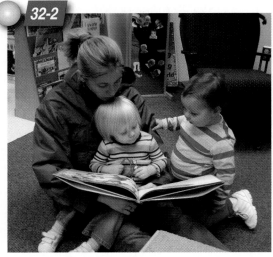

32-2

Being exposed to other parents and children means adults can find new ways to work with children.

Objectives

The purpose of parent involvement is to promote an exchange of ideas and information. Parents can gain by

- developing an understanding of child growth and development
- gaining confidence in their parenting roles
- learning about their children's experiences at the center
- understanding their children by observing other children
- learning new ways of positively interacting with children, 32-2
- becoming informed about community resources
- fostering the children's and parent's ability to interact with each other
- extending learning from the center into the home
- understanding how a partnership between center and home can promote the children's development

Family involvement can be encouraged using several methods. Some of these include written communication, class videos, parent-teacher conferences, advisory committees, and discussion groups. Newsletters are also

a way to extend learning from the center to the home. When parents see how their involvement can benefit their children, they are more likely to participate. This will promote parent-child communication.

Written Communication

Three popular forms of written communication are newsletters, letters, and daily news flashes. **Newsletters** most often include information concerning a variety of subjects. They are shared on a regular basis. **Letters** most often address only one subject and are sent out as needed. A **daily news flash** contains bits of news that parents can discuss with their children. These forms of communication are often written or printed on paper. However, e-mail is also an option that parents and teachers can use for effective communication.

Written communications are popular for one important reason. They require less time and energy for the teacher than meetings or multiple telephone calls. If a letter is sent out

---

Cross-Curricular Activity

Language Arts
Collect examples of preschool parent newsletters and other communications sent home to parents. Make a copy of the communications for each student. Have students review the examples for

evidence of simple, clear writing; accurate spelling and grammar; and concise and useful information. Ask them to correct any mistakes and change any areas that could use improvement. Allow time for students to discuss their changes in class.

Open-Door Policy

In order to encourage the development of positive parent/staff relationships and prevent the abuse of children in child care, talk with parents about program's open-door policy at the time their children are enrolled. This policy gives parents the freedom to visit the center at any time. As a care provider, you should encourage parents to speak freely about their concerns and suggestions for the care of their children.

regarding an upcoming event, the teacher need only compose one letter and then print copies of that letter for all parents.

Families also like written communication for the same reason. A newsletter can be read over a weekend, during lunch hour, or while commuting. This saves parents time and energy as well.

Use the active, not passive, voice when you write newsletters. The active voice states the subject did something. The passive voice says the subject was acted upon. For example, the active voice would say "Reza read books and painted pictures." The passive voice would say "Reading books and painting pictures were Reza's main activities."

Keep your communications short, clear, and simple for all parents. Short messages are appreciated by busy parents. Simple, clear writing prevents misinterpretation of the message.

Newsletters

A newsletter serves as a link between home and center. In most centers, the newsletter is produced and sent out on a regular basis, 32-3. A center might send out newsletters on the first Monday of each month. Other centers, depending on budgets and resources, might send out newsletters on a biweekly basis. If most parents have e-mail accounts, programs can send newsletters by e-mail to lower their costs.

32-3

A newsletter can be written quickly using a computer.

Discuss

Why should you use the active voice when writing newsletters? Give examples of active voice sentences.

Enrich

Have students debate the pros and cons of sending home a regular parent newsletter by means of e-mail. Students should take a poll of parents of young children to discover their viewpoint on the topic.

Resource

Happy-Gram, color transparency CT-27, TR

Workplace Connection

If a parent newsletter is not already part of the child care lab program, have students make a sample newsletter. Students can use a desktop publishing program for an easy-to-use format for the newsletter. Have students select a title such as *(Program Name) News*

and Notes. Prepare a heading with the school contact information and date. Select some suitable clip art to create interest. Ask student volunteers to write, proofread, type, and edit the articles and print the newsletter.

Note

When should you use a newsletter and when will a letter suffice? Letters can be sent to inform parents of upcoming events and suggestions and can be specific in nature. Newsletters can briefly highlight the most recent activities and include mention of upcoming ones on a calendar of events.

Resource

Family Letters, Activity B, SAG

Activity

Have students list events that occurred in the child care lab this year that would make appropriate items for a newsflash. Ask students to design a simple poster for the bulletin board where the daily newsflash could be posted.

A newsletter may include the following:

- review of special activities
- special classroom-related activities for children to do in the home
- guidance tips
- upcoming special events at the center
- short articles of interest
- summaries of books or articles related to parenting
- nutritious recipes
- child development information
- a want-ad section
- a help-wanted section asking for parent volunteers
- upcoming community events of interest to young children and their families
- a "meet the staff" section
- recognition for parent contributions
- a parent exchange section
- reminders of center policies
- welcome for new families and teacher
- classroom celebrations and birthdays
- classroom needs

The design of a newsletter can also allow for a blank section. This section can be used by the teacher to write a brief, personal note. This should be a positive note about the child. For instance, a teacher may write, "I'm so pleased with James; he has learned how to tie his shoes."

Another section could also be provided for parents. After reading the newsletter, families might write their comments and/or thoughts. Perhaps they could respond to the newsletter or submit ideas or information for future issues. This way, the newsletter can be a two-way communication tool.

Letters

Letters are another useful written communication tool. Letters can be used to touch base with one parent or an entire group of parents. Letters are often one page long and sent as needed. Parent letters can serve as a supplement to newsletters.

The first letter sent to families should introduce the teachers and staff. This letter can also address classroom goals, rules, and expectations. The first letter should also welcome family members to observe and/or take part in center activities.

After the first letter, subsequent letters should include the current theme. Special center activities should be noted, along with the goals. New songs and fingerplays should be written out with the accompanying music or actions that go with them. Field trip sites, dates, and times should be included. Parents should also be thanked for any favors. Home learning activities for the parents to do with their child should be shared. Include with these activities a rationale for their use. This will make families feel involved in their child's education. An example of a parent letter is shown in 32-4.

At times, you may choose to send home a special letter during the week. This letter should outline something special the children did on a special day. It may be an event, such as a field trip, or an activity within the classroom, 32-5. This letter can promote a learning experience between parents and children.

Daily News Flash

Parents and teachers may be too busy for daily in-depth, face-to-face communication. A daily news flash can be an effective tool for communicating with parents. The flash may contain news about special occasions or interesting events such as the following:

- This morning we made blueberry muffins and ate them at snacktime.
- Erica lost her tooth today during lunch.
- Mrs. Huth is the new center cook.
- Henry is the name of the center's pet gerbil.
- Toby has a new baby brother named Ivan.
- We learned a new song today about apples.

Portfolio Project

Have students write a sample letter to indicate their skill in this form of parent communication. Ask students to select a theme or topic they have taught or supervised in the child care lab and write a letter to inform the parents about the activities their children will experience. Be sure to include some at-home activity suggestions for the parents and children to do together. Keep the length of your letter to one side of a letter-sized sheet of paper. Have students file a copy of the letter in their portfolio.

32-4

Dear Families,

Our curricular emphasis next week is "Eating Well: Foods for Good Health." This will be a continuation of our Self-Awareness unit. We have previously explored how our bodies work and the importance of exercise.

The children will be involved in a wide variety of experiences. We will play "fruit basket upset," make collages of foods that are good for us, play "grocery store," participate in having a "pickle party," paint with onions and potatoes, and enjoy tasting a variety of fruits. Thursday will be a very special day—our trip to Connell's Orchard! The children will watch apples being washed, dried, sorted, bagged, and boxed. We will taste "Connell Reds" and drink some delicious apple cider. After the trip, we will write a language experience chart.

Center Activities
Our learning experiences will focus on "Foods for Good Health." Activities will include
- preparing and eating mini-pizzas (with smiley faces of pepperoni and green peppers)
- creating mosaics of eggshells
- having a play restaurant in our dramatic play area
- acting out a "Good Breakfast" version of *The Three Bears* (which the children heard last week)
- making applesauce
- mixing colors with eyedroppers
- reading "Bread and Jam for Frances"

Home/School Connection
Activities you can do at home to reinforce the concepts learned at the center include
- visiting a grocery store, identifying foods in MyPyramid for Kids: grains; vegetables; fruits; milk; meat & beans; and oils
- looking through old magazines, cutting out pictures, and making a collage of "Good Foods" for the whole family
- reading labels with your child, especially focusing on fat and sugar (in their many forms) content within certain foods
- encouraging your child to try new foods (you can, too)
- allowing your child to help in the kitchen
- involving your child in planning what to eat for a meal

Here's to healthful eating!

Sincerely,

Miss Judy

Use detailed, descriptive language when writing a family letter. It is an inexpensive way to keep all families informed.

Discuss

How can a letter such as the one in 32-4 encourage parent-child communication about the upcoming week's activities? How can a child benefit from the reinforcement he or she might receive at home?

Reflect

Letters can be an effective way to communicate with parents. What information would you want to include in your first letter to parents?

Discuss

What is the difference between a letter and a daily news flash? What information is contained in a daily news flash? Which of these forms of communication might be more effective when dealing with a very busy parent?

Workplace Connection

Unexpected events at school might cause confusion and distress for children. Have students discuss situations that might require a special letter to be sent home. Have them offer suggestions that might be included in the letter. Example: an unexpected fire drill or severe weather drill may make children anxious and fearful of returning to school. A letter may help parents explain the need for the drill to their children, reassure children they will always be there to pick them up, and explain their teacher will make sure they are safe.

Activity

Have students
practice using video-
recording equipment in
the classroom so they
can develop proficiency
in recording and editing
events in the child
care lab. Contact your
school's technology
department for advice
and suggestions on
using the equipment.

Discuss

What can parents gain
from parent-teacher
conferences about their
children? How does the
teacher benefit from
conferences?

Note

Remind students that
Appendix B, *Develop-
mental Traits of Children
from Birth to Age 12*,
might be helpful informa-
tion to review for parent
conferences. Students
will need developmental
checklists filled out for
each child in their class.

32-5

We went to the apple orchard today.
We rode in a big yellow bus.
We saw many trees with apples on them.
We observed the beauty of apples on the trees.
The guide showed us four parts of an apple—
    stem, skin, meat, and core.
We tasted green, yellow, and red apples.
Tomorrow we will make applesauce.

To: Families
From: Miss Libby
Activity: Field Trip to the Apple Orchard

This letter is intended to promote discussion between families and children.

The daily news flash may be posted at the center's main entrance, on a classroom door, or on a bulletin board. Some teachers even use a computer screen to share this information on a daily basis. Others have been successful in videotaping classroom experiences and sharing them using a television monitor.

Class Videos

Prepare videos of the children involved in activities that can be checked out and shared with families. You may want to tape special days such as birthdays and other holiday celebrations. Tapes of favorite fingerplays and stories can also be interesting. Families enjoy tapes of children participating in theme-related activities. Tape them in the dramatic play area acting out stories, building with blocks, preparing foods, and experimenting with creative media.

Parent-Teacher Conferences

Parent-teacher conferences are one way to involve parents in their children's center program. Conferences help parents and teachers develop a shared understanding of the child. Parents will share what children are like at home. Teachers will share what children are like at the center. When these two viewpoints are shared, staff and parents can see themselves as a team sharing developmental information, 32-6. Plans can then be made to better meet the needs of the children.

Parent-teacher conferences can be a way to bridge a culture gap between home

32-6

Through parent-teacher conferences, the parent can gain insight into how best to work with a child at home.

Workplace Connection

Invite an administrator in your school to discuss the need for parent-teacher conferences. How are the conferences conducted for high school students similar to those for young children? How can teachers make parents feel like an important partner in their child's education?

Based on past experience, what situations in parent-teacher conferences cause the most challenges for teachers? How can you prepare to meet those challenges? Have students write a list of additional questions to ask prior to the visit.

and center. Parents from other cultures may be unfamiliar with the American approach to early childhood education. They may not understand what is expected of their children or how to help the children succeed. To help these parents, teachers can explain the program goals, schedule, and competencies the children will gain. Parents can explain how their culture views the role of early childhood education. Teachers can use this information to better understand the family and make learning experiences more culturally relevant for the children.

There are three phases to parent-teacher conferences. The first phase is planning. The second phase is the individual conference. The final phase is the follow-up.

Planning

Planning includes setting basic rules that will help you work successfully with the parents. Before the conference, spend time planning. A good conference does not just happen. It needs to be carefully planned if you are to win the respect of the parents. The responsibility for the success of the conference lies largely on you as the teacher.

Conferences provide an opportunity to review each child's progress and plan future goals. This time should provide an objective review of the child's total development. Begin the planning phase by gathering assessment materials and samples of the child's work. Gather records on the child's emotional, social, cognitive, and physical development. This information can most often be obtained from developmental checklists and from anecdotal records.

Some teachers use planning sheets to prepare for conferences. After reviewing all anecdotal records and developmental records, this information is recorded on the planning sheet. Included are the following:

- daily routines
- types of play
- activity preferences

- fine-motor skills
- gross-motor skills
- social-emotional development
- relationships with children and adults
- cognitive development
- language development
- eating habits
- sleeping habits

The planning sheet is divided into sections. For instance, one section might cover these routines: dressing, cleanup, rest patterns, eating, and toileting, 32-7.

Be prepared to share children's portfolios with their parents. Begin by collecting notes, developmental assessments, and observations. Then continue by collecting some of the children's artwork to share with the parents. Make sure that the child's name and date are on each piece. Photographs, tape recordings, and notes can also be useful. If developmentally appropriate, ask each child

---

32-7

Routines

Dressing:
_____ needs _____ some _____ much help
no help

Cleanup:
_____ accepts _____ helpful _____ needs
prompting

Nap time:
_____ accepts _____ resists

Eating:
_____ good _____ fair _____ finicky eater

Toileting needs:
_____ needs _____ some _____ much help
no help

If you use a planning sheet, you may wish to divide notes into sections.

Discuss

What are the three phases to parent-teacher conferences? When planning for a parent-teacher conference, what assessment materials and samples would you want to gather?

Activity

Ask students to write a brief essay about their understanding of planning for conferences and what they would do to plan for a parent-teacher conference. Allow time for students to read and discuss their essays in class.

Discuss

Why should the child's portfolio be an important part of the parent-teacher conference? Should portfolios be handed out to parents at the conference or should they be saved until the end of the school year? Explain.

Workplace Connection

Have students interview area preschool teachers and other early childhood education professionals to discover how often planning sheets are used to prepare for conferences. If possible, obtain samples of the different types of planning sheets. Have students write a brief report of their findings. Allow time for students to share their reports with the class.

Enrich

Debate the pros and cons of conducting a parent-teacher conference in the child's own home. Are there any programs you know about that offer this option for busy parents?

Activity

Ask students to draft a letter to parents explaining the purpose of the parent-teacher conference. Allow time for students to share their letters with the class.

Note

A sample parent-teacher conference letter and questionnaire, in addition to other templates, can be downloaded for use at the Education World™ Web site at **www.education-world. com/tools_templates/ index.shtml**.

to tell you a story about a picture. Record the story as the child speaks.

Video recordings are also popular for use in parent-teacher conferences. A week or two before a conference, videotape each child engaging in classroom activities. Allow three to five minutes per child. Review the tape before the conference, and note the start and stop numbers for each child.

Parent Availability

A brief letter can be sent home explaining the purpose of the parent-teacher conference. Tell parents that conferences are a routine part of communication. It is a time to share progress, thoughts, and ideas. Moreover, it is a time to ask questions and provide information that may be helpful to teachers. Include in the letter the date(s) the conferences will be held. See 32-8.

These dates should accommodate parents' schedules whenever possible. Before

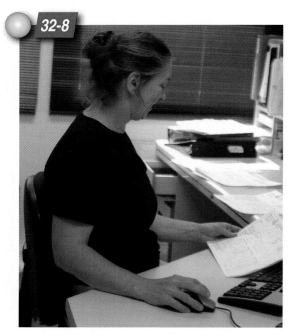

32-8

Many parents will sign up eagerly for parent-teacher conferences. For others, a phone call might be necessary to set up an appointment.

you begin scheduling parents for specific time slots, ask about their availability on the scheduled date(s). Try to schedule conferences for the times parents find most convenient. Your teaching schedule may also make it difficult to find times for conferences. You might try scheduling conferences

- during nap time (teachers can alternate conferences and supervising nap time)

- before or after program hours

- by hiring a substitute teacher for one day each month

- by hiring a substitute teacher for lunchtime if working parents can come at this time

- by dismissing center activities for a day every two to three months (this may not be a desirable option if parents cannot find alternate care)

Generally, each conference should last about half an hour. Allot 10 minutes between conferences. This will give you a chance to record any needed information. It will also provide time if a conference runs longer than planned. If families have two or more children at the center, it is considerate to schedule consecutive conferences. When evening conferences are scheduled, provide child care for the children.

Another option is to schedule parent-teacher conferences in the family's home. Dual-worker or single-parent families may find this appointment most convenient. Teachers can learn more about the child's home environment from this visit. This scheduling is most costly because it involves time and expense for the teacher to travel to the homes. As a result, not many centers offer this alternative.

A scheduled home visit can be valuable for the teacher. Seeing the child's home environment can provide a better understanding of the child. The teacher can observe parent-child interactions as well as the home environment.

Service Learning Activity

If area preschool and child care centers must schedule parent-teacher conferences after school or in the evening, consider having the child care students offer to provide babysitting and child care during the conferences. Contact the area programs to discover if they are interested in the students' services. Students may also be needed to provide child care for their own school district parent-teacher conferences. Contact the school superintendent and school principals to coordinate a child care service project.

First Impressions

The first impression you make with children's parents is important. Be prepared. Have your notes outlined, including what you would like to discuss. Use your notes during the conference. This will show the parents you are well prepared.

As you think through the conference, keep in mind you will set the tone for it. If you are nervous and anxious, parents will likely feel the same way. If you are calm, parents will likely be calm, too. Your goal is to set the proper tone for a successful meeting.

Questions

You may ask parents questions during the conference to help them think. For instance, invite them to share how their children act at home and what their children's interests are. It is best to plan your questions before the meeting.

Ask open-ended questions if you want more than a yes or no answer. The "w" questions are many times the most successful. These include *why, what, when,* and *where. How* is also considered a "w" question. Make sure to provide parents opportunities to share and ask questions.

The Setting

The conference setting can greatly influence success. Find an area in the center that is private with adult-sized chairs and a table. No interruptions should occur during the conference. To ensure this, place a sign on the door that states a parent-teacher conference is in session and must not be interrupted. If the conference is scheduled in an office, take the telephone off the hook or arrange for messages to be taken.

When an office is used, set chairs in a grouping that will help create a feeling of a partnership. Likewise, avoid sitting behind a desk. This places you in the position of authority. This will decrease the feeling of a partnership.

The Conference

Always begin and end the conference with a positive comment. Parents always enjoy hearing something positive about their child. As you share the comment, try to be relaxed. If you are tense, the parents will be aware of it.

Be prepared to assume the role of a good listener. Good listening involves using your eyes, ears, and heart. This is critical for effective communication. Use positive nonverbal body language. Show interest by maintaining eye contact and encouraging facial expressions.

Avoid making general statements. "Tommy is doing fine" or "Jodi is doing well in school" does not give parents much information. Rather, be specific. For instance, you might say, "Travis has really improved in the area of routines. He no longer needs assistance with his clothing when preparing to go outside. At transition time, he takes care of his personal needs in the bathroom. At nap time, he accepts the center's rest pattern. Likewise, he no longer needs encouragement to help during cleanup. In fact, I am so pleased, for he is even encouraging other children to assist."

Watch how you word your comments. As you speak, put yourself in the parents' place. Try to imagine the effects of your remarks. You must evaluate the child's progress without being critical. To do this, always try to use a positive expression. See 32-9.

During the meeting, watch for signs of emotion. These signs may include gestures, changes in tone of voice, or expression. If the parent appears uncomfortable, provide reassurance that all information will be kept confidential.

Questions Parents Ask

"How is Divina doing?" "Does Kelly behave at the center?" "Is Kris ready for kindergarten?" All these questions are common for parents to ask. Each question can

Reflect

Four-year-old Sergio has been having trouble playing cooperatively with other children. He has been threatening children who will not let him use some play equipment and has been heard to say, "You better watch out or else you're gonna get it!" What open-ended questions related to this behavior will you ask Sergio's parents during their conference?

Discuss

Why might new child care teachers have feelings of anxiety and nervousness when dealing with parents? What strategies can help new teachers handle these emotions in order to have successful parent-teacher conferences?

Activity

Ask child care students to interview their parents about parent-teacher conferences they attended when the students were young. What information did parents find particularly useful? What do they most remember about the conference itself?

Portfolio Project

Have students search for information on how to conduct a parent-teacher conference. Have them use the information to write a *Parent-Teacher Conference Survival Guide.* Include suggestions for scheduling the conference; setting up the area where the conference will be held; wearing professional attire; and gathering the materials needed for the conference. How much of the conference time should be allotted to parents' responses and questions? Include suggestions both from print or Internet sources. Have students file a copy of the *Survival Guide* in their portfolio.

Reflect

Mr. and Mrs. Fletcher think you should spend more time working with their daughter because she's so bright and is probably smarter than all the other children in the class. What professional and respectful response should be made to the Fletchers?

Enrich

Ask student volunteers to role-play a teacher answering a parent's questions about their child at a parent-teacher conference. Have other students make sure positive responses are given in answer to the questions.

Discuss

How is interrupting a parent a sign of disrespect? How can *active listening* be useful during conferences?

32-9

Language Expressions

Negative Expressions	More Positive Expressions
troublemaker	disturbs others at story time
below age	performs at his own level
lazy	is capable of doing more
stubborn	insistent in having his own way
mean	finds it difficult to get along with others
clumsy	is not physically well coordinated
selfish	needs to learn to share with others
show-off	tries to get others' attention
messy	works too quickly

Practice using positive phrases when talking to others. Such phrases are much more acceptable than negative phrases.

have several answers. When planning for the conference, be prepared for these questions. Questions may be phrased differently, but they basically include

- Is my child happy in child care?
- How can I help at home?
- Does he or she get along with others?
- Does he or she respect others' property rights?
- How long does he or she nap?
- Does he or she eat a nutritious diet?
- Is he or she making progress in all developmental areas?
- With whom does he or she play?
- Does he or she have any special abilities or needs?

Be prepared to answer these questions with positive comments. Instead of labeling a child based on behavior, explain actions using positive expressions.

Listening

Most people can listen to 400 words per minute but only speak 131 words. Based on this difference, a good listener does not jump ahead of the speaker. Give parents time to finish their stories or thoughts.

While a parent is talking, show interest and alertness. Avoid preparing an answer while listening. The parent's last sentence may be a source of new information. This may put an entirely different slant on what was previously shared.

Never interrupt a parent. Also, avoid quibbling over words. Instead, focus intently on what the parent is trying to say. Also focus on areas of agreement. This will encourage more friendly, open communication from the parent. See 32-10.

32-10

Listen attentively to parents during meetings. You may learn vital information that will help you work with their children.

Cross-Curricular Activity

Language Arts
After reviewing the list of negative language expressions and suggested positive alternatives in 32-9, *Language Expressions*, ask students to write down positive ways to say each of the following: *she's spoiled; he's hyper;* *she is such a brat; the children were bouncing off the wall and no one, including your child, would listen; Wendy is always snotty to Michelle; Rafael is obnoxious after naptime; Buddy drives me crazy.* Allow time for students to share their positive phrases with the class.

Working with Parents

Some parents are more difficult to work with than others. For example, a timid parent may be speechless at the start of a meeting. To reassure the parent, be friendly. As you speak, provide the parent with several sincere compliments. Second meetings are often much easier for timid parents.

Health and Safety

Parent Conferences

According to federal standards, early childhood providers should regularly schedule conferences with parents of children enrolled at the facility. Topics of primary discussion during conferences include

- a review of a child's strengths and abilities
- a review of the child's development
- a discussion about appropriate disciplinary practices
- a review of the child's health including special health conditions, developmental delays, nutrition, or sleeping problems

During the conference, parents and care providers must sign the child's updated health record. Generally, conferences for children six years and under are held every six months.

The worried parent always needs reassurance. This parent can often be identified by hand twirling, handkerchief twisting, or finger drumming. If the parent expresses concern regarding the child's developmental progress, provide reassurance. Often parents are unaware of unevenness of a child's development. They may also be unaware of the "spurts" that can occur in a short period of time.

A parent who is egotistical often enters feeling self-confident and smiling. The parent will want to talk about what a wonderful child he or she has and what a wonderful parent he or she is. With this parent, it is very important to remember the ego is a precious possession and to comment on the parent's skills.

The critical parent can be hard to work with if not handled properly. This parent has expert opinions on teaching the children in the center. Be accepting. That is, do not show disapproval or surprise as the parent talks. Never argue with this parent or any other. Arguing only arouses resistance and bad feelings. Arguments will not benefit the child. Successful conferences depend on your relationship with parents.

Professional Behavior

Always model professional behavior. If a parent makes a negative comment about another teacher, ignore it. Your attitude should always be positive toward your colleagues. Do not bring up or respond to negative comments about other children or parents.

Ending a Conference

Just as a conference should begin on a positive note, it should also end on one. Summarize major areas that have been discussed. Begin by repeating positive comments made at the beginning of the conference. Note areas that may need attention, including the agreed upon goals and action. Then restate your goals at the center as well as what the parent(s) can do at home. End the conference by again

Reflect

You have just informed Jeronda's mother that she is having trouble learning colors and shapes. Jeronda's mother wants to know if Cherie, their next door neighbor, is also having these problems. What is your professional response?

Activity

Have students conduct a role-play session in which a teacher meets with a timid parent during a parent-teacher conference. Conduct additional role-play sessions for dealing with a worried, an egotistical, and a critical parent. Have students critique the teacher role-play to make sure professional behavior is modeled at all times.

Discuss

How would you handle a parent that is always calling you and criticizing your teaching methods? What would you say to this parent? Have students give examples.

Workplace Connection

Remind students that the parent-teacher conference should be focused on the children and their needs. Occasionally, parents have a need to discuss their personal life, problems, and worries. Although the teacher should be sensitive to the needs of the parents, and can use such personal information to help understand the children, she or he is not a trained psychologist or social worker and should refrain from offering advice for handling personal problems. The well-prepared teacher should have a list of resources to suggest to parents who may have a need for them.

Resource

Parent-Teacher Conference Summary Form, reproducible master 32-2, TR

Discuss

What is involved in a conference follow-up? Who benefits from this strategy? How can teachers efficiently handle individual parent communications without being overwhelmed?

Resource

Checklist for a Good Conference, reproducible master 32-3, TR

making a constructive, pleasant comment. Let the parents know how appreciative you are of having an opportunity to share their children's progress with them.

Invite the parents to visit the center any time. Thank them for sharing. Stress the importance of shared information and common goals. Then walk them to the door. Leave them with a statement of encouragement or reassurance. You may say "Thank you for coming today. We both have shared information and have a better understanding of Marena. Since our last conversation, she has shown growth in all developmental areas. We will work together in encouraging her to become more independent."

Follow-Up

The follow-up involves touching base again with the parents to make sure actions agreed on in the conference are being followed. It should also include a report of the progress made since the conference. A parent-teacher conference should allow for sharing of information. Just as parents will learn, so will you, the teacher. Specifically, you may learn answers to the following:

- the child's reaction to the center, including likes and dislikes

- how the child spends time outside the center

- what home responsibilities the child has

- special interests the child has shown at home

- the status of the child's health

- who the child prefers to play with in the home as well as in school

Record conference notes in the child's folder. Make a point of calling or sending a note to parents, sharing any progress the child has made. See 32-11. Some teachers schedule time each week to contact parents. Each week they contact a few parents by phone or with a brief note. Over the course of

Take the time to write a quick note or make a quick phone call to parents. They will appreciate the update.

a month, each parent hears from the teacher regarding his or her child.

Home Visits

Visiting the child's home is another method for working successfully with families. **Home visits** allow the teacher to enter the child's world by spending time together in the family's home. The face-to-face contact provides the teacher with firsthand insights. This helps the teacher understand the "whole child."

Entering the child's world provides helpful information on the cultural background and daily life of individual families. The teacher

---

Meeting Special Needs

Pair special learners with student volunteers to complete *Checklist for a Good Conference,* reproducible master 32-3, TR. Have students conduct the mock conference twice so students get a chance to role-play the teacher and the parent. Have students fill out the checklist to record and evaluate each role-play session. Spend additional time discussing any information that is difficult for special learners to understand.

observes the child's physical environment and meets other family members and pets. The teacher also learns how the family interacts with the child in the home. Parents can communicate more comfortably in their own home. They are also reassured as they learn of the teacher's interest and concern. Because of the visit, the child feels special. Seeing the teacher in his or her own home builds feelings of trust and intimacy.

Home visits are beneficial for teachers and parents. However, they are primarily for the child. Head Start, Early Start, and other programs use home visits as a routine part of the teacher-family partnership.

Discussion Groups

Another method for involving parents in their children's education is group discussion. Through discussion, parents become familiar with child growth and development concepts. They also learn to notice some crisis points in the family cycle and learn to understand their own roles better.

When conducting discussions, remember that adults

- need to integrate new information with what they already know
- tend to take errors personally
- prefer self-designed learning experiences
- like straightforward "how-to" approaches
- must be physically comfortable
- learn a great deal from interacting with others
- enjoy learning when many senses are used

Group discussions are useful for studying new ideas. Discussions allow several people to take part. Through discussion, individual thinking is challenged. As the group exchanges experiences during discussion, individuals have the chance to study and review their own experiences. They are made to think through their positions. Chart 32-12 lists techniques for helping parents relax in a discussion group.

32-12

Techniques to Help Parents Relax

- Place items of interest on the walls for parents to look at.
- Provide refreshments for parents to eat and drink.
- Play soft background music.
- Provide name tags on which parents can write their name as well as their child's name.
- Arrange the chairs in a circle.
- Greet parents individually as they enter.
- Introduce parents to each other.

Parents are not immune to being nervous when visiting the school. Listed here are several methods for helping parents relax prior to a group discussion.

Group discussion also has disadvantages. First, it most often takes a long time. Other methods, such as a film or lecture, are generally faster. If the group is not handled properly, the discussion may wander. See 32-13.

Preparation

Arrange the room so participants can easily talk face to face. A circle or horseshoe arrangement is usually best. Coffee, tea, punch, and/or water should be available for parents when they arrive. If all the parents do not know each other, hand out name tags. These tags should include the child's name under the parent's name. This will allow parents to identify parents of their children's friends. You may also ask parents to introduce themselves before the discussion begins. To encourage the parents to talk, you may want to begin with a short DVD or CD addressing the subject to be discussed.

Several problems may arise. Some parents may not feel comfortable taking part. When this happens, ask a question that requires a response. For example, you may ask, "John, how do you feel?" Also, you can build on a previous comment by saying, "John, earlier you said you

Discuss

What types of programs might benefit best from offering parent discussion groups? Why should the leader of a discussion group have experience conducting parent groups?

Reflect

Imagine you are inviting parents to a group discussion on bullying. You will need to direct the discussion and be able to answer questions. What preparations should you make for this discussion? What information will you need to start the discussion and handle questions?

Resource

Family Discussion Groups, Activity C, SAG

Cross-Curricular Activity

Language Arts
You have just determined the need for a series of parent discussions. Have students write a letter to the director, principal, or superintendent stating your request to start the program and include reasons why the groups are

needed. Write your letter using clear, concise statements supported by facts and any statistics that can be used to prove your need to hold the discussion groups. The letter should reflect a professional viewpoint and use correct writing style, grammar, spelling, and form.

Note

Parents who do not have Internet access, cannot afford parenting magazine subscriptions, or are too busy to visit the local library may benefit from a lending library in the child care center. Placing the library in a visible and accessible location may encourage parents to learn about growth and development. This can help parents be more effective in their parenting role.

Enrich

Ask students to review 32-13, *Advantages and Disadvantages of Discussion*. Have students hold a debate about the advantages and disadvantages of using discussion groups as a method for involving parents in their children's education.

Reflect

What ways do you think are the most effective when trying to involve parents in their children's education? Why? Have student volunteers share responses with the class.

32-13

Advantages and Disadvantages of Discussion

Advantages
- Ideas can be carefully studied.
- Many people can take part.
- Parent educators can note if parents understand the discussion.
- People are forced to think through their problems.
- Disagreement is clarified or agreement is reached.

Disadvantages
- It is time-consuming.
- Parents may pool misinformation.
- Parents expecting to be told what to do may dislike this method.
- Parents can come to the wrong conclusion.
- Tension and emotions may be aroused.

Before you decide to schedule a group discussion, study the advantages and disadvantages. Will your concerns be best addressed by such a discussion?

were opposed to physical punishment. Why do you think you feel this way?"

Another problem that occurs quite often is that small groups begin debating among themselves. If this happens, you will need to redirect the group's attention by asking them to share their comments with the whole group.

Other Methods of Involvement

There are many other ways to involve parents in their children's education. These other methods are not as detailed as meetings and discussion groups. However, they are useful in their own way. These methods include a lending library, family resource center, traveling backpack, problem-solving file, bulletin boards, documentation boards, sunshine calls, and theme bags.

Lending Library

A lending library is one way to share parenting information, 32-14. If space is not available for a parent library, a few shelves in the director's office can be used. Current books and magazines that relate to parenting should be included in the library. Available reading materials can be mentioned during daily parent contacts, at conferences, in newsletters, and/or on the parent bulletin board.

Family Resource Center

Early childhood centers play another important role in meeting the needs of families. This role is to provide referrals and resources. Families need access to information on child development, child guidance, and community services. Books, brochures, professional articles, and other media may be available. Some communities even have free magazines related to families. Government pamphlets on nutrition, health, and safety are available to everyone.

However, many families are not aware of where to find all this information. To meet this need, some centers provide a room or space designed as a family resource center.

32-14

A lending library for parents should be well organized and inviting.

Service Learning Activity

Consider starting a Backpacks for Readers Program at a local elementary school. First and second grade students who are reading below grade level can be paired with high school reading buddies. The children meet with their reading buddy before school and read a book. Then the book is sent home in a backpack for the child to read with a parent. The reading buddies check out the progress each day and decide whether the book goes home again or if a new book should be chosen.

Other centers provide information boards, shelves, or files.

Centers also provide parents information on community services. If they are not informed, families may not realize they are eligible for some of these services. Often centers provide applications and flyers on some of the programs. Included may be information on

- home visiting programs that provide parent education and support
- WIC (Women, Infants and Children), a federal nutritional supplement program for pregnant women, new mothers, and infants
- food stamps—food purchasing help for low-income families
- nutrition, meal planning, and infant feeding
- earned income tax credit for low-income working families
- service programs such as Big Brothers and Big Sisters
- medicaid, a health care benefit for low-income families
- dependent care tax credit for some costs related to child care
- hospital programs that support new parents
- health clinics and dental screenings
- agencies that work with families in crisis, such as domestic violence and drug addiction
- counseling and emergency housing
- child care resources and referral agencies
- Federal housing assistance for low-income families
- family service programs from the Department of Health, Department of Human Services, licensing agency, or public library

Traveling Backpack

Another method for involving parents in their children's education is the **traveling backpack**. On a rotating basis, the children can choose their favorite books, music cassettes, puzzles, or games. Some teachers even encourage them to include paper and writing tools. When the children take home the backpack, they can share these items with their parents.

Problem-Solving File

Some child care directors use a **problem-solving file** to help parents. This file contains information on problems parents may face. Reading materials such as journal articles and newspaper clippings related to each problem are filed in folders. Topics you may wish to include in a problem-solving file are listed in 32-15. The file can be publicized through newsletters and at parent meetings.

Bulletin Board

Making a parent bulletin board is a convenient way to communicate with parents. Post meeting dates, newspaper clippings, and other center information, 32-16. Inform parents of local events, library resources, and educational television programs. Offer tips for choosing toys, books, and nutritious snacks. Attach a pocket for handouts on parenting issues such as biting, bed wetting, and thumbsucking. You may also include information on childhood diseases, immunizations, safety, and child development issues.

Hang the bulletin board in the most visible and well-traveled area of the center. Cover it with paper or attractive fabric. Change the background color often. This alerts parents to updated information on the board.

Sunshine Calls

Sunshine calls create positive parent-teacher relationships and foster two-way communication. A **sunshine call** is a telephone call made by a teacher to a parent to communicate praise and support for the

Discuss

What activities could you suggest for a traveling backpack that would encourage parents and children to work together on language development? What activities and materials would you include for math experiences?

Vocabulary

Have a student volunteer define the term *problem-solving file.* Give an example of how a problem-solving file may be useful when answering telephone calls from parents with questions about their child.

Note

When assigning students the job of assembling a problem-solving file, consider any copyright infringements from copying books; newspaper, journal, and magazine articles; and other printed material. If an original article cannot be filed because it would ruin the book or magazine to tear it out, contact the publisher for permission to copy the material for educational use only.

Workplace Connection

Ask students to assemble a problem-solving file. Consider asking the child care lab parents for their input. Ask students to design a short letter to survey parents for the topics they would like to see covered in the file. Gather articles, brochures, magazines, pamphlets, videos, etc. that they no longer need and would consider contributing to the file. A parent volunteer may also be needed to help collect materials from the other parents and help get the file set up.

Resource

Class Problem-Solving File, reproducible master 32-4, TR

Vocabulary

Have a student volunteer define the term *sunshine call.* What is the role of a sunshine call in creating positive parent relationships?

Discuss

Why might some parents get nervous at receiving a call from their child's teacher? What are the guidelines a teacher should follow when using the telephone?

32-15

Topics for a Problem-Solving File

Allowance	Language development
Behavior problems	Lying
Biting	Nightmares
Child abuse	Nutrition
Childhood diseases	Play
Children's products	Safety
Cognitive development	School readiness
Crying	Selecting toys
Death	Self-esteem
Disabilities	Separation anxiety
Discipline	Sibling relationships
Diversity	Single-parent families
Divorce	Speech problems
Emotional development	Stepfamilies
Fine-motor skills	Stress
Friendships	Teething
Giftedness	Technology
Gross-motor skills	Television
Guidance	Thumbsucking
Handedness	Toileting issues

Today, parents are concerned about many topics that affect their children. A problem-solving file is a useful resource.

32-16

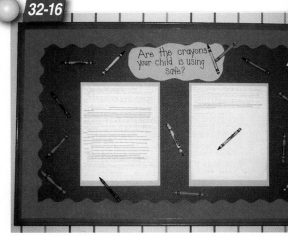

A parent bulletin board can be set up outside the classroom door to announce topics of interest and messages to parents.

child. The purpose of this call is to share with parents something outstanding or interesting the child has done recently. It also informs the parents of the teacher's interest in and knowledge of their child. For instance, Mrs. Barr may call Mr. Ross to let him know his child has just learned to ride a tricycle, jump rope, or tie shoelaces.

Some parents have had poor school experiences. When these parents were in school, a call from the teacher usually meant they had done something wrong. Such calls often focused on a social or learning problem. As a result, these parents may be alienated.

Done well, sunshine calls can help dispel some of these negative attitudes and help build good feelings toward the teacher and center. The goal of sunshine calls should be to build feelings of cooperation.

Sunshine calls are valuable for the parent, teacher, and child. For the teacher and parent, the value of sunshine calls lies in the two-way communication that occurs. For the child, the call is a pleasant event. The teacher has taken a personal interest in him or her. A sunshine call, however, should not replace regularly scheduled parent-teacher conferences.

There are several guidelines that must be followed when using the telephone.

- Plan the conversation by carefully choosing what to say.

- Keep the call to about five minutes in length.

- Begin the conversation by asking the parent if it is a convenient time to talk. If it is not, arrange a time to call back.

- Put the parent at ease immediately by telling the reason for the call.

- Share positive statements about the child.

Putting Technology to Use

Ask students to select a topic from 32-15, *Topics for a Problem-Solving File.* Have students conduct an Internet search for informative articles on the subject they selected. Students should also make a resource list of Web sites that pertain to their topic. Have students add their Web resource list and a copy of the articles to the class problem-solving file. Students should continue to update the file throughout the year.

- Whenever possible, also give the parent a word of praise or thanks.

Some adults are at ease with a telephone conversation. Thus, the conversation may be quite relaxed. Also, many teachers and parents are more at ease on the phone than when they talk face-to-face.

Theme Bags

For teaching parents how to promote children's learning at home, some teachers use **theme bags** to involve parents. These bags are in the form of a traveling backpack. Included for the parent is a letter of introduction that includes the purpose of the bag along with the contents. The specific value of the activities are described in terms of the child's development. The letter also includes specific suggestions for successfully involving their children in the activities.

Games, puppets, storybooks, songs, and charts can all be included. You may even send home a tape recorder to have the parents record their children's favorite stories. Be creative. Study your theme and brainstorm a list of related activities that can be shared at home. Then determine which ones would be the most successful for parents to introduce.

Volunteers

Parents want to be involved in their children's education. Many parents feel a need to develop a sense of connection with their child's classroom. This is why teachers and directors need to make an effort to involve parents. One way to do this is through volunteer programs.

Some teachers hesitate to include parents in their program plans. Their objections include the following:
- Parents may not have the time needed to devote to volunteer efforts.
- Parents may criticize the program.

- Parents may not have effective child guidance skills.
- Parents may want to take over classroom responsibilities.
- Children may act up when their parents are present.
- Parents may discuss confidential information outside of school.

These concerns are all worthwhile. However, most can be addressed by carefully recruiting and then training volunteers. Each volunteer, in turn, will gain a great deal, including
- personal satisfaction
- a better understanding of child development and child guidance
- an understanding of how children learn
- an understanding of what activities are appropriate for young children
- an understanding of his or her own child by observing him or her playing with other children
- an experience of being part of a teaching team

Recruiting

The best volunteers are those who have an interest in working with young children. Perhaps they would have enjoyed teaching as a profession. Still others are interested in presenting the best experiences to their children. These people are interested in supporting the center and learning more about young children. Many parents have talents or interests that could be useful to your program. A letter that can be used to recruit parents is shown in 32-17. Parent volunteers are usually interested in what the job entails and what they need to know. Finally, they are interested in the day or dates, time, and length of time they will be needed.

Parent volunteers must be dependable, fond of children, and healthy. In order to take part in a program, parents need some type of orientation.

Vocabulary

Have a student volunteer define the term *theme bags*. How do theme bags involve parents in their child's education?

Discuss

What themes and activities can students suggest for theme bags that are not already part of the curriculum? How can theme bags extend a lesson beyond the classroom? Give examples.

Reflect

Mrs. Miller has a college degree in early childhood education. She is now staying home to raise her four-year-old son Brad, who is enrolled in your preschool, and would like to volunteer to help out in the classroom. What are the advantages of having Mrs. Miller volunteer? What disadvantages, if any, do you foresee?

Portfolio Project

Contact area child care centers to arrange for students to observe a class on the day a volunteer will be present. Students should document the classroom activities, noting the assistance given by the volunteer. Have the student interview the teacher to determine the extent volunteers are used with the programs at the center. Students should write a brief essay to be filed in their portfolios on the value of parent volunteers and their understanding of the role of volunteers in early childhood classrooms.

Resource

Suggestions for Parent Volunteers, reproducible master 32-5, TR

Enrich

Divide students into two groups. Have students debate the pros and cons of teachers allowing parents to volunteer in their child's classroom.

Reflect

What information do you think should be included in an orientation for classroom parent volunteers? Have student volunteers share their responses with the class.

32-17

To: Parents

From: Cindy Mirro, Director

To help us provide a quality early childhood program, parents as classroom resources or volunteers are needed from time to time. If you are interested, please check those tasks with which you would like to assist.

_____ Sharing a hobby or job

_____ Repairing books

_____ Repairing toys and equipment

_____ Coordinating and assisting with field trips

_____ Assisting with celebrations

_____ Caring for classroom pets during holidays

_____ Assisting with public relations activities

_____ Supervising art experiences

_____ Assisting with field trips

_____ Cooking with the children

_____ Editing the newsletter

_____ Reading stories to children

_____ Sharing a musical hobby or vocation

_____ Participating in your child's birthday celebration

_____ Organizing the fall family picnic

_____ Organizing the spring family picnic

_____ Making puppets, doll clothes, and/or dramatic play costumes

_____ Serving on a parent advisory board

_____ Serving as a librarian

_____ Serving as a secretarial aide

_____ Other (specify): _____

_____

Please return this note to the basket in my office. If you have any questions, please contact me.

_____   _____
Parental Signature   Date

Written communication is effective when recruiting volunteers for the center.

Workplace Connection

Ask an adult who has a special talent or hobby to visit the child care class and demonstrate the hobby. Students are to observe the presentation "through the eyes of a child" and ask questions a child may have about the presentation. Students should offer suggestions to make the presentation effective at a child's level. Prepare the guest in advance by explaining the students will critique the presentation to make them more effective teachers.

Orientation

To get the most from volunteers, plan a training session. During this session, share staff expectations of them, including classroom limits and state licensing rules. As you discuss these duties, make the parents feel welcome. In addition, prepare a list of guidelines for parent volunteers as shown in 32-18.

If you have not met parents before the orientation session, be prepared to make a good impression. Studies show that first impressions are lasting impressions. The tone for an entire relationship is often set in the first four minutes.

First, begin by making the parents feel comfortable. Welcome them. Offer them chairs. Begin the orientation by explaining how important volunteers are in a center.

Resource

Volunteer Orientation, Activity A, OG

Reflect

Ask students to review 32-18, *Suggestions for Parent Volunteers.* Are there any other suggestions you can think of adding to the list for parent volunteers?

Resource

Teacher Hotline, Activity D, SAG

32-18

Suggestions for Parent Volunteers

General participation. Remember the children always come first. Share your interest in the children in the following ways:

- Provide praise with such statements as "I like your painting," "Thanks for hanging your coat on the hanger," or "You are good at helping with cleanup."
- State your suggestions positively by telling what the child should do. For example, instead of saying "Don't put the puzzle on the floor," tell the child where to place the puzzle. Say "Place the puzzle on the table."
- When talking with the children, get down at their level by squatting or sitting. As the child speaks, give him or her your full attention.
- Speak with other adults only when necessary.
- Avoid doing for a child what he or she can do for himself or herself. In other words, always stress independence. Let children put on their own coats, boots, etc. Assist only when absolutely needed so the children gain independence.
- Avoid discussing the children outside the center.

At story time
- Sit in the circle with the children.
- Allow interested children to crawl on your lap.
- Show your interest in the story by listening attentively.
- If you are asked to read, hold the book so all the children can see.

At the easel
- Children need to wear a smock while painting.
- Only one child should use each side of the easel at a time.
- Encourage the children to replace the brushes in the proper container. (There is one brush for each container of paint.)
- Show an interest in the children's work, but do not interpret it for them. Do not ask children what they have made.
- After children finish painting, print their names in the upper left-hand corners of their work. Capitalize only the first letter of each name.
- Hang finished paintings on the drying rack.
- At the end of the day, encourage the children to take their artwork home.

At music time
- Participate with the children.
- Reinforce the head teacher's actions.
- Show your enjoyment of the music.

Parent volunteers need guidance when they begin their work at the center.

Workplace Connection

Have students demonstrate their knowledge on the topic of parent volunteers by answering the questions that follow. Why is it important to include licensing information when giving parent volunteers an orientation to the early childhood classroom? Should parent volunteers have to submit to a criminal record background check and a health physical? What reminders should be given to parents whose child will be present in the class while they are volunteering? What will you share with the volunteer about showing favoritism to certain children? Allow time for students to discuss their responses in class.

Discuss

What do you think are some questions volunteers might have about helping in the classroom? What information should be included on a parent helper schedule?

Reflect

How would you feel if you were a parent attending an orientation and the teacher did not remember your name after he or she had heard it several times? What are some ways in which a teacher can recall parents' names?

Activity

Have students write a practice thank-you note to a parent or classroom volunteer to demonstrate their skill at this task. Have students exchange their notes with another student for a constructive critique.

Parents feel good when you remember their names. As you meet each parent, pay attention to his or her name. If you do not hear it, ask the person to repeat it. Say the name to yourself. Memory experts claim that by repeating the name to yourself, you will improve recall by 30 percent. See 32-19.

Whenever possible, use the parent's name in conversation. Through repetition, you will engrave the parent's name in your memory. Studies show people recall faces better than names. Another way to recall parents' names is to observe their faces. Concentrate on one trait such as the nose, eyes, or cheekbones. Then associate the names to their faces. By remembering the parents' names, you will make them feel important.

Schedule

Parents will only return to the classroom if they feel needed. Post a parent helper schedule such as the one shown in 32-20. This will help detail your expectations. Also ask volunteers if there are any questions you can answer.

Thank-You Notes

Send each parent a thank-you note after he or she has volunteered. Share at least one positive comment related to his or her participation. This gesture will show your appreciation. It will also encourage parents to volunteer again.

32-19

Parents and teachers both benefit by wearing name tags. These help everyone learn names more quickly.

Putting Technology to Use

Have students conduct an Internet search to learn about memory recall exercises. In what ways may memory be assessed? What are the current social beliefs regarding the ability to improve one's memory? What are some examples of memory tasks that could be practiced to increase memory function? Have students write a brief report of their findings. Allow time for students to try to demonstrate some of the memory tasks in class.

32-20

Parent Volunteer Schedule

Time	Teacher— Judy Tenario	Teacher— Lisa Sung	Parent— Rita Ulesich	Parent— Georgia Suski
Before class	Set up equipment for special free play activities. Welcome volunteers.	Set up equipment for activities other than dirt-and-water play; special, and paint activities.	Place paper on easels. Put out paint.	Fill water table.
9:00	Welcome children. Supervise free choice of activities.	Welcome children. Supervise free choice of play activities.	Supervise painting.	Supervise water table.
10:00	Serve snack.	Supervise handwashing.	Put away easels and join snack table.	Put away dirt-and-water play equipment and help with handwashing. Assist with snack.
10:30	Help with equipment or story as needed.	Read story.	Assist Judy in putting away equipment.	Assist with story and quiet time.
10:45	Help with special activity, or on alternate days, introduce it.	Introduce special activity, or on alternate days, help with it.	Assist with special activity.	Help with special activity.
11:00	Supervise movement activity.	Put away equipment from special activity.	Assist with movement activity.	Assist with movement activity.
11:15-11:45	Do dishes and pick up classroom.	Supervise playground.	Supervise playground.	Supervise playground.

Have duties outlined for parent volunteers for the days they work.

Resource

Getting Family Involved, Activity A, SAG

Discuss

Ask students to review 32-20, *Parent Volunteer Schedule.* What other duties could parent volunteers assist with in the classroom?

Resource

Family Involvement Purposes, Activity B, OG

Meeting Special Needs

Review the special learners' chapter outlines to determine if the students have any questions about the concepts or content of this chapter. Review the chapter objectives and ask the students to evaluate their progress in meeting these objectives. Ask the students to summarize, orally or in writing, what they learned from this chapter.

Summary

An alliance between teachers and parents is important. Parents play the key role in the physical, emotional, cognitive, and social development of their children. They are the children's primary teachers, as well as partners with the center staff. Involving them in the early childhood program, then, makes sense.

Involve parents in their children's school program by keeping in touch with them. Set aside time for communication, particularly at the beginning and end of the day. Conduct parent-teacher conferences during which you can get to know parents on a one-on-one basis. Hold discussion groups so all parents can share ideas and get to know one another. Communicate often using these methods: telephone, newsletters, letters, informal contacts, and e-mail (if it is available).

Parents can assume many roles in the classroom as volunteers. With their help, new activities that are impossible without adult assistance can be introduced.

Review and Reflect

1. What is needed to establish and maintain an alliance between parents and caregivers?
2. List four objectives for involving parents in the center program.
3. Name two points to consider when using written communication.
4. Newsletters should _____.
    A. include a review of special classroom activities and upcoming events
    B. be negative in nature
    C. be long and detailed
    D. All the above.

5. What are the three phases of the parent-teacher conference?
6. True or false. About five minutes should be allowed for each parent-teacher conference.
7. What is the purpose of scheduling a 10-minute break after each parent-teacher conference?
8. The "w" questions are often the most successful for getting information from parents. What are these questions?
9. True or false. Always begin a parent-teacher conference with a positive comment.
10. Rewrite the following negative expressions as more positive expressions.
    A. Selfish.
    B. Show-off.
    C. Lazy.
    D. Clumsy.
11. When talking with a parent, avoid preparing a(n) _____ while listening.
12. During a conference, worried parents always need _____.
    A. to be ignored
    B. refreshments
    C. reassurance
    D. None of the above.
13. What are three advantages of making a home visit?
14. True or false. Adults tend to take errors personally.
15. List two advantages of group discussions.
16. Disadvantages of group discussions include _____.
    A. too many people can take part
    B. the discussion may wander
    C. parents will take over the discussion
    D. All the above.
17. What is the purpose of a lending library?
18. A _____ file contains information on difficulties parents with children may face.

Review and Reflect Answer Key

1. regular communication
2. (List four:) develop an understanding of child growth and development; gain confidence in their parenting roles; learn about their children's experiences at the center; understand their children by observing other children; learn new ways of positively interacting with children; become informed about community resources; foster the children's and parent's ability to interact with each other; extend learning from the center into the home; understand how a partnership between center and home can promote the children's development
3. Use the active voice; keep communications short, clear, and simple.
4. A
5. planning, conducting the conference, follow-up
6. false
7. This allows time to record any important information and also allows time if the conference runs slightly longer than planned.

8. why, what, when, where, and how
9. true
10. A. needs to learn to share with others
    B. tries to get others' attention
    C. is capable of doing more
    D. is not physically well coordinated
11. answer
12. C

19. A sunshine call _____.
    A. is made by a teacher to a parent
    B. is made to share with parents something positive about their children
    C. can help dispel some negative feelings parents may have about school
    D. All the above.
20. Who makes the best volunteer?
21. Send each parent a _____ after he or she has volunteered.

Apply and Explore

1. Make a list of questions that parents most often ask teachers. Design answers for these questions based on the contents of this chapter.
2. Discuss ways you might build a positive relationship with
   A. a shy parent
   B. a worried parent
   C. an angry parent
   D. an unconcerned parent
3. Brainstorm a list of discussion topics for a parents' group.
4. Identify two advantages for child care teachers who work as partners with parents.
5. Develop a list of materials that could be included in a portfolio for a four-year-old child.
6. Role-play parent-teacher conferences with each type of parent described in the chapter.
7. Brainstorm community sources for pamphlets and other publications for a parent resource center.
8. Role-play and discuss the following circumstances, which you might experience while making a home visit.
   A. A mother begins talking negatively about her child.
   B. The mother appears embarrassed for you to see the home.
   C. The father speaks limited English and the mother is very uncomfortable.
   D. The child takes his sibling's toy and the mother slaps him.

Cross-Curricular Link

Language Arts

1. Interview several early childhood teachers and find out the strategies they use for developing alliances with parents.

2. Interview a child care teacher about parent-teacher conferences. Share your findings in an oral report.

Writing

3. Write a parent letter about an upcoming field trip to an ice cream factory. Use the active voice.

Reading

4. Collect parent newsletters from several centers. Analyze their design and content. Then, based on your analysis, design a newsletter for the A-B-C Learning Center.

Workplace Link

Contact early childhood programs in your area to learn the role that parent communication plays in the programs. Do the centers send out timely newsletters and notes about classroom activities? Do the centers schedule regular parent-teacher conferences, and if so, how often? Are parents consulted in decisions about field trips, holiday celebrations, or program changes?

16. B
17. A lending library is a useful way to share parenting information.
18. problem-solving
19. D
20. The best volunteer is a person who is interested in working with young children.
21. thank-you note

13. (List three:) Home visits provide helpful information on the cultural background and daily life of individual families. The teacher observes the child's physical environment and meets other family members and pets. The teacher learns how the family interacts with the child in the home. Parents can communicate more comfortably in their own home. Parents are reassured as they learn of the teacher's interest and concern. The child feels special. Seeing the teacher in his or her own home builds feelings of trust and intimacy.
14. true
15. (List two:) group discussions are useful for studying new ideas; they allow several people to take part; individual thinking is challenged; individuals have the chance to study and review their own experiences; they are made to think through their positions

Discuss

Look at the body language and actions of the teacher in the chapter opening photo. Do you think she is happy about her career choice? Why or why not?

Discuss

Look over the chapter objectives before reading the chapter to get a sense of the material to be covered. What skills can you learn from studying this chapter?

33

A Career for You in Early Childhood Education

After studying this chapter, you will be able to

- explain how interests, abilities, values, and family responsibilities affect career choices.
- compile your résumé.
- write a cover letter.
- list various methods for seeking employment.
- list questions to ask during an interview.
- prepare a teaching portfolio.
- explain the basic interviewing process.
- describe illegal questions and how to respond to them.
- describe the rights and responsibilities of employees and employers.
- summarize the importance of finding balance among family, work, and community roles.

Terms to Know

self-assessment

values

professional priorities

résumé

cover letter

networking letter

hidden job market

networking

teaching portfolio

attitude

confidentiality

role

role strain

Preparing for your future is both rewarding and exciting. Choosing a career and job hunting are important, challenging tasks. To be successful, they must be approached in a thoughtful manner. Successful candidates often treat job hunting as a full-time job. They commit themselves to the process 100 percent. They approach the hunt with a plan.

Many early childhood teachers have been successful using several types of job searching techniques. One method has been to apply directly to the employer or center director. This contact may be in the form of an e-mail request for an application, a visit to the center, or a telephone call. Usually people make these contacts just before their courses to meet state licensing guidelines or early childhood certification are completed.

Answering newspaper ads is one more way to seek employment. Check the want ads on a daily basis. If you notice an appealing position, contact the center director at once. If a telephone number is listed, a call can be made. Many times, positions need to be filled immediately. Therefore, do not waste any time in making a contact.

Choosing a Career

Choosing your life's work is a challenging responsibility. As you begin the process of selecting a career, you may be thinking, "What do I want to do with my life?" Only a few people seem to know from an early age what career they will pursue. Most people find this a difficult question to answer. It is a decision best made with much care and thought, 33-1. People often begin choosing a career by doing a self-assessment.

Self-assessment is the process of examining your interests, abilities, values, and professional priorities. As you consider these factors, you will gain important self-knowledge for use in choosing a career. You will ask yourself many questions, and your answers will help you determine whether a career working with young children is for you.

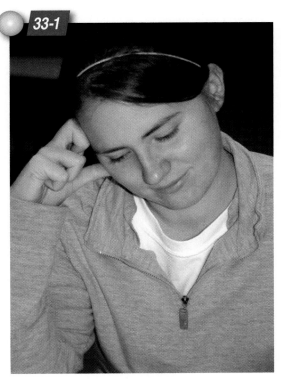

33-1

Many teens spend a great deal of time reflecting on the future and what careers they will pursue.

Vocabulary

Review the *Terms to Know.* Ask students to look up unfamiliar terms in the glossary before reading the chapter.

Reflect

If you are reading this chapter at the end of the child care course, what have you learned about the early childhood profession that would encourage you to seek higher-level training? What are your career goals, if any, in a career working with children?

Vocabulary

Have students define *self-assessment.* How is conducting a self-assessment related to a possible future career choice?

Meeting Special Needs

Provide an outline of the chapter with all the chapter headings for special learners. Students should fill in each section of the outline as the material is covered in class with a sentence or two about the content. Review the special learners' IEPs to decide if any modifications should be made in presenting the chapter content.

Discuss

How is a self-assessment question about your hobbies related to a future career choice? How do your preferences for working with people, information, or objects relate to future career possibilities?

Resource

Assessing Your Abilities, Activity A, SAG

Discuss

How do aptitude tests and skills assessments help you explore career choices? How can these tests help eliminate some career possibilities?

Resource

Reel In a Child Care Career, transparency master 33-2, TR

Interests

Interests usually play a large role in career choices. For the most part, people seek to prepare themselves for a career they will enjoy. The Chinese philosopher Confucius offered important advice concerning career decisions. He said if you choose a job you love, you will never need to work a day in your life. You will feel fulfilled and believe you are doing something worthwhile.

Determining what work you will enjoy can be challenging. Begin this process by analyzing your interests. Start by asking yourself the following basic questions:

- How do you spend your time? What are your hobbies?

- Do you enjoy learning? Which courses in school have you found most interesting?

- Do you prefer working independently or working with others?

- Do you prefer working with people, information, or objects?

- Which career fields do you find most exciting?

Gaining experience in a career field can help you make or confirm a career decision. For example, volunteering, working part-time, or doing an internship can help you explore early childhood as a career option. As a result of this experience, you might decide you are not suited to be a child care or early education teacher. On the other hand, you may feel more strongly than ever that working with young children is a good career option for you.

You can also assess your interests by learning more about other careers. Research a few careers you are considering. What responsibilities does each job entail? Are these tasks you would enjoy? Interview a professional employed in the field to learn more. You might be able to arrange a *job shadowing* experience where you can spend an entire day with an employee at his or her job.

This experience can give you an overview of the job duties and rewards.

Abilities

A second part of self-assessment is analyzing your abilities. Abilities have a direct influence on job performance—you are more likely to succeed in a job you can do well. Having interests and abilities in similar areas is not uncommon. You are more likely to be interested in tasks you are good at, and you may work harder to develop abilities in areas that interest you. It is also possible to have abilities that differ from your interests.

What abilities do you have? Perhaps you are well aware of your abilities. These may be areas in which you have always excelled. Other abilities may seem less obvious. You might discover these abilities through tests given by a guidance or career counselor. Common names for these tests are *aptitude tests* and *skills assessments*. Taking these tests can help you identify careers for which you might be suited.

You can also ask close friends and trusted adults for their insight. They may comment "You're so good with children," "You relate to people so easily," or "You solve problems well." These comments can help you identify areas of strength.

Developing a solid foundation of basic skills will help you in any career. This foundation includes skills in human relations, teamwork, leadership, communication (writing, speaking, and listening), computers, mathematics, problem solving, decision making, time management, stress management, and planning. With these basic skills, chances are you will become a successful employee in your chosen career, 33-2.

In addition, you will need some career-specific abilities. These relate more closely to the demands of a particular job. Effective early childhood teachers need the abilities that will help them carry out

Meeting Special Needs

Have students with special needs find out what postsecondary training and education is available to meet their own specific learning style and needs. Have them contact the guidance and counseling department for assistance in locating programs that provide assistance in meeting education and career goals. Students should discuss realistic expectations with the special education staff, school psychologist, social worker, parents, teachers, and advocates. Students should also review the job market for opportunities suited to their individual skills and abilities.

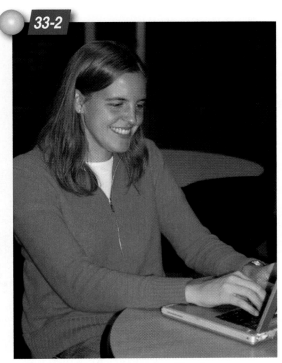

Developing your computer skills will make you a more valuable employee in almost any career you choose.

their responsibilities as described in earlier chapters of this book. Some of these abilities include the following:

- planning developmentally appropriate themes, lessons, activity areas, schedules, and routines

- leading group activities and assisting children in activity areas as needed

- matching guidance and communication techniques to children's developmental ages

- setting and enforcing needed limits for children's health, safety, and healthy development

- providing comfort, nurturance, affection, and effective praise

- offering constant supervision to all children throughout all daily activities

- demonstrating appropriate physical care techniques (such as diapering, feeding, dressing, toileting, and hand washing) to keep children safe and healthy

Abilities needed by professionals in other child-related careers may differ somewhat from those that teachers need. For example, a child care director needs budgeting, recordkeeping, planning, organizing, leading, and supervising abilities. Learning more about particular careers will help you find out what career-specific abilities are needed.

How do the abilities you have now compare to those you will need in your chosen career? You may have many of the needed abilities already, but there may be others you still need to develop. If a career deeply interests you, it may be worthwhile to identify ways to build the needed skills. Taking additional classes to learn more about the subject can help. Ask a teacher, guidance counselor, supervisor, or other trusted adult to help you identify other ways to develop the needed abilities.

Values

First, you will want to take a look at your **values**. These are your beliefs, feelings, and ideas about what is important. Values influence your decisions and actions. Each person is an individual with unique thoughts, feelings, experiences, and beliefs. These differences are often reflected in the values people hold. For example, some people desire popularity, wealth, and material possessions most. Others find education, career, family life, or friendships more meaningful. Each person can value any combination of priorities in any order of importance. That is what makes values truly personal.

As you examine your values, you will better understand the importance of various people, objects, and ideas in your life. Choosing a career that aligns with your values greatly increases your chances of

Discuss

Joanne has a special rapport with children and really enjoys working with them. However, she is unorganized, rarely turns in assignments, and does not control large group activities well. She performs poorly on tests and has a poor attendance record. With only these facts, would you recommend that Joanne plan to attend college to study child development?

Vocabulary

Have a student volunteer define *values*. Discuss how identifying your values can help you define a career choice.

Discuss

What math and computer skills are needed for those interested in a career in early childhood education? Would these skills be needed for an individual who does not want to attend college but is only seeking a job as a preschool or child care center aide?

Resource

Values Are Personal, reproducible master 33-1, TR

Portfolio Project

Have students review all the courses they have taken since starting high school. Ask them to evaluate each course related to a future career in early childhood education or other work associated with children. Write next to each course how it contributes to a career with children. Are they able to make connections with all their courses to a future child care career? Have them look over the portfolio they have assembled for this course and make note of all the projects and samples that are related to English, math, social studies, science, art, music, health, and physical education.

Enrich

Have student volunteers debate the role of professional priorities in having a fulfilling career.

Vocabulary

Define *résumé*. How is writing a résumé similar to a self-assessment?

Discuss

Although Adrienna wants to be a kindergarten teacher, she knows that as soon as she graduates from high school she is expected to get a job to contribute to the family finances. Her single mother has three more children to raise and get through school. How have Adrienna's family obligations impacted her career choices?

happiness and career success. Such a career will enhance your life by allowing you to focus on what matters most to you.

Closely related to values are **professional priorities**. These are global aspects of work that are important to a person's satisfaction. Which of the following are professional priorities for you?

- helping or providing service to others
- feeling a sense of accomplishment
- working as a team member
- having a leadership role
- gaining recognition
- earning a high salary
- being competitive
- working independently
- making a contribution to society through your work

In addition to these professional priorities, what others can you identify? When you think of a fulfilling career, what characteristics come to mind? List your professional priorities on a sheet of paper. Compare your list to those commonly found among workers in your chosen career field. Figure 33-3 shows professional priorities commonly shared by successful child care teachers.

Professionals in child-related careers other than teaching may have professional priorities that differ somewhat. For example, successful directors are likely to list managing, organizing, and leading among their priorities.

Examining your values and professional priorities will help you determine whether working with young children will be a satisfying career choice for you. This part of self-assessment can also help you narrow the objective to work with young children into a more specific career goal. With a specific career in mind, you can seek the needed education, training, and experiences to qualify you to work in that career.

33-3

Professional Priorities of Child Care Teachers

Successful child care teachers commonly share the following professional priorities:

- **Independence:** working on their own
- **Creativity:** trying out their own ideas
- **Responsibility:** making their own decisions and solving problems
- **Achievement:** gaining a feeling of accomplishment
- **Relationships:** providing service to others and working with coworkers in a friendly noncompetitive environment
- **Sharing knowledge:** teaching and guiding young children to learn new concepts

How do your professional priorities compare to those of early childhood teachers?

Résumés

To prepare for your job search, first prepare a résumé. A **résumé** is a brief summary of your qualifications, skills, and experience. It should be tailored to the type of job for which you're applying. The purpose of a résumé is to secure an interview and/or inform a potential employer of your qualifications and experience. If your résumé is effective, you will receive invitations to interview from potential employers.

Résumés also serve many other purposes. First, a résumé may serve as your own self-inventory. Having an objective list of your background and skills can be quite helpful when looking for a job. It can also serve as a starting point in an interview. A well-written résumé will give the employer information on which to base the interview. After the interview, your résumé will help the employer recall your experiences as well as the interview.

Putting Technology to Use

Have students conduct an Internet search for information on preparing a résumé and answer the following questions: What is an objective? How should it be stated? How can you show your experiences and skills with more clarity by using action words? How can you stress work experience when you are a recent graduate? Have students prepare a list of résumé-writing tips to incorporate into their own résumés.

Preparing a Résumé

A well-prepared résumé plays an important role in your job search. First, it instantly creates a favorable impression of you. Second, it creates a desire on the part of the employer to meet you. In many cases, it is your ticket to a job interview.

All résumés contain key information about the applicant: name, current address, e-mail address, and a telephone number or cell phone number are always included. If you are applying for jobs outside your hometown, include the area code with your telephone or cell phone number.

Remember, your résumé represents you. Be accurate and neat. Use simple words and write in a clear, concise manner. Include your educational background, employment objective, paid and volunteer work experience, professional activities, interests, and references. Organize the experience section so your strongest experience comes first even if it was not the most recent. Always be descriptive. For instance, if you want to share that you are a hard worker, create a statement that will deliver that message: "Worked 20 hours per week during the past two semesters."

Using a résumé as a tool, your goal should be to present yourself as an active, well-rounded person. The résumé should have an easy-to-read format. Also be sure to correct all misspellings, grammar errors, and typing errors. An example of a résumé is shown in 33-4.

Helpful Hints

Directors will quickly look at a résumé to find out if you have enough educational background and experience to qualify for the position. If your experience appears to meet the requirements of the job description, the résumé is read more closely. At this time, most employers will look for gaps in your employment dates, the amount of space given to earlier jobs, and the emphasis on education.

Are there gaps in your job history? These gaps may make directors wary of problems in your job history. They may signal that you were unemployed between jobs. You may choose to leave out a job on your résumé because it does not apply to the position you seek. Perhaps you were unemployed for a legitimate reason, such as returning to school. Be sure to explain such gaps in your cover letter.

When you give the time of your employment, be sure to specify the month and year of the starting and ending date of each job. Listing only years can be confusing to directors. Such a listing can also give the impression that gaps in employment are being concealed. Be honest in your résumé. Center directors are experienced at dissecting résumés. Avoid omitting facts.

A good résumé should reflect progress in a career over the years. Also, directors are more interested in an applicant's most recent accomplishments. Therefore, the most recent job experience should be emphasized. Some résumé writers devote more space to an earlier teaching position. This usually means one of two things. It may simply be due to poor judgment. It could mean the applicant has updated an old résumé by simply adding a few lines about the new job. Overall, these errors convey a lack of ambition and/or poor planning on the part of the applicant. These errors may not always rule out an applicant from an interview. However, they do signal that the applicant needs to be closely reviewed during this process.

The director will also review a résumé to see if there is too much stress on education and non-job factors. When an applicant has been out of school for several years, the résumé should stress work experience. Applicants who stress postsecondary honors may be focusing too much on the past. If the

Resource

Résumé Outline, reproducible master 33-3, TR

Activity

Raul will be going to college in the fall. He has not held any paid jobs during high school, but he has volunteered for babysitting at his church. He helps serve meals at a homeless shelter one night a week. He acted as a student aide for the science department for two years. Have students explain how Raul can present or describe these activities in a way that showcases his skills and abilities as he applies for a position as a summer camp counselor.

Resource

Résumé Writing, color transparency CT-28, TR

Putting Technology to Use

Have students review some of the résumé software programs available. How does the software assist the writer? What features are usually included in the programs? What is the usual cost of a software package? Do students think the software is worth the price? Have them explain their reasoning in oral reports to the class.

Resource

Résumé Checklist,
reproducible master
33-4, TR

Activity

Have students use
the résumé given and
recreate it in different
styles. Discuss the
differences among the
various samples and
have the class vote on
a favorite. Why do they
think employers would
react positively to this
style of résumé?

Discuss

Does the informa-
tion presented on
this résumé give you
any ideas for what to
include on your own
résumé? What are
some other ideas for
activities or interests to
include? What should
not be included?

33-4

Sharon Kaminski

University Address:
University of Wisconsin-Stout
Tainter Hall
Menomonie, WI 54751
(715) 555-1111

Home Address:
109 Liberty Street
Valders, WI 54362
(414) 555-4422

Objective
To obtain a position teaching two-, three-, or four-year-old children.

Education
University of Wisconsin-Stout
- Graduating June, 20XX with a Bachelor of Science in Early Childhood Education.
- 3.83 (out of 4.0) cumulative grade point average.
- Dean's List: 20xx-present.

Valders High School
- Graduated June, 20xx.
- Activities: member of National Honor Society and school band; captain of women's volleyball team.

Experiences
Wee Care Child Care Center, Atlanta, Georgia, June, 20XX-September, 20XX
- Assisted head teacher with all program activities during the summer session.
- Created new teaching aids for art, science, music, and social studies activities.
- Supervised adult volunteers.

Course Assistant, Early Childhood Department at University of Wisconsin-Stout, September, 20XX-June, 20XX
- Coordinated teacher education resource room: maintained files, ordered materials, and designed room layout.

Valders Public Schools, September, 20xx-June, 20xx
- Assisted kindergarten teacher with special activities: coordinated and supervised holiday parties, prepared teaching aids, and maintained classroom centers.

Activities
International Relations Council, University of Wisconsin-Stout
- Delegate to State Model United Nations.

Dean's Student Advisory Council, University of Wisconsin-Stout
- Advised Dean on students' activities. Coordinated special school events including Parents Weekend.

Student Ambassador, University of Wisconsin-Stout.
- Visited community high schools to recruit students for the University of Wisconsin-Stout.

Interests
Alpine and cross-country skiing, reading, gourmet cooking.

References available upon request.

Résumés should be neatly organized and evenly spaced.

Cross-Curricular Activity

English
Have students contact an English teacher at your school to determine if the school has a writing manual or other guide for résumé writing. Have students arrange to visit a class that is working on professional writing, including résumé writing, for tips in preparing their own résumés.

applicant stresses more non-job factors, this may indicate where his or her real interests lie.

Students who are recent graduates have a special challenge. How can you stress work experience if you have little or none? Do not overlook any previous unpaid work experience. Any practice teaching or volunteer work in your field of study can be included on your résumé. Any involvement in professional organizations related to your field of study such as an affiliate of the National Association for the Education of Young Children (NAEYC) may also be included. You may wish to explain any leadership roles you assumed or any skills you developed that will help you on the job.

Poor computer or writing skills and grammatical errors will always reflect badly on the applicant. Basic mistakes may cripple your job search. In fact, some highly qualified applicants have failed to obtain interviews because of poor writing skills. It is always wise to ask a friend who has outstanding writing skills to proofread any résumés before you send them to an employer.

Cover Letters

A **cover letter** is a letter of introduction that is usually included when sending a résumé. The main purposes of the letter are to capture the employer's attention and to request an interview. This letter is important. A mistake some job applicants make is putting too little effort into writing the cover letter.

Remember the basics while preparing your cover letter. Follow a business letter format. As with the résumé, use proper grammar and punctuation. Write each cover letter separately. Avoid writing one generic cover letter that can be used to apply for any job. This gives the impression you're not interested enough to write a tailored letter. It also fails to stand out to the reader.

Keep in mind no one in the early childhood community is called *Sir, Madam,* or *Whom It May Concern*. If necessary, call to obtain the name of the center director or the person responsible for hiring. Address the cover letter to this person.

Your cover letter is an opportunity to "sell yourself" to the employer. The cover letter should not be a summary of your résumé. It should convince the person hiring to read and consider your résumé.

Keep the cover letter short. A few paragraphs should be enough. Tell how you learned of the opening or how you are familiar with the center. Explain why you want to be considered for the position. Describe your interests, aptitudes, and abilities related to the job. Close by telling the employer what action—for instance, a phone call or interview—you would like him or her to take. Be polite in your request and thank the person for reviewing your cover letter and résumé. Sign the letter *Yours truly,* or *Sincerely,* and your name.

Reread your letter several times for content, typing, and grammatical errors. Have several other people proofread the letter for you, too. In one study, seventy-six percent of recruiters said they would not consider an applicant whose résumé contained errors. A mistake could make a poor impression of you. See 33-5.

Avenues for Seeking Employment

Early childhood job seekers may use a number of methods to find employment. These methods include mailing cover letters with résumés and placing or answering ads in the newspaper. Career fairs and networking provide other opportunities to search for positions. Successful applicants also do not overlook the hidden job market.

Make sure your cover letter and résumé are forwarded to the proper person. Find out the name of the individual who is responsible for hiring and address your letter to that person.

Vocabulary

Have a student volunteer define *cover letter*. Why is a well-written cover letter essential for job hunters?

Discuss

Why is it important to have someone proofread your résumé and cover letter before sending them out? What can result from failing to do this?

Resource

Guidelines for Cover Letters, reproducible master 33-5, TR

Workplace Connection

Contact your school principal, dean, or other administrator who may have recent cover letters from job applicants to share. Make sure that personal identification information is blocked out before showing the letters to your students. Ask the administrator to point out any cover letters that particularly caught his or her attention and resulted in a job offer. Ask students to evaluate those letters that they feel need improvement and suggest the improvements to be made.

Enrich

Have students debate
the pros and cons of
placing a newspaper
ad for a position or
placing an ad on the
Internet. What costs are
involved? How long will
the ads appear?

Discuss

How can a cover letter
help you stand out from
the crowd? What are
some common mis-
takes made in writing a
cover letter?

Enrich

Have student vol-
unteers role-play a
telephone call response
to a newspaper job ad.
How should the con-
versation begin? What
important points should
be covered? How can
students become more
comfortable making
these calls?

33-5

615 Market St.
Menomonie, WI 54362
August 1, 20XX

Alex Briones, Director
Child Development Center
1318 Hillcrest Road
Springfield, MA 56789

Dear Mr. Briones:

While searching for job positions on the Internet, I read your advertisement for a teacher. I am interested in obtaining a position in the child care field and in relocating to Springfield, Massachusetts.

I hold a certificate in early childhood education. My interest in early childhood education as a profession started while I was in middle school. Since then, I have cared for children, assisted with the preschool program at my church, and worked in an after-school program in a local center. These experiences convinced me of my interests, skills, and enthusiasm for working with young children.

My résumé is enclosed for your consideration. You will see that both my experience and education match the qualifications outlined in your advertisement.

Thank you for considering me for a position in your center. This is exactly the type of opportunity I am seeking. If you would like to schedule an interview or have any questions, please call me at 789-555-5748 or e-mail me at chak@uwstout.edu.

Sincerely,

Kim Cha

Kim Cha

Include a cover letter with your résumé when responding to newspaper ads.

Newspaper Ads and the Internet

Answering newspaper ads and responding to announcements on the Internet can be helpful when looking for work. As a job seeker, make a habit of reading the ads every day, 33-6. Newspaper ads are alphabetized. Ads for child care center staff may be listed under different areas. Therefore, study the entire section. Examples of titles related to child care include *child care teacher, infant teacher, toddler teacher, preschool teacher, early childhood teacher, school-age child care teacher, program coordinator, curriculum specialist,* and *activities director*. If you are looking for an administrative position, look closely for descriptions such as *director, administrator,* or *coordinator*.

Putting Technology to Use

Have students research the trend to post résumés online on Web sites such as **www.careerbuilder.com** and **www.monster.com**. Have students answer the following questions: How do these sites assist in locating jobs? What services do these sites offer? What is the pricing for these services? How willing are you to pay for a professionally written résumé and cover letter?

Many new child care teachers find their first jobs through newspaper ads.

If an ad appeals to you, respond according to the instructions given in the ad. Some ads contain telephone numbers. In this case, do not wait; call right away. Telephone numbers are most often included when a position must be filled as soon as possible.

If a phone number is not given, send your résumé with a cover letter to the address or post office box listed.

If an advertisement does not ask for your salary requirements, do not mention them in your letter. By including a salary figure, you could be screened out and not have the chance to interview. Some ads state the exact

salary or range they will pay. For instance, an ad might note the exact dollar figure per hour or a range of several thousand dollars. Many times when a range is provided, the ad might state that salary is open "based on experience" or "based on educational background." See 33-7.

Internet Job Search

Have you ever thought about knocking on doors using the Internet? By using an Internet browser, you can search for a job. Job hunting on the information superhighway can be fun and rewarding. Although you may begin with a goal in mind, chances are you may encounter better contacts than you expected. On the Internet, there are thousands of Web sites that will offer you assistance. A Web site will provide you addresses.

Joining a chat room or discussion group in your field is another way to find a job. Some professional associations sponsor list servers or message boards and use net news groups.

Networking Letter

Like a cover letter, a **networking letter** should be carefully written. It should be sent to an assortment of people in the field of early childhood education who you know personally or who are referred to you. The purpose of the networking letter is to inform them you are available for employment. After receiving the letter, these individuals could pass your name

Head Teacher at the Sheboygan Early Childhood Center. Applicant must hold a two-year certificate from an accredited institution of higher learning. Salary range from $2,200-$3,000 per month.
Call 1-414-555-4598 or
e-mail: eccenter@sheboygan.edu

Newspaper ads give a short summary of the open position.

Reflect

If you were to respond to an ad that asks for salary requirements, what would you say? How would you find out if you were requesting an appropriate amount?

Discuss

If you see an ad for a job that sounds ideal for you, but the stated salary is lower than you hoped for, what would you do? What is the value of applying for a job if you're not sure you would accept it?

Activity

Have students practice writing networking letters. How should a job hunter introduce himself or herself in a networking letter?

Putting Technology to Use

Have students investigate the possibility of joining an Internet chat room or message board for finding a job. Have students answer the following questions: How do you locate chat rooms on the Internet in your career area? How do you join? Describe some of the dialogue you see in the chat room. How helpful do you think chat rooms are for providing job-seeking networking?

Activity

Have students review the qualifications for the position listed in Figure 33-8. What types of activities do they think should be documented in their résumés or portfolios to demonstrate their qualifications?

Discuss

Explain *passive job search technique*. How successful do you think this strategy is in comparison to an active search?

Activity

Have students contact the career or college placement office of a local college or university to discover the types of services they offer to graduates for career placement. Do the placement centers actively work with recruiters and potential job applicants, or do they simply post a list of current job opportunities?

on to the appropriate people. They could also provide you with valuable insight into possible employment opportunities.

Placing Ads

Newspaper ads, ads in professional journals, or ads on the Internet can help you make your availability known. They are quite helpful if you are moving to another area. For example, you may want to work as a child care teacher in New York City after graduation, but you live in Chicago. You could place an ad in the *New York Times* in the positions wanted section of the paper.

Before placing an ad, write, e-mail, or call to find out the cost. The cost of placing an ad varies depending on the city, circulation of the paper, size of the ad, and the number of days it will run. Often, charges are either on a per word or per line basis. Depending on

your budget and the costs of advertising, you may have to limit the length of your ad.

Placing a position wanted ad is a passive job search technique. It requires employers to seek you out. However, most employers will actively pursue only the most qualified candidates. Therefore, this method works best for those people who are experienced. It is best to also use active job search techniques.

College or School Placement Offices

Most early childhood certificate and degree programs provide a placement service. The purpose of this service is to find positions for graduates. Placement offices are usually located on campus. Employers are encouraged to call in, send, or e-mail job information for the office to post, 33-8. Likewise, employers are

---

33-8

Position:
Head Teacher, Child Care Program
Full-Time Position
Yearly contract renewal for a maximum of three years

Date Available:
August, 20XX

Job Responsibilities:
Head Teacher in early childhood center. Plan and implement a developmentally appropriate curriculum for three- and four-year-old children. Supervise a teacher's aide and volunteers from a local community college. Assist Director in applying for accreditation. Plan and implement parent meetings, conferences, and related activities.

Qualifications:
- B.S. degree in Early Childhood Education is required, graduate work preferred.
- Must be certified to teach preschool in Texas.
- Experience in assessment, curriculum development, and program evaluation.
- Demonstrated excellence in teaching young children for a minimum of three years.
- Demonstrated ability to interact positively with people and work cooperatively with other staff members, parents, students, volunteers, and children.
- Must be able to organize and coordinate activities with volunteers.
- Must be able to motivate children in a creative environment.
- Must be able to demonstrate initiative and continuous professional development.

Notices posted in school placement offices often give a comprehensive summary of the open position.

Workplace Connection

Have students locate and attend a job fair held in your area or on a college campus. What types of occupations are represented at the fair? What information is available from potential employers? Ask students to take notice of the attendees at the fair and observe their attire and attitude as they meet with professionals.

given help finding qualified graduates when they contact the office.

As a student, chances are you will be asked to prepare a portfolio. This portfolio will include samples of materials on paper or on a computer disk. Regardless of the format used, this file will usually include a standard form prepared by the college or school placement service. The form lists your current address, schools attended, degree earned, and past work experiences. In addition, your file will contain your résumé and letters of recommendation from faculty and/or previous employers.

The Hidden Job Market

Many job candidates are most successful when they focus their efforts on the **hidden job market**. These are jobs advertised informally through personal contacts. Many child care positions are never listed in help wanted ads, in early childhood journals, or with placement offices. Rather, these jobs are filled through word of mouth. To find out about such openings, you as a job seeker should contact center directors personally. This can be done through a letter, a telephone call, or e-mail. Some candidates have met with success by arranging a visit to the center and then asking about job openings. Even if no position is open at the time of the visit, some applicants have been called later when jobs become available.

Get to know early childhood staff workers in the community. One way to do this is to join the local chapter of the NAEYC. When you attend meetings, try to meet as many people as possible. Always let them know of your job search and when you will be available. In addition, become active in the organization. Volunteer for committees. Show the membership you are willing to work and are professionally motivated.

Networking

Networking is a process of building relationships with people who can help you. It is an important skill to develop. Networking is the job-seeker's most powerful tool. Almost 80 percent of positions are found through some type of networking with others.

One way to have your résumé considered is to have recommendations from respected people in the field. To find these people, you need to go where they are. Attend meetings of early childhood organizations, workshops, conferences, seminars, open houses, job fairs, and center tours. Since networking is a process, it usually takes several contacts to build a relationship. These contacts may be person-to-person meetings, phone conversations, e-mail contacts, voice mail, letters, and notes.

Maintaining a Filing System

Keep a file of all the centers or schools you have contacted, 33-9. Make a photocopy of each cover letter you send or maintain copies on a computer disk. You may also prepare

33-9

Keeping your job search information organized and up-to-date is important.

Vocabulary

Have a student volunteer define *hidden job market*. What is the role of the hidden job market in helping secure a job?

Enrich

Have students debate the following statement: Networking is the most powerful tool for a job seeker.

Note

Remind students that when asking a parent, teacher, employer, or other individual who knows them well to write a letter of recommendation, they should give the person a copy of their most recent résumé with a clearly defined job objective. This will help the person write a recommendation focused more toward their goal.

Putting Technology to Use

Have students conduct an Internet search for information on membership in professional organizations for early childhood education and answer the following questions: What organizations exist in your area that involve active participation, including meetings, workshops, and networking? What organizations provide newsletters or journals on early childhood education topics? Which have formal meetings? How might membership in these organizations affect your possible employment potential?

Discuss

What does it mean to say that employers want to hire *self-directed* people? Give some examples of occasions when you were self-directed during this course.

Activity

Have students look over Figure 33-10, *Positive Traits of Early Childhood Teachers*, and select five of the traits that they feel best represent them. Have them write a two-sentence explanation or description of activities that demonstrate each trait that could be brought up in an interview.

Resource

Interview Inventory, reproducible master 33-6, TR

index cards or a file on your computer for each contact. If you get a call from a director, you should quickly be able to retrieve the information and refresh your memory on the open position. To assist in this process, always keep a record of the school's name, address, telephone number, contact person, and date the contact letter was mailed.

If you have answered an ad, you may want to attach a copy of the ad to your cover letter or index card. When you receive a response (whether negative or positive), record this on your cover letter or index card. Make notes of interviews, thank-you notes, and other contacts on each letter or card as well.

Preparing for an Interview

Job offers only happen during or after an interview. Interviews are the single most important aspect of a job search. It is an opportunity to convey information about yourself.

When preparing for an interview, think positively. Picture yourself walking into the interview confident and relaxed. Get in the habit of being enthusiastic. Remember, enthusiasm is catching. It indicates appreciation and interest. Often, if you are enthusiastic, the interviewer will also share this feeling.

Employers want to hire self-directed people with a wide range of skills. They want people who are dependable, enthusiastic, and committed to the child care profession. They also want people who work hard and learn fast. They want people who manage their time well and who look for extra work when their work is done. In order to run a quality center, directors need to hire people who are resourceful.

Chart 33-10 outlines traits employers seek when hiring people to work in early childhood centers. In preparation for an interview, read the statements and check those that match qualities you would be able

33-10

Positive Traits of Early Childhood Teachers

- Flexible
- Energetic
- Self-confident
- Enthusiastic
- Mature
- Willing to do extra work
- Patient
- Cooperative
- Easy to get along with
- A fast learner
- A good time manager
- Creative
- Cheerful
- Positive
- Resourceful
- Dependable
- A good planner
- Committed to teaching
- Open to new ideas
- Self-disciplined
- Dedicated to hard work
- Motivated
- Self-reliant
- Thorough
- Self-directed
- Friendly
- Nurturing
- Possessing a good sense of humor
- Possessing strong interpersonal skills

Deciding which of these traits fit you will help you focus on your best traits and skills during an interview.

to bring to a position. Completing this task will bolster your own self-image. The exercise will help you get a clear picture of your skills. It will also prepare you to make a persuasive presentation during an interview.

Preparing Your Questions

In nearly all interviews, applicants are given the opportunity to ask questions. Thus, smart applicants always prepare questions for an interview. Learn everything you can about the center. You might form questions by talking to teachers who have taught at the center or asking questions of parents who have children attending the center. You can get general information about the center from the local Chamber of Commerce. Some questions you may wish to ask during an interview include

---

Portfolio Project

If students haven't already filed examples of evaluations of their teaching from the child care lab, have them select those evaluations that best represent their skills and abilities. If they have mastered a skill or improved a weakness from an earlier lesson, they may consider filing evaluations

that demonstrate this. If they have participated in a child care internship or work program, they should be sure to include evaluations from those activities. Remind students to be selective in the content of their portfolios to demonstrate their strengths and minimize their weaknesses.

- What is the educational philosophy of your center?

- To what extent may I implement my own ideas?

- Is the staff encouraged to attend conferences? If so, how often may a staff member attend, and who pays the fees?

- What audiovisual equipment is provided by the school?

- How often are parent conferences scheduled?

- Does the center send home a weekly parent letter or monthly newsletter? If so, who is responsible for writing and editing them?

Asking questions tells the interviewer you are serious about a job. Take time to practice your questions, eye contact, and posture.

The Interview

When you go to a job interview, arrive on time. Remember to take your driver's license or state ID card, Social Security card, résumé, portfolio, and list of questions for the interviewer. Give special thought to your appearance. You want to make a good impression. Make sure your hair is well groomed and attractively styled. Choose conservative jewelry, accessories, and shoes. For females, makeup should be applied lightly. Be sure your clothes are clean and neat. Choose clothes that are one step above those you would wear on the job. Avoid overdressing, but don't wear a T-shirt and jeans, either. Let your appearance tell the interviewer you are professional and can fit into the workplace.

At the interview, use body language to show interest. Make eye contact, smile, and greet the employer with a firm handshake. Many interviewers begin an interview simply by introducing themselves and welcoming you to the center. This is usually followed by small talk that might include the weather or a center activity. After this, you will probably be told information about the job. The interviewer may then ask you structured questions concerning your education or experience. Be enthusiastic; smile, nod and give nonverbal feedback to the interviewer. Provide full, focused answers and use the interviewer's name from time to time as you speak. Avoid answering a question with "no" or "yes." Instead say "no, but" and "yes, and." After all questions have been answered, the interviewer will ask you if you have any questions. At this point, you can ask those questions you prepared beforehand. Avoid asking questions about vacation time, benefits, and breaks. The interviewer may think your main concern is with nonwork functions.

Follow the lead of the interviewer. Throughout the interview, listen with an intelligent, intent look on your face. When necessary, ask questions that will help you better understand the job. Other tips for successful interviewing are listed in 33-11.

Be careful not to volunteer negative information about your former employer or yourself. Employers are seeking positive people to work for them. If you were not happy in a previous job or jobs, you may not be happy with this job either. Thus, it is vital not to mention anything negative. Focus on the position.

Throughout the interviewing process, you will need to sell your positive qualities. When asked what you did during your practicum, student teaching, or last job, do not recite the daily schedule or curriculum. Instead, state specific things you did to improve the center or classroom. For example, you might tell about how you made protective education part of the curriculum. Perhaps you revised the format for parent letters and reorganized the children's library.

Interview Questions

Prospective employers usually decide before the interview what information they

Enrich

Ask students what information they would want about a child care facility or program before they interviewed there. Have them select a program from your area and imagine they are going to participate at an interview in this facility. Tell them to investigate the information they think is significant.

Discuss

What information can you give about a former position? What information should you avoid sharing about the position or former fellow employees?

Resource

A Job Application, Activity C, SAG

Putting Technology To Use

Have students search the Internet for Web sites that offer tips on filling out job applications. Have students make lists of helpful tips and use a publishing program to create booklets to pass out to job hunters. Make sure the booklet contains a bibliography of the Web sites referenced.

Discuss

What type of questions should you avoid during an interview? What questions should you save for later in the interview after you have found out what the job requires?

Reflect

The following question is popular in job interviews: *What do you think a former employer or teacher would say about you?* What answer would you give to this question in an interview?

Resource

Interview Questions, Activity A, OG

33-11

Tips for a Successful Interview

- Be on time.
- Present your best appearance.
- Extend your hand to greet the interviewer with a firm handshake.
- Use the interviewer's name and smile as you speak.
- Bring your résumé and teaching portfolio with you.
- Remain relaxed and friendly.
- Listen carefully.
- Convey a positive attitude.
- Show your enthusiasm.
- Stress your strengths.
- Use active verbs while speaking.
- Personalize your questions.
- Respond to questions carefully.
- Be truthful; if you do not know an answer, say so.
- Provide more than a "yes" or "no" response to questions, but be concise.
- Thank the interviewer for his or her consideration at the end of the interview.
- Send a thank-you note.

The interview is your chance to make a good impression. Following these tips will help you.

33-12

Interviewers often prepare questions for the applicant ahead of time. They may record the applicant's answers during the interview.

need to share with you about a job. Job expectations, duties, and benefits are often included. Specific questions that you may be asked are also recorded, 33-12. The following questions are often included:

- Will you please share your educational background?
- What philosophy of education did that center have?
- What type of course work did you have?
- Do you have previous job experience? If so, describe your positions.
- Why are you looking for a new job?
- What are the most important characteristics of a teacher of young children?

- Use three words to describe your personality.
- What are some of your negative qualities? What is the biggest mistake you ever made?
- How would you describe your teaching style?
- Where do you see yourself professionally 10 years from today? Describe that job.
- Why are you interested in this job?

In addition, any of the following questions may also be asked:

- What is the value of children's play?
- How would you handle a child that is always hitting others?
- How would you plan a developmentally appropriate curriculum?
- How do you think your references described you when they were contacted?
- How would you handle transitions?
- How would you relate to parents?
- What is most annoying about children?

Portfolio Project

One of the possible interview questions from the textbook asks students to describe their teaching styles. Ask students to write a brief description of their teaching styles from their experiences in the child care lab; internship or work program employment; or other employment in the field. Have them look at evaluations from teachers and supervisors and include remarks that show what others think of their teaching styles. Have them include examples that demonstrate their style and approach to education.

- On what basis do you plan curriculum for young children?
- What would you do if a child kicked you and said "I don't like you"?

Employers who have had training in interviewing techniques may ask the following questions to find out more about your performance in your previous position:

- What disappointments did you face in your last teaching position?
- In what areas did your supervisor criticize you?
- In what areas did your supervisor compliment you?
- For what things did you need guidance or help from your supervisor?

Questions will also be asked to determine your level of motivation.

- Why did you select teaching young children as a career?
- Why did you apply for this job?
- What is your long-term career objective?
- What are you looking for in this position that you have not had in past positions?
- What type of position would you like to hold in three years? Ten years?

It is not unusual for an interviewer to ask "What are your weaknesses?" If this happens, sit quietly for a moment. It is always a mistake to quickly answer a question off the top of your head. Give each question some thought, then form a response in your mind. Then respond carefully and positively. Do not put yourself down while answering this question. Rather, share your growth by saying something like "I have really developed skills in classroom control" or "My parent interaction skills really grew during the last few weeks of my student teaching." Or express your weaknesses in a positive way: "I care too much about the children," "I take my work too seriously," or "I try too many new ideas."

Often the interviewer may end the interview with a final question. You may be asked, "Was there anything that you were afraid that I was going to ask?" If this occurs, remain calm. Sometimes interviewees will share a question that they feared. Then an interviewer could raise the question.

Teaching Portfolio

Bring along your teaching portfolio to demonstrate your growth and success. Your **teaching portfolio** tells a story. It should serve as a professional snapshot of your efforts, progress, and achievements. Your portfolio should contain evidence of your competence. Chart 33-13 contains the contents of a teaching portfolio.

Offer to share your teaching portfolio. You may say "I brought along my teaching portfolio. I would like to share the contents with you." While sharing the contents, use descriptions to support your materials. Explain why you chose each piece to include in the portfolio.

Exercise care so your portfolio does not take the form of a scrapbook. This type of portfolio should include your philosophy of teaching. One way to organize a portfolio is to have a table of contents with two major subheadings. The first subheading could be labeled *Background Information*. Your résumé and background information on your teaching experience could be included. Also include information on your teaching goals, letters of recommendation, and teachers' evaluations of your work.

The second subheading could be labeled *Teaching Artifacts*. This section of the portfolio should focus on the actual process and outcomes of teaching. Lesson plans, unit and theme plans, videos, anecdotal records, photographs, parent letters, and examples of teacher-made materials could be included.

Discuss

If the question *What do you find annoying about children?* is asked during an interview, how can you make a positive response that is realistic and shows that you know how to handle the annoyance? Example: if you don't like that children cry when their parents leave, explain successful strategies that reduce the crying time and distract the child.

Activity

The question *Where do you see yourself in five years or in ten years?* may be asked during an interview. Have students write a brief scenario of their ideal professional life and career advancement. What challenges will they face to achieve this ideal?

Vocabulary

Have a student volunteer define *teaching portfolio*. What is the role of the teaching portfolio during a job interview?

Workplace Connection

Ask students to conduct a survey among students and teachers in the school to discover the most difficult-to-answer questions from their own job interview experiences. Have the students compile a list of the most interesting questions and take turns answering the questions in a creative manner. Remind them that sometimes questions have no relation to the job because the interviewer is just trying to determine how the applicant will react under pressure. Creativity often scores high points in an interview, but students should be wary about trying to be too funny or entertaining during the interview.

Discuss

What is the difference between *teaching background* and *artifacts* in a portfolio? Why should you avoid a "scrapbook look" to your portfolio?

Enrich

Have students role-play responding respectfully but appropriately when asked illegal questions during an interview. One scenario might be a potential employer asking the interviewee about possible family planning.

Resource

Preparing for Interviews, reproducible master 33-7, TR

33-13

Teaching Portfolio

- Table of contents
- Résumé
- Official transcripts
- Copies of certifications, licenses, or CDA Credential certificate
- Letters of recommendation
- Anecdotal records
- Critical incident journals
- Photographs of bulletin boards and room arrangements you designed
- Parent letters
- Sample lesson plans and block plans
- Curriculum units and themes you have developed
- Photographs of activities with descriptions
- Teachers' evaluations
- Videotapes of a good teaching lesson
- Teacher-made materials
- Statement of educational philosophy and teaching goals
- Extracurricular activities

Keep the contents of your portfolio updated to reflect the progress of your career.

Legal Problems in Interviewing

At both the state and federal level, it is illegal to discriminate on the basis of age, sex, national origin, race, or religion. Most employers do not intend to use information obtained from an interview in order to discriminate. However, such information could affect the hiring decision. Therefore, it is illegal for an employer to ask questions about an applicant's race, national origin, or religion.

Interviewers are limited in the questions that can be asked. For example, a parent of small children cannot be asked how the children will be cared for while he or she is working. Likewise a parent cannot be asked about a spouse's employment or salary.

Women cannot be asked if they are planning to have a family or are currently pregnant. Interviewers are also forbidden to ask applicants their marital status or the number of children they have. Chart 33-14 lists questions that may be asked. To prevent discrimination, all applicants for a job should be asked the same questions during an interview.

Despite the fact that they are illegal, you may still find yourself being asked some of these questions. Some prospective employers may purposely ask such questions to discriminate. Others, however, may simply ask them in an effort to get to know you better or make you feel at ease. These interviewers may not even know that the questions they ask are illegal.

If you are ever asked an illegal question, it is up to you to decide what the intent of the interviewer was. Based on your judgment, use discretion and tact to handle the situation. You may decide to simply answer the question. If you believe the person's intent was to discriminate, and then you are offered the job, you may ask why the question was asked. If the person's answer concerns you, you may decide to decline the job offer.

You may also choose to not answer the question. Do not accuse the person of discrimination. Instead, you may say simply and calmly "I am sorry, but I am not required to answer that question."

Ending the Interview

An interview can be ended with words and/or through actions. Verbally, the interviewer may thank you for coming to signal the end of the interview. Nonverbally, the interviewer may sit up straight or stand up. This gesture means the interview is over. At this point, the interviewer has obtained all the information from you that is needed. Respond by thanking the interviewer for his or her time. See 33-15.

Workplace Connection

Have students review the items listed for a teaching portfolio in Figure 33-13 and answer the following questions: What items do you already have in your portfolio? What items will you still need to acquire? What items are not on the list but should be included in your portfolio because they help demonstrate your skills, abilities, attitudes, and philosophies?

33-14

Interview Questions

Subject	Legal Inquiries
Age	Only a question to determine if you meet state licensing requirements related to age Date of birth
Arrest record	Nothing
Marital status	Nothing
Convictions	Only convictions that would affect the job position
Education	Only questions related to training and experience related to the position
Family	Only questions related to meeting work schedule
Disabilities	Only questions about disabilities that would affect job performance
National origin	Only questions about ability to read, speak, and write the language the job requires
Organizations	Only questions about participation in professional organizations related to your ability to perform the job
Pregnancy	Only questions about anticipated absences from work
Religion	Only questions about anticipated absences from work

Interviewers are not allowed to ask questions that may result in discrimination.

Many people are disappointed when they learn they were not successful in getting the position. If you feel this way, do not think something is wrong with you. It is not unusual to feel depressed or feel a slip in your self-esteem. These feelings will pass.

Thank-You Letters

Always write a brief letter thanking the people who interviewed you. Sending a thank-you letter establishes good will and strengthens your candidacy. This simple courtesy is observed by as few as 10 percent of job seekers. In the letter, mention the secretaries, if appropriate. Also, your letter will serve as a reminder to those you met. Even if you are not hired for that position, the interviewer may remember you for future openings. He or she may even pass your name to someone else who is searching for a child care employee.

More people are sending thank-you letters to interviewers by e-mail. In today's era of electronic communication, this is quite acceptable to most employers. Whether you use e-mail or regular mail, the key is to be prompt. Always send your thank-you letter within two days of the interview.

33-15

Be sure to leave the interviewer with a positive impression of you.

Discuss

What message are you sending to a prospective employer when you e-mail or mail a thank-you note within two days after a job interview? How might this courtesy benefit you in the future?

Note

Have students practice the basic skills of writing letters in the appropriate format and addressing envelopes correctly. These skills are sometimes overlooked in the electronic age of e-mail communication.

Resource

Know How to Job Hunt, Activity B, SAG

Cross-Curricular Activity

Social Studies
Have students conduct an Internet search for information on Federal Equal Employment Opportunity (EEO) Laws. Some information may be accessed at **www.eeoc.gov**. What laws make up the United States government's protection of workers' rights? What areas of discrimination fall under the jurisdiction of the Equal Employment Opportunity Commission? What current initiatives of the EEOC are helping promote and provide employment for youth, people with disabilities, and displaced workers?

Discuss

How can knowing your employee rights and responsibilities make you a better employee? Explain what is meant by *employer's rights*.

Activity

Write the first paragraph under *Section I: Ethical Responsibilities to Children*, from Appendix A, *Principles from the Code of Ethical Conduct*, on the board or overhead projector. Ask students to explain and give examples of each of the harmful practices listed.

Resource

Rights Balance Responsibilities, transparency master 33-8, TR

These letters should be sent to everyone who was involved in the interview process. In addition to thanking them, you can restate your interest in the position and re-emphasize your qualifications. Point out the match between the job requirements and your experience. Also provide any important information that you did not share in the cover letter, résumé, or interview.

Employee Rights and Responsibilities

As an employee, you have certain rights that are protected by law. You also have other rights that are granted by your employer through personnel policies. Rights come with responsibilities, however. Some of a child care teacher's responsibilities are defined by law. Others have been set by NAEYC in the Code of Ethical Conduct. (See the Appendix at the back of this book for more information about the Code of Ethical Conduct.)

Knowing your employee rights helps you ensure those rights are respected. Employees desire a work environment in which their rights are honored. Similarly, being aware of your responsibilities helps you to be the best employee possible. When you understand what is expected of you, you can comply with all program policies and state child care licensing requirements.

Following these guidelines will ensure that your work contributes to the quality of the program and builds the program's reputation.

In many ways, your employee rights parallel responsibilities your employer has to you. For example, it is your employer's responsibility to make sure your right to a safe workplace is met in accordance with federal and state laws. Likewise, your employee responsibilities parallel rights of your employer. For example, your employer

Health and Safety

Employee Health Appraisals

As part of protecting the health and safety of young children, all early childhood staff members who work 40 hours or more per month should have regular health appraisals. The first screening takes place prior to working with children. Additional screenings take place every two years. These health appraisals include

- a complete health history
- physical, dental, vision, and hearing exams
- tuberculosis test
- a review of immunization status with immunization boosters given as needed
- a review of occupational health concerns as related to functioning on the job, such as back problems that might interfere in caring for children

In addition to regular health appraisals, it is strongly recommended that early childhood teachers have yearly influenza vaccinations.

has the right to receive a full day's work in exchange for a full day's pay. It is your responsibility as an employee to provide this work in a manner that meets the employer's expectations.

Workplace Connection

If possible, obtain a copy of an employee handbook from a local child care facility. Have students examine it for rights and responsibilities of both employee and employer. If a handbook cannot be obtained, ask students to list the rights they would expect as employees of a child care center. What rights and responsibilities do they think the employer should be entitled to from their employees? How can knowing these provide the basis for a respectful and productive employee-employer relationship?

Employee Rights

Employers have an ethical responsibility to create a quality workplace. The employer should strive to offer a supportive early childhood environment where both children and adults can reach their potential. This type of environment will encourage you to focus on your work and find satisfaction in it, 33-16.

In addition, your employer's policies may grant you other rights. When you begin a new position, ask for a copy of the employee handbook or other personnel papers. This information should outline your employee rights and responsibilities as defined by the employer. These are in addition to any rights and responsibilities protected by law.

Most importantly, you are entitled to be treated fairly by your employer as outlined in the handbook. All employees should be treated equally according to the terms set forth by the employer. Make it a point to familiarize yourself with the handbook so you can obtain all the benefits to which you are entitled and adhere to the employer's rules and expectations.

Early childhood programs have an ethical responsibility to provide a job orientation program for new hires. *Job orientation programs* are activities designed to acquaint you with the workplace. You should receive an overview of the program, its policies and procedures, and your employer's expectations of you. Any other training needed for your position should be part of the orientation period.

Another ethical practice is supportive supervision for employees. Your supervisor should assist you by answering questions, solving problems, and recommending areas for improvement. Early childhood programs should provide ongoing training to meet licensing requirements and improve the quality of the program. Workshops or classes that may be offered include curriculum, technology, parent involvement, health, safety, and communication skills. Supervision and ongoing training promote professional growth and job satisfaction.

In addition to employer-granted rights, many employee rights are protected by federal and state laws, 33-17. Employers have an obligation to understand and adhere to these laws. Your employer has a legal responsibility to observe all federal and state labor laws. In addition, all applicable federal and state payroll, wage, and income tax laws must be followed. You have legal rights regarding some aspects of employee benefits and insurance. Federal laws give you the right to work in an environment free from discrimination and sexual harassment. You have the right to a safe work environment. In specified medical and family situations, your employer must allow you to take up to 12 weeks unpaid leave per year and hold your job (or an equivalent job) until your leave ends. These are only a few examples—you have many other employee rights that are protected by law.

33-16

Early childhood teachers are happiest and most effective in a quality work environment.

Vocabulary

Have students define *job orientation programs*. Why is providing a job orientation part of the ethical responsibility of the employer?

Reflect

Benny was hired a month ago and is concerned that his employer is not satisfied with his job performance. The director is always popping into Benny's classroom for little visits several times each week. What would you say to Benny to alleviate his fears? What would you recommend he do if he is worried about his job performance?

Discuss

What is the benefit to the employee when the employer holds workshops or in-service opportunities for continuing education? Can an employer require attendance at these meetings as a provision of employment?

Putting Technology to Use

Have students investigate information about taxes at the Internal Revenue Service Web site, **www.irs.gov**. Some students don't understand how much of their paychecks will be taken for taxes when they get their first jobs. Also have students practice filling out W-4 forms, which are available in PDF format on the site. Explain withholding allowances.

Discuss

Why are attendance issues so critical for child care centers? What can receiving a licensing violation for being understaffed mean to a center?

Activity

Have students survey area child care centers to discover their workplace clothing requirements. Are jeans or shorts acceptable at any of the centers surveyed?

Note

You may wish to review with students what circumstances constitute sexual harassment. Information can be found at **www.eeoc.gov**.

33-17

Employee Rights Protected by Law

- Labor, pay, tax, and benefit administration procedures in accordance with laws
- Equal pay for equal work regardless of gender
- Freedom from workplace discrimination
- Freedom from sexual harassment
- Safe workplace
- Reasonable workplace accommodations for disabled workers
- Right to take specified unpaid leave to attend to covered family and medical conditions

This list is only a sampling of the many employee rights that are protected by state and federal laws.

Employee Responsibilities

When you accept an early childhood teaching position, you agree to fulfill certain responsibilities. You agree to do the job for which your employer is paying you. First and foremost, you are responsible for complying with all center policies and state childcare licensing requirements. You must also adhere to the ethical standards of the profession, as set forth in NAEYC's Code of Ethical Conduct.

An early childhood teacher's role is to provide the children with developmentally appropriate, responsive care. Your employer has a responsibility to create a quality work environment. You have a responsibility to maintain and contribute to the quality of the program. To do this, you must have good attendance and be punctual. You should also have a professional appearance, model a positive attitude, and maintain confidentiality. When necessary, you are also responsible for seeking help from your supervisor.

Attendance and Punctuality

Your employer has the right to expect a full day's work from you in exchange for the pay you earn. You have a responsibility to maintain good work attendance and be punctual. The director, staff members, and parents count on you to be at work every day. You should arrive a few minutes early each day or at least be on time.

Being even a few minutes late also causes extra work and stress for your coworkers and director. State licensing rules and regulations specify required adult-child ratios at all times. This means the director must try to make other arrangements to cover your classroom in case you are absent or late. If no one can cover for you, this places your program at risk for noncompliance. The center can receive a licensing violation for being understaffed. Legally, the center can also be at risk if a child is seriously injured when required ratios are not met. Repeated violations can cause a center to lose its license. In addition to legal responsibilities, you have an ethical obligation to the families and children you serve, as well as to your coworkers and director.

For these reasons, repeated absenteeism or tardiness is a serious performance problem. Many programs have attendance and tardiness policies. If you fail to follow these policies, you are likely to be fired from your job. Even if no written attendance policies are in place, you can lose your job as a result of repeated attendance problems.

Professional Appearance

You have an ethical obligation to your employer to maintain a professional appearance. You must represent your program in a professional manner. In large part, parents, children, visitors, and coworkers will base their initial impressions of you on your appearance. To illustrate, parents may feel a teacher wearing a casual

Workplace Connection

Have students investigate the following: Does your state require child care workers and educators in licensed facilities to obtain continuing education credit each year? If so, how many hours are required? How do employees obtain and document these credits? Are licensed centers required to offer classes or workshops for their employees? Are they required to pay for the employees to attend continuing education?

two-piece outfit is more intelligent and nurturing than a teacher wearing blue jeans. People may equate your grooming and dress with how seriously you take your work. These assessments may not be accurate, but they occur nevertheless.

Looking professional requires good grooming and avoiding extremes in hairstyles and clothing. Being well groomed involves both cleanliness and neatness, 33-18. Follow good hygiene practices, such as showering or bathing daily. Keep your hair clean, groomed, and simply styled. If you have long hair, try to keep it out of your face. Tying your hair back while working with young children will prevent children from pulling it. This also prevents loose hair from falling into the children's faces.

33-18

Child care directors should present a neat, clean appearance with their dress and grooming.

When you work with young children, you will need comfortable, washable clothing that allows for easy movement. Avoid tight or restrictive clothing in which it is difficult to move. Your clothes should be clean and neat. Clothing should not be wrinkled, frayed, stained, or ripped.

Male and female teachers alike often prefer washable slacks because these are comfortable yet convey a professional appearance. Most early childhood programs consider jeans, sweatpants, shorts, and spandex leggings unacceptable. Females can wear skirts or dresses, but skirts and dresses can be less comfortable for playing with children outside or on the floor.

Sweaters or shirts should be washable, casual business attire. T-shirts are often considered inappropriate, especially those with crude sayings or graphics. Tube, halter, sleeveless, cropped, and low-cut tops are always inappropriate for the early childhood workplace.

For directors, more dressy business attire may be appropriate, depending on the program. Directors interact more with parents, visitors, and teachers than directly with children. Male directors might wear dress slacks, shirt, and tie, with a jacket for more formal occasions. Female directors might wear dresses, skirts, and pantsuits.

Positive Attitude

Much of your success as a child care professional will depend on your attitude. Your **attitude** is your outlook on life—the ways in which you think about or act toward others. Finding great pleasure in teaching requires a positive attitude. This attitude enables you to see the potential in any child, parent, staff member, situation, or idea. Instead of seeing limitations, you seek opportunities.

People with a positive attitude want to do well. They take responsibility for their decisions. Teachers who have a positive attitude view working with young children as

Activity

Have students look through clothing catalogs to find examples of acceptable clothing to wear as a child care professional. Have students create a bulletin board using images cut from the catalogs.

Note

When taking your students on a field trip to a child care center, it is a good idea to require them to dress in a manner consistent with what is required at the center. Although jeans and T-shirts may be acceptable for school attire, the center may discourage the students from dressing so casually for what is, in effect, a professional visit.

Reflect

How can having a positive attitude affect others? Give examples of personal incidents or situations where having a positive attitude led to success.

Portfolio Project

Have students review their school attendance records for the last several years, paying particular attention to absences and tardies, and answer the following questions: What does your attendance say about your attitude toward work? How would a potential employer interpret your readiness for employment? Have students write a paragraph that shows their understanding of the relationship of good attendance to successful job performance. Have them refer to their attendance records, if applicable, as examples of positive attitude.

Vocabulary

Have a student volunteer define *confidentiality*. Why is keeping confidentiality an ethical consideration for child care employees?

Reflect

Jonathan's mother has told you not to worry about his repeated bruises because he is very clumsy and always falling. What is your legal responsibility as a mandated reporter in this situation?

Discuss

What is the difference between gossiping and showing concern? Why is gossiping with or about coworkers a bad idea? How is this true of any job, including those that do not require confidentiality?

a chance for continuous learning. They seek knowledge about child development, guidance, and curriculum. These teachers are easy to recognize on the job. They welcome suggestions on improving their skills for working with young children. Employers enjoy workers who demonstrate a positive attitude.

Confidentiality

As a teacher of young children, you will have access to a wide range of privileged information. You may see personal records and learn private information about others. For example, you may know which children do and do not receive child care tuition assistance. Daniel's parents may share with you personal information about their divorce to help you work with Daniel in the most understanding way. You may know that Juana's mother has cancer, and Kevin may tell you about his father leaving the family.

In most cases, you must keep sensitive personal information private. This is called keeping **confidentiality**. It means not sharing this information with others beyond what is required by your work. Keeping confidentiality protects and shows respect for children, families, coworkers, and the program itself.

Confidentiality does have some limits. For example, you can and should share information about children and families with certain coworkers for reasons relevant to the job. For example, you should inform other staff members who work with a child about the child's special medical, physical, or learning needs. This information helps the staff provide appropriate care and learning experiences. Likewise, you may need to inform your director about the unethical practices of a coworker after you have tried unsuccessfully to resolve the matter with that person. This information helps the director keep the children healthy and safe.

Child abuse and neglect present another exception to confidentiality. The law requires that cases of abuse and neglect be reported to

the proper state agency. If you suspect neglect or abuse, follow your program's policy for making this report. Your legal responsibility as a mandated reporter outweighs your responsibility to keep private information. In this case, you are required by law to break confidentiality.

In most other cases, it is unacceptable to break confidentiality. For example, you should not gossip with your coworkers, friends, or family members about the children and families at the center. Do not talk to parents about other families or children in the program. Avoid discussing the personal matters of coworkers. These practices are unethical. If parents learn you have broken confidentiality, they may feel betrayed. Their resulting suspicion could cause long-term damage to the reputations of you and your program. Broken trust can strain coworker relationships and undermine teamwork.

Some centers ask their employees to sign confidentiality agreements. These agreements protect the confidentiality of a program's families, children, and fellow employees. A confidentiality agreement should specify with whom various types of information can and cannot be shared. If an employee violates this agreement, the employee loses his or her job.

At times, knowing which information to keep private can be challenging. It is always best to err on the side of caution. When considering whether to share personal or private information about other people, always ask yourself the questions in 33-19. Base your decision on your answers to these questions.

Terminating Employment

You will have many jobs during the course of your lifetime. Job changes are common today. Employee turnover is high for all age groups.

Workplace Connection

Present the following problem to students: While in the grocery store checkout lane, you overhear two of your coworkers discussing the family situation of a little girl in their class. The girl's father is in jail and the family is now on public assistance. What is your responsibility concerning the situation? What should you do first? If your first attempt does not work, what should you do next? Why should you be concerned with what child care coworkers do on their own time?

33-19

Deciding When to Share Private Information

- What is my purpose for sharing the information? Does my disclosure help the child or family in any important way?
- With whom am I sharing the information? Does this person have a need or right to know?
- Whose privacy is involved? How might this person feel about me sharing this information with others? If I am unsure, have I asked him or her?
- How would my supervisor feel about me sharing this information? If I am unsure, have I asked him or her?
- How might sharing this information negatively affect my current position and my career? Is the disclosure legally or ethically important enough to take these risks?

Answering these questions can help you decide whether it is a good idea to share confidential information you possess.

There are many reasons why people leave their jobs. Some of these reasons include the following:

- desire for better pay or fringe benefits
- desire for better working conditions or hours
- seeking more opportunities for advancement
- looking for new challenges and responsibilities
- making better use of personal skills and abilities
- a conflict with supervisors or coworkers at current job
- transportation problems
- company layoffs, restructuring, downsizing, or closings

A change in their personal lives can lead to a job change. For example, a person may need to change jobs if a spouse is transferred to another city. A family move can lead to a job change. Marriage, divorce, death, or the birth of children can create new job requirements. Others leave their jobs to further their education. Sometimes health problems can dictate a job or environment change.

Before a job change is made, it is important to think through your options. Is this the best course of action at this time? Carefully weigh the pros and cons of leaving your current job for another job.

If you decide a job change is needed, resist the urge to leave your old job immediately. Instead, start looking for a new job before leaving your current job, if at all possible. Be sure you have enough money set aside to carry you over to your next paycheck. If you do not have enough money in savings, you may want to keep your current job until you find a better one.

Guidelines for Leaving a Job

There is a right way to leave your job. You want to leave under the best possible circumstances. Inform your employer before you tell your coworkers. Do so at least two weeks prior to your leaving. This allows your employer time to find your replacement.

Give notice to your employer in person, but also provide a written *letter of resignation*. A resignation letter is appropriate in most situations. This letter should state your last day of work and why you are leaving. It can be brief, but it should be positive. Thank your employer for the opportunity to work there. Describe how you have benefited from your job. You might offer to train your replacement, if appropriate.

During the two weeks before you leave, continue to do your job as you always have. If you work directly with children, prepare them for your departure. Be pleasant to your coworkers as you may work with them again

Discuss

How could a conflict with coworkers or supervisors affect your job performance? What family issues may cause you to seek a new job?

Activity

Ask students to research on the Internet to find out the current job turnover rate for child care workers. What reasons are given to explain the rate of turnover?

Discuss

How can a high job turnover rate affect a child care center? How might it affect the children at the center?

Putting Technology to Use

Have students conduct an Internet search for information on labor or professional unions for child care workers and answer the following questions: What is the primary role of child care worker unions? What unions exist for child care workers? Have they been successful in their initiatives? How do they encourage memberships? What can unions offer to child care workers beyond what employers can offer?

Vocabulary

Have students define *role* and list their current roles and responsibilities.

Discuss

Who may suffer from role strain? Why? Do students ever suffer from role strain?

Reflect

As an early childhood educator, a family member, and possibly a parent, you will have personal and job-related needs and responsibilities. What can you do to ensure success and balance in all your roles?

Resource

Balancing Multiple Roles, Activity D, SAG

in a different job. Do not complain about your current job, nor brag about your new one. Thank coworkers for their help and friendship.

Balancing Multiple Roles

One of the most challenging tasks for workers is to balance their many roles. A **role** is a set of responsibilities that accompanies a position you hold in life. Each person has several roles. For example, some of these roles include wage-earner, spouse, parent, son or daughter (and other family relationships), friend, citizen, and volunteer. Every role has demands and responsibilities. Achieving harmony among various roles is challenging but important.

Many adults feel **role strain**, a type of stress created by being unable to successfully balance multiple roles. Anyone can feel role strain, but it is most common in single-parent and dual-career families. In these families, parents arrive home from a day's work and must assume home-care and parenting tasks in the evening, 33-20. Errands must also be squeezed into evening and weekend hours. Working parents often feel they are juggling too many responsibilities with too little time to devote to them. Too many times, their personal and relationship needs go unmet. Having unmet needs adds to the level of stress they feel.

Even as a young person, you have several roles. You are a son or daughter, student, friend, community member, and perhaps also a worker or volunteer. As a family member, you may be expected to help with family tasks, attend family events, and spend quality time with the family (such as evening meals). As a student, you have homework, tests, and projects to complete. Extracurricular activities, such as clubs or sports, bring additional roles.

Friends will want you to spend time with them. Volunteer or part-time work creates even more demands on your time.

Making time for all these roles can be an enormous challenge. Learning to manage your time is a valuable tool. Planning can help you meet your most important duties. Although you might like to, you will not always be able to say yes to everything. Being able to set priorities will help you decide which things to let go. Learning to say no in a positive, unapologetic way will be useful, too.

Staying healthy will help you meet your many obligations. Getting adequate rest, nutrition, and physical activity will allow you to feel your best. You also need personal time to relax, think, and plan. Strengthening relationships with family and friends will promote your social and emotional development.

To succeed in a child care career, you will need to strike a balance among your many roles. The way in which you do this will likely be as unique as you are. However, finding this balance matters more than exactly how you achieve it.

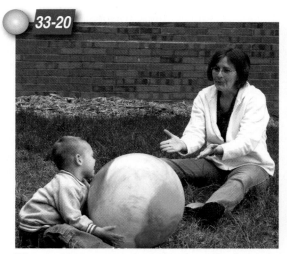

33-20

When working parents come home, they often find their children are eager to spend time with them.

Meeting Special Needs

Review the special learners' chapter outlines to determine if the students have any questions about the concepts or content of this chapter. Review the chapter objectives and ask the students to evaluate their progress in meeting these objectives. Ask the students to summarize, orally or in writing, what they have learned from this chapter.

Summary

Choosing a career involves a process of self-assessment. As part of this process, you must examine your interests and abilities, as well as values and professional priorities. Your answers to many important questions can help your childhood position decide if you are well suited to a career in teaching.

Searching for an early childhood career is a rewarding but sometimes frustrating experience. During your search for a position, you can learn a great deal about yourself. A well-organized search is never boring!

While each person's search differs, there are some general guidelines to follow. Start with a résumé. Include a cover letter. Use your résumé when you meet with or talk to prospective employers.

When you obtain an interview, be prepared. Bring your teaching portfolio. Prepare yourself for the interviewer's questions. Also write questions of your own to ask the interviewer. Conduct yourself in a professional manner and show your enthusiasm for working with young children. Send a thank-you letter after the interview to everyone who was involved.

Once you are hired for a position, you gain employee rights and responsibilities. It is important for you to fully understand both your rights and your responsibilities. Knowing your rights helps you receive the full benefits to which you are entitled. Understanding your responsibilities allows you to do your work as your employer expects.

Balancing multiple roles is challenging but important. Many conflicting demands will arise, but you can prioritize which demands to fulfill and which to let go. Many skills can help you in this process. Achieving a healthy role balance will promote your success as an early education professional!

Review and Reflect

1. Why are interests and abilities important considerations in choosing a career?
2. Explain the differences between values and professional priorities
3. A _____ should include a list of your qualifications, skills, and job experience.
4. How can a recent graduate stress job experience on his or her résumé?
5. True or false. Some highly qualified job applicants may not obtain job interviews because of poor writing skills.
6. If you notice an ad for an appealing position, _____.
   A. wait a few weeks and then contact the center director
   B. contact the center director at once
   C. place your own ad in hopes that the center director will contact you
   D. None of the above.
7. What is the major disadvantage of placing a position wanted ad?
8. What is the hidden job market?
9. What steps might you take to learn about job openings through the hidden job market?
10. When preparing for an interview, _____.
    A. think positively
    B. put the interview out of your mind until the time it is scheduled
    C. it's best if you are nervous
    D. None of the above.
11. Asking questions about a job shows the interviewer you are _____ about the position.
    A. desperate
    B. serious
    C. undecided
    D. None of the above.
12. True or false. For a job interview, you should always choose clothes that are one step above those you would wear on the job.

5. by listing all unpaid work experience, such as lab work, volunteer work in field of study, involvement in professional organizations
6. B
7. Placing an ad in the position wanted section of the newspaper is a passive job search technique that requires the employer to seek you out. This usually works best for those people who have a great deal of experience.
8. jobs advertised informally through personal contacts
9. contact center directors personally, join local chapters of professional organizations, network
10. A
11. B
12. true
13. B
14. portfolio
15. true
16. Sending a thank-you letter establishes goodwill and strengthens your candidacy. Your letter will serve as a reminder to those you have met. A thank-you letter is considered a professional courtesy.
17. Employee rights are almost always parallel to an employer's responsibilities. An employer must create or accept the conditions that lead to the employee's right being respected.

Review and Reflect Answer Key

1. Workers are most satisfied and have the most success in careers that interest them and in careers for which they have the abilities needed to perform the tasks of the job.
2. While values relate more to an individual's beliefs, ideas, and feelings about what is important in life, professional priorities are aspects of the job that are important to a person's satisfaction.
3. résumé
4. true

18. (List four employee rights and four employee responsibilities: Student response.)

19. Keeping confidentiality shows respect for children, families, coworkers, and the program itself.

20. Balancing multiple roles means to achieve harmony between the demands of various positions a person fills in life. Meeting the responsibilities of each role requires individuals to prioritize and plan carefully.

13. If an interviewer asks you what your weaknesses are, you should _____.
   A. answer quickly
   B. think for a moment before answering
   C. refuse to answer
   D. None of the above.

14. Your teaching _____ tells a story about your efforts, progress, and achievements.

15. True or false. It is illegal to discriminate on the basis of an applicant's religion.

16. Why should you write a thank-you letter to your interviewer following a job interview?

17. How do employee rights relate to employer responsibilities?

18. List four employee rights and four employee responsibilities.

19. Explain why keeping confidentiality is important for professionals in early childhood.

20. What does it mean to balance multiple roles?

Apply and Explore

1. Prepare a résumé. When you finish, ask your teacher for suggestions on how you might improve it.

2. Prepare a teaching portfolio. Practice describing the contents to a friend.

3. Attend a meeting of a local chapter of NAEYC. Talk with a variety of the members to learn about their work.

Cross-Curricular Link

Language Arts

1. Role-play a job interview with a classmate.

Math

3. Visit the Web site www.salary.com. Compare the salaries for early childhood and childcare teachers throughout the country.

Technology

5. Visit the Web site of the American Job Bank (www.ajb.org), which is sponsored by the Department of Labor. Search the database for early childhood jobs.

Workplace Link

Contact the guidance department of your school and arrange to take an aptitude test and self-assessment. Your school may have computer programs that combine both. Go over your results and determine if your skills and aptitudes are suitable for a career working with children. Discuss the results with your guidance counselor. Ask for additional advice regarding courses to take and opportunities for higher learning. Also explore information about internships, job shadowing, and job placement.

Appendix A
Principles from the Code of Ethical Conduct National Association for the Education of Young Children

Section I: Ethical responsibilities to children

- Above all, we shall not harm children. We shall not participate in practices that are emotionally damaging, physically harmful, disrespectful, degrading, dangerous, exploitative, or intimidating to children. *This principle has precedence over all others in this Code.*
- We shall care for and educate children in positive emotional and social environments that are cognitively stimulating and that support each child's culture, language, ethnicity, and family structure.
- We shall not participate in practices that discriminate against children by denying benefits, giving special advantages, or excluding them from programs or activities on the basis of their sex, race, national origin, religious beliefs, medical condition, disability, or the marital status/family structure, sexual orientation, or religious beliefs or other affiliations of their families.
- We shall involve all of those with relevant knowledge (including families and staff) in decisions concerning a child, as appropriate, ensuring confidentiality of sensitive information.

- We shall use appropriate assessment systems, which include multiple sources of information, to provide information on children's learning and development.
- We shall strive to ensure that decisions such as those related to enrollment, retention, or assignment to special education services will be based on multiple sources of information and will never be based on a single assessment, such as a test score or a single observation.
- We shall strive to build individual relationships with each child; make individualized adaptations in teaching strategies, learning environments, and curricula; and consult with the family so that each child benefits from the program. If after such efforts have been exhausted the current placement does not meet a child's needs, or the child is seriously jeopardizing the ability of other children to benefit from the program, we shall collaborate with the child's family and appropriate specialists to determine the additional services needed and/or the placement option(s) most likely to ensure the child's success.
- We shall be familiar with the risk factors for and symptoms of child abuse and neglect, including physical, sexual, verbal, and emotional abuse and physical, emotional, educational, and medical neglect. We shall know

667

and follow state laws and community procedures that protect children against abuse and neglect.

- When we have reasonable cause to suspect child abuse or neglect, we shall report it to the appropriate community agency and follow up to ensure that appropriate action has been taken. When appropriate, parents or guardians will be informed that the referral will be or has been made.
- When another person tells us of his or her suspicion that a child is being abused or neglected, we shall assist that person in taking appropriate action to protect the child.
- When we become aware of a practice or situation that endangers the health, safety, or well-being of children, we have an ethical responsibility to protect children or inform parents and/or others who can.

Section II: Ethical responsibilities to families

- We shall not deny family members access to their child's classroom or program setting unless access is denied by court order or other legal restriction.
- We shall inform families of program philosophy, policies, curriculum, assessment system, and personnel qualifications, and explain why we teach as we do—which should be in accordance with our ethical responsibilities to children (see Section I).
- We shall inform families of and, when appropriate, involve them in policy decisions.
- We shall involve the family in significant decisions affecting their child.
- We shall make every effort to communicate effectively with all families

in a language that they understand. We shall use community resources for translation and interpretation when we do not have sufficient resources in our own programs.

- As families share information with us about their children and families, we shall consider this information to plan and implement the program.
- We shall inform families about the nature and purpose of the program's child assessments and how data about their child will be used.
- We shall treat child assessment information confidentially and share this information only when there is a legal need for it.
- We shall inform the family of injuries and incidents involving their child, of risks such as exposures to communicable diseases that might result in infection, and of occurrences that might result in emotional stress.
- Families shall be fully informed of any proposed research projects involving their children and shall have the opportunity to give or withhold consent without penalty. We shall not permit or participate in research that could in any way hinder the education, development, or well-being of children.
- We shall not engage in or support exploitation of families. We shall not use our relationship with a family for private advantage or personal gain, or enter into relationships with family members that might impair our effectiveness in working with their children.
- We shall develop written policies for the protection of confidentiality and the disclosure of children's records. These policy documents shall be made available to all program personnel and families. Disclosure of children's records beyond family members, program personnel, and consultants having an obligation of confidentiality shall require familial consent (except in cases of abuse or neglect).
- We shall maintain confidentiality and shall respect the family's right to privacy,

refraining from disclosure of confidential information and intrusion into family life. However, when we have reason to believe that a child's welfare is at risk, it is permissible to share confidential information with agencies, as well as with individuals who have legal responsibility for intervening in the child's interest.

- In cases where family members are in conflict with one another, we shall work openly, sharing our observations of the child, to help all parties involved make informed decisions. We shall refrain from becoming an advocate for one party.
- We shall be familiar with and appropriately refer families to community resources and professional support services. After a referral has been made, we shall follow up to ensure that services have been appropriately provided.

Section III: Ethical responsibilities to colleagues

Responsibilities to co-workers

- We shall recognize the contributions of colleagues to our program and not participate in practices that diminish their reputations or impair their effectiveness in working with children and families.
- When we have concerns about the professional behavior of a co-worker, we shall first let that person know of our concern in a way that shows respect for personal dignity and for the diversity to be found among staff members, and then attempt to resolve the matter collegially and in a confidential manner.
- We shall exercise care in expressing views regarding the personal attributes or professional conduct of co-workers. Statements should be based on firsthand knowledge, not hearsay, and relevant to the interests of children and programs.
- We shall not participate in practices that discriminate against a co-worker because of sex, race, national origin, religious beliefs or other affiliations, age, marital status/family structure, disability, or sexual orientation.

Responsibilities to employers

- We shall follow all program policies. When we do not agree with program policies, we shall attempt to effect change through constructive action within the organization.
- We shall speak or act on behalf of an organization only when authorized. We shall take care to acknowledge when we are speaking for the organization and when we are expressing a personal judgment.
- We shall not violate laws or regulations designed to protect children and shall take appropriate action consistent with this Code when aware of such violations.
- If we have concerns about a colleague's behavior, and children's well-being is not at risk, we may address the concern with that individual. If children are at risk or the situation does not improve after it has been brought to the colleague's attention, we shall report the colleague's unethical or incompetent behavior to an appropriate authority.
- When we have a concern about circumstances or conditions that impact the quality of care and education within the program, we shall inform the program's administration or, when necessary, other appropriate authorities.

Responsibilities to employees

- In decisions concerning children and programs, we shall draw upon the education, training, experience, and expertise of staff members.

- We shall provide staff members with safe and supportive working conditions that honor confidences and permit them to carry out their responsibilities through fair performance evaluation, written grievance procedures, constructive feedback, and opportunities for continuing professional development and advancement.
- We shall develop and maintain comprehensive written personnel policies that define program standards. These policies shall be given to new staff members and shall be available for review by all staff members.
- We shall inform employees whose performance does not meet program expectations of areas of concern and, when possible, assisted in improving their performance.
- We shall conduct employee dismissals for just cause, in accordance with all applicable laws and regulations. We shall inform employees who are dismissed of the reasons for their termination. When a dismissal is for cause, justification must be based on evidence of inadequate or inappropriate behavior that is accurately documented, current, and available for the employee to review.
- In making evaluations and recommendations, we shall make judgments based on fact and relevant to the interests of children and programs.
- We shall make hiring, retention, termination, and promotion decisions based solely on a person's competence, record of accomplishment, ability to carry out the responsibilities of the position, and professional preparation specific to the developmental levels of children in his/her care.
- We shall not make hiring, retention, termination, and promotion decisions based on an individual's sex, race, national origin, religious beliefs or other affiliations, age, marital status/family structure, disability, or sexual orientation. We shall be familiar with and observe laws and regulations that pertain to employment discrimination.
- We shall maintain confidentiality in dealing with issues related to an employee's job performance and shall respect an employee's right to privacy regarding personal issues.

Section IV: Ethical responsibilities to community and society

- We shall communicate openly and truthfully about the nature and extent of services that we provide.
- We shall apply for, accept, and work in positions for which we are personally well-suited and professionally qualified. We shall not offer services that we do not have the competence, qualifications, or resources to provide.
- We shall carefully check references and shall not hire or recommend for employment any person whose competence, qualifications, or character makes him or her unsuited for the position.
- We shall be objective and accurate in reporting the knowledge upon which we base our program practices.
- We shall be knowledgeable about the appropriate use of assessment strategies and instruments and interpret results accurately to families.
- We shall be familiar with laws and regulations that serve to protect the children in our programs and be vigilant in ensuring that these laws and regulations are followed.
- When we become aware of a practice of situation that endangers the health,

safety, or well-being of children, we have an ethical responsibility to protect children or inform parents and/or others who can.

- We shall not participate in practices that are in violation of laws and regulations that protect the children in our programs.
- When we have evidence that an early childhood program is violating laws or regulations protecting children, we shall report the violation to appropriate authorities who can be expected to remedy the situation.
- When a program violates or requires its employees to violate this Code, it is permissible, after fair assessment of the evidence, to disclose the identity of that program.
- When policies are enacted for purposes that do not benefit children, we have a collective responsibility to work to change these practices.
- When we have evidence that an agency that provides services intended to ensure children's well-being is failing to meet its obligations, we acknowledge a collective ethical responsibility to report the problem to appropriate authorities or to the public. We shall be vigilant in our follow-up until the situation is resolved.
- When a child protection agency fails to provide adequate protection for abused or neglected children, we acknowledge a collective ethical responsibility to work toward the improvement of these services.

©2005 National Association for the Education of Young Children. These excerpts from an official position statement of the National Association for the Education of Young Children are reprinted by permission.

Appendix B

Developmental Traits of Children from Birth to Age 12*	
Birth to Two Years	
Motor Skills	
1 Month	Moves reflexively. Does not control body movements. Needs support for head. Without support, head will flop backward and forward. Lifts head briefly from the surface in order to turn head from side to side when lying on tummy. Twitches whole body when crying. Keeps hands fisted or slightly open. May hold object if placed in hand, but drops it quickly.
2 Months	Can keep head in midposition of body when lying on tummy. Can hold head up for a few minutes. Can turn head when lying on back. Cycles arms and legs smoothly. Movements are mainly reflexive, but may begin to become voluntary. Grasps objects in reflex movements, but grasps are becoming voluntary. May hold object longer, but still drops object after a few seconds. Uses improved vision to look at objects more closely and for a longer time.
3 Months	Shows active body movements. Can move arms and legs together. Turns head vigorously. Can lift head when lying on tummy. Can sit briefly with support. Follows moving objects with eyes.
4 Months	On tummy, can lift head and chest from surface using arms for support. On tummy, may roll from side to side. Can maintain a sitting position for several minutes if given proper support. Begins to use mitten grasp for grabbing objects near the hands. Looks from object to hands to object. Swipes at objects, gradually improving aim.

Motor Skills *(continued)*	
5 Months	On back, can lift head and shoulders off surface. Can roll from tummy to back. When supported under arms, stands and moves body up and down, stamping feet alternately. Helps when being pulled to a sitting position. Can sit supported for 15 to 30 minutes with a firm back. Reaches for objects such as an activity gym with good coordination and aim. Begins to grasp objects with thumb and fingers. Grabs objects with either hand. Transfers objects from one hand to the other, dropping objects often.
6 Months	Rolls from back to tummy. On tummy, moves by pushing with legs and reaching with arms. Gets up on hands and knees, but then may fall forward. Is able to stand while supported. May be able to sit for short periods of time. Reaches with one arm and grasps object with hand, then transfers the object to other hand, then reaches for another object. Learns to drop an object at will. Holds an object in both hands. Sits in a tripod position using arms for support.
7 Months	Crawls awkwardly, combining movements on tummy and knees. Likes to bounce when in standing position. May be able to pull self to a standing position. Can lean over and reach while in sitting position. Has mastered grasping by using thumb in opposition to fingers. Holds an object in each hand. Brings objects together with banging noises. Keeps objects in hands most of the time. Fingers, manipulates, and rattles objects repeatedly.
8 Months	Sits alone steadily for longer periods of time. Crawls. Achieves sitting position by pushing up with arms. Learns pincer grasp, using just the thumb and forefinger. Is able to pick up small objects and string.
9 Months	Sits alone. May try to crawl up stairs. May be able to move along furniture, touching it for support. Uses index finger to point, lead, and poke.
10 Months	Likes to walk holding caregiver's hands. Climbs on chairs and other furniture. Stands with little support. Can release grasped object instead of dropping it.
11 Months	Stands alone. Is able to stand and pick up objects. Likes to grasp feeding utensils and cup. May carry spoon to mouth in feeding attempt. Takes off shoes and socks.

	Motor Skills *(continued)*
12 Months	Climbs up and down stairs. May show preference for one hand. May be able to take off clothes. Walks with one hand held.
13 to 15 Months	Builds a tower consisting of 2 one-inch cubes. Turns pages in a book 2 or 3 at a time. Walks without assistance. While walking, cannot maneuver around corners or stop suddenly. Scribbles vigorously.
16 to 18 Months	Walks up steps. Walks well while carrying or pulling a toy. Hurls a ball. Can place 6 round pegs in pegboard.
19 to 22 Months	Walks up stairs independently, one at a time. Completes a 3-piece formboard. Places 4 rings on post in random order. Rolls, pounds, squeezes, and pulls clay. Kicks backward and forward. Jumps in place.
22 to 24 Months	Attempts to stand on balance beam. Builds tower of 6 cubes. Runs without falling. Pedals a tricycle. Kicks a large ball.
	Cognitive Skills
1 Month	Prefers to look at human faces and patterned objects. Listens attentively to sounds and voices. Cries deliberately for assistance; also communicates with grunts and facial expressions. Is comforted by the human voice and music.
2 Months	Coordinates eye movements. Shows obvious preference for faces to objects. Makes some sounds, but most vocalizing is still crying. Shows some interest in sounds and will stop sucking to listen.
3 Months	Is able to suck and look at the same time, thus doing two controlled actions at once. Discovers hands and feet as an extension of self. Searches with eyes for sounds. Begins cooing one syllable, vowel-like sounds—*ooh, ah, aw*. Laughs out loud.
4 Months	Likes to repeat enjoyable acts like shaking a rattle. Enjoys watching hands and feet. Looks at an object, reaches for it, and makes contact with it. Makes first consonant sounds—*p, b, m, l*. Smiles and coos when caregiver talks to him or her. Explores toys by grasping, sucking, shaking, and banging.

Cognitive Skills *(continued)*	
5 Months	Recognizes and responds to own name. Smiles at self in mirror. Can recognize people by their voices. Babbles spontaneously.
6 Months	Grabs at any and all objects in reach. Studies objects intently, turning them to see all sides. Varies volume, pitch, and rate while babbling. Acquires sounds of native language in babbles.
7 Months	Anticipates events. Enjoys looking through books with familiar pictures. May begin to imitate an act. May say *mama* or *dada* but does not connect words with parents. Produces gestures to communicate. Points to desired object.
8 Months	Likes to empty and fill containers. Begins putting together a long series of syllables. May label object in imitation of its sounds, such as *choo-choo* for train. Finds objects that are totally hidden.
9 Months	Responds appropriately to a few specific words. Likes to look for contents in a container.
10 to 12 Months	Speaks first recognizable word. Links specific acts or events to other events. Can point to body parts. Likes to look at pictures in a book. Puts nesting toys together correctly. Begins to find familiar objects that are not in view but have permanent locations (looks for cookies after being told he or she can have one). Waves good-bye.
13 to 15 Months	Identifies family members in photographs. Gives mechanical toy to caregiver to activate toy. Has an expressive vocabulary of 4 to 10 words; most refer to animals, food, and toys.
16 to 18 Months	Demonstrates knowledge of absence of familiar person (points to door, says "gone"). Enjoys cause-effect relationships (banging drum, splashing water, turning on TV). Has expressive vocabulary of 10 to 20 words.
19 to 24 Months	Sorts shapes and colors. Mimics adult behaviors. Points to and names objects in a book. Points to body parts upon request. Has expressive vocabulary of 20 to 50 words. Refers to self by name. Recognizes self in photo or mirror.
Social-Emotional Skills	
1 Month	Reacts to discomfort and pain by crying for assistance. Recognizes a parent's voice. Is comforted by the human face. Makes eye contact.

Social-Emotional Skills *(continued)*	
2 Months	Is able to show distress, excitement, contentment, anger and delight. Can quiet self by sucking. Looks at a person alertly and directly. Prefers to look at people over objects. Quiets in response to being held. Shows affection by looking at a person while kicking, waving arms, and smiling.
3 Months	Shows feelings of security when held or talked to. Senses that the hands and feet are extensions of self. Whimpers when hungry, chortles when content. Communicates with different sounds and facial expressions. Responds with total body to a familiar face. Tries to attract attention of caregiver. Watches adults' facial expressions closely.
4 Months	Expresses delight. May form an attachment to one special object. Responds to continued warmth and affection. Shows increased pleasure in social interactions. Enjoys social aspects of feeding time. Becomes unresponsive if left alone most of waking hours. Laughs when tickled.
5 Months	May begin to show fearful behavior as separateness is felt. Distinguishes between familiar and unfamiliar adults. Builds trust when cries are answered; becomes anxious and demanding when cries are unanswered. May be able to play the peek-a-boo game.
6 Months	Enjoys playing with children. Responds to affection and may imitate signs of affection. Likes attention and may cry to get it. May begin clinging to a primary caregiver. Desires constant attention from caregiver. Laughs when socializing. Smiles at familiar faces and stares solemnly at strangers.
7 Months	May show more dependence on caregiver for security. Has increased drive for independence but senses frightening situations. Shows desire for social contacts. Thoroughly enjoys company of siblings. Begins to have a sense of humor. Expresses anger more dramatically.
8 Months	Exhibits fear of strangers. May anticipate being left and become disturbed. Values quick display of love and support from caregiver. Likes to explore new places, but wants to be able to return to caregiver. Enjoys playing with own image in a mirror. Definitely prefers caregiver to strangers. Is more aware of social approval or disapproval.

	Social-Emotional Skills *(continued)*
9 Months	May show fear of heights; may be afraid to crawl down from a chair. May show a fear of new sounds. Shows interest in play activities of others. Likes to play games like pat-a-cake. Recognizes the social nature of mealtimes. Performs for others, repeats act if applauded.
10 Months	Cries less often. Expresses delight, happiness, sadness, discomfort, and anger. May be able to show symbolic thought by giving love to a stuffed toy. Is more aware of and sensitive to other children. Enjoys music and may mimic movements others make to music. Fears strange places.
11 Months	May not always want to be cooperative. Recognizes the difference between being good and being naughty. Seeks approval and tries to avoid disapproval. Imitates movements of other adults and children. Likes to say *no* and shake head to get response from a caregiver. Tests caregivers to determine limits. Objects to having his or her enjoyable play stopped.
12 Months	May reveal an inner determination to walk. Begins to develop self-identity and independence. Shows increased negativism. May have tantrums. Enjoys playing with siblings. Likes to practice communication with adults. Continues to test caregiver's limits. May resist napping.
13 to 15 Months	Shows pride in personal accomplishments. Likes to exhibit affection to humans and to objects. Prefers to keep caregiver in sight while exploring environment. Demands personal attention. May show fear of strangers. Shows negativism. Becomes frustrated easily. Enjoys solitary play. Shows preference for family members over others. Demands personal attention
16 to 18 Months	Is emotionally unpredictable and may respond differently at different times. Is unable to tolerate frustration. May reveal negativism and stubbornness. May exhibit fear of thunder, lightning, large animals, and strange situations. Is very socially responsive to parents and caregivers. Responds to simple requests. May punch and poke peers as if they were objects. Is unable to share.

	Social-Emotional Skills *(continued)*
19 to 21 Months	May become possessive of toys, hiding them from others. Likes to claim things as "mine." Gives up items that belong to others upon request. Begins to show empathy for another child or adult. Continues to desire personal attention. Indicates awareness of a person's absence by saying "bye-bye." May enjoy removing clothing and is not embarrassed about being naked. Reveals a sense of trust in adults. Plays contentedly alone if near adults. Likes to play next to other children, but does not interact with them. Is able to play some simple interacting games for short periods of time.
22 to 24 Months	Displays signs of love for parents and other favorite people. Is easily hurt by criticism. Shows the emotions of pride and embarrassment. May show some aggressive tendencies, such as slapping, biting, hitting. May assume an increasingly self-sufficient attitude. Wants own way in everything. May dawdle but desires to please adults. Is more responsive to and demanding of adults. Still prefers to play alone, but likes to be near others. Engages in imaginative play related to parents' actions. Uses own name in reference to self when talking to others. Is continually testing limits set by parents and caregivers. Likes to control others and give them orders.

Two- and Three-Year-Olds

	Gross-Motor Skills
24 to 29 Months	Runs without falling. Pedals a tricycle. Kicks a large ball. Jumps in place. Plays on swings, ladders, and other playground equipment with fair amount of ease. Throws ball without falling. Bends at waist to pick up object from floor. Walks up and down stairs, both feet on step, while holding onto railings. Stands with both feet on balance beam.
30 to 36 Months	Walks on tiptoes. Performs a standing broad jump 8½ inches. Attempts to balance on one foot. Walks to and picks up a large ball. Balances on one foot for 5 seconds. Catches a large ball with arms. Walks up stairs with alternating feet. Rides a tricycle. Performs 1 to 3 hops with both feet together.
37 to 48 Months	Walks toe-to-heel for four steps. Balances on one foot for 8 seconds. Catches a beanbag while standing. Performs 1 to 3 hops on one foot. Catches a bounced ball with hands.

Fine-Motor Skills	
24 to 29 Months	Inserts key into lock. Turns pages in a book one at a time. Strings large beads. Copies a vertical line. Copies a horizontal line. Builds a tower consisting of 6 to 7 cubes. Uses two or more cubes to make a train. Uses one hand consistently for most activities. Holds scissors correctly. Opens and closes scissors.
30 to 36 Months	Builds a tower consisting of 8 cubes. Copies a circle. Imitates building a three-block bridge. Snips paper with scissors.
37 to 48 Months	Pours liquid from a pitcher. Copies a cross. Builds a tower of 9 to 10 cubes. Completes simple puzzles. Wiggles thumb. Folds paper twice (in imitation). Draws a person with three parts. Cuts a 5-inch piece of paper in two. Traces a diamond. Cuts along a 5-inch line within ½ inch of the line.
Self-Help Skills	
24 to 29 Months	Cooperates in dressing. Removes shoes, socks, and pants. Pulls on simple garments. Unzips zipper. Unsnaps snap. Verbalizes toilet needs. Usually remains dry during the day.
30 to 36 Months	Seldom has bowel accidents. Unbuttons large buttons. Closes snaps. Sits on toilet without assistance. Puts on shoes. Pours well from a pitcher. Uses a knife for spreading.
37 to 48 Months	Washes and dries face and hands. Unbuckles belt. Usually remains dry at night. Turns faucet on and off.

Expressive Language Skills	
24 to 29 Months	Combines two or more words (*boy hit*). Yes/no questions marked only by intonation (*Mommy go? You see me?*). *No* and *not* used to negate entire sentence (*No eat; Mommy no; No sit down*). Preposition *in* used (*Go in house; Ball in box*). Uses plural (*More cookies; cats*).
30 to 36 Months	Uses negative elements *no*, *can't*, and *don't* after subject (*I can't eat; Mommy, don't go*). Use of different modifiers: qualifiers (*some, a lot, all*); possessives (*mine, his, hers*); adjectives (*pretty, new, blue*). Overgeneralization of regular past with an *ed* (*He eated it; I woked up*).
37 to 48 Months	Preposition *on* used (*book on table; sit on chair*). Possessives used (*mommy's coat; daddy's car*). *When* questions appear. Negatives *cannot* and *do not* appear. Uses double negatives with a negative pronoun (*nobody, nothing*) or adverb (*never, nowhere*). Examples include "I can't do nothing" or "I don't never get to go." Joins sentences with two clauses (*Then it broke and we didn't have it anymore*).

Language Comprehension Skills	
24 to 29 Months	Child answers routine questions (*What is that? What is your name? What is he doing?*). Points to six body parts on doll or self. Provides appropriate answers to yes/no questions that deal with the child's environment (*Is mommy sleeping? Is daddy cooking?*). Comprehends pronouns: *I, my, mine, me*.
30 to 36 Months	Follows two-step directions. Provides appropriate answers for *where* (place) questions that deal with familiar information (*Where does daddy work? Where do you sleep?*). Comprehends pronouns: *she, he, his, him*, and *her*.
37 to 48 Months	Provides appropriate answers for *whose* questions (*Whose doll is this?*). Provides appropriate answers for *why* (cause or reason) questions (*Why is the girl crying?*). Provides appropriate answers for *who* (person or animal) questions (*Who lives at the North Pole?*). Understands the pronouns *you* and *they*. Provides appropriate answers for *how* questions (*How will mother bake the pie?*).

Math Readiness	
30 to 36 Months	Gives "just one" upon request. Comprehends concepts *light* and *heavy* in object manipulation tasks. Comprehends size concepts *big* and *tall* in object manipulation tasks. Comprehends spatial concepts *on, under, out of, together*, and *away from* in object manipulation tasks.

	Math Readiness *(continued)*
37 to 48 Months	Gives "just two" upon request. Distinguishes between *one* and *many*. Understands the quantity concept *empty* in object manipulation tasks. Understands *smaller*; points to smaller objects. Understands *largest*. Counts while correctly pointing to 3 objects. Understands quantity concepts *full*, *more*, and *less* in object manipulation tasks. Comprehends spatial concepts *up*, *top*, *apart*, and *toward* in object manipulation tasks. Comprehends spatial concepts *around*, *in front of*, *in back of*, *high*, and *next to* in object manipulation tasks.
	Social Skills
24 to 29 Months	Likes to play near other children, but is unable to play cooperatively. Becomes a grabber, and may grab desired toys away from other children. Does not like to share toys. Has not learned to say *please* but often desires the toys of other children. Likes to give affection to parents. May pull hair or bite before giving up a desired possession.
30 to 36 Months	Continues to have a strong sense of ownership but may give up a toy if offered a substitute. May learn to say *please* if prompted. Has increased desire to play near and with other children. May begin cooperative play. Distinguishes between boys and girls. Likes to be accepted by others. Enjoys hiding from others. Likes to play with adults on a one-to-one basis. Enjoys tumble play with other children and caregivers.
37 to 48 Months	Is learning to share and take turns. Follows directions and takes pride in doing things for others. May act in a certain way to please caregivers. Makes friends easily. Seeks status among peers. May attempt to comfort and remove cause of distress of playmates. Seeks friends on own initiative. Begins to be choosy about companions, preferring one over another. Uses language to make friends and alienate others.
	Emotional Development
24 to 29 Months	Continues to be self-centered. May exhibit increasing independence one minute and then run back to security of parents the next. Likes immediate gratification of desires and finds it difficult to wait. May exhibit negativism. Continues to seek caregiver approval for behaviors and accomplishments. Displays jealousy. May develop fear of dark; needs reassurance.

Emotional Development *(continued)*	
30 to 36 Months	May display negative feelings and occasional bad temper. May exhibit aggressiveness. May dawdle but insists on doing things for self. Likes to dress self and needs praise and encouragement when correct. Feels bad when reprimanded for mistakes. Desires caregiver approval. Wants independence but shows fear of new experiences. May reveal need for clinging to security object. Needs an understanding, orderly environment. May have trouble sleeping if the day's events have been emotional.
37 to 48 Months	Is usually cooperative, happy, and agreeable. Feels less frustrated because motor skills have improved. May still seek comfort from caregivers when tired or hungry. Learns more socially acceptable ways of displaying feelings. May substitute language for primitive displays of feelings. May show fear of dark, animals, stories, and the "bogeyman."

Four- and Five-Year-Olds

Gross-Motor Skills

4 Years	Catches beanbag with hands. Hops on one foot. Walks down stairs with alternating feet. Throws ball overhand. Carries a cup of liquid without spilling. Rides bicycle with training wheels. Balances on one foot for 10 seconds. Skips with alternating feet. Walks backward toe-to-heel for four consecutive steps. Builds elaborate structures with blocks.
5 Years	Marches to music. Jumps from table height. Climbs fences. Attempts to jump rope. Attempts to skate. Walks forward, backward, and sideways on balance beam. Catches ball with hands.

Fine-Motor Skills

4 Years	Builds a 3-block bridge from a model. Completes a 6- to 8-piece puzzle. Folds paper diagonally (three folds). Copies a square. Paints and draws freely.
5 Years	Copies a triangle. Prints first name. Prints simple words. Dials telephone numbers correctly. Models objects with clay. Colors within lines. Draws recognizable people, houses, and vehicles.

Self-Help Skills	
4 Years	Laces shoes. Buckles belt. Cuts with knife. Dresses and undresses with supervision. Distinguishes front and back of clothing. Zips separating zipper.
5 Years	Dresses and undresses without assistance. Washes self. Puts shoes on correct feet. Unbuttons back buttons.
Language Skills	
4 Years	Understands *has/doesn't have* and *is/is not*. Identifies *penny*, *nickel*, and *dime*. Follows three commands in proper order (*clear the table, wash the table, and get ready to go outdoors*). Understands the pronoun *we*. Uses irregular verb forms (*ate*, *ran*, *went*). Uses regular tense (*ed*) verbs. Uses third person present tense verbs (*runs*, *shops*). Speaks fluently with a 1500-word vocabulary. Forms sentences of 4 to 8 words. Asks many *when*, *why*, and *how* questions. Tells simple jokes.
5 Years	Uses third person irregular verbs (*He has a ball.*) Uses compound sentences. (*I went to the grocery store and I went to my grandmother's.*) Uses descriptions in telling a story. Uses some pronouns correctly. Uses words to describe sizes, distances, weather, time, and location. Asks the meaning of words. Recalls the main details of a story. Recognizes some verbal absurdities. Tells original stories. Has a 2000-word vocabulary.
Math Readiness Skills	
4 Years	Understands the concepts *beside*, *bottom*, *backward*, and *forward* in object manipulation tasks. Understands size concepts *short*, *fat*, and *thin* in object manipulation tasks. Counts 1 to 4 chips and correctly answers questions such as "How many altogether?" with cardinal number. Says correct number when shown 2 to 6 objects and asked "How many?" Can rote count 1 through 9. Understands the concepts of *triangle* and *circle*. Understands the concepts *tallest* and *same size*.

Math Readiness Skills *(continued)*	
5 Years	Understands *square* and *rectangle*. Understands the concept of *same shape*. Understands the position concepts *first* and *last* in object manipulation tasks. Understands position concept *middle*. Rote counts 1 through 20. Recognizes the numerals 1 through 10. Writes the numerals 1 through 5. May count 1 to 20 objects correctly.
Social-Emotional Development	
4 Years	May seem less pleasant and cooperative than at age 3. May be more moody, tries to express emotions verbally. Strives for independence; resents being treated like a baby. May be stubborn and quarrelsome at times. Resents directions; may think he or she knows it all and can do it all. Learns to ask for things instead of snatching things from others. Is increasingly aware of attitudes and asks for approval. Needs and seeks parental approval often. Has strong sense of family and home. May quote parents and boast about parents to friends. Becomes more interested in friends than in adults. Shares possessions and toys, especially with special friends. Suggests taking turns but may be unable to wait for his or her own turn. Likes to play with friends in cooperative play activities.
5 Years	Shows increased willingness to cooperate. Is more patient, generous, and conscientious. Expresses anger verbally rather than physically. Is more reasonable when in a quarrel. Develops a sense of fairness. Likes supervision, accepts instructions, and asks permission. Has a strong desire to please parents and other adults. Still depends on parents for emotional support and approval. Is proud of mother and father. Delights in helping parents. May act protective of younger siblings. Shapes ideas of gender roles by watching parents' behavior. Is increasingly social and talkative. Is eager to make friends and develop strong friendships. May pick a best friend. Prefers cooperative play in small groups. Prefers friends of same age and gender. Stays with play groups as long as interests hold. Learns to respect the property of friends.

Six to 12 Years of Age	
Physical Development	
6 Years	Body becomes more slender with longer arms and legs; babyhood physique continues to disappear. Loses baby teeth, which are replaced by the first permanent teeth. Is constantly active. Prefers running over walking. May have frequent minor tumbles and scrapes.
7 to 8 Years	May look lanky due to thin body and long arms and legs. Becomes better coordinated; movements become more fluid and graceful. Develops improved sense of balance and timing. Enjoys sports, especially boisterous games. Enjoys skating, skipping, and jumping rope. Able to handle simple tools. Girls are developing faster than boys.
9 to 10 Years	Continues to improve coordination. Improves sense of balance and timing. May develop particular physical skills. Enjoys organized games. Can run, kick, throw, catch, and hit. Further refines fine-motor skills. Is able to use hands skillfully in building models, learning handcrafts, or using tools. Enjoys drawing. Spends a lot of time and energy playing physical games. Girls may start adolescent growth spurt.
11 to 12 Years	Likes to test strength and daring. Becomes very conscious of overall appearance. Boys may grow little in height. Girls may experience growth spurt. Girls may begin menstruation.
Cognitive Development	
6 Years	Asks more complex questions and wants detailed answers. Concentrates on doing one activity for longer period of time. Has improved memory. Has better understanding of the concept of *time*. Is inquisitive and eager to learn in school. May begin to understand concepts of *seriation*, *conservation*, *reversibility*, and *multiple classification*. Usually can distinguish between fantasy and reality. Can understand and follow rules. Begins reading, writing, and math at school.

Cognitive Development *(continued)*	
7 to 8 Years	Accepts idea of rules and knows harm might result if rules are not followed. Understands concept of *time*. Has longer attention span. Understands value of money and may be ready for an allowance. Favors reality; is less interested in fairy tales. Beings to show interest in collectiing certain objects. Likes to help teachers. Enjoys reading animal stories and science fiction stories. May show interest in stories about children of other countries. Refines concepts of *seriation*, *conservation*, *reversibility*, and *multiple classification*. Begins to understand cause and effect.
9 to 10 Years	Is able to consider more than one conclusion to problems or choices. Understands more about truth and honesty. Likes to act in a more adult manner. Is still enthusiastic about learning. Likes games that involve mental competition. Enjoys quizzing parents and impressing them with new facts. Shows increasing capacity for self-evaluation. Enjoys mysteries and secrets. May show less interest in TV programs. May continue to show interest in collecting certain objects. Has vocabulary of about 5400 words. Has better use of language and is able to converse well with adults. Uses more abstract words.
11 to 12 Years	Is able to detect problems in daily situations and work out solutions. Grasps math concepts and applies them to daily activities. May like group projects and classes based on cooperative effort. Likes active learning, reading aloud, reciting, and science projects. May allow peer relationships to affect schoolwork. Has vocabulary of about 7200 words. May enjoy lengthy conversations with teachers. May enjoy long periods of solitude to think or to work on projects like building models. May show interest in reading; mysteries, adventure stories, and biographies are favorites. Understands concepts of *seriation*, *conservation*, *reversibility*, and *multiple classification*. Applies logic to problem solving. Uses language to discuss feelings.
Emotional and Social Development	
6 Years	Becomes more socially independent; chooses own friends. May feel less jealous of siblings as outside interests become more important. Is still egocentric, but is becoming interested in group activities. May still have a hard time waiting and taking turns. Wants desperately to be right and to win. Tattles often to check sense of right and wrong. Wants all of everything, making choices is difficult. May have nightmares. Often expresses sense of humor in practical jokes and riddles. Begins to see others' points of view. Learns to share and take turns.

Emotional and Social Development *(continued)*	
7 Years	May seem withdrawn and moody. Likes to spend time alone or in the background. May feel that everyone is against him or her. Wants and needs approval of adults and peers. Is very conscientious; strives hard to please. Is sensitive and hurt by criticism.
8 Years	Shows more spirit; is willing to try just about anything. May turn to tears and self-criticism upon failure, but recovers quickly. Is able to get along well with others. Chooses companions of same gender and age. Is very sensitive to what others think. Shows intense interest in groups. Wants to look and act like peers. Enjoys group activities in organizations and in own secret clubs. Chooses a best friend, but may change best friends often.
9 Years	Is relatively quiet. Worries about everything. Is sensitive to criticism. Forms groups with others of same gender. Complains a lot. Has definite likes and dislikes. Begins a new drive for independence; resents being "bossed" by parents. Knows right from wrong; will accept blame when necessary, but offers excuses. Shows increased interest in friends and decreased interest in family. Is interested in group activities and concerns. Often competes with others.
10 Years	Is happy with life in general. Likes people and is liked by others. Is dependable and cooperative. Obeys adults easily and naturally. Likes to accept responsibility and tries to do things well. Likes praise and encouragement. Still has strong group spirit, but it may be diminishing. May begin to show more loyalty to a best friend than to the group, especially girls. May enjoy being part of a team. Likes teacher attention and approval.
11 to 12 Years	Is less self-centered. May express great enthusiasm. Likes to plan and carry out activities with a group. Is willing to reach out to others for friendship. Has improved social skills. May show more tact, especially with friends. Is patient and friendly with younger children. If puberty has begun, may become moody and show signs of emotional turmoil. Has strong desire to conform to peers in dress and behavior. Likes team games. Is becoming interested in opposite gender; girls more interested than boys.

*The items listed are based on average ages when various traits emerge. Many children may develop certain traits at an earlier or later age.

Adapted from *Parents and Their Children* by Verdene Ryder, Goodheart-Willcox Company, Inc., 2006.

Acknowledgments

Through the long months of revising this manuscript, there were many individuals whose encouragement, support, and expertise helped me immeasurably. My sincere thanks to all of them.

First, I would like to dedicate this book to my grandchildren, Jeffrey, Eva, Vivian, Marena, and Evan Herr. They are fascinating and constantly remind me just how much young children know and learn. Also, I want to dedicate the book to Elijah and Quinten Anger, two special friends.

To my husband, Dr. James Herr, who has supported and nurtured me throughout this process.

To my sons, John and Mark, who by their development and accomplishments have reinforced the value of the book's content and the importance of nurturing young children. They have more than earned all the credit and appreciation that I can give them; both have become independent, productive, and fascinating young adults.

To May and Molly Herr, my daughters-in-law, who share my love of young children.

To Dr. Karen Zimmerman and Dr. Judy Jax, who saw a need for this textbook.

To Deb Hass, Vicki Weber, Shirley Gebhart, and Betsy Hartford, my secretaries, who so ably transcribed my writing.

To Deanna Applehans, Sara Anger, Sandy Duncan, Karen Maggio, and Sue Unger for their professional support and friendship.

To Moe Hendricks, the Director of the Child and Family Study Center, whose professional conversations, cooperation, creativity, and enthusiasm kept me focused on my writing.

To Kathy Preusse, Jami Lynch, Heidi Anderson, Melissa Seehaver, Marcia Wolf—staff in the Child and Family Study Center—for allowing me to photograph the children in their developmentally appropriate programs.

To Sue Dunkley, who allowed me to photograph in her centers.

To Pat Crittendon, Jill Klefstad, Julia Lorenz, Judy Gifford, Kari Merritt, Linda Vanderloop, Rachel Wegner, Tonya Jones, Maggie Olson, Michael Kennan, Christian Hahn, Susan Justice, Vicki Rempfer, Jan Nickerson, Cassie Roost, Amanda Kowalski, Tanisha Soles, Matthew Steffes, Nicki Malinoski, Lindsy Barnhart, Stacy Bair, Andrew Farrar, Nicole Stopera, Marian Marion, Dawn Tenneyson-Grimm, Terri Swim, Robin Muza, Paula Noll, Connie Weber, Karen Benkowski, Carla Ahman, Gina Schafer, Megan Shaw, Dr. Esther Fahm, Dr. Mary Thompson, Donna Dixon, Eileen Zenk, Margaret Brunn, Paula Noll, Peg Saienga, Lori Register, Patti Herman, Janet Massa, Teresa Mitchell, Rita Devery, Dr. Priscilla Huffman, Candy Jordon, Carla Ahmann, Dianne Carriveau, Linda DeMore, Dr. Joan Herwig, Elaine Staaland, Janet Mafet, Cari Parent, Joanne Fruit, Dr. Penny Warnert, Nancy Graese, Nan Olson, Angela La Bonne Kaiser, Paulette Fontaine, Paula Iverson, Jeannette Daines, Sally Olm, Phyllis Barilla, Lori Pioske, Elizabeth Kaster, Jill Behnke, and my parents, Melba and Herb Knutsen, for their support and encouragement throughout this process.

To Yvonne Libby, a former colleague and coauthor on other publications.

To Chancellor Charles Sorensen, Vice Chancellor Julie Furst-Bowe, Vice Chancellor Dr. Janice Coker, and Mary-Hopkins-Best, the Interim Dean of the School of Education, for their continuous support of the early childhood program.

To Martin Springer and Kathy Rucker Schaffer for assistance with photography.

To Gladys Earl, Assistant Professor in the Food and Nutrition Department, who contributed recipes for use in the text.

Finally, to all the early childhood majors at the University of Wisconsin-Stout and the children in the Child and Family Study Center who have facilitated my thinking for the content of this book.

Photo Credits

Children's World Learning Center, 22-3
Corbis, Chapter 2 Opener
Dole Food Company (www.dole5aday.com), 26-5
Fotosearch, Part 1 opener, Chapter 6 opener, Chapter 8 opener, Chapter 21 opener, Chapter 28 opener, Part 5 opener, Chapter 30 opener, Chapter 33 opener
©**Gideon Mendel/Corbis,** Chapter 2 opener
©**2007 JupiterImages Corporation,** 31-8, 31-11, 31-12, 31-18, 32-10, 32-11
Landscape Structures, Inc., 31-13

Lillian Vernon Corporation, 23-4, 23-5, 25-4, 30-8
Macander, Jo Ann, Thornridge High School, 23-1
Mississippi Development Authority, 10-14
New Horizon Child Care, 9-20, 9-21.
The Kids on the Block, Columbia Maryland, 31-21
USDA Center for Nutrition Policy and Promotion, 12-3
US Potato Board (www.potatohelp.com), 17-6

Glossary

A

abrasion. A scrape that damages a portion of the skin, such as a skinned knee, scratched arm, or rope burn. (13)

acceleration. Process in which a gifted child is assigned to a class with older children. (31)

accredited. Having a certification that states a set of standards has been met. (2)

acoustic material. Material used to deaden or absorb sounds. Carpets, drapes, bulletin boards, pillows, stuffed toys, and sand are examples. (9)

active listening. Listening to what is said, then repeating it. (14)

activity patterns. Levels of movements in infants. (5)

acquired immunodeficiency syndrome (AIDS). A disease caused by the human immunodeficiency virus. The virus breaks down the body's immune system, leaving the body vulnerable to disease. (13)

adult-centered program model. A structured curriculum format for school-age child care that has a high level of adult direction. (30)

allergen. A substance, such as dust, pollen, mold, or food, that causes a negative reaction in some people's bodies. (12)

allergy. The body's negative reaction to a substance, possibly including rashes, swelling, or sneezing. (12)

amblyopia. The result of a muscle imbalance caused by disuse of an eye. Often called *lazy eye.* (31)

ambulatory. Being able to move from place to place. (31)

anecdotal records. Notes kept by the teacher concerning children's play. (3)

animal stories. Books giving animals some human qualities. Usually, the animal has some unusual success or ability. (20)

anaphylactic shock. Extreme allergic reaction that causes shock symptoms and possibly death. (12)

arthritis. Condition brought on by inflammation that produces swelling of joints and surrounding tissues. (31)

articulation. The ability to speak in clearly pronounced sounds. (7)

articulation problems. Omissions, distortions, or substitutions of vowels or consonants or both. (31)

assessment. A process that involves observing, recording, and documenting children's individual capabilities over time. This information is the basis for curriculum decisions when planning for one child or groups. (3)

asthma. A chronic inflammatory disorder of the airways that causes labored breathing, gasping, coughing, and wheezing. (13)

attachment. The strong emotional connection that develops between people. (5)

attention deficit disorder (ADD). Condition in which a child has an unusually short attention span; is considered a learning disability. (31)

attention deficit hyperactivity disorder (ADHD). Form of ADD that includes hyperactivity and impulsiveness; is considered a learning disability. (31)

attitude. Your outlook on life; the way in which you think about or act toward others. (33)

audiovisual board. A smooth wall board that serves as a bulletin board, chalkboard, and movie screen. (9)

auditory discrimination skills. The ability to detect different sounds by listening. (27)

auditory learner. A child who learns best through hearing. This child is the first to hear a fly in the classroom or a snow plow outdoors. (18)

auditory signals. Informing children of a change through the use of sound, such as a bell, timer, Autoharp®, tambourine, or piano. (17)

augmentative communication device. Device designed to help facilitate communication with a child who is unable to speak understandably. (31)

au pair. A person from a foreign country who lives with a family and provides child care in exchange for room, board, and transportation. (1)

autism. A behavioral disorder in which children are unable to interact with others socially because of ritualistic and compulsive behavior. Their language development is also atypical. (31)

Autoharp®. A simple chording instrument used to accompany singing. (27)

B

behavioral disorder. A condition that affects an individual's social and emotional functions, such as attention deficit disorder, hyperactivity, conduct disorder, or autism.

behavioral expectations. Limits that children are expected to follow. (28)

behaviors. Any visible activities done by the child. (18)

bentonite. A clay product used as a thickening agent for powdered tempera paint. (19)

block plan. A written overall view of the curriculum. (18)

body percussion. Musical movement activities such as stomping feet, clapping hands, patting thighs, and snapping fingers. (27)

bridging. A process of placing two blocks vertically a space apart, then adding a third block. (19)

burn. An injury caused by heat, radiation, or chemical agents, generally classified by degree or depth. (13)

C

cardinality. The concept that the last number in a counting sequence tells how many objects exist in a set. (23)

cautious. Slower to make decisions. (18)

cephalocaudal principle. Principle of development stating that development tends to proceed from the head downward. According to this principle, the child first gains control of the head, then the arms, then the legs. (4)

cerebral palsy. Condition resulting from damage to the brain and characterized by lack of control of voluntary movements. (31)

chalk painting. Art activity in which chalk is dipped into water and used to draw on construction paper. (19)

chalk talk. Storytelling method using drawings on chalkboard, tagboard, or newsprint. (20)

chant. Song that has word patterns, rhymes, and nonsense syllables in one to three tones repeated in a sequence. (27)

checking-in services. Program assigning workers to call children in self-care to make sure there are no problems. (2)

checklist. Form of assessment designed to record the presence or absence of specific traits or behaviors. (3)

child care centers. Full-day child care facilities that focus on basic nutritional, social, emotional, intellectual, and physical needs. (2)

child-centered program model. A curriculum format for school-age child care that allows children an opportunity to self-select activities. (30)

Child Development Associate (CDA) Credential. A national credential that requires postsecondary courses in child care education and a minimum number of hours of child care experience. To be eligible for this credential, a person must be eighteen years of age and have a high school diploma. (1)

chronic health needs. Needs for special care caused by an illness that persists over a period of time. (31)

chronological age. Age determined by a birth date. (10)

classification. The process of mentally grouping objects or ideas into categories or classes based on some unique feature or common attribute. (8, 23)

closed wound. An injury to the tissue directly under the skin surface but not involving a break in the skin, such as a bruise. (13)

closed-ended questions. Questions requiring few decision-making skills and most often answered with *yes* or *no*. Also referred to as *single-answer questions*. (24)

closure. The way an activity will end. (18)

coaching. Teaching skill that provides children with ideas for difficult situations. (21)

cognitive development. Growth in the mental processes used to gain knowledge, such as thought, reasoning, and imagination. (4)

collage. A selection of materials mounted on a flat surface. (19)

color blindness. The inability to see a color. This problem, also referred to as *color deficiency*, is hereditary. (31)

color deficiency. The inability to see a color. This problem, also referred to as *color blindness*, is hereditary. (31)

communicable diseases. Illnesses that can be passed on to other people. (13)

compassion. Being aware of others' distress and wanting to help them. (8)

concept. A generalized idea or notion. (18)

concrete operations. The use of logic based on what has been experienced or seen. (4)

conditions of performance. List of tools a child will use, including puzzles, paper, scissors, beads, or any other materials and/or equipment found in early childhood settings. This list can also include what the child will be denied. (18)

confidentiality. The keeping private of sensitive personal information involving other people. (33)

conflict. Two or more forces that oppose each other. (21)

congenital. Describing a condition caused before birth but not necessarily hereditary. (31)

consequence. A result that follows an action or behavior. (14)

conservation. Concept that change in position or shape of substances does not change the quantity. (8)

consumable supplies. Supplies that, in most cases, are used up and cannot be used again. (10)

contactants. Objects that make contact with the body through touch. (31)

content and process-centered approach. A teaching philosophy in which learning is seen as a constant process of exploring and questioning the environment with hands-on curriculum stressed. (18)

conventions of print. Standardized spelling, word spacing, and upper- and lowercase letters in writing. (22)

cool colors. Colors, such as blue and green, that make a room appear larger and create a feeling of openness. (9)

co-op. Group of people or groups who unite so they have more buying power. (10)

cooperative play. Type of play in which two or more children interact with one another. At this stage socio-dramatic play begins. (21)

cover letter. A letter of introduction that is usually included when sending a résumé to a prospective employer. (33)

crawling. A skill in the motor sequence occurring shortly after the infant learns to roll onto the stomach. It occurs when the infant's abdomen is on the ground. (5)

creeping. Movement in which infants support their weight on their hands and knees, moving their arms and legs to go forward. (5)

cubbies. Top sections of lockers used to store finished artwork, library books, parent letters, and other valuable items. (9)

culture. A group's ideas and ways of doing things—such as traditions, language, beliefs, and customs—that become a learned pattern of social behavior. (25)

custodial care. Type of child care that focuses primarily on meeting the child's physical needs. (2)

cystic fibrosis. A chronic hereditary disease that involves persistent and serious lung infections; failure to gain weight; and loose, foul-smelling stools. (31)

D

daily news flash. A written communication tool used by centers to inform parents about program or center news. Parents can use this news to bring about verbal interaction with their children. (32)

dawdling. Eating slowly or having a lack of interest in food; sometimes used as an attempt to gain attention. (17)

deferred imitation. Watching another person's behavior, then acting out that behavior. This occurs between eighteen and twenty-four months. (5)

desensitized. Describing a process in which a doctor injects small amounts of an allergen into the body over time building immunities to an irritant. (31)

development. Change or growth in a human being. Development is usually measured in terms of physical, intellectual, social, and emotional growth. (4)

developmental age. A child's skill and growth level compared to what is thought of as typical for that age group. (10)

developmentally appropriate practice (DAP). A set of guidelines that focus on the outcomes of learning activities. (1)

developmental milestones. Characteristics and behaviors considered normal for children in certain age groups. (3)

diabetes. A disease in which the body cannot properly control the level of sugar in the blood. (12)

direct guidance. Physical and verbal actions, such as facial and body gestures, that influence behavior. (14)

direct learning experience. Learning experience planned with a specific goal in mind. (18)

disinfecting. The process of eliminating germs from surfaces. (13)

dramatic play. A form of play in which a child imitates others. (21)

draw and tell. Storytelling method using drawings made on chalkboard, tagboard, or newsprint. Also called *chalk talk*. (20)

E

early childhood. The period of life from birth to nine years of age. (1)

ecology. Study of the chain of life, focusing on water, land, air, grass, trees, birds, and insects. (25)

egocentric. Quality of people believing everyone thinks as they do. (6)

elimination. Bowel or bladder release. (17)

emergent curriculum. Child-centered curriculum that "emerges" from the children's interest and experiences. It involves both the participation of teachers and children in decision making.

emetic. A substance used for emergency poisonings. When swallowed, it will induce vomiting. (11)

emotional abuse. Abuse of a child's self-concept by parents or guardians through such acts as providing insufficient love, guidance, and/or support. (11)

empathy. The ability to understand the feelings of others. (8)

empty set. A set without any members, such as a set of tables without legs or a set of children with beards. (23)

encouraging. A guidance strategy teachers use to recognize a child's efforts and improvements. (14)

enrichment. A process to broaden the range of experiences with special curriculum. (31)

entrepreneur. A person who starts his or her own business. (1)

epilepsy. A convulsive disorder caused by damage to the brain causing a person to have periodic seizures. (13)

ethics. A guiding set of moral principles, either those held personally or those determined by a professional organization for its members. (1)

expansion. Technique that involves taking a child's mispronounced words and correctly expanding them into sentences. (6)

expressive language. The ability to produce language forms; used to express a person's thoughts to others. (6)

F

fairy tales. Books having a theme of achievement. The characters or heroes of these stories must perform difficult tasks in order to succeed. (20)

family child care home. Child care that is provided in a private home. (2)

family life stories. Books containing the theme of social understanding. (20)

farsighted. Able to see objects in the distance more clearly than those that are close. (8)

feeding-in. A strategy where a teacher helps a child learn language by providing the child's language for him or her. (6)

feely box. A box with a circle cut in it large enough for children to put their hands into and identify different objects and materials placed inside by touch. (24)

felt board. A board covered with felt or flannel that is used as a background for placing felt characters and props to tell a story. (20)

field-independent. Children who are more independent and prefer to work on their own. They enjoy competition as well as individual recognition. (18)

field-sensitive. Children who are more interactive with others; volunteering, assisting, and helpful, they also try to gain attention. (18)

fine-motor development. The ability to coordinate the small muscles in the arms, fingers, and wrists to complete tasks such as grasping, holding, cutting, drawing, and writing. (4)

first aid. Immediate treatment given for injuries, including those that are life-threatening. (13)

first-degree burn. Burn to the top layer of skin. It is the least severe of all burns. Signs include redness or mild discoloration, pain, and mild swelling. (13)

flannel board. A board covered with felt or flannel that is used as a background for placing felt characters and props to tell a story. (20)

flexible limits. Limits that can be adapted to the needs of an individual or a situation. (16)

flipcharts. Stories drawn on large tagboard cards used for storytelling. (20)

foodborne illness. An illness caused by eating food that contains harmful bacteria, toxins, parasites, or viruses. (13)

frustration. Feelings of defeat or discouragement causing tension. (15)

functional stage of play. Second stage of material use. During this stage, a child will use a prop as it was intended while playing with other children. (21)

G

gender roles. Behaviors expected of girls or boys. (6)

gerontology. The study of older adults. (25)

giftedness. Having exceptional skills in one or more of six areas: creative or productive thinking, general intellectual ability, leadership ability, psychomotor ability, specific academic aptitude, and/or visual or performing arts. (31)

glaucoma. Condition caused by failure of the eye fluid to circulate in the proper way, resulting in increased pressure on the eye. Over time, this pressure can destroy the optic nerve. (31)

grand mal seizure. A reaction, or seizure, caused by epilepsy. During a grand mal seizure, a person will lose consciousness, jerk, thrash, or become stiff. (13)

gross-motor development. Improvement of the skills involving arms, legs, and whole body movements. Examples include running, jumping, throwing, and climbing. (4)

guidance. Direct and indirect actions used by an adult to help children develop socially acceptable behavior. (14)

H

hand-eye coordination. Muscle control that allows the hand to do a task in the way the eye sees it done. (22)

head lice. Small bugs that make their homes on the hair and scalp and feed on human blood. (13)

Head Start. A program developed by the federal government to strengthen the academic skills of children from low-income homes, and designed mainly for four- and five-year-olds. (2)

hearing impairment. Term that refers to a problem in one or more parts of the ear, which usually prevents a child from hearing adequately. (31)

hemophilia. Genetic blood disease in which the blood cannot clot normally. (31)

hidden job market. Jobs advertised informally through word of mouth. (33)

hitching. Movement that occurs after an infant is able to sit without support. From this position, infants move their arms and legs, sliding their buttocks across the floor. (5)

home visits. Experiences that allow the teacher to enter the child's world by spending time together in the family's home. (32)

human immunodeficiency virus (HIV). A virus that breaks down the body's immune system, eventually causing the disease AIDS. (13)

hyperopia. Difficulty in seeing things that are close. Also referred to as *farsightedness*. (31)

I

ignoring. Avoiding an acknowledgment to a child's inappropriate behavior if the behavior is not dangerous. (14)

imaginative stage of play. The third and final stage of material use. Children in this stage do not need real props; they are able to think of substitutes. (21)

I-message. A verbal statement that explains the effect of a child's behavior on others without placing blame. (14)

impulsive. Quick to make decisions. (18)

incest. Sexual abuse by a relative. (11)

incidental learnings. Learning experiences that happen during the course of an average day. (25)

inclusion. Term used to refer to an education setting in which children with and without special needs are integrated. (31)

indirect guidance. Outside factors influencing behavior, such as the layout of the center. (14)

indirect learning experience. Learning experience that occurs on the spur of the moment. (18)

individual transition. Quietly informing a particular child of a change, such as cleaning up or going to the snack table. (17)

Individualized Education Plan (IEP). A written strategy for learning designed to ensure that each child with special needs is educated in the most appropriate manner for him or her. (31)

Individualized Family Service Plan (IFSP). Strategy developed when a preschool age child is diagnosed as having a disability. It includes the family's needs in regard to enhancing the child's development, goals for the child, services to be provided to the child and/or family, and a plan for transitioning the child to other services and regular education. (31)

Individuals with Disabilities Education Act (IDEA). Federal law requiring all states to provide education for children who are developmentally delayed. (31)

induce. To produce on purpose. (17)

infant. Term used to refer to a child from birth through the first year of life. (4)

ingestants. Foods, drugs, or anything taken through the mouth. (31)

inhalants. Airborne substances that are inhaled. (31)

initial assessment. An assessment done when a child enrolls or at the beginning of the year to determine what skills children have mastered or where they are in their development. (3)

injectables. Chemicals or drugs injected into the body. (31)

insulin. A hormone that is needed to keep sugar in the blood at a proper level. As insulin is released into the body, the blood sugar level drops. (12)

insulin reaction. An imbalance in blood sugar levels that occurs in a person with diabetes when the amount of insulin is not properly adjusted. (31)

internal. Under the skin. (31)

irritability. Tendency to feel distressed. (5)

isolation area. Special room or space in the center for children who become ill or show signs of a communicable disease. (9)

L

laboratory schools. Schools located on a postsecondary or college campus with a primary purpose of training future teachers and serving as a study group for research. (2)

language comprehension. An understanding of language. Sometimes referred to as *receptive* or *inner language*. (6)

latchkey children. Term used to describe children left in self-care; also refers to children left in the care of a sibling under age 15. (30)

lazy eye. An eye disorder that is the result of a muscle imbalance caused by disuse of the eye. The correct name is *amblyopia*. (31)

learning disability. Problems with one or more basic skills of learning. Poor memory skills, trouble following directions, or poor coordination may be signs. (31)

learning objective. Outcome of an activity that is used to plan teaching strategies. (18)

lesson plan. A written plan outlining specific actions and activities that will be used to meet goals. (18)

letters. Written communication most often addressing only one subject and sent out on an "as needed" basis. (32)

leukemia. A form of cancer that affects the blood-forming organs and the blood. This cancer can cause a sharp increase in the number of white blood cells in the bloodstream. (31)

level of performance. The minimum standard of achievement and how well one might want the child to do. (18)

licensing specialist. A person employed by a state to ensure that the state's child care rules and regulations are followed. (1)

limits. Guides to actions and behaviors that reflect the goals of the center. (11)

listening. Giving full attention to another person or people. (14)

logical consequences. Consequence deliberately set up by an adult to show what will happen if a limit is not followed. (14)

loudness. Term describing the amount of energy or volume used when speaking. (31)

M

malnutrition. A lack of proper nutrients in the diet that happens when a nutrient is absent or lacking from the diet; caused by an unbalanced diet, poor food choices, or the body's inability to use certain nutrients properly. (12)

manipulative stage of play. First stage of material use; stage at which children will begin to handle props. (21)

manuscript writing. A simple form of calligraphy not requiring the sustained muscle control that cursive writing does. This writing involves unconnected letters made of simple, separate strokes. (22)

matching. A form of classification involving putting like objects together. (23)

maturation. Sequence of biological changes in a child giving the child new abilities. (4)

middle childhood. The span of years between ages six and twelve. (8)

modeling. Verbal and nonverbal actions by one person, setting an example for others. (14) Showing the children the appropriate behavior to use during their socio-dramatic play. (21)

molestation. Sexual contact made by someone outside the family with a child. (11)

mono painting. Art activity in which a piece of paper is placed over a finger painting. The two papers are patted together, then pulled apart. (19)

Montessori approach. Schools provide children freedom within limits by a rather structured approach, and a fixed method in which materials are presented. (2)

moral development. Process of acquiring the standards of behavior considered acceptable by a society. (8)

morality. Understanding and using accepted rules of conduct when interacting with others. (8)

morning meetings. Class meetings that promote a caring community at toddler, preschool, kindergarten, and school-age levels by creating and modeling a democratic environment. (25)

motivation. In a lesson plan, a method of gaining children's attention. (18)

motor sequence. Order in which a child is able to perform new movements. Motor sequence depends on the development of the brain and nerves. (5)

multicultural. Representing a variety of racial and ethnic groups. (10)

multiple intelligences. Theory developed by Howard Gardner that emphasizes different kinds of intelligences used by the human brain. Each intelligence functions separately, but all are closely linked. According to Gardner, a potential intelligence will not develop unless it is nurtured. (4)

myopia. Visual difficulty in seeing things that are far away. Also referred to as *nearsightedness*. (31)

MyPyramid. A set of online tools developed by the U.S. Department of Agriculture (USDA) to help plan nutritious diets to fit individual needs. (12)

N

nanny. A child care worker who usually provides care in the child's home and may receive food and housing in addition to wages. (1)

National Association for the Education of Young Children (NAEYC). One of the most respected professional organizations for people who work with young children. (1)

natural consequences. Experiences that follow naturally as a result of a behavior. (14)

nearsighted. The ability to see close objects more clearly than those at a distance. (8)

neglect. Form of child abuse in which the child is not given the basic needs of life. Neglected children may be deprived of proper diet, medical care, shelter, and/or clothing. (11)

networking. A process of building relationships with people who can help you. (33)

networking letter. A letter sent to an assortment of people who you know personally or who are referred to you to inform them that you are available for employment. After receiving the letter, these individuals could pass your name on to the appropriate people or provide you with valuable insight into possible employment opportunities. (33)

neurons. Specialized nerve cells. (4)

newsletters. Written communications most often including information concerning a variety of subjects. (32)

nonaccidental physical injury. Physical abuse inflicted on the child on purpose; the most visible type of child abuse. (11)

nonverbal behavior. Communication through actions and facial expressions rather than words. (14)

numerals. Number symbols, each of which represents an amount. (23)

nutrients. Chemical substances found in foods that are needed for growth and maintenance of health. (12)

nutrition. The science of food and how the body uses foods taken in. (12)

nutrition concepts. Basic concepts that will help children develop good lifetime healthful eating habits. (26)

O

obesity. A major health problem caused by overeating. A condition in which the body weight is 20 percent or more above the normal weight for a given height. (8)

object permanence. An understanding that objects continue to exist even if a person cannot see them. (5)

omission. Implication that some groups have less value than other groups in our society caused by not mentioning or including a group in teaching. (25)

one-to-one correspondence. The understanding that one group has the same number as another. (23)

ongoing assessment. Type of assessment after an initial assessment that measures a child's continuing progress or development over time. (3)

onlooker. A person who watches others' behavior but does not participate in it. (15)

open wound. An injury involving a break in the skin, such as a cut or scrape. (13)

open-ended questions. Questions promoting discussion and requiring decision-making skills. (24)

operation. The manipulation of ideas based on logic rather than perception. (8)

overeating. The intake of more food than is needed by the body to function properly, often causing health and emotional problems. (12)

overfamiliarity. Lack of interest in a particular toy shown by children who are given the same toy day after day. (29)

overstimulated. Overexcited. (15)

P

pantomiming. Telling a story with body movements rather than words. (27)

parallel play. A type of play in which children play by themselves but stay close by other children. All the children may be involved in similar activities, but play between and among the children does not exist. (21)

parent cooperatives. Child care programs that are formed and run by parents who wish to take part in their children's preschool experience. (2)

parent involvement. Patterns of program participation by parents in early childhood settings that are related to their parenting roles. Volunteering in programs, home teaching, and helping with fundraising are examples. (32)

parquetry blocks. Geometric pieces that vary in color and shape used to teach shape concepts. (23)

participation chart. A tool used to gather information on specific aspects of children's behavior. (3)

passive voice. Sentence in which the object of the sentence is placed before the subject. (7)

passivity. Term for describing the level of involvement with a child's surroundings, such as withdrawing from a new person or event. (5)

perceptions. Ideas formed about a relationship or object as a result of what is learned through the senses. (25)

personification. Giving human traits to nonliving objects, such as dolls or puppets. (21)

persuading. Encouraging children to act or behave in a certain way by appealing to their basic wants and needs. (14)

petit mal seizure. An epileptic condition in which the person may have a few muscles twitch briefly or may become confused with the surroundings. These seizures are milder than grand mal seizures. (13)

phrase method. Method of teaching songs using short sections of a long song, having children repeat these sections. These sections are increased until the children know the entire song. (27)

phrase/whole combination method. Method of teaching a song stressing key phrases with rhythmic movement or visual props. (27)

physical age. Age determined by a birth date. (10)

physical development. Physical body changes in a growing individual, such as changes in bone thickness, size, weight, vision, and coordination. (4)

pica. A craving for nonfood items such as paper, soap, rags, and toys. (17)

picture books. Books having single words or simple sentences and simple plots. (20)

pitch. The lowness or highness of a speaking voice. (31)

Plasticene®. An oil-based, commercially manufactured modeling compound available in many bright colors. (19)

policy. A course of action chosen that controls future decisions, such as a center's health policy. (13)

portable kitchen. Kitchen created in the classrooms by placing the ingredients, tools, and other equipment on a low table so all children can watch. Also, portable appliances such as an electric skillet or a hot plate are used rather than a stove. (26)

portfolio. A collection of materials that shows a person's abilities, accomplishments, and progress over time. (3)

positive reinforcement. Molding children's behavior by rewarding positive behavior. (14)

practical life experiences. Experiences in the Montessori curriculum that stress independence for children. (2)

praising. Giving children recognition for their accomplishments. (14)

prekindergarten (PK). The full range of early childhood programs including school-based programs for three- and four-year-olds, preschool, child care, Head Start, and home-based child care. (1)

preoperational stage. Period between ages two and seven during which children learn to classify groups and use symbols and internal images. (4)

preschooler. Term referring to children ages three to six years. (4)

privacy law. A law designed to protect children. It states that a child's records cannot be given to anyone other than parents without the parents' permission. (11)

privately sponsored programs. Child care programs sponsored by a house of worship, hospital, charitable organization, or an individual. (2)

problem-solving file. File containing helpful information on problems parents may face. (32)

professional priorities. Global aspects of work that are important to a person's satisfaction. (33)

program goals. Broad statements of purpose that reflect the end result of education. They state what is important. (18)

projection. A type of play allowing children to place feelings and emotions they feel onto another person or an object, such as a puppet. Through this play, a child may share his or her inner world. (21)

prompting. Making a verbal or nonverbal suggestion that requires a response; used either to stop an unacceptable action or start an acceptable one. (14)

prop box. Box containing materials and equipment needed for certain roles in socio-dramatic play. (21)

props. Items that relate to the story and would attract children's attention. (20)

prosocial behaviors. Acts of kindness that benefit others, such as helping, sharing, and cooperating. (14)

prosthesis. An artificial limb, such as an arm, a hand, or a leg. (31)

proximodistal principle. Principle noting that development of the body occurs in an outward direction. The spinal cord develops before outer parts of the body; arms develop before hands; hands develop before fingers. (4)

publicly sponsored programs. Child care programs funded by the government, school district, and/or division of social services. (2)

puppetry. Using puppets in play. (21)

puppets. Figures designed in likeness to an animal or a human, used to enact stories, actions, or thoughts. (21)

R

rabies. A disease caused by a viral infection of the nervous system and brain. Rabies is transmitted through the saliva of a rabid animal. (13)

rating scale. Tool used to record the degree to which a quality or trait is present. (3)

rational counting. Attaching a number to a series of grouped objects. (23)

recognizing. The ability to relate past and present experiences and classify items; made possible by using the senses to learn from repeated experiences. (23)

redirecting. Diverting or turning a child's attention in a different direction. (14)

referral. Directing a parent to obtain a diagnosis from a professional when a problem exists with a child. (31)

reflex. An automatic body response to a stimulus. At birth, an infant's physical abilities are limited to reflexes. (5)

rehearsal. The repetition of information after it is used. (8)

resource people. Center guests or field trip hosts. (28)

résumé. Brief summary of a person's qualifications, skills, and job experience. The purpose of a résumé is to secure an interview and/or inform a potential employer of a person's qualifications and experience. (33)

reviews. Lists and descriptions of books, which can be found in public libraries. (20)

rheumatoid arthritis. Common form of juvenile arthritis that can also strike adults. General fatigue, loss of appetite, aching joints, and a stiffness of joints are the first signs of the disease. (31)

role. A set of responsibilities that accompanies a position you hold in life. (33)

role-playing. A type of play allowing children to mimic the actions of others, such as wife, husband, mommy, daddy, doctor, or police officer. (21)

role strain. A type of stress created by being unable to successfully balance multiple roles. (33)

rote counting. Reciting numbers in their proper order. (7)

routines. Everyday experiences such as dressing, undressing, eating, napping, toileting, and changing activities. (17)

S

salt painting. Art activity using salt mixed with colored tempera in shakers. (19)

sanitizing. Process of removing dirt or soil and a small amount of bacteria from surfaces. (13)

schemata. Mental representations or concepts. (4)

school-age child care programs. Programs often sponsored by schools, houses of worship, or child care centers that provide care for children before and/or after school. (2)

school-age years. Another name given to middle childhood. (8)

science. The study of natural processes and their products. (24)

science table. A table used to display items related to the science area. (24)

second-degree burn. Burn causing damage to underlying layers of skin, requiring medical treatment. This burn is marked by pain, blistering, swelling, and discoloration. (13)

self-assessment. The process of examining your interests and abilities, as well as values and professional priorities. (33)

self-concept. Qualities a child believes he or she possesses. A result of beliefs, feelings, and perceptions a child has of himself or herself as part of the world. (6)

self-esteem. The belief that you are worthwhile as a person. (8)

sensorimotor stage. Period between birth and two years of age during which infants use all their senses to explore and learn. (4)

sensory table. Table in the sensory area that gives children the opportunity to experience the sensations related to water and sand. It also allows them practice in social situations. Also known as a water or sand table. (9)

sensory training. Learning from impressions received from the five senses. (2)

separation anxiety. A child's difficulty in separating from parents, often occurring between 9 and 18 months of age. (5)

sequencing. The process of ordering real-life objects from shortest to tallest or tallest to shortest. (23)

seriation. The ability to arrange items in an increasing or decreasing order based on weight, volume, or size. (8)

set. A group of objects that are alike in some way and, therefore, belong together. (23)

sexism. Any action, attitude, or outlook used to judge a person based only on the sex of that person. (20)

sexual abuse. Abuse that involves adults using children for their own sexual pleasure, including rape, fondling, incest, pornography, and indecent exposure. (11)

shape. The outline of an object. (23)

single-answer questions. Questions requiring few decision-making skills and most often answered with *yes* or *no*. Also referred to as *closed-ended questions*. (23)

skywriting. Demonstrating the correct way to make a letter by writing it in the air. (22)

social comparison. Process where people define themselves in terms of the qualities, skills, and attributes they see in others. (8)

social-emotional development. Growth in the two related areas of social and emotional skills. Social development involves learning to relate to others. Emotional development involves refining feelings and expressions of feelings. (4)

socio-dramatic play. Social play in which several children play together as they imitate others. (21)

solitary play. Independent play. (21)

sorting. A form of classification involving the process of physically separating objects based on unique features. (23)

spatial relationships. The position of people and objects in space relative to each other. (23)

specific task assessment. Giving children set activities to determine skill and/or needs. (23)

spectator toys. Toys requiring little action on the child's part, such as battery-powered cars and talking dolls. (10)

spice painting. Art activity in which children spread glue on a piece of paper, and then shake spices onto the paper. (19)

spina bifida. A condition in which the bones of the spine fail to grow together, resulting in paralysis. (31)

spiral curriculum. A curriculum based on the fact that as children grow, their circle of interests becomes larger. (18)

staff room. Room in a child care center provided for staff to spend work-related time away from the classroom. (9)

stationary equipment. Permanently installed equipment in the playground, such as jungle gyms, slides, and tree houses. (9)

statute. Formal document drawn up by elected officials. (11)

stereotypes. Preset ideas about people based on one characteristic such as sex, ethnicity, age, or religion. (20)

storybooks. Books that contain pictures but have more complex plots than picture books. (20)

storytelling. Reciting a story or reading aloud from a book. (20)

stranger anxiety. Fear of strangers, which infants begin to experience between seven and nine months of age. (29)

stress. The body's reaction to physical or emotional factors, often taking the form of tension. (15)

string painting. Type of art activity in which heavy yarn or string is dipped in paint and pulled across a piece of paper. (19)

stuttering. Speech disorder that is often characterized by repetition, hesitation, and prolongation. (7)

sudden infant death syndrome (SIDS). The death of a healthy infant due to unexplained causes. (29)

suggesting. Placing thoughts for consideration into children's minds. (14)

sunshine calls. Telephone calls made by teachers to parents to communicate praise and support for children. (32)

synapses. Connections between nerve cells that pass messages in the brain. (4)

T

teachable moment. An unexpected event the teacher can use as a learning opportunity. (18)

teaching portfolio. A collection of materials that tell a story about your efforts, progress, and achievements. (33)

telegraphic speech. Two-word phrases used by toddlers when they first learn to combine words. (5)

temperament. Quality and intensity of children's emotional reactions to their environment, such as passivity, irritability, and activity patterns. (5)

texture painting. Using liquid tempera paints mixed with sand, sawdust, or coffee grounds. (19)

theme. One main topic or concept around which the classroom activities are planned. (18)

theme bags. A child's backpack filled with games, puppets, storybooks, songs, and charts and including a letter of introduction for the parents. (32)

theme walks. Simple field trips taken in and around the center based on a theme. (28)

theory. A principle or idea that is proposed, researched, and generally accepted as an explanation. (4)

third-degree burn. Burn that destroys the skin layer and nerve endings, requiring prompt medical attention. (13)

time-out. A guidance technique used when a child's behavior cannot be ignored. It involves excusing the child from interacting with others so he or she can calm down and gain self-control. (14)

toddler. Term used to refer to a child from the first year until the third birthday. The term is used because of the awkward walking style of children in this age group. (4)

traffic pattern. The way in which people move through the classroom area, affecting its arrangement. (9)

transitions. Changing from one activity to another and/or moving from one place to another. (17)

traveling backpack. A backpack in which children take home their favorite books, music cassettes, puzzles, or games to share with their parents. (32)

U

undernutrition. Not eating enough food to keep a healthful body weight and activity level. (12)

unit-based program model. A curriculum format for school-age child care that revolves around curriculum themes that reflect the children's interests. (30)

universal infection and control precautions. Processes practiced to prevent accidental exposure to any microorganism that can cause infection. (13)

universal pre-kindergarten (UPK). A state-sponsored program designed to introduce three- and four-year-old children to a literary-rich environment. (2)

V

values. Your beliefs, feelings, and ideas about what is important. (33)

vendors. People and companies who sell products and supplies. (10)

verbal environment. All the communication that occurs within a setting, including verbal and nonverbal communication. (14)

vision impairment. Any eye or nerve problem that prevents a person from seeing normally. (31)

visual documentation. Collecting or photographing samples of a child's work that portrays learning and development. (3)

visual learner. A child who depends a great deal on the sense of sight. This child will notice small visual changes in the environment. (18)

visual perception. The coordination of the eye and hand. (8)

voice flexibility. The changes of pitches and loudness levels in a speaker's voice that often reflect the speaker's emotions. (31)

voice-quality disorders. Disorders in which the quality of a speaker's voice is affected; includes harshness, breathiness, nasality, and hoarseness. (31)

W

warm colors. Colors including red, yellow, and orange that make a room appear smaller. (9)

warning. Reminding children to follow classroom rules, stating the misbehavior and the consequences. (14)

web. Drawn chart that outlines major concepts related to a theme. (18)

whole song method. Method used to teach short, simple songs by having the children listen and then sing along. (27)

windows of opportunity. Specific spans of time for the normal development of certain skills. (4)

wound. Damage to the surface of the skin or body tissue. (13)

Index

A

D